University Casebook Series

CONSTITUTIONAL LAW, INDIVIDUAL RIGHTS IN (1970) with 1973 Supplement

Gerald Gunther, Professor of Law, Stanford University.
Noel T. Dowling, late Professor of Law, Columbia University.

CONTRACT LAW AND ITS APPLICATION (1971)

Addison Mueller, Professor of Law, University of California, Los Angeles.
Arthur I. Rosett, Professor of Law, University of California, Los Angeles.

CONTRACT LAW, STUDIES IN (1970)

Edward J. Murphy, Professor of Law, University of Notre Dame.
Richard E. Speidel, Professor of Law, University of Virginia.

CONTRACTS AND CONTRACT REMEDIES, Fourth Edition (1957)

The late Harold Shepherd, Professor of Law Emeritus, Stanford University, and
Harry H. Wellington, Professor of Law, Yale University.

CONTRACTS AND CONTRACT REMEDIES, Second Edition (1969)

John P. Dawson, Professor of Law, Harvard University, and
Wm. Burnett Harvey, Professor of Law, Indiana University.

CONTRACTS, Second Edition (1972) with Statutory Supplement

E. Allan Farnsworth, Professor of Law, Columbia University.
William F. Young, Jr., Professor of Law, Columbia University.
Harry W. Jones, Professor of Law, Columbia University.

CONTRACTS (1971) with Statutory and Administrative Law Supplement

Ian R. Macneil, Professor of Law, University of Virginia.

CONVEYANCES, Second Edition (1941)

Marion R. Kirkwood, Professor of Law Emeritus, Stanford University.

COPYRIGHT, Unfair Competition, and Other Topics Bearing on the Protection of Literary, Musical, and Artistic Works (1960)

Benjamin Kaplan, Professor of Law, Harvard University, and
Ralph S. Brown, Jr., Professor of Law, Yale University.

CORPORATE FINANCE (1972)

Victor Brudney, Professor of Law, Harvard University.
Marvin A. Chirelstein, Professor of Law, Yale University.

CORPORATION LAW, with Statutory Supplement (1973)

Detlev F. Vagts, Professor of Law, Harvard University.

CORPORATIONS, Fourth Edition—Unabridged (1969) with Case Supplement and Special Supplement

William L. Cary, Professor of Law, Columbia University.

CORPORATIONS, Fourth Edition—Abridged (1970) with Case Supplement and Special Supplement

William L. Cary, Professor of Law, Columbia University.

CORPORATIONS (1972)

Reprinted with Conard, Knauss & Siegels' Enterprise Organization.

CORPORATIONS, see also Enterprise Organization

CORRECTIONAL PROCESS (1971) (Pamphlet)

Reprinted from Miller, Dawson, Dix and Parnas's Criminal Justice Administration & Related Processes.

CREDITORS' RIGHTS, Fifth Edition (1957)

The late John Hanna, Professor of Law Emeritus, Columbia University, and The late James Angell MacLachlan, Professor of Law Emeritus, Harvard University.

CREDITORS' RIGHTS AND CORPORATE REORGANIZATION, Fifth Edition (1957)

The late John Hanna, Professor of Law Emeritus, Columbia University, and The late James Angell MacLachlan, Professor of Law Emeritus, Harvard University.

CREDITORS' RIGHTS AND SECURED TRANSACTIONS, 1967

William E. Hogan, Professor of Law, Cornell University.
William D. Warren, Professor of Law, Stanford University.

CRIMINAL LAW (1973)

Fred E. Inbau, Professor of Law, Northwestern University.
James R. Thompson, U. S. Attorney for the Northern District of Illinois.
Andre A. Moenssens, Professor of Law, University of Richmond.

CRIMINAL PROCEDURE (1974)

Fred E. Inbau, Professor of Law, Northwestern University.
James R. Thompson, U. S. Attorney for the Northern District of Illinois.
James B. Haddad, First Assistant State's Attorney, Cook County, Illinois.
James B. Zagel, Chief, Criminal Justice Division, Office of Attorney General of Illinois.
Gary L. Starkman, Assistant U. S. Attorney, Northern District of Illinois.

CRIMINAL JUSTICE, THE ADMINISTRATION OF, CASES AND MATERIALS ON, Second Edition (1969)

Francis C. Sullivan, Professor of Law, Louisiana State University.
Paul Hardin III, Professor of Law, Duke University.
John Huston, Professor of Law, University of Washington.
Frank R. Lacy, Professor of Law, University of Oregon.
Daniel E. Murray, Professor of Law, University of Miami.
George W. Pugh, Professor of Law, Louisiana State University.

CRIMINAL JUSTICE ADMINISTRATION AND RELATED PROCESSES (1971) with Supplement

Frank W. Miller, Professor of Law, Washington University.
Robert O. Dawson, Professor of Law, University of Texas.
George E. Dix, Professor of Law, University of Texas.
Raymond I. Parnas, Professor of Law, University of California, Davis.

CRIMINAL LAW (1969)

Lloyd L. Weinreb, Professor of Law, Harvard University.

CRIMINAL LAW AND ITS ADMINISTRATION (1940), with 1956 Supplement

The late Jerome Michael, Professor of Law, Columbia University, and Herbert Wechsler, Professor of Law, Columbia University.

CRIMINAL LAW AND PROCEDURE, Fourth Edition (1972)

Rollin M. Perkins, Professor of Law, University of California, Hastings College of the Law.

CRIMINAL PROCESS (1969)

Lloyd L. Weinreb, Professor of Law, Harvard University.

DAMAGES, Second Edition (1952)

The late Charles T. McCormick, Professor of Law, University of Texas, and The late William F. Fritz, Professor of Law, University of Texas.

DECEDENTS' ESTATES (1971)

Max Rheinstein, Professor of Law Emeritus, University of Chicago.
Mary Ann Glendon, Professor of Law, Boston College Law School.

DECEDENTS' ESTATES AND TRUSTS, Fourth Edition (1971)

John Ritchie III, Professor of Law, University of Virginia,
Neill H. Alford, Jr., Professor of Law, University of Virginia, and
Richard W. Effland, Professor of Law, Arizona State University.

DECEDENTS' ESTATES AND TRUSTS (1968)

Howard R. Williams, Professor of Law, Stanford University.

DOMESTIC RELATIONS (1970), with Statutory Supplement

Monrad G. Paulsen, Dean of the Law School, University of Virginia.
Walter Wadlington, Professor of Law, University of Virginia.
Julius Goebel, Jr., Professor of Law Emeritus, Columbia University.

DOMESTIC RELATIONS: STATUTORY MATERIALS

Monrad G. Paulsen, Dean of the Law School, University of Virginia.
Walter Wadlington, Professor of Law, University of Virginia.

DOMESTIC RELATIONS—Civil and Canon Law (1963)

Philip A. Ryan, Professor of Law, Georgetown University, and
Dom David Granfield, Associate Professor, Catholic University of America.

DYNAMICS OF AMERICAN LAW, THE: Courts, the Legal Process and Freedom of Expression (1968)

Marc A. Franklin, Professor of Law, Stanford University.

ENTERPRISE ORGANIZATION (1972)

Alfred F. Conard, Professor of Law, University of Michigan.
Robert L. Knauss, Dean of the School of Law, Vanderbilt University.
Stanley Siegel, Professor of Law, University of Michigan.

ENVIRONMENTAL PROTECTION, SELECTED LEGAL AND ECONOMIC ASPECTS OF (1971)

Charles J. Meyers, Professor of Law, Stanford University.
A. Dan Tarlock, Professor of Law, Indiana University.

EQUITY, Fifth Edition (1967)

The late Zechariah Chafee, Jr., Professor of Law, Harvard University, and
Edward D. Re, Professor of Law, St. John's University.

EQUITY, RESTITUTION AND DAMAGES (1969)

Robert Childres, Professor of Law, Northwestern University.

ESTATE PLANNING PROBLEMS (1973)

David Westfall, Professor of Law, Harvard University.

ETHICS, see Legal Profession

EVIDENCE, Second Edition (1972)

David W. Louisell, Professor of Law, University of California, Berkeley.
John Kaplan, Professor of Law, Stanford University.
Jon R. Waltz, Professor of Law, Northwestern University.

EVIDENCE, Sixth Edition (1973) with Statutory Supplement

John M. Maguire, Professor of Law Emeritus, Harvard University.
Jack B. Weinstein, Professor of Law, Columbia University.
James H. Chadbourn, Professor of Law, Harvard University.
John H. Mansfield, Professor of Law, Harvard University.

EVIDENCE (1968)

Francis C. Sullivan, Professor of Law, Louisiana State University.
Paul Hardin, III, Professor of Law, Duke University.

FEDERAL COURTS, Fifth Edition (1970) with 1973 Supplement

The late Charles T. McCormick, Professor of Law, University of Texas.
James H. Chadbourn, Professor of Law, Harvard University, and
Charles Alan Wright, Professor of Law, University of Texas.

FEDERAL COURTS AND THE FEDERAL SYSTEM, Second Edition (1973)

The late Henry M. Hart, Jr., Professor of Law, Harvard University.
Herbert Wechsler, Professor of Law, Columbia University.
Paul M. Bator, Professor of Law, Harvard University.
Paul J. Mishkin, Professor of Law, University of California, Berkeley.
David L. Shapiro, Professor of Law, Harvard University.

FEDERAL RULES OF CIVIL PROCEDURE, 1973 Edition

FEDERAL TAXATION, see Taxation

FREE ENTERPRISE AND ECONOMIC ORGANIZATION, Fourth Edition (1972)

Louis B. Schwartz, Professor of Law, University of Pennsylvania.

FUTURE INTERESTS AND ESTATE PLANNING (1961) with 1962 Supplement

The late W. Barton Leach, Professor of Law, Harvard University, and
James K. Logan, Dean of the Law School, University of Kansas.

FUTURE INTERESTS (1958)

The late Philip Mechem, Professor of Law Emeritus, University of Pennsylvania.

FUTURE INTERESTS (1970)

Howard R. Williams, Professor of Law, Stanford University.

HOUSING (THE ILL-HOUSED) (1971)

Peter W. Martin, Professor of Law, Cornell University.

INJUNCTIONS (1972)

Owen M. Fiss, Professor of Law, University of Chicago.

INSURANCE (1971)

William F. Young, Professor of Law, Columbia University.

INTELLECTUAL PROPERTY (1960–71) (Prepared for use as a supplement to Kaplan & Brown: Copyright, Unfair Competition and Other Topics (1972)

Albert P. Blaustein, Professor of Law, Rutgers University, Camden.
Robert A. Gorman, Professor of Law, University of Pennsylvania.

INTERNATIONAL LAW, See also Transnational Legal Problems and United Nations Law

INTERNATIONAL LEGAL SYSTEM (1973) with Documentary Supplement

Noyes E. Leech, Professor of Law, University of Pennsylvania.
Covey T. Oliver, Professor of Law, University of Pennsylvania.
Joseph Modeste Sweeney, Dean of the School of Law, Tulane University.

INTERNATIONAL TRADE AND INVESTMENT, REGULATION OF (1970)

Carl H. Fulda, Professor of Law, University of Texas.
Warren F. Schwartz, Professor of Law, University of Virginia.

INTERNATIONAL TRANSACTIONS AND RELATIONS (1960)

Milton Katz, Professor of Law, Harvard University, and
Kingman Brewster, Jr., President, Yale University.

INTRODUCTION TO THE STUDY OF LAW (1970)

E. Wayne Thode, Professor of Law, University of Utah.
J. Leon Lebowitz, Professor of Law, University of Texas.
Lester J. Mazor, Professor of Law, University of Utah.

INTRODUCTION TO LAW, see also Legal Method, also On Law in Courts, also Dynamics of American Law

JUDICIAL CODE: Rules of Procedure in the Federal Courts with Excerpts from the Criminal Code, 1973 Edition

The late Henry M. Hart, Jr., Professor of Law, Harvard University, and Herbert Wechsler, Professor of Law, Columbia University.

JURISPRUDENCE (Temporary Edition Hard Bound) (1949)

Lon L. Fuller, Professor of Law, Harvard University.

JUVENILE COURTS (1967)

Hon. Orman W. Ketcham, Juvenile Court of the District of Columbia.
Monrad G. Paulsen, Dean of the Law School, University of Virginia.

JUVENILE JUSTICE PROCESS (1971) (Pamphlet)

Reprinted from Miller, Dawson, Dix & Parnas's Criminal Justice Administration & Related Processes.

LABOR LAW, Seventh Edition (1969) with Statutory Supplement and 1973 Case Supplement

Archibald Cox, Professor of Law, Harvard University, and
Derek C. Bok, President, Harvard University.

LABOR LAW (1968) with Statutory Supplement

Clyde W. Summers, Professor of Law, Yale University.
Harry H. Wellington, Professor of Law, Yale University.

LABOR RELATIONS (1949)

The late Harry Shulman, Dean of the Law School, Yale University, and
Neil Chamberlain, Professor of Economics, Columbia University.

LAND FINANCING (1970)

Norman Penney, Professor of Law, Cornell University.
Richard F. Broude, Professor of Law, Georgetown University.

LAW, LANGUAGE AND ETHICS (1972)

William R. Bishin, Professor of Law, University of Southern California.
Christopher D. Stone, Professor of Law, University of Southern California.

LEGAL DRAFTING (1951)

Robert N. Cook, Professor of Law, University of Cincinnati.

LEGAL METHOD, Second Edition (1952)

Noel T. Dowling, late Professor of Law, Columbia University,
The late Edwin W. Patterson, Professor of Law, Columbia University, and
Richard R. B. Powell, Professor of Law, University of California, Hastings College of the Law.
Second Edition by Harry W. Jones, Professor of Law, Columbia University.

LEGAL METHODS (1969)

Robert N. Covington, Professor of Law, Vanderbilt University.
E. Blythe Stason, Professor of Law, Vanderbilt University.
John W. Wade, Professor of Law, Vanderbilt University.
The late Elliott E. Cheatham, Professor of Law, Vanderbilt University.
Theodore A. Smedley, Professor of Law, Vanderbilt University.

LEGAL PROFESSION (1970)

Samuel D. Thurman, Dean of the College of Law, University of Utah.

Ellis L. Phillips, Jr., Professor of Law, Columbia University.

The late Elliott E. Cheatham, Professor of Law, Vanderbilt University.

LEGISLATION, Third Edition (1973)

Horace E. Read, Vice President, Dalhousie University.

John W. MacDonald, Professor of Law, Cornell Law School.

Jefferson B. Fordham, Professor of Law, University of Utah, and

William J. Pierce, Professor of Law, University of Michigan.

LOCAL GOVERNMENT LAW (1949)

Jefferson B. Fordham, Professor of Law, University of Utah.

MENTAL HEALTH PROCESS (1971) (Pamphlet)

Reprinted from Miller, Dawson, Dix & Parnas's Criminal Justice Administration & Related Processes.

MODERN REAL ESTATE TRANSACTIONS, Second Edition (1958)

Allison Dunham, Professor of Law, University of Chicago.

MUNICIPAL CORPORATIONS, see Local Government Law

NEGOTIABLE INSTRUMENTS, see Commercial Paper

NEW YORK PRACTICE, Third Edition (1973)

Herbert Peterfreund, Professor of Law, New York University.

Joseph M. McLaughlin, Dean of the Law School, Fordham University.

OIL AND GAS, Second Edition (1964)

Howard R. Williams, Professor of Law, Stanford University,

Richard C. Maxwell, Professor of Law, University of California, Los Angeles, and

Charles J. Meyers, Professor of Law, Stanford University.

ON LAW IN COURTS (1965)

Paul J. Mishkin, Professor of Law, University of California, Berkeley.

Clarence Morris, Professor of Law, University of Pennsylvania.

OWNERSHIP AND DEVELOPMENT OF LAND (1965)

Jan Krasnowiecki, Professor of Law, University of Pennsylvania.

PARTNERSHIP PLANNING (1970) (Pamphlet)

William L. Cary, Professor of Law, Columbia University.

PATENT, TRADEMARK AND COPYRIGHT LAW (1959)

E. Ernest Goldstein, Professor of Law, University of Texas.

PLEADING & PROCEDURE: STATE AND FEDERAL, Third Edition (1973)

David W. Louisell, Professor of Law, University of California, Berkeley, and

Geoffrey C. Hazard, Jr., Professor of Law, Yale University.

UNIVERSITY CASEBOOK SERIES — Continued

POLICE FUNCTION (1971) (Pamphlet)

Reprinted from Miller, Dawson, Dix & Parnas's Criminal Justice Administration and Related Processes.

PROCEDURE—Biography of a Legal Dispute (1968)

Marc A. Franklin, Professor of Law, Stanford University.

PROCEDURE—CIVIL PROCEDURE (1961)

James H. Chadbourn, Professor of Law, Harvard University, and
A. Leo Levin, Professor of Law, University of Pennsylvania.

PROCEDURE—CIVIL PROCEDURE, Third Edition (1973)

Richard H. Field, Professor of Law, Harvard University, and
Benjamin Kaplan, Professor of Law, Harvard University.

PROCEDURE—CIVIL PROCEDURE, Second Edition (1970)

Maurice Rosenberg, Professor of Law, Columbia University.
Jack B. Weinstein, Professor, of Law, Columbia University.
Hans Smit, Professor of Law, Columbia University.

PROCEDURE—FEDERAL RULES OF CIVIL PROCEDURE, 1971 Edition

PROCEDURE PORTFOLIO (1962)

James H. Chadbourn, Professor of Law, Harvard University, and
A. Leo Levin, Professor of Law, University of Pennsylvania.

PRODUCTS AND THE CONSUMER: DECEPTIVE PRACTICES (1972)

W. Page Keeton, Dean of the School of Law, University of Texas.
Marshall S. Shapo, Professor of Law, University of Virginia.

PRODUCTS AND THE CONSUMER: DEFECTIVE AND DANGEROUS PRODUCTS (1970)

W. Page Keeton, Dean of the School of Law, University of Texas.
Marshall S. Shapo, Professor of Law, University of Virginia.

PROPERTY, Third Edition (1972)

John E. Cribbet, Dean of the Law School, University of Illinois,
The late William F. Fritz, Professor of Law, University of Texas, and
Corwin W. Johnson, Professor of Law, University of Texas.

PROPERTY—PERSONAL (1953)

The late S. Kenneth Skolfield, Professor of Law Emeritus, Boston University.

PROPERTY—PERSONAL, Third Edition (1954)

The late Everett Fraser, Dean of the Law School Emeritus, University of Minnesota—Third Edition by
Charles W. Taintor II, late Professor of Law, University of Pittsburgh.

PROPERTY—REAL—INTRODUCTION, Third Edition (1954)

The late Everett Fraser, Dean of the Law School Emeritus, University of Minnesota.

PROPERTY—REAL PROPERTY AND CONVEYANCING (1954)

Edward E. Bade, late Professor of Law, University of Minnesota.

PROPERTY, REAL, PROBLEMS IN (Pamphlet) (1969)

Edward H. Rabin, Professor of Law, University of California, Davis.

PUBLIC UTILITY LAW, see Free Enterprise, also Regulated Industries

RECEIVERSHIP AND CORPORATE REORGANIZATION, see Creditors' Rights

REGULATED INDUSTRIES (1967) with Statutory Supplement

William K. Jones, Professor of Law, Columbia University.

RESTITUTION, Second Edition (1966)

John W. Wade, Professor of Law, Vanderbilt University.

SALES AND SECURITY, Fourth Edition (1962), with Statutory Supplement

George G. Bogert, James Parker Hall Professor of Law Emeritus, University of Chicago.

The late William E. Britton, Professor of Law, University of California, Hastings College of the Law, and

William D. Hawkland, Professor of Law, University of Illinois.

SALES AND SALES FINANCING, Third Edition (1968) with Statutory Supplement

John Honnold, Professor of Law, University of Pennsylvania.

SECURITY, Third Edition (1959)

The late John Hanna, Professor of Law Emeritus, Columbia University.

SECURITIES REGULATION, Third Edition (1972) with 1973 Statutory and Case Supplement

Richard W. Jennings, Professor of Law, University of California, Berkeley.
Harold Marsh, Jr., Professor of Law, University of California, Los Angeles.

SOCIAL WELFARE AND THE INDIVIDUAL (1971)

Robert J. Levy, Professor of Law, University of Minnesota.
Thomas P. Lewis, Professor of Law, Boston University.
Peter W. Martin, Professor of Law, Cornell University.

TAXATION, FEDERAL, Sixth Edition (1966) with 1972 Supplement

Erwin N. Griswold, Solicitor General of the United States.

TAXATION, FEDERAL ESTATE AND GIFT, 1961 Edition with 1973 Supplement

William C. Warren, Professor of Law, Columbia University, and
Stanley S. Surrey, Professor of Law, Harvard University.

TAXATION, FEDERAL INCOME (1972)

James J. Freeland, Professor of Law, University of Florida.
Richard B. Stephens, Professor of Law, University of Florida.

TAXATION, FEDERAL INCOME, Volume I, Personal Tax (1972); Volume II, Corporate and Partnership Taxation (1973)

Stanley S. Surrey, Professor of Law, Harvard University.
William C. Warren, Professor of Law, Columbia University.
Paul R. McDaniel, Professor of Law, Boston College Law School.
Hugh J. Ault, Professor of Law, Boston College Law School.

TORT LAW AND ALTERNATIVES: INJURIES AND REMEDIES (1971)

Marc A. Franklin, Professor of Law, Stanford University.

TORTS, Second Edition (1952)

The late Harry Shulman, Dean of the Law School, Yale University, and Fleming James, Jr., Professor of Law, Yale University.

TORTS, Fifth Edition (1971)

The late William L. Prosser, Professor of Law, University of California, Hastings College of the Law.
John W. Wade, Professor of Law, Vanderbilt University.

TRADE REGULATION, Fourth Edition (1967) with 1970 Supplement

Milton Handler, Professor of Law, Columbia University.

TRADE REGULATION, see Free Enterprise

TRANSNATIONAL LEGAL PROBLEMS (1968) with 1973 Documentary Supplement

Henry J. Steiner, Professor of Law, Harvard University.
Detlev F. Vagts, Professor of Law, Harvard University.

TRIAL ADVOCACY (1968)

A. Leo Levin, Professor of Law, University of Pennsylvania.
Harold Cramer, Esq., Member of the Philadelphia Bar, (Maurice Rosenberg, Professor of Law, Columbia University, as consultant).

TRUSTS, Fourth Edition (1967)

George G. Bogert, James Parker Hall Professor of Law Emeritus, University of Chicago.
Dallin H. Oaks, President, Brigham Young University.

TRUSTS AND SUCCESSION, Second Edition (1968)

George E. Palmer, Professor of Law, University of Michigan.

UNFAIR COMPETITION, see Competitive Process and Business Torts

UNITED NATIONS IN ACTION (1968)

Louis B. Sohn, Professor of Law, Harvard University.

UNITED NATIONS LAW, Second Edition (1967) with Documentary Supplement (1968)

Louis B. Sohn, Professor of Law, Harvard University.

WATER RESOURCE MANAGEMENT (1971) with 1973 Supplement

Charles J. Meyers, Professor of Law, Stanford University.
A. Dan Tarlock, Professor of Law, Indiana University.

WILLS AND ADMINISTRATION, 5th Edition (1961)

The late Philip Mechem, Professor of Law, University of Pennsylvania, and
The late Thomas E. Atkinson, Professor of Law, New York University.

WORLD LAW, see United Nations Law

University Casebook Series

EDITORIAL BOARD

CASES

ON

UNITED NATIONS LAW

Edited by

LOUIS B. SOHN

Bemis Professor of International Law
Law School of Harvard University

SECOND EDITION

(Revised)

Brooklyn
THE FOUNDATION PRESS, INC.
1967

Sohn Cs. United Nations Law 2d Ed. UCB
2nd Reprint—1976

PREFACE

In the spring of 1950, the editor of this casebook published his first collection of materials on world organization, entitled *Cases and Other Materials on World Law*. In that earlier book an attempt was made to bring together the basic materials on the principal international organizations for the period from 1920 to 1950. While special attention was paid to the problems of the United Nations, a large proportion of materials related to other international organizations.

A completely revised version of that casebook was published in 1956 under the title *Cases on United Nations Law*. Unlike the previous volume, the new casebook centered on the work of the United Nations, and contained only incidental references to the work of other international organizations. It was no longer a general reference book on world law, but an introduction to the constitutional law of the United Nations. The new title indicated clearly this change in emphasis.

At the very moment at which the 1956 volume was published, the United Nations was faced with two great crises—Hungary and Suez—and made its first venture into "peace-keeping" through international military forces. The new tool was tempered in Lebanon and the Congo, and more limited versions were employed on several other situations. The problem of division of powers between the United Nations and regional organizations which first appeared in the Guatemalan Question in 1954 led to numerous conflicts after 1960. Finally, the constantly escalating situation in Viet-Nam presented the United Nations with a frustrating problem. In the meantime, the growth in United Nations membership to more than 120 Members, the dominance of the Afro-Asian group in the General Assembly and the financial crisis caused by the high expenses of the peace-keeping operations led to a change in the role of the Assembly and to a reconsideration of the distribution of powers between the various organs of the United Nations.

In order to take all these events into account, it proved necessary to revise the casebook completely. More than half of the casebook contains new materials. Old cases had to make room for new ones, and the scope of the casebook had to be further restricted. Several chapters in the old casebook have been completely omitted from the new one, and new emphasis has been placed on problems of the maintenance of international peace and security. It is hoped that a supplementary volume will be published later, dealing with matters for which there was no room in the present casebook.

Many of the old cases have been drastically revised to make them more "teachable." The number of notes has been greatly increased and selected bibliographies have been added to practically every case.

Those documents of the United Nations which are of a constitutional character and need to be resorted to frequently by anyone studying the principal cases are contained in a companion volume entitled *Basic Documents of the United Nations.* This arrangement facilitates simultaneous consideration of the text itself and of the materials which interpret it.

While the editor is solely responsible for the final product, he wishes to acknowledge the many helpful suggestions received from his colleagues and more than twenty "generations" of students. Most of the materials included in the new volume have been pre-tested in mimeographed form on several groups of students, and have been revised in accordance with their reactions.

The editor's thanks go also to the Secretariat of the United Nations which has generously furnished him with all the necessary documents.

LOUIS B. SOHN

August 1967
Cambridge, Massachusetts

TABLE OF CONTENTS

CHAPTER III. MEMBERSHIP—Continued

TABLE OF CONTENTS

CHAPTER VI. MAINTENANCE OF INTERNATIONAL PEACE AND SECURITY

DOCUMENTS, CITATIONS AND ABBREVIATIONS

1. United Nations Documents and Publications

Most documents of the United Nations (UN) are published first in mimeographed form. Each of these documents bears a symbol referring to the main organ under whose auspices it has been issued; often also to any subsidiary organ issuing it or for which it was prepared; sometimes to a further subdivision of a subsidiary organ; and finally to the consecutive number of the particular document. Each part of the document symbol is separated from others by the so-called slash (/).

The document symbols for the main organs are: A (General Assembly), S (Security Council), E (Economic and Social Council), T (Trusteeship Council), and ST (Secretariat). Separate primary symbols were given also to a few subsidiary organs, e. g., the Atomic Energy Commission (AEC) and the Disarmament Commission (DC). In documents of the main organs, the second part of a symbol contains the consecutive number of the document (e. g., A/2437), which is sometimes preceded by an L, e. g., E/L.86 (indicating a document of limited distribution), or an R (indicating a restricted document distributed to Governments only).

If the document has been issued by a subsidiary organ, its symbol is inserted between the symbol of the main organ and the number; e. g., A/CN.4/3 indicates the third document of the fourth Commission of the General Assembly (the International Law Commission). The principal symbols of subsidiary organs are: C (Committee), CN (Commission), AC (Ad Hoc Committee), and CONF (Conference). Some committee documents, especially older ones, bear symbols indicating the functions of the committee, e. g., HQC (Headquarters), CR (Credentials), ECAFE (Economic Commission for Asia and the Far East), PET (Petitions); BUR (General Committee of the General Assembly). Sometimes a document comes from a subcommittee of a subsidiary organ (SC or Sub.), and its symbol is inserted before the consecutive number, e. g., E/CN.4/Sub.2/121.

If a document constitutes an addition to a previous document or contains a correction of a previous document, it receives the same number as the older document, with the additional symbol Add. or Corr.; e. g., E/AC.32/L.43/Add.3. A new edition of a document, containing all corrections and revisions, is sometimes issued; it bears the number of the old document, with the addition of Rev. (e. g., S/1745/Rev.1).

The records of meetings are either verbatim (VR) or summary (SR); e. g., A/AC.18/SR.45. Most of them exist only in a mimeographed form, but the official records (OR) of the principal organs, and of the main committees of the General Assembly have been print-ed. Their main symbols are: GAOR (General Assembly, Official Records), ESCOR (Economic and Social Council, Official Records), SCOR (Security Council, Official Records), and TCOR (Trusteeship Council, Official Records). In this book, the sessions of the General Assembly, of the Economic and Social Council, and of the Trusteeship Council, and the years of the Security Council records are indicated by Roman numerals; if there are several parts of a session, or several series of the Security Council records, these are indicated by Arabic numerals. Thus "GAOR, III.1, C.1" indicates the Official Records of the First Committee of the First Part of the Third Session of the Gen-eral Assembly; while "SCOR, I.2" indicates the Official Records of the Security Council, First Year, Second Series. Where the Official Records have been issued in pamphlet form, they are cited either by the number of the Records (No.) or by the number of the meeting (Mtg.).

Various reports submitted to the principal organs of the United Nations and some more voluminous documents are published in Sup-plements (Supp.) or Special Supplements (Spec. Supp.) to the Official Records. For instance, the Annual Report of the Secretary-General on the Work of the Organization is ordinarily published as Supp. 1 to the Official Records of each session of the General Assembly. The resolutions of each session of the General Assembly, and those of the Economic and Social Council and the Trusteeship Council, were first published in separate volumes, but are now published as Supplements. Many of the mimeographed documents considered by the principal organs during their discussions are reprinted in the Annexes to the Official Records; in the recent volumes of Annexes, the documents are grouped by Agenda Items under which they were discussed. For such documents it is desirable to indicate not only their original number, but also the pages of the Annexes to the Official Records on which they have been reprinted.

The documents of the San Francisco Conference of 1945, i. e., the United Nations Conference on International Organization (UNCIO), are referred to by their consecutive number and the number of the Commission and Committee which issued them; e. g., UNCIO Doc. 933, IV/2/42. They have been reprinted, in 22 volumes, in the "Documents of the United Nations Conference on International Organization" (UNCIO Documents). The principal documents are also reproduced in "The United Nations Conference on International Organization, Selected Documents" (US Department of State Pub. 2490, Conference Series 83). The first American drafts of the Charter may be found in "Postwar Foreign Policy Preparation, 1939–1945" (US, DOS Pub. 3580, General Foreign Policy Series 15), pp. 472, 526, 577, 582, 595. An excellent history of the role of the United States in the preparation of the Charter may be found in Ruth B. RUSSELL and Jeanette E. MUTHER, A History of the United Nations Charter (Washington, D. C., 1958), 1140 pp.

The Secretariat of the United Nations issues seventeen series of studies and reports on a variety of subjects. These publications (UN Pub.) are referred to by the year of issue, number of the series and the consecutive number of the publication; e. g., the "Systematic Survey of Treaties for the Pacific Settlement of Disputes, 1928–1948", a legal publication (series V), was published as UN Pub. 1949 V. 3. A complete catalogue of all United Nations printed publications was published in 1966 under the title "United Nations Publications, 1966" (UN Doc. ST/CS/SER.J/7), 119 pp.

Treaties registered or filed with the United Nations Secretariat are published in the United Nations Treaty Series (UNTS).

There are two types of indexes to the documents of the United Nations. The documents prior to 1949 are listed in their numerical order and indexed by subjects in the "Check List of United Nations Documents." This List is divided into twelve main parts, each dealing with a different organ of the United Nations; e. g., Part 5, No. 1, deals with the first five sessions of the Economic and Social Council. (Not all the volumes of the List have been published and there are still considerable gaps in this part of the index.) The documents published since 1950 have been indexed in the "United Nations Document Index," issued monthly. This Index contains not only a numerical list of all documents issued in a particular month by the United Nations and all the specialized agencies, but also a subject-index of these documents; a cumulative issue of this subject index is issued at the end of each year. There are also separate indexes to the Proceedings of the General Assembly, session by session, starting with the fifth session in 1950. (For prior sessions, consult mimeographed documents, issued in series A/INF/–, under the title "Disposition of Agenda Items of the . . . Session".)

Current summaries of United Nations debates and developments are contained in the "United Nations Monthly Chronicle" and in the "Yearbook of the United Nations" (UN Yearbook), which are both published by the UN Department of Public Information (DPI). Excellent summaries may be found also in the quarterly "International Organization," published in Boston by the World Peace Foundation.

A systematic survey of United Nations practice from 1945 to 1954, arranged by articles of the Charter, has been published in five volumes by the Secretariat of the United Nations in 1955 under the title "Repertory of Practice of United Nations Organs" (cited as UN Repertory;

UN Pub. 1955.V.2). An additional volume, containing a table of contents and a subject index, was published in 1957. There are also two supplements, published, respectively, in 1958 (2 volumes) and 1963–64 (3 volumes), covering the United Nations practice up to 31 August 1959. No serious student of the United Nations can do without these volumes.

A separate survey of the work of the Security Council is contained in the "Repertoire of the Practice of the Security Council, 1946–1951" (UN Pub. 1954.VII.1), 514 pp. Three supplements cover the period from 1952 to 1963.

2. Abbreviations

The following special abbreviations are used in this volume:

ABAJ --------------- American Bar Association Journal

AFDI --------------- Annuaire français de droit international

AJCL --------------- American Journal of Comparative Law

AJIL --------------- American Journal of International Law

Annals ------------- Annals of the American Academy of Political and Social Science.

APSR --------------- American Political Science Review

ARUNA ------------ Annual Review of United Nations Affairs

ASDI --------------- Annuaire suisse de droit international

ASIL Procgs. ------ American Society of International Law, Proceedings

ASJG --------------- Acta Scandinavica Juris Gentium (English and French Supplement to Nordisk Tidsskrift for International Ret).

AUrugDI ---------- Anuario Uruguayo de Derecho Internacional

Australian YBIL --- Australian Yearbook of International Law

AVR --------------- Archiv des Völkerrechts.

BFSP -------------- British and Foreign State Papers.

BYBIL ------------- British Year Book of International Law.

Canadian YBIL ---- Canadian Yearbook of International Law.

DSB --------------- United States, Department of State Bulletin.

GOODRICH-HAM-
  BRO (II) -------- Leland M. Goodrich and E. Hambro, Charter of the United Nations, Commentary and Documents (2d ed.; Boston, 1949).

GOODRICH-SI-
  MONS ----------- Leland M. Goodrich and Anne P. Simons, The United Nations and the Maintenance of International Peace and Security (Washington, 1955).

Grotius Soc. Trans-
  actions ---------- The Grotius Society, Transactions for the Year

HUDSON, Int. Leg. Manley O. Hudson, International Legislation: A Collection of the Texts of Multipartite International Instruments of General Interest, 1919–1945 (Washington, 1931–1950), 9 vols.

ICJ Reports -------- ICJ, Reports of Judgments, Advisory Opinions and Orders (issued in pamphlets which are collected in annual volumes).

ICLQ .... International and Comparative Law Quarterly.
IDI Annuaire ...... Annuaire de l'Institut de Droit International.
ILA Report .... International Law Association, Report of . . .
                     Conference.
ILQ .... International Law Quarterly (London).
Indian JIL .... Indian Journal of International Law.
Int. Affairs .... International Affairs.
Int. Conc. .... International Conciliation (Carnegie Endowment for
                     International Peace, New York).
Int. Org. .... International Organization (World Peace Foundation,
                     Boston).
Int. Relations ...... International Relations (David Davies Memorial In-
                     stitute of International Studies, London)
IRD .... Internationales Recht und Diplomatie
Japanese AIL ...... Japanese Annual of International Law
JDI .... Journal du droit international (Clunet)
JIR .... Jahrbuch für internationales Recht
KELSEN, UN Law . Hans Kelsen, The Law of the United Nations: A
                     Critical Analysis of its Fundamental Problems (New
                     York, 1950).
Nederlands TIR .... Nederlands Tijdschrift voor Internationaal Recht
Nordisk TIR .... Nordisk Tidsskrift for International Ret (including
                     Acta Scandinavica Juris Gentium)
OPPENHEIM-LAU-
TERPACHT
   (VIII) .... L. Oppenheim, International Law, Vol. I (8th ed. by
                     H. Lauterpacht, 1955).
ÖZÖR .... Österreichische Zeitschrift für öffentliches Recht.
PCIJ .... Permanent Court of International Justice. (Publi-
                     cations are cited by series and number.)
RCADI .... Recueil des Cours de l'Académie de Droit Interna-
                     tional (The Hague).
RDerI .... Revista de derecho internacional (Havana).
RDI .... Revue de droit international (Paris).
RDILC .... Revue de droit international et de législation com-
                     parée (Brussels).
RDIMO .... Revue de droit international pour le Moyen-Orient.
RDISDP .... Revue de droit international, de sciences diplomatiques
                     et politiques (Geneva).
REgDI .... Revue égyptienne de droit international
REspDI .... Revista española de derecho internacional
RGDIP .... Revue générale de droit international public (Paris).
RIFDG .... Revue internationale française du droit des gens
                     (Paris).
RiDI .... Revista di diritto internazionale.
RIIA .... Royal Institute of International Affairs.
RJPIC .... Revue juridique et politique, indépendance et coopér-
                     ation.
SJIR .... Schweizerisches Jahrbuch für internationales Recht.
SOHN, World Law . Sohn, Cases and Materials on World Law (Brooklyn,
                     1950).

Swiss RWA .... Swiss Review of World Affairs
UN, A Bibliography
   of the Charter ...... UN, A Bibliography of the Charter of the United Nations (Headquarters Library, Bibliographical Series No. 3; UN Doc. ST/LIB/SER.B/3; UN Pub. 1955. I.7).
UN Repertory ...... UN, Repertory of Practice of United Nations Organs, 5 vols. (UN Pub. 1955.V.2), with supplements.
UNTS .... United Nations Treaty Series.
US, DOS, Pub. ...... US, Department of State, Publication.
US, EAS .... US, Executive Agreements Series (discontinued in 1946).
UST .... US, Treaties and Other International Agreements (published in annual volumes; previously published as a part of US Statutes at Large).
US, TIAS .... US, Treaties and Other International Acts Series (published in pamphlet form).
US, TS .... US, Treaty Series (discontinued in 1946).
WILCOX-MARCY ... F. O. Wilcox and C. M. Marcy, Proposals for Changes in the United Nations (Washington, 1955).
YBWA .... Year Book of World Affairs (London).
ZaöRV .... Zeitschrift für ausländisches öffentliches Recht und Völkerrecht.
ZöR .... Zeitschrift für öffentliches Recht.

In citing various periodicals the following additional abbreviations have been used:

Ass'n .... Association.
B. .... Bar
J. .... Journal
L. .... Law
Q. .... Quarterly
R. .... Review
YB .... Year Book or Yearbook
Z. .... Zeitschrift

The following other abbreviations have also been used in this volume:

C. .... Committee
ESC .... Economic and Social Council
GA .... General Assembly
ICJ .... International Court of Justice
ILC .... International Law Commission
OAS .... Organization of American States
SC .... Security Council
TC .... Trusteeship Council
UK .... United Kingdom
US OR USA .... United States of America
USSR .... Union of Soviet Socialist Republics

†

CASES

ON

UNITED NATIONS LAW

Chapter I

CHARTER INTERPRETATION

STATEMENT OF COMMITTEE IV/2 OF THE
SAN FRANCISCO CONFERENCE

Report of Committee IV/2 of the United Nations Conference on International
Organization, San Francisco, 12 June 1945. UNCIO Doc. 933,
IV/2/42(2), p. 7; 13 UNCIO Documents, p. 703, at 709–10.

In the course of the operations from day to day of the various
organs of the Organization, it is inevitable that each organ will interpret such parts of the Charter as are applicable to its particular functions. The process is inherent in the functioning of any body which
operates under an instrument defining its functions and powers. It
will be manifested in the functioning of such a body as the General
Assembly, the Security Council, or the International Court of Justice.
Accordingly, it is not necessary to include in the Charter a provision
either authorizing or approving the normal operation of this principle.

Difficulties may conceivably arise in the event that there should be
a difference of opinion among the organs of the Organization concerning the correct interpretation of a provision of the Charter.
Thus, two organs may conceivably hold and may express or even act
upon different views. Under unitary forms of national government
the final determination of such a question may be vested in the highest court or in some other national authority. However, the nature
of the Organization and of its operation would not seem to be such
as to invite the inclusion in the Charter of any provision of this
nature. If two member states are at variance concerning the correct
interpretation of the Charter, they are of course free to submit the
dispute to the International Court of Justice as in the case of any
other treaty. Similarly, it would always be open to the General
Assembly or to the Security Council, in appropriate circumstances,
to ask the International Court of Justice for an advisory opinion concerning the meaning of a provision of the Charter. Should the Gen-

eral Assembly or the Security Council prefer another course, an *ad hoc* committee of jurists might be set up to examine the question and report its views, or recourse might be had to a joint conference. In brief the members or the organs of the Organization might have recourse to various expedients in order to obtain an appropriate interpretation. It would appear neither necessary nor desirable to list or to describe in the Charter the various possible expedients.

It is to be understood, of course, that if an interpretation made by any organ of the Organization or by a committee of jurists is not generally acceptable it will be without binding force. In such circumstances, or in cases where it is desired to establish an authoritative interpretation as a precedent for the future, it may be necessary to embody the interpretation in an amendment to the Charter. This may always be accomplished by recourse to the procedure provided for amendment.

NOTE. The adoption of this document was preceded by the following debate on 28 May and 7 June 1945 [UNCIO Docs. 664, IV/2/33, pp. 1–2, and 873, IV/2/37(1); 13 UNCIO Documents, pp. 633–34, 653–54]:

28 May 1945: "The Secretary announced that the question for discussion was how and by what organ or organs of the Organization the Charter should be interpreted. This question was originally raised before Committee II/2 by the Belgian Delegation and was referred by that Committee to Committee IV/2. . . .

"It was suggested at the outset of the discussion that some articles of the Charter might give rise to a conflict of jurisdiction. Therefore, it was felt that this Committee should determine the proper interpretative organ for the several parts of the Charter.

"During the course of the debate, it was apparent that certain delegations favored constituting the General Assembly as the competent organ. Other delegations were in favor of allowing the Court to perform this function. It was suggested that either a joint conference be called along the lines suggested in Article 12 of the Statute of the Court, or a committee of experts be nominated to determine questions of interpretation. It was also pointed out that the Court should be called upon to render advisory opinions in these matters.

"It was pointed out that the Statute of the Court was to form part of the Charter and only the Court could interpret its own statute. By analogy, it was argued that the General Assembly was the logical body to interpret the provisions of the Charter which did not clearly pertain to any other organ, such as the Court. In this connection, it was argued that the power to interpret was tantamount to the power to legislate, and this was the function of the General Assembly, as the democratic body of the new organization.

"The Chairman observed that a certain amount of interpretation would be a normal and even daily necessity in the application of the provisions of the Charter and this normal situation would be necessarily disposed of by the appropriate organ. Should a conflict arise or a particular difficulty present itself, expert advice could be sought; but over and above these normal situations requiring interpretation, were those situations which called for an authentic and constitutional interpretation, the results of which might be tantamount to a revision of the Charter. This latter category was thought to require the same treatment as that required for amending the Charter.

"Some members of the Committee felt that it was not necessary to insert any provisions in the Charter relating to any of the categories of interpretation for the reason that practice would determine the method of interpretation much in the same manner as under the Covenant. Others wished provisions in the Charter relating to those categories of interpretation which include articles giving rise to disagreement or requiring an authentic and legislative interpretation. Still others wished that a definite organ be constituted under a provision of the Charter to act as the official organ of interpretation."

7 June 1945: The Committee had before it a report of a subcommittee which was composed of delegates of Belgium, France, Norway, UK, USA, and Yugoslavia. "The question was raised whether or not the Charter should provide a procedure for resolving disagreements over the interpretation of the Charter between organs, such as referral to the International Court of Justice, or, in the event the Court refused jurisdiction, to pursue the amendment procedure in Chapter XI. It was pointed out that such a definite procedure was not practicable and that flexibility was preferable.

"The Delegate of Belgium disapproved of according equal weight to opinions of the Court and an *ad hoc* interpreting committee and suggested that organs should refer their interpretation disputes to the Court in the interest of objectivity and uniformity of jurisprudence. Several delegates on the other hand observed that the Court and an *ad hoc* committee each perform a function of equal weight: The Court deciding disagreements of a serious nature where time is not a factor; the committee deciding everyday routine disagreements where time is a factor.

"*Decision: The Committee decided to reject the Belgian suggestion of referring interpretation disagreements on the Charter between organs to the Court as an established procedure.*

"Thereafter the Committee adopted the report of Subcommittee IV/2/B."

NEED FOR GREATER USE BY THE UNITED NATIONS AND ITS ORGANS OF THE INTERNATIONAL COURT OF JUSTICE

1.　*Resolution 171A (II) of the General Assembly,*
14 November 1947.

GAOR, II, Resolutions (A/519), p. 103.

The General Assembly,

Considering that it is a responsibility of the United Nations to encourage the progressive development of international law;

Considering that it is of paramount importance that the interpretation of the Charter of the United Nations and the constitutions of the specialized agencies should be based on recognized principles of international law;

Considering that the International Court of Justice is the principal judicial organ of the United Nations;

Considering that it is also of paramount importance that the Court should be utilized to the greatest practicable extent in the progressive development of international law, both in regard to legal issues be-tween States and in regard to constitutional interpretation,

Recommends that organs of the United Nations and the specialized agencies should, from time to time, review the difficult and important points of law within the jurisdiction of the International Court of Justice which have arisen in the course of their activities and involve questions of principle which it is desirable to have settled, including points of law relating to the interpretation of the Charter of the United Nations or the constitutions of the specialized agencies, and, if duly authorized according to Article 96, paragraph 2, of the Charter, should refer them to the International Court of Justice for an advisory opinion.

NOTE. This resolution was based on an Australian proposal. A/C.6/165 (8 October 1947); GAOR, II, Sixth C., pp. 314–15. In the discussion of that proposal in the Sixth Committee of the General Assembly, the Soviet delegate (Mr. Rodionov) declared that the Australian proposal "indicated a desire to alter the Charter by interpretative methods. The Australian draft resolution gave the International Court of Justice a prior right in interpreting the United Nations Charter. The delegation of the USSR considered such a recommendation to be contrary to the Charter and therefore illegal.

"It was stated in Article 96 of the Charter that the General Assembly and the Security Council 'may request the International Court of Justice to give an advisory opinion on any legal question' and that similar action might be taken by other organs of the United Nations and specialized agencies with the authorization of the General Assembly.

"Under Article 65 of its Statute, the International Court of Justice 'may give an advisory opinion' on any question. Thus, both Articles referred merely to the permissive and not the obligatory nature of requests to the International Court of Justice for advisory opinions. Nothing was said about it being obligatory to ask the International Court for advisory opinions on questions relating to the interpretation of the United Nations Charter. The adoption of the Australian draft resolution would be tantamount to the insertion [of] a new provision in the Charter: in other words, it would mean a violation and modification of the Charter. Such a violation of the Charter would be yet another blow dealt it, and would serve only to weaken and undermine the United Nations.

"An attempt to give the International Court of Justice the right to interpret [the] Charter had already been made in 1945 at the San Francisco Conference. At that time the Belgian representative had proposed that the International Court of Justice be given the right to interpret the Charter. On 7 June 1945, the Legal Committee of the San Francisco Conference decided to reject the Belgian proposal—which was that differences between United Nations organs on the interpretation of the Charter should be referred to the International Court—and did not include the proposal in the

Charter. The present draft resolution now urged the adoption of the provision which had been turned down at San Francisco, giving the International Court the right to interpret the Charter. Any changes in the Charter should be effected, not by means of a resolution, but in accordance with Chapter XVIII of the Charter, which clearly defined the procedure for adopting new amendments to the Charter (Article 108).

"It was noticeable that several attempts had recently been made to modify the Charter, without explicitly announcing the intention to do so, but under the guise of various resolutions and recommendations. This particular draft resolution was one such attempt. Any attempts to weaken the rights and powers of the organs authorized by the Charter—in particular the Security Council—or to modify the Charter—under the guise of various resolutions and recommendations—must inevitably lead to the undermining of the United Nations and the destruction of the democratic principles enshrined in the Organization at its founding and incorporated in its Charter. The proposed modification of the Charter was harmful both in form and in substance. The Australian representative, in defending his draft resolution, cited the example of various Anglo-Saxon countries in which the Supreme Court possessed the exclusive right to interpret the country's constitution. Each country, of course, had a right to determine its own constitutional procedures; but there was no legal justification for insisting that the Charter should be refashioned in accordance and in conformity with the constitutional procedure of individual countries. The USSR delegation opposed the adoption of the Australian draft resolution as being clearly illegal." *Idem*, pp. 96–97.

The Rapporteur of the Sixth Committee, Mr. Kaekenbeeck, explained in his report [A/459 (11 November 1947); GAOR, II, Plenary, p. 1559, at 1560–61)] that:

"(a) The draft resolution as submitted applies to all organs of the United Nations authorized by Article 96, paragraph 1, or in conformity with Article 96, paragraph 2, of the Charter, to request advisory opinions of the Court, and to all specialized agencies which are or may be so authorized, under Article 96, paragraph 2.

"(b) The points of law upon which advisory opinions may be requested are points of law arising from concrete cases dealt with by the said organs and agencies within the scope of their competence.

"(c) In order to avoid the risk of conflicts between the attitude adopted by an organ of the United Nations in a concrete case and an advisory opinion of the Court which might be subsequently requested, it is desirable that requests for opinions should, as far as possible, be submitted while the matter is still pending, and preferably at an early stage.

"(d) The organs of the United Nations and the specialized agencies are, of course, in no way relieved of the task of interpreting provisions on which their activity depends. The sole object of the Court's advisory opinions is to enlighten and guide them in the accomplishment of that task. The recommendation is, moreover, limited to cases the interpretation of which involves questions of principle. It does not therefore, propose that all points of law should be referred to the Court indiscriminately. There is no question of the Court's being flooded with futile or hypothetical questions. The aim is to recommend a limited but perfected use of the machinery for requesting advisory opinions from the Court to constructive ends in conformity with the objects of the Charter.

"It has been further pointed out in the Sixth Committee that the first resolution does not create any obligation to request advisory opinions but merely recommends that the possibility provided by Article 96 of the Charter and article 65 of the Statute of the Court should be made use of in appropriate cases.

"Finally, the opinion was expressed, but rejected by the Committee, that the Court was not competent to interpret the Charter. An amendment to this effect was proposed by the Polish delegation, but rejected with only six votes in favour.

"It was explained that the question here was not, as in the Belgian proposal at San Francisco, to make the Court the constitutional organ for interpreting the Charter. The only question involved was rather whether the Charter or the Statute of the Court prevents consultative opinions from being requested or given because they relate to a point of interpretation of the Charter. Clearly, neither the Charter nor the Statute of the Court contains any restriction of that kind. On the contrary, the final report of Committee IV (2) of San Francisco on the interpretation of the Charter (document 750), expressly records that if two Member States are at variance concerning the correct interpretation of the Charter, they are of course free to submit the dispute to the International Court of Justice, as in the case of any other treaty. Similarly, it should always be open to the General Assembly or to the Security Council, in appropriate circumstances, to ask the International Court of Justice for an advisory opinion concerning the meaning of a provision of the Charter. Hence on points of interpretation of the Charter, as on other legal points, organs of the United Nations may request advisory opinions; just as specialized agencies may consult the Court on the interpretation of their organic provisions in accordance with such provisions."

2. *Discussion in the General Assembly, 14 November 1947.*

GAOR, II, Plenary, pp. 859–95.

Mr. LANGE (Poland): On behalf of the Polish delegation, I wish to present an amendment to the first resolution contained in the report of the Sixth Committee. The amendment refers to a point which was raised a moment ago and commented on extensively by the Rapporteur. I should like to indicate that, in general, my delegation is in favour of the proposal contained in the first resolution. Our objection is directed only to a portion of the fifth paragraph, which reads as follows:

"*Recommends* that organs of the United Nations and the specialized agencies should, from time to time, review the difficult and important points of law within the jurisdiction of the International Court of Justice which have arisen in the course of their activities and involve questions of principle which it is desirable to have settled, including points of law relating to the interpretation of the Charter of the United Nations or the constitutions of the specialized agencies . . . ."

My delegation proposes that the words "including points of law relating to the interpretation of the Charter of the United Nations or the constitutions of the specialized agencies . . ." be deleted.
. . .

Our reason for proposing this amendment is that, first, we have legal doubts as to whether the giving of advisory opinions concerning the interpretation of the Charter of the United Nations really falls within the jurisdiction of the International Court of Justice; and, secondly, we have grave doubts as to the political wisdom of such a procedure.

I shall first mention and briefly explain the legal doubts. An opinion contrary to ours has been presented very learnedly by the Rapporteur, whose authority in matters of international law is recognized by all of us. However, I must say that, in this case, his arguments have not convinced me.

Reference is made to this question in two Articles of the Charter and in two Articles of the Statute of the International Court of Justice. Article 92 of the Charter establishes the International Court of Justice as the principal judicial organ of the United Nations, and also states that the Statute of the Court is an integral part of the Charter.

Consequently, I may quote from the Statute of the International Court of Justice as if it were part of the Charter. The Charter itself, in Article 96, says that "The General Assembly or the Security Council may request the International Court of Justice to give an advisory opinion on any legal question." In the second paragraph, it extends the right to certain other organs, to request an advisory opinion under other conditions, but it is not necessary to refer to that at this moment.

In the Statute of the Court itself, we have two Articles, which refer to the jurisdiction of the Court. In Article 36, paragraph 2, we have jurisdiction over legal questions which, among others, also involve questions of international law. However, in cases of Member States bringing certain legal questions for opinion to the International Court of Justice, the organs of the United Nations may ask for advisory opinions under Article 65, which states that "The Court may give an advisory opinion on any legal question at the request of whatever body may be authorized by or in accordance with the Charter . . .".

It is argued that the words "any legal question" obviously include questions concerning the interpretation of the Charter. I am not able to share this extensive interpretation of the words "any legal question," but in the whole context, if you study it, you always find that they mean certain specific legal disputes between Member States which are brought before the International Court for opinion, either directly by those States or by such organs of the United Nations as handle such disputes.

I think it rather a far-fetched interpretation to include in the meaning of the words "any legal question" interpretations of the Charter, which is, if I may say so, the basic constitution of the United Nations, and the constitution on the basis of which the International Court of Justice also operates. We believe that, unless the Charter explicitly states that in doubtful cases an organ like the International Court of Justice is entitled to interpret the Charter, we have to keep to a restrictive interpretation of the provisions and not include an interpretation of the Charter under the words "any legal question."

In certain countries—not all by any means—supreme courts have the right to interpret the constitution, usually in the form of passing judgment on constitutionality of acts of the legislature. In such cases, this right is usually explicitly stipulated in the constitutions of such countries. I may argue by analogy, and say that, in the absence of any such explicit stipulation, it clearly must follow that it was not the intention of the authors of the Charter, and of those Governments which signed the Charter at that time, to include the question of interpretation of the Charter within the jurisdiction of the International Court of Justice.

Indeed, let us consider what would be the consequence of adopting the interpretation which has been submitted to us. I think that the consequence would be to change the whole structure of the United Nations and to place the International Court of Justice in the position of an organ which, in a certain way, is superordinate to the other organs of our Organization. This would happen, particularly, if we were to accept the wording of the resolution at present before us, which requests a review from time to time with regard to important and difficult points of law, including the interpretation of the Charter.

What is proposed is not that we go there sporadically in certain cases of doubt, but that we do so systematically and from time to time, every year, every half year, or some such period of time. If we adopt that proposal, then we shall really establish the International Court of Justice in a special superordinate position within the structure of our Organization, a position which clearly was not intended by the Charter. On this ground, we doubt not only our legal ability to do so, but also the political wisdom.

Mr. EVATT (Australia): . . . The representative of Poland divides his argument into two points. He asks, "Can we do it; is there power to have advisory opinions on the interpretation of the Charter asked of the Court?" Secondly, he asks, "Is it wise to do it?"

I say quite clearly that we have power to do it, and it is quite proper to make this recommendation, leaving it of course to the discretion of each organ of the United Nations to act as it thinks fit in the circumstances of the case.

First, then, is there the power to do it? Article 96 of the Charter says that the General Assembly or the Security Council may request the International Court of Justice to give an advisory opinion on—what?—on any legal question. There is no restriction whatever as to the legal question. Why should it be interpreted to exclude questions as to the meaning of the Charter of the United Nations?

As a matter of fact, Article 103 of the Charter is the supreme law of the United Nations because Article 103 states: "In the event of a conflict between the obligations of the Members of the United Nations under the present Charter and their obligations under any other international agreements, their obligations under the present Charter shall prevail." Therefore, the Charter is not only the legal measure of the obligations of those States who joined the United Nations, but the supreme law. Any other international agreement which is inconsistent with the Charter must yield to it.

Under Article 36 of the Statute of the International Court of Justice, to which Mr. Lange referred, it is provided that the jurisdiction of the Court in legal disputes covers such matters as the interpretation of a treaty. The most obvious example of a multi-lateral treaty is the Charter of the United Nations itself and the interpretation of that Charter is obviously, I submit, a question of law. Therefore, by reason of Article 96 of the Charter, it would be competent, legally, for the General Assembly, the Security Council or any other organ of the United Nations, or any other specialized agency authorized by the General Assembly, to ask questions of the International Court of Justice as to the meaning of the Charter.

I entirely agree with the Rapporteur's view of the law. May I point out that the delegation of the Union of Soviet Socialist Republics, in document A/474 which is before the members of the General Assembly, has made available to us the report of the special committee of jurists which worked on this problem in San Francisco. They addressed their minds to this very question and they said in this document, "Similarly, it would always be open to the General Assembly or to the Security Council, in appropriate circumstances, to ask the International Court of Justice for an advisory opinion concerning the meaning of a provision of the Charter."

The very legal point which is now raised was dealt with by this distinguished sub-committee of jurists, after which the terms of the Charter were approved. This document thus shows quite clearly that the right of the various organs of the United Nations to ask questions as to the meaning of the Charter is established.

Then Mr. Lange comes to the second point: Should we do it? He fears—and I do not know why he should be frightened—that the Court might become a body superior to other organs of the United Nations. Why should that fear be entertained? After all, the court of fifteen jurists is selected by the Security Council and the General Assembly and, if any body is entitled to give a legal opinion as to the meaning of an international instrument or an international treaty or of this Charter, surely such a body is the most competent tribunal in the world so to do. That cannot be denied.

The question now assumes this form. There are questions arising from time to time, questions that are important and difficult. They raise questions of principle affecting the operation of these respective organs. Why should they not have the opportunity, and why should they not, in appropriate circumstances, have the duty of asking some authoritative body for an expression of opinion as to the legal meaning of the Charter?

We have had debate after debate in the present General Assembly, and especially in the First Committee, upon questions in relation to which acute differences of opinion as to the meaning of the Charter have arisen. What has been done has, on the one hand, been alleged to constitute a breach of the Charter, and, has on the other hand, been alleged to be actually in conformity with the Charter.

Who is to determine that? It is quite true that, in the ordinary administrative policies of each organ, the Assembly determines these questions, or without determining them, it assumes a certain determination and goes on to do its work.

This is similar with regard to various Councils like the Security Council and other bodies. The question of domestic jurisdiction arises over and over again in the Security Council; and surely, it would be of some help to the Security Council if these matters could be looked at regularly to see whether any guidance cannot be obtained from the International Court as to the meaning of the Charter and its application to the particular problems which arise from time to time in that organ, or in the organs of the General Assembly.

When a decision is given, it is purely advisory. As is proposed, it is not to be an order to be enforced against anybody. It is an advisory opinion given to the organ that asks for it. It does not compel action. It would be an expression of opinion of the supreme tribunal of the world, so far as international law is concerned. I submit that this would be helpful to the United Nations in its work. At any rate, after the most careful consideration, the Committee dealing with this problem was of the opinion that, first, the Court was competent to do this and, second, that it was desirable in the interest of the United Nations to do so.

It is not a proposal, I submit, aimed at any particular problem or directing attention to anything which is pending in the General Assembly or any matter of that kind. It is simply a recommendation to the effect that the various organs should look into this situation regularly, and if there are questions of law, including questions arising under the Charter and its interpretation, which are difficult, important and involve questions of principle, those are very classical examples of cases where advice would be of value to the organs and to the United Nations.

Mr. VYSHINSKY (USSR): . . . The majority in the Sixth Committee took the position expressed in the Australian resolution, and by doing so supported the proposals designed to give the International Court the right to interpret the Charter. This would really mean that, whenever a question regarding the interpretation of a particular paragraph of the Charter arises in the General Assembly or the Security Council, the International Court will, in fact, be placed above the General Assembly and the Security Council.

What is really involved in giving the International Court the right to interpret the Charter? What will be the consequences if the International Court delivers interpretations of the Charter? It will mean that the General Assembly will either have to accept the interpretation given by the International Court as binding on itself—and that is essentially the intention of the authors of the Australian resolution—or, alternatively, it will have to reject the International Court's interpretation. If, having received the International Court's interpretation, or, in other words, its advisory opinion on some question connected with the interpretation of the Charter, the General Assembly rejects the interpretation because it does not agree with the International Court, then the question will arise as to why, in such a case, the General Assembly applied to the International Court? Why did it apply to the International Court, if it subsequently disregards the Court's opinion or considers it wrong? If the General Assembly considers that it will finally be able to decide whether the International Court's recommendations or interpretation are right or wrong, there would, of course, be no reason in such a case to apply to the International Court. It would then be enough to refer the problem to some *ad hoc* committee of jurists, which would, of course, suffer much less discredit than the International Court if its opinion were heard but not taken into account. It is said that long ago in Turkey, the system was that the judge heard the witnesses, but acted directly contrary to their testimony. I think that a similar system survives in a number of other countries which are still at that primitive stage in the development of justice which characterises the whole history of mankind and the history of civilization and jurisprudence law in various countries. We cannot, however, put ourselves in the position of the Turkish judge in the case of the International Court of Justice, or place the Court in the position of a rather unreliable witness.

Thus, if the General Assembly asks the International Court for an opinion or for an interpretation of some Article of the Charter, and then rejects this interpretation, this would only serve to discredit the International Court and, I think, the General Assembly itself. If, on the other hand, the General Assembly agrees with the Court's interpretation, that will mean that the International Court is able to decide matters more correctly than the General Assembly, and if we admit that the International Court should and can decide matters more correctly than the General Assembly, could we not then refer all the General Assembly's business for decision to the International Court? Would that not be more consistent? Why should we, a less well-qualified Assembly, undertake to settle matters that can be better decided by a more highly qualified body—the fifteen judges who are members of the International Court? That is why I consider a rule such as that which the Australian resolution is now seeking to put through the General Assembly to be incompatible with the dignity of the General Assembly, the Security Council and the International Court of Justice.

We objected to this recommendation through our representatives on the Sixth Committee, because we consider that the adoption of a recommendation based on the Australian suggestion would, apart from everything else, be a direct violation of the Charter. Indeed, what legal grounds are there for introducing a new rule giving the International Court the right to interpret the Charter? I would ask you to name the relevant Article of the Charter. Mr. Evatt has spoken here. Unless I am mistaken, I only heard him refer to Article 65, Article 36 and, I think, Article 96. Article 36, however, says that the International Court has the right to give interpretations of treaties, but not of the Charter. We are then asked: "Is the Charter not a treaty?" Of course, the Charter is a treaty in the broad, everyday meaning of the word, but in the legal sense there is a difference between the Charter and a treaty. If there were no such difference, there would be no reason for speaking of the Charter and of treaties separately. But such a difference does exist. If the Charter can be called a treaty, it is a treaty of a special kind, a treaty *sui generis*. This special nature is indicated, in the first place, by the fact that it has been adopted, not by two parties, three parties or five parties, but that it is of such a multilateral and all-embracing character that it has none of the features of an agreement in the usual sense of that term. . . .

Thus, there remains Article 36 of the Charter, which defines the competence of the International Court of Justice with absolute exactitude. I maintain that Article 36 of the Charter says nothing at all about the International Court's right to interpret the Charter. I would remind you of the opinion expressed by the experts of the Preparatory Commission at San Francisco, to the effect that when an organ has to apply the Charter, it must also interpret it. In this connexion it is easy to understand why the Charter does not say that the International Court may interpret the Charter. Moreover, an interpretation of the Charter should not be confused with an advisory opinion. An advisory opinion is one thing, and an interpretation is another. It is one thing to interpret the law, and another to consult special experts or a special body about a particular law.

We certainly have Article 65, which gives various bodies the right to ask the International Court for an advisory opinion, but the words used are "an advisory opinion on any legal question". Hence, if you now assert, on this basis, that the International Court has the right to give advisory opinions on the Articles of the Charter, this must mean—neither more [nor] less—that you consider the interpretation of the Articles of the Charter and of the Charter itself to be synonymous with an advisory opinion on a legal question. It would be hard, however, to imagine the real meaning of the words being more distorted than is being done in the present case. In talking about advisory opinions on legal questions it must be remembered that the interpretation of the Articles of the Charter is far from being a purely legal matter, and advisory opinions on legal matters certainly are not what is called interpretations of the Charter.

Let us take a concrete example analogous with the questions which are now being raised here. We are arguing about the Interim Committee, or so-called "Little Assembly". We are told that the Interim Committee is being or has been established under Article 22 of the Charter. Sir Hartley Shawcross then says: "You do not agree with this, you say it is a violation of the Charter; then let us go to the International Court and let the Court say whether or not we, the General Assembly, have violated the Charter." But that is a ridiculous way of putting the question. In the first place, it is not for the International Court to decide whether the General Assembly is right or wrong in taking a particular decision. It is not even for the Court to say whether a particular delegation is right or wrong in opposing a particular decision. That is no business of the International Court, for we meet here to discuss matters on a free and equal footing, without any threat of being held morally, legally or politically responsible before any court whatsoever, even before the International Court of Justice. The fact of the matter is, however, that in the first place, the interpretation of the Charter is not essentially a matter of legal interpretation. If you ask whether Article 22 of the Charter has been properly applied to the Interim Committee, what answer can the jurists give? They will reply that Article 22 says that the General Assembly may establish subsidiary organs. The General Assembly considers that this Committee is a subsidiary organ. Hence, Article 22 has not been violated. That is the line of reasoning a jurist will take. A politician, however, would argue differently. He would say that morally you can certainly appeal to Article 22, but this formal exercise of your right and formal application of that Article is politically wrong, since it is contrary to the spirit and letter of the Charter, to which every decision taken by the General Assembly should conform. The question whether Article 22 can properly be applied in this case cannot be decided by a legal analysis of that Article. The Article says nothing as to how exactly the expression "subsidiary organs" should be construed or whether the Interim Committee is a subsidiary organ. This question cannot be decided by giving the Articles of the Charter a legal interpretation distinct from their political interpretation. It is no mere coincidence that Mr. Dulles himself, in speaking from this rostrum in support of the establishment of an Interim Committee, divided all the arguments for and against into two categories, the legal and the political. I maintain, therefore, that there is nothing jurists can do here, for this is not a legal but a political question; it is a legal question only in so far as we have here a violation of the spirit of the Charter as expressed in legal formulæ, of the procedure for amending the Charter as laid down in its Articles, etc. Those who say that the judges of the International Court should deal with interpretations of the Charter are forgetting the rule that the judges who are members of the International Court should be least of all susceptible to political tendencies.

If the judges of the International Court were to begin investigating, for instance, the dispute between Albania and the United Kingdom from the political angle, I would know beforehand that their verdict would be against Albania, because the political sympathies of these judges, who represent various Governments, are, unfortunately, the same as those of the representatives of those Governments in the General Assembly, and the attitude of most of those representatives is clearly not one for which we can muster much enthusiasm. If, however, the judges were to consider the question from the legal point of view, I would be prepared to rely on their competence. Hence, neither legal nor, *a fortiori*, political, considerations would justify giving the International Court of Justice the right to interpret the Charter, for the interpretation of the Charter is not so much a legal as a political matter. That is shown, for instance, by the question of the legality or illegality of the establishment of a commission for Greece to control and supervise sovereign States—Yugoslavia, Albania or Bulgaria. That is why the International Court of Justice cannot be instructed to interpret the Charter from a legal point of view and still less from a political one. Moreover, it is inadmissible that any body should be given the right to control the activities of the General Assembly or the Security Council. I affirm that the Australian resolution is not in conformity either with the meaning, spirit or principles of our Organization, or with the principle of the sovereignty of each Member of this Organization, or with everything connected with the concept of interpreting the Charter, that is, with our practical work. The matter has even gone so far that it is proposed that the International Court should, by interpreting the Charter of the United Nations, participate in the formulation of the basic principles which it would seem desirable to have established for the future. What does that mean? It means that the International Court is to be brought into the practical work of our Organization in working out principles for future guidance, that is to say, in dealing with basic political questions. Apparently, the International Court is to be brought into the welter of politics and, consequently, of political conflict which is concentrated, and inevitably so, upon the organs of the United Nations. This trend has nothing in common with the real purposes and principles of the International Court as they are laid down in the Charter. It represents an attempt to smash the Charter and its principles.

That is why the USSR delegation feels obliged to oppose the Australian draft resolution and vote against it.

Mr. AMADO (Brazil): . . . Political organs, such as the General Assembly and the Security Council, are not competent to decide on disputes of a judicial nature. They run the risk of losing their prestige if they persist in doing so. When a conflict can be settled in a satisfactory manner through an international tribunal, it is wise, even from the political point of view, not to settle it by political methods.

May I be allowed to quote here the words spoken by President Aranha in the Security Council on 3 April 1947 in connexion with incidents that took place in the Corfu Channel. He said: "The Security Council is not and cannot be a tribunal. It is *par excellence* the political and executive organ of the United Nations. Ours is not a judicial function, nor do we meet here as international judges."

It is therefore essential that the organs of the United Nations, upon which rests the duty of finding solutions to international disputes, should refer them, if they are of a legal character, to the International Court of Justice in accordance with the provisions of the Charter.

Of course, we cannot deny the difficulty that is so often experienced in defining what constitutes a legal dispute as contrasted to a political dispute. There are no precise criteria in the matter.

Certain States have often tried to limit the Court's judicial competence by submitting a list of questions that, in their opinion, cannot be resolved by arbitration or recourse to law. Nevertheless, it is comforting to see that this list grows shorter daily. My country did not hesitate—and history will place this to its credit—to submit to arbitration, some years ago, even questions relating to frontiers, which closely touch upon her national sovereignty. But now it is for the international organs dealing with a dispute to examine, in the first instance, whether such a dispute lies within the competence of the International Court of Justice. Should these political organs have any doubts in this respect, they can always ask the Court's opinion, and if this latter holds that the dispute is of a judicial nature, they should ask the Court to resolve it.

Every organ of the United Nations has the right to interpret the Charter; we all know this, and the representative of the USSR, with his usual eloquence, has just reminded us once more of this fact. The International Court of Justice is not the only body possessing the privilege of interpreting the Charter. This, from the constitutional point of view, is all that can be said regarding the competence of the International Court of Justice in this matter. The resolution which the Sixth Committee has adopted bestows no exclusive rights upon it. This resolution changes nothing with regard to the principle of objective justice which governs our Organization. Its aim is only to recommend that the organs of the United Nations and the specialized agencies make better use of facilities that are recognized by the Charter as being at their disposal; the resolution in no way modifies the law, and contains nothing that is unconstitutional. We are merely expressing the desire that a practice which has been followed until now be modified in favour of another which is likely to yield more satisfactory results.

There can be no doubt that the organs of the United Nations have the right, if they so desire, to ask for the advisory opinion of the International Court of Justice on the interpretation of the text of a treaty, and the Charter is nothing but a treaty; if not, what is it? We are merely expressing the wish that organs of the United Nations should make more frequent use of this facility, because we think they have not done so sufficiently up to now. In the past, the International Court of Justice has not been consulted in cases where such consultation might have yielded very good results; this is obvious when we look back at the history of the years that immediately followed the First World War.

This recommendation will not give a compulsory character to what according to the Charter is optional; its only aim is to encourage the more frequent use of an existing faculty.

Certain States fear that the Court, if it interprets the Charter, will do so too strictly by applying legal rules to political matters. Experience of the interpretation of the Covenant of the League of Nations by the Permanent Court of International Justice leads us to think that the International Court of Justice, like its predecessor, will show a sufficiently wide comprehension of the political nature of our Charter. We must avoid anarchy in the interpretation of the Charter; we must not take undue advantage of the flexibility of its provisions. A minimum of stability is necessary as a basis for every kind of organization. Flexibility has its advantages. Everybody can interpret the Charter—the Security Council does so every day—but flexibility may become a source of weakness, as present circumstances demonstrate. As in the intellectual sphere, flexibility may be both a virtue and a failing. If we wish to avoid anarchy in the interpretation of the Charter, we must not exaggerate. To achieve this object, to attain a minimum of security and certainty, the path we must follow is to ask for an objective and impartial opinion of the Court in very controversial cases.

In signing the Charter, the States have agreed to surrender part of their sovereignty; they have created organs endowed with certain powers. It is important that such organs should function normally and that they should not seek to make politics predominate over legality.

We are not dreamers, we do not want to rush forward headlong, we are hastening slowly—*festina lente*; but we believe in our Organization. It is in the strengthening of the International Court of Justice that we place part of our hopes.

[At the end of the debate, the resolution was adopted by 45 votes to 6, with 3 abstentions.]

CERTAIN EXPENSES OF THE UNITED NATIONS

Advisory opinion of the International Court of Justice, 20 July 1962.
ICJ Reports, 1962, p. 151, at 184–97.

Separate Opinion of Judge Sir Percy SPENDER . . .

Words communicate their meaning from the circumstances in which they are used. In a written instrument their meaning primarily is to be ascertained from the context, the setting, in which they are found.

The cardinal rule of interpretation that this Court and its predecessor has stated should be applied is that words are to be read, if they may so be read, in their ordinary and natural sense. If so read they make sense, that is the end of the matter. If, however, so read they are ambiguous or lead to an unreasonable result, then and then only must the Court, by resort to other methods of interpretation, seek to ascertain what the parties really meant when they used the words under consideration (Competence of the General Assembly regarding Admission to the United Nations, I.C.J. Reports 1950, p. 8, and Polish Postal Service in Danzig, P.C.I.J., Series B, No. 11, p. 39).

This injunction is sometimes a counsel of perfection. The ordinary and natural sense of words may at times be a matter of considerable difficulty to determine. What is their ordinary and natural sense to one may not be so to another. The interpreter not uncommonly has, what has been described as, a personal feeling towards certain words and phrases. What makes sense to one may not make sense to another. Ambiguity may lie hidden in the plainest and most simple of words even in their natural and ordinary meaning. Nor is it always evident by what legal yardstick words read in their natural and ordinary sense may be judged to produce an unreasonable result.

Moreover the *intention* of the parties at the time when they entered into an engagement will not always—depending upon the nature and subject-matter of the engagement—have the same importance. In particular in the case of a multilateral treaty such as the Charter the intention of its original Members, except such as may be gathered from its terms alone, is beset with evident difficulties. Moreover, since from its inception it was contemplated that other States would be admitted to membership so that the Organization would, in the end, comprise "all other peace-loving States which accept the obligations contained in the Charter" (Article 4), the intention of the framers of the Charter appears less important than intention in many other treaties where the parties are fixed and constant and where the nature and subject-matter of the treaty is different. It is hardly the intention of those States which originally framed the Charter which is important except as that intention reveals itself in the text. What is important is what the Charter itself provides; what—to use the words of Article 4—is "contained in . . . the Charter".

It is, I venture to suggest, perhaps safer to say that the meaning of words, however described, depends upon subject-matter and the context in which they are used.

In the interpretation of a multilateral treaty such as the Charter which establishes a permanent international mechanism or organization to accomplish certain stated purposes there are particular considerations to which regard should, I think, be had.

Its provisions were of necessity expressed in broad and general terms. It attempts to provide against the unknown, the unforeseen and, indeed, the unforeseeable. Its text reveals that it was intended— subject to such amendments as might from time to time be made to it—to endure, at least it was hoped it would endure, for all time. It was intended to apply to varying conditions in a changing and evolving world community and to a multiplicity of unpredictable situations and events. Its provisions were intended to adjust themselves to the ever changing pattern of international existence. It established international machinery to accomplish its stated purposes.

It may with confidence be asserted that its particular provisions should receive a broad and liberal interpretation unless the context of any particular provision requires, or there is to be found elsewhere in the Charter, something to compel a narrower and restricted interpretation.

The stated purposes of the Charter should be the prime consideration in interpreting its text.

Despite current tendencies to the contrary the first task of the Court is to look, not at the *travaux préparatoires* or the practice which hitherto has been followed within the Organization, but at the terms of the Charter itself. What does it provide to carry out its purposes?

If the meaning of any particular provision read in its context is sufficiently clear to satisfy the Court as to the interpretation to be given to it there is neither legal justification nor logical reason to have recourse to either the *travaux préparatoires* or the practice followed within the United Nations.

The Charter must, of course, be read as a whole so as to give effect to all its terms in order to avoid inconsistency. No word, or provision, may be disregarded or treated as superfluous, unless this is absolutely necessary to give effect to the Charter's terms read as a whole.

The purpose pervading the whole of the Charter and dominating it is that of maintaining international peace and security and to that end the taking of effective collective measures for the prevention and removal of threats to the peace.

Interpretation of the Charter should be directed to giving effect to that purpose, not to frustrate it. If two interpretations are possible in relation to any particular provision of it, that which is favourable to the accomplishment of purpose and not restrictive of it must be preferred.

A general rule is that words used in a treaty should be read as having the meaning they bore therein when it came into existence. But this meaning must be consistent with the purposes sought to be achieved. Where, as in the case of the Charter, the purposes are directed to saving succeeding generations in an indefinite future from the scourge of war, to advancing the welfare and dignity of man, and establishing and maintaining peace under international justice for all time, the general rule above stated does not mean that the words in the Charter can only comprehend such situations and contingencies and manifestations of subject-matter as were within the minds of the framers of the Charter (cf. Employment of Women during the Night, P.C.I.J., Series A/B, No. 50, p. 377).

The wisest of them could never have anticipated the tremendous changes which politically, militarily, and otherwise have occurred in the comparatively few years which have elapsed since 1945. Few if any could have contemplated a world in thraldom to atomic weapons on the scale of today, and the dangers inherent in even minor and remote events to spark wide hostilities imperilling both world peace and vast numbers of mankind. No comparable human instrument in 1945 or today could provide against all the contingencies that the future should hold. All that the framers of the Charter reasonably could do was to set forth the purposes the organization set up should seek to achieve, establish the organs to accomplish these purposes and confer upon these organs powers in general terms. Yet these general terms, unfettered by man's incapacity to foretell the future, may be sufficient to meet the thrusts of a changing world.

The nature of the authority granted by the Charter to each of its organs does not change with time. The ambit or scope of the authority conferred may nonetheless comprehend ever changing circumstances and conditions and embrace, as history unfolds itself, new problems and situations which were not and could not have been envisaged when the Charter came into being. The Charter must accordingly be interpreted, whilst in no way deforming or dislocating its language, so that the authority conferred upon the Organization and its various organs may attach itself to new and unanticipated situations and events.

All canons of interpretation, however valuable they may be, are but aids to the interpreter. There are, as this Court's predecessor acknowledged, many methods of interpretation (Territorial Jurisdiction of the International Commission on the River Oder, P.C.I.J., Series A, No. 23, p. 26). The question whether an unforeseen, or extraordinary, or abnormal development or situation, or matter relating thereto, falls within the authority accorded to any of the organs of the Organization finds its answer in discharging the essential task of all interpretation —ascertaining the meaning of the relevant Charter provision in its context. The meaning of the text will be illuminated by the stated purposes to achieve which the terms of the Charter were drafted. . .

In the proceedings on this Advisory Opinion practice and usage within the United Nations has been greatly relied upon by certain States . . . as establishing a criterion of interpretation of relevant Charter provisions. . . .

The proposition advanced was that it is a general principle that a treaty provision should be interpreted in the light of the subsequent conduct of the contracting parties—words which echo those to be found in the Advisory Opinion of the Permanent Court in Interpretation of the Treaty of Lausanne (P.C.I.J., Series B, No. 12, 1925, p. 24)—and that the uniform practice pursued by the organs of the United Nations should be equated with the "subsequent conduct" of contracting parties as in the case of a bilateral treaty. . . .

The practice of the parties in interpreting a constitutive instrument, it was submitted, was a guide to that instrument's true meaning. . .

It is of course a general principle of international law that the subsequent conduct of the parties to a bilateral—or a multilateral—instrument may throw light on the intention of the parties at the time the instrument was entered into and thus may provide a legitimate criterion of interpretation.

So the conduct of *one* party to such an instrument—or to a unilateral instrument—may throw light upon *its* intentions when entering into it whilst that of *both*—or *all*—parties may have considerable probative value in aid of interpretation.

There is, however, as the late Judge Sir Hersch Lauterpacht has pointed out, an element of artificiality in the principle, and care must be taken to circumscribe its operation. This element of artificiality is greatly magnified when the principle is sought to be extended from the field of bilateral instruments to that of multilateral instruments of an organic character and where the practice (or subsequent conduct) relied upon is that, not of the parties to the instrument, but of an organ created thereunder.

In any case subsequent conduct may only provide a criterion of interpretation when the text is obscure, and even then it is necessary to consider whether that conduct itself permits of only one inference

(Brazilian Loans Case, P.C.I.J., Series A/B, Nos. 20/21, p. 119). Except in the case where a party is by its conduct precluded from relying upon a particular interpretation, with which type of case we are not presently concerned, it can hardly control the language or provide a criterion of interpretation of a text which is not obscure.

I find difficulty in accepting the proposition that a practice pursued by an *organ* of the United Nations may be equated with the subsequent conduct of *parties* to a bilateral agreement and thus afford evidence of intention of the parties to the Charter (who have constantly been added to since it came into force) and in that way or otherwise provide a criterion of interpretation. Nor can I agree with a view sometimes advanced that a common practice pursued by an organ of the United Nations, though *ultra vires* and in point of fact having the result of amending the Charter, may nonetheless be effective as a criterion of interpretation.

The legal rationale behind what is called the principle of "subsequent conduct" is I think evident enough. In essence it is a question of evidence, its admissibility and value. Its roots are deeply embedded in the experience of mankind.

A man enters into a compact usually between himself and another. The meaning of that compact when entered into whether oral, or in writing, may well be affected, even determined, by the manner in which both parties in practice have carried it out.

That is evident enough. Their joint conduct expresses their common understanding of what the terms of their compact, at the time they entered into it, were intended to mean, and thus provides direct evidence of what they did mean.

That conduct on the part of both parties to a treaty should be considered on the same footing is incontestable. It provides a criterion of interpretation.

It is however evident enough—despite a flimsy and questionable argument based upon what appears in Iranian Oil Company (I.C.J. Reports 1952, pp. 106–107)—that the subsequent conduct of one party alone cannot be evidence in its favour of a common understanding of the meaning intended to be given to the text of a treaty. Its conduct could, under certain conditions to which I have in the Case concerning the Temple of PreahVihear (I.C.J. Reports 1962, p. 128) made brief reference, preclude it as against the other party to the treaty from alleging an interpretation contrary to that which by its conduct it has represented to be the correct interpretation to be placed upon the treaty. Short of conduct on its part amounting to preclusion, it may also, if the other party to the treaty acknowledges that the interpretation so placed upon it by the first party is correct, provide evidence in favour of the first party, depending on the weight the acknowledgment merits, and thus also provide a criterion of interpretation.

As in the field of municipal law, multilateral compacts were a later development; as also were multilateral treaties in the field of international law, particularly those of the organizational character of the Charter.

In the case of multilateral treaties the admissibility and value as evidence of subsequent conduct of one or more parties thereto encounter particular difficulties. If all the parties to a multilateral treaty where the parties are fixed and constant, pursue a course of subsequent conduct in their attitude to the text of the treaty, and that course of conduct leads to an inference, and one inference only, as to their common intention and understanding at the time they entered into the treaty as to the meaning of its text, the probative value of their conduct again is manifest. If however only one or some but not all of them by subsequent conduct interpret the text in a certain manner, that conduct stands upon the same footing as the unilateral conduct of one party to a bilateral treaty. The conduct of such one or more could not of itself have any probative value or provide a criterion for judicial interpretation.

Even where the course of subsequent conduct pursued by both parties to a bilateral treaty or by all parties to a multilateral treaty are in accord and that conduct permits of only one inference it provides a criterion of interpretation only when, as has already been indicated, the text of the treaty is obscure or ambiguous. It may, however, depending upon other considerations not necessary to be here dealt with, provide evidence from which to infer a new agreement with new rights and obligations between the parties, in effect superimposed or based upon the text of the treaty and amending the same. This latter aspect of subsequent conduct is irrelevant for present consideration since no amendment of the Charter may occur except pursuant to Article 108 of the Charter.

When we pass from multilateral treaties in which the parties thereto are fixed and constant to multilateral treaties where the original parties thereto may be added to in accordance with the terms of the treaty itself we move into territory where the role and value of subsequent conduct as an interpretive element is by no means evident.

The Charter provides the specific case with which we are concerned. The original Members of the Charter number less than half the total number of Member States. If the intention of the original Members of the United Nations, at the time they entered into the Charter, is that which provides a criterion of interpretation, then it is the subsequent conduct of *those* Members which may be equated with the subsequent conduct of the parties to a bilateral or multilateral treaty where the parties are fixed and constant. This, it seems to me, could add a new and indeterminate dimension to the rights and obligations of States that were not original Members and so were not privy to the intentions of the original Members.

However this may be, it is not evident on what ground a practice consistently followed by a majority of Member States not in fact accepted by other Member States could provide any criterion of interpretation which the Court could properly take into consideration in the discharge of its judicial function. The conduct of the majority in following the practice may be evidence against them and against those who in fact accept the practice as correctly interpreting a Charter provision, but could not, it seems to me, afford any in their favour to support an interpretation which by majority they have been able to assert.

It is not I think permissible to move the principle of subsequent conduct of parties to a bilateral or multilateral treaty into another field and seek to apply it, not to the *parties* to the treaty, but to an *organ* established under the treaty.

My present view is that it is not possible to equate "subsequent conduct" with the practice of an organ of the United Nations. Not only is such an organ not a party to the Charter but the inescapable reality is that both the General Assembly and the Security Council are but the mechanisms through which the Members of the United Nations express their views and act. The fact that they act through such an organ, where a majority rule prevails and so determines the practice, cannot, it seems to me, give any greater probative value to the practice established within that organ than it would have as conduct of the Members that comprise the majority if pursued outside of that organ. .   .   .

Apart from a practice which is of a peaceful, uniform and undisputed character accepted in fact by all current Members, a consideration of which is not germane to the present examination, I accordingly entertain considerable doubt whether practice of an organ of the United Nations has any probative value either as providing evidence of the intentions of the original Member States or otherwise a criterion of interpretation. As presently advised I think it has none.

If however it has probative value, what is the measure of its value before this Court?

An organ of the United Nations, whether it be the General Assembly, the Security Council, the Economic and Social Council, the Secretariat or its subsidiary organs, has in practice to interpret its authority in order that it may effectively function. So, throughout the world, have countless governmental and administrative organs and officials to interpret theirs. The General Assembly may thus in practice, by majority vote, interpret Charter provisions as giving it authority to pursue a certain course of action. It may continue to give the same interpretation to these Charter provisions in similar or different situations as they arise. In so doing action taken by it may be extended to cover circumstances and situations which had never been contemplated by those who framed the Charter. But this would not, for reasons which have already been given, necessarily involve any departure from the terms of the Charter.

On the other hand, the General Assembly may in practice construe its authority beyond that conferred upon it, either expressly or impliedly, by the Charter. It may, for example, interpret its powers to permit it to enter a field prohibited to it under the Charter or in disregard of the procedure prescribed in the Charter. Action taken by the General Assembly (or other organs) may accordingly on occasions be beyond power.

The Charter establishes an Organization. The Organization must function through its constituted organs. The functions and authorities of those organs are set out in the Charter. However the Charter is otherwise described the essential fact is that it is a multilateral treaty. It cannot be altered at the will of the majority of the Member States, no matter how often that will is expressed or asserted against a protesting minority and no matter how large be the majority of Member States which assert its will in this manner or how small the minority. . . .

In practice, if the General Assembly (or any organ) exceeds its authority there is little that the protesting minority may do except to protest and reserve its rights whatever they may be. If, however, the authority purported to be exercised against the objection of any Member State is beyond power it remains so.

So, if the General Assembly were to "intervene in matters which are essentially within the domestic jurisdiction of any State" within the meaning of Article 2(7) of the Charter, whatever be the meaning to be given to these words, that intervention would be the entering into a field prohibited to it under the Charter and be beyond the authority of the General Assembly. This would continue to be so, no matter how frequently and consistently the General Assembly had construed its authority to permit it to make intervention in matters essentially within the domestic jurisdiction of any States. The majority has no power to extend, alter or disregard the Charter.

Each organ of the United Nations, of course, has an inherent right to interpret the Charter in relation to its authority and functions. But the rule that they may do so is not in any case applicable without qualification. Their interpretation of their respective authorities under the Charter may conceivably conflict one with the other. They may agree. They may, after following a certain interpretation for many years, change it. In any case, their right to interpret the Charter gives them no power to alter it.

The question of constitutionality of action taken by the General Assembly or the Security Council will rarely call for consideration except within the United Nations itself, where a majority rule prevails. In practice this may enable action to be taken which is beyond power. When, however, the Court is called upon to pronounce upon a question whether certain authority exercised by an organ of the Organization is within the power of that organ, only legal considerations may be invoked and *de facto* extension of the Charter must be disregarded.

COMPETENCE OF THE GENERAL ASSEMBLY FOR THE ADMISSION OF A STATE TO THE UNITED NATIONS

Advisory Opinion of the International Court of Justice, 3 March 1950.
ICJ Reports, 1950, p. 4, at 15–19, 23–24.

Dissenting Opinion of Judge ALVAREZ . . . First of all it must be made perfectly clear that the Court has competence to interpret the Charter of the United Nations like any other instrument, without any limitations whatever.

It has been contended that the Court was not competent to interpret this treaty. That is not correct. Moreover, the Court has already taken an opportunity of asserting its competence in this respect (ICJ Reports 1947–1948, p. 61).

Legal texts can be interpreted by anyone; but when such an interpretation is made by an authorized organ, such as the General Assembly of the United Nations or the International Court of Justice, it presents a great practical value and creates precedents.

Because of the progressive tendencies of international life, it is necessary to-day to interpret treaties, as well as laws, in a different manner than was customary when international life showed few changes. This interpretation must be made in such a way as to ensure that institutions and rules of law shall continue to be in harmony with the new conditions in the life of the peoples.

There are two considerations which support this assertion. First, we observe that national courts, in their interpretation of private law, seek to adapt it to the exigencies of contemporary life, with the result that they have modified the law, sometimes swiftly and profoundly, even in countries where law is codified to such an extent that it is necessary to-day to take into consideration not only legal texts, but also case-law. It is the same, *a fortiori,* in the interpretation of international matter, because international life is much more dynamic than national life.

Again, because of this very dynamism, the political aspect of questions is tending to have precedence over the juridical aspect. We have a very important concrete illustration of this tendency. According to traditional international law, the state of war still exists between **the** Allies and Germany, since no peace treaty has yet been signed with the latter State. But this situation is considered unacceptable, and efforts are being made to bring it to an end.

It is therefore necessary to establish a theory, a technique of interpretation. This process will reveal great differences between the old system and the new one which will have to be applied henceforward.

The old system possessed the following characteristics:

A. No distinction was made between treaties: the same rules of interpretation were applied in all cases.

B. Those who interpreted the treaties were slaves, so to speak, of the wording. When the wording was clear, it had to be applied literally, without taking into account the possible consequences.

C. When a text was not clear, recourse was had to the *travaux préparatoires*.

D. The interpretation of a given text, notably of a treaty, was, so to speak, immutable. No change could be made, even if the matter considered had undergone modifications.

The new system of interpretation must present other characteristics:

(A) Distinctions must be made between different kinds of treaties. A bilateral treaty concerning an ordinary question, such as extradition, cannot be interpreted in the same way as a political treaty. Three categories of treaties must be specially recognized: peace treaties, in particular those affecting world peace; treaties creating principles of international law; and treaties creating an international organization, notably the world organization. All these possess both a political and a psychological character.

Peace treaties are dictated by material force; and those creating principles of international law, or international organizations, are created by the majority of the participating States, for the new signatories can only accept what has already been done. Consequently, these three categories of treaties are not to be interpreted literally, but primarily having regard to their purposes.

(B) The text must not be slavishly followed. If necessary, it must be vivified so as to harmonize it with the new conditions of international life.

When the wording of a text seems clear, that is not sufficient reason for following it literally, without taking into account the consequences of its application. Multilateral treaties are not drafted with the help of a dictionary, and their wording is often the result of a compromise which influences the terms used in the text.

In the case of the Polish Postal Service in Danzig, the Permanent Court of International Justice (PCIJ, Series B, No. 11, p. 39) decided that the words of a treaty must be interpreted according to their normal meaning, unless the interpretation would thus lead to unreasonable or absurd consequences.

It is necessary to add that to-day the same method must be observed when the provisions of a clause appear to run counter to the purposes of the institution concerned or to the new conditions of international life.

There is a decisive argument applicable to this question. It has long been held that treaties contained, implicitly, the clause *rebus sic stantibus*, according to which, when the fundamental conditions in which a treaty was made have become modified, the treaty ceases to have effect. The correctness of this clause is so manifest that it has recently been carried over from international to private law.

For the same reason, it must be recognized that even the clear provisions of a treaty must not be given effect, or must receive appropriate interpretation, when, as a result of modifications in international life, their application would lead to manifest injustice or to results contrary to the aims of the institution. For, otherwise, marked discrepancies would result between the written text and the reality; and that would be inadmissible.

But there is more: it is possible, by way of interpretation, to attribute to an institution rights which it does not possess according to the provisions by which it was created, provided that these rights are in harmony with the nature and objects of the said institution. Thus, for instance, in its Advisory Opinion of April 11th, 1949, on the Reparation for Injuries suffered by the United Nations, the International Court of Justice declared that, having in view the nature and objects of that institution, it was entitled to claim damages suffered not only by itself but by its agents in the performance of their duties. This Court has therefore attributed to the United Nations a right which was not expressly conferred on that Organization by the Charter and which, according to traditional international law, appertains solely to States. The Court, in so doing, created a right and, as I have already shown, it was entitled to do so.

A fortiori, the Court has the power to limit rights, or to give them an effect other than that prescribed by the literal text where the circumstances mentioned above make it necessary to do so.

(C) It will be necessary in future—unless in exceptional cases—when interpreting treaties, even those which are obscure, and especially those relating to international organizations, to exclude the consideration of the *travaux préparatoires,* which was formerly usual. The value of these documents has indeed progressively diminished, for different reasons: (*a*) they contain opinions of all kinds; moreover, States, and even committees, have at times put forward some idea and have later abandoned it in favor of another; (*b*) when States decide to sign a treaty, their decision is not influenced by the *travaux préparatoires*, with which, in many cases, they are unacquainted; (*c*) the increasing dynamism of international life makes it essential that the texts should continue to be in harmony with the new conditions of social life.

It is therefore necessary, when interpreting treaties—in particular, the Charter of the United Nations—to look ahead, that is to have regard to the new conditions, and not to look back, or have recourse to *travaux préparatoires*. A treaty or a text that has once been established acquires a life of its own. Consequently, in interpreting it we must have regard to the exigencies of contemporary life, rather than to the intentions of those who framed it.

(D) The interpretation of treaties must not remain immutable; it will have to be modified if important changes take place in the matter to which it relates.

It results from the foregoing considerations, that it is possible, by way of interpretation, to effect more or less important changes in treaties, including the Charter of the United Nations. That causes surprise to those who believe that this document is unchangeable, but such modifications are the natural consequence of the dynamism of international life. We have to choose between the maintenance of texts as immutable, even if they lead to unreasonable consequences, and the modification of these texts, if that becomes necessary. There cannot be any doubt as to the choice.

If the International Court of Justice were able by its judgments and advisory opinions to establish a doctrine of the limitation of the rights of States and a doctrine of the misuse of rights, and in addition a new doctrine concerning the interpretation of treaties, it would be rendering important services to international law and to the cause of peace.

. . .

Dissenting Opinion of Judge AZEVEDO . . . First of all, the commentator [the interpreter of the Charter] is struck by the very unusual stress put by the Charter on the aims and principles of the Organization; by a unanimous vote, the signatories also stressed that the obligations assumed by the Members must be carried out in good faith.

That is why the interpretation of the San Francisco instruments will always have to present a teleological character if they are to meet the requirements of world peace, co-operation between men, individual freedom and social progress. The Charter is a means and not an end. To comply with its aims one must seek the methods of interpretation most likely to serve the natural evolution of the needs of mankind.

Even more than in the applications of municipal law, the meaning and the scope of international texts must continually be perfected, even if the terms remain unchanged. This proposition is acceptable to any dogmatic system of law, and even to those who hold that law should be autonomous and free from the interference of forces, tendencies or influences alien to its proper sphere.

Literal interpretation will not prevail, even through the sinister adage *fiat justitia pereat mundus*. The aims of the United Nations must be served so that mankind may flourish.

SOUTH–WEST AFRICA CASES

Judgment of the International Court of Justice, 18 July 1966.
ICJ Reports, 1966, p. 6, at 352–53.

Dissenting Opinion of Judge JESSUP: . . . The task of interpretation in this case requires the Court to ascertain what meaning must be given to certain important provisions of the Covenant of the League of Nations, and of the Mandate for South West Africa.

At the outset:

" . . . one must bear in mind that in the interpretation of a great international constitutional instrument, like the United Nations Charter, the individualistic concepts which are generally adequate in the interpretation of ordinary treaties do not suffice.[1]" (Separate opinion of Judge de Visscher, Status of South West Africa, I.C.J. Reports 1950, p. 189.)

In particular it is true that one cannot understand or analyze the proceedings of a great international conference like those at Paris or San Francisco if one regards it as essentially the same as a meeting between John Doe and Richard Roe for the purpose of signing a contract for the sale of bricks.

"But lawyers who are trained in the methods of interpretation applied by an English court should bear in mind that English draftsmanship tends to be more detailed than continental, and it receives, and perhaps demands a more literal interpretation. Similarly, diplomatic documents, including treaties, do not as a rule invite the very strict methods of interpretation that an English court applies, for example, to an Act of Parliament." (The Law of Nations by J. L. Brierly, 6th ed., 1963, by Sir Humphrey Waldock, p. 325.)

It may be agreed that there are dangers in dealing with multipartite treaties as "international legislation," but if municipal law precedents are invoked in the interpretative process, those precedents dealing with constitutional or statutory construction are more likely to be in point than ones dealing with the interpretation of contracts.

DRAFT ARTICLES ON THE LAW OF TREATIES

Adopted by the International Law Commission, 18–19 July 1966.
UN Doc. A/6348 (9 August 1966), pp. 13–14.

Article 27. *General Rule of Interpretation*

1. A treaty shall be interpreted in good faith in accordance with the ordinary meaning to be given to the terms of the treaty in their context and in the light of its object and purpose.

---

[1] One recalls the famous apothegm of Chief Justice Marshall in McCulloch v. Maryland (4 Wheat. 407): "We must never forget that it is a constitution we are expounding."

2. The context for the purpose of the interpretation of a treaty shall comprise, in addition to the text, including its preamble and annexes:

(a) any agreement relating to the treaty which was made between all the parties in connexion with the conclusion of the treaty;

(b) any instrument which was made by one or more parties in connexion with the conclusion of the treaty and accepted by the other parties as an instrument related to the treaty.

3. There shall be taken into account, together with the context:

(a) any subsequent agreement between the parties regarding the interpretation of the treaty;

(b) any subsequent practice in the application of the treaty which establishes the understanding of the parties regarding its interpretation;

(c) any relevant rules of international law applicable in the relations between the parties.

4. A special meaning shall be given to a term if it is established that the parties so intended.

Article 28.   *Supplementary Means of Interpretation*

Recourse may be had to supplementary means of interpretation, including the preparatory work of the treaty and the circumstances of its conclusion, in order to confirm the meaning resulting from the application of article 27, or to determine the meaning when the interpretation according to article 27:

(a) leaves the meaning ambiguous or obscure; or

(b) leads to a result which is manifestly absurd or unreasonable.

Article 29.   *Interpretation of Treaties in Two or More Languages*

1. When a treaty has been authenticated in two or more languages, the text is equally authoritative in each language, unless the treaty provides or the parties agree that, in case of divergence, a particular text shall prevail.

2. A version of the treaty in a language other than one of those in which the text was authenticated shall be considered an authentic text only if the treaty so provides or the parties so agree.

3. The terms of the treaty are presumed to have the same meaning in each authentic text. Except in the case mentioned in paragraph 1, when a comparison of the texts discloses a difference of meaning which the application of articles 27 and 28 does not remove, a meaning which as far as possible reconciles the texts shall be adopted.

NOTE. In reading the cases which follow keep in mind the following questions:

1. Which questions should be considered by the International Court of Justice and which by other organs of the United Nations?

2. In particular, should the Court consider legal questions which are closely related to political issues or as to which United Nations Members are in strong disagreement? In what cases should the Court refuse to give an opinion?

3. What is in fact the difference between advisory opinions of the Court and its judgments?

4. Which of the methods of interpretation discussed in this Chapter are actually followed by the Court and by the other organs of the United Nations?

5. Do the methods of interpretation used by the Court differ from those employed by other organs of the United Nations?

Chapter II

INTERNATIONAL STATUS OF THE UNITED NATIONS

SAN FRANCISCO STATEMENTS

NOTE. The records of the San Francisco Conference throw very little light on the international status of the United Nations.

On 23 May 1945, the following discussion took place in Committee IV/2 of the Conference:

"The Committee discussed the question whether the Charter should include an article concerning the international or juridical status of the Organization. The following Belgian proposal was commented on by several delegates: 'The Parties to the present Charter recognize that the Organization they are setting up possesses international status, together with the rights this involves.' In favor of the proposal it was urged that since international status for the Organization was implied in certain parts of the Charter, a specific provision should be made. The League of Nations had found it necessary to arrange for a status enabling it to lease property and make contracts, and provision had been made for international status of UNRRA.

"One delegate felt that the proposal needed clarification, since the Organization might have the necessary status to contract and hold property under internal law, particularly in the state where its seat would be established, without having an international status like that of states. Another delegate expressed the view that the international legal status of the Organization should be defined later by the General Assembly. The suggestion was made by another delegate that 'juridical' rather than 'international' personality or status would be a better term, as susceptible of definition in such a way as to distinguish it from the status enjoyed by states in international law. A further suggestion was that the Charter should enumerate with some exactness the incidents of the legal status the Organization would possess." UNCIO Doc. 554, IV/2/28; 13 UNCIO Documents, pp. 622–23.

After a report from a subcommittee, the Committee approved the following statement in its final report:

"The Committee recommends for inclusion in the Charter the following text:

" 'The Organization shall enjoy in the territory of each of its members such legal capacity as may be necessary for the exercise of its functions and the fulfillment of its purposes.'

"It is to be noted that this provision is conceived in very general terms. It is confined to a statement of the obligation incumbent upon each member State to act in such a way that the Organization enjoys in its territory a juridical status permitting it to exercise its functions. The Organization must be able, in its own name, to contract, to hold movable and immovable property, to appear in court. These are only examples. The Committee has preferred to express no opinion on the procedures of internal law necessary to assure this result. These procedures may differ according to the legislation of each member State. It is possible that among the majority of them it may be indispensable that the Organization be recognized as a juridical personality.

"As regards the question of international juridical personality, the Committee has considered it superfluous to make this the subject of a text. In effect, it will be determined implicitly from the provisions of the Charter taken as a whole." UNCIO Doc. 933, IV/2/42(2), p. 8; 13 UNCIO Documents, p. 703, at 710.

REPARATION FOR INJURIES SUFFERED IN THE SERVICE OF THE UNITED NATIONS

Advisory Opinion of the International Court of Justice, 11 April 1949. ICJ Reports, 1949, pp. 174–88, 198–99, 216, 217–19.

On December 3rd, 1948, the General Assembly of the United Nations adopted the following Resolution:

"Whereas the series of tragic events which have lately befallen agents of the United Nations engaged in the performance of their duties raises, with greater urgency then ever, the question of the arrangements to be made by the United Nations with a view to ensuring to its agents the fullest measure of protection in the future and ensuring that reparation be made for the injuries suffered; and

"Whereas it is highly desirable that the Secretary-General should be able to act without question as efficaciously as possible with a view to obtaining any reparation due; therefore

"The General Assembly

"Decides to submit the following legal questions to the International Court of Justice for an advisory opinion:

" 'I. In the event of an agent of the United Nations in the performance of his duties suffering injury in circumstances involving the responsibility of a State, has the United Nations, as an Organization, the capacity to bring an international claim against the responsible *de jure* or *de facto* government with a view to obtaining the reparation due in respect of the damage caused (*a*) to the United Nations, (*b*) to the victim or to persons entitled through him?

" 'II. In the event of an affirmative reply on point I (*b*), how is action by the United Nations to be reconciled with such rights as may be possessed by the State of which the victim is a national?' . . . "

. . .

It will be useful to make the following preliminary observations:

(*a*) The Organization of the United Nations will be referred to usually, but not invariably, as "the Organization".

(*b*) Questions I (*a*) and I (*b*) refer to "an international claim against the responsible *de jure* or *de facto* government". The Court understands that these questions are directed to claims against a State, and will, therefore, in this opinion, use the expression "State" or "defendant State".

(c) The Court understands the word "agent" in the most liberal sense, that is to say, any person who, whether a paid official or not, and whether permanently employed or not, has been charged by an organ of the Organization with carrying out, or helping to carry out, one of its functions—in short, any person through whom it acts.

(d) As this question assumes an injury suffered in such circumstances as to involve a State's responsibility, it must be supposed, for the purpose of this Opinion, that the damage results from a failure by the State to perform obligations of which the purpose is to protect the agents of the Organization in the performance of their duties.

(e) The position of a defendant State which is not a member of the Organization is dealt with later, and for the present the Court will assume that the defendant State is a Member of the Organization.

The questions asked of the Court relate to the "capacity to bring an international claim"; accordingly, we must begin by defining what is meant by that capacity, and consider the characteristics of the Organization, so as to determine whether, in general, these characteristics do, or do not, include for the Organization a right to present an international claim.

Competence to bring an international claim is, for those possessing it, the capacity to resort to the customary methods recognized by international law for the establishment, the presentation and the settlement of claims. Among these methods may be mentioned protest, request for an enquiry, negotiation, and request for submission to an arbitral tribunal or to the Court in so far as this may be authorized by the Statute.

This capacity certainly belongs to the State; a State can bring an international claim against another State. Such a claim takes the form of a claim between two political entities, equal in law, similar in form, and both the direct subjects of international law. It is dealt with by means of negotiation, and cannot, in the present state of the law as to international jurisdiction, be submitted to a tribunal, except with the consent of the States concerned.

When the Organization brings a claim against one of its Members, this claim will be presented in the same manner, and regulated by the same procedure. It may, when necessary, be supported by the political means at the disposal of the Organization. In these ways the Organization would find a method for securing the observance of its rights by the Member against which it has a claim.

But, in the international sphere, has the Organization such a nature as involves the capacity to bring an international claim? In order to answer this question, the Court must first enquire whether the Charter has given the Organization such a position that it possesses, in regard to its Members, rights which it is entitled to ask them to respect. In other words, does the Organization possess international personality? This is no doubt a doctrinal expression, which has sometimes given rise to controversy. But it will be used here to mean that if the Organization is recognized as having that personality, it is an entity capable of availing itself of obligations incumbent upon its Members.

To answer this question, which is not settled by the actual terms of the Charter, we must consider what characteristics it was intended thereby to give to the Organization.

The subjects of law in any legal system are not necessarily identical in their nature or in the extent of their rights, and their nature depends upon the needs of the community. Throughout its history, the development of international law has been influenced by the requirements of international life, and the progressive increase in the collective activities of States has already given rise to instances of action upon the international plane by certain entities which are not States. This development culminated in the establishment in June 1945 of an international organization whose purposes and principles are specified in the Charter of the United Nations. But to achieve these ends the attribution of international personality is indispensable.

The Charter has not been content to make the Organization created by it merely a centre "for harmonizing the actions of nations in the attainment of these common ends" (Article 1, para. 4). It has equipped that centre with organs, and has given it special tasks. It has defined the position of the Members in relation to the Organization by requiring them to give it every assistance in any action undertaken by it (Article 2, para. 5), and to accept and carry out the decisions of the Security Council; by authorizing the General Assembly to make recommendations to the Members; by giving the Organization legal capacity and privileges and immunities in the territory of each of its Members; and by providing for the conclusion of agreements between the Organization and its Members. Practice—in particular the conclusion of conventions to which the Organization is a party—has confirmed this character of the Organization, which occupies a position in certain respects in detachment from its Members, and which is under a duty to remind them, if need be, of certain obligations. It must be added that the Organization is a political body, charged with political tasks of an important character, and covering a wide field namely, the maintenance of international peace and security, the development of friendly relations among nations, and the achievement of international co-operation in the solution of problems of an economic, social, cultural or humanitarian character (Article 1); and in dealing with its Members it employs political means. The "Convention on the Privileges and Immunities of the United Nations" of 1946 creates rights and duties between each of the signatories and the Organization (see, in particular, Section 35). It is difficult to see how such a convention could operate except upon the international plane and as between parties possessing international personality.

In the opinion of the Court, the Organization was intended to exercise and enjoy, and is in fact exercising and enjoying, functions and rights which can only be explained on the basis of the possession of a large measure of international personality and the capacity to operate upon an international plane. It is at present the supreme type of international organization, and it could not carry out the intentions of its founders if it was devoid of international personality. It must be acknowledged that its Members, by entrusting certain functions to it, with the attendant duties and responsibilities, have clothed it with the competence required to enable those functions to be effectively discharged.

Accordingly, the Court has come to the conclusion that the Organization is an international person. That is not the same thing as saying that it is a State, which it certainly is not, or that its legal personality and rights and duties are the same as those of a State. Still less is it the same thing as saying that it is "a super-State", whatever that expression may mean. It does not even imply that all its rights and duties must be upon the international plane, any more than all the rights and duties of a State must be upon that plane. What it does mean is that it is a subject of international law and capable of possessing international rights and duties, and that it has capacity to maintain its rights by bringing international claims.

The next question is whether the sum of the international rights of the Organization comprises the right to bring the kind of international claim described in the Request for this Opinion. That is a claim against a State to obtain reparation in respect of the damage caused by the injury of an agent of the Organization in the course of the performance of his duties. Whereas a State possesses the totality of international rights and duties recognized by international law, the rights and duties of an entity such as the Organization must depend upon its purposes and functions as specified or implied in its constituent documents and developed in practice. The functions of the Organization are of such a character that they could not be effectively discharged if they involved the concurrent action, on the international plane, of fifty-eight or more Foreign Offices, and the Court concludes that the Members have endowed the Organization with capacity to bring international claims when necessitated by the discharge of its functions.

What is the position as regards the claims mentioned in the request for an opinion? Question I is divided into two points, which must be considered in turn.

Question I (*a*) is as follows:

"In the event of an agent of the United Nations in the performance of his duties suffering injury in circumstances involving the responsibility of a State, has the United Nations, as an Organization, the capacity to bring an international claim against the responsible *de jure* or *de facto* government with a view to obtaining the reparation due in respect of the damage caused (*a*) to the United Nations . . . ? "

The question is concerned solely with the reparation of damage caused to the Organization when one of its agents suffers injury at the same time. It cannot be doubted that the Organization has the capacity to bring an international claim against one of its Members which has caused injury to it by a breach of its international obligations towards it. The damage specified in Question I (*a*) means exclusively damage caused to the interests of the Organization itself, to its administrative machine, to its property and assets, and to the interests of which it is the guardian. It is clear that the Organization has the capacity to bring a claim for this damage. As the claim is based on the breach of an international obligation on the part of the Member held responsible by the Organization, the Member cannot contend that this obligation is governed by municipal law, and the Organization is justified in giving its claim the character of an international claim.

When the Organization has sustained damage resulting from a breach by a Member of its international obligations, it is impossible to see how it can obtain reparation unless it possesses capacity to bring an international claim. It cannot be supposed that in such an event all the Members of the Organization, save the defendant State, must combine to bring a claim against the defendant for the damage suffered by the Organization.

The Court is not called upon to determine the precise extent of the reparation which the Organization would be entitled to recover. It may, however, be said that the measure of the reparation should depend upon the amount of the damage which the Organization has suffered as the result of the wrongful act or omission of the defendant State and should be calculated in accordance with the rules of international law. Amongst other things, this damage would include the reimbursement of any reasonable compensation which the Organization had to pay to its agent or to persons entitled through him. Again, the death or disablement of one of its agents engaged upon a distant mission might involve very considerable expenditure in replacing him. These are mere illustrations, and the Court cannot pretend to forecast all the kinds of damage which the Organization itself might sustain.

Question I (*b*) is as follows:

. . . "has the United Nations, as an Organization, the capacity to bring an international claim . . . in respect of the damage caused . . . (*b*) to the victim or to persons entitled through him? "

In dealing with the question of law which arises out of Question I (*b*), it is unnecessary to repeat the considerations which led to an affirmative answer being given to Question I (*a*). It can now be assumed that the Organization has the capacity to bring a claim on the international plane, to negotiate, to conclude a special agreement and to prosecute a claim before an international tribunal. The only legal question which remains to be considered is whether, in the course of bringing an international claim of this kind, the Organization can recover "the reparation due in respect of the damage caused . . . to the victim . . .".

The traditional rule that diplomatic protection is exercised by the national State does not involve the giving of a negative answer to Question I (*b*).

In the first place, this rule applies to claims brought by a State. But here we have the different and new case of a claim that would be brought by the Organization.

In the second place, even in inter-State relations, there are important exceptions to the rule, for there are cases in which protection may be exercised by a State on behalf of persons not having its nationality.

In the third place, the rule rests on two bases. The first is that the defendant State has broken an obligation towards the national State in respect of its nationals. The second is that only the party to whom an international obligation is due can bring a claim in respect of its breach. This is precisely what happens when the Organization, in bringing a claim for damage suffered by its agent, does so by invoking the breach of an obligation towards itself. Thus, the rule of the nationality of claims affords no reason against recognizing that the Organization has the right to bring a claim for the damage referred to in Question I (*b*). On the contrary, the principle underlying this rule leads to the recognition of this capacity as belonging to the Organization, when the Organization invokes, as the ground of its claim, a breach of an obligation towards itself.

Nor does the analogy of the traditional rule of diplomatic protection of nationals abroad justify in itself an affirmative reply. It is not possible, by a strained use of the concept of allegiance, to assimilate the legal bond which exists, under Article 100 of the Charter, between the Organization on the one hand, and the Secretary-General and the staff on the other, to the bond of nationality existing between a State and its nationals.

The Court is here faced with a new situation. The questions to which it gives rise can only be solved by realizing that the situation is dominated by the provisions of the Charter considered in the light of the principles of international law.

The question lies within the limits already established; that is to say it presupposes that the injury for which the reparation is demanded arises from a breach of an obligation designed to help an agent of the Organization in the performance of his duties. It is not a case in which the wrongful act or omission would merely constitute a breach of the general obligations of a State concerning the position of aliens; claims made under this head would be within the competence of the national State and not, as a general rule, within that of the Organization.

The Charter does not expressly confer upon the Organization the capacity to include, in its claim for reparation, damage caused to the victim or to persons entitled through him. The Court must therefore begin by enquiring whether the provisions of the Charter concerning the functions of the Organization, and the part played by its agents in the performance of those functions, imply for the Organization power to afford its agents the limited protection that would consist in the bringing of a claim on their behalf for reparation for damage suffered in such circumstances. Under international law, the Organization must be deemed to have those powers which, though not expressly provided in the Charter, are conferred upon it by necessary implication as being essential to the performance of its duties. This principle of law was applied by the Permanent Court of International Justice to the International Labour Organization in its Advisory Opinion No. 13 of July 23rd, 1926 (Series B., No. 13, p. 18), and must be applied to the United Nations.

Having regard to its purposes and functions already referred to, the Organization may find it necessary, and has in fact found it necessary, to entrust its agents with important missions to be performed in disturbed parts of the world. Many missions, from their very nature, involve the agents in unusual dangers to which ordinary persons are not exposed. For the same reason, the injuries suffered by its agents in these circumstances will sometimes have occurred in such a manner that their national State would not be justified in bringing a claim for reparation on the ground of diplomatic protection, or, at any rate, would not feel disposed to do so. Both to ensure the efficient and independent performance of these missions and to afford effective support to its agents, the Organization must provide them with adequate protection.

This need of protection for the agents of the Organization, as a condition of the performance of its functions, has already been realized, and the Preamble to the Resolution of December 3rd, 1948 [*supra*, p. 249], shows that this was the unanimous view of the General Assembly.

For this purpose, the Members of the Organization have entered into certain undertakings, some of which are in the Charter and others in complementary agreements. The content of these undertakings need not be described here; but the Court must stress the importance of the duty to render to the Organization "every assistance" which is accepted by the Members in Article 2, paragraph 5, of the Charter. It must be noted that the effective working of the Organization—the accomplishment of its task, and the independence and effectiveness of the work of its agents—require that these undertakings should be strictly observed. For that purpose, it is necessary that, when an infringement occurs, the Organization should be able to call upon the responsible State to remedy its default, and, in particular, to obtain from the State reparation for the damage that the default may have caused to its agent.

In order that the agent may perform his duties satisfactorily, he must feel that this protection is assured to him by the Organization, and that he may count on it. To ensure the independence of the agent, and, consequently, the independent action of the Organization itself, it is essential that in performing his duties he need not have to rely on any other protection than that of the Organization (save of course for the more direct and immediate protection due from the State in whose territory he may be). In particular, he should not have to rely on the protection of his own State. If he had to rely on that State, his independence might well be compromised, contrary to the principle applied by Article 100 of the Charter. And lastly, it is essential that—whether the agent belongs to a powerful or to a weak State; to one more affected or less affected by the complications of international life; to one in sympathy or not in sympathy with the mission of the agent—he should know that in the performance of his duties he is under the protection of the Organization. This assurance is even more necessary when the agent is stateless.

Upon examination of the character of the functions entrusted to the Organization and of the nature of the missions of its agents, it becomes clear that the capacity of the Organization to exercise a measure of functional protection of its agents arises by necessary intendment out of the Charter.

The obligations entered into by States to enable the agents of the Organization to perform their duties are undertaken not in the interest of the agents, but in that of the Organization. When it claims redress for a breach of these obligations, the Organization is invoking its own right, the right that the obligations due to it should be respected. On this ground, it asks for reparation of the injury suffered, for "it is a principle of international law that the breach of an engagement involves an obligation to make reparation in an adequate form"; as was stated by the Permanent Court in its Judgment No. 8 of July 26th, 1927 (Series A., No. 9, p. 21). In claiming reparation based on the injury suffered by its agent, the Organization does not represent the agent, but is asserting its own right, the right to secure respect for undertakings entered into towards the Organization.

Having regard to the foregoing considerations, and to the undeniable right of the Organization to demand that its Members shall fulfil the obligations entered into by them in the interest of the good working of the Organization, the Court is of the opinion that, in the case of a breach of these obligations, the Organization has the capacity to claim adequate reparation, and that in assessing this reparation it is authorized to include the damage suffered by the victim or by persons entitled through him.

The question remains whether the Organization has "the capacity to bring an international claim against the responsible *de jure* or *de facto* government with a view to obtaining the reparation due in respect of the damage caused (*a*) to the United Nations, (*b*) to the victim or to persons entitled through him" when the defendant State is not a member of the Organization.

In considering this aspect of Question I(*a*) and (*b*), it is necessary to keep in mind the reasons which have led the Court to give an affirmative answer to it when the defendant State is a Member of the Organization. It has now been established that the Organization has capacity to bring claims on the international plane, and that it possesses a right of functional protection in respect of its agents. Here again the Court is authorized to assume that the damage suffered involves the responsibility of a State, and it is not called upon to express an opinion upon the various ways in which that responsibility might be engaged. Accordingly the question is whether the Organization has capacity to bring a claim against the defendant State to recover reparation in respect of that damage or whether, on the contrary, the defendant State, not being a member, is justified in raising the objection that the Organization lacks the capacity to bring an international claim. On this point, the Court's opinion is that fifty States, representing the vast majority of the members of the international community, had the power, in conformity with international law, to bring into being an entity possessing objective international personality, and not merely personality recognized by them alone, together with capacity to bring international claims.

Accordingly, the Court arrives at the conclusion that an affirmative answer should be given to Question I (*a*) and (*b*) whether or not the defendant State is a Member of the United Nations.

Question II is as follows:

"In the event of an affirmative reply on point I (*b*), how is action by the United Nations to be reconciled with such rights as may be possessed by the State of which the victim is a national?"

The affirmative reply given by the Court on point I (*b*) obliges it now to examine Question II. When the victim has a nationality, cases can clearly occur in which the injury suffered by him may engage the interest both of his national State and of the Organization. In such an event, competition between the State's right of diplomatic protection and the Organization's right of functional protection might arise, and this is the only case with which the Court is invited to deal.

In such a case, there is no rule of law which assigns priority to the one or to the other, or which compels either the State or the Organization to refrain from bringing an international claim. The Court sees no reason why the parties concerned should not find solutions inspired by goodwill and common sense, and as between the Organization and its Members it draws attention to their duty to render "every assistance" provided by Article 2, paragraph 5, of the Charter.

Although the bases of the two claims are different, that does not mean that the defendant State can be compelled to pay the reparation due in respect of the damage twice over. International tribunals are already familiar with the problem of a claim in which two or more national States are interested, and they know how to protect the defendant State in such a case.

The risk of competition between the Organization and the national State can be reduced or eliminated either by a general convention or by agreements entered into in each particular case. There is no doubt that in due course a practice will be developed, and it is worthy of note that already certain States whose nationals have been injured in the performance of missions undertaken for the Organization have shown a reasonable and co-operative disposition to find a practical solution.

The question of reconciling action by the Organization with the rights of a national State may arise in another way; that is to say when the agent bears the nationality of the defendant State.

The ordinary practice whereby a State does not exercise protection on behalf of one of its nationals against a State which regards him as its own national, does not constitute a precedent which is relevant here. The action of the Organization is in fact based not upon the nationality of the victim, but upon his status as agent of the Organization. Therefore it does not matter whether or not the State to which the claim is addressed regards him as its own national, because the question of nationality is not pertinent to the admissibility of the claim.

In law, therefore, it does not seem that the fact of the possession of the nationality of the defendant State by the agent constitutes any obstacle to a claim brought by the Organization for a breach of obligations towards it occurring in relation to the performance of his mission by that agent.

For these reasons,

The Court is of opinion

On Question I (a):

(i) unanimously,

That, in the event of an agent of the United Nations in the performance of his duties suffering injury in circumstances involving the responsibility of a Member State, the United Nations as an Organization has the capacity to bring an international claim against the responsible *de jure* or *de facto* government with a view to obtaining the reparation due in respect of the damage caused to the United Nations.

(ii) unanimously,

That, in the event of an agent of the United Nations in the performance of his duties suffering injury in circumstances involving the responsibility of a State which is not a member, the United Nations as an Organization has the capacity to bring an international claim against the responsible *de jure* or *de facto* government with a view to obtaining the reparation due in respect of the damage caused to the United Nations.

On Question I (b):

(i) by eleven votes against four,

That, in the event of an agent of the United Nations in the performance of his duties suffering injury in circumstances involving the responsibility of a Member State, the United Nations as an Organization has the capacity to bring an international claim against the responsible *de jure* or *de facto* government with a view to obtaining the reparation due in respect of the damage caused to the victim or to persons entitled through him.

(ii) by eleven votes against four,

That, in the event of an agent of the United Nations in the performance of his duties suffering injury in circumstances involving the responsibility of a State which is not a member, the United Nations as an Organization has the capacity to bring an international claim against the responsible *de jure* or *de facto* government with a view to obtaining the reparation due in respect of the damage caused to the victim or to persons entitled through him.

On Question II:

By ten votes against five,

When the United Nations as an Organization is bringing a claim for reparation of damage caused to its agent, it can only do so by basing its claim upon a breach of obligations due to itself; respect for this rule will usually prevent a conflict between the action of the United Nations and such rights as the agent's national State may possess, and thus bring about a reconciliation between their claims; moreover, this reconciliation must depend upon considerations applicable to each particular case, and upon agreements to be made between the Organization and individual States, either generally or in each case.

. . .

Dissenting Opinion by Judge HACKWORTH. . . . It is stated in the majority opinion that the Charter does not expressly provide that the Organization should have capacity to include, in "its claim for reparation", damage caused to the victim or to persons entitled through him, but the conclusion is reached that such power is conferred by necessary implication. This appears to be based on the assumption that, to ensure the efficient and independent performance of missions entrusted to agents of the Organization, and to afford them moral support, the exercise of this power is necessary.

The conclusion that power in the Organization to sponsor private claims is conferred by "necessary implication" is not believed to be warranted under rules laid down by tribunals for filling lacunæ in specific grants of power.

There can be no gainsaying the fact that the Organization is one of delegated and enumerated powers. It is to be presumed that such powers as the Member States desired to confer upon it are stated either in the Charter or in complementary agreements concluded by them. Powers not expressed cannot freely be implied. Implied powers flow from a grant of expressed powers, and are limited to those that are "necessary" to the exercise of powers expressly granted. No necessity for the exercise of the power here in question has been shown to exist. There is no impelling reason, if any at all, why the Organization should become the sponsor of claims on behalf of its employees, even though limited to those arising while the employee is in line of duty. These employees are still nationals of their respective countries, and the customary methods of handling such claims are still available in full vigour. The prestige and efficiency of the Organization will be safeguarded by an exercise of its undoubted right under point I(a) *supra*. Even here it is necessary to imply power, but, as stated above, the necessity is self-evident. The exercise of an additional extraordinary power in the field of private claims has not been shown to be necessary to the efficient performance of duty by either the Organization or its agents.

But we are presented with an analogy between the relationship of a State to its nationals and the relationship of the Organization to its employees; also an analogy between functions of a State in the protection of its nationals and functions of the Organization in the protection of its employees.

The results of this liberality of judicial construction transcend, by far, anything to be found in the Charter of the United Nations, as well as any known purpose entertained by the drafters of the Charter.

These supposed analogies, even assuming that they may have some semblance of reality, which I do not admit, cannot avail to give jurisdiction, where jurisdiction is otherwise lacking. Capacity of the Organization to act in the field here in question must rest upon a more solid foundation. . . .

Dissenting Opinion by Judge BADAWI PASHA. . . . According to the rules in force, the Organization has the capacity to make international claims, when one of its agents (in the widest sense) has suffered injury in the performance of his duty, for the damage referred to in Question I(a). This damage may include the damage suffered by the victim, in so far as this was provided for in the contract of service. But there is nothing to prevent temporary agents, mediators or members of commissions from entering into contracts for reparation due to them in the event of injury sustained in the performance of their duties, whenever the nature of their duties or missions obliges them to expose themselves to danger in the territories of States where they may have to perform these duties or carry out these missions.

This form of reparation will be for the interested parties more direct, more effective and more immediate than any right of making an international claim that might be accorded to the Organization on their behalf. . . .

Dissenting Opinion by Judge KRYLOV. I agree with the Court's Opinion to the effect that the United Nations Organization has the right to bring an international claim with a view to obtaining reparation for damage caused to the Organization itself; i. e., I reply in the affirmative to Question I(a) put to the Court by the General Assembly. It is beyond doubt that the Organization is entitled to defend its patrimony; in particular, to claim compensation for direct damage caused to itself, including disbursements in cases where an official of the Organization has suffered injury in the performance of his duties: for example, funeral expenses, medical expenses, insurance premiums, etc. In my opinion an affirmative reply to Question I(a) fully meets the practical requirements referred to by the Secretary-General of the United Nations.

I agree in a large measure with the arguments used in the dissenting opinions of Judges Hackworth and Badawi Pasha, and I believe that the United Nations Organization is not entitled, according to the international law in force, to claim compensation for injuries suffered by its agents.

The majority of the Court has founded this right to bring a claim on the right of functional protection exercised by the Organization in regard to its officials and—more generally—its agents.

I entirely associate myself with the desire unanimously expressed by the General Assembly of the United Nations in the recital clauses of its Resolution of December 3rd, 1948, of "ensuring to its agents the fullest measure of protection . . . .".

But I consider that this aim should be attained *proprio modo*, i. e., by the elaboration and conclusion of a general convention. I think that the problem should be approached in the same way as in the Convention concerning the Privileges and Immunities of the Organization, of representatives of governments and of the officials of the Organization.

To affirm, in the Court's Opinion, a right of the Organization to afford international protection to its agents as an already existing right, would be to introduce a new rule into international law and—what is more—a rule which would be concurrent with that of diplomatic protection which appertains to every State vis-à-vis its nationals.

The alleged new rule of functional protection will give rise to conflicts or collisions with the international law in force. The Court is not entitled to create a right of functional protection which is unknown in existing international law.

The Court itself states that it is confronted with a "new situation", but it considers itself authorized to reason—if I may so express it— *de lege ferenda.*

I am also unable to associate myself with the following affirmations of the majority of the Court. The Court considers that it may understand the term "agent" in the very widest sense. I think that the term "agent" must be interpreted restrictively. The representatives of the governments accredited to the Organization and the members of the different delegations are not agents of the Organization. Nor are the representatives of the governments in the different commissions of the United Nations agents of that Organization.

The conflict between the existing rules of international law (diplomatic protection of nationals) and the rules declared by the Court to be in existence—i. e., the rules of functional protection—is still further intensified by the fact that the majority of the Court even declares that the protection afforded by the United Nations Organization to its agent may be exercised against the State of which the agent is a national. We are thus far outside the limits of the international law in force.

I have not lost sight of the fact that the protection afforded by the United Nations is only functional, i. e., it is only asserted in cases where the agent of the organization is "performing his duties", but the conflict between the two methods of protection—that of the United Nations Organization and that of the State—nevertheless subsists.

It should also be observed that the relations between a State and its nationals are matters which belong essentially to the national competence of the State. The functional protection proclaimed by the Court is in contradiction with that well-established rule.

I therefore feel justified in asserting that the protection by the United Nations Organization of its agents could not be well founded from the standpoint of the international law in force, even if we are considering the relations between the United Nations and its Members.

Still less is it possible to assert this right of the United Nations Organization vis-à-vis non-member States. It is true that paragraph 6 of Article 2 of the Charter lays down that States which are not members of the United Nations should act in accordance with the Principles of the Organization (Chapter I of the Charter) "so far as may be necessary for the maintenance of international peace and security". But this paragraph has very little connexion with the right of the

United Nations to bring an international claim with a view to obtaining reparation for damage.

It is true that the non-member States cannot fail to recognize the existence of the United Nations as an objective fact. But, in order that they may be bound by a legal obligation to the Organization, it is necessary that the latter should conclude a special agreement with these States.

I associate myself with the concern of the majority of the Court to find appropriate legal means whereby the United Nations may attain its objects—i. e., in the present case, protect its agents. But, as I have already said, we must found the right of the Organization to bring an international claim in order to protect its agent on the express consent of the States, either by the preparation and conclusion of a general convention, or by agreements concluded between the Organization and the respective States in each individual case.

In my view, the Court cannot sanction by its Opinion the creation of a new rule of international law, particularly in the present case, where the new rule might entail a number of complications.

The majority of the Court has in view the functional protection of an agent of the United Nations Organization, even as against the national State of the agent. But it has not borne in mind, for example, the opposite—and possible—situation in which the said State may find it desirable and necessary to protect the agent against the acts of the Organization itself.

The Court can only interpret and develop the international law in force; it can only adjudicate in conformity with international law. In the present case, the Court cannot found an affirmative reply to Question I(*b*) either on the existing international convention or on international custom (as evidence of a general practice), or again, on any general principle of law (recognized by the nations).

[Individual opinions by Judges Alvarez and Azevedo and the statement of dissent by Judge Winiarski are omitted.]

NOTE.—1. On the basis of this advisory opinion, the Secretary-General of the United Nations presented the following proposals to the General Assembly (A/955; GAOR, IV, Sixth C., Annex, pp. 19–20):

"The advisory opinion of the Court gives an adequate legal basis for the consideration of further action. The Secretary-General proposes that the General Assembly should accept the advisory opinion of the Court as an authoritative expression of international law on the questions considered.

"Assuming such acceptance of the advisory opinion, the following questions remain to be decided: (1) Should the United Nations proceed to present claims for the deaths or injury of its agents in cases in which the responsibility of a State may appear to be involved? (2) What procedure should be followed in the presentation of such claims? (3) What policy should be followed with respect to damages?

"Question (1). The Secretary-General is strongly of the opinion that the United Nations should proceed to present claims for the deaths or injury of its agents in cases in which the responsibility of a State may appear to be involved. It is of the highest importance for the functioning of the Organization that its agents receive the requisite protection. Where the breach of the obligation of a State to afford protection has taken place and the Organization or its agent has suffered material damage, adequate compensation should be requested in order to ensure respect for such obligations in the future. In this connexion, attention is called to the comment by the Acting Mediator for Palestine in his final report to the Security Council, dated 26 July 1949: 'The United Nations effort in Palestine has been costly in casualties as well as in monetary expenditure. Ten members of the Organization, including the Mediator, have lost their lives over a period of fourteen months, and twice that many have been wounded. Some of these lives have been lost under conditions which would appear fully to justify the United Nations in holding the Governments concerned liable for the deaths.' Moreover, a claim for reparations is an asset of the Organization, and every effort needs to be made to protect and realize upon them, as in the case of other assets.

"Question (2). It must be emphasized that the opinion of the Court deals only with the general questions of the right of the United Nations to put forth claims. The Court did not, and could not by the terms of the request for an advisory opinion, go into the question whether any particular State was responsible in any specific case.

"In his memorandum to the third session, the Secretary-General stated that he 'assumes that the General Assembly will not desire to consider itself as a fact-finding body or judicial tribunal for determining the facts in these matters, or for the assessment of responsibility in individual cases. He considers that these must be determined elsewhere, as far as individual cases are concerned, that is to say, either by direct negotiations between the appropriate organ of the United Nations and the State or authority concerned, or by an arbitral tribunal'. The Secretary-General assumes that the General Assembly will continue to adhere to this view.

"In his judgment, the Secretary-General, as chief administrative officer of the Organization, is the appropriate organ for the presentation and settlement of the claims here involved. The Secretary-General has acted on behalf of the Organization in the prosecution of all other claims, and there is no apparent reason for differentiation here.

"Subject to the General Assembly's approval, the Secretary-General proposes to adopt the following procedure: Determine which of the cases appear likely to involve the responsibility of a State; consult with the Government of the State of which the victim was a national in order to determine whether that Government has any objection to the presentation of a claim or desires to join in submission; present, in each such case, an appropriate request to the State involved for the initiation of negotiations to determine the facts, and the amount of reparations, if any, involved. In the event of differences of opinion between the Secretary-General and the State concerned which cannot be settled by negotiation, it would be proposed that the differences be submitted to arbitration. The arbitral tribunal would be composed of one arbitrator appointed by the Secretary-General, one appointed by the State involved, and a third to be appointed by mutual agreement of the two arbitrators, or, failing such agreement, by the President of the International Court of Justice.

"Lastly, the Secretary-General would propose to make an annual report to the General Assembly on the status of such claims, and proceedings in connexion with them.

"*Question (3)*. The Secretary-General considers that negotiations for settlement of these claims would be facilitated by allowing him discretion with respect to the elements of damage which should be included in any claim and the amount of reparation to be requested, or eventually accepted. He would be guided by the following principles in presentation and settlement:

"The reparations requested should be reasonably adequate to compensate the Organization and the victim or the persons entitled through him.

"The State involved should be given appropriate assurances that it would not be subject to multiple claims by the United Nations, the victim, and the State of the victim's nationality for the same damages;

"The Secretary-General would not advance any claim for exemplary damages."

2. On 1 December 1949, the General Assembly adopted Resolution 365 (IV), authorizing "the Secretary-General, in accordance with his proposals, to bring an international claim against the Government of a State, Member or non-member of the United Nations, alleged to be responsible, with a view to obtaining the reparation due in respect of the damage caused to the United Nations and in respect of the damage caused to the victim or to persons entitled through him and, if necessary, to submit to arbitration, under appropriate procedures, such claims as cannot be settled by negotiation". It also authorized him "to take the steps and to negotiate in each particular case the agreements necessary to reconcile action by the United Nations with such rights as may be possessed by the State of which the victim is a national". GAOR, IV, Resolutions (A/1251), p. 64.

3. In 1950, the Secretary-General reported to the General Assembly that he had "addressed a letter to the Minister for Foreign Affairs of Israel requesting a formal apology to the United Nations for the murder of the Mediator in territory under the control of the Israeli Government, the continuation and intensification of the government's efforts to apprehend and bring to justice the perpetrators of the crime, and the payment to the United Nations of the sum of $54,628 as reparation for the monetary damage borne by the United Nations [i.e., $28,040 for funeral expenses and $26,580 for administrative expenses]. It was stated in the letter that, in view of the decision of the widow of the late Mediator not to present a claim for pecuniary redress with regard to the damage suffered by her on account of the death of Count Bernadotte, the monetary reparation demanded was limited to the pecuniary damage suffered by the United Nations in connexion with the murder of the Mediator. The claim by the United Nations was based upon three elements of responsibility: failure to exercise due diligence and to take all reasonable measures for the prevention of the assassination; liability of the government for actions committed by irregular forces in territory under the control of the Israeli authorities; and failure to take all the

measures required by international law and by the Security Council resolution of 19 October 1948 to bring the culprits to justice.

"The Israeli Government replied to the Secretary-General by a letter dated 14 June 1950. With respect to the Secretary-General's contention that the government had failed to exercise due diligence in the protection of the Mediator, the Israeli Government stated: 'It is clear that the government would have done wiser had it been more precise in acquainting itself with the real desires and attitude of Count Bernadotte and not allowed the matter to rest on inferences, however strong, which led to the belief that an armed escort was not desired in view of his special position as United Nations Mediator.' As regards the complaint that the government had failed to take all the measures which would have been required to apprehend the culprits, the Israeli Government admitted that a number of gaps and omissions had been established in the police inquiry following the assassination. It was stated in the letter that the Israeli Government had decided, without admitting the validity of all the legal contentions put forward on behalf of the United Nations, to take the action requested in the Secretary-General's letter. Accordingly, a remittance of $54,628 was enclosed as reparation for the damage borne by the United Nations. Furthermore, the government expressed to the United Nations 'its most sincere regret that this dastardly assassination took place on Israeli territory, and that despite all its efforts the criminals have gone undetected', and added that 'these facts are deeply deplored'. With regard to the continuation and intensification of the government's efforts to apprehend the culprits, the Israeli Government stated that 'the government is forced to the conclusion that nothing fresh is likely to emerge from a re-examination of the crime, carried out on the basis of the existing material, both that on the police file and that assembled by the army. This does not, however, imply that the government regards the case as closed, but that the course of further investigation will depend on the nature and value of any fresh evidence that may come to light'.

"On 22 June 1950, the Secretary-General replied to the Government of Israel. After expressing his regret that the efforts so far made by that government had not resulted in the apprehension and trial of the perpetrators of the crime, the Secretary-General stated that the payment of indemnity, the expression of regret and the report on the steps taken to date, which were included in the Israeli Government's letter, constituted substantial compliance with the claim submitted in the Secretary-General's letter of 21 April 1950." A/1347; GAOR, V, Annexes, Agenda Item 50, pp. 2–3.

4. In 1951, the Secretary-General submitted a claim to Jordan in connection with the death of Mr. Bakke, a member of the UN Secretariat. "After setting forth the circumstances in which Mr. Bakke was shot by Arab Legion soldiers while he was driving a United Nations vehicle in the Mount Scopus area near Jerusalem, the Secretary-General stated that the international responsibility of the Jordan Government rested upon the following elements: violation of the Agreement concerning the demilitarization of Mount Scopus; violation of the obligations owed by Jordan to the United Nations to facilitate the Mediator's mandate and to furnish adequate protection to the Mediator and his staff; and failure to take the necessary measures to bring the culprits to justice. Accordingly, the Secretary-General requested a formal apology to the United Nations, a report on the measures taken in connexion with the incident, and payment of the sum of $US 36,803.76 as

reparation for the monetary damage suffered by the Organization, and of the sum of 22,000 Norwegian kroner (or $US 3,080) for the damage suffered by Mr. Bakke's mother." A/1851, p. 2. In its reply to this letter, Jordan "disclaimed responsibility for the death of Mr. Bakke. . . . Whilst expressing its regret and condemnation of the incident, the Jordan Government stated that the shooting had started from the Israeli side during the passage of the United Nations convoy which included the jeep driven by Mr. Bakke, that he had been hit by a stray bullet, and that the shot was not fired by a member of the Arab Legion. The Jordan Government expressed the hope that it would be relieved of all financial claim connected with the incident." When the Secretary-General proposed that the controversy be submitted to arbitration, Jordan stated that "[t]he terms of the General Assembly resolution 365 (IV) referred to in your above-quoted letter presuppose the prior establishment of guilt or responsibility, which in the present case is completely absent". It asked the Secretary-General "to reconsider the case and to release it of all financial responsibility". The Secretary-General replied "that, on the basis of the information available to the United Nations, he was unable to release the Jordan Government from all financial liability in connexion with the matter and reiterated the proposal that the claim should be submitted to arbitration. It was also pointed out that, contrary to the Jordan Government's statement about the prior establishment of guilt or responsibility 'the purpose of an arbitration tribunal would be precisely to determine whether the Government of Jordan has international responsibility and, if so, what reparation should be awarded to the United Nations. . . .' " In view of the unwillingness of the Jordan Government to settle the claim, the Secretary-General asked the General Assembly for guidance. A/2180; GAOR, VII, Annexes, Agenda Item 57, pp. 1–2.

In the Sixth Committee of the General Assembly the following objections were raised to any action by the General Assembly in this field: "that the cases in question involved the United Nations directly, and the Organization should not be judge and party at the same time; that the claims presented by the Secretary-General were for damages under private law and should be brought before national courts; that the General Assembly could not impose arbitration on States unwilling to agree to it and could not even recommend to States to submit to arbitration their controversies with the Secretary-General; and that the submission to arbitration presupposed an admission of responsibility on the part of a State against which the Secretary-General had brought a claim." In reply, it was stated: "that the United Nations had authority to do what any party to a controversy could do, i.e., ask the other party to arbitrate the matter at issue; that under the Swedish draft resolution the General Assembly would not force States to arbitrate against their will, but would simply recommend that they do so if no settlement could be reached by direct negotiations; that the acceptance of arbitration was not an admission of responsibility and did not prejudge the substance of the case; and that those were international claims and could not be brought before national courts." A/2353; GAOR, op. cit., pp. 3–4. The General Assembly in Resolution 690 (VII) of 21 December 1952, merely recommended that the claims presented by the Secretary-General should "be settled by the procedures envisaged in resolution 365 (IV)." GAOR, VII, Supp. 20 (A/2361), p. 64.

After further efforts to arrange for an arbitration proved unsuccessful, and following an exchange of views between a representative of the Secretary-General and the Minister of Foreign Affairs of Jordan, the Secretary-General in January 1954 "proposed the establishment of a board of inquiry composed of two representatives of the Jordan Government and two representatives of the United Nations. It was suggested that the board should establish the facts and circumstances concerning the death of Mr. Bakke and submit recommendations to the two parties for the settlement of the claim." In his reply the Minister for Foreign Affairs of Jordan stated "that in his conversations with the Secretary-General's representative he had agreed to nothing more than a fact-finding committee. He pointed out that the Jordan Government did not admit any liability in the case and that any finding of the committee would not in any way prejudice the point of view of Jordan. The Minister regretted therefore that he was unable to accept the proposals made by the Secretary-General." GAOR, IX, Supp. 1 (A/2663), p. 102. When, however, the Secretary-General proposed that a fact-finding committee be established, the Minister of Foreign Affairs of Jordan answered "that, as a result of careful investigation, including hearing of witnesses, it had been established to the satisfaction of the Jordan Government that Mr. Bakke had not been shot by a member of the Arab Legion. It was therefore the opinion of the Jordan Government that there was no necessity, as far as it was concerned, for further investigations, whether by means of a fact-finding committee or otherwise." GAOR, X, Supp. 1 (A/2911), p. 109.

5. Difficulties have arisen also with respect to the claim brought by the Secretary-General against Egypt in connexion with the deaths of two United Nations observers, Lieutenant-Colonel Quéru and Captain Jeannel, who were killed by Saudi Arabian troops under Egyptian command. See A/2180 (12 Sept. 1952); GAOR, Annexes (VII) 57, p. 2; GAOR, IX, Supp. 1 (A/2663), p. 102; GAOR, X, Supp. 1 (A/2911), p. 109.

6. The issue of responsibility of the United Nations for acts of its personnel was raised in the Congo Case and was settled by an exchange of letters between the Secretary-General and the Belgian Government. According to the letter from the Secretary-General, of 20 February 1965:

"A number of Belgian nationals have lodged with the United Nations claims for damage to persons and property arising from the operations of the United Nations Force in the Congo, particularly those which took place in Katanga. The claims in question have been examined by United Nations officials assigned to assemble all the information necessary for establishing the facts submitted by the claimants or their beneficiaries and any other available information.

"The United Nations has agreed that the claims of Belgian nationals who may have suffered damage as a result of harmful acts committed by ONUC personnel, not arising from military necessity, should be dealt with in an equitable manner.

"It has stated that it would not evade responsibility where it was established that United Nations agents had in fact caused unjustifiable damage to innocent parties.

"It is pointed out that, under these principles, the Organization does not assume liability for damage to persons or property, which resulted solely from military operations or which, although caused by third parties, gave rise to claims against the United Nations; such cases are therefore excluded from the proposed compensation.

"Consultations have taken place with the Belgian Government. The examination of the claims having now been completed, the Secretary-General shall, without prejudice to the privileges and immunities enjoyed by the United Nations, pay to the Belgian Government one million five hundred thousand United States dollars in lump-sum and final settlement of all claims arising from the causes mentioned in the first paragraph of this letter.

"The distribution to be made of the sum referred to in the preceding paragraph shall be the responsibility of the Belgian Government." S/6597, Annex I (6 August 1965).

The agreement entered into effect on 17 May 1965, after its approval by the Belgian Legislative Chambers. *Idem*, Annex II. The Soviet Union protested against this agreement; it considered that this action was "unlawful" and "a reward for brigandage"; and that "the Belgian Government should itself bear full moral and material responsibility for all consequences of its aggression against the Republic of the Congo." It expressed the view that the Secretary-General should "take immediate steps to cancel the agreement." S/6589 (3 August 1965). The Secretary-General replied that:

"It has always been the policy of the United Nations, acting through the Secretary-General, to compensate individuals who have suffered damages for which the Organization was legally liable. This policy is in keeping with generally recognized legal principles and with the Convention on Privileges and Immunities of the United Nations. In addition, in regard to the United Nations activities in the Congo, it is reinforced by the principles set forth in the international conventions concerning the protection of the life and property of civilian population during hostilities as well as by considerations of equity and humanity which the United Nations cannot ignore.

. . .

"Of approximately 1,400 claims submitted by Belgian nationals, the United Nations accepted 581 as entitled to compensation.

"As regards the role of the Belgian Government, it was considered that there was an advantage for the Organization both on practical and legal grounds that payment to the Belgian claimants whose claim has been examined by the United Nations should be effected through the intermediary of their government. This procedure obviously avoided the costly and protracted proceedings that might have been necessary to deal with the 1,400 cases submitted and to settle those in which United Nations responsibility was found.

"Following consultations, the Belgian Government agreed to act as an intermediary and also agreed that the payment of a lump sum amounting to $1.5 million would constitute a final and definite settlement of the matter. At the same time, a number of financial questions which were outstanding between the United Nations and Belgium were settled. Payment was effected by offsetting the amount of $1.5 million against unpaid ONUC assessments amounting approximately to $3.2 million.

"Similar arrangements are being discussed with the governments of other countries, the nationals of which have similarly suffered damage giving rise to United Nations liability. About 300 unsettled claims fall within this category.

"In making these arrangements, the Secretary-General has acted in his capacity of chief administrative officer of the Organization, consistently with the established practice of the United Nations under which claims addressed to the Organization by private individuals are considered and settled under the authority of the Secretary-General." S/6597, pp. 1–2 (6 August 1965).

Agreements similar to the one with Belgium were concluded by the United Nations with other States the nationals of which suffered injuries because of the United Nations activities in the Congo. See, e. g., the exchanges of letters with Switzerland and Greece, of 3 and 20 June 1966, respectively; UN, Statement of Treaties and International Agreements Registered . . . in the Secretariat, June 1966, pp. 9, 11 (ST/LEG/SER.A/ 232).

Chapter III

MEMBERSHIP

Section 1. Admission to Membership

ORIGINAL MEMBERS OF THE UNITED NATIONS AND ADMISSION OF NEW MEMBERS

NOTE.—1. Article 3 of the Charter provides that "The original Members of the United Nations shall be the states which, having participated in the United Nations Conference on International Organization at San Francisco, or having previously signed the Declaration by United Nations of January 1, 1942, sign the present Charter and ratify it in accordance with Article 110."

Under this Article the following fifty States, which took part in the San Francisco Conference, became original members of the United Nations: Argentina, Australia, Belgium, Bolivia, Brazil, the Byelorussian SSR, Canada, Chile, China, Colombia, Costa Rica, Cuba, Czechoslovakia, Denmark, the Dominican Republic, Ecuador, Egypt (after 1958 the United Arab Republic), El Salvador, Ethiopia, France, Greece, Guatemala, Haiti, Honduras, India, Iran, Iraq, Lebanon, Liberia, Luxembourg, Mexico, the Netherlands, New Zealand, Nicaragua, Norway, Panama, Paraguay, Peru, the Philippines, Saudi Arabia, South Africa, Syria, Turkey, the Ukrainian SSR, the Union of Soviet Socialist Republics, the United Kingdom, the United States, Uruguay, Venezuela, and Yugoslavia. Poland, which did not participate in the San Francisco Conference because at that time two governments were contending for recognition, was subsequently allowed to sign the Charter and became an original member as one of the States which have previously signed the United Nations Declaration of 1942.

2. Article 4 of the Charter contains the following provisions about admission of new members: "Membership in the United Nations is open to all other peace-loving states which accept the obligations contained in the present Charter and, in the judgment of the Organization, are able and willing to carry out these obligations.—The admission of any such state to membership in the United Nations will be effected by a decision of the General Assembly upon the recommendation of the Security Council."

Between 1946 and 1950 the following nine States were admitted to the United Nations: Afghanistan, Burma, Iceland, Indonesia, Israel, Pakistan, Sweden, Thailand, and Yemen. No States were admitted between 1951 and 1954, despite the fact that there were some twenty-five applicants.

3. The reasons for the failure of most of the applicant States to gain admission for many years are diverse. Several of them have received more than seven favorable votes in the Security Council and the General Assembly has expressed itself in favor of their admission. The failure of the Security Council to submit recommendations in respect of these States has been the source of debate every year in the General Assembly and its Committees as well as in the Security Council. It has also been the basis of two requests to the International Court for advisory opinions.

At the San Francisco Conference in 1945 some representatives considered that membership in the United Nations should be universal. The majority, however, refused to open the United Nations widely to accession by any State. In particular, it was felt that certain States should not be admitted to the United Nations. This view found expression in the interpretative commentary proposed by the Delegation of Mexico and approved by the Conference in plenary session. This commentary reads: "It is the understanding of the Delegation of Mexico that paragraph 2 of Chapter III cannot be applied to the states whose regimes have been established with the help of military forces belonging to the countries which have waged war against the United Nations, as long as those regimes are in power." (See UNCIO Doc. 1210, P/20, 1 UNCIO Documents, pp. 615–16, 620. Since this statement was clearly directed against the Franco regime, Spain refrained until 1955 from presenting an application for membership.

In 1946 when the applications of eight States were before the Security Council, the United States representative proposed that a "broad and far-sighted action be taken to extend the membership." He suggested the admission of all the States then applicants, but in view of Soviet opposition this proposal was withdrawn. Some representatives, bearing in mind the Corfu Channel incidents and the situation on the border between Albania and Greece, expressed doubts as to whether the Albanian Government was peace-loving and able and willing to carry out the obligations of the Charter. On the basis of available information, five representatives were not satisfied that the Mongolian People's Republic was capable of fulfilling the obligations of the Charter. Representatives pointed out that only the USSR maintained diplomatic relations with that country and only the USSR and China had accorded recognition to it. Consequently, neither Albania nor the Mongolian People's Republic obtained the seven votes necessary for a recommendation. Transjordan, Portugal and Ireland received more than the seven needed votes, but the USSR cast a negative vote (a veto) on the ground that those countries maintained no diplomatic relations with it. In addition, the USSR claimed that the proof of Transjordan's independence was unsatisfactory and in any case, the mandate had been illegally surrendered; and that Portugal and Ireland had remained neutral during the war. Only Afghanistan, Iceland and Sweden were recommended for membership by the Security Council. SCOR, I.2, Nos. 4–5, pp. 41–140.

The General Assembly admitted the three applicants recommended by the Security Council, and requested that the Security Council re-examine the applications of the five States which did not secure a recommendation. Resolutions 34(I) and 35(I); GAOR, I.2, Resolutions (A/64/Add. 1), p. 61.

On 18 August 1947, Yemen and Pakistan received a favourable recommendation from the Security Council, but the five States previously rejected together with a further five applicants failed to receive such a recommendation. After the rejection of these ten applications, the United States proposed that the Security Council should request the General Assembly to consider these applications and should agree in advance to recommend immediately to the General Assembly the admission of any of the ten applicants "which the General Assembly shall consider qualified for admission." Though the United States opposed certain of these applicants, it was "ready and willing to rely on the judgment of the fifty-five Members of this Organization for a just and wise decision." But the Soviet representative deemed the proposed procedure to be "a direct contradiction of the procedure provided by the Charter," and the US proposal was withdrawn.

At the end of September, following the entry into force of the peace treaties with them, the applications of Hungary, Italy, Roumania and Bulgaria were revived and that of Finland was considered for the first time. The USSR and Poland argued that the Potsdam Agreement bound the United States, the United Kingdom and the USSR to support the applications of all five, as that Agreement provided that "The conclusion of Peace Treaties with recognized democratic Governments in these States will also enable the three Governments to support applications from them for membership of the United Nations." [See Protocol of the Proceedings of the Berlin Conference, 2 August 1945; British Parliamentary Papers, Misc. No. 6 (1947), Cmd. 7087, p. 12.] The USSR stated that all five countries were willing and able to fulfil the obligations of the Charter, but added that it was impossible to consider any one of them separately from the others. Australia, the United States and the United Kingdom objected to voting on the applications *en bloc* and on the vote which followed all five applications failed. The USSR vetoed those of Italy and Finland; Bulgaria, Hungary and Roumania failed to secure seven favorable votes. SCOR, II, Nos. 90–2, pp. 2408–79.

As a result, the General Assembly at its second regular session requested the opinion of the International Court of Justice on the interpretation of Article 4 of the Charter. Resolution 113B (II), 17 November 1947; GAOR, II, Resolutions (A/519), p. 18.

CONDITIONS OF ADMISSION OF A STATE TO MEMBERSHIP IN THE UNITED NATIONS

Advisory Opinion of the International Court of Justice, 28 May 1948.
ICJ Reports, 1948, pp. 57–115.

On November 17th, 1947, the General Assembly of the United Nations adopted the following Resolution:

The General Assembly,

"Considering Article 4 of the Charter of the United Nations,

"Considering the exchange of views which has taken place in the Security Council at its Two hundred and fourth, Two hundred and fifth and Two hundred and sixth Meetings, relating to the admission of certain States to membership in the United Nations,

"Considering Article 96 of the Charter,

"Requests the International Court of Justice to give an advisory opinion on the following question:

" 'Is a Member of the United Nations which is called upon, in virtue of Article 4 of the Charter, to pronounce itself by its vote, either in the Security Council or in the General Assembly, on the admission of a State to membership in the United Nations, juridically entitled to make its consent to the admission dependent on conditions not expressly provided by paragraph 1 of the said Article? In particular, can such a Member, while it recognizes the conditions set forth in that provision to be fulfilled by the State concerned, subject its affirmative vote to the additional condition that other States be admitted to membership in the United Nations together with that State?' . . . "

Before examining the request for an opinion, the Court considers it necessary to make the following preliminary remarks:

The question put to the Court is divided into two parts, of which the second begins with the words "In particular", and is presented as an application of a more general idea implicit in the first.

The request for an opinion does not refer to the actual vote. Although the Members are bound to conform to the requirements of Article 4 in giving their votes, the General Assembly can hardly be supposed to have intended to ask the Court's opinion as to the reasons which, in the mind of a Member, may prompt its vote. Such reasons, which enter into a mental process, are obviously subject to no control. Nor does the request concern a Member's freedom of expressing its opinion. Since it concerns a condition or conditions on which a Member "makes its consent dependent", the question can only relate to the statements made by a Member concerning the vote it proposes to give.

It is clear from the General Assembly's Resolution of November 17th, 1947, that the Court is not called upon either to define the meaning and scope of the conditions on which admission is made dependent, or to specify the elements which may serve in a concrete case to verify the existence of the requisite conditions.

The clause of the General Assembly's Resolution, referring to "the exchange of views which has taken place . . . ", is not understood as an invitation to the Court to say whether the views thus referred to are well founded or otherwise. The abstract form in which the question is stated precludes such an interpretation.

The question put is in effect confined to the following point only: are the conditions stated in paragraph 1 of Article 4 exhaustive in character in the sense that an affirmative reply would lead to the conclusion that a Member is not legally entitled to make admission dependent on conditions not expressly provided for in that Article, while a negative reply would, on the contrary, authorize a Member to make admission dependent also on other conditions.

Understood in this light, the question, in its two parts, is and can only be a purely legal one. To determine the meaning of a treaty provision—to determine, as in this case, the character (exhaustive or otherwise) of the conditions for admission stated therein—is a problem of interpretation and consequently a legal question.

It has nevertheless been contended that the question put must be regarded as a political one and that, for this reason, it falls outside the jurisdiction of the Court. The Court cannot attribute a political character to a request which, framed in abstract terms, invites it to undertake an essentially judicial task, the interpretation of a treaty provision. It is not concerned with the motives which may have inspired this request, nor with the considerations which, in the concrete cases submitted for examination to the Security Council, formed the subject of the exchange of views which took place in that body. It is the duty of the Court to envisage the question submitted to it only in the abstract form which has been given to it; nothing which is said in the present opinion refers, either directly or indirectly, to concrete cases or to particular circumstances.

It has also been contended that the Court should not deal with a question couched in abstract terms. That is a mere affirmation devoid of any justification. According to Article 96 of the Charter and Article 65 of the Statute, the Court may give an advisory opinion on any legal question, abstract or otherwise.

Lastly, it has also been maintained that the Court cannot reply to the question put because it involves an interpretation of the Charter. Nowhere is any provision to be found forbidding the Court, "the principal judicial organ of the United Nations", to exercise in regard to Article 4 of the Charter, a multilateral treaty, an interpretative function which falls within the normal exercise of its judicial powers.

Accordingly, the Court holds that it is competent, on the basis of Article 96 of the Charter and Article 65 of the Statute, and considers that there are no reasons why it should decline to answer the question put to it.

In framing this answer, it is necessary first to recall the "conditions" required, under paragraph 1 of Article 4, of an applicant for admission. This provision reads as follows:

"Membership in the United Nations is open to all other peace-loving States which accept the obligations contained in the present Charter and, in the judgment of the Organization, are able and willing to carry out these obligations."

The requisite conditions are five in number: to be admitted to membership in the United Nations, an applicant must (1) be a State; (2) be peace-loving; (3) accept the obligations of the Charter; (4) be able to carry out these obligations; and (5) be willing to do so.

All these conditions are subject to the judgment of the Organization. The judgment of the Organization means the judgment of the two organs mentioned in paragraph 2 of Article 4, and, in the last analysis, that of its Members. The question put is concerned with the individual attitude of each Member called upon to pronounce itself on the question of admission.

Having been asked to determine the character, exhaustive or otherwise, of the conditions stated in Article 4, the Court must in the first place consider the text of that Article. The English and French texts of paragraph 1 of Article 4 have the same meaning, and it is impossible to find any conflict between them. The text of this paragraph, by the enumeration which it contains and the choice of its terms, clearly demonstrates the intention of its authors to establish a legal rule which, while it fixes the conditions of admission, determines also the reasons for which admission may be refused; for the text does not differentiate between these two cases and any attempt to restrict it to one of them would be purely arbitrary.

The terms "Membership in the United Nations is open to all other peace-loving States which . . ." and *"Peuvent devenir Membres des Nations unies tous autres États pacifiques"*, indicate that States which fulfil the conditions stated have the qualifications requisite for admission. The natural meaning of the words used leads to the conclusion that these conditions constitute an exhaustive enumeration and are not merely stated by way of guidance or example. The provision would lose its significance and weight, if other conditions, unconnected with those laid down, could be demanded. The conditions stated in paragraph 1 of Article 4 must therefore be regarded not merely as the necessary conditions, but also as the conditions which suffice.

Nor can it be argued that the conditions enumerated represent only an indispensable minimum, in the sense that political considerations could be superimposed upon them, and prevent the admission of an applicant which fulfils them. Such an interpretation would be inconsistent with the terms of paragraph 2 of Article 4, which provide for the admission of *"tout État remplissant ces conditions"*—"any *such* State". It would lead to conferring upon Members an indefinite and practically unlimited power of discretion in the imposition of new conditions. Such a power would be inconsistent with the very character of paragraph 1 of Article 4 which, by reason of the close connexion which it establishes between membership and the observance of the principles and obligations of the Charter, clearly constitutes a legal regulation of the question of the admission of new States. To warrant an interpretation other than that which ensues from the natural meaning of the words, a decisive reason would be required which has not been established.

Moreover, the spirit as well as the terms of the paragraph preclude the idea that considerations extraneous to these principles and obligations can prevent the admission of a State which complies with them. If the authors of the Charter had meant to leave Members free to import into the application of this provision considerations extraneous to the conditions laid down therein, they would undoubtedly have adopted a different wording.

The Court considers that the text is sufficiently clear; consequently, it does not feel that it should deviate from the consistent practice of the Permanent Court of International Justice, according to which there is no occasion to resort to preparatory work if the text of a convention is sufficiently clear in itself.

The Court furthermore observes that Rule 60 of the Provisional Rules of Procedure of the Security Council is based on this interpretation. The first paragraph of this Rule reads as follows:

"The Security Council shall decide whether in its judgment the applicant is a peace-loving State and is able and willing to carry out the obligations contained in the Charter, and accordingly whether to recommend the applicant State for membership."

It does not, however, follow from the exhaustive character of paragraph 1 of Article 4 that an appreciation is precluded of such circumstances of fact as would enable the existence of the requisite conditions to be verified.

Article 4 does not forbid the taking into account of any factor which it is possible reasonably and in good faith to connect with the conditions laid down in that Article. The taking into account of such factors is implied in the very wide and very elastic nature of the prescribed conditions; no relevant political factor—that is to say, none connected with the conditions of admission—is excluded.

It has been sought to deduce either from the second paragraph of Article 4, or from the political character of the organ recommending or deciding upon admission, arguments in favour of an interpretation of paragraph 1 of Article 4, to the effect that the fulfilment of the conditions provided for in that Article is necessary before the admission of a State can be recommended or decided upon, but that it does not preclude the Members of the Organization from advancing considerations of political expediency, extraneous to the conditions of Article 4.

But paragraph 2 is concerned only with the procedure for admission, while the preceding paragraph lays down the substantive law. This procedural character is clearly indicated by the words "will be effected", which, by linking admission to the decision, point clearly to the fact that the paragraph is solely concerned with the manner in which admission is effected, and not with the subject of the judgment of the Organization, nor with the nature of the appreciation involved in that judgment, these two questions being dealt with in the preceding paragraph. Moreover, this paragraph, in referring to the "recommendation" of the Security Council and the "decision" of the General Assembly, is designed only to determine the respective functions of these two organs which consist in pronouncing upon the question whether or not the applicant State shall be admitted to membership after having established whether or not the prescribed conditions are fulfilled.

The political character of an organ cannot release it from the observance of the treaty provisions established by the Charter when they constitute limitations on its powers or criteria for its judgment. To ascertain whether an organ has freedom of choice for its decisions, reference must be made to the terms of its constitution. In this case, the limits of this freedom are fixed by Article 4 and allow for a wide liberty of appreciation. There is therefore no conflict between the functions of the political organs, on the one hand, and the exhaustive character of the prescribed conditions, on the other.

It has been sought to base on the political responsibilities assumed by the Security Council, in virtue of Article 24 of the Charter, an argument justifying the necessity for according to the Security Council as well as to the General Assembly complete freedom of appreciation in connexion with the admission of new Members. But Article 24, owing to the very general nature of its terms, cannot, in the absence of any provision, affect the special rules for admission which emerge from Article 4.

The foregoing considerations establish the exhaustive character of the conditions prescribed in Article 4.

The second part of the question concerns a demand on the part of a Member making its consent to the admission of an applicant dependent on the admission of other applicants.

Judged on the basis of the rule which the Court adopts in its interpretation of Article 4, such a demand clearly constitutes a new condition, since it is entirely unconnected with those prescribed in Article 4. It is also in an entirely different category from those conditions, since it makes admission dependent, not on the conditions required of applicants, qualifications which are supposed to be fulfilled, but on an extraneous consideration concerning States other than the applicant State.

The provisions of Article 4 necessarily imply that every application for admission should be examined and voted on separately and on its own merits; otherwise it would be impossible to determine whether a particular applicant fulfils the necessary conditions. To subject an affirmative vote for the admission of an applicant State to the condition that other States be admitted with that State would prevent Members from exercising their judgment in each case with complete liberty, within the scope of the prescribed conditions. Such a demand is incompatible with the letter and spirit of Article 4 of the Charter.

For these reasons,

THE COURT,

by nine votes to six,

is of opinion that a Member of the United Nations which is called upon, in virtue of Article 4 of the Charter, to pronounce itself by its vote, either in the Security Council or in the General Assembly, on the admission of a State to membership in the United Nations, is not juridically entitled to make its consent to the admission dependent on conditions not expressly provided by paragraph 1 of the said Article;

and that, in particular, a Member of the Organization cannot, while it recognizes the conditions set forth in that provision to be fulfilled by the State concerned, subject its affirmative vote to the additional condition that other States be admitted to membership in the United Nations together with that State. . . .

Judges Basedevant, Winiarski, McNair, Read, Zoričić and Krylov, Court, have availed themselves of the right conferred on them by Article 57 of the Statute and appended to the opinion a statement of their individual opinion.

Judges Basedevant, Winiariski, McNair, Read, Zoričić and Krylov, declaring that they are unable to concur in the opinion of the Court, have availed themselves of the right conferred on them by Article 57 of the Statute and appended to the opinion a statement of their dissenting opinion. . . .

Individual Opinion by M. ALVAREZ. I do not agree with the method adopted by the Court in giving the opinion for which it has been asked by the General Assembly of the United Nations.

The Court has inferred from the enumeration of the conditions prescribed in Article 4, paragraph 1, of the Charter for the admission of a State to membership in the United Nations, that nothing else can be adduced to justify a negative vote. This question cannot be answered merely by a clarification of the texts, nor by a study of the preparatory work; another method must be adopted and, in particular, recourse must be had to the great principles of the new international law.

More changes have taken place in international life since the last great social cataclysm than would normally occur in a century. Moreover, this life is evolving at a vertiginous speed: inter-State relations are becoming more and more various and complex. The fundamental principles of international law are passing through a serious crisis, and this necessitates its reconstruction. A new international law is developing, which embodies not only this reconstruction, but also some entirely new elements. . . .

I hold that in this connexion the Court has a free hand to allow scope to the new spirit which is evolving in contact with the new conditions of international life: there must be a renewal of international law corresponding to the renewal of this life.

With regard to the interpretation of legal texts, it is to be observed that, while in some cases preparatory work plays an important part, as a rule this is not the case. The reason lies in the fact that delegates, in discussing a subject, express the most varied views on certain matters and often without a sufficient knowledge of them; sometimes also they change their views without expressly saying so. The preparatory work on the constitution of the United Nations Organization is of but little value. Moreover, the fact should be stressed that an institution, once established, acquires a life of its own, independent of the elements which have given birth to it, and it must develop, not in accordance with the views of those who created it, but in accordance with the requirements of international life. . . .

Before giving the opinion asked of it by the General Assembly of the United Nations, the Court has had to make up its mind as to the legal or political character of the question put.

The traditional distinction between what is legal and what is political, and between law and politics, has to-day been profoundly modified. Formerly, everything dependent on precepts of law was regarded as legal and anything left to the free will of States was regarded as political.

Relations between States have become multiple and complex. As a result, they present a variety of aspects: legal, political, economic, social, etc.; there are, therefore, no more strictly legal issues. Moreover, many questions regarded as essentially legal, such as the interpretation of a treaty, may, in certain cases, assume a political character, especially in the case of a peace treaty. Again, many questions have both a legal and a political character, notably those relating to international organization.

A new conception of law in general, and particularly of international law, has also emerged. The traditionally *juridical* and *individualistic* conception of law is being progressively superseded by the following conception: in the first place, international law is not strictly juridical; it is also political, economic, social and psychological; hence, all the fundamental elements of traditional individualistic law are profoundly modified, a fact which necessitates their reconstruction. In the next place, strictly individualistic international law is being more and more superseded by what may be termed the *law of social interdependence*. The latter is the outcome, not of theory, but of the realities of international life and of the juridical conscience of the nations. The Court is the most authoritative organ for the expression of this juridical conscience, which also finds expression in certain treaties, in the most recent national legislative measures and in certain resolutions of associations devoted to the study of international law.

This *law of social interdependence* has certain characteristics of which the following are the most essential: (*a*) it is concerned not only with the delimitation of the rights of States, but also with harmonizing them; (*b*) in every question it takes into account all its various aspects; (*c*) it takes the general interest fully into account; (*d*) it emphasizes the notion of the *duties* of States, not only towards each other but also towards the international society; (*e*) it condemns the abuse of right; (*f*) it adjusts itself to the necessities of international life and evolves together with it; accordingly, it is in harmony with policy; (*g*) to the rights conferred by strictly juridical law it adds that which States possess to belong to the international organization which is being set up.

Far therefore from being in opposition to each other, law and policy are to-day closely linked together. The latter is not always the selfish and arbitrary policy of States; there is also a collective or individual policy inspired by the general interest. This policy now exercises a profound influence on international law; it either confirms it or endows it with new life, or even opposes it if it appears out of date. It is also one of the elements governing the relations between States when no legal precepts exist.

It is however always necessary to differentiate between juridical and political elements, particularly from the standpoint of the Court's jurisdiction.

The United Nations Charter makes the Court one of its organs (Art. 7), and Article 92 lays down that it is its principal judicial organ. The Statute of the present Court, like that of the old, indicates that its task is to hear and determine legal questions, and not political questions. The advisory opinions for which it may be asked must also relate to legal questions (Articles 36, No. 3, and 96 of the Charter; Article 65 of the Statute of the Court).

When a question is referred to the Court, the latter therefore must decide whether its dominant element is legal, and whether it should accordingly deal with it, or whether the political element is dominant and, in that case, it must declare that it has no jurisdiction.

In the questions which it is called upon to consider, the Court must, however, take into account all aspects of the matter, including the political aspect when it is closely bound up with the legal aspect. It would be a manifest mistake to seek to limit the Court to consideration of questions solely from their legal aspect, to the exclusion of other aspects; it would be inconsistent with the realities of international life.

It follows from the foregoing that the constitutional Charter cannot be interpreted according to a strictly legal criterion; another and broader criterion must be employed and room left, if need be, for political considerations.

The Court has decided that the question on which its advisory opinion has been asked is a legal one because it concerns the interpretation of the Charter of the United Nations, which is a treaty.

In reality, this question is both legal and political, but the legal element predominates, not so much because it is a matter of interpreting the Charter but because it is concerned with the problem whether States have a *right* to membership in the United Nations Organization if they fulfil the conditions required by the Statute of the Organization. The question is at the same time a political one, because it is the States comprising the Security Council and those belonging to the General Assembly which determine whether these conditions are, or are not, fulfilled by the applicant.

As regards the essential conditions to be fulfilled by every State desiring to be admitted to membership in the United Nations Organization, these are prescribed in Article 4, paragraph 1, of the Charter. These conditions are exhaustive because they are the only ones enumerated. If it had been intended to require others, this would have been expressly stated.

Moreover, having regard to the nature of the universal international society, the purposes of the United Nations Organization and its mission of universality, it must be held that all States fulfilling the conditions required by Article 4 of the Charter have a *right* to membership in that Organization. The exercise of this right cannot be blocked by the imposition of other conditions not expressly provided for by the Charter, by international law or by a convention, or on grounds of a political nature.

Nevertheless, it has to be judged in each case whether the conditions of admission required by the Charter are fulfilled. The units which may form this judgment are the States composing the Security Council and the members of the General Assembly. They must be guided solely by considerations of justice and good faith, i. e., they must confine themselves to considering whether the applicant fulfils the conditions required by Article 4, paragraph 1. In actual fact, however, these States are mainly guided by considerations of their own policy and, consequently, if not directly, at all events indirectly, they sometimes require of an applicant conditions other than those provided for in Article 4, since they vote against its admission if such other conditions are not fulfilled. That is an abuse of right which the Court must condemn; but at the present time no sanction attaches to it save the reprobation of public opinion.

Nevertheless, cases may arise in which the admission of a State is liable to disturb the international situation, or at all events the international organization, for instance, if such admission would give a very great influence to certain groups of States, or produce profound divergencies between them. Consequently, even if the conditions of admission are fulfilled by an applicant, admission may be refused. In such cases, the question is no longer a legal one; it becomes a political one and must be regarded as such. In a concrete case of this kind, the Court must declare that it has no jurisdiction.

A claim by a Member of the United Nations Organization, which recognizes the conditions of Article 4 of the Charter to be fulfilled by an applicant State, to subject its affirmative vote to the condition that other States be admitted to membership together with this applicant, would be an act contrary to the letter and spirit of the Charter. Nevertheless, such a claim may be justified in exceptional circumstances, for instance, in the case of applications for admission by two or more States simultaneously brought into existence as the result of the disappearance of the State or colony of which they formed part. It is natural in that case that their admission should be considered simultaneously. . . .

Individual Opinion by M. AZEVEDO. I agree with the findings of the Court, and the purpose of the following remarks is merely to

explain certain reasons which I should like to add to the opinion.
. . .

That a Court should be asked for an opinion on theoretical questions
may seem strange. But it must not be forgotten that the International
Court of Justice has a double character: that of tribunal, and that of
counsellor. And it is quite fitting for an advisory body to give an answer *in abstracto* which may eventually be applied to several *de facto*
situations: *minima circumstantia facti magnam diversitatem juris.*

It is true that Manley Hudson made the point that the Permanent
Court never deviated from the facts (*The Permanent Court of International Justice,* 1933, para. 470, pp. 495–496, and note 69), but he admits too that in Advisory Opinion No. 1 the question had already been
decided by the International Labour Office, and that the request for
the opinion had as its sole purpose the establishment of a criterion for
the future (Hudson, *op. cit.,* p. 497, P.C.I.J., Series B., No. 1, p. 14).

Any request—apart from a quite artificial attitude, which cannot be
presumed—always arises from or is influenced by facts, but it is also
possible to eliminate the concrete elements, so as to reveal an isolated
point of doctrine.

In the original report by Lapradelle, in 1920, an abstract request was
already contemplated in connexion with the distinction between a
"point", on the one hand, which was always limited to a question of
pure, theoretical law, and, on the other hand, a "dispute", which had
arisen from a concrete disagreement, already in existence.

Such a distinction therefore corresponds to the idea held by the
founders of the Court, and it was clearly indicated in the plan proposed
in 1920 by the Brazilian jurist Clovis Bevilacqua. It is for all these
reasons that the Permanent Court could say:

"There seems to be no reason why States should not be able to ask
the Court to give an abstract interpretation of a treaty; rather would
it appear that this is one of the most important functions which it can
fulfil." (P.C.I.J., Series A., No. 7, pp. 18–19; Series B., No. 1, p. 24
[17].)

It is even preferable that the Court should ignore disputes that have
given rise to any particular question. The Court would not then be led
to incur responsibility by departing from its normal duty; the Court
would thus leave a wider field of appreciation open to the body which
would have to apply the convention without slighting the prestige of
the tribunal. . . .

By applying an objective criterion faithfully, any legal question
can be examined without considering the political elements which may,
in some proportion, be involved.

Objection to the political aspect of a case is familiar to domestic
tribunals in cases arising from the discretionary action of governments, but the Courts always have a sure means of rejecting the *non*

liquet and of acting in the penumbra which separates the legal and the political, in the endeavour to protect individual rights.

In my country, an eminent jurist who was also a member of this Court, Ruy Barbosa, examined the problem fully in the light of comparative law (*Direito do Amazonas ao Acre*, Rio de Janeiro, 1910); it is particularly interesting to see in his work how, for instance, the history of the Washington Court from the beginning of the country's autonomous existence, through the war of Secession, until 1937, and the adoption of the *New Deal* by Franklin Roosevelt, affords useful information.

The decisions known as the "Insular Cases" have been ably commented on. C. F. Randolph, for instance, states that "these may be momentous political questions without the precincts of the Court; within, they are simple judicial questions". (*The Law and Policies of Annexation*, p. 105.) . . .

In the present case, the legal question is clearly apparent, and the Court can decide it without enquiring whether hidden political motives have been introduced or not, in the same way as the old Court has done in the Opinion No. 23[13]:

"The Court . . . is called upon to perfom a judicial function, and . . . there appears to be no room for the discussion and application of political principles or social theories . . . " (Series B., No. 13, p. 23.)

Passing to the examination of the particular case, and dismissing the notion of the universality of the United Nations, an ideal which has not yet become a guiding rule for the admission of new Members, the following question must first be considered: whether there exists, or not, a subjective right to be admitted to this international society.

In favour of an affirmative answer, it has been suggested that the notion of an obligation in favour of third parties should be applied by analogy; such a notion has been adopted in several treaties, and also by various international groups, such as the Industrial Property Group, to which each country is free to adhere, such adherence being sufficient for the country to begin to enjoy its rights and assume its obligations.

But here the act involved is not unilateral, but manifestly bilateral; and it is complete only when the request for admission has been accepted by the principal organs of the United Nations.

Such a request is binding only on the applicant, and even if it is founded on the existence of the qualifications required by the Charter, the candidate cannot himself judge whether the conditions are fulfilled in conformity with Article 4. This is the task of the Organization, which may, or may not, accept the proposal by a judgment which it alone can render.

Therefore it is not a question of right, but simply of interest, which may, however, be transformed later by the judgment in question.

The conditions for admission, as deliberately laid down, are so broad and flexible that the recommendations and decisions relating thereto necessarily contain a strong arbitrary element.

It would be difficult to say that any one of the required conditions has a purely objective character, and that it could be appraised algebraically; and despite the place allotted to the word "judgment", it is precisely in the matter of the peace-loving nature of a State that a wide scope has been given to the political views of those who are called upon to pronounce themselves.

Motives of all kinds, tending to unite or separate men and countries, will slip through the remaining loopholes; all kinds of prejudices, and even physical repugnance will find a way of influencing the decision, either by an act of the will or even through the action of the subconscious. Each appraisal will be psychologically determined according to the criterion applied by each voter.

It would be vain to require in practice that the representatives of States should act exclusively according to ideal and abstract considerations, seeing that at the basis of every social organization, there are only men, whose virtues and faults, individually or collectively, are almost the same.

The philosophical quarrel of the "universals" has not succeeded, through the centuries, in giving any other basis to human groups, in spite of the effect of nominalist, realist and conceptualist doctrines on legal personality, or on the institutional organism.

In short, all political considerations may intervene in determining the judgment of the organs of the United Nations regarding the qualifications laid down in Article 4 of the Charter. Hence, objections that have been raised regarding the protection of the rights of man, the attitude of countries during the last war, the extent of diplomatic relations, etc., may, in principle, justify the rejection of an application.

The idea arose in the San Francisco Conference itself, which approved, by acclamation, a proposal that countries whose governments had been established with the aid of the military force of countries that had fought against the United Nations, should be held not to fulfil the required conditions.

A direct reference to democratic institutions was avoided, roughly in the terms adopted at the Teheran Conference of 1943 (Goodrich and Hambro, *Charter of the United Nations*, p. 80), in order not to intervene in or even meddle with the domestic affairs of a country; but the report itself, which expressed such fears, did not fail to stress that such an appraisal might be made when judgment as to the required qualifications was given. (U.N.C.I.O., Committee I/2, Doc. 1160, Vol. VII, p. 316.)

On the other hand, it must be admitted that the examination of candidatures has been limited by determining all the requirements that a candidate was obliged to fulfil; this was a *minimum* considered necessary to prevent arbitrary acts. . . .

The examination of all the documents leads to the conclusion that exhaustive interpretation has been current in the practice of the organs of the United Nations, the Members of which have reciprocally made complaints on the subject of requirements lying outside the scope fixed by Article 4. It has never been asserted that a country fulfilling all the legal conditions might nevertheless not be admitted, because other conditions were not fulfilled; on the other hand, it has always been stated that the absence of such qualifications prevented the fulfilment of the conditions prescribed by a provision that it was desired not to infringe.

And if I were not faced with an abstract question, and, consequently, if I had to take facts into account, I should consider that allegations which might be the basis of the first question asked have not been proved.

Having established that the required conditions are fixed, it might still be possible—having regard to the doctrine of the relativity of rights already accepted in international law (P.C.I.J., Series A., No. 7, p. 30; and No. 24, p. 2; Series A./B., No. 46, p. 167)—to admit a kind of censorship for all cases in which there has been a misuse or, at any rate, abnormal use of power in the appreciation of the exhaustive list of qualities—even granting a wide scope to political considerations.

Any legal system involves limitations and is founded on definite rules which are always ready to reappear as the constant element of the construction, whenever the field of action of discretionary principles, adopted in exceptional circumstances, is overstepped.

This is a long-established principle, and has served, during centuries, to limit the scope of the principle *qui suo jure utitur neminem laedit.*

The concept of the misuse of rights has now been freed from the classical notions of *dolus* and *culpa;* in the last stage of the problem an enquiry into intention may be discarded, and attention may be given solely to the objective aspect; i. e., it may be presumed that the right in question must be exercised in accordance with standards of what is normal, having in view the social purpose of the law. (*Cf.* Swiss Civil Code, Art. 2; Soviet, Art. 1; and Brazilian, Art. 160.)

There are even restrictions on arbitrary decision. It would, no doubt, be difficult to fix limits *a priori,* though examples might easily be given; e. g., could Switzerland be regarded as a non-peace-loving country? Could policy override the law to such an extent?

In another field, it might also be asked how the United Nations could continue to function if the reservation in the Charter regarding domestic jurisdiction was subject to no control.

But here there would be no need to seek for reasons; for the Court has before it a theoretical opinion. In any case, it would be a very difficult task to perform, because the Members voting are not bound to state their reasons.

Of course, if they choose to express their motives, they themselves would open the way to the examination of the restrictions, by transforming an abstract act into a causal act (as sometimes happens in private law in the case of certain forms of bonds), in such a way that an enquiry would be possible into the existence and authenticity of a particular cause. The *falsa demonstratio* may thus vitiate the act when it is subordinated to a certain motive.

It is true that it has been maintained that the statement of reasons is not merely an act of courtesy, but the fulfilment of a duty which enables the Assembly to know the reasons for a refusal. But if the great majority of the Members of the United Nations hold that the Security Council's recommendation is a condition *sine qua non* for the admission of a Member by the Assembly, it would be useless for the latter to verify the reasons that the Council might have had for not reporting favourably on the application.

The request for an opinion is not confined to a general point. It also contains a particular question, namely, the hypothetical case in which an affirmative vote is made subject to simultaneous admission of other States. Such an attitude has been alleged directly or indirectly, clearly or in a disguised manner, on several occasions.

But there is no question of a simple example or corollary, which would make a special reply superfluous; on the contrary, the second question is, from its nature, not wholly included in the first. There is a change of plane from the individual to the collective, and this is not legally justified, if arbitrary action is excluded; there is a change from the consideration of the qualities inherent in a certain candidate, to circumstances foreign to that candidate and concerned with the interests of third parties.

Once it is admitted that a State has proved that it has all the required qualifications, a refusal to accept its application might be considered tantamount to a violation, not only of an interest, but of a right already established, the acceptance of the State having been recognized, by final judgment, to be fully justified.

The most weighty reasons, such as the validity of a prior international undertaking, even if that undertaking bound all the Members of the United Nations, could not, in any case, justify the abandonment of a rule of law as an act of retortion. It would, in law, be equally abnormal to refuse admission in order to avoid acting unjustly towards a third party, or to defend oneself against action considered to be arbitrary, as it would be to demand compensatory advantages from a candidate.

Having completely covered the question in its true limits, a judge will have fulfilled his duty if he gives a legal answer as to the law, independent of facts and without commenting on the attitude of any particular State (P.C.I.J., Series B., No. 13, p. 24).

If he does so, he will not hinder the political activity of the organs that are responsible for the maintenance of peace; for elements of expediency, manifest or hidden, can always be considered when reasonable use is made of the wide possibilities opened by Article 4 of the Charter. Respect for law must never constitute a reason for disturbing international harmony, nor cause an upheaval in the life of any society.

Dissenting Opinion of Judges BASDEVANT, WINIARSKI, Sir ARNOLD McNAIR and READ. We regret that, while we concur in the opinion of the majority of the members of the Court as to the legal character of the first question, as to the power of the Court to answer it and the desirability of doing so, and as to the competence of the Court to give any interpretation of the Charter thereby involved, we are unable to concur in the answer given by the majority to either question, and we wish to state our reasons for not doing so. . . .

In our opinion, it is impossible to regard the first question as one which relates solely to the statements or the arguments which a Member of the United Nations may make or put forward in the Security Council or in the General Assembly when those organs are considering a request for admission, and not to the reasons on which that Member bases its vote. The Court is asked whether a Member is "juridically entitled to make its consent to the admission" dependent on conditions not provided for by paragraph 1 of Article 4. Its consent to admission is expressed by its vote. It is therefore the vote that is in question, as is confirmed by the expression "subject its affirmative vote" used in the second question, which is complementary to the first. But it would be a strange interpretation which gave a Member freedom to base its vote upon a certain consideration and at the same time forbade it to invoke that consideration in the discussion preceding the vote. Such a result would not conduce to that frank exchange of views which is an essential condition of the healthy functioning of an international organization. It is true that it is not possible to fathom the hidden reasons for a vote and there exists no legal machinery for rectifying a vote which may be cast contrary to the Charter in the Security Council or the General Assembly. But that does not mean that there are no rules of law governing Members of the United Nations in voting in either of these organs; an example is to be found in paragraph 1 of Article 4 prohibiting the admission of a new Member which does not fulfil the qualifications specified therein. This distinction, which it has been attempted to introduce between the actual vote and the discussion preceding it, cannot be accepted; it would be inconsistent with the actual terms of the question submitted to the Court, and its recognition would involve the risk of undermining that respect for good faith which must govern the discharge of the obligations contained in the Charter (Article 2, paragraph 2). . . .

The resolutions which embody either a recommendation or a decision in regard to admission are decisions of a political character; they emanate from political organs; by general consent they involve the examination of political factors, with a view to deciding whether the applicant State possesses the qualifications prescribed by paragraph 1 of Article 4; they produce a political effect by changing the condition of the applicant State in making it a Member of the United Nations. Upon the Security Council, whose duty it is to make the recommendation, there rests by the provisions of Article 24 of the Charter "primary responsibility for the maintenance of international peace and security"—a purpose inscribed in Article 1 of the Charter as the first of the Purposes of the United Nations. The admission of a new Member is pre-eminently a political act, and a political act of the greatest importance.

The main function of a political organ is to examine questions in their political aspect, which means examining them from every point of view. It follows that the Members of such an organ who are responsible for forming its decisions must consider questions from every aspect, and, in consequence, are legally entitled to base their arguments and their vote upon political considerations. That is the position of a member of the Security Council or of the General Assembly who raises an objection based upon reasons other than the lack of one of the qualifications expressly required by paragraph 1 of Article 4.

That does not mean that no legal restriction is placed upon this liberty. We do not claim that a political organ and those who contribute to the formation of its decisions are emancipated from all duty to respect the law. The Security Council, the General Assembly and the Members who contribute by their votes to the decisions of these bodies are clearly bound to respect paragraph 1 of Article 4, and, in consequence, bound not to admit a State which fails to possess the conditions required in this paragraph. . . .

When a Member of the United Nations imports into the examination of an application for admission a consideration which is foreign to the qualifications of paragraph 1 of Article 4, what he does is not the same thing as it would be if the Charter made such a consideration a qualification additional to those already required. That would involve amending the Charter, and there can be no question of that. The Member is merely introducing into the discussion, as he has a right to do, a political factor which he considers of importance and on which he is entitled to rely but which the other Members are equally entitled to consider and decide whether to accept or reject, without being legally bound to attach any weight to it; whereas on the other hand they would be legally bound to give effect to an objection based on the duly established lack of one of the qualifications specified in paragraph 1 of Article 4.

While the Members of the United Nations have thus the right and the duty to take into account all the political considerations which are in their opinion relevant to a decision whether or not to admit an applicant for membership or to postpone its admission, it must be remembered that there is an overriding legal obligation resting upon every Member of the United Nations to act in good faith (an obligation which moreover is enjoined by paragraph 2 of Article 2 of the Charter) and with a view to carrying out the Purposes and Principles of the United Nations, while at the same time the members of the Security Council, in whatever capacity they may be there, are participating in the action of an organ which in the discharge of its primary responsibility for the maintenance of international peace and security is acting on behalf of all the Members of the United Nations.

That does not mean the freedom thus entrusted to the Members of the United Nations is unlimited or that their discretion is arbitrary.

For these reasons, our view is that the first question should be answered as follows:

A Member of the United Nations which is called upon, in virtue of Article 4 of the Charter, to pronounce itself by its vote, either in the Security Council or in the General Assembly, on the admission of a State which possesses the qualifications specified in paragraph 1 of that Article, is participating in a political decision and is therefore legally entitled to make its consent to the admission dependent on any political considerations which seem to it to be relevant. In the exercise of this power the Member is legally bound to have regard to the principle of good faith, to give effect to the Purposes and Principles of the United Nations and to act in such a manner as not to involve any breach of the Charter. . . .

If it is agreed (as we have already submitted) that a Member of the United Nations is legally entitled to refuse to vote in favour of admission by reason of considerations foreign to the qualifications expressly laid down in Article 4, paragraph 1, this interpretation applies equally to the second question.

A consideration based on the desire that the admission of the State should involve the contemporaneous admission of other States is clearly foreign to the process of ascertaining that the first State possesses the qualifications laid down in Article 4, paragraph 1; it is a political consideration. If a Member of the United Nations is legally entitled to make its refusal to admit depend on political considerations, that is exactly what the Member would be doing in this case.

If the request for an opinion involved the Court in approving or disapproving the desire thus expressed by a Member of the United

Nations to procure the admission of other States at the same time as the applicant State, it would only be possible to assess this political consideration from a political point of view. But such an assessment is not within the province of the Court. An opinion on this subject would not be an opinion on a legal question within the meaning of Article 96 of the Charter and Article 65 of the Statute. It is one thing to ask the Court whether a Member is legally entitled to rely on political considerations in voting upon the admission of new Members; that is a legal question and we have answered it. It is quite another thing to ask the Court to assess the validity of any particular political consideration upon which a Member relies; that is a political question and must not be answered.

Nevertheless, as we have said, a Member of the United Nations does not enjoy unlimited freedom in the choice of the political considerations that may induce it to refuse or postpone its vote in favour of the admission of a State to membership in the United Nations. It must use this power in good faith, in accordance with the Purposes and Principles of the Organization and in such a manner as not to involve any breach of the Charter. But no concrete case has been submitted to the Court which calls into question the fulfilment of the duty to keep within these limits; so the Court need not consider what it would have to do if a concrete case of this kind were submitted to it.

[Dissenting opinion by M. ZORICIĆ is omitted.]

Dissenting Opinion by M. KRYLOV.—To my regret, I am unable for the following reasons to concur in the opinion of the Court. . . .

Appearances are deceptive: though framed in a legal form, it is a question put with a definitely political purpose; it is political in conception; though abstract in form, it is a concrete question which expressly refers in one of its paragraphs to the "exchange of views which has taken place in the Security Council at its 204th, 205th and 206th Meetings"; though impersonal in form, it is a question designed to censure the reasons given by a permanent member of the Security Council.

It has been suggested that the request couched in abstract terms is not of a political character, that the Court is not called upon to consider the reasons which may [underlie] the request and, lastly, that the Court is bound only to envisage the question in the abstract form in which it has been presented by the General Assembly.

I cannot share this view. I hold that it is impossible to eliminate the political elements from the question put to the Court and only to consider it as presented in an abstract form. The reply to the question should refer to concrete cases which have been considered by the Security Council and General Assembly. The legal criteria should be examined in the light of the political grounds on which, in actual fact, the attitude of Members of the United Nations was based. . . .

In view of the fact that the admission of new Members is dependent on political decisions of the Security Council and General Assembly, I should have preferred that the Court should have abstained from giving a reply which might, in the nature of things, be utilized in the political dispute which has been going on for a year and a half in the Security Council and General Assembly and have refused to give an advisory opinion.

My view would seem to be borne out by the fact that, during the eighteen years of its activities, the Permanent Court of International Justice was never once asked to give an advisory opinion regarding any article of the Covenant of the League of Nations *in abstracto*. It may be noted, by way of example, that in three of its opinions, the Permanent Court had to deal with articles of the Covenant, but in each of these opinions—(1) Nationality Decrees in Tunis and Morocco; (2) the Status of Eastern Carelia, and (3) the Frontier between Turkey and Iraq—the Court was considering concrete situations. The interpretation of Articles 5, 15 and 17 of the Covenant was in close connexion, in all these opinions, with the concrete situation.

It is easy to explain why this was so. Quite obviously, it was not desired to involve the Permanent Court in political disputes.

I must even go further: not once did the Permanent Court adjudge any case *ex aequo et bono*, that is to say, it always kept within the limits of existing law, of strict legality.

In the present case, the question put to the Court is couched in abstract form. The Court's opinion will have a quasi-legislative effect, and this, as will be shown later, is in no way desirable. From the standpoint under consideration, the practice of the Permanent Court should be taken into account by the Court: the interpretation of the Charter *in abstracto* is not desirable.

Whereas the Permanent Court, in interpreting the Covenant of the League of Nations, sought to consider concrete situations, or existing disputes, the Court, in the present case, is about to make a pronouncement, with quasi-legislative effect, concerning decisions to be taken by the political organs of the United Nations. The Court's answer will amount to a definition of the competence of the organs of the United Nations which decide the question of the admission of a new State to membership in the United Nations. In practice, the terms of opinions of the Permanent Court have always been complied with. But the Permanent Court never had before it a question of such importance formulated *in abstracto*. In the present case, it may be asked whether the political organs of the United Nations, acting under conditions which cannot even be foreseen at the present time, might not one day depart from the precepts of the Court's opinion. International justice must keep within the framework of international law and must not encroach on the political sphere.

I would refer, in this connexion, to the last article by Professor
Manley Hudson, a former judge of the Permanent Court, in the
first number of the *American Journal of International Law* for 1948.
This distinguished author says in this article (pp. 15–19) that it
must be borne in mind that in some cases it may be a disservice to
the Court to urge that it shall deal with disputes in which legal relations between the parties are subordinated to political considerations
involved. Speaking of requests for advisory opinions, Professor Hudson suggests that caution must be exercised in cases where a request for an opinion has to do with questions relating to the powers
of organs of the United Nations. I think as he does that in this case
the Charter should be interpreted rather by the political organs
themselves than by opinions of the Court. The Court's activity must
not be "artificially stimulated".

Thus I conclude that it would be better if the Court were to assert its right not to answer the question put, and to state its grounds
for so doing (Article 65 of the Statute says: "the Court *may* give
an advisory opinion . . .").

Since the Court has decided to give an opinion and is content to
answer the question in the artificially narrow form in which it has
been framed, I find myself obliged to avail myself of my right to extend the scope of the question and to express my opinion on the legal
import of Article 4 of the Charter. . . .

The authoritative texts of Article 4 of the Charter show some
differences of wording. The English text, and the Russian text,
which closely follows it, say that membership in the United Nations
is open to States which have the qualifications required by Article 4.
The French, Spanish and Chinese texts better express the general
principle of the constitution of the United Nations, a principle which
is not purely and simply that of universality ("peuvent *devenir Membres des Nations unies* . . .") ("Podran *ser Miembros de las
Naciones Unidas* . . ."). It is true that *all* (applicant) States
may become Members of the United Nations ("*Peuvent devenir Membres des Nations unies* tous *États* . . ." *candidats*) but only if
they satisfy the criteria of Article 4 of the Charter. Certainly the
five texts all express the same idea, namely, that the qualifications
required by Article 4 are necessary in order to become a Member of
the United Nations. But these texts by no means imply that the
presence of these requisite qualifications necessarily leads to the admission of the applicant State to the United Nations.

The same conclusion emerges from an analysis of the report of
the Rapporteur of Committee I/2 of the San Francisco Conference.
According to this report (U.N.C.I.O., Vol. 7, p. 315), the admission of
a new Member must be submitted for examination by the Organization. The Committee did not enumerate the elements to be considered
in this examination. It only mentioned the main criteria. This

means that the enumeration of criteria in Article 4 of the Charter is not exhaustive. In forming a judgment as to the desirability of admitting a new Member—that is to say, in exercising its discretionary powers with regard to such admission—the Organization may be guided by considerations "of any nature", i. e., not merely legal but also political considerations. This demonstrates the true legal meaning of paragraph 1 of Article 4 of the Charter.

The affirmation that the qualifications required by Article 4 of the Charter are exhaustive in character, implies that Members of the United Nations taking part in the vote in the Security Council and General Assembly must be exclusively guided by considerations which can be "connected" with the five conditions enumerated in Article 4. But this is definitely contrary to the interpretation given by the Report of Committee I/2.

Again, this requirement does not to my mind appear to serve any purpose. A member of the United Nations, called upon to vote on the admission of a State, is legally entitled to vote according to its own appreciation of the situation. It is not obliged to give reasons for its vote; it may vote without giving any reasons and such a vote is not subject to any control. What purpose then would be served by a censure of the reasons invoked by Member States in the Security Council or General Assembly? The recommendation to the effect that the real reasons for a vote must be "connected" with the allegedly exhaustive criteria of Article 4 might result in hypocritical declarations being made by some Members of the United Nations Organization.

The Court, in its opinion, declares that it does not follow from the exhaustive character of paragraph 1 of Article 4 that "an appreciation is precluded of such circumstances of fact as would enable the existence of the requisite conditions to be verified". The opinion states that in this connexion no relevant political factor is excluded. This means that, in a concrete case, Members have a right of discretionary and political appreciation. But in that case, one is forced to the, in my view, inevitable conclusion that this right of discretionary appreciation is implicitly sanctioned by Article 4 of the Charter and that the enumeration of criteria in that Article is not exhaustive. Otherwise, this right of appreciation would have no basis.
. . . .

Finally, I come to the question of the vote which has—wrongly, I think—been described as a "conditional vote". A vote may be affirmative or negative; or a Member may also abstain from voting. But a "conditional vote" is meaningless in law. Obviously, as has already been said, the question put by the General Assembly refers not to the "vote" but to the reasons for it.

The concrete case envisaged by the question put to the Court is the admission of five ex-enemy States which was discussed by the Security Council. The delegates of the majority of Members of the

Council wished to admit two ex-enemy States (Italy and Finland) and were unwilling to admit three others (Bulgaria, Hungary and Roumania). The U.S.S.R. delegate in the Security Council post-poned his affirmative vote in favour of Italy and Finland because he was not sure of the admission of the three others to membership. Was this delegate legally justified in so doing? The majority of the delegates in the Security Council, in interpreting Article 4, held that that Article did not warrant such a proceeding and even forbade it. It would not seem that there is anything to justify such an interpreta-tion. No doubt, the application of each State must be considered sep-arately on its own merits. But it is possible to imagine several ap-plicant States being admitted together and such a vote is by no means precluded by Article 4 of the Charter.

Such a proceeding is especially warranted when it is a question of admitting States whose applications are presented in identical cir-cumstances; for instance, in a case where several newly created States succeed to a State which has ceased to exist.

In the particular case, the applications for admission to the United Nations of the five ex-enemy States were considered to be worthy of support, after the conclusion of the Peace Treaties of Paris of 1947, not only by the participants in the Conference of Potsdam of 1945 but also by all parties to these peace treaties. All these applica-tions should have been treated in the same manner, that is to say, that all these applicant States should have been admitted simultane-ously. As I have stated above, there was no warrant for an unjusti-fied discrimination between the five candidates on the ground of their domestic régime. In this specific, concrete, and even unique case— having regard to the Potsdam Agreement and to the above-mentioned peace treaties—the suggestion made by the delegate of the Soviet Union was not contrary to Article 4 of the Charter, and could not be regarded as illegal. As I have stated, a block vote is not forbid-den by the Charter and accordingly it is legal; it is a legitimate pro-ceeding. Accordingly, there is no need for me to consider wheth-er the clause approved at Potsdam and repeated in the Peace Treaties of 1947 is inconsistent with Article 103 of the Charter.

It follows that the right of appreciation, sanctioned by Article 4 of the Charter, may be exercised by Members of the United Nations in various circumstances in connexion with the admission of new Members. It goes without saying that, in utilizing this right of ap-preciation in respect of an applicant State, each Member of the Organization must be guided by legal and political considerations which accord with the Purposes and Principles of the United Nations and that it must exercise its right in all good faith.

Accordingly, I give the following reply to the question (that is to say to two parts of the question) put by the General Assembly:

A Member of the United Nations, which is called upon, in virtue of Article 4 of the Charter, to pronounce itself by its vote, either in the Security Council or in the General Assembly, on the admission of a State to membership in the United Nations, is entitled to declare during the discussion and before the vote, that it takes into account in voting: (1) the legal criteria prescribed in paragraph 1 of the said Article and (2) the political considerations consistent with the Purposes and Principles of the United Nations.

NOTE.—1. During the first part of the third session of the General Assembly in 1948, the advisory opinion of the International Court of Justice was considered by the *Ad Hoc* Political Committee. In the debate the following positions were taken concerning the effect of that opinion (GAOR, III. 1, *Ad Hoc* Political C., pp. 65–78):

"Mr. Vyshinsky (USSR) expressed the view that there was in fact no advisory opinion of the International Court of Justice. The International Court of Justice consisted of fifteen members. The document before the Committee represented the opinion of nine of those members, two of whom— Mr. Alvarez of Chile and Mr. Azevedo of Brazil—had submitted individual concurring opinions, which differed from those of the majority on the most important issue of whether political considerations could be invoked in addition to the legal conditions provided by paragraph 1 of Article 4. Consequently, on that crucial question the majority of nine was reduced to a minority of seven, and the decision of that minority could not be accepted as a decision of the International Court of Justice.

"Apart from that majority of nine, of whom two dissented on the most important question, the International Court of Justice had been divided into a minority group of four who had dissented on the crucial question already mentioned and a smaller group of two, which had shared the views of the minority of four on all essential issues. . . .

"The minority of four, together with the minority of two and Mr. Alvarez and Mr. Azevedo, had expressed the opinion that the compelling requirements of Article 4 did not bar additional political considerations, which must, in fact, guide a political organ such as the Security Council. Those eight judges had denied that there was any contradiction between the legal and political standards to be applied.

"The USSR went further. It held that, since law was in the last analysis nothing but the tool for the implementation [of] policy, political considerations could not be divorced from strictly legal conditions in deciding a question as important as the admission of new Members. In such a question, political interests were too closely linked with legal requirements to permit of a genuine separation of the two; a decision was not reached on legal or political grounds alone, but on a combination of both factors. The eight judges had been of the opinion that it was the right and even the duty of every Member of the United Nations, when voting on a question of admission to membership, to be guided not only by the legal standards laid down in Article 4 but by political considerations as well. . . .

"The majority of the judges of the Court had also declared that the motives for the non-admission of a State to membership in the United Nations were not subject to control, because freedom of opinion and judgment was a sovereign right. Each Member of the United Nations had at least one unqualified right which was the right to adopt decisions without being accountable for them to anyone whatsoever. That was the view of the majority of the judges of the Court, which had recognized that political reasons could be invoked in deciding upon the admission of new Members.

"Although the nine members of the International Court of Justice were quite sure on that point, two of its members, Judges Alvarez and Azevedo, had taken an independent position, the opinion of Judge Alvarez being that the traditional distinction between law and politics had been modified. Today, he had said, there were no more strictly legal issues, but simply many questions regarded as essentially legal, such as the interpretation of a treaty which, in certain cases, might assume a political character. That, Mr. Vyshinsky added, was directly relevant to the arguments he had presented. There was no contradiction but rather a close link between law and politics.

"The opinions expressed were not those of Soviet lawyers but of two of the most renowned experts on international law in Latin America. The USSR delegation went further than they did in some respects, for it maintained that law had no independent role, but always represented the policy of the master or ruling class of which it was the tool. . . .

"Mr. Vyshinsky drew five conclusions. First, in deciding on the question of admission of new Members, a Member of the United Nations must be guided by the conditions set forth in paragraph 1 of Article 4 of the Charter, which constituted the legal or juridical basis for the settlement of the question of the admission of new Members.

"Secondly, every Member of the United Nations, which participated in the voting with respect to the admission of new Members, was a party to a political decision, and it therefore had every right to make its agreement to such admission conditional upon considerations of a political character. In this it must act in good faith in the spirit of the purposes and principles of the United Nations as a whole.

"Thirdly, the conditions set forth in paragraph 1 of Article 4 in respect to the admission of new Members were necessary conditions in deciding the question of admission. However, those essential conditions did not exclude the possibility of political considerations being taken into account as well.

"Fourthly, in estimating criteria for admission, every Member of the United Nations, and of the Security Council in particular, was free to make its own decisions and its motives were not to be questioned or be subject to control, because that was a matter for the particular Member's political conscience.

"Finally, the requirement that the same approach should be adopted to the question of the admission of several States which had complied with the requirements of Article 4, was in accordance with the principles of the United Nations and of the sovereign equality of States. It was therefore not contradictory to the principles of the Charter to set forth other political requirements, such as the requirement of the simultaneous admission of several States, all of which complied with the same conditions and had a similar status.

"Mr. Vyshinsky added that in advancing these ideas, the USSR delegation took the position that the application of legal considerations must necessarily always be guided by political interests, provided that there was good faith in respect of the principles of the United Nations. . . .

"Mr. COHEN (USA) . . . The representative of the USSR had challenged the reasoning of the Court, as he had every right to do; but he had also questioned the existence of the opinion of the Court, and there he was on slippery ground. It was for the Court to decide what its opinion was, and there could be no doubt what the Court had decided. The Court was not required to agree on all the arguments in order to make a decision.

"The situation appeared to have reached a stalemate. On the one hand, the attitude of the USSR was unyielding. On the other hand, the majority of the Members of the United Nations was powerless in the face of the USSR veto. That majority was confirmed in its position by the advisory opinion emitted by the proper international tribunal. In the circumstances, it was not surprising that members of the General Assembly should feel deep concern at the continued frustration of the majority's desire to take action to give a moral basis to the right of the United Nations to speak for the world community of nations.

"The United States delegation sympathized with that sentiment and with the desire for remedial action. On 17 September 1947, the Secretary of State had declared that the United States was willing to accept the elimination of the unanimity requirement with regard to the admission of new Members, and it had thenceforward maintained that position, and would continue to do so. At the second regular session of the Assembly the United States delegation had stated that it would not exercise its right of veto in the Security Council to exclude from membership any of the applicants then under consideration which the Assembly found qualified for membership."

2. On the basis of a report by the *Ad Hoc* Committee, the General Assembly recommended that "each Member of the Security Council and of the General Assembly, in exercising its vote on the admission of new Members, should act in accordance with" the opinion of the Court; and asked the Security Council to reconsider the applications of certain States, taking into account the circumstances in each particular case. Resolution 197 (III), A–I, 8 December 1948; GAOR, III.1, Resolutions (A/810), pp. 30–36.

3. In the discussion before the *Ad Hoc* Political Committee Argentina had proposed a draft resolution that a Security Council decision should be deemed to be a recommendation in favour of admission if the application received seven or more affirmative votes. The Assembly could also decide, it was proposed, to admit an applicant which was the subject of an unfavorable recommendation. After discussion this resolution was withdrawn. GAOR, III.1, *Ad Hoc* Political Committee, pp. 52–156. At the plenary meeting of 8 December 1948, the representatives of the United States and the United Kingdom announced they would not use the veto to block the admission of a member receiving seven affirmative votes. GAOR, III.1, Plenary Meetings, pp. 773, 797.

4. In its report to the General Assembly of 15 July 1948, on the problem of voting in the Security Council, the Interim Committee of the General Assembly had recommended that a decision in the Security Council to recommend the admission of a State to membership in the United Nations should be adopted by a vote of any seven members. A/578; GAOR, III, Supp. No. 10, pp. 4, 16. On the basis of this report, on 14 April 1949 the General Assembly adopted a resolution recommending "to the permanent members of the Security Council that they seek agreement among themselves upon

what possible decisions by the Security Council they might forbear to exercise their veto, when seven affirmative votes have already been cast in the Council, giving favorable consideration to a list of such decisions" contained in the report of the Interim Committee, which list included recommendations for admission to membership. Resolution 267 (III); GAOR, III.2, Resolutions (A/900), p. 7.

5. At the 4th session of the General Assembly Argentina submitted the following draft resolution (A/AC.31/L.18; GAOR, IV, *Ad Hoc* Political Committee, Annex, Vol. I, p. 7):

"Whereas Committee 1 of Commission II of the San Francisco Conference approved the following interpretation of the powers of the Assembly with regard to the admission of new Members and directed that it should be included in its minutes as the only interpretation which should be given of that power:

" 'Admission of new Members

" '(Chapter V, section B, paragraph 2 of the Dumbarton Oaks Proposals)

" 'The Committee considered a revision of the text of this paragraph which was under consideration by the Co-ordination Committee in order to determine whether the power of the Assembly to admit new Members on recommendation of the Security Council was in no way weakened by the proposed text.

" 'The Committee was advised that the new text did not, in the view of the Advisory Committee of Jurists, weaken the right of the Assembly to accept or reject a recommendation for the admission of a new Member, or a recommendation to the effect that a given State should not be admitted to the United Nations.

" 'The Committee agreed that this interpretation should be included in its minutes as the one that should be given to this provision of the Charter, and on this basis approved the text as suggested by the Co-ordination Committee.'

"Whereas Commission II, and later the Conference, approved the decision of Committee II/1,

"'The General Assembly

"Decides to submit the following questions to the International Court of Justice for an advisory opinion:

"I. Does the last part of the second paragraph of the interpretation of the powers of the Assembly as approved by Committee II/1, by Commission II and finally by the Conference in plenary session and reading 'or a recommendation to the effect that a given State should not be admitted to the United Nations' refer to a *recommendation* by the Security Council to the effect that a given State should not be admitted to the United Nations?

"If the reply to the foregoing question is in the affirmative, does this mean that the Security Council can make a recommendation *against* admission?

"II. The third paragraph of the interpretation of the powers of the Assembly quoted above reads: 'The Committee agreed that this interpretation should be included in its minutes as the one that should be given to this provision of the Charter, and on this basis approved the text as suggested by the Co-ordination Committee.'

"Is this interpretation the only authentic interpretation that can be given to the above-mentioned provision of the Charter?

"III. If this interpretation is not the only authentic interpretation, is there any provision *in the Charter* which affords legal support for the view that the recommendation to which Article 4 refers must always be positive?

"IV. Must the decision to which Article 4, paragraph 2, refers be to the same effect as the Security Council's recommendation—positive or negative —or is the General Assembly completely free to decide?

"V. If the reply to the foregoing question is in the affirmative, is it absolutely essential that the Security Council should adopt a resolution in the form of a positive or negative recommendation, or is it sufficient that the Security Council should have taken cognizance of the request and should have had an opportunity to express its opinion, even if for any reason it has not expressed such opinion?

"VI. Is the admission of new Members a purely legal question or may the General Assembly be guided by political considerations in exercising its powers of decision?"

After some discussion, the representative of Argentina presented a revised draft which proposed that only one question be put to the Court; this proposal was accepted by the General Assembly on 22 November 1949. Resolution 296 J (IV); GAOR, IV, Resolutions (A/1251), p. 21.

COMPETENCE OF THE GENERAL ASSEMBLY FOR THE ADMISSION OF A STATE TO THE UNITED NATIONS

Advisory Opinion of the International Court of Justice, 3 March 1950.
ICJ Reports, 1950, pp. 4–34.

On November 22nd, 1949, the General Assembly of the United Nations adopted the following Resolution:

"The General Assembly,

"Keeping in mind the discussion concerning the admission of new Members in the *Ad Hoc* Political Committee at its fourth regular session,

"Requests the International Court of Justice to give an advisory opinion on the following question:

" 'Can the admission of a State to membership in the United Nations, pursuant to Article 4, paragraph 2, of the Charter, be effected by a decision of the General Assembly when the Security Council has made no recommendation for admission by reason of the candidate failing to obtain the requisite majority or of the negative vote of a permanent Member upon a resolution so to recommend?' " . . .

The Request for an Opinion calls upon the Court to interpret Article 4, paragraph 2, of the Charter. Before examining the merits of the question submitted to it, the Court must first consider the objections that have been made to its doing so, either on the ground that it is not competent to interpret the provisions of the Charter, or on the ground of the alleged political character of the question.

So far as concerns its competence, the Court will simply recall that, in a previous Opinion which dealt with the interpretation of Article 4, paragraph 1, it declared that, according to Article 96 of the Charter and Article 65 of the Statute, it may give an Opinion on any legal question and that there is no provision which prohibits it from exercising, in regard to Article 4 of the Charter, a multilateral treaty, an interpretative function falling within the normal exercise of its judicial powers (ICJ Reports, 1947–1948, p. 61).

With regard to the second objection, the Court notes that the General Assembly has requested it to give the legal interpretation of paragraph 2 of Article 4. As the Court stated in the same Opinion, it "cannot attribute a political character to a request which, framed in abstract terms, invites it to undertake an essentially judicial task, the interpretation of a treaty provision".

Consequently, the Court, in accordance with its previous declarations, considers that it is competent on the basis of Articles 96 of the Charter and 65 of its Statute and that there is no reason why it should not answer the question submitted to it. . . .

The Request for an Opinion envisages solely the case in which the Security Council, having voted upon a recommendation, has concluded from its vote that the recommendation was not adopted because it failed to obtain the requisite majority or because of the negative vote of a permanent Member. Thus the Request refers to the case in which the General Assembly is confronted with the absence of a recommendation from the Security Council.

It is not the object of the Request to determine how the Security Council should apply the rules governing its voting procedure in regard to admissions or, in particular, that the Court should examine whether the negative vote of a permanent Member is effective to defeat a recommendation which has obtained seven or more votes. The question, as it is formulated, assumes in such a case the non-existence of a recommendation.

The Court is, therefore, called upon to determine solely whether the General Assembly can make a decision to admit a State when the Security Council has transmitted no recommendation to it.

Article 4, paragraph 2, is as follows:

"The admission of any such State to membership in the United Nations, will be effected by a decision of the General Assembly upon the recommendation of the Security Council."

The Court has no doubt as to the meaning of this text. It requires two things to effect admission: a "recommendation" of the Security Council and a "decision" of the General Assembly. It is in the nature of things that the recommendation should come before the decision.

The word "recommendation", and the word "upon" preceding it, imply the idea that the recommendation is the foundation of the decision to admit, and that the latter rests upon the recommendation. Both these acts are indispensable to form the judgment of the Organization to which the previous paragraph of Article 4 refers. The text under consideration means that the General Assembly can only decide to admit upon the recommendation of the Security Council; it determines the respective roles of the two organs whose combined action is required before admission can be effected; in other words, the recommendation of the Security Council is the condition precedent to the decision of the Assembly by which the admission is effected.

In one of the written statements placed before the Court, an attempt was made to attribute to paragraph 2 of Article 4 a different meaning. The Court considers it necessary to say that the first duty of a tribunal which is called upon to interpret and apply the provisions of a treaty, is to endeavour to give effect to them in their natural and ordinary meaning in the context in which they occur. If the relevant words in their natural and ordinary meaning make sense in their context, that is an end of the matter. If, on the other hand, the words in their natural and ordinary meaning are ambiguous or lead to an unreasonable result, then, and then only, must the Court, by resort to other methods of interpretation, seek to ascertain what the parties really did mean when they used these words. As the Permanent Court said in the case concerning the *Polish Postal Service in Danzig* (PCIJ, Series B, No. 11, p. 39):

"It is a cardinal principle of interpretation that words must be interpreted in the sense which they would normally have in their context, unless such interpretation would lead to something unreasonable or absurd."

When the Court can give effect to a provision of a treaty by giving to the words used in it their natural and ordinary meaning, it may not interpret the words by seeking to give them some other meaning. In the present case the Court finds no difficulty in ascertaining the natural and ordinary meaning of the words in question and no difficulty in giving effect to them. Some of the written statements submitted to the Court have invited it to investigate the *travaux préparatoires* of the Charter. Having regard, however, to the considerations above stated, the Court is of the opinion that it is not permissible, in this case, to resort to *travaux préparatoires.*

The conclusions to which the Court is led by the text of Article 4, paragraph 2, are fully confirmed by the structure of the Charter, and particularly by the relations established by it between the General Assembly and the Security Council.

The General Assembly and the Security Council are both principal organs of the United Nations. The Charter does not place the Security Council in a subordinate position. Article 24 confers upon it "primary responsibility for the maintenance of international peace and security", and the Charter grants it for this purpose certain powers of decision. Under Articles 4, 5, and 6, the Security Council co-operates with the General Assembly in matters of admission to membership, of suspension from the exercise of the rights and privileges of membership, and of expulsion from the Organization. It has power, without the concurrence of the General Assembly, to reinstate the Member which was the object of the suspension, in its rights and privileges.

The organs to which Article 4 entrusts the judgment of the Organization in matters of admission have consistently interpreted the text in the sense that the General Assembly can decide to admit only on the basis of a recommendation of the Security Council. In particular, the Rules of Procedure of the General Assembly provide for consideration of the merits of an application and of the decision to be made upon it only "if the Security Council recommends the applicant State for membership" (Article 125 [137]). The Rules merely state that if the Security Council has not recommended the admission, the General Assembly may send back the application to the Security Council for further consideration (Article 126[138]). This last step has been taken several times: it was taken in Resolution 296(IV), the very one that embodies this Request for an Opinion.

To hold that the General Assembly has power to admit a State to membership in the absence of a recommendation of the Security Council would be to deprive the Security Council of an important power which has been entrusted to it by the Charter. It would almost nullify the role of the Security Council in the exercise of one of the essential functions of the Organization. It would mean that the Security Council would have merely to study the case, present a report, give advice, and express an opinion. This is not what Article 4, paragraph 2, says.

The Court cannot accept the suggestion made in one of the written statements submitted to the Court, that the General Assembly, in order to try to meet the requirement of Article 4, paragraph 2, could treat the absence of a recommendation as equivalent to what is described in that statement as an "unfavourable recommendation", upon which the General Assembly could base a decision to admit a State to membership.

Reference has also been made to a document of the San Francisco Conference, in order to put the possible case of an unfavourable recommendation being voted by the Security Council: such a recommendation has never been made in practice. In the opinion of the Court, Article 4, paragraph 2, envisages a favourable recommendation of the Security Council and that only. An unfavourable recommendation would not correspond to the provisions of Article 4, paragraph 2.

While keeping within the limits of a Request which deals with the scope of the powers of the General Assembly, it is enough for the Court to say that nowhere has the General Assembly received the power to change, to the point of reversing, the meaning of a vote of the Security Council.

In consequence, it is impossible to admit that the General Assembly has the power to attribute to a vote of the Security Council the character of a recommendation when the Council itself considers that no such recommendation has been made.

For these reasons,

THE COURT,

by twelve votes to two,

is of the opinion that the admission of a State to membership in the United Nations, pursuant to paragraph 2 of Article 4 of the Charter, cannot be effected by a decision of the General Assembly when the Security Council has made no recommendation for admission, by reason of the candidate failing to obtain the requisite majority or of the negative vote of a permanent Member upon a resolution so to recommend. . . .

Dissenting Opinion by M. ALVAREZ . . . We have before us a case which involves the interpretation of the Charter of the United Nations; it refers therefore to a new question of international law.

This case must not be decided in accordance with the precepts of traditional or classic international law, which were established on an *individualistic* basis and have hitherto prevailed, but rather in accordance with the *new international law,* which is now emerging. . . .

I hold that the role of the General Assembly in the admission of new Members is an active role, for it is the Assembly which effects the admission.

According to paragraph 2 of Article 4 of the Charter, the Assembly effects the admission of States which fulfil the conditions laid down in that article, but it is necessary that the Security Council should have recommended the State requesting admission.

Two situations may arise:

A.   The State seeking admission has failed to obtain the requisite number of votes in the Security Council. In that case, its admission cannot be recommended to the General Assembly. The resulting situation resembles that which occurs in regard to the election of Members of the International Court of Justice: in order that a judge may be elected, he must have obtained the requisite majority both in the Security Council and in the General Assembly; if he does not secure the required majority in the Council, he cannot be elected.

B.   The State seeking admission has obtained the requisite number
of votes in the Council, but one of the permanent Members has opposed the recommendation, in other words, has made use of the *veto*.
This is the case which we must specially consider.   I think that the
General Assembly may appraise the veto.

The right of veto has been provided by paragraph 3 of Article 27 of
the Charter of the United Nations.   But, if we examine the provisions
of Chapters V, VI, VII and VIII to which it refers, we see that when
this right was created the only objects in view were matters concerning the maintenance of peace and international security.   Article 24
states that the Members of the United Nations Organization confer on
the Security Council a primary responsibility for the maintenance of
international peace and security.   The article thus establishes something closely resembling the former "European Directorate" created
after the Napoleonic wars, but with a universal scope.   The creation
of such a body is certainly fitting and justifiable, having regard to the
primary role played by the Great Powers in case of conflict.   It is entirely natural that the Security Council should be unable to adopt decisions in matters so grave as those of peace and security against the
opposition of a Great Power, for the latter would then be obliged to
take part, contrary to its will, in the proposed measures, and that
would be a very dangerous situation.

But the exercise of this right of veto must be kept within proper
limits.   The literal text of Article 27, which established this right, is
clear, if taken in isolation; but it is no longer clear if we have regard
to the nature and objects of the United Nations Organization.

To decide that the right of veto may be freely exercised in every
case in which the Security Council may take action would mean deciding that the will of a single Great Power could frustrate the will
of all the other Members of that Council and of the General Assembly,
even in matters other than the maintenance of peace and security;
and that would reduce the U.N.O. to impotence.

Even if it is admitted that the right of veto may be exercised freely
by the permanent Members of the Security Council in regard to the
recommendation of new Members, the General Assembly may still
determine whether or not this right has been *abused* and, if the answer is in the affirmative, it can proceed with the admission without
any recommendation by the Council.

It has been argued that the Security Council is alone competent to
appraise the use made by one of its permanent Members of the right
of veto, and that this is shown by the practice which has become established.   I cannot agree with that opinion either: the General Assembly is entitled not only to ask the Council for what reason it has
failed to recommend a State seeking admission, but also to determine
whether or not this right of veto has been abused.

According to Articles 10 and 11 of the Charter, the General Assembly may make recommendations to the Security Council; *a fortiori* it may make observations to that Council whenever it sees fit. It is not necessary that the Assembly should have been endowed with such a right in express terms, for it is a necessary consequence of its powers.

The above solution is consistent both with the spirit of the Charter of the United Nations and with the requirements of common sense.

It is consistent with the spirit of the Charter by the terms of which the U.N.O. has a universal role, with the consequence that all members of the international community which fulfill the conditions laid down in Article 4 should be admitted to the United Nations; these States have a *right* to be admitted.

The solution is also consistent with the requirements of common sense because, if it were admitted that the right of veto could be freely exercised, the result might be—as has just been pointed out—that a State whose request for admission had been approved by all the Members of the Security Council except one and by all the Members of the General Assembly would nevertheless be unable to obtain admission to the United Nations because of the opposition of a single country; a single vote would thus be able to frustrate the votes of all the other Members of the United Nations; and that would be an absurdity.

[In his dissenting opinion, M. AZEVEDO laid stress on the difference between "recommendations" and "decisions", and interpreted Article 27 restrictively. His conclusion was that "the word 'decision', as it has been used in Article 27, cannot be extended to a 'recommendation' of the Security Council addressed to another organ to which has been left the 'decision' in a certain case, even if the recommendation is necessary. Even if we preferred that Article 27 should exceed the specific powers of the Security Council [enumerated in Article 24], and go so far as to include the case of the admission of new Members, we should be justified in considering such a question as depending upon 'procedure'. . . . Therefore, if, in the report from the Security Council, the General Assembly observes that the applicant State has obtained the votes of any seven Members of the Council, it may freely decide to accept or reject the applicant. On the other hand, if the application has not obtained seven favourable votes, the Assembly would be under obligation to take note of the absence of a recommendation preventing any final discussion."]

NOTE.—1. In 1949, regardless of the 1948 opinion of the Court, the USSR proposed the simultaneous admission to membership of all thirteen applications then pending, but the Security Council rejected this Soviet proposal. SCOR, IV, No. 42, pp. 2–3, 45.

After various attempts to solve the deadlock, a Committee of Good Offices established by the General Assembly succeeded in persuading the major powers to modify their positions. It reported to the tenth session of the General Assembly in 1955 that the "permanent members, although continuing to adhere to their positions on the question of admission, conveyed the impression that such adherence was not necessarily immutable in view of the current evolution of the international atmosphere." A/2973; GAOR, Annexes (X) 21, pp. 1–2. On 8 December 1955 the General Assembly adopted a resolution requesting "the Security Council to consider, in the light of the general opinion in favour of the widest possible membership of the United Nations, the pending applications for membership of all those eighteen countries about which no problem of unification arises." Resolution 918(X); GAOR, X, Supp. 19 (A/3116), p. 8. In the Security Council, on 13 December 1955, the Soviet Union vetoed the admission of fifteen applicants (including South Korea and South Vietnam), after China vetoed the admission of the Mongolian People's Republic. A day later agreement was reached in the Security Council on the admission of sixteen applicants, after Japan and the Mongolian People's Republic were eliminated from the "package". SCOR, X, Mtgs. 701–705. The General Assembly on the same day took final action to admit the sixteen applicants, and membership of the United Nations thus increased to 76. Resolution 995(X); GAOR, X, Supp. 19(A/3116), p. 50. The final package included the following States: Albania, Austria, Bulgaria, Cambodia, Ceylon, Finland, Hungary, Ireland, Italy, Jordan, Laos, Libya, Nepal, Portugal, Romania and Spain.

The following States were admitted thereafter: in 1956—Japan, Morocco, Sudan and Tunisia; in 1957—Ghana and Malaya; in 1958—Guinea; in 1960—Cameroon, Central African Republic, Chad, Congo (Brazzaville), Congo (Leopoldville), Cyprus, Dahomey, Gabon, Ivory Coast, Malagasy Republic, Mali, Niger, Nigeria, Senegal, Somalia, Togo and Upper Volta; in 1961—Mauritania, Mongolia, Sierra Leone and Tanganyika; in 1962—Algeria, Burundi, Jamaica, Rwanda, Trinidad and Tobago, and Uganda; in 1963—Kenya, Kuwait and Zanzibar (which combined in 1964 with Tanganyika into the United Republic of Tanzania); in 1964—Malawi, Malta and Zambia; in 1965—Gambia, the Maldive Islands and Singapore; in 1966—Barbados, Botswana, Guyana and Lesotho.

2. In January 1957 the USSR proposed joint admission of the Democratic People's Republic of Korea and the Republic of Korea, and of the Democratic Republic of Viet-Nam and the Republic of Viet-Nam, but this proposal was rejected by the General Assembly. GAOR, XI, Special Political C., pp. 79–80, 105–6. Later the USSR vetoed in the Security Council proposals to admit only the Republics of Korea and Viet-Nam. SCOR, XII, Mtgs. 789–90 (9 September 1957); SCOR, XIII, Mtgs. 842–43 (9 December 1958). In 1966 The German Democratic Republic applied for membership in the United Nations, and suggested that the German Federal Republic be admitted at the same time. A/6283 and S/7192 (10 March 1966), and A/6443 and S/7508 (26 September 1966). The German Federal Republic contended that "the Soviet Zone of Germany" is not eligible for membership because "(1) it fails to meet the United Nations definition of a state and (2) it constantly violates the human rights guaranteed by the U.N. General Assembly." 14 The Bulletin. . . issued by the Press and Information Office of the German Federal Government, No. 12 (22 March 1966), p. 2.

OTHER MEMBERSHIP QUESTIONS

NOTE.—1. The Charter limits membership in the United Nations to "states". But what is a "state"? According to Article 1 of the Inter-American Convention on Rights and Duties of States (6 Hudson, Int.Leg. 622) a State "should possess the following qualifications: (a) a permanent population; (b) a defined territory; (c) government; and (d) capacity to enter into relations with the other states." Are those the only necessary qualifications? For a bibliography on the subject, see SOHN, World Law, p. 172.

Is the capacity of a State to enter into relations with other States, and to carry out the obligations contained in the Charter of the United Nations, affected by its size? See the statement of the President of the Security Council (Mr. Yost, USA) in connection with the admission of the Maldive Islands (with a population of 98,000 in 1965), 20 September 1965, SCOR, XX, Mtg. 1243. As many as seventy "mini-states" might apply for admission to the United Nations in the next twenty years.

2. Can a component unit of a federation be considered as a State? With respect to the component Republics of the USSR, see, e. g., Samuel DOBRIN, "Soviet Federalism and the Principle of Double Subordination," 30 Grotius Soc. Transactions (1944), pp. 260–83; Edward DOLAN, "The Member-Republics of the U.S.S.R. as Subjects of the Law of Nations," 4 ICLQ (1955), pp. 629–36; Louis B. SOHN, "Multiple Representation in International Assemblies," 40 AJIL (1946), pp. 71–99; N. S. TIMASHEFF, "The United Nations Charter: Legal Aspects of the Grant of Three Seats to Russia in the United Nations Charter," 14 Fordham L.R. (1945), pp. 180–90; and Alfred VERDROSS, "Die Völkerrechtssubjektivität der Gliedstaaten der Sovjetunion," 1 ÖZÖR (1946), pp. 212–8.

3. Is the membership of a State in the United Nations contingent upon the maintenance of a substantial identity of territory or population? If a State, a member of the United Nations, becomes divided into two or more States by reason of constitutional reform, secession or the like, which unit, if any, retains the membership in the United Nations? Is there any difference between the results of secession or dismemberment for this purpose? What are the criteria for determining this question as between the two or more competing units?

If two or more members of the United Nations confederate, is the resultant unit automatically a member of the United Nations? Could it have more than one vote?

In 1947, by the terms of a United Kingdom statute, the India Independence Act (10 & 11 Geo. 6, Ch. 30), the two independent Dominions of India and Pakistan were constituted out of the territory and population of a United Nations Member, formerly known as India. Pursuant to Section 9 of the statute, provision was made that the Dominion of India should assume the membership of all international organizations and that the Dominion of Pakistan should take such steps as might be necessary to apply for membership of such international organizations as it chose to join. See India Independence (International Arrangements) Order, 14 August 1947, Governor-General's Order No. 17; reproduced as Annex I of UN Doc. A/C.6/161. In a telegram to the United Nations, Pakistan claimed automatic membership, but intimated that if this right was not conceded, she would submit an application to the Security Council. A Secretariat opinion given by the Assistant Secretary-General in charge of Legal Affairs, Dr. Ivan Kerno, and approved by the Secretary-General was made public on 12 August 1947. It concluded that the partition of India was a situation "in which part of an existing state breaks off to form a new state." "In such a situation," continued the opinion, "the territory which breaks off is a new state, with none of the treaty rights and obligations of the parent state; the remaining portion retains its 'international personality' and all treaty rights and obligations remain in force." It also concluded that new credentials should be requested for the Indian representatives. See New York Times, 13 August 1947, p. 11. This opinion, though intended only for departmental use, resulted in the filing of an application by Pakistan which was subsequently approved by both the Council and the General Assembly. The right of the Dominion of India to retain membership without a new application was not contested. On 24 September 1947, Mr. Arce (Argentina) expressed the view in the First Committee of the General Assembly that Pakistan "was already a Member of the United Nations, since with India it inherited the original membership held by the previous Indian Government. The division had been achieved in a legal fashion without war or revolution. . . . If the United Nations had decided that, since India and Pakistan were new States, both Governments should submit applications, he would have no objection to that procedure." GAOR, II First C., pp. 3–4. The application of Pakistan was approved at the same meeting of the First Committee, but as a result of Mr. Arce's comments it was decided to ask the Sixth Committee for its opinion, on the understanding that such opinion was for future use and had no bearing on the present case. The conclusions of the Rapporteur, Mr. Kaeckenbeeck (Belgium), concurred in by the Sixth Committee, were as follows:

"1. That, as a general rule, it is in conformity with legal principles to presume that a State which is a member of the United Nations does not cease to be a Member simply because its constitution or its frontier have been subjected to changes, and that the extinction of the State as a legal personality recognized in the international order must be shown before its rights and obligations can be considered thereby to have ceased to exist.

"2. That when a new State is created, whatever may be the territory and the populations which it comprises and whether or not they formed part of a State Member of the United Nations, it cannot under the system of the Charter claim the status of a Member of the United Nations unless it has been formally admitted as such in conformity with the provisions of the Charter.

"Beyond that, each case must be judged according to its merits." GAOR, II, Sixth C., pp. 37–44, 304–10.

On the question of Pakistan's application see also O. SCHACHTER, "The Development of International Law through the Legal Opinions of the United Nations Secretariat", 25 BYBIL (1948), pp. 91, 101–9; Lionel H. LAING, "Admission of Indian States to the United Nations," 43 AJIL (1949), pp. 144–54.

With respect to the membership of Malaysia in the United Nations and other similar cases, see the memorandum of the Office of Legal Affairs of the United Nations, 19 September 1963. UN Juridical Yearbook, 1963, pp. 161–64. See also the memorandum by the Secretary of the United Nations on the succession of States in relation to membership in the United Nations, 3 December 1962. A/CN.4/149 and Add. 1; ILC Yearbook, 1962, Vol. II, pp. 101–5. Cf., ibid., p. 124.

4. Rule 58 of the Rules of Procedure of the Security Council requires a State applying for membership to submit "a declaration made in a formal instrument that it accepts the obligations contained in the Charter". What constitutes a formal instrument? Would the United Nations be bound to take any steps to verify the constitutionality of such a declaration in terms of the internal law of the applicant State? Would subsequent participation of that state in the work of the United Nations cure any constitutional defects in such a declaration? For a discussion of a similar problem in the League of Nations, see M. O. HUDSON, "The Argentine Republic and the League of Nations," 28 AJIL (1934), pp. 125–33; C. FAIRMAN, "Competence to Bind the State to an International Engagement," 30 AJIL (1936), pp. 439, 446–9.

5. On 10 April 1948, Mr. Austin (US) suggested in the Security Council that States which were prevented by a veto from becoming United Nations members should be given "a voice in the General Assembly." SCOR, III, No. 54, p. 17. At the fifth session of the General Assembly, El Salvador proposed that the States which received seven or more favorable votes in the Security Council be invited to send observers to sessions of the General Assembly and its Committees "in order to enable them to express their views and furnish information whenever consulted by the delegation of any Member State." A/1585, 2 December 1950; GAOR, V, Annexes, Agenda Item 19, pp. 3–4. This proposal was rejected by 21 votes to 11, with 16 abstentions. Secretary of State Dulles made a proposal in January 1954 that a special "associate membership" be created for such States, which would authorize them "to take part in the proceedings, to express their views, and to record their votes." US SENATE, Review of the United Nations Charter: Hearing before a Subcommittee of the Committee on Foreign Relations (83d Congress, 2d session, 1954), p. 20. See also WILCOX-MARCY, pp. 101–2.

Does the Charter permit the establishment of such an associate membership?

Such associate status should be distinguished from the accreditation by non-members of permanent observers at the United Nations headquarters; as to the latter see the memorandum of the Office of Legal Affairs of the United Nations, 22 August 1962, UN Juridical Yearbook, 1962 (Provisional Edition, ST/LEG/8), pp. 236–37. The Secretary-General of the United Nations has suggested that "countries not at present represented in New York should be enabled to maintain contact with the world body and be able to listen to its deliberations. In this way, they too would obtain an exposure, now denied them to the currents and cross-currents of opinion in the world Organization." Introduction to the Annual Report of the Secretary-General on the Work of the Organization, 1963–64 [GAOR, XIX, Supp. 1A (A/5801/Add.1], p. 11. He repeated this suggestion in 1965 and 1966. Introduction to the Annual Report of the Secretary-General on the Work of the Organization, 1964–65 [GAOR, XX Supp. 1A (A/6001/Add.1)], p. 11; *idem*, 1965–66 [GAOR, XXI, Supp. 1A (A/6301/Add.1)], p. 14.

6. Though Article 92 of the Charter makes the Statute of the International Court of Justice "an integral part of the present Charter," Article 93, paragraph 2, of the Charter allows non-member States to become parties to the Statute "on conditions to be determined in each case by the General Assembly upon the recommendation of the Security Council." Under this pro-

vision four States became parties to the Statute: Switzerland in 1948, Liechtenstein in 1950, San Marino and Japan in 1954. (Japan became a member of the United Nations in 1956.)

The conditions were the same for all applicants. For instance, in Resolution 91(I) of the General Assembly of 11 December 1946 (GAOR, I.2, Resolutions, pp. 182–3) Switzerland was asked to deposit with the Secretary-General an instrument containing:

"(a) Acceptance of the provisions of the Statute of the International Court of Justice;

"(b) Acceptance of all the obligations of a Member of the United Nations under Article 94 of the Charter;

"(c) An undertaking to contribute to the expenses of the Court such equitable amount as the General Assembly shall assess from time to time after consultation with the Swiss Government."

For comments on this resolution, see M. HAGEMANN, "Der Beitritt der Schweiz zum Statut des internationalen Gerichtshofes und die schweizerische Neutralität," 5 SJIR (1948), pp. 117–54; M. O. HUDSON, "The Twenty-Fifth Year of the World Court," 41 AJIL (1947), pp. 7–9; *idem*, "Switzerland and the International Court of Justice," 41 AJIL (1947), pp. 866–71; *idem*, "Twenty-Sixth Year of the World Court," 42 AJIL (1948), pp. 5–7; KELSEN, UN Law, pp. 79–82, 489–506.

Under Article 4 of the Statute of the Court, the General Assembly laid down on 8 October 1948 the following conditions for the participation by a State which is a party to the Statute but is not a member of the United Nations in the election of judges (Resolution 264(III); GAOR, III.1, Resolutions, p. 181):

"1. That such a State shall be on an equal footing with the Members of the United Nations in respect to those provisions of the Statute which regulate the nominations of candidates for election by the General Assembly;

"2. That such a State shall participate, in the General Assembly, in electing the members of the Court in the same manner as the Members of the United Nations;

"3. That such a State, when in arrears in the payment of its contribution to the expenses of the Court, shall not participate in electing the members of the Court in the General Assembly if the amount of its arrears equals or exceeds the amount of the contribution due from it for the preceding two years. The General Assembly may, nevertheless, permit such a State to participate in the elections, if it is satisfied that the failure to pay is due to conditions beyond the control of that State (see Charter, Article 19)."

Section 2. Withdrawal, Suspension and Expulsion of Members

WITHDRAWAL FROM MEMBERSHIP

NOTE.—1. Unlike the Covenant of the League of Nations, the Charter contains no provision for withdrawal. The Covenant allowed a Member to withdraw "after two years' notice of its intention so to do," provided that it has fulfilled at the time of its withdrawal "all its international obligations and all its obligations" under the Covenant (Article 1, paragraph 3). More

than one-fourth of the Members actually withdrew from the League in accordance with this procedure. For a bibliography on this subject, see SOHN,
World Law, pp. 250–1.

2. An explanation of the reasons for omitting a provision on withdrawal
from the Charter is contained in the report of Committee I/2 of the San
Francisco Conference, which was properly approved by Commission I and
by the Conference itself. UNCIO Docs. 1178, 1179(1) and 1210; 1 UNCIO
Documents, pp. 619–20; 6 *idem*, p. 249; 7 *idem*, pp. 327–9. The report was
as follows:

"The questions of withdrawal, expulsion and suspension have the following problem in common:

"Can a member State cease to be a member, either on its own initiative, or
as a result of measures taken against it by the Organization?

"The arguments against withdrawal were: (1) that it would be contrary
to the conception of universality. (However, universality, as we have seen,
has only general acceptance as an ideal or an objective); (2) that withdrawal would give recalcitrant members the possibility of securing concessions from the Organization by threatening to leave it; (3) that withdrawal
would be a means of escape from fulfilling obligations by leaving the Organization.

"During the discussion two theses for the insertion of the right of withdrawal in the Charter were brought forward: The first recommended a
clause providing for withdrawal, pure and simple; the second one suggested
the adoption of a clause which would permit withdrawal only in the well-de-
fined cases: 1) when the rights and obligations of a member are altered by
an amendment which he does not approve of and which he is not in a position
to accept and 2) when an amendment duly accepted by the necessary majority of the Assembly or of a special Conference fails to secure the ratifications
necessary to bring such amendment into force.

"After weighing the arguments presented in support of these two theses,
the Committee declared itself against the insertion in the Charter of a withdrawal clause.

"Some delegates repeated their statement that they were fundamentally
opposed to even the idea of withdrawal, being in favor of universality, and
they considered it only natural to vote against insertion in the Charter of a
clause providing for withdrawal.

"Many of them were of the opinion that although, in exceptional circumstances such as those envisaged in some of the proposals, the option of withdrawal seemed admissible and in keeping with the spirit of the Charter, it
could not be generally recognized without certain drawbacks. Even if limited to specific conditions—which, moreover, it would be difficult to determine
restrictively—any express mention of withdrawal in the Charter would run
the risk of representing the withdrawal of certain members as something
normal or probable, whereas, on the contrary, if the Charter should work
reasonably well, particularly as regards revision, this would be unnecessary.
After discussing the matter at length, the Committee arrived at the opinion
that no withdrawal clause should be inserted in the Charter and that its idea
could be expressed by the following text, which it was decided to insert in
the report:

" 'The Committee adopts the view that the Charter should not make express provision either to permit or to prohibit withdrawal from the Organization. The Committee deems that the highest duty of the nations which will become Members is to continue their cooperation within the Organization for the preservation of international peace and security. If, however, a Member because of exceptional circumstances feels constrained to withdraw, and leave the burden of maintaining international peace and security on the other Members, it is not the purpose of the Organization to compel that Member to continue its cooperation in the Organization.

" 'It is obvious, particularly, that withdrawals or some other forms of dissolution of the Organization would become inevitable if, deceiving the hopes of humanity, the Organization was revealed to be unable to maintain peace or could do so only at the expense of law and justice.

" 'Nor would a Member be bound to remain in the Organization if its rights and obligations as such were changed by Charter amendment in which it has not concurred and which it finds itself unable to accept, or if an amendment duly accepted by the necessary majority in the Assembly or in a general conference fails to secure the ratification necessary to bring such amendment into effect.

" 'It is for these considerations that the Committee has decided to abstain from recommending insertion in the Charter of a formal clause specifically forbidding or permitting withdrawal.' "

When this report was discussed in the plenary session of the Conference, Mr. GROMYKO (USSR) made the following statement:

"The Soviet Delegation feels that the expression 'and leave the burden of maintaining international peace and security on the other Members', contained in the above . . . Report, is defective and in no way can the Delegation agree to it.

"The opinion of the Soviet Delegation is that it is wrong to condemn beforehand the grounds on which any state may find it necessary to exercise its right of withdrawal from the Organization. Such right is an expression of state sovereignty and should not be reviled, in advance, by the International Organization.

"May I cite as an example of unconditional acknowledgement of this right of sovereign states Article 17 of the Constitution of U.S.S.R., which reads as follows: 'To every Union Republic is reserved the right freely to secede from U.S.S.R.' It is common knowledge that this right is a most striking manifestation of democracy on which the organization of the Soviet State is founded. The U.S.S.R. is formed on the basis of voluntary accession to the Union with a right of free withdrawal from it.

"It would be still less justifiable to condemn in advance the reasons for a state's withdrawal from the International Organization, which is also founded on voluntary participation of sovereign states. To deny or to revile such a right would be a violation of principles of democracy and of sovereignty.

"Further the same paragraph of the above-mentioned Report states:

" 'It is obvious, however, that withdrawal or some other form of dissolution of the Organization would become inevitable if, deceiving the hopes of humanity, the Organization was revealed to be unable to maintain peace or could do so only at the expense of law and justice.'

"The Soviet Delegation cannot agree to this assertion either.

"The presence of the above-cited sentence in an official document of the Conference can only discredit the International Organization, since it makes the Organization responsible for any withdrawal of any state, regardless of the motives of such withdrawal.

"The Soviet Delegation have already expressed their opinion on this matter, but unfortunately due weight has not been given to their arguments. Therefore, the Soviet Delegation reaffirming their point of view deem it necessary to make this statement to the plenary session and request that their statement be attached to the record of this session." UNCIO Doc. 1210; 1 UNCIO Documents, pp. 619–20.

WITHDRAWAL OF INDONESIA

NOTE.—1. After Malaysia was elected to the Security Council on 29 December 1964 Indonesia notified the United Nations on 31 December 1964 that it would withdraw from the United Nations if Malaysia should be seated in the Council. By a letter of 20 January 1965, the Minister of Foreign Affairs of Indonesia informed the Secretary-General of the United Nations that his government "has taken the decision to withdraw from the United Nations." He explained that:

"My Government was fully aware of the great weight and impact of such a decision, but in the circumstances which have been created by colonial powers in the United Nations so blatantly against our anti-colonial struggle and indeed against the lofty principles and purposes of the United Nations Charter, my Government felt that no alternative had been left for Indonesia but withdrawal from the United Nations. Summing up and balancing all the considerations in their negative and positive aspects we have come to the conclusion that our decision may become the catalyst to reform and re-tool the United Nations in spirit and in deed, lest the present atmosphere of complacency shown by the neo-colonial Powers may undermine the lofty principles of the United Nations and consequently the decline of the United Nations as an international body for collective security and harmonious co-operation may become irrevocable. . . .

"This decision of my Government is of course a revolutionary one, unprecedented as it may be. This however, was taken for the good of the United Nations itself, which in our view need a strong reminder from time to time. It might even be, that this decision of my Government could well entail a beneficial effect for the speedy solution of the problem of 'Malaysia' itself. Arrogance displayed so far for a settlement based on previous agreements might be dissolved, in the general desire for the just solution of burning and acute problems in South-East Asia as a whole.

"As to your personal appeal, Mr. Secretary-General, that Indonesia should not withdraw from its co-operation with the United Nations, I want to assure you that Indonesia still upholds the lofty principles of international co-operation as enshrined in the United Nations Charter. This, however, can be implemented outside as well as inside the United Nations body.

"Indonesia has been active in the field of international co-operation for a better world and it will continue to do so. However, due to the serious reasons I mentioned above, Indonesia has decided at this stage and under the present circumstances to withdraw from the United Nations and in addition also from specialized agencies like the FAO, UNICEF and UNESCO." A/5857 (21 January 1965).

2. In his reply, the Secretary-General pointed out that the position taken by the Indonesian Government "has given rise to a situation in regard to which no express provision is made in the Charter. It is to be recalled, however, that the San Francisco Conference adopted a declaration relating to the matter." Consequently, he issued the Indonesian letter as a document of both the Security Council and the General Assembly, the two bodies concerned with membership questions, transmitted it to all Members of the United Nations, and over a period of a month held consultations with many Members of the Organization. After noting Indonesia's statement on upholding the principles of international co-operation, the Secretary-General expressed "both the profound regret which is widely felt in the United Nations that Indonesia has found it necessary to adopt the course of action outlined in your letter and the earnest hope that in due time it will resume full co-operation with the United Nations." A/5899 (26 February 1965).

3. Commenting on Indonesia's withdrawal, the United Kingdom on 8 March 1965 noted that:

"Without prejudice to their views as to the circumstances which might legally justify a Member State in withdrawing from the United Nations, Her Majesty's Government wish to place formally on record their conviction that the reason for withdrawal advanced in the letter of 20 January from the First Deputy Prime Minister and Minister for Foreign Affairs of Indonesia —namely the election of a non-permanent member of the Security Council which the Government of Indonesia unilaterally considers as not fulfilling the requirements of Article 23 of the Charter—is not a circumstance so exceptional in nature as to justify the Government of Indonesia in withdrawing from the Organization.

"Her Majesty's Government would at the same time wish to draw attention to the terms of Article 2, paragraph 6, of the Charter which provides that 'the Organization shall ensure that States which are not Members of the United Nations act in accordance with [the] principles [contained in Article 2 of the Charter] so far as may be necessary for the maintenance of international peace and security.' Amongst these principles, which are declaratory of general international law binding upon all States, are the principles obliging States to settle their international disputes by peaceful means and to refrain in their international relations from the threat or use of force against the territorial integrity or political independence of any State, or in any other manner inconsistent with the purposes of the United Nations. Since the Organization and its Members are obligated to act in accordance with the principle contained in Article 2, paragraph 6, of the Charter, and since the principles contained in Article 2 of the Charter constitute general principles of international law binding upon all States, Her Majesty's Government wish to place formally on record their view that a State which has expressed an intention to withdraw from the Organization nevertheless remains bound to observe the fundamental principles embodied in Article 2 of the Charter relative to the maintenance of international peace and security." A/5910 (12 March 1965).

4. The Italian Government, in a *note verbale* of 13 May 1965, voiced "its apprehension over the disquieting consequences for the United Nations resulting from the absence of any mention in the Charter of such an important point as withdrawal or recession of a Member State from the Organization. Authoritative sources have appropriately stressed the existence of a 'declaration' adopted by the San Francisco Conference concerning the withdrawal of Member States from the United Nations. The declaration in question appears, however, to be not entirely adequate in so far as it does not contain any definition of the circumstances which might justify the withdrawal or recession of a Member State, nor does it specify any procedure for determining those circumstances in the future. Lastly, the document does not indicate any procedure whereby the withdrawal of a Member State may be considered effective. It is hoped, therefore, that in the near future it will be possible to undertake an appropriate study of the problem in general terms.

"The Italian Government has duly taken note of the declaration on the basis of which 'Indonesia still upholds the lofty principles of international co-operation as enshrined in the United Nations Charter.' In effect, the principles of the United Nations Charter now form part of customary international law and of general international law and no State which withdraws from the Organization may evade some fundamental obligations laid down in the Charter. Similarly, it is to be assumed that the United Nations will retain its full authority under Article 2, paragraph 6, and consequently under Chapter VII of the Charter, which are applicable to relations between the United Nations and States which are not Members of the Organization. Even though the principle of respect for the sovereignty of States should be observed and safeguarded, it is nevertheless also true that, in joining the United Nations, States have implicitly renounced a part of their sovereign capacities which might have been contrary to the principles proclaimed by the San Francisco Charter and which might have prevented the attainment of the aims stated in the Charter. It is now generally acknowledged that these principles must be considered an integral part of the constitutional structure of modern democratic States. This is explicitly confirmed by the norms which have been adopted on that subject in various post-war constitutions, including some which have major political and legal significance and major doctrinal importance. For example, article II of the Constitution of the Italian Republic states, *inter alia*: 'Italy .   .   . agrees, provided that it enjoys parity with other States, to any limitations on sovereignty required to establish an order which will ensure peace and justice between nations; and promotes and fosters international organizations directed towards this purpose.'

"Finally, one aspect of particular importance in the event of withdrawal or recession of a Member State concerns the obligations assumed under multilateral conventions adopted within the framework of the United Nations and to which the State acceded as a Member of the Organization. It is indeed to be assumed that such obligations stand regardless of whether the State continues to be part of the Organization or not. Adherence to the aforesaid conventions is, in fact, effected by means of a definite act of will expressed on each occasion in the form stipulated by international law. It cannot therefore be admitted that withdrawal or recession from the Organization in itself puts an end to the obligations assumed under a regular international agreement. In the event of a State not wishing to carry out such obligations after its withdrawal or recession from the Organization, it must make its intention clear in the form stipulated by the convention itself." A/5914 (17 May 1965).

5. Neither the Security Council nor the General Assembly took any formal action on the Indonesian letter. On 1 March 1965, the necessary "administrative actions" were taken by the Secretariat to deal with the consequences of Indonesia's withdrawal. Thus the Indonesian name-plate and flag were removed from the United Nations premises, and Indonesia ceased to be listed as a Member of the Organization, or of United Nations principal and subsidiary organs of which it had been a member solely by virtue of its membership in the United Nations itself. Furthermore, the name of Indonesia did not appear in resolution 2118 (XX) of 21 December 1965, whereby the Assembly fixed the scale of assessments of Member States for the financial years 1965, 1966 and 1967 (nor was it assessed in the same resolution as a non-member for the expenses of certain organs in which non-members participate). UN Press Release GA/3210 (28 Sept. 1966), p. 2.

6. On 19 September 1966, the Indonesian Government notified the Secretary-General that it had decided "to resume full co-operation with the United Nations and to resume participation in its activities starting with the twenty-first session of the General Assembly." A/6419 (19 September 1966). After consulting with the Members of the United Nations, the President of the General Assembly announced on 28 September 1966 that the Government of Indonesia was of the opinion that Indonesia's absence from the United Nations "was based not upon withdrawal from the United Nations but upon a cessation of co-operation." He noted that the "action so far taken by the United Nations would not appear to preclude this view. If this is also the general view of the membership, the Secretary-General would give instructions for the necessary administrative actions to be taken for Indonesia to participate again in the proceedings of the Organization. It may be assumed that, from the time that Indonesia resumes participation, it will meet in full its budgetary obligations. If it is the general view that the bond of membership has continued throughout the period of non-participation, it would be the intention of the Secretary-General to negotiate an appropriate payment with the representatives of Indonesia for that period and to report the outcome of his negotiations to the Fifth Committee for its consideration." As no objections were raised, the President assumed "that it is the will of the membership that Indonesia should resume full participation in the activities of the United Nations." Consequently, he invited the representatives of Indonesia to take their seats in the General Assembly. UN Press Release GA/3210 (28 Sept. 1966), p. 3; 3 UN Monthly Chronicle, No. 9 (Oct. 1966), pp. 11–12.

7. For comments on the general question of withdrawal and on the special problem of Indonesia's withdrawal, see Elias BLUTH, "Retiro voluntario de un Estade miembro de la Organizacion de las Naciones Unidas: El caso de Indonesia," 3 AUrugDI (1964), pp. 363–87; Fernand DEHOUSSE, "Le droit de retrait aus Nations Unies," 1 Revue belge de droit international (1965), pp. 30–48; 2 *idem* (1966), pp. 8–27; N. FEINBERG, "Unilateral Withdrawal from an International Organization," 39 BYBIL (1965), pp. 189–219; Francesco Carlo GENTILE, "Il recesso dalle Nazioni Unite," 6 Comunità Internazionale (1951), pp. 464–81; George E. GLOS, "Termination of

Membership in the United Nations," 2 University of Malaya L.Rev. (1960),
pp. 226–45; Hans KELSEN, "Withdrawal from the United Nations," 1
Western Political Q. (1948), pp. 29–43; F. L. LAURIA, "Il recesso dall'Or-
ganizzazione delle Nazioni Unite: Il caso dell'Indonesia," 20 Diritto internazionale (1966), pp. 153–74; Frances LIVINGSTONE, "Withdrawal from
the United Nations: Indonesia," 14 ICLQ (1965), pp. 637–46; H. N.
MORSE, "The New Secession: A Study of the Legal Right to Withdraw from
the United Nations," 21 South Dakota B. J. (1953), pp. 14–17; Lucien
NIZARD, "Le retrait de l'Indonésie des Nations Unies," 11 AFDI (1965), pp.
498–528; Mario SCERNI, "Aspetti giuridici del ritiro dalle Nazioni Unite,"
20 Comunità Internazionale (1965), pp. 227–44; Nagendra SINGH, Termination of Membership of International Organisations (London, 1958), pp.
92–98.

SUSPENSION AND EXPULSION

NOTE.—1. In its report to the San Francisco Conference (UNCIO Doc.
1178, I/2/76(2); 7 UNCIO Documents, pp. 329–32), Committee I/2 dealt
not only with the question of withdrawal but also with suspension and expulsion. It summarized the discussion as follows: "When this question was
brought before the whole Committee, the members in favor of expulsion
explained that the primary purposes of the Organization were peace and
security, not universality. Expulsion would only apply to Member States
which were admittedly incorrigible and which violated the principles contained in the Charter in a grave or persistent manner. So far as such States
were concerned, the attitude which would be adopted towards them by the
Organization would have to be stated quite plainly. In the case of a State
the exercise of whose rights and privileges was suspended, to maintain its
status as a member might prevent the Organization from taking sufficiently
severe action against it; and, failing the power of expulsion, a Member State
might be able to take concerted action with a non-member State in order to
impede the working of the Organization. It was wrong to say that expulsion,
as opposed to suspension, would release a State from all obligations imposed
on Member States. In point of fact, by virtue of the principles contained in
the Charter, it would still be bound by various obligations devolving upon
non-member States in so far as such obligations affected the maintenance of
peace. It was likewise wrong to say that such a measure was irremediable.
Expulsion, though conclusive in character, could not be an obstacle to subsequent re-admittance if this were justified by circumstances.

"Those in favor of omitting any reference to expulsion in the Charter
maintained that this would be incompatible with the concept of universality,
which pre-supposed that all States would eventually be admitted to membership in the Organization. It would entail more drawbacks for the Organization itself than for the State concerned. It would set up a center in opposition to the Organization around which other discontented States would rally.
It would force Member States to break off all relations, diplomatic or otherwise, with the State which had been expelled. It would prevent any reconciliation between the Organization and the State expelled, and, whatever might
be said, its results would be less severe than those of suspension.

"On condition that the terms of the Dumbarton Oaks Proposals were extended somewhat, this would fulfil all the purposes of expulsion without re-

leasing the penalized State from its obligations, as expulsion would, or closing the door to subsequent reconciliation.

"At the meeting of Committee I/2 held on May 25th, a proposal providing for inclusion of expulsion in the Charter was approved by a simple majority, but failed to obtain the support of two-thirds of the delegates present and voting.

"The Committee was led to reconsider this decision, which was referred back to it by the Steering Committee on a point of procedure. In the course of this new discussion it appeared that expulsion would have a certain justification in the fact that repeated violations of the Charter often involve, for the guilty Government, the approval of its entire people. A nation led into such convictions would obviously no longer be qualified as 'peace-loving' and would therefore lack the essential quality for participation in the Organization.

"In face of this argument, those opposed to expulsion added that they were not in favor of imposing their point of view upon the majority favoring the text of the Dumbarton Oaks Proposals, and the final vote therefore concludes with the inclusion in the Charter of an expulsion clause in the following form:

" 'The Organization may expel from the Organization any member which persistently violates the principles contained in the Charter.'

"Certain delegates voted against this decision in loyalty to the principle of universality.

"The question of suspension, as can be seen, was associated from the beginning with that of expulsion. Likewise when the Committee had failed to give the expulsion clause a two-thirds majority it then adopted, by a large majority, a text extending suspension to all cases of serious or persistent violation. However, once the expulsion clause was definitely accepted by the Committee, the withdrawal of the words 'or who have violated the principles of the Charter in a serious and persistent fashion' was considered opportune, which led the Committee at its second meeting on June 17, to adopt unanimously the original text quoted and repeated here:

" 'The Organization may at any time suspend from the exercise of the rights or privileges of membership any member of the Organization against which preventive or enforcement action shall have been taken by the Security Council. The exercise of these rights and privileges may be restored in accordance with the procedure laid down in Chapter ——, paragraph ——.' "

2.   The question of expulsion arose in the League of Nations when the Soviet Union attacked Finland in 1939. After the Assembly approved on 14 December 1939 a finding of a Special Committee that it was "impossible to argue that the operations of the Soviet forces in Finland do not constitute resort to war within the meaning of the Pact of Paris or Article 12 of the Covenant of the League of Nations," the Council of the League of Nations resolved on the same day that: ". . . by its act, the Union of Soviet Socialist Republics has placed itself outside the League of Nations. It follows that the Union of Soviet Socialist Republics is no longer a Member of the League." See 20 LNOJ (1939), pp. 506, 531–41. On the validity of this action, see Leo GROSS, "Was the Soviet Union Expelled from the League of Nations?", 39 AJIL (1945), pp. 35–44.

3.   While no State has been expelled from the United Nations, Portugal was expelled in 1963 from membership in the Economic Commission for Africa.

ESC Resolution 974 D III (XXXVI), 24 July 1963; ESCOR, XXXVI, Supp. 1 (E/3816), p. 3. A few days later the Economic and Social Council decided that "the Republic of South Africa shall not take part in the work of the Economic Commission for Africa until the Council, on the recommendation of the Economic Commission for Africa, shall find that conditions for constructive co-operation have been restored by a change in its racial policy." ESC Resolution 974 D IV, 30 July 1963; ESCOR, op. cit., p. 4. See Louis B. SOHN, "Expulsion or Forced Withdrawal from an International Organization," 77 Harvard L.R. (1964), pp. 1381–1425.

Section 3.   Representation

CHINESE REPRESENTATION QUESTION

NOTE.—1. In September 1949, the victorious communist forces proclaimed the establishment of the Central People's Government of the People's Republic of China, and in December 1949 the National Government transferred its seat to the island of Formosa (Taiwan). 5 Chronology of International Events (1948–9), pp. 610, 814–5.

On 18 November 1949, the Chinese Communist Government requested that the United Nations immediately deprive the Nationalist delegation "of all rights to further represent the Chinese people in the United Nations." A/1123. (Several similar communications were received by the United Nations in later years; see, e. g., A/1364 and A/1364/Add.1.)

On 25 November 1949, the delegations of the five countries of the Soviet bloc refused to participate in the consideration by the First Committee of the General Assembly of the question of "threats to the political independence and territorial integrity of China" on the ground that this question was submitted to the Assembly "by the Kuomitang ex-Government which had no right to claim that it represented the Chinese people and certainly had no authority over China with the exception of a small slice of territory." GAOR, IV, First Committee, pp. 339–40. Nevertheless, the Committee continued to debate the matter, and on the basis of its report the General Assembly adopted two resolutions on the subject, one of which called upon all States "to respect the political independence of China" and "to respect the right of the people of China now and in the future, to choose freely their political institutions and to maintain a government independent of foreign control." Resolutions 291–2 (IV), 8 December 1949; GAOR, IV, Resolutions (A/1251), pp. 13–14.

On 10 January 1950, the USSR submitted to the Security Council a draft resolution proposing that the Council should decide "not to recognize the credentials of the representative" of the National Government "and to exclude him from the Security Council." SCOR, V, No. 1, p. 3. After the rejection of this proposal, the Soviet representative walked out of the Council and did not return to it until 1 August 1950. Similar proposals were made by delegates from communist States in other organs of the United Nations and in various specialized agencies; for a list see US SENATE, Military Situation in the Far East: Hearings before the Committee on Armed Services and the Committee on Foreign Relations (82d Congress, 1st session, 1951), pp. 3204–10.

2. In March, 1950, the Secretary-General of the United Nations made public a memorandum on the legal aspects of representation of States in the United Nations. For the text of the memorandum and the Chinese reply thereto, see pp. 107, 111, below. With respect to his further efforts to solve this problem, see Trygve LIE, In the Cause of Peace (New York, 1954), pp. 257–274.

3. On 1 August 1950, Mr. Malik (USSR), as President of the Security Council made "a ruling that the representative of the Kuomitang group seated in the Security Council does not represent China and cannot therefore take part in the meetings of the Security Council." This ruling was immediately challenged and was overruled by a vote of 8 to 3 (India, USSR, Yugoslavia). SCOR, V, No. 22, pp. 1–10.

4. In the meantime, the general question was raised as to the organ competent to decide who should represent a particular State in the United Nations. On 13 January 1950, India proposed that the Security Council insert in its rules of procedure the following new Rule 17–A: "Where the right of any person to represent, or to continue to represent, a State on the Security Council, or at a meeting of the Security Council, is called in question on the ground that he does not represent, or has ceased to represent, the recognized government of that State, the President of the Council shall, before submitting the question to the decision of the Council, ascertain (by telegraph if necessary) and place before the Council, so far as available, the views of the governments of all the other Member States of the United Nations on the matter." UN Doc. S/1447; SCOR, V, Supp. for Jan.–May 1950, pp. 2–3. The Council's Committee of Experts rejected this proposal and suggested that "the question under consideration was of such a nature that the General Assembly should be the organ of the United Nations to initiate the study and to seek uniformity and co-ordination with regard to the procedure governing representation and credentials." S/1457; SCOR, V, Supp. for Jan.–May 1950, pp. 16–8. A similar suggestion was made on 30 May 1950 by the General Conference of UNESCO. A/1344; GAOR, V, Annexes, Agenda Item 61, p. 3. Accordingly, the Cuban delegation proposed that the fifth session of the General Assembly should deal with the matter; it explained that "the item proposed for the General Assembly's consideration does not refer only to the formal problem of credentials, but to the problem that arises with regard to the legality of the representation of a Member State; that is, when the United Nations has to decide which government has the right to represent that State in the Organization. The Charter makes no provision for such a situation, nor do the rules of procedure of the main organs give any standards by which it may concretely and specifically be solved." It added that the "distinction between credentials and representation is an undeniable legal and political reality. Credentials merely accredit the powers conferred by a government on its representatives; representation, on the other hand, is the right of a government to act on behalf of the State. Consequently, the objections lodged against credentials with those who have to decide on the validity of those credentials do not necessarily affect the legality of the representation of the government that has issued them. Nevertheless, objections made to the representation which a government claims or invokes necessarily and directly affect the competence or right of that government to act and to be represented as such on behalf of the State." A/1308 (4 August 1950); GAOR, Annexes (V) 61, pp. 2–3. The Assembly

referred the matter to its *Ad Hoc* Political Committee. For the various proposals discussed by that Committee and for the resolution adopted on the subject by the General Assembly, see pp. 113–18, below.

Does the General Assembly have the power to adopt in this field a decision which other organs of the United Nations will be bound to follow? See 1 Repertory of UN Practice, pp. 267–72.

5. The same session of the Assembly was also confronted at its opening meeting with an Indian proposal that the Communist Government of China "shall be entitled to represent the Republic of China in the General Assembly"; and with two separate Soviet proposals asking the Assembly to decide "that the representatives of the Kuomintang group cannot take part in the work of the General Assembly and its organs because they are not the representatives of China," and "to invite the representatives of the People's Government to take part in the work of the General Assembly and its organs." All these proposals were rejected by the General Assembly, which instead adopted a Canadian proposal to establish a Special Committee on the subject and, pending a decision on the report of this Committee, to allow the representatives of the National Government of China to sit in the Assembly with the same rights as other representatives. GAOR, V, Plenary, pp. 2–16. The Special Committee reported that it was "unable to make any recommendations on the question" (A/1923), and the Assembly merely noted this report. Resolution 501 (V), 5 November 1951; GAOR, V, Supp. 20A (A/1775/Add.1), p. 2.

At the sixth session, the General Assembly adopted a recommendation of its General Committee "to postpone consideration" for the duration of the session "of any further proposals to exclude representatives of the National Government of China from the Assembly or to seat representatives of the Central People's Government of the People's Republic of China to represent China in the Assembly." A/1950 (10 November 1951); GAOR, VI, Annexes, Agenda Item 7, pp. 14–5; GAOR, VI, Plenary, pp. 99–104. Similar action was taken by the next sessions of the General Assembly, from the seventh to the fifteenth. See, e. g., Resolution 609 (VII), 25 October 1952, GAOR, VII, Supp. 20 (A/2361), p. 1; and Resolution 1493 (XV), 8 October 1960, GAOR, XV, Supp. 16 (A/4684), p. 61. See also 1 UN Repertory, pp. 249–53; 2 *idem*, pp. 11–14; 3 *idem*, pp. 190–92, 517–19; 4 *idem*, pp. 321–23; *idem*, Supp. 1, Vol. I, pp. 111–12, 247, and Vol. II, pp. 68–69, 128–29.

6. Mr. Gross (US), speaking in the Security Council on 12 January 1950, stated that "the United States Government considers that the Soviet Union draft resolution [directed at unseating the representative of the National Government] presents to the Council a procedural question involving the credentials of a representative of a member. Accordingly, a vote against the motion by my Government could not be considered as a veto, even assuming that seven members of the Council vote in favour of the resolution. I wish to make it clear that my Government will accept the decision of the Security Council on this matter when made by an affirmative vote of seven members." SCOR, V, No. 2, p. 6. On the other hand, Mr. Tsiang (China) expressed the view that the question which the Soviet Union delegation has raised is not a question of credentials, but a question of representation. It is, therefore, not a question of mere procedure; it is a political question of the utmost importance." Id., p. 8.

In June 1951, US Secretary of State Acheson testifying before a Senate committee stated that if the United States should find itself in the minority in the Security Council on the question of representation of China, the International Court of Justice should be asked "what the significance of a [negative] vote of a permanent member on this matter is"; he added later that he expected that the decision of the Court on this question "would be respected by all members of the Security Council." US SENATE, Military Situation in the Far East: Hearings before the Committee on Armed Services and the Committee on Foreign Relations (82d Congress, 1st session, 1951), pp. 1935, 2024, 2049, 2088, 2143, 2160.

On 8 July 1954 Secretary of State Dulles stated in a news conference that the question of representation of China is an "important matter" requiring a two-thirds vote in the General Assembly and "in the Security Council it is a matter which is properly subject to veto." 31 DSB (1954), p. 87.

Consider the following questions: Should this problem of veto on the credentials (or representation) question be referred to the International Court of Justice? What might the Court's opinion be?

7. The question of voting procedure on the representation question was discussed in the General Assembly in 1961 and 1965. On both occasions the General Assembly decided that "any proposal to change the representation of China is an important question," requiring a two-thirds vote. Resolution 1668 (XVI), 15 December 1961, GAOR, XVI, Supp. 17 (A/5100), p. 66; and Resolution 2025 (XX), 17 November 1965, GAOR, XX, Supp. 14 (A/6014), p. 2. For a summary of the 1965 discussion, see p. 118, below.

LEGAL ASPECTS OF PROBLEMS OF REPRESENTATION IN THE UNITED NATIONS

1. *Memorandum Prepared for the Secretary-General, February 1950.*

S/1466; SCOR, V, Supp. for Jan.–May 1950, pp. 18–23.

The primary difficulty in the current question of the representation of Member States in the United Nations is that this question of representation has been linked up with the question of recognition by Member States.

It will be shown here that this linkage is unfortunate from the practical standpoint, and wrong from the standpoint of legal theory.

From a practical standpoint, the present position is that representation depends entirely on a numerical count of the number of Members in a particular organ which recognize one government or the other. It is quite possible for the majority of Members in one organ to recognize one government, and for the majority of Members in another organ to recognize the rival government. If the principle of individual recognition is adhered to, then the representatives of different governments could sit in different organs. Moreover in organs like the Security Council, of limited membership, the question of representation may be determined by the purely arbitrary fact of the particular governments which happen to have been elected to serve at a given time.

From the standpoint of legal theory, the linkage of representation in an international organization and recognition of a government is a confusion of two institutions which have superficial similarities but are essentially different.

The recognition of a new State, or of a new government of an existing State, is a unilateral act which the recognizing government can grant or withhold. It is true that some legal writers have argued forcibly that when a new government, which comes into power through revolutionary means, enjoys, with a reasonable prospect of permanency, the habitual obedience of the bulk of the population, other States are under a legal duty to recognize it. However, while States may regard it as desirable to follow certain legal principles in according or withholding recognition, the practice of States shows that the act of recognition is still regarded as essentially a political decision, which each State decides in accordance with its own free appreciation of the situation. . . .

Various legal scholars have argued that this rule of individual recognition through the free choice of States should be replaced by collective recognition through an international organization such as the United Nations (e. g. Lauterpacht, *Recognition in International Law*). If this were now the rule then the present impasse would not exist, since there would be no individual recognition of the new Chinese Government, but only action by the appropriate United Nations organ. The fact remains, however, that the States have refused to accept any such rule and the United Nations does not possess any authority to recognize either a new State or a new government of an existing State. To establish the rule of collective recognition by the United Nations would require either an amendment of the Charter or a treaty to which all Members would adhere.

On the other hand membership of a State in the United Nations and representation of a State in the organs is clearly determined by a collective act of the appropriate organs; in the case of membership, by vote of the General Assembly on recommendation of the Security Council, in the case of representation, by vote of each competent organ on the credentials of the purported representatives. Since, therefore, recognition of either State or government is an individual act, and either admission to membership or acceptance of representation in the Organization are collective acts, it would appear to be legally inadmissible to condition the latter acts by a requirement that they be preceded by individual recognition.

This conclusion is clearly borne out by the practice in the case of admission to membership in both the League of Nations and in the United Nations.

In the practice of the League of Nations, there were a number of cases in which Members of the League stated expressly that the admission of another State to membership did not mean that they recognized such new Member as a State (e. g., United Kingdom in the case of Lithuania; Belgium and Switzerland in the case of the Soviet Union; Colombia in the case of Panama). [A number of writers such as Scelle, Fauchille, Anzillotti, Malbone Graham, contended that admission to the League constituted an implied recognition by all Members. In the words of Lauterpacht (*Recognition in International Law,* page 401): "Actual practice did not substantiate these postulated implications of admission".]

In the practice of the United Nations there are, of course, several instances of admission to membership of States which had not been recognized by all other Members, and other instances of States for whose admission votes were cast by Members which had not recognized the candidates as States. For example, Yemen and Burma were admitted by a unanimous vote of the General Assembly at a time when they had been recognized by only a minority of Members. A number of the Members who, in the Security Council, voted for the admission of Transjordan [Jordan] and Nepal, had not recognized these candidates as States. Indeed, the declarations made by the delegation of the Soviet Union and its neighbours that they would not vote for the admission of certain States (e. g. Ireland, Portugal and Transjordan [Jordan]), because they were not in diplomatic relations with these applicants, were vigorously disputed by most other Members, and led to the request for an advisory opinion of the International Court of Justice by the General Assembly.

The Court was requested to answer the question, whether a Member, in its vote on the admission to membership of another State, was "juridically entitled to make its consent to the admission dependent on conditions not expressly provided" by paragraph 1 of Article 4 of the Charter. One of the conditions which had been stated by Members had been the lack of diplomatic relations with the applicant State. The Court answered the question in the negative. At its third session the General Assembly recommended that each Member act in accordance with the opinion of the Court.

The practice as regards representation of Member States in the United Nations organs has, until the Chinese question arose, been uniformly to the effect that representation is distinctly separate from the issue of recognition of a government. It is a remarkable fact that, despite the fairly large number of revolutionary changes of government and the larger number of instances of breach of diplomatic relations among Members, there was not one single instance of a challenge of credentials of a representative in the many thousands of meetings which were held during four years. On the contrary, whenever the reports of credentials committees were voted on (as in the sessions of the General Assembly), they were always adopted unanimously and without reservation by any Members.

The Members have therefore made clear by an unbroken practice that:

(1) A Member could properly vote to accept a representative of a government which it did not recognize, or with which it had no diplomatic relations, and

(2) Such a vote did not imply recognition or a readiness to assume diplomatic relations.

In two instances involving non-members, the question was explicitly raised: the cases of granting the Republic of Indonesia and Israel the right to participate in the deliberations of the Security Council. In both cases, objections were raised on the grounds that these entities were not States; in both cases the Security Council voted to permit representation after explicit statements were made by members of the Council that the vote did not imply recognition of the State or government concerned.

The practice which has been thus followed in the United Nations is not only legally correct but conforms to the basic character of the Organization. The United Nations is not an association limited to like-minded States and governments of similar ideological persuasion (as is the case in certain regional associations). As an Organization which aspires to universality, it must of necessity include States of varying and even conflicting ideologies.

The Chinese case is unique in the history of the United Nations, not because it involves a revolutionary change of government, but because it is the first in which two rival governments exist. It is quite possible that such a situation will occur again in the future and it is highly desirable to see what principle can be followed in choosing between the rivals. It has been demonstrated that the principle of numerical preponderance of recognition is inappropriate and legally incorrect. Is any other principle possible?

It is submitted that the proper principle can be derived by analogy from Article 4 of the Charter. This Article requires that an applicant for membership must be able and willing to carry out the obligations of membership. The obligations of membership can be carried out only by governments which in fact possess the power to do so. Where a revolutionary government presents itself as representing a State, in rivalry to an existing government, the question at issue should be which of these two governments in fact is in a position to employ the resources and direct the people of the State in fulfilment of the obligations of membership. In essence, this means an inquiry as to whether the new government exercises effective authority within the territory of the State and is habitually obeyed by the bulk of the population.

If so, it would seem to be appropriate for the United Nations organs, through their collective action, to accord it the right to represent the State in the Organization, even though individual Members of the Organization refuse, and may continue to refuse, to accord it recognition as the lawful government for reasons which are valid under their national policies.

2. *Reply to the Secretariat Memorandum on Problems of Representation.*

Letter from the Permanent Representative of China to the United Nations, 15 March 1950. S/1470; SCOR, V, Supp. for Jan.–May 1950, pp. 23–26.

China's struggle for freedom and national independence has a number of fronts—the Formosa front, the Hainan front, the mainland front with a number of sectors, and the United Nations front.

The United Nations front is moral in nature and is of vital importance. Success or failure on the United Nations front affects the decisions on the other fronts. Your memorandum is a deliberate attack on China's United Nations front. In time, it will be recognized as also an attack on the cause of freedom throughout the world.

So long as the National Government of China continues to exist and fight the Communists, the latter are in no position to throw their full energies into expansion in South East Asia. If the National Government of China should cease to struggle against Communism in China, the Chinese Communists would then be able to throw their full power into South East Asia. There can be no question that the spread of Communism in Asia would hasten the coming of a third world war. For this reason the United Nations, founded to preserve world peace, should lend its influence to support the National Government of China. If it is too much to expect you to use your influence against Communism, it is certainly not too much to expect you to remain at least neutral in this world struggle. . . .

On the technical side your memorandum asserts that it is wrong to link the question of representation with the question of recognition by Member States. International law has nothing direct to say for or against this linkage. As practised in the League of Nations as well as in the United Nations, this linkage is the general rule; the few cases of non-operation of linkage which your memorandum cited, have been the exceptions. The Soviet Union delegation, in voting on admission of new Members, specifically stressed the linkage between admission and recognition. In spite of the advisory opinion of the International Court of Justice, the Soviet Union veto on a number of applications for membership holds today. The deputy representative of the United States to the United Nations, in his Press statement of 8 March, made it clear that the United States Government would continue to support my delegation and to vote against admission of a Communist delegation for the specific reason that the United States continued to recognize the National Government of China.

Your memorandum proposes a new criterion, namely, "whether the new government exercises effective authority within the territory of the State and is habitually obeyed by the bulk of the population". The individual governments, in deciding to accord recognition to, or withhold recognition from a new government, must take into consideration the very criterion that you suggest for deciding on representation. In fact, recognition and representation are based on similar considerations. The linkage between recognition and representation is only natural and inevitable.

If you wish to institute "an inquiry as to whether the new government exercises effective authority within the territory of the State and is habitually obeyed by the bulk of the population", the only possible procedure, consistent with the principles of the Charter, is a fair and free election. In spite of appearances, the Communist régime in China does not have the support of the Chinese people. Its ideology and programme are un-Chinese. Internationally, the Communist régime is regarded by the Chinese people as a puppet régime. Today, the opposition to the Communist régime is stronger than it was a year ago. Before long the world will hear more about the hatred of the Chinese people for the Communists.

Article 100 of the Charter states *inter alia:* "They [The Secretary-General and the staff] shall refrain from any action which might reflect on their position as international officers responsible only to the Organization". The impartiality of the Secretary-General and his staff in all questions under controversy is one of the essential foundations of the United Nations. In the present instance you have supplied argument against my delegation and in favour of the Soviet Union delegation. You have destroyed public confidence in the impartiality of the Secretariat. . . .

The Secretariat is free to circulate data papers to furnish background information on any question under debate. Your memorandum is, however, certainly not a data paper and was not circulated in the way that data papers are usually circulated, that is, simultaneous distribution to all members of the body for which the data paper is prepared.

My government does not wish to put a narrow interpretation to Article 99 of the Charter, which is the only Article that assigns a sphere of political action to the Secretary-General. That Article authorizes the Secretary-General to "bring to the attention of the Security Council any matter which in his opinion may threaten the maintenance of international peace and security". Nobody can believe that the question of Chinese representation "may threaten the maintenance of international peace and security". Even if it were such a matter, you should not have circulated a secret memorandum to a limited number of the delegates to the Security Council, excluding the delegation which is most directly concerned.

For these reasons, your memorandum and the mode of its circulation constitute bad law.

Today, with such bad politics and bad law, you have intervened against the interests of my country; tomorrow you can do the same thing against the interests of other countries. The organization of international security is vitiated by an element of insecurity at its very centre, particularly for the smaller and weaker countries.

RECOGNITION BY THE UNITED NATIONS OF THE REPRESENTATION OF A MEMBER STATE

1. *Draft Resolution proposed by Cuba, 7 October 1950.*

A/AC.38/L.6; GAOR, Annexes (V) 61, p. 5.

The General Assembly,

Considering:

That questions which arise regarding the representation of a Member State in the United Nations cannot be definitely settled in accordance with the rules at present established and that there is a danger that conflicting decisions may be reached by its various organs,

That it is in the interest of the proper functioning of the Organization that there should be uniformity in the procedure applicable when there are doubts regarding the representation of a Member State or when the representation of a Member State is challenged in any organ of the United Nations,

That, in virtue of its composition, the General Assembly is the only organ of the United Nations which is in a position to express the general opinion of all Member States in matters affecting the functioning of the organization as a whole;

1. Recommends that questions arising in connexion with the representation of a Member State in the United Nations should be decided in the light of:

(a) effective authority over the national territory;

(b) the general consent of the population;

(c) ability and willingness to achieve the Purposes of the Charter, to observe its Principles and to fulfill international obligations of the State; and

(d) respect for human rights and fundamental freedoms;

2. Resolves that when it is necessary to take a decision regarding the legitimacy of the representation of a Member State, the matter shall be referred to the General Assembly for decision;

3. Declares that decisions taken by the General Assembly in accordance with this resolution shall not affect the direct relations of individual Member States with the State, the representation of which has been the subject of such decisions;

4. Requests the Secretary-General to transmit the present resolution to the organs and specialized agencies of the United Nations for such action as may be appropriate.

2. *Amendments to the Cuban Draft Resolution proposed by China, 23 October 1950.*

A/AC.38/L.22; GAOR, Annexes (V) 61, p. 6.

Add the following paragraph at the end of the preamble:

"That the recognition of a new representation of a Member State should not be premature and should be guided strictly by the principles and provisions of the Charter of the United Nations and the Stimson Doctrine of Non-Recognition."

Amend paragraphs 1, 2 and 3 as indicated by italics:

"1. Recommends that questions arising in connexion with the representation of a Member State in the United Nations should be decided in the light of:

(a) effective authority over the national territory, *established without the intervention of any other State, independent of foreign control and domination, and not as a result of foreign aggression, direct or indirect;*

(b) the general consent of the population, *expressed through freely conducted or internationally supervised or observed elections;*

(c) ability and willingness to achieve the Purposes of the Charter, to observe its Principles and to fulfil the international obligations of the State, *not having been an accomplice of aggression or given aid and sympathy to an aggressor so proclaimed by the United Nations; and not having committed acts of aggression;*

(d) respect for human rights and fundamental freedoms, *as defined by the United Nations Universal Declaration of Human Rights:*

"2. Resolves that when it is necessary to take a decision regarding the legitimacy of the representation of a Member State, the matter shall be referred to the General Assembly for decision *as a question of importance and that the General Assembly shall appoint a Commission of Investigation to ascertain the facts relating to each one of the items under paragraph 1, and to report to the General Assembly for consideration;*

"3. Declares that decisions taken by the General Assembly in accordance with this resolution shall affect *neither* the direct relations of individual Member States with the State, the representation of which has been the subject of such decisions, *nor the application of regional agreements concerning recognition."*

3.   *Draft Resolution proposed by the United Kingdom,*
20 October 1950.

A/AC.38/L.21 ; GAOR, Annexes (V) 61, p. 6.

The General Assembly,

Considering:

That there is no uniformly agreed principle for determining the right of the Government of a Member State to represent it in the United Nations and that there is a danger that conflicting decisions on this subject may be reached by the various organs of the United Nations and in the Specialized Agencies,

That it is in the interest of the proper functioning of the Organization that there should be uniformity in the criteria to be applied in determining whether a given Government is entitled to represent a Member State or when the representation of a Member State is challenged in any organ of the United Nations,

That, in virtue of its composition, the General Assembly is the only organ of the United Nations in which consideration can be given to the views of all Member States in matters affecting the functioning of the Organization as a whole;

1.   Recommends that where the question of the representation of a Member State arises in consequence of internal processes or changes which have taken place in that State the right of a Government to represent the Member State concerned in the United Nations should be recognized if that Government exercises effective control and authority over all or nearly all the national territory, and has the obedience of the bulk of the population of that territory, in such a way that this control, authority and obedience appear to be of a permanent character;

2.   Resolves that when any question arises regarding the right of a Government to represent a Member State in the United Nations, the matter shall be referred to the General Assembly for consideration, but without thereby precluding action by any other organ of the United Nations which is called upon to take a decision on the matter during the period before the Assembly meets;

3.   Recommends that the view taken by the General Assembly concerning the right of a Government to represent a Member State should be acted upon by Member States in other organs of the United Nations and in the Specialized Agencies;

4.   Declares that decisions taken by the General Assembly in accordance with this resolution shall not of themselves affect the direct relations of individual Member States with the State, the representation of which has been the subject of such decisions;

5.   Requests the Secretary-General to transmit the present resolution to the organs and Specialized Agencies of the United Nations for such action as may be appropriate.

4. *Draft Resolution proposed by a Sub-Committee of the* Ad Hoc
   Political Committee of the General Assembly,
   21 November 1950.

A/1578, p. 5; GAOR, Annexes (V) 61, p. 9.

The General Assembly,

Considering:

That difficulties may arise regarding the representation of a Member State in the United Nations and that there is a risk that conflicting decisions may be reached by its various organs,

That it is in the interest of the proper functioning of the Organization that there should be uniformity in the procedure applicable whenever more than one authority claims to be the government entitled to represent a Member State in the United Nations, and this question becomes the subject of controversy in the United Nations,

That, in virtue of its composition, the General Assembly is the organ of the United Nations in which consideration can best be given to the views of all Member States in matters affecting the functioning of the Organization as a whole;

1. Recommends:

(a) That whenever more than one authority claims to be the government entitled to represent a Member State in the United Nations, and this question becomes the subject of controversy in the United Nations, it should be considered in the light of the Purposes and Principles of the Charter and the circumstances of each case;

(b) That the following should be among the factors to be taken into consideration in determining any such question:

(i) The extent to which the new authority exercises effective control over the territory of the Member State concerned and is generally accepted by the population;

(ii) The willingness of that authority to accept responsibility for the carrying out by the Member State of its obligations under the Charter;

(iii) The extent to which that authority has been established through internal processes in the Member State.

2. Recommends that when any such question arises, it should be considered by the General Assembly, or by the Interim Committee if the Assembly is not in session;

3. Recommends that the decision reached by the General Assembly or its Interim Committee concerning any such question should be taken into account in other organs of the United Nations and in the specialized agencies;

4. Declares that decisions reached by the General Assembly or its Interim Committee concerning any such question shall not of them-

selves affect the direct relations of individual Member States with the State, the representation of which has been the subject of such decisions;

5. Requests the Secretary-General to transmit the present resolution to the other organs of the United Nations and to the specialized agencies for such action as may be appropriate.

NOTE. In the *Ad Hoc* Political Committee, an Egyptian proposal to delete sub-paragraph 1(b) of this Draft Resolution was approved by 27 votes to 13, with 14 abstentions; at the same time a few other changes were made in the draft. GAOR, V, *Ad Hoc* Political Committee, pp. 364–90. The General Assembly restored paragraph 2 which was eliminated by the Committee. GAOR, V, Plenary, p. 675.

5. Resolution 396 (V) of the General Assembly, 14 December 1950.

GAOR, V, Supp. 20 (A/1775), p. 24.

The General Assembly,

Considering that difficulties may arise regarding the representation of a Member State in the United Nations and that there is a risk that conflicting decisions may be reached by its various organs,

Considering that it is in the interest of the proper functioning of the Organization that there should be uniformity in the procedure applicable whenever more than one authority claims to be the government entitled to represent a Member State in the United Nations, and this question becomes the subject of controversy in the United Nations,

Considering that, in virtue of its composition, the General Assembly is the organ of the United Nations in which consideration can best be given to the views of all Member States in matters affecting the functioning of the Organization as a whole,

1. Recommends that, whenever more than one authority claims to be the government entitled to represent a Member State in the United Nations and this question becomes the subject of controversy in the United Nations, the question should be considered in the light of the Purposes and Principles of the Charter and the circumstances of each case;

2. Recommends that, when any such question arises, it should be considered by the General Assembly, or by the Interim Committee if the General Assembly is not in session;

3. Recommends that the attitude adopted by the General Assembly or its Interim Committee concerning any such question should be taken into account in other organs of the United Nations and in the specialized agencies;

4. Declares that the attitude adopted by the General Assembly or its Interim Committee concerning any such question shall not of it-

self affect the direct relations of individual Member States with the State concerned;

5. Requests the Secretary-General to transmit the present resolution to the other organs of the United Nations and to the specialized agencies for such action as may be appropriate.

REPRESENTATION OF CHINA: 1965 DISCUSSION

Summary of the discussion in the General Assembly, November 1965. Annual Report of the Secretary-General on the Work of the Organization, 1965–66 [GAOR, XXI, Supp. 1 (A/6301)], pp. 35–37.

A request for the inclusion of an item "Restoration of the lawful rights of the People's Republic of China in the United Nations" was made by a letter dated 25 August 1965 from Albania, Algeria, Burundi, Cambodia, Congo (Brazzaville), Cuba, Ghana, Guinea, Mali and Romania. On 13 September Syria asked to be included in the list of those proposing the item.

An explanatory memorandum of 7 September 1965 stated *inter alia* that "the restoration to the People's Republic of China of its lawful rights in the United Nations and in all its subsidiary bodies constitutes a categorical imperative" because the present representation of China at the United Nations was "unlawful" and because the exclusion of the Peking Government was contrary to the desired universality of the Organization. The exclusion also disregarded the recommendation contained in the final declaration of the Second Conference of Heads of States or Governments of Non-Aligned Countries held at Cairo in October 1964. Furthermore, the refusal to restore the rights was contrary to the conditions for admission contained in the Charter, as the Government of the People's Republic of China had clearly expressed itself in favour of the peaceful settlement of disputes and other differences between independent States and had proved that it desired peace and peaceful co-existence. It also supported the right to self-determination of "the peoples struggling against colonial Powers". Moreover the existence of the People's Republic of China was a political reality, proved by the fact that an ever-increasing number of States had extended diplomatic recognition to it. Finally, the solution of any important international problem without the participation of the People's Republic of China was inconceivable, especially since it had become a nuclear Power.

The item was discussed at eleven plenary meetings of the General Assembly from 8 to 17 November 1965. Fifty representatives took part in the debate or spoke to explain their vote. Legal arguments centred around interpretations of the provisions of the Charter concerning new Members; recognition of Governments; accreditation of representatives; interpretation of Article 18 defining an "important question" and stipulating consequently a two-thirds majority vote;

the criteria required by the Charter for membership; and finally, the question whether the expressed wish of the People's Republic of China to participate in the work of the Organization was a necessary condition for its seating. Political arguments centred around the question of the realities of the present time and the possible results of the absence of the People's Republic of China on the effectiveness of the United Nations in its efforts to ensure world peace.

The arguments put forward by those favouring the seating of the People's Republic of China may be summarized as follows: the People's Republic of China was not a candidate for admission to the United Nations, but was the only Government representative of the people of a member country, namely China. When the Charter of the United Nations provided that China would assume special responsibilities as a permanent member of the Security Council, it referred to a State and not to a Government. Unlike individual States, the Organization did not have the sovereign privilege to recognize Governments, but only to ensure that their representatives were duly accredited. Consequently, seating the representatives of the People's Republic of China was not an important question within the meaning of that term as employed in the Charter. Furthermore, settlement of present political problems was strongly hampered by the absence of representatives of a country whose population amounted to one-quarter of that of the world. That country in addition had become a nuclear Power. Settlement of the problems of South-East Asia and of disarmament were the kind of issues which could not be solved without the presence of the People's Republic of China in the United Nations, and particularly in the Security Council.

The opponents of any change in representation of China argued on the basis of resolution 1668 (XVI) which stated that any proposal to change the representation of China was an important question under the terms of Article 18 of the Charter. They stated in addition that the Republic of China was a member in good standing and therefore should not be expelled or suspended. The Peking Government, on the other hand, had flouted the purposes and principles of the Charter and therefore did not qualify to be seated. The representative of the Republic of China emphasized that the present delegation represented all of the Chinese people. If any lawful rights were to be restored, they must be restored to the Chinese people of the mainland, who had been denied the enjoyment of every fundamental human freedom. Other representatives insisted that the People's Republic of China, far from accepting the provisions of the Charter, had reversed the position and laid down its own conditions for membership, which were unacceptable. They argued that the People's Republic of China opposed the United Nations in principle and also in its most important goals. The presence of the People's Republic of China, far from strengthening the United Nations, would seriously impede the functioning of its organs, especially the Security Council.

Between the two above positions, a number of opinions were expressed, all tending to the view that some kind of representation for the Republic of China should be assured. Some representatives, such as the representative of Jamaica, agreed that the People's Republic of China exercised *de facto* control over the overwhelming majority of the Chinese people and that it was therefore entitled not only to a seat in the organs of the United Nations, but to the permanent seat of China on the Security Council. However, they voiced the opinion that the Taipei Government had effective control over that "island province", that it was therefore not a government-in-exile, and that some type of membership should be provided for it. Others, such as the United Kingdom, made it clear that their vote in favour of seating the People's Republic of China left the question of the sovereignty over Formosa, and hence the question of its representation, undetermined.

Two draft resolutions were submitted to the Assembly: (1) An eleven-Power draft resolution, sponsored by Australia, Brazil, Colombia, Gabon, Italy, Japan, Madagascar, Nicaragua, Philippines, Thailand and United States, provided that the Assembly reaffirm the validity of resolution 1668 (XVI) of 15 December 1961, which stated that, "in accordance with Article 18 of the Charter of the United Nations, any proposal to change the representation of China is an important question" and accordingly required a two-thirds majority vote; and (2) a twelve-Power draft resolution, sponsored by Albania, Algeria, Cambodia, Congo (Brazzaville), Cuba, Ghana, Guinea, Mali, Pakistan, Romania, Somalia and Syria, which contained two operative paragraphs, the first providing that the Assembly "restore all its rights to the People's Republic of China" including the right to represent China in the United Nations and the second that the Assembly "expel forthwith the representatives of Chiang Kai-Shek from the place which they unlawfully occupy at the United Nations and in all the organizations related to it". An amendment to this draft resolution by the representative of Ceylon would have replaced the two operative paragraphs by the wording: *"Decides* that the representatives of the People's Republic of China be seated in the United Nations and all its organs". In proposing this amendment, the representative of Ceylon stated that the draft resolution "quite unnecessarily goes on to condemn those who have so far represented the entity of China . . . ." and that in that form it "is likely to embarrass . . . . quite a few of those who may feel strongly that China should immediately be restored to its lawful rights". The representative of Mauritania proposed orally the omission of the second paragraph of the draft resolution, which referred to expulsion. The Cambodian representative, requesting Mauritania and Ceylon not to press their proposals, stated that "one paragraph cannot stand without the other", that the sponsors had "stinted no effort to give it a balance which might gain the support of all", and that its deletion would "create a misunderstanding to the benefit of those who oppose the restoration of the lawful rights of the People's Republic of China".

After both these amendments had been withdrawn on 17 November, the Assembly was called upon to vote first on the eleven-Power draft resolution. This draft resolution was adopted by a vote of 56 in favour and 49 against, with 11 abstentions. Subsequently, the twelve-Power draft resolution received 47 votes in favour and 47 against, with 20 abstentions. Consequently, the representation of China in the United Nations remained unchanged.

NOTE. Consider the following statements:

1. William P. BUNDY, Assistant Secretary of State for Far Eastern Affairs [54 DSB (1966), p. 310, at 316–17]:

"Some nations at the U.N. hope that Communist China's seating would have a moderating effect on its policies. They advance the thesis that, not being included in the U.N., Peking feels rejected and acts with considerably less restraint than if it were a member with a member's obligations.

"We respect those who hold this view, but we cannot agree with it. It seems to us a rationalistic view that ignores the deep-seated historic and ideologic reasons for Peking's current attitudes. Nor does this theory—the 'neurosis' theory if you will—explain Peking's behavior toward other Communist nations or its behavior in Afro-Asian groupings to which Communist China has been fully welcomed. I return again to Professor Fairbank's description of China's 'long background of feeling superior to all outsiders and expecting a supreme position in the world.' Surely this, alongside ideologic differences, lies at the root of the Sino-Soviet split, of Communist China's disruptive behavior in Afro-Asian groupings, and of the heavy-handedness of Communist China's policy from Indonesia to Burundi.

"Moreover, we must consider Peking's price for entering the U.N. On September 29, 1965, Chen Yi, the Chinese Communist Premier, made the following demands:

1. The expulsion of the Republic of China from the U.N.

2. The complete reorganization of the U.N.

3. The withdrawal of the General Assembly resolution condemning Peking as an aggressor in the Korean conflict.

4. The branding of the United States as an aggressor in that conflict.

"These are obviously unacceptable conditions.

"The Republic of China, for example, is one of the original signatories of the United Nations Charter and has lived up to its obligations as a U.N. member in good faith. More than 13 million people live on the Island of Taiwan. This is a larger population than that of 83 members of the United Nations. The United States for many years has had close and friendly relations with the Republic of China, and since 1954 we have been bound by treaty to join with it in the defense of Taiwan. It would be unthinkable and morally wrong to expel the Government of the Republic of China from the U.N. to meet this demand of Peking's.

"One must also consider the attitude of Communist China toward conflict, not only where its own interests are directly concerned but even in cases where they are not. Had Communist China been in the United Nations, could there have been a cease-fire resolution on the India-Pakistan conflict in September and could Secretary-General U Thant have received any mandate to bring that conflict to a halt? Peking's critical comment on the Tashkent proceedings is a clear answer. We are dealing with a nation that, at least as far as we can now see, will attempt as a matter of principle to put a monkey wrench into every peacemaking effort which may be made in the world.

"Finally, there is the psychological factor: whether the admission to the U.N. of a nation that is dedicated to violent revolution and currently supporting North Viet-Nam's aggression against South Viet-Nam and threatening India in seeking to exacerbate and extend the Indo-Pakistan conflict would, in fact, not encourage Peking to think it is on the right track while deeply discouraging other nations which are resisting Peking's pressures and seeking to maintain their own independence.

"It continues, therefore, to be U.S. policy to support the position of the Republic of China in the U.N. For our part, we will also continue to oppose the admission of Communist China."

2. Senator Edward M. KENNEDY [112 Congressional Record, No. 116 (20 July 1966), pp. 15660–62]: "In past years we have undertaken an enormous diplomatic effort to convince our allies and the neutral nations that the admission of mainland China is detrimental to the best interest of the free world.

"There is little doubt that this yearly effort has been costly to us. We have expended precious diplomatic capital. Not all nations—indeed it can be said that less than a majority—today view China's admission to the U.N. as disastrous as we do. We have retained their support in other ways, in some instances yielding to these member states on other issues. In most instances we have been forced to send our emissaries to argue a position again and again to nations that find our position quite unrealistic in the light of world events—even nations living on the rim of China. Perhaps this annual diplomatic activity was justifiable in the past. But its continuation depends on a new judgment that success on this issue is worth the price we have been paying. I am no longer convinced that our best interests continue to lie in this direction. I do not believe that an unyielding negative approach to the China question serves the best interests of the United States, Formosa, our Asian friends, or the United Nations in the world today. . . .

"The major concern of the United States is, or should be, the commitment we have to our friends on Formosa, that, regardless of international events, their presence and the voice of the 12 million Nationalist Chinese citizens will be preserved in the United Nations. It appears that we are endangering that commitment by our continued emphasis on obstructing the usual China resolutions. All of the resolutions that have been proposed to date have called for the expulsion of Formosa. Thus, in this diplomatic effort, we have allowed others to choose the issue and control the setting. Our position has been purely defensive. Many of our traditional allies—Great Britain, France, India, the Scandinavian countries, to mention but a few—have opted in the past for the exclusion of Formosa and the presence of Red China. And the roll call on this question over the years has shown our position to be deteriorating; our persuasion less compelling. . . .

"I would suggest that if we are to preserve the presence of Formosa in the United Nations, we would be well advised to take the initiative in drafting and supporting a resolution that would allow both the presence of China as well as the retention of Formosa. While it is quite likely that this proposal would be considered unacceptable at first, by both Formosa and China, I feel it has many advantages that would serve our position well. First, we would, in effect, be placing the burden of China's absence from the U.N. on the Chinese themselves as well as their supporters in that body, should China object to our attempts or subsequently refuse the invitation of the member states.

"Second, we would be shifting the emphasis of the annual discussion from the question of why China should be included or excluded, to the question of the preservation of Formosa.

"Finally, we would be informing the United Nations that we are prepared to labor for the goal of the United Nations being a universal body, with representation for all the people of the world.

"The question of preserving Formosa, and our support for universality in the U.N. will, I am sure, have an impact on the many small nations of the General Assembly. Many of the new U.N. members should be asked if they are anxious to negate this principle by continuing to move for the expulsion of a fellow member. Formosa is a country of 12 million people. She is one of the most advanced economies in Asia, having just raised her per capita income by 50 percent in 10 years. She carries on over a billion dollars in world trade and has formal diplomatic relations with 57 nations. There are few new member nations in the U.N. of this size or growth with such comparable success in the world scene. What can guarantee these new states their own presence in a world body if Formosa can be so easily expelled?

"Mr. President, I would not take it upon myself to state what any specific resolution should contain, or whether or not is should be combined with other matters of U.N. representation or membership. There have been situations in the past where former single states split and the United Nations had to handle the admissions problem. This occurred in 1947 when Pakistan separated from India, and in 1961 when Syria withdrew from the United Arab Republic.

"In the China case, however, we have an additional complexity that must be recognized. The Nationalist Government holds one of the five permanent seats on the Security Council. Those in the past who have supported the usual resolutions for the entry of the People's Republic of China to the U.N., have assumed that China would be entitled to take the Formosan seat on the Security Council, also. I would be strongly opposed to this development at this time, and view the possibility of this occurring as another substantial reason for a U.S. initiative on this question. . . .

"I would suggest, therefore, that part of the United States effort also be directed toward a review of the current Security Council arrangements. The five permanent members of the Council—the United States, U.S.S.R., Great Britain, France, and China—were entitled to their favored position on the basis of their leadership of victory in World War II. The world, and the powers that affect the world, have changed considerably since that time. We are now committed to our former enemies. We have had serious confrontations and differences with our former allies. It would seem only appropriate that the basic Security Council composition reflect who has the most potential to preserve peace today, rather than who won the war 20 years ago.

"Without endorsing any one solution to the Security Council problem, certain alternatives can be suggested, that I am sure are apparent to those expert in these matters.

"The basic Security Council problem centers on which China should have the permanent China seat and the accompanying veto power. The most obvious solution is that neither China be seated on the Council permanently at this time. This could be accomplished by a revision of the Charter reducing the number of permanent seats from five to four.

"More realistic, perhaps, would be the retention of the five permanent seats, with the fifth position going to one of the dominant underdeveloped states of the southern half of the world—such as India.

"This move would reflect the concern of the U.N. in the developing world while recognizing that world power and a voice in peace is not a function of armaments alone. India represents the great experiment of our generation—a struggle toward freedom and democracy against all the negative forces generated by problems of population, poverty, underdeveloped resources, and geography. To the extent that such a proposal for one nation would be unacceptable to others, this fifth seat with its permanent seat privileges could rotate among developing world members.

"The Covenant of the League of Nations contained a provision allowing for the expansion of the League's Council, without constant amendment to the covenant. Similarly, the Charter of the U.N. could be so amended to introduce the needed flexibility in Council membership. This would allow for future representation of China on the Council, if she displayed by her behavior after admission that she deserved such a position. This basic change in the Charter could also be accompanied by revisions in the veto procedure, as for example reserving the use of the veto only on binding decisions of the Council with majority votes controlling the nonbinding recommendations of the Council to the General Assembly [or to member states].

"The point remains, however, that regardless of the construction of the U. S. proposal, our efforts and the abilities of our statesmen should be directed toward new approaches to old problems. We should be exercising, in international affairs, the same ingenuity with which we have attacked our problems on the domestic scene."

3. See also Lincoln P. BLOOMFIELD, "China, the United States, and the United Nations," 20 Int.Org. (1966), pp. 653–76; Louis B. SOHN, "China, the U. N., and the U. S.," 6 War/Peace Report, No. 4 (April 1966), pp. 10–11; UNITED NATIONS ASSOCIATION OF THE UNITED STATES OF AMERICA, China, the United Nations and United States Policy (New York, 1966), 64 pp.

OTHER QUESTIONS OF REPRESENTATION

NOTE.—1. In 1956 doubts were expressed as to the validity of the credentials of the representatives of Hungary issued by the Government which was established after the suppression of the revolution in that country. The representatives of Hungary were permitted to take part in the debates of the General Assembly on the basis of Rule 29 of the Assembly's Rules of Procedure, which provides for the provisional seating of any representative whose credentials have been challenged, "until the Credentials Committee has reported and the General Assembly has given its decision," but at the sessions of the General Assembly from the eleventh to the seventeenth the General Assembly approved reports of the Credentials Committee which merely stated that "the Committee takes no decision regarding the credentials submitted on behalf of the representatives of Hungary." See, e. g., A/3536 (13 February 1957), GAOR, Annexes (XI) 3, pp. 1–2; A/5395 (20 December 1962), GAOR, Annexes (XVII) 3, pp. 1–2; UN Repertory, Supp. 2, Vol. II, pp. 7–8. This procedure was abandoned in 1963.

2. Concerning the difficulties caused in 1958 by the change of Government in Iraq and the dissolution of the Arab Union, see UN Repertory, Supp. 2, Vol. II, pp. 281–82.

3. The United Nations was confronted with a difficult situation in September 1960, when Mr. Kasa-Vubu, the Chief of State of the Republic of the Congo (Leopoldville), dismissed Mr. Lumumba, the Prime Minister, and appointed a new government; the Parliament conferred full powers on Mr. Lumumba; the Chief of State suspended the Parliament; and Mr. Mobutu, the Chief of Staff of the Army, announced the formation of a third government, which was later accepted by the Chief of State. The Credentials Committee of the General Assembly had to determine the validity of the credentials issued by the various governments. The Committee approved a proposal by the United States that the General Assembly accept the credentials issued by the Head of the State. Those supporting this decision noted that "the latest credentials dated 8 November 1960 bore the signature of Joseph Kasa-Vubu, President of the Republic, who was undeniably the Chief of State of the Republic of the Congo (Leopoldville) and that rule 27 of the rules of procedure provided that credentials 'shall be issued either by the Head of the State or Government or by the Minister for Foreign Affairs'. It was considered that it would be an intervention in the domestic affairs of the Republic of the Congo to question the validity of a document issued by the Chief of State. It was pointed out that President Kasa-Vubu had been heard as Chief of State by the General Assembly without objection at its 912th plenary meeting, and that he had requested that the credentials of the delegation of which he was the Chairman be approved without delay." In opposing the decision, the representative of the USSR observed that "the credentials referred to in the United States draft resolution were illegal because they had not been drawn up in accordance with the *Loi fondamentale* of the Republic of the Congo (Leopoldville): there had been no approval by the Chambers of the Parliament and the person who had countersigned Mr. Kasa-Vubu's signature was not a Minister of the legal Government of the Republic of the Congo." A/4578 (17 November 1960); GAOR, Annexes (XV) 3, pp. 1–3. The General Assembly approved the report of the Credentials Committee by 53 votes to 24, with 19 abstentions. GAOR, XV, Plenary, pp. 978–79. See

also Annual Report of the Secretary-General on the Work of the Organization, 1960–1961 [GAOR, XVI, Supp. 1 (A/4800)], pp. 12–25.

4. In 1963 Algeria, Liberia and the USSR raised in the Credentials Committee the question of the validity of credentials submitted by the Government of South Africa which, in their view, "was not representative of the people of South Africa." A/5676/Rev. 1 (14 December 1963); GAOR, Annexes (XVIII) 3, p. 2. The issue was raised again in the Credentials Committee in 1965. According to the report of that Committee [A/6208 (20 December 1965); GAOR, Annexes (XX) 3, pp. 2–3]:

"The representative of the USSR, referring to the credentials of the representatives of the Government of South Africa, stated that at least four fifths of the people of that country, who were its true rulers, were victims of unprecedented colonialist oppression, racial discrimination and terror on the part of those in power and were deprived of their most elementary rights and freedoms through the policies of *apartheid,* which had repeatedly been condemned by the United Nations and by world public opinion. He therefore considered that the representatives of the Government of South Africa could not legitimately represent the people of South Africa in the United Nations. Similar views were expressed by the representatives of Madagascar, Syria and the United Arab Republic, all of whom stated that they could not recognize as valid the credentials of the representatives of the Government of South Africa.

"The representatives of Australia, Costa Rica, Guatemala, Iceland and the United States of America all expressed their Government's abhorrence of the South African Government's policy of *apartheid.* Like so many other Governments, they had categorically condemned that policy in various United Nations organs. However, in the view of those representatives, this question was quite separate from that of the credentials of the representatives of the Government of South Africa. The Committee, in their opinion, was merely called upon to examine the credentials and to ensure that they had been issued by the proper authorities in accordance with rule 27 of the rules of procedure of the General Assembly. The following views were also expressed by certain of those representatives: that there was a distinct advantage in having the South African delegation present in the various organs of the United Nations so that it could learn at first hand how strong and impassioned were the feelings of Member States concerning *apartheid;* that were the Committee to judge the legality of Governments on the basis of whether they represented the will of the majority, or on the basis of the observance of human rights and political freedom in their countries, it would find many Governments which failed to fulfil these criteria.

"On the other hand, some representatives took the view that the function of the Committee was not merely to examine whether credentials were properly signed but to ensure that those who had signed them were the rightful representatives of the people; that, in their opinion, was not the case in so far as concerned the representatives of the present Government of South Africa which maintained itself in power by force.

"The representative of the United Arab Republic, speaking on behalf of his delegation and the delegations of Madagascar and Syria, and for the reasons they had given earlier, formally moved that 'the Credentials Committee decide not to recognize as valid the credentials of the representatives of the present Government of South Africa'. The representative of the USSR stated that his delegation also wished to join the sponsors of the motion.

"The motion was rejected by 5 votes to 4."

On the basis of a proposal by a group of African States, the General Assembly adopted a resolution going beyond the decision of the Credentials Committee and applying to South Africa the formula previously adopted in the case of Hungary; it decided, by 53 votes to 42, with 9 abstentions, "to take no decision on the credentials submitted on behalf of the representatives of South Africa." Resolution 2113 (XX), 21 December 1965; GAOR, XX, Supp. 14 (A/6014), p. 4.

Chapter IV

SECURITY COUNCIL

Section 1. Members of the Security Council

NOTE.—1. The original text of Article 23 of the Charter fixed the number of members of the Security Council at eleven; unlike Article 4 of the League of Nations Covenant, it provided no procedure for increasing that number. An amendment of the Charter was required in order to increase the number of members to fifteen; that amendment was adopted in 1963 and came into force on 31 August 1965. The Charter grants permanent seats on the Security Council to the Republic of China, France, the Union of Soviet Socialist Republics, the United Kingdom of Great Britain and Northern Ireland, and the United States of America. The General Assembly by a two-thirds majority elects the non-permanent members of the Security Council for a term of two years. Until 1965 three such members were elected annually; after that date the number of members elected annually was increased to five. (As a transitional measure seven members were elected in 1965, but two of them were chosen for one year only.) To ensure constant rotation the Charter provides that no non-permanent member shall be eligible for immediate re-election. In choosing the non-permanent members, the General Assembly is enjoined to pay due regard "in the first instance to the contribution of Members of the United Nations to the maintenance of international peace and security and to the other purposes of the Organization, and also to equitable geographical distribution." While the General Assembly does not seem to pay too much respect to the first injunction, it applies quite vigorously the principle of geographical distribution.

2. The following table shows the way in which seats have been allotted to various groups of Members during the 1946–1965 period:

	Latin America I	Latin America II	Common-wealth	Middle East	Western Europe	Eastern Europe (and Asia)
1946	Brazil	Mexico	Australia	Egypt	Netherlands	Poland
1947	Brazil	Colombia	Australia	Syria	Belgium	Poland
1948	Argentina	Colombia	Canada	Syria	Belgium	Ukrainian SSR
1949	Argentina	Cuba	Canada	Egypt	Norway	Ukrainian SSR
1950	Ecuador	Cuba	India	Egypt	Norway	Yugoslavia
1951	Ecuador	Brazil	India	Turkey	Netherlands	Yugoslavia
1952	Chile	Brazil	Pakistan	Turkey	Netherlands	Greece
1953	Chile	Colombia	Pakistan	Lebanon	Denmark	Greece
1954	Brazil	Colombia	New Zealand	Lebanon	Denmark	Turkey
1955	Brazil	Peru	New Zealand	Iran	Belgium	Turkey
1956	Cuba	Peru	Australia	Iran	Belgium	Yugoslavia
1957	Cuba	Colombia	Australia	Iraq	Sweden	Philippines
1958	Panama	Colombia	Canada	Iraq	Sweden	Japan
1959	Panama	Argentina	Canada	Tunisia	Italy	Japan

	Latin America I	Latin America II	Common- wealth	Middle East	Western Europe	Eastern Europe (and Asia)
1960	Ecuador	Argentina	Ceylon	Tunisia	Italy	Poland
1961	Ecuador	Chile	Ceylon	UAR	Liberia	Turkey
1962	Venezuela	Chile	Ghana	UAR	Ireland	Romania
1963	Venezuela	Brazil	Ghana	Morocco	Norway	Philippines
1964	Bolivia	Brazil	Ivory Coast	Morocco	Norway	Czechoslovakia
1965	Bolivia	Uruguay	Ivory Coast	Jordan	Netherlands	Malaysia

3. This allocation of seats has led to two main difficulties: (1) the Members from Southeast Asia and Africa did not have their own non-permanent seat, though they have sometimes occupied the Commonwealth seat; (2) the Eastern European seat was originally allocated to members of the Soviet bloc, but later it has been occupied instead by Yugoslavia, Greece, and even Turkey (which has previously sat on the Council as a Middle Eastern State). For debates on this subject, see GAOR, II, Plenary, pp. 749–50; IV, Plenary, p. 103; VI, Plenary, p. 236; VIII, Plenary, pp. 218–19.

The tenth session of the General Assembly was confronted by a clash between the Asian and Eastern European groups, when first Poland and later Yugoslavia were confronted with an attempt by the Philippines to obtain the Eastern European seat vacated by Turkey. After 35 unsuccessful ballots a compromise was reached, assuring the election of Yugoslavia on condition that after one year Yugoslavia will resign and the Philippines will be elected for the remainder of the two-year term. This compromise was not accepted officially by the Assembly, but Yugoslavia was elected on the thirty-sixth ballot. GAOR, X, Plenary, pp. 494–501. Yugoslavia resigned at the end of 1956 "for reasons that are well known," and the General Assembly elected the Philippines to fill the vacancy. GAOR, Annexes (XI) 68, p. 1. A similar procedure was followed in several other cases between 1960 and 1965.

4. When the General Assembly adopted the amendment to the Charter increasing the number of the non-permanent members of the Security Council to ten, it also agreed that these members "shall be elected according to the following pattern: (a) Five from African and Asian States; (b) One from Eastern European States; (c) Two from Latin American States; (d) Two from Western European and other States." Resolution 1991 A (XVIII), 17 December 1963; GAOR, XVIII, Supp. 15 (A/5515), pp. 21–22. Accordingly, after the 1965 election, the Security Council included the following non-permanent members: Argentina, Bulgaria, Japan, Jordan, Mali, the Netherlands, New Zealand, Nigeria, Uganda and Uruguay.

Sohn Cs. United Nations Law 2d Ed. UCB—9

Section 2.   Origin of the Veto

VOTING IN THE SECURITY COUNCIL

1.   *United States Tentative Proposals for a General International Organization.*

Draft of 18 July 1944, which formed the basis of the Dumbarton Oaks Conversations.
US Department of State, Postwar Foreign Policy Preparation,
1939–1945 (Washington, 1949), pp. 595, 599.

1.   Each state member of the executive council should have one vote.

2.   Decisions with respect to the following matters should be taken by a majority vote including the concurring votes of all member states having continuing tenure, except as provided for in paragraphs 4 and 5 below:

a.   the assumption on its own initiative or on reference to it of jurisdiction over a dispute;

b.   the terms of settlement of disputes;

c.   the negotiations for a general agreement on the regulation of armaments and armed forces;

d.   the determination of threats to the peace, of breaches of the peace, and of acts obstructing measures for the maintenance of security and peace; and

e.   the institution and application of measures of enforcement.

3.   Other decisions should be taken by a simple majority vote.

4.   In all decisions any state member of the executive council should have the right to abstain from voting, but in such case the abstaining member should be bound by the decision.

5.   Provisions will need to be worked out with respect to the voting procedure in the event of a dispute in which one or more of the members of the council having continuing tenure are directly involved.

2.   *Memorandum for the President on the Voting Procedure in the Security Council.*

Approved by the President, 15 November 1944. US Department of State,
Postwar Foreign Policy Preparation, 1939–1945
(Washington, 1949), pp. 657–58.

Background

There are three issues involved in this connection, as follows:

1.   Size of majority.

2.   Unanimity of permanent members.

3.   Procedure in the event that one of the permanent members is a party to a dispute.

The Russians took the position that the Council should make decisions by a simple majority vote; that unanimity of the permanent members should be required, except on procedural questions; and that the unanimity rule should prevail even when one of the permanent members is a party to a dispute.

The British took the position that the Council's decisions should be by a two-thirds majority vote, except that procedural questions might be settled by a simple majority vote; that unanimity of the permanent members should be required on all substantive matters; and that parties to a dispute should not vote.

The Chinese position was similar to the British.

In accordance with your instructions, our delegation took a position similar to the British, except that we expressed our willingness to accept either a simple majority or a two-thirds majority.

In the course of the Dumbarton discussions, in order to meet the conflicting views, proposals were tentatively made that decisions should require the affirmative votes of seven members, rather than of six members as would be the case under a simple majority rule, or of eight members as would be the case under a two-thirds rule; and that unanimity of the permanent members should be required on all substantive matters, except that in decisions of the Council relating to pacific settlement of disputes (Section A of Chapter VIII) parties to a dispute should not vote. These proposals were not accepted, although they were favorably regarded by Sir Alexander Cadogan and his associates and by Dr. Koo and his associates.

Recommendation

It is recommended that this government accept the formula embodied in the attached draft of a proposal on this subject and seek to obtain the acceptance of that formula by Soviet Russia and the United Kingdom.

The proposed formula is essentially along the lines of the compromise solution discussed at Dumbarton Oaks. It provides that parties to a dispute should abstain from voting in those decisions of the Council which relate to the investigation of disputes, to appeals by the Council for peaceful settlement of disputes, and to recommendations by the Council as to methods and procedures of settlement. It retains the unanimity rule for decisions relating to the determination of the existence of threats to the peace or breaches of the peace and to the suppression of such threats or breaches.

This proposal should be acceptable to this country, since no party to a dispute would sit as a judge in its own case so long as judicial or quasi-judicial procedures are involved, but would participate fully in procedures involving political rather than judicial determination. It should be acceptable to Soviet Russia because it meets her desire that no action be taken against her without her consent.

Proposal for Section C of the Chapter on the Security Council

[Text identical with that read by Secretary Stettinius at Yalta; see No. 1 of next document.]

3. *Statement by Secretary of State Stettinius on the American Position on Voting in Security Council.*

Made at the Crimea (Yalta) Conference, 6 February 1945. US Department of State, Postwar Foreign Policy Preparation, 1939–1945 (Washington, 1949), pp. 659–60, 664–65. See also US Department of State, Foreign Relations of the United States, The Conferences at Malta and Yalta, 1945 (Washington, 1955), pp. 44–93, 567, 590–91, 660–67, 682–86, 711–13, 994–96.

1. *Review of Status of this Question*

It was agreed at Dumbarton Oaks that certain matters would remain under consideration for future settlement. Of these, the principal one was that of voting procedure to be followed in the Security Council.

At Dumbarton Oaks, the three Delegations thoroughly explored the whole question. Since that time the matter has received continuing intensive study by each of the three Governments.

On December 5, 1944, the President sent to Marshal Stalin and to Prime Minister Churchill a proposal that this matter be settled by making Section C, Chapter VI of the Dumbarton Oaks proposals read substantially as follows:

"1. Each member of the Security Council should have one vote.

"2. Decisions of the Security Council on procedural matters should be made by an affirmative vote of seven members.

"3. Decisions of the Security Council on all other matters should be made by an affirmative vote of seven members including the concurring votes of the permanent members; provided that, in decisions under Chapter VIII, Section A and under the second sentence of paragraph 1 of Chapter VIII, Section C, a party to a dispute should abstain from voting."

2. *Analysis of the American Proposal*

(a) We believe that our proposal is entirely consistent with the special responsibilities of the great powers for the preservation of the peace of the world. In this respect our proposal calls for unqualified unanimity of the permanent members of the Council on all major decisions relating to the preservation of peace, including all economic and military enforcement measures.

(b) At the same time our proposal recognizes the desirability of the permanent members frankly stating that the peaceful adjustment of any controversy which may arise is a matter of general world interest in which any sovereign member state involved should have a right to present its case.

We believe that unless this freedom of discussion in the Council is permitted, the establishment of the World Organization which we all so earnestly desire in order to save the world from the tragedy of another war would be seriously jeopardized. Without full and free discussion in the Council, the Organization, even if it could be established, would be vastly different from the one we have contemplated.

The paper which we have placed before the other two delegations [see Annex, below] sets forth the text of the provisions which I have read and lists specifically those decisions of the Council which, under our proposals, would require unqualified unanimity and, separately, those matters in the area of discussion and peaceful settlement in which any party to a dispute would abstain from casting a vote.

3. *Reasons for the American Position*

From the point of view of the United States Government there are two important elements in the matter of voting procedure.

First, there is the necessity for unanimity among the permanent members for the preservation of the peace of the world.

Second, it is of particular importance to the people of the United States that there be provision for a fair hearing for all members of the organization, large and small.

We believe that the proposals submitted by the President to Marshal Stalin and Prime Minister Churchill on December 5 of last year provide a reasonable and just solution and satisfactorily combine these two main considerations.

It is our earnest hope that our two great Allies will find it possible to accept the President's proposal.

Annex

Principal Substantive Decisions on Which the Security Council Would Have to Vote: U. S. Paper of 15 January 1945, Referred to in Statement by Secretary Stettinius

Under the voting formula proposed by the President, all of the decisions listed below would require the affirmative votes of 7 members of the Security Council, including the votes of the permanent members. The only exception would be that, in the event that a permanent member is a party to a dispute or a situation before the Council, that member would not cast its vote in decisions listed under "Promotion of Peaceful Settlement of Disputes" (Category III below).

I. Recommendations to the General Assembly on

1. Admission of new members;
2. Suspension of a member;
3. Expulsion of a member;
4. Election of the Secretary General.

II.   Restoration of the rights and privileges of a suspended member.

III.   Promotion of peaceful settlement of disputes, including the following questions:

1.   Whether a dispute or a situation brought to the Council's attention is of such a nature that its continuation is likely to threaten the peace;

2.   Whether the Council should call on the parties to settle or adjust the dispute or situation by means of their own choice;

3.   Whether the Council should make a recommendation to the parties as to methods and procedures of settlement;

4.   Whether the legal aspects of the matter before it should be referred by the Council for advice to the international court of justice;

5.   Whether, if there exists a regional agency for peaceful settlement of local disputes, such an agency should be asked to concern itself with the controversy.

IV.   Removal of threats to the peace and suppression of breaches of the peace, including the following questions:

1.   Whether failure on the part of the parties to a dispute to settle it by means of their own choice or in accordance with the recommendations of the Security Council in fact constitutes a threat to the peace;

2.   Whether any other actions on the part of any country constitute a threat to the peace or a breach of the peace;

3.   What measures should be taken by the Council to maintain or restore the peace and the manner in which such measures should be carried out;

4.   Whether a regional agency should be authorized to take measures of enforcement.

V.   Approval of special agreement or agreements for the provision of armed forces and facilities.

VI.   Formulation of plans for a general system of regulation of armaments and submission of such plans to the member states.

VII.   Determination of whether the nature and the activities of a regional agency or arrangement for the maintenance of peace and security are consistent with the purposes and principles of the general organization.

NOTE.—1.   The voting formula proposed by the United States was accepted by the Soviet Union at Yalta and it became, with only a few minor drafting amendments, Article 27 of the Charter.   At the San Francisco Conference, however, various difficulties arose as to the interpretation of this provision and, in particular, with respect to the question whether a permanent member could by its veto prevent completely even a preliminary discussion by the Security Council of a dispute submitted to it.   This question was finally settled at a conference at Moscow between Premier Stalin and Mr. Hopkins, a special representative of President Roosevelt. See Ruth B. RUSSELL, A History of the United Nations Charter (Washington, D. C., 1958), pp. 713–42; Robert E. SHERWOOD, Roosevelt and Hopkins (New York, 1948), pp. 910–12; US Department of State, Postwar Foreign Policy Preparation, 1939–1945 (Washington, 1949), p. 449. The agreement on the subject was incorporated into a statement of the five permanent members of the Security Council of 7 June 1945; for the text of that statement, see Section 5 of Part II of the BASIC DOCUMENTS.

2. For a list of cases in which negative votes were cast in the Security Council, see 2 UN Repertory, pp. 92–6; *idem*, Supp. 1, Vol. I, pp. 274–75; *idem*, Supp. 2, Vol. II, pp. 312–13; Arlette MOLDAVER, "Repertoire of the Veto in the Security Council, 1946–1956," 11 Int. Org. (1957), pp. 261–74. For an analysis of some of the early cases, see Norman J. PADELFORD, "The Use of the Veto," 2 Int. Org. (1948), pp. 227–46. While most vetoes were cast by the USSR, a few were cast also by China, France and the United Kingdom.

Section 3.   Abstention From Voting

ABSTENTION FROM VOTING BY PARTIES TO A DISPUTE

Statement by Dr. Yuen-li Liang (China) before the Committee of Experts of the Security Council, 16 April 1946.   UN Doc. S/Procedure/61/Rev. 1; 24 BYBIL (1947), p. 349.

. . . There is no question as to the necessity for the concurring votes of the permanent members in any of the decisions called for under Article 34. This is clear from the terms of the Yalta formula and the Statement of the Sponsoring Governments.

The Yalta formula, however, also provides that when a State is party to a dispute it shall abstain from voting in the decisions of the Council under Chapter VI of the Charter concerning such dispute. This requirement for abstention, in the case of a permanent member being a party to a dispute, obviously does not affect the requirement that the remaining permanent members must concur in the decisions.

It is also clear that the abstention requirement laid down in Article 27, Paragraph 3, is not intended to apply to all matters arising under Article 35, Paragraph 1. Thus when a State brings to the attention of the Security Council, by reason of the general interest of that State as a Member of the United Nations, a matter which it considers might endanger international peace and security, the requirement for abstention shall not apply to such member in any of the decisions of the Council provided for in Article 34. In exercising such a general right, the position of the State bringing the matter to the attention of the Security Council is similar to that of the Secretary-General under Article 99.

With respect to the requirement for abstention, however, the distinction between disputes and situations should not extend to those cases in which one State complains that its specific rights have been infringed upon or their enjoyment directly endangered by the action of one or more other States, and alleges that a dispute, the continuance of which endangers international peace and security, has arisen. Should the other State or States directly involved make the allegation that a situation has arisen as distinct from a dispute, such an attempted distinction shall not affect the requirement for abstention laid down in Article 27, Paragraph 3, of the Charter.

The specific function of the Security Council in connection with the pacific settlement of disputes and situations endangering the maintenance of international peace and security is laid down in Article 36 which states that "The Security Council may at any stage of a dispute of the nature referred to in Article 33 or of a situation of like nature, recommend appropriate procedures or methods of adjustment." The terms of this Article indicate that the action contemplated is not based upon a prior determination whether a matter is a dispute or a situation, but upon whether the matter brought before the Council is of such a nature that its continuance is likely to endanger the maintenance of international peace and security. It is clear that Article 36 makes no distinction between disputes and situations insofar as the function of the Council in making recommendations is concerned.

At the time of the Yalta Conference, the authors of the voting formula had before them only the text of the Dumbarton Oaks Proposals. An examination of these Proposals reveals that the paragraph corresponding to Article 36(1) of the Charter, namely Chapter VIII, Section A, Paragraph 5, refers only to disputes and not to situations. In embodying the abstention clause into the voting formula, therefore, it was clearly the intention of the authors to exclude from voting those states involved directly in a matter whose continuance might endanger international peace and security. However, as the term used to describe such matters was "dispute" in the text of the Dumbarton Oaks Proposals, it was only logical that the term used in the Yalta formula was "parties to a dispute". There is further evidence of the fact that the term "parties to a dispute" was meant to include "parties directly concerned in a situation" in cases where the Security Council has to make the determination provided for in Article 34 of the Charter. In a statement issued on 5 March 1945, Mr. Stettinius, then Secretary of State said: "This means that no nation, large or small, if a party to a dispute, would participate in the decisions of the Security Council on questions like the following: '(b) Whether the dispute or situation is of such a nature that its continuation is likely to threaten the peace.' "

As stated above, the text of the Yalta formula was drafted on the basis of the text of the Dumbarton Oaks Proposals in which the term "situation" did not appear in connection with the specific function of the Council relative to pacific settlement, as laid down in Chapter VIII, Section A, Paragraph 5. At San Francisco this Section of the

Dumbarton Oaks Proposals was extensively revised while the text of the Yalta formula remained untouched. Among the many modifications made in Section A of Chapter VIII was the insertion of the term "or of a situation of like nature" in paragraph 5 of that section. The Summary Report of the Twelfth Meeting of Committee III/2 reveals that the words "or of a situation of like nature" were intended to give effect to the Australian amendment which proposed that the Security Council should be permitted to deal with both a dispute or a situation the continuance of which was likely to endanger the peace. Thus it is clear that the insertion of the term "or of a situation of like nature" in Article 34 with reference to the specific function of the Security Council as regards pacific settlement, was never intended to be the basis of a differentiation between the duty of States to abstain from voting in a dispute to which they are parties and the absence of such a duty in the case of situations in which they are directly concerned.

The abstention clause in Article 27(3) of the Charter is an embodiment of the principle that, so far as the process of pacific settlement calls for the appreciation by the Council of a question presented to it, a State shall not at once be judge and party in its own cause. If a matter brought to the attention of the Council is sufficiently grave so that the Council considers that its continuance may endanger international peace and security, it may make such a decision exclusive of the votes of the States directly involved. If this decision is in the affirmative, the Security Council may recommend appropriate procedure or methods of adjustment by virtue of a decision which is again exclusive of the votes of the States directly involved. This requirement for abstention, however, does not flow from the fact that the States directly involved are parties to a dispute as distinct from being parties to a situation. Rather it is derived from the necessity for effective action on the part of the Council on the one hand, and the principle that no State shall be judge and party in its own cause on the other.

If the interpretation is accepted that, with respect to the requirement for abstention, a distinction exists between parties to a dispute and parties directly concerned in a situation, then when a matter is brought to the attention of the Security Council involving a permanent member, that matter can never be considered a dispute within the meaning of the Charter, unless that permanent member chooses to have it so considered. Furthermore, to make the determination of whether a dispute or situation exists subject to the veto power of a permanent member, is to defeat the clear intention of the Yalta formula and to render meaningless the distinction made therein between voting procedures applicable to pacific settlement and voting procedures applicable to enforcement action.

NOTE. Suppose that the following rule of procedure had been proposed to the Security Council:

"Should the Security Council consider a dispute provided for by Article 33 of the Charter, a party to the dispute shall abstain from voting in accordance with paragraph 3 of Article 27 of the Charter.

"Should the Security Council consider a situation provided for by Article 34 or any other dispute which does not fall under Article 33, all the members of the Security Council are entitled to participate in voting.

"The decision of whether the question under consideration by the Security Council is of a procedural nature and also of whether the question under consideration is a dispute or situation and whether this dispute is of the nature referred to in Article 33 of the Charter shall be regarded as accepted if it is voted for by seven members of the Security Council including the concurring votes of all the permanent members of the Security Council."

Would such a rule be consistent with the Charter and the San Francisco Declaration of the Sponsoring Powers?

RESTRICTIONS IMPOSED BY EGYPT ON THE PASSAGE OF SHIPS THROUGH THE SUEZ CANAL: ABSTENTION OF PARTIES TO THE DISPUTE

Discussion in the Security Council, 16 and 27 August 1951. SCOR, VI, Mtg. 553, pp. 23–5; Mtg. 555, pp. 1–4, 15–6.

Mahmoud FAWZI Bey (Egypt): . . . I take it that the representatives of such members of the Council as France, the Netherlands, the United Kingdom and the United States, which are parties to this dispute will, in conformity with the last part of Article 27 of the Charter, abstain from voting. I am not making a full list; I am just giving a few illustrations of what members of the Council I have in mind when I cite this part of Article 27 of the Charter.

That there is a dispute is clear from the fact that Israel and other countries, some of which have in vain tried to hide behind Israel, are disputing the right of Egypt to impose the present restrictions on the passage of some war materials to Israel through the Suez Canal. Allow me to recall in this respect the definition of "dispute" given by Mr. Bevin at the 19th meeting of the Security Council, when he said that "if a State makes a charge against another State and the State against which it is made repudiates it or contests it, then there is a dispute".

Another definition of "dispute" is laid down in document A/578 [GAOR, III, Supp. 10, pp. 7–8], dated 15 July 1948, embodying the report of the Interim Committee to the General Assembly, which in part recommends:

"In deciding, for the purposes of Article 27, paragraph 3, whether a matter brought before the Security Council by a State or States is a dispute or a situation, the Security Council shall hold that a dispute arises

"(a) Whenever the State or States bringing the matter before the Security Council allege that the actions of another State or States, in respect of the first State or States constitute a breach of an international obligation

"(b) . . . and the State or States which are the subject of these allegations contest, or do not admit, the facts alleged or inferences to be drawn from such allegations."

That such countries as France, the Netherlands, the United Kingdom and the United States—to which we might add, because of its protest, Turkey—are parties to the present dispute is undeniable. Much of the context of this dispute conclusively proves it, as do, in particular, the attitudes, the statements and the protests of these countries, five of them. Up to today, the Netherlands has protested to the Egyptian Government no less than three times; Turkey, at least once; the United Kingdom, at least ten times; the United States, twelve times; and France, twenty-two times. Most of the protests were lodged with the Egyptian Government even while the hostilities in Palestine were still taking place. In each and all of these protests, the position is unequivocally taken by the complaining country that it is a directly interested party which is disputing the right of Egypt to impose the restrictions in question. It is, therefore, distinctly evident that a dispute exists between Egypt and those countries on the interpretation of the Armistice Agreement, the Suez Canal Convention and international law, including the Charter of the United Nations. They contend that Egypt has violated these two treaties and the law of nations, whereas Egypt contends that it is within its legitimate rights and acting in conformity with the stipulations and provisions of the Armistice Agreement, the Suez Canal Convention and the principles of international law.

I should also like to call the Council's attention to the proposal introduced in the Interim Committee by the United States—United Nations document A/AC.18/SC.3/4. The proposal reads in part:

"The abstention clause in Article 27, paragraph 3 of the Charter embodies the principle that in the pacific settlement of a matter a State shall not be both judge and party in its own cause. The requirement for abstention does not flow from the fact that the States primarily involved are parties to a dispute as distinguished from being parties to a situation. Rather it is derived from the principle of justice that no State shall be judge and party in its own cause.

"When the issue comes up in the Security Council, the basic question which each member of the Council must answer for himself in deciding how he should vote is: 'Is this a matter on which State X should abstain, because if it did not abstain it would be acting as a judge in a case in which it is implicated?'"

The United States proposal stated further: "It is the view of the United States that the application of this simple principle affords a proper guide on which to base its vote whenever this issue arises in the Security Council".

We shall see about that.

This fundamental and Charterwise principle—namely, that no State shall be judge and party—should apply and command our respect in all cases, whether there are two or more parties to a question. Furthermore, the Council cannot rightly subscribe to any attempt to defeat the *raison d'être* of this principle by claiming that it would at times impede the Council from discharging its duties. The duties of the Council are only and exclusively those which conform to the principles of justice and the United Nations Charter. Any betrayal of these principles could not form part of the Council's duties and do not form part of the Charter. . . .

Sir Gladwyn JEBB (UK): In his statement . . . the representative of Egypt suggested that the matter which is now before the Council is technically a dispute, and that the delegations of France, the Netherlands, Turkey, the United Kingdom and the United States—and indeed, I understood him to say very probably other members of the Council as well—are all parties to that dispute and must, therefore, under Article 27, paragraph 3, of the Charter, abstain from voting. . . .

Two main points are at issue, as we see it. Firstly, there is the technical question whether this matter is a dispute within the meaning of the Charter and, if so, whether the five delegations mentioned are parties to it, and whether Article 27, paragraph 3, of the Charter consequently applies. Secondly, there is the broader question, which was also raised by the Egyptian representative, namely, whether the five delegations ought to abstain on general principles, even if they are not strictly obliged to do so by Article 27, paragraph 3. I think I have put the point correctly.

As regards the technical question, the representative of Egypt first claimed that this matter was manifestly a dispute. Let us suppose, for the sake of argument, that it is technically a dispute. But what really matters is the question who the parties to the dispute are. On this point I think it can be clearly shown that the contention of the Egyptian representative is not correct. He referred to the two proposed definitions of a dispute, neither of which, incidentally, has ever been adopted by the Security Council itself. But even if one of them had been adopted, the effect would have been that, if a State came to the Security Council with a complaint or accusation against another State, and if the State against which the complaint or accusation had been made rejected it, then there would be a dispute between them. It is of course possible that more than two States might be involved. The complaint or accusation might be brought to the Council by a group of States, and might be brought against more than one State. In the present instance, however, only two States are concerned. The matter has been brought before the Council by the Government of Israel and the complaint is directed against the Government of Egypt. The dispute, if there is a dispute, is between Israel and Egypt, and between nobody else.

I should be quite prepared to admit that any one of the five delegations mentioned by the representative of Egypt might have asked the Security Council to deal with the restrictions which the Egyptian Government has imposed on shipping using the Suez Canal. . . . We have not, however, done so. If we had done so, the basis for our action would have had to have been quite different from the basis of the action of the Government of Israel. If there were any dispute within the meaning of the Charter between one of the five delegations mentioned and Egypt, the Armistice Agreement and the whole question of Palestine would be quite irrelevant. The plain fact is, however, that none of our five delegations has brought this matter to the attention of the Security Council.

So much for the technical position. I shall now deal with the broader question and with the Egyptian representative's suggestion that if our delegations vote on the draft resolution which is now before the Council we shall in some sense, as I think he said, be acting as judge and party in our own cause. Those were his words: "judge and party". There is, however, no precise analogy between the Security Council and a court of law. The Security Council is an organ established under the United Nations Charter with the primary responsibility, as we all know, of maintaining international peace and security. Its primary duty is, therefore, to take any action which may be required in order to fulfil this task. It is almost inevitable that in many, if not all, questions which come before the Council, a number of States members of the Council will be concerned to a greater or less degree, even though they may not be parties to the dispute with which the Council is dealing. In itself, this is certainly no reason why they should be debarred from voting. In the present case, I need only say that our five delegations do not feel that the concern which each of us may have in securing the removal of the present restrictions is such as to warp our judgment or prevent us from expressing an opinion which we feel to be just and reasonable. But quite apart from this, if the Egyptian representative's argument were accepted the result would be to paralyze the Security Council in dealing with many of the matters which are brought before us. Any question affecting international peace and security is certain to be of concern to most, if not to all, members of the Security Council, and all of their interests are bound to be more or less closely affected by it.

One result of accepting the Egyptian contention would be that the Council would not be able to take a decision in the area of peaceful settlement of disputes when a universally accepted principle, such as the freedom of the seas, was involved. All members of the Council are interested in upholding this principle, and all of them, according to the Egyptian argument as we see it, would therefore be debarred from voting if the principle were violated and if the Council were required to uphold the principle.

To summarize, it can, I think, easily be shown that the Egyptian argument would produce quite incongruous results. The effect of it would be to enable any State against which a complaint was made in the Security Council to ensure that the Council should be unable to take any action at all. All that is necessary is that the State concerned should do sufficient damage to the interests of at least five members of the Council so that it could then claim that their interests were directly involved and that, therefore, they should not vote. The Security Council would then not be able to take certain types of decisions as regards what might be a completely valid complaint by a Member of the United Nations.

We have, therefore, come to the conclusion that Article 27, paragraph 3, in no way debars us from voting on the draft resolution before the Council. On the contrary, to read such an interpretation into the Article would be, as we see it, to paralyze the Security Council so as to prevent it handling many controversies which, under the plan of the Charter, should come before it.   .   .   .

Mahmoud FAWZI Bey (Egypt):   .   .   .   The representative of the United Kingdom has attributed to me a statement   .   .   .   that not only the sponsors of the draft resolution now before us, but also other members of the Security Council as well, were interested parties. I take it, however, that he meant only the members to which I actually referred, namely, the three sponsors, the Netherlands and Turkey. His contention that we can extend the description of "interested" to almost everyone in the world, to almost every State in the world is, to say the least, a very carefree contention. If we were to apply his criterion, there would never be an application of paragraph 3, Article 27 of the Charter. We would never find any party to which we could apply the description or definition of an interested party. The question of what is an interested party is a matter to be investigated. I mentioned those five countries because they actually have material interests involved in the question and, furthermore, because each and every one of them has presented protests on many occasions to the Egyptian Government against the restrictions applied in the Suez Canal on the passage of some war materials to Israel. How can we validly say that these countries are not parties? I do not see how there can be any doubt that they are.

The representative of the United Kingdom even went so far as to imply—I hope I did not misunderstand him, or perhaps I should hope I did misunderstand him—that whether or not they are parties is a matter almost entirely, if not entirely, left to their own appraisal or appreciation.   .   .   .

Article 27 is   .   .   .   an essential part of the Constitution of the United Nations known as the Charter. It stipulates essential rights for the Members of the United Nations. It stipulates the basic protection which has existed throughout the ages—even before the United Nations or any such thing as the League of Nations had ever been heard of—that a party shall not be, at the same time, a judge.

I am very disappointed, I must confess, to note the persistent desire of some of the members of the Security Council to indulge in the very doubtful luxury of being, at the same time, judges and parties. I was clinging to the hope that France, the Netherlands, Turkey, the United Kingdom and the United States of America would give the Charter its due and would, by deciding to abstain from voting and by not wanting to be at the same time parties and judges in relation to the present dispute, pay respect, as they should, to the traditions of international law. However, this hope has evidently been frustrated. The only choice left to me in this connexion, therefore,—apart from other issues in relation to which I reserve the right of my Government—is to submit to the Council the following draft resolution:

"Considering the debate in the Security Council on the restrictions imposed by Egypt in relation to the passage through the Suez Canal of some war materials to Israel,

"Considering the claim by Egypt that, according to paragraph 3 of Article 27 of the Charter, France, the Netherlands, Turkey, the United Kingdom and the United States of America must abstain from voting,

"Considering that this claim by Egypt is contested by the members of the Security Council mentioned in the preceding paragraph,

"The Security Council

"Resolves to request the International Court of Justice to give its advisory opinion on the following question:

" 'In the light of the Charter of the United Nations, particularly paragraph 3 of Article 27, and in view of the debate in the Security Council, are France, the Netherlands, Turkey, the United Kingdom and the United States of America obliged to abstain from voting on the question of the restrictions imposed by Egypt in relation to the passage through the Suez Canal of some war materials to Israel?' "

. . .

[As Egypt was not at the time of this discussion a member of the Council, and no member of the Council was willing to sponsor its draft resolution, that resolution was not put to the vote. A resolution calling upon Egypt "to terminate the restrictions on the passage of international commercial shipping and goods through the Suez Canal" was adopted by the Security Council on 1 September 1951 by 8 votes to none, with 3 abstentions (China, India, USSR). The five members mentioned in the Egyptian draft resolution all took part in this vote and voted in favor of the final resolution. SCOR, VI, Mtg. 555, pp. 2–3.]

NOTE.—1. The full text of the definition of a "dispute", prepared by the Interim Committee of the General Assembly (GAOR, III, Supp. 10, pp. 7–8) for the purpose of applying Article 27, paragraph 3, is as follows:

"(1) In deciding, for the purpose of Article 27, paragraph 3, whether a matter brought before the Security Council by a State or States is a dispute or a situation, the Security Council shall hold that a dispute arises:

"(a) If the State or States bringing the matter before the Security Council, and the State or States whose conduct is impugned, agree that there is a dispute.

"(b) Whenever the State or States bringing the matter before the Security Council allege that the actions of another State or States in respect of the first State or States constitute a breach of an international obligation or are endangering or are likely to endanger the maintenance of international peace and security, or that such actions demonstrate preparation to commit a breach of international obligations or to endanger the maintenance of international peace and security, and the State or States which are the subject of these allegations contest, or do not admit, the facts alleged or inferences to be drawn from such allegations.

"(2) Further, if a State bringing before the Security Council a matter of the nature contemplated under paragraph (1) above, alleges that another State is violating the rights of a third State, and the latter supports the contention of the first State, then the third State shall also be deemed to be a party to the dispute.

"(3) Nothing in this definition shall prevent the Security Council from deciding that a dispute exists in circumstances not covered by the above definition."

2. In the Corfu Channel Case the question arose whether a party to a dispute can vote on a decision which is "a purely procedural one," and not a decision "under Chapter VI." The decision in question related to the appointment by the Security Council, as "a preliminary step in the consideration of the incidents in the Corfu Channel," of a subcommittee of three members "to examine all the available evidence" and to make a report to the Security Council "on the facts of the case." SC Resolution 19 (1947), 27 February 1947; SCOR, II, Resolutions and Decisions, 1947, pp. 2–3. The PRESIDENT of the Security Council (Mr. F. van Langenhove, Belgium) ruled that the United Kingdom representative was entitled to vote. He stated:

"Article 27 of the Charter is quite definite; it does not debar members of the Security Council who are parties to a dispute from voting, except with regard to decisions to be taken by the Council 'under Chapter VI.' But Chapter VI does not mention decisions of the kind which we have now to take. We have to establish a purely advisory sub-committee, whose only task will be to assist the Council in the submission of facts; this body will take no decisions; it will confine itself to formulating conclusions intended to help the Council in taking a decision. The sole function of the future sub-committee will be to facilitate the Council's work by classifying information submitted to the Council; there is no question in this case of undertaking an investigation. . . .

"In so far as it sanctions an exception to the voting order, Article 27, paragraph 3, must, where applicable, be interpreted strictly; it cannot be stretched to cover cases which are not mentioned in Chapter VI of the Charter. If we study the various Articles of Chapter VI we shall see that the establishment of a sub-committee, such as that proposed by the Australian resolution, is not amongst the decisions and recommendations mentioned in that Chapter."

Mr. EL-KHOURI (Syria) pointed out that in order "to come within the provisions of Article 34, an investigation must be aimed at discovering whether the dispute or situation is likely to endanger the maintenance of international peace and security. I think the proposal of the Australian delegation for the formation of the sub-committee was not directed towards this end. The proposed sub-committee will not be created in order to find out whether the existing situation between these two States in question would be likely to endanger the maintenance of international peace and security, but simply to clarify certain ambiguities in the statements which we have heard from both parties."

Mr. GROMYKO (USSR) objected to this ruling, contending that no "point of order" was involved, that decisions "cease to be decisions of a procedural nature from the moment the Council begins to take a decision regarding investigation," and that a decision to investigate facts is a decision about an investigation. Nevertheless, in order not to hinder the appointment of the sub-committee, he did not request a separate vote on the question whether this was a matter of procedure, and he abstained on the final vote on the resolution which was adopted by eight votes (including the United Kingdom), with three abstentions. SCOR, II, pp. 425–32.

ADMISSION OF ISRAEL TO MEMBERSHIP: ABSTENTION BY A PERMANENT MEMBER

1. *Discussion in the Security Council, 4 March 1949.*

SCOR, IV, No. 17, pp. 8–9, 14–15.

Mr. AUSTIN (USA): . . . I move the following resolution [S/1276]:

"The Security Council,

"Having received and considered the application of Israel for membership in the United Nations,

"Decides in its judgment that Israel is a peace-loving State and is able and willing to carry out the obligations contained in the Charter, and

"Recommends to the General Assembly that it admit Israel to membership in the United Nations." . . .

A vote was taken by show of hands, as follows:

In favour: Argentina, Canada, China, Cuba, France, Norway, Ukrainian Soviet Socialist Republic, Union of Soviet Socialist Republics, United States of America.

Against: Egypt.

Abstaining: United Kingdom.

The resolution was adopted by 9 votes to 1, with 1 abstention.

The PRESIDENT [Mr. A. Alvarez, Cuba]: In accordance with the principle established by the Security Council on resolutions subject to the unanimity rule, abstention by a permanent member of the Council does not render the Council's decision invalid. I therefore declare the United States draft resolution to be adopted.

Mr. ARCE (Argentina): I do not wish to comment on the President's statement that the Council, having adopted the draft resolution by more than the seven votes required by the Charter, has decided to recommend Israel's admission to membership in the United Nations. I wish, however, to go on record as stating that, contrary to the view held by some, if not by practically all the permanent members of the Council, this resolution has not been supported by the five permanent members of the Council as required in Article 27, paragraph 3, of the Charter. While the President has referred to an established principle, I do not believe that the Security Council can establish principles to modify the Charter whenever it thinks fit.

Mahmoud FAWZI Bey (Egypt): For reasons similar to those expounded by the representative of Argentina, I wish to express my doubt as to certain interpretations of the way in which Article 27, paragraph 3, of the United Nations Charter should be applied.

Mr. MALIK (USSR): I would merely like to draw the Council's attention to the fact that, in accordance with the established practice of the Security Council, when a permanent member of the Council abstains from voting, such action is not interpreted in the way that some are now endeavouring to interpret it.

2. *Discussion in the* Ad Hoc *Political Committee of the General Assembly, 3–4 May 1949.*

GAOR, III.2, *Ad Hoc* Political C., pp. 181–3, 200–1.

[When the General Assembly was considering the recommendation of the Security Council to admit Israel] Sir Mohammed ZAFRULLAH KHAN (Pakistan) raised a preliminary question. The Committee was proceeding on the assumption that the Security Council had recommended the admission of Israel to membership in the United Nations. The record of the voting in the Security Council, however, disclosed that one of the permanent members, the United Kingdom, had registered an abstention. Accordingly, the provision of Article 27 of the Charter had not been observed. Paragraph 3 of that Article provided that decisions of the Security Council on other than procedural matters—and the admission of Israel was not a procedural matter—should be made "by an affirmative vote of seven members including the concurring votes of the permanent members". Although the result of the voting had been nine votes in favour of admission of Israel, those nine votes had included the affirmative votes of only four of the permanent members of the Council. One non-permanent member had voted against the recommendation and one permanent member had abstained. Thus, the vote had not been interpreted in accordance with the requisite conditions set forth in Article 27.

He was aware that the Security Council had proceeded on the basis of a practice it was trying to establish whereby the abstention of a permanent member in decisions of a substantive nature was not to be treated as a veto. Paragraph 3 of Article 27, however, did not mention the veto; it merely stipulated that the concurring votes of the permanent members must be included in the seven or more affirmative votes necessary for the adoption of substantive decisions. Moreover, regardless of the interpretation placed by the Security Council in its own practice on the abstention of a permanent member, the General Assembly was not bound by any action taken by the Council which failed to comply with the explicit terms of Article 27. . . .

In view of those considerations, the Committee had before it no Security Council decision which had been taken in accordance with the conditions laid down in the Charter. Should any member of the Committee not agree with him on that subject, it would be necessary to clarify the interpretation of Article 27. That could be done either by referring the matter to the International Court of Justice with a request for an advisory opinion, or by sending the recommendation back to the Security Council in accordance with rule 126 of the rules of procedure. Surely, the General Assembly could take no decision until it had dispelled all doubt concerning the regularity of the Council's recommendation to admit Israel to membership. . . .

Sir Terence SHONE (UK) recalled the argument advanced at the preceding meeting by the representative of Pakistan to the effect that the Security Council's recommendation on the admission of Israel was invalid because it failed to comply with the terms of paragraph 3 of Article 27. While he did not wish to debate the legal interpretation of that Article, Sir Terence did wish to emphasize certain other considerations which should be borne in mind.

In addition to the laws and rules which governed the conduct of the various United Nations organs, they had established certain practices which had acquired great force. Since July 1946, a practice had been created in the Security Council whereby a permanent member could, by abstaining from the vote, permit the Council to take action which that member did not affirmatively support, provided that such action had been approved by the affirmative votes of seven members. That procedure had been explicitly sanctioned by all five permanent members on various occasions. It should be noted, specifically, that during the discussion on the question of Indonesia in July 1947, the then President of the Council, the representative of Syria, had stated: "I think it is now jurisprudence in the Security Council—and the interpretation accepted for a long time—that an abstention is not considered a veto, and the concurrent votes of the permanent members mean the votes of the permanent members who participate in the voting. Those who abstain intentionally are not considered to have cast a veto. That is quite clear." . . .

Irrespective of the strictly legal position, it was unwise to abandon a practice whereby the permanent members of the Council were attempting to avoid hampering decisions by exercising their veto. However, the United Kingdom delegation was not anxious to prevent the Assembly from examining the whole question. Its position had been made clear when it had abstained from voting on the Security Council's recommendation to admit Israel to the United Nations. It had abstained on the grounds that it did not wish to use its privileged vote to block the admission of any State which obtained the requisite majority.

NOTE. In more than seventy cases, decisions of the Security Council on non-procedural matters were adopted despite abstention by one or more of the permanent members. For a list of such decisions, see 2 UN Repertory, pp. 97–103; *idem*, Supp. 1, Vol. I, p. 276; *idem*, Supp. 2, Vol. II, p. 314. In addition, on two occasions in 1946 and for several months in 1950, the representative of the USSR absented himself from meetings of the Council. Later he challenged the validity of the decisions of the Council taken in his absence, while other members of the Council considered that an absence should be treated in the same way as an abstention. 2 *idem*, pp. 82–3. See also Leo GROSS, "Voting in the Security Council: Abstention from Voting and Absence from Meetings," 60 Yale L.J. (1951), pp. 209–57; Yuen-li LIANG and Kwen CHEN, "Abstention and Absence of a Permanent Member in Relation to the Voting Procedure in the Security Council," 44 AJIL (1950), pp. 694–708; Myres S. McDOUGAL and Richard N. GARDNER, "The Veto and the Charter: An Interpretation for Survival," 60 Yale L.J. (1951), pp. 258–92.

Section 4. Voting on "Procedural" Questions and "Double Veto"

SPANISH QUESTION: THE AUSTRALIAN DRAFT RESOLUTION

Discussion in the Security Council, 26 June 1946. SCOR, I.1, No. 2, pp. 326, 379, 380, 388, 400–401, 413–432.

[During the consideration by the Security Council of the Spanish Question, a special Sub-Committee was appointed, by 10 votes to none, with one absention (USSR), "to examine the statements made before the Security Council concerning Spain, to receive further statements and documents, and to conduct such inquiries as it may deem necessary, and to report to the Security Council." Resolution 4 (1946), 29

April 1946; SCOR, I, Resolutions and Decisions, 1946, p. 8. This Sub-Committee recommended:

"(a) The endorsement by the Security Council of the principles contained in the declaration by the Governments of the United Kingdom, the United States of America and France, dated 4 March 1946;

"(b) The transmitting by the Security Council to the General Assembly of the evidence and reports of this Sub-Committee, together with the recommendation that, unless the Franco regime is withdrawn and the other conditions of political freedom set out in the declaration are, in the opinion of the General Assembly, fully satisfied, a resolution be passed by the General Assembly recommending that diplomatic relations with the Franco regime be terminated forthwith by each Member of the United Nations; . . . "

A draft resolution approving these recommendations was not adopted by the Security Council, as a permanent member (USSR) voted against it. The Polish representative then proposed the adoption of the following draft resolution:

"The Security Council

"Declares that the existence and activities of the Franco regime in Spain have led to international friction and endangered international peace and security;

"Calls upon, in accordance with the authority vested in it, all Members of the United Nations who maintain diplomatic relations with the Franco Government to sever such relations immediately;

"Expresses its deep sympathy to the Spanish people; hopes and expects that the people of Spain will regain the freedom of which they have been deprived with the aid and contrivance of Fascist Italy and Nazi Germany; and

"Is convinced that the day will come soon when it will be able to welcome the Spanish nation into the Community of the United Nations."

This draft resolution was rejected by 7 votes to 4. The Australian representative presented therefore the following draft resolution:

"Whereas the Security Council on 29 April 1946 appointed a Sub-Committee to investigate the situation in Spain;

"Whereas the investigation of the Sub-Committee has fully confirmed the facts which led to the condemnation of the Franco regime by the Potsdam and San Francisco Conferences, by the General Assembly at the first part of its first session and by the Security Council by resolution of the date above-mentioned; and

"Whereas the Sub-Committee was of the opinion that the situation in Spain is one the continuance of which is likely to endanger the maintenance of international peace and security,

"The Security Council decides that without prejudice to the rights of the General Assembly under the Charter, the Council shall keep the situation in Spain under continuous observation and shall maintain it upon the list of matters of which it is seized, in order that it will be at all times ready to take such measures as may become necessary to maintain international peace and security. Any member of the Security Council may bring up the matter for consideration by the Council at any time."

After a short discussion the President submitted the text to the vote of the Council.]

A vote was taken by show of hands, as follows:

In favour: Australia, Brazil, China, Egypt, France, Mexico, Netherlands, United Kingdom, United States of America.

Against: Poland, Union of Soviet Socialist Republics.

The PRESIDENT (Mr. Castillo Nájera, Mexico): The amended draft resolution is carried.

Mr. GROMYKO (USSR): I consider the President's statement that the resolution was adopted to be the result of a misunderstanding. The resolution failed to be adopted because one of the permanent members of the Security Council voted against it. One of the non-permanent members also voted against it.

This resolution is not of a procedural character. It concerns questions of substance which—I stress the point—have already been voted upon once. Some members of the Council wished to raise once again old questions which had already been voted upon. That is their affair. They have a perfect right to do so. But it does not follow that because these questions are raised once again they become procedural questions. For this reason, I positively declare that this resolution was not approved. It was rejected and must be so regarded.

If there should be any objection to this statement hereafter, I should ask the Security Council to decide whether this is a question of substance or a question of procedure. On the decision and interpretation which will be given will depend the subsequent solution of the question and the subsequent procedure.

The PRESIDENT: The main question of the resolution is that the item be kept on the agenda. That is a question of procedure. If, in the opinion of the representative of the USSR there is something of substance in the remainder of the resolution, he can point it out and we shall discuss it. Eventually, when the question arises as to whether the remainder is of substance or procedure, it will be necessary to have the affirmative votes of the five permanent members, and if it is opposed now it is useless to discuss it further. . . .

Mr. VAN KLEFFENS (Netherlands): I think that Mr. Gromyko is perfectly entitled to have a vote on the question as to whether this is a matter of procedure or of substance.

If I may state my own opinion, it seems to me that there can hardly be any doubt at all that this is a question of procedure. The resolution has been admirably drafted by the drafting committee, and it falls into two sections. The first gives a sort of preamble, or a foreword which simply states facts. It states no opinion, but records that which exists and which is incontrovertible.

First it states that the Security Council appointed a Sub-Committee.

Secondly, it states that the investigation of the Sub-Committee fully confirmed the facts.

Thirdly it states that the Sub-Committee was of a certain opinion, which nobody can call into question, because the report is before us and that is exactly what it states.

Then there is the second section, *"Therefore resolves . . ."* And what is resolved? It is resolved that certain things, without prejudice to certain rights, may be done at any time. I think there is no question that this touches on matters of substance; it remains entirely on the surface of the question and does not go into the core of it at all.

Therefore, I believe that this is a matter of procedure, but at this point I should like to observe that this debate has an importance which, I think, goes beyond the question at issue.

It is true, as the President reminded us, that if the question as to whether this is a matter of procedure or of substance is put to the vote, the affirmative vote of the five permanent members of this Council is required. That is what we all read in the statement by the delegations of the four sponsoring Governments on voting procedure, a statement which they made at San Francisco on 7 June last year. In its last paragraph they said that should such a matter as we now have before us, arise—that is, a choice as to whether the matter is one of procedure or of substance—the decision regarding that question must be taken by a vote of seven members of the Security Council, including the concurring votes of the permanent members.

We have just voted by a majority, which perhaps is not operative—but that is not the question—that this is a thing of procedure. If this veto is exercised, we come to the extraordinary position that a vast majority of the Council says this is a matter of procedure, but it is not a matter of procedure, because one member votes against it.

. . .

I think, and I believe that is the importance of this question, that this whole discussion only goes to show into what impossible situations this veto right leads us. I shall not go into it further, but I think it is well worth pondering whether, as experience leads us along and shows us how this system works, it should not be revised, at some future time perhaps, if we can gain still more experience. I shall not say more about it at this stage.

Mr. EVATT (Australia): This is a very important turn in the discussion. The first point, as Mr. van Kleffens pointed out, is whether this proposal now approved by nine votes, with two dissenting, one a permanent member, is a procedural vote. That is the first point. Normally the President would rule on that, and I entirely agree with Mr. van Kleffens; I do not think it is arguable that this is a decision other than a question of procedure alone. All the preliminary statements leading up to the operative part of the resolution are merely recitals, and then comes the operative part which keeps the situation in Spain on the list of matters before the Council. There can be no better illustration of a procedural question. So I submit that if someone says it is not a procedural matter, the first step we should take is to vote on that, and on whether the President's ruling is correct or not.

It is quite true, as Mr. van Kleffens has said, if that vote takes place and there is a dissenting vote from a permanent member, the further question will arise if the veto extends to the question as to whether the matter is procedure or substance. Then the Council is up against an impasse. . . .

I understand from what the President said that he regards this as a question of procedure. Then the next step under the rules is to take a vote. If that is objected to—I understand it is but I am not sure whether it is or not—but if it is objected to, then the first question is to decide whether that ruling is correct. And that step must be taken before the final situation envisaged by Mr. van Kleffens arises.

What was placed in a document at San Francisco does not govern the interpretation of the Charter. It is not contained in the Charter. It does not bind the Security Council, but I do not wish to say anything more about it now. Those of us who opposed the veto principle in certain respects at San Francisco carefully guarded lest that [statement] should be held as authoritative and binding.

But I do suggest that the first thing to do is to affirm the President's ruling that the resolution is procedural and then it may not be contended that if we so affirm the veto will not operate. I do not know if that is intended, but it is a very serious matter. I submit we should act in accordance with the rules and dispose of this matter this afternoon, and therefore the question is whether the President's ruling that this is a procedural question should be affirmed or not. If the vote goes a certain way, we might have to deal with that situation.

In any event, I take it the matter will probably remain on the agenda of the Security Council, but I suggest that we should first vote as a Council on the correctness of the President's ruling, which seems to me demonstrably correct.

Mr. GROMYKO (USSR): I believe that Mr. van Kleffens is sincere in saying that, in principle, he does not like the provision regarding unanimity of the permanent members of the Security Council. I believe this statement is sincere. But what is the use of discussing today the question of who likes some provisions of the Charter of the Organization and who does not? Perhaps I, too, do not quite like some of the provisions and should like them to be improved and made perfect. But what is the use of discussing this question now? It is a waste of time. I realize that the purpose is to say a few words on this question, but there is no practical sense in it.

In stating that the question on which we have just voted is one of procedure, the President said that the main point in the resolution is that of leaving on the agenda the question of the situation in Spain. If that is so, let us isolate this question from the resolution and vote upon it separately. I shall have no objections to regarding the vote on the question of retaining the Polish representative's statement as a vote on the question of procedure. But this is not the only question in the resolution. There are a number of other points which cannot in any way be regarded as procedural. If we isolate the question of retaining the Polish representative's statement on the agenda and vote upon it separately, I think we shall be able to find a way out of the situation. . . .

At present, all the points are mixed together. How can one mix procedural questions with non-procedural questions and then declare the resolution to be one of procedure? Such a method will not lead us to a correct and unanimous decision.

I repeat, if the President and other members of the Security Council insist that this resolution is to be regarded as one of procedure, if my proposal to separate this question and the resolution is not adopted, I shall insist that a vote be taken as to whether the resolution is to be regarded as procedural or non-procedural. . . .

The PRESIDENT: To make it clear, I am going to ask Mr. Gromyko if he thinks the whole resolution is a question of procedure or one of substance, or merely the part on whether to take out or retain the item on the agenda.

Mr. GROMYKO (USSR): I shall state my position as follows: If this resolution is voted upon as a whole, and it has already been voted upon, I shall vote against its adoption. As it is not a question of procedure, it will consequently not be adopted.

If there are any objections to the statement that the resolution is not a procedural one, it will be necessary to take a vote on my question as to whether the resolution is procedural or non-procedural.

To get out of the difficult situation that has arisen, I have submitted a proposal that the procedural questions be separated from the non-procedural ones and voted and decided upon separately. First of all there arises the question of retaining on the agenda of the Security Council the statement made by the Polish representative. The President declares this to be the main question. Very well, perhaps other members of the Council will agree that it is the main question. But there is no doubt as to this question being one of procedure. Very well, then, let us vote upon it separately. We shall get out of the deadlock that has arisen, and we shall not have any difficulties. We shall take a joint decision. As regards the other points of the resolution, they must be dropped because they are non-procedural.

In view of my objection to these points, in view of the fact that they are questions of substance which we have already discussed and voted upon, why not take the opportunity to reach a correct, joint decision, if the President considers that the question touched upon at the end of the resolution is really the main question? I am prepared to agree that it is the main question. But it is not the only question.

The PRESIDENT: I agree that I have separated the point about the retention or withdrawal of the Spanish question from the agenda. A resolution has been submitted to the vote and has been accepted by nine members and rejected by two, one of them a permanent member. I cannot put the same resolution to the vote again, even if it is divided, but I have anticipated the question of retaining the items separately. I am not going to discuss the matter further as it does not work. I cannot put the same resolution again to the vote as it has been rejected, although it was accepted by nine members of the Council.

There is a proposal by the Australian representative that the opinion of the Council be asked as to whether the resolution is a question of procedure or not. I was going to put that to the vote when the representative of the USSR said that he had submitted an amendment first. But, as I see it, he referred to dividing the resolution into two parts. I thought he only wanted to change the terms of my proposal which was: "Those in favour of the ruling by the President that it is a question of procedure", into: "Those who consider that it is a question of substance". But now I find that he wants to come back to a resolution which has already been decided upon, and I want to know, in order to see whether this resolution can be carried, if it is a matter of procedure or of substance.

According to the rules of this Council, my ruling is going to be voted on and it is necessary to have the concurring vote of the five permanent members. I am going to propose that because I find that the resolution has been accepted by nine members against the vote of two, but one of them, a permanent member, had the right of veto and exercised it. I still want to know whether the resolution is a question of procedure or one of substance. There is a doubt, and the decision must be accepted by the five permanent members. We shall also have to put to the vote, or discuss, the maintenance of the item on the agenda, and then will come the time for Mr. Gromyko to make the amendment he wants. I think I have explained myself very clearly.

Mr. EVATT (Australia): Is the President going to put to the Council, under rule 29 of the provisional rules of procedure, the question of whether his ruling is right or not?

The PRESIDENT: Yes.

Mr. EVATT (Australia): It is impossible to consider amendments. The question is whether our ruling is effective or not; whether our decision is one of procedure. As rule 29 says, when a point of order is raised, the President shall immediately state the ruling. If it is challenged, as Mr. Gromyko has challenged it, the President shall submit this ruling to the Security Council for immediate decision and it shall stand, unless overruled.

The PRESIDENT: I made all these explanations to Mr. Gromyko for his information, and in accordance with rule 29 we can immediately take a vote. Those who are in favour of the ruling that this is a question of procedure, please raise their hands.

A vote was taken by show of hands, as follows:

In favour: Australia, Brazil, China, Egypt, Mexico, Netherlands, United Kingdom, United States of America.

Against: France, Union of Soviet Socialist Republics.

Abstaining: Poland.

Mr. GROMYKO (USSR): What conclusion does the President draw from this vote?

The PRESIDENT: The conclusion that I draw is that in accordance with the present circumstances, if it is to be decided whether a question is one of procedure or substance, it is necessary to accept one or another alternative by seven votes, but the five permanent members must concur. Here we have two of the permanent members deciding, against the others, that it is a question of substance.

Mr. PARODI (France): . . . I am of the opinion that, in so far as this resolution records that the inquiry made by the Sub-Committee confirms certain facts, it represents a decision of substance on a *de facto* situation and that therefore this part of the resolution deals with a point which is not a point of procedure. On the other hand, the decision to keep the question on the list of subjects under consideration appears to me to be a question of procedure; when the resolution says, "in order that it will be at all times ready to take such measures as may become necessary to maintain international peace and security", it is merely explaining what went before and thus represents a question of procedure. The last part of the resolution which says that "Any member of the Security Council may bring the matter up for consideration by the Council at any time" is likewise a question of procedure.

I apologize for not giving this explanation at a time when it would have been more helpful.

Mr. VAN KLEFFENS (Netherlands): The President has just given a ruling to the effect that when a question is to be decided as to whether a matter is one of procedure or substance, the affirmative votes of the five permanent members of the Security Council are required.

I wish to observe, and I refer to what Mr. Evatt and myself said a little while ago, that this is not a matter which rests upon the Charter itself. It is a matter which we have seen expressed in a very weighty document emanating from the five Powers having permanent seats on this Council, but it is not a matter which finds its source and foundation in the Charter. I think the position is a little difficult because this statement was made in San Francisco, and the most we can say about it, although some may express reservations, is that it was to a greater or lesser extent acquiesced in.

We are now exactly in the position which I allowed myself to point out previously; this question ends on a very jarring note because of this ruling, and I presume that the President will be the first to admit that no grounds for it may be found in the Charter but only in the memorandum of the five Powers having permanent seats on the Council. . . .

Mr. GROMYKO (USSR): I shall divide my present statement into two parts: in the first part, I shall try to answer the rather belated question put by Mr. Parodi; in the second part, I shall deal with the conclusion which the President drew as to the result of the vote.

Mr. Parodi asks what there is of a non-procedural character in this resolution. I shall recapitulate what there is of a non-procedural character: first, the statement that the situation in Spain is one that is merely likely to endanger peace in the future, that is to say that it may lead to the danger of war, is of a non-procedural character. This thesis is contrary to the position adopted by the USSR delegation and some other delegations, which maintain that the situation in Spain constitutes a threat to peace at the present time. What is there of a procedural character in this?

Secondly, the beginning of the last paragraph contains the statement that the retention of the Spanish question on the agenda of the Security Council does not affect the rights of the General Assembly to examine this question, referring apparently to the next session of the General Assembly. Moreover, this statement is interpreted to mean that the General Assembly may examine the Spanish question and take action whether or not that question is sent to the General Assembly by the Security Council; that is to say, whether or not the Security Council has the Spanish question under consideration when the General Assembly is in session. What is there of a procedural character in that? This is the same question on which we have already voted once. Is it not clear that there is nothing of a procedural character here? But further on there is a procedural question regarding the retention on the agenda of the Security Council of the proposal submitted by Mr. Lange. A question of procedure is affected and I submitted a proposal on this question.

I consider that the President's conclusion corresponds, of course, to the result of the vote. The resolution was not adopted as a result of my objection, supported by another member of the Security Council. As is known, all the permanent members of the Security Council are bound by the Declaration of the Four Powers at San Francisco, to which France adhered. Consequently, the five permanent members of the Security Council plus a non-permanent member, Mr. Lange, consider and cannot fail to consider that this resolution was not adopted, because, I repeat, all the permanent members are bound by the above-mentioned Declaration.

Thus, even if we assume that a simple majority is required for adoption—which is not so in fact, a qualified majority being required for this purpose—nevertheless, out of eleven members minus five permanent members of the Security Council and one non-permanent member, that is to say, minus six, there remain only five members of the Security Council who can juridically vote for the approval of the resolution as a procedural one. I proceed on the assumption that all five would vote for it. Therefore, there is no juridical basis for the adoption of the resolution, and the President's conclusion is, of course, correct. The resolution was not adopted.

Mr. EVATT (Australia): As I understand it the position is this. In spite of the decision to adopt this proposal recommended by the Sub-Committee by nine votes to two, in spite of the fact that the President's ruling that it was a procedural matter was upheld by the Council with only two dissenting votes, the President now rules, as a result of those two dissenting votes, that it is not a question of procedure.

I understand that the President takes Mr. Gromyko's decision as binding the Council because he dissents from the President's ruling, affirmed by the majority of the Council, that it is a question of procedure. I do not think this situation should be allowed to pass unnoticed, and Mr. van Kleffens has already expressed sentiments about it, with which I entirely agree. I do not think this afternoon is the right occasion for any further debate upon the precise interpretation, because it is perfectly true that the sponsoring Powers at San Francisco gave a ruling to that effect; but, as Mr. van Kleffens pointed out, that ruling was not accepted by any authority at San Francisco; not accepted by any committee, not accepted by any commission, and not accepted by the Conference in open session, and protests against its accuracy were made.

But the ruling the President made this afternoon is, I think, most important. We cannot proceed with the business, because Mr. Gromyko, ever since this matter was decided ninety or one hundred minutes ago, has in one form or another objected to the decision of the Council; nor can he now put forward amendments to this proposal.

The position will have to be reviewed. I understood the President to say that he regarded this matter as still being before the Security Council, and it might be that this ruling will become important.

I am not going to enter into the merits of the question, whether it is procedural or not. The overwhelming majority of the members of this Council think it is a question of procedure. Mr. van Kleffens has expressed the view, with which I entirely agree, that if you look at the real essence of the proposal to see if it alters any rights, or whether it simply decides how the Security Council is to approach the question in the future—the method of proceeding—then this resolution does not. But it is no use having an overwhelming majority with you if any representative of a permanent member, simply by saying that he thinks that the interpretation is different, can make his view prevail. If that is the Charter, it does not matter if the permanent Court says the opposite; even the judgment of the Court would not bind the permanent member. The judges of the permanent Court might say: "That is wrong", but the permanent member, according to that ruling, can say, not only "I can veto the decision of the Council", but "I can determine the question which I will veto." That, of course, is a very significant and important thing, if it is so. .   .   .

Mr. LANGE (Poland): I regret very much that the problem of Spain has been utterly mixed up, and I might say, messed up, with all kinds of legal points. At an earlier discussion I had the opportunity of pointing out that, however important legal rules are, they should be the servants of our purposes, and not our masters.

The question of the veto right and other matters are very important, and I have nothing against certain members carrying on campaigns for or against the veto right, but I think that if it has to be done, we ought to have a separate session or discuss it at the General Assembly, where it properly belongs.

I want to beseech you not to let the question of Spain get mixed up with other things that are not directly concerned with the matter under discussion. The situation is this. We have some doubts whether the resolution was legally amended. There were also some divergent views as to whether the veto taken on the procedural question was effective or not.

I propose that without any precedent for the future, or any prejudice in the matter itself, we just agree to disagree, each one of us holding our views on the question of interpretation of Article 27 of the Charter, and on the question of whether the declaration of the four sponsoring Powers is binding or not. Just let us keep our private views about it, without any precedents or anyone being bound by it. But since there is a doubt as to whether the resolution is validly accepted or not, I think we can all agree without precedent and prejudice, to put the last portion of it, which is undoubtedly procedural, to the vote once more. If somebody wants to make an amendment, as the representative of the USSR does, we can vote on it too. It will take us three minutes and I think with this procedure we shall be finished within ten minutes. . . .

[After further discussion the Security Council adopted the following resolution:

"Whereas the Security Council on 29 April 1946 appointed a Sub-Committee to investigate the situation in Spain,

"And whereas the investigation of the Sub-Committee has fully confirmed the facts which led to the condemnation of the Franco regime by the Potsdam and San Francisco Conferences, by the General Assembly at the first part of its first session, and by the Security Council by resolution of the date above mentioned,

"The Security Council decides to keep the situation in Spain under continuous observation and maintain it upon the list of matters of which it is seized in order that it will be at all times ready to take such measures as may become necessary to maintain international peace and security. Any member of the Security Council may bring the matter up for consideration by the Council at any time."]

NOTE. Other aspects of the Spanish Question are discussed on pp. 291–321, below.

REQUEST TO THE GENERAL ASSEMBLY TO CONSIDER THE GREEK QUESTION

Discussion in the Security Council, 15 September 1947. SCOR, II, No. 89, pp. 2368–69, 2390–2405.

Mr. JOHNSON (USA): I should like to make a statement on behalf of my delegation in which I shall not make any attempt to go further into the substance of this question. My remarks are simply procedural.

One of the subjects on the agenda of the General Assembly, which opens its second regular session tomorrow, is the Greek question. This matter is clearly one of great importance and one which is bound to engage the full attention of the Assembly. I feel convinced that every delegation present at the Assembly will hope that some way may be found whereby the United Nations can exert its influence effectively to bring about an improvement in the situation in the Balkans.

In the view of my delegation and of my Government, all the efforts of the members of the Assembly should be devoted to this end. All of the Member nations represented here in the Security Council are also members of the Assembly, and it seems fitting that the Security Council should do its part to help the Assembly in its efforts to bring about an improvement in the Balkan situation.

The Assembly is not free to exert all the powers given to it under the Charter in a situation of this nature as long as the Council is exercising its functions in respect of a given question, unless the Council requests the Assembly to do so.

My Government and my delegation feel that it would be most appropriate for the Council, in a spirit of co-operation and in deference to a co-ordinate organ of the United Nations, to welcome the exercise by the General Assembly of its full powers with respect to matters relating to the maintenance of international peace and security. This surely is the spirit which the framers of the Charter had in contemplation when they wrote Article 12 of the Charter.

In following this course, the Security Council would not only be indicating its high hopes and its confidence that the General Assembly could find a solution where the Security Council itself had been unable to do so, but would be making a further contribution to the successful solution of the matter by itself retaining jurisdiction. In so doing, the Council avoids the necessity of terminating the Subsidiary Group of the Commission of Investigation concerning Greek Frontier Incidents which is now in the area. The Council would, therefore, be able to exert some influence towards the stabilization of the situation pending the General Assembly's decision as to what, if any, recommendations to the parties concerned, to the Security Council or to the Members of the United Nations it might decide and desire to make.

The draft resolution which I should like to place before the Council reads as follows:

"The Security Council, pursuant to Article 12 of the Charter,

"(a) Requests the General Assembly to consider the dispute between Greece on the one hand, and Albania, Yugoslavia and Bulgaria on the other, and to make any recommendations with regard to that dispute which it deems appropriate under the circumstances;

"(b) Instructs the Secretary-General to place all records and documents in the case at the disposal of the General Assembly." . . .

The PRESIDENT (Mr. Gromyko, USSR): . . . I think that the Council is ready to take a vote on the United States draft resolution. We shall follow the procedure defined in paragraph 3 of Article 27 of the Charter of the United Nations. . . .

Mr. JOHNSON (USA): My delegation is obliged to challenge the ruling of the President that our draft resolution concerns a matter of substance rather than of procedure. It seems to me that the resolution is clearly procedural. All the Council is asked to do here is to request another organ of the United Nations to consider and take action in a dispute which has been brought to the United Nations. There is no colour of substance to this resolution. It relates to the internal procedure of the United Nations and to relations between its various organs. In this resolution the Council is not attempting in any way to indicate a view with regard to the merits of the dispute. In the view of my delegation it cannot be considered as a matter of substance to be covered by paragraph 3 of Article 27 of the Charter.

The PRESIDENT: Speaking as the representative of the Union of Soviet Socialist Republics, I cannot accept the interpretation of this question given by the United States representative. The resolution submitted by the United States delegation deals with the substance of the Greek question, especially if one takes into account the implications of this resolution.

As President of the Security Council I have to say that whether the question is one of procedure or of substance is not subject to the ruling of any President. The Security Council has to take a special decision on this question. At the appropriate moment I shall make an additional explanation on this point. . . .

[After a proposal to postpone the voting was defeated, the discussion was continued as follows:]

The PRESIDENT: We cannot take a vote on the United States resolution without knowing what we are taking a decision on, whether on a question of substance or on a question of procedure. I have already said that I did not make a ruling on the question as to whether the United States resolution is one of a procedural character or one of substance. I expressed my opinion as the President. The United States representative and some other representatives did not agree with my opinion. I have already stated that the question as to whether any proposal is one of a procedural character or one of substance is not subject to a ruling of any President of the Security Council. The President can only make a ruling on a point of order. The President cannot decide that the question is one of substance or procedure.

Mr. LANGE (Poland): Since you are going to vote on the question as to whether the resolution before us is a matter of procedure or substance, I should like to express briefly the opinion of my delegation. The opinion of my delegation is that it is a matter of substance. We consider matters of procedure to be matters of internal procedure of the Council. Here, however, we have a proposal that the Council ask another organ of the United Nations for an opinion, although it is really outside of the Council, and we therefore cannot consider this a matter of internal procedure. In addition, I think the importance of the proposal has also to be taken into consideration. As I have stated before, in the view of our delegation the adoption of this proposal would mean really relinquishing our responsibility, and if I may use a colloquial term, it would also mean, so to speak, "passing the buck" to another organ of the United Nations. It seems to me that it is a question of too grave an importance to be considered a pure matter of procedure.

Mr. NISOT (Belgium): I propose that we take a vote immediately on the United States draft resolution. I would request you, Mr. President, to be good enough to ask the Council whether, as I have suggested, the draft resolution in question should be voted upon at once. This is my definite motion.

Mr. JOHNSON (USA): I should like to support that request. I see no reason whatever why the United States resolution, which is simple and clear and is understood by everyone at this table, should not be voted on now. Then, Mr. President, you would declare the result of that vote, whether it is passed or not passed. If it is not passed you would give your reason. If that reason should involve a question of whether or not it is procedural or substantive, that matter could then be put to the vote. That has been the practice in the past, and I see no reason for departing from it now.

This discussion has not been necessary, and I think that as the proposer of this resolution my delegation has the right to ask that it be voted on.

The PRESIDENT: The proposal of the Belgian representative does not have precedence over any other proposal. According to rule 33 of the provisional rules of procedure of the Security Council,

"The following motions shall have precedence in the order named over all principal motions and draft resolutions relative to the subject before the meeting:

"1.   to suspend the meeting;

"2.   to adjourn the meeting;

"3.   to adjourn the meeting to a certain day or hour;

"4.   to refer any matter to a committee, to the Secretary-General or to a rapporteur;

"5.   to postpone discussion of the question to a certain day or indefinitely; or

"6.   to introduce an amendment.

"Any motion for the suspension or for the simple adjournment of the meeting shall be decided without debate."

These proposals shall have precedence; not the Belgian proposal. This is my ruling. When I make rulings I quote them. When I do not make rulings I do not quote them.

Mr. NISOT (Belgium): Mr. President, I am sorry that I cannot agree to your interpretation. I would renew the request which I made to you to be good enough to consult the Security Council immediately to find out whether or not the United States draft resolution should be voted upon at once.

The PRESIDENT: I made a ruling on this matter. I consider that a decision on the Belgian proposal, which is to take a decision on the

American resolution before taking a decision on whether it is of a procedural character or not, cannot be taken now because it does not have precedence over other proposals. I repeat that this is my ruling. If the majority of the members of the Council do not agree, they may overrule it. . . .

Mr. NISOT (Belgium): Mr. President, I challenge the ruling you have just given, and for the third time I would request you to be good enough to get the Council's opinion on the Belgian proposal to ascertain whether the United States proposal should be voted upon at once or not.

The PRESIDENT: Those who contest my ruling may overrule me. I made a ruling, and if the Council does not agree with it, it may overrule me. I shall put to the vote my ruling: that before taking a decision on the United States resolution, we have to decide whether or not this resolution deals with procedural or substantive matters.

A vote was taken by show of hands, and the ruling was rejected by 8 votes to 2, with 1 abstention.

Votes for: Poland, Union of Soviet Socialist Republics.

Votes against: Australia, Belgium, Brazil, China, France, Syria, United Kingdom, United States of America.

Abstention: Colombia.

The PRESIDENT: If the proposal to take a decision on the United States draft resolution still stands, the Council may take a decision on this resolution. Before taking a vote, I shall make certain explanations as the President and as the representative of the Union of Soviet Socialist Republics.

When the Charter of the United Nations was being prepared at the San Francisco Conference, a great deal of discussion took place, especially among the delegations of the United States, the United Kingdom, the Union of Soviet Socialist Republics and China, and later the delegation of France joined us. This discussion related to the procedure which the Security Council must follow when the question arises as to whether a proposal is of a procedural or of a substantive nature.

I am not going to speak extensively about the positions taken at that time by the five delegations, but I wish to remind the representatives of the four other delegations which took part in the discussion, as well as all others who wish to know the real situation among the five Governments, that a decision was reached whereby if a question arises as to whether a certain proposal is of a procedural character or a substantive character, the affirmative decision that the proposal is procedural can be taken only when there are concurrent votes of all five permanent members of the Security Council. This agreement among the five Governments was expressed in a special statement approved by all five Governments. I should like to quote the appropriate provision of this statement. It reads: "Should, however, such a matter arise, the decision regarding the preliminary question"—I repeat, "the preliminary question"—"as to whether or not such a matter is procedural must be taken by a vote of seven members of the Security Council, including the concurring votes of the permanent members."

Two conclusions may be said to follow from this statement. The first one is that the question of whether a certain proposal is of procedural character or one of substance is regarded, according to this agreement, as a "preliminary question". A preliminary question in all languages in the world—I hope in English and French—means a preliminary question, and a decision on it should be taken before a decision is taken on the proposal itself.

The second conclusion is that the affirmative decision on this preliminary question may be taken only when there are the concurrent votes of the permanent members of the Security Council.

I have not added anything myself. I have quoted the agreement reached at the San Francisco Conference and stated absolutely obvious rules established by this agreement.

I must note with regret that the representatives of the United States, the United Kingdom, China and France acted contrary to this agreement reached at San Francisco by the five Powers. Of course this agreement is not binding upon the other, non-permanent members of the Security Council, but it is binding with respect to the permanent members. They acted contrary to this agreement. Possibly they do not agree with this agreement, but I have heard nothing from the Governments of the United States or the United Kingdom or the other Governments to the effect that they denounce this agreement. They have not negotiated with the Government of the Union of Soviet Socialist Republics on this question; they have not directed any request to the USSR Government on this question. They did not make their position known; they did not keep to the position they took at the San Francisco Conference.

The Security Council as a whole cannot, nor can any member or group of members of the Council, make any agreement invalid by any decisions. This fact relates not only to this agreement but to any agreement concluded between sovereign States.

Sir Alexander CADOGAN (UK): Up to now I have not spoken as I did not wish to prolong this discussion, but since the representative of the USSR has just said or implied that I have in some way gone back on the declaration of San Francisco, which he read out, I should just like to say one word.

I fully accept the principle of that statement which was read to us by the representative of the Soviet Union. He seized on one word, one adjective, "preliminary", and he tried to interpret that to mean that before one can vote on a resolution or a proposal, one must first vote on whether it is substantive or procedural. I do not remember that that has ever been done in the Council at all. I can remember, for instance, a case where a difference of opinion of this kind occurred; that is, the Spanish question. That question was raised after the actual resolution or proposal had been voted upon. But "preliminary" in that sense does not mean that on every occasion one must vote first on the question of whether it is substantive or procedural. That is a governing consideration, of course, but it cannot mean that one has to take a vote of that kind before voting on any proposal. It has never been done to my knowledge.

Mr. PARODI (France): I should like to add a word in support of the United Kingdom's representative's statement to explain the vote just taken.

The question as to whether a resolution contains a point of substance or of procedure can sometimes be a very delicate problem. It is only after a motion has been voted upon that one can tell if it should be defined whether it is a procedural or a substantive point. To explain: when a resolution is submitted and it is supported by seven members, including the five permanent members, no purpose is served by asking whether it is a procedural matter or a point of substance. It is, therefore, logical to begin by voting on the motion itself and to decide later whether it is a procedural or substantive matter.

Mr. NISOT (Belgium): What the French representative has just said proves that there is nothing to prevent us from complying with the decision just taken by the Council, namely, to take an immediate vote on the United States proposal.

I would ask the President to put this proposal to the vote immediately in conformity with the resolution we have just taken. . . .

The PRESIDENT: The Council will now vote on the United States draft resolution.

A vote was taken by show of hands. There were 9 votes in favour and 2 against. The resolution was not adopted, one of the votes against being that of a permanent member of the Council.

Votes for: Australia, Belgium, Brazil, China, Colombia, France, Syria, United Kingdom, United States of America.

Votes against: Poland, Union of Soviet Socialist Republics.

The PRESIDENT: Since I, as President, as well as representative of the USSR, consider the United States resolution to be one of substance, I rule that this resolution is rejected because one of the permanent members of the Security Council voted against it.

There is disagreement on this question and, naturally, we have to take another decision, which in fact we should have taken before the decision on the United States resolution itself. That is, a decision as to whether the United States resolution deals with procedure or with substance.

Mr. NISOT (Belgium): I shall limit myself for the moment to saying that I cannot agree with your interpretation of the vote on the resolution which we have just passed.

Mr. JOHNSON (USA): As I had occasion to say when this point was raised before, the United States delegation cannot accept the ruling of the President. For reasons already stated, we consider this to be a motion of procedure, and I would ask the President to accept the challenge which my delegation has put forward and to submit the matter again to be voted upon by the Council.

The PRESIDENT: We now have to take a decision on the question as to whether the United States resolution deals with procedure or with substance. The vote is upon the proposal that the question is one of procedure.

A vote was taken by show of hands. There were 8 votes in favour, 2 against and 1 abstention. The proposal was not adopted, one of the votes against being that of a permanent member of the Council.

Votes for: Australia, Belgium, Brazil, China, Colombia, France, United Kingdom, United States of America.

Votes against: Poland, Union of Soviet Socialist Republics.

Abstention: Syria. . . .

The PRESIDENT: . . . I consider that the proposal is rejected since one of the permanent members of the Security Council voted against it. I ask the Council to consider my statement as a ruling of the President.

Colonel HODGSON (Australia): What the President is in effect relying on is an agreement between the five permanent members at San Francisco that is nowhere in the Charter. It was never put up to the other fifty members. It does not bind this Council. It does not bind the United Nations. I, for one, do not see how it can apply here now.

The PRESIDENT: I have said already that the agreement to which I made reference, and which I quoted, does not bind any countries other than the five permanent members of the Security Council. I tried to explain that the agreement binds only the five Powers which agreed to that document.

Mr. LANGE (Poland): I quite agree with the view of the representative of Australia and the view of the President that this agreement does not bind the other members of the Council. For this reason I think that in deciding on the President's ruling we cannot invoke that agreement. I do not think it is absolutely necessary to go into the matter of that agreement because the Charter provides us with a very clear statement.   Article 27 of the Charter reads in part as follows:

"2.   Decisions of the Security Council on procedural matters shall be made by an affirmative vote of seven members.

"3.   Decisions of the Security Council on all other matters shall be made by an affirmative vote of seven members including the concurring votes of the permanent members   .   .   ."

Obviously, whether the matter is procedural or not is not a procedural matter.   Consequently, paragraph 3 of Article 27 applies, and I think there is no need to invoke in any way, or even discuss the agreement among the five permanent members.

The PRESIDENT: I make the ruling that the last proposal, the proposal to consider the United States resolution to be of a procedural character, was rejected since one of the permanent members of the Security Council voted against it.   Until I am overruled, this ruling stands.

Mr. JOHNSON (USA): I think there is no doubt that under the existing agreements and under the Charter the President has been within his technical rights in deciding that this matter was, from his point of view, not a question of procedure.

I must, however, in the name of my Government protest against the use by the Union of Soviet Socialist Republics of its power in this case.   What the President has done, in effect, is to frustrate the will of this Council, which I think has been freely expressed: that the Assembly be free to make recommendations in this case without prejudice to the issue.   I therefore must now propose a simple draft resolution to this effect:

"The Security Council

"(a) Resolves that the dispute between Greece on the one hand, and Albania, Yugoslavia and Bulgaria on the other, be taken off the list of matters of which the Council is seized; and

"(b) Requests that the Secretary-General be instructed to place all records and documents in the case at the disposal of the General Assembly."

The Council must do that, and there can be no doubt that that would be a procedural vote.   Furthermore, the Council will realize that by so doing it is destroying the Subsidiary Group which is now operating in Greece, but we must free the great Assembly of the United Nations to discuss and make recommendations in this matter, if it sees fit.   This will not ask for recommendations.   It will be entirely up to the Assembly.

I move this resolution and ask that it be voted on at once, if there is no discussion.

The PRESIDENT: The United States representative protests. If I follow his example it will lead us too far; we shall renew the discussion on the Greek question and on its substance.

As to the new United States draft resolution, as I have already stated, as the USSR representative, I cannot agree with a proposal to remove this question from the agenda of the Security Council. I gave the reasons why we consider that such a decision would not be in accordance either with the interests of the Security Council as an organ of the United Nations or with the interests of the General Assembly. My attitude towards such a proposal is definitely negative.

. . .

A vote was taken by show of hands, and the resolution was adopted by 9 to 2.

Votes for: Australia, Belgium, Brazil, China, Colombia, France, Syria, United Kingdom, United States of America.

Votes against: Poland, Union of Soviet Socialist Republics.

The PRESIDENT: Nine in favour, two against; the resolution is adopted, and the Greek Question is accordingly removed from the agenda of the Security Council. We have exhausted the second question on the agenda.

NOTE. For a discussion of other aspects of the Greek Question, see pp. 351, 321, below.

CZECHOSLOVAK QUESTION: APPOINTMENT OF A SUB-COMMITTEE

Discussion in the Security Council, 29 April, 21–26 May 1948. SCOR, III, Nos. 63, 71, 73 and 74.

Mr. SOBOLEV (Assistant Secretary-General in charge of Security Council Affairs): The draft resolution reads:

"Whereas the attention of the Security Council has been drawn by a Member of the United Nations, in accordance with Articles 34 and 35 of the Charter, to the situation in Czechoslovakia, which may endanger international peace and security; and the Security Council has been asked to investigate this situation; and

"Whereas, during the debate which took place in the Council, the existence of further testimonial and documentary evidence in regard to such situation has been announced;

"Whereas the Security Council considers it advisable that such further testimonial and documentary evidence should be heard,

"Therefore, to this end and without prejudice to any decisions which may be taken in accordance with Article 34 of the Charter,

"The Security Council resolves to appoint a sub-committee of three members and instructs this sub-committee to receive or to hear such evidence, statements and testimonies, and to report to the Security Council at the earliest possible time." . . .

Mr. GROMYKO (USSR): I consider that this draft resolution is not of a procedural nature, but concerns the substance of the question. The voting procedure to be followed should, therefore, be that which applies to draft resolutions concerned with matters of substance. Possibly the representative of Belgium holds another opinion and he is entitled to do so, but I venture to disagree with his interpretation.

As there is a divergence of opinion among us on this matter, I propose that we should first decide whether or not this is a procedural matter.

Mr. AUSTIN (USA): In the opinion of the United States, the draft resolution before the Security Council to establish a sub-committee is clearly a procedural decision. It is a decision under Article 29 of the Charter, not under Chapter VI. The Charter contains a clear indication that this type of matter is procedural. Article 29 is one of the five articles in the portion of Chapter V of the Charter entitled "Procedure." Consequently, under the language of the Charter, a Security Council decision pursuant to Article 29 must be considered as procedural.

We should also note that the Four-Power Statement itself recognizes the establishment of a subsidiary organ as a procedural decision. Part I, paragraph 2 of the statement provides:

"For example, under the Yalta formula a procedural vote will govern the decisions made under the entire Section D of Chapter VI."— This section of the Dumbarton Oaks proposal is equivalent to Articles 28 to 32 inclusive of the Charter and of course includes Article 29.— "This means that the Council will, by a vote of any seven of its members, . . . establish such bodies or agencies as it may deem necessary for the performance of its functions."

It is quite obvious that this express provision in Part I of the Four-Power Statement was intended to cover a situation such as is now before us. If it does not cover this situation it has no meaning whatever.

The adoption of this draft resolution would mean no more than a continuance by the Security Council of its consideration of the Czechoslovak question with the assistance of a sub-committee composed of its own members. The use of such a subsidiary organ to assist the Security Council in the performance of its functions is expressly provided for in Article 29 of the Charter.

The decision before us now is almost an exact parallel to the decision we took in the Corfu case on 27 February 1947. At that time we established a committee to facilitate the work of the Security Council, to analyze the facts, to obtain additional facts from the parties, and to report back to the Security Council. The decision of the Security Council on that motion was that such a motion was not a substantive decision under Chapter VI of the Charter. The issue arose when the representative of the United Kingdom, who was a party to the dispute, asked for a ruling on whether the decision was a procedural one under Article 27(2), in which case he could exercise his vote, or a decision under Article 27(3) of the Charter, in which case, being a party to the dispute, he was required to abstain. The President ruled that the decision was not one under Chapter VI of the Charter and that the United Kingdom was therefore entitled to vote.

The President held that the setting up of a sub-committee did not fall within the scope of Chapter VI of the Charter. Presumably the President determined, in accordance with the suggestions of other members, that the decision was being taken under Article 29. Mr. Gromyko urged that it was a decision for an investigation under Article 34 and protested the President's ruling, but he did not formally challenge it. The United Kingdom was permitted to vote, and the resolution was carried by eight votes, with the Union of Soviet Socialist Republics abstaining.

The decision in that case was either a decision under Article 29 of the Charter or under Article 34 of the Charter. If it was under Article 34, the United Kingdom should not have voted. If it was under Article 29, the matter was procedural and it was therefore legitimate for the United Kingdom to vote. The decision to allow the United Kingdom to vote was clearly a decision that a motion to set up a sub-committee is procedural in nature, not substantive. It is a clear precedent for the issue before us.

We believe that it is beyond question that the motion before us is a procedural matter and should be determined by the votes of any seven members of the Security Council. . . . .

Mr. GROMYKO (USSR): It is clear that a difference of opinion has arisen between us as to whether this draft resolution is or is not of a procedural nature. I affirm that it is of a non-procedural character. This resolution does not provide for the creation of any subsidiary organ such as is contemplated in Part I, paragraph 2, of the Four-Power San Francisco Declaration, to which France later adhered, but falls under Part I, paragraph 4, of that Declaration.

I consider that this resolution, if adopted, would necessitate investigations. The United States representative, or any other representative, may define the action to be taken on the strength of the resolution as the clarification of facts and not as investigations, but I call it *investigations*. The United States representative will not convince me of the contrary.

This means that there is disagreement between us on this point. I am not interested in how the resolution will be styled or how the committee will be named by those who desire to establish it and to carry out investigations, but I am concerned with the substance of the question of the proposed committee and the activities which it will have to undertake in virtue of the resolution if it is adopted.

In view of the disagreement which has arisen, we should follow the procedure adopted on several occasions in the past. We should follow the San Francisco Declaration of the Five Powers, to which I have already referred. The last paragraph of that Declaration reads as follows—I quote:

"In this case"—and this refers to the position described in previous paragraphs which, for the time being, I will ignore, quoting only the last paragraph, which is in direct relation to the question under discussion—"it will be unlikely that there will arise in the future any matters of great importance on which a decision will have to be made as to whether a procedural vote would apply. Should, however, such a matter arise"—and such a question has in fact arisen—"the decision regarding the preliminary question as to whether or not such a matter is procedural must be taken by a vote of seven members of the Security Council, including the concurring votes of the permanent members."

I repeat: *"including the concurring votes of the permanent members."*

That is the voting procedure. This Declaration—and there is no need for me to remind you of it—is in itself an obligation binding on the part of the United States of America, the United Kingdom, China, France and the Union of Soviet Socialist Republics. This obligation we have accepted, we still accept it and we cannot but abide by it in the future. It is a part of the general obligations accepted by these countries in connexion with the drafting and ratification of the Charter.

. . .

Mr. EL–KHOURI (Syria): I wish to comment on whether this matter is a substantive or procedural one. The statement of the representative of the Soviet Union was correct in that this agreement in San Francisco did take place in that form. But I do not consider it to mean that any obviously procedural question should be voted upon as a substantive question and be subject to the veto. It was left to the decision and judgment of the representatives of the permanent members of the Security Council to be careful not to bring up such questions and complicate the business of the Security Council in that way. Otherwise, a permanent member could say that any procedural question is a substantive one, and it would cast its vote against the majority, and the Security Council would not be able to accomplish anything.

In this case, having regard for common sense and the conduct of business of the Security Council, I consider that the constitution of sub-committees for the purpose of studying, fact-finding and reporting on a matter to the Security Council is a procedural matter. It is not a decision on substance. In the past, I have said that, if we make this study through a sub-committee, it will give us the opportunity either to dismiss the case altogether, in that it is out of our competence or that it is not well-founded and nothing has been proved, or to take other measures.

This is the conduct of business which makes it obligatory for the Security Council to take such steps. Therefore, I hope that no obstruction will be based on this point. It would then be a precedent for other matters, and the work of the Security Council would become more and more complicated. I consider this matter as a procedural one, and I shall vote in favour of its being treated as such. . . .

Mr. ARCE (Argentina): . . . Good sense has been mentioned and indeed, this is merely a matter of good sense. It is obvious that we are dealing with a question of procedure, and I cannot understand what reason the USSR representative can have had for presenting the matter otherwise.

It is public knowledge that I think, speak, write, and work by every means at my disposal against the veto, and an excellent opportunity is now offered to me to speak again against this provision of the Charter. If the Security Council were to accept the view that the question under discussion is one of substance and not of procedure, the unfitting and unjustifiable nature of the privilege granted to the five great Powers would really be clearly shown. Not only would the inconsistency with legal principles be apparent, but also the inconsistency with good sense. With regard to good sense, to which the representative of Syria referred a few moments ago and to which I refer now, I would like to point out that good sense, like common sense, is apt to be the least common of all senses.

I do not admit the value of the statement of the four great Powers as a precedent. Nevertheless, it is a very interesting study because it contains contradictions from beginning to end, and because there is sufficient evidence in it to show that the countries which accepted the veto at San Francisco were certainly ingenuous. I must point out that the statement of the four great Powers was neither included in the Charter, nor accepted by the San Francisco Conference, nor even annexed to its records. That statement bound the four great Powers, and perhaps the representative of the USSR can ask them to fulfil the obligation contracted; but it in no way bound or binds the other fifty-three nations (France adhered to the statement later) because that very statement shows that the four great Powers did not know how to answer the twenty-three questions put to them by the medium and smaller Powers. Not knowing what to reply, they drafted that document, which shows very well how two or three pages can be written without saying anything at all. . . .

It has been mentioned during the discussion . . . that Article 29 empowers the Council to establish such subsidiary organs as it deems necessary for the performance of its functions. What has not been said is that there is no lack of arguments when there is a desire to argue; and there has been lack of a speaker to maintain that this Article refers only to the committees of the Security Council, such as the Committee on the Admission of New Members, the Committee of Experts, etc. If that were the case, I might well defeat the announced intention of the USSR representative by proposing that one of these already existing committees, say the Committee of Experts, be requested to report to us on the possibility of obtaining fresh information on the case in question. Could such a proposal be vetoed? Of course not.

But I am not going to make such a proposal, for we are members of an organ of the United Nations, and the world is watching us; such a proposal would be a farce which I, for my part, cannot entertain. I will confine myself to stating that just as the Security Council set up the Committee of Experts, so it can appoint three of its members to collect information on the Czechoslovak case which has been brought before the Council before we begin to discuss the case itself, to give it due consideration or to adopt a resolution regarding it.

I must add that the Charter offers us an interpretation that may have been overlooked by the distinguished representative of the USSR for all I know, but which I consider conclusive. The Charter is a single document, and the legal interpretation of all such documents of public law must be made in accordance with known and predetermined rules, one of which is the coordination of the various provisions. In the Security Council, there is no established procedure for settling any doubt as to whether a question is procedural or not; but in the General Assembly there is such procedure.

Indeed, Article 18 of the Charter states that when the General Assembly is in doubt as to whether a question is important or not (a majority of two-thirds being required in the former case and a simple majority in the latter) the decision shall be made by a simple majority. This is good sense, for otherwise, if a two-thirds majority were necessary even to decide whether a question is important or not, the Assembly would never reach a decision in these cases. Now Article 18 is a part of the Charter, even though it is not mentioned in the statement of the four great Powers. It is a part of the legal document that binds all States Members of the United Nations.

Consequently, I maintain that if there is any doubt as to whether paragraph 2 or paragraph 3 of Article 27 is applicable, the majority required to settle that doubt is only any seven votes, so that there may be some conformity between the provisions governing the Security Council and those governing the General Assembly. . . .

The PRESIDENT (Mr. Parodi, France): We will now take a vote on the draft resolution submitted at the last meeting on the Czechoslovak question. This resolution provides for the appointment of a sub-committee to receive and hear evidence. It has been submitted by the Chilean delegation and taken up in accordance with the rules of procedure, by the Argentine representative.

As you will remember, at that meeting, a procedural discussion took place as to how the vote on this resolution should be treated: whether it should be regarded as a vote on a question of procedure or on a question of substance.

Two courses are now open to me: either to ask you to vote at once on the draft resolution, considering only later on how the vote taken should be interpreted, or to ask you to decide in advance, before the vote is taken, how the President would have to interpret it.

I propose to ask you to follow the second procedure and to decide first how the vote is to be interpreted; we shall then proceed to vote. I shall therefore ask you to vote first on the following question: is the vote on the draft resolution to be considered as a procedural vote?

Mr. GROMYKO (USSR): I agree that we should first settle the preliminary question as to whether or not this is a procedural resolution.

If there are still any objections to my contention that this is a non-procedural resolution, I agree that that preliminary question should be settled first.

The PRESIDENT: I would like to add that the procedure I have chosen, in this case, shall not constitute any kind of precedent, and will leave future Presidents entirely free to choose, in other cases, between this course and the other one that I mentioned a few minutes ago.

I shall therefore put the following question to the vote: is the vote on the draft resolution to be considered as a vote on a question of procedure?   .   .   .

General McNAUGHTON (Canada): I hold the view that the resolution submitted by the representative of Argentina on behalf of Chile is strictly a procedural matter.

As has already been stated in this debate, Article 29 of the Charter is specific on the question of setting up a sub-committee of the Security Council to aid the Council in examining the case. Article 29 reads: "The Security Council may establish such subsidiary organs as it deems necessary for the performance of its functions."   .   .   .

In our opinion, as I have said, the question of procedure is completely covered by Article 29. The decision involved is clearly procedural and not substantive. As the provision of the Charter in this case is specific and clear, the Four-Power Declaration, in our view, is therefore irrelevant.   Supposing, however, for the purpose of argument only, that the Four-Power Declaration were applicable in this case, then the Declaration, in our view, should, like other documents, be considered as a whole, as has been pointed out by the representative of the United Kingdom, and not merely applied in regard to those paragraphs which suit a particular argument.   Chapter I, paragraph 8 of this Declaration is just as applicable as chapter II, paragraph 2.   It is stated in paragraph 8 that:

"It is not to be assumed, however, that the permanent members any more than the non-permanent members will use their veto power wilfully to obstruct the operation of the Council."

Unfortunately, this portion of the Declaration has been more honoured by one of the permanent members of the Security Council in the breach than in the observance.   Where one portion of this Declaration has been violated as in this particular case, the validity of the document as a whole is certainly brought into question.

The representative of the Argentine gave us a timely reminder at our last meeting on this question that fifty-three Members of the United Nations are not bound in any sense by the provisions of the Four-Power Declaration and for its part the Canadian Government certainly does not consider itself bound by this Declaration. . . .

Perhaps, as an additional argument, I might refer the attention of the permanent members .   .   .   to the provisions of Article 103 which states that:

"In the event of a conflict between the obligations of the Members of the United Nations under the present Charter and their obligations under any other international agreement, their obligations under the present Charter shall prevail."

If the Four-Power Declaration is regarded by the permanent members as in some sense constituting an international agreement, then surely the obligations, under the Charter, of the permanent members of the Security Council shall, as stated in Article 103, prevail over any obligations assumed under the Four-Power Declaration or "any other international agreement."

Mr. GROMYKO (USSR): Paragraph 2 of the San Francisco Five-Power Declaration stipulates that decisions concerning the establishment of subsidiary organs of the Security Council can be taken by a procedural vote.   But paragraph 4 of the same Declaration stipulates that any decision concerning an investigation, not to mention decisions which should or may be taken after an investigation, relates to non-procedural matters and as such can only be taken by a vote of seven members, including the five concurring votes of the permanent members.

The organ envisaged in the Chilean resolution is said to come under paragraph 2 of the San Francisco Declaration.   The delegation of the

Soviet Union does not agree with this assertion. It is an organ for the purpose of investigation and everyone realizes that this is so. Consequently, a decision regarding the establishment of such an organ must be taken by a non-procedural vote.

It appears that some members of the Council consider such a decision to be a procedural one. The delegation of the Soviet Union, on the other hand, considers it to be a non-procedural one. In these circumstances we must be guided by the last paragraph of the San Francisco Declaration which stipulates that in case of a divergence of views on the preliminary question, an affirmative decision can be taken only if the votes of the permanent members concur. . . .

The Canadian representative has quoted a provision in the Five-Power Declaration declaring that permanent members should not abuse their right. But perhaps we differ in our approach to the question whether this or that permanent member of the Security Council is abusing his right. Perhaps the Canadian representative considers that the USSR delegation is abusing this right. But we cannot share that view. We consider that in rejecting all attempts to interfere in Czechoslovakia's internal affairs, we are defending the perfectly legitimate rights and interests of the people of Czechoslovakia and of the Czechoslovak State.

The Canadian representative attempts to prove that the San Francisco Five-Power Declaration can be regarded as an international agreement and that the obligations assumed under it must, according to the Charter, take a secondary place in comparison with the obligations under the Charter. We cannot agree with this interpretation because it is wrong and erroneous. The San Francisco Declaration deals precisely with the interpretation of the Charter. It is not an agreement under which the Five Powers have assumed obligations in addition to those assumed under the Charter. The Declaration is an interpretation of the provisions of the Charter. It would therefore be altogether unjustifiable to set the obligations assumed under the Five-Power Declaration against those assumed under the Charter.

I am not prepared to listen to the moralizing of the Canadian representative as to whether or not the delegation of the USSR is abusing its right. The delegation of the USSR will use its rights as it thinks fit in accordance with the terms of the Charter. It is not prepared to take lessons from the Canadian representative. I have already said, and I say so again, that the delegation of the Soviet Union will not digress one single iota from the obligations assumed under the San Francisco Declaration. I can only tell the Canadian representative that it is better not to waste time on such moralizing. Whether anyone likes it or not, we are accustomed to fulfil our obligations, including those assumed under the San Francisco Declaration.

Mr. TARASENKO (Ukrainian SSR): . . . What is the issue with which this resolution deals? Does it really deal with questions which have no substantive significance? I say it does not; this resolution proposes an investigation which involves a number of States, and on the basis of which a serious decision will have to be taken. The statements which we have heard here, in the course of many meetings of the Security Council, have made the nature of the accusations abundantly clear. It has become clear that the United Kingdom representative, the United States representative and a number of representatives of other States, have levelled a series of grave but absolutely unfounded accusations at the Republic of Czechoslovakia and the Government of the Union of Soviet Socialist Republics. Other countries of Eastern Europe are also involved in these charges. Is it possible, in view of those facts, to say that the resolution deals with mere formalities? No, for here we have to consider accusations levelled at a number of States, and this is no matter of procedure but, in fact, a serious question of substance.

We have heard it argued here that a number of States do not consider themselves bound by the Five-Power Declaration. I must, however, remind you that the Declaration was the outcome of an agreement reached by the five Great Powers, and has as much legal force and validity as many other agreements reached by the same five Powers during the war. No one now contests the legality of those agreements; the character they bear is fully legal.

Moreover, that Declaration forms, so to speak, an organic and inseparable part of the United Nations Charter, and without it, the United Nations Organization itself would not have been created. What, in fact, does the Declaration proclaim? It proclaims that the Great Powers had reached a mutual understanding which made possible the creation of the United Nations. There can be no doubt that if no agreement had been reached among the Great Powers, the United Nations would not have come into being.

But for the Declaration, neither the representative of Argentina nor the representative of Canada might be sitting here today. Attainment of agreement among five Powers is a significant fact which must be taken into account. On the basis of that fact we can judge the Declaration signed by the five Great Powers, which formed the foundation stone of the United Nations. It would be easy to discard it today, but we have no right to do so, even if anyone among us wished it; even if it was in the interests of any delegation to discard it. No delegation has the right to repudiate that document unilaterally.

Now I have a question to put to the representatives of the United States and the United Kingdom. Do their Governments consider themselves bound by agreements signed by the five Great Powers even when they do not coincide with their temporary interests at any given moment? I stress the word "temporary", because the Five-Power Declaration reflects the vital interests of the peoples of the five nations concerned. It reflects the principle of long-term co-operation. And if at some stage, for one reason or another, the agreement embarrasses one or another of the States concerned, that does not mean that it does not correspond to the interests of that State and nation. That is why I used the phrase "temporary interests" when putting my question.

The attempt made here to set aside the Declaration when voting on the resolution before us is quite illegal, as it runs counter to the spirit and the letter of the agreement reached by the five Powers and is contrary to the spirit of the Charter itself since the Declaration is an inseparable part of the Charter. . . .

Mr. AUSTIN (USA): I understand that the question propounded by the representative of the Ukrainian SSR was substantially this: Do the United States and the United Kingdom consider their agreements binding even when those agreements do not coincide with their temporary interests and convenience? That question was asked after this distinguished representative had presented a case of a substantive question before the Security Council. His remarks referred to the charges that have been made here, whereas the pending resolution does not refer to them at all. The operative paragraph of the pending resolution, which, we claim, raises only a procedural question, reads as follows:

"Resolves to appoint a sub-committee of three members and instructs this sub-committee to receive or to hear such evidence, statements and testimonies and to report to the Security Council at the earliest possible time."

That is strictly a procedural matter, as appears in the Charter. It is an exercise of the power created by Article 29, one of the Articles appearing under the heading "Procedure." The Charter itself declares that this is a procedural matter; reason declares that it is a procedural matter.

However, assuming that one cannot say that it is beyond question a procedural matter, assuming that there is an issue as far as that point is concerned, I wish to have the record repeat the attitude of the United States toward the statement to which the distinguished representative of the Ukrainian SSR refers as a binding agreement. I shall repeat, in order to keep straight the record of the United States delegation's position on this matter, a statement made by Mr. Dulles on a previous occasion. At the 113th meeting of the First Committee of the General Assembly on 18 November 1947, Mr. Dulles said:

"There are two special aspects of the matter as to which perhaps the position of the United States ought to be indicated. The first is our attitude toward the four-Power statement on voting procedure made at San Francisco on 7 June 1945, to which France also adhered. That statement, by its terms, was a statement of general attitude."

. . .

"It did not purport to be an agreement, much less an agreement binding in perpetuity. The views therein expressed were only partly made explicit in the Charter, and to the extent that they were not so made explicit, the views were never accepted by the San Francisco Conference as a whole. The statement was based on certain assumptions which, in the light of developments, have proved incorrect"— just as they are now proving incorrect. "Thus, the statement said: 'It is not to be assumed, however, that the permanent members would use their veto power wilfully to obstruct the operation of the Council.'

"It was further assumed that action under Chapter VI to investigate the facts or to ask States to settle their differences would be apt to initiate a so-called chain of events leading to action under Chapter VII. Also, it was assumed that it would be 'unlikely that there will arise in the future any matters of great importance on which a decision will have to be taken as to whether a procedural vote would apply'. None of these three assumptions has been borne out by events.

"In view of all these considerations, we believe that the parties to the San Francisco statement are free to explore the question of whether—and if so, how—better voting procedure can be put into operation. We feel that if better voting procedures can be found, the United States would not be prevented from seeking to achieve them merely because that might involve an attitude not in all respects identical with the attitude taken by the United States on 7 June 1945. We do not, however, abandon that earlier attitude until the matter is further explored and until we are satisfied as to precisely what is the better attitude to be taken."

That is the position of the United States delegation right now. We do not abandon the attitude we took in that statement; we stand upon it. You may call it what you like: if it is an agreement, we stand by the agreement; if it is a statement, we stand by the statement.

. . .

Mr. GROMYKO (USSR): . . . I must repeat once more that we do not intend to deviate by one iota from the obligations assumed by the Union of Soviet Socialist Republics under the San Francisco Five-Power Declaration. We shall abide by the obligations with consistency, whether any one else likes it or not. . . .

It has been said that the Declaration contains a special paragraph expressing the hope of the five Powers that the permanent members of the Security Council will not use their right of veto too frequently. Such a paragraph does exist. No one denies its existence in the document, and it retains its significance as a paragraph giving expression to the wish that the permanent members of the Security Council should make the least possible use of the veto. The fault, however, lies not with the USSR, but with those States which work up situations in which it becomes necessary to resort to the veto. Those States are the ones to be blamed. . . .

I have listened carefully to Mr. Austin's speech. Naturally I cannot in any case agree with his interpretation of the Chilean resolution. But there is another part of the United States representative's statement which deserves attention. He recognizes that the United States is bound by the San Francisco Declaration, though he makes certain reservations, which run contrary to the obligations assumed under the Declaration. He does, however, recognize that the Declaration is still in force, and is binding upon the delegation of the United States as well as upon the other delegations. This means that when the Chilean resolution and the question as to whether it is procedural come under discussion, the permanent members of the Security Council cannot—I repeat, they cannot—support the proposal to consider that resolution as procedural. Hence it becomes quite clear that the proposal to consider the Chilean resolution as procedural cannot be adopted. . . .

Mr. ARCE (Argentina): . . . I have given my opinion . . . that this Declaration [of the five Great Powers] may perhaps be indirectly connected with the Charter as regards the five Great Powers, but that it has absolutely nothing to do with the United Nations.

To finish with the subject, I wish to add that this Declaration is not even an agreement reached between the Governments of those five countries, but is merely a statement, such as might be issued by any of the other countries if we agreed to draft it in one of the adjoining rooms. My own view is that it does not bind the five Great Powers either, and consequently I was struck by the fact that the representatives of Great Britain and the United States persist in saying that their countries are bound by it; it seems to me that they are forgetting the rule of international law according to which even treaties formally signed and ratified by the parliaments concerned may be revoked when the conditions under which agreement was reached have changed. How can it be maintained that a mere statement which is not even in the form of an agreement should not now be revoked? . . .

The PRESIDENT: . . . You have before you a draft resolution submitted by the Chilean and Argentine delegations, which proposes to set up a committee to hear the evidence and to report to the Security Council. The vote to be taken on this draft resolution raises the question of procedure we have just been discussing. As I pointed out at the last meeting which we devoted to this matter, there are two methods of proceeding. I could ask you to vote immediately on the resolution and interpret the vote afterwards, and you would have to decide on the question of procedure at the same time; or I could ask you to settle the question of procedure first. As I stated the other day, it is the second which I have chosen.

I favour this second method because the ruling I might have to give as President would not be in accordance with the views held by the majority of the Council's members. In these circumstances, I would prefer the question to be settled beforehand, rather than to announce the result of the vote on the resolution and then to have to reconsider my ruling if it were not accepted by the Council. . . .

I shall now put to the vote the question whether the vote to be taken on the draft resolution shall be considered a procedural vote. I shall then interpret the result of this vote. My interpretation, which I shall explain briefly, may be contested. In that way we shall be able to decide the question of procedure.

I shall then call for a vote on the resolution and shall interpret the results of it, according to the ruling given in your first decision.

I now put to the vote the following question: Should the vote to be taken on the draft resolution be considered a procedural vote?

A vote was taken by show of hands as follows:

In favour: Argentina, Belgium, Canada, China, Colombia, Syria, United Kingdom, United States of America.

Against: Ukrainian Soviet Socialist Republic, Union of Soviet Socialist Republics.

Abstaining: France.

The PRESIDENT: I shall now interpret the vote which has taken place, taking as my basis the following considerations.

In the first place, the President, as a representative of a permanent member of the Security Council, cannot ignore the San Francisco Declaration. This is confirmed by some precedents. The President in those cases was not necessarily a representative of the permanent members. On one occasion at least, the President was a representative of a non-permanent member, yet the provisions of the Declaration were taken into account.

I consider two passages in the San Francisco Declaration to be applicable in the present difficulty. One is the final statement of the text which provides that, should the question arise whether a matter is procedural or substantive in character, ". . . the decision regarding the preliminary question as to whether or not such a matter is procedural must be taken by a vote of seven members of the Security Council, including the concurring votes of the permanent members". The United Kingdom representative—if I have understood him correctly—expressed the opinion that the final provision of the San Francisco Declaration must be interpreted as applying to doubtful cases, and that interpretation would seem to accord with the text of the last part of the Declaration to which I have just referred. For the present, I shall not offer any comment on that interpretation.

With regard to the other parts of the Declaration which could be applied to the case now before the Council, paragraph 2 of part I states that a procedural vote will govern the establishment of "such bodies or agencies as it"—that is, the Council—"may deem necessary for the performance of its functions". Paragraph 4, part I, on the other hand, provides that certain decisions, which in themselves might be procedural, must be considered substantive because of the "major political consequences" which they might have, and it is further specified that "This chain of events begins"—for instance— "when the Council decides to make an investigation . . ." I had wondered whether, in this paragraph, the word "investigation" could not be interpreted as applying to the sending of a commission to conduct an inquiry on the spot, and whether, therefore, a distinction might not be drawn between that and an investigation to be carried out directly by a subsidiary organ of the Security Council.

However, if we refer to paragraph 5 of part I of the Declaration, we find the following: "To illustrate: in ordering an investigation, the Council has to consider whether the investigation—which may involve calling for reports, hearing witnesses, dispatching a commission of inquiry, or other means—might not further aggravate the situation".

In those circumstances, I consider that the word "investigation" which appears in the first line of that paragraph, is used in its widest meaning, and I think it applies to the situation now before us.

Therefore, whatever the interpretation of paragraph 5, part I, it seems in any case that the question may appear doubtful and that, in the circumstances, the final provision of the Declaration, according to which the concurring vote of the five permanent members is necessary to decide whether a question is a matter of procedure, retains its importance.

For these various reasons, I interpret the vote which has just taken place as a decision to consider the vote on the resolution as one of substance.

I would add that I have interpreted the last paragraph in accordance with the practice which has become established here, namely, that the abstention of a member does not prevent a decision being taken by the Council. It was because a permanent member had cast a negative vote that I have given this ruling.

Mr. ARCE (Argentina): I am very sorry, but I must object to the ruling the President has just given. Moreover, I wish to point out that various Presidents of this body have frequently stated that when determining a question like this, the Council's decision did not set a precedent. This is a very wise statement, since the interpretation of the Charter cannot be dependent on the composition of the Council at any given time. . . .

Sir Alexander CADOGAN (UK): I wish to say a word or two to make my position clear. In the circumstances in which we find ourselves and in the position in which the President finds himself, I do not think the President's ruling on the main point is wrong, because there is a difference as to whether this question is one of procedure or one of substance. My Government hold by the last paragraph of the San Francisco Declaration, which directs that that preliminary question must be decided by a vote of seven members including the votes of the five permanent members.

I feel very strongly, however, that the difference is one which ought not to have arisen. The question ought never to have been raised because, to my mind, it is perfectly clear that this is a question of procedure under the Charter, in accordance with our rules of procedure, and in accordance with the Declaration of San Francisco itself.
. . .

I agree that, taking the Declaration as a whole and pushing it to the last degree, there is that last paragraph on which the representatives of the USSR and the Ukrainian SSR wholly depend, ignoring the other parts which seem to me to point in a different direction. I think that if Mr. Gromyko leans too heavily on the San Francisco Declaration, he may find one day that it will crack under his weight. . . .

The PRESIDENT: I shall put my ruling to the vote of the Council.

Mr. VAN LANGENHOVE (Belgium): Might I ask the President what voting procedure will be followed in the coming vote?

The PRESIDENT: The question should certainly be put, since it is probable that the Security Council itself will have to decide it. Rule 30 of our rules of procedure reads as follows:

"If a representative raises a point of order, the President shall immediately state his ruling. If it is challenged, the President shall submit his ruling to the Security Council for immediate decision and it shall stand unless overruled."

If my interpretation of this text is correct, what I should put to the vote is the annulment of the ruling I have given.

Mr. GROMYKO (USSR): I should like to clear up the question raised half-humorously by the Belgian representative. The President's ruling is, of course, correct. That ruling was made in accordance with the San Francisco Declaration.

But if, instead of having the French representative as President, we had another President, say, the Syrian representative, who disagreed with the Five-Power Declaration—though I do not know how he would act if he were President—and if that President made a ruling inconsistent with the Five-Power Declaration, that ruling would not be legally valid. If the representative of any country were presiding over the Security Council and, in spite of the fact that one of the permanent members of the Council had voted against the proposal to consider the Chilean resolution as procedural, ruled that the resolution was procedural after all, his ruling would be legally invalid.

How else could it be? The alternative would be that the question as to whether the resolution was procedural or non-procedural would, by the process of voting, by various stages be reduced to a point of order, which would be an absurdity.

I should like to add that no vote which the Security Council can now take, even if, shall we say, the representative of Argentina insists on a vote on the President's ruling, can weaken or annul the presidential ruling. Otherwise, the question as to whether the Chilean resolution was substantive or procedural would be reduced to a point of order. Is it not clear that such a situation would make no sense from the point of view of fact, logic, or anything else?

The PRESIDENT: When I replied to the representative of Belgium a moment ago, I considered that rule 30 of the rules of procedure was applicable, as I think we are dealing here with a point of order. If the Council thinks otherwise, I should at once put to the vote the interpretation which I have given.

But if we are dealing with a point of order—as I think we are— I feel I must, as I said before, put to the vote the annulment of my ruling, in conformity with rule 30. Nevertheless, I should point out that in certain other cases of disagreement, it was the President's ruling which was put directly to the vote. . . .

Mr. ARCE (Argentina): Rule 30 of our rules of procedure makes no distinction, and it cannot be conceded that the President's ruling may be challenged on some occasions and not on others. I therefore maintain that four members of the Council challenge the President's ruling, and consequently my objection should be put to the vote.

If the position becomes ridiculous, it will not be our fault, but the result of the attitude of certain delegations; or else of the obscurity of the Charter or of our rules of procedure.

The PRESIDENT: We must solve this difficulty. I shall first of all ask for your opinions on the following: In applying rule 30 of our rules of procedure, if the ruling given by the President is to be overruled, must this be done by means of a positive vote against it and in favour of the annulment?

Mr. EL-KHOURI (Syria): I think that rule 30 of the provisional rules of procedure is clear. It states that if the ruling of the President is challenged " . . . . The President shall submit his ruling to the Security Council for immediate decision. . . ." That means, the ruling, and not the challenge, should have the required majority in order for it to stand.

Mr. GROMYKO (USSR): I think that we are wasting our time on such verbal tightrope-walking, and my remark is directed more particularly at the representatives of Syria and Argentina. Was the representative of Syria born yesterday? Does he not know that whenever a presidential ruling is challenged in the Security Council, the question is put in such a way as to establish who is against the ruling, and not who is for it?

We should perhaps ask the Secretary-General to refresh our memories on the point by producing a few dozen records containing the appropriate rules for the guidance of Presidents in questions of dispute. It might help the representatives of Syria and Argentina, and perhaps some others, to see the matter more clearly. If it were thought useful, it might be as well to ask the Secretary-General to bring with him a whole collection of documents and records.

I should like to draw the President's attention to the last clause of rule 30, which reads: ". . . it shall stand unless overruled".

The PRESIDENT: In reply to what the representative of Syria has just said, I would point out that the French text of rule 30 differs from the English. The translation is not a literal one. The English text says: ". . . the President shall submit his ruling to the Security Council for immediate decision and it shall stand unless overruled". This appears somewhat self-contradictory, unlike the French text, which states, not that the President submits his decision to the Security Council, but that he refers his ruling to the Security Council for immediate decision. I admit I prefer the French text since it avoids the contradiction in the English. [The French text of Rule 30 reads: "Si un représentant soulève une question d'ordre, le Président se prononce immédiatement sur ce point. S'il y a contestation, le Président en réfère au Conseil de sécurité pour décision immédiate et la règle qu'il a proposée est maintenue, à moins qu'elle ne soit annulée."]

To enable the Security Council to give its verdict, I shall put the question to the vote in the following form: Is it agreed that I should put to the vote the proposal that my ruling should be annulled?

Mr. GROMYKO (USSR): It seems to me that if we go on in this way, each proposal will be followed by another and still more far-fetched proposal and so on *ad infinitum*. The situation will tend to become like that described in Zeno's famous sophism about Achilles and the tortoise. In theory, Achilles should have caught up with the tortoise, but in practice he was never able to do so; when Achilles covered a hundred yards, the tortoise covered only one yard; when he covered one yard, the tortoise did only one-hundredth of a yard, and so on without end.

It seems to me that the matter should be conducted according to precedent. If anybody disagrees with the President's ruling, the question must be put in the following way: "Who wishes the President's ruling to be overridden?" and not "Who wishes the President's ruling to be maintained?"

If I am not mistaken, the President's second proposal corresponds in meaning to the second alternative. Perhaps he would be kind enough to put his proposal in more precise terms and clarify it.

Mr. ARCE (Argentina): We have already spoken of the ignorance of representatives, but I have just discovered a further piece of wisdom: when the person opposing the view one maintains is right, one should admit it. I think that the representative of the USSR is right in this case, and consequently I shall vote in accordance with the President's decision.

The PRESIDENT: In my opinion we are in a far worse predicament than Achilles, for after all, Achilles did succeed in catching up with the tortoise, whereas there is a danger that we shall never finish if every time I wish to put a question, a decision must first of all be taken on the way in which I must put it.

The question submitted to the Council is essentially one connected with the application of the San Francisco Declaration. My interpretation was made in accordance with the Declaration which the permanent members adopted at San Francisco. I shall put the question to the vote in the following form, for I consider it the only way out of our difficulty: Will those who object to my interpretation raise their hands?

A vote was taken by show of hands, as follows:

In favour of rejecting the President's ruling: Argentina, Belgium, Canada, China, Colombia, Syria.

Against rejecting the President's ruling: Ukrainian Soviet Socialist Republic, Union of Soviet Socialist Republics.

Abstaining: France, United Kingdom, United States of America.

The result of the vote was 6 votes in favour of rejecting the President's ruling, 2 against, and 3 abstentions.

The President's ruling stood, the motion for its rejection having failed to obtain the affirmative votes of seven members.

Mr. GROMYKO (USSR): I wish to ask whether the representative of China really voted against the President's ruling or whether it was a misunderstanding?

Mr. HSU (China): I wish to explain why I voted against the President's ruling. I did so because I felt that the ruling was not correct, not because I do not consider China to be bound by the Declaration.

Mr. GROMYKO (USSR): I wish to say a few words in connexion with the Chinese representative's last statement.

It is my opinion that the Chinese representative is, beyond any doubt, acting inconsistently with the obligations assumed by the Chinese Government at the San Francisco Conference. The Chinese Government has no right—I repeat, has no right—to act contrary to the Five-Power Declaration. The obligations assumed by the five Great Powers form part of their obligations under the Charter. Only irresponsible persons can act in such a way.

What grounds can China have for renouncing her obligations at a time when all other permanent members of the Security Council are abiding by them? To say that the Chinese representative, if you please, does not like the President's ruling, is not sufficient reason to vote against it. To vote against the presidential ruling is to vote against the Declaration which bears the signature of the Chinese delegation at San Francisco.

Mr. HSU (China): I think it is very unfortunate that this question which has already been decided, has again been raised. It is especially unfortunate, since, if it is to be discussed, the ruling of the President must again be involved. I have such a great respect for the President that I do not like to have to repeat again and again that I do not agree with him.

It is clear that I have not said that China does not want to abide by the Declaration of San Francisco. However, can the representative of the Union of Soviet Socialist Republics see this point: that in the interpretation of the Declaration, we may have different views? That does not mean that, if one member has a wrong interpretation, another member has to work on that basis.

I voted against the President's ruling simply because I considered that the interpretation given by the President was not correct. The essential point on which the President based his ruling was that what has been called for is an investigation. Anyone can readily see that there may be honest differences of opinion as to this. I feel that the draft resolution before the Security Council clearly indicates that what is called for is a sub-committee to be set up for a specific question; it is not a matter of ordering an investigation.

In any case, I think Mr. Gromyko can admit that there may be differences of opinion. I voted against the President's ruling entirely for the reason I have stated. . . .

The PRESIDENT: . . . I shall put to the vote the draft resolution submitted by the delegations of Chile and Argentina, and shall then interpret the vote in accordance with the decision arrived at as a result of our discussion. . . .

A vote was taken by show of hands, as follows:

In favour: Argentina, Belgium, Canada, China, Colombia, France, Syria, United Kingdom, United States of America.

Against: Ukrainian Soviet Socialist Republic, Union of Soviet Socialist Republics.

The resolution was not adopted, one of the votes against being that of a permanent member of the Council.

Mr. AUSTIN (USA): . . . The representative of the Union of Soviet Socialist Republics, in his last remarks before we began to vote, referred to my remarks as if he had misunderstood them. I want to clarify that so that the record will be accurate. I did not say that the United States considered itself bound by the statement made in San Francisco—whether it is called a statement or an agreement—but I said exactly the opposite. I did not say that we would not change our attitude towards the veto as set forth in the San Francisco statement. I said that we had not changed our attitude. We feel free, however, to do so. We feel free to change our attitude, and I reserve the right of my Government to do so whenever that course seems advisable. . . .

The United States is not prepared to admit that the use of the so-called double veto can in any way change the Charter, change the law of Article 29. While the double veto might prevent—as it has done in this case—the Security Council from acting at the time when it is used, it cannot transform the character of any question treated in the Charter as procedure, that is, it cannot change it into one having a substantive character.

Consequently, I wish, in the name of my Government, to declare that the United States does not recognize this act as a precedent. I claim that what we have done is not a precedent which goes beyond the point of the ruling of the President, that it does not constitute a transformation of the true character of this type of resolution, and that if such a situation should arise again, we would feel free, notwithstanding the decision taken today, to claim that a procedural matter under the Charter is involved, and to take exactly the same course we have taken today. . . .

Sir Alexander CADOGAN (UK): I have only a short comment to make on the proceedings at our last meeting at which we dealt with this question, when, by exercising his double veto, the representative of the Union of Soviet Socialist Republics obstructed the desire of the rest of the Security Council to examine the evidence that is available on this subject.

I am rather surprised that he did so. I should have thought that it would have been better and more appropriate for any such evidence to be examined methodically in a small sub-committee, rather than that we should have to discuss it all here in the Security Council itself. But, doubtless, he has his reasons for his preference.

I cannot refrain from saying that I am shocked at his misuse of the double veto. I repeat, my Government stands by the San Francisco Declaration, although I do not know how it will be affected by the Union of Soviet Socialist Republics representative's use of one of its paragraphs to nullify another paragraph of the same document.

At this rate, there might never again be a procedural vote, as, according to his theory, the representative of the Soviet Union could on any occasion declare, at his own discretion, that the question at issue was not procedural.

NOTE.—1. No further action was taken by the Security Council with respect to the Czechoslovak Question.

2. What is a "point of order"? Should the Security Council be guided by the following interpretation adopted by the Special Committee on Methods and Procedures of the General Assembly in 1949 [GAOR, IV, Supp. 12 (A/937), p. 11]:

"It is the opinion of the Special Committee that a valid point of order may relate to the manner in which the debate is conducted, to the maintenance of order, to the observance of the rules of procedure, or to the manner in which Chairmen exercise the powers conferred upon them by the rules. Thus, within the scope of the General Assembly's rules of procedure, representatives are enabled to direct the attention of the presiding officer to violations or misapplications of the rules of procedure by other representatives or by the presiding officer himself. Points of order may also refer to legitimate requests for information, to material arrangements (temperature of the room, seating, interpretation system), to documents, translations and so on."

RECOMMENDATIONS OF THE GENERAL ASSEMBLY ON THE PROBLEM OF VOTING IN THE SECURITY COUNCIL

NOTE. The question of voting procedure in the Security Council was first discussed in 1946 during the second part of the first session of the General Assembly on the basis of an Australian proposal. GAOR, I.2, First C., pp. 84–100, 102–26, 210–9, 284–93; *idem*, Plenary, pp. 1231–64. The General Assembly adopted then, by 36 votes to 6, with 11 abstentions, Resolution 40(I), reading as follows (GAOR, I.2, Resolutions [A/64/Add. 1], p. 64):

"The General Assembly,

"Mindful of the Purposes and Principles of the Charter of the United Nations, and having taken notice of the divergencies which have arisen in regard to the application and interpretation of Article 27 of the Charter:

"Earnestly requests the permanent members of the Security Council to make every effort, in consultation with one another and with fellow members of the Security Council, to ensure that the use of the special voting privilege of its permanent members does not impede the Security Council in reaching decisions promptly;

"Recommends to the Security Council the early adoption of practices and procedures, consistent with the Charter, to assist in reducing the difficulties in the application of Article 27 and to ensure the prompt and effective exercise by the Security Council of its functions; and

"Further recommends that, in developing such practices and procedures, the Security Council take into consideration the views expressed by Members of the United Nations during the second part of the first session of the General Assembly."

At its second session, the General Assembly was confronted with an Argentine proposal for a convocation of a General Conference under Article 109 of the Charter to amend the privilege of the veto. A/351; GAOR, II, First C., p. 529. Without a vote on this proposal, the General Assembly by 38 votes to 6, with 11 abstentions, adopted a United States suggestion that the Interim Committee of the General Assembly "consider the problem of voting in the Security Council." GA Resolution 117(II), 21 Nov. 1947; GAOR, II, Resolutions (A/519), p. 23. On the basis of the Committee's report, the General Assembly approved Resolution 267(III), the text of which is reproduced below.

The UN Repertory (Vol. I, pp. 265–6) contains the following summary of the arguments with respect to the authority of the General Assembly to adopt recommendations on the voting procedure in the Security Council:

"In the discussion preceding the adoption of these resolutions the view was expressed, on the one side, that under Article 10 the General Assembly had the authority to discuss questions relating to the powers and functions of any organ of the United Nations and to make recommendations on those questions to the Members of the United Nations and to the Security Council. It was, therefore, unquestionably the duty of the General Assembly to examine how the Security Council carried out its functions and powers, particularly under Article 24. The Security Council had complete power over its own rules and procedures, but the General Assembly had the right to examine the problem of the voting in the Security Council and to make recommendations with regard to this problem. Consequently, it was entirely appropriate for the General Assembly to recommend certain methods with regard to the smooth and effective practices and procedures of the Security Council in order to ensure the prompt and effective exercise of its functions. If the General Assembly had an opinion regarding the working of the Organization, it was its duty to speak its mind: it would be a denial by the General Assembly of its rights and a neglect of its duty if it failed to take notice of any defects in the working of the United Nations or if it refrained from expressing its opinion on the way in which those defects could be remedied.

"On the other side it was argued that, while Article 10 authorized the General Assembly to make any recommendations as regards the powers and functions of the Security Council as well as of other organs of the United Nations, the Security Council under Article 30 had the exclusive right to adopt its own rules of procedure. The methods of the voting in the Security Council were part of its own procedure and remained essentially within its own competence. Therefore, whatever resolution might be adopted on this question by the General Assembly, it could only take effect when implemented by the Security Council. Unless such a resolution of the General Assembly was accepted by all the members of the Security Council, the chance of having a resolution of the General Assembly fully implemented would remain uncertain.

"It was further argued that the proposed recommendations concerning the voting procedure in the Security Council represented an effort to eliminate the voting formula of Article 27 and to break the fundamental principles of the Charter. They constituted further attempts to undermine the principle of unanimity of the permanent members of the Security Council, were incompatible with the relevant provisions of the Charter and aimed at substituting a new procedure for that provided for in the Charter. The recommendations were, therefore, tantamount to a revision of the Charter by circumventing Articles 108 and 109. It was also pointed out in this connexion that essential questions relating to the maintenance of international peace and security could not be settled by voting and could not be decided automatically by a simple majority."

THE PROBLEM OF VOTING IN THE SECURITY COUNCIL

Resolution 267 (III) of the General Assembly, 14 April 1949; GAOR, III.2,
Resolutions (A/900), pp. 7–10.

The General Assembly,

Having considered the report of its Interim Committee on the problem of voting in the Security Council, and

Exercising the authority conferred upon it by Article 10 of the Charter to discuss any question within the scope of the Charter or relating to the functions of any organ of the United Nations and to make recommendations to the Members of the United Nations and to the Security Council thereon.

1. Recommends to the members of the Security Council that, without prejudice to any other decisions which the Security Council may deem procedural, the decisions set forth in the attached Annex be deemed procedural and that the members of the Security Council conduct their business accordingly.

2. Recommends to the permanent members of the Security Council that they seek agreement among themselves upon what possible decisions by the Security Council they might forbear to exercise their veto, when seven affirmative votes have already been cast in the Council, giving favourable consideration to the list of such decisions contained in conclusion 2 of part IV of the report of the Interim Committee;

3. Recommends to the permanent members of the Security Council, in order to avoid impairment of the usefulness and prestige of the Council through excessive use of the veto:

(a) To consult together wherever feasible upon important decisions to be taken by the Security Council;

(b) To consult together wherever feasible before a vote is taken if their unanimity is essential to effective action by the Security Council;

(c) If there is not unanimity, to exercise the veto only when they consider the question of vital importance, taking into account the interest of the United Nations as a whole, and to state upon what ground they consider this condition to be present;

4. Recommends to the Members of the United Nations that in agreements conferring functions on the Security Council such conditions of voting within that body be provided as would to the greatest extent feasible exclude the application of the rule of unanimity of the permanent members.

ANNEX

Decisions deemed procedural

Decision to postpone consideration of or voting on a recommendation of a State for membership until the next occasion for the consideration of applications.

Submission to the General Assembly of any questions relating to the maintenance of international peace and security.

Request to the General Assembly that the General Assembly make a recommendation on a dispute or situation in respect of which the Security Council is exercising the functions assigned to it in the Charter.

Consent to notification by the Secretary-General to the General Assembly or to Members of the United Nations of any matters relative to the maintenance of international peace and security which are being dealt with by the Security Council.

Consent to notification by the Secretary-General to the General Assembly or to Members of the United Nations of any matters relative to the maintenance of international peace and security with which the Security Council ceases to deal.

Request to the Secretary-General for the convocation of a special session of the General Assembly.

Approval of credentials of representatives of members of the Security Council.

Approval of annual reports to the General Assembly.

Submission and approval of special reports to the General Assembly.

Organization of the Security Council in such manner as to enable it to function continuously.

Arrangement of the holding of periodic meetings.

Holding of meetings at places other than the seat of the United Nations.

Establishment of such subsidiary organs as the Security Council deems necessary for the performance of its functions.

Steps incidental to the establishment of a subsidiary organ: appointment of members, terms of reference, interpretation of terms of reference, reference of questions for study, approval of rules of procedure. However, the approval of the terms of reference of such subsidiary organs should require the unanimity of the permanent members if the subsidiary organ were given authority to take steps which, if taken by the Security Council, would be subject to the veto, or if the conferring of such authority would constitute a non-procedural decision.

Adoption of rules of procedure: Decisions to adopt rules of procedure and decisions in application of the provisional rules of procedure, not contained elsewhere in the list:

(1) Overruling of ruling of the President on a point of order (rule 30).

(2) Order of principal motions and draft resolutions (rule 32).

(3) To suspend the meeting; to adjourn the meeting; to adjourn the meeting to a certain day or hour; to postpone discussion of the question to a certain day or indefinitely (rule 33).

(4) Order in which amendments to motions or draft resolutions are to be voted upon (rule 36).

(5) Request to members of the Secretariat or to other persons for information or for other assistance (rule 39).

(6) Publication of documents in any language other than the official languages (rule 47).

(7) To hold a meeting in private (rule 48).

(8) To determine what records shall be kept of a private meeting (rule 51).

(9) To approve important corrections to the records (rule 52).

(10) To grant access to the records of private meetings to authorized representatives of other Members of the United Nations (rule 56).

(11) To determine which records and documents shall be made available to other Members of the United Nations, which shall be made public, and which shall remain confidential (rule 57).

Adoption of the method of selecting the President.

Participation without vote of Members of the United Nations not members of the Security Council in the discussion of any question brought before the Security Council whenever the Security Council considers that the interests of those Members are specially affected.

Invitation to a Member of the United Nations which is not a member of the Security Council or to any State which is not a Member of the United Nations to participate without vote in the discussion relating to a dispute to which it is a party.

Enunciation of conditions for such participation of a State which is not a Member of the United Nations.

Decision whether a State not a Member of the United Nations has accepted the conditions deemed just by the Security Council for participation under Article 32 of the Charter.

Approval of credentials of representatives of States invited under Articles 31 and 32 of the Charter and rule 39 of the provisional rules of procedure.

Decision to remind Members of their obligations under the Charter.

Establishment of procedures for the hearing of disputes or situations.

Request for information on the progress or the results of resort to peaceful means of settlement.

Deletion of a question from the list of questions of which the Security Council is seized.

Decision to consider and discuss a dispute or a situation brought before the Security Council (adoption of the agenda).

Decision whether a State not a Member of the United Nations has accepted, for the purposes of the dispute which it desires to bring to the attention of the Security Council, the obligations of pacific settlement provided in the Charter.

Invitation to a Member of the United Nations not a member of the Security Council to participate in the decisions of the Security Council concerning the employment of contingents of that Member's armed forces.

Approval of rules of procedure and organization of the Military Staff Committee.

Request for assistance from the Economic and Social Council.

Decision to avail itself of the assistance of the Trusteeship Council to perform those functions of the United Nations under the Trusteeship System relating to political, economic, social and educational matters in the strategic areas.

Decision to dispense, on grounds of security, with the assistance of the Trusteeship Council.

Request of the Security Council for the appointment of a joint conference for the purpose of choosing one name for each vacant seat in the International Court of Justice.

Fixation of a period within which those members of the International Court of Justice who have already been elected shall proceed to fill the vacant seats by selection from among those candidates who have obtained votes either in the General Assembly or in the Security Council.

Fixation of the date of the election to fill vacancies in the International Court of Justice.

NOTE.—The suggestions of the Interim Committee with respect to decisions to be included in the Annex to this Resolution were based on the following criteria [A/578 (15 July 1948); GAOR, III, Supp. 10, p. 2]:

"(a) That all decisions of the Security Council adopted in application of provisions which appear in the Charter under the heading 'Procedure' are procedural, and, as such, are governed by a procedural vote. . . .

"(b) That all decisions which concern the relationship between the Security Council and other organs of the United Nations, or by which the Security Council seeks the assistance of other organs of the United Nations, relate to the internal procedure of the United Nations, and, consequently, are subject to a procedural vote. . . .

"(c) That all decisions of the Security Council which relate to its internal functioning and the conduct of its business are procedural and consequently are to be taken by a procedural vote. . . .

"(d) That certain decisions of the Security Council, which bear a close analogy to decisions included under the above-mentioned criteria, are procedural and are therefore subject to a procedural vote. . . .

"(e) That certain decisions of the Security Council . . . which are instrumental in arriving at or in following up a procedural decision, are procedural. . . . "

In paragraph 2 of this Resolution, the General Assembly recommended that veto should not be used with respect to decisions enumerated in conclusion 2 of part IV of the report of the Interim Committee. In that conclusion (*idem*, p. 16), the Interim Committee suggested that the following decisions of the Security Council "should be adopted by the vote of any seven members, whether the decisions are considered procedural or non-procedural":

1. Recommendation to the General Assembly on the admission of a State to membership in the United Nations.

2. Whether a matter is or is not procedural within the meaning of Article 27, paragraph 2.

3. Whether any matter before the Security Council falls within one of the categories which the Interim Committee and the General Assembly recommend should be determined by the vote of any seven members of the Security Council.

4. To determine whether a question is a situation or a dispute for the purposes of Article 27, paragraph 3.

5. Whether any member of the Security Council is a party to a dispute before the Security Council for the purposes of Article 27, paragraph 3.

6. Determination as to whether a question is a situation or a dispute for purposes other than those of Article 27, paragraph 3.

7. Determination of the parties to a dispute for purposes other than those of Article 27, paragraph 3.

8. To call upon the parties to a dispute to settle their dispute by peaceful means of their own choice in accordance with Article 33, paragraph 1.

9. To invite the parties to a dispute to continue or to resume their efforts to seek a solution of their dispute in accordance with Article 33, paragraph 1.

10. Investigation of any dispute or any situation which might lead to international friction or give rise to a dispute, in order to determine whether the continuance of the dispute or situation is likely to endanger the maintenance of international peace and security.

11. Determination whether the continuance of a dispute or situation is likely to endanger the maintenance of international peace and security.

12. Recommendation of appropriate procedures or methods of adjustment of a dispute of the nature referred to in Article 33, or of a situation of like nature.

13. Recommendation that a legal dispute should be referred by the parties to the International Court of Justice in accordance with the provisions of the Statute of the Court.

14. Whether a dispute referred to the Security Council in accordance with Article 37, paragraph 1, is in fact likely to endanger the maintenance of international peace and security.

15. Recommendation of such terms of settlement as the Security Council may consider appropriate for a dispute referred to the Security Council in accordance with Article 37, paragraph 1.

16. Recommendation at the request of all the parties to a dispute with a view to pacific settlement of the dispute.

17. Recommendation to encourage the development of pacific settlement of local disputes through regional arrangements or regional agencies.

18. Recommendation of the Security Council on conditions on which a State which is not a Member of the United Nations may become a party to the Statute of the International Court of Justice.

19. Recommendation on the conditions under which a State which is a party to the Statute but is not a Member of the United Nations may participate in electing members of the Court.

20. Determination of conditions under which the International Court shall be opened to States other than the States parties to the Statute of the International Court.

21. Recommendation concerning the participation of States which are parties to the Statute but are not Members of the United Nations in the amendment of the Statute.

The Interim Committee arrived at this enumeration "by considering whether the decision, if taken by a vote of any seven members of the Security Council, would improve the functioning of that body and permit it, promptly and effectively, to fulfil its responsibilities under the Charter." *Idem*, p. 3.

With respect to the implementation of its proposals, the Interim Committee suggested that "the General Assembly should recommend that the members of the Security Council consider the items enumerated in part IV, A, paragraph 1, of the report [i. e., those included in the Annex to Resolution 267 (III)] as procedural, and conduct their business accordingly. This would apply to the positions which the members of the Security Council take on the question whether or not any of these items is procedural, in case this question is raised; to the manner in which any member of the Security Council, when acting as President, interprets the result of a vote on such a question; and, finally, to the manner in which the members of the Security Council vote if the ruling made by the President is challenged.

"In connexion with the interpretation of the Charter, several delegations, whose Governments were not parties to the statement of the four sponsoring Governments at San Francisco, declared that their Governments did not consider themselves bound by that statement. But even if a Member considers itself bound by this statement, the view of the majority of the members of the Interim Committee is that this constitutes no obstacle to the application of the recommendation made in the preceding paragraph. According to part II, paragraph 2, of the statement, the question whether a given matter is procedural or not shall be decided by a non-procedural vote. This preliminary vote, however, clearly should not, in the opinion of these members, apply to the matters termed procedural in part I of that statement, nor to those matters for which the Charter itself contains an indication of the voting procedure, as these are covered by part II, paragraph 1, of the statement." *Idem,* pp. 15–16.

INVASION OF TAIWAN (FORMOSA) QUESTION: INVITATION TO THE PEOPLE'S REPUBLIC OF CHINA TO ATTEND MEETINGS OF THE SECURITY COUNCIL

Discussion in the Security Council, 29 September 1950. SCOR, V, Nos. 48 and 49.

[On 25 August 1950, the President of the Security Council (Mr. Malik, USSR) brought to the attention of the Council a cablegram from the Central People's Government of the People's Republic of China charging that the transfer of the United States' 7th Fleet to the strait between Taiwan and the mainland of China constituted a "direct armed aggression on the territory of China."

Mr. TSIANG (China) objected to the placing of the item on the agenda merely "on the strength of a telegram from a man who calls himself the 'Foreign Minister' of some country." Nevertheless, the question was placed on the agenda, and the representative of USSR proposed that representatives of the People's Republic of China be invited to attend the meetings of the Security Council during the discussion of this question. SCOR, V, Nos. 34–35.

When the Security Council returned to this question on 28 September 1950, Mr. TSIANG (China) pointed out (SCOR, V, No. 47, pp. 18–19) that:

"The first part of the San Francisco Declaration contains an enumeration of the matters which the four sponsoring States considered to be procedural. Among the matters enumerated in that paragraph is this item: 'Establish such bodies or agencies as it may deem necessary for the performance of its functions.' That is one of the items which the four sponsoring Powers considered to be procedural. However, in connexion with the Czechoslovak question, that part was not interpreted in that manner. That question was discussed at the 303rd meeting of the Security Council held on 24 May 1948. At that meeting the representative of Argentina proposed that a committee should be set up to hear evidence and report to the Security Council. There is an instance of the Security Council attempting to set up an organ for the performance of its functions. On that occasion, in spite of this specific mention in paragraph 2 of the San Francisco Agreement, the representative of the Soviet Union claimed that it was a matter of substance. The President, on that occasion, was the representative of France, who accepted the point of view of the Soviet Union representative and decided that it was a matter of substance.

"In connexion with the question before the Council, there are in fact two matters involved. One matter is postponement, and that is procedural. I do not claim that is a matter of substance. But there is the other matter, namely, the invitation of a representative of the puppet regime of Peiping to take part in the Council's discussions. That is not provided for in the San Francisco Declaration. The San Francisco Declaration refers to the invitation of someone who is not a member of the Council; China is a member of the Council. The point cannot be covered by reference to that paragraph.

"Furthermore, I should like to call the attention of the Council to the proceedings of its 483rd meeting, held on 4 August 1950, which is very recent. At that meeting we were discussing the question of whether to extend an invitation to the representatives of North Korea and South Korea. On that occasion the representative of the Soviet Union who is now present made a statement to the Council. I take this statement from the record of the 483rd meeting held on 4 August 1950. On that occasion Mr. Malik said the following:

" 'Usually, too, the President of the Security Council, with the permission of the Council—with the permission of all its members—invites the countries concerned, as well as the parties to the conflict which is being discussed by the Council to attend the Council's meetings. In the event of any objections, the Security Council duly considers the matter and comes to a decision upon it.

" 'The Soviet Union delegation considers this a question of substance and not of procedure, since it concerns peace and war.'

"There we have a question of the invitation to be extended to North and South Korea. The very representative of the Soviet Union who is with us today contended on that occasion that it was a question of substance and not of procedure.

"Here the Council has the question of inviting a second representative from the same country, which touches upon the right of representation in the Security Council. My contention that this is a question of substance is certainly more justified than the Soviet Union contention of 4 August. I therefore request that the procedure to be adopted on this occasion should be in accordance with the San Francisco Declaration; in other words, this question, whether one of substance or procedure, should be put to the vote of the Council."

On 29 September 1950, the Council first adopted, paragraph by paragraph, the following draft resolution (S/1836):

"The Security Council,

"Considering that it is its duty to investigate any situation likely to lead to international friction or to give rise to a dispute, in order to determine whether the continuance of such dispute or situation may endanger international peace and security, and likewise to determine the existence of any threat to peace,

"Considering that, in the event of a complaint regarding situations or facts similar to those mentioned above, the Council may hear the complainants,

"Considering that, in view of the divergency of opinion in the Council regarding the representation of China and without prejudice to this question, it may, in accordance with rule 39 of the rules of procedure, invite representatives of the Central People's Government of the People's Republic of China to provide it with information or assist it in the consideration of these matters,

"Having noted the declaration of the People's Republic of China regarding the armed invasion of the Island of Taiwan (Formosa);

"Decides

"(a) To defer consideration of this question until the first meeting of the Council held after 15 November 1950;

"(b) To invite a representative of the said Government to attend the meetings of the Security Council held after 15 November 1950 during the discussion of that Government's declaration regarding an armed invasion of the Island of Taiwan (Formosa)."

When the President of the Council (Sir Gladwyn Jebb, UK) asked for a vote on the resolution as a whole, the vote was as follows:

In favour: Ecuador, France, India, Norway, Union of Soviet Socialist Republics, United Kingdom of Great Britain and Northern Ireland, Yugoslavia.

Against: China, Cuba, United States of America.

Abstaining: Egypt.

This decision led to the following discussion:]

The PRESIDENT: In my opinion, the resolution is adopted. There were 7 votes in favour, 3 against and one abstention.

Mr. TSIANG (China): I think that the opinion of the President is a mistake. The votes against the draft resolution included my vote. Since, in the opinion of my delegation, operative paragraph (b) of the draft resolution is a question of substance, my opposition to the draft resolution should be considered as a veto.

On this question there always appears to be a difference of opinion. It is for this very contingency that the San Francisco Declaration provided for a preliminary vote on whether a matter is a question of substance or one of procedure. That preliminary vote must have the concurrent votes of the five permanent members of the Council. The difference of opinion on such a point is immaterial. It is because of the difference of opinion that we have the provision in the San Francisco Declaration. . . .

In the history of the Security Council, to the best of my recollection, there have been three occasions on which the "double veto" was cast.

The first occasion was at the 49th meeting on 26 June 1946, in connexion with the Spanish question. At that meeting the President of the Council was the representative of Mexico. The representative of Australia, Mr. Evatt, presented a draft resolution on behalf of a drafting committee which had been appointed by the Council. The draft resolution was to the effect that the Security Council should keep the situation in Spain under continuous observation, and should maintain it upon the list of matters of which it was seized. That was the question at issue.

When the draft resolution was declared adopted by the President, following the casting of nine affirmative votes, Mr. Gromyko stated that the President had made a mistake. According to him, the resolution failed to be adopted because one of the permanent members of the Security Council had voted against it. The President admitted that, in order to determine whether the question was one of substance or of procedure, it would be necessary to have the affirmative votes of the five permanent members.

During that discussion there were some very important statements made by various representatives. For example, on that occasion Mr. Gromyko said:

"If there should be any objection to this statement . . ."—
that it was one of substance—"I should ask the Security Council to decide whether this is a question of substance or a question of procedure. On the decision . . . which will be given will depend the subsequent solution of the question and the subsequent procedure."

The representative of the Netherlands, Mr. van Kleffens, a noted authority on the Charter and international law, admitted that Mr. Gromyko was legally correct.

On the occasion, the President, the representative of Mexico, ruled that the resolution had been adopted. Mr. Gromyko challenged that ruling and it was put to a vote. The result of the vote was as follows: there were eight votes in favour of the President's ruling, two against and one abstention. What did the President on that occasion decide after that vote? He decided that his ruling was overruled by the Council, in spite of the fact that it received eight affirmative votes to two against. That is a precedent which the Council must consider.

There is a second occasion on which the "double veto" was cast, and that was in connexion with the Greek question, at the 202nd meeting of the Security Council held on 15 September 1947. At that meeting Mr. Gromyko was President of the Council.

The delegation of the United States presented a draft resolution to the effect that the Security Council should request the General Assembly to consider the dispute between Greece, on the one hand, and Albania, Yugoslavia and Bulgaria on the other, and to make any recommendations with regard to that dispute which it might deem appropriate under the circumstances.

Immediately before the vote was taken, the President ruled that the Council should follow the procedure defined in paragraph 3 of Article 27 of the Charter. Thereupon Mr. Johnson, representing the United States, challenged the ruling of the President—that is, the ruling of Mr. Gromyko—on the ground that the draft resolution concerned was a matter of procedure rather than one of substance. Mr. Johnson insisted that the draft resolution was purely procedural. There was a difference of opinion in regard to whether it was a matter of procedure or of substance.

In reply to the statement of Mr. Johnson, Mr. Gromyko made the following statement. I quote from the record:

"As President of the Security Council, I have to say that whether the question is one of procedure or of substance is not subject to the ruling of any President. The Security Council has to take a special decision on this question. At the appropriate moment I shall make an additional explanation on this point."

Mr. Gromyko later made that additional statement, and I quote:

"We cannot take a vote on the United States resolution without knowing what we are taking a decision on, whether on a question of substance or on a question of procedure. I have already said that I did not make a ruling on this question as to whether the United States resolution is one of a procedural character or one of substance. I expressed my opinion as the President. The United States representative and some other representatives did not agree with my opinion. I already stated that the question as to whether any proposal is one of a procedural character or one of substance is not subject to a ruling of any President of the Security Council. The President can only make a ruling on a point of order. The President cannot decide that the question is one of substance or procedure."

On that occasion again, in spite of the fact that the large majority of the Council considered the matter to be a question of procedure, the vote of Mr. Gromyko alone made it a question of substance, and it was so treated on the second vote.

In the history of the Security Council, the delegation of the Soviet Union has cast more than forty vetoes. Does the Council consider that my claim to veto this proposal is less justified than the forty vetoes cast by the Soviet Union? I claim and insist that because of the lack of my concurrence in the vote, this resolution has not been adopted. . . .

Sir Benegal RAU (India): The question before us is whether operative paragraph (b) of the Ecuadorian resolution is a procedural matter or not. It is quite clear from the preamble to the resolution that the invitation proposed to be extended to the representative of the Central People's Government of the People's Republic of China is meant to be issued under rule 39 of our rules of procedure. These rules are made under Article 30 of the Charter, which is one of a group of Articles—Articles 28 to 32 inclusive—occurring in Chapter V of the Charter under the heading "Procedure." The matter may therefore be said to be doubly procedural, that is to say, procedural by virtue of the provisions of the Charter and procedural by virtue of our rules of procedure. Again, the preamble to the resolution expressly states that the invitation is without prejudice to the question of the representation of China. . . .

In other words, the invitation does not involve any decision as to which of the two Governments claiming to represent China is the one entitled to representation. That point is to be left undecided.

It will be noted that under rule 39: "The Security Council may invite members of the Secretariat or other persons . . . to supply it with information. . . ." An invitation under this rule does not therefore involve any political decisions. It is on the same footing as an invitation to any member of our Secretariat. No one will, I hope, contend that an invitation to a member of our Secretariat is a non-procedural matter. . . .

Mr. CHAUVEL (France): The French delegation has no intention of questioning the San Francisco Declaration, to which it subscribed, but it does not think that the resolution we have just voted on is in fact a question of substance. The resolution deals with problems which merely follow upon the inclusion on the agenda of the "Complaint of armed invasion of Taiwan (Formosa)." It therefore appears that a question of substance could have been raised in relation to the question of whether that complaint was admissible. Such a question was not raised, and the present occasion seems to me to be both late and hardly suitable for it. . . .

My meaning is that, at a certain time, there could have been discussion of the question of ascertaining whether the complainant was qualified to make a complaint and that, if the complaint itself was receivable, the question of substance would have arisen. But that question cannot be raised today, because what we are discussing today results only from the inclusion of the complaint in our agenda. The decision on the substance was taken at the very time of so including it.

Mr. MALIK (USSR): The examples of the application of the San Francisco Declaration, to which the representative of the Kuomintang group has referred, have no bearing whatsoever on the question we are considering, and cannot be taken into account. They are invalid. All the cases he has quoted had, in fact, a direct bearing on questions of substance and not on questions of procedure.

The resolution on the Spanish question which he mentioned in referring to the San Francisco Declaration dealt with the substance of the question. A proposal was made that the Security Council should decide to refer the question to the General Assembly, and the draft resolution outlined a programme of action by the General Assembly on the question. In other words, a question of substance was involved. It is quite obvious that, in the event of the resolution being adopted by the Council, the question was a question of substance for a delegation which did not approve of this programme of action which the Security Council had laid down in advance. In my opinion, it would not occur to anyone to regard a question of this kind as a procedural question, since the draft resolution contained a programme which was advocated by the Security Council by stating its views on the substance of the question and by requesting the General Assembly to consider the substance of the question on the lines the Security Council regarded as desirable. How can a proposal of this kind be treated as a question of procedure? There are absolutely no grounds for so treating it, either in law or from the standpoint of the provisions of the Charter. References to this case are therefore completely irrelevant.

The second case which the representative of the Kuomintang group quoted was the Greek question. This case occurred at the meeting of the Security Council on 15 September 1947. There was a United States draft resolution proposing that the General Assembly should consider the dispute in Greece. Here, again, the substance of the question was involved. The draft resolution, which was submitted for the Security Council's consideration, laid down in advance the lines on which it would be desirable for the General Assembly to consider that question. In other words, it dealt with the substance of the question. What connexion had this with procedure?

There are thus no grounds for referring to these cases in an attempt to justify the application of the San Francisco Declaration to the present instance.

The attempt to quote the case of the Czechoslovak question is also irrelevant. For what took place when the Czechoslovak question was under discussion? A group of States, hostile to the Czechoslovak people and the people's democracy which has been set up in Czechoslovakia, decided without any justification and in violation of Article 2, paragraph 7 of the Charter—which prohibits intervention in the domestic matters of a State—to submit to the Security Council a proposal for the establishment of a commission with broad powers to be sent to Czechoslovakia, that is to a sovereign State, and there to do as it wished: investigate, inspect or explore.

Has anything of the kind been seen or heard before? What standards of international law or what Articles of the Charter permit the Security Council to adopt such decisions, namely, that the Security Council, at the wish of a group which commands a majority under certain conditions, may force upon the Council a decision to send a specially selected and arbitrarily established commission to any State, granting it the broadest powers and authorizing it to examine State documents, interfere in domestic affairs, study anything it may please or, more correctly, anything which may please those who have sent it.

I ask, since when have such questions been regarded as procedural matters? If we were to adopt this point of view, we might find to-morrow that a group of States, united in some political or military bloc or other in the Security Council, could adopt as a procedural matter decisions to set up commissions to be sent to any country in the world with broad powers, even including interference in the constitutional affairs of the State. . . .

The reference to the fact that the USSR representative in the Security Council has used the veto forty times is also unfounded. In all those instances the veto was used in regard to questions of substance. It was used strictly in accordance with the Charter and the principle of the rule of unanimity of the five great Powers which are permanent members of the Security Council, in voting upon questions of substance. All this has nothing to do with procedure. . . .

Thus, the position of the USSR Government and the USSR delegation in regard to all the questions to which reference has been made here has been correct, just and fully in accordance with the Charter. Those precedents therefore provide no justification for barring the legal representative of the legal Government of China from being heard here in the Security Council on the question which that Government has brought before the Council: the armed invasion of Taiwan.

The Security Council has taken that question under consideration, and it is the Council's duty to consider it in strict conformity with the Charter, with the rules of procedure, with precedents and practice. That is, its duty is to hear both parties. One of these parties—the United States of America, against which the complaint has been made, is here at this table; the other party, which lodged the complaint, the Government of the People's Republic of China, must be invited and must be given the right to be heard here, at this table, in accordance with the Charter and with the accepted standards of international law.

This is how matters actually stand.

With the support of a number of his patrons, the representative of the Kuomintang group has illegally usurped China's right to occupy its legitimate place at the Security Council table, and is continuing to occupy that place illegally. While occupying that place, he is abusing it; he is guided not by the Charter, the rules of procedure, the Security Council's normal practice and precedents, but solely by hostility towards the Government of the People's Republic of China manifested by the attempt to debar the legal representative of that Government from being present here, in accordance with the decision taken by the majority of the Security Council, when the question of the armed invasion of Taiwan is considered.

Such a position cannot of course be taken seriously, and it is impossible to agree with it.

At one of our previous meetings the representative of the Kuomintang group said that the régime he represents controls Formosa's population of 8 million people. But every member of the Security Council, every one present at this meeting, and every individual with common sense and a modicum of education, is aware that the Central People's Government of the People's Republic of China controls the biggest State in the world, one having a population of 475 million people.

What right has any member of the Security Council to debar that Government from sending its legal representative here to state its complaint before the Security Council concerning the question which has already been included in the Council's agenda at the request of that Government, and which the Council has agreed to consider?

In view of these considerations the USSR delegation is of the opinion that there are no grounds for the claim made by the representative of the Kuomintang group that, through making references to the San Francisco Declaration, the legal representative of the People's Republic of China can be debarred from coming here to attend meetings at which that question will be discussed. The representative of India has explained in detail that the question of representation is not involved, but merely that of attendance at meetings at which the question will be discussed. . . .

Mr. GROSS (USA): In spite of the fact that my delegation is strongly opposed to this motion and voted against it, I believe that it would be a most undesirable precedent for the Security Council to accept the proposition that an invitation to an outside party to attend Security Council meetings is a substantive matter which is subject to the great Power veto. In our opinion, this resolution involves clearly a procedural question.

The Charter of the United Nations and the Four-Power Declaration of San Francisco and the precedents of the Security Council themselves seem to us solidly to support the conclusion that a motion of this kind is procedural. In the first place, rule 39 of the Security Council's provisional rules of procedure provides for such an invitation, and this is by its nature procedural. Rule 39 itself was of course adopted under Article 30 of the Charter. Article 30 of the Charter is under the heading of "procedure", designated explicitly as such in the Charter itself.

In the second place, with regard to the precedents of the Security Council, in the case of Czechoslovakia, when Mr. Tsiang of China was President of the Council and when the Soviet Union representative voted in the negative, the Council decided to invite the representative of Chile to the Council table.

Also in the case of Czechoslovakia, the Council decided under rule 39 in favour of inviting Mr. Papanek to the Council table. Here again the Soviet Union cast a negative vote.

In the Indonesian case, when Mr. El-Khouri of Syria was President, the Council voted to invite the representative of the Indonesian Republic to participate in the discussion. France and the United Kingdom voted against this resolution, and the President of the Council stated: "I consider this to be a procedural point and I therefore declare the proposal adopted." There were eight votes in favour.

Furthermore, the San Francisco Four-Power Declaration, to which reference has been made by my Chinese colleague, explicitly provides in part I, paragraph 2, that decisions to adopt or alter rules of procedure shall be procedural questions, as well as decisions under Article 32 of the Charter, with which we are not here concerned.

The United States has always taken the position that part II of the San Francisco Declaration cannot be taken as altering or rendering illusory part I of that statement. Decisions which part I states are procedural cannot, we think, properly be labelled substantive by action of a permanent member of the Security Council under part II. Any such resort to the San Francisco Declaration would, in the opinion of my Government, be inappropriate.

Finally, the General Assembly itself has considered the question before us and has given its opinion in resolution 267 (III) that decisions in application of the rules of procedure of the Security Council, and in particular decisions under rule 39 of the rules of procedure, are procedural in their nature. The General Assembly recommended, as the members of the Council will recall, that the members of the Security Council consider questions of this nature procedural and, quoting from the General Assembly resolution, "that the members of the Security Council conduct their business accordingly." It is in accordance with that recommendation of the Council [Assembly] that my delegation is acting here today.

The representative of China has made reference to the string of Soviet Union vetoes which have so abused the principle and objective of unanimity upon which the so-called great Power veto is based. But we all know that it was precisely this Soviet Union abuse of the veto in this organ, including particularly the Soviet Union abuses of the "double veto" procedures, which led the Interim Committee and the General Assembly to make the recommendation to which I have just referred, and which is designed to prevent in the future just those abuses.

Almost all delegations represented here agreed to and supported the recommendations contained in that resolution. I recall, with particular pride, that the Chinese delegation not only supported that resolution but joined with the United States in sponsoring the draft resolution in the General Assembly. The General Assembly adopted the resolution by a very large majority, as we all will recall, and my Government continues to support the position which it took in sponsoring and voting in favour of that resolution.

My delegation—as I need hardly repeat—voted against the motion to which I am now addressing myself. We do not think, for the reasons which I have stated, that it is appropriate at this time to invite the Chinese communist representatives to this forum for the purpose envisaged in the resolution. But despite our feeling in that regard, we believe firmly that the majority of the Council has the right under the Charter and the precedents to take that decision as a procedural matter. .   .   .

Mr. TSIANG (China): I should like to reply to certain points that were made by some of the representatives.

The representative of France thought, if I understood him correctly, that the question would be substantive if taken from the angle of the receivability of this complaint. If I were to put it on that ground, namely, that the complainant does not have the qualities to complain, that would indeed be substance. However, the representative of France went on to say that such a question should have been raised at the time the question was placed on the Security Council's agenda and that it is now too late to raise it.

On 29 and 31 August 1950 when this question was about to be placed on the agenda, I made the very point that the French representative thought that I should have made. The statements I made on those occasions were mainly based on the fact that the party making the complaint had neither the juridical nor the factual right to make that complaint. I went on to say that the origin and character of the puppet régime was such that it could not possibly represent China in any way. On that occasion I did not even attempt to use my right of veto, because it is my understanding that the placing of an item on the agenda is not subject to veto. .   .   .

In regard to the statement made by the representative of the United States I shall only make a brief reference to one point. He brought up the recommendations of the General Assembly in regard to the restraint which one was to exercise in the use of the veto. I acknowledge that that has great importance in our discussion. However,

I should like to know whether the recommendations of the General Assembly have been accepted by all of the five permanent members of the Security Council and whether the Council can count upon those recommendations being acted upon henceforth by all the five permanent members of the Security Council?

In the General Assembly and in the Interim Committee my delegation undoubtedly did try to promote a restraint in the use of the veto. However, a decision of that kind, if applied at all, should be applied to all five permanent members. If it is not applied by all, then it cannot be applied by any particular party.

I would not arbitrarily say that the opinions of all my colleagues are *ipso facto* wrong, just because they differ from mine. After listening to this debate, however, I am convinced that I am entitled to veto section (b) of the operative part of this resolution, and I insist that a preliminary vote on that question should be taken now.

I should like to add one sentence. In so far as the recommendations of the General Assembly are concerned, I should like to say that no specific point is to be found among the recommendations covering the question at issue, because those recommendations do not cover the question of inviting a second representative from the same country.

The PRESIDENT: . . . The Council will now vote on whether it regards the vote taken this morning on the Ecuadorean resolution as procedural.

A vote was taken by show of hands, as follows:

In favour: Ecuador, Egypt, France, India, Norway, Union of Soviet Socialist Republics, United Kingdom of Great Britain and Northern Ireland, United States of America, Yugoslavia.

Against: China.

Abstaining: Cuba.

The PRESIDENT: The proposal is therefore adopted; there were 9 votes in favour, 1 against and 1 abstention.

Mr. TSIANG (China): The San Francisco Declaration regulates a vote of this kind. The relevant statement reads as follows: " . . . the decision regarding the preliminary question as to whether or not such a matter is procedural must be taken by a vote of seven members of the Security Council, including the concurring votes of the permanent members."

The vote just taken did not have the concurring vote of my delegation, and therefore the proposal that the matter is procedural was not adopted.

The PRESIDENT: The position is that a vote which is regarded as procedural by no less than nine members of the Security Council, for what seems to me, and I suggest, to all reasonable people, to be patently valid reasons, is pronounced as substantive by one of our permanent members.

I think that if such a situation as this is allowed to stand, a very grave precedent will have been created which may well impede the whole functioning of the United Nations in the future. I do not believe, therefore, that in the general interests of all of us it should be allowed to stand, and I consequently rule as President that, notwithstanding the objection of our Chinese colleague, the vote which the Council took this morning on the Ecuadorean resolution is procedural.

Mr. TSIANG (China): I have a point of order. I think the ruling of the President is *ultra vires*. In the history of the Council, votes of this kind have taken place several times. On the Spanish question, in spite of the fact that eight members thought it was procedural and two members, the representatives of the Soviet Union and the Ukrainian Soviet Socialist Republic, thought it was substantive, the President had to declare that it was a question of substance.

I do not wish to argue this business any further; but in the first place, I want to protest against the arbitrary ruling of the President. In the second place, I offer to the Security Council a proper and legal way of settling the question by sending it to the International Court of Justice and asking that body for an advisory opinion.

I would put this question to the International Court of Justice: in view of the statement of 7 June 1945 by delegations of four sponsoring governments on voting procedure in the Security Council and in view of the precedents of the Council, is the claim of the representative of China to veto paragraph (b) of the operative part of the proposal of Ecuador of 29 September 1950 justified?

I promise this Council in advance that my government and my delegation will accept the advisory opinion of the International Court of Justice. In making this offer, I hope that the members of the Council will notice the great concession on the part of my government. According to the agreement, the veto is not subject to any judicial review. I offer this Council the possibility of a judicial review, and I do not insist that the precedent set by me today should be followed by the other permanent members of the Council; I propose that the Council should solve this question itself.

In the interests of the proper institutional development of this body, I should think that this magnanimous offer on my part would be accepted by the Security Council. I should like to point out that my offer is not a manoeuvre or a matter of tactics because, since this resolution does not come into operation until 15 November 1950, there remains time to obtain an advisory opinion from the International Court of Justice before that date. There is no intention on our part to perpetrate a manoeuvre or tactic on a matter of this kind. In the participation of my delegation in the work of all of the organs of the

United Nations, it has never once tried to win a substantial advantage by any tactical manoeuvre. Therefore, I hope that the members of the Council will appreciate both the real import and the value of this offer I am making.

The PRESIDENT: As I understand it, the President's ruling has not been challenged, though it has been qualified as arbitrary. We may therefore take it that the ruling stands.

The question of the reference to the International Court of Justice is, I think, a separate matter on which no doubt the Council would wish to have a short time for reflection. I suggest that we postpone consideration of that matter, unless it is the desire of the Council to consider it now.

Mr. TSIANG (China): There is an element of misunderstanding which I should like to clear up first of all.

When I offered to submit this question to the International Court of Justice, it was obvious that I could not agree that the present ruling should stand. The question to be submitted to the International Court of Justice is precisely that ruling. The Council therefore can reject or accept my offer; that is up to it. However, if the Council deems it worth while to accept my offer, it must be accepted on the condition that the question remains in suspense until the Court has rendered its advisory opinion.

I am surprised that the President of the Security Council could tell us that an offer to submit a question to the International Court of Justice could be brushed aside and that, in the meantime, his decision should stand. You who believe that you have used a right should have the courage to submit this question to the International Court of Justice. I believe that I am right. I have the courage to submit this question to the International Court of Justice for settlement. I announce in advance that if the advisory opinion is against me, I will accept it.

For an organ of the United Nations to refuse to resort to the Court and to insist on abiding by a decision which one of its members considers arbitrary and in view of the fact that such submission to the Court does not in the meantime hamper the due process of work— such an attitude is unworthy of this great institution of ours.

The PRESIDENT: In that case I am afraid I can only interpret the Chinese representative's remarks as a challenge to my ruling. As the representatives know, rule 30 of the provisional rules of procedure reads as follows:

"If a representative raises a point of order, the President shall immediately state his ruling. If it is challenged, the President shall submit his ruling to the Security Council for immediate decision and it shall stand unless overruled."

The President's ruling has been challenged and must stand unless it is overruled. Therefore, subject to whatever the Chinese representative or any other representative wishes to state, I shall put that challenge to the vote.

The representative of China wishes to speak on a point of order.

Mr. TSIANG (China): The President and the other representatives in the Council know very well that a matter of this kind is not subject to a Presidential ruling. The President and the other representatives know full well that the device of a Presidential ruling is a clever but unsound manoeuvre, because the President knows he has seven votes to uphold his ruling. I think such tactics are unworthy of the great responsibility which rests on this body.

The PRESIDENT: We may all have our own views as to what constitutes a manoeuvre, and likewise we may all have our own views as to what constitutes action which is in the best interest of the United Nations. I shall therefore put to the vote the challenge to my ruling and ask those members who are in favour of overruling my decision to please raise their hands.

A vote by show of hands was taken as follows:

In favour: None.

Against: None.

Abstaining: None.

The PRESIDENT: Since there is no vote in favour of overruling my decision, it stands.

Mr. TSIANG (China): I did not choose to participate in a vote which is in itself illegal. I wish to have it recorded that the President's action is arbitrary and that the decisions he has arrived at are illegal and therefore invalid.

The PRESIDENT: All I can say is that the views of the representative of China in regard to the arbitrariness and illegality of my action are well known; but they do not seem to be shared by anybody else.

Mr. GROSS (USA): I think it may be appropriate that I should explain the position of my delegation on this matter.

It falls to our lot to discuss this question involving, as the President very correctly pointed out, a matter of great importance to the future orderly processes of the United Nations, with regard to a case wherein, on the merits, the United States delegation feels very strongly that the action which has been taken by the Council at this time in inviting the Chinese Communists to take seats at the Council table during the consideration of the Formosa complaint is neither an appropriate nor a desirable action. It would have been a happier process to have discussed the policy questions involved in the problem now before the Council—that is, the double veto—in a different context. I think I may be forgiven for saying that, precisely because the attitude of my delegation toward the veto in connexion with the question with which the Council has dealt earlier today, with regard to the invitation to the Chinese Communists to attend the meetings of the Council, is well known, the views of my delegation with regard to the matter of the double veto we are dealing with at this time are entitled to whatever weight the other representatives may wish to give to them as objective and disinterested. Without further preface, I should like to explain my own participation in the vote just taken which upheld the ruling of the President that the motion on which the Council had voted was procedural.

In taking that position, as I remarked earlier today, my delegation is acting in accordance with the recommendation of the General Assembly made a year ago. A year ago, following careful study by the Interim Committee, the General Assembly adopted a resolution, to which I have referred earlier, and which dealt with this matter. As the representative of China said a little while ago, it is quite obvious that it is assumed that the recommendation of the General Assembly will be complied with by all the members of the Council. That being so, and precisely for that reason, my delegation is anxious to comply with that recommendation and give it the weight to which we think it is entitled.

The recommendation, we submit, must be taken in connexion with the San Francisco Declaration and with rule 39 of our own rules of procedure. As I remarked earlier on, the resolution of the General Assembly deals specifically with the point before us. After recommending that a list of decisions, including decisions taken under rule 39, be deemed procedural by members of the Council, the resolution recommends that the members of the Security Council should govern themselves and "conduct their business accordingly."

Reference to the report of the Interim Committee will indicate that the words I have just quoted—that the members of the Security Council should conduct their business accordingly, that is, in accordance with the recommendations of the resolution—were intended to apply to the positions taken by members of the Security Council on the question whether or not any of these items is procedural, in case this question is raised; to the manner in which any member of the Security Council, when acting as President, interprets the result of a vote on such a question; and, finally, to the manner in which the members of the Council vote if the ruling made by the President is challenged.

I think that each of these three elements is present here, and I think that each has found compliance on the part of my delegation this afternoon. The United States believes that the words contained in the General Assembly resolution "that the members of the Security Council conduct their business accordingly" were intended as a recommendation to individual members of the Council to prevent any effort of a permanent member by use of the double veto to exercise a veto on a matter about which there is no reasonable doubt that it falls within one of the thirty-five categories of decisions which are listed in the General Assembly resolution. Since in our opinion there is no room for any reasonable doubt, my delegation has conducted itself in accordance with the General Assembly resolution.

The United States Government believes that paragraph 1 of General Assembly resolution 267 (III) properly recommends a procedure whereby seven members of the Security Council can exercise the power to take a decision on matters falling within these thirty-five categories, as the Charter intended that they should be able to do, and that it prevents the attempted use of the double veto with respect to these items. My government believes that the General Assembly resolution, in recommending this use of the power of the majority, should be interpreted as implying that it should be used with discretion and should not itself be abused; the United States is prepared to conduct itself in a way likely to accomplish that objective.

As the United States delegation has previously indicated in this Council, we feel that the course of action which the General Assembly has recommended to the members of the Council is consistent with the Charter and with the Four-Power Declaration of San Francisco. Section II, paragraph 2 of the San Francisco Declaration was never intended, and cannot properly be construed, as giving the five permanent members of the Security Council the right to use the device of the double veto to determine unilaterally as non-procedural, matters which according to the Charter, or by agreement contained in part I of the San Francisco Declaration, are procedural.

It is the policy of the United States to restrict the use of the veto by extending, wherever possible, by example, by precedent or by agreement, the area of Security Council action in which the veto is not applicable. This policy has been determined in the full knowledge that in taking this position the United States was working to restrict its own right of veto. It has been our view that in the long run the proper functioning of the United Nations is much more important to any of the permanent members than the power to obstruct the proper functioning of the Security Council.

The results of applying the law of the Charter, as I said at the outset of my remarks, in the present instance, where it is against our own interests, are not pleasant, but if we do not apply that law now in these circumstances, we cannot expect others to apply it when it is not in their interests to do so. In the present state of the world, it is not difficult to see that the unlimited power of the veto and the double veto in the Security Council would be dangerous to security.

My delegation has therefore deemed it appropriate to state its position with regard to the ruling and the reasons for which we believe the President's ruling was properly upheld by the Council. .   .   ..

Mr. MALIK (USSR): The USSR delegation is not entirely satisfied with the decision taken on the Ecuadorean delegation's proposal, having regard to the fact that consideration of the question of armed invasion of Taiwan is thereby delayed for a considerable period.

As the Security Council is aware, the USSR delegation made every effort to ensure a satisfactory solution of the question of inviting a representative of the People's Republic of China and to ensure that the Council took the just decision in issuing an immediate invitation to a representative of the People's Republic of China so that the latter might be given a hearing at the meetings of the Security Council when the question of armed invasion of Taiwan was considered.

When, however, the resolution introduced by the USSR delegation proposing the immediate invitation of a representative of the People's Republic of China was twice rejected, the USSR delegation thought it desirable to vote in favour of the Ecuadorean draft resolution, which provides for the invitation of a representative of the People's Republic of China to the meeting of 15 November 1950 and to meetings held after that date when the question of armed invasion of Taiwan is discussed. It did so with particular regard to the fact that that decision was adopted by seven votes, and that its adoption thus to a large extent depended upon the vote of the USSR delegation, which felt it necessary under the circumstances, to support and vote for this proposal, in order to ensure that the representative of the legal Government of the People's Republic of China should have an opportunity of attending meetings of the Security Council at which the question of armed invasion of Taiwan is discussed; that question, as you know, was referred to the Security Council by the Central Government of the People's Republic of China.

As regards the very lengthy statement made here by the United States representative today, the USSR delegation is of the view that the United States representative's statement went far beyond the question under discussion here today.

In view of this, the delegation of the Soviet Union reserves the right to express its views on the United States representative's statement after it has had an opportunity of studying it more thoroughly in the verbatim record of the Security Council.

Mr. GROSS (USA): In the light of the comment by the representative of the Soviet Union that any remarks of mine may have been outside the framework of the problem which is under discussion here, I deem it appropriate to say simply that the United States position is based upon what we consider to be the application of the law of the Charter which has been developed in the present instance, as we understand it.

Of course we consider that any interpretation regarding the power or responsibility in respect of voting in the Security Council applies equally to all permanent members of the Council or it applies to none. I wanted to make that statement so as to leave no doubt in anyone's mind regarding the significance of the statement which I made earlier.

QUESTION OF LAOS: APPOINTMENT OF A SUBCOMMITTEE

1. *Telegram from the Minister of Foreign Affairs of Laos to the Secretary-General of the United Nations, 4 September 1959.*

United Nations Doc. S/4212; SCOR, XIV, Suppl. for July-Sept. 1959, pp. 7–8.

Since 16 July 1959, foreign troops have been crossing the frontier and engaging in military action against garrison units of the Royal Army stationed along the northeastern frontier of Laos. These garrison units have been obliged to evacuate several posts and to engage in numerous defensive actions. It is obvious that these attacks would not have taken place if the attackers had not come from outside the country and would not have continued if the attackers had not been receiving reinforcements and supplies of food and munitions from outside. As a result of these attacks, losses have been suffered by the Royal Army. On 30 August a new attack, more violent than the previous ones, was launched against the posts of Muong Het and Xieng Kho. Elements from the Democratic Republic of Viet-Nam took part in the attack, which was supported by artillery fire from the other side of the frontier. In the face of this flagrant aggression, full responsibility for which rests with the Democratic Republic of Viet-Nam, Laos requests the assistance of the United Nations, of which it is a Member; it is doing so under Article 1, paragraph 1, and Article 11, paragraph 2, of the Charter. In particular, the Royal Government requests that an emergency force should be dispatched at a very early date in order to halt the aggression and prevent it from spreading.

2. *Discussion in the Security Council, 7 September 1959.*

SCOR, XIV, Mtgs. 847–48.

Mr. LODGE (USA): . . . Once again the United Nations confronts an appeal which puts us to the test. It is an appeal for help from Laos, a small State of recent membership in the United Nations. The appeal tells of threats to its integrity and independence by forces from outside its own borders. Clearly, we cannot ignore this appeal. It calls for action of some kind, and this Council must decide what this action should be.

The United States believes that there is no doubt at all that aggression is being committed. The newspapers are full of it. It is common knowledge. We realize, of course, that there may be those around this table who do not agree. But, certainly there can be no doubt about one fact, and that is that the Government of Laos believes that it has been the victim of aggression, and that when the Government of any Member State, large or small, appeals to the Security Council, the Security Council cannot turn a deaf ear and pass by on the other side. The telegram from the Foreign Minister of Laos, in and of itself, is *prima facie* evidence of the need for the Security Council to act, and to act quickly.

For this reason, the United States, in co-operation with other members of the Security Council, has introduced a draft resolution [S/4214]. To keep the parliamentary situation clear, I hereby move its adoption.

[The text of the proposed resolution was as follows:

"The Security Council,

"Decides to appoint a subcommittee consisting of Argentina, Italy, Japan and Tunisia, and instructs this subcommittee to examine the statements made before the Security Council concerning Laos, to receive further statements and documents and to conduct such inquiries as it may determine necessary and to report to the Security Council as soon as possible."]

Now, the language of this resolution is virtually identical with language which has been used before, notably in the action under Article 29 of the Charter, in the Spanish case in 1946 [39th meeting]. In that case the vote in the Security Council was 10 for, none against, and 1 abstention; and the member who abstained was the then representative of the Soviet Union, Mr. Gromyko, who is now the Foreign Minister of the Soviet Union. This resolution is squarely within the provisions of Article 29 of the Charter. It is a step which is necessary for the Council to take in the performance of its functions in this case. It will be a subsidiary organ which will in effect provide for the continuation of the Council's consideration of this subject.

This draft resolution has the great advantage that it enables the Security Council to react without undue delay to this appeal from a small country. This draft resolution should, in a short time, result in finding facts which will be of value to the whole Council. This draft resolution does not close any doors and does not put anybody up against a stone wall. This draft resolution is a constructive way of dealing with a menacing situation and of dampening down flames which are spurting up dangerously.

Finally, members should understand that if the Security Council shrinks from taking this very modest step the alternative courses of action may be much more far-reaching, much harder to control and much more dangerous.

This draft resolution will have a good effect if it is voted promptly. But if we present to the world a spectacle of hair-splitting and haggling, its effect will be much reduced.

For these reasons, we think that the Council should enact this draft resolution promptly. In fact, I hope that we will not hesitate to hold a night meeting if need be so that we may do our full duty to the world and once again inspire the confidence of world opinion in the United Nations. . . .

Mr. SOBOLEV (USSR): Before this proposal is put to the vote, I think we must say a few words about the nature of the proposal before the Security Council. An effort was made to depict this joint draft resolution submitted by France, the United Kingdom and the United States—there is no indication of the subject, as the draft resolution has no title—as procedural in character, which would mean that the vote would be on a procedural matter. In other words, the voting procedure would be such that the unanimity of the permanent members would not be required for the adoption of the resolution. Of course, those who referred to the procedural nature of the resolution did not go so far as to make an explicit statement to this effect. But naturally, that was what they meant when they said that the draft resolution was procedural.

We must, I think, make it clear at the outset that this draft resolution is not procedural. It relates to the substance of the question now before the Security Council and, if adopted by the Council, might have far-reaching consequences. As, however, the question of its procedural character has been raised, it might be useful to refer to the practice of the Security Council.

Mr. Lodge cited one case from the practice of the Security Council, a case in which a resolution to establish a committee or sub-committee on the Spanish question was adopted with one of the permanent members abstaining. This case, which did indeed occur, does not depart from the established voting procedure in the Security Council because, when a permanent member abstains, its vote does not count.

There are, however, other precedents for consideration by the Security Council of proposals to appoint individuals or to establish various kinds of committees, commissions, and sub-committees, all of which might be classified as "subsidiary organs". In these cases the Security Council has invariably followed the practice of treating the question of establishing a sub-committee or committee of that kind not as a procedural but as a substantive matter. And the vote on such a question has been considered a vote on a substantive matter, in other words, as being subject to the unanimity rule contained in Article 27 of the Charter.

In order to substantiate my statements, I shall refer to the valuable document entitled Repertoire of the practice of the Security Council 1946–1951, prepared for us by the Secretariat. This volume contains accounts of cases, of which it may be useful to remind the Security Council, since they are precedents applicable to the case before us.

For example, Case 19 on page 190 reads as follows:

"At the 194th meeting on 25 August 1947, in connexion with the Indonesian question (II), the representative of the USSR submitted several amendments to a joint Australian-Chinese draft resolution, one of which provided for the establishment of a commission composed of the States members of the Security Council 'to supervise the implementation of the decision of the Security Council of 1 August'. The amendments were not adopted. There were 7 votes in favour, 2 against (one vote against being that of a permanent member) and 2 abstentions."

In this case, then, there is a direct statement that the proposal was not adopted because one permanent member of the Security Council voted against it; in other words, the matter was considered substantive and not procedural.

Case 13 on page 189 reads as follows:

"At the 70th meeting on 20 September 1946, in connexion with the Ukrainian complaint against Greece, the representative of the United States proposed to establish a commission of three individuals nominated by the Secretary-General to investigate the facts relating to the border incidents along the frontiers between Greece, on the one hand, and Albania, Bulgaria and Yugoslavia on the other, and to submit to the Security Council a report on the facts disclosed by its investigation. The draft resolution was not adopted. There were 8 votes in favour, 2 against (one vote against being that of a permanent member), and 1 abstention."

You will note that this case, too, dealt with the submission of a proposal to establish a commission, or what is termed in English a "fact-finding commission". The proposal was not adopted by the Council because one of the permanent members of the Council voted against it; in other words, the vote on the proposal was not procedural but substantive, and the unanimity rule was applied.

I do not wish to burden the Council with a list of other precedents. The Secretariat has been very meticulous in this respect and has assembled all the available cases. Unless I am mistaken, in no case has a proposal for the establishment of a commission or committee by the Security Council in connexion with a question such as the one now before us been considered procedural. In every case such a proposal has been considered substantive and the unanimity rule has been applied to the vote on it, as provided in Article 27 of the Charter.

What is the proposal now before us? We are asked to appoint a sub-committee consisting of Argentina, Italy, Japan and Tunisia, and to instruct this sub-committee to examine the statements made before the Security Council concerning Laos, to receive further statements and documents and to conduct such inquiries as it, that is, the sub-committee, may determine necessary. In short, the sub-committee is to be given "carte blanche" ; it may take any action it wishes.

What precisely will the sub-committee do? The sponsors of the resolution do not make this clear, but give the sub-committee "carte blanche". For example, the sub-committee is instructed to examine the statements made before the Security Council concerning Laos and to receive documents; it will, for instance, have before it the request by the Laotian Government for the dispatch of an emergency force to Laos. Under this resolution, if adopted, the sub-committee must examine the Laotian request and submit a report to the Security Council.

Can this really be regarded as a procedural matter, when the sub-committee is to consider the question of dispatching an emergency force? The sub-committee will have before it the request I have mentioned or, if it does not, it may receive such a request and others of the same kind. Moreover, this request and many of the statements made in the Security Council contain accusations of aggressive activities by a sovereign State. Under the terms of the resolution, the sub-committee will examine these accusations and determine whether or not, in its opinion, aggression has been committed. And since it is free to conduct "such inquiries as it may determine necessary", obviously it will conduct such inquiries.

In short, attempts to represent this sub-committee as technical, "innocuous", procedural and so forth are groundless. The committee will unquestionably have great political significance, and in taking a decision on the resolution, the Security Council must apply the procedure laid down in the Charter for the adoption of decisions of this sort.

There is another document I can use to illustrate the position in regard to this question. This sub-committee is essentially a sub-committee for investigation. Whatever it is called, the fact remains that the sub-committee will conduct an investigation in Laos. The question of the possible consequences of an investigation by the Security Council was given special attention at the San Francisco Conference in the earliest stages of the United Nations. At the time the voting procedure in the Security Council was being worked out, a close study was made of various cases and of the line the Security Council should follow in those cases. For instance, the declaration of 7 June 1945 of the four sponsoring Governments (the Soviet Union, the United States of America, the United Kingdom and China) at the San Francisco Conference, with which France later associated itself, deals with the question of investigations.

Paragraph 4 of this declaration points out: ". . . decisions and actions by the Security Council may well have major political consequences . . . .".

There is no doubt that the decision we are being called upon to take today may have major political consequences.

". . . and may even initiate a chain of events which might, in the end, require the Council under its responsibilities to invoke measures of enforcement under Section B, Chapter VIII. This chain of events begins when the Council decides to make an investigation, or determines that the time has come to call upon States to settle their differences, or makes recommendations to the parties."

I should like to repeat this phrase: "This chain of events begins when the Council decides to make an investigation."

The declaration continues:

"It is to such decisions and actions that unanimity of the permanent members applies, with the important proviso, referred to above, for abstention from voting by parties to a dispute."

Thus, this basic document defining voting procedure in the Security Council specifically states that a vote on an investigation requires the unanimity of the permanent members of the Council.

I would remind the representatives of France, the United Kingdom and the United States of this document. They can scarcely deny that the adoption of a decision such as the one we have to take today is a decision regarding an investigation.

To sum up, I should like it to be clear to the members of the Council that the vote on the draft resolution before the Security Council is a vote on a substantive matter and is subject to the unanimity rule.

Should anyone have any doubt on this score, the four-Power declaration, with which France associated itself, indicates in its concluding sentence the procedure for resolving such doubt:

"Should, however, such a matter arise, the decision regarding the preliminary question as to whether or not such a matter is procedural must be taken by a vote of seven members of the Security Council, including the concurring votes of the permanent members."

In other words, if there is any doubt that the question is procedural, the Council has no alternative but to decide the question by the procedure I have just mentioned, which was approved by all the Members of the United Nations at San Francisco.

I shall, therefore, put the question—does anyone have any doubt that this resolution is not procedural?

The PRESIDENT (Mr. Ortona, Italy): I think I may point out that many of the speakers have already expressed their opinion on whether the draft resolution is procedural or not. In any case, I think that the question which has been raised by the Soviet representative could more properly be taken up after the vote on the draft resolution which has been submitted by the United States representative together with the representatives of France and the United Kingdom. This is a practice which has some precedent within this Council and it seems to me that it is a sensible and reasonable one. Here we have a draft resolution submitted by one of the representatives together with two others. I think that the first step for us should be to proceed to the vote on this draft resolution.

Mr. SOBOLEV (USSR): The past practice of the Security Council has varied and there have been a number of cases in which the Council, before voting on a proposal or a draft resolution, has taken a decision on whether the vote was to be of a procedural or a substantive character. Such a vote took place, for example, on 24 May 1948 [303rd meeting], when a preliminary decision was taken on whether the vote on the draft resolution under discussion would or would not be procedural.

In order, therefore, to avoid any later procedural difficulties, I request the President to settle the question of the voting procedure immediately, before the draft resolution is put to the vote. In other words, I request that a vote should be taken on the question whether the vote on the draft resolution is to be considered a procedural vote. I request that a vote should be taken on that question and the voting procedure should be in accordance with the four-Power declaration which I have just read out.

The PRESIDENT: I would like to note again that the cases in which the votes on the draft resolution have been taken first are quite numerous and I think that they outnumber the cases of the reverse order by at least one. But in any case, I think that I understand correctly that the Soviet representative wants me to put to a formal vote the question whether the draft resolution under consideration is a procedural one, and we shall proceed accordingly. I will now put to the vote of the Council the following question: Should the vote on this draft resolution be considered a procedural one? . . .

Mr. LODGE (USA): Just a parliamentary inquiry. Those who think that the draft resolution is procedural should vote "yes", and those who think it is not procedural should vote "no". Is that correct?

The PRESIDENT: Yes. Those who believe that it is a procedural matter will say "yes" and raise their hands.

A vote was taken by a show of hands.

In favour: Argentina, Canada, China, France, Italy, Japan, Panama, Tunisia, United Kingdom of Great Britain and Northern Ireland, United States of America.

Against: Union of Soviet Socialist Republics.

The PRESIDENT: The result of the vote is as follows: 10 in favour and 1 against. Therefore, the resolution should be considered procedural. It is the interpretation of the Chair, shared by the overwhelming majority of the members, that the draft resolution falls clearly under Article 29 of the Charter which reads:

"The Security Council may establish such subsidiary organs as it deems necessary for the performance of its functions."

Since this Article appears under the heading of "Procedure", this cannot mean anything but that all matters included in it are of a procedural nature. The Charter itself declares, consequently, that this is a procedural question and must be voted accordingly under Article 27, paragraph 2. In the previous practice the Security Council has always considered the establishment of subsidiary organs as a matter of procedure. The Chair can act only in accordance with the Charter and the rules of procedure, and this is my ruling.

Mr. SOBOLEV (USSR): The President's interpretation of the vote is at variance with the Charter of the United Nations, at variance with the procedure laid down in the four-Power declaration issued at the San Francisco Conference on 7 June 1945 and at variance with the whole practice of the Security Council. I mentioned some examples of that practice a few moments ago.

I have just quoted from the four-Power declaration of 7 June 1945 in which the four Powers, with the adherence of France, established the procedure for deciding the preliminary question whether a procedural vote might be taken in a particular case. That procedure provides that such a vote shall be subject to the unanimity rule, in other words, the adoption of an affirmative decision shall require the concurring votes of all the permanent members.

In the vote which has just taken place, a vote on this very question which is dealt with in the declaration and to which the procedure I have mentioned applies, the Soviet Union, a permanent member of the Security Council, voted "against".

Consequently, the President's interpretation is at variance with the Charter, with the declaration of which I have just spoken and with the practice of the Security Council. Hence I protest against his ruling. I consider that he has announced the results of the vote incorrectly. The vote on the draft resolution, which he intends to put to the vote, will be a vote not on a procedural matter but on a matter of substance, to which the unanimity rule is applicable.

I am surprised at the attitude of the representatives of the United States, the United Kingdom and France, who were parties to the San Francisco declaration of 7 June 1945. How can they consider this ruling, this announcement by the President, to be in accordance with the Charter, with the practice of the Security Council and, most important of all, with the four-Power declaration?

In short, the President's interpretation of the vote is illegal. It is at variance with the Charter, it is at variance with the four-Power declaration to which France subscribed, and it is at variance with the practice of the Security Council. For these reasons, it is null and void. . . .

Sir Pierson DIXON (UK): Mr. President, before we proceed to the vote, I should like to explain why I considered as correct your ruling that the draft resolution is subject to a procedural vote.

The issue raises matters to which we attach considerable importance affecting the practice of the Security Council. The representative of the Soviet Union has sought to show that because on a number of occasions in the past the Council has failed to adopt draft resolutions providing for the establishment of commissions of investigation by virtue of the unanimity rule the draft resolution now before the Council must fail unless it has the support of the five permanent members. This is not so. We are considering not a proposal to establish an investigating body, but a proposal under Article 29 of the Charter for the Council to establish a sub-committee of itself. The point at issue, therefore, is whether the establishment by the Security Council of a sub-committee of itself is a procedural or substantive decision. . . .

The representative of the Soviet Union also referred to the last sentence of the San Francisco declaration and argued that this is a case when the question of whether a matter is procedural must be decided by a vote of seven members of the Security Council, including the concurring votes of the permanent members. We should also read paragraph 1 of part II of the declaration which immediately precedes that paragraph. It says:

"In the opinion of the delegations of the sponsoring Governments, the draft charter"—as it then was—"itself contains an indication of the application of the voting procedures to the various functions of the Council."

The second paragraph of part II on which the Soviet representative relied was therefore clearly intended to apply only when the Charter did not give any guidance; it was intended to apply to those cases where there was genuine doubt as to whether a matter was procedural or substantive. In the present case, Article 29 of the Charter gives a clear indication, namely, that, as a matter of procedure and administrative convenience, the Security Council can appoint such sub committees of its members as is now proposed.

It is for these reasons, which I felt obliged to give in some detail, that in my view your ruling, Mr. President, was entirely correct and the representative of the Soviet Union was not entitled to claim that the question of whether the draft resolution was procedural should be settled in accordance with the practice under the San Francisco declaration which provided for a different set of circumstances. . . .

The PRESIDENT: After the exhaustive comments that we have heard from the last speakers, I think that it would be only natural for me to limit myself to a very brief statement concerning the remarks that the representative of the Soviet Union has directed to me and to my ruling. I think that his remarks fall mainly into three categories. One is the observance of the past practice. Another is my abidance by the Charter. The third is the San Francisco declaration.

As far as concerns the first category that I mentioned, I think that the past practice, and more recent than that mentioned by the representative of the Soviet Union, shows that there has been at least one case similar to the one to which my ruling applies. As reported in the Repertory of Practice of United Nations Organs,

"At the 507th meeting the President . . . asked the Council to vote on whether the Ecuadorian draft resolution voted upon that morning was a procedural matter. There were 9 votes in favour, 1 against and 1 abstention, the vote against being that of a permanent member, and the President declared adopted the proposal to consider the matter procedural." [Vol. II, p. 80.]

As far as concerns my abidance by the Charter, I wish to reiterate that my interpretation is based on the firm conviction that the draft resolution which has been submitted falls clearly within the scope of Article 29 of the Charter. This view appears to be shared by the great majority of members of the Council. Since this Article appears under the heading of "Procedure", this cannot mean anything but that all matters included in it are procedural. The Charter declares, by consequence, that this is a procedural question and must be voted accordingly under Article 27, paragraph 2.

Furthermore, I would add that I also was guided in my ruling by the conviction that the tasks entrusted to the sub-committee established under the resolution clearly define the nature of this body and of its work. It should not itself conduct investigations or make recommendations. The sub-committee should collect information and present the facts in order to clarify the present situation and to enable the Council itself to make decisions. Rule 40 of the rules of procedure of the Council states:

"Voting in the Security Council shall be in accordance with the relevant Articles of the Charter . . ."
It is the purport of the Articles of the Charter that has guided my decision.

As far as the third category is concerned, I repeat that the Chair can act only in accordance with the Charter and with the rules of procedure. Any other document cannot be binding if its interpretation might run contrary to the Charter itself.

It is not my intention, after so many comments have been heard around this table on the San Francisco declaration, to enter now on any argument about the validity of the San Francisco statement on voting procedure to which speakers have been referring, but I feel obliged to stress again that this document cannot be interpreted in a way inconsistent with the Charter, which is the only document to which we must adhere in any case and to which I have tried to adhere most strictly in my decision.

The PRESIDENT: If there are no other speakers I should like to proceed now to take a vote on the draft resolution submitted by

France, the United Kingdom and the United States [S/4214]. Since I see no objection, we will now proceed to the vote.

A vote was taken by a show of hands.

In favour: Argentina, Canada, China, France, Italy, Japan, Panama, Tunisia, United Kingdom of Great Britain and Northern Ireland, United States of America.

Against: Union of Soviet Socialist Republics.

The PRESIDENT: There are 10 votes in favour, 1 against, and no abstentions. I consider therefore the draft resolution adopted.

Mr. SOBOLEV (USSR): The President has just said that he considers the draft resolution adopted. However, his statement is not in accordance with the procedure for voting in the Security Council laid down in the Charter. A vote against this resolution, which deals with a question of substance, was cast by one of the permanent members of the Security Council, the Soviet delegation. Therefore, in accordance with the Security Council's rules of procedure and with the Charter, this resolution cannot be regarded as adopted, and, needless to say, a resolution on which the voting was illegal cannot be regarded as having any legal force. The fact that the voting on the resolution was contrary to the Charter and the Council's rules of procedure means that the resolution is not binding on anyone.

The resolution was adopted on the basis of an illegal procedure to which the majority of the Council's members have subscribed. This illegal procedure was followed in violation of the San Francisco declaration. Although the President stated that, as far as he is concerned, and perhaps as far as the other members of the Council are concerned, this declaration is not binding, the fact that it exists and that it was recognized at San Francisco by the States that signed the Charter means that it forms part of the procedure and principles governing the work of the Security Council and the United Nations as a whole.

The San Francisco declaration is an interpretation of the Charter and cannot be opposed to the Charter, since it is an interpretation upon which formal agreement was reached. It is the only document adopted at the conference concerned with the interpretation of specific provisions of the Charter, and by virtue of that fact those parts of it which relate to the Charter are as important as the Charter itself.

It is clear from today's proceedings in the Security Council that the action taken here today followed a preconceived plan. The Council began by violating its rules of procedure, as we pointed out at the very outset. It went on by breaking with the San Francisco declaration and ended by flagrantly violating a number of basic provisions of the Charter—the provisions dealing with voting.

All those who are genuinely concerned to ensure that the United Nations functions in accordance with the Charter and its principles should ponder the implications of this practice on the part of the Security Council. I think nobody can doubt that the decision just taken by the Security Council sets a very dangerous precedent which may have far-reaching repercussions on all the activities of the United Nations.

We are witnessing a first step towards a revision of the Charter, a revision in practice and in fact. I believe that this will give many Members of the United Nations room for thought. If today the Security Council's rules of procedure can be broken, if one of the fundamental documents defining the basis of the Security Council's work— the San Francisco declaration—can be violated, we must consider what the next stage will be, what fate lies in store for the United Nations Charter.

The Soviet delegation wishes to state once again that it regards this resolution as non-existent, illegal and hence not binding upon anyone.

The PRESIDENT: The representative of the Soviet Union has spoken serious and grave words. They strike, I would say, a note dissenting from the one I had hoped to see prevail in this meeting today when I recalled to the members of the Council that we were here to implement that part of the Charter which speaks of us as "a centre for harmonizing the actions of nations in the attainment of these common ends".

However, I do realize that every member is entitled to his own opinions and certainly to express them. I have already explained to the Council and to the representative of the Soviet Union what has been my guidance in my ruling, and I can only reiterate that I have done that in good faith and consistent with the purposes of the Charter. It is my duty to underline that the resolution has been adopted by the vote of ten members and that my ruling has been supported. Therefore I have no doubt in my mind that the resolution is valid.

Mr. LODGE (USA): Let me first express gratification that this resolution has been adopted, and by such a very large vote. There is no question whatever that it has been legally adopted and that there is absolutely no flaw at all in its status. I am confident that the four nations mentioned in the resolution will immediately address themselves to the work prescribed in the resolution and I am sure that this will have an excellent effect on opinion throughout the world and will receive and merit the applause of all those who value the rights of small nations. . . .

I would like to make a few more remarks on this subject to summarize the position of the United States both on our procedure today and on the four-Power declaration. The United States has consistently taken the view that the so-called double veto cannot be used to make substantive a matter declared by the four-Power statement to be procedural. This was clearly expressed before the Council by Ambassador Gross, the United States representative, on 29 September 1950, nearly ten years ago, in these words:

"Section II, paragraph 2 of the San Francisco declaration was never intended, and cannot properly be construed, as giving the five permanent members of the Security Council the right to use the device of the double veto to determine unilaterally as non-procedural, matters which according to the Charter, or by agreement contained in Part I of the San Francisco declaration, are procedural." [507th meeting, pp. 9 and 10.]

That was ten years ago, but that continues to be the view of the United States.

This resolution which we have just adopted establishes a sub-committee of the Council to receive statements and documents and to conduct such inquiries as it may determine necessary. We regard such action as a normal and accepted procedure by which the Council can make its work more orderly and efficient. This is truly, and I am quoting from the Charter now, a subsidiary organ which the Council deems necessary for the performance of its functions, which is the precise situation covered by Article 29.

Such a subsidiary organ is specifically considered procedural in the Charter in Article 29, which says:

"The Security Council may establish such subsidiary organs as it deems necessary for the performance of its functions."

It is also procedural under rules 28 and 33 of the rules of procedure.

.   .   .

This matter is procedural under Part I, paragraph 2, of the four-Power declaration.   .   .   .   And it is procedural under General Assembly resolution 267 (III) which reads:

"The General Assembly   .   .   .

"1.   Recommends to the members of the Security Council that, without prejudice to any other decisions which the Security Council may deem procedural, the decisions set forth in the attached annex be deemed procedural and that the members of the Security Council conduct their business accordingly;"

And one of the decisions referred to was: "Establishment of such subsidiary organs as the Security Council deems necessary for the performance of its functions." That is a vote of the General Assembly which states categorically that what we have just done is procedural. Let me call the attention of the Council to the fact that the authority to refer "any matter to a committee" in the Council's rules of procedure is found in rule 33 which gives the order of precedence of obviously procedural motions, and I am quoting, "over all principal motions and draft resolutions relative to the subject".

It is both illogical and contrary to the fundamental intention of the Charter that the Security Council should be prevented by a double veto from obtaining assistance from subsidiary organs which it deems necessary for the performance of its functions. But beyond that, in the resolution which we have adopted, the Council stands on a precedent of long standing in reaffirming that establishment of such a sub-committee is a matter under Article 29. I refer, of course, to the Spanish case in 1946. The draft resolution submitted today by three members is in substance taken verbatim from the operative paragraph of the resolution adopted on the Spanish question on 29 April 1946. The resolution adopted by the Council on the Spanish question was a revision of an earlier draft which had called specifically for an investigation under Article 34. But in introducing the revised resolution its sponsor, who was the representative of Australia, said that the draft had cut out the idea of a formal investigation under Article 34 so as to enable the proposed body to be brought in under Article 29 as a subsidiary organ. At that time the Australian representative clearly drew this distinction, and his interpretation was never explicitly challenged, and was in fact reinforced by subsequent statements by the representative of Australia in explaining the intent and scope of the resolution, including the statement that it was up to the sub-committee itself to decide "how and when and where the inquiry is to be made". Furthermore, the Spanish sub-committee is listed in the Repertoire of the practice of the Security Council under Article 29. That is how it is officially listed and you can verify that. A sub-committee which was established under Article 29 in 1946 can be established under the same Article in 1959.

Now, as a matter of fact, the Soviet Union has already tacitly conceded that under circumstances similar to those pertaining today, the Council can determine a resolution to be procedural without the concurring votes of all the permanent members. I will tell you when that happened. That happened when the Council, on 29 September 1950, considered the agenda item, "Complaint of armed aggression against Taiwan (Formosa)". The Security Council decided an issue in that case against the negative vote of one of the permanent members and the Soviet Union made no complaint. Because its political interests are different now, the Soviet Union takes an entirely different point of view from that which it took in 1950.

Now in contrast to that, let me point out that the United States has consistently taken the position since 1946 that resolutions of the type which we have today, setting up sub-committees of the Security Council, are procedural questions under Article 29. We took that position in the Spanish case, in the Corfu Channel case and in the Czech case. In the Czech case, which the Soviet Union has cited to support its position, the Council will remember that a majority of the members of the Council voted that the resolution was procedural. The United States made an explicit reservation to that effect and announced that regardless of the decision at that time, we would feel free to act in the future on the basis that resolutions establishing sub-committees were procedural.

But even more important than this, the United States concurred during the complaint relating to the Taiwan discussion in 1950, that the resolution was procedural and that a negative vote of a permanent member could not prevent it from being procedural. And we did this even though we were opposed to and voted against the resolution. That is the side we were on. Ambassador Gross, the United States representative, said:

"The results of applying the law of the Charter, as I said at the outset of my remarks, in the present instance, where it is against our interests, is not pleasant, but if we do not apply that law now in these circumstances, we cannot expect others to apply it when it is not in their interests to do so." [507th meeting, p. 10.]

That was our position then and that is our position now. There is no cloud of any kind on the resolution which we have just adopted.

Mr. SOBOLEV (USSR): The statement just made by the United States representative compels me to make certain comments.

The United States representative said that Part I, paragraph 2, of the San Francisco declaration lists those actions of the Security Council which are procedural in nature. He specifically quoted the part of the paragraph which says that the Council will, by a vote of any seven of its members, that is to say by a procedural vote, "establish such bodies or agencies as it may deem necessary for the performance of its functions". There is such a provision and there have indeed been cases in which the Council has established bodies for the performance of its functions on the basis of a vote of that kind in view of the procedural nature of the bodies concerned. We can cite, for example, the Committee of Experts on Rules of Procedure of the Security Council and the Committee on the Admission of New Members, and there may well have been others. But I would point out to Mr. Lodge, that reference to committees and commissions is made not only in this part of the declaration. He is very well aware that reference to the establishment of commissions, and hence of committees (since "commission" is the generic term for commissions, committees, sub-committees—the precise title is immaterial) is found not only in this part, not only in paragraph 2 of the declaration, but also in paragraph 5. It is in this paragraph that reference is made to actions taken by the Council in connexion with questions of peace and security. And this is of the essence. When paragraph 2 of the declaration, like Article 29 of the Charter, says that the Security Council will "establish such bodies or agencies as it may deem necessary for the performance of its functions", it is referring to bodies, to committees, sub-committees or commissions, which have no connexion with questions of peace and security, that is, with matters within the scope of Chapters VI and VII of the United Nations Charter. The San Francisco declaration is absolutely clear on this point. . . .

Therefore, we cannot consider the committee or sub-committee proposed in the resolution as a subsidiary body established in accordance with Article 29 of the Charter. This body is being set up in connexion with the Security Council's obligations under Chapters VI and VII of the Charter, that is, in connexion with the performance of its functions in the maintenance of international peace and security. And the establishment of such a body is subject to the voting procedure laid down in the Charter, that is to say, it must be treated as a vote on a substantive question to which the unanimity rule applies. This is completely in keeping with the Council's entire previous practice. But what occurred in the Council today constitutes a departure from its previous practice, a break with the San Francisco declaration—for which the sponsors of that declaration, the United States, the United Kingdom and France, are responsible. It also constitutes a violation of the Charter—for which the majority of the Security Council's members are responsible. The resolution adopted today is illegal, as it was adopted in violation of the Charter.

NOTE.—1. The Sub-Committee spent a month in Laos, at the invitation of the Laotian Government. In its report, the Sub-Committee emphasized the distinction between "inquiry" and "investigation", and stated that its task was confined to an inquiry, or "fact-finding", i. e., that "it must receive information on the facts from the Government concerned, rather than seek facts itself on its own initiative," and that it "should not make recommendations." S/4236 (5 November 1959), p. 7; SCOR, XIV, Suppl. for Oct.-Dec. 1959, pp. 10, 14. The Sub-Committee reached the following conclusions:

"According to the documents presented to the Sub-Committee by the Laotian authorities it appears that, especially since 16 July 1959, military actions have taken place on Laotian territory against Laotian army posts and units. According to the same documents these actions increased progressively, reaching their maximum intensity between 30 August and the middle of September, particularly in the Province of Sam Neua, along the River Ma and in the area of Sam Teu.

"According to a document of the Laotian Government, presented to the Sub-Committee on 15 October 1959, the military situation especially in the two provinces of Sam Neua and Phong Saly appears to reflect a regression after 15 September, and the general scope of the military actions has taken the characteristics of guerilla activity, scattered practically throughout the territory of the Kingdom.

"Generally speaking, the Sub-Committee considers that although there were actions of different scope and magnitude, all of them—throughout the four periods (from 16 July to 11 October)—were of a guerrilla character.

"From the statements of the Laotian authorities, and from those of some witnesses, it appears, however, that certain of these hostile operations must have had a centralized coordination.

"Practically all witnesses (forty out of forty-one) stated that the hostile elements received support from the territory of the Democratic Republic of Viet-Nam consisting mainly of equipment, arms, ammunition, supplies, and the help of political cadres. The same emerges from the official Laotian documents submitted and from some of the material exhibits.

"Hostile elements seemed centered around former members of the *Unités Combatantes du Pathet Lao* previously integrated in 1957, the 2nd Battalion of Pathet-Lao, which deserted from the Plaine des Jarres on 11 May 1959, and sections of the frontier minorities (Thais, Meos and a few Khas). According to a document presented to the Sub-Committee by the Laotian Government, participation of regular army units from the Democratic Republic of Viet-Nam were reported during the attacks of the River Ma area on 30 August. The Laotian Government states in another document presented to the Sub-Committee on 15 October, that after 15 September, these units re-crossed the border into North Viet-Nam, excepting those who occupied the section of Laotian territory between the left bank of the River Ma and the frontier. Witnesses reported that in certain cases there had been participation of armed elements with ethnic Viet-Namese characteristics, but they did not identify them as belonging to North Viet-Namese regular army units. The body of information submitted to the Sub-Committee did not clearly establish whether there were crossings of the frontier by regular troops of the Democratic Republic of Viet-Nam." (S/4236, pp. 30–31; SCOR, XIV, Suppl. for Oct.-Dec. 1959) pp. 10, 33–34.

2. For comments on the problem of the "double veto", see Leo GROSS, "The Double Veto and the Four-Power Statement on Voting in the Security Council," 67 Harvard L.R. (1953), pp. 251–80, and "The Question of Laos and the Double Veto in the Security Council," 54 AJIL (1960), pp. 118–31; E. JIMÉNEZ DE ARÉCHAGA, Voting and the Handling of Disputes in the Security Council (New York, 1950), pp. 1–17; Marion K. KELLOGG, "The Laos Question: Double What Veto?" 45 Virginia L. Rev. (1959), pp. 1352–60; A. W. RUDZINSKI, "The So-Called Double Veto," 45 AJIL (1951), pp. 443–61. See also 67 Harvard L.R. (1954), No. 8, pp. vii–xiii.

Chapter V

GENERAL ASSEMBLY

Section 1.   Voting on Important Questions

VOTING ON A RECOMMENDATION TO THE SECURITY
COUNCIL ON ADMISSION OF NEW MEMBERS

Discussion in the General Assembly, 1 February 1952;
GAOR, VI, Plenary, pp. 463-9.

[On 30 January 1952, the First Committee approved by 21 votes to 12, with 25 abstentions a Soviet draft resolution proposing that the General Assembly should note "the increasing general sentiment in favour of the universality of the United Nations," and recommend "that the Security Council reconsider the applications" of thirteen States "and consider the application of Libya." A/2100; GAOR, VI, Annexes, Agenda Item 60, p. 8.   When this draft resolution II was debated in the General Assembly, the following question arose:]

Mr. URRUTIA HOLGUIN (Colombia): Colombia has always supported the principle of universality. Unfortunately, draft resolution II submitted by the Union of Soviet Socialist Republics does not make for unversality. . . .

[T]his draft would finally close the doors of the United Nations to countries other than those named in the list which it contains.

For these reasons, the Colombian delegation will do more than abstain: it will vote against the draft resolution, for we feel it would be most dangerous if this draft resolution, which, I repeat, in our opinion destroys the principle of universality, were passed simply because of a large number of abstentions.

Moreover, we consider that since there can be no subject more important than the admission of new Members, no draft resolution on these lines can be adopted unless two-thirds of the Members present and voting in the Assembly vote for it. Accordingly, if the case should arise, we should want a ruling from the President on this point. . . .

Mr. MICHALOWSKI (Poland): . . .   The representative of Colombia, for obvious reasons, raised here the question of the two-thirds majority in our voting. I wish to state emphatically our opposition to this false interpretation of the principles of the Charter and of our procedure in regard to this draft resolution. Article 18 of the Charter, and also the identically worded rule 84 [85] of the rules of procedure, by no means require a two-thirds majority of the votes for the adoption of this draft resolution. According to these Articles, a two-

232

thirds majority is needed for "the admission of new Members to the United Nations". The USSR draft resolution does not mean the admission of new Members. It is a recommendation to the Security Council that it should reconsider once more thirteen applications and consider one application for the first time, namely that of Libya. Only if the Security Council were to reconsider these applications and were to send a recommendation to the General Assembly in accordance with Article 4 would a two-thirds majority be needed to accomplish the formal admission of these States.

The desire to apply the rule concerning the two-thirds majority to this recommendation does not find any basis in the provisions of the Charter or in the rules of procedure. There are no precedents for this either. On the contrary, all the resolutions during the past years which have recommended a reconsideration of any candidatures have been adopted by a simple majority. Therefore the Polish delegation considers that, for the adoption of the USSR draft resolution, a simple majority of the representatives present and voting is sufficient, in accordance with Article 18, paragraph 3, of the Charter and rule 85 of the rules of procedure. This effort to find a new interpretation is a fresh manoeuvre in order to prevent the admission of fourteen countries to our Organization. . . .

Mr. GROSS (USA): I wish to raise a point of order in connexion with the application of the rules of procedure. It is not clear to my delegation whether a formal request has been made for the application of the two-thirds requirement of the rules of procedure. In any event, I wish now formally to propose the application of the two-thirds rule and, with the permission of the Chair, I should like three minutes in which to explain the reasons in support of that motion.

It seems to my delegation that either rule 84 [85] or rule 85 [86] applies to this situation, and we believe that rule 84 [85] applies to it. We think that this is a question involving "the admission of new Members to the United Nations". What other significance can the USSR draft resolution have if it does not raise an important question regarding the admission of new Members? Unless it involves a recommendation to the Security Council to consider favourably and recommend the admission of the applicants listed in the draft resolution, it means nothing at all. It would merely be a repetition in different language of the Peruvian draft resolution which the Assembly adopted earlier today.

The USSR representative and all the speakers who have indicated their intention to vote for the USSR draft resolution have explained that the reason for doing so and the underlying purpose of the USSR draft resolution is to obtain a declaration of policy from the General Assembly that all the applicants listed in the draft resolution should be admitted to membership. It is a declaration of policy of the most serious import, as has been demonstrated and admitted by the USSR representative himself. Moreover, it involves a fundamental interpretation by the General Assembly of Article 4 of the Charter.

If it is not an important question it is not a question at all. Even if—and I conclude with this comment—rule 84 [85] does not apply, even if this is not a question involving the admission of new Members, it is, for the reasons I have just stated, an important question.

It is obviously, therefore, at least under rule 85 [86], the type of question which the General Assembly by a majority vote may in its discretion consider to be a category of questions additional to those specified in rule 84 [85] and thus subject to a two-thirds majority procedure.

The representative of Poland, I think, requires correction. If I understood him correctly, he said that in the past resolutions regarding a recommendation on membership have been adopted by a simple majority and the two-thirds question has not been raised. A careful survey of the history of the matter from 1948 until 1950 will show to the Members of the Assembly that all membership resolutions have been adopted or rejected by a vote of well over two-thirds of the membership. It is for that reason—and I am confident for that reason alone—that the two-thirds question has not been raised previously.

The PRESIDENT [Mr. Luis Padilla Nervo, Mexico]: . . . My opinion is that rule 84 [85], constituting as it does an exception to the general rule that the Assembly's decisions shall be taken by a simple majority except on the questions specifically mentioned in rule 84 [85] and on any other questions which the Assembly considers important enough to require a two-thirds majority in accordance with rule 85 [86]—my opinion, I repeat, is that the reference in rule 84 [85] to the admission of new Members applies to substantive decisions taken by the Assembly on this subject.

I cannot judge the draft resolution on which we are about to vote except by its actual text. As you are aware, the text states in the preamble that it is the judgment of the Organization which will determine whether the States are able to carry out the obligations laid down in the Charter and whether they are prepared to submit their international complaints or disputes for settlement by the measures established under international law. And, in its operative part, it recommends that the Security Council should consider these applications.

My opinion therefore is that rule 84 [85] does not apply to this draft resolution. However, I do not wish to state this in the form of a ruling from the Chair. In accordance with the United States representative's motion, I think that in this case, in order to avoid establishing any dangerous precedents for the future, it would be better for the Assembly to settle the matter and express its opinion on the majority required only in this particular case.

Accordingly, the Assembly will have to decide whether, in its view, this draft resolution, to be adopted, requires a two-thirds majority of the Members present and voting. . . .

It was decided by 29 votes to 21, with 5 abstentions, that the adoption of draft resolution II required a two-thirds majority of the Members present and voting.

The PRESIDENT: We shall now proceed to vote upon draft resolution II. A roll-call vote has been requested, and the General Assembly has just decided that a two-thirds majority is required for adoption. . . .

The result of the vote was 22 in favour, 21 against, with 16 abstentions.

Draft resolution II was not adopted, having failed to obtain the required two-thirds majority.

Prince WAN WAITHAYAKON (Thailand): I wish to explain my vote on the procedural question. It depended on the interpretation to be attached to draft resolution II. It is true that in form it is a recommendation to the Security Council for reconsideration of the applications from the countries enumerated, but I put to myself the question whether that meant a recommendation to the Security Council for a completely free reconsideration. My reading of the draft resolution is that it is in fact a recommendation to the Security Council for a favourable reconsideration, and that is why I think it is a substantive and important question and therefore requires a two-thirds majority. Had it been a mere recommendation for a free reconsideration by the Security Council I would have voted differently.

NOTE.—1. Similar questions with respect to voting on "important" matters arose also in several other cases; e. g., with respect to resolutions relating to the Treatment of Indians in South Africa (held to require a two-thirds majority), South West Africa (held to be an "important" question), Libya (held not to require a two-thirds majority), information from non-self-governing territories (at the second session held to require a two-thirds majority, and at the eighth session held to require a simple majority only), and amendments to the Statute of the UN Administrative Tribunal (held to require a simple majority). 1 UN Repertory, pp. 575–86; *idem*, Supp. 1, Vol. I, pp. 199–201.

2. The following problems have also arisen as to voting in the General Assembly:

(a) What majority is required for the adoption of amendments to proposals or parts of proposals relating to important questions. See GA, Rules of Procedure, R. 86; Report of the Secretary-General of 11 September 1950 (A/1356), GAOR, Annexes (V) 49, pp. 1–6; 1 UN Repertory, pp. 568–9, 592–3.

(b) Is the majority required for a decision to be calculated on the basis of all the votes cast by "members present and voting", including those who abstained, or only on the basis of the number of affirmative and negative votes? See GA, Rules of Procedure, R. 88; 1 UN Repertory, pp. 569–70.

(c) What questions are "budgetary questions" and require, in consequence, decisions by a two-thirds majority? See 1 UN Repertory, pp. 591–2.

(d) After the results of a vote in the General Assembly have been announced, can a member request that his vote be "corrected"? Can this be done, in particular, if such a correction would affect the outcome of the vote as announced? See the report of the Secretary-General of 30 September 1955, A/2977; and the report of the Sixth Committee of 22 November 1955, A/3040; GAOR, Annexes (X) 51, pp. 1–10, 13–15.

3. See also Allan HOVEY, Jr., "Voting Procedure in the General Assembly," 4 Int.Org. (1950), pp. 412–7; Ernest L. KERLEY, "Voting on Important Questions in the United Nations General Assembly," 53 AJIL (1959), pp. 324–40; F.A. VALLAT, "Voting in the General Assembly of the United Nations," 31 BYBIL (1954), pp. 273–98.

VOTING ON A QUESTION RELATING TO THE APPLICABILITY
OF CHAPTER XI OF THE CHARTER TO NEW MEMBERS
OF THE UNITED NATIONS

Discussion in the General Assembly, 20 February 1957, GAOR, XI,
Plenary, pp. 1153–1166.

[The question of voting on questions relating to non-self-governing territories was considered at several sessions of the General Assembly. See, e. g., 1 UN Repertory of Practice, pp. 582–86. The issue arose again at the eleventh session of the General Assembly in connection with Draft Resolution VI of the Fourth Committee relating to the establishment of an *Ad Hoc* Committee "to study the application of the provisions of Chapter XI of the Charter in the case of Members newly admitted to the United Nations." A/3531 and Add.1 (13 and 20 February 1957); GAOR, Annexes (XI) 34, p. 20.]

Mrs. AHMAN (Sweden): The very fact that a full debate in the plenary meeting on draft resolution VI has been requested and agreed to indicates the importance of this question. The Swedish delegation feels that the question with which draft resolution VI deals is of such importance that the rule of the two-thirds majority should be applied to it.

During the debate in the Fourth Committee, most of the speakers underlined the importance of the subject with which this draft resolution deals. The representative of Iraq, who opened the debate at the 615th meeting of the Committee, began by saying:

"We are beginning a debate of a crucial and perhaps unparalleled importance. Rarely has the Fourth Committee been faced with a question that raises such vital and far-reaching issues. The whole concept of the sacred trust inherent in Chapter XI of the Charter will come under review. . . . The problem before us, therefore, goes beyond the immediate interests of one or more Member States: it touches on matters of fundamental principles and affects every aspect of the work that has been accomplished in the last eleven years."

At the 619th meeting of the Committee, the Polish representative observed that the problem facing the Committee was a very serious one since it involved the obligations of Member States resulting from the Charter, and the sovereign rights of States. The representative of Guatemala stated at the 621st meeting of the Committee that, owing to the importance of the matter and the questions of principle it raised, it was necessary once again to consider the interpretation of certain aspects of Chapter XI of the Charter, and to decide how its provisions applied to the case in point. . . .

Although this accent on the importance of the draft resolution with which we are now concerned has been very noticeable all through our debates, there were actually a few speakers in the Fourth Committee who tried to play down its importance by representing the draft resolution as a purely procedural one which did not affect the substance of the matter. Those attempts have not convinced my delegation. True, the draft resolution is procedural in the sense that it proposes a procedure, it sets up machinery. If this yardstick is to be applied, the resolutions, in the past, setting up the Special Committee on Information and its successors, and the Committee on Factors, were also procedural ones. The General Assembly apparently did not think so at that time.

When the Special Committee on Information was set up in 1947, the Assembly expressly decided that the rule concerning a two-thirds majority vote should be applied. The following year, when the Committee was renewed, the Rapporteur of the Fourth Committee pointed out that a two-thirds majority was required, and there was no objection from the Assembly. In 1949, there was no discussion of the two-thirds rule, but the resolution was, in effect, adopted by a two-thirds majority. Again, in 1952, the Rapporteur suggested that the draft resolution on the renewal of the Committee on Information was such as to require a two-thirds majority and nobody objected.

When the Committee on Factors was first set up in January 1952, there was an inconclusive discussion on the applicability of the two-thirds majority rule. However, in effect, the vote was by a two-thirds majority. At its seventh session, the General Assembly appointed a new Committee on Factors, and on that occasion the vote was made subject to Article 18, paragraph 2, of the Charter at the request of one delegation.

The Swedish delegation thinks it is obvious that the Assembly should follow those precedents, which are closely related to the case now before the Assembly. They were not considered procedural, and the draft resolution before us cannot be termed procedure with any more justification.

The creation of the *ad hoc* committee, proposed in draft resolution VI, is not an end in itself. The committee has to have a specific task, and this task is laid down in the terms of reference given to it. Those

terms of reference necessarily concern the substance of the matter.
The purpose in setting up the committee is to have a study made of
the application of Chapter XI of the Charter in the case of Members
newly admitted to the United Nations, and in particular of the replies to the Secretary-General's letter of 24 February 1956 by which
the new Members were required to inform him whether they were
responsible for the administration of any of the territories referred
to in Article 73. This most certainly involves the obligations of Member States resulting from the Charter, and the sovereign rights of
States, to use once more the words of the Polish representative in the
Fourth Committee. . . .

We ought to have enough respect for the fundamental law of our
Organization not to allow a simple majority to open the door to interpretations of the Charter which affect the sovereign rights of Member States, and which constitute, in fact, amendments to the Charter.

I formally move that draft resolution VI be considered an important
question within the provisions of Article 18, paragraph 2, requiring
a two-thirds majority. I should like the vote on this motion to be
taken by roll-call. . . .

Mr. BOZOVIC (Yugoslavia): A motion has just been made by the
representative of Sweden to the effect that draft resolution VI entitled
"General question relating to the transmission of information under
Article 73e of the Charter" should be voted upon by a two-thirds majority. The motion has been supported by the argument that the draft
resolution concerns an important question within the terms of Article
18, paragraph 2, of the Charter or an important question within the
terms of our rules of procedure.

The question whether draft resolutions or, it may be more correct
to say, some draft resolutions, relating to the application of Chapter
XI of the Charter should or should not be voted upon by a two-thirds
majority is, as everyone in this Assembly knows, not a new one. It
has been raised in the past and, significantly enough, almost always
in cases where the interests of one or more Administering Powers were
involved. In this case, I submit that the reason is the same.

The report of the Fourth Committee contains seven draft resolutions concerned with matters relating to non-self-governing peoples—
to hundreds of millions of peoples. By singling out one of them and
declaring it important, the representative of Sweden clearly implies
that the other draft resolutions are unimportant. It is easy to understand the reasons why the representaive of Sweden seems to consider
these resolutions unimportant. I must confess, in all sincerity, that
the arguments on the basis of which she has singled out one of these
draft resolutions is not quite clear to me.

First of all it seems to me that the manner in which the question
has been raised is not the most appropriate one. In our view, we are
not concerned here with the question whether the problems discussed

by the General Assembly are important or not because we believe that
all issues which are debated here are important. The problem is what
working procedure we should apply in regard to some categories of
questions dealt with in the Charter and on what basis action can be
taken by the General Assembly in respect of them. In our opinion, the
answer to this question should be sought in the Charter and in the
rules of procedure.

Article 18, paragraph 2, says:

"2. Decisions of the General Assembly on important questions
shall be made by a two-thirds majority of the Members present and
voting. These questions shall include: . . . " and then there is
an enumeration of different categories of questions which have to be
voted on, in any case, by a two-thirds majority. Of course it is possible that, owing to some ambiguity, the English text of the Charter
might have misled the representative of Sweden. The part of Article
18, paragraph 2, which I have just read says "These questions shall
include . . . " and this is followed by the enumeration. This
has apparently led the representative of Sweden to believe that the
enumeration included in paragraph 2 of Article 18 is not exhaustive.

The English text of the Charter is not the only official text and if,
in a legal document which is valid in two or more languages, one is
open to doubt, and another is precise, then the interpretation has to be
taken from the more precise text. The French text says:

"2. Les décisions de l'Assemblée Générale sur les questions importantes sont prises à la majorité des deux-tiers des membres présents
et votant. Sont considérées comme questions importantes: . . . "
This is the part which concerns us. It means that the decisions on
important questions are made by a two-thirds majority and then the
definition of important questions follows: "Sont considérées comme
questions importantes: . . . " This means that the enumeration
of questions which should be considered as important, according to
the Charter, is exhaustive. If that were not the case, there would be
no need whatsoever to have Article 18, paragraph 3, in the Charter:
paragraph 3 provides that the General Assembly can add to the enumeration additional categories of questions to be decided by a two-
thirds majority. In other words, if, as has been claimed in the past,
paragraph 2 of Article 18 had not given an exhaustive list of questions for which a two-thirds majority was categorically required and
is required, why would the framers of the Charter, which is reputed
to be a concise document, have taken the trouble of adding another
paragraph providing for decisions on other questions?

Here again the English text of the Charter might be misleading.
Paragraph 3 says: "Decisions on other questions" and [the] representative of Sweden might have asked herself, "What other questions?"
Of course she is not the only one to be confused in this respect because
one of the best commentators on the Charter, Mr. Hans Kelsen, says:

"The words 'other questions' are ambiguous. They may mean questions other than important ones, that is to say, unimportant questions, the enumeration in paragraph 2—in conformity with the wording in this paragraph—being not exhaustive. But they may also mean: questions other than those enumerated in paragraph 2. Then this enumeration is exhaustive."

It seems that the same thoughts were entertained by the drafters of our rules of procedure. If the representative of Sweden would glance at rule 87 of the rules of procedure, she would find an answer to the question put forth by Mr. Kelsen.

According to Kelsen, and according to our interpretation of the Charter, which we consider to be correct and outside of procedural wranglings, rule 87 means that the drafters of the rules of procedure considered that paragraph 2 of Article 18 was exhaustive. In this connexion, Kelsen said:

"If the enumeration of paragraph 2 is considered to be exhaustive, only two problems are possible: it may be doubtful whether a concrete matter falls within the categories enumerated; or whether a matter about which there is no doubt that it does not fall within these categories, falls within a category which should be added to those enumerated in paragraph 2. If the enumeration of 'important' questions is exhaustive, the question as to whether the decision on a concrete matter requires a two-thirds majority can be answered only by deciding that the question does, or does not, fall within the categories enumerated in paragraph 2, or if there is no doubt that the concrete question"—in this case, the question under draft resolution VI—"does not fall within these categories, by deciding that the category within which this concrete question falls shall be added. All questions are to be decided, according to paragraph 3, by a simple majority. But, if the enumeration of paragraph 2 is exhaustive, it is not possible"— and I stress this—"it is not possible to determine that the decision on a concrete matter which does not fall within the enumerated categories, requires a two-thirds majority (because it is important), without determining, at the same time, that the category in which this matter falls shall be added to those enumerated in paragraph 2."

In the light of what I have just quoted, as well as in the light of the fact that the representative of Sweden requested that a two-thirds majority vote be applied, the question may arise whether the matter dealt with in draft resolution VI falls within one of the categories enumerated in Article 18, paragraph 2, of the Charter, or in rule 85 of the rules of procedure; if the answer is "Yes", then within which of them. . . .

I shall now refer to Article 18, paragraph 3, which states: "Decisions on other questions"—other than those enumerated in paragraph 2 of the same Article—". . . . shall be made by a majority of the members present and voting." These other questions—and I repeat this, in citing rule 87 of the rules of procedure, which states: "other than those provided for in rule 85", which is the exact reproduction of Article 18, paragraph 2—include the "determination of additional categories of questions to be decided by a two-thirds majority."

From this text, it clearly appears that the General Assembly may add, and has the right to add, to the enumeration in paragraph 2 important, additional categories of questions to be decided by a two-thirds majority vote. This Article, as can be seen, does not entitle the General Assembly to add to the enumeration in paragraph 2 additional, individual questions, as the representative of Sweden would like to interpret it, if such questions do not fall within one of the categories of questions mentioned in paragraph 2, or previously added as a category to that enumeration.

This was the opinion of one of the earlier Presidents of the General Assembly. Summing up the debate on the question of the treatment of persons of Indian origin in the Union of South Africa, the President of the General Assembly concluded that the terms of Article 18, paragraph 3, referred not to individual questions, but to categories of questions. The decision then that the two-thirds majority rule should apply to the question of the treatment of persons of Indian origin was based upon the interpretation that it belonged to the category of questions related to the maintenance of international peace and security.

So far as we are concerned, there is no doubt whatsoever that Article 18, paragraph 3, under which the General Assembly would presumably have to decide, means that the General Assembly is entitled only to add additional categories of questions, but it is not entitled by the Charter to add individual questions to those enumerated in paragraph 2.

Contrary to the view held by some delegations, we have always believed that questions relating to non-self-governing peoples are important, and I am happy to note that the representative of Sweden has just declared that she holds the same view. But the reason why we have not requested that a vote should always be taken by a two-thirds majority, with regard to this question, is that it was our wish to adhere to the Charter and to avoid amending the Charter provisions through manoeuvring of a procedural character.

The Charter has left these questions out of Article 18, paragraph 2, and we wish to respect this provision of the Charter. We do not, of course, deny the right of other delegations to do it, provided their actions are in conformity with the Charter.

The idea of the representative of Sweden would, of course, be in conformity with the Charter if it translated the opinion just expressed: that all of the questions relating to colonial territories are important, and if she, according to her opinion, requested the addition of new categories of questions relating to the application of Chapter XI as a whole. In that case, I can assure my colleagues that the vote of my delegation would be different from the vote that we are going to cast in connexion with the Swedish proposal. However, the manner in which the proposal was drafted is, so far as we are concerned, outside of the scope of the Charter—I would not like to say contrary to the Charter—and, therefore, my delegation will have to oppose the proposal. . . .

Mr. PACHACHI (Iraq): . . . It has been established beyond any doubt that matters relating to Non-Self-Governing Territories— that is to say, matters falling within the scope of Chapter XI of the Charter—should be decided by a simple rather than a two-thirds majority vote, irrespective of whether the question under consideration is important or not. This opinion is based on legal texts, on precedent, and—we submit, in all humility—on common sense. . . .

Let me take first Article 18, paragraph 2, of the Charter. It is our contention that the list of categories of questions enumerated in that paragraph is exhaustive, despite the appearance of the unfortunate word "include." This word has created some confusion in the past— as, indeed, it still does today. Doubts have arisen whether the enumeration appearing in paragraph 2 of Article 18 provides a definition of the term "important questions" or merely gives examples of some— but not all—of the categories of "important questions." This confusion and these doubts disappear, however, when we look at the French text—which, I understand, the representative of Yugoslavia read at the 656th meeting.

As the representative of Yugoslavia said on a similar occasion more than three years ago, in choosing between two equally authentic texts, the text that is more precise should be preferred over the doubtful and ambiguous text—which, in this case, is the English text.

If any doubt still remains on this point, it should be dispelled by reading paragraph 3 of Article 18. It will be noted that the reference in this paragraph is not to other important questions, but rather to other categories of questions which may be voted on by a two-thirds majority if the Assembly so desires. That is to say, the Assembly, in taking such a decision, will not be called upon to pronounce on the importance of any question, because in reality it cannot justifiably do so, since the question of importance is necessarily a relative one and is often a matter of individual opinion. What is important to us might be less important to others—and vice versa.

Furthermore, as Professor Hans Kelsen said, everything that is considered by this world organization is important, and the distinction appearing in Article 18 was not due to a desire to differentiate between important and unimportant questions, but rather "to differentiate decisions which require a two-thirds majority and decisions which require only a simple majority". Therefore, a decision taken in accordance with Article 18, paragraph 3, will not and cannot be a decision on the relative importance of single questions; it is a decision on

whether additional categories of questions other than those specifically mentioned in paragraph 2 of Article 18 shall be subjected to the two-
thirds-majority rule.

Two main conclusions must be drawn from reading these texts.
First, the only questions automatically requiring a two-thirds majority
are those enumerated in paragraph 2 of Article 18.   .   .   .   The
second conclusion is that, by deciding not to invoke the two-thirds-majority rule, the Assembly would not be pronouncing itself on the importance of the question under discussion, but would merely be determining whether or not an additional category should come under the
two-thirds-majority rule. It is therefore wrong to claim that, merely
because a question is regarded as important, it should be decided by a
two-thirds majority, so long as it is not specifically mentioned in Article 18, paragraph 2. Our attitude on this, I submit, should be based
on past experience.

Let us look now at the precedents which we have. The debate at
the eighth session provides us with a clear and useful guide. Despite
the admitted importance of the questions discussed during that session
of the General Assembly, namely the question of the factors that should
be taken into account in determining whether the people of a Territory had or had not attained a full measure of self-government and the
question of the cessation of the transmission of information on Puerto
Rico, these two questions were decided by a simple majority, although
their importance and significance could not have escaped the attention
of the majority of the Assembly that voted in favour of the simple-
majority rule. In its wisdom, the Assembly decided that, since those
questions did not belong to any categories specifically mentioned in
Article 18, paragraph 2, there was no reason why it should restrict
its rights and freedom of action by invoking the two-thirds-majority
rule.

It is hard for us to believe that the Assembly should deviate
from this wise course now and change its opinion with regard to the
draft resolution now before the Assembly.

If it is a question of importance, then surely no one, and least of
all the proposer of the motion, can seriously claim that a procedural
act such as the setting up of an *ad hoc* committee is more important
than the adoption of the list of factors, or a decision on whether the
people of a Non-Self-Governing Territory have attained a full measure
of self-government.

Let us look at the draft resolution before us, particularly with the
inclusion of the amendments submitted by the four Powers. In it,
the General Assembly recalls certain resolutions which have been recalled many times in the past. It decides to set up an *ad hoc* committee for the sole purpose of studying—and I stress the word "studying", because there is nothing in the draft resolution that gives the
slightest hint or indication of anything other than a study—the ap-

plication of certain provisions of the Charter which, it is commonly agreed, need further elucidation. In the name of logic and common sense, how can anyone suggest now that this simple, straight-forward and entirely procedural draft resolution should be considered as more important than the two resolutions, one on factors and the other on Puerto Rico, which were adopted at the eighth session? I feel sure that all of the thirty-four delegations which voted for the simple-majority procedure at the eighth session will have even more reason to do so at this session in respect of a draft resolution that is admittedly less important than the two which were adopted at the eighth session.

The inescapable conclusion is that the proposer of the motion is not really interested in deciding whether this is an important question or not. The aim is clear and simple in all its naked crudeness. It is to defeat the draft resolution and thus frustrate and obstruct the will of the majority of the Assembly. The important question, and, indeed, the ultimate aim, is to paralyse the Assembly and place its future decisions on Chapter XI at the mercy of a minority which has consistently denied the rights of the Assembly and viewed colonial questions, as, rather, the exclusive concern of the Administering Powers.

I need hardly stress the importance of the decision we are about to take on this procedural matter. The consequences for Chapter XI, and all the machinery so elaborately constructed over the years, might well be catastrophic. Therefore, I appeal to all those who have laboured continually to breathe life into the declaration regarding Non-Self-Governing Territories, to all those who have upheld the rights and prerogatives of this Assembly, to all those who believe that the United Nations has an important and constructive role to play in the progress of dependent peoples—I appeal to them all to reject this proposal. . . .

Mr. SERRANO (Philippines): I understand that we are confined to the procedural question whether the draft resolution presented to this Assembly by the Fourth Committee should require a simple-majority or a two-thirds-majority vote. In order to settle this procedural question we must determine whether the question to be decided upon is important or not, within the meaning of Article 18 of the Charter.

I must state that I approach this procedural question with great caution, even with trepidation. I have noted with deep regret certain statements made by our colleagues in this Assembly to the effect that those who are taking the position that this matter requires a two-thirds-majority vote, appear to be taking a step that would frustrate the obligations to be assumed by an Administering Power in connexion with a Non-Self-Governing Territory. I hope that this question, although procedural, will be viewed with great objectivity and that any accusations with regard to the existence of ulterior motives as far as the vote is concerned, will be completely dismissed.

As far as my delegation is concerned, we view with great concern the question of the responsibilities of an Administering Member in so far as a Non-Self-Governing Territory is concerned. But, I must also state that this question cannot be pressed with the passion of prejudice. It is important that we view this delicate question in the light of the Charter and that justice should be observed.

In this connexion we have been reminded of precedents, in determining whether or not the question is an important one. We are also reminded of the meaning of Article 18 of the Charter. At this point, I must state in all candour that I do not find the interpretation of Article 18 of the Charter a very difficult matter. The Article simply states, in paragraph 2, that "decisions on important questions shall be made by a two-thirds majority". It then proceeds to list some of these important questions. It is an elementary rule of law that, so far as the principle of construction is concerned, whenever a general provision is followed by a specification of cases, that specification shall be construed as being merely an illustration of the general rule.

It must follow that the statements here relating to the maintenance of international peace and security, the election of the non-permanent members of the Security Council, the admission of new Members, election to important organs of the United Nations, and questions relating to the operation of the Trusteeship System and the suspension of privileges and rights of all Members, are merely illustrations of the important questions within the meaning of paragraph 2 of this Article. They are not designed or intended to be exhaustive in character.

This view is strengthened by the provision of paragraph 3 of Article 18, which envisages situations or cases which are in addition to those enumerated in paragraph 2, but the voting on those questions, of course, should be by a simple majority.

Going back to the precedents, I understand that at the eighth session some kind of decision was taken by this Assembly on the cases of Puerto Rico and other islands to the effect that in any question relating to a Non-Self-Governing Territory a simple-majority vote would be sufficient. Assuming that this is intended to be a precedent—and I am not quite prepared to agree that it is intended to be a precedent—should it apply to this case or could it be made to apply to this case? I hold the view that it cannot apply, because when we speak of a question relating to any matter pertaining to a Non-Self-Governing Territory there is an assumption that the Territory is non-self-governing. That is the assumption, and the only thing that is intended by the rule which has governed the action of this Assembly relates to the discharge of the responsibilities of the Administering Power with respect to the Non-Self-Governing Territory.

For instance, if the question arises whether the Administering Power has promoted to the utmost the welfare of the inhabitants of the

Non-Self-Governing Territory, if the question arises whether the Administering Power has sought to ensure the political, economic, social and educational advancement of the people of the Non-Self-Governing Territory or whether it has sought to promote the political institutions of the Non-Self-Governing Territory, then it is a question which pertains to a Non-Self-Governing Territory and therefore the simple-majority rule shall apply.

Is this the case at issue before us, in so far as the draft resolution is concerned? I must state, in all candour, that it is not, because the draft resolution before us envisages an *ad hoc* committee which would study the application of the provisions of Chapter XI to new Member States admitted to the United Nations. The purpose, therefore, of this *ad hoc* committee is to determine whether certain Members of the United Nations have an obligation under the Charter to administer certain Non-Self-Governing Territories. It is a question not only whether an Administering Power has failed to comply, but whether it has complied, with certain specific obligations in connexion with Non-Self-Governing Territories. It is a fundamental question whether a State assumes those responsibilities under the Charter or not. That is the primary question involved in the draft resolution recommended by the Fourth Committee. Therefore, in my opinion, the precedents which have been mentioned here, far from being applicable to this case, cannot apply to it. This is how I, with my legal training, analyse this question.

On the other hand, apart from the fact that mention has been made quite extensively in the Fourth Committee of the unprecedented importance of the creation of this *ad hoc* committee, we must not fail to consider the committee's terms of reference. I note that the draft resolution gives the *ad hoc* committee the authority "to study the application of the provisions of Chapter XI of the Charter". If it were merely a question of creating an *ad hoc* committee, I would say without hesitation that it was a procedural question. But if you examine the terms of reference, simple as they appear to be since the committee is called upon only "to study the application of the provisions of Chapter XI" to certain Member States, and if you press the terms of reference to their logical conclusion, you will note that in the discharge of its duties this *ad hoc* committee may come to grips with the constitutional rights of Member States. It is quite likely that it will tread on very dangerous ground. In discharging its duties, the *ad hoc* committee may come up against the question of the equality and sovereignty of States Members of the United Nations. And again, if the *ad hoc* committee decides that a particular State falls within the provisions of Article 73 of the Charter, you can see what tremendous responsibilities will be placed on the shoulders of that Member State—the responsibilities enumerated in Article 73 of the Charter. That is the tremendous importance of the *ad hoc* committee which this draft resolution seeks to create. For this reason, we hold the view that, even as we would wish and we would bend every effort to see to it that the Administering Power should, in fact, discharge its responsibilities under the Charter scrupulously, we cannot apply that principle until it is a clear case that that State has in fact assumed its responsibilities under Article 73. We are aware that the question is in doubt and that this draft resolution merely seeks to determine which Member States fall under the provisions of the Article, but we are constrained to hold the view that although the creation of the *ad hoc* committee is in itself procedural, the discharge of the committee's tasks will require it to undertake terrible responsibilities. Because of that, we believe that the question is an important one and should be decided by a two-thirds majority in this Assembly. . . .

The PRESIDENT: The Swedish proposal is to the effect that draft resolution VI shall be considered an important question within the provisions of Article 18, paragraph 2, requiring a two-thirds majority. I will now ask the Assembly to vote on this motion; a roll-call vote has been requested.

A vote was taken by roll-call.

The Netherlands, having been drawn by lot by the President, was called upon to vote first.

In favour: Netherlands, New Zealand, Norway, Pakistan, Paraguay, Peru, Philippines, Portugal, Spain, Sweden, Thailand, Turkey, Union of South Africa, United Kingdom of Great Britain and Northern Ireland, United States of America, Uruguay, Venezuela, Argentina, Australia, Austria, Belgium, Brazil, Canada, Chile, China, Colombia, Cuba, Denmark, Dominican Republic, Ecuador, Finland, France, Iceland, Ireland, Israel, Italy, Japan, Luxembourg.

Against: Poland, Romania, Saudi Arabia, Sudan, Syria, Tunisia, Ukrainian Soviet Socialist Republic, Union of Soviet Socialist Republics, Yemen, Yugoslavia, Afghanistan, Albania, Bulgaria, Burma, Byelorussian Soviet Socialist Republic, Ceylon, Czechoslovakia, Egypt, El Salvador, Ethiopia, Greece, Guatemala, Haiti, India, Indonesia, Iran, Iraq, Jordan, Lebanon, Liberia, Libya, Mexico, Morocco, Nepal.

Abstaining: Nicaragua, Bolivia, Cambodia, Costa Rica, Honduras, Laos.

The proposal was adopted by 38 votes to 34, with 6 abstentions.

[While Draft Resolutions I–V and VII were approved by large majorities, the vote on Draft Resolution VI was 35 in favor, 35 against, and 5 abstentions. It was, therefore, rejected.]

NOTE. When the question of the voting procedure applicable to resolutions of the General Assembly on matters concerning non-self-governing territories was raised again at the twelfth session of the General Assembly, the Secretary-General presented a working paper to the Sixth Committee summarizing the practice of the United Nations. A/C.6/L.408 (13 November

1957); GAOR, Annexes (XII) 35, pp. 19–26. At the same session of the General Assembly suggestions were made for obtaining an opinion on the subject from the International Court of Justice, or at least from the Sixth Committee. *Idem,* pp. 16–17, 29–30. The General Assembly decided that the two-thirds majority rule should be applied to one of the resolutions then before it and the resolution was defeated. GAOR, XII, Plenary, pp. 516–17. At the thirteenth session, in 1958, the General Assembly decided not to act on a similar resolution after the issue of voting majority was raised. GAOR, XIII, Plenary, p. 584.

Section 2. Weighted Voting

REPRESENTATION AND VOTING IN THE GENERAL ASSEMBLY

Excerpts from Francis O. WILCOX, Representation and Voting in the United Nations General Assembly (US Senate, Committee on Foreign Relations, Subcommittee on the United Nations Charter, Staff Study No. 4; 1954), pp. 1–23. Footnotes omitted.

I. *Introductory Comments*

It is a curious fact that while public opinion in the United States has been deeply disturbed over the veto and the problem of voting in the U. N. Security Council, there has been relatively little interest in the problem of voting in the General Assembly. This remains true in spite of the fact that the prestige and influence of the Security Council have been on the wane and the star of the General Assembly has been rising.

As the charter was drafted, voting power in the Security Council, where decisions on all substantive questions require the concurring votes of the five permanent members, is heavily weighted in favor of the great powers. In the General Assembly, where all states have an equal voice, the scales are balanced in favor of the smaller nations. The great powers were willing to accept such an arrangement at the San Francisco Conference because they believed their interests would be adequately protected by their right of veto in the Security Council. At the time this seemed a reasonable assumption. The Security Council was charged with the primary responsibility for the mainte- nance of peace and it was in that body that the really important deci- sions of the U. N. were to be taken. The General Assembly, which possessed only the power of recommendation, was destined, they be- lieved, to be an organ of lesser political significance.

This estimate of the situation proved wrong. Gradually, as the tension between the Soviet bloc and the free world has increased, the importance of the Security Council—when compared with that of the General Assembly—has declined. During the past few years that organ has been greatly handicapped by the excessive use of the veto on the part of the Soviet Union. . . . .

Given this shift of power within the U. N. structure, the importance of a reconsideration of the voting procedures in the General Assembly becomes apparent.　Thus far relatively few suggestions for changes in the existing system have been made.　In any event, it will be helpful to examine briefly present voting practices in the General Assembly and then turn to the proposals that have been advanced to amend the charter in this regard.

II.　*Present Voting Practices in the General Assembly*

In the past, international organizations ordinarily have been based on two fundamental principles: the legal equality of states and unanimity in voting.　In practice this has meant that nations like Luxembourg and Iceland, with very small populations, have participated in international assemblies on a basis of legal equality with large nations like the United States, China, and India.　"Russia and Geneva have equal rights," declared Chief Justice Marshall in 1825, and this principle of state equality applied to international conferences (as well as to international commerce).

It has meant, too, that whenever the decision stage has been reached at an international conference, any small state, as well as any large one, has been in a position to block action on substantive questions by casting a negative vote.　Sometimes little countries have responded to the pressure of other states and have abandoned their opposition; at other times they have prevented conferences from arriving at decisions which, but for their opposition, might have been unanimously approved.

At the San Francisco Conference the framers of the U. N. Charter accepted the first of these principles but rejected the second.　.　.　.

The fundamental proposition, expressed in article 2, that the U. N. is based on the sovereign equality of all its members is reiterated in article 18.　Each member is given one vote.　.　.　.

With respect to the principle of unanimity, the charter turns its back upon the past.　No doubt the experience of the League of Nations was, in large part, responsible for this departure.　Article 5 of the League Covenant, in effect, gave every member of the League a veto by providing that, with certain exceptions, "decisions at any meeting of the Assembly or of the Council shall require the agreement of all the members of the League represented at the meeting."　This requirement by no means paralyzed the League Assembly.　It did, however, hamper its activity and on some occasions prevented it from reaching important decisions strongly advocated by a majority of the members.

Article 18 of the charter provides for votes on two types of questions.　The first category includes the so-called important questions which require a two-thirds majority.　The second category includes all other questions and these call for a simple majority.　It will be noted that the majority required under the article is a majority of the members "present and voting."   Members abstaining from the vote are considered as not voting.

By a simple majority the General Assembly may decide that further categories of questions—in addition to those enumerated in article 18—are of sufficient importance to require a two-thirds vote.   It can also modify or abolish these additional categories by a majority of the members present and voting.

The two-thirds majority for the handling of important questions seems to have worked fairly well in practice.   No doubt it has served as a deterrent to hasty and ill-considered action by the General Assembly.   On the other hand, it has not prevented action on any measure desired by a large majority of U. N. members.   During the first 6 years of the United Nations, there were some 18 instances in which draft resolutions (or portions of resolutions), received a simple majority in the committees of the General Assembly but were not adopted because they failed to secure the necessary two-thirds vote in the Assembly itself.

The principal effect of article 18 is to reject the veto with respect to General Assembly votes.   This is a move in the direction of democracy in world affairs in that it decreases the negative power of individual states.   At the same time it increases the positive power of groups of states which may wish to band together to accomplish their objectives within the U. N. system.   .   .   .

The principle of one-state-one-vote results in glaring inequalities in the General Assembly.   Only 9 states can boast a population of 40 million or more.   Some 26 states have a population of 5 million or under, including Iceland with 146,000 and Luxembourg with 300,000.   Three countries—China, India and the Soviet Union—contain more than half the total U. N. population of roughly 1,800 million.

Under the circumstances, it is theoretically possible to secure a majority of 31 votes which represent only a little over 5 percent of the population of U. N. members.   A vote of the 21 smallest countries—representing only about 2.3 percent of the U. N. population—could prevent the two-thirds majority needed for the approval of "important" resolutions.   On the other hand, if a contest should arise between the large and small states, a two-thirds majority could be rolled up by 40 of the smallest nations with a population of only about 11 percent.

Clearly, this is a hypothetical danger which probably will never arise in practice in the extreme form referred to above.   U. N. members are unlikely ever to divide on important issues merely because of population differences.   Even so, these figures illustrate the lack of balance which exists between population and voting strength; a very small minority of the U. N. population is in a position to control decisive votes and to frustrate the will of the majority.

Similar inequalities exist with respect to national wealth, productivity, national territory, and other factors.   The U. S. S. R., for example, has a total area of 8,700,000 square miles. This is more than 1,000 times the area of El Salvador. An even greater margin of difference exists with respect to the gross national product. According to the best estimates available some 6 U. N. members had a gross national product of less than $200 million in 1952 or 1953. In contrast, the gross national product of the United States is estimated at $363 billion for 1953. The comparable figure for the Soviet Union is $100 billion, for the United Kingdom, $45 billion, and for France, $39 billion. . . .

The situation has been complicated further by the development of what has come to be known as bloc voting in the General Assembly. By pooling or combining their voting strength on particular issues groups of small states are able to exert an influence far out of proportion to either their population or their political importance.

While this tendency toward bloc voting has developed considerably since 1945, the lineup in the General Assembly varies a great deal depending upon the issue. The five Communist states will invariably be found on the same side. The seven Arab countries often vote as a unit particularly with respect to Israeli-Arab problems and resolutions having to do with dependent areas. In most cases two-thirds of the 20 Latin American states will be found in the same camp.

On the other hand, there is no predictable solidarity among the countries of Western Europe. The Benelux states (Luxembourg, Belgium, and the Netherlands) vote together on some issues as do the Scandinavian countries. The seven British Commonwealth nations rarely vote as a unit. Nevertheless, during the past few years, the free world countries have demonstrated a remarkable unity whenever the most vitial issues are up for a vote. The 52 to 5 vote on the Uniting for Peace Resolution in 1950 is a case in point.

An interesting example of what the small states can do when they are effectively organized emerged during the third session of the General Assembly when the resolution providing for the use of Spanish as one of the working languages of the U. N. was approved by a vote of 32–20 with 5 abstentions. In that case, the small states successfully opposed the permanent members. Latin America and the Arab countries, with a few supporting votes, outvoted the United States, China, three of the British Commonwealth nations, and all of Europe, including the United Kingdom. . . .

III. *Attempts in Past to Change Methods of Voting and Representation*

For a long time the states of the international community have been groping for a satisfactory voting formula that will prove more workable in practice and still be compatible with the principle of state sovereignty. The real need is to find a measuring stick which will reflect in terms of voting power the glaring inequalities in power and importance which now exist among the nations of the world. A brief review of experience to date may be helpful in determining whether a more effective formula can now be developed.

In a number of international organizations extra voting power has been given to states with colonial possessions. This practice was adopted early in the life of the Universal Postal Union and persists to-day. Thus for voting purposes Portuguese colonies in West Africa form a separate country as do the Portuguese colonies in East Africa, Asia, and Oceania. Such an arrangement may have its commendable features in granting some voting power to people who have not yet attained their independence. No one would argue, however, that a formula which gives more votes to Portugal than to India and China together is a very good index of the relative importance of the members.

In some cases, also, attempts have been made to relate the financial contributions of members to their voting power. This was true of the former International Institute of Agriculture established in Rome in 1905. The convention setting up the Institute created five classes of membership with the number of votes allotted to states in each category increasing in arithmetical progression. The contributions of states in the various categories increased in geometric progression.

Article 10 established the various categories as follows :

Groups of nations	Number of votes	Units of assessment
I	5	16
II	4	8
III	3	4
IV	2	2
V	1	1

More successful perhaps are the attempts which have been made to relate voting power to the varying interests of states in a particular problem. The International Sugar Council and the International Wheat Council are cases in point. The new International Sugar Agreement (1953), for example, provides that a total of 2,000 votes are to be apportioned among the Council members, divided equally between the exporting and importing countries. In general, the number of votes assigned to each importing state is related to that state's average imports. Countries like Saudi Arabia and Jordan, with relatively small imports, have 15 votes. The largest importing countries, the United Kingdom and the United States, have 245 votes each. The 1,000 votes allocated to the exporting countries are assigned in much the same fashion.

Decisions of the Sugar Council, in general, are taken by a majority of the votes cast by the exporting states and a majority of the votes cast by the importing states. In all voting, decisions taken by a majority of the importing countries must include the votes of at least one-third of the importing states present and voting. This special proviso results in increasing the voting power of the smaller importing nations whose total votes are only slightly larger than the combined total assigned to the United States and the United Kingdom.

Of a somewhat similar character are the complicated voting procedures used by the International Bank for Reconstruction and Development and the International Monetary Fund. In these organizations, the voting power of each member reflects its proportionate share of the total capital to which the members as a whole have subscribed. As of June 30, 1953, for example, Panama had subscribed to less than 0.005 percent of the bank's capital and was entitled to 252 votes out of a total of 103,865. The United States, on the other end of the spectrum, having subscribed to 35.13 percent of the capital was assigned 32,000 votes, or approximately one-third of the total.

Up to the present time, population has been rarely used in international organizations as a factor in determining voting strength. The new European Consultative Assembly, which is the deliberative organ of the Council of Europe, appears to be one of the few current exceptions to the rule. Article 26 of the Statute of the Council of Europe provides that member states shall be entitled to the number of representatives given below:

Belgium	6	Netherlands	6
Denmark	4	Norway	4
France	18	Sweden	6
Irish Republic	4	United Kingdom	18
Italy	18		
Luxembourg	3	Total	87

It will be seen that while voting strength in the Consultative Assembly is based roughly on population, the scale nevertheless remains weighted in favor of the small states. Thus, Luxembourg with population of less than one one-hundredth that of France nevertheless has one-sixth the number of votes. Moreover, a two-thirds vote is required for all resolutions approved by the Assembly. This means that even if the three largest states—France, Italy, and the United Kingdom—supported a proposal, their combined votes (54) would still be short of the total of 58 necessary for approval.

On the whole it has not been easy to induce states to depart from the principle of one-state-one-vote. It has been done in a few cases where international organizations have been set up to deal with special problems.　It remains for the future, however, to develop a satisfactory voting formula that will be workable in the General Assembly and at the same time acceptable to the members of the U. N.

IV.　*Mr. Dulles' Proposal for Weighted Voting*

In 1950, in his book entitled War or Peace, John Foster Dulles set forth a proposal for weighted voting in the General Assembly.　While his suggestions were general in character they merit careful study, first because they embrace some interesting possibilities, and second because his is the only proposal of its kind which has emerged from official or semiofficial sources.

Mr. Dulles points out that in the Congress we have two ways of voting.　In the Senate each State, regardless of size, has two votes.　New York with its 15 million people, and Nevada with its 150,000, have equal voting strength.　In the House of Representatives, however, where representation is based on population, New York has 45 votes to Nevada's 1.

"I would not abolish in the United Nations," he writes [pp. 191–4], "an Assembly vote which, like that of our Senate, reflects the sovereign equality of all nations and gives them all an equal vote.　But there might be introduced, in addition, a system of 'weighted' voting so that the result would indicate, roughly, a verdict in terms also of ability to play a part in world affairs.　Then it should be provided that decisions on important matters would require a simple majority, rather than two-thirds, under each of the two voting procedures."

Mr. Dulles apparently has in mind other factors in addition to population.　The weight of the General Assembly's recommendations, he contends, would be far greater than they are at present if votes reflected "not merely numbers but also ability to contribute to the maintenance of international peace and security."

This point he stressed again on January 18, 1954, in his statement before the Senate Foreign Relations Committee's special subcommittee on the U. N. Charter.　"If the General Assembly is to assume greater responsibilities," he said, "then should there not be some form of weighted voting, so that nations which are themselves unable to assume serious military or financial responsibilities cannot put those responsibilities on other nations?　Should there be, in some matters, a combination vote whereby affirmative action requires both a majority of all the members, on the basis of sovereign equality, and also a majority vote, on some weighted basis, which takes into account population, resources, and so forth?"

Mr. Dulles' proposal has a great deal of merit.　In the first place, it would not disturb existing machinery.　It is designed to fit into the present organization without any major alterations or adjustments. Mr. Dulles does not suggest the creation of a second Assembly, nor even the need for additional delegates. He merely proposes that each vote in the General Assembly be tallied twice; the first tally would correspond to the present sovereign-state arrangement with each state casting one vote; in the second tally additional votes would be awarded to states depending upon their ability—because of population, productive capacity, armed strength, etc.—to contribute to the maintenance of world peace. A simple majority under each of the two procedures would be necessary for the General Assembly to reach a decision.

This double-barreled vote would have a double-barreled effect. It would not take away from the small nations their ability to protect their vital interests in the United Nations. So long as they could command a simple majority of the votes—and the large majority of U. N. members are relatively small nations—they could prevent decisions which might prove inimical to them. At the same time it would place in the hands of the larger states a potential veto which they could exercise in order to block what they might consider irresponsible action on the part of the smaller countries.

Moreover, if this kind of balanced-weighted voting were introduced, it would equip the General Assembly to assume full responsibility for such organizational matters as the selection of the Secretary General and the admission of new members to the U. N. As things stand now, this responsibility is shared with the Security Council where the negative vote of a permanent member has often blocked action for long periods of time.

Few people would question the logic of bestowing upon the permanent members added weight in connection with important organizational decisions. But it is certainly not logical to permit any single state, by the use of the veto, to tie the hands of the United Nations with respect to such issues. This dilemma could be resolved if the interests of the great powers were reflected by an appropriate system of weighted voting in the General Assembly. In such an event the responsibility of the Security Council with respect to such matters might well be brought to an end.

As ingenious as Mr. Dulles' plan is, it raises certain extremely difficult questions. Would the smaller nations agree to any proposal which reduces the relative importance of their role in the General Assembly? At the San Francisco Conference they bitterly resented the privileged position given to the great powers in the United Nations. By the same token would they not now resist any adverse readjustment in the balance of power that was so carefully worked out at San Francisco?

More important still, what criteria would be used in computing the voting strength of the different members? Population? Literacy? Territorial possessions? National wealth? Productive capacity? Financial contribution to the U. N.? World trade? Military strength? Willingness to contribute to the maintenance of world peace? And if several of these factors should be used, how much importance should be attached to each?

It is here that we encounter the crux of the problem of weighted voting. From a mathematical point of view, it would be far simpler to use a single criterion, such as population, and apportion the votes accordingly. But the differences between the states are so vast that any single factor would result in a false picture of the relative importance of various countries in the world and would concentrate voting power in the hands of a few states in an unrealistic way.

If, for example, an attempt is made to award votes directly in proportion to total population then we find that two states, India and China, would be entitled to nearly one-half the voting power in the General Assembly, and Burma would have six times as many votes as Norway. If military strength is our standard, considerably more than half the votes would go to the United States and the Soviet Union. On the other hand, if world trade is the measuring stick, Great Britain would receive a relatively large number of votes and the Soviet Union would be rather far down the scale.

The problem of weighted voting must be approached realistically. Clearly the small countries, which have been used to the principle of legal equality, are not going to underwrite any system of voting which gives the great powers 50 or 100 votes to their 1. They might, however, agree to a system which is far less discriminatory from their point of view.

The problem then, would seem to be one of agreeing upon two or three criteria—such as population, national production and contribution to the U. N.—and balancing them in such a way as to reflect, on a considerably reduced scale, the relative importance of the various countries in the organization. It might then be possible to set up 4 or 5 categories of states, as in the case of the International Institute of Agriculture, with each state receiving from 1 to 5 votes, depending upon its importance.

Any proposal for weighted voting in the General Assembly should also take into consideration the unique position of the Soviet Union which, together with its two constituent republics, Byelorussia and the Ukraine, already possesses three votes. The difficulty of removing voting power which has already been granted is apparent. Nevertheless, before any new formula is fixed, it would seem desirable to offset, insofar as that is possible, the initial advantage given to the Soviet Union at San Francisco.

At present, the chief weakness of Mr. Dulles' proposal is at once its greatest strength. If it were spelled out in detail it might stir up a hornet's nest of opposition. So long as it remains couched in general terms, it will probably command the support of a great many people.

V.   *United Nations Contributions and Voting Power*

It has been suggested by at least one delegation that voting power should be directly related to a state's contribution to the U. N. budget. In 1950, the New Zealand delegate to the First Committee of the General Assembly (Mr. Doidge) called attention to the "obvious elements of absurdity" that are involved in according to a small nation the same voting power accorded a country with a population of 200 million.

"Equally"—he said—"there is much unreality in giving to a member without armed forces and one without any desire or willingness to supply armed forces even for common defense the same voting power as to those which do possess armed forces and have from time to time, by the devotion of the lives of their citizens, proved their willingness to undertake those international duties which are correlative to all international rights."

Mr. Doidge then went on to point up the complexity of the problem, suggesting that "voting must be based on many considerations and not on population alone." "Perhaps," he remarked—"a voting power to each member roughly equal to the proportion which its financial contribution to the funds of the United Nations bears to the total contribution would provide a system of rough justice and efficiency."

Since the United Nations is based upon the principle of sovereign equality—which implies equal obligations as well as equal rights— there would seem to be some logic in Mr. Doidge's suggestion. In some organizations with small expenditures, members contribute to the budget on an equal or nearly equal basis. No member of the International Telecommunications Union, for example, pays more than 5 percent of the budget, and the highest contribution in the Universal Postal Union is approximately 8 percent.

But the United Nations, with a much larger budget than any other international organization, constitutes a special case. In 1954 only 16 states contributed more than 1 percent each of the budget. Nine countries contributed as little as 0.04 percent each. The 5 permanent members contributed nearly 70 percent of the total with the United States assessed for 33.33 percent, the Soviet Union roughly 14 percent, the

United Kingdom 10 percent, France and China approximately 5.5 percent each.

If these figures were translated into proportional voting terms, they would mean that the United States, with one-third of the votes, would be in a position to block any important resolution proposed in the General Assembly. They would mean that the five permanent members—assuming they were in agreement to do so—could always command a two-thirds majority. They would mean that the United States, the United Kingdom, and France would have a simple majority of the votes in their pockets before any voting began.

Such an arrangement would be open to serious objection. It would draw an invidious distinction between rich and poor countries. Even more important, as the United States delegation to the U. N. has repeatedly pointed out, it would be most unfortunate if any single state were to be placed in a position where it could exert undue influence over the organization. Given the tremendous differences that exist among U. N. members with respect to their capacity to pay, the contributions scale would seem to be an even less reliable criterion than population for determining voting strength.

On the other hand, from the point of view of the United States, if any reshuffling of voting power is contemplated, the financial angle certainly should not be ignored. It is a well-known fact that some of the loudest advocates of state equality show much less enthusiasm for that principle when it comes to the question of apportioning the expenses of an international organization. The Latin American countries, for example, are strong supporters of the principle of the legal equality of all states. Yet the United States, which has only 1 vote out of 21 in the inter-American system, bears more than half the expenses of the Organization of American States.

Perhaps the relationship between legal equality and financial responsibility has not been stressed enough in the United Nations. It is suggested that if an arrangement can be worked out to give some additional voting strength to states which do their best to meet their financial responsibilities it might have at least one salutary effect; it might encourage some states to increase their contributions and thus make possible a revision of the contributions scale. . . .

VI. *Population and Voting Strength*

In addition to the suggestions outlined above, a number of proposals have been advanced relating to representation and voting by organizations that advocate the establishment of some kind of supra-national agency endowed with additional authority to meet present-day world problems. For the most part, these proposals would make drastic inroads upon the concept of national sovereignty. They would either subject the United Nations to a thorough overhaul or else replace it altogether. . . .

The most fully developed of these plans are the so-called Clark-Sohn proposals [Grenville Clark and Louis B. Sohn, Peace Through Disarmament and Charter Revision, July 1953]. . . . .

Representation in the General Assembly, under the Clark-Sohn plans would be based solely on population. Each member of the U. N. would be entitled to 1 representative for each 5 million population or major fraction thereof. Small states with a population of more than 100,000 and not more than 2,500,000 would be entitled to 1 representative and members with large populations would be limited to 30 representatives. Nations with a population of 100,000 or less—such as San Marino and Monaco—would be entitled to a delegate with the right to participate in the discussion but without the right to vote.

[These suggestions have been considerably modified in later Clark-Sohn proposals; see pp. 282–290, below.]

Somewhat similar to the Clark-Sohn proposals are the recommendations of the British Parliamentary Group for World Government. In their so-called plan A [Report of the Second London Parliamentary Conference on World Government, pp. 101–107] they call for the creation of a world legislative body made up of two chambers, the upper chamber consisting of "one representative of each nation state appointed in a manner to be determined by that state." The intention here apparently is to provide for some continuity with the present General Assembly. The group also argues that such an arrangement would "tend to secure the representation of some valuable men and women who were not willing to submit themselves to popular suffrages."

In contrast to the upper house, the lower chamber would consist of representatives of member states "in numbers proportionate to population." This would reflect in some degree the balance achieved by the Senate and the House in the Congress of the United States. While the British Parliamentary Group does not spell out their plan in any detail, they evidently contemplate placing an upper limit upon the number of representatives from any state. In a note dealing with the lower chamber they point out that "the reason for weighting the representation is to avoid the overwhelming preponderance of the nations with the largest population, and thus make it more attractive to join."

In suggesting a double-vote system based on the sovereign equality of states and some form of weighted representation, the British Parliamentary Group approach somewhat the proposal of Mr. Dulles. The principal difference would seem to be that Mr. Dulles does not suggest changing the simple unicameral character of, or the method of representation in, the present General Assembly. He would secure his double vote by mathematical rather than physical changes. . . .

VII. *Regionalism and Voting Strength*

Still another approach to the problem emerged in 1948 from the Committee to Frame a World Constitution [Preliminary draft of a World Constitution, University of Chicago, 1948]. This committee, which conducted its studies at the University of Chicago, used the concept of regionalism as a basis for representation in a world assembly. The formula which they devised was designed to accomplish two major objectives: (1) To deemphasize national boundary lines and minimize the importance of the nation state; and (2) to develop a method of representation based on population, yet weighted in favor of those countries with the richest experience in democratic government.

Under the committee's proposal a Federal convention would be convened consisting of delegates elected directly by the member states, one delegate for each million of population or major fraction thereof. This body would then subdivide into 9 electoral colleges, corresponding to 9 regions of the world, for the purpose of nominating and electing a President and the members of the world council or legislature. The council would be made up of 9 members from each region with 18 elected at large, or a total of 99. Representatives would vote as individuals rather than as members of instructed delegations.

The nine regions are delineated in the draft constitution as follows:

(1) The continent of Europe and its islands outside the Russian area, together with the United Kingdom if the latter so decides, and with such overseas English- or French- or Cape Dutch-speaking communities of the British Commonwealth of Nations or the French Union as decide to associate (this whole area here tentatively denominated "Europa");

(2) The United States of America, with the United Kingdom if the latter so decides, and such kindred communities of British, or Franco-British, or Dutch-British or Irish civilization and lineage as decide to associate (Atlantis);

(3) Russia, European and Asiatic, with such east Baltic or Slavic or south Danubian nations as associate with Russia (Eurasia);

(4) The Near and Middle East, with the states of north Africa, and Pakistan if the latter so decides (Afrasia);

(5) Africa, south of the Sahara, with or without the South African Union as the latter may decide;

(6) India, with Pakistan if the latter so decides;

(7) China, Korea, Japan, with the associate archipelagoes of the north- and mid-Pacific (Asia Major);

(8) Indochina and Indonesia, with Pakistan if the latter so decides, and with such other mid- and south-Pacific lands and islands as decide to associate (Austrasia);

(9) The Western Hemisphere south of the United States (Columbia).

It will be noted that some of these regions would have a greater representation in proportion to population than others. Thus Asia Major (China, Japan, Korea), with about 25 percent of the world's population, would receive 11 percent of the total representation, while Columbia (Latin America) would have the same number of representatives with only about 7 percent of the population. The three regions of the Western World—Europa, Atlantis, and Columbia—with about a fifth of the world's population, would be given one-third of the representation.

Admittedly, this device of grouping kindred nations or cultures together into regions for representation and voting purposes would have certain theoretical advantages which some of the other proposals would not have. Certainly no single region, and no bloc of 2 or 3 regions, could dominate the world assembly or prevent the approval of desirable measures. Moreover, the formula provides a basis for representation other than mere population statistics without undue discrimination against any area of the world.

Space will not permit an analysis of the plan's weak points. Obviously it is a very complex proposal which assumes that people and governments are willing to move much further in the direction of world government and regionalism that is probably the case. There is little in the experience of the United Nations to date that would indicate that states are ready to pool their voting power with their neighbors on a purely regional basis. Proximity does not necessarily result in compatibility between states. . . .

IX. *Representatives Voting as Individuals*

One common feature of the so-called supranational proposals is the proposition that representatives to a world assembly should be popularly elected and should cast their votes as individuals. . . .

The arguments against such an arrangement in an organization of sovereign states are apparent. The first has to do with the relations between democratic countries and totalitarian systems. Democratic delegates might possibly vote as individuals but it is inconceivable that the representatives of totalitarian states would ever be in a position to do so.

In the second place, the lack of discipline would be harmful to United Nations programs. What good would come from our delegation voting for a General Assembly resolution if, after it was passed, our Government refused to support it?

Finally, with the conduct of diplomacy as complicated as it is, states find it extremely difficult to develop a unified, cohesive foreign policy even under the best of conditions. It would seem unlikely that most governments and the people they represent would want to abdicate their responsibility for the conduct of foreign relations to persons voting as "individuals" and thus beyond their control in an international organization.

X.   *Concluding Comments*

In spite of the growing importance of voting in the General Assembly, this remains one of the great unexplored areas of the charter. Very little research has been done on this problem; very few practical suggestions have been made for improving the present situation. . . .

Summarizing what has been said above, however, two conclusions seem inescapable. In the first place, there are striking inequalities among the 60 U. N. members with respect to population, armed strength, national income, territory, contribution to the U. N. and other factors. The present system of awarding one vote to each state thus confers upon the smaller countries a voting strength far out of proportion to their influence in world affairs.

In the second place, if any departure is made from the principle of one-state-one-vote it will have to be a modest one with a relatively low ceiling placed on the voting power of the great nations. For the small states, having been in a favorable voting position for many years, can be expected to put up a vigorous fight to block any proposal which would serious alter what is in effect their privileged status in the General Assembly.

This does not mean that a satisfactory quid pro quo could not be arranged. It would appear that the problem of weighted voting is closely related to the further revision of the charter. The small states, in other words, might be persuaded to make significant concessions in this respect if the General Assembly is given sufficient authority to take vigorous and effective action on behalf of world peace.

There is presented below, by way of illustration, an approach to the problem of weighted voting which is based, in part, on past experience and which does not constitute a drastic departure from present procedures. The idea is not final in form; rather it is presented as a tentative suggestion in order to stimulate further discussion of an important issue.

It is suggested in this illustration, in line with Mr. Dulles' proposal outlined above, that the vote of each state in the General Assembly be counted twice; once on the basis of one vote for each state and the second time on the basis of a weighted formula. A majority of each of the votes would be required for the General Assembly to reach a decision.

In the weighted voting formula here presented, only two criteria are taken into account; a state's population and its contribution to the United Nations. Each state would be awarded from 2 to 10 votes with the scale running from 1 to 5 for each criterion. Votes would be awarded for population in accordance with the following scale: States under 1 million would receive 1 vote; 1 to 5 million, 2 votes; 5 to 20 million, 3 votes; 20 to 100 million, 4 votes; and over 100 million, 5 votes. For U. N. contributions the scale would be: States contributing less than $20,000 to the regular U. N. budget would receive 1 vote; $20,000 to $100,000, 2 votes; $100,000 to $500,000, 3 votes; $500,000 to $2 million, 4 votes; and all over $2 million, 5 votes.

ILLUSTRATIVE WEIGHTED VOTING FORMULA—UNITED NATIONS GENERAL ASSEMBLY VOTING STRENGTH IN ORDER OF POPULATION, FINANCIAL CONTRIBUTION, AND COMBINED WEIGHTED VOTES

Population Vote

Rank	Country	Population (thousands)	Vote	Per-cent of population vote
1	China	463,493	5	2.87
2	India	367,000	5	
3	United States	156,981	5	
4	U. S. S. R.	151,663	5	
5	United Kingdom	*122,537	5	
6	France	*91,128	5	
7	Indonesia	78,163	4	2.30
8	Pakistan	75,842	4	
9	Brazil	54,477	4	
10	Ukraine	30,960	4	
11	Mexico	26,922	4	
12	Poland	24,977	4	
13	Egypt	21,425	4	
14	Turkey	20,934	4	
15	Philippines	20,631	4	
16	Iran	19,798	3	1.73
17	Thailand	19,193	3	
18	Burma	18,859	3	
19	Argentina	18,054	3	
20	Yugoslavia	16,729	3	
21	Ethiopia	15,000	3	
22	Canada	14,430	3	
23	Union of South Africa	12,912	3	
24	Czechoslovakia	12,340	3	
25	Afghanistan	12,000	3	
26	Colombia	11,768	3	
27	Netherlands	10,377	3	
28	Peru	8,864	3	
29	Belgium	8,706	3	
30	Australia	8,649	3	
31	Greece	7,761	3	
32	Sweden	7,125	3	
33	Saudi Arabia	7,000	3	

Contribution Vote

Rank	Country	Contribution (dollars)	Vote	Percent of contribution vote
1	United States	13,765,290	5	3.05
2	U. S. S. R.	5,843,950	5	
3	United Kingdom	4,047,400	5	
4	France	2,374,750	5	
5	China	2,321,060	5	
6	India	1,404,200	4	
7	Canada	1,362,900	4	
8	Ukraine	776,440	4	
9	Australia	722,750	4	
10	Poland	714,490	4	2.44
11	Sweden	681,450	4	
12	Brazil	578,200	4	
13	Argentina	578,200	4	
14	Belgium	569,940	4	
15	Netherlands	516,250	4	
16	Czechoslovakia	433,650	3	
17	Denmark	322,140	3	
18	Union of South Africa	322,140	3	
19	Mexico	309,750	3	
20	Pakistan	309,750	3	
21	Turkey	268,450	3	
22	Indonesia	247,800	3	
23	Byelorussia	206,500	3	
24	Norway	206,500	3	
25	New Zealand	198,240	3	1.83
26	Egypt	194,110	3	
27	Philippines	185,850	3	
28	Yugoslavia	181,720	3	
29	Colombia	169,330	3	
30	Venezuela	161,070	3	
31	Cuba	140,420	3	
32	Chile	136,290	3	
33	Iran	115,640	3	

Combined Vote

Rank	Country	Vote	Percent of combined vote
1	China	10	2.96
	U. S. S. R.	10	
	United Kingdom	10	
	United States	10	
	France	10	
2	India	9	2.66
3	Brazil	8	2.37
	Poland	8	
	Ukraine	8	
4	Argentina	7	2.07
	Australia	7	
	Belgium	7	
	Canada	7	
	Egypt	7	
	Indonesia	7	
	Mexico	7	
	Netherlands	7	
	Pakistan	7	
	Philippines	7	
	Sweden	7	
	Turkey	7	
5	Byelorussia	6	1.78
	Chile	6	
	Colombia	6	
	Cuba	6	
	Czechoslovakia	6	
	Iran	6	
	Union of South Africa	6	
	Venezuela	6	
	Yugoslavia	6	

No.	Country	Figure	Votes	Ratio
34	Chile	5,932	3	
35	Cuba	5,927	3	
36	Byelorussia	5,568	3	
37	Venezuela	5,280	3	
38	Iraq	5,100	3	
39	Yemen	4,500	2	
40	Denmark	4,334	2	
41	Syria	3,381	2	
42	Ecuador	3,350	2	
43	Norway	3,327	2	
44	Haiti	3,200	2	
45	Bolivia	3,089	2	
46	Guatemala	2,938	2	
47	Uruguay	2,365	2	1.15
48	Dominican Republic	2,236	2	
49	New Zealand	1,995	2	
50	El Salvador	1,986	2	
51	Liberia	1,643	2	
52	Israel	1,607	2	
53	Honduras	1,513	2	
54	Paraguay	1,464	2	
55	Lebanon	1,320	2	
56	Nicaragua	1,128	2	
57	Costa Rica	850	1	
58	Panama	841	1	.57
59	Luxembourg	301	1	
60	Iceland	148	1	
	Total	2,012,026	175	

No.	Country	Figure	Votes	Ratio
34	Greece	86,730	2	
35	Peru	74,340	2	
36	Thailand	74,340	2	
37	Uruguay	74,340	2	
38	Israel	70,210	2	
39	Burma	53,690	2	
40	Iraq	49,560	2	
41	Ethiopia	41,300	2	
42	Afghanistan	33,040	2	
43	Syria	33,040	2	1.22
44	Saudi Arabia	28,910	2	
45	Guatemala	28,910	2	
46	Bolivia	24,780	2	
47	El Salvador	24,780	2	
48	Luxembourg	24,780	2	
49	Dominican Republic	20,650	2	
50	Lebanon	20,650	2	
51	Panama	20,650	2	
52	Costa Rica	16,520	1	
53	Ecuador	16,520	1	
54	Haiti	16,520	1	
55	Honduras	16,520	1	
56	Iceland	16,520	1	
57	Liberia	16,520	1	
58	Paraguay	16,520	1	
59	Nicaragua	16,520	1	.61
60	Yemen	16,520	1	
	Total	41,300,000	164	

Group	Country	Votes	Ratio
6	Afghanistan	5	
	Burma	5	
	Denmark	5	
	Ethiopia	5	
	Greece	5	
	Iraq	5	1.48
	New Zealand	5	
	Norway	5	
	Peru	5	
	Saudi Arabia	5	
	Thailand	5	
7	Bolivia	4	
	Dominican Republic	4	
	El Salvador	4	
	Guatemala	4	
	Israel	4	1.18
	Lebanon	4	
	Syria	4	
	Uruguay	4	
8	Ecuador	3	
	Haiti	3	
	Honduras	3	
	Liberia	3	
	Luxembourg	3	.89
	Nicaragua	3	
	Panama	3	
	Paraguay	3	
	Yemen	3	
9	Costa Rica	2	
	Iceland	2	.59
	Total	339	

*Aggregate figure, including non-self-governing territories and dependencies. In this illustrative formula, France, a permanent member of the Security Council is awarded 5 votes even though her total population falls below the 100 million suggested for the first category of states.

Several observations may be made about this kind of illustrative weighted voting system.

1. It would increase the relative voting strength of certain countries—particularly the great nations—but it would not materially alter the balance of power in the General Assembly.

2. The Latin American and the Arab States would lose somewhat, as indeed they would in almost any system of weighted voting that could be devised. Thus, the 20 Latin American states, with a total of 91 out of the 338 votes in the General Assembly, would command only 27 percent of the votes instead of the strategic one-third they now control. The 6 Arab States would drop from 10 percent to roughly 8 percent.

3. Unless the votes of the Ukraine and Byelorussia were discounted somewhat, as suggested earlier in this study, the Soviet bloc would pick up voting strength. The 5 Communist states now control 8 percent of the votes; under the illustrative schedule they would claim 11 percent. The so-called neutralist states of India, Indonesia, and Burma would also add slightly to their voting power.

4. Two other groups of states, generally inclined to support American policy, would either hold their own or else gain voting strength. The 12 NATO states in the U. N. would continue to hold roughly one-fifth of the votes. The seven British Commonwealth countries would increase their total from 11.6 percent to 15 percent.

5. If other criteria, such as national income, productivity and foreign trade, are taken into account, the states of Western Europe and the British Commonwealth countries would improve their relative standings somewhat. The more complicated the formula, however, the more opposition it is likely to encounter.

6. In this chart the votes are calculated on the basis of the contribution of each member to the *regular* U. N. budget. Clearly, this is not the most satisfactory measuring stick. It would be far better—though perhaps not very practical—if a schedule could be devised that would reflect the ability and the willingness of U. N. members to contribute manpower, military equipment and supplies, as well as bases and other facilities toward the maintenance of world peace.

. . .

Voting in the General Assembly is grimly serious business. Any significant realinement of votes might have an adverse impact upon our policy—either now or at some time in the unpredictable future.

Before we urge the principle of weighted voting, therefore, we must make certain, through a careful analysis of the facts, that such a move is in our national interest. We must make sure that we are not opening a Pandora's box from which a host of unpleasant results might flow to plague us in the years to come.

Clearly, any formula that would result in a substantial decrease in voting power for the 20 Latin American countries would be open to grave objections on our part. Generally speaking, these nations have been the most consistent supporters of our policy in the United Nations and we hope they will remain so.

Our national position on this issue must also be conditioned by the probability that a number of states—including the relatively great powers of Germany, Japan, and Italy—may be admitted to the U. N. within the next few years. With a possible increase in membership that may run as high as 30 percent, Assembly voting patterns could undergo drastic changes.

Up to the present time, the United States has been able to retain its position of leadership in the General Assembly through the logic of its argument and the justice of its cause. In a political organiza-tion where each state has one vote, we have been able to rally the small countries to the cause of the free world.

Theoretically, there may be logical reasons for supporting a sys-tem of weighted voting for the General Assembly. From a practical point of view, however, it might be better to let well enough alone.

NOTE. For recent writings on weighted voting, see Elizabeth Mc-INTYRE, "Weighted Voting in International Organizations," 8 Int.Org. (1954), pp. 484–97; Catherine Senf MANNO, "Selective Weighted Voting in the United Nations General Assembly: Rationale and Method," 20 *idem* (1966), pp. 37–62; Alan de RUSETT, "Large and Small States in Interna-tional Organization: Present Attitudes to the Problem of Weighted Voting," 30 Int. Affairs (1954), pp. 463–74, and "The Need for a New Approach to the Question of Weighting Votes in the General Assembly," 31 *idem* (1955), pp. 192–202; H. A. SCHWARZ-LIEBERMANN von WAHLENDORF, Mehrheitsentscheid und Stimmenwägung (Tübingen, 1953), 286 pp.; Cath-erine SENF, "A Proposal for Weighting Votes in the UN Assembly," *in* COMMISSION TO STUDY THE ORGANIZATION OF PEACE, Charter Review Conference (New York, 1955), pp. 107–29; Louis B. SOHN, "The Role of the General Assembly and the Problem of Weighted Voting," *in* COMMISSION TO STUDY THE ORGANIZATION OF PEACE, *op. cit.,* pp. 77–106. For earlier writings, see SOHN, World Law, pp. 316–47.

THE INTERNATIONAL APPORTIONMENT PROBLEM

Statement by Richard N. Gardner, Deputy Assistant Secretary of State for International Organization Affairs, 23 April 1965. 52 DSB (1965), pp. 701–11.

Of all our preoccupations these last 4 years in the field of international organization the one which best illustrates the relevance of law and legal skills has been our effort to adapt the decisionmaking procedures of the United Nations and its family of agencies to take adequate account of world power realities.

The Secretary of State himself called special attention to this problem in his Hammarskjold Lecture at Columbia University on January 10, 1964. He pointed out that a two-thirds vote could now be put together in the General Assembly, at least in theory, by members representing only 10 percent of the population of U.N. members and 5 percent of contributions to the regular budget. He noted that the rapid and radical expansion of the organization may require some adaptation of procedures if the U.N. is to remain relevant to the real world and therefore effective in that world.

The reason for our preoccupation with this subject is obvious. The United Nations has grown from 51 to 114 members in the last 20 years. A parallel increase has taken place in the membership of the specialized and affiliated agencies. U.N. membership may reach a total of 125 to 130 before it finally levels off.

What makes this extraordinary increase in membership particularly significant from a constitutional point of view is the simultaneous increase in the U.N.'s capacity to act. The United States has played a leading role in the strengthening of the action responsibilities of the United Nations system in both peacekeeping and development. We want to continue to play this role in the years ahead.

It is obvious that, as the U.N. develops an increasing capacity to act, there will be increasing concern with the procedures by which this capacity is exercised. The manifest disproportion between voting power and real power is now a central preoccupation of persons concerned with the future of the world organization. Unless we can find ways to allay the anxieties felt on this subject in the United States and in other countries, it will be increasingly difficult to use the U.N. in the years ahead for important tasks of peacekeeping and development.

To be sure, it is important not to overstate the problem which is inherent in the present constitutional situation. As Dag Hammarskjold reminded us some years ago in an annual report to the General Assembly [U.N. doc. A/3594/Add. 1], the members of the United Nations may have equal votes but they are far from having equal influence:

"The criticism of 'one nation, one vote,' irrespective of size or strength, as constituting an obstacle to arriving at just and representative solutions, tends to exaggerate the problem. The General Assembly is not a parliament of elected individual members; it is a diplomatic meeting in which the delegates of member states represent governmental policies, and these policies are subject to all the influences that would prevail in international life in any case."

Anyone who believes that United States influence in the United Nations is measured by the fact that it has less than one-hundredth of the votes in the General Assembly fails completely to understand the realities of power as they are reflected in the world organization. These realities include the fact that the United States is the principal contributor to the U.N.'s regular budget, is by far the largest supporter of the U.N.'s peacekeeping and development programs, and is making by far the largest individual contribution to the defense and development of the non-Communist world. On U.N. decisions of vital importance to the United States, the voting of other countries has been considerably influenced by U.S. views.

Nevertheless, after these and other qualifications are made, it remains true that the present procedures do need to be improved in the light both of the growth of U.N. membership and the growth of U.N. responsibilities. The last UNESCO [United Nations Educational, Scientific and Cultural Organization] Conference, for example, voted a budget by a large majority of votes which represented less than 30 percent of the funds that had to be raised to make the budget a reality. And at the United Nations Conference on Trade and Development in Geneva last spring there was a disturbing tendency of the 75 (now 77) less developed countries to use their automatic two-thirds majority to vote recommendations for action in trade and development over the opposition of the very minority of developed countries to whom the recommendations were addressed.

On the whole, the majority of small countries have not behaved as irresponsibly as the pessimists have predicted. We hope in the years ahead that the "revolution of rising expectations" will be matched by an "evolution of rising responsibility." But we cannot base our participation in the U.N. on hope alone. Sound procedural adaptations can help make this hope a reality. . . .

The sovereign equality of states is one of the fundamental principles of international law. In the words of a famous case decided many years ago by the U.S. Supreme Court: "Russia and Geneva have equal rights." Article 2, paragraph 1, of the United Nations Charter declares that the United Nations is based on the principle of sovereign equality.

The sovereign equality of states, however, has never meant the equal right to participate in the decisionmaking process of international organizations. The composition of the Security Council and other councils, the veto provision, the amendment process—these and other provisions of the charter all accord special privileges to certain members. So the structure of the United Nations from the very beginning recognized the need to reconcile the principle of sovereign equality with the uneven disposition of real power and real responsibility for implementing U.N. decisions. Appropriate means of balancing these considerations were also incorporated in the constitutions of the specialized agencies.

Quite apart from charter provisions, procedures have been developed over the years to adapt decisionmaking procedures to power realities. In the last several years this central problem has occasioned a vast amount of staff work in our own and other governments—and a considerable amount of discussion and negotiation in the U.N. system.

We have explored with other nations many different procedures for rationalizing the decisionmaking process. We recognize that no one procedure is appropriate for all cases:

—Certain procedures may be appropriate for the voting of General Assembly resolutions which merely manifest the views of members and have no binding legal effect.

—Other procedures may be appropriate when the General Assembly is exercising its mandatory power to assess.

—Still other procedures may be appropriate in specialized agencies lending substantial sums of money for exchange stabilization or economic development.

So our search for adequate procedures has been undertaken on a case-by-case basis with special regard for the peculiarities of each case. . . .

To put it another way, we are persuaded of the need to protect the interests of ourselves and other large and middle powers in the United Nations vehicle. But we do not want to do this by draining all the gasoline out of the motor. We prefer to keep the gasoline in—and to keep the vehicle on the road through the introduction of "power steering."

How can "power steering" be built into the United Nations vehicle? Diplomats and scholars have explored six main approaches to this problem:

1. *Weighted Voting*

Most public discussion of the international apportionment question has focused on proposals to introduce weighted voting in the General Assembly and in the conferences of the major U.N. agencies.

Weighted voting exists, of course, in the four financial agencies of the United Nations system—the International Monetary Fund, the International Bank for Reconstruction and Development, the International Finance Corporation, and the International Development Association. In each of these voting power is roughly proportionate to financial contribution. Weighted voting is also employed in the main international commodity arrangements, where it is related to the size of participating countries' trade in the particular commodity. Except for these financial and trade arrangements, it is not otherwise employed in the United Nations system.

But most U.N. members, while willing to employ weighted voting for decisions on the disbursement of loans or the administration of commodity agreements, are not prepared to introduce this system across the board to cover recommendations of the General Assembly and other bodies.

The obvious practical impediment to the introduction of weighted voting in the General Assembly is that it would require amendment of the U.N. Charter—and therefore the approval not only of the Soviet Union, France, and other members of the Security Council but also of two-thirds of the membership of the General Assembly. In the present state of international relations, it is hard to imagine the permanent members of the Council and two-thirds of the Assembly agreeing on any formula which would assign different weights to their share in the decisionmaking process.

The most likely consequence of pressing for a charter review conference to consider weighted voting, as some have urged, would be to provide a golden opportunity for the Communist countries and others to press for amendments diminishing the powers that the U.N. has developed under the charter during the last 20 years and that have generally promoted the objectives of U.S. foreign policy.

Even if it were possible to amend the charter to provide for weighted voting, it is not at all certain that our national interest would be served by the result. No system of weighted voting could conceivably be negotiated which did not weigh population as a major factor. It is questionable whether such an arrangement would suit a country like ours, which has only 6 percent of the world's population and which, together with its NATO allies, has only 16 percent. If population were a primary criterion, India with its 450 million people and China with its 700 million people might well end up with more votes than the United States.

Of course, it is always possible to construct hypothetical systems of weighted voting congenial to our interests, based mainly on such factors as literacy, per capita income, and military power. But such systems are simply not negotiable—at least, not in the foreseeable future.

The Department of State in 1962 conducted a study of various weighted-voting formulas based on population and contributions to the U.N. budget. When these formulas were applied to 178 key votes that took place in the General Assembly between 1954 and 1961, it was found that, while they would have somewhat reduced the number of resolutions passed over U.S. opposition, they would have reduced much more the number of resolutions supported by the United States and passed over Communist opposition. The same conclusion was reached in projecting these formulas to 1970, having regard to further increases in membership.

The results of this study reflect the fact that the desire for political independence and economic progress has put most U.N. members on the same side as the United States on most important matters—particularly where action is involved as well as talk.

We have therefore concluded that any system of weighted voting taking population substantially into account—and, I repeat, no weighted voting system would be negotiable that failed to do this—would help Communist countries more than ourselves, by making it easier for them to achieve a blocking one-third vote on U.N. actions for peace and welfare that are in the interest of the United States and other nations of the non-Communist world.

2. *Dual Voting*

Dual voting—or a system of double majorities—has recently been advanced by some commentators as a possible answer. Benjamin Cohen, for example, has proposed that General Assembly decisions on substantive matters should be made in the future by a two-thirds majority of members present and voting, *provided* that the majority includes two-thirds of the members of the Security Council.

Dual voting has two great advantages as compared with weighted voting:

—It does not offend directly the "one nation, one vote" principle.

—It does not require a complicated negotiation involving national prestige in which different weights have to be assigned to different members.

But most members of the United Nations would probably feel that the introduction of dual voting on all substantive matters would require charter amendment. It is doubtful that a sufficient consensus on the desirability of dual voting presently exists for such an amendment to be approved.

It is always possible, of course, that dual voting might be introduced in selected areas of U.N. decisionmaking. At the U.N. Conference on Trade and Development in Geneva last year the non-Communist industrial countries, in the closing weeks of the conference, proposed a system of dual voting for the new U.N. trade machinery. Under this proposal, decisions on certain important matters in the periodic Trade and Development Conference were to be taken by a two-thirds majority, including a majority of developed countries and a majority of less developed countries; in the Trade and Development Board such decisions would be taken by a plain majority, including a majority of developed countries and a majority of less developed countries.

This proposal found some support not only among developed countries but also among less developed countries, some of whom recognized the futility of voting self-serving resolutions without the concurrence of at least a majority of those countries to whom the recommendations were addressed.

But the idea involved too great a change in existing procedures to gain approval at Geneva. And some of the Western industrial countries even developed second thoughts on the proposal—on the grounds that special voting procedures of this kind might cause greater significance to be attached to U.N. recommendations than they were prepared to accept.

3. *Bicameralism*

Bicameralism in one form or other is an approach to the international apportionment problem offering greater possibilities in the short run than either weighted or dual voting.

In its extreme form bicamerlism would mean treating the Security Council and the General Assembly as an "Upper House" and a "Lower House" and requiring that decisions on some or all matters would have to be passed by both of them. For example, the veto could continue to apply to enforcement action; but voluntary peacekeeping operations and perhaps recommendations in other areas could be adopted by two-thirds of the General Assembly and by 7 of the 11 members of the Security Council (9 members of the enlarged Council of 15).

. . .

4. *Committees With Selective Representation*

Probably the most promising method yet devised for building greater responsibility into United Nations decisionmaking is that of committees with selective representation.

The basic concept was provided in the charter provision for a Security Council with 11 members, including the 5 permanent members which bear the principal responsibility for the maintenance of peace and security. The same concept is embodied in the charters of a number of the specialized agencies—for example, in the Governing Body of the International Labor Organization, the 10 members of chief industrial importance have permanent seats.

Even where no specific provision is made for permanent seats for a certain category of members, elections to the executive boards of U.N. agencies have normally taken account of the special responsibilities of members in the particular functional area of cooperation, whether it be telecommunications, weather forecasting, or medical research. Presumably this will continue to be true in the future as well.

In the case of the Security Council the charter itself declares that "due regard" should be "specially paid, in the first instance to the contribution of Members of the United Nations to the maintenance of international peace and security and to the other purposes of the Organization" as well as to equitable geographic distribution. This provision has not received the attention it deserves. It would enhance the effectiveness of an enlarged Council if this consideration could be adequately reflected in Council elections in the years ahead.

The members of the United Nations have found committees with selective representation particularly useful in the financial field. The General Assembly's Advisory Committee on Administration and Budgetary Questions bears responsibility for examining and reporting on the Secretary-General's U.N. budget estimates. The United States has supported the effective operation of this small 12-man body, which is not merely representative of the major geographic groups in the United Nations but also reflects comparative contributions to the U.N. budget. We have sought to strengthen the authority of similar groups in the specialized agencies, and we believe members might usefully consider the possibility of creating such groups in agencies which do not have them.

We also favor use of a committee with selective representation in the peacekeeping field. Our working paper to the Committee of 21 last September proposed that the General Assembly establish a standing Special Finance Committee. The composition of this committee would be similar to that of the present Working Group of 21—it would include the permanent members of the Security Council and a relatively high percentage of those member states in each geographic area that are large financial contributors to the United Nations. The General Assembly, in apportioning expenses for peacekeeping operations, would act only on a recommendation from the committee passed by a two-thirds majority of the committee's membership.

One great advantage of the committee approach is that it does not require amendment of the U.N. Charter or the constitutions of the various specialized agencies. The proposed Special Finance Committee for peacekeeping operations, for example, could be constituted under and governed by firm rules of procedure by the General Assembly. In effect, the Assembly would be adopting a self-denying ordinance to act only upon proposals first adopted in this new suborgan.

5. *Informal Relations With International Secretariats*

Informal relations with the international secretariats may also provide a useful approach. Obviously, the Secretary-General of the United Nations and the heads of the specialized and affiliated agencies engage in a continuous process of consultation with the membership. In these consultations they naturally take account of the differing responsibilities which the members have for supporting the work of their organizations.

During the United Nations Operation in the Congo, for example, the Secretariat systematically consulted an advisory committee of countries that contributed military personnel. More informally, consultation was carried on with key contributors of services and money. For example, the United States and other major contributors were in frequent touch with the Secretary-General and his staff in New York and with the chief of the U.N. Congo operation in Léopoldville. This was a truly international undertaking. At the same time, its conduct reflected the views of the major supporters of the operation. . . .

6. *Conciliation*

The most recent, and perhaps the most original, procedural innovation in U.N. decisionmaking is the conciliation procedure established by the last General Assembly for the new U.N. machinery in the field of trade and development.

The need for the conciliation procedure became apparent during the United Nations Conference on Trade and Development at Geneva. In the closing days of UNCTAD . . .   there was an encouraging disposition to reach a consensus on some subjects. But there were also instances when the voting bloc of less developed countries passed resolutions over the opposition of the minority of industrial countries on matters involving important economic interests.

Some delegates argued that this was no cause for concern, since the resolutions were recommendations only—and any resolutions of the new trade machinery would be recommendations only. But the United States and other countries pointed out that the currency of such recommendations would be hopelessly debased if they failed to reflect a substantial consensus among all countries, including particularly the countries bearing the principal responsibility for implementing them.

Trade questions have traditionally been dealt with among nations by negotiation—not legislation. Undoubtedly there is a constructive role for institutions whose primary purpose is to articulate through recommendations the measures which should be undertaken by both developed and less developed countries to deal with the trade problems of the latter. But such institutions can only operate through a process of persuasion.

Persuasion is assisted when delegates seek a consensus through conciliation and express that consensus in resolutions. If it is not assisted, it may even be set back by the passage of self-serving resolutions by automatic majorities. Public opinion in the industrial countries is likely to react adversely to recommendations that are passed over the opposition of the industrial countries but call for concessions by them.

What is wanted, in the last analysis, is not voting, but results. Because this was recognized by most delegations, a last-minute agreement was reached at Geneva that the new UNCTAD machinery should contain procedures . . .   designed to establish a process of conciliation to take place before voting and to provide an adequate basis for the adoption of recommendations with regard to proposals of a specific nature for action substantially affecting the economic or financial interests of particular countries.

The task of working out these procedures was left to a special committee appointed by the Secretary-General of the United Nations. I had the privilege of serving as the U.S. expert on this committee. The conciliation procedure which the committee devised will operate in the periodic Conference, in the Trade and Development Board, and in its committees.

Under this procedure, conciliation can be initiated and voting suspended on any resolution, upon the motion of a very small number of countries (10 in the Conference, 5 in the Board, and 3 in committees) or upon the motion of the president of the Conference or chairman of the Board.

The initiation of conciliation is automatic. However, guidelines are provided defining the kind of resolutions which are appropriate for the conciliation procedure.

Following a motion for conciliation, a conciliation group is appointed with adequate representation of countries interested in the subject matter. If the conciliation group cannot reach agreement at the same session of the Conference or Board, it reports to the next session of the Conference or Board, whichever comes first.

If the conciliation group has reached agreement, the agreed resolution can be voted. If it has not, a decision can be taken continuing conciliation for a further period, or the original proposal, or some variant thereof, can be voted in the normal way.

In the event that a vote is taken after unsuccessful conciliation, the resolution will cite the report of the conciliation group (which may contain minority as well as majority views), and the records of the United Nations will show how the members voted on the resolution.

These procedures offer important benefits to all U.N. members:

—For the minority of developed countries, they provide some safeguard against the voting of unacceptable resolutions by automatic majorities and a "cooling off" period of 6 months or more during which efforts at compromise can be sought through quiet diplomacy.

—For the majority of less developed countries, they afford a means of engaging the developed countries in a sustained debate during which the developed countries explain the reasons for their opposition to proposals of the majority.

It is too early to see just how the conciliation procedure will work in practice, but we may hazard one prediction: The main value of the new procedures may be less in their actual use than in the subtle way in which their mere existence influences member governments in the direction of compromise rather than voting on disagreed proposals.

This catalog of procedures for coping with the international apportionment problem should serve to indicate four things:

—First, that the United States and other countries are very much aware of the need to adapt U.N. procedures to take account of power realities.

—Second, that a wide variety of alternative procedures can be developed to come to grips with the problem.

—Third, that the most practical of these procedures can be put into effect without amendment of the U.N. Charter or of the constitutions of other U.N. agencies.

—Fourth, that a great process of procedural adaptation and innovation is already underway throughout the U.N. system.

Of course, procedures in and of themselves are only part of the problem. What is really required is widespread recognition of the common interest in basing U.N. decisions on an adequate consensus— a consensus which includes the support of most of the countries bearing the principal responsibilities for action.

Will such a recognition be forthcoming? The cynic may ask why the majority of small countries should accept any restraint on the use of their voting power. The answer is clear enough.

If United Nations procedures cannot be adapted to take account of power realities, the large and middle powers will increasingly pursue their national interests outside the U.N. system.

If, on the other hand, the necessary procedural adjustments can be carried out, the United Nations and its agencies will be able to assume increasing responsibilities for action in both peacekeeping and development.

This is the fundamental reason why the important procedural adjustments now underway in the United Nations serve the enlightened long-term interests of all its members.

————————

RECONCILING POWER WITH THE SOVEREIGN EQUALITY OF STATES

Excerpt from COMMISSION TO STUDY THE ORGANIZATION OF PEACE, New Dimensions for the United Nations: The Problems of the Next Decade (New York, 1966), pp. 13–18.

One of the first steps that will enable the United Nations to take binding decisions is to make an adjustment between the principle of one vote for each state and the fact that some nations are able to make a greater contribution than others to international society.

. . . .

The rapid increase in United Nations membership, including so many new states of varying sizes and degrees of development, raises the problem of how the Organization can give maximum justice and equality both to the great and to the small, and how it can operate responsibly and effectively.

The United Nations is based on the principle of the sovereign equality of all of its Members. This principle must be preserved. The very smallest Member state must know that it has the equal protection of the law—that it has the protection of the Organization from aggression and direct or indirect interference in its internal affairs. It must have an equal right to protest against injustice. It must have an equal right in the General Assembly to address itself to world problems. Certainly a small power represented by an able statesman may at times make a contribution of ideas greater than that of a major power.

Nevertheless, some nations are more able than others to put authority and resources back of a particular decision of the Organization. In time of danger only a few can put overwhelming physical force back of the Organization to support its resistance to aggression. These nations are entitled to feel that their contributions are given due recognition.

There are different kinds and degrees of contributions. Some nations pay the larger share of peacekeeping costs. Some invest the most money in the World Bank and the International Development Association. Some contribute the major facilities for the development of the resources of outer space, including satellite communications and weather reporting. Some make available research reactors through the International Atomic Energy Agency. Some contribute the most troops for peacekeeping operations. The nod of a few nations can determine disarmament.

The Commission to Study the Organization of Peace is optimistic that equality and power can be harmonized in many kinds of United Nations activity. The phrase "weighted voting" is popularly used to define a means for this adjustment. A rich variety of weighted voting now exists in the United Nations family and in regional agencies. Certainly "invisible" weighted voting is apparent in the General Assembly. It is false to say that the vote of Costa Rica is comparable to that of the United States, or that of Malta to that of the United Kingdom. Obviously individual great powers influence more votes than do individual smaller ones. A nation's influence may be greater in certain circumstances than in others. On the other hand, taken as a group the small nations with able leadership may greatly modify the attitudes of the great powers.

The other five major organs of the United Nations either by provision of the Charter or by agreement of the Members give added weight to the great powers. The assignment of special privileges to these states is more marked in the Security Council, where five great powers are assigned permanent seats with the right of veto. The Trusteeship Council, so composed as to maintain a balance between the trust powers and the non-colonial powers, also gives a seat to each of five permanent members of the Security Council. Although the Charter does not guarantee them permanent seats on the Economic and Social Council, the United States, the United Kingdom, the Soviet Union and France have always been elected to it. The International Court of Justice has always included nationals of the five permanent members of the Security Council among its fifteen judges. And in the Secretariat, it is generally understood that nationals of the major powers are assured a certain number of the higher level posts. The quota system provides a greater number of Secretariat jobs for nationals of the major powers.

Some of the Specialized Agencies, such as the World Bank, the Monetary Fund, the International Development Association, and the International Finance Corporation have adopted formal weighted voting systems based upon capital subscriptions.

The regional institutions of the European Community have developed some very sophisticated decision-making procedures which give extra weight to the larger members' votes (France, Germany, Italy) and, in most cases, require majorities which would allow any two (but not any one) member to block action. Most European states have also accepted a weighted voting system in the Council of Europe.

A system of weighted voting must be kept flexible. Power shifts. Nations grow and decline. Some nations may be powerful in some aspects of life, but not in others. Consequently, the systems of weighted voting in United Nations bodies must never be frozen. The weakness of the Security Council is that it is inflexible. Unless the Charter is revised, five great powers and five alone will forever hold permanent seats with the right of veto.

The General Assembly is the one body of the United Nations proper in which all states are represented, each with one vote. In twenty years, the Assembly has grown to become the paramount body of the Organization. Its main strength is due to the fact that in all areas outside of peace and security the Charter gives it the major role in the Organization. It is the representative body in which all nations have their say. It is the place where all problems may be discussed and processes of peaceful change set in motion. Part of its strength derives from the weakening of the Security Council by the frequent use of the veto. As a result, circumstances have enabled the General Assembly to exercise important decision-making functions probably beyond what was anticipated, but not beyond what was provided by the framers of the Charter. Nevertheless, with the addition of so many new and inexperienced states fear has arisen in responsible quarters that the General Assembly might not be able to make balanced and responsible judgments on many important issues.

. . .

The Commission believes this problem can be met head on.

As the one universal body of the United Nations, the General Assembly should be recognized and strengthened as the acknowledged center of all United Nations activity. In every political society, there must be a central organ. It must be the most inclusive and the most democratic, in which all participants have an equal voice. It must be able to take decisions in all of the Organization's concerns. The General Assembly is this body in the United Nations.

The Commission suggests a revision of the procedures of the General Assembly so that it may be so organized as to be able to function continuously. Obviously, this does not mean that the General Assembly will be in continuous plenary session. It does mean that there is a certain amount of work that will be carried on by committees when the Assembly is not in session. It also means that on very brief notice the Assembly may be called into plenary session.

Indeed, there might be three types of Assembly meetings throughout the year. Inevitably, there would be annual plenary sessions at which prime ministers and foreign ministers could meet to discuss outstanding problems, take decisions involving the lawmaking process, conduct elections and adopt the budget. Other plenary sessions might be attended by lesser delegates and heads of mission and would deal with the Assembly's agenda which is divided among its seven Main Committees. A third type of meeting is described in the recommendation that follows

The Commission suggests that the day-by-day work of the General Assembly be conducted more and more by representative committees of limited size which could be in continuous session.

These committees would have several advantages. The membership of each could be limited in number. The committees could be weighted in favor of those Members with the greatest interest or responsibility in the issue involved. At times they could be weighted in favor of the major powers and blocs and yet be so flexible in composition as to permit additions and subtractions as the need arose. For illustration, a budget committee obviously would have larger representation from the approximately 6 per cent of the Members of the United Nations that pay approximately 70 per cent of the bills. The criteria for selection on such committees may include general weighting by population, financial contribution, and other evidence of power and influence or geographical areas; or general political association. The increased work load of the General Assembly necessitates that such committees be standing committees and when necessary remain in continuous session. Such committees could be given power to act, and make decisions of policy, within the fields of their respective competence, and with the Assembly's general directives.

Other advantages of the special committees are that they would be small enough to transact business with greater efficiency and would be able to travel and meet as necessary whether or not the plenary Assembly was in session.

There is precedent for these committees. The Committee of 24 on anti-colonialism and the Committee of 33 on peacekeeping operations are two outstanding illustrations. The Charter expressly authorizes the General Assembly to establish "subsidiary organs." (Article 22).

The General Assembly's President would not only preside at plenary meetings but supervise the day-by-day work of the committees of the Assembly.

What would be the relationship of the three Councils to this re-organized Assembly? The role of the Trusteeship Council has to a considerable extent been taken over by the Committee of 24 on anti-colonialism. The Economic and Social Council, strengthened as is suggested in the latter part of this Report, is also subordinate to the General Assembly under Article 60 of the Charter. It could well have a closer relationship to the General Assembly in practice. As such, it could function as one of the standing committees of the General Assembly. It meets the requirements of a special committee as described above. It is limited in number and its membership is selected to represent the major economic systems of the world. The Security Council while given independent functions by the Charter must report on its activity to the General Assembly.

The Commission proposes that a special committee of the Assembly be created to consider a revision of its procedures for the gradual accomplishment of the above objectives. Like many recommendations the Commission has made in this Report, it could be accomplished without revision of the Charter.

The Commission further recommends that more of the Assembly's decisions be made by dual voting processes. "Dual voting" refers to those decision-making arrangements in which two or more organs, acting separately, must approve a measure before it is adopted. At the present time, the General Assembly and the Security Council engage in dual voting in the selection of the judges of the International Court of Justice and the Secretary-General and in the admission of new Members.

Another kind of dual voting might be provided by the requirement that certain kinds of decisions should be taken concurrently by a majority of the appropriate limited representative committee and by two-thirds of the plenary session of the General Assembly.

However, our discussion must not stop short of an examination of the possibility of weighted voting when the General Assembly is taking important lawmaking decisions. . . . Several proposals have been made for the establishment of a bicameral system in the United Nations. It has been suggested that the General Assembly's vote be tallied twice on matters involving important decisions. In one tally each state would be counted equally, as is now the practice. In a second tally plural votes would be granted the larger states with a ceiling. The decision, to be valid, would have to secure a simple or in some matters a two-thirds majority in each tally, somewhat as legislation in the United States Congress must pass both the Senate based on equality and the House of Representatives based on population. A single roll call in the Assembly could be tallied simultaneously in several different ways through the newly-installed electronic voting process.

Another suggestion has been that the United Nations have an advisory committee made up of members of national parliaments, which could evolve into a second house or chamber of the General Assembly. The advisory committee would take the form of an International Parliamentary Conference, similar to the Conference of the Interparliamentary Union which has functioned since 1890. It would consist of three representatives from each national parliament and additional representation to a possible maximum of twenty-five based on population and contribution to the expenses of the Organization. The Parliamentary Conference would meet concurrently with the General Assembly to advise it on budgetary and financial matters, to consider the Annual Report of the Secretary-General and to maintain liaison with the national parliaments. The Assembly delegates would look for advice from the parliamentary representatives on decisions they take in the General Assembly and for support of these decisions back home.

Other ingenious methods tantamount to a bicameral system have been suggested. The Commission believes that all should be studied with a view to an early solution.

CLARK-SOHN PROPOSAL

Excerpt from G. CLARK and L. B. SOHN, World Peace Through World Law: Two Alternative Plans (3d ed., Cambridge, Mass., 1966), pp. 399–402.

1. The General Conference of the World Disarmament and World Development Organization shall consist of Representatives from all the Members of the Organization and from the non-self-governing and trust territories under their administration.

2. For the purpose of determining the number of Representatives in the General Conference from the respective Members of the Organization, the Members shall be divided into seven categories as follows:

a. From each of the four Members having the largest populations there shall be thirty Representatives.

b. From each of the ten Members having the next largest populations there shall be twelve Representatives.

c. From each of the fifteen Members having the next largest populations there shall be eight Representatives.

d. From each of the twenty Members having the next largest populations there shall be six Representatives.

e. From each of the thirty Members having the next largest populations there shall be four Representatives.

f. From each of the forty Members having the next largest populations, there shall be three Representatives.

g. From each of the remaining Members there shall be one Representative.

3. The apportionment of Representatives pursuant to the foregoing formula shall be made by the General Conference upon the basis of world censuses. The first census shall be taken within ten years after the coming into force of this Treaty and subsequent censuses shall be taken in every tenth year thereafter, in such manner as the Conference shall direct. The Conference shall make a reapportionment of the Representatives within two years after each such census.

4. The non-self-governing and trust territories under the administration of Members of the Organization shall be represented in the General Conference in accordance with decisions made from time to time by the Conference. In determining the total number of Representatives from these territories, the Conference shall be guided by the principle that the number of such Representatives shall bear the same proportion to the number of Representatives in the Conference from the Members of the Organization as the population of these territories bears to the population of the Members. In allotting such Representatives to the various territories, the Conference shall take into account their respective populations and progress toward independent statehood or self-government.

5. Until the first apportionment of Representatives shall be made by the General Conference upon the basis of the first world census, the apportionment of Representatives in the Conference shall be as follows:

a. The People's Republic of China, India, the Union of Soviet Socialist Republics, and the United States of America—thirty Representatives each.

b. Brazil, France, the Federal Republic of Germany, Indonesia, Italy, Japan, Mexico, Nigeria, Pakistan, and the United Kingdom of Great Britain and Northern Ireland—twelve Representatives each.

c. Argentina, Burma, Canada, Ethiopia, Iran, the Republic of Korea, the Philippines, Poland, Romania, Spain, Thailand, Turkey, the United Arab Republic, the Democratic Republic of Viet-Nam, and Yugoslavia—eight Representatives each.

d. Afghanistan, Algeria, Australia, Ceylon, the Republic of China, Colombia, Congo (Leopoldville), Czechoslovakia, the Democratic Republic of Germany, Kenya, the People's Republic of Korea, the Federation of Malaysia, Morocco, Nepal, the Netherlands, Peru, South Africa, Sudan, Tanzania, and the Republic of Viet-Nam—six Representatives each.

e. Austria, Belgium, Bulgaria, Cambodia, Cameroun, Chile, Cuba, Denmark, Ecuador, Finland, Ghana, Greece, Guatemala, Haiti, Hungary, Iraq, the Malagasy Republic, Malawi, the Mali Republic, Portugal, Saudi Arabia, Southern Rhodesia, Sweden, Switzerland, Syria, Tunisia, Uganda, Upper Volta, Venezuela, and Yemen—four Representatives each.

f. Albania, Bolivia, Burundi, the Central African Republic, Chad, Congo (Brazzaville), Costa Rica, Dahomey, the Dominican Republic, El Salvador, Guinea, Honduras, Ireland, Israel, the Ivory Coast, Jamaica, Jordan, Laos, Lebanon, Liberia, Libya, Mauritania, Mauritius, Mongolia, New Zealand, Nicaragua, Niger, Norway, Panama, Paraguay, Rwanda, Senegal, Sierra Leone, Somalia, the South Arabian Federation, Togo, Trinidad and Tobago, Uruguay, the West Indies Federation, and Zambia—three Representatives each.

g. Cyprus, Gabon, Gambia, Guiana, Iceland, Kuwait, Luxembourg, the Maldive Islands, Malta, and Samoa (Western)—one Representative each.

h. All the non-self-governing and trust territories as a group—six Representatives.

6. Representatives shall be chosen for terms of four years, such terms to begin at noon on the third Tuesday of September in every fourth year; except that the first Representatives shall be chosen as soon as practicable after the coming into force of this Treaty and shall serve from the date upon which they convene, pursuant to paragraph 1 of Article 14 of this Treaty, until noon on the third Tuesday of September in the fourth calendar year thereafter.

7. For the first three terms after the coming into force of this Treaty, the Representatives from each Member of the Organization shall be chosen by its national legislature, except to the extent that such legislature may prescribe the election of the Representatives by popular vote. For the next three terms, not less than half of the Representatives from each Member of the Organization shall be elected by popular vote and the remainder shall be chosen by its national legislature, unless such legislature shall prescribe that all or part of such remainder shall also be elected by popular vote; provided that any Member entitled to only one Representative during this three-term period may choose its Representative either through its national legislature or by popular vote as such legislature shall determine. Beginning with the seventh term, all the Representatives of each Member of the Organization shall be elected by popular vote. The General Conference may, however, by a two-thirds vote of all the Representatives in the Conference, whether or not present or voting, postpone for not more than eight years the coming into effect of the requirement that not less than half of the Representatives shall be elected by popular vote; and the Conference may also by a like majority postpone for not more than eight years the requirement that all the Representa-

tives shall be elected by popular vote. In all elections by popular vote held under this paragraph, all persons shall be entitled to vote who are qualified to vote for the members of the most numerous branch of the national legislatures of the respective nations.

8. The Representatives of the non-self-governing and trust territories shall be chosen in such manner as the General Conference shall determine, taking into account that the right of the peoples of the respective territories to participate directly in the selection of their Representatives should be recognized to the maximum extent possible.

9. Any vacancy among the Representatives of any Member of the Organization shall be filled in such manner as the national legislature of such Member may determine; and any vacancy among the Representatives of the non-self-governing or trust territories shall be filled in such manner as the General Conference shall determine. A Representative chosen to fill a vacancy shall hold office for the remainder of the term of his predecessor.

TABLE SHOWING PROPOSED INITIAL REPRESENTATION IN THE GENERAL CONFERENCE OF THE WORLD DISARMAMENT AND WORLD DEVELOPMENT ORGANIZATION

This illustrative Table sets forth the representation in the General Conference which each nation would have under the proposed representation formula as applied to estimated populations as of July 1, 1970.

Member Nations	Population (Estimate for 1 July 1970)	Rank Relative to Population	Interim Number of Representatives
China, People's Rep. of	845,000,000	1	30
India	525,000,000	2	30
USSR	248,000,000	3	30
USA	214,000,000	4	30
Indonesia	115,000,000	5	12
Pakistan	113,000,000	6	12
Japan	101,000,000	7	12
Brazil	96,000,000	8	12
Nigeria	63,000,000	9	12
Germany, Fed. Rep. of	62,000,000	10	12
United Kingdom	56,000,000	11	12
Italy	52,000,000	12	12
France	51,000,000	13	12
Mexico	46,000,000	14	12
Philippines	37,000,000	15	8
Thailand	35,300,000	16	8
Turkey	35,000,000	17	8
Poland	33,500,000	18	8
Korea, Rep. of	33,400,000	19	8
UAR (Egypt)	33,000,000	20	8
Spain	32,500,000	21	8
Burma	29,000,000	22	8
Iran	23,500,000	23	8
Ethiopia	23,400,000	24	8
Argentina	23,000,000	25	8
Canada	22,000,000	26	8
Viet-Nam, Dem. Rep. of	21,500,000	27	8
Yugoslavia	20,500,000	28	8
Romania	19,900,000	29	8
South Africa	19,800,000	30	6
Germany, Dem. Rep. of	18,600,000	31	6
Viet-Nam, Rep. of	18,500,000	32	6
Afghanistan	18,000,000	33	6
Colombia	17,500,000	34	6
Congo (Leopoldville)	17,400,000	35	6
Morocco	15,600,000	36	6
Sudan	15,100,000	37	6
Czechoslovakia	14,700,000	38	6
China, Rep. of	14,500,000	39	6
Algeria	13,300,000	40	6
Peru	13,200,000	41	6
Netherlands	13,000,000	42	6
Malaysia, Fed. of	12,900,000	43	6
Ceylon	12,800,000	44	6
Australia	12,700,000	45	6
Korea, People's Rep. of	12,500,000	46	6
Tanzania	11,500,000	47	6

Member Nations	Population (Estimate for 1 July 1970)	Rank Relative to Population	Interim Number of Representatives
Kenya	10,600,000	**48**	6
Nepal	10,500,000	49	6
Hungary	10,400,000	50	4
Venezuela	10,200,000	51	4
Belgium	9,600,000	52	4
Portugal	9,500,000	53	4
Chile	9,300,000	54	4
Greece	9,000,000	55	4
Bulgaria	8,600,000	56	4
Uganda	8,500,000	57	4
Ghana	8,400,000	58	4
Cuba	8,200,000	59	4
Sweden	7,900,000	60	4
Iraq	7,800,000	61	4
Austria	7,500,000	62	4
Saudi Arabia	7,200,000	63	4
Malagasy Rep. (Madagascar)	7,100,000	64	4
Switzerland	6,700,000	65	4
Cambodia	6,500,000	66	4
Syria	6,300,000	67	4
Yemen	6,200,000	68	4
Ecuador	5,900,000	69	4
Upper Volta	5,800,000	70	4
Mali Republic	5,700,000	71	4
Guatemala	5,200,000	72	4
Cameroun	5,000,000	73	4
Denmark	4,950,000	74	4
Haiti	4,900,000	75	4
Finland	4,800,000	76	4
Southern Rhodesia	4,700,000	77	4
Tunisia	4,600,000	78	4
Malawi (Nyasaland)	4,300,000	79	4
Zambia (Northern Rhodesia)	4,250,000	80	3
Dominican Republic	4,200,000	81	3
Ivory Coast	4,000,000	82	3
Bolivia	3,975,000	83	3
Niger	3,950,000	84	3
Norway	3,900,000	85	3
Senegal	3,850,000	86	3
Guinea	3,800,000	87	3
Rwanda	3,400,000	88	3
El Salvador	3,350,000	89	3
Burundi	3,300,000	90	3
Israel	3,050,000	91	3
Chad	3,000,000	92	3
New Zealand	2,900,000	93	3
Ireland	2,875,000	94	3
Uruguay	2,850,000	95	3
Somalia	2,800,000	96	3
Lebanon	2,700,000	97	3
Dahomey	2,600,000	98	3
Honduras	2,500,000	99	3
Sierra Leone	2,275,000	100	3
Laos	2,250,000	101	3
Paraguay	2,225,000	102	3
Albania	2,150,000	103	3
Jordan	2,100,000	104	3
Nicaragua	1,925,000	105	3

Member Nations	Population (Estimate for 1 July 1970)	Rank Relative to Population	Interim Number of Representatives
Jamaica	1,900,000	106	3
Libya	1,875,000	107	3
Togo	1,850,000	108	3
Costa Rica	1,750,000	109	3
Central African Republic	1,450,000	110	3
Panama	1,400,000	111	3
South Arabian Federation	1,275,000	112	3
Mongolia	1,250,000	113	3
Liberia	1,150,000	114	3
Trinidad and Tobago	1,125,000	115	3
Mauritania	1,000,000	116	3
Congo (Brazzaville)	950,000	117	3
Mauritius	850,000	118	3
West Indies Federation	750,000	119	3
Guyana	725,000	120	1
Cyprus	650,000	121	1
Gabon	500,000	122	1
Kuwait	450,000	123	1
Gambia	350,000	124	1
Luxembourg	340,000	125	1
Malta	330,000	126	1
Iceland	205,000	127	1
Samoa (Western)	150,000	128	1
Maldive Islands	100,000	129	1
	3,615,500,000		730
Non-self-governing or trust territories	28,400,000		6
TOTAL	3,643,900,000		736

NOTE. This proposal constitutes an important part of a plan for a new international organization which would assist the United Nations in maintaining peace, in enforcing a disarmament treaty, and in the economic development of the developing nations. It provides in effect for a second chamber of the United Nations, as major decisions of the General Conference would be subject to revocation by the General Assembly or the Security Council of the United Nations. Alternatively, a similar scale could be adopted for the General Assembly itself, for a new representative body of the United Nations under a revised Charter, or for a consultative parliamentary body established by a resolution of the General Assembly as its subsidiary organ.

In their comment on an earlier draft of this proposal the authors have pointed out that over a period of years they "have studied many plans for determining representation by various formulas that would take account of such factors as relative literacy, relative wealth as measured by per capita income, etc." They have concluded, however, that "the introduction of any such other factors would raise so many complications and involve such uncertain and invidious distinctions that it is wiser to hold to the less elaborate formula herein proposed." CLARK and SOHN, World Peace Through World Law: Two Alternative Plans (3d ed., Cambridge, Mass., 1966), p. xxi. They add that:

"The principles governing the proposed representation plan are: (1) that every member Nation, however small, should be entitled to some representation; (2) that there should be a reasonable upper limit upon the representation of even the largest member Nation; and (3) that, subject to these provisions, representation should be apportioned by groups of nations according to their relative populations without attempting to reflect any such factors as relative natural resources, productive capacity, trade or literacy. . . .

"The proposed plan is avowedly a compromise as between two main factors,—the factor of relative populations and the factor of the independent statehood of the individual separate nations. It will be seen, however, that it is a compromise which gives major weight to the factor of independent statehood as demonstrated by the fact that the twelve most populous nations, with a combined population far greater than the combined population of the eighty-seven smaller nations, would, nevertheless, have a representation considerably less than that of the smaller nations. In fact, upon the basis of estimated populations as of July 1, 1965, the eighty-seven smaller nations with a combined population of 891 million would have 311 Representatives, whereas the twelve largest nations with a combined population of 2186 million would have only 240 Representatives. While it is clearly recognized that this plan results in heavy overrepresentation in relation to population of the smaller and middle-sized nations, this overrepresentation is deemed advisable in order to recognize the separate existence of the various national states, some of them very old, with their distinct histories and traditions.

"It may be argued that the plan goes too far in respect of not giving weight to the population factor. A slight consideration makes it clear, however, that no plan of representation proportionate to or even closely related to population would be either practicable or possibly acceptable. For example, an apportionment of Representatives in strict accordance with relative populations would entitle the largest nation, the People's Republic of China with its estimated 720 million people in 1965, to have 4000 times as many Representatives as Iceland with its estimated 180 thousand people in 1965. And if one assumes that even the smallest nations should have one Representative, it is plain that any plan even nearly related to population would result in a General Assembly of impracticable size.

"In short, while the proposed plan takes into important account relative populations, it would be inaccurate to say that it is based upon or is even closely related to that factor.

"The plan also takes into account certain very practical considerations relating to acceptability, of which the following are the most important: (1) that it is, in practice, essential to allot the same maximum representation to the United States and the Soviet Union, for the simple reason that neither could possibly accept a plan under which the other was given a larger voice; and in this age, it is impossible to deny the same maximum representation to the two great Asian nations—mainland China and India—which by tremendous margins have the largest populations in the world; (2) that it would be unwise and unacceptable to distinguish between the eight middle-sized nations, since neither France, West Germany, Italy nor the United Kingdom would consent to less representation than the others and, this being assumed, the same representation should not be denied to the considerably larger nations in this category, namely, Brazil, Indonesia, Japan and Pakistan; and (3) that once this principle of equal representation within each of the first two categories is accepted, it should also be applied to the other four categories.

"In summary, the proposed apportionment seeks: (a) the utmost practical degree of fairness to all the nations; and (b) general acceptability in the sense that, on due consideration, all the various nations would perceive that the plan is impartially conceived without intention to prefer or prejudice any particular nation or group of nations. As in the case of proposed solutions to other thorny problems, however, the authors do not presume to say that this is the only or the perfect solution. What they can say is that the proposal is the result of years of consideration of many other alternative plans, all of which, on analysis, seemed to present more serious objections than this proposal." *Idem*, pp. 25–27.

Chapter VI

MAINTENANCE OF INTERNATIONAL PEACE AND SECURITY

Section 1. Testing the Original Powers of the United Nations

SPANISH QUESTION

NOTE. The problem of the relations between the United Nations and Spain occupied the United Nations from the very beginning. The Franco regime had been helped to power by the Axis States and during the war, though remaining neutral, had maintained a close relationship with them. At the San Francisco Conference, during the discussion in the First Commission on membership, on 19 June 1945, the delegate of Mexico had stated that "It is the understanding of the Delegation of Mexico that paragraph 2 of Chapter III cannot be applied to the States whose regimes have been established with the help of military forces belonging to the countries which have waged war against the United Nations, as long as those regimes are in power." The Commission approved this interpretation by acclamation and incorporated it in the report to the Conference, which approved it without dissent. See UNCIO Doc. 1167, I/10, pp. 17–29; 6 UNCIO Documents, pp. 124–136; 1 *idem*, pp. 615, 620.

On 2 August 1945, at the end of the Potsdam Conference, Marshal Stalin, President Truman and Prime Minister Attlee signed a protocol of the proceedings which included the following statement: "The three Governments, so far as they are concerned, will support applications for membership from those States which have remained neutral during the war and which fulfil the qualifications set out above [of Article 4 of the United Nations Charter]. The three Governments feel bound, however, to make it clear that they for their part would not favour any application for membership put forward by the present Spanish Government, which, having been founded with the support of the Axis Powers, does not, in view of its origins, its nature, its record and its close association with the aggressor States, possess the qualifications necessary to justify such membership." British Parliamentary Papers, Misc. No. 6 (1947), Cmd. 7087, p. 12; Report of the Sub-Committee on the Spanish Question [SCOR, I.2, Special Supp. (S/75)], p. 38.

On 9 February 1946, the General Assembly endorsed these two statements and recommended that "the Members of the United Nations should act in accordance with the letter and the spirit of these statements in the conduct of their future relations with Spain." Resolution 32(I); GA Resolutions, I.1 (A/64), p. 39.

On 4 March 1946, France, the United Kingdom and the United States made a joint declaration: "It is agreed that so long as General Franco continues in control of Spain, the Spanish people cannot anticipate full and cordial association with those nations of the world which have, by common effort, brought defeat to German Nazism and Italian Fascism, which aided the present Spanish regime in its rise to power and after which the regime was patterned.

"There is no intention of interfering in the internal affairs of Spain. The Spanish people themselves must in the long run work out their own destiny. In spite of the present regime's repressive measures against orderly efforts of the Spanish people to organize and give expression to their political aspirations, the three Governments are hopeful that the Spanish people will not again be subjected to the horrors and bitterness of civil strife.

"On the contrary, it is hoped that leading patriotic and liberal-minded Spaniards may soon find means to bring about a peaceful withdrawal of Franco, the abolition of the Falange, and the establishment of an interim or caretaker government under which the Spanish people may have an opportunity freely to determine the type of Government they wish to have and to choose their leaders. Political amnesty, return of exiled Spaniards, freedom of assembly and political association and provision for free public elections are essential. An interim government which would be and would remain dedicated to these ends should receive the recognition and support of all freedom-loving peoples.

"Such recognition would include full diplomatic relations and the taking of such practical measures to assist in the solution of Spain's economic problems as may be practicable in the circumstances prevailing. Such measures are not now possible. The question of the maintenance or termination by the Governments of France, the United Kingdom and the United States of diplomatic relations with the present Spanish regime is a matter to be decided in the light of events and after taking into account the efforts of the Spanish people to achieve their own freedom." 14 DSB (1946), p. 412; Report of the Sub-Committee on the Spanish Question [SCOR, I.2, Special Supp. (S/75)], pp. 38–9.

In April 1946, the representative of Poland, invoking Articles 2(6), 34 and 35 of the Charter, requested the Security Council to place on its agenda "the situation arising from the existence and activities of the Franco regime in Spain." S/32 and S/34; SCOR, I.1, Supp. 2, pp. 54–55.

1.   *Discussion in the Security Council, 17–29 April 1946.*

SCOR, I.1, No. 2, pp. 154–200, 216–245.

Mr. LANGE (Poland): In the name of the Government of the Republic of Poland, I wish to draw the attention of the Security Council to a situation which is causing international friction and which presents a serious danger to international peace and security. This situation arises out of the existence and activities of the fascist Franco regime in Spain.

The fact is well known and generally and officially recognized today that the Franco regime was brought into power against the will of the Spanish people by the armed forces of the Axis Powers which waged war against the United Nations. The Franco regime is the creation of the enemies of the United Nations. It is the lone alien survivor of the Axis in a world of international peace and justice to which the United Nations is committed, a dangerous remnant of the enemies which they defeated at such tremendous cost of blood and wealth.   .   .   .

[After referring to the San Francisco decision on Spain and to the General Assembly Resolution 32(I), Mr. Lange continued as follows:]

Thus, the fact that the Franco regime was put into power by Fascist Italy and Nazi Germany was universally accepted by all the United Nations. No further evidence to support this charge is required. By this act alone it was established that the question of the Franco regime is not an internal affair of interest to Spain alone but an international problem which concerns all the United Nations. . . .

We are not interested in the purely domestic affairs of Spain. It was not interest in the domestic affairs of Roumania, Hungary and Bulgaria which prompted us to destroy the enemy regimes of these countries and to set up a system of government committed to the maintenance of peace and capable of maintaining that peace. These countries were Axis satellites; so is the fascist regime in Spain; and I demand that you draw your proper conclusions.

The fascist regime in Spain is a problem not only of the past; it is a serious problem of the present. Unless appropriate action is taken by this Council, it will become a fateful problem for the future. For Franco's regime in Spain, following the defeat of Italy, Germany and Japan by the United Nations, continues to maintain and to serve the purpose of the Axis. It continues to exist as a centre of fascist infection and a springboard for war which once more may spread all over the world.

Under the Franco regime Spain continues to be an armed camp. The former American Ambassador in Madrid, Norman Armour, on his return from Spain on 22 December 1945, declared that the Franco Government maintains a standing army of from 600,000 to 700,000 men. I should like to add that never in the course of her history did Spain have as large an army as she has at present.

Manufacture of arms flourishes, and sections of the Spanish border with France have been heavily fortified. Tank traps have been built on the roads; bridges and passes across the Pyrenees are mined.

And finally, a month ago, the fascist Government in Spain started to mass military forces along the French border. I have before me a memorandum on the concentration of fascist Spanish troops in the Pyrenees, submitted to our delegation by General Sarabia, Minister for War of the Spanish Republic. According to this document, 200,-000 men are massed in Catalonia alone. . . .

The constant intrigues of the Franco regime against the French Republic, which last year regained her freedom from the double oppression of the German tyranny and of fascist traitors at home, finally compelled the Government of France, whose distinguished representative sits among us, to close the frontier between France and Spain. The closing of the frontier implies interruption of railway traffic, stoppage of postal and telegraphic services and of the passage of persons across the border.

I submit for the consideration of the Council the following question: When borders between two countries are hermetically sealed, when one Government assembles large aggregations of troops along the border of another country, does this not constitute international friction likely to endanger the maintenance of international peace and security? If your answer is in the negative then I do not know what international friction is. Do we have to wait until guns are being fired, until bombs are dropped, until men are killed and cities destroyed, in order to proclaim that the situation is one of international friction?

I urge and beseech you not to deal lightly with situations such as this. This is international friction. This is danger to international peace and security. And I am sure that all the members of this Council will share my view that the responsibility for this danger rests not upon the Government of the French Republic, but upon the fascist regime placed in power by the Axis against the will and the heroic resistance of the Spanish people. . . .

This is a situation of the nature referred to in Article 34 of our Charter, one which has already led to international friction and which most seriously endangers international peace and security. Article 35 gives us the right to take up the question. Article 1 of the Charter specifies the purposes of the United Nations and Article 2 enumerates the principles which must be followed in pursuit of these purposes. Paragraph 6 of Article 2 declares:

"The Organization shall ensure that States which are not Members of the United Nations act in accordance with these principles so far as may be necessary for the maintenance of international peace and security."

The fascist regime in Spain does not act in accordance with the principles of the United Nations, nor has it ever given any evidence that it intends to do so. It endangers the maintenance of international peace and security. It is, therefore, the duty of our Organization to insure that any nation, whether a Member or not, does not endanger international peace and security. . . .

In the name of the Government of the Republic of Poland, I call upon you to fulfil your duty and to adopt the following resolution:

"The Security Council

"Declares that the existence and activities of the Franco regime in Spain have led to international friction and endangered international peace and security;

"Calls upon, in accordance with the authority vested in it under Articles 39 and 41 of the Charter, all Members of the United Nations who maintain diplomatic relations with the Franco Government to sever such relations immediately;

"Expresses its deep sympathy to the Spanish people; hopes and expects that the people of Spain will regain the freedom of which they have been deprived with the aid and contrivance of Fascist Italy and Nazi Germany, and

"Is convinced that the day will come soon when it will be able to welcome the Spanish nation into the community of the United Nations."

Mr. VAN KLEFFENS (Netherlands): . . . I cannot say that on the basis of the evidence that has been placed before us, much of which is purely conjectural, a case has been made out justifying a verdict that the Franco regime is endangering international peace and security. If the French Government chose to close the frontier, that surely is not sufficient evidence. It only shows that the French Government has been moved to stop traffic across the frontier, inasmuch as the movement of Spanish troops has admittedly taken place after and not before the closing of the frontier.

I have not heard the Polish delegation say one word which pointed with any degree of certainty or even probability to fundamental offensive action on the part of the Spanish armed forces, and I must say that whatever my feeling concerning the Franco regime, I do not think it is so foolish as to take offensive action. . . .

I therefore come to the conclusion that there is not sufficient ground for the Council to take any measures. I do not think that the resolution adopted by the first session of the General Assembly with regard to Spain is a good reason for the Security Council now to take measures against that regime. Clearly, the Assembly's resolution did not call for any measures to be taken by the Council. We may not like the Franco regime, and we may not admit Spain as a Member of the United Nations as long as the Franco regime is in power there, but that does not mean that we must take positive action against that regime or that we are entitled to do so.

If we are to interfere in Spanish affairs on the basis of such evidence as has been placed before us, I think we would establish a most regrettable and harmful precedent for all sorts of ill-founded intervention. We are discussing the matter fully, and that is certainly useful. The Franco regime is, as I said, a disturbing factor in this postwar world which does Spain no good as a nation. But I cannot see that there are valid grounds, in the light of the Charter, to go beyond discussion.

So long as Franco does not really threaten international peace and security, whether Spain wants to keep that regime or not is a matter for Spain and for Spain alone. It is, in my opinion, in the language of the Charter, a matter which is essentially within Spain's domestic jurisdiction. . . .

Sir Alexander CADOGAN (UK): . . . The representative of any Member of the United Nations is at liberty, either individually or jointly with his colleagues, to express his country's disapproval of the regime in force in any other country.

It is perfectly within their rights in the United Nations for Members to go further and declare they will not support the admission to the United Nations of a country subjected to such a regime, but before the Council embarks on collective action, it must be sure that it does so in conformity with the Charter and that its action is calculated to achieve the desired result.

Previous speakers have called attention to paragraph 6 of Article 2 of the Charter, but I must point out that that paragraph is immediately followed by a further statement, in paragraph 7, to the effect that nothing in this Charter authorizes the United Nations to intervene in matters which are essentially within the domestic jurisdiction of any State. The nature of the regime in any given country is indisputably a matter of domestic jurisdiction.

But those who drafted the Charter wisely made one exception to this rule, designed to meet the case where a regime such as the Nazi regime in Germany might be of so aggressive a nature as plainly to threaten the peace and security of other countries. The paragraph I have quoted also lays down that this principle, that is to say, the principle of non-intervention in matters of domestic jurisdiction, shall not prejudice the application of enforcement matters [i. e., measures] under Chapter VII. That is the Chapter of the Charter which deals with enforcement measures and the first Article of that Chapter, Article 39, governs the whole Chapter. It lays down that "The Security Council shall determine the existence of any threat to the peace, breach of the peace, or act of aggression and shall make recommendations", or decide on methods "to maintain or restore international peace and security".

The Polish representative has not sought to show that there is a case for the application of Chapter VII. He bases his appeal on Articles 34 and 35 of the Charter, which form part of Chapter VI. Therefore, it would appear that in spite of his reference to the "existence . . . of the Franco regime in Spain", what he claims is that the Spanish Government has taken or is taking measures which, in the words of Article 34, might "lead to international friction or give rise to a dispute."

That is the question actually submitted to the Council, and I must say that I do not find the evidence submitted sufficiently convincing.

. . .

Now as regards the resolution which the representative of Poland has submitted, it would appear that the only thing the Council could do under Chapter VI in regard to a situation such as that defined in Article 34 would be, under Article 36, to "recommend appropriate procedures or methods of adjustment".

The only operative part of the Polish resolution is that which requires Members of the United Nations to sever diplomatic relations with the Spanish Government immediately. The severance of diplomatic relations is one of the first enforcement measures prescribed in Chapter VII of the Charter, which is not invoked here, and can only be invoked if the Council determines "the existence of any threat to the peace, breach of the peace, or act of aggression".

I cannot admit that the case so far made against the Spanish Government has established the existence of such a threat to the peace, breach of the peace, or act of aggression, and I do not therefore consider it appropriate to ask now for a collective severance of diplomatic relations. Nor, in view of what I have just said, can I think that such a step would be wise. . . .

Mr. GROMYKO (USSR): . . . It has been claimed that the Polish statement constitutes interference in the domestic affairs of Spain, and that such interference is prohibited under Article 2, paragraph 7, of the Charter. Such assertions are, however, ill-founded and a distortion of the true facts. The Charter indeed contains a provision with reference to non-interference on the part of the United Nations in the domestic affairs of any State. But it is clearly stated in the Charter that interference by the United Nations in the domestic affairs of a State should not take place in normal circumstances, that is to say, when the internal situation in any State does not constitute a threat to international peace and security. The Charter admits and provides for the necessity of taking definite measures with regard to States when their internal situation constitutes a threat to international peace and security. This is also clearly stated in Article 2 of the Charter. So the Charter leaves no doubt whatever under which circumstances the United Nations cannot and should not intervene in the internal affairs of sovereign States and under which circumstances the United Nations both can and should take certain measures required by the situation arising even out of the internal affairs of a State when these internal affairs constitute a menace to international peace and security. . . .

Peace-loving humanity will not understand a refusal on the part of the Security Council to take decisive measures to prevent the hydra of fascism, which has been decapitated a number of times by the United Nations, from rearing another head elsewhere. I hope the Security Council will correctly appraise the situation in Spain and the serious threat it represents for future peace, and that the Council will support the proposal submitted by the Polish representative. Such a decision would be in conformity with the decision adopted by the Berlin Conference of the Heads of State of the three great Powers and with the resolution taken by the General Assembly during the first part of its first session, defining the general principles by which States Members of the United Nations should be guided in determining their relations with the present fascist regime in Spain. Such a decision would be in conformity with the spirit and letter of the United Nations Charter and with the high purposes and principles proclaimed by our Organization, and would also serve to back the democratic forces in Spain. It would be in conformity with the interests of the Spanish people, since it would help them to rid themselves of the fascist regime in Spain and take a worthy place in the family of the peace-loving peoples of the world. . . .

Colonel HODGSON (Australia): . . . Now, at the outset, the question of domestic jurisdiction has been raised. We have one important limitation in this Council, imposed by Article 2 of the Charter. It expressly forbids us to intervene in a matter which is essentially one of domestic jurisdiction. As a general rule, it follows that we cannot make recommendations concerning the government of any country. Now the Australian Government places great stress on that limitation. It believes it is one of the most valuable, one of the very few safeguards for the protection of small nations. The large nations, the five permanent members, are, of course, safeguarded always by their right to veto.

Prima facie, then, this question is one of domestic jurisdiction. But the line between what is of international concern and what is of domestic concern is not fixed, it is mutable. It seems reasonably clear that a government of fascist origin may, by its actions, by its policy, both at home and abroad, in conjunction with reactionary groups of other countries, seriously threaten international peace. For example, Hitlerite Germany actively pursued a domestic policy deliberately aimed at international friction.

The mere existence of a fascist government as such does not, therefore, give us the right to discuss it. We have to have an investigation and proof that its policy and activities are of international concern, and therefore within the ambit of the Charter. . . .

Now, the Polish representative brought his case under Chapter VI. But Chapter VI calls for investigation. It requires investigation before we can take any action. We have to take a decision and ascertain facts. But he jumps straight away into Chapter VII, Articles 39 and 41, which operate only against a proved aggressor.

The Australian viewpoint has been consistent throughout. We have demanded investigation and evidence and proved facts before reaching decisions. . . .

We want an investigation into three questions. . . .

First, is it a matter of international concern and not merely of domestic jurisdiction?

Secondly, is the situation a cause of international friction?

If the answer to that question is affirmative, the following question arises: Thirdly, is it endangering international peace and security?

If the answer to these questions is negative, we can take no further action. If the answer is affirmative, then, and then only, can this Council decide what can and should be done. . . .

So, I am going to propose an amendment to the Polish resol\
.   .   .   for the establishment of a sub-committee of this Council
investigate and examine the facts.   .   .   .

Mr. GROMYKO (USSR):   .   .   .   The statement by Dr. Lange,
the representative of Poland, and also the discussions which have tak-
en place in the Security Council   .   .   .   leave no room for doubt that
the fascist regime of Franco at present existing in Spain is indeed a
serious danger to international peace and security.

In view of this fact, there is no need to set up any kind of commission to study the question.   In the presence of an abundance of facts
and evidence which confirm the rightness of the accusation brought
against the fascist regime of Franco by the representative of Poland,
the setting up of a commission might have a negative effect on world
public opinion, as well as on democratic forces in Spain itself.   It would
be impossible to justify the setting up of such a commission in the
eyes of the public opinion of the world, which demands the complete
severance of relations with the Franco regime, and not delays, for
which it is impossible to find any justification.   For these reasons I
declare myself opposed to the proposal to set up a commission.

[The following resolution was adopted at the 39th meeting by 10
votes, the USSR abstaining:

"The attention of the Security Council has been drawn to the situation in Spain by a Member of the United Nations acting in accordance
with Article 35 of the Charter, and the Security Council has been
asked to declare that this situation has led to international friction
and endangers international peace and security.

"Therefore the Security Council, keeping in mind the unanimous
moral condemnation of the Franco regime in the Security Council,
and the resolutions concerning Spain which were adopted at the United
Nations Conference on International Organization at San Francisco
and at the first General Assembly of the United Nations; and the
views expressed by members of the Security Council regarding the
Franco regime,

"Hereby resolves: to make further studies in order to determine
whether the situation in Spain has led to international friction and
does endanger international peace and security, and if it so finds, then
to determine what practical measures the United Nations may take.

"To this end, the Security Council appoints a Sub-Committee of five
of its members and instructs this Sub-Committee to examine the statements made before the Security Council concerning Spain, to receive
further statements and documents, and to conduct such inquiries as
it may deem necessary, and to report to the Security Council before
the end of May."

Representatives of Australia, Brazil, China, France and Poland were
appointed to the Sub-Committee.]

2. *Report of the Sub-Committee on the Spanish Question, 31 May 1946.*

SCOR, I.2, Special Supp., pp. 1–6.

The Sub-Committee's examination of the facts of the case has been based mainly upon documents received from Members of the United Nations in response to a request to them to supply all relevant information and also in response to inquiries on specific questions. A public announcement was made that the Committee would welcome information from any sources and it was in response to this general invitation that an extensive submission was also made by the Spanish Republican Government. The Sub-Committee approached its task with an earnest endeavor, first, to ascertain the relevant facts and then to apply the laws of the Charter to the facts as ascertained.

There can be no question that the situation in Spain is of international concern. That fact is sufficiently evidenced by the resolution of the first part of the first session of the General Assembly in London, the resolution of the Security Council and the joint declaration of the United States, United Kingdom and France dated 4 March 1946.

It is also plain that the facts established by the evidence before the Committee are by no means of essentially local or domestic concern to Spain. What is imputed to the Franco regime is that it is threatening the maintenance of international peace and security and that it is causing international friction. The allegations against the Franco regime involve matters which travel far beyond domestic jurisdiction and which concern the maintenance of international peace and security and the smooth and efficient working of the United Nations as the instrument mainly responsible for performing this duty. . . .

On the basis of the material placed before it, the Sub-Committee has come to the following conclusions:

(a) In origin, nature, structure and general conduct, the Franco regime is a Fascist regime patterned on, and established largely as a result of aid received from Hitler's Nazi Germany and Mussolini's Fascist Italy.

(b) During the long struggle of the United Nations against Hitler and Mussolini, Franco, despite continued Allied protests, gave very substantial aid to the enemy Powers. First, for example, from 1941 to 1945 the Blue Infantry Division, the Spanish Legion of Volunteers and the Salvador Air Squadron fought against Soviet Russia on the Eastern front. Second, in the summer of 1940 Spain seized Tangier in breach of international statute, and as a result of Spain maintaining a large army in Spanish Morocco large numbers of Allied troops were immobilized in North Africa.

(c) Incontrovertible documentary evidence establishes that Franco was a guilty party, with Hitler and Mussolini, in the conspiracy to wage war against those countries which eventually in the course of the world war became banded together as the United Nations. It was part of the conspiracy that Franco's full belligerency should be postponed until a time to be mutually agreed upon.   .   .   .

There is also extensive evidence, chiefly from underground sources but which is considered by the Sub-Committee to be authentic and credible, even if not susceptible of proof in all its details, indicating that the Franco regime continues to practice those methods of persecution of political opponents and police supervision over its people which are characteristic of Fascist regimes and which are inconsistent with the principles of the United Nations concerning the respect for human rights and for the fundamental freedoms.

The Sub-Committee gave close attention to evidence regarding the military strength and plans of Franco Spain, the production of war materials in Spain and, in general, the preparations for war on the part of Franco Spain. Various estimates were obtained of the strength of the naval, military and air forces and of the para-military organizations in the country and regarding the building of fortifications. The number of men under arms is far larger than might be expected in any peace-loving and non-aggressive country. Further, the activities on the French frontier seemed to indicate the possibility of expectation of conflict by Franco Spain. However, it must be remembered that it is the very essence of military dictatorships to maintain large armies for the purpose of suppressing internal opposition.

The Sub-Committee examined the circumstances of the recent closing of the Franco-Spanish frontier. While there is no clear evidence that the closing of the frontier was the result of any immediate threat of military action as between France and Spain, it is plain that a state of tension was thereby brought into existence and international friction accentuated. In reply to a question addressed to it by the Secretary-General, at the request of the Sub-Committee, the French Government furnished the following information in relation to the closing of the frontier:

"The decision of the French Government to close the Franco-Spanish frontier was taken following upon the increasing difficulties which arose, at the close of hostilities in Europe, in the relations of France and the Franco Government, the maintenance of which, after the collapse of the totalitarian regime, appears to be a challenge to the victorious democracies.

"The sentiments of justified mistrust which the methods and political tendencies of the dictatorial Spanish regime evoked in French public opinion were still more accentuated at the end of 1945 by the revelations concerning Franco collusion with the Axis Powers. In a note of 12 December 1945, addressed to London and Washington, the French Government suggested that the British and United States Governments should study the most appropriate measures to hasten the end of the present regime in Spain, which had been implicitly condemned by the Allies at Potsdam on 2 August 1945. For this purpose, France suggested a joint rupture of relations with Franco, being of the opinion that the democratic nations should not continue to give him the support which the maintenance of diplomatic and commercial relations actually gave him.

"It was in the same spirit that, on 17 January 1946, the National Constituent Assembly invited the Provisional Government of the Republic, by a motion adopted with an imposing majority, to prepare to break off relations with the Spanish Government. While the French diplomatic action did not have the reception which might have been expected, the Franco authorities accentuated the repressive measures against the Republicans inside Spain. They caused one of them, Cristino Garcia, to be executed, a man in whose fate French public opinion took a very great interest, on account of the active part which he had played in France during the battles for the liberation.

"Coming after other repressive measures which had already given rise to indignation, this act was the occasion for the Constituent Assembly, on 24 January 1946, to renew the motion which it had previously voted. It was in these circumstances that the Government of the Republic decided, on 26 February, pending the adoption of concerted measures with the Allies, to close the frontier with effect as from 1 March 1946."

Such evidence as was available regarding the training and equipment of the Spanish army and the existing state of its armaments would not justify a finding that Spain was at the present time preparing for an act of aggression.

Nevertheless, having regard to the proved conspiracies of Franco with Hitler and Mussolini, the maintenance in Spain of large forces, and the other evidence before us, it is plain that Franco Spain might again become a ready instrument of aggressive warfare. The fact that there are two rival Spanish Governments in existence is in itself a potential danger to the peace, inasmuch as there is always the possibility of civil strife and the possibility of intervention by other countries. The strategic situation and resources of Spain, coupled with the declared unfitness of Franco Spain for membership in the United Nations, means that at the present time the United Nations system of security will be dangerously incomplete. . . .

The first crucial point to be considered is whether the situation in Spain is of such a kind as to justify direct executive action by Security Council itself under Chapter VII of the Charter which deals with various types of enforcement action which Members are obligated to take at the direction of the Security Council.

The original complaint to the Security Council by Poland was aimed at placing the Spanish question on the agenda of the Council, and Articles 34 and 35 of the Charter alone were mentioned. But the resolution subsequently placed before the Security Council by Poland suggested action based upon the enforcement powers conferred upon the Security Council under Articles 39 and 41 of the Charter. Both these Articles are in Chapter VII.

The Polish draft resolution before the Security Council asserted that the existence and activities of the Franco regime "have led to international friction and endanger international peace and security." But these are not the conditions which must be satisfied before the Security Council has jurisdiction, under Articles 39 and 41, to decide to call upon Members of the United Nations to apply the enforcement measures set out in Articles 41 and 42. Before direct action under Article 41 or 42 can be ordered, the Charter requires that the Security Council must determine, under Article 39, the existence of a threat to the peace or a breach of the peace, or an act of aggression.

In the first place, the question is whether the evidence justifies a positive and affirmative finding under Article 39.

The juridical meaning of Article 39 is that the Security Council has to measure the situation as at the moment of the proposed action on its part, it being the clear intention of the Charter that the Security Council should only call for direct enforcement measures, which include the actual waging of war, provided it is affirmatively satisfied that a threat to the peace, or a breach of the peace, or an act of aggression has actually come into existence.

A very sharp instrument has been entrusted to the Security Council by the United Nations under Chapter VII of the Charter, and the Security Council must be careful that this instrument is not blunted nor used in any way which would strain the intentions of the Charter or which would not be applicable in all similar cases.

In the opinion of the Sub-Committee the Security Council cannot, on the present evidence, make the determination required by Article 39. No breach of the peace has yet occurred. No act of aggression has been proved. No threat to the peace has been established. Therefore, none of the series of enforcement measures set out in Articles 41 and 42 can at the present time be directed by the Security Council.

. . .

Nevertheless, in the opinion of the Sub-Committee, the matters brought before the Security Council in relation to Franco Spain are of so serious a nature that the Security Council, in discharging its primary responsibility for the maintenance of international peace and security, should not allow them to pass from its notice simply because it is unable to take the direct enforcement measures proposed in the Polish draft resolution.

Chapter VI of the Charter empowers the Security Council to examine "any situation which might lead to international friction" in order to determine whether the continuation of the situation is "likely to endanger the maintenance of international peace and security." In the opinion of the Sub-Committee, the Spanish situation is one which has already led to international friction. The investigation has convinced the Sub-Committee, not only that international friction has occurred, but that it is almost bound to recur.   .   .   .

The Sub-Committee finds that the present situation in Spain, though not an existing threat within the meaning of Article 39, is a situation the continuance of which is in fact likely to endanger the maintenance of international peace and security. The situation in Spain thus falls to be dealt with by the Security Council under Chapter VI of the Charter, which covers measures of peaceful settlement and adjustment.

The Security Council is empowered under Article 36 to recommend appropriate procedures or methods of adjustment of such a situation. It is not vested with executive authority, as in the case of Chapter VII, but it has the duty of devising methods of adjustment adequate to meet the given situation.

Moreover, while the Security Council exercises a primary duty in regard to the maintenance of international peace and security, the General Assembly is also vested by the Charter with power to deal with such situations. The General Assembly has power under Article 14 to make recommendations as to the peaceful adjustment of any situation and it is only when the Security Council is actually handling a situation itself that the General Assembly cannot exercise this power. Furthermore, the General Assembly's powers of recommendation under Article 10 cover all matters within the scope of the Charter, including the purposes of the Charter set out in paragraph 2 of Article 1, which is to take appropriate measures to strengthen universal peace.
.   .

The conclusions to which the Sub-Committee has come are as follows:

(a) Although the activities of the Franco regime do not at present constitute an existing threat to the peace within the meaning of Article 39 of the Charter and therefore the Security Council has no jurisdiction to direct or to authorize enforcement measures under Article 40 or 42, nevertheless such activities do constitute a situation which is a potential menace to international peace and security and which therefore is a situation "likely to endanger the maintenance of international peace and security" within the meaning of Article 34 of the Charter.

(b) The Security Council is therefore empowered by paragraph 1 of Article 36 to recommend appropriate procedures or methods of adjustment in order to improve the situation mentioned in (a) above.

The final question is what action should be recommended by the Sub-Committee to the Security Council. After considering carefully what would be effective and appropriate measures to meet the particular case, and having regard to the important powers of the General Assembly under Article 10 of the Charter, the Sub-Committee recommends as follows:

(a) The endorsement by the Security Council of the principles contained in the declaration by the Governments of the United Kingdom, the United States and France, dated 4 March 1946.

(b) The transmitting by the Security Council to the General Assembly of the evidence and reports of this Sub-Committee, together with the recommendation that unless the Franco regime is withdrawn and the other conditions of political freedom set out in the declaration are, in the opinion of the General Assembly, fully satisfied, a resolution be passed by the General Assembly recommending that diplomatic relations with the Franco regime be terminated forthwith by each Member of the United Nations.

(c) The taking of appropriate steps by the Secretary-General to communicate these recommendations to all Members of the United Nations and all others concerned.

[The Polish representative on the Sub-Committee made the following reservations to this Report:

"The functions of the Security Council are preventive as well as repressive. The Security Council is free, within the purposes and principles of the Organization, to determine whether a situation is a threat to the peace in the sense of Article 39. The Charter does not demand that such a situation, in order to be recognized as a threat to the peace, be an immediate danger of a breach of peace or act of aggression within the next few days, weeks or even months. Potential, as well as imminent, dangers can be construed as a threat to the peace in the sense of Article 39. To affirm otherwise would mean that no action by the Security Council is possible in situations like that of Mussolini before the imminent invasion of Abyssinia or that of Hitler before the first bombs were dropped on Polish cities. Unless threats to the peace are taken care of by the Security Council at an early stage while they still are potential and easy to remove, the United Nations may find themselves in face of situations beyond their power to control.

"The enumeration in Article 41 of the Charter of steps such as interruption of postal, telegraphic and radio communications and the severance of diplomatic relations indicates clearly that potential threats to the peace are also covered by Article 39. If only imminent threats to the peace were envisaged in Article 39, measures short of economic and military sanctions would be meaningless.

"For the reasons indicated, the Polish representative cannot agree with the statement that the activities of the Franco regime do not represent a threat to the peace within the meaning of Article 39 of the Charter and that the Security Council has no jurisdiction to direct, in this case, severance of diplomatic relations. While he supports the recommendations of the Sub-Committee he does so without prejudice to the rights of the Security Council." SCOR, I.2, Special Supp., p. 6.]

3. *Discussion in the Security Council on the Report
of the Sub-Committee, 6–18 June 1946.*

SCOR, I.1, No. 2, pp. 311–381.

Mr. EVATT (Australia): . . . It will be noticed that the majority of the Sub-Committee take the view that the situation in Spain is not of the kind described in Chapter VII: that is, that there is no existing threat to peace. As a consequence of that decision, the question has been raised whether or not the proposed action by the Council would be contrary to the provisions of Article 2, paragraph 7 of the Charter, namely that the United Nations cannot intervene in a matter essentially within the jurisdiction of a State. Now, in my opinion, this argument springs from fallacious logic and it should be pointed out quite clearly that Article 2, paragraph 7 of the Charter does not say that the United Nations shall not intervene in any matter which does not fall within Chapter VII. What it does say is that the United Nations shall not intervene in a matter essentially within the domestic jurisdiction of a State. When considering this point we can forget about Chapter VII. We should concern ourselves only with the terms of Article 2, paragraph 7 and ask ourselves whether or not this question is essentially within the domestic jurisdiction of Spain. That is a question of fact. It depends upon the circumstances of the particular case.

At the San Francisco Conference, together with other colleagues sitting at this Council with me today, I had some share in the final drafting of Article 2, paragraph 7, and I should like to quote from the memorandum presented by my delegation to the First Committee of Commission I at that Conference:

"Once a matter is recognized as one of legitimate international concern, no exception to the general rule is needed to bring it within the powers of the Organization. The general rule itself ceases to apply as soon as the matter ceases to be one of domestic jurisdiction."

Therefore, the Security Council must determine that point. The Security Council has to look at the facts of this particular situation and ask itself whether the situation is essentially within the domestic jurisdiction of Spain.

What are the facts? The facts are that there is a situation the continuance of which, in the finding of the Sub-Committee, is likely to endanger the maintenance of international peace and security. That situation has already led to strong expressions of concern and disapproval by various Governments and to the closing of a frontier. There is a record of past participation in the Second World War and of recent action hindering the victorious Allies in removing vestiges of Nazism. Various Governments, Members of the United Nations, have already broken off diplomatic relations and recognized a rival Government. All this is a matter of vital international concern. The situation, I submit, is the complete antithesis of an essentially domestic situation.

Then, as to the action proposed, the recommended measures are the breaking off of diplomatic relations by all Members of the United Nations. This is a form of action completely within the control of the various nations and it is within their sole discretion to adopt this measure. The matter of diplomatic relations with other countries belongs to the sphere of external and international relationships. Further, the termination of diplomatic relations is the normal action taken by nations to express their disapproval or to make their protest against the international actions of another nation. Again, the proposed action follows directly from the decision taken in the course of international deliberations during the past year seeking to exclude Franco Spain from membership in the United Nations. Inasmuch as the United Nations, which is the organized family of nations, has already denied membership to Franco Spain, it is completely logical and consequential for it not to maintain diplomatic relations with a regime, which according to the United Nations' own decision can never become a member of that Organization.

Then, I turn to the purpose of the action in order to demonstrate that this matter is not essentially one of domestic concern. The object is to remove a danger to international peace and a cause of international friction. It is true that this international objective may be served by a withdrawal of the Franco regime, but how that change is to be brought about is entirely a matter for the Spanish Government and people. The United Kingdom, the United States of America and France, in favouring such a change last March, expressed the hope that Franco himself would peacefully withdraw. So long as he remains, there is likely to be an international situation of concern to the United Nations because, in the view of the Sub-Committee, it is one likely to endanger the maintenance of international peace and security.

Therefore, first, the nature of the situation; secondly, the action proposed; and thirdly, the objective to be obtained by that action, are all international in character and in no wise essentially domestic. The argument, therefore, that the United Nations and the Security Council, or any other Members of the United Nations, cannot touch this matter because it only affects internal affairs in Spain is unsubstantiated and should be rejected. . . .

Mr. GROMYKO (USSR): The material collected by the Sub-Committee from the States which are Members of the United Nations and from the Spanish Republican Government of Giral fully confirms the correctness of the accusations brought against the Franco regime by the representative of Poland in his letters dated 8 and 9 April 1946, to the Secretary-General. Numerous facts put forward in the documents in question confirm that the existence of the fascist regime in Spain is a serious threat to the maintenance of peace and that the situation in Spain should therefore not be regarded as a purely Spanish affair. This situation, which is fraught with serious consequences for peace, cannot fail to be a matter deserving careful consideration by the Security Council with the object of taking the necessary measures provided for in the Charter of the United Nations. . . .

Those who assert that the fascist regime in Spain is not a real menace to peace repeat the discredited arguments which were advanced regarding the fascist regime of Mussolini. Before the war many people pointed out that Mussolini was unable to begin war in Europe, as though he who joins the initiator of aggression is not also an aggressor. Mussolini, as is known, immediately became the partner of Hitler when the latter started a military conflagration in Europe. Must we again wait until fascist aggression becomes a reality? The Security Council, being an organ whose task is to take practical measures to forestall the danger of war and aggression, should treat with the utmost seriousness the question raised by the representative of Poland and take effective and speedy practical measures to remove the menace to peace which the existence of fascism in Spain constitutes.

A first measure capable of contributing effectively to a solution of the Spanish problem would be the rupture of diplomatic relations with Franco by all the Member States of the United Nations. The situation in Spain is such that it not only demands moral condemnation of the Franco regime but also calls for practical action in conformity with the Charter of the United Nations. Otherwise the Security Council will not carry out its tasks which are dictated by the existing situation; it will resemble a forum for discussing the question and not an organ of high authority, making decisions for the purpose of removing the menace to peace which has arisen.

Lastly, I wish to dwell on the conclusions of the Sub-Committee, which also include proposals to the Security Council. While bringing forward a considerable array of facts confirming that the Franco regime is a menace to peace, the Sub-Committee nevertheless has not dared to draw the right conclusion from all the material it has used. It is stated in the Sub-Committee's proposal that the situation in Spain does not at present constitute a threat to peace and that this situation does not come under the definition of Article 39 of the Charter.

Such a conclusion is incorrect. It is due to a restrictive interpretation of Article 39. The Sub-Committee came to the conclusion that the situation in Spain constituted merely a potential threat to peace. In introducing the idea of a potential threat to peace, the Sub-Committee renounced the precise sense of Article 39. Such a conclusion may be the basis for an incorrect and dangerous doctrine, capable of diminishing the significance of the relevant Articles of the Charter, in so far as the action of the Security Council on the strength of these Articles is concerned. The outcome is that a real threat to peace would exist only if fascist Spain took practical action of a military nature. But this would not be merely a threat to peace; it would be an act of aggression.

On the basis of the first conclusion, the Sub-Committee drew a second incorrect conclusion to the effect that the Security Council has not the right or, as the Sub-Committee expresses it, the jurisdiction to take decisions regarding the severance of diplomatic relations with Franco, that is, to act in conformity with Article 41 of the Charter.

In the Sub-Committee's conclusion there is another important, but incorrect proposal. I refer to the Sub-Committee's recommendation not to take a decision in the Security Council regarding the severance of diplomatic relations with Franco, but to recommend the taking of such a decision by the General Assembly, having in mind, probably, the next session of the Assembly. This proposal has two drawbacks:

First, it is by nature contradictory. On the one hand, the Sub-Committee considers that the Security Council has not the right, in the present case, to take a decision regarding the severance of relations with Franco, and it does so on the basis of the previously mentioned incorrect assertion that the situation in Spain does not at present constitute a threat to peace. On the other hand, the Sub-Committee considers the severance of relations with Franco to be necessary, even with the reservations that are made in the last variant of the resolution proposed today, while recommending, however, that the severance should be effected by the General Assembly. The contradictory nature of this proposal is obvious.

Secondly, in asserting that the Security Council has not the right, in the present case, to take a decision regarding the severance of relations with Franco, and in recommending that the Assembly should take such a decision, the Sub-Committee seems, in regard to the present question, to confuse the functions of the Security Council and the General Assembly. The Security Council has the primary responsibility for the maintenance of peace, and precisely for this reason the Security Council should, and is appointed to, decide the question of the measures to be taken regarding the Franco regime. The Security Council is precisely the organ which should take the decision regarding action in connexion with questions dealing with the maintenance of peace. This is clearly indicated in the relevant Articles of the Charter defining the tasks and functions of the Security Council. This is entirely consonant not only with the functions and tasks of the Security Council, but also with the character of the organization of its work as a permanently functioning organ. The Security Council has the necessary powers for this, which are provided, in particular, by Article 24, paragraph 1 of the Charter. The Sub-Committee's proposal is contrary to this Article.

The Security Council, as the organ appointed to safeguard the maintenance of peace and security, ought not to shirk taking a decision to carry out practical and speedy measures in respect to the Franco regime. To refer the Spanish question to the General Assembly would mean that the Security Council shirked carrying out it[s] direct responsibilities. A decision to refer the Spanish question to the Assembly would be incompatible with the authority of the Security Council. It would merely contribute to the undermining of its authority.

NOTE. At the 47th meeting of the Security Council (18 June 1946), a resolution approving the recommendations of the Sub-Committee was rejected, the vote being nine votes in favor, one abstention and the USSR against. The original Polish resolution was also rejected, by seven votes to four. At the 49th meeting (26 June 1946), after an Australian draft resolution was "double vetoed" (see Chapter IV, above), the Security Council, considering that "the investigation of the Sub-Committee has fully confirmed the facts which led to the condemnation of the Franco regime" by various conferences and the General Assembly, decided "to keep the situation in Spain under continuous observation and maintain it upon the list of matters of which it is seized in order that it will be at all times ready to take such measures as may become necessary to maintain international peace and security." SCOR, I.1, No. 2, pp. 378–81, 388, 437, 441–42; SCOR, I, Resolutions and Decisions of the Security Council, 1946 (S/INF/2/Rev. 1 [I]), p. 9. At the 78th meeting of the Security Council (30 October 1946), the representative of Poland stated that his delegation intended "to present to the General Assembly resolutions containing certain recommendations on this problem." Since according to Article 12 of the Charter, the General Assembly was "not free to make recommendations on a matter on which the Council exercises its functions," he proposed "that this Spanish question be taken off the list of matters of which the Council is seized." SCOR, I.2, No. 20, pp. 487–8. At the 79th meeting (4 November 1946), he presented a formal proposal to that effect which was adopted unanimously. The Council also decided that "all records and documents of the case be put at the disposal of the General Assembly." SCOR, I.2, No. 21, p. 498.

On 31 October 1946, as a result of a joint request by the delegations of Belgium, Czechoslovakia, Denmark, Norway and Venezuela, the General Assembly included on the agenda the question of the relations between Spain and the United Nations and referred it to the First Committee. UN Doc. A/BUR/45; GAOR, I.2, First C., p. 351; *idem*, Plenary, p. 925.

The General Assembly had before it a number of proposals. One Polish proposal was as follows:

"[The] General Assembly recommends that each Member of the United Nations terminate, forthwith, diplomatic relations with the Franco regime.

"The General Assembly expresses its deep sympathy to the Spanish people. The General Assembly hopes and expects that in consequence of this action the people of Spain will regain the freedom of which they were deprived with the aid and contrivance of Fascist Italy and Nazi Germany. The General Assembly is convinced that the day will come soon when it will be able to welcome a free Spain into the community of the United Nations." A/C.1/24 (1 Nov. 1946); GAOR, I.2, First C., pp. 352–53.

According to another Polish proposal, the General Assembly would recommend that "the Franco Government be barred from membership and participation in any of the organs and agencies mentioned." A/C.1/25 (1 Nov. 1946); GAOR, *op. cit.*, p. 353.

A Byelorussian draft resolution went further, as under it the General Assembly would recommend that "each Member of the United Nations terminate diplomatic and economic relations with Franco Spain, such action to include the suspension of communications by rail, sea, air, post and telegraph." A/C.1/35 (4 Nov. 1946); GAOR, *op. cit.*, p. 353.

The following elaborate proposal was made by the United States: "The peoples of the United Nations, at San Francisco, Potsdam and London condemned the Franco regime in Spain and decided that, as long as that regime remains, Spain may not be admitted to the United Nations.

"The peoples of the United Nations assure the Spanish people of their enduring sympathy and of the cordial welcome awaiting them when circumstances enable them to be admitted to the United Nations.

"Therefore the General Assembly,

"Convinced that the Franco Fascist Government of Spain, which was imposed by force upon the Spanish people with the aid of the Axis powers and which gave material assistance to the Axis powers in the war, does not represent the Spanish people, and by its continued control of Spain is making impossible the participation of the Spanish people with the peoples of the United Nations in international affairs;

"Recommends that the Franco Government of Spain be debarred from membership in international agencies set up at the initiative of the United Nations, and from participation in conference or other activities which may be arranged by the United Nations or by these agencies, until a new and acceptable government is formed in Spain.

"The General Assembly further,

"Desiring to secure the participation of all peace-loving peoples, including [the] people of Spain, in the community of nations,

"Recognizing that it is for the Spanish people to settle the form of their government;

"Places on record its profound conviction that in the interest of Spain and of world co-operation the people of Spain should give proof to the world that they have a government which derives its authority from the consent of the governed; and that to achieve that end General Franco should surrender the powers of government to a provisional government broadly representative of the Spanish people, committed to respect freedom of speech, religion, and assembly and to the prompt holding of an election in which the Spanish people, free from force and intimidation and regardless of party, may express their will; and

"Invites the Spanish people to establish the eligibility of Spain for admission to the United Nations." A/C.1/100 (2 Dec. 1946); GAOR, *op cit.*, pp. 354–55.

4. *Discussion in the First Committee of the General Assembly,*
2–9 December 1946.

GAOR, I.2, First C., pp. 225–54, 262–71, 293–306.

Mr. LANGE (Poland) pointed out that the problems arising from the existence and activities of the Franco regime had been repeatedly before the United Nations. . . .

The answer to the Spanish question was simple. While the Organization had emerged as a result of the joint efforts of the United Nations in their struggle against the Axis Powers and their satellites, there still existed in Spain a surviving partner of the Axis which was a nest of fascist activities and a shelter for nazis and traitors. The Franco regime had become a rallying point for those who had seen their aims defeated by the United Nations and who placed their hopes in a new war to recoup their political fortunes. The Spanish question was a painful thorn in the living flesh of the United Nations; the Organization as well as world peace and security would be menaced unless definite and final action was taken. . . .

The representative of Poland strongly emphasized that in a world organized under the auspices of the United Nations on the basis of human rights and fundamental freedoms, there was no room for a surviving partner of the fascist Axis. Moral condemnation of fascism was not sufficient; action had to be taken. There was no truth in the argument that positive action against the Franco regime would actually strengthen it. On the contrary, what strengthened Franco was the conviction that the United Nations did not intend to act or were incapable of doing so.

The case presented by the Franco situation was so clear and solution was so easy that, if the Organization was unable to take action in this case, it would fail to take any measures in all other cases, and the world would lose confidence in the Organization. . . .

Mr. CASTRO (El Salvador) observed that the twenty Latin American Republics and other countries had firm ties with Spain, and while there might be differences of opinion for political, ideological or other reasons, it should be remembered above all other considerations that the peoples were related by a common language, blood and religion. The case should be considered with impartiality and accordingly he would refer only to actual historical facts.

Firstly, the present Spanish Government was not a result of the war since the civil war in Spain had ended before the beginning of the world war. It should not be forgotten that this civil war was principally Spanish and that less than ten per cent of the million or more men involved were German or Italian. Once the German and Italian forces had been withdrawn, the Spanish people could have overthrown the Franco Government if it had been the will of the majority, but on the contrary the present Government had existed for seven years. The Polish resolution called for an interference in the internal affairs of Spain, an intervention which was prohibited by paragraph 7 of Article 2 of the Charter. . . .

Another fact that should be recognized was that the Franco Government had not had an opportunity of being heard. While he did not want to pass judgment on the disagreement between the Spanish Government and the Union of Soviet Socialist Republics, this had prejudiced the Spanish case, and he wished to explain that the Spanish Government retained normal relations with many other States. The consequence of the Polish resolution to break off relations with Spain would be to produce a desperate situation in Spain which would lead to revolution and civil war.

The United Nations should seek a peaceful atmosphere for a juridical comment [*afin de pouvoir apprécier la situation en toute justice*], rather than to cultivate differences, remembering that the United Nations included many governments and ideologies of all forms and types. It would be incongruous to overthrow the Franco regime in a neutral nation after having kept Hirohito as a leader to help the Japanese people's progress towards democracy.

The Government of El Salvador had traditionally opposed the intervention of one State in the internal affairs of another. It had defended this principle of non-intervention at the Inter-American Conferences at Havana in 1928 and Montevideo in 1933. Twenty-one American Republics had signed the declaration at Montevideo which provided that no State had the right to intervene in the internal or external affairs of another. While each State had the right to decide on its relations with another, when the United Nations recommended that its Members break off diplomatic relations with Spain, it was a clear case of collective intervention to which El Salvador was opposed. . . .

Mr. MORA (Uruguay) . . . The Sub-Committee created by the Security Council to investigate the Spanish situation, had called attention to the fact that the Franco regime "continues to use persecution methods against political adversaries and police control of the people, which were characteristic of the fascist regimes and which are incompatible with the principles of the United Nations on the respect of human rights and fundamental freedoms". The indefinite continuation of that regime was a latent menace to internal and external peace.

The General Assembly must, therefore, by use of its authority, assume a serene but firm attitude, which would end such a situation. The Government of Uruguay did not extemporize concepts to apply to this special case. It fundamentally adhered to the deeply held convictions which it had expressed at several conferences and as often as necessary.

In accordance with paragraph 6, Article 2, of the Charter of the United Nations "the Organization shall ensure that States which are not members of the United Nations act in accordance with these principles so far as may be necessary for the maintenance of international peace and security" and the basic point of these principles is the reaffirmation of faith in fundamental human rights, and in the dignity and worth of human peoples.

Under Article 13, paragraph 1(*b*), of the Charter, the General Assembly could make recommendations for the purpose of assisting in the realization of rights and fundamental freedoms for all men, "without distinction as to race, sex, language or religion".

Therefore, in the opinion of the Government of Uruguay, the General Assembly should assist in the fostering of those rights and essential freedoms in order that they might be made effective in Spain. To this end, the Assembly should formulate an explicit recommendation.

As opposed to the old world, the new should be guided by the idea of the interdependency of nations and human solidarity. It would be regrettable if the Organization, which had been called upon to deal with this problem, were to evade the responsibility clearly imposed upon it by the very words and spirit of the San Francisco Charter.

. . .

Mr. WOLD (Norway) emphasized that enough resolutions had been adopted in this case and that what the people were asking for was action in order to aid the Spanish people in regaining their freedom and establishing a constitutional government without civil war. Individual action by Members against Franco Spain was not sufficient, a common line of action should be adopted and positive steps taken against Franco. The peace-loving and democratic peoples of the United Nations would not understand if nothing were done. He then referred to the report of the Sub-Committee which had found the Franco regime to be a potential menace to international peace and security, on the basis of conclusive documentary evidence.

The findings of the Sub-Committee had not been challenged in the Security Council or later and since the situation was still the same, this report was a sound basis for discussion. The question before the Committee should not be whether action should be taken, but what action the United Nations was going to take.

Certain arguments have been put forward by the opponents of collective action against Spain:

(1) *The competence of the General Assembly had been denied on the basis of Article 39 of the Charter which gave the power of recommendations to the Security Council in such matters.* Mr. Wold referred to Articles 10 and 14 of the Charter which undoubtedly rendered the General Assembly competent to make recommendations on matters within the scope of the Charter.

(2) *Any action taken by the United Nations was to be considered as an intervention in the internal affairs of Spain under Article 2, paragraph 7.* If such was the correct interpretation of the Charter, there would be no room for considering even a resolution against the Franco regime, and the unanimous decision taken in London would run contrary to the principles of the Charter. But it should be recalled that the Franco regime had been established through foreign military intervention, and consequently the action proposed to the General Assembly should be considered as a peaceful adjustment of the Spanish situation.

(3) *The General Assembly should be careful about judging the form of government of a State in view of the principle that States are free to choose their own form of government.* Such argument lost sight of the fact that the Franco regime had been established with the help of the fascist aggressors.

(4) *A severance of diplomatic relations with Spain would lead to nothing.* So far, no action had been decided upon and the impression had been created that the United Nations would never be able to reach agreement on united action against Franco. This was all the more to be deplored as the Spanish press and radio showed how great was the concern and interest demonstrated by Franco regarding possible action by the United Nations.

The representative of Norway thought that the severance of diplomatic relations would have a great moral effect in Spain and would result in reinforcing the democratic forces within Spain. . . .

Mr. ALFARO (Panama) wished to examine the Spanish problem from a legal point of view:

(1) In barring Franco Spain from membership in the United Nations, the latter had done more than break relations with Franco, since they had formally declared that they would not maintain any relations with him as long as his regime had not been replaced by a democratic one. Therefore, it was not consistent to hesitate now over some action likely to produce the desired change in regime.

(2) The word *intervention* had been misused and misinterpreted. The principle of non-intervention had blinded the Members to realities and prevented them from seeing that the favoured system that they had set up in San Francisco was based on collective action or intervention in order to consolidate the peace and the security of the nations as well as the freedom and dignity of men. The essence of the United Nations is collective action. The Security Council which acts on behalf of fifty-four nations does nothing else but take collective action, and the General Assembly acts in the same manner when it makes a resolution with regard to one or more nations. *Intervention* was a word used in bygone days when big Powers resorted to unilateral action such as military occupation or punitive expeditions in order to assure their political control of certain countries.

As far as the Western hemisphere was concerned, that era was past history. The policy of intervention had been done away with gradually at Havana in 1928, and finally in Montevideo in 1933. The Conference of Montevideo laid down, as far as the Western hemisphere was concerned, the principles of non-intervention and of the respect of the sovereignty of all nations big and small. But these principles did not prevent the system of collective action built up in San Francisco from working in the interest of peace or of human rights.

Article 2, paragraph 7, of the Charter, frequently quoted, did not prevent either collective action from being taken to enforce the principles set forth in the Charter. To deny the United Nations the right to act collectively would be tantamount to destroying the very purposes on which it was based. The principle of collective action had been repeatedly reaffirmed in the Charter in Articles 39, 41, 42 and also in Article 2, paragraph 6. It had also been adopted in no equivocal terms at the Conferences of Buenos Aires in 1936, Lima in 1938, and Mexico in 1945. Therefore, the word *intervention* should not be used but rather the word *inter-dependence* should be applied to the relations between nations of the world.

(3) On the other hand, severance of diplomatic relations with Spain was not an act of intervention since it was a well-known principle of international law that the independence of States did not depend on their being recognized by other countries. Recognition or severance of diplomatic relations rested within the national jurisdiction of every State. . . .

Sir Hartley SHAWCROSS (UK) approved the United States resolution as the means most likely to rid Spain of Franco and return the Spanish people to the community of nations with a truly democratic regime. He emphasized that his delegation's belief that the United Nations ought not to intervene more actively was not because the United Kingdom had any delusions about the Franco Government or any lack of sympathy for the Spanish people which suffered under its yoke. The Spanish people should be left in no doubt as to the contempt with which their present government was regarded, or as to the resolute refusal of the rest of the world to admit them into the community of nations while that government remained in power. The United States resolution contained that message. . . .

The United Kingdom delegation believed that nothing had done more to maintain Franco in power than the fear of foreign intervention, the threat of starvation, and the danger of civil strife. If the Spanish people were relieved of these fears, the prospects for the Franco regime would be considerably diminished.

Breaking diplomatic relations was not considered to be in the interests of the Spanish people because it would remove channels of information and of humanitarian intervention. Nor was his Government prepared to agree to economic sanctions. These sanctions might receive ready approval from countries which were not diplomatically or economically affected, but his Government could not accept responsibility for a course of action which would dislocate food supplies and drastically interfere with world trade.

Even if diplomatic or economic sanctions were wise, he declared, at the present stage of development of the United Nations, interference in the domestic affairs of other Governments would set a very grave precedent.   No matter was more obviously the exclusive concern of the people of a State than the form of its own government.   Since the Security Council had expressly refrained from declaring that the Spanish question constituted a threat to the peace, his Government maintained it to be a domestic matter.   He suggested the important Panamanian proposal on the rights and duties of States might help to clarify the meaning of the domestic jurisdiction clause in the Charter.   In the meantime he felt that to interfere and make an exception, in what was alleged to be a "very special" case, would only lead to the temptation to intervene in other, no doubt, "very special" cases.

If the Spanish people truly loved liberty and democracy, they would ultimately work out their own salvation.   The people of Spain must be made to realize that under their present regime they were outcasts from the community of nations.   When they had established, under free election, a democratic government, the United Nations, individually and collectively, would extend to them help in the great political and economic problems they would have to solve.   .   .   .

Mr. GROMYKO (USSR) pointed out that the greatest task of the United Nations was to secure peace and security for the peoples of the world.   This could not be successfully accomplished unless they fought against the warmongers and primarily against the remnants of fascism.   For this reason they had attributed great importance to the Spanish problem.   The Franco regime had been condemned by the United Nations at its first organizational meeting in San Francisco, at Potsdam and at London, and was now being considered again by the present Assembly.   Such attention could only be explained by the fact that this problem had become of international concern.   .   .   .

There were two very important facts which stressed the importance of taking action against the Franco regime.   Firstly, the grave problem of the existence of two Spanish governments, both recognized by a number of Members of the United Nations, must be solved.   It was obvious that the United Nations must uphold the Republican government of the Spanish people and the democratic forces trying to rid themselves of this last remnant of fascism.   Secondly, Mr. Gromyko recalled the grave situation explained by the representative of France in the Security Council which compelled the French Government to close their Spanish frontier.   This was an act of great international importance and signified friction between these two States.

In the light of the previous United Nations decisions and the above facts, the United Nations could not confine itself to a decorative resolution, for the time had come for action which would be in accord with the gravity of the situation, and which would assist the Spanish people in freeing themselves from fascism.

Unfortunately, however, all delegations did not share this viewpoint and attempts were made to introduce irrelevant juridical considerations. . . .

Article 2, paragraph 7, and warnings that practical measures would lead to civil war, were both being used as pretexts for inaction. It had been claimed in the Security Council that the General Assembly should take action, but now it was being stated in the General Assembly that the matter was within the competence of the Security Council. The General Assembly had the power and right to consider and take a decision on this problem, and a policy of inaction would have grave consequences. . . .

[A resolution prepared by a Special Sub-Committee was approved by the Committee on 9 December 1946, with several amendments, by 23 votes to 4, with 20 abstentions. The matter was again discussed at the plenary meetings of the General Assembly on 12 December 1946, and the resolution was approved by 34 votes to 6 (Argentina, Costa Rica, Dominican Republic, Ecuador, El Salvador, Peru), with 13 abstentions (Afghanistan, Canada, Colombia, Cuba, Egypt, Greece, Honduras, Lebanon, Netherlands, Saudi Arabia, Syria, Turkey, Union of South Africa). GAOR, I.2, Plenary, p. 1222.]

5.   *Resolution 39(I) of the General Assembly, 12 December 1946.*

GAOR, I.2, Resolutions (A/64/Add.1), pp. 63–4.

The peoples of the United Nations, at San Francisco, Potsdam and London, condemned the Franco regime in Spain and decided that, as long as that regime remains, Spain may not be admitted to the United Nations.

The General Assembly, in its resolution of 9 February 1946, recommended that the Members of the United Nations should act in accordance with the letter and the spirit of the declarations of San Francisco and Potsdam.

The peoples of the United Nations assure the Spanish people of their enduring sympathy and of the cordial welcome awaiting them when circumstances enable them to be admitted to the United Nations.

The General Assembly recalls that, in May and June 1946, the Security Council conducted an investigation of the possible further action to be taken by the United Nations. The Sub-Committee of the Security Council charged with the investigation found unanimously:

"(a) In origin, nature, structure and general conduct, the Franco regime is a fascist regime patterned on, and established largely as a result of aid received from, Hitler's Nazi Germany and Mussolini's Fascist Italy.

"(*b*) During the long struggle of the United Nations against Hitler and Mussolini, Franco, despite continued Allied protests, gave very substantial aid to the enemy Powers. . . .

"(*c*) Incontrovertible documentary evidence establishes that Franco was a guilty party with Hitler and Mussolini in the conspiracy to wage war against those countries which eventually in the course of the world war became banded together as the United Nations. It was part of the conspiracy that Franco's full belligerency should be postponed until a time to be mutually agreed upon."

The General Assembly,

Convinced that the Franco Fascist Government of Spain, which was imposed by force upon the Spanish people with the aid of the Axis Powers and which gave material assistance to the Axis Powers in the war, does not represent the Spanish people, and by its continued control of Spain is making impossible the participation of the Spanish people with the peoples of the United Nations in international affairs;

Recommends that the Franco Government of Spain be debarred from membership in international agencies established by or brought into relationship with the United Nations, and from participation in conferences or other activities which may be arranged by the United Nations or by these agencies, until a new and acceptable government is formed in Spain.

The General Assembly,

Further, desiring to secure the participation of all peace-loving peoples, including the people of Spain, in the community of nations,

Recommends that if, within a reasonable time, there is not established a government which derives its authority from the consent of the governed, committed to respect freedom of speech, religion and assembly and to the prompt holding of an election in which the Spanish people, free from force and intimidation and regardless of party, may express their will, the Security Council consider the adequate measures to be taken in order to remedy the situation;

Recommends that all members of the United Nations immediately recall from Madrid their Ambassadors and Ministers plenipotentiary accredited there.

The General Assembly further recommends that the States Members of the Organization report to the Secretary-General and to the next session of the Assembly what action they have taken in accordance with this recommendation.

NOTE. On 4 July 1947, the Secretary-General reported to the General Assembly that: thirty States had no diplomatic relations with the Franco Government at the time of the adoption of Resolution 39(I); nineteen States had no ambassadors or ministers plenipotentiary accredited to Spain at that time; three States had recalled ambassadors (El Salvador, the Netherlands and United Kingdom); Liberia declared that it would adhere to the resolution; the Dominican Republic announced that it would give proper consideration to the resolution; and Argentina merely acknowledged the communication from the Secretary-General asking for information about the action taken. GAOR, II, Supp. 1 (A/315), p. 3.

Various measures were taken by several specialized agencies of the United Nations to exclude Spain from their membership. *Idem*, p. 4.

When the Spanish question came up for consideration again at the second session of the General Assembly in 1947, a proposal to reaffirm the previous resolution failed to gain a two-thirds majority. The General Assembly, however, expressed "its confidence that the Security Council will exercise its responsibilities under the Charter as soon as it considers that the situation in Spain so requires." Res. 114(II), 17 Nov. 1947; GAOR, II, Resolutions (A/519), p. 21. This resolution was brought to the attention of the President of the Security Council by a letter from the Secretary-General of 3 December 1947. The letter was placed on the provisional agenda for the Council's 327th meeting (25 June 1948). In the debate on the adoption of the agenda the President, Mr. El-Khouri (Syria) said: "[T]his request was made to the Security Council by the General Assembly, and it should be considered by the Security Council. I agreed to put it on the agenda today in order to consult the Council, and to find out if the Council thinks that there is anything in Spain which would require the consideration or involve the responsibility of the Security Council under the Charter. For my part, I consider that nothing of the sort is involved. . . . I do not believe that there is anything more to do than to take note of this letter of the Secretary-General. . . . " This item of the provisional agenda was not adopted, though Mr. Gromyko (USSR) protested that the Council "should discuss the Spanish situation to decide whether to adopt any decisions on the substance of the question, and if so, what decision." SCOR, III, No. 90, pp. 1–9.

At the second part of the third session of the General Assembly in May 1949, the representative of Poland presented a draft resolution proposing that the General Assembly should recommend that "all Members of the United Nations should as a first step forthwith cease to export to Spain arms and ammunition as well as all warlike and strategic material." A/C.1/452 and A/860 (11 May 1949); GAOR, III.2, Plenary, Annexes, p. 84. This proposal was rejected by the First Committee by 39 votes to 6, with 11 abstentions. GAOR, III.2, First C., pp. 240–244.

On the other hand, Bolivia, Brazil, Colombia and Peru proposed that the Assembly decide, "without prejudice to the declarations contained in the resolution of 12 December 1946, to leave Member States full freedom of action as regards their diplomatic relations with Spain." Certain Governments, they said, had interpreted the failure of the second Assembly to reaffirm the 1946 resolution "as virtually revoking the clause in the previous resolution which recommended the withdrawal of heads of mission with the rank of ambassador or minister plenipotentiary accredited to the Spanish Government." A/C.1/450 and A/852 (9 May 1949); GAOR, III.2, Plenary, Annexes, pp. 58–61. Though this draft resolution was approved by the First Committee by 25 votes to 16, with 16 abstentions, it failed to secure in the General Assembly the two-thirds vote necessary for approval. GAOR, III.2, Plenary, p. 501.

A similar attempt the next year was successful, and on 4 November 1950 the following resolution was adopted by 38 votes to 10, with 12 abstentions:

"The General Assembly,

"Considering that: . . .

"The establishment of diplomatic relations and the exchange of Ambassadors and Ministers with a government does not imply any judgment upon the domestic policy of that government,

"The specialized agencies of the United Nations are technical and largely non-political in character and have been established in order to benefit the peoples of all nations, and that, therefore, they should be free to decide for themselves whether the participation of Spain in their activities is desirable in the interest of their work,

"Resolves:

"1.   To revoke the recommendation for the withdrawal of Ambassadors and Ministers from Madrid, contained in General Assembly resolution 39(I) of 12 December 1946;

"2.   To revoke the recommendation intended to debar Spain from membership in international agencies established by or brought into relationship with the United Nations, which recommendation is a part of the same resolution adopted by the General Assembly in 1946 concerning relations of Members of the United Nations with Spain." Resolution 386(V); GAOR, V, Supp. 20 (A/1775), p. 16.

Spain soon obtained full membership in most of the specialized agencies, and on 14 December 1955 Spain was admitted to the United Nations together with fifteen other Members. GA Resolution 995(X); GAOR, X, Supp. 19 (A/3116), p. 50.

With respect to the various aspects of this case, see Santiago TORRES BERNARDEZ, L'Espagne et les organisations internationales (Saarbrücken, 1960), pp. 89–320.

GREEK QUESTION

NOTE.   In a letter of 21 January 1946 to the President of the Security Council, the representative of the USSR requested that the situation which had arisen in Greece be discussed in the Security Council. He stated that the presence of British troops in Greece "has been turned into a means of bringing pressure to bear upon the political situation inside the country, pressure which has not infrequently been used by reactionary elements against the democratic forces of the country." SCOR, I.1, Supp. 1, pp. 73–74.

The representative of the United Kingdom stated before the Security Council that British troops and administrators had been requested to go to Greece by the Greek Government. The representative of Greece was invited to participate in the Council's discussion and stated that neither the civil nor the military authorities of Great Britain had at any time sought to intervene in any manner in the internal affairs of Greece, and that the continued presence of British military forces in Greece was regarded as indispensable. A statement by the President taking note of the various statements made terminated discussion of the question. SCOR, I.1, No. 1, pp. 81, 88, 89, 171–72.

By a telegram of 24 August 1946 to the Secretary-General, the Minister of Foreign Affairs of the Ukrainian SSR brought to the attention of the Security Council under Article 34 of the Charter a situation which had "arisen in the Balkans" "as a result of the irresponsible policy of the present Greek Government". This was caused, he alleged, by "numerous border incidents on the Greek-Albanian frontier which are being provoked by the Greek armed units with the connivance and encouragement of the Greek authorities". He also alleged "persecution by the Greek Government of national minorities in Macedonia, Thrace, and Cyprus". The principal factor conducive to this situation, he continued, was "the presence of British troops in Greece and the direct intervention of British military representatives in the internal affairs of this Allied country in behalf of aggressive monarchist elements". S/137; SCOR, I.2, Supp. 5, pp. 149–51.

This telegram was placed on the provisional agenda for the 54th meeting on 28 August 1946. The Netherlands representative questioned whether the Ukrainian complaint could be admitted on the agenda in the form in which it had been presented. He considered it "a series of unsubstantiated accusations against two Members of the United Nations. The wealth of invectives which characterizes the complaint cannot take the place of what, in my view, should at least be some initial evidence." SCOR, I.2, No. 4, p. 33. The representative of the United Kingdom pointed out that the charge had been brought up on a former occasion and that the United Kingdom was at that time exonerated. If the charge was to be brought up again, "it seems to me," he said, "only reasonable to ask that some facts should be produced to substantiate this charge." *Idem*, p. 35. After some hesitation the telegram was placed on the agenda at the 59th meeting of the Council (3 September 1946). The representatives of the Ukrainian SSR and Greece were invited to take seats at the Council table, and the representative of Albania, not a member of the United Nations, was invited to make a factual statement before the Council. In the course of a prolonged debate several draft resolutions were proposed. One presented by the representative of the USSR would, in effect, have the Security Council confirm as fact the allegations of the Ukrainian SSR and, *inter alia,* call upon the Greek Government to cease "provocative activities" and "terminate the persecution of national minorities"; this proposal received only two favourable votes. SCOR, I.2, No. 13, pp. 334–35; No. 16, pp. 408–9. The representative of the United States proposed the establishment of a commission of three individuals "to investigate the facts relating to the border incidents along the frontier between Greece on the one hand and Albania, Bulgaria and Yugoslavia on the other. . . . " This resolution received eight favourable votes but was vetoed by the USSR. *Idem*, p. 412. A resolution proposed by the Netherlands failed to secure seven favourable votes. *Idem*, p. 409. Following the rejection of a Polish proposal that the situation be kept under observation and retained on the list of matters with which the Council is seized, the President ruled that the question was no longer on the Council's agenda. *Idem*, pp. 420–22. The question was reopened by Greece in December 1946.

The Governments of Albania, Bulgaria and Yugoslavia requested that they be invited to attend the meetings of the Council when the questions raised by Greece were discussed. S/207, S/208, S/209; SCOR, I.2, Supp. 10, pp.

191–2. On 10 December 1946 the Council considered the procedural question of allowing these States to participate in the debate. There was general agreement that Greece and Yugoslavia should be invited to participate in terms of Article 31 of the Charter, since they were Members of the United Nations. Several members were of the opinion that the other States could only be invited to participate under Article 32 which presupposes a finding by the Council of the existence of a dispute. The Council agreed on the following compromise:

"The representatives of Greece and of Yugoslavia are invited to participate in the discussion without vote.

"The representatives of Albania and Bulgaria are invited to enable the Security Council to hear such declarations as they may wish to make.

"Should the Security Council find at a later stage that the matter under consideration is a dispute, the representatives of Albania and Bulgaria will be invited to participate in the discussion without vote." SCOR, I.2, No. 24, pp. 558–9.

The representatives of all four States took their seats at the Council table at the 83rd meeting, and at the next meeting of the Council it was decided to invite Albania and Bulgaria to participate in the discussion without vote on condition that those States accept, for the purposes of this case, the obligations regarding pacific settlement provided for in the Charter; these obligations were duly accepted. SCOR, I.2, No. 26, pp. 608, 613; No. 27, pp. 615–6.

1. *Letter from the Acting Chairman of the delegation of Greece to the Secretary-General, 3 December 1946.*

S/203; SCOR, I.2, Supp. 10, pp. 169–172.

Under instructions from my Government, I have the honour to request you, in virtue of Article 34 and of Article 35, paragraph 1, of the Charter, to be so good as to submit to the Security Council, for early consideration, a situation which is leading to friction between Greece and her neighbours, by reason of the fact that the latter are lending their support to the violent guerrilla warfare now being waged in northern Greece against public order and the territorial integrity of my country. This situation, if not promptly remedied, is, in the opinion of my Government, likely to endanger the maintenance of international peace and security.

In particular, the Greek Government desires to draw the attention of the Security Council to the urgent necessity for an investigation to be undertaken on the spot, in order that the causes of this situation may be brought to light. They are confident that, in this way, the charges brought by them may be confirmed authoritatively, and means provided for the settlement of the question. .   .   .

There is conclusive evidence that the whole guerrilla movement against Greece is receiving substantial support from the countries adjacent to Greece's northern boundaries, and particularly from Yugoslavia, and that this support takes the following forms:

(i) Groups of men are being trained and organized in foreign territory; they are then sent into Greece, together with consignments of war material.

(ii) Armed bands or isolated members of such bands are crossing the boundary-line in both directions under the protection and guidance of the frontier authorities of the neighbouring countries.

(iii) Greek fugitives from justice and anarchists are being received and cared for in foreign territory, and are being incited by propaganda to carry on subversive activities in Greece.

It is to be noted that Bulgaria and Albania bear a similar responsibility for the activities of the hostile bands operating on Greece's northern frontiers. . . .

The situation to which the events referred to have given rise is seriously hampering the Greek Government's efforts to promote the economic rehabilitation of the country, and is tending to create causes of friction with neighbouring countries with which Greece desires, and is firmly decided, to live in peace and in a spirit of sincere collaboration.

2. *Resolution adopted by the Security Council, 19 December 1946.*

SCOR, I.2, No. 28, pp. 700–01.

Whereas there have been presented to the Security Council oral and written statements by the Greek, Yugoslav, Albanian and Bulgarian Governments relating to disturbed conditions in northern Greece along the frontier between Greece on the one hand and Albania, Bulgaria and Yugoslavia on the other, which conditions, in the opinion of the Council, should be investigated before the Council attempts to reach any conclusions regarding the issues involved:

The Security Council

Resolves:

That the Security Council under Article 34 of the Charter establish a Commission of Investigation to ascertain the facts relating to the alleged border violations along the frontier between Greece on the one hand and Albania, Bulgaria and Yugoslavia on the other;

That the Commission be composed of a representative of each of the members of the Security Council as it will be constituted in 1947;

That the Commission shall proceed to the area not later than 15 January 1947, and shall submit to the Security Council at the earliest possible date a report of the facts disclosed by its investigation. The Commission shall, if it deems it advisable or if requested by the Security Council, make preliminary reports to the Security Council;

That the Commission shall have authority to conduct its investigation in northern Greece and in such places in other parts of Greece, in Albania, Bulgaria, and Yugoslavia as the Commission considers should be included in its investigation in order to elucidate the causes and nature of the above-mentioned border violations and disturbances;

That the Commission shall have authority to call upon the Governments, officials and nationals of those countries, as well as such other sources as the Commission deems necessary, for information relevant to its investigation;

That the Security Council request the Secretary-General to communicate with the appropriate authorities of the countries named above in order to facilitate the Commission's investigation in those countries;

That each representative on the Commission be entitled to select the personnel necessary to assist him and that, in addition, the Security Council request the Secretary-General to provide such staff and assistance to the Commission as it deems necessary for the prompt and effective fulfilment of its task;

That a representative of each of the Governments of Greece, Albania, Bulgaria and Yugoslavia be invited to assist in the work of the Commission in a liaison capacity;

That the Commission be invited to make any proposals that it may deem wise for averting a repetition of border violations and disturbances in these areas.

3. *Report to the Security Council by the Commission of Investigation concerning Greek frontier incidents, 27 May 1947.*

S/360/Rev. 1; SCOR, II, Spec. Supp. 2, Vol. I, pp. 152-7.

Before coming to its actual proposals, the Commission felt it would be useful to recapitulate in brief the situation along Greece's northern border which those proposals were designed to alleviate and remedy. First, there were the allegations by the Greek Government that its three northern neighbors were assisting the guerrilla warfare in Greece. Secondly, there was the present disturbed situation in Greece which was a heritage from the past and the causes of which were to be found in Greece's tragic experience during the war, in her occupation by the Italians, Germans and Bulgarians, in the guerrilla warfare waged during the occupation and the political bitterness and economic difficulties to which the war gave rise.

Next to be mentioned is the refusal of most of the countries concerned to accept as final their frontiers as at present defined. Some of those claims had been advanced in a perfectly legitimate manner before the forum of the United Nations or other competent international bodies but their reiteration had undoubtedly aggravated an already dangerous situation.

Furthermore, in the case of the Macedonian question, claims had been ventilated not before the United Nations but in speeches by representatives of individual governments or in government controlled organs of the press. The exploitation of the Macedonian question in that manner was in the Commission's opinion, a positive threat to the peace of the Balkans and could only add to existing tension and suspicion and increase national passions which, far from being decreased as a result of the experience of the war, had been sharpened by their identification in many cases with political ideas.

Also to be mentioned was the presence in Greece, on the one hand, and Yugoslavia, Bulgaria and Albania on the other, of political refugees from each other's territory, many of whom had taken part in the political struggles which had raged in their own countries both during and since the war. Some of those refugees had been quartered near the frontier of the country from which they came. Some again had, during their exile, engaged in political and military activities, and all too many lived in the hope that there would be some violent turn of the tide which would enable them to return to their homes under the conditions they chose. Others of those refugees had been victims of panic, flight and would, if given a free choice, gladly return to their homes. The continued presence of all of them under the conditions in which they lived at the time was, however, all too clearly a serious contributory factor to the existing situation.

Lastly, the violence and scale of the propaganda used by some of the protagonists in their relations with each other could not escape the notice of the Commission during its stay in the four countries. Such propaganda had always served to inflame passions which were already running high.

Faced by such circumstances it would be idle to believe that the situation in northern Greece could be solved by a stroke of the pen but the proposals which follow were framed in the spirit of Chapter VI of the Charter of the United Nations with a view, first, to prevent any aggravation of the situation, and, secondly, to alleviate it and eventually to restore it to normal.

The Commission did not make any suggestions in matters which were essentially within the domestic jurisdiction of the countries concerned as they would be contrary to the provisions of paragraph 7 of Article 2 of the Charter. However, in the event that the Greek Government should decide to grant a new amnesty for political prisoners and guerrillas, the Commission suggested that the Security Council make known to the Greek Government its willingness, if that Government so requested it, to lend its good offices in order to secure by all possible means the realization of that measure.

The following were the Commission's proposals:

A. The Commission proposed to the Security Council that it recommend to the Governments of Greece, on the one hand, and Albania, Bulgaria and Yugoslavia, on the other, that they do their utmost to establish normal good-neighbourly relations, abstain from all action direct or indirect likely to increase or maintain the tension and unrest in the border areas, and rigorously refrain from any support, overt or covert, of elements in neighbouring countries aiming at the overthrow of the lawful Governments of those countries. If subjects of complaint arose, they should not be made the object of propaganda campaigns, but referred either through diplomatic channels to the government concerned, or should that resource fail, to the appropriate organ of the United Nations. In the light of the situation investigated by it, the Commission believed that in the area of its investigation, future cases of support of armed bands formed on the territory of one State and crossing into the territory of another State, or of refusal by a government in spite of the demands of the State concerned to take all possible measures on its own territory to deprive such bands of any aid or protection, should be considered by the Security Council as a threat to the peace within the meaning of the Charter of the United Nations.

B. In order to provide effective machinery for the regulation and control of their common frontiers, the Commission proposed that the Security Council recommend to the Governments concerned that they enter into new conventions along the lines of the Greco-Bulgarian Convention of 1931, taking into account the needs of the existing situation.

C. For the purpose of restoring normal conditions along the frontiers between Greece, on the one hand, and Albania, Bulgaria and Yugoslavia on the other, and thereby assisting in the establishment of good neighbourly relations, the Commission recommended the establishment of a body with the following composition and functions:

(a) The body should be established by the Security Council in the form of either a small commission or a single commissioner. If the body was a small commission it should be composed of representatives of governments. If the body was to consist of a commissioner he and his staff should be nationals of States who are neither permanent members of the Security Council nor have any direct connexion or interest in the affairs of the four countries concerned.

(b) The commission or commissioner should have the necessary staff to perform its functions, including persons able to act as border observers and to report on the observance of the frontier conventions referred to in recommendation B, the state of the frontier area, and similar matters.

(c) The commission or commissioner should have the right to perform its functions on both sides of the border and the commission or commissioner should have the right of direct access to the four Governments of Albania. Bulgaria, Yugoslavia and Greece. The functions and duties of the commission or commissioner should be:

(i) To investigate any frontier violations that should occur;

(ii) To use its good offices for the settlement, through the means mentioned in Article 33 of the Charter, of:

a.   Controversies arising from frontier violations;

b.   Controversies directly connected with the application of the frontier conventions envisaged in paragraph B;

c.   Complaints regarding conditions on the border which might be brought by one Government against another.

(iii) To use its good offices to assist the Governments concerned in the negotiation and conclusions of the frontier conventions envisaged in recommendation B;

(iv) To study and make recommendations to the Governments concerned with respect to such additional bilateral agreements between them for the pacific settlement of disputes relating to frontier incidents or conditions on the frontier as the Commission might consider desirable;

(v) To assist in the implementation of recommendation D below; to receive reports from the four governments with respect to persons who had fled from any one of such countries to any of the others, to maintain a register for their confidential use of all such persons and to assist in the repatriation of those who wished to return to their homes, and in connexion with those functions, to act in concert with the appropriate agency of the United Nations;

(vi) To report to the Security Council every three months, or whenever they thought fit.

It was recommended that that body should be established for a period of at least two years, before the expiration of which the necessity for its continued existence should be reviewed by the Security Council.

D. The Commission recognized that owing to the deep-rooted causes of the present disturbances and to the nature of the frontiers, it was physically impossible to control the passage of refugees across the border. As the presence of those refugees in any of the four countries was a disturbing factor, each Government should assume the obligation to remove them as far away as possible from the area from which they came as it was physically and practically possible.

Those refugees should be placed in camps or otherwise segregated. The Governments concerned should undertake to ensure that they should not be permitted to indulge in any political or military activity.

The Commission would also strongly recommend that, if practicable, the camps containing the refugees should be placed under the supervision of some international body authorized by the United Nations to undertake the task.

In order to ensure the return of genuine refugees only, their re-entry in their country of origin should take place only after (1) arrangements with the Government of such country had been made and (2) notification to the commission or commissioner or to the international United Nations body if such was established. The Commission here pointed out the desirability of the Governments concerned encouraging the return of refugees to their homes.

E. The Commission proposed that the Security Council recommend to the Governments concerned that they study the practicability of concluding agreements for the voluntary transfer of minorities. In the meantime, minorities in any of the countries concerned desiring to emigrate should be given all facilities to do so by the Government of the State in which they were residing at the time. The arrangements of any such transfers could be supervised by the commission or commissioner who would act as a registration authority for any person desiring to emigrate.

NOTE. The proposals of the Commission set out above were those approved by the majority of its members, namely Australia, Belgium, Brazil, China, Colombia, Syria, UK and USA. The USSR and Polish delegations did not approve these proposals. S/360/Rev. 1; SCOR, II, Special Supp. No. 2, Vol. I, p. iii. The delegation of the USSR made the following statement:

"The delegation of the Soviet Union objects to the proposals put forward . . . on the Greek question for the following reasons:

"1. The above-mentioned proposals are in no way derived from the facts and documents gathered by the Commission during the investigation of the situation in northern Greece and on her northern frontiers, but are based merely on the unfounded assertions of the Greek Government regarding aid to the guerrillas by the northern neighbours of Greece.

"2. The proposals admit the possibility of frontier incidents, conflicts and even acts of aggression in the future in the relations between Greece, on the one hand, and Yugoslavia, Bulgaria and Albania on the other, although the Commission has no grounds whatever for proposals of such a nature.

"3. The proposals contemplate measures concerning not only Greece but Yugoslavia, Bulgaria and Albania as well although it is evident from the documents at the disposal of the Commission that there is a tense situation in Greece and that disorders are taking place there not only in the northern part but throughout the country, and that the tense situation and disorders in Greece are due to internal causes.

"4. The establishment of a permanent frontier commission or body representing the Security Council, as contemplated in the proposals, and also the conclusion of conventions and agreements between Greece, Yugoslavia, Bulgaria and Albania, is tantamount to a limitation of the sovereign rights of these States in settling their relations among themselves." *Idem*, p. 156.

The Polish delegation raised the following objections:

"1. The measures as a whole seem ineffectual since they take into account only the symptoms and not the causes of the troubles existing in northern Greece and along her northern frontiers. The fact that the measures proposed are ineffectual could easily prejudice the prestige of the United Nations.

"2.   Some of the measures proposed do not seem to take into account the fact that diplomatic relations do not exist between Greece on the one hand and Bulgaria and Albania on the other.

"3.   Concerning proposal C, which suggests the establishment of a permanent body of control, this measure appears inadequate for the following reasons:

"(a) Such a body of control would prejudice the sovereign rights of Greece as well as those of Albania, Bulgaria and Yugoslavia.

"(b) It would constitute a measure of coercion towards Albania, Bulgaria and Yugoslavia. This measure would be in no way justified by the results of the Commission's investigation. Therefore, instead of improving the existing difficulties it could quite well do the opposite.

"The Polish delegation considers that the choice of recommendations for the solution of the problems which form the object of the inquiry should be left to the Security Council." *Idem*, pp. 156–7.

4.   *Discussion in the Security Council, 27 June–25 July 1947.*

SCOR, II, Nos. 51–64, pp. 1126–1547.

[The report of the Commission was brought before the Security Council at the 147th meeting. In the course of the debate which followed several draft resolutions were presented. The United States proposed that the Council adopt the proposals made by the Commission, making some changes, however, in the powers to be granted to the Commission envisaged in the report. S/391; SCOR, II, No. 51, pp. 1124–6. At the 170th meeting (29 July 1947), this draft as amended received nine favourable votes but was vetoed by the USSR.

On the other hand, the USSR had submitted a draft resolution proposing that the Security Council should consider it to be established that the investigation "confirmed the connexion between the incidents and the general hostile policy pursued by the present Greek Government towards Greece's neighbours", that the internal situation in Greece was "the fundamental factor responsible for the strained situation in the northern frontier areas of Greece", that the Greek Government had not only failed to check but had encouraged and justified provocative acts against Yugoslavia, Albania and Bulgaria", and "that the state of affairs prevailing in Greece .   .   .   is to a considerable extent the result of foreign intervention in the internal affairs of Greece"; and that it should recommend that the Greek Government "take steps to put an end to the frontier incidents", that diplomatic relations between Greece and the three other countries be restored to normal, and "that the Greek Government put through the necessary measures guaranteeing the elimination of all discrimination against citizens belonging to the Macedonian and Albanian ethnic groups on Greek territory;" and that it further recommend that "foreign troops and foreign military personnel be recalled from Greece", and appoint a commission for the supervision of foreign economic assistance to Greece to "ensure that such assistance is used only in the interests of the Greek people." S/404; SCOR, II, No. 55, pp. 1254–5.

This draft resolution was rejected on 4 August 1947 by nine votes to two. SCOR, II, No. 69, p. 1730. Subsequent resolutions proposed by Australia and the United States which would have the Security Council determine that there was a threat to the peace and which would invoke powers of the Security Council under Articles 39 and 40 of the Charter, were vetoed by the USSR. SCOR, II, No. 79, pp. 2094, 2098–9. At the 202d meeting on 15 September 1947, the representative of the United States stated that the Greek question had been placed on the agenda of the General Assembly. At the same meeting, after a United States proposal to refer the matter to the General Assembly was "double vetoed," a resolution was passed removing this "dispute" from the Security Council's agenda. SCOR, II, No. 89, p. 2405. (With respect to the "double veto" discussion in this case, see Chapter IV, Section 4, above.)

During the consideration of these resolutions, and of the amendments thereto, several legal questions were raised, and the following discussions took place:]

Mr. DENDRAMIS (Greece): On behalf of the Greek people, I should like to thank the Commission of Investigation for the way in which it has done its work. As a result of its conscientious labour, the Security Council has before it an objective report, which will enable it to take decisions in conformity with the principles of the Charter. . . .

The Security Council has the main responsibility for ensuring that all States Members or non-members of the United Nations will refrain from all threats to, and all breaches of, the peace. When a dispute likely to disturb the peace is brought to the attention of the Council, the latter has the right to hold an inquiry and, if the inquiry reveals the existence of a threat to the peace or a breach of the peace, it is the Council's duty to "call upon the parties concerned to comply with such provisional measures as it deems necessary". The parties, for their part, must apply the terms of settlement which the Council may consider appropriate. It is the duty of each State member of the Council to see to it that the measures adopted by the latter are effective for the re-establishment of peace. . . .

Mr. VAN LANGENHOVE (Belgium): [One of the objections raised against the recommendations of the Commission] considers the establishment of a frontier commission, acting under authority of the Security Council, to be contrary to the sovereignty of the States concerned, and in particular to their sovereign right of freely regulating their mutual relations. The same defect is alleged to affect the procedure whereby these States are to conclude with one another treaties and agreements, as suggested in the text of the recommendations. Perhaps I misunderstand the purport of this particular argument, but I cannot conceal my surprise at seeing it invoked once again in the present state of development of the law of nations. Without there being any need in this connexion to refer to the precedents of the Permanent Court of International Justice, it will suffice to recall here that the right to accept international restrictions has always been considered, in theory and in practice, one of the essential attributes of sovereignty. It is precisely because they are sovereign that States can bind themselves by treaty and legally accept restrictions on their liberty. To contest the power of any State to take such action would be to deny its sovereignty. To recommend States to cooperate with an international commission does not, therefore, mean that it is proposed to infringe their sovereign rights. They are not even being asked to submit to limitations of which contemporary history provides few examples. There can, thus, be no talk here of methods which are coercive or contrary to State sovereignty, any more than such terms could be applied to recommendations for the conclusion of treaties between the States concerned. . . .

Mr. MEVORAH (Bulgaria): . . . Under Chapter VI of the Charter, the Council is only called upon to make recommendations, whereas the actual settlement of the dispute is left to the parties concerned. The Council may recommend a procedure to be followed in order to put an end to a conflict, but the application of this procedure requires the consent of the parties concerned. In this lies the difference between the *decisions* of the Council taken under Chapter VII and the *recommendations* provided for in Chapter VI. In the case of the former, the Council does not require the consent of the parties; it lays down the measures to be taken. In the case of the latter, it takes into consideration the sovereignty of the States and confines itself to acting as a mediator, to conciliation (Article 33, paragraph 1), to recommendations (Article 36, paragraph 1), and to calling upon the parties (Article 33, paragraph 2).

The establishment of the proposed commission represents more than a recommendation; this is a decision to be imposed regardless of the consent of the parties. Judging by the powers and privileges to be conferred on it, nothing less than a control commission is being planned. I would even say that it would be a commission exercising guardianship.

This commission is not only to take cognizance of facts; it is also to have power to settle disputes. Apparently the Balkan States are to be placed in a position of subordination to a commission appointed without their consent. Thus, this commission would have the right to demand reports from the four Governments, to move from one territory to another without requesting authorization from the Governments concerned and to enter into direct contact with officials of the said Governments. It would maintain observers on the frontier, perhaps on both sides of this frontier. Under the United States draft resolution the Council would even be able subsequently to confer more extensive rights upon it. The establishment of the commission would, as I have just said, place us in the position of wards—and this would indeed be contrary to the principles of the Charter.

The fact that the establishment of the proposed commission would limit the sovereignty of the four Balkan States was not denied, not even by the United Kingdom representative who sought to justify such a limitation by referring to Articles 25 and 36. But I think his reasoning is faulty, since Article 25 stipulates that States Members of the United Nations should "agree to accept and carry out the decisions of the Security Council. . . ." As has been pointed out above, however, it is only under Chapter VII that the Council takes decisions, and, in cases such as ours, considered under Chapter VI which only refers to recommendations, Article 25 is not applicable. If the word "recommendation", which is used in Chapter VI, has any meaning, it can only denote something which is not obligatory, which may be accepted or refused.

It is therefore absolutely incorrect to speak of the possibility of limiting a State's sovereignty on the basis of Chapter VI. Admittedly under the Charter it is possible to override the sovereignty of States; but the Charter is very careful to limit this possibility to the far more serious cases provided for in Chapter VII. Everybody values the Charter—that is taken for granted; but that being so, its terms should not be contravened under the pretext of an inadmissibly "broad" interpretation.

The representative of Belgium, on the contrary, wishes to protect the principle of the sovereignty of States; but he thinks that a suggestion to the Balkan States that they should come to terms, coupled with an offer of the Council's good offices if required, cannot be regarded as an infringement of sovereignty; he adds, elegantly, that precisely because they are sovereign can States bind themselves by treaty and properly accept restrictions of their liberty. All this is perfectly true and that is why, in my first speech, I declared myself ready to accept any suggestions or recommendations. In this case, however, we are concerned with a commission with extensive powers, a commission which is not being proposed to us, but which it is desired to impose upon us, and this without our previous consent and even against our will. Would it be a proof of our sovereignty if we allowed something we do not wish to be forced upon us?

With regard to the utility of the proposed commission, it seems certain that it is likely not to appease passions but, on the contrary, to excite them. The commission's presence would make it possible to exaggerate the importance of the least incidents, even those not of a political nature. Incidents such as occur every day on all the frontiers of the world would be transformed into political affairs by the presence of the commission. Fabrications and "cooked-up" evidence would be inevitable; the Press would publish comments and thus stir up misunderstandings. There would naturally be voluminous correspondence; misunderstandings and dissension would arise within the commission, and also between the commission and Governments. Finally, a commission such as that proposed in the report would constitute a clumsy and costly body, which it would be better to avoid on principle.

The commission's intervention would offend the feelings of the four countries. No terms of reference, however detailed and clear, could adequately determine the relations between the commission and the four Governments; hence, friction and misunderstandings would often arise. . . .

Mr. [H. V.] JOHNSON (USA): . . . The representative of Bulgaria maintained that Chapter VI authorizes the Council to make recommendations only, and these recommendations would have to be accepted by all the parties to the dispute.

The principle involved in that observation arose at the time the Council was considering a letter from the Chairman of the Council of Foreign Ministers concerning the Statute of Trieste, and is reported in the Official Records of the Security Council, Second Year, No. 3. At the ninety-first meeting on 10 January 1947, Mr. Sobolev, acting for the Secretary-General, informed the Council that he had been instructed by the Secretary-General to submit to the Security Council, a statement "with regard to the legal issues raised in connexion with the consideration by the Council of the three instruments relating to the Free Territory of Trieste."

The legal questions raised are:

"1. The authority of the Security Council to accept the responsibilities imposed by these instruments, and

"2. The obligation of Members of the United Nations to accept and carry out the decisions of the Security Council pursuant to these instruments."

In the memorandum which was read by Mr. Sobolev, it was stated:

"It has been suggested that it would be contrary to the Charter for the Security Council to accept the responsibilities proposed to be placed on it by the Permanent Statute for the Free Territory of Trieste and the two related instruments. This position has been suggested on the ground that the powers of the Security Council are limited to the specific powers granted in Chapters VI, VII, VIII, and XII of the Charter, and that these specific powers do not vest the Council with sufficient authority to undertake the responsibilities imposed by the instruments in question.

"In view of the importance of the issue raised, the Secretary-General has felt bound to make a statement which may throw light on the constitutional questions presented. Paragraph 1 of Article 24 provides: 'In order to ensure prompt and effective action by the United Nations, its Members confer on the Security Council primary responsibility for the maintenance of international peace and security, and agree that in carrying out its duties under this responsibility the Security Council acts on their behalf.' The words 'primary responsibility for the maintenance of international peace and security' coupled with the phrase 'acts on their behalf' constitute," stated Secretary-General Lie, "a grant of power sufficiently wide to enable the Security Council to approve the documents in question and to assume the responsibilities arising therefrom."

"Furthermore, the records of the San Francisco Conference," continued Mr. Lie in this statement, "demonstrate that the powers of the Council under Article 24 are not restricted to the specific grants of authority contained in Chapters VI, VII, VIII, and XII. In particular, the Secretary-General wishes to invite attention [of the Council] to the discussion at the fourteenth meeting of Committee III/1 at San Francisco wherein it was clearly recognized by all the representatives that the Security Council was not restricted to the specific powers set forth in Chapters VI, VII, VIII, and XII." The Secretary-General cited, in particular, document 597, Committee III/1/30 of the San Francisco Conference.

"It will be noted that this discussion concerned a proposed amendment to limit the obligation of Members to accept decisions of the Council solely to those decisions made under the specific powers. In the discussion"—at the Committee meeting—"all the delegations which spoke, including both proponents and opponents of this amendment, recognized that the authority of the Council was not restricted to such specific powers. It was recognized in this discussion that the responsibility to maintain peace and security carried with it a power to discharge this responsibility. This power, it was noted, was not unlimited,"—of course—"but subject to the purposes and principles of the United Nations, as embodied in the first two Articles of the Charter.".   .   .

Mr. GROMYKO (USSR):   .   .   .   I should like to draw the Security Council's attention to a point which was incidentally raised in the course of the discussion: How are we to evaluate the Council's decision on this matter? It is clear that any decision on this question is a decision taken in conformity with Chapter VI of the Charter, relating to the pacific settlement of disputes. This means that any decision we may take in the Council on this question will be in the nature of a recommendation and will have nothing in common with the decisions provided for in Article 25 of the Charter. I think it advisable to emphasize this idea, mainly in connexion with the elucidation given at the last meeting of the Council by the United States representative. In his reply to the representative of Bulgaria the United States representative gave an explanation which was at variance with the Charter.

In connexion with the Trieste question, in the matter of appointing a governor for Trieste, the United States representative attempted to prove that the powers and functions of the Security Council are not confined only to the chapters referred to in Article 24 of the Charter of the United Nations, in which the functions and powers of the Council are defined. I should like to draw your attention to the fact that the question which arose in connexion with the discussion of the appointment of a governor for Trieste is the problem not of the nature of the Security Council's decisions, but of the extent of the Security Council's powers. This puts the matter on an absolutely different plane and the reference to a memorandum of the Secretary-General, Mr. Trygve Lie, offers no confirmation, as this memorandum deals with an absolutely different question, the question of the extent and scope of the Security Council's powers, and not with the nature of the Security Council's decisions. .   .   .

Colonel HODGSON (Australia): .   .   .   [C]ertain action proposed in the United States resolution has been challenged on the ground that it is invalid.   .   .   .

The argument—which was submitted first by the representative of Bulgaria and supported by the representatives of Albania and Yugoslavia, and by a speech of the representative of the USSR—indicated that we can adopt only recommendations under Chapter VI; we cannot take action such as is contemplated in the setting up of a commission. It is argued that such action can be taken only under Chapter VII, when the Security Council finds that there is a breach of the peace. "In this case", they say, "as we have not found that there is a breach of the peace, we are confined to Chapter VI; we can only recommend, and a recommendation is not a decision. Yet a decision is required if the parties are to be bound under Article 25." Therefore, they say they are not bound to accept that action.   .   .   .

[In] Chapter VI itself and in other places in the Charter, we find ample justification for all the action proposed in the United States resolution. That has never been denied; even the first time the question arose, this Council decided to investigate. Indeed, we are bound to investigate because, before we decide that the continuation of a situation does endanger international peace and security, we must make a finding to that effect; otherwise we cannot do anything.   .   .   .

A decision to investigate—and that has never been challenged—is surely more than a recommendation. Under Chapter VI we can take many decisions. This resolution on the setting up of a commission has two purposes, confers two main powers: the power of investigation and the power of conciliation and mediation. If you give a body a certain power, that connotes that you give it authority to carry out that power. Authority is inherent in that power. Otherwise, what point would there be in this Council having the right to investigate, if the investigating body were not clothed with authority to act, authority, for example, to move about the frontiers; authority to examine witnesses; authority to examine officials of the country concerned; the very authority given in this resolution?

Further, the right to investigate also connotes a right to continue investigation, and that was never challenged when we set up the original Commission of Investigation. It is a strange thing that, for the first time, it should be challenged now. That is a decision, and not a recommendation; therefore, Article 25 does apply.

This Council could even take a decision to set up a conciliation commission. It could even take a decision to set up an arbitration commission in this case, if it wished. Those are all decisions, they are not recommendations; the Council has such power.

Under Article 28, we know that even the Security Council could go to Greece and hold meetings. Under Article 29 of the Charter, the Security Council has the right to establish subsidiary organs to carry out its function of maintaining international peace and security.

For all those reasons, there is ample justification for setting up the proposed body. Moreover, it is our right and duty to set up this body and to clothe it with the necessary powers; otherwise, the will of this Council would be completely stultified in any action it contemplated under Chapter VI. . . .

Mr. JOHNSON (USA): . . . The United States delegation feels strongly that the establishment of a commission with the purposes outlined in our resolution is entirely within the powers of the Security Council, under the Charter. Not only is it within the powers of the Security Council, but it is within its duties.

I think it is generally admitted that the primary role of the Security Council is to be the guardian organ of the United Nations for international peace and security. Under Article 34 of the Charter, the Security Council itself could go to the region which we have been discussing and conduct investigations. It follows, therefore, that it can set up a subsidiary organ to perform those functions. To argue that, in setting up such an organ, it would have the power only to recommend to countries that the commission should be allowed to function, and that those countries could refuse to accept it and to cooperate with it, or refuse to give it facilities, would seem to me to undermine the very foundations of the Charter and would stultify whatever influence and power the Security Council might have for the preservation of international peace. It is a totally unacceptable doctrine, in the view of the United States delegation.

Such a refusal of any Member of the United Nations or of any country which, for the purposes of a particular question, had accepted the stipulations of the Charter, would lay it open . . . to much graver charges and action under another Chapter of the Charter. . . .

Mr. VILFAN (Yugoslavia): . . . I shall confine myself to-day to three brief comments, all bearing on the interpretation of Article 34 of the Charter.

First of all, I should like to make a remark on a matter of principle. It appears to me that at the present stage when the United Nations has been in existence only two years, it would be wise to keep to the strictest possible interpretation of the Charter. If we start inter-preting the spirit of certain Articles, we risk raising disputes instead of creating unity among the United Nations.

It has been emphasized today that we should not limit ourselves to the literal interpretation of the Charter's Articles; I am in com-plete agreement. But if we are going to examine the exact spirit and purport of certain Articles of the Charter, it would seem to me better to retrace the history of these Articles and see how they were worked out and voted on at the San Francisco Conference.

Article 34 of the Charter has a history. Amongst others, an amend-ment was submitted by Bolivia on 5 May 1945. With your permission I shall read this amendment:

"The Security Council should be empowered to investigate any dis-pute or situation which may lead to international friction or give rise to a dispute, *and to propose the means which it considers neces-sary and to determine the measures which will be chosen in order to prevent the continued existence of the dispute or situation from en-dangering international peace, security and justice.*"

If you analyse the contents of this amendment, you will see that it corresponds exactly to what the United States resolution now pro-poses; the latter provides for everything suggested by the Bolivian delegation, namely permanent inquiry, and the possibility of taking decisions and of determining what are here called "the measures".

What was the fate of the Bolivian amendment? At the San Fran-cisco Conference, this amendment was rejected; in other words, it was not found desirable to give such a categorical nature to measures assigned to the Security Council in Chapter VI of the Charter as is provided by the United States resolution under discussion today. While I agree that an Article of the Charter should not be interpreted literally, I do not think we should go so far as to interpret this Ar-ticle as meaning something which was expressly rejected by the San Francisco Conference.

Finally, with the object of interpreting Chapter VI of the Charter properly, I have tried to ascertain the opinion of the United States Government. That opinion was expressed, at the time, by the Chair-man of the United States delegation to the San Francisco Conference; it is to be found in the report submitted to the President of the United States by the Chairman of that delegation.

What then was the character of the measures provided by Chap-ter VI of the Charter according to the interpretation, I repeat, of the

Chairman of the United States delegation?   On page 79 of this report, dated 26 June 1945 and addressed to the President of the United
States, the following passage occurs:

"It is to be noted that the Members of the Organization agree to
carry·out the decisions of the Security Council 'in accordance with
the present Charter'. Thus the precise extent of the obligations of
Members under Article 25 can be determined only by reference to
other provisions of the Charter, particularly Chapters VI, VII, VIII,
and XII (Article 24, paragraph 2). Decisions of the Security Council
take on a binding quality only as they relate to the prevention or suppression of breaches of the peace. With respect to the pacific settlement of disputes, the Council has only the power of recommendation."

It seems to me that this is an express and clear statement that the
measures assigned to the Security Council—which, by virtue of
Chapter VI, debates them—are solely in the nature of recommendations and are not decisions.   .   .   .

[Continuing his argument two days later, the Yugoslav representative added the following points:]

The United States resolution and the amendments contemplate a
commission set up in advance which would be imposed upon the States
concerned and which would be empowered to undertake investigations.

My Government's opinion is that, under the Charter, such a commission cannot be set up: Chapter VI of the Charter provides for investigation only as a method of procedure, and any decision taken by
the Security Council regarding an investigation is a decision *pro foro
interno*.

I shall not embark now on a detailed analysis of Chapter VI of the
Charter and of its Articles. You will remember the discussion which
arose in the Council two days ago. An attempt was made to justify
a commission of this kind by invoking the various Articles of Chapter
VI. I could summarize the result of this discussion very briefly. I
shall quote the words of the representative of France who, after a long
discussion during which attempts were made to find justification, in
all the Articles of Chapter VI, for the establishment of this commission, said the following—I shall read the text of the English interpretation for I have not a French text before me: "If we maintain
the literal interpretation of the text, we cannot in any way get out of
the difficulty."

Thus, the result of the discussion which lasted a whole afternoon
was that it was impossible, on the grounds of the text of Chapter VI,
to establish a commission with the competence provided for in the
United States resolution and in the amendments to that resolution.

Attempts were made to give an interpretation of this text, and I
have already said that, if it is desired to interpret a text, the best
method is to retrace its history. I have quoted an example. I could

give others, for there are plenty more to choose from. But I do not think that this is necessary.

I shall ask only one question today: if not only the history of the text precludes such an interpretation, but if even the actual text of the Charter is absolutely contrary to the establishment of such a commission, what will be done? Of course I am thinking of Article 2, paragraph 7 of the Charter . . . [I]f we translate the last provision of Article 2, paragraph 7 into positive terms, we should say: the Charter restricts the sovereignty of States only in the case of the measures provided for in Chapter VII.

It is obvious, however, that the existence of a commission such as that provided for in the United States resolution restricts the sovereignty of the States concerned. That is why the United States proposal is contrary not only to the letter of Chapter VI, but to the very principles of the Charter.

These are, briefly, the reasons why our Government thinks that a commission such as this cannot be established if we wish to remain faithful to the Charter.

But I should like to dispel a misunderstanding. We are not returning to this question for the pleasure of entering upon a procedural quibble. I do not think that this has been understood, for otherwise I cannot understand why we are told: "If you do not accept the commission under Chapter VI, it will be set up under Chapter VII."

I repeat that we have no wish to quibble; we wish to defend the principles of the Charter in this matter. This is not only a procedural question, but a question of substance.

The authors of the Charter clearly established a distinction between two kinds of procedure: that provided for by Chapter VI and that provided for by Chapter VII. In drawing up the measures contained in Chapter VI, they took special care not to restrict the sovereignty of States. It was only in connexion with a serious situation that they thought fit to restrict this sovereignty.

I should like to quote once more a document of which I spoke at the hundred and sixty-third meeting, the report to the President of the United States in which the following appears on page 86:

"Every assistance is provided to the nations themselves to settle their troubles peacefully. The right of the Security Council to intervene develops by carefully graduated stages only as it becomes necessary to do so for the maintenance of peace."

This means that the Charter has deliberately provided for successive stages: it has provided for a first phase, in which the sovereignty and independence of States are respected, and during which any possible agreement is left, so to speak, to mature as a fruit of the independent and free will of the States concerned.

I think, gentlemen, that you will detract greatly, not to say entirely, from the moral value of your decisions, if you do not take into account this difference between the Chapters of the Charter.   .   .   .

Mr. JOHNSON (USA): I do not agree with the interpretation of the representative of Yugoslavia regarding the intent of our resolution, nor do I agree with him in what seems to be his interpretation of the Charter.   .   .   .

Chapter VI of the Charter contains two Articles, Articles 33 and 34 which, in my opinion, are complementary and are not interdependent. Article 33 imposes a moral and—if one may say so—a legal obligation on individual Members of the United Nations, obligations which flow basically from Articles 1 and 2 of the Charter.   Paragraph 2 of Article 33 stipulates that, if the Members of the United Nations who may have causes of difference, have not, without any prodding from this Council whatsoever, fully performed their moral duty to obey the injunction contained in paragraph 1 of Article 33, then the Security Council, when it deems necessary, should call upon the parties to settle their dispute by the peaceful means stipulated in Article 33, paragraph 1.

However, the Security Council, when told in Article 33 that it ".   .   .   shall   .   .   ." after consideration ".   .   .   when it deems necessary, call upon the parties to settle their dispute by such means," has also other means at its disposal for carrying out its duties under the Charter as the guardian of international peace.   It is Article 34, which confers full and complete authority on the Security Council to investigate any dispute or any situation which might lead to international friction or give rise to a dispute.

If, in order to make such an investigation, the Security Council feels it necessary to go itself to the territory of some Member State, or to the territory of some non-member State, which for the purposes of the dispute has accepted its obligations, the Security Council has the right to ask that State for certain facilities and for co-operation.   The actual implementation of that request may entail certain inconveniences to the State granting it, but those inconveniences are to be expected, if they are necessary for carrying out the purposes of the Charter.

This does not mean that the Security Council, the United Nations or any individual Member of the United Nations desires to impair the sovereignty of that State.   Any treaty entered into between two States may, in some degree, impair the sovereignty of those States.   All the Members of the United Nations, when they accepted the Charter, agreed to accept a certain diminution of their sovereignty under certain circumstances and for certain purposes.

In my honest opinion, if the interpretation which has just been given by the representative of Yugoslavia of what may or may not be done by the Council under Chapter VI is accepted, it would mean a complete nullification of Article 34. It would mean that Chapter VI, for all practical purposes, consists of Articles 33, 36 and 37. I do not think that anything that the Yugoslav representative has said, nor anything that has been said at the Council table since the discussion of the United States resolution began, has in any way convinced me that our resolution exceeds the bounds of Chapter VI.

The Council certainly has powers and rights of conciliation, and unless the doctrine just proposed by the representative of Yugoslavia is rejected, it would have no power under Article 34 to make investigations. The Council has the power to make those investigations whether or not the country being investigated likes it; that is the fundamental issue. The representative of Yugoslavia claims that the Council can set up a commission to make investigations in Yugoslavia under Chapter VI only if Yugoslavia consents. I think that is completely erroneous as an interpretation of the Charter, and it would nullify the whole operative intent of Chapter VI. . . .

There is a clear distinction between conciliation and investigation. . . . It is obviously the duty of the Security Council to attempt to conciliate opposing parties under certain conditions. It is equally obvious that, under the Charter, it is the duty of those opposing parties at least to lend an ear to the admonitions of the Council. Thirdly, it is obvious that the Council cannot force two opposing parties to conciliate their views. Conciliation implies voluntary will on the part of those who oppose each other; and it is suggested only that the Security Council, in the spirit of the Charter, might act as a catalytic agent.

As regards functions of investigation, however, the situation is entirely different. There the Council has a duty—or may have a duty—to the entire United Nations which would override the consideration of the desires of any individual State.

I shall not attempt to argue in detail because I do not feel competent to do so at this moment, but I totally reject the interpretation given to Article 34 by the representative of Yugoslavia. I should like to point out to the representative of Yugoslavia, however, that consistent with what we believe to be the real intent and meaning of Chapter VI, judged in the light of its history and its formation, and even in the light of the statement of the Secretary of State to which he referred, Article 34 gives the Security Council the right to investigate any dispute regardless of whether or not the State investigated approves or likes it; and other stipulations of the Charter impose on the State being investigated the duty to accept the investigation whether or not it likes it, and to co-operate loyally.

That Article does not confer on the Security Council, operating under Chapter VI, any power of sanction or any power of enforcement. Article 34 gives the Security Council the means to find out the facts behind any situation which it may determine to investigate, so that those facts can be brought before the Council in order that it may decide upon the necessary action to be taken under whichever Article or Chapter of the Charter may be appropriate. But I do not think that the Council can accept that it may be frustrated in making an investigation simply by the will of one Member of the United Nations who does not desire to be investigated. That interpretation is not inconsistent with any interpretation of Chapter VI which has been given by any authorized spokesman of the United States. I agree that the Security Council cannot order any action or take any form of sanctions for violation of the Charter under Chapter VI. It can, however, determine what violation has taken place, and it may choose to do so by an investigation. If any Member refuses to co-operate in an investigation which has been ordered by a formal act of the Council, the Council can take no action, but it can initiate action against that State for violation of the Charter. . . .

Mr. MEVORAH (Bulgaria): . . . [A very amiable gentleman asked me the following question:] "Why do you not want a commission? This proves that your conscience is not quite clear." . . .

A commission is something very serious. It presupposes a body composed of many persons, requiring many vehicles and many drivers, and causing a great deal of worry; a body attracting numbers of correspondents and also arousing many misunderstandings. We already know what a commission is. We tell you frankly that we have had enough of them. We should be left in peace, because we have problems to solve. We are preoccupied with many matters at the present time. We are concerned above all with the economic problems which weigh upon our country as a result of the war and of two years of drought which have impoverished us.

Suppose, nevertheless, that you decide to set up a commission: this commission would move about in our territory; it would travel along our frontiers; according to what I read in the proposals, its agents would have the right to put their noses in everywhere without our having the right to keep them out; and this would inevitably give rise to complications and misunderstandings; witnesses would be summoned to appear before the commission; they would provide information; their evidence would have to be scrutinized to see if it was reliable or if it had been "cooked"; there would be charges and counter-charges; in fact, big politics would be carried on through this commission and above all, this would happen on our own soil. . . .

If the commission was only to spend a short time in our country, in Greece and in Yugoslavia, it would not be so bad: the commission would get to know our country, and for our part, we should be able to make ourselves known. But the commission is to settle down in our country and will be like a guest invited with good grace but to whom one would like to say, in the long run, that he has outworn his welcome. The commission is to last two years, with the possibility of a further extension. It is obvious that this would weigh on our daily life, like this Allied Control Commission which we have had, which we still have, and to which we are to some extent subordinated, since it was imposed on us by law and since we are forced by law to apply to it for many things, even for little things.

If this were an absolute necessity, we should say: it is most disagreeable, but we must put up with it. But I do not think that such necessity exists.

In the first place, it is desired to conduct an investigation. But an investigation is made of a *fait accompli*: if anything is happening, an investigation is made in order to discover the truth. But to institute a commission to investigate events which might or will take place in the future is beyond all normal logic; we no longer have a commission of investigation. And if this commission is assigned considerable powers and, in particular, has the right of enforcing its decisions on certain points, it is obvious that we shall really be in a state of tutelage. . . .

Of course, we are told: "We offer you our good offices," but it is also added: "We expect you to accept them." This is a "recommendation," but we are told: "If you do not accept, we shall draw our own conclusions." We therefore really have a recommendation which is imposed and must be accepted, and whoever would have the audacity not to accept it is liable to have his refusal interpreted in a disagreeable sense.

Thus, you see that these are measures with coercive force, and that, in the final analysis, this commission is a compulsory one and will be imposed on our authorities. We may be a small country, but even small countries have their susceptibilities, and we want to be absolutely free. That is why we protest against the establishment of the commission. . . .

Mr. GROMYKO (USSR): . . . I want to make a few supplementary remarks on a question which requires some clarification. I mean the question of the interpretation of Security Council decisions taken in connexion with the pacific settlement of disputes under Chapter VI of the United Nations Charter.

We are witnessing an attempt by the representatives of certain Governments to prove to us that decisions taken under Chapter VI of the Charter, or, at least, some of these decisions, have the same force as decisions taken under Chapter VII of the Charter. That is a wrong point of view, and is not consonant with the United Nations Charter.

Is it really possible to prove that the decisions taken by the Council for the pacific settlement of disputes are of a compulsory nature, when Chapter VI of the Charter directly states that the Security Council makes recommendations under that Chapter? It is quite impossible to prove such a thing.

In pursuance of the powers and functions assigned to it, the Security Council has to consider disputes and situations and to adopt decisions adjusted to the degree of gravity of those disputes and situations. If these situations and disputes are classified according to their gravity, we shall have, first, the preliminary measures, including investigations, then recommendations for pacific settlement and, lastly, measures which the Security Council must take when it finds there is a threat to the peace, a breach of the peace or an act of aggression.

It is obvious that a Security Council decision to conduct an investigation falls into the category of preliminary measures for pacific settlement, whereas decisions which the Security Council has to take under Chapter VII of the Charter relate to disputes and situations which may constitute or do constitute a threat to the peace.

Incidentally, not even all the decisions taken under Chapter VII of the Charter are compulsory. As we know, Article 39 of the Charter (Chapter VII) provides that the Security Council may make recommendations to States even under Chapter VII. The chief difference between Chapter VII and Chapter VI is that all Security Council decisions taken under Chapter VI bear the character merely of recommendations.

What would happen if we took the view advocated here by the United States representative? We should inevitably come to the conclusion that the Security Council adopts decisions which are binding, both as regards final measures, to be taken in connexion with the existence of a threat to the peace or a breach of the peace, and as regards preliminary measures for investigation. Need it be shown that such a concept is contrary to the letter and spirit of the United Nations Charter? The idea that Security Council decisions to conduct an investigation are obligatory is contrary to Chapter VI of the Charter. . . .

It is sometimes said that this is a question of interpretation: one person may adopt one interpretation and another may follow a different interpretation. That is wrong. This is not a question of interpretation. Regardless of how any of us interpret it, we must follow the Charter and act in conformity with the Charter. No interpretation which may be favoured by one member of the Council, or five members of the Council or eleven members of the Council can alter the Charter.

While the Charter exists in the form in which it was adopted at the Conference and ratified by the States, we should adhere to it and not try by giving interpretations, to by-pass it or act as it suits us— one way in 1945 and a different way in 1947. If we follow such a policy, our work in the Security Council will have no sound foundation and it will be difficult for us to work normally.

If we attempt to by-pass a clear Charter provision by using an interpretation, what can we say about other United Nations bodies?

If the Security Council sets such an example in its work, the example may be followed by other bodies.

Thus, the USSR delegation cannot share the view of certain representatives that decisions in connection with the pacific settlement of disputes (under Chapter VI of the Charter) are of a compulsory character. If we take that path, we shall inevitably reach the conclusion that, if a State does not fulfil certain recommendations, some other measures must automatically be applied to it. The question then arises: what other measures? Obviously, compulsory measures. But, in that event, the whole of Chapter VI regarding the pacific settlement of disputes loses its significance and meaning. All that should be left in the Charter, then, is Chapter VII, which provides for taking compulsory decisions. Such is the absurd conclusion to which this concept leads.

On one point, we can agree with those who defend this concept; we can agree with them that, in the case also of Council decisions for the pacific settlement of disputes, i. e., in the case of recommendations, States which do not comply with those recommendations bear a moral responsibility. No one will deny this. But that is a different matter. . . .

Mr. JOHNSON (USA): . . . [The] Council, in interpreting Chapter VI, must consider it in the light of other portions of the Charter. It is perfectly true that Chapter VI is the Chapter providing for pacific settlement of disputes. If, however, the Council is to fulfil its role as a conciliator and also as the guardian of the peace, it must have certain operating powers. Otherwise, it could not move; it could do nothing. Those powers, in my opinion, are given in Article 34. If the situation is such that the Council thinks it must have further information before it can make the recommendations to the interested States which are provided for in Article 33 and in other Articles of Chapter VI, then Article 34, in the powers which it confers on this Council, stands by itself and separate from any other Article in Chapter VI. To my mind, it can hardly be questioned that the Council has the power to make investigations, and that under Article 29 of the Charter it has the power to set up a subsidiary organ to perform such an investigation if the Council itself is not able, in a physical sense, to perform it.

There remains only the question of the measure and degree of obligation which the Members of the United Nations are under, within the purview of Chapter VI, to co-operate with such an investigation. That obligation, I believe, is imposed in Article 25. I do not think it can be denied that, under Chapter VI, certain forms of decisions can be taken; and that, under Article 25, it is the duty of the Members of the United Nations to conform to those decisions. . . .

[If] we accept the thesis first propounded at the hundred and sixty-sixth meeting by the representative of Yugoslavia, it will amount to a complete nullification of any power of action which the Security Council might be able to take under Chapter VI.

I believe that our interpretation is sound. I repeat that I do not think it confers upon the commission which would be created any power of action, by way of sanctions, within any of the countries. It confers only the right to assess certain facts, under certain conditions which are to be laid down, and to report those facts to the Security Council for its action.

Furthermore, if any of the countries concerned had violated Article 25 or any other Article of the Charter in connexion with this arrangement and if anything were to be done about it, the Security Council would have to proceed to affirmative action. I am not claiming that any power of sanctions exists under this Article. However, it does lay non-complying States open to serious charges, which may be brought before the Security Council and acted upon, charges of non-compliance with their own obligations under the Charter to cooperate with the Security Council in its decisions. The Security Council can make such decisions under Chapter VI. . . .

The PRESIDENT [Mr. Lange, Poland]: We have digressed slightly from our subject into a discussion of certain legal principles involved in the interpretation of the Charter. I thought the matter was sufficiently important to give the representatives an opportunity to express their views.

I have refrained from expressing my own views. Although I hold very definite opinions on this subject, I thought it wise to overcome the temptation—sometimes a strong one—to express them, partly because I did not want to prolong the discussion and partly because the discussion seemed to me, to a certain degree, academic.

It is clear, according to the Charter, that there are certain actions which the Council can take which have a legal and binding force. There are other actions which are recommendations. The controversy was in the way the difference of interpretation was drawn. But there is one point I should like to make, and in doing so I express the views of all the members of the Council, whatever they are—I do not want to enter into that question now—: any action of the Council which is merely a recommendation without legal binding force, has, for all practical purposes, consequences which are not very different from actions which do have legal binding force. I believe that the moral and political authority of this Council and its decisions, whatever the legal character, is so great that no Member State will ever wish not to carry out the decision of this Council.

NOTE.—1. With respect to the power of the Security Council to investigate, see Ernest L. KERLEY, "The Powers of Investigation of the United Nations Security Council," 55 AJIL (1961), pp. 892–918.

2. On 12 March 1947, President Truman in a message to the Congress announced the so-called "Truman Doctrine," namely, that "it must be the

policy of the United States to support free peoples who are resisting attempted subjugation by armed minorities or by outside pressure," and that, in pursuance of this policy, the United States must provide assistance to Greece and Turkey. 16 DSB (1947) p. 829, at 831. This assistance was authorized on 22 May 1947 by Public Law 75, 80th Congress, 1st Session (61 US Statutes at Large, Part I, p. 103), and was implemented by aid agreements concluded with Greece on 20 June 1947 (7 UNTS, p. 267) and with Turkey on 12 July 1947 (7 UNTS, p. 299). Article 10 of the agreement with Greece read as follows:

"Any or all assistance authorized to be provided pursuant to this Agreement will be withdrawn:

"(1) If requested by the Government of Greece representing a majority of the Greek people;

"(2) If the Security Council of the United Nations finds (with respect to which finding the United States waives the exercise of any veto) or the General Assembly of the United Nations finds that action taken or assistance furnished by the United Nations make the continuance of assistance by the Government of the United States pursuant to this Agreement unnecessary or undesirable;

"(3) Under any of the other circumstances specified in section 5 of the aforesaid Act of Congress or if the President of the United States determines that such withdrawal is in the interest of the United States; or

"(4) If the Government of Greece does not take reasonable steps to effectuate those measures proposed in its note of June 15, 1947 or subsequently agreed upon which are essential to reconstruction and recovery in Greece."

Similar provisions were included in Article VI of the Agreement with Turkey, except for the omission of the phrase "representing a majority of the [Turkish] people" in subparagraph (1) and the omission of the whole subparagraph (4).

On 20 August 1947, the United States delegation submitted to the second session of the General Assembly an item entitled "Threats to the political independence and territorial integrity of Greece." A/344. The Soviet Union opposed the inclusion of this item on the agenda, "stating that that request could not be justified. There was no threat to the political independence and territorial integrity of Greece from her neighbours to the north; there was, rather, a situation made more difficult every day by the interference of foreign Governments in the internal affairs of Greece, a situation which was aggravated by the presence of British troops." The General Committee decided, however, by 12 votes to 2, to recommend the inclusion of this item. GAOR, II, General C., pp. 5–6. The General Assembly approved the inclusion by 38 votes to 6, with 9 abstentions. GAOR, II, Plenary, pp. 299–300.

After an extensive debate in the First Committee, a draft resolution proposed by the United States was considerably amended. It was approved by the General Assembly on 21 October 1947 by 40 votes to 6, with 11 abstentions. GAOR, II, Plenary, pp. 461–2. For its text see No. 5, below.

5. *Resolution 109(II) of the General Assembly, 21 October 1947.*

GAOR, II, Resolutions (A/519) pp. 12–14.

1.   Whereas the peoples of the United Nations have expressed in the Charter of the United Nations their determination to practise tolerance and to live together in peace with one another as good neighbours and to unite their strength to maintain international peace and security; and to that end the Members of the United Nations have obligated themselves to carry out the purposes and principles of the Charter,

2.   The General Assembly of the United Nations,

Having considered the record of the Security Council proceedings in connexion with the complaint of the Greek Government of 3 December 1946, including the report submitted by the Commission of Investigation established by the Security Council resolution of 19 December 1946 and information supplied by the Subsidiary Group of the Commission of Investigation subsequent to the report of the Commission;

3.   Taking account of the report of the Commission of Investigation which found by a majority vote that Albania, Bulgaria and Yugoslavia had given assistance and support to the guerrillas fighting against the Greek Government,

4.   Calls upon Albania, Bulgaria and Yugoslavia to do nothing which could furnish aid and assistance to the said guerrillas;

5.   Calls upon Albania, Bulgaria and Yugoslavia on the one hand and Greece on the other to co-operate in the settlement of their disputes by peaceful means, and to that end recommends:

(1) That they establish normal diplomatic and good neighbourly relations among themselves as soon as possible;

(2) That they establish frontier conventions providing for effective machinery for the regulation and control of their common frontiers and for the pacific settlement of frontier incidents and disputes;

(3) That they co-operate in the settlement of the problems arising out of the presence of refugees in the four States concerned through voluntary repatriation wherever possible and that they take effective measures to prevent the participation of such refugees in political or military activity;

(4) That they study the practicability of concluding agreements for the voluntary transfer of minorities;

6.   Establishes a Special Committee:

(1) To observe the compliance by the four Governments concerned with the foregoing recommendations;

(2) To be available to assist the four Governments concerned in the implementation of such recommendations;

7. Recommends that the four Governments concerned co-operate with the Special Committee in enabling it to carry out these functions;

8. Authorizes the Special Committee, if in its opinion further consideration of the subject matter of this resolution by the General Assembly prior to its next regular session is necessary for the maintenance of international peace and security, to recommend to the Members of the United Nations that a special session of the General Assembly be convoked as a matter of urgency;

9. Decides that the Special Committee

(1) Shall consist of representatives of Australia, Brazil, China, France, Mexico, the Netherlands, Pakistan, the United Kingdom and the United States of America, seats being held open for Poland and the Union of Soviet Socialist Republics;

(2) Shall have its principal headquarters in Salonika and with the co-operation of the four Governments concerned shall perform its functions in such places and in the territories of the four States concerned as it may deem appropriate;

(3) Shall render a report to the next regular session of the General Assembly and to any prior special session which might be called to consider the subject matter of this resolution, and shall render such interim reports as it may deem appropriate to the Secretary-General for transmission to the Members of the Organization; in any reports to the General Assembly the Special Committee may make such recommendations to the General Assembly as it deems fit;

(4) Shall determine its own procedure, and may establish such subcommittees as it deems necessary;

(5) Shall commence its work within thirty days after the final decision of the General Assembly on this resolution, and shall remain in existence pending a new decision of the General Assembly.

10. The General Assembly

Requests the Secretary-General to assign to the Special Committee staff adequate to enable it to perform its duties, and to enter into a standing arrangement with each of the four Governments concerned to assure the Special Committee, so far as it may find it necessary to exercise its functions within their territories, of full freedom of movement and all necessary facilities for the performance of its functions.

NOTE. The USSR and Poland refused to take part in the activities of the Special Committee. A/574; GAOR, III.1, Supp. No. 8, p. 2. See also, GAOR, II, Plenary Meetings, p. 460.

On 27 November 1948 the General Assembly passed a second resolution on the Greek question. It noted "the conclusions of the Special Committee and, in particular, its unanimous conclusion that, despite the aforesaid resolution of the General Assembly, 'the Greek guerrillas have continued to receive aid and assistance on a large scale from Albania, Bulgaria and Yugoslavia, with the knowledge of the Governments of those countries' ", and "that a continuation of this situation 'constitutes a threat to the political independence and territorial integrity of Greece and to peace in the Balkans' and 'that the conduct of Albania, Bulgaria and Yugoslavia has been inconsistent with the purposes and principles of the Charter of the United Nations.' " It considered "that the continued aid given by Albania, Bulgaria and Yugoslavia to the Greek guerillas endangers peace in the Balkans, and is inconsistent with the purposes and principles of the Charter of the United Nations" and called upon "Albania, Bulgaria and Yugoslavia to cease forthwith rendering any assistance or support in any form to the guerillas in fighting against the Greek Government, including the use of their territories as a base for the preparation or launching of armed action." It recommended "to all Members of the United Nations and to all other States that their Governments refrain from any action designed to assist directly or through any other Government any armed group fighting against the Greek Government." Resolution 193 (III); GAOR, III.1, Resolutions (A/810), pp. 18–21. At the same time the General Assembly rejected a Soviet draft resolution that the General Assembly should consider it to be established that "the situation which has arisen in Greece . . . is the result of increased foreign interference in the domestic affairs of Greece," and that "the activities of the Special Committee have led to a further aggravation of the situation"; that it should recommend that "the Government of Greece . . . take the necessary measures to ensure the removal of any discrimination in regard to citizens of Macedonian or Albanian nationality living in the territory of Greece" and "that all foreign troops and foreign military personnel be withdrawn from Greece"; and finally that it should "terminate the activities of the Special Committee." A/729; GAOR, III.1, Plenary, Annexes, p. 395.

In a further resolution, passed on 18 November 1949, the General Assembly referred to the reports of the Special Committee "and in particular its unanimous conclusions that: (i) Albania and Bulgaria have continued to give moral and material assistance to the Greek guerrilla movement, Albania being the principal source of material assistance; (ii) There has been an increase in the support afforded to the guerrillas from certain States not bordering upon Greece, particularly Romania." It considered "that the active assistance given to the Greek guerrillas by Albania in particular, by Bulgaria and by certain other States, including Romania, in disregard of the Assembly's recommendations, is contrary to the purposes and principles of the United Nations Charter and endangers peace in the Balkans", and "that further foreign assistance to the Greek guerrillas resulting in the launching of new armed action against Greece from adjacent territory would seriously increase the gravity of the danger to the peace and would justify the Special Committee in recommending, pursuant to paragraph 8 of resolution 109 (II), the convocation, as a matter of urgency, of a special session of the General Assembly in order to give consideration to further steps necessary for the removal of this danger to the peace." It recommended "to all Members of the United Nations and to all other States: . . . to refrain from the direct or indirect provision of arms or other materials of war to Albania and Bulgaria until the Special Committee or another competent United Nations organ has determined that the unlawful assistance of these States to the Greek guerrillas has ceased; [and] to take into account, in their relations with Albania and Bulgaria, the extent to which those two countries henceforth abide by the recommendations of the General Assembly in their relations with Greece." Resolution 288 A (IV); GAOR, IV, Resolutions (A/1251), pp. 9–10.

The Special Committee was continued for a further year by Resolution 382 (V) of the General Assembly of 1 December 1950, which noted that "although a certain improvement has taken place in the situation on the northern frontiers of Greece, there nevertheless remains a threat to the political independence and territorial integrity of Greece." GAOR, V, Supp. 20 (A/1775), p. 14. On 7 December 1951, the General Assembly decided to discontinue the Special Committee but added that "the situation in the Balkans may require prompt establishment of observation as contemplated in resolution 377 A (V), section B." It therefore resolved "to request the Peace Observation Commission [created by the so-called "Uniting for Peace" Resolution, p. 491, below] to establish a Balkan Sub-Commission composed of not less than three nor more than five members . . . with authority: (a) To despatch such observers as it may deem necessary to any area of international tension in the Balkans on the request of any State or States concerned, but only to the territory of States consenting thereto; (b) To visit, if it deems necessary, any area in which observation requested under subparagraph (a) is being conducted." Resolution 508 (VI); GAOR, VI, Supp. 20, (A/2119), pp. 9–10. A Balkan Sub-Commission was established by the Peace Observation Commission on 23 January 1952. A/CN.7/6. By letter dated 26 November 1953 addressed to the Secretary-General, the representative of Greece suggested that the number of military observers in Greece might henceforth be limited to three and that complete discontinuance of the military observation mission might be possible as early as 31 July 1954 in view of the improved relations between Greece and Albania and Bulgaria. A/CN.7/SC.1/52. By a further letter of 14 May 1954 the representative of Greece suggested that the mission of the United Nations military observers in Greece might be discontinued from 1 August 1954. A/CN.7/SC.1/55. On 28 May the Sub-Commission so decided. See GAOR, IX, Supp. 1 (A/2663), p. 29.

For comments on the Greek Question, see C. E. BLACK, "Greece and the United Nations," 63 Political Science Quarterly (1948), pp. 551–68; Loy W. HENDERSON, "The Greek Situation," 18 DSB (1948), pp. 272–78; Harry N. HOWARD, "The United Nations and the Problem of Greece," 17 *idem* (1947), pp. 279–89, 347–61, 443–62, 1097–1149; 21 *idem* (1949), pp. 407–31; Jean HUGONNOT, "Les origines et la signification de la crise grecque," 11 Politique étrangère (1946), pp. 71–94; YUGOSLAVIA, OFFICE OF INFORMATION, Book on Greece (Belgrade, 1948), 228 pp.

INDONESIAN QUESTION

NOTE. 1. The Indonesian Question was first submitted to the Security Council by the Ukrainian SSR on 21 January 1946, which complained that "military operations directed against local population have been carried on" in Indonesia "by regular British troops," and that this situation constituted "a threat to international peace and security." SCOR, I.1, Supp. 1, p. 76. It was contended by the United Kingdom and the Netherlands that the British troops were sent to Indonesia by the Allied Supreme Command, with the full consent of the Netherlands, to round up Japanese troops and rescue more than 200,000 internees; that when they were attacked by local inhabitants, the British troops had been compelled to defend themselves; that there was neither a "dispute" nor danger to international peace; and that a United Nations commission could not be sent to investigate and deal with problems arising within a sovereign power. None of the proposed resolutions obtained more than two votes and the President declared the matter closed. Report of the Security Council to the General Assembly, Jan.– July 1946 (A/93; GAOR, I.2, Supp. 1), pp. 37–46.

2. The conflict which followed the return of British and later Dutch forces to Indonesia ended on 15 November 1946 with the initialling by the Netherlands and the Republic of Indonesia of the Linggadjati Agreement, in which the former extended *de facto* recognition to the government of the Republic. The agreement also envisioned the creation of two other states— Great East (the Celebes, the Sunda Islands and the Moluccas) and Borneo— which together with the Republic would be federated into a United States of Indonesia, which in turn would be part of a Netherlands Union under the Netherlands Crown. These principles were incorporated into the final agreement signed at Batavia on 25 March 1947. 18 DSB (1948), pp. 325–27. Hostilities between Netherlands and Republican forces, however, continued and the situation was brought before the Security Council.

3. On 30 July 1947, the Australian representative to the Security Council brought to the attention of the Security Council "the hostilities which are at present in progress in Java and Sumatra between armed forces of the Netherlands and of the Republic of Indonesia, and which have been the subject of *communiqués* by their respective army commanders during the past ten days." The Australian Government considered that "these hostilities constitute a breach of the peace under Article 39" and urged that "the Council should take immediate action to restore international peace and security." In order to prevent an aggravation of the situation, the Australian Government proposed that "the Security Council as a provisional measure and without prejudice to the rights, claims or position of the parties concerned, should call upon the Governments of the Netherlands and the Republic of Indonesia to cease hostilities forthwith and to commence arbitration in accordance with article 17 of the Linggadjati Agreement between the Netherlands and the Government of the Republic of Indonesia signed at Batavia on 25 March 1947." S/449; SCOR, II, Supp. 16, p. 149. In that article the Netherlands Government and the Government of the Republic of Indonesia agreed that they "shall settle by arbitration any dispute which might arise from this agreement and which cannot be solved by joint consultation in conference between those delegations. In that case a chairman of another nationality with a deciding vote shall be appointed by agreement between the delegations or, if such agreement cannot be reached, by the President of the International Court of Justice." RIIA, Docs. on Int. Affairs, 1947–48, pp. 739, 742.

4. On the same day the Council also received a letter from the permanent liaison officer of the Indian Government with the United Nations in which he drew the "attention of the Council, under Article 35, paragraph 1, to the situation in Indonesia." He noted the large-scale military action, which Dutch forces had launched against the Indonesian people without warning. In the opinion of the Indian Government, this situation endangered the maintenance of international peace and security, and was covered by Article

34. He requested the Security Council "to take the necessary measures provided by the Charter to put an end to the present situation." S/447; SCOR, II, Supp. 16, p. 150.

1. *Discussion in the Security Council, 31 July–1 August 1947.*

SCOR, II, Nos. 67–68; pp. 1616–46, 1657–95.

Colonel HODGSON (Australia): At midnight on 20–21 July, large-scale fighting commenced on the islands of Java and Sumatra between the armed forces of the Netherlands and of the Republic of Indonesia. The Australian Government immediately took action, in consultation with other Members of the United Nations, to persuade the belligerents to cease hostilities and to seek a solution of their disputes by negotiation and mediation in accordance with the purposes and principles set forth in the Charter, by the peaceful means which Members are bound to use in the first instance, under Article 33.

Unfortunately, however, all efforts by individual Governments, all offers of mediation have so far been unavailing. Hostilities continue, and my Government has felt it imperative to bring the situation to the attention of the Council without further delay. . . .

It is our hope that the Council will not attempt to reach any decision as regards the merits of the case and will confine its deliberation to deciding on a course of action to bring about a cessation of hostilities.

We feel that the Council should proceed with its work even though one or more of the Governments concerned may not be in a position to participate immediately. I understand that representatives of the Netherlands and India are present in the Council chamber and may be authorized to participate if invited. I am not sure whether the same is true of the Republic of Indonesia, but I am certain that neither the members of the Council nor the other countries concerned, least of all the Republic of Indonesia, would wish to see any delay or procrastination. . . .

Mr. VAN LANGENHOVE (Belgium): . . . The Security Council has before it communications from the representatives of India and Australia. These communications represent an initiative taken by two States Members of the United Nations who invoke certain provisions of the Charter in their appeal to the Council. For this reason alone, these communications seem to be admissible and thus to qualify for inclusion in the Council's agenda.

This decision on admissibility does not, however, prejudge the Council's competence in any way. By admitting their admissibility, the council in no way decides whether the subject of the communications thus placed on the agenda does or does not fall within its competence. In this particular case, we are concerned with a matter which has just been referred to the Council.

But, I repeat, communications are admissible. Otherwise, failure to place them on its agenda would mean that the Council could not even consider whether their subject was within its competence and hence whether it could proceed to an examination of their substance.

The PRESIDENT [Mr. Lange, Poland]: I should like to make it clear that the adoption of this item on the agenda does not in any way prejudge either the competence of the Security Council in the matter or any of the merits of the case.

The agenda was adopted.

[The PRESIDENT, at the request of the Belgian representative, ruled that according to Article 31 of the Charter, the Netherlands and India were entitled to participate in the Security Council's debates on this issue even though neither was at that time a member of the Council. They were invited to take their seats at the Council's table.]

Colonel HODGSON (Australia): I assume that, after granting the right to participate to the Netherlands and India, the Council would also immediately authorize the sending of an invitation to the Government of Indonesia to participate in a similar manner. We do not know whether Indonesia has a representative available, but, at least, the invitation should be sent immediately.

Mr. VAN KLEFFENS (Netherlands): I wish to thank the members of the Security Council for the opportunity accorded us to present our point of view, without vote. I take the liberty of asking to be heard at this early stage because the question of admitting representatives of the Republic of Indonesia to this Council table seems to me to prejudge the whole question at issue before the Council at this time.

What is the Republic of Indonesia? I wish to remind the Council that this is a misleading name. Indonesia is that whole archipelago reaching from Sumatra in the west to New Guinea in the east, in which at the present moment there is not only the Republic of Indonesia which comprises geographically only the islands of Java and Sumatra and is not designed to comprise any more than that—but there are also the States of Eastern Indonesia—comprising Celebes, the Moluccas, the Lesser Sunda Islands, and a number of other islands in the east of the archipelago—and the State of Borneo. These two States, together with the Republic of Indonesia—which, I can not repeat often enough, comprises only the islands of Java and Sumatra—are destined to be affiliated, associated, and federated into something which, according to the Agreement of Linggadjati—with which the Council, I take it, is familiar—is to be called the "United States of Indonesia". The State-to-be, and no other state in those regions, is, according to that Agreement which bears the signature of the representative of the Republic of Indonesia, to be a sovereign, democratic State on a federal basis.

The Republic of Indonesia is not a sovereign State any more than the State of Eastern Indonesia or of Borneo. It never has been a sovereign State. It is a political entity to be affiliated ultimately with the two other States I have named, and to be part of a federation. It has a Government which is only *de facto*. But the government of what? Of a sovereign State? No, not of a sovereign State, but a State in the nature of—I mention this with all due respect to these States with which the Republic of Indonesia, plus Eastern Indonesia and Borneo, is comparable—let us say, New York or Utah or New South Wales or Parahiba in Brazil, or a state of the United States of Venezuela. Since that is so, I submit there is no justification for asking a political entity of that kind to be admitted to this Council table.   .   .   .

Colonel HODGSON (Australia): .   .   .   It is with a deep sense of responsibility that the Australian Government has drawn the attention of the Council under Article 39 of the Charter of the United Nations to the situation in Indonesia. We had certainly hoped that circumstances would never arise which would make it necessary for Chapter VII to be invoked, and we have done so only after making strenuous attempts, in consultation with other Governments, particularly the United Kingdom, the United States and India, to bring about a solution by negotiation and mediation.

However, although the parties to any dispute are bound to seek a solution by mediation and negotiation under Article 33, all attempts to bring the parties together have failed, and it is felt that further delay is not justified because of the loss of life being sustained. The events of the last few days have been most disturbing to the Australian Government. Not only is Indonesia adjacent to our territory, but we are bound by the closest possible economic and commercial ties with this important area. Therefore, we not only share the concern which all Members of the United Nations must have in the restoration of peace and security, but we feel that the interests of Australia are especially affected by the dispute between the Government of the Republic of Indonesia and the Government of the Netherlands, as the result of which hostilities have been in progress in Java and Sumatra during the last ten days.

We feel further that we have a responsibility to bring this situation to the attention of the Council, for it is one of international concern and already has far-reaching repercussions. It affects the well-being and stability of the whole of the South-west Pacific and South-east Asia in which we are directly concerned.

This is the first time a case has been brought before the Council under Chapter VII. Under Article 39, we are alleging a breach of the peace. There are no precedents as to what constitutes a breach of the peace, but we assume that this means a breach of international peace and applies to cases where hostilities are occurring, but where it is not alleged that one particular party is the aggressor or has committed an act of aggression.

That hostilities are in progress is now well established. The Security Council should take cognizance of the substance and reality of what is taking place. There have been large-scale military operations involving the use of naval units, aircraft and tanks, and regular *communiqués* have been issued by the respective commanders. . . .

The Council should also note that the hostilities proceeding are not merely police action but are in fact warfare; that is, in international law, armed conflict between two States. It can be clearly established that the Republic of Indonesia does constitute a State.

First, the original Netherlands-Indonesian Draft Agreement of 15 November was negotiated and initialled by representatives of the two Governments, the Netherlands and the Republic of Indonesia.

Secondly, the Government of the Republic of Indonesia has been recognized by the Netherlands Government as exercising *de facto* authority over Java, Madura and Sumatra by the Linggadjati Agreement, article I.

Thirdly, the Republic of Indonesia has been given *de facto* recognition by a number of other Governments including the United Kingdom, United States, India, members of the Arab League and Australia. We understand also that Egypt, Syria, and Iraq have given diplomatic recognition, and that Egypt and Syria have concluded treaties of friendship with the new State. Indeed, the Arab League as far back as 18 November of last year, proposed that the Arab States should consider recognizing the Republic.

Lastly, in the Linggadjati Agreement under article XVII, there is provision for the President of the International Court of Justice to nominate the Chairman of an arbitration body. This is significant. As the members are aware, only States may be parties in cases before that Court. . . .

On previous occasions when a dispute has been brought to the attention of the Council, the Australian delegation has constantly taken the attitude that there should be a full investigation of the facts under Article 34 of the Charter before the Council made a determination or decided to take action.

However, we have also made it clear that the application of the principle of investigation should be considered in the light of each case which comes before the Council. The present situation is completely different from any previous case which has arisen. Hostilities are being carried on. The parties in this dispute have not only admitted the fact that hostilities are in progress but, as I have already mentioned, have issued official *communiqués* regarding them. Investigation is not required to establish the crucial fact, and before the Security Council determines further action, it is essential to call a halt to hostilities which are each day taking their toll of human life and destruction of property. . . .

In the opinion of my Government, therefore, the appropriate measures of a provisional nature which this Council should take are: (1) demand for cessation of hostilities; (2) arbitration under article XVII of the Linggadjati Agreement.

To that end, the Australian delegation submits the following resolution to the Security Council:

"The Security Council,

"Noting with concern the hostilities in progress between the armed forces of the Netherlands and of the Republic of Indonesia, and

"Having determined that such hostilities constitute a breach of the peace under Article 39 of the Charter of the United Nations,

"Calls upon the Governments of the Netherlands and of the Republic of Indonesia, under Article 40 of the Charter of the United Nations, to comply with the following measures, such measures to be without prejudice to the rights, claims or position of either party:

"(a) To cease hostilities forthwith, and

"(b) To settle their disputes by arbitration in accordance with article XVII of the Linggadjati Agreement, signed at Batavia on 25 March 1947."

. . . We are not in any way prejudging the issue. We are not condemning anybody. We ask only for cessation of hostilities so that independent arbitration can decide on the merits of the case, and so that further destruction of life and property can be avoided. . . .

With regard to the point raised concerning a representative of the Republic of Indonesia, if the Council is prepared to adopt a resolution along the lines we have proposed, some members will probably consider that there is no need to wait for a representative of the Republic of Indonesia to be present here.

As the representative of the Netherlands said, the membership of the United Nations is certainly based on the equality of sovereign States; yet many of them fail by that test. But nowhere in the Charter is it said that this Council cannot act in a dispute between States, and certainly when a State is involved which is already internationally recognized and indeed has received a very wide international recognition.

For those reasons, I leave in the hands of the Council the question as to whether or not, at this stage, the Council should invite a representative of the Republic of Indonesia. If the Council does extend such an invitation, I suggest that the invitation should be extended under Article 32 of the Charter, that is, on the same terms and conditions as those of the invitations extended to Albania and Bulgaria [in the Greek Case]—namely, that the Republic of Indonesia accepts the obligations of settlement provided for in the Charter of the United Nations.

Mr. EL-KHOURI (Syria): . . . The Government of the Netherlands concluded with the Republic of Indonesia an Agreement which was signed on 2 March 1947. The following day the Government of the Netherlands submitted to the Secretariat of the United Nations a copy of that Agreement to be registered in the United Nations in pursuance of Article 102 of the Charter, which reads, "Every treaty and every international agreement entered into by any Member of the United Nations after the present Charter comes into force shall as soon as possible be registered with the Secretariat and published by it."

We believe that the Government of the Netherlands considered that Agreement which it concluded with Indonesia as an international agreement. It could not have been described as an international agreement unless it had been concluded between two independent States, each independent of the other. When this Agreement was published and made known to the world, all the world considered that Indonesia would be recognized as independent.

My Government, as well as the other Governments of the Arab League, recognized the independence of Indonesia after it had been recognized by the Netherlands Government. Our recognition was based on their recognition in accordance with the Agreement which was registered in the United Nations as an international treaty. This is our first point.

The second point is that neither the Charter nor our rules of procedure stipulate that any State, to be considered a State, should have complete independence. We know that some States of the world do not have complete independence; they are independent, but not completely so, by virtue of certain agreements and certain treaties which bind them to other nations or to the United Nations, and which limit their independence to a certain extent. But that does not alter their independence and deprive them of the right to be treated as independent States. For this reason we consider that Indonesia should be considered an independent State and should have the right to enjoy the same privileges as other States.

Mr. JOHNSON (USA): I wonder if it is necessary for the Council to take a legal decision this afternoon on the question of the participation of the Indonesian so-called Republic. Could not the Council invite that territory to send a representative who would be available for consultation by the Council? Later, if it became necessary during the course of the discussion of the case which has been brought up by the Indian and Australian representatives, the Council might finally make a juridical decision; but it does not seem to me that the Council need give up the advantage of having a representative of that territory here. It would be an advantage from the point of view both of allowing that group of people a spokesman and of making it possible to consult them in some way. I make these remarks as an inquiry.

The PRESIDENT: In reply to the representative of the United States, according to rule 39 we can invite anybody we wish for consultation. A State which participates in a dispute must be invited according to Article 32 of the Charter, under certain conditions which the Security Council may lay down. It is quite possible to adopt the procedure of inviting a representative of the Indonesian Republic and leaving until later the matter of deciding his legal status, and the legal basis of the representation. There would be no objection to that. We do not need to settle the question of the legal status of the Indonesian Republic just now; but I should like once more to urge the Council to take a decision on the cessation of hostilities.

Mr. TSIANG (China): My delegation is of the opinion that the resolution submitted by our colleague from Australia meets the requirements of the case exactly and completely. It does not attempt to judge. In fact, it expressly excludes prejudging the rights, claims or position of either party. It calls on this Council to perform its primary duty—a duty which it cannot escape—to stop the fighting and to solve the dispute by peaceful means.

Now, I have a modest suggestion which I would request our colleague from Australia to consider. Would he be willing to add at the end of paragraph (b) the phrase "or by other peaceful means"? I suggest that phrase not because I am opposed to the present formulation but in order to cover possible contingencies. . . .

Colonel HODGSON (Australia): My delegation welcomes that suggestion. . . .

Mr. GROMYKO (USSR): . . . [We] can at any time, even now, take a decision to put an end to hostilities, but it is absolutely necessary to consider the Indonesian situation, and to do so from the right angle. In any case, such questions as to whether it is necessary to set up arbitration or choose some other means in order to establish normal relations between the Indonesian Republic and the Netherlands, or whether a decision merely to put an end to hostilities is or is not sufficient, call for detailed consideration by the Council. Urgency and inexcusable haste are two different things. We cannot, under the pretext of suiting our action to the urgency of the matter, confine ourselves to the discussion of purely formal and unimportant measures. . . .

The PRESIDENT: Before calling upon the representative of the Netherlands, I should like to make a suggestion.

The resolution consists of two parts: a proposal to cease hostilities, and a proposal for the settlement of the dispute. Quite a number of representatives expressed some doubt as to whether we could make a decision on the second point without going into the details in an extensive debate.

I think that everybody who spoke agreed with the first point. The representative of Australia also expressed his willingness to have considered for the moment the first part of the resolution, which includes the preamble and the point about the cessation of hostilities. I should like to take up this proposal, because I think it will facilitate our debate. I think it is a point which we might settle today, and we could then postpone the discussion of the rest of the resolution to the next meeting.

I should also like to suggest to the representative of Australia that, if we consider only the part of the resolution contained in point (a), then it might be better to use, instead of the words "to cease hostilities forthwith", "to cease hostilities immediately". Whether or not we add something, or what we do about the settlement of the dispute, would be discussed at the next meeting.

Mr. VAN KLEFFENS (Netherlands): Even if that procedure is followed, I am very anxious to be heard. I shall endeavour to show the Council that, although this is admittedly a case of military action, it is a form of military action with which this Council has no concern. . . .

The chief characteristic of the Republic has been—and this is very pertinent to the discussion in progress here—that it had no authority at home; it was not obeyed. . . .

Moreover, undisciplined troops and lawless armed bands continued to range the countryside, living on the population of the land by terrorizing the inhabitants. . . .

The average native has had more than enough of this. The people of Java are not an industrial proletariat. They are small landowners, as there is a law which forbids any white person to have land there—a law which we made years and years ago, to be quite correct in 1870, in order that the land should belong to the inhabitants. These people are peaceful folk, like everybody here in the United States or in the country of any other member, and they ask for protection. . . .

All we care about is that anarchy, chaos and lawlessness should cease and that the great masses of the people, on behalf of whom we act as the guardians of their security and true liberty, should at last be enabled again to live in peace.

This is not war. The best words we have been able to find for it— but I do not wish to quarrel about words—were "police action". I repeat that we do not wage war against the Republic. We shall be quite happy to continue negotiations with the Republic, but we cannot go on with a Government which is divided within itself, is not obeyed by those under its *de facto* authority, and is generally evasive, unconstructive, and unco-operative. . . .

Let us now analyse the relevant portions of the Charter against this background. The Charter was designed I think to operate between sovereign States. Article 2, paragraph 1 of the Charter says, "The Organization is based on the principle of the sovereign equality of all its Members."

I beg to observe that no State which is not a sovereign State is eligible for membership. Let me add that Committee 1 of the San Francisco Conference, in its report to Commission I, stated that sovereign equality includes the following element: " . . . 2. That each State enjoys the right inherent in full sovereignty."

There is on the side of the Republic of Indonesia no question of full sovereignty. The sovereign Power—and I think this has never been disputed yet—is the Netherlands, whose Government has difficulties with one of its constituent elements, not with an external element. We therefore contend:

First, the Charter is not applicable to what is now happening in Java and Sumatra; and

Secondly, that while it seems to us that that contention is adequate to rule out action of any kind, including an affirmative vote on the Australian draft resolution now before us, we consider, in addition, that this is a matter essentially within the domestic jurisdiction of the Netherlands. Article 2, paragraph 7 of the Charter reads as follows:

"Nothing contained in the present Charter shall authorize the United Nations to intervene in matters which are essentially within the domestic jurisdiction of any State or shall require the Members to submit such matters to settlement under the present Charter; but this principle shall not prejudice the application of enforcement measures under Chapter VII."

Now, I come to Chapter VII. Assuming purely and simply for argument's sake that the Charter is applicable—which I deny—to what is now taking place in Java and Sumatra, where then, I ask, is there any danger to international peace or security, let alone breaches of the peace or acts of aggression in the sense of the Charter? In what countries outside the Netherlands' territory are there any signs of danger to peace caused by this action? . . .

The Charter has its limitations. The Security Council has no right to extend its limits. If the Council thinks that the Charter is inadequate, let the United Nations write a better Charter. But let the Council not overstep the boundaries laid down in that Charter as it now, fortunately or unfortunately, is at present. As long as the text of the Charter is what it is today, it must be applied as it is. Some of us may regret that, but it is well-known the Charter was never meant to be a cure for all the evils and ills in this world.

In one of his earlier statements this afternoon, I heard the representative of Australia mention that this was a matter of international concern. When I had the honour and privilege of being the representative of my country on the Security Council, I had occasion to hear that expression. I heard it, if I recall, in the course of the discussion of the Spanish question about a year ago. I had occasion then to say that I could not warn the Council enough against the loose use of that expression. It does not figure in the Charter, and it is an easy way to let the Council assume responsibilities for which it has not been instituted. There are many matters of international concern which do not fall within the terms of the Charter. . . .

Last year when the matter of British troops in Indonesia came up for discussion in the Security Council, I remember very well what I said on that occasion. The Council decided it had found no reason for taking action; and this was based very largely on considerations identical with or akin to those which I have just advanced. . . .

[On 1 August 1947, the discussion was continued under a new President, Mr. EL–KHOURI (Syria).]

Mr. JOHNSON (USA): . . . I had suggested to the representative of Australia that I should like to offer an amendment to his resolution which, if the Council approved it, would, I believe, accomplish the purpose of exhorting the parties to this dispute to cease hostilities and to settle their disputes by arbitration or by any other peaceful method. I believe that such a resolution, if approved and passed by the Council, would be a fitting complement to the offer of good offices which we have now made and which the Netherlands Government has accepted, and which we hope may be rapidly implemented.

In this amendment to the Australian resolution, which I shall read in a moment—I have copies for the members of the Council—there is no mention of any Article of the Charter, and there is no commitment regarding the sovereignty of the Netherlands over the region in question. All of those questions are left open and without prejudice to any determination which the Council may later reach.

The amendment as it now reads—which I shall give to the President and the other members—is as follows:

"The Security Council,

"Noting with concern the hostilities in progress between the armed forces of the Netherlands and of the Republic of Indonesia,

"Calls upon the parties,

"(a) To cease hostilities forthwith, and

"(b) To settle their disputes by arbitration or by other peaceful means."

I respectfully submit that amendment to the judgment of the Council. My delegation believes that if we can pass that simple statement quickly, we may then go into the legal issues involved at a subsequent time, when our various delegations on this Council will have had the time to study and to think of all of the indications [implications] which might follow our adopting any one of the juridical principles.

Mr. GROMYKO (USSR): . . . Mr. van Kleffens told us at great length that the Netherlands had, in his view, been obliged to undertake military operations because the Government of the Indonesian Republic had failed to fulfil the obligations which it undertook under the Agreement of 25 March 1947 to which I have referred.

According to Mr. van Kleffens' reasoning, we might draw the very odd inference that when a Government which has concluded an agreement with another Government fails in some respect to carry out provisions of the agreement, the Government which is carrying out the agreement or claims to be doing so, has the right to start military operations against the State accused of not carrying out the agreement. How can such an assertion be accepted? Clearly, such an assertion is quite inadmissible, for it would mean justifying and encouraging aggression. . . .

Mr. van Kleffens yesterday drew our attention to the fact that the Netherlands hopes to end military operations soon, i. e., to score a victory over the forces of the Indonesian Republic. That means that mediation, or any other procedure which may be chosen for settling the questions outstanding between the Netherlands and the Indonesian Republic, would place the Netherlands in a more advantageous position, simply because its troops had been victorious over the forces of the Indonesian Republic and had occupied its important productive economic and strategic centres. It is in these circumstances that we are recommended to use mediation, arbitration and other peaceful means of settling the various questions between the Netherlands and the Indonesian Republic and so by-pass the United Nations.

We all know the meaning of negotiations between two countries, when one country has occupied the other's territory. . . .

In conclusion, on behalf of the USSR delegation, I beg to submit the following motion:

"The Security Council

"Considers it necessary that the troops of both sides, the Netherlands and the Indonesian Republic, should be immediately withdrawn to the previous positions which they occupied before the beginning of military operations." . . .

I consider this proposal to be an addition to the text of the Australian resolution, which is acceptable to the USSR delegation in the form in which it was submitted to the Security Council yesterday. The USSR delegation considers that the addition of such a paragraph would improve the Australian resolution and would bring the eventual decision of the Security Council into conformity with the seriousness of the situation in Indonesia. . . .

Mr. LANGE (Poland): . . . I should like to urge the Council very earnestly to take at least one action today: either to adopt the recommendation calling for a cessation of hostilities; or to decide, if it so believes, that the representative of the Netherlands is correct in his contention that the matter is outside the competence of the Council. I believe the matter is of sufficient importance for us to decide today whether it is within our competence to recommend a cessation of hostilities; and, if it is, to make such a recommendation.

The PRESIDENT [Mr. El-Khouri, Syria] . . . The representative of Poland has spoken about the question of the competence of the Council in this matter. Had any motion in regard to competence been submitted, I would have given it priority, because it would then have been necessary to decide first whether or not the Security Council was competent to deal with this question. If that had been decided affirmatively, we should then have proceeded to any other recommendation that might have been made. The fact is, however, that the question of competence has simply been mentioned by some of the speakers in the course of the discussion. If any member has submitted a formal proposal stating that this matter was outside the competence of the Security Council and that therefore this item ought to be deleted from the Council's agenda, that proposal would have received priority over any other. However, no such proposal has been made.

I shall therefore call for further discussion on the proposal of the Australian delegation, as amended by the delegations of the United States and the Union of Soviet Socialist Republics. The vote on that proposal will, after all, reveal the views of the members on the question of competence. Those who believe that the matter is within the competence of the Council may vote affirmatively or negatively on the Australian resolution; however, those who believe that the matter is outside the competence of the Council will certainly vote against the resolution. . . .

Colonel HODGSON (Australia): . . . At one stage it was thought that this Council might, for the first time in its history, reach a speedy solution. But that seemed to be too much for some representatives. I sense a feeling of timidity lest we are going too fast. My delegation does not believe that we are going too fast; but, to avoid all those technicalities, on behalf of my delegation, I accepted the amendment to the Australian resolution which was proposed by the United States of America, subject, of course, to the reservation that my colleagues who supported the Australian resolution yesterday were also in agreement with the United States proposal. . . .

Mr. PARODI (France): . . . I do not quite see on what grounds the Security Council is competent to deal with the Indonesian question. . . .

We cannot be competent to deal with this question unless there is a threat to the peace. The events taking place in Java and Sumatra might constitute such a threat either if—being considered to be of an internal nature—they were liable to give rise to international complications, on account of their repercussions on external affairs (I do not think that that is so; and, in any case, since no information to this effect has been provided, I cannot with my present knowledge consider that it is so) or if, upon examination of the facts themselves, we were to consider them as acts of war between two distinct and sovereign States.

The explanations given yesterday show that, with regard to the second alternative—the existence of two sovereign States—the answer is, to say the least extremely doubtful. . . .

On the other hand, if the Council considers that . . . [legal or technical questions] can and should be left aside completely, I would understand and I would support the proposed decision provided it were submitted fully and very clearly. . . . First of all, I want us to state clearly that we are completely leaving aside the problem of the Security Council's competence and that we should make it plain that the appeal we are making is an appeal on humanitarian grounds, and not on legal or political grounds. In addition, I think we should go further, and since this delicate legal question has been raised and since it is an essential one, we should take steps to settle it. I should like the Security Council to decide to submit our difficulty to the International Court of Justice and to obtain an opinion as to whether or not the Council is competent, in this matter, to take a decision beyond the appeal proposed to us now. . . .

Mr. VAN KLEFFENS (Netherlands): . . . I desire to say a few words with regard to asking for the opinion of the International Court of Justice. We, in our capacity of a Member State, cannot do so under the Statute of the Court, that applies to any other Member State, as advisory opinions can be requested only by a body authorized to that effect by or in accordance with the Charter of the United Nations. The Security Council or certain other organs can, but a Member State cannot.

I wish to point out again that this Council implicitly declares itself competent to deal with this question if it does not make in the body of the resolution a certain reservation to the effect that its competence is at least doubtful. I need not say more at the moment.

[The Australian resolution, as amended by the United States and Poland, was passed on 1 August 1947 (while the resolution proposed by the USSR was rejected). As adopted, the Council's resolution read as follows (S/459; SCOR, II, No. 72, p. 1839):

"The Security Council,

"Noting with concern the hostilities in progress between the armed forces of the Netherlands and the Republic of Indonesia,

"Calls upon the parties:

"(a) To cease hostilities forthwith, and

"(b) To settle their disputes by arbitration or by other peaceful means and keep the Security Council informed about the progress of the settlement."]

NOTE. On 3 August 1947, the representative of the Netherlands stated that his Government, although persisting in its denial of the Council's jurisdiction in this matter, fully understood the Council's desire to see the use of arms come to an end. Accordingly, it had instructed the Lt. Governor-General of the Netherlands Indies to enter into contact with the Republican authorities to arrive at a cessation of hostile action on both sides. S/466 (4 August 1947).

Another discussion of the question of inviting a representative from Indonesia took place in the Security Council on 12 August 1947. The President of the Council (Mr. El-Khouri, Syria) summarized the issues as follows:

"As to the determination or definition of sovereignty and of the degree of sovereignty which the Indonesian Republic now possesses, I think that is not for us to consider. We have nothing to do with that. We are not defining sovereignties now. Sovereignty has several prerogatives; I think the Indonesian Republic may be enjoying some of them and may not be enjoying others. However, the invitation to participate in this discussion and to study the problem now presented to the Security Council does not necessitate that this State should enjoy all the prerogatives and exercise all the functions of sovereignty. The word 'State,' which appears in Article 32, does not indicate what type of State is being referred to.

"There are the United States of America and there is the State of Michigan. The latter has a certain amount of sovereignty. It has sovereignty in legislation; for instance, the State of Michigan can make laws, levy taxation and exercise other sovereign rights. But in regard to currency or foreign representation, it does not have sovereign rights.

"We do not know what prerogatives of sovereignty are exercised by Indonesia. For that reason I prefer not to go into details in this matter. We are here to restore peace to a troubled area, and we have started restoring that peace by adopting, at the hundred and seventy-third meeting, the resolution which appears in document S/459. Now we consider that the presence of representatives from Indonesia would be necessary and helpful for the just solution of this problem. For that reason I shall put to the vote only the question of extending an invitation to the representatives of the Indonesian Republic to appear before the Security Council during the discussion of this question, without any definition or determination of the sovereignty of that Republic.

"I should like to add that an invitation to the representatives of the Indonesian Republic to participate in this discussion would not bind any State to recognize the independence or sovereignty of the Indonesian Republic. The invitation would be extended simply in connexion with the work of the Security Council. Every State would have complete liberty either to recognize or not to recognize the sovereignty or independence of the Indonesian Republic. We are not now discussing the admission of the Indonesian Republic to membership in the United Nations; we are simply discussing an invitation to the representatives of the Republic to participate in the discussion of the matter before the Council. We shall now vote on the question of inviting the representatives of the Indonesian Republic on the basis which I have indicated."

The Security Council approved this proposal by 8 votes to 3 (Belgium, France, UK). SCOR, II, No. 74, pp. 1918–40.

On 15 August 1947, the representative of the Netherlands in the Security Council made a protest against "the Council being led step by step towards the assertion of full jurisdiction which it so manifestly does not possess." But, at the same time, to show that the Netherlands Government's attitude was not "purely negative," he was authorized to say that "the Netherlands Government is prepared to propose to the Republic of Indonesia that each— the Republic of Indonesia and the Netherlands—designate one State, the two States so designated to be asked to appoint one other State which is considered by them to be completely impartial. This impartial State, if it is willing, would then send a number of its nationals to Indonesia to enquire into the situation, to supervise the implementation of the cease-fire order, and to see what conditions obtain there." The Netherlands Government also suggested that "all the career consuls stationed in Batavia should jointly and immediately—so as to lose no time whatsoever, because the situation has an element of the greatest urgency—draw up a report on the present situation on the islands of Java, Sumatra and Madura." SCOR, II, No. 77, p. 2006, at 2012–13.

On 25 August 1947 the Soviet Union proposed a resolution providing that the Council establish a commission composed of the States Members of the Security Council to supervise the implementation of the decision of the Security Council of 1 August. Although there were seven votes in its favour, the proposal was not adopted as one permanent member (France) voted against it. SCOR, II, No. 83, p. 2199. The Council then adopted the following Australian-Chinese proposal (S/513; SCOR, II, No. 82, p. 2173, n. 3 and No. 83, p. 2200):

"Whereas the Security Council on 1 August 1947 called upon the Netherlands and the Republic of Indonesia to cease hostilities forthwith, and

"Whereas communications have been received from the Governments of the Netherlands and of the Republic of Indonesia advising that orders have been given for the cessation of hostilities, and

"Whereas it is desirable that steps should be taken to avoid disputes and friction relating to the observance of the cease-fire orders, and to create conditions which will facilitate agreement between the parties,

"The Security Council

"1. Notes with satisfaction the steps taken by the parties to comply with the resolution of 1 August 1947;

"2. Notes with satisfaction the statement issued by the Netherlands Government on 11 August, in which it affirms its intention to organize a sovereign, democratic United States of Indonesia in accordance with the purposes of the Linggadjati Agreement;

"3. Notes that the Netherlands Government intends immediately to request the career consuls stationed in Batavia jointly to report on the present situation in the Republic of Indonesia;

"4. Notes that the Government of the Republic of Indonesia has requested appointment by the Security Council of a commission of observers;

"5. Requests the Governments members of the Council who have career consular representatives in Batavia to instruct them to prepare jointly for the information and guidance of the Security Council reports on the situation in the Republic of Indonesia following the resolution of the Council on 1 August 1947, such reports to cover the observance of the cease-fire orders and the conditions prevailing in areas under military occupation or from which armed forces now in occupation may be withdrawn by agreement between the parties;

"6. Requests the Governments of the Netherlands and of the Republic of Indonesia to grant to the representatives referred to in paragraph 5 all facilities necessary for the effective fulfilment of their mission;

"7. Resolves to consider the matter further should the situation require."

At the same meeting the Security Council rejected another Australian draft resolution which proposed the creation of a Commission of three Arbitrators, one to be selected by each of the parties and one by the Security Council. S/512; SCOR, II, No. 82, p. 2147, n. 1 and No. 83, p. 2209. In its place the Security Council adopted the following United States resolution (S/514; SCOR, II, No. 82, p. 2179, n. 1 and No. 83, p. 2209):

"The Security Council,

"Resolves to tender its good offices to the parties in order to assist in the pacific settlement of their dispute, in accordance with paragraph (b) of the resolution of the Council of 1 August 1947. The Council expressed its readiness, if the parties so request, to assist in the settlement through a committee of the Council consisting of three members of the Council, each party selecting one, and the third to be designated by the two so selected."

At its next meeting, on 26 August, the Security Council rejected a resolution submitted by Belgium requesting the International Court of Justice to give an advisory opinion on the Council's competence to deal with the Indonesian question. S/517; SCOR, II, No. 83, p. 2193, n. 1 and No. 84, p. 2224.

On the other hand, at the same meeting, a Polish draft resolution reminding the parties of the Council's resolution of 1 August 1947 and calling on the parties to the conflict "to adhere strictly" to it was accepted by a vote of ten in favour, with one abstention (the United Kingdom). S/521; SCOR, II, No. 84, p. 2224, n. 1 and p. 2232.

The representative of the Netherlands, in a letter of 3 September 1947 to the Secretary-General, stated that his Government maintained its position as to the Council's jurisdiction, but believed that the tendency of the resolutions of 25 and 26 August was acceptable. This statement was based on the premise "that the Indonesian Republic will cease all hostile action in word and in deed." S/537; SCOR, II, No. 92, p. 2481.

The Netherlands Government selected the Belgian Government to represent it on the Good Offices Committee; the Republic of Indonesia selected Australia, and Australia and Belgium together chose the United States as the third government to be represented.

On 21 October 1947 the Security Council received the first report of the Consular Committee, which was composed of the consuls-general of Australia, Belgium, China, France, the United Kingdom, and the United States. That report ended with the following summary:

"Cease-fire orders were duly given, but there was no confidence on the part of either Dutch or Indonesians that the other side would carry them out, and no attempt was made by either side to come to an agreement with the other about means of giving effect to the orders.

"While the Republican Government ordered its troops to remain in their positions and to cease hostilities, the Netherlands East Indies Government considered it incumbent upon it to proceed with the restoration of law and order within the limits of the lines laid down by it.

"The rapid Netherlands advance bypassed considerable Republican forces, which remained in their positions in accordance with the Republican cease-fire order, while they were subject to mopping-up operations by troops under Netherlands command in accordance with the Netherlands interpretation of the order. The Republican Government directed its forces to defend themselves and to oppose movements within Netherlands-held territory. The different interpretations of the cease-fire order by each side thus made it impossible for the order to be observed.

"Apart from actions involving regular forces, a considerable amount of banditry, including murder, arson and looting, is still being carried on by irregular bands. . . ." S/586/Rev. 1; SCOR, II, Special Supp. 4, p. 23.

After rejecting several proposals for withdrawal of forces to pre-war lines, the Security Council passed the following resolution on 1 November 1947 (S/594; SCOR, II, No. 103, p. 2723):

"The Security Council,

"Having received and taken note of the report of the Consular Commission, dated 14 October 1947, indicating that the Council's resolution of 1 August 1947, relating to the cessation of hostilities, has not been fully effective;

"Having taken note that, according to the report, no attempt was made by either side to come to an agreement with the other about the means of giving effect to that resolution;

"Calls upon the parties concerned forthwith to consult with each other, either directly or through the Committee of Good Offices, as to the means to be employed in order to give effect to the cease-fire resolution and, pending agreement, to cease any activities or incitement to activities which contravene that resolution, and to take appropriate measures for safeguarding life and property;

"Requests the Committee of Good Offices to assist the parties in reaching agreement on an arrangement which will ensure the observance of the cease-fire resolution;

"Requests the Consular Commission, together with its military assistants, to make its services available to the Committee of Good Offices;

"Advises the parties concerned, the Committee of Good Offices and the Consular Commission that its resolution of 1 August should be interpreted as meaning that the use of the armed forces of either party by hostile action to extend its control over territory not occupied by it on 4 August 1947 is inconsistent with the Council's resolution of 1 August 1947; and

"Invites the parties, should it appear that some withdrawals of armed forces be necessary, to conclude between them as soon as possible the agreements referred to in its resolution of 25 August 1947."

The Committee of Good Offices on 24 December 1947 addressed an informal message to the parties containing suggested terms for a truce agreement. S/649/Rev. 1; SCOR, III, Special Supp. 1, p. 49. A truce agreement between the Netherlands and the Republic of Indonesia was signed on board the U.S.S. Renville on 17 January 1948.

The negotiations leading to the Renville Agreement are described in the report of the Committee of Good Offices, which was presented to the Security Council on 10 February 1948. S/649/Rev. 1; SCOR, III, Special Supp. 1, pp. 1–20. See also SCOR, III, Nos. 16–35, pp. 140–43.

2. *The Renville Agreement, 17 January 1948.*

S/649/Rev. 1, SCOR, III, Special Supp. 1, pp. 72, 76–77.

[The main part of the Renville Agreement provided for an immediate cease-fire, the establishment of demilitarized zones, and the supervision of the arrangements by the military assistants of the Committee of Good Offices. The Agreement was accompanied by the following statements of principles:]

PRINCIPLES FORMING AN AGREED BASIS FOR THE POLITICAL DISCUSSIONS

The Committee of Good Offices has been informed by the delegation of the Kingdom of the Netherlands and by the delegation of the Republic of Indonesia that, the truce agreement having been signed, their Governments accept the following principles on which the political discussions will be based:

1. That the assistance of the Committee of Good Offices be continued in the working out and signing of an agreement for the settlement of the political dispute in the islands of Java, Sumatra and Madura, based upon the principles underlying the Linggadjati Agreement.

2. It is understood that neither party has the right to prevent the free expression of popular movements looking toward political organizations which are in accord with the principles of the Linggadjati Agreement. It is further understood that each party will guarantee the freedom of assembly, speech and publication at all times, provided that this guarantee is not construed so as to include the advocacy of violence or reprisals.

3. It is understood that decisions concerning changes in administration of territory should be made only with the full and free consent of the populations of those territories and at a time when the security and freedom from coercion of such populations will have been ensured.

4. That, on the signing of the political agreement, provision be made for the gradual reduction of the armed forces of both parties.

5.   That as soon as practicable after the signing of the truce agreement, economic activity, trade, transportation and communications be restored through the co-operation of both parties, taking into consideration the interests of all the constituent parts of Indonesia.

6.   That provision be made for a suitable period of not less than six months nor more than one year after the signing of the agreement, during which time uncoerced and free discussion and consideration of vital issues will proceed.   At the end of this period, free elections will be held for self-determination by the people of their political relationship to the United States of Indonesia.

7.   That a constitutional convention be chosen according to democratic procedure to draft a constitution for the United States of Indonesia.

8.   It is understood that if, after signing the agreement referred to in paragraph 1, either party should ask the United Nations to provide an agency to observe conditions at any time up to the point at which sovereignty is transferred from the Government of the Netherlands to the Government of the United States of Indonesia, the other party will take this request into serious consideration.

The following four principles are taken from the Linggadjati Agreement:

9.   Independence for the Indonesian peoples.

10.   Co-operation between the peoples of the Netherlands and Indonesia.

11.   A sovereign state on a federal basis under a constitution which will be arrived at by democratic processes.

12.   A union between the United States of Indonesia and other parts of the Kingdom of the Netherlands under the King of the Netherlands.

ADDITIONAL PRINCIPLES FOR THE NEGOTIATIONS
TOWARDS A POLITICAL SETTLEMENT

Accepted by the parties on 19 January 1948. S/649/Rev. 1; SCOR, III,
Special Supp. 1, p. 67.

1.   Sovereignty throughout the Netherlands Indies is and shall remain with the Kingdom of the Netherlands until, after a stated interval, the Kingdom of the Netherlands transfers its sovereignty to the United States of Indonesia.   Prior to the termination of such stated interval, the Kingdom of the Netherlands may confer appropriate rights, duties and responsibilities on a provisional federal government of the territories of the future United States of Indonesia.   The United States of Indonesia, when created, will be a sovereign and independent State in equal partnership with the Kingdom of the Netherlands in a Netherlands-Indonesian Union at the head of which shall be the King of the

Netherlands. The status of the Republic of Indonesia will be that of a state within the United States of Indonesia.

2. In any provisional federal government created prior to the ratification of the constitution of the future United States of Indonesia, all states will be offered fair representation.

3. Prior to the dissolution of the Committee of Good Offices, either party may request that the services of the Committee be continued to assist in adjusting differences between the parties which relate to the political agreement and which may arise during the interim period. The other party will interpose no objection to such a request; this request would be brought to the attention of the Security Council of the United Nations by the Government of the Netherlands.

4. Within a period of not less than six months or more than one year from the signing of this agreement, a plebiscite will be held to determine whether the populations of the various territories of Java, Madura and Sumatra wish their territory to form part of the Republic of Indonesia or of another state within the United States of Indonesia, such plebiscite to be conducted under observation by the Committee of Good Offices should either party, in accordance with the procedure set forth in paragraph 3 above, request the services of the Committee in this capacity. The parties may agree that another method for ascertaining the will of the populations may be employed in the place of a plebiscite.

5. Following the delineation of the states in accordance with the procedure set forth in paragraph 4 above, a constitutional convention will be convened, through democratic procedures, to draft a constitution for the United States of Indonesia. The representation of the various states in the convention will be in proportion to their populations.

6. Should any state decide not to ratify the constitution and desire, in accordance with the principles of articles 3 and 4 of the Linggadjati Agreement, to negotiate a special relationship with the United States of Indonesia and the Kingdom of the Netherlands, neither party will object.

NOTE. The truce arrangements were put into effect promptly, and some 35,000 Republican troops were evacuated from the Netherlands-controlled territory. Political discussions for the implementation of the Renville Agreement did not, however, meet with success, despite the valiant efforts of the Committee of Good Offices. See the reports of the Committee, S/729, S/786, S/787, S/842, S/848/Add.1, S/918, S/919, S/1085, S/1117, S/1129/Add. 1; SCOR, III, Supp. for June 1948, pp. 11, 25, 41, 91, 122, Supp. for July 1948, pp. 89, 90, and Supp. for Dec. 1948, pp. 1, 122, 224.

In a highly successful surprise attack on 19 December 1948, the Netherlands forces occupied almost all principal cities in the territory of the Republic and captured practically all members of the Indonesian Government.

3. *Security Council Debate on the Resumption of Hostilities,*
22 December 1948–28 January 1949.

SCOR, III, No. 132, pp. 24–27; No. 133, pp. 6–41; SCOR, IV, No. 6, pp. 7–9;
No. 9, pp. 10–19; No. 20, pp. 7–9; No. 21, pp. 11–14.

[On 24 December 1948, the Security Council adopted a resolution
calling upon the parties: "(a) To cease hostilities forthwith;" and
"(b) Immediately to release the President of the Republic of Indonesia
and other political prisoners" taken since the resumption of hostilities;
and instructing the Committee of Good Offices to report at once on
recent developments. SCOR, III, Resolutions and Decisions of the
Security Council, 1948 [S/INF/2/Rev. 1(III)], p. 12. During the debate on this resolution the following arguments were heard before the
Security Council:]

Mr. VAN ROIJEN (Netherlands): . . . This brings me to the
last subject I have to deal with: the question of the competence of the
Security Council. . . . We have nothing to hide, but this should
not be taken as a recognition on our part of the competence of the
Security Council further to deal with this matter. Since negotiations
with the Republic have definitely broken down, and the Committee of
Good Offices unfortunately has not succeeded in its task, what is the
situation with which the Security Council is now confronted? In the
opinion of the Netherlands Government it is the following.

The Committee's good offices were accepted by the Netherlands in
August 1947 in a spirit of accommodation and in the hope of reaching
an agreement. We made it very clear on that occasion that we did so
because we were motivated by a spirit of good will and were desirous
of promoting a solution, but that we could not admit even by implication that the competence of the Security Council was valid in this
matter. Notwithstanding the constant and admirable efforts of the
Committee of Good Offices and the endless patience with which the
Netherlands authorities have tried, for nearly three years, to reach an
understanding and have endured breaches of the agreement already
reached, the Committee's good offices have, to our regret, as I have
already said, failed to produce a result. The Council now has to face
the very serious question whether it can take any further action with
regard to the Indonesian case. In our opinion, the answer to this question must undoubtedly be in the negative because the Council, according to the letter and spirit of the Charter, is not competent to deal with
this matter. . . .

In the first place, the Charter was designed to operate between sovereign States. For instance, Article 2, paragraph 1 says that "The
Organization is based on the principle of the sovereign equality of all
its Members." Now, it is beyond doubt that the Republic of Indonesia,
whatever its present status may be, is not a sovereign State. This was

expressly recognized by the Government of the Republic itself in the first of the six additional principles of the Renville Agreement. . . .

In the second place, it follows from this very principle which was subscribed to by the Republic of Indonesia that this is a matter essentially within the domestic jurisdiction of the Netherlands. Article 2, paragraph 7 . . . constitutes one of the cornerstones of the Charter. It is one of the guarantees that, without prejudice to the pledges made by individual States in the interests of world cooperation, they still retain full authority within their own borders. Therefore every Member of the United Nations, whether large or small, is master in its own house within the limits of the Charter.

In its short history the United Nations has not always abstained from intervening in the domestic affairs of Member States. But I submit that this is an extremely dangerous tendency and that the sooner it is stopped, the better it will be, because there is no telling where it may lead us. Some of us have the most serious objections to the policies followed by other Members of the United Nations, objections in regard to social conditions prevailing in some countries or in regard to the lack of freedom of the individual in certain other States. These objections have been voiced in the General Assembly and in its Committees. But voicing an opinion on the situation in other States and taking a decision on it, are two very different matters. The first is a perfectly legitimate and often even praiseworthy occupation, whereas the latter is, as I have said, distinctly contrary to the Charter.

In the third place, under the Charter the Security Council can take action only when international peace and security are endangered. It is evident that the events in Indonesia, however regrettable they may seem, do not constitute a danger to the maintenance of international peace and security in the sense of Articles 33 and 34, let alone a threat to the peace or breach of the peace or act of aggression in the sense of Article 39 of the Charter. What happened in Indonesia was not a breach of international peace, but rather a breach of internal peace. Breaches of internal peace, whether they are labeled strikes, mutiny, revolution, rebellion, or whatever other name may be applied to a given situation, are and remain the exclusive responsibility of the Members of the United Nations on the territory of which those unfortunate occurrences take place. Repression of terrorism on the part of lawless elements, counteraction against over 1,100 violations of the truce, restoration of order and security in certain parts of Java and Sumatra, do not present a threat to international peace and security.

This fact also disposes of the final clause of Article 2, paragraph 7, which limits the protection of domestic jurisdiction by these words: ". . . but this principle shall not prejudice the application of the enforcement measures under Chapter VII."

Since there exists no threat to the peace, breach of the peace or act of aggression, as required for the application of Chapter VII, paragraph 7 of Article 2 applies in full force without the limitation contained in its final clause.

I fully understand the interest which countries like Australia, India, the Philippines and other adjacent territories take in the solution of the Indonesian question. But that does not entitle the Security Council to intervene in what was and still is an internal conflict within the limits of the Kingdom of the Netherlands. In support of this contention, I could cite many authorities on the Charter. I shall limit myself to one only, and to one whom I choose because he is a distinguished representative of one of the interested countries.

Referring to Article 2, paragraph 7 of the Charter, Mr. Hasluck, of Australia, in his book *Workshop of Security,* which appeared this year, states: "I am not convinced that a matter ceases to be a matter essentially within the domestic jurisdiction of a State simply because there is international concern about it."

The author then gives the following example: "The United States fiscal policy is a matter of the liveliest international concern at the moment, but it is still a matter of domestic jurisdiction."

The author then criticizes the Security Council for having dealt with the Indonesian question without deciding beforehand whether that question came within its jurisdiction.

On the ground of what I have said, I must conclude, with regard to the competence of the Security Council, that the Indonesian question is outside that competence, first, because the Charter deals only with relations between sovereign States; secondly, because this is a matter within the domestic jurisdiction of the Netherlands; and, thirdly, because the situation does not endanger international peace and security. . . .

Colonel HODGSON (Australia): . . . I must say this about the real merits of this question of the competence of the Council. . . . I can sum this up in a few words. In international law, a State has defined territory, it has an organization of government controlling that territory and the people resident therein, is independent of foreign control, is substantially recognized by other States, and is capable of making international agreements. That is a broad definition, and Indonesia answered to all these attributes. Even by the original Linggadjati Agreement, the Netherlands Government itself recognized Indonesia as having *de facto* sovereignty and as being *de facto* a State. The United States of America, the United Kingdom, Egypt, Lebanon, India and several others I could mention all recognized Indonesia as a *de facto* State. Some of them had even entered into international agreements with Indonesia.

Last year we were confronted with a breach of the peace and we brought the original resolution under Chapter VII, Article 39, of the Charter, calling upon the parties to do certain things. But, in deference to various members, we cut out the words "Article 39" to avoid, as our Chinese colleague said, the long procedural wrangle. At that time, with all that loss of life and property and pillage and destruction going on, and at a time when the Council was called upon before the world to do something, we had one representative solemnly proposing that, like Pontius Pilate, we should wash our hands of the whole thing and refer it to the International Court of Justice to see if we had jurisdiction. Of course, the Council rejected that, and rightly so, and on 1 August passed the first of its resolutions on this question—the resolution which has already been quoted during the course of this debate.

That order was for a cease-fire and for the peaceful settlement of the dispute. Now, there are two things about that. While the Netherlands Government was maintaining its point of view about the incompetence of the Security Council, the representative of the Netherlands solemnly came to this Council table and said before the world that his Government would observe and act on that resolution in good faith. That solemn undertaking has been violated. But there is more in it than that. The Council did make a decision, and did pass that resolution, irrespective of whether or not it had competence. That was a decision of the Council.

I shall quote Article 25 because yesterday the representative of the Netherlands said before this Council that his country was going on in the full knowledge of what it was doing and prepared to take all consequences. The first consequence is this: Article 25 of the Charter states:

"The Members of the United Nations agree to accept and carry out the decisions of the Security Council in accordance with the present Charter."

We thus have the first clear-cut deliberate violation of the Charter by a Member. As I shall show, two other decisions were violated, and the consequences must be—if the Council faces up to the matter—expulsion from the United Nations. On 26 August the Council passed several resolutions. These resolutions established a consular commission of observers; secondly, a Committee of Good Offices; and, thirdly, they reaffirmed the cease-fire order. On 30 August, the representatives of the Netherlands accepted these resolutions and indicated the full co-operation of the Netherlands in the Committee of Good Offices. My delegation believes, on the basis of the evidence we have, that that pledge was violated. . . .

This is not merely a question of international interest; it is not merely a question of international concern. It is a question which directly affects the whole of South East Asia, and it affects my country. It causes strife and strikes and turmoil; it causes a loss of vital raw materials which are essential for world rehabilitation; it causes the loss of trade and commerce; it gives cause for the growth of extremist forces to take charge in areas vital to our well-being. The repercussions in the territory of the Netherlands East Indies are such that they may well, as the representative of the United States said yesterday, cause a big breach in international peace. Therefore, we are bound to take action. . . .

Mr. MALIK (USSR): . . . The Netherlands representative's allegations that the Security Council is not competent to discuss the question of aggression of the Netherlands Government against the Indonesian Republic are obviously without foundation. The Indonesian question has long been an international problem and the Netherlands Government cannot pretend that it is a Dutch domestic concern. The Republican Government has been recognized *de facto* by the Netherlands under the Linggadjati Agreement. The Security Council invited the Government of the Republic to take part in the discussion of the dispute between the Republic and the Netherlands, thereby formally recognizing the Republic as an entirely equal party to the dispute.

The Indonesian Republic was officially proclaimed in August 1945 and possesses all the principal attributes of an independent sovereign State. It has territory, a people, a government, armed forces, and so forth. Its relations with the Netherlands have gone far beyond the stage of a domestic dispute and have become an international problem.

Dutch colonial aggression loosed against the Republic is without doubt a breach of the peace and represents a threat to peace and security throughout Eastern Asia. From the standpoint of international law, it is an armed conflict between two States and none of the references made by the Netherlands Government to so-called police measures can alter the international nature of the conflict. The Security Council is fully justified and competent to consider the Indonesian question and to take a decision on it. . . .

[On 28 December 1948, the Security Council adopted the following resolution (S/1164; SCOR, III, No. 136, pp. 51, 67):

"The Security Council,

"Noting that the Netherlands Government has not so far released the President of the Republic of Indonesia and other political prisoners, as required by the resolution of 24 December 1948,

"Calls upon the Netherlands Government to set free these political prisoners forthwith and report to the Security Council within 24 hours of the adoption of the present resolution."

At the same meeting a Colombian resolution was adopted which sidestepped Netherlands objections to supervisory functions being allocated to the Committee on Good Offices by requesting the consular representatives in Batavia to send a report "for the information and guidance of the Security Council" on the observance of cease-fire orders and conditions prevailing in areas under military occupation.

S/1160 and S/1165; SCOR, III, No. 136, pp. 80, 82–3 and Supp. for Dec. 1948, p. 319.

Thereupon both the Committee of Good Offices and the Consular Commission requested the Council to "clarify" their status and jurisdiction. S/1189 and S/1190; SCOR, IV, Supp. for Jan. 1949, pp. 6, 16, and 17–18.

On 20–23 January 1949, delegates of the governments of Afghanistan, Australia, Burma, Ceylon, Egypt, Ethiopia, India, Iran, Iraq, Lebanon, Pakistan, Philippines, Saudi Arabia, Syria and observers from China, Nepal, New Zealand and Siam (Thailand) attended a Conference on Indonesia in New Delhi.

The Conference expressed "the opinion that the Dutch military action launched on 18 December 1948, constitutes a flagrant breach of the Charter of the United Nations and defiance of the efforts of the Security Council and its Committee of Good Offices to bring about a peaceful settlement", and recommended specific terms of settlement, the performance of which was to be supervised by the Committee of Good Offices or an alternate body. The resolution of the Conference further requested that "in the event of either party to the dispute not complying with the recommendations of the Security Council, the Security Council shall take effective action under the wide powers conferred upon it by the Charter, to enforce the said recommendations. Member States of the United Nations represented at this Conference pledge their full support to the Council in the application of any of these measures". S/1222; SCOR, IV, Supp. for Jan. 1949, p. 57.

On 28 January 1949, the Security Council approved the following resolution, most paragraphs being carried by seven votes to none, Argentina, France, Ukrainian SSR and USSR abstaining (S/1234; SCOR, IV, No. 9, pp. 20–23 and Supp. for Feb. 1949, p. 1):

"The Security Council,

"Recalling its resolutions of 1 August 1947, 25 August 1947, and 1 November 1947, with respect to the Indonesian Question;

"Taking note with approval of the reports submitted to the Security Council by its Committee of Good Offices for Indonesia;

"Considering that its resolutions of 24 December 1948 and 28 December 1948 have not been fully carried out;

"Considering that continued occupation of the territory of the Republic of Indonesia by the armed forces of the Netherlands is incompatible with the restoration of good relations between the parties and with the final achievement of a just and lasting settlement of the Indonesian dispute;

"Considering that the establishment and maintenance of law and order throughout Indonesia is a necessary condition to the achievement of the expressed objectives and desires of both parties;

"Noting with satisfaction that the parties continue to adhere to the principles of the Renville Agreement and agree that free and democratic elections should be held throughout Indonesia for the purpose of establishing a constituent assembly at the earliest practicable date, and further agree that the Security Council should arrange for the observation of such elections by an appropriate agency of the United Nations; and that the representative of the Netherlands has expressed his government's desire to have such elections held not later than 1 October 1949;

"Noting also with satisfaction that the Government of the Netherlands plans to transfer sovereignty to the United States of Indonesia by 1 January 1950, if possible, and, in any case, during the year 1950;

"Conscious of its primary responsibility for the maintenance of international peace and security, and in order that the rights, claims and position of the parties may not be prejudiced by the use of force;

"1. Calls upon the Government of the Netherlands to insure the immediate discontinuance of all military operations, calls upon the Government of the Republic simultaneously to order its armed adherents to cease guerrilla warfare, and calls upon both parties to co-operate in the restoration of peace and the maintenance of law and order throughout the area affected.

"2. Calls upon the Government of the Netherlands to release immediately and unconditionally all political prisoners arrested by it since 17 December 1948 in the Republic of Indonesia; and to facilitate the immediate return of officials of the Government of the Republic of Indonesia to Jogjakarta. . . .

"3. Recommends that, in the interest of carrying out the expressed objectives and desires of both parties to establish a federal, independent, and sovereign United States of Indonesia at the earliest possible date, negotiations be undertaken as soon as possible by representatives of the Government of the Netherlands and representatives of the Republic of Indonesia with the assistance of the Commission referred to in paragraph 4 below on the basis of the principles set forth in the Linggadjati and Renville Agreements, and taking advantage of the extent of agreement reached between the parties regarding the proposals submitted to them by the United States representative on the Committee of Good Offices on 10 September 1948; and in particular, on the basis that:

"(a) The establishment of the Interim Federal Government which is to be granted the powers of internal government in Indonesia during the interim period before the transfer of sovereignty shall be the result of the above negotiations and shall take place not later than 15 March 1949;

"(b) The elections which are to be held for the purpose of choosing representatives to an Indonesian Constituent Assembly should be completed by 1 October 1949; and "(c) The transfer of sovereignty over Indonesia by the Government of the Netherlands to the United States of Indonesia should take place at the earliest possible date and in any case not later than 1 July 1950;

"Provided that if no agreement is reached by one month prior to the respective dates referred to in sub-paragraphs (a), (b), and (c) above, the Commission referred to in paragraph 4(a) below or such other United Nations agency as may be established in accordance with paragraph 4(c) below, shall immediately report to the Security Council with its recommendations for a solution of the difficulties.

"4.   (a) The Committee of Good Offices shall henceforth be known as the United Nations Commission for Indonesia. The Commission shall act as the representative of the Security Council in Indonesia and shall have all of the functions assigned to the Committee of Good Offices by the Security Council since 18 December, and the functions conferred on it by the terms of this resolution. The Commission shall act by majority vote, but its reports and recommendations to the Security Council shall present both majority and minority views if there is a difference of opinion among the members of the Commission.

"(b) The Consular Commission is requested to facilitate the work of the United Nations Commission for Indonesia by providing military observers and other staff and facilities to enable the Commission to carry out its duties under the Council's resolutions of 24 and 28 December 1948 as well as under the present resolution, and shall temporarily suspend other activities.

"(c) The Commission shall assist the parties in the implementation of this resolution, and shall assist the parties in the negotiations to be undertaken under paragraph 3 above and is authorized to make recommendations to them or to the Security Council on matters within its competence. Upon agreement being reached in such negotiations, the Commission shall make recommendations to the Security Council as to the nature, powers, and functions of the United Nations agency which should remain in Indonesia to assist in the implementation of the provisions of such agreement until sovereignty is transferred by the Government of the Netherlands to the United States of Indonesia.

"(d) The Commission shall have authority to consult with representatives of areas in Indonesia other than the Republic, and to invite representatives of such areas to participate in the negotiations referred to in paragraph 3 above.

"(e) The Commission or such other United Nations agency as may be established in accordance with its recommendation under paragraph 4(c) above is authorized to observe on behalf of the United Nations the elections to be held throughout Indonesia and is further authorized, in respect of the Territories of Java, Madura and Sumatra, to make recommendations regarding the conditions necessary (a) to ensure that the elections are free and democratic, and (b) to guarantee freedom of assembly, speech and publication at all times, provided that such guarantee is not construed so as to include the advocacy of violence or reprisals.

"(f) The Commission should assist in achieving the earliest possible restoration of the civil administration of the Republic. To this end it shall, after consultation with the parties, recommend the extent to which, consistent with reasonable requirements of public security and the protection of life and property, areas controlled by the Republic under the Renville Agreement (outside of the Jogjakarta area) should be progressively returned to the administration of the Government of the Republic of Indonesia, and shall supervise such transfers. The recommendations of the Commission may include provision for such economic measures as are required for the proper functioning of the administration and for the economic well-being of the population of the areas involved in such transfers. The Commission shall, after consultation with the parties, recommend which if any Netherlands forces shall be retained temporarily in any area (outside of the Jogjakarta area) in order to assist in the maintenance of law and order. If either of the parties fails to accept the recommendations of the Commission mentioned in this paragraph, the Commission shall report immediately to the Security Council with its further recommendations for a solution of the difficulties.

"(g) The Commission shall render periodic reports to the Council, and special reports whenever the Commission deems necessary.

"(h) The Commission shall employ such observers, officers and other persons as it deems necessary.

"5.   Requests the Secretary-General to make available to the Commission such staff, funds and other facilities as are required by the Commission for the discharge of its functions.

"6.   Calls upon the Government of the Netherlands and the Republic of Indonesia to co-operate fully in giving effect to the provisions of this resolution."

During the debate on this resolution (SCOR, IV, No. 6, pp. 6–9; No. 9, pp. 6–19) the following statements were made:]

Mr. JESSUP (USA): .   .   .   In the first place, we are convinced that there is no question but that the Council must continue to concern itself with the Indonesian question.   .   .   .   As matters stand, I think the majority of the members of the Council will agree that we have an obligation to continue our efforts to assist in arriving at a solution as a whole. The time has passed for a piecemeal approach.

A second basic premise of ours is that there were and are two parties before us. Discussions concerning the legal inequality in their status have not at any point prevented the Council from dealing with them as parties. The fact that they both in good faith signed an agreement under the auspices of our agency is sufficient, apart from any other consideration, to establish both as parties with which we can legitimately concern ourselves, as we have done hitherto. As we understand the factual situation at the moment, however, it is necessary for the Council to seek to re-establish the position of one of the parties to a point where it can resume *bona fide* negotiations with the other. Naturally, the Council cannot accept the contention that, in its present situation, the Government of the Republic is able to enter upon negotiations in any real sense of the word. Clearly, it must be enabled to negotiate with the Netherlands freely and thus have a voice in the discussion of the future of Indonesia.

In the third place, we do not believe that the Security Council can place the seal of its approval on the results of the recent military action. We all know that the Dutch troops will have to be withdrawn if the ultimate goal of creating a sovereign United States of Indonesia is to be achieved. . . .

In the fourth place, we consider that the negotiations should be assisted by an agency of the Security Council. Both parties have heretofore accepted such assistance; we assume they will continue to accept it. . . .

Mr. VAN ROIJEN (Netherlands): . . . Now, I urge every member of the Security Council to ask himself this question: Is there a more drastic and incisive interference possible in the internal affairs of a State than for the Council to take in hand the decisions about the setting up of a specific government, and about the transfer of sovereignty over seventy-five million people? Has the Council ever gone to that length with regard to any other State? Does any member seriously contend that this remains within the limits of the obligations which the Governments accepted when signing the Charter at San Francisco? . . .

Even if the competence of the Security Council to deal with the Indonesian question, which we deny, were fully conceded by us and by all others, even then the Council would be barred by the Charter from interfering in this way in our domestic affairs. . . .

If this resolution is adopted, this provision [Article 2, paragraph 7], which is one of the cornerstones of the United Nations Charter, will from now on be a dead letter.

In order to prevent such a danger to the future of the United Nations and its Members, may I once again, on behalf of my Government, urge the Council to submit to the International Court of Justice the question of whether the Council is competent to deal with the Indonesian question. . . .

There is another fundamental objection closely connected with that of the transfer to the Security Council of essential rights. Sub-paragraph 4(a) of the draft resolution provides that in the future the

United Nations Commission for Indonesia should take its decisions by a majority vote. Since there is on the Commission one member chosen by the Netherlands and one member chosen by the Republic of Indonesia, the decisive vote would as a rule lie with the third member, the United States of America. This is not changed by the provision that minority opinions can be brought to the knowledge of the Security Council. Thus, the real effect of the resolution would be that the Netherlands would, during the interim period, hand over fundamental rights, constituting part of its sovereignty over Indonesia, to the United States of America. Such a concession, I submit, cannot be asked from any State. . . .

I have [made] it clear that we have fundamental objections to the basic principles contained in certain paragraphs of the draft joint resolution. The paragraphs or provisions to which we have those fundamental objections are:

1. Paragraph 2, which provides for the reinstallation of the Government of the Republic of Indonesia in Jogjakarta;

2. The final sub-paragraph of paragraph 3, which empowers the Commission and the Council to deal with the establishment of a federal interim government, the holding of elections and the transfer of sovereignty;

3. The last sentence of sub-paragraph 4(a), laying down the majority rule for decisions of the Commission;

4. Sub-paragraph 4(f), which empowers the Commission to make recommendations to the Council for the return of certain areas to the Republican Government and for the withdrawal of Netherlands troops, and which implicitly authorizes the Council to make decisions on these points. . . .

In the rest of the resolution, there are many things which are difficult for us to accept and many which we should like to see changed. But we realize that each party must make sacrifices, and we shall therefore formulate no objections to the rest of the resolution. My Government will carry out this resolution, if it is adopted by the Security Council, to the extent to which it is compatible with the responsibility of the Netherlands for the maintenance of real freedom and order in Indonesia, a responsibility which at this moment no one else can take over from us.

[In the following letter of 2 March 1949 to the Security Council, the Netherlands Government outlined the course of action it proposed to take (S/1274; SCOR, IV, Supp. for March 1949, pp. 35–38):

"The Netherlands Government has in the past weeks given thorough consideration to the resolution of the Security Council of 28 January 1949, and to the question how the Netherlands could best contribute towards the achievement of the aims set forth in that resolution.

"The Netherlands Government will cooperate with the UNCI in the same way as it has cooperated with the Committee of Good Offices in the past, to promote discussions to attain as quickly as possible the goal which is common to all parties.   .   .   .

"In order to carry into effect the wish repeatedly expressed by the Security Council on the subject and in order to render possible a prompt beginning of the discussions, the Netherlands Government has lifted the remaining restrictions on the liberty of movement of the Republican leaders, which means that they remain subject only to the general regulations applicable to everyone in the matter of travel and residence which for military purposes are at this time still in force in certain parts of Indonesia.   .   .   .

"In order to carry into effect the aims set out above the Netherlands Government has extended invitations to all interested parties to take part in a round table conference to be held at The Hague at the earliest possible date, preferably on 12 March 1949. The task of this conference should be to devise arrangements for an accelerated transfer of sovereignty over Indonesia, for the simultaneous establishment of the Netherlands-Indonesian Union, to draft the financial, economic and military agreements pertaining thereto, and to make arrangements for the interim period, which would include the institution of a Federal Interim Government.

"Invitations to this conference have been extended to all interested parties, notably among others to the President of the Republic of Indonesia, and to the Chairman of the Federal Consultative Assembly. The United Nations Commission for Indonesia has equally been invited to attend the conference, so that it may render its valuable assistance to achieve positive results.   .   .   .

"The invited Indonesian parties are entirely free to decide on the size and composition of their delegations. No rules have been laid down for voting, since the Netherlands Government is convinced that no settlement can be carried into effect which is not freely accepted by all parties present.   .   .   .

"It will be necessary to form a Federal Government for the whole of Indonesia, which will command sufficient authority to take over sovereignty from the Netherlands and to bind Indonesia to the execution of agreements entered into. This is all the more necessary as the transfer of sovereignty will under the plan take place before the holding of elections, in the same way as happened in several other Asiatic countries.

"It will be up to Indonesia itself to decide how this federal government will be constituted, taking due account of the relative importance of the different groups of the population. In this connection, a reasonable basis of negotiations may be found in the oral note of the United States Member of the Committee of Good Offices submitted informally to the Netherlands Delegation on 10 September 1948, providing for a representation of the Republican territories by one-third and of the Federal territories by two-thirds of the total number. Furthermore, the principal minority groups in Indonesia should be appropriately represented.

"It is impossible for the Netherlands Government to fix unilaterally a date for the transfer of sovereignty over Indonesia, since this depends also upon the wishes of the other parties concerned. The Netherlands Government trusts, however, that if the present plan is adopted, it should be possible by a determined effort to reach an agreement by 1 May 1949, after which, as far as the Netherlands are concerned, a period of about six weeks would still be needed for the ratification in accordance with the provisions of its constitution. . . .

"It follows from the foregoing that the result of the plan outlined will be to transfer sovereignty over Indonesia more than one year earlier than foreseen in the Security Council's resolution. The Netherlands Government's plan, therefore, goes even further towards meeting the desire of Indonesian nationalism for independence than the Security Council's resolution. . . .

"It is not the intention of the Netherlands Government to divest itself prematurely of its responsibility in Indonesia. Hence, it will be prepared to assist the new state for a limited period after the transfer of sovereignty, but only if the USI takes the initiative to request such assistance which will, therefore, in no way be thrust upon it; the future relationship between the two countries should be based upon the real and voluntarily recognized common interests of both parties.

"The Netherlands Government is fully aware of the seriousness of the Indonesian question and of its responsibility in that respect. In the plan outlined above it is making a bold new approach to the whole problem, which should result in a considerably accelerated achievement of its aim with regard to Indonesia, which, it cannot be repeated too often, is the same as that of the Security Council and of the Indonesians. It, therefore, appeals to the Council to further the realization of this plan which, in the present circumstances, offers the quickest and most effective way of establishing a democratic USI and a durable and voluntary co-operation between the Netherlands and Indonesia."

When the Security Council was considering the question whether this Netherlands statement constituted adequate compliance with the Council's resolution of 28 January 1949, the following comment was made by the Belgian representative on 11 March 1949:]

Mr. VAN LANGENHOVE (Belgium):   . . . According to some people, it would seem that, after the adoption of the last resolution of the Council, the Netherlands refused to comply with an injunction directing them to free the peoples of Indonesia. However, such an injunction does not exist and cannot exist for two reasons: first of all, the Charter does not confer such powers on the Security Council, even in those matters where its competence is unquestionable, which is not the case here. Even when the Council has grounds to do so, when it is acting by virtue of Chapter VII, its power to take a decision, to enjoin, is under Article 39, limited to the measures specified in Articles 41 and 42. Articles 41 and 42, however, refer not to the substance of the dispute, but to the means of coercion for maintaining or restoring international peace and security.

With regard to the settlement of the substance of a question, the Council can only make recommendations, and it could not be otherwise. To acknowledge the Council's right to decide on the liberation of the peoples of Indonesia, or of any other people, would be the equivalent of granting it the authority to settle the fate of a territory, to determine likewise its allegiance, in a word, to settle categorically the question whether a State should or should not be dismembered, or whether a new State should or should not be created.

It was never the intention of the authors of the Charter to confer such powers on the Security Council. Nowhere in the Charter can any provision be found from which it can be concluded that the Members of the United Nations, of whom only five are protected by the veto, have consented to placing their destiny, and even their very existence, in the hands of the Council.

At the San Francisco Conference I had the honour of participating in the debates of the Committee which drew up the provisions in question. From those discussions I retain the very clear impression that the States which were not destined to exercise the right of veto would never have admitted any such concept.

Need I add that I quoted Chapter VII only to make what I had to say even clearer, since that Chapter of the Charter is the one which confers most powers on the Council? In fact, I never meant to suggest by that reference that, at this juncture, the Council would be legally justified in resorting to this Chapter and that this would be a politically expedient moment to do so. .   .   .

Mahmoud FAWZI Bey (Egypt): .   .   . When the representative of Belgium says that there could be no such injunction to tell the Netherlands to emancipate the people of Indonesia, I have two ways of approaching this point. One way is to recall that under the Charter, we still have the principle of self-determination. The other way is to remind ourselves that the Republic of Indonesia is not being created and could not have been created by this Security Council or any other organ of the United Nations. It has been and it is there, and it has been recognized by the Netherlands inside and outside the United Nations.

In other instances, the Egyptian delegation has firmly maintained the view that the United Nations is not competent, has no authority to ordain the existence of States, to partition States, or to do such things in international life, but when we now tell one country not to kill thousands of people and throw millions of people of another country into misery, this is not ordaining the existence of a State; this is not creating a new State. The Republic of Indonesia, I repeat, has been and still is there, whether some reactionaries like it or not. And by reactionaries, I mean those—I hope, decreasing—numbers in colonial countries who are still clinging to an irredeemable past and who want to draw us into it and stop time from moving.

NOTE. On 25 March 1949, the Security Council adopted a Canadian draft directive approving the Netherlands proposal for a Round Table Conference and directed the Commission for Indonesia to assist in its preparation. SCOR, IV, No. 24, p. 5.

The First Interim Report of the Commission was submitted to the Security Council on 4 August 1949. It set out the agreements reached between the parties on (1) the restoration of the Republican Government to its capital; (2) the cessation of hostilities and the arrangements to implement the cease-fire order; and (3) the time and conditions for the conference at The Hague.

On 8 November 1949, the Commission submitted a special report on the Round Table Conference held at The Hague from 23 August to 2 November 1949. The Commission informed the Council that the Conference had "reached agreement on all issues before it" and that, under the agreements reached, the Netherlands, by 30 December 1949 at the latest, would unconditionally transfer complete sovereignty to the "Republic of the United States of Indonesia." The Commission further stated that it "would continue to carry out its functions in accordance with its terms of reference, and would observe in Indonesia the implementation of the agreements reached at the Round Table Conference." S/1417; SCOR, IV, Special Supp. 6, pp. 33, 37.

The agreements between the Netherlands and the Republic of Indonesia concluded on 2 November 1949 came into force on 27 December 1949, and the transfer of sovereignty took effect on that day. For the text of the various agreements, see 69 UNTS, pp. 200–397.

The Commission on 3 April 1951 submitted a further report to the Security Council (S/2087; SCOR, VI, Special Supp. 1, pp. 2–3, 29):

"The Commission is glad to report that, in general, the implementation of the agreements did not necessitate its intervention. In most cases the parties settled their problems in direct discussions, either through the diplomatic channels of their respective High Commissariats in Djakarta and The Hague, or through the Conference of Ministers of the Netherlands-Indonesian Union. As regards financial, economic, social and cultural affairs, the Commission was able to limit itself to taking note of the results achieved by the parties at the first and second sessions of the Union Conference.

"The Commission was more actively associated with problems arising from the military and political provisions of the Round Table Conference Agreements. Apart from the general provision of article VI of the covering resolution, certain special provisions concerning the duties of the Commission were included in the Hague Agreements. It was specified, for instance, that the Commission or its successor would be given the opportunity to co-operate in the repatriation of the Royal Netherlands Army from Indonesia, and that plebiscites to ascertain the wishes of the population with regard to the future status of their respective territories in the federal structure might be recommended by the Commission or by another United Nations organ and that the Commission or another United Nations organ would supervise such plebiscites.

"In the exercise of its functions, the Commission relied on information submitted to it by the parties, upon its own observation and upon reports received from its military observers.   .   .   .

"The Commission has the honour to inform the Security Council that, as the military problems are now virtually solved, as no other matters have been submitted to it by the parties, and as no items remain on its agenda, it has decided that, while continuing to hold itself at the disposal of the parties, it will adjourn *sine die.*"

4. *Problems Arising out of the Creation of a Unitary Republic of Indonesia*

[The metamorphosis of the "Republic of the United States of Indonesia" into the unitary "Republic of Indonesia" is described as follows in a report of the Commission for Indonesia (S/2087, 13 April 1951); SCOR, VI, Special Supp. 1, pp. 9–13, 21–29):]

Provisions concerning rights of self-determination were also included in the agreements signed at The Hague on 2 November 1949. Article 2 of the Agreement on Transitional Measures provided in particular that:

"1.   The division of the Republic of the United States of Indonesia into component states shall be established finally by the Constituent Assembly in conformity with the provisions of the Provisional Constitution of the Republic of the United States of Indonesia, with the understanding that a plebiscite will be held among the population of territories thereto indicated by the Government of the Republic of the United States of Indonesia upon the recommendation of the United Nations Commission for Indonesia or of another organ of the United Nations, under supervision of the United Nations Commission for Indonesia or the other United Nations organ referred to, on the question whether they shall form a separate component state.

"2.   Each component state shall be given the opportunity to ratify the final constitution. In case a component state does not ratify that constitution, it will be allowed to negotiate about a special relationship toward the Republic of the United States of Indonesia and the Kingdom of the Netherlands."

This article allowed means for the exercise of the so-called "external right of self-determination", namely the right of Indonesian territories to dissociate themselves from the Republic of the United States of Indonesia and to enter into special relationship with both Indonesia and the Netherlands.

Even prior to the signing of the Provisional Constitution there were indications of a movement for the liquidation of the *negaras* in Java and Madura and for the inclusion of these territories in the Republic of Indonesia. Following the transfer of sovereignty, this movement was greatly accelerated and was also active in Sumatra, Borneo and other adjoining islands. On 15 February 1950, President Sukarno, addressing the first meeting of Parliament, referred to the position of member states in the Federation in the light of the popular demand for the abolition of the federal Provisional Constitution of the country. He stressed the temporary nature of the structure of the Republic of the United States of Indonesia and the provisional character of the Constitution, and announced the Government's intention to introduce in Parliament a draft Bill to be based on article 44 of the Constitution "to channel the claims and demands of the people along legal and peaceful ways". This Bill was eventually promulgated by the President on 7 March 1950, as the Emergency Law "on the procedure of political reforms of the territory of the Republic of the United States of Indonesia".

The Emergency Law of 7 March provided that the initiative to realize "political reforms" could be taken by each state, by the Government of the Republic of the United States of Indonesia, or by a territory without the status of a state; such initiative should be approved by the population of the territory concerned, directly, through a plebiscite, or by a majority vote of a council of representatives specially elected for that purpose. However, a number of exceptions to the above principle were provided for and actually no plebiscites were held. A "political reform" might be (a) the liquidation of a state through the transfer of all authority and power directly to the Government of the Republic of the United States of Indonesia; (b) the liquidation of a state by incorporation into another state; (c) the fusion of several states into one; or (d) the partition of a state and incorporation into several other states.

The "political reforms" started immediately with the promulgation of the Emergency Law and, on 9 March, by decree of the Federal Government, the territories of East Java, Central Java, Madura, Padang and Sabang were incorporated into the Republic of Indonesia. This process continued during March and April and by the beginning of May 1950, all states and territories, with the exception of East Sumatra and East Indonesia, had joined the Republic of Indonesia. Negotiations between the Governments of the Republic of the United States of Indonesia (acting also on behalf of East Sumatra and East Indonesia) and the Republic of Indonesia, which followed these developments, led to an agreement on 19 May concerning the establishment of a unitary State.

While not questioning that these reforms in the first place pertained to the Government of the Republic of the United States of Indonesia, the Netherlands High Commissioner, in a letter addressed to the Commission on 25 May, expressed his Government's concern over safeguarding the right of self-determination as laid down in article 2 of the Agreement on Transitional Measures. The Netherlands Government asked how the right of self-determination could be carried into effect in a unitary State. In the view of the Netherlands Government, article 2 of the Agreement on Transitional Measures imposed on the United Nations Commission for Indonesia "a task of its own in that the recommendations of holding a plebiscite under its supervision among the population of areas which in its opinion are qualified therefore must emanate from it". The Netherlands Government indicated that the result of a possible plebiscite was less important than the safeguarding of the principle itself.

The Commission forwarded the High Commissioner's letter to the Indonesian Government on 3 June and expressed confidence that plans for the creation of a unitary State for the whole of Indonesia would not interfere in any way with the right of self-determination of the people or with the obligations of the Government under the terms of the Round Table Conference agreements.

In a letter addressed to the Commission on 8 June the Indonesian Prime Minister expressed the view that the right of self-determination of the peoples in Indonesia was to be guaranteed by establishing autonomous provinces or communities; he further stated that preparations were being made to hold general elections to a constituent assembly as stipulated in the Provisional Constitution; the constituent assembly, together with the government, would enact the final constitution "displaying the real democratic features of the unitary state".

At a ceremony held on 15 August 1950 in the Indonesian House of Representatives, in the presence of the members of the diplomatic corps accredited in Djakarta and the members of the Commission, President Sukarno proclaimed the establishment of the Republic of Indonesia as a unitary State. . . .

The movement towards the liquidation of the *negaras* and the establishment of a unitary State met with some opposition in the Negara Indonesia Timur (East Indonesia). . . .

On 25 April, a group of people, including fugitives from Makassar, seized authority in the city [of Ambon], while the local council announced the formation of a "South Moluccas Republic" (comprising Amboina, Buru, Ceram and other adjoining islands). The "Republic" proclaimed its separation from the East Indonesian State which "was no longer capable of maintaining its status as a component State," and from the Republic of the United States of Indonesia "which had acted in contravention of the resolutions of the Round Table Conference and of the Provisional Constitution". . . .

On 9 May, the Indonesian Government made known its decision to leave the solution of the South Moluccas affair to the Minister of Defence, who on 22 May announced that action would be taken to free "the Indonesian people in the South Moluccas from political and military adventurers". On 13 July, armed forces of the Republic of the United States of Indonesia landed on the island of Buru and later in the month on the island of Ceram. While operations in Buru led to the immediate restoration of control to the Indonesian Government, the operations in Ceram continued for some time. . . .

Subsequently, the Commission appealed to the Indonesian Government to halt the military operations in the South Moluccas and further to explore the possibility of a peaceful settlement by accepting the Commission's offer of good offices. In its letter dated 6 October, the Commission pointed out that in making this appeal it was prompted by humanitarian considerations. . . .

The Indonesian Government, however, did not accept the Commission's offer. In a letter dated 9 October it reiterated its view that the Commission's intervention, instead of achieving any favourable results would on the contrary encourage the rebels; it would also create the impression that the Indonesian Government was unable to discharge its domestic responsibilities without outside assistance. The Indonesian Government expressed the hope that the military operations in Amboina would be successfully concluded within a short time, and stated that extreme care was being taken by the Indonesian forces to ensure the safety of the civilian population. It also informed the Commission that upon the conclusion of the operations it intended to grant to the province of South Moluccas an "appropriate measure of autonomy". . . .

In these circumstances, and acting under its terms of reference, the Commission felt obliged to report to the Security Council on 11 October 1950 its attempts to bring about a peaceful settlement of the South Moluccas problem and their failure.

In forwarding a copy of its report to the Indonesian Foreign Minister, the Commission pointed out that its only purpose was to assist in the peaceful settlement of the difficulties in the South Moluccas, and that in its opinion its offer of good offices opened a way for negotiations, while leaving the Indonesian Government entirely free to decide upon its final position in the matter. At the same time, the Commission released for publication its correspondence with the Indonesian Government relating to this matter. . . .

Although fighting on the island of Amboina and on other adjoining islands continued for some time, the South Moluccas rebellion virtually came to an end with the occupation of the city of Ambon.

NOTE. For comments on the developments in Indonesia, see J. Foster COLLINS, "The United Nations and Indonesia," 459 Int.Conc. (1950), pp. 115–200; Günter DECKER, Republik Maluku Selatan: Die Republik der Süd-Molukken (Göttingen, 1957), 239 pp.; Rupert EMERSON, "Reflections on the Indonesian Case," 1 World Politics (1948), pp. 59–81; William HENDERSON, Pacific Settlement of Disputes: The Indonesian Question, 1946–1949 (New York, 1954), 89 pp.; George M. KAHIN, Nationalism and Revolution in Indonesia (Ithaca, N.Y., 1952), pp. 213–55, 332–50, 391–469; Leslie H. PALMIER, Indonesia and the Dutch (London, 1962), 194 pp.; Whitney T. PERKINS, "Sanctions for Political Change: The Indonesian Case," 12 Int.Org. (1958), pp. 26–42; Ulrich SCHEUNER, "Die Entstehung des indonesischen Staates, 3 AVR (1951), pp. 44–67; A. Arthur SCHILLER, The Formation of Federal Indonesia, 1945–1959 (The Hague, 1955), pp. 18–25, 337–42; Alastair M. TAYLOR, Indonesian Independence and the United Nations (Ithaca, N.Y., 1960), 503 pp.; G. H. J. VAN DER MOLEN, "Indonesia and the Republic of the South Moluccas," 1 Int.Rels. (1958), pp. 393–400; Charles WOLF, Jr., The Indonesian Story, New York, (1948), 201 pp.

HYDERABAD QUESTION

NOTE. After India became independent and the British Crown relinquished its suzerainty over the Indian princes, the Government of India and the Nizam of Hyderabad concluded a "Standstill Agreement," leaving in Indian hands temporarily the control of external affairs, defense and communications, in accordance with prior agreements and arrangements with the Crown. The Agreement provided expressly that nothing contained therein "shall include or introduce paramountcy functions or create any paramountcy relationship." It also contained the following provision: "Nothing herein contained shall impose any obligation or confer any right on the Dominion (i) to send troops to assist the Nizam in the maintenance of internal order, or (ii) to station troops in Hyderabad territory except in time of war and with the consent of the Nizam which will not be unreasonably withheld, any troops so stationed to be withdrawn from Hyderabad territory within 6 months of the termination of hostilities." Finally, any dispute between the parties were to be "referred to the arbitration of two arbitrators, one appointed by each of the parties, and an umpire appointed by those arbitrators."

On 21 August 1948 the "Secretary to the Government of the Nizam of Hyderabad and Berar in the Department of External Affairs" sent a cablegram to the President of the Security Council reciting that "The Government of Hyderabad, in reliance on Article 35, paragraph 2, of the Charter of the United Nations, requests you to bring to the attention of the Security Council the grave dispute which has arisen between Hyderabad and India, and which, unless settled in accordance with international law and justice, is likely to endanger the maintenance of international peace and security. Hyderabad has been exposed in recent months to violent intimidation, to threats of invasion, and to crippling economic blockade which has inflicted cruel hardship upon the people of Hyderabad and which is intended to coerce it into a renunciation of its independence. The frontiers have been forcibly violated and Hyderabad villages have been occupied by Indian troops. The action of India threatens the existence of Hyderabad, the peace of the Indian and entire Asiatic Continent, and the principles of the United Nations. The Government of Hyderabad is collecting and will shortly present to the Security Council abundant documentary evidence substantiating the present complaint. Hyderabad, a State not a Member of the United Nations, accepts for the purposes of the dispute the obligations of pacific settlement provided in the Charter of the United Nations. . . ." S/986; SCOR, III, Supp. for September 1948, p. 5.

In a further cablegram of 12 September 1948 he urged that the matter be given immediate consideration by the Security Council "[i]n view of the officially proclaimed intention of India as announced by its Prime Minister to invade Hyderabad, and in view of actual preparations for imminent invasion." S/998; *ibid.*, p. 6. The following day he cabled that "[t]he invasion of our country is now taking place and hostilities have broken out in various parts of Hyderabad. Any further delay must aggravate the most dangerous situation. S/1000; *ibid.*, pp. 6–7. The Security Council met on 16 September 1948 in Paris, where the third session of the General Assembly was to be held a few days later, and by eight votes, with three abstentions, decided to put the matter on the agenda. SCOR, III, No. 109, p. 11.

1. *Discussion in the Security Council, 16–28 September 1948.*

SCOR, III, Nos. 109, 111–12.

N. MOIN NAWAZ JUNG (Hyderabad): . . . The very existence of my country is now being defended on the field of battle against a brutal invasion which has shocked the conscience of the world and which has rallied to the defence of the principles of the United Nations even those who, not having had an opportunity of listening to our own plea in defence of our right to live, have been inclined to justify the claims of India. But we are conscious that a great and most significant portion of the task of defending Hyderabad will have to be performed here, before this high organ of the United Nations and before the public opinion of the world. For the world has been stirred to deepest apprehensions by this premeditated act of war emanating from a State which has based the claim to its own independence on high spiritual ideals of non-violence. The world has listened before to the shrill explanations of the invader pointing to disorder and anarchy which its liberating army was about to remove. . . . Sherman tanks are liberating the people, and the planes of the Royal Indian Air Force are bombing the population of Hyderabad in order to restore law and order. . . .

It will be recalled that on 21 August 1948, Hyderabad first brought the dispute between India and Hyderabad before the Security Council under Article 35, paragraph 2, of the Charter which enables a State not a Member of the United Nations to bring to the attention of the Security Council or of the General Assembly any dispute to which it is a party. On 13 September 1948, India committed an act of aggression by invading the independent State of Hyderabad.

Our case is that the United Nations is confronted with the most determined and most serious onslaught on its principles since the Organization was set up; that this breach of the Charter is not the result of a sudden eruption of passion but is due to a premeditated plan, the implications of which have been carefully weighed and deliberately accepted; that the action taken by the Dominion of India constitutes a denial of the principles of independence and equality, as laid down in the Charter; that the cause of Hyderabad has now been identified with those principles; that it is within the province and in the power of the United Nations to prevent the accomplishment of the criminal design; and that action—swift, authoritative, and determined—must be taken to prevent and to stop this threat to international peace and justice. We most assuredly desire our case to be heard by the United Nations fully and in all its aspects. We have put before the Security Council two printed volumes of memoranda and documents substantiating our complaint. We shall give the Security Council every assistance in our power for any further investigation or inquiry that may be necessary. But the Council will realize that time is limited; that mechanized forces, fully equipped, are operating on our territory, and that there is extreme danger in any avoidable delay. Every hour is now of the essence of the matter. The situation demands immediate action by the Security Council not only under Chapter VI of the Charter relating to the peaceful settlement of disputes, but also under Chapter VII which bears on the action of the Security Council for enforcing its decisions for safeguarding the peace of the world. In that Chapter, Article 39 of the Charter enjoins upon the Security Council the duty to determine the existence of any threat to the peace, breach of the peace, or act of aggression, and that it shall take appropriate action. Who can doubt that these conditions are now present? Who can doubt that a case has arisen for the Security Council to call upon the parties to comply with provisional measures contemplated by Article 40 of the Charter and intended, without prejudice to the rights, claims or position of the parties concerned, to prevent an aggravation of the situation?

While, therefore, our first desire, at the present stage of this dispute, is that the Security Council should take such action as is obviously called for by the actual hostilities and aggression now in progress, we hope that the Council will consider, investigate fully, and make recommendations upon the dispute between Hyderabad and the Dominion of India in relation to the situation as it existed when the dispute was first brought before the Security Council under Article 35, paragraph 2, of the Charter. That situation was in itself of such gravity as to make the appeal of Hyderabad to the United Nations imperative. The economic life of a peaceful people was being strangled by a systematic blockade admittedly adopted as an instrument of political coercion.   .   .   .

The guiding motive has been to coerce the Government of Hyderabad to renounce the independence of its country and to make it, politically and internationally, part of India. The independence of Hyderabad and its complete legal right to independence have been fully conceded by Great Britain, whose suzerainty over Hyderabad came to an end on 15 August 1947. In an official statement of the British Viceroy, made to the rulers and representatives of the Indian State on 25 July and reproduced in the White Book on Indian States published by the Government of India in July 1948, the Viceroy used language, couched in deliberate and solemn terms, which admits of no uncertainty. He said:

"The Indian Independence Act releases the States from all their obligations to the Crown. The States have complete freedom; technically and legally they are independent. . . ."

In the same speech he emphasized that the withdrawal of British paramountcy enabled the Indian States "to regain complete sovereignty". The fact of that right to independence has been given repeated and emphatic expression by other official spokesmen of the British Government. It has been occasionally admitted by the representatives of the Indian Government themselves. . . .

At this moment we desire and pray the Security Council, in the first instance, to use all its powers under the Charter and under all the applicable Chapters of the Charter, to put a halt to the invasion and to bring about the withdrawal of the invading troops. This, clearly, is a matter for instantaneous action, and it brooks no delay. When this has been done, we shall look to the Security Council for an inquiry into our complaint as presented prior to the invasion and, if our complaint is found to be justified, for action calculated to remove a most serious threat to international peace, to the principles of the Charter, and to the safety and well-being of Hyderabad. . . .

Subject to that overriding necessity of taking immediate action for the restoration of peace, we are ready and willing to answer in detail the objections, of a jurisdictional and legal nature, which have been raised against the right of the Security Council to entertain our complaint and our right to bring it before the Security Council.

Thus, it has been said, that this is a matter which is exclusively within the domestic jurisdiction of India. In our view, this assertion of the Government of India is tantamount to a claim that India has already annexed Hyderabad and that the territory of Hyderabad has become part of India. Only then would it be possible in law for the Government of India to maintain that the matter is essentially one within the domestic jurisdiction of India.

We have submitted, in the general presentation of the case of Hyderabad—and we stand by that statement—that even if the intolerable acts of coercion by means of systematic blockade, official intimidation and repeated assaults upon the frontiers of Hyderabad, had not taken place, the fact of the official claim that a dispute between Hyderabad and India, relating largely to the interpretation of an agreement freely concluded between them, is a domestic matter of India, that very fact would in itself be sufficient to bring the entire situation to the attention of the Security Council.

It has also been maintained that the bringing of the dispute before the Security Council is wrong in law on the ground that in the "Standstill" Agreement of 29 November 1947, Hyderabad has temporarily renounced the right to conduct its foreign relations, including the submission of disputes to an international agency. As I will submit presently, this argument was totally unfounded when it was first put forward following upon our submission of the case to the Security Council on 21 August 1948. Today the appeal to that argument by the State which, by the act of aggressive war, has torn the "Standstill" Agreement to shreds, is, to say the least, incongruous.

.   .   .

Sir Ramaswami MUDALIAR (India): .   .   .   The Security Council is at present engaged in determining facts which may lead it to the conclusion either that Hyderabad is competent to come before the Security Council or that it is not. .   .   .

I wish to make it quite clear that in my Government's view Hyderabad is not competent to bring any question before the Security Council; that it is not a State; that it is not independent; that never in all its history did it have the status of independence; that neither in the remote past nor before August 1947, nor under any declaration made by the United Kingdom, nor under any act passed by the British Parliament, has it acquired the status of independence which would entitle it to come in its own right to present a case before the Security Council. .   .   .

If .   .   .   I deny the competence of any area to come before the Security Council on a matter like this, it is because my Government and I are convinced that if the Articles of the Charter are not properly read, appreciated and respected, if opportunity is given to any particular area which does not possess the characteristics of a State to lay what it considers its grievances before the Security Council, the utility of the United Nations will be considerably impaired and great damage will be done to the cause of peace itself.

It is from that point of view—not purely from a legalistic point of view—that I venture to put forward the case of my Government that Hyderabad has not the status to come and present any case before this Council. It has to be remembered that the case of Hyderabad was presented on 21 August, that the very gruesome tale that has been mentioned to this Council—the aggression of my country, the invasion by my country of poor Hyderabad, the mechanized forces that are marching in dealing death and destruction on their way— that this story has no bearing at all on the application which Hyderabad made on 21 August before ever any such incident arose. .   .   .

I shall, if necessary, and at the proper time, state that both legally and technically and, even more—and I consider this fundamentally important—politically, Hyderabad can never be independent territory and that the Security Council can never recognize it as an independent territory or State. .   .   .   We shall publish all the documents we can to show how Hyderabad is not competent to come before this council, and that will take some time. Therefore, I suggest that we be given time, until Monday, to present our documents and to make our statement of the case before this august body. . . .

[When the Council resumed the discussion two days later, the President referred to a number of press reports and broadcast statements concerning the situation in Hyderabad which, he said, they had all seen, since they last discussed the question.]

Mr. Zahir AHMED (Hyderabad): With the permission of the President, I desire to make a brief statement to the Security Council on the situation which has arisen since the last meeting of the Council.

No instructions emanating directly from the Nizam have reached our delegation. It appears from reports in the Press that the Nizam has ordered the cessation of hostilities; that the forces of Hyderabad have surrendered; that Indian troops have entered the capital; that a Military Governor of Hyderabad has been appointed, and that martial law has been proclaimed throughout the country. In addition, the news has been circulated—and the Council will probably hear a statement on this—to the effect that the Nizam has given instructions to the Hyderabad delegation not to press the complaint before the Security Council.

In the absence of any direct, official instructions to the delegation of Hyderabad, the Council may not wish to dismiss the matter from the agenda at this stage. The situation is confused and the Council may find it convenient to postpone the discussion for a few days. . . .

Sir Ramaswami MUDALIAR (India): . . . We have . . . received a telegram which we have tried, somewhat unsuccessfully, to communicate to the Hyderabad delegation. The telegram reads as follows:

"Our Agent-General in Hyderabad wishes the following message passed immediately to Nawab Moin Nawaz Jung, President of the Hyderabad delegation to the United Nations. Begins: Dated 18 September 1948, addressed to Nawab Moin Nawaz Jung, President Hyderabad delegation United Nations, Plaza Hotel, Paris: 'I order you to withdraw the Hyderabad case from the Security Council. Signed, Nizam VII'." . . .

I also have a message from my Government regarding the present position in Hyderabad. The members of the Security Council may wish to know what the position really is. The telegram reads as follows:

"Evidently position in regard to Hyderabad has been greatly misunderstood. Hyderabad's complaint was not withdrawn under pressure from us. . . ."

This has reference to reports in some newspapers in England to the effect that the complaint was withdrawn under pressure and as part of the surrender terms.   My Government states emphatically that that was not the case; that there was no question of our asking the Nizam to withdraw the petition, but that the action was taken by the Nizam himself.

The telegram continues:

".   .   .   Long before Indian Army reached Hyderabad, Nizam dismissed his Government which had made the reference to the Security Council.   Again before our Army reached Hyderabad, Nizam announced the withdrawal of the complaint.   The Indian Army entered Secunderabad with the consent of His Exalted Highness the Nizam.   The Nizam's State forces are co-operating with the Indian Army in maintaining law and order in the State.   Old civil administration also functioning as before and fully co-operating with our Army.   Hardly any changes have been made.   For the present our Army Commander is in formal charge to tide over the period of transition and to maintain order.   .   .   ."

Our position has been that our troops had to enter Hyderabad in order to prevent atrocities which were being committed on Hyderabad soil; to prevent border incidents; to prevent repercussions in the provinces adjoining Hyderabad and indeed in the rest of the Dominion of India.   That our forces have entered without much trouble is an indication not of the lack of preparedness of the other side, but of the overwhelming good will which the people of Hyderabad extended to our forces.   That is the position at the present time.

I do not know what the desire of the Security Council will be in this matter.   However, we have already taken the position that Hyderabad is not competent to bring a complaint of this kind before the Security Council, and the instructions which the Nizam has issued to the Hyderabad delegation—which none of us, I believe, has any reason to doubt, although the Hyderabad delegation states that it has not yet received those instructions— in my opinion conclude the matter.   .   .   .

Mr. JESSUP (USA): The Government of the United States, in this situation, as in all situations, views with very deep regret resort to force for the adjustment of a difference.   The use of force does not alter legal rights.   I believe that we would all be unanimous on this point.   The Government of India does not predicate any rights upon the use of force.   From this point of view, therefore, it seems to me that the situation has not been materially affected by the events of the last hours nor has it been substantially changed from what it was when the Security Council took it under consideration at our last meeting.   .   .   .

My Government noted with interest, a number of days ago, a press report of a proclamation of the Indian Army Command to the people of Hyderabad, in which the following statement was made:

"As soon as our task is completed, the people of Hyderabad will be given the opportunity to decide their future both as regards internal government and relations with India."

The Government of the United States has no doubt that the Government of India, in giving effect to this declaration, will bear in mind that not only the members of the Security Council but all the Members of the United Nations will watch with interest the developments in Hyderabad, with the hope and with the expectation that the outcome of this affair will demonstrate loyal support of the principles contained in the Charter of the United Nations.   .   .   .

Sir Ramaswami MUDALIAR (India):   .   .   .   [The] representative of the United States drew the attention of this Council to a message in the proclamation issued by the Commander. If the Council will bear with me, I should like to read the whole of that paragraph as it is relevant to an understanding of the objective of my Government in this matter. This is what the paragraph says:

"As soon as our task has been completed, the people of Hyderabad will be given an opportunity to decide their future, both as regards their internal government and their relationship with India. We shall be here no longer than may be absolutely necessary for the effective restoration of normal conditions of life, in which every citizen may go about his business without fear, and for the establishment of a government which will maintain the rule of law and conform to the will of the people. Till then the administration will be carried on by my operational Commander in collaboration with the Civil Administrator whom the Government of India have appointed to work with me.   .   .   ."

We have .   .   .   repeatedly said that the will of the people will determine the relationship of Hyderabad with the Dominion of India and the form of government which they wish for their own Dominion. I think that is the general desire—I hope it is the general desire, and I am sure it is the general desire—of all the members of the Security Council and all the Members of the United Nations.

At San Francisco we drew up a Charter beginning with the words, "We the peoples of the United Nations"—not the Governments, not the potentates, but the people of the United Nations. India, which signed the Charter, wants to observe that Charter and is most anxious that the will of the people should be ascertained and that their will should prevail.

I do not know what is the intention with reference to the item on the agenda and when it will be taken off. I gather that the Hyderabad delegation has not so far received any official instructions. But we are agreeable to this, that while we maintain the domestic character of the dispute, we would nevertheless be prepared, as an earnest of our desire to work in harmony with the United Nations, to report in due course to the Security Council full details of the steps which we propose to take for the restoration of order and for the ascertaining of and giving effect to the will of the Hyderabad people. We are willing to place all our cards on the table and voluntarily, apart from the question of the jurisdiction of the Council, to be seized of the matter, to give every co-operation which will be of help to the Security Council in understanding the position as it develops. Our Government is anxious to see that the will of the people of Hyderabad prevails in this matter.   .   .   .

Mr. ARCE (Argentina): I shall make no attempt to conceal my surprise at these events and, if I may say so, at the attitude of the Council. Only two or three days ago, the Indian representative promised us all the necessary information to enable us to decide upon the competence of the Council and on other matters connected with this subject. He stated that the Council had no competence, and we naturally expected proof of this contention. It was also natural that he should promise to produce documents in support of his case.

He has, however, today preferred to mention facts which we know more or less correctly from press reports. He has furnished none of the arguments he promised; he has not proved that the Council is not competent to deal with the matter, and he has not examined the merits of the case.

However, as the Council does not appear to be disposed to remove the question from the agenda, I trust that we shall hear those arguments later.

The Indian representative has repeated emphatically what he said the other day regarding the proclamation issued by the officer commanding the Indian troops in Hyderabad territory. This proclamation, made during the march on the capital of Hyderabad, reminds me of a former Italian song sung by Mussolini's troops when they were advancing on Addis Ababa. I believe it was called *Faccetta nera* (little dark faces), and naturally, in this song the troops promised the people of Abyssinia that they would obtain all they wanted as soon as Italy had gained control.

The Indian representative has also told us that the Nizam, the ruler of Hyderabad, and his people, were co-operating with the Indian Army, since the civil administration at once began to work with the military and civil administrations imposed by India. I do not find it difficult to accept this statement. In fact, I am sure it is perfectly true, for it is rather hard to refuse co-operation when it is demanded with a loaded pistol and a foot on your neck.   .   .   .

Mr. UMAÑA BERNAL (Colombia):   .   .   . I do not quite understand what attitude the Council would adopt in the future should the State and Government of Hyderabad disappear completely. I therefore thought it appropriate, in case for any reason this question should not again be discussed, or in case it should in any way be considered as closed, to put on record, in the name of my delegation, the reservations we should have to make in connexion with such a solution.

Without going deeply into the question, it must be said that the disappearance of the Government and State of Hyderabad would seriously compromise two of the fundamental principles on which the United Nations is based, namely: the condemnation of any forcible acquisition of territory, and the self-determination of peoples.

In the name of my Government, therefore, I think it desirable to declare that we should make this explicit reservation before accepting any solution which implied that this matter could not be discussed by the Council. . . .

[The discussion was resumed by the Council at its next meeting eight days later (28 September). Copies of a cablegram addressed to the Secretary-General from the Nizam of Hyderabad had been distributed to the Members of the Council. The Nizam therein requested the Secretary-General "to note that the complaint made by my Government to the Security Council has been withdrawn by me. I would add for your information that, on 17 September 1948, the Ministry at whose instance the said complaint was made resigned and I personally assumed the charge of my State. The delegation to the Security Council which had been sent at the instance of the said Ministry has now ceased to have any authority to represent me or my State." S/1011; SCOR, III, Supp. for Sept. 1948, p. 7. The Council also had before it the following note, dated 24 September, from the Hyderabad delegation to the President of the Security Council:

"The delegation of Hyderabad views with satisfaction the attitude adopted by the Security Council at its meeting of 20 September. We understand the view of the Security Council to be that the invasion of Hyderabad by India, being an act of force, can confer no legal rights upon India; that the Council took note of the declaration of the Indian representative that the sole purpose of the intervention of India was to restore order and to create conditions for a free expression of the will of the people of Hyderabad; and that the Council retains the question of Hyderabad on its agenda.

"The events which have occurred since the last meeting of the Security Council have shown that the Government of India and the Indian occupation authorities in Hyderabad are determined not to act in accordance with the declaration of the representative of India. They have introduced most important constitutional and administrative changes not related in any way to the avowed purpose of maintaining internal order. They have compelled the Nizam to surrender complete power to the Indian military commander. They have removed the principal administrative officers in most districts of Hyderabad. They have assumed full military control of the country. They have issued instructions to the Agents-General of Hyderabad abroad to suspend their activities. It is clear that the occupation is being used for effecting purposes entirely alien and, in fact, contrary, to its alleged purpose and inconsistent with the declaration of the Indian representative to the Security Council. In addition there are reports, substantiated from Indian sources, that a regime of victimization and persecution has already begun.

"In these circumstances it is imperative that a meeting of the Security Council be called to review the situation and to put a stop to the extension of the scope of the *fait accompli* with which the Council has been presented. It is possible that, in view of the strict censorship and complete blackout of impartial news, the Security Council may find it desirable to appoint its own observers for the purpose of keeping itself informed of the trend of events in Hyderabad." S/1015; *ibid.,* p. 9.]

The PRESIDENT [Sir Alexander Cadogan, UK]: . . . From these documents, [S/1011 and S/1015, quoted above], the Security Council will have seen that there may be some doubt, in the present circumstances, as to what I would call the validity of the credentials of the representatives of Hyderabad. In the normal course, before opening the discussion on this question, with the consent of the Security Council, I should have invited the representatives of the two parties to come to the table. Before I do that, however, in view of the doubt which has been cast on the credentials of the representatives of Hyderabad, I would ask the Security Council to consider that particular point, and I should like to ask the members whether they think that, in these circumstances, the representative of Hyderabad should be invited to take part in the discussion in the same way and on the same terms as at our former discussions of this question.
. . .

Mr. TSIANG (China): Whatever we may decide to do with this item on the agenda, it is very clear to my delegation that we should not invite the delegation of Hyderabad to the Security Council table.

Mr. EL–KHOURI (Syria): At the end of the cablegram from the Nizam of Hyderabad [S/1011], it is stated that the representatives of Hyderabad here have ceased to represent the Nizam or his State. I think that if the cablegram comes from an authentic source, it can be used to substantiate the theory expressed by the representative of China.

However, I do not believe that the Security Council should base its resolutions on cablegrams which, in our view, may not come from a truly authentic source. . . .

We do not know the circumstances or the conditions which govern the position there. For this reason, in order to be assured of the correctness of the situation as it has been described, I think it would be wise for the Security Council to find some source of information in

Hyderabad which could supply accurate information and be responsible to the Security Council. In this way, the Security Council could be sure that the situation is as it has been described and that the Nizam of Hyderabad has decided to back these people and has done what he is said to have done. The representative of Hyderabad has sent this letter which makes many things clear, but I do not think it would be fair for the Security Council to drop the matter without making investigations in order that the facts might be substantiated. There is no hurry, and it would be safer for us to make certain inquiries on the matter.

We might charge some representative in Hyderabad with the duties of being an observer or something like that in order that he could communicate with the Security Council. For instance, we might select a representative of one of the States represented on the Security Council to give us information gathered on the spot. Why should we press the matter without having authentic and convincing information on the subject? In case of any doubt, we should try to dispel that doubt.

Mr. ARCE (Argentina): . . . It is a legal maxim that admission of guilt makes proof unnecessary. There is no need to seek further facts or to carry out an investigation. I would not object in any way to the Syrian representative's proposal if its purpose was to check something; but since representatives of India have stated at Council meetings and elsewhere that their country invaded Hyderabad for one reason or another, and since we know that the Government of India has proclaimed martial law in the State of Hyderabad and has assumed civil and military control, then I must say that as long as the Nizam does not appear in person before us, unaccompanied by anyone who would force him to follow instructions from the Government of India, I shall not give credence to any letter or cable bearing his signature. . . .

It appears entirely clear to me that the Security Council must request the Government of India to withdraw its troops from Hyderabad and re-establish the former Government there. It must ask the Government of India to observe the provisions of the Charter and settle its disputes with the State of Hyderabad by talks and peaceful negotiations, and, as a last resort, bring the case before the Council. If that is not done, Hyderabad will have experienced—I repeat it again, even at the risk of being insulted or being blamed in the Press—the same fate as Ethiopia. . . .

I believe that the only definite steps we can take are, either to investigate events by means at our own disposal, or, if we are satisfied with the Press reports and the statements made by the representatives of the Government of India, take the measures prescribed to us by the Charter. . . .

The PRESIDENT: The difficulty in which the Chair finds itself is this: rule 14 of our rules of procedure says: "Any Member of the United Nations not a member of the Security Council and any State not a Member of the United Nations, if invited to participate in a meeting or meetings of the Security Council, shall submit credentials for the representative appointed by it for this purpose."

Some time ago the representative of Hyderabad submitted credentials signed by the Nizam of Hyderabad. I have now received a letter, of which the Council has already cognizance, signed, it seems to me, by the same ruler. That letter, as I have already indicated, says:

"The delegation to the Security Council which had been sent at the instance of the said Ministry has now ceased to have any authority to represent me or my State."

I do not know that the authenticity of this letter has been questioned. What is stated or implied, I think, is that the writer of this letter, when he wrote it, was not a free agent; that is to say, that events have led up to a situation in which he has written that letter, not of his own free will but under some kind of compulsion. Unless I can get any further guidance from the Council at this moment, I would make a suggestion to the members, and that is that they should call both parties to the table to discuss that point of the validity of this letter. I would suggest that the representative of India would normally and regularly appear as the representative of India. But, for the moment, as we have not yet resolved the validity or otherwise of the credentials of the representative of Hyderabad, he should appear, as he could appear under rule 39 of the rules of procedure, as an individual, and as an individual representative, and would be entitled to take part in the discussion only of this preliminary point of the validity of his credentials. He would not be entitled to take part in a discussion of the question, and, indeed, we could not, I think, continue with any discussion of the substance of the question until we have resolved this preliminary point: whether or not he is entitled to sit as authorized by the Charter and to take part in the discussion of the Security Council. . . .

[On the invitation of the President, Sir Ramaswami Mudaliar, representative of India, and the Nawab Moin Nawaz Jung (Hyderabad) took their places at the Security Council table.]

Nawab MOIN NAWAZ JUNG (Hyderabad): . . . The question which, in our view, is a proper matter for the Security Council to decide is, assuming that these communications have been sent by and on the authority of the Nizam, whether the ruler of the State has acted as a free agent. We know, and the Security Council knows, that the Nizam has divested himself of all powers of government in favour of the Indian Commander. . . .

This, it will be noted, is not a case of one Government withdrawing the credentials issued by its predecessor. It is, in fact, the case of an invader which has been successful in withdrawing the credentials of a delegation issued by the lawful Government. . . .

[W]e refute the assertion that the troops of India entered on our soil for the sake of maintaining order. There is no one in this room who deep in his heart does not know that the claim that the invasion was undertaken for the sake of maintaining order in Hyderabad is but a pretext, or that the lawlessness and the excesses of the private volunteer army are a gross and deliberate exaggeration, and that the war on Hyderabad was planned and determined as part of the national policy in pursuance of the idea of creating a uniform and unified India. It would be consistent with the respect for world opinion and the United Nations and, we believe, also with respect for the dignity of India to admit that fact openly and sincerely. There were no disorders in Hyderabad, no communal strife and no excesses, even after the invasion had begun and after it had stirred up resentment and bitterness among the people of Hyderabad. . . . .

This, then, is the first task of the United Nations in this matter: to put an effective stop to the annexation of Hyderabad which is now going on. The normal administrative and constitutional life of the country must be restored, and observers of the United Nations must ensure that the pretext of restoring order does not deprive Hyderabad of its freedom at the very time when the United Nations is considering the situation which has arisen.

The far-reaching changes which are being introduced have a profound and immediate bearing upon the question of the plebiscite to determine the future relations between Hyderabad and India. The offer of a plebiscite was made by the Government of Hyderabad as early as June 1948. It was repeated, with all necessary emphasis, in the statement of the case of Hyderabad when it was submitted to the Security Council. We said therein:

"The Government of Hyderabad offered that the question of accession in matters of Defence, External Affairs and Communications, as defined by the parties, should be submitted for determination by a plebiscite on the basis of adult suffrage under the supervision of the United Nations". . . .

But there must be a true plebiscite, not a mockery under the pressure of Indian military power and of imported Indian administrators. The ordinary constitutional government of the country must be restored and conditions created for a free plebiscite.

The United Nations can take effective steps to ensure that result. International practice has by now developed a satisfactory machinery for that purpose. But it is essential that, pending the setting-up of that machinery, impartial observers be appointed to report on the conditions and the administration of the country. It is clearly impossible for the Security Council to limit itself to information supplied by the Indian authorities alone. In addition, a specific undertaking must be obtained from the Dominion of India that in the period between now and the restoration of the civil administration of the country by Hyderabad authorities, there will be no attempt at persecution for alleged political offences, victimization, and other forms of persecution, nor interference with state property. This, too, must be assured through the presence of impartial observers. . . .

Sir Ramaswami MUDALIAR (India): . . . In a broadcast that the Nizam made on 23 September, he stated:

"Several delegations calling themselves Hyderabad's delegations have been carrying on a campaign against India's so-called misdeeds, which, in fact, have merely restored my freedom to deal with Hyderabad's destinies in a manner consistent with the traditions of the Asafjah dynasty and the best interests of Hyderabad. In November last . . . a small group which had organized a quasi-military organization hostile to Hyderabad's best traditions surrounded the house of my then Prime Minister, the Nawab of Chhatari, in whose wisdom I had complete confidence, and the house of Sir Walter Monckton, my constitutional adviser, and thus by duress compelled the Nawab of Chhatari and other trusted ministers to resign. This group, with Kasim Razvi at its head . . . took possession of the State, spread terror into all elements of society, Muslims and non-Muslims, that refused to bend their knees to it." . . .

When that happened the Nizam became not a free agent but a person under the control of a set of gangsters . . .

Today, when he has been released from the *razakars* and in a position to take his own view of the situation, to look after himself and his dynasty, to look after his people, to bring about the happy relations which were disturbed and more than disturbed during the last eight months, the Nizam is sweetly, suavely, and simply alleged by the gentleman opposite not to be a free agent. What justification is there for making such an allegation? What proof has been brought by the honourable gentleman opposite to show that the Nizam is not a free agent? . . .

I submit that for the first time since the last eight or ten months, the Nizam has acted as an independent agent. I submit that he has come to the conclusion that this matter should not be further pursued in the best interests of himself, in the best interests of his dynasty, and in the best interests of the people of Hyderabad who are one with the people of the rest of the Dominion of India, and in the best interests of the State. . . .

The Security Council has therefore to consider whether any further useful purpose would be served by keeping this matter on the agenda; whether, with the genuine withdrawal of the case . . . by His Exalted Highness the Nizam, the cause of peace will not be better served by dropping the matter. . . .

NOTE. Discussion of this question was then adjourned. On 6 October 1948, Sir Ramaswami Mudaliar, the delegate of India, wrote to the President of the Security Council: "On September 16th Council provisionally placed Hyderabad's complaint on agenda merely for discussion whether Hyderabad was competent to make complaint. Since then complaint, such as it was, has been withdrawn and India showed at meeting of September 28th that the Nizam's withdrawal was voluntary. Position therefore is that complaint which Hyderabad had never any right to make now stands expressly withdrawn. There was never any dispute or situation endangering international peace, and never any act of aggression by India. Each time case comes before Council, on however narrow an issue, various individuals abuse opportunity and insult India on a completely false version of facts. This is naturally causing deepest resentment in India. The Council will appreciate that, in these circumstances, there no longer exists any reason for the Government of India to maintain a delegation in Paris for dealing with the Hyderabad question. . . ." S/1089, p. 2 (25 Nov. 1948). On the same day, Sir Mohammed Zafrullah Khan, the representative of Pakistan, in a letter to the President, requested that Pakistan be permitted to participate in the discussion under Article 31 of the Charter. S/1027. On 20 November 1948 he wrote again to the President stating that "Reports received . . . show that the situation in Hyderabad continues to deteriorate and that urgent action by the Security Council is needed to remedy the situation." He therefore requested "that the Security Council may be pleased to take up and deal with the Hyderabad-India case at a very early date." S/1084; SCOR, III, Supp. for Nov. 1948, p. 14. The question was then placed on the provisional agenda for the 382nd meeting of the Security Council. In a letter of 24 November, however, Mrs. Pandit informed the President that the Indian delegation "has in fact been withdrawn and there is no one now in Paris with authority from my Government" to deal with the Hyderabad question. S/1089. At the 382nd meeting (25 Nov. 1948), a proposal by the representative of Colombia "that examination of this item on the agenda be postponed to a future meeting of the Council" was accepted. Mr. El-Khouri, the representative of Syria, complained at the next meeting (2 Dec. 1948), that that question had not been included in the provisional agenda for the day. "The Indian delegation", he said, "stated that it did not have adequate representation for that meeting. But surely that does not mean that all meetings should be postponed for that reason!" SCOR, III, No. 128, p. 6. The agenda finally adopted for this meeting did not include the Hyderabad question. *Ibid.*, p. 7. In a letter of 6 December 1948 the representative of Pakistan made a further request "that a meeting of the Security Council may be called at as early a date as may be convenient," to deal with this question. S/1109; SCOR, III, Supp. for Dec. 1948, p. 119.

In a letter of 12 December the head of the Hyderabad delegation wrote to the President of the Security Council saying:

". . . [R]eliable information has come to our knowledge which no longer permits us to leave the Security Council in doubt as to the fact that neither at the time when the alleged instructions to withdraw the complaint from the United Nations were issued nor at any subsequent period till the present day has the Nizam been a free agent able to express without constraint the will of the State.

"It now appears clear that instructions in the matter were given under duress, and that the Nizam is now held virtually in the position of a prisoner of the Indian military authorities who have occupied the country by force of arms. . . .

"In view of this, we consider it our duty to reassert, in most emphatic terms, the authority of our delegation as originally appointed and its continued right and obligation to defend the interests of Hyderabad before the United Nations. Should that authority be challenged from any quarter, then, in our submission, the question before the Security Council is in the first instance one of fact. It must be ascertained by the Security Council to what extent, if any, the Nizam has been a free agent since the invasion of Hyderabad and the occupation of the capital by Indian troops. At the meeting of the Security Council held on 28 September 1948 the representative of India put forward the astonishing and, in the face of it, absurd assertion that the Nizam became a free ruler only since the invasion. It will be for the Indian Government, by agreeing to an investigation of this matter through a commission sent by the Security Council to Hyderabad, to assist in arriving at the true facts of the situation.

"The second question which requires elucidation in this connexion is one of law, namely, to what extent the Security Council can consider as valid the instructions, ordering the withdrawal of a complaint lodged before the United Nations, of the head of a State invaded and occupied by an aggressor. That question, which could be properly answered by the International Court of Justice, is of vital importance not only for Hyderabad but also, we believe, for the United Nations and we trust that the Security Council will not fail to take appropriate action in this regard." S/1118; *ibid.*, pp. 209–10.

The following day the representative of India wrote to the President attaching a "brief factual report on the present situation in Hyderabad . . . without prejudice to the question of the competence of the Council, regarding which India's position has been repeatedly made clear." S/1124; *ibid.*, p. 211. The question was placed on the agenda of the 384th meeting of the Council (15 Dec. 1948). When the representative of Pakistan, Sir Mohammed Zafrullah Khan, announced that his argument "would at the very least occupy two full meetings", the Council decided to postpone the hearing to a later meeting, and it was not until the 425th and 426th meetings on May 19th and 24th of the following year that he made his statement to the Council.

A letter from the Indian representative of 18 May 1949 (S/1324; SCOR, IV, Supp. for May 1949, p. 3) emphasized "that there never was any dispute or situation in Hyderabad likely to endanger the maintenance of international peace and security or to lead to international friction; and since the withdrawal of the complaint by the Nizam of Hyderabad, there has never been even the semblance of any such dispute or situation. It is only a dispute or situation of such an international character that can be dealt with by the Security Council under the Charter. Pakistan is, therefore, not competent to invoke the jurisdiction of the Security Council on this question.

"All matters relating to Hyderabad are now regularly dealt with by the Government of India as matters of domestic jurisdiction; questions are put and answers are given on all such matters in the Indian Constituent Assembly, to which the Government of India is responsible."

2. *Discussion in the Security Council, 19–24 May 1949.*

SCOR, IV, Nos. 28–29.

[The President of the Council asked the Indian representative to speak first on the question of the Council's competence.]

Sir Benegal N. RAU (India):   .   .   .   This case started as a complaint by Hyderabad on 21 August 1948 under Article 35, paragraph 2 of the Charter of the United Nations. That Article reads:

"A State which is not a Member of the United Nations may bring to the attention of the Security Council or of the General Assembly any dispute to which it is a party if it accepts in advance, for the purposes of the dispute, the obligations of pacific settlement provided in the present Charter."

Members of the Council will notice that the Article opens with the words "A State". Hyderabad has never been a State in the international sense, as I shall explain presently. India contended and still contends that Hyderabad was not competent to appeal to the Security Council under the Article in question.

While the issue of competence thus raised was pending, India was forced to take certain action in Hyderabad to put an end to the prolonged lawlessness and disorder which were disturbing not only Hyderabad itself but also the adjoining districts of India. When I say lawlessness and disorder, I am not using an idle phrase.   .   .   .

[T]he action which India was forced to take was not directed against the people of Hyderabad, or even against the ruler, but against a fascist clique which had usurped power and was misusing it in a manner that threatened the tranquility of India as well as Hyderabad itself. As soon as these men resigned and the Nizam was free to assume charge, he withdrew the complaint which they had made to the United Nations.

I ask, is there anything of international significance in all this? Do not let us be led away by words.   This complaint is not really made by Hyderabad, but by certain individuals who had once usurped a little brief authority in Hyderabad and have now lost it. They have ceased to represent the ruler; they never represented the people. Whatever dispute or situation they created in Hyderabad has now come to an end, and conditions are gradually settling down to normal.

.   .   .   .

The future of the State and its relationship with India are matters which have been left to be decided by the people. Arrangements are in train for convening a constituent assembly for this purpose. Electoral rolls based on adult franchise are under preparation. It is hoped that all arrangements for elections to the constituent assembly will be completed by this autumn.   .   .   .

It has, however, been contended by some persons that it [Hyderabad] became an independent State as the result of the Indian Independence Act. It is on this footing that its position has sometimes been thought to be similar to that of Indonesia. There is not the slightest analogy between the two cases. The Indonesian Republic has been granted *de facto* recognition as a State by several countries —by the United States of America, by the United Kingdom, by Egypt, by India, and by other countries—but no country has ever recognized Hyderabad either *de jure* or *de facto* as an independent State. . . .

Indonesia is not in the heart of the Netherlands as Hyderabad and the other Indian States are in the heart of India. As someone has said, "You can live without your appendix and be the healthier for it, but you cannot live without your heart." I should like to make this perfectly clear, that India cannot possibly recognize any of these Indian States lying within its borders as independent, any more than the United States of America can allow the independence of its southern states. Let us not forget that the trouble in Burma started with a claim of independence by a certain State of the Union. With this object lesson before it, India cannot possibly agree to be dismembered or disintegrated by allowing any of these Indian States to claim international statehood. Hyderabad was not a State in the international sense before the Indian Independence Act; it is not one now by virtue of the stand-still agreement and the arrangements that followed it; and it cannot be one at any time in the future if India is to live. We cannot defy or ignore geography.

It follows that any dispute with Hyderabad is not an international dispute. All matters relating to Hyderabad are now dealt with regularly by the Government of India as matters of domestic concern. Questions are put and answers are given in all such matters in the Indian Constituent Assembly to which the Government of India is responsible. . . . Any genuine grievance of the Muslims in any part of India can be voiced by any Muslim or other member in the Constituent Assembly, which is at once a safeguard against incorrect or exaggerated statements and a means of prompt redress where the facts call for redress. . . .

Sir Mohammed ZAFRULLAH KHAN (Pakistan): . . . [I]t is a very naive simplification of this problem to say that India, out of its own necessities or considerations of its own security, was compelled to take this action and that, the action having been completed, there is nothing more to do about it. I am sure that the narration of events will convince the members of the Security Council that India's action, by whatever name it might be described on one side or the other, was entirely unjustified; that it amounted to a breach of international peace; and that it constitutes a threat to the maintenance of peace and a continuation of aggression which calls for redress. . . .

The Prime Minister of the United Kingdom, Mr. Attlee, speaking on the Indian Independence Bill in the House of Commons on 10 July 1947, said:

"With the ending of the treaties and agreements, the States regained their independence. It is the hope of His Majesty's Government that all States will, in due course, find their appropriate place within one or other of the Dominions within the British Commonwealth. But, until the constitution of the Dominions has been framed in such a way as to include the States as willing partners, there must be a less organic form of relationship between them and there must be a period before a comprehensive system can be worked out."

What does that mean? It means that the States would be independent, that it was hoped that they would choose to accede either to one Dominion or to the other, but that time must be given for them to make the decision and, in any case, they must make that decision to come in with one or the other willingly. It obviously meant, therefore, that if they did not come in, they would continue to be independent. They might find it awkward, in actual fact, to continue that independence; by force of their geographical situation—as the representative of India has said—for lack of resources, or, in the case of many of them, lack of size, etc.—but the juridical position was perfectly clear. . . .

Now has the State a choice as to what relationship it would have with India? And if it has a choice and the people, as the result of this plebiscite, record their decision in favour of independence, will India recognize that decision or will it not?

Sir Benegal N. RAU (India): . . . So far as independence is concerned, I think it has been made clear that India will not recognize any of the Indian States within its borders as independent, in the same way as which, in the old days, no Indian State was regarded as independent. However, there are two choices open: the State can decide to accede, which carries with it the privileges of membership in the legislature, and so on; or it need not accede—but it will be subject to having its external affairs looked after by India. So far as independence is concerned, India's position is quite clear. Within those limits, it is open to the State to say either "We shall accede" or "we shall remain outside"—but, in that latter case, it will be in the same position in which it was in the days before 1947. . . .

Sir Mohammed ZAFRULLAH KHAN (Pakistan): . . . India has gone on to contend that the dispute, if any, between Hyderabad and India is a domestic matter. I presume that the representative of India intended to invoke Article 2, paragraph 7, of the Charter—although, curiously enough, all that he submitted in that connexion was emphasized by the use of the words "today" and "now": that is to say, today Hyderabad has been left no choice; now, Hyderabad has become a domestic matter. But if Hyderabad was independent before

12 September of last year, then the mere fact that its independence
has been destroyed does not make the dispute a domestic matter for
India. If that were so, then, after every annexation by one State of
territory belonging to another State, once the annexation had been
completed as the result of military action—I shall describe it in no
harsher terms—the State that had gained the accession might say:
"Well, this is now a domestic matter. Today, it is a domestic matter.
The territory is part of our territory, and there is no trouble about it."
.   .   .

With all respect, and in spite of what the representative of India
sought by his own statement to urge   .   .   .—namely, that the relationship of Hyderabad with the Union of India be left to be determined
by the free vote of the people of Hyderabad—I must submit that if that
assertion is to mean anything at all, if it is not to be reduced to an
absurdity, it must mean that the people shall decide whether Hyderabad shall accede or remain independent. If there is still some doubt
in the mind of the Council as a whole, or in those of some members
of the Council, with regard to the competence of the Security Council to deal with this matter, I submit that this is pre-eminently a
case on which the Security Council should seek the advisory opinion
of the International Court of Justice, under Article 96 of the Charter,
as it undoubtedly has the right to do.   .   .   .

Then, in case the Council decided to seek the opinion of the International Court, and if the opinion of the Court showed that the Council was competent to intervene in the matter—and the facts do dis-
close, as I submit, that an aggression has been committed for which
there was no justification while the matter was pending before the
Security Council—then the Council is duty bound, under the Charter,
to take appropriate steps to restore the *status quo* so far as it is capable of being restored. Very often when, in human relationships, a
situation has developed in a certain direction, it is not possible to restore the *status quo* completely, and perhaps it would be impossible
to do so with regard to this matter; but as far as it is possible to do
so, it should be done.

However, perhaps the Security Council is in doubt with regard to
the matter.   .   .   . In that case, the Security Council has the
means of ascertaining the facts for itself. If the Council is convinced,
on such evidence as is available or on such evidence as it might procure, that an aggression has been committed, it is the Council's duty
to take action to have the *status quo* restored. We again arrive, then,
at the central matter of the dispute: whether Hyderabad shall accede
to the Dominion of India or shall remain independent. On that question, I submit, the Government of India has in the past repeatedly expressed its willingness for settlement by means of a reference to the
people themselves. It is obvious, however, that the people, under the
circumstances which I have detailed, and under the kind of regime
which has been imposed upon them and which may continue to be im-

posed upon them until their views are to be ascertained, cannot possibly be expected to express their views freely. That plebiscite should take place under the guidance, supervision and control of the United Nations; that is to say, now that the matter is before the Security Council, of the Security Council.

[After the conclusion of Sir Mohammed Zafrullah Khan's statement, the President invited Members of the Council to speak. None of them expressed a desire to do so and the meeting was adjourned. Since then there has been no further discussion of the question by the Council, though the question has been retained on the agenda. See Summary Statement on Matters of Which the Security Council Is Seized (S/7382, 5 July 1966), pp. 61–63.]

NOTE.—1. By a firman of 24 November 1949 the Nizam of Hyderabad declared that the Constitution of India, shortly to be adopted, should be the Constitution for the State of Hyderabad. On 26 January 1950, the date of the inauguration of the Republic of India, he was sworn in as *Rajpramukh* of Hyderabad State, taking the oath of loyalty to the Indian Constitution. Nevertheless, when India was reorganized on linguistic lines in 1956, the State of Hyderabad was abolished and its territory was divided among the neighboring Indian States.

For comments on this case, see Taraknath DAS, "The Status of Hyderabad during and after British Rule in India," 43 AJIL (1949), pp. 57–72; Clyde EAGLETON, "The Case of Hyderabad before the Security Council," 44 AJIL (1950), pp. 277–302; Muhammad HAMIDULLAH, "Der Fall Haiderabad im Lichte des Völkerrechts," *in* Mensch und Staat: Festschrift für Herbert Kraus (Kitzingen/Main, 1954), pp. 57–72; V. P. MENON, The Story of the Integration of the Indian States (Bombay, 1956), pp. 314–89; Wilfred C. SMITH, "Hyderabad: Muslim Tragedy," 4 Middle East J. (1950), pp. 27–51.

2. While the Hyderabad Case involved the incorporation into India of a State with predominantly Hindu population which was ruled by a Moslem prince, the *Kashmir* Case related to the accession to India of a State with predominantly Moslem population which was ruled by a Hindu prince. When raiders from Pakistan threatened the rule of the Maharajah of Jammu and Kashmir, he acceded to India and asked for military help. India promised to the people of Kashmir that "once the soil of the State had been cleared of the invader and normal conditions restored, its people would be free to decide their future by the recognized democratic method of a plebiscite or referendum which, in order to ensure complete impartiality, might be held under international auspices." India asked the Security Council to order Pakistan to stop giving the invaders direct and indirect military aid. S/628 (2 January 1948), reprinted in S/1100 (9 Nov. 1948), Annex 28; SCOR, III, Supp. for Nov. 1948, pp. 139–44. Pakistan denied the charges and contended that massacres of the Moslem population of Kashmir by the forces of the Maharajah led to an uprising and the establishment of the Azad (Free) Kashmir Government, the forces of which were joined by Moslem refugees, independent tribesmen and other persons from Pakistan. Pakistan asked the Council to appoint a Commission which would arrange for a cessation

of fighting and a plebiscite. S/646 (16 Jan. 1948), reprinted in S/1100 (9 Nov. 1948), Annex 6; SCOR, III, Supp. for Nov. 1948, pp. 67–87. India claimed that, even apart from accession, it was entitled to come to the aid of a legitimate government, while Pakistan cannot be allowed to help the insurgents. SCOR, III, Nos. 1–15, pp. 275–76. While the parties agreed to the establishment of a Commission, which was able to arrange for a cessation of hostilities, no agreement could be reached on the modalities of the plebiscite to be conducted in Kashmir. S/1430/Rev. 1 (9 Dec. 1949/22 March 1950); SCOR, IV, Special Supp. 7, pp. 19–63. Efforts at mediation by a special United Nations Representative for India and Pakistan, first Sir Owen Dixon and later Dr. Frank P. Graham, did not result in the settlement of the dispute. For the last report on the subject, see S/2967 (27 March 1953); SCOR, VIII, Special Supp. 1, pp. 2–23. Another unsuccessful attempt to settle the dispute was made in 1957. GAOR, XII, Supp. 2 (A/3648), pp. 46–72; GAOR, XIII, Supp. 2 (A/3901), pp. 8–29. An uneasy truce was supervised throughout this period by the United Nations Military Observer Group in India and Pakistan. New fighting occurred in 1965, but on request of the Security Council a cease-fire went into effect on 22 September 1965. At a meeting held in Tashkent, with the assistance of the Soviet Union, the parties agreed to withdraw their forces to the old cease-fire line and to restore normal relations. GAOR, XXI, Supp. 1(A/6301), pp. 9–17.

For comments on the Kashmir Case, see J. S. BAINS, India's International Disputes: A Legal Study (Bombay, 1962), pp. 62–86; Lord BIRWOOD, Two Nations and Kashmir (London, 1956), 227 pp.; Michael BRECHER, The Struggle for Kashmir (Toronto, 1953), 211 pp.; W. Norman BROWN, The United States and India and Pakistan (2d ed., Cambridge, Mass., 1963), pp. 180–203; Taraknath DAS, "The Kashmir Issue and the United Nations," 65 Political Science Q. (1950), pp. 264–82; Rudolf GEIGER, Die völkerrechtliche Lage Kaschmirs (Munich Diss., 1963), 84 pp.; Sisir GUPTA, "Issues and Prospects in Kashmir," 21 India Quarterly: A Journal of International Affairs (1965), pp. 253–84; M. M. R. KHAN, The United Nations and Kashmir (Groningen, 1955), 213 pp.; Josef KORBEL, Danger in Kashmir (Princeton, N.J., 1954), 351 pp.; Rajbans KRISHEN, Kashmir and the Conspiracy against Peace (Bombay, 1951), 108 pp.; Alastair LAMB, The Kashmir Problem: A Historical Survey (New York, 1967), 163 pp.; Sylvain LOURIE, "The United Nations Military Observer Group in India and Pakistan," 9 Int.Org. (1955), pp. 19–31; V. P. MENON, The Story of the Integration of the Indian States (Bombay, 1956), pp. 390–415; T. B. MILLAR, "Kashmir, the Commonwealth, and the United Nations," 17 Australian Outlook (1963), pp. 54–73; A. G. NOORANI, The Kashmir Question (Bombay, 1964), 125 pp.; Phillips TALBOT, "Kashmir and Hyderabad," 1 World Politics (1949), pp. 321–32; David W. WAINHOUSE and others, International Peace Observation (Baltimore, Md., 1966), pp. 357–73.

3. Another complaint against India was brought to the Security Council in 1961, when Portugal charged that India has launched a full scale attack on *Goa* and other Portuguese territories in India, and asked the Security Council to stop India's aggression and to order an immediate cease-fire and the withdrawal of Indian troops from Portuguese soil. S/5030 (18 Dec. 1961); SCOR, XVI, Supp. for Oct.–Dec. 1961, p. 295. India contended that Portugal had refused to negotiate concerning the transfer of the territories to India,

in disregard of the declaration of the General Assembly on colonialism [Resolution 1514 (XV) of 14 Dec. 1960]; that the Portuguese territories were acquired by the use of force some 450 years ago; that India never accepted this illegal acquisition; that there was no legal frontier between these territories and India; and that, consequently, India did not commit any aggression by coming to the assistance of the local population which was in revolt against Portugal. The representative of the United States, Mr. Stevenson, stated that the action by India constituted a clear violation of Article 2, paragraph 4, of the Charter, and that the United Nations, if it is to survive, "cannot condone the use of force in this instance and thus pave the way for the forceful solutions of other disputes which exist in Latin America, in Africa, in Asia and in Europe"; the United Nations "cannot apply a double standard with regard to the principle of resort to force." The Soviet delegate, Mr. Zorin, on the other hand, argued that the Council should condemn Portugal for not carrying out the declaration of the General Assembly on colonialism which was binding on it, and thereby was causing "a threat to peace and security in various parts of the world." SCOR, XVI, Mtg. 987, pp. 7–27. A draft resolution, presented by the United States, the United Kingdom, France and Turkey, proposed that the Council should deplore the use of force by India, and call for a cease-fire and the withdrawal of Indian forces; it received seven votes but was vetoed by the Soviet Union. Another resolution, presented by Ceylon, Liberia and the United Arab Republic, suggested that the Council should determine that the Portuguese enclaves constitute a threat to international peace, and call upon Portugal "to terminate hostile action and to co-operate with India in the liquidation of her colonial possessions in India"; it was rejected by seven votes to four. Commenting on these decisions, Mr. Stevenson (USA) stated that he found "the attitude of some other members of the Council profoundly disturbing and ominous because we have witnessed tonight an effort to rewrite the Charter, to sanction the use of force in international relations when it suits one's own purposes. This approach can only lead to chaos and to the disintegration of the United Nations." SCOR, XVI, Mtg. 988, pp. 21–27. In 1963, four Goan petitioners made an attempt to present to the General Assembly the case for self-determination of Goa, but the Fourth Committee did not allow them to finish their statements. GAOR, XVIII, Fourth Committee, pp. 534–39; GOA FREEDOM MOVEMENT, Goan Petitioners in the United Nations (1964), 70 pp. See also the Portuguese letter of 15 October 1965 (A/6051); GAOR, Annexes (XX) 9, pp. 2–3. For a Portuguese selection of comments, see NATIONAL SECRETARIAT OF INFORMATION, The Invasion and Occupation of Goa in the World Press (Lisbon, 1962), 636 pp. On the other hand, see J. S. BAINS, India's International Disputes (Bombay, 1962), pp. 195–208. See also Maurice FLORY, "Les implications juridiques de l'affaire de Goa," 8 AFDI (1962), pp. 476–91.

THE PALESTINE QUESTION

NOTE.—1. Since ancient times, Palestine has been the subject of conquests and reconquests by her stronger neighbors: Egyptians, Assyrians, Babylonians, Persians, Macedonians, Romans, Byzantines, Arabs, Western European crusaders, and finally (in 1516) Turks. Since 1897 the Zionist movement, created by Theodor Herzl, laid claims to Palestine on behalf of the

Jewish people who were the main inhabitants of that land for more than a thousand years prior to 70 A.D., when the Romans punished a rebellion by destruction of Jerusalem, which was followed by complete dispersion of the remainder of the Jews after another rebellion in 137 A.D.

2. On 2 November 1917, the British Government issued the so-called Balfour Declaration (contained in a letter from the British Foreign Secretary to Lord Rothschild), conveying "a declaration of sympathy with the Jewish Zionist aspirations" and announcing that "His Majesty's Government view with favour the establishment in Palestine of a national home for the Jewish people, and will use their best endeavours to facilitate the achievement of this object, it being clearly understood that nothing shall be done which may prejudice the civil and religious rights of existing non-Jewish communities in Palestine, or the rights and political status enjoyed by Jews in any other country." GAOR, II, Supp. 11, Vol. II, p. 18. British troops occupied Palestine in 1917–8, and by agreement between the Allied Powers, Palestine was assigned to the United Kingdom as a mandated territory. The terms of the mandate were confirmed by the Council of the League of Nations on 24 July 1922 in accordance with Article 22 of the Covenant of the League, and the British Government agreed to exercise the Mandate "on behalf of the League of Nations." The preamble of the Mandate reproduced the terms of the Balfour Declaration, and the Mandatory was given the responsibility "for placing the country under such political, administrative and economic conditions as will secure the establishment of the Jewish national home, as laid down in the preamble, and the development of self-governing institutions, and also for safeguarding the civil and religious rights of all the inhabitants of Palestine, irrespective of race and religion." Article 6 of the Mandate also provided that the "Administration of Palestine, while ensuring that the rights and position of other sections of the population are not prejudiced, shall facilitate Jewish immigration under suitable conditions and shall encourage . . . close settlement by Jews on the land, including State lands and waste lands not required for public purposes." *Idem*, pp. 18–21; 1 HUDSON, International Legislation, p. 109. When the Mandate came into force the population of Palestine consisted of about 650,000 Arabs and 84,000 Jews. With the approval of the Council, the area east of the river Jordan was separated from Palestine and became a separate mandated territory (Transjordan). GAOR, *op.cit.*, pp. 21–2.

3. While the Jewish community considered the Balfour Declaration as implying the evolution of Palestine into a Jewish State, the British Government contended that it only promised that a Jewish Home "should be founded *in Palestine*," and that this term means "not the imposition of a Jewish nationality upon the inhabitants of Palestine as a whole, but the further development of the existing Jewish community, with the assistance of Jews in other parts of the world, in order that it may become a centre in which the Jewish people as a whole may take, on the grounds of religion and race, an interest and a pride." Statement by Winston Churchill, Secretary of State for Colonies, 3 June 1922; British Parliamentary Papers, Cmd., 1700, pp. 18–9; reproduced in GAOR, II, Supp. 11, Vol. I, p. 20. The Arabs, on the other hand, based their position on their centuries old possession and occupation of the country and on certain pledges given by the British Government in an exchange of correspondence between Sir Henry McMahon and Sherif Hussein of Mecca and later statements by various official British

spokesmen. The Arabs considered that Palestine was included among the territories to which independence was pledged; the British Government denied, however, this interpretation of these documents. *Idem*, pp. 33–5; GAOR, II, *Ad Hoc* C. on the Palestine Question, pp. 272–3.

4. Serious Arab riots took place in Palestine in 1920–1, 1929, 1933 and 1936–8, and a Royal Commission, under the chairmanship of Lord Peel, finding the claims of the Arab and Jewish communities entirely irreconcilable, recommended partition in 1937. British Parliamentary Papers, Cmd. 5479, pp. 380–96. As the Jewish State contemplated by the Peel Commission would have contained an Arab minority amounting to 49 per cent, another Commission, under the chairmanship of Sir John Woodhead, proposed the allocation of a smaller area to Jews and temporary retention of the Mandate over areas with mixed population. *Idem*, Cmd. 5854. After this proposal was rejected, a White Paper in May 1939 announced as the objective of the British Government "the establishment within ten years of an independent Palestine State . . . in which Arabs and Jews share in government in such a way as to ensure that the essential interests of each community are safeguarded." At the same time, Jewish immigration was to be limited to 75,000 over a five-year period and "no further immigration will be permitted unless the Arabs of Palestine are prepared to acquiesce in it." Finally, no further transfer of Arab land to Jews would be allowed in certain zones. *Idem*, Cmd. 6019, pp. 5–6, 10–2. The Jewish community refused to accept the White Paper, and after the end of the war in 1945 acts of terrorism started to multiply and illegal immigration reached new heights. The United States exerted pressure on the British Government to grant 100,000 immigration certificates to displaced European Jews, and a joint Anglo-American Committee of Inquiry was appointed to investigate the situation. The Committee endorsed the relaxation of immigration restrictions, and recommended that "Palestine shall be neither a Jewish nor an Arab State," but that it should "ultimately become a State which guards the rights and interests of Moslems, Jews, and Christians alike." *Idem*, Cmd. 6808, pp. 2–4. A new British proposal (the Morrison Plan) suggested the division of the country into four areas, two smaller ones to be administered by the Mandatory and two larger ones to be made autonomous and to be controlled, respectively, by the Arabs and the Jews under general supervision of a Central Government; the control of immigration to each province was to be exercised by the Central Government on the basis of recommendations of each province which were to be followed so long as the absorptive capacity of the province was not exceeded. *Idem*, Cmd. 7044, pp. 3–8. This proposal was rejected by both sides, and a similar fate met also another British proposal for a five-year period of British trusteeship, to be terminated when agreement was reached between a majority of the Arab representatives and a majority of Jewish representatives in a proposed Constituent Assembly. *Ibid.*, pp. 11–4.

5. The British Government announced in February 1947 that they were "not prepared to continue indefinitely to govern Palestine themselves merely because Arabs and Jews cannot agree upon the means of sharing its government between them;" and on 2 April 1947 they asked the General Assembly of the United Nations "to make recommendations, under Article 10 of the Charter, concerning the future government of Palestine," and suggested the convocation of a special session of the Assembly "for the purpose of constituting and instructing a special committee" to prepare a preliminary study

for the consideration of the next regular session of the Assembly. A/286 (3
April 1947); GAOR, First Special Session, Vol. I, p. 183. Five Arab States
then requested that the special session consider also an additional item, namely "the termination of the Mandate over Palestine and the declaration of its
independence." A/287–91 (21–23 April 1947); GAOR, *op.cit.*, pp. 183–6.
The General Committee refused, however, to include the Arab item on the
Assembly's agenda, and this decision was confirmed by the General Assembly
by 24 votes to 15, with 10 abstentions. *Ibid.*, pp. 59–60. The First Committee
of the General Assembly granted a hearing to the Jewish Agency for Palestine and to the Arab Higher Committee; it also was informed by the British
Government that, while they would welcome a just solution acceptable to both
parties, they would not accept the responsibility "for enforcing a solution
which is not accepted by both parties and which we cannot reconcile with our
conscience." *Idem*, Vol. III, pp. 183–4. The General Assembly, by a vote of
45 to 7, appointed a special committee not including the five permanent members of the Security Council, with "the widest powers to ascertain and record
facts, and to investigate all questions and issues relevant to the problem of
Palestine." Resolution 106 (S–1), 15 May 1947; GAOR, First Special Session, Resolutions (A/310), p. 6. On the same day, the General Assembly
called "upon all Governments and peoples, and particularly upon the inhabitants of Palestine, to refrain, pending action by the General Assembly on
the report of the Special Committee on Palestine, from the threat or use of
force or any other action which might create an atmosphere prejudicial to
an early settlement of the question of Palestine." *Idem*, p. 7. Though the
Arab Higher Committee refused to cooperate with the United Nations Special
Committee on Palestine (UNSCOP), representatives of the Arab States tes-
tified before the Committee. GAOR, II, Supp. 11, Vol. I, p. 7. The Committee presented two sets of recommendations: (1) a plan of partition with
economic union and international trusteeship for the City of Jerusalem, supported by seven members; and (2) a plan for a federal state, supported by
three members. *Idem*, pp. 47–64, and Document 1, below.

1.   *Report of the United Nations Special Committee
on Palestine, 3 September 1947.*

GAOR, II, Supp. 11 (A/364), Vol. I, pp. 29–35, 39–62.

The Jewish case

The Jewish case, as herein considered, is mainly the case advanced
by the Jewish Agency which, by the terms of the Mandate, has a special status with regard to Jewish interests in Palestine.

The Jewish case seeks the establishment of a Jewish State in Palestine, and Jewish immigration into Palestine both before and after
the creation of the Jewish State, subject only to the limitations imposed by the economic absorptive capacity of that State. In the Jewish case, the issues of the Jewish State and unrestricted immigration
are inextricably interwoven. On the one hand, the Jewish State is
needed in order to assure a refuge for the Jewish immigrants who are
clamoring to come to Palestine from the displaced persons camps and
from other places in Europe, North Africa and the Near East, where

their present plight is difficult. On the other hand, a Jewish State would have urgent need of Jewish immigrants in order to affect the present great numerical preponderance of Arabs over Jews in Palestine. The Jewish case frankly recognizes the difficulty involved in creating at the present time a Jewish State in all of Palestine in which Jews would, in fact, be only a minority, or in part of Palestine in which, at best, they could immediately have only a slight preponderance. Thus, the Jewish case lays great stress on the right of Jewish immigration, for political as well as humanitarian reasons. Special emphasis is therefore placed on the right of Jews to "return" to Palestine.

Aside from connections based on biblical and historical sources as to this right, the Jewish case rests on the Balfour Declaration of 1917 and on the Mandate for Palestine, which incorporated the Declaration in its preamble and recognized the historic connection of the Jewish people with Palestine and the grounds for reconstituting the Jewish National Home there.

It is the Jewish contention that the mandatory Power in Palestine became a trustee for the specific and primary purpose of securing the establishment of the Jewish National Home by means of Jewish immigration, which must be facilitated, and by close settlement of the Jews upon the land, which must be encouraged subject to certain safeguards.

In their view, the Mandate intended that the natural evolution of Jewish immigration, unrestricted save by economic considerations, might ultimately lead to a commonwealth in which the Jews would be a majority.

They regard the pledges to the Jews in the Balfour Declaration and the Mandate as international commitments not to the Jews of Palestine alone, who were at the time only a small community, but to the Jewish people as a whole, who are now often described as the "Jewish nation".

They contend that there has been no change in conditions since these intentions were expressed, for the existence of an Arab majority was a fact well understood at the time when the legal and political commitments of the Mandate were originally made.

The Jews, it is urged, have built in Palestine on the basis of faith in the international pledges made to the Jewish people and they cannot be halted in midstream.

(*a*) The Jewish immigrants to Palestine, who are said to be merely returning to their homeland, are portrayed as having been primarily responsible for developing the economy of the country, for establishing an infant industry, for cultivating theretofore waste lands, for instituting irrigation schemes and for improving the standard of living of Palestine Arabs as well as Jews.

(b) The immigrant Jews displace no Arabs, but rather develop areas which otherwise would remain undeveloped.

They contend that no time limit was suggested for immigration or settlement. The Mandate, it is claimed, was to be terminated only when its primary purpose, the establishment of the Jewish National Home, had been fulfilled. That Home will be regarded as having been established only when it can stand alone, for there can be no security for it unless it is free from Arab domination. Any proposed solution, therefore, should ensure the existence and continued development of the Jewish National Home in accordance with the letter and the spirit of the international pledges made.

(a) The establishment of the Jewish Home and State will, it is claimed, do no political injustice to the Arabs, since the Arabs have never established a government in Palestine.

(b) In the Jewish Home and State the Arab population, which, as a result of accelerated Jewish immigration will have become a minority population, will be fully protected in all its rights on an equal basis with the Jewish citizenry.

Appraisal of the Jewish case

Under the preamble of the Mandate, the Principal Allied Powers agreed, for the purpose of giving effect to the provisions of Article 22 of the Covenant of the League of Nations, to entrust to a mandatory Power the administration of the territory of Palestine. They also agreed that this mandatory should be responsible for putting into effect the Balfour Declaration. Article 2 of the Mandate made the mandatory responsible for placing the country under such political, administrative and economic conditions as would assure:

(a) The establishment of a Jewish National Home, as laid down in the preamble, and

(b) The development of self-governing institutions.

The obligation to assure the establishment of a Jewish National Home was qualified by article 6, which made the mandatory Power responsible for the facilitation of immigration and the encouragement of close settlement on the land.

There has been great controversy as to whether the obligations relating to the National Home and self-governing institutions were equal in weight, and also as to whether they were consistent with each other. Opinions have been expressed that between these two obligations the Mandate recognizes no primacy in order of importance and no priority in order of execution, and that they were in no sense irreconcilable. According to other opinions, however, the primary purpose of the Mandate, as expressed in its preamble and in its articles, was to promote the establishment of a Jewish National Home, to which the obligation of developing self-governing institutions was subordinated.

The practical significance of the controversy was that, if the country were to be placed under such political conditions as would secure the development of self-governing institutions, these same conditions would in fact destroy the Jewish National Home. It would appear that, although difficulties were anticipated, when the Mandate was confirmed it was not clearly contemplated that these two obligations would prove mutually incompatible. In practice, however, they proved to be so. The conflict between Arab and Jewish political aspirations, intensified by the growth of Arab nationalism throughout the Arabic-speaking countries and by the growth of anti-Semitism in some European countries, excluded any possibility of adjustment which would allow the establishment of self-governing institutions. Had self-governing institutions been created, the majority in the country, who never willingly accepted Jewish immigration, would in all probability have made its continuance impossible, causing thereby the negation of the Jewish National Home.

It is part of the Jewish case that any restriction on immigration, other than economic considerations, is illegal and in violation of the provisions of the Mandate. Article 6 of the Mandate made the mandatory Power responsible for facilitating Jewish immigration under suitable conditions, while insuring that the rights and position of other sections of the population were not prejudiced. No other restriction was provided thereon.

By 1922, the mandatory construed article 6 to mean that Jewish immigration could not be so great in volume as to exceed whatever might be the economic capacity of the country to absorb new arrivals. This interpretation was accepted by the Executive of the Zionist Organization and, thus, by construction, a restriction of the general terms of the article was established.

The Jewish contention, that the Mandate intended that the natural evolution of Jewish immigration might ultimately lead to a commonwealth in which Jews would be a majority, raises the question as to the meaning of "National Home".

The notion of the National Home, which derived from the formulation of Zionist aspirations in the 1897 Basle program has provoked many discussions concerning its meaning, scope and legal character, especially since it has no known legal connotation and there are no precedents in international law for its interpretation. It was used in the Balfour Declaration and in the Mandate, both of which promised the establishment of a "Jewish National Home" without, however, defining its meaning. The conclusion seems to be inescapable that the vagueness in the wording of both instruments was intentional. The fact that the term "National Home" was employed, instead of the word "State" or "Commonwealth", would indicate that the intention was to place a restrictive construction on the National Home scheme from its very inception. This argument, however, may not be conclusive since "National Home", although not precluding the possibility of establishing a Jewish State in the future, had the advantage of not shocking public opinion outside the Jewish world, and even in many Jewish quarters, as the term "Jewish State" would have done.

What exactly was in the minds of those who made the Balfour Declaration is speculative. The fact remains that, in the light of experience acquired as a consequence of serious disturbances in Palestine, the mandatory Power, in a statement on "British Policy in Palestine," issued on 3 June 1922 by the Colonial Office, placed a restrictive construction upon the Balfour Declaration.

The statement recognized for the first time "the ancient historic connection" of the Jews with Palestine, and declared that they were in Palestine "as of right and not on sufferance". It, however, excluded in its own terms "the disappearance or subordination of the Arabic population, language or customs in Palestine" or "the imposition of Jewish nationality upon the inhabitants of Palestine as a whole", and made it clear that in the eyes of the mandatory Power the Jewish National Home was to be founded in Palestine and not that Palestine as a whole was to be converted into a Jewish National Home.

It should be noted here that this construction, which restricted considerably the scope of the National Home, was made prior to the confirmation of the Mandate by the Council of the League of Nations and was formally accepted at the time by the Executive of the Zionist Organization, in its capacity as the "appropriate Jewish agency" provided for in article 4 of the Mandate.

Nevertheless, neither the Balfour Declaration nor the Mandate precluded the eventual creation of a Jewish State. The Mandate in its Preamble recognized, with regard to the Jewish people, the "grounds for reconstituting their National Home". By providing, as one of the main obligations of the mandatory Power the facilitation of Jewish immigration, it conferred upon the Jews an opportunity, through large-scale immigration, to create eventually a Jewish State with a Jewish majority.

Both the Balfour Declaration and the Mandate involved international commitments to the Jewish people as a whole. It was obvious that these commitments were not limited only to the Jewish population of Palestine, since at the time there were only some 80,000 Jews there.

This would imply that all Jews in the world who wish to go to Palestine would have the right to do so. This view, however, would seem to be unrealistic in the sense that a country as small and poor as Palestine could never accommodate all the Jews in the world.

When the Mandate was approved, all concerned were aware of the existence of an overwhelming Arab majority in Palestine. Moreover, the King-Crane Report, among others, had warned that the Zionist program could not be carried out except by force of arms. It would seem clear, therefore, that the provisions of the Mandate relating to the Jewish National Home could be based only on the assumption that sooner or later the Arab fears would gradually be overcome and that Arab hostility to the terms of the Mandate would in time weaken and disappear.

This seems to have been the basic assumption, but it proved to be a false one, since the history of the last twenty-five years has established the fact that not only the creation of a Jewish State but even the continuation of the building of the Jewish National Home by restricted immigration could be implemented only by the use of some considerable force. It cannot be properly contended that the use of force as a means of establishing the National Home was either intended by the Mandate or implied by its provisions. On the contrary, the provisions of the Mandate should preclude any systematic use of force for the purpose of its application. In its preamble, the Mandate states that the Principal Allied Powers agreed to entrust Palestine to a mandatory Power for the purpose of giving effect to the provisions of Article 22 of the Covenant of the League of Nations. The guiding principle of that Article was the well-being of peoples not yet able to stand by themselves.

It has been suggested that the well-being of the indigenous population of Palestine might be ensured by the unfettered development of the Jewish National Home. "Well-being" in a practical sense, however, must be something more than a mere objective conception; and the Arabs, thinking subjectively, have demonstrated by their acts their belief that the conversion of Palestine into a Jewish State against their will would be very much opposed to their conception of what is essential to their well-being. To contend, therefore, that there is an international obligation to the effect that Jewish immigration should continue with a view to establishing a Jewish majority in the whole of Palestine, would mean ignoring the wishes of the Arab population and their views as to their own well-being. This would involve an apparent violation of what was the governing principle of Article 22 of the Covenant.

That the Jews have performed remarkable feats of development in Palestine cannot be denied. The fact remains, however, that there may be serious question as to the economic soundness of much of this achievement, owing to the reliance on gift capital and the political motivation behind many of the development schemes with little regard to economic considerations.

That Jews would displace Arabs from the land if restrictions were not imposed would seem inevitable, since, as land pressures develop, the attraction of Jewish capital would be an inducement to many Arabs to dispose of their lands. Some displacement of this nature has already occurred.

It would appear that the clear implication of the Jewish contention that the National Home can be safeguarded from Arab domination only when it can stand by itself is that an independent Jewish State in all or part of Palestine is the only means of securing the promise of the Mandate for a Jewish National Home. Even a bi-national State, on a parity basis, unless there were extensive international guarantees, would not seem to meet the Jewish contention.

The Jewish assurance that no political injustice would be done to the Arabs by the creation of a Jewish State in Palestine, since the Arabs have never established a government there, gains some support from the fact that not since 63 B.C., when Pompey stormed Jerusalem, has Palestine been an independent State. On the other hand, the fact remains that today in Palestine there are over 1,200,000 Arabs, two-thirds of the population, who oppose a Jewish State and who are intent on establishing an independent Arab State.

Any solution assuring the continued development of the Jewish National Home in Palestine would necessarily involve continued Jewish immigration, the postponement of independence, and also administration by a third party, at least until the Jewish people become a majority there. Such a solution would have to be enforced, in view of the opposition of the Arab population. Many Jews contend that, if given the opportunity, the Jews alone could defend a Jewish State. Even this, however, envisages the possibility of a violent struggle with the Arabs.

The Arab case

The Arab case as here set forth is based mainly on the contentions made by the representatives of the Arab Higher Committee before the first special session of the General Assembly and by the representatives of the Arab States at that session, at Beirut and Geneva.

The Arab case seeks the immediate creation of an independent Palestine west of the Jordan as an Arab State. It rests on a number of claims and contentions which are summarized below.

The Arabs emphasize the fact of an actual Arab numerical majority, in the ratio of two to one in the present population of Palestine.

They postulate the "natural" right of the Arab majority to remain in undisputed possession of the country, since they are and have been for many centuries in possession of the land. This claim of a "natural" right is based on the contention that the Arab connection with Palestine has continued uninterruptedly from early historical times, since the term "Arab" is to be interpreted as connoting not only the invaders from the Arabian Peninsula in the seventh century, but also the indigenous population which intermarried with the invaders and acquired their speech, customs and modes of thought in becoming permanently Arabized.

The Arabs further stress the natural desire of the Arab community to safeguard its national existence from foreign intruders, in order that it may pursue without interference its own political, economic and cultural development.

The Arabs also claim "acquired" rights, based on the general promises and pledges officially made to the Arab people in the course of the First World War, including, in particular, the McMahon-Hussein correspondence of 1915–1916 and the Anglo-French Declaration of 1918. The "Hogarth Message", the Basset letter, and the "Declaration to the Seven" are regarded as further support for the Arab claim to an independent Palestine.

(a) In the Arab view, these undertakings, taken collectively, provide a firm recognition of Arab political rights in Palestine which, they contend, Great Britain is under a contractual obligation to accept and uphold—an obligation thus far unfulfilled.

(b) It is also their contention that these promises and pledges of Arab freedom and independence were among the main factors inspiring the Arabs to revolt against the Ottoman Empire and to ally themselves with Great Britain and the other allies during the First World War.

The Arabs have persistently adhered to the position that the Mandate for Palestine, which incorporated the Balfour Declaration, is illegal. The Arab States have refused to recognize it as having any validity.

(a) They allege that the terms of the Palestine Mandate are inconsistent with the letter and spirit of Article 22 of the Covenant of the League of Nations for the following reasons:

(1) Although paragraph 4 of Article 22 stipulated that certain communities had reached a stage of development where their existence as "independent nations" could be provisionally recognized, subject only to a limited period of tutelage under a mandatory Power in the form of administrative advice and assistance until such time as these communities would be able to stand alone, the Palestine Mandate violated this stipulation by deliberately omitting immediate provisional recognition of the independence of the territory and by granting to the mandatory Power in article 1 of the Mandate "full powers of legislation and administration".

(2) The wishes of the Palestine community had not been "a principal consideration in the selection of the Mandatory", as provided for in Article 22, paragraph 4 of the Covenant.

(b) The principle and right of national self-determination were violated.

(c) The Arab States were not Members of the League of Nations when the Palestine Mandate was approved, and are not, therefore, bound by it.

Although the terms of the Palestine Mandate are, in the Arab view, illegal and invalid and, therefore, Jewish immigrants have had no legal right to enter the country during the period of the Mandate, the Arab position regarding such Jews is that their presence has to be recognized as a *de facto* situation.

Appraisal of the Arab case

That the Arab population is and will continue to be the numerically preponderant population in Palestine, unless offset by free and substantial Jewish immigration, is undisputed. The Arab birth rate is considerably higher than the Jewish birth rate. Only large-scale Jewish immigration, strongly assisted by capital and efforts from outside Palestine, can provide the basis for the attainment of numerical parity between Arabs and Jews in the population.

The Arabs of Palestine consider themselves as having a "natural" right to that country, although they have not been in possession of it as a sovereign nation.

The Arab population, despite the strenuous efforts of Jews to acquire land in Palestine, at present remains in possession of approximately 85 per cent of the land. The provisions of the land transfer regulations of 1940, which gave effect to the 1939 White Paper policy, have severely restricted the Jewish efforts to acquire new land.

The Arabs consider that all of the territory of Palestine is by right Arab patrimony. Although in an Arab State they would recognize the right of Jews to continue in possession of land legally acquired by them during the Mandate, they would regard as a violation of their "natural" right any effort, such as partition, to reduce the territory of Palestine.

The desire of the Arab people of Palestine to safeguard their national existence is a very natural desire. However, Palestinian nationalism, as distinct from Arab nationalism, is itself a relatively new phenomenon, which appeared only after the division of the "Arab rectangle" by the settlement of the First World War. The National Home policy and the vigorous policy of immigration pursued by the Jewish leadership has sharpened the Arab fear of danger from the intruding Jewish population.

With regard to the promises and pledges made to the Arabs as inducement for their support of the Allies in the First World War, it is to be noted that apparently there is no unequivocal agreement as to whether Palestine was included within the territory pledged to independence by the McMahon-Hussein correspondence. In this connexion, since the question of interpretation was raised Great Britain has consistently denied that Palestine was among the territories to which independence was pledged.

These promises were examined in 1939 by a committee consisting of British and Arab representatives which was set up for that purpose during the Arab-British Conference on Palestine. That committee considered the McMahon correspondence and certain subsequent events and documents which one party or the other regarded as likely to shed light on the meaning or intention of the correspondence. It examined, *inter alia*, the so-called Sykes-Picot Agreement, the Balfour Declaration, the "Hogarth Message", the "Declaration to the Seven", General Allenby's assurance to the Amir Feisal, and the Anglo-French Declaration of 7 December 1918.

In its report the committee stated that the Arab and the United Kingdom representatives had been "unable to reach agreement upon an interpretation of the correspondence". The United Kingdom representatives, however, informed the Arab representatives that the Arab contentions, as explained to the committee, regarding the interpretation of the correspondence, and especially their contentions relating to the meaning of the phrase "portions of Syria lying to the west of the districts of Damascus, Hama, Homs and Aleppo have greater force than has appeared hitherto". Moreover, the United Kingdom representatives informed the Arab representatives that "they agree that Palestine was included in the area claimed by the Sherif of Mecca in his letter of 14 July 1915, and that unless Palestine was excluded from that area later in the correspondence, it must be regarded as having been included in the area in which Great Britain was to recognize and support the independence of the Arabs. They maintain that on a proper construction of the correspondence, Palestine was in fact excluded. But they agree that the language in which its exclusion was expressed was not so specific and unmistakable as it was thought to be at the time".

With regard to the various statements mentioned [previously], the above committee considered that it was beyond its scope to express an opinion upon their proper interpretation, and that such opinion could not in any case be properly formed unless consideration had also been given to a number of other statements made during the war. In the opinion of the committee, however, it was evident from these statements that "His Majesty's Government were not free to dispose of Palestine without regard for the wishes and interests of the inhabitants of Palestine, and that these statements must all be taken into account in any attempt to estimate the responsibilities which— upon any interpretation of the correspondence—His Majesty's Government have incurred towards those inhabitants as a result of the correspondence".

With regard to the "Hogarth Message", the Arab representatives explained that they relied strongly on a passage in the message delivered to King Hussein of the Hejaz in 1918, to the effect that Jewish settlement in Palestine would be allowed only in so far as would be consistent with the political and economic freedom of the Arab population.

It is noteworthy that the "Hogarth Message" was delivered to King Hussein in January 1918, that is, two months after the Balfour Declaration was made. There is a clear difference between the Balfour

Declaration itself, which safeguarded only the civil and religious rights of the existing non-Jewish communities, and the "Hogarth Message", which promised political freedom to the Arab population of Palestine.

A Memorandum presented by Amir Feisal to the Paris Peace Conference, however, would indicate that the special position of Palestine was recognized in Arab circles. He said:

"The Jews are very close to the Arabs in blood and there is no conflict of character between the two races. In principle we are absolutely at one. Nevertheless, the Arabs cannot risk assuming the responsibility of holding level the scales in the clash of races and religions that have, in this one province, so often involved the world in difficulties. They would wish for the effective superposition of a great trustee, so long as a representative local administration commended itself by actively promoting the material prosperity of the country."

It was also Amir Feisal who, representing and acting on behalf of the Arab Kingdom of the Hejaz, signed an agreement with Dr. Weizmann, representing and acting on behalf of the Zionist Organization. In this agreement, Feisal, subject to the condition that the Arabs obtained independence as demanded in his Memorandum to the British Foreign Office of 4 January 1919, accepted the Balfour Declaration and the encouragement of Jewish immigration into Palestine. The Feisal-Weizmann agreement did not acquire validity, since the condition attached was not fulfilled at the time.

The Peel Commission, in referring to the matter, had noted in its report that "there was a time when Arab statesmen were willing to consider giving Palestine to the Jews, provided that the rest of Arab Asia was free. That condition was not fulfilled then, but it is on the eve of fulfilment now".

With regard to the principle of self-determination, although international recognition was extended to this principle at the end of the First World War and it was adhered to with regard to the other Arab territories, at the time of the creation of the "A" Mandates, it was not applied to Palestine, obviously because of the intention to make possible the creation of the Jewish National Home there. Actually, it may well be said that the Jewish National Home and the *sui generis* Mandate for Palestine run counter to that principle.

As to the claim that the Palestine Mandate violates Article 22 of the Covenant because the community of Palestine has not been recognized as an independent nation and because the mandatory was given full powers of legislation and administration, it has been rightly pointed out by the Peel Commission:

"(*a*) That the provisional recognition of 'certain communities formerly belonging to the Turkish Empire' as independent nations is permissible; the words are 'can be provisionally recognized', not 'will' or 'shall';

"(b) That the penultimate paragraph of Article 22 prescribes that the degree of authority to be exercised by the mandatory shall be defined, at need, by the Council of the League;

"(c) That the acceptance by the Allied Powers and the United States of the policy of the Balfour Declaration made it clear from the beginning that Palestine would have been treated differently from Syria and Iraq, and that this difference of treatment was confirmed by the Supreme Council in the Treaty of Sèvres and by the Council of the League in sanctioning the Mandate."

With regard to the allegation that the wishes of the Palestine community had not been the principal consideration in the selection of the mandatory Power, it should be noted that the resolutions of the General Syrian Congress of 2 July 1919, in considering under certain conditions the possibility of the establishment of a mandate over the Arab countries, gave Great Britain as a second choice, the United States of America being the first. This choice was also noted by the King-Crane Commission.

There would seem to be no grounds for questioning the validity of the Mandate for the reason advanced by the Arab States. The terms of the Mandate for Palestine, formulated by the Supreme Council of the Principal Allied Powers as a part of the settlement of the First World War, were subsequently approved and confirmed by the Council of the League of Nations.

The spirit which prevailed at the creation of the Mandate for Palestine was explained by Lord Balfour at the opening of the eighteenth session of the Council of the League of Nations as follows:

"The mandates are not our creation. The mandates are neither made by the League, nor can they, in substance, be altered by the League. . . .

"Remember that a mandate is a self-imposed limitation by the conquerors on the sovereignty which they obtained over conquered territories. It is imposed by the Allied and Associated Powers themselves in the interests of what they conceived to be the general welfare of mankind; and they have asked the League of Nations to assist them in seeing that this policy should be carried into effect. But the League of Nations is not the author of the policy, but its instrument. It is not they who have invented the system of mandates; it is not they who have laid down the general lines on which the three classes of mandates are framed. Their duty, let me repeat, is to see, in the first place, that the terms of the mandates conform to the principles of the Covenant, and in the second place, that these terms shall, in fact, regulate the policy of the mandatory Powers in the mandated territories.

"Now, it is clear from this statement, that both those who hope and those who fear that what, I believe, has been called the Balfour Declaration is going to suffer substantial modifications, are in error. The fears are not justified; the hopes are not justified. . . . The general lines of policy stand and must stand." . . .

[*Main Proposals:*]

General

Proposals for the solution of the Palestine question propounded at various times by official and unofficial sources during the past decade may be broadly classified as of three main categories:

(i) The partition of Palestine into two independent states, one Arab and one Jewish, which might either be completely separate or linked to the extent necessary for preserving, as far as possible, economic unity;

(ii) The establishment of a unitary State (with an Arab majority, unless a Jewish majority is created by large-scale Jewish immigration);

(iii) The establishment of a single State with a federal, cantonal or bi-national structure, in which the minority would, by such political structure, be protected from the fear of domination.

The following is a brief summary of the main proposals which have been put forward, including those advanced prior to the creation of this Committee as well as those submitted to it. . . .

[*Proposals of the Jewish Agency for Palestine*]

(a) That Palestine be established as a Jewish commonwealth integrated in the structure of the democratic world;

(b) That the gates of Palestine be opened to Jewish immigration;

(c) That the Jewish Agency be vested with the control of immigration into Palestine and the necessary authority for the upbuilding of the country. . . .

[*Proposals of the Arab States*]

(a) That Palestine should be a unitary State, with a democratic constitution and an elected legislative assembly,

(b) That the constitution should provide, *inter alia*, guarantees for (i) the sanctity of the Holy Places and, subject to suitable safeguards, freedom of religious practice in accordance with the *status quo;* (ii) full civil rights for all Palestine citizens, the naturalization requirement being ten years' continuous residence in the country; (iii) protection of religious and cultural rights of the Jewish community, such safeguards to be altered only with the consent of the majority of the Jewish members in the legislative assembly,

(c) That the constitution should provide also for (i) adequate representation in the legislative assembly of all important communities, provided that the Jews would in no case exceed one-third of the total number of members; (ii) the strict prohibition of Jewish immigration and the continuation of the existing restrictions on land transfer, any change in these matters requiring the consent of a majority of the Arab members of the legislative assembly; (iii) the establishment of a Supreme Court which would be empowered to determine whether any legislation was inconsistent with the constitution. . . .

Recapitulation

All the proposed solutions have aimed at resolving, in one manner or another, the Palestinian dilemma: the reconciliation of two diametrically opposed claims, each of which is supported by strong arguments, in a small country of limited resources, and in an atmosphere of great and increasing political and racial tension and conflicting nationalisms.

Some of the solutions advanced have been more in the nature of palliatives than solutions. Confronted with the virtual certainty that no solution could ever be devised that would fully satisfy both conflicting parties, and probably not even one party except at the expense of determined opposition by the other, arrangements have at times been suggested such as the continuation of the Mandate or the establishment of a Trusteeship, which, in the nature of the case, could be only temporary

It is not without significance that only since the rise of nazism to power in Germany, with the resultant mass movement of Jews to Palestine, has the Palestine question become sufficiently acute to require the devising of solutions outside the framework of the normal evolution of an "A" Mandate. Thus, all of the significant solutions devised for Palestine are of comparatively recent origin.

Every practicable solution today, even the most extreme, is confronted with the actual fact that there are now in Palestine more than 1,200,000 Arabs and 600,000 Jews, who, by and large, are from different cultural milieux, and whose outlook, languages, religion and aspirations are separate.

The most simple solutions, naturally enough, are the extreme solutions, by which is meant those which completely reject or ignore, or virtually so, the claims and demands of one or another party, while recognizing in full the claims of the other. The Special Committee has rejected such solutions. . . .

Following the rejection of the extreme solutions in its informal discussions, the Committee devoted its attention to the bi-national State and cantonal proposals. It considered both, but the members who may have been prepared to consider these proposals in principle were not impressed by the workability of either. It was apparent that the bi-national solution, though attractive in some of its aspects, would have little meaning unless provision were made for numerical or political parity between the two population groups, as provided for in the proposal of Dr. J. L. Magnes. This, however, would require the inauguration of complicated mechanical devices which are patently artificial and of dubious practicality.

The cantonal solution, under the existing conditions of Arab and Jewish diffusion in Palestine, might easily entail an excessive fragmentation of the governmental processes, and in its ultimate result, would be quite unworkable.

Having thus disposed of the extreme solutions and the bi-national and cantonal schemes, the members of the Committee, by and large, manifested a tendency to move toward either partition qualified by economic unity, or a federal-State plan. In due course, the Committee established two informal working groups, one on partition under a confederation arrangement and one on the federal State, for the purpose of working out the details of the two plans.   .   .   .

[Plan of Partition with Economic Union]

The basic premise underlying the partition proposal is that the claims to Palestine of the Arabs and Jews, both possessing validity, are irreconcilable, and that among all of the solutions advanced, partition will provide the most realistic and practicable settlement, and is the most likely to afford a workable basis for meeting in part the claims and national aspirations of both parties.

It is a fact that both of these peoples have their historic roots in Palestine, and that both make vital contributions to the economic and cultural life of the country. The partition solution takes these considerations fully into account.

The basic conflict in Palestine is a clash of two intense nationalisms. Regardless of the historical origins of the conflict, the rights and wrongs of the promises and counter-promises, and the international intervention incident to the Mandate, there are now in Palestine some 650,000 Jews and some 1,200,000 Arabs who are dissimilar in their ways of living and, for the time being, separated by political interests which render difficult full and effective political co-operation among them, whether voluntary or induced by constitutional arrangements.

Only by means of partition can these conflicting national aspirations find substantial expression and qualify both peoples to take their places as independent nations in the international community and in the United Nations.

The partition solution provides that finality which is a most urgent need in the solution. Every other proposed solution would tend to induce the two parties to seek modification in their favour by means of persistent pressure. The grant of independence to both States, however, would remove the basis for such efforts.

Partition is based on a realistic appraisal of the actual Arab-Jewish relations in Palestine. Full political co-operation would be indispensable to the effective functioning of any single-State scheme, such as the federal-State proposal, except in those cases which frankly envisage either an Arab or a Jewish-dominated State.

Partition is the only means available by which political and economic responsibility can be placed squarely on both Arabs and Jews, with the prospective result that, confronted with responsibility for bearing fully the consequences of their own actions, a new and important element of political amelioration would be introduced. In the proposed federal-State solution, this factor would be lacking.

Jewish immigration is the central issue in Palestine today and is the one factor, above all others, that rules out the necessary co-operation between the Arab and Jewish communities in a single State. The creation of a Jewish State under a partition scheme is the only hope of removing this issue from the arena of conflict.

It is recognized that partition has been strongly opposed by Arabs, but it is felt that that opposition would be lessened by a solution which definitively fixes the extent of territory to be allotted to the Jews with its implicit limitation on immigration. The fact that the solution carries the sanction of the United Nations involves a finality which should allay Arab fears of further expansion of the Jewish State.

In view of the limited area and resources of Palestine, it is essential that, to the extent feasible, and consistent with the creation of two independent States, the economic unity of the country should be preserved. The partition proposal, therefore, is a qualified partition, subject to such measures and limitations as are considered essential to the future economic and social well-being of both States. Since the economic self-interest of each State would be vitally involved, it is believed that the minimum measure of economic unity is possible, where that of political unity is not.

Such economic unity requires the creation of an economic association by means of a treaty between the two States. The essential objectives of this association would be a common customs system, a common currency and the maintenance of a country-wide system of transport and communications.

The maintenance of existing standards of social services in all parts of Palestine depends partly upon the preservation of economic unity, and this is a main consideration underlying the provisions for an economic union as part of the partition scheme. Partition, however, necessarily changes to some extent the fiscal situation in such a manner that, at any rate during the early years of its existence, a partitioned Arab State in Palestine would have some difficulty in raising sufficient revenue to keep up its present standards of public services.

One of the aims of the economic union, therefore, is to distribute surplus revenue to support such standards. It is recommended that the division of the surplus revenue, after certain charges and percentage of surplus to be paid to the City of Jerusalem are met, should be in equal proportions to the two States. This is an arbitrary proportion but it is considered that it would be acceptable, that it has the merit of simplicity and that, being fixed in this manner, it would be less likely to become a matter of immediate controversy. Provisions are suggested whereby this formula is to be reviewed.

This division of customs revenue is justified on three grounds: (1) The Jews will have the more economically developed part of the country embracing practically the whole of the citrus-producing area which includes a large number of Arab producers; (2) the Jewish State would, through the customs union, be guaranteed a larger free trade area for the sale of the products of its industry; (3) it would be to the disadvantage of the Jewish State if the Arab State should be in a financially precarious and poor economic condition.

As the Arab State will not be in a position to undertake considerable development expenditure, sympathetic consideration should be given to its claims for assistance from international institutions in the way of loans for expansion of education, public health and other vital social services of a non-self-supporting nature.

International financial assistance would also be required for any comprehensive irrigation schemes in the interest of both States, and it is to be hoped that constructive work by the Joint Economic Board will be made possible by means of international loans on favourable terms. . . .

The primary objectives sought . . . are, in short, political division and economic unity: to confer upon each group, Arab and Jew, in its own territory, the power to make its own laws, while preserving to both, throughout Palestine, a single integrated economy, admittedly essential to the well-being of each, and the same territorial freedom of movement to individuals as is enjoyed today. The former necessitates a territorial partition; the latter, the maintenance of unrestricted commercial relations between the States, together with a common administration of functions in which the interests of both are in fact inextricably bound together.

The territorial division with the investment of full political power in each State achieves, in turn, the desire of each for statehood and, at the same time, creates a self-operating control of immigration. Although free passage between the States for all residents is provided, each State retains exclusive authority over the acquisition of residence and this, with its control over land, will enable it to preserve the integrity of its social organization.

The Economic Union is to be administered by a Joint Economic Board, in the composition of which a parity of interest in the two States is recognized by equal representation from them. But in relation to such necessary and convenient services, day-to-day rulings are imperative; and since in the present circumstances it cannot be expected that in joint matters they would easily agree, the principle of arbitral decision is introduced by adding to the Board three independent outside persons to be chosen by the United Nations. It is obvious that, while such a device is an accepted mode of adjusting economic disputes, it would be unacceptable as a general method of making political decisions. This limits, therefore, the functions with which the Board can be clothed and confines them to such neutral services as communications or to a function which, though carrying a political quality, is dictated by the necessities of the overriding interest of unity.

In these respects the scheme may be contrasted with that of the federal State presented by three members of the Committee. In the later, paramount political power, including control over immigration, is vested at the centre; but the attempt to introduce parity through equal representation in one chamber of the legislature is nullified by the predominance of Arab majority influence in the ultimate decision. But even were an independent element to be introduced, the administration would break down because of the wide political field in which it would operate. If that field were reduced to the subjects dealt with by the Board under the Economic Union scheme, apart from the question of majority determination, the difference in substance between the two plans would lie in the failure of the federal scheme to satisfy the aspirations of both groups for independence.

The Arab State will organize the substantial majority of Arabs in Palestine into a political body containing an insignificant minority of Jews; but in the Jewish State there will be a considerable minority of Arabs. That is the demerit of the scheme. But such a minority is inevitable in any feasible plan which does not place the whole of Palestine under the present majority of the Arabs. One cannot disregard the specific purpose of the Mandate and its implications nor the existing conditions, and the safeguarding of political, civil and cultural rights provided by the scheme are as ample as can be devised.

But in the larger view, here are the sole remaining representatives of the Semitic race. They are in the land in which that race was cradled. There are no fundamental incompatibilities between them. The scheme satisfies the deepest aspiration of both: independence. There is a considerable body of opinion in both groups which seeks the course of co-operation. Despite, then, the drawback of the Arab minority, the setting is one from which, with good will and a spirit of co-operation, may arise a rebirth, in historical surroundings, of the genius of each people. The massive contribution made by them throughout the centuries in religious and ethical conceptions, in philosophy, and in the entire intellectual sphere, should excite among the leaders a mutual respect and a pride in their common origin.

The Jews bring to the land the social dynamism and scientific method of the West; the Arabs confront them with individualism and intuitive understanding of life. Here then, in this close association, through the natural emulation of each other, can be evolved a synthesis of the two civilizations, preserving, at the same time, their fundamental characteristics. In each State, the native genius will have a scope and opportunity to evolve into its highest cultural forms and to attain its greatest reaches of mind and spirit. In the case of the Jews, that is really the condition of survival. Palestine will remain one land in which Semitic ideals may pass into realization.

At the same time there is secured, through the constitutional position of Jerusalem and the Holy Places, the preservation of the scenes of events in which the sentiments of Christendom also centre. There will thus be imposed over the whole land an unobjectionable interest of the adherents of all three religions throughout the world; and so secured, this unique and historical land may at last cease to be the arena of human strife. . . .

[Minority Proposal for a Federal State]

The basic assumption underlying the views herein expressed is that the proposal of other members of the Committee for a union under artificial arrangements designed to achieve essential economic and social unity after first creating political and geographical disunity by partition, is impracticable, unworkable, and could not possibly provide for two reasonably viable States.

Two basic questions have been taken into account in appraising the feasibility of the federal-State solution, viz., (a) whether Jewish nationalism and the demand for a separate and sovereign Jewish State must be recognized at all costs, and (b) whether a will to co-operate in a federal State could be fostered among Arabs and Jews. To the first, the answer is in the negative, since the well-being of the country and its peoples as a whole is accepted as outweighing the aspirations of the Jews in this regard. To the second, the answer is in the affirmative, as there is a reasonable chance, given proper conditions, to achieve such co-operation.

It would be a tragic mistake on the part of the international community not to bend every effort in this direction. Support for the preservation of the unity of Palestine by the United Nations would in itself be an important factor in encouraging co-operation and collaboration between the two peoples, and would contribute significantly to the creation of that atmosphere in which the will to co-operate can be cultivated. In this regard, it is realized that the moral and political prestige of the United Nations is deeply involved.

The objective of a federal-State solution would be to give the most feasible recognition to the nationalistic aspirations of both Arabs and Jews, and to merge them into a single loyalty and patriotism which would find expression in an independent Palestine.

The federal State is also in every respect the most democratic solution, both as regards the measures required for its implementation and in its operation, since it requires no undemocratic economic con-

trols, avoids the creation of national minority groups, and affords an opportunity for full and effective participation in representative government to every citizen of the State. This solution would be most in harmony with the basic principles of the Charter of the United Nations.
. . .

As a condition prior to the grant of independence, the constitution of the proposed independent federal State of Palestine shall include, in substance, the following provisions:

1. The governmental structure of the independent federal State of Palestine shall be federal and shall comprise a federal Government and the governments of the Arab and Jewish states respectively.

2. Among the organs of government there shall be a head of State and an executive body, a representative federal legislative body, a federal court and such other subsidiary bodies as may be deemed necessary.

3. The federal legislative body shall be composed of two chambers.

4. Election to one chamber of the federal legislative body shall be on the basis of proportional representation of the population as a whole.

5. Election of members to the other chamber of the federal legislative body shall be on the basis of equal representation of the Arab and Jewish citizens of Palestine.

6. The federal legislative body shall be empowered to legislate on all matters entrusted to the federal Government.

7. Legislation shall be enacted when approved by majority votes in both chambers of the federal legislative body.

8. In the event of disagreement between the two chambers with regard to any proposed legislation, the issue shall be submitted to an arbitral body. That body shall be composed of one representative from each chamber of the federal legislative body, the head of State, and two members, other than members of the federal court, designated by that court for this purpose; these members shall be so designated by the court with regard to Arabs and Jews as to ensure that neither the Arab nor the Jewish community shall have less than two members on the arbitral body. This arbitral body shall first attempt to resolve the disagreement by mediation, but in the event mediation fails, the arbitral body shall be empowered to make a final decision which shall have the force of law and shall be binding.

9. The head of the independent federal State of Palestine shall be elected by a majority vote of the members of both chambers of the federal legislative body sitting in a joint meeting convened for this purpose, and shall serve for such term as the constitution may determine. . . .

NOTE. At its second session, the General Assembly established an *Ad Hoc* Committee on the Palestinian Question, under the chairmanship of Mr.

Evatt (Australia), to consider the UNSCOP report. Three sub-committees were appointed: (1) Sub-Committee 1 to draw up a detailed plan based on the majority proposals of UNSCOP; (2) Sub-Committee 2 to draw up a plan for the recognition of Palestine as an independent State in accordance with the Arab proposals; and (3) a conciliation sub-committee. The Chairman was authorized to appoint the members of the sub-committees, and he appointed to each sub-committee only those who were supporting the proposals considered by that sub-committee. GAOR, II, *Ad Hoc* C. on the Palestinian Question, pp. 136–9. Sub-Committee 1 approved the UNSCOP plan of partition with economic union, with some changes (e.g., transferring to the Arab State the city of Jaffa and some areas in the south which UNSCOP included in the Jewish State). *Idem,* pp. 242–64. This text was adopted by the *Ad Hoc* Committee by 25 votes to 13, with 17 abstentions. GAOR, *op. cit.,* p. 223. In plenary session some delegations changed their votes (Belgium, France, Haiti, Liberia, Luxembourg, Netherlands, New Zealand, Paraguay and the Philippines), and a two-thirds majority was obtained for the resolution; the final vote was 33 to 13 (Afghanistan, Cuba, Egypt, Greece, India, Iran, Iraq, Lebanon, Pakistan, Saudi Arabia, Syria, Turkey and Yemen), with 10 abstentions (Argentina, Chile, China, Colombia, El Salvador, Ethiopia, Honduras, Mexico, UK and Yugoslavia). GAOR, II, Plenary, p. 1425. For excerpts from Resolution 181 (II), see Document 2, below. Sub-Committee 2 made three proposals: on the establishment of a unitary State in Palestine, on refugees, and on reference to the International Court of Justice of certain legal questions (for text, see Document 3, below). Some of these questions raised the issue of the jurisdiction of the General Assembly to adopt the partition plan; for a discussion of these questions, see Document 4, below. A last-minute attempt by the Arab States to shift to a federal solution found little support in the Assembly. GAOR, II, Plenary, pp. 1411–13, 1417–21.

2. *Resolution 181 (II) of the General Assembly, 29 November 1947.*

GAOR, II, Resolutions (A/519), pp. 131–50. This Resolution was based on the Report of Sub-Committee 1.

The General Assembly,

Having met in special session at the request of the Mandatory Power to constitute and instruct a Special Committee to prepare for the consideration of the question of the future government of Palestine at the second regular session;

Having constituted a Special Committee and instructed it to investigate all questions and issues relevant to the problem of Palestine, and to prepare proposals for the solution of the problem; and

Having received and examined the report of the Special Committee including a number of unanimous recommendations and a plan of partition with economic union approved by the majority of the Special Committee;

Considers that the present situation in Palestine is one which is likely to impair the general welfare and friendly relations among nations;

Takes note of the declaration by the Mandatory Power that it plans to complete its evacuation of Palestine by 1 August 1948;

Recommends to the United Kingdom, as the Mandatory Power for Palestine, and to all other Members of the United Nations the adoption and implementation, with regard to the future government of Palestine, of the Plan of Partition with Economic Union set out below;

Requests that

(a) The Security Council take the necessary measures as provided for in the Plan for its implementation;

(b) The Security Council consider, if circumstances during the transitional period require such consideration, whether the situation in Palestine constitutes a threat to the peace. If it decides that such a threat exists, and in order to maintain international peace and security, the Security Council should supplement the authorization of the General Assembly by taking measures, under Articles 39 and 41 of the Charter, to empower the United Nations Commission, as provided in this resolution, to exercise in Palestine the functions which are assigned to it by this resolution;

(c) The Security Council determine as a threat to the peace, breach of the peace or act of aggression, in accordance with Article 39 of the Charter, any attempt to alter by force the settlement envisaged by this resolution;

(d) The Trusteeship Council be informed of the responsibilities envisaged for it in this Plan;

Calls upon the inhabitants of Palestine to take such steps as may be necessary on their part to put this Plan into effect;

Appeals to all Governments and all peoples to refrain from taking any action which might hamper or delay the carrying out of these recommendations.

PLAN OF PARTITION WITH ECONOMIC UNION

PART I.   FUTURE CONSTITUTION AND GOVERNMENT OF PALESTINE

A.   TERMINATION OF MANDATE, PARTITION AND INDEPENDENCE

1.   The Mandate for Palestine shall terminate as soon as possible but in any case not later than 1 August 1948.

2.   The armed forces of the Mandatory Power shall be progressively withdrawn from Palestine, the withdrawal to be completed as soon as possible but in any case not later than 1 August 1948. . . .

The Mandatory Power shall use its best endeavours to ensure that an area situated in the territory of the Jewish State, including a seaport and hinterland adequate to provide facilities for a substantial immigration, shall be evacuated at the earliest possible date and in any event not later than 1 February 1948.

3.   Independent Arab and Jewish States and the Special International Regime for the City of Jerusalem, set forth in Part III of this Plan, shall come into existence in Palestine two months after the evacuation of the armed forces of the Mandatory Power has been completed but in any case not later than 1 October 1948.   .   .   .

B.   STEPS PREPARATORY TO INDEPENDENCE

1.   A Commission shall be set up consisting of one representative of each of five Member States. The Members represented on the Commission shall be elected by the General Assembly on as broad a basis, geographically and otherwise, as possible.

2.   The administration of Palestine shall, as the Mandatory Power withdraws its armed forces, be progressively turned over to the Commission, which shall act in conformity with the recommendations of the General Assembly under the guidance of the Security Council. The Mandatory Power shall to the fullest possible extent co-ordinate its plans for withdrawal with the plans of the Commission to take over and administer areas which have been evacuated.

In the discharge of this administrative responsibility the Commission shall have authority to issue necessary regulations and take other measures as required.

The Mandatory Power shall not take any action to prevent, obstruct or delay the implementation by the Commission of the measures recommended by the General Assembly.

3.   On its arrival in Palestine the Commission shall proceed to carry out measures for the establishment of the frontiers of the Arab and Jewish States and the City of Jerusalem in accordance with the general lines of the recommendations of the General Assembly on the partition of Palestine.   .   .   .

4.   The Commission, after consultation with the democratic parties and other public organizations of the Arab and Jewish States, shall select and establish in each State as rapidly as possible a Provisional Council of Government. The activities of both the Arab and Jewish Provisional Councils of Government shall be carried out under the general direction of the Commission.

If by 1 April 1948 a Provisional Council of Government cannot be selected for either of the States, or, if selected, cannot carry out its functions, the Commission shall communicate that fact to the Security Council for such action with respect to that State as the Security Council may deem proper, and to the Secretary-General for communication to the Members of the United Nations.

5.   Subject to the provisions of these recommendations, during the transitional period the Provisional Councils of Government, acting under the Commission, shall have full authority in the areas under their control, including authority over matters of immigration and land regulation.

6. The Provisional Council of Government of each State, acting under the Commission, shall progressively receive from the Commission full responsibility for the administration of that State in the period between the termination of the Mandate and the establishment of the State's independence. . . .

8. The Provisional Council of Government of each State shall, within the shortest time possible, recruit an armed militia from the residents of that State, sufficient in number to maintain internal order and to prevent frontier clashes.

This armed militia in each State shall, for operational purposes, be under the command of Jewish or Arab officers resident in that State, but general political and military control, including the choice of the militia's High Command, shall be exercised by the Commission.

9. The Provisional Council of Government of each State shall, not later than two months after the withdrawal of the armed forces of the Mandatory Power, hold elections to the Constituent Assembly which shall be conducted on democratic lines. . . .

10. The Constituent Assembly of each State shall draft a democratic Constitution for its State and choose a provisional government to succeed the Provisional Council of Government appointed by the Commission. The Constitutions of the States shall . . . include *inter alia* provisions for:

(a) Establishing in each State a legislative body elected by universal suffrage and by secret ballot on the basis of proportional representation, and an executive body responsible to the legislature.

(b) Settling all international disputes in which the State may be involved by peaceful means in such a manner that international peace and security, and justice, are not endangered.

(c) Accepting the obligation of the State to refrain in its international relations from the threat or use of force against the territorial integrity or political independence of any State, or in any other manner inconsistent with the purposes of the United Nations.

(d) Guaranteeing to all persons equal and non-discriminatory rights in civil, political, economic and religious matters and the enjoyment of human rights and fundamental freedoms, including freedom of religion, language, speech and publication, education, assembly and association.

(e) Preserving freedom of transit and visit for all residents and citizens of the other State in Palestine and the City of Jerusalem, subject to considerations of national security, provided that each State shall control residence within its borders. . . .

12. During the period between the adoption of the recommendations on the question of Palestine by the General Assembly and the termination of the Mandate, the Mandatory Power in Palestine shall maintain full responsibility for administration in areas from which it

has not withdrawn its armed forces. The Commission shall assist the Mandatory Power in the carrying out of these functions. Similarly the Mandatory Power shall co-operate with the Commission in the execution of its functions.

13.　With a view to ensuring that there shall be continuity in the functioning of administrative services and that, on the withdrawal of the armed forces of the Mandatory Power, the whole administration shall be in the charge of the Provisional Councils and the Joint Economic Board, respectively, acting under the Commission, there shall be a progressive transfer, from the Mandatory Power to the Commission, of responsibility for all the functions of government, including that of maintaining law and order in the areas from which the forces of the Mandatory Power have been withdrawn.

14.　The Commission shall be guided in its activities by the recommendations of the General Assembly and by such instructions as the Security Council may consider necessary to issue.

The measures taken by the Commission, within the recommendations of the General Assembly, shall become immediately effective unless the Commission has previously received contrary instructions from the Security Council.　.　.　.

PART III.　CITY OF JERUSALEM　.　.　.

The City of Jerusalem shall be established as a *corpus separatum* under a Special International Regime and shall be administered by the United Nations. The Trusteeship Council shall be designated to discharge the responsibilities of the Administering Authority on behalf of the United Nations.　.　.　.

The Trusteeship Council shall, within five months from the approval of the present plan, elaborate and approve a detailed Statute of the City which shall contain *inter alia* the substance of the following provisions:

1.　*Government machinery: Special objectives.*

The Administering Authority in discharging its administrative obligations shall pursue the following special objectives:

(a) To protect and to preserve the unique spiritual and religious interests located in the City of the three great monotheistic faiths throughout the world, Christian, Jewish and Moslem; to this end to ensure that order and peace, and especially religious peace, reign in Jerusalem.

(b) To foster co-operation among all the inhabitants of the City in their own interests as well as in order to encourage and support the peaceful development of the mutual relations between the two Palestinian peoples throughout the Holy Land; to promote the security, well-being and any constructive measures of development of the residents, having regard to the special circumstances and customs of the various peoples and communities.

2. Governor and administrative staff.

A Governor of the City of Jerusalem shall be appointed by the Trusteeship Council and shall be responsible to it. He shall be selected on the basis of special qualifications and without regard to nationality. He shall not, however, be a citizen of either State in Palestine.

The Governor shall represent the United Nations in the City and shall exercise on their behalf all powers of administration, including the conduct of external affairs. He shall be assisted by an administrative staff classed as international officers in the meaning of Article 100 of the Charter and chosen whenever practicable from the residents of the City and of the rest of Palestine on a non-discriminatory basis. A detailed plan for the organization of the administration of the City shall be submitted by the Governor to the Trusteeship Council and duly approved by it.

3. Local autonomy.

(a) The existing local autonomous units in the territory of the City (villages, townships and municipalities) shall enjoy wide powers of local government and administration.

(b) The Governor shall study and submit for the consideration and decision of the Trusteeship Council a plan for the establishment of special town units consisting, respectively, of the Jewish and Arab sections of new Jerusalem. The new town units shall continue to form part of the present municipality of Jerusalem.

4. Security measures.

(a) The City of Jerusalem shall be demilitarized; its neutrality shall be declared and preserved, and no para-military formations, exercises or activities shall be permitted within its borders.

(b) Should the administration of the City of Jerusalem be seriously obstructed or prevented by the non-co-operation or interference of one or more sections of the population, the Governor shall have authority to take such measures as may be necessary to restore the effective functioning of the administration.

(c) To assist in the maintenance of internal law and order and especially for the protection of the Holy Places and religious buildings and sites in the City, the Governor shall organize a special police force of adequate strength, the members of which shall be recruited outside of Palestine. The Governor shall be empowered to direct such budgetary provision as may be necessary for the maintenance of this force.

3. *Draft Resolution Proposing the Reference of Certain Legal Questions to the International Court of Justice.*

Proposal of Sub-Committee 2, of 11 November 1947, which was rejected by *Ad Hoc* Committee on the Palestinian Question. A/AC.14/32; GAOR, II, *Ad Hoc* C. on the Palestinian Question, pp. 299–301.

The General Assembly,

Considering that the Palestine question raises certain legal issues connected, *inter alia,* with the inherent right of the indigenous population of Palestine to their country and to determine its future, the pledges and assurances given to the Arabs in the First World War regarding the independence of Arab countries, including Palestine, the validity and scope of the Balfour Declaration and the Mandate, the effect on the Mandate of the dissolution of the League of Nations and of the declaration by the Mandatory Power of its intentions to withdraw from Palestine,

Considering that the Palestine question also raises other legal issues connected with the competence of the United Nations to recommend any solution contrary to the Covenant of the League of Nations or the Charter of the United Nations, or to the wishes of the majority of the people of Palestine,

Considering that doubts have been expressed by several member states concerning the legality under the Charter of any action by the United Nations, or by any member state or group of member states, to enforce any proposal which is contrary to the wishes, or is made without the consent, of the majority of the inhabitants of Palestine,

Considering that these questions involve legal issues which so far have not been pronounced upon by any impartial or competent tribunal, and it is essential that such questions be authoritatively determined before the United Nations can recommend a solution of the Palestine question in conformity with the principles of justice and international law,

Resolves to request the International Court of Justice to give an advisory opinion under Article 96 of the Charter and Chapter IV of the Statute of the Court on the following questions:

(*a*) Whether the indigenous population of Palestine has not an inherent right to Palestine and to determine its future constitution and government;

(*b*) Whether the pledges and assurances given by Great Britain to the Arabs during the First World War (including the Anglo-French Declaration of 1918) concerning the independence and future of Arab countries at the end of the war did not include Palestine;

(*c*) Whether the Balfour Declaration, which was made without the knowledge or consent of the indigenous population of Palestine, was valid and binding on the people of Palestine, or consistent with the earlier and subsequent pledges and assurances given to the Arabs;

(*d*) Whether the provisions of the Mandate for Palestine regarding the establishment of a Jewish National Home in Palestine are in conformity or consistent with the objectives and provisions of the Covenant of the League of Nations (in particular Article 22), or are compatible with the provisions of the Mandate relating to the development of self-government and the preservation of the rights and position of the Arabs of Palestine;

(*e*) Whether the legal basis for the Mandate for Palestine has not disappeared with the dissolution of the League of Nations, and whether it is not the duty of the Mandatory Power to hand over power and administration to a Government of Palestine representing the rightful people of Palestine;

(*f*) Whether a plan to partition Palestine without the consent of the majority of its people is consistent with the objectives of the Covenant of the League of Nations, and with the provisions of the Mandate for Palestine;

(*g*) Whether the United Nations is competent to recommend either of the two plans and recommendations of the majority or minority of the United Nations Special Committee on Palestine, or any other solution involving partition of the territory of Palestine, or a permanent trusteeship over any city or part of Palestine, without the consent of the majority of the people of Palestine;

(*h*) Whether the United Nations, or any of its Member States, is competent to enforce or recommend the enforcement of any proposal concerning the constitution and future Government of Palestine, in particular, any plan of partition which is contrary to the wishes, or adopted without the consent of, the inhabitants of Palestine,

Instructs the Secretary-General to transmit this resolution to the International Court of Justice, accompanied by all documents likely to throw light upon the questions under reference.

4. *Discussion in the Ad Hoc Committee on the Palestinian Question, 20–24 November 1947*

GAOR, II, *Ad Hoc* C. on the Palestinian Question, pp. 5–10, 153–96.

Mr. HUSSEINI (Arab Higher Committee) [stated that the] case of the Arabs of Palestine was based on the principles of international justice; it was that of a people which desired to live in undisturbed possession of the country where Providence and history had placed it. The Arabs of Palestine could not understand why their right to live in freedom and peace, and to develop their country in accordance with their traditions, should be questioned and constantly submitted to investigation.

One thing was clear: it was the sacred duty of the Arabs of Palestine to defend their country against all aggression. The Zionists were conducting an aggressive campaign with the object of securing by force a country which was not theirs by birthright. Thus there was self-defence on one side and, on the other, aggression. The *raison d'être* of the United Nations was to assist self-defence against aggression. . . .

The solution lay in the Charter of the United Nations, in accordance with which the Arabs of Palestine, who constituted the majority, were entitled to a free and independent State. Mr. Husseini welcomed the recent declaration by the representative of the United Kingdom that the Mandate should be terminated and its termination followed by independence, and expressed the hope that the British Government would not on that occasion, as in the past, reverse its decision under Zionist pressure.

Regarding the manner and form of independence for Palestine, it was the view of the Arab Higher Committee that that was a matter for the rightful owners of Palestine to decide. Once Palestine was found to be entitled to independence, the United Nations was not legally competent to decide or to impose the constitutional organization of Palestine, since such action would amount to interference with an internal matter of an independent nation. . . .

In conclusion, Mr. Husseini said that he had not commented on the Special Committee's report because the Arab Higher Committee considered that it could not be a basis for discussion. Both schemes proposed in the report were inconsistent with the United Nations Charter and with the Covenant [of the] League of Nations. The Arabs of Palestine were solidly determined to oppose with all the means at their command any scheme which provided for the dissection, segregation or partition of their country or which gave to a minority special and preferential rights or status. Although they fully realized that big Powers could crush such opposition by brute force, the Arabs nevertheless would not be deterred, but would lawfully defend with their life-blood every inch of the soil of their beloved country. . . .

Sir Alexander CADOGAN (UK) regretted that no progress had been possible in the direction of conciliation between the two peoples most directly concerned with the future of Palestine. The absence of that conciliation created exceptional difficulty, since it could hardly be imagined that the proposals of Sub-Committee 1 should be acceptable to the Arab population, or that the proposals of Sub-Committee 2 would be acceptable to the Jewish population of Palestine.

It had been the hope of the United Kingdom Government that the United Nations would be able to find a solution which the United Kingdom had failed to find. Without entering into a discussion of the merits of the proposals made by the two Sub-Committees, Sir

Alexander desired to refer to the part assigned to his Government in the implementation of those proposals. . . .

The United Kingdom . . . could not play a major part in the implementation of a scheme which was not acceptable to both Arabs and Jews, but it would not wish to impede the implementation of a recommendation of the General Assembly. The United Kingdom Government had assumed that the General Assembly would take full account of the risk of strife in Palestine and of the need to provide means of filling the gap left by the decision of the Mandatory Power that its troops should not be used to enforce the decision of the United Nations. . . .

[T]he Sub-Committee proposed that the administration of Palestine during the transitional period should be entrusted to a United Nations commission. No better way could be found of creating confusion and disorder in Palestine than by the establishment of an authority which would operate concurrently with the existing mandatory administration. It must be made clear that the United Kingdom Government would insist upon its undivided control of Palestine as long as it continued to hold the Mandate.

In determining the date on which it would relinquish the Mandate, the United Kingdom Government would give proper consideration to any arrangements which might have been made by the United Nations for the establishment of a provisional regime to succeed the Mandate. There was, however, no reason to suggest that it must await the approval of the Security Council before relinquishing the Mandate. . . .

The United Kingdom Government would not participate in any scheme which was not acceptable to both Arabs and Jews. If a scheme of partition were approved and a United Nations commission set up, the Palestine Government would, when the time came, hand over its authority to that commission. The commission could, if it desired, transfer its authority to local bodies.

The British authorities would do everything possible to expedite the withdrawal of any British troops which might remain after authority had been relinquished to the United Nations commission. In the event of any attempt being made to interfere with or delay that withdrawal, it might prove necessary for those troops to take action for the maintenance of order. Those were the only circumstances in which they could be used. . . .

The United Kingdom Government would announce in due course a date upon which the British civil administration would be considered at an end. After that date, apart from the British authorities who would be exercising strictly limited functions in certain areas, there would be no regularly constituted authority. If the Committee were able to recommend a way in which the gap thus created could be filled, it should be possible without great difficulty to make arrangements consequent upon the subsequent stages of British military withdrawal from Palestine. . . .

Mr. PRUSZYNSKI (Poland), speaking as Chairman of Sub-Committee 1, stated that that Sub-Committee's report had been amended in the light of the statement made by the representative of the United Kingdom. . . . He proposed to reply to the questions submitted in writing by various representatives in connexion with the plan of Sub-Committee 1. . . . He thought the first two questions asked by the representative of Pakistan, were closely connected and should be answered together. Those questions were first, what Articles of the Charter gave the General Assembly and the Security Council the right to exercise all the powers which the plan conferred upon those organs and, secondly, from what source the United Nations commission would receive the power to exercise executive, legislative and administrative functions.

Mr. Pruszynski indicated what he thought to be the legal basis of the plan proposed by Sub-Committee 1; in his view, however, the powers the commission needed were not as wide as suggested by the second question.

The situation was that the Mandatory Power had notified its decision to terminate the Mandate and to withdraw from Palestine. It had requested the General Assembly to make recommendations for the future government of the country. It had, however, made it clear that it did not wish to participate in the implementation of a solution which did not meet with the approval of both Jews and Arabs. Neither of the plans submitted satisfied that condition and it was highly improbable that such a plan could be drawn up. Since the United Kingdom had stated that it was prepared to transfer its powers only to an organ of the United Nations, the United Nations was obliged to establish such an organ.

The commission contemplated in the plan of Sub-Committee 1 was not to act as the government of Palestine but solely as the body through whose agency the administration of the country would be transferred to the provisional councils of government, which would exercise authority until a permanent government was set up. The commission would have to see that the General Assembly's recommendations were implemented by the provisional councils.

With regard to the General Assembly's right to make recommendations, Mr. Pruszynski cited the report of Committee II of the San Francisco Conference, where it was stated that the General Assembly would have power to discuss any question within the scope of the Charter and to make recommendations to the Security Council and Member States. That power included the right to recommend measures for the pacific settlement of any dispute which might endanger the general welfare or friendly relations between States. The official records of the debates of Committee II confirmed the fact that the authors of the Charter intended that the General Assembly should have very wide powers of recommendation. Consequently, if in the General Assembly's opinion partition of Palestine and the establishment of two independent States was the best solution of the problem, the General Assembly could make a recommendation to the Mandatory Power and to the Members of the United Nations in that sense.

Obviously, the General Assembly should exercise that power in conformity with the principles of Chapter I of the Charter. The General Assembly's decision would be based on the principles of justice and international law, the equality of rights of peoples and their right to self-determination. Such a recommendation would not be contrary to the principle of the sovereignty of States or of respect for the territorial integrity or political independence of States because, in international law, Palestine could not be considered as a State.

The General Assembly's competence to examine the Palestinian question was based on Articles 10 and 14 of the Charter.

The United Kingdom, when it had approached the Assembly, had considered that that body could make recommendations on the future government of Palestine under Article 10 of the Charter according to which the Assembly could discuss any question within the scope of the Charter and make recommendations to Members of the United Nations or to the Security Council. The only questions excluded were those under examination by the Security Council or outside the scope of the Charter. The question to be decided was essentially that of the future government of a territory whose population was not yet self-governing. The fact that that question was within the competence of the United Nations was amply demonstrated by the declaration of the purposes of the United Nations contained in Article 1 of the Charter; it was also demonstrated by the declaration regarding non-self-governing territories contained in Chapter XI and by the provisions of Chapter XII concerning the international trusteeship system, particularly Articles 77 and 79, which laid down the procedure to be followed for placing mandated territories under United Nations trusteeship. Those Articles had been included in the Charter for the purpose of emphasizing that the United Nations should assume the responsibilities of the League of Nations in respect of peoples who had not yet become independent.

Article 14 of the Charter could also be considered relevant to the situation in Palestine, and the General Assembly could make recommendations by virtue of that Article.

To sum up, the problem of the future of Palestine was a question which came within the scope of the Charter; consequently the General Assembly, under Articles 10 and 14 of the Charter, could discuss that question and make such recommendations as it deemed suitable.

The power of the Security Council to make recommendations in the event that one of the parties refused to organize a provisional council

of government . . . was based on Article 34, by virtue of
which the Security Council could investigate any situation which
might lead to international friction. The right of the Security Council to give instructions to the United Nations commission . . .
was based on sub-paragraph (a) of the seventh paragraph of the Sub-
Committee's draft resolution, which provided that the General Assembly should request the Security Council to take the necessary measures for the implementation of the plan; it was also based on Article
10 of the Charter. . . .

Mr. Pruszynski turned next to the third question, namely, whether
the Sub-Committee had examined the other questions of a legal nature raised by the representatives of the Arab States and, if so, what
its conclusions were. He replied that the question had not been examined, but that it was impossible to dispute the validity of the Mandate
conferred by the League of Nations and confirmed by the terms of
Article 80 of the Charter. Although the functions of the League of
Nations had come to an end, that did not mean that all control was
thereby abolished. That responsibility now rested with the United
Nations.

The fourth question was whether the Sub-Committee had considered the question of aid to Jewish refugees and displaced persons and,
if so, what its conclusions were. Mr. Pruszynski pointed out that the
question had been considered from one standpoint only, namely, how
to establish a Jewish State and solve the Palestine problem. . . .

With regard to the fifth question, namely, whether the Sub-Committee had considered the question of the viability of the two proposed
States, Mr. Pruszynski said that the Sub-Committee had accepted the
conclusions contained in the report of the Special Committee.

The sixth question was what principles the Sub-Committee had
taken as a basis in determining the proposed boundaries and whether
those principles had been applied impartially to the proposed Arab
and Jewish States. Mr. Pruszynski replied that the Sub-Committee
had given equal consideration to Arab and to Jewish interests. Moreover, if the Arab State found itself in a difficult situation, the repercussions would be felt in the Jewish State too. It was impossible to
establish boundaries which would be absolutely equitable. The dominant consideration in mapping the boundaries had been to establish
two national States containing as few minorities as possible. That
was why the Sub-Committee had altered the boundaries proposed by
the Special Committee and had included the city of Jaffa in the Arab
State, thus reducing the Arab minority by 80,000.

The seventh question bore on the numbers of Arab and Jewish inhabitants in the proposed Jewish State and in each of its sub-districts.
Mr. Pruszynski stated that the sub-districts were of no great importance in themselves; but according to the figures given in the
report of the Special Committee [it] had been estimated on the basis

of official figures up to the end of 1946, [that] there would be 498,000 Jews and 327,000 non-Jews, Arabs or others in the Jewish State contemplated by the Sub-Committee.

In reply to the eighth question, namely whether the Palestinian Bedouin had been included in the Sub-Committee's estimate of the population, and whether those Bedouin would be citizens of the Jewish or of the Arab State, Mr. Pruszynski stated that purely nomadic tribes had not been included. He believed the nomad question would decrease in importance as civilization developed in that area.

The ninth question concerned the considerations which had induced the Sub-Committee to include in the Jewish State land belonging to 54 villages in the Arab State. Mr. Pruszynski pointed out that the question was very complex. It should be noted nevertheless that although the boundary line cut through the land of 54 villages, it followed the boundaries of 450 others. It appeared impossible to map boundaries without cutting through the lands of some villages. The plan of the Special Committee envisaged the division of 37 villages. Other villages had been divided for special reasons, such as, for example, the construction of a reservoir in the common interests of both communities. In all countries, land sometimes had to be expropriated. Generally speaking, however, it was only a small proportion of the land belonging to a given village that would have to be cut off. The Jewish Agency had given the Sub-Committee an assurance that not only would the right of transit be observed, but also that Arabs would not have to pay higher taxes on land in the Jewish State than they would in the Arab State.

The tenth question concerned the means whereby the Sub-Committee's recommendations would be put into effect in the event that the Arabs resident in the area of the proposed Arab State refused to co-operate in the establishment of that State, and the forces which would be used to maintain order in that area. Would the militia of the Jewish State be used for that purpose? Mr. Pruszynski stated in reply that he believed the Arab population to be mature enough to take part in the establishment of an independent State even though that State did not have the frontiers that the Arabs might desire. However, if the United Nations commission were obliged itself to set up a government, it would appeal to the Security Council, which would have the duty of taking steps to maintain order and security. There was absolutely no question of using the Jewish militia to maintain order in the Arab State.

In reply to the eleventh question, concerning the meaning of the word "militia" and the responsibilities which the United Nations would incur if it established and armed the proposed militias, Mr. Pruszynski pointed out that according to the dictionary, a militia was an armed force raised from among the people. It was something half-way between a police force and an army. The word presented no ambiguity.

The twelfth question concerned the possible right of appeal against decisions of the governor of Jerusalem with respect to disagreements concerning religious and other rights in the Holy Places. Mr. Pruszynski stated that the governor would be responsible to the Trusteeship Council, to which an appeal could be made. The exact terms of the statute had not been studied. Since the City of Jerusalem would be under the authority of the United Nations, provisions could be drawn up to meet the wishes of Member States.

In reply to the thirteenth question, namely, what measures the Sub-Committee proposed for dealing with the deadlock which would arise if the General Assembly and the Security Council could not agree on the functions of the United Nations commission, Mr. Pruszynski said that there was no reason to anticipate a deadlock. Should the situation demand it, the commission would refer the matter to the Security Council.

Mr. JAMALI (Iraq) did not wish to insist on legal issues. . . . He would point out, however, that the General Assembly had power only to discuss a question and make a recommendation concerning it, whereas the action which was being proposed was of a much weightier character.

The problem under discussion could not be dealt with under Article 14 of the Charter, since what was being proposed was not the peaceful adjustment of a situation but the imposition by force of a settlement contrary to the wishes of the people concerned. In view of the stand taken by the Arabs, it was shirking the issue to speak of peaceful settlement. The Arab population would fight for its independence. Sub-Committee 1 proposed that a large number of Arabs should become citizens of a Jewish State. The Arab community, like any other living organism, would take steps to defend its rights. If the General Assembly adopted the plan for partition, it would have to use force to carry it out. The United Kingdom representative had stated that his country was not prepared to furnish troops; if the United Nations felt that a solution must be imposed by force, it must decide what means were to be employed and what armed forces were to be organized. . . .

Mr. [H. V.] JOHNSON (USA) expressed agreement with the statement made by the Chairman of Sub-Committee 1 that the plan presented by the Sub-Committee was legal under the Charter. There was nothing in the Charter which prevented an immediate transition from a Class A mandate to independence. Under the proposals of Sub-Committee 1, the work of the United Nations would be of short duration, with the exception of its supervision of Jerusalem. The role of the United Nations would be to assist in the actual transfer of authority from the Mandatory Power to the independent States. In practice, the United Nations commission, while retaining the responsibility, would have to transfer the practical duties of administration immediately to the provisional councils of government. It was not contemplated that there would be a gap during which there would be no effective governmental authority.

A most difficult situation had been created by the declaration of the Mandatory Power that it could not take part in the implementation of a plan which did not have the approval of the two peoples of Palestine, a condition impossible of fulfilment. He could not agree with the statement of the representative of New Zealand that the Mandatory Power was being given the sole responsibility for implementation. The members of Sub-Committee 1 . . . had endeavoured to avoid that situation. They had been assured that the Mandatory Power would not prevent the carrying out of the implementation programme.

The Mandatory Power had requested the United Nations to make recommendations for the future government of Palestine and had unilaterally declared that it was relinquishing its responsibility. Hence any legal objections to the action of the General Assembly must be formal in character. The United States delegation would support the proposals of Sub-Committee 1 which, in its view, met the request of the Mandatory Power.

In formulating proposals for the implementation of the majority plan contained in the report of the Special Committee, members of Sub-Committee 1 had reached unanimity on every point. It was the earnest hope of the United States delegation that a large majority of the Members of the United Nations would approve the plan of the Sub-Committee and co-operate in its implementation. The plan was sufficiently flexible to afford adjustment to any situation which might confront the commission or the joint economic board in Palestine. It offered protection for the Holy Places and religious interests of the three great religions.

The United Nations was the proper forum for the solution of the Palestine problem. Those Governments which supported partition, realizing its imperfections but nevertheless believing in its justice and workability, would contribute to the solution of one of the most difficult political problems in the world. In the view of the United States delegation, no Member of the United Nations would attempt to defy the decision of the United Nations. In that sense, the greatest test of its integrity was being offered to the United Nations. . . .

Mr. TSARAPKIN (USSR) recalled that the situation in Palestine and the unsatisfactory manner in which the Mandate had been carried out had often disturbed world public opinion. . . .

Finally, in February 1947, Mr. Bevin, the United Kingdom Foreign Secretary, had been obliged to admit that the terms of the Mandate could not be carried out in practice and that the undertakings given to the Arabs and the Jews were incompatible. That was undoubtedly the reason why the United Kingdom Government had requested the United Nations to find a solution to the problem.   .   .   .

The intention of the United Kingdom not to co-operate in carrying out a plan recommended by the General Assembly unless both parties agreed would give those who wished to prevent the execution of such a plan an opportunity to obstruct a just and impartial solution proposed by the General Assembly.

That was why the USSR delegation considered the attitude of the United Kingdom to be bad, harmful, fraught with danger and obstructive to action by the United Nations. If that was its position, the United Kingdom had had no need to submit the matter to the United Nations; it could merely have suggested to the Arabs and the Jews that they should draw up an agreement themselves. The Government of the United Kingdom asked the United Nations to take steps to solve the Palestinian question, and in the same breath made reservations which rendered its request meaningless. Such an attitude could not be regarded as normal or compatible with the principles of international co-operation which the United Kingdom delegation was so fond of invoking.

In the opinion of the USSR Government, a Member of the United Nations which really desired to see the Palestinian question settled justly and quickly should accept the necessary responsibilities unconditionally. The Mandatory Power, more than any other, was under an obligation to carry out the decision adopted by the United Nations and to take action required to enforce it. The statements made by the United Kingdom delegation must therefore be rejected as contrary to the obligations assumed by the Mandatory Power, which was a Member of the United Nations.   .   .   .

Mr. Tsarapkin dealt with the question of the Assembly's powers in regard to the solution of the Palestinian problem. It was surprising and deplorable that those powers should have been called in question. Neither the United Kingdom when it had made its request to the United Nations, nor the representatives who had attended the special session of the Assembly, nor the members of the Special Committee had had any doubts on that score. Such doubts as were being expressed in the *Ad Hoc* Committee were completely unjustified, because Article 10 of the Charter gave the General Assembly the right and the duty to discuss the Palestinian question. It was in complete accordance with the provisions of Article 10 that the special session had been called, the Special Committee established and the Palestinian question considered by the General Assembly. Any recommendations which the Assembly made would have sound juridical foundations.

The doubts expressed by certain States were based not on legal but on political grounds. In particular, the Mandatory Power was attempting to avoid its responsibilities in the matter of Palestine and any co-operation in solving the problem, despite the moral and political obligations of a Mandatory Power conscious of its responsibilities.

With regard to the two plans, the delegation of the USSR was in favour of the plan drawn up by Sub-Committee 1 on the basis of the majority plan contained in chapter VI of the report of the Special Committee, for that plan gave both the Arab and the Jewish people an opportunity to organize their national life as they desired. It was based on the principles of the equality of peoples and the right of self-determination, principles on which the USSR had based its domestic policy and on which it was in duty bound to base its international policy. . . .

Mr. CHAMOUN (Lebanon) . . . expressed agreement with the view that the United Nations was attempting to make a decision for which it had no sovereign powers, and without consultation of the will of the people concerned. A United Nations commission should go to Palestine for the purpose of conducting a referendum there, not to set up the machinery of government against the will of the people.

Statements had been made in the Committee that it was within the legal competence of the General Assembly to delegate powers to the proposed commission, but no member had indicated the Article or principle of the Charter from which the General Assembly had derived its power. Article 10 of the Charter stated merely that the General Assembly could make recommendations to the Members of the United Nations, and Article 14 merely gave it the right to take certain limited measures for the peaceful adjustment of any situation. But it was not empowered to take substantive measures which would bind the future of a nation.

Under Articles 10, 12 and 14 of the Charter, the General Assembly could make recommendations to the United Kingdom concerning the future government of Palestine. But the powers which Sub-Committee 1 proposed for the United Nations commission were a violation of the Charter. The United Kingdom had drawn attention to risks in the plan. In reply, it had been stated that in practice the commission would not physically carry out its powers, but would act as a repository for the powers of the Mandate. Quoting the proposed functions of the commission from the Sub-Committee's report, Mr. Chamoun pointed out that the commission would have complete administrative authority, including the control of immigration and land regulations, in Palestine. . . .

Mr. Chamoun challenged the argument that because the Arabs had attained sufficient political maturity, they would not rebel against a decision of the United Nations. It was not a sign of political immaturity if a people, after appealing to the principles of the Charter and to every sentiment of justice and equity, and after being denied the right to self-determination, rebelled against that denial. It was useless to state that no Member nation would challenge a decision of the United Nations when the decision itself flouted the Charter.

There was no justification for partition against the will of a people. It would have to be imposed by force. Mr. Chamoun asked how partition would be implemented when it was well known that the majority of the inhabitants of Palestine would never accept it. He quoted from the report of the King-Crane Commission, which had stated that partition against the will of the overwhelming majority in Palestine would be devoid of juridical and ethical bases, even if imposed by force. The people of Palestine would have the right to rebel against a decision of the United Nations which was devoid of legal foundation in the Charter and devoid of moral foundation in divine and human law.

[When the Committee took a vote on the Arab draft resolution (Document 3, above), sub-paragraphs i–vii were rejected by 25 votes to 18, with 11 abstentions; paragraph viii, relating to the competence of the United Nations to enforce the partition plan, was rejected by 21 votes to 20, with 13 abstentions. GAOR, II, *Ad Hoc* C. on the Palestinian Question, p. 203. No request was made, therefore, for an advisory opinion of the Court on this subject.]

NOTE. Resolution 181 (II) was brought to the attention of the Security Council in December 1947, but the Council refused to take any action on it at that time. SCOR, II, No. 106, pp. 2776–89. The United Nations Palestine Commission was confronted with the refusal of the Mandatory Power to let the Commission come to Palestine and the accelerated collapse of law and order in Palestine, and on 16 February 1948 it asked the Security Council to provide it with an adequate non-Palestinian military force. SCOR, III, Spec. Supp. 2, pp. 10–19.

5. *Discussion in the Security Council, 24 February 1948.*

SCOR, III, Nos. 16–35, pp. 264–92.

Mr. AUSTIN (USA): The Security Council is now confronted with the complex problem of Palestine as presented to us in General Assembly resolution 181 (II) of 29 November 1947 and the two reports from the Palestine Commission. .   .   .

While we are discussing the problem of Palestine, it is of primary importance to the future of the United Nations that the precedent to be established by the action taken in this case should be in full accord with the terms of the Charter under which we operate. The interpretation of the terms of the Charter given in the Palestine issue will seriously affect the future actions of the United Nations in other cases.

Let us now turn to the first and most important document before us, namely, the General Assembly resolution of 29 November 1947. The recommendations of the General Assembly have great moral force which applies to all Members, regardless of the views they hold or the votes they may have cast on any particular recommendation. Similarly, the Security Council, although not bound under the Charter to accept and carry out General Assembly recommendations, is nevertheless expected to give great weight to them.

Attempts to frustrate the General Assembly's recommendation by the threat or use of force, or by incitement to force, on the part of States or people outside Palestine, are contrary to the Charter. Members of the Council may recall that when the representative of the United States expressed the views of my Government to the General Assembly on the Palestine question on 11 October 1947, he said:

"We assumed that there would be Charter observance. The life of this Union depends upon obedience to the law. If any Member should violate its obligations to refrain in its international relations from the threat or use of force, the Security Council itself must act."

The resolution of the General Assembly makes three separate requests of the Security Council. The first is that the Security Council "take the necessary measures as provided for in the plan for its implementation". To determine what these measures are, it is necessary to turn to the plan itself. It will be seen that these are: To give guidance to the Palestine Commission; to take such action as the Security Council may deem proper with respect to either the Jewish or the Arab State if by 1 April 1948 a provisional council of government cannot be selected for that State, or, if selected, cannot carry out its functions; to issue such instructions to the Commission as the Security Council may consider necessary; to receive and consider periodic progress reports, special reports and the final report of the Palestine Commission; to give sympathetic consideration to the application for membership in the United Nations made by either the Arab or the Jewish State when a certain stage in the plan has been achieved.

We believe it is clear that the Security Council can undertake the above-mentioned measures. It is further clear from the terms of the resolution of 29 November 1947 that the Palestine Commission is bound by whatever instructions the Security Council gives to it pursuant to the General Assembly's requests.

We come now to the two following requests of the General Assembly as set forth in the resolution of 29 November. These invoke the wide peace-keeping powers of the Security Council under the Charter. The second request in the resolution asks the Security Council to consider whether " . . . during the transitional period . . . the situation in Palestine constitutes a threat to the peace".

The third request of the General Assembly asks that the Security Council "determine as a threat to the peace, breach of the peace or act of aggression, in accordance with Article 39 of the Charter, any attempt to alter by force the settlement envisaged by this resolution".

I am sure that every member of this body is deeply concerned with the tragic events which have taken place in Palestine since 29 November last. Our hearts are saddened by the internecine hostilities, the interracial strife, and the interreligious conflict, which in these past three months have stained the soil of the Holy Land with the blood of Briton, Jew and Arab. If these conditions continue, the Security Council must consider whether or not the situation in Palestine is a threat to international peace. The Security Council would have to do this even if the resolution of 29 November had never been written, because under the Charter it must take steps "to prevent or remove any threat to the peace, breach of the peace or act of aggression".

In considering whether or not the situation in Palestine is a threat to international peace, the Security Council should consult with the United Kingdom, which as Mandatory Power, is responsible for the protection of Palestine and the maintenance of internal order therein.

The second and third requests of the General Assembly's resolution, mentioned above, raise constitutional questions of the Security Council's powers under the Charter. What are the powers of the Security Council?

The Security Council is given the responsibility under the Charter to "determine the existence of any threat to the peace, breach of the peace or act of aggression". If it makes such a determination with respect to the situation in Palestine, the Security Council is required by the Charter to act. Its finding and subsequent action might arise either in connexion with incursions into Palestine from the outside or from such internal disorder as would itself constitute a threat to international peace.

If the Security Council finds that a threat to international peace or breach of the peace exists, the Charter authorizes it to follow various lines of action. It is empowered to make recommendations, or to take "provisional measures" under Article 40, or to impose economic and other non-military sanctions under Article 41, or to take military measures under Article 42. The Security Council is required to follow one or more of these lines of action. It may pursue these lines of action in any sequence it deems proper.

Although the Security Council is empowered to use, and would normally attempt to use, measures short of armed force to maintain the peace, it is authorized under the Charter to use armed force if it considers other measures inadequate. A finding by the Security Council that a danger to peace exists places all Members of the United Nations, regardless of their views, under obligation to assist the Security Council in maintaining peace. If the Security Council should decide that it is necessary to use armed force to maintain international peace in connexion with Palestine, the United States would be ready to consult under the Charter with a view to such action as may be necessary to maintain international peace. Such consultation would be required in view of the fact that agreement has not yet been reached making armed forces available to the Security Council under the terms of Article 43 of the Charter.

The Security Council is authorized to take forceful measures with respect to Palestine to remove a threat to international peace. The Charter of the United Nations does not empower the Security Council to enforce a political settlement whether it is pursuant to a recommendation of the General Assembly or of the Security Council itself.

What this means is this: The Security Council, under the Charter, can take action to prevent aggression against Palestine from outside. The Security Council, by these same powers, can take action to prevent a threat to international peace and security from inside Palestine. But this action must be directed solely to the maintenance of international peace. The Security Council's action, in other words, is directed to keeping the peace and not to enforcing partition.

The United States Government believes that the first of the three requests made by the General Assembly to the Security Council under its resolution of 29 November 1947 can properly be complied with by the Security Council. With respect to the second and third requests of the General Assembly's resolution, the Security Council must act, if necessary, to preserve international peace and security or to curb and repel aggression as provided in the Charter. . . . .

[The] first special report of the Palestine Commission to the Security Council on the problem of security, dated 16 February 1948, . . . does not allege that a threat to the peace, breach of the peace or act of aggression has occurred in Palestine. It reports facts which, if accepted or substantiated by the Security Council, would appear to lead to the conclusion that a threat to international peace is present in that situation. With this special report before it, the Security Council must, in our opinion, look into the matter immediately to determine whether such a danger exists.

The report looks ahead to what it considers will happen in the future, and clearly implies that a threat to the peace and a breach of the peace will occur if the Commission continues its effort to carry out the General Assembly's resolution. Perhaps the most emphatic illustration is found in the conclusion of the report, section VIII, paragraph 5 of which reads as follows:

"It is the considered view of the Commission that the security forces of the Mandatory Power, which at the present time prevent the situation from deteriorating completely into open warfare on an organized basis, must be replaced by an adequate non-Palestinian force which will assist law-abiding elements in both the Arab and Jewish communities, organized under the general direction of the Commission, in maintaining order and security in Palestine, and thereby enabling the Commission to carry out the recommendations of the General Assembly. Otherwise, the period immediately following the termination of the Mandate will be a period of uncontrolled, widespread strife and bloodshed in Palestine, including the City of Jerusalem. This would be a catastrophic conclusion to an era of international concern for that territory." . . .

Although we do not wish to place specific resolutions before the Security Council at this early stage of the discussion, my government believes we should have in mind the desirability of the following specific steps which the Security Council might take at once: (1) to accept the tasks which the General Assembly asked the Security Council to accept in its resolution of 29 November 1947 on Palestine, subject to the authority of the Security Council under the Charter; (2) to establish a committee of the Security Council, comprising the five permanent Members, to look at once into the question of the possible threats to international peace arising in connexion with the Palestine situation and to consult with the Palestine Commission, the Mandatory Power and representatives of the principal communities of Palestine concerning the implementation of the General Assembly resolution; (3) to call upon all Governments and peoples, particularly in and around Palestine, to take all possible action to prevent or reduce the disorders now occurring in Palestine. . . .

Mr. EL-KHOURI (Syria): . . . Under the pressure of time, the General Assembly advanced and adopted in a rush its resolution of 29 November, giving no attention to the proposals which were submitted for more adequate and more pacific solutions.

The General Assembly did not care even to discuss and vote upon the legal contentions frequently and repeatedly submitted by various delegations with a view to obtaining, under Article 96 of the Charter, an advisory opinion from the International Court of Justice, although this demand for an advisory opinion was discussed and defeated in the *Ad Hoc* Committee on the Palestinian Question by a close vote of 21 to 20, and would, therefore, in the circumstances, have been an appropriate matter to be discussed and voted upon by the General Assembly.

Three meetings were scheduled for 26 November in order to terminate discussion of this item and to vote upon it. But when, during the morning meeting, the sponsors of the plan of partition realized that certain representatives had declared in their speeches that they would vote against the draft resolution and that others had declared their intention of abstaining, they manoeuvred to adjourn the afternoon meeting and to cancel the evening meeting. They realized, it seems, that their scheme would be definitely rejected if put to the vote on that day. Through a suggestion by the President and a vote of 24 to 21, they cancelled the evening meeting also. In this way they secured a two-day recess, fixing the next meeting for Friday, 28 November.

In the meantime influence was being vigorously brought to bear on the Governments of certain Member States in an attempt to change their attitude and to have them cast affirmative votes instead of negative votes or abstentions. The manoeuvres were completed on 29 November, and certain States were brought into line. Other delegations, which had declared their intention of abstaining, were also won over. There is no doubt whatsoever that had the delegations been left to vote according to their declarations at the meeting of 26 November, the partition scheme would have been condemned to failure.

After the resolution was passed by that artificial majority, it was subjected to severe and caustic criticism by the world Press and many impartial jurists. Twenty-four delegations, representing two-thirds of the total population of the Member States of the United Nations amounting to about 1,000 million inhabitants, refused to support the resolution by flatly rejecting it or by abstaining from voting for it. Many representatives, even of those who supported the scheme, discredited and condemned it severely.

Aware of its incapacity to enforce such an aggressive measure, the General Assembly shifted the burden of its implementation to the Security Council. . . .

The Security Council is an independent organ of the United Nations, endowed with complete liberty to act within the provisions of the Charter, irrespective of any recommendations or instructions given to it by any other body. The recommendations of the General Assembly, therefore, are legitimately subject to reconsideration by the Security Council, to be scrutinized as to their correctness and their compliance with the powers assigned to the General Assembly and to the Security Council by the Charter. . . .

The General Assembly is not intended to be a central government of the world empowered with unlimited authority to create States and to violate the integrity of countries. Nor is it allowed to impose government regimes under specified constitutional forms, nor to dictate economic unions between States, nor to detach territories and cities and put them under permanent trusteeships. It is not legally entitled to appoint commissions, delegating to them powers and prerogatives which the General Assembly itself does not possess. Finally, it has no right to ask the Security Council to take charge of the implementation of an illegal resolution.

The General Assembly is bound to act within the limits of the Charter provisions; it is not free to act arbitrarily or capriciously. The Charter is an international treaty which must be respected by all its signatories. Palestine is a mandated territory, and the question concerning it cannot be treated beyond the stipulations governing mandated territories. Such territories can only be declared independent and left free to determine their regime of government through a constituent assembly representing all the population. In the cases of populations of such territories attaining maturity for independence, they will be helped by applying the Trusteeship System, by virtue of a trusteeship agreement concluded in accordance with Article 79 of the Charter. The newly invented measures adopted by that artificial majority of the General Assembly not only violate the letter and spirit of the Charter; they cannot find even a fictitious justification, resting on any historical precedent, any existing practice or any elementary rule of common sense.

The partition of India was cited as an example. That partition, however, was accomplished by mutual consent of both parties—majority and minority—who are both original inhabitants of the country, and neither of them foreign and intruding newcomers, as in the case of Palestine.

Democracy is defined as the government of the people, where the wishes of the majority should prevail and the political and social rights of the minority should be guaranteed and lawfully protected. Under this rule, the right of self-determination is to be exercised by the freely expressed and openly exhibited wishes of the majority. This is the principle universally respected by all countries and applying actually or potentially to all. Why must the Palestinians alone make an exception to this fundamental rule of human society? Is it because foreign groups of Jews do not wish to live peacefully with the Arabs? With what right does a foreign religious minority dictate its wishes upon the majority of the lawful owners of the country in determining the political and social organism of that country? . . .

I spoke before on the limitations of the General Assembly in relation to the Security Council. The General Assembly is also limited in authority and capacity in relation to the Mandatory. The United Kingdom, as Mandatory of Palestine, requested the General Assembly merely to make recommendations as to the future government of that country. It is obvious that the United Kingdom did not act under its obligations to help the inhabitants of Palestine to attain independence by creating, during the long period of its mandate, the governmental organs necessary for the assumption of power; nor had it submitted an agreement under Article 79 of the Charter for a further delay to complete its obligations. Its behaviour in this respect was not in conformity with the provisions of its mandate nor with the stipulations of the Charter. . . .

The proper procedure for the Security Council is to study this resolution and determine whether it is justified in taking this charge upon itself.

In the first place, the recommendations of the General Assembly are not imperative on those to whom they are addressed. We have numerous precedents during the short past life of the General Assembly: the dispute between India and the Union of South Africa, the Balkan situation, the Interim Committee, the Korean question, the admission of new Members. . . .

The Security Council is requested by the General Assembly to endorse a Commission of five Members nominated by the President, who by so doing by-passed rule 82 of the rules of procedure concerning elections by secret ballot. This Commission will be exercising an illegal and usurped authority. Its members are called to replace the Mandatory Power during the transitional period by promulgating regulations, establishing councils of governments, appointing high commands of militia forces, supervising the military activities, convoying forces from the Security Council, exercising sovereign authority in Palestine and so on, without being trustees holding a trusteeship agreement, which is the only way by which the General Assembly may create any authority in the Non-Self-Governing Territories.

In such circumstances the Security Council cannot back the application of this illegally constituted Commission.

The sponsors of the partition scheme cited Article 22 of the Charter as justifying the creation of this Commission. . . .

It is to be asked here: Is the administration of any country, one of the functions of the General Assembly, to be delegated to a subsidiary organ? These functions are defined in the Charter and none of them refers even tacitly to such authority, except the Trusteeship System in Chapter XII, which was not applied in this case.

They also quoted Articles 10 and 14 of the Charter. . . .

It is obvious from Article 10 that the competence of the General Assembly is limited to discussing and making recommendations within the scope of the Charter, but not outside that scope. . . .

Article 14 authorizes the General Assembly to recommend peaceful adjustments and peaceful settlements within the limits of the purposes and principles of the United Nations, not to recommend measures of a warlike nature, challenging the Arabs in particular and the Moslem world in general to resort to arms in self-defence. Further, the General Assembly is authorized to make recommendations with respect to the pacific settlement of disputes, as outlined in Chapter VI of the Charter. However, the recommendations of the General Assembly stated that Articles 39 and 41 of the Charter should be applied, these Articles appearing in Chapter VII. This means that the General Assembly is making recommendations not for a peaceful settlement, but for enforcement, which the General Assembly is not entitled to do.

The purposes of the United Nations, as set forth in Article 1, are to develop friendly relations among the nations and remove threats to peace, not create threats to peace and hostile relations among nations. . . .

The demand addressed by the Commission to the Security Council, to provide and dispatch to Palestine a considerable or adequate international force to suppress any opposition to the implementation of the recommendations of the General Assembly, has no justification in the Charter of the United Nations. I fail to find in this Charter any text which implies, directly or indirectly, that the General Assembly has the authority to enforce its own recommendations by military force. If this were to be the case, then the recommendations would cease to be recommendations and would become orders or governmental laws.

The General Assembly is not a world government. It is not vested with executive power over the peoples of the world. Had it been a central government of the world, it would have been required to execute its orders and make its laws respected. But it is obvious that the General Assembly is not a government. It only gives advice, and the parties to whom advice is addressed accept it when it is rightful and just, and when it does not impair their fundamental rights. If the recommendations are not accepted, it will have no effect on the prestige of the United Nations. For a government which fails to observe its own laws may collapse, but not an international organization composed of individual sovereign nations, as the General Assembly is, which is not in any sense a government.

The use of international force by the Security Council is clearly defined in the chapter devoted to this topic, where it is laid down when and how such a force is to be used and what steps should be taken by the Security Council to accomplish its purpose.

Chapter VII is the part of the Charter dealing with this question. We do not find in it, or anywhere else in the Charter, the least reference to the use of force by the Security Council or by the General Assembly for the preserving of public order in any country. The use of force is allowed to the Security Council only for the maintenance or restoration of international peace and security by suppressing aggression by one State against another. I say international, and not local, peace and order in any country. Public order has been disturbed and continues to be so in Greece, North China, India, Pakistan and elsewhere on a very large scale. Nobody thought of applying to the Security Council for military help to keep law and order in any of those areas. The Security Council is requested by the General Assembly to act in the case of Palestine within its capacity as defined in this Chapter. Any request by the General Assembly or by any other organ beyond that capacity, is unacceptable.

Consequently, the Commission's application for international force under the present conditions has no justification in the functions of the Security Council and should be rejected. Furthermore, it cannot be claimed that any situation or dispute is hereby brought to the attention of the Security Council against any State, in accordance with Article 35 of the Charter referred to above. No application of this nature, allowing the Security Council to take steps in the matter, exists.

It is equally obvious that no measures of sanction or of any other kind could be taken against any State under Chapter VII by the Security Council before being seized of a formal accusation made by a competent party, and before an examination of the complaint is made in the presence of both sides, with a view to substantiating the accusation.

NOTE.   On 5 March 1948, the Security Council refused to accept a United States proposal that it "accept, subject to the authority of the Security Council under the Charter, the requests addressed by the General Assembly to it" in Resolution 181 (II); only five members voted for the proposal, while six members abstained. SCOR, III, Nos. 36–51, p. 40. Instead, the Council, by 8 votes, with three abstentions (Argentina, Syria, United Kingdom), adopted a resolution calling on the permanent members to consult and to make recommendations to the Council regarding the instructions to be given to the Palestine Commission; it also made an appeal "to all Governments and peoples, particularly in and around Palestine, to take all possible action to prevent or reduce such disorders as are now occurring in Palestine." S/691 (5 March 1948); SCOR, III, Nos. 36–51, p. 43. Though the five permanent members seem to have agreed that the Council "should take further action by all means available to bring about the immediate cessation of violence and the restoration of peace and order in Palestine," the United States suddenly proposed that an international trusteeship should be established for Palestine, and that the implementation of the partition plan be suspended. *Idem*, pp. 141–3, 167–8. On 1 April 1948, the Security Council, pursuant to a recommendation of four permanent members adopted two resolutions. In the first one, adopted unanimously, the Security Council: "in the exercise of its primary responsibility for the maintenance of international peace and security," noted "the increasing violence and disorder in Palestine" and expressed the belief "that it is of the utmost urgency that an immediate truce be effected in Palestine;" called upon "the Jewish Agency for Palestine and the Arab Higher Committee to make representatives available to the Security Council for the purpose of arranging a truce between the Arab and Jewish communities of Palestine;" emphasized "the heavy responsibility which would fall upon any party failing to observe such a truce;" and called upon "the Arab and Jewish armed groups in Palestine to cease acts of violence immediately." In the second one, adopted by 9 votes, with 2 abstentions (USSR and Ukrainian SSR), the Security Council requested the Secretary-General to convoke a special session of the General Assembly "to consider further the question of the future government of Palestine." S/714, I and II (1 April 1948); SCOR, III, No. 52, pp. 33–5; SCOR, Supp. for April 1948, pp. 4–5. As the President of the Council did not succeed in bringing about a truce agreement between the parties, the Council adopted on 17 April 1948 a detailed resolution calling for cessation of military activities.

6.   *Resolution of the Security Council, 17 April 1948.*

S/723; SCOR, III, Supp. for April 1948, pp. 7–8.

Considering the Council's resolution of 1 April 1948 and the conversations held by its President with the representatives of the Jewish Agency for Palestine and the Arab Higher Committee with a view to arranging a truce between Arabs and Jews in Palestine;

Considering that, as stated in that resolution, it is of the utmost urgency to bring about the immediate cessation of acts of violence in Palestine, and to establish conditions of peace and order in that country;

Considering that the United Kingdom Government, so long as it remains the Mandatory Power, is responsible for the maintenance of peace and order in Palestine and should continue to take all steps necessary to that end; and that, in so doing, it should receive the co-operation and support of the Security Council in particular as well as of all the Members of the United Nations;

The Security Council:

1. Calls upon all persons and organizations in Palestine and especially upon the Arab Higher Committee and the Jewish Agency to take immediately, without prejudice to their rights, claims, or positions, and as a contribution to the well-being and permanent interest of Palestine, the following measures:

(a) Cease all activities of a military or para-military nature, as well as acts of violence, terrorism and sabotage;

(b) Refrain from bringing and from assisting and encouraging the entry into Palestine of armed bands and fighting personnel, groups and individuals, whatever their origin;

(c) Refrain from importing or acquiring or assisting or encouraging the importation or acquisition of weapons and war materials;

(d) Refrain, pending further consideration of the future government of Palestine by the General Assembly, from any political activity which might prejudice the rights, claims, or positions of either community;

(e) Co-operate with the Mandatory authorities for the effective maintenance of law and order and of essential services, particularly those relating to transportation, communications, health, and food and water supplies;

(f) Refrain from any action which will endanger the safety of the Holy Places in Palestine and from any action which would interfere with access to all shrines and sanctuaries for the purpose of worship by those who have an established right to visit and worship at them.

2. Requests the United Kingdom Government, for so long as it remains the Mandatory Power, to use its best efforts to bring all those concerned in Palestine to accept the measures set forth under paragraph 1 above and, subject to retaining the freedom of action of its own forces, to supervise the execution of these measures by all those concerned, and to keep the Security Council and the General Assembly currently informed on the situation in Palestine.

3. Calls upon all Governments and particularly those of the countries neighbouring Palestine to take all possible steps to assist in the implementation of the measures set out under paragraph 1 above, and particularly those referring to the entry into Palestine of armed bands and fighting personnel, groups and individuals and weapons and war materials.

NOTE.—1. On 23 April 1948, the Council established a Truce Commission for Palestine, composed of representatives of three members of the Security Council which then had career consular officers in Jerusalem (i. e., Belgium, France and US) "to assist the Security Council in supervising the implementation by the parties" of the resolution of April 17. SCOR, III, No. 62, p. 33.

2. A special session of the General Assembly met on 19 April 1948. It considered various trusteeship proposals, both with respect to Palestine as a whole and with respect to the City of Jerusalem. On 14 May 1948, by 31 votes to 7, with 16 abstentions, it adopted Resolution 186 (S–2), terminating the Palestine Commission and authorizing the appointment of a United Nations Mediator in Palestine, with the following functions (GAOR, Second Special Session, Supp. 2, p. 5):

"(a) To use his good offices with the local and community authorities in Palestine to:

"(i) Arrange for the operation of common services necessary to the safety and well-being of the population of Palestine;

"(ii) Assure the protection of the Holy Places, religious buildings and sites in Palestine;

"(iii) Promote a peaceful adjustment of the future situation of Palestine;

"(b) To co-operate with the Truce Commission for Palestine appointed by the Security Council in its resolution of 23 April 1948;

"(c) To invite, as seems to him advisable, with a view to the promotion of the welfare of the inhabitants of Palestine, the assistance and co-operation of appropriate specialized agencies of the United Nations, such as the World Health Organization, of the International Red Cross, and of other governmental or non-governmental organizations of a humanitarian and non-political character."

Count Folke Bernadotte (Sweden), Vice-President of the International Red Cross, was appointed as Mediator on 20 May 1948.

3. The Mandate expired at midnight on May 14 and the Jewish community immediately established the State of Israel which was promptly recognized by several States, including the United States. Simultaneously the Arab States declared that "peace and order have been completely upset in Palestine" and this constitutes "a serious and direct threat to peace and security within the territories of the Arab States themselves"; considering further that "the security of Palestine is a sacred trust for them, and out of anxiousness to check the further deterioration of the prevailing conditions and to prevent the spread of disorder and lawlessness into the neighbouring Arab lands, and in order to fill the vacuum created by the termination of the Mandate and the failure to replace it by any legally constituted authority, the Arab Governments find themselves compelled to intervene for the sole purpose of restoring peace and security and establishing law and order in Palestine." S/745 (15 May 1948); SCOR, III, Supp. for May 1948, p. 83, at 87.

4. On 22 May 1948, the Security Council failed to adopt a United States resolution asking it to determine that "the situation in Palestine constitutes a threat to the peace within the meaning of Article 39 of the Charter"; there were 5 votes in favor and 6 abstentions. It adopted, however, a resolution asking for a cease-fire within thirty-six hours. SCOR, III, No. 72, pp. 54, 66.

5. The Arab States having refused to comply with this resolution, the Soviet Union proposed that the Council should consider that "as a result of these events the situation in Palestine constitutes a threat to peace and security within the meaning of Article 39 of the Charter" and should order immediate cessation of hostilities. S/794/Rev. 2 (29 May 1948); SCOR, Supp. for May 1948, pp. 101–2. Instead, the Council adopted on 29 May 1948 a milder British resolution calling for a four-week truce and for limitations on immigration to Palestine (as requested by the Arab States); but, at the same time the Council warned the parties about future application of Chapter VII if either of them should reject the resolution. *Idem,* pp. 103–4, and Document 7, below.

7.   *Resolution of the Security Council, 29 May 1948.*

S/801; SCOR, III, Supp. for May 1948, pp. 103–4.

The Security Council,

Desiring to bring about a cessation of hostilities in Palestine without prejudice to the rights, claims and position of either Arabs or Jews,

Calls upon all Governments and authorities concerned to order a cessation of all acts of armed force for a period of four weeks;

Calls upon all Governments and authorities concerned to undertake that they will not introduce fighting personnel into Palestine, Egypt, Iraq, Lebanon, Saudi Arabia, Syria, Transjordan and Yemen during the cease-fire;

Calls upon all Governments and authorities concerned, should men of military age be introduced into countries or territories under their control, to undertake not to mobilize or submit them to military training during the cease-fire;

Calls upon all Governments and authorities concerned to refrain from importing war material into or to Palestine, Egypt, Iraq, Lebanon, Saudi Arabia, Syria, Transjordan and Yemen during the cease-fire;

Urges all Governments and authorities concerned to take every possible precaution for the protection of the Holy Places and of the City of Jerusalem, including access to all shrines and sanctuaries for the purpose of worship by those who have an established right to visit and worship at them;

Instructs the United Nations Mediator for Palestine in concert with the Truce Commission to supervise the observance of the above provisions, and decides that they shall be provided with a sufficient number of military observers;

Instructs the United Nations Mediator to make contact with all parties as soon as the cease-fire is in force with a view to carrying out his functions as determined by the General Assembly;

Calls upon all concerned to give the greatest possible assistance to the United Nations Mediator;

Instructs the United Nations Mediator to make a weekly report to the Security Council during the cease-fire;

Invites the States members of the Arab League and the Jewish and Arab authorities in Palestine to communicate their acceptance of this resolution to the Security Council not later than 6 p. m. New York Standard Time on 1 June 1948;

Decides that if the present resolution is rejected by either party or by both, or if, having been accepted, it is subsequently repudiated or violated, the situation in Palestine will be reconsidered with a view to action under Chapter VII of the Charter;

Calls upon all Governments to take all possible steps to assist in the implementation of this resolution.

NOTE. After various difficulties were removed by the Mediator, the truce entered into force on 11 June 1948. An appeal by the Security Council for the prolongation of the truce beyond the original four weeks was rejected by the Arabs, hostilities were resumed, the Arab armies were defeated, and Israel succeeded in extending its boundaries beyond those allotted to her in the partition resolution. The United States asked again for a determination under Article 39 of the Charter and for provisional measures under Article 40 [S/890 (13 July 1948); SCOR, III, No. 95, pp. 40–1], and this resolution was adopted with some changes on 15 July 1948.

8. Resolution of the Security Council, 15 July 1948.

S/902; SCOR, III, Supp. for July 1948, pp. 76–7.

The Security Council,

Taking into consideration that the Provisional Government of Israel has indicated its acceptance in principle of a prolongation of the truce in Palestine; that the States members of the Arab League have rejected successive appeals of the United Nations Mediator, and of the Security Council in its resolution of 7 July 1948, for the prolongation of the truce in Palestine; and that there has consequently developed a renewal of hostilities in Palestine:

Determines that the situation in Palestine constitutes a threat to the peace within the meaning of Article 39 of the Charter;

Orders the Governments and authorities concerned, pursuant to Article 40 of the Charter of the United Nations, to desist from further military action and to this end to issue cease-fire orders to their military and para-military forces, to take effect at a time to be determined by the Mediator, but in any event not later than three days from the date of the adoption of this resolution;

Declares that failure by any of the Governments or authorities concerned to comply with the preceding paragraph of this resolution would demonstrate the existence of a breach of the peace within the meaning of Article 39 of the Charter requiring immediate consideration by the Security Council with a view to such further action under Chapter VII of the Charter as may be decided upon by the Council;

Calls upon all Governments and authorities concerned to continue to co-operate with the Mediator with a view to the maintenance of peace in Palestine in conformity with the resolution adopted by the Security Council on 29 May 1948;

Orders as a matter of special and urgent necessity an immediate and unconditional cease-fire in the City of Jerusalem to take effect 24 hours from the time of the adoption of this resolution, and instructs the Truce Commission to take any necessary steps to make this cease-fire effective;

Instructs the Mediator to continue his efforts to bring about the demilitarization of the City of Jerusalem, without prejudice to the future political status of Jerusalem, and to assure the protection of and access to the Holy Places, religious buildings and sites in Palestine;

Instructs the Mediator to supervise the observance of the truce and to establish procedures for examining alleged breaches of truce since 11 June 1948, authorizes him to deal with breaches so far as it is within his capacity to do so by appropriate local action, and requests him to keep the Security Council currently informed concerning the operation of the truce and when necessary to take appropriate action;

Decides that, subject to further decision by the Security Council or the General Assembly, the truce shall remain in force, in accordance with the present resolution and with that of 29 May 1948, until a peaceful adjustment of the future situation of Palestine is reached;

Reiterates the appeal to the parties contained in the last paragraph of its resolution of 22 May and urges upon the parties that they continue conversations with the Mediator in a spirit of conciliation and mutual concession in order that all points under dispute may be settled peacefully.

NOTE.—1. Both sides complied promptly with this resolution and the truce came into effect on 18 July 1948. To prevent its violation, the Security Council on 19 August 1948 adopted a supplementary resolution informing "the governments and authorities concerned that:

"(a) Each party is responsible for the actions of both regular and irregular forces operating under its authority or in territory under its control;

"(b) Each party has the obligation to use all means at its disposal to prevent action violating the truce by individuals or groups who are subject to its authority or who are in territory under its control;

"(c) Each party has the obligation to bring to speedy trial, and in case of conviction to punishment, any and all persons within their jurisdiction who are involved in a breach of the truce;

"(d) No party is permitted to violate the truce on the ground that it is undertaking reprisals or retaliations against the other party;

"(e) No party is entitled to gain military or political advantage through violation of the truce." SCOR, III, Resolutions and Decisions of the Security Council, 1948 [S/INF/2/Rev. 1 (III)], p. 24.

Despite many violations, the truce arrangements remained in force until they were superseded by a series of armistice agreements in 1949. These agreements, concluded through the intermediary of Mr. Ralph J. Bunche, Acting Mediator after the assassination of Count Bernadotte, provide for United Nations supervision of their execution and an elaborate machinery has been instituted for that purpose. For the texts of these agreements, see 42 UNTS, pp. 251, 287, 303, 327; SCOR, IV, Spec. Supps. 1–4. Many questions arising out of the violations of these armistice agreements have come before the Security Council and in several cases the Council adopted resolutions condemning the activities of the parties; see, e. g., the reports of the Security Council to the General Assembly, 1953–4 and 1954–5, GAOR, IX, Supp. 2, pp. 6–44, and GAOR, X, Supp. 2, pp. 6–15; and S/6003 (8 Oct. 1964), SCOR, XIX, Supp. for Oct.-Dec. 1964, pp. 12–14.

2. The General Assembly, at its third session, established a Conciliation Commission for Palestine consisting of three Member States (France, Turkey and the United States), with three main functions: "to assist the governments and authorities concerned to achieve a final settlement of all questions outstanding between them"; to prepare detailed proposals for a permanent international regime for the territory of Jerusalem which "should be placed under effective United Nations control"; and "to facilitate the repatriation, resettlement and economic and social rehabilitation of refugees." Resolution 194 (III), 11 Dec. 1948; GAOR, III.1, Resolutions (A/810), pp. 21–5. Since then little progress has been made in these three areas; the refugees are being assisted in the meantime by the United Nations Relief and Works Agency for Palestine Refugees in the Near East, established by Resolution 302 (IV) of the General Assembly, of 8 Dec. 1949; GAOR, IV, Resolutions (A/1251), pp. 23–5.

3. In later negotiations great reliance was placed by the Arab States on Israel's acceptance of the original 1947 boundaries, subject to necessary territorial adjustments and the settlement of other outstanding questions, in the so-called Lausanne Protocol of 12 May 1949. With respect to the circumstances surrounding this document, see the reports of the Conciliation Commission of 13 June 1949, 22 Sept. 1949, and 2 Sept. 1950; GAOR, IV, *Ad Hoc* Political Committee, Annex, Vol. II, pp. 5–13; GAOR, V, Supp. 18 (A/1367/Rev. 1), pp. 2–21.

4. For comments on the Palestine problem, see Benjamin AKZIN, "The United Nations and Palestine," 1948 Jewish Yb. of Int. L. pp. 87–114; Lewis M. ALEXANDER, "The Arab-Israel Boundary Problem", 6 World Politics (1954), pp. 322–37; ANGLO-AMERICAN COMMITTEE OF INQUIRY ON JEWISH PROBLEMS, Report, April 20, 1946 (Washington, 1946; US, DOS Pub. 2536), 92 pp.; ARAB OFFICE, Palestine: The Solution: The Arab Proposals and the Case on Which They Rest (Washington, D. C., 1947), 19 pp.; David BROOK, Preface to Peace: The United Nations and the Arab-Israeli Armistice System (Washington, 1964), 151 pp.; J. CHLALA, "Le problème palestinien devant l'O.N.U., 1947–1949", 5 REgDI (1949), pp. 102–130; Richard CROSSMAN, Palestine Mission: A Personal Record (New York, 1947), 210 pp.; Bartley C. CRUM, Behind the Silken Curtain: A Personal Account of Anglo-American Diplomacy in Palestine and the Middle East (New York, 1947), 297 pp.; Clyde EAGLETON, "Palestine and the Constitutional Law of the United Nations", 42 AJIL (1948), pp. 397–99; A. S. EBAN, "The United Nations and the Palestine Question", 2

World Affairs (N.S.; 1948), pp. 124–35; Rony E. GABBAY, A Political Study of the Arab-Jewish Conflict: The Arab Refugee Problem: A Case Study (Geneva, 1959), 611 pp.; Jorge GARCÍA—GRANADOS, The Birth of Israel (New York, 1949), 291 pp.; Charles R. GELLNER, The Palestine Problem: An Analysis, Historical and Contemporary (Washington, 1947; US, Library of Congress, Legislative Reference Service, Public Affairs Bulletin, No. 50), 188 pp.; GREAT BRITAIN, The Political History of Palestine under British Administration: Memorandum . . . presented . . . to the United Nations Special Committee on Palestine (New York, 1947), 40 pp., and UN Doc. A/AC.14/8; Sami HADAWI, Palestine: Questions and Answers (Arab Information Center, New York, 1961), 85 pp.; HEBREW UNIVERSITY OF JERUSALEM, Israel and the United Nations (New York, 1956), pp. 65–155; J. C. HUREWITZ, The Struggle for Palestine (New York, 1950), 404 pp.; J. C. HUREWITZ, "The United Nations Conciliation Commission for Palestine", 7 Int. Org. (1953), pp. 482–97; Elmo H. HUTCHINSON, Violent Truce (New York, 1956), 199 pp.; ISRAEL OFFICE OF INFORMATION, Israel's Struggle for Peace (New York, 1960), 187 pp.; J. and D. KIMCHE, A Clash of Destinies: The Arab-Jewish War and the Founding of the State of Israel (New York, 1960), 287 pp.; Arthur KOESTLER, Promise and Fulfilment: Palestine 1917–1949 (New York, 1949), 335 pp.; Larry L. LEONARD, "The United Nations and Palestine", 454 Int. Conc. (Oct. 1949), pp. 607–786; Yuen-li LIANG, "The Palestine Commission", 42 AJIL (1948), pp. 649–56; J. L. MAGNES, "Jewish-Arab Cooperation in Palestine", 16 Political Q. (1945), pp. 297–306; Paul MOHN, "Jerusalem and the United Nations", 464 Int. Conc. (Oct. 1950), pp. 421–471; NATION ASSOCIATES, The Palestine Problem and Proposals for Its Solution; Memorandum Submitted to the General Assembly of the United Nations, April 1947 (New York, 1947), 133 pp.; Don PERETZ, Israel and the Palestine Arabs (Washington, D. C., 1958), 264 pp.; William R. POLK, David M. STAMLER and Edmund ASFOUR, Backdrop to Tragedy: The Struggle for Palestine (Boston, Mass., 1957), 399 pp.; Simon H. RIFKIND and others, The Basic Equities of the Palestine Problem (New York, 1947), 107 pp.; Jacob ROBINSON, Palestine and the United Nations: Prelude to Solution (Washington, D. C., 1947), 269 pp.; Kermit ROOSEVELT, "The Partition of Palestine: A Lesson in Pressure Politics", 2 Middle East J. (1948), pp. 1–16; Shabtai ROSENNE, Israel's Armistice Agreements with the Arab States: A Juridical Interpretation (Tel Aviv, 1957), 93 pp.; ROYAL INSTITUTE OF INTERNATIONAL AFFAIRS, Great Britain and Palestine, 1915–1945 (London, 1946), 177 pp.; Frank C. SAKRAN, Palestine Dilemma: Arab Rights versus Zionist Aspirations (Washington, D. C., 1948) 230 pp.; Fayez A. SAYEGH, The Arab-Israeli Conflict (2d ed.; Arab Information Center, New York, 1964) 69 pp.; Joseph B. SCHECHTMAN, The Arab Refugee Problem (New York, 1952), 137 pp.; Benjamin SHWADRAN, "The Palestine Conciliation Commission", 1 Middle Eastern Affairs (1950), pp. 271–85; Susan STRANGE, "Palestine and the United Nations", 3 Yb. of World Affairs (1949), pp. 151–68; Carl H. VOSS, The Palestine Problem Today: Israel and Its Neighbors (Boston, Mass., 1953), 64 pp.; David W. WAINHOUSE and others, International Peace Observation: A History and Forecast (Baltimore, 1966), pp. 242–76; Günther WEISS, "Die Entstehung des Staates Israel", 13 ZaöRV (1950–51), pp. 146–72; Sumner WELLES, We Need not Fail (Boston, 1948), 151 pp.; J. ZASLOFF, Great Britain and

Palestine: A Study of the Problem before the United Nations (Munich. 1952), 187 pp.

THE KOREAN QUESTION

NOTE.—1. Korea became a Japanese protectorate in November 1905 and was formally annexed by Japan in August 1910. By a declaration issued at the Cairo Conference on 1 December 1943, China, the United Kingdom and the United States expressed their determination that "in due course Korea shall become free and independent." "Korea's Independence," US, DOS, Pub. 2933, p. 16. This Declaration was incorporated by reference in the Potsdam Declaration and in the Instrument of Japanese Surrender. By a military decision, the Soviet forces were authorized to accept the surrender of Japanese troops north of the 38th parallel in Korea, while the Japanese troops south of that parallel were to surrender to United States forces. At the Moscow Conference, in December 1945, the following agreement was reached with respect to Korea *(idem,* pp. 18–19):

"(1) With a view to the re-establishment of Korea as an independent state, the creation of conditions for developing the country on democratic principles and the earliest possible liquidation of the disastrous results of the protracted Japanese domination in Korea, there shall be set up a provisional Korean democratic government which shall take all the necessary steps for developing the industry, transport and agriculture of Korea and the national culture of the Korean people.

"(2) In order to assist the formation of a provisional Korean government and with a view to the preliminary elaboration of the appropriate measures, there shall be established a Joint Commission consisting of representatives of the United States command in southern Korea and the Soviet command in northern Korea. In preparing their proposals the Commission shall consult with the Korean democratic parties and social organizations. The recommendations worked out by the Commission shall be presented for the consideration of the Governments of the Union of Soviet Socialist Republics, China, the United Kingdom and the United States prior to final decision by the two Governments represented on the Joint Commission.

"(3) It shall be the task of the Joint Commission, with the participation of the provisional Korean democratic government and of the Korean democratic organizations to work out measures also for helping and assisting (trusteeship) the political, economic and social progress of the Korean people, the development of democratic self-government and the establishment of the national independence of Korea.

"The proposals of the Joint Commission shall be submitted, following consultation with the provisional Korean Government, for the joint consideration of the Governments of the United States, Union of Soviet Socialist Republics, United Kingdom and China for the working out of an agreement concerning a four-power trusteeship of Korea for a period of up to five years. . . ."

2. The principal South Korean political organizations refused to accept the Moscow decision to establish a trusteeship for Korea, while the North Korean parties agreed to it. The Soviet Commander in North Korea then

proposed that the Joint Commission created by the Moscow agreement should consult only "those democratic parties and organizations which uphold fully the Moscow Decision on Korea." *Idem,* p. 29. An agreement was reached in June 1947 on consultations with all organizations which agreed to cooperate with the Commission. *Idem,* pp. 38–45. When, however, lists were prepared by both sides of the organizations which should be consulted, the Soviet list excluded most South Korean organizations with an alleged membership of 15,200,000. *Idem,* p. 54. The United States then proposed elections in each zone for choosing representatives for a national provisional legislature, the number of representatives to be chosen in each zone reflecting the proportion between the population of these zones, and asked for a four-power conference to consider this proposal. *Idem,* pp. 55–6. When the Soviet Union refused to consider these proposals, the United States announced its intention to submit the case to the United Nations. *Idem,* p. 59. The Soviet Union then proposed that all foreign troops should withdraw from Korea at the beginning of 1948. "Korea, 1945 to 1948," US, DOS, Pub. 3305, p. 49.

3. On 17 September 1947, the United States asked for the inclusion on the agenda of the second session of the General Assembly of the item: "The problem of the independence of Korea." Despite Soviet objections, the General Assembly accepted the recommendation of the General Committee to include the item in its agenda. GAOR, II, General C., pp. 19–20; Plenary, pp. 275–99. The members of the Soviet bloc contended that the Korean question related to the liquidation of the consequences of the Second World War and that its consideration was, therefore, prohibited by Article 107 of the Charter; the question was also beyond United Nations competence because a special international agreement on the Korean question established special organs for dealing with this problem. On the other side, it was argued that Article 107 did not apply to this question as Korea was not an enemy state; that the Moscow agreement on Korea would be taken into account during Assembly discussions; that the Allied Powers had not succeeded in concluding peace treaties and had not fulfilled their commitment to restore independence to Korea; and that the General Assembly was competent, under Article 14 of the Charter, to consider "any situation, regardless of origin," and to recommend measures for its peaceful adjustment. GAOR, II, Plenary, Vol. I, pp. 275–82; First C., pp. 252, 256, 271, 291; Plenary, Vol. II, pp. 841, 848, 851. Having been defeated on the jurisdictional issue, the Soviet Union proposed that elected representatives of the Korean people from both parts of Korea be invited to take part in the discussion of the question. This proposal was rejected on the ground that the elective character of the Korean representatives should first be assured through an election in Korea to be held under the supervision of a United Nations Commission; instead an American proposal for such supervised elections was approved by the First Committee and the General Assembly, Resolution 112 (II); for text, see Document 1, below.

4. A similar action with respect to another divided country was taken by the General Assembly in 1951, when it established a commission to investigate the situation in the two parts of Germany in order to ascertain "whether conditions in these areas are such as to make possible the holding of genuinely free and secret elections throughout these areas." Resolution 510 (VI), 20 Dec. 1951; GAOR, VI, Supp. 20 (A/2119), pp. 10–11. For the reports of the Commission, see A/2122 and Add.1 and 2 (5 May, 3 June and 11 Aug. 1952).

1. *Resolution 112(II) of the General Assembly,*
14 November 1947.

GAOR, II, Resolutions (A/519), pp. 16–18.

A.   Inasmuch as the Korean question which is before the General
Assembly is primarily a matter for the Korean people itself and concerns its freedom and independence, and

Recognizing that this question cannot be correctly and fairly resolved without the participation of representatives of the indigenous
population,

The General Assembly

1.   Resolves that elected representatives of the Korean people be
invited to take part in the consideration of the question;

2.   Further resolves that in order to facilitate and expedite such
participation and to observe that the Korean representatives are in
fact duly elected by the Korean people and not mere appointees by
military authorities in Korea, there be forthwith established a United
Nations Temporary Commission on Korea, to be present in Korea,
with right to travel, observe and consult throughout Korea.

B.   The General Assembly,

Recognizing the urgent and rightful claims to independence of the
people of Korea;

Believing that the national independence of Korea should be re-
established and all occupying forces then withdrawn at the earliest
practicable date;

Recalling its previous conclusion that the freedom and independence
of the Korean people cannot be correctly or fairly resolved without
the participation of representatives of the Korean people, and its
decision to establish a United Nations Temporary Commission on
Korea (hereinafter called the "Commission") for the purpose of facilitating and expediting such participation by elected representatives
of the Korean people,

1.   Decides that the Commission shall consist of representatives of
Australia, Canada, China, El Salvador, France, India, Philippines,
Syria, Ukrainian Soviet Socialist Republic;

2.   Recommends that the elections be held not later than 31 March
1948 on the basis of adult suffrage and by secret ballot to choose
representatives with whom the Commission may consult regarding
the prompt attainment of the freedom and independence of the Korean
people and which representatives, constituting a National Assembly,
may establish a National Government of Korea. The number of representatives from each voting area or zone should be proportionate to
the population, and the elections should be under the observation of
the Commission;

3. Further recommends that as soon as possible after the elections, the National Assembly should convene and form a National Government and notify the Commission of its formation;

4. Further recommends that immediately upon the establishment of a National Government, that Government should, in consultation with the Commission: (a) constitute its own national security forces and dissolve all military or semi-military formations not included therein, (b) take over the functions of government from the military commands and civilian authorities of north and south Korea, and (c) arrange with the occupying Powers for the complete withdrawal from Korea of their armed forces as early as practicable and if possible within ninety days;

5. Resolves that the Commission shall facilitate and expedite the fulfilment of the foregoing programme for the attainment of the national independence of Korea and withdrawal of occupying forces, taking into account its observations and consultations in Korea. The Commission shall report, with its conclusions, to the General Assembly and may consult with the Interim Committee (if one be established) with respect to the application of this resolution in the light of developments;

6. Calls upon the Member States concerned to afford every assistance and facility to the Commission in the fulfilment of its responsibilities;

7. Calls upon all Members of the United Nations to refrain from interfering in the affairs of the Korean people during the interim period preparatory to the establishment of Korean independency, except in pursuance of the decisions of the General Assembly; and thereafter, to refrain completely from any and all acts derogatory to the independence and sovereignty of Korea.

NOTE. The Soviet Union refused to accept this decision of the Assembly and to cooperate with the United Nations Temporary Commission on Korea. The Commission was able to supervise elections only in South Korea; for its report see GAOR, III, Supp. 9 (A/575 and Add.1–4), in 5 parts. On the basis of that report, the General Assembly adopted Resolution 195 (III) declaring the Government of the Republic of Korea, established in the southern part, as the only lawful government in Korea; it also established a new Commission on Korea to assist in the unification of Korea. For text, see Document 2, below. The Commission was continued by Resolution 293 (IV), of 21 Oct. 1949, which requested that the Commission, in addition to its previous duties, should "observe and report any developments which might lead to or otherwise involve military conflict in Korea." GAOR, IV, Resolutions (A/1251), p. 15.

2. *Resolution 195(III) of the General Assembly, 12 December 1948.*

GAOR, III.1, Resolutions (A/810), pp. 25–27.

The General Assembly,

Having regard to its resolution 112(II) of 14 November 1947 concerning the problem of the independence of Korea,

Having considered the report of the United Nations Temporary Commission on Korea (hereinafter referred to as the "Temporary Commission"), and the report of the Interim Committee of the General Assembly regarding its consultation with the Temporary Commission,

Mindful of the fact that, due to difficulties referred to in the report of the Temporary Commission, the objectives set forth in the resolution of 14 November 1947 have not been fully accomplished, and in particular that unification of Korea has not yet been achieved,

1. Approves the conclusions of the reports of the Temporary Commission;

2. Declares that there has been established a lawful government (the Government of the Republic of Korea) having effective control and jurisdiction over that part of Korea where the Temporary Commission was able to observe and consult and in which the great majority of the people of all Korea reside; that this Government is based on elections which were a valid expression of the free will of the electorate of that part of Korea and which were observed by the Temporary Commission; and that this is the only such Government in Korea;

3. Recommends that the occupying Powers should withdraw their occupation forces from Korea as early as practicable;

4. Resolves that, as a means to the full accomplishment of the objectives set forth in the resolution of 14 November 1947, a Commission on Korea, consisting of Australia, China, El Salvador, France, India, the Philippines and Syria, shall be established to continue the work of the Temporary Commission and carry out the provisions of the present resolution, having in mind the status of the Government of Korea as herein defined, and in particular to:

(a) Lend its good offices to bring about the unification of Korea and the integration of all Korean security forces in accordance with the principles laid down by the General Assembly in the resolution of 14 November 1947;

(b) Seek to facilitate the removal of barriers to economic, social and other friendly intercourse caused by the division of Korea;

(c) Be available for observation and consultation on the further development of representative government based on the freely-expressed will of the people;

(d) Observe the actual withdrawal of the occupying forces and verify the fact of withdrawal when such has occurred; and for this purpose, if it so desires, request the assistance of military experts of the two occupying Powers;

5. Decides that the Commission:

(a) Shall within thirty days of the adoption of the present resolution, proceed to Korea, where it shall maintain its seat;

(b) Shall be regarded as having superseded the Temporary Commission established by the resolution of 14 November 1947;

(c) Is authorized to travel, consult and observe throughout Korea;

. . .

7. Calls upon the Member States concerned, the Government of the Republic of Korea, and all Koreans to afford every assistance and facility to the Commission in the fulfilment of its responsibilities;

8. Calls upon Member States to refrain from any acts derogatory to the results achieved and to be achieved by the United Nations in bringing about the complete independence and unity of Korea;

9. Recommends that Member States and other nations, in establishing their relations with the Government of the Republic of Korea, take into consideration the facts set out in paragraph 2 of the present resolution.

NOTE. On 25 June 1950, the United States and the Commission on Korea notified the United Nations that North Korean forces had invaded the territory of the Republic of Korea. SCOR, V, No. 15, pp. 1–2. A meeting of the Security Council was held on the same day and, in the absence of the Soviet representative (who left the Security Council in January 1950 because of the Chinese representation question), a resolution was adopted determining that the North Korean action constituted a breach of the peace and asking for withdrawal of North Korean forces (for text, see Document 3, below). On 27 June 1950, the Council recommended that members furnish assistance to the Republic of Korea (for text, see Document 4, below), and on 7 July 1950 the Council established "a unified command under the United States" (for text, see Document 5, below). Finally, the Council decided on 31 July 1950 to vest in the Unified Command responsibility for the relief and support of the civilian population of Korea. S/1657; SCOR, V, Resolutions and Decisions, 1950 (S/INF/5/Rev.1), pp. 6–7. The validity of these resolutions was challenged after the return of the Soviet representative in August 1950; for a discussion of this question, see Document 6, below.

3. *Resolution of the Security Council, 25 June 1950.*

S/1501; SCOR, V, Resolutions and Decisions, 1950 (S/INF/5/Rev.1), pp. 4–5.

The Security Council,

Recalling the finding of the General Assembly in its resolution of 21 October 1949 that the Government of the Republic of Korea is a lawfully established government having effective control and jurisdiction over that part of Korea where the United Nations Temporary Commission on Korea was able to observe and consult and in which the great majority of the people of Korea reside; and that this Government is based on elections which were a valid expression of the free will of the electorate of that part of Korea and which were observed by the Temporary Commission; and that this is the only such Government in Korea;

Mindful of the concern expressed by the General Assembly in its resolutions of 12 December 1948 and 21 October 1949 of the consequences which might follow unless Member States refrained from acts derogatory to the results sought to be achieved by the United Nations in bringing about the complete independence and unity of Korea; and the concern expressed that the situation described by the United Nations Commission on Korea in its report menaces the safety and well being of the Republic of Korea and of the people of Korea and might lead to open military conflict there;

Noting with grave concern the armed attack upon the Republic of Korea by forces from North Korea,

Determines that this action constitutes a breach of the peace,

I. Calls for the immediate cessation of hostilities; and

Calls upon the authorities of North Korea to withdraw forthwith their armed forces to the 38th parallel;

II. Requests the United Nations Commission on Korea

(a) To communicate its fully considered recommendations on the situation with the least possible delay;

(b) To observe the withdrawal of the North Korean forces to the 38th parallel; and

(c) To keep the Security Council informed on the execution of this resolution;

III. Calls upon all Members to render every assistance to the United Nations in the execution of this resolution and to refrain from giving assistance to the North Korean authorities.

4. Resolution of the Security Council, 27 June 1950.

S/1511; SCOR, V, Resolutions and Decisions, 1950 (S/INF/4/Rev.1), p. 5.

The Security Council,

Having determined that the armed attack upon the Republic of Korea by forces from North Korea constitutes a breach of the peace;

Having called for an immediate cessation of hostilities; and

Having called upon the authorities of North Korea to withdraw forthwith their armed forces to the 38th parallel; and

Having noted from the report of the United Nations Commission for Korea that the authorities in North Korea have neither ceased hostilities nor withdrawn their armed forces to the 38th parallel, and that urgent military measures are required to restore international peace and security; and

Having noted the appeal from the Republic of Korea to the United Nations for immediate and effective steps to secure peace and security,

Recommends that the Members of the United Nations furnish such assistance to the Republic of Korea as may be necessary to repel the armed attack and to restore international peace and security in the area.

5. *Resolution of the Security Council, 7 July 1950.*

S/1588; SCOR, V, Resolutions and Decisions, 1950 (S/INF/5/Rev.1), p. 5.

The Security Council,

Having determined that the armed attack upon the Republic of Korea by forces from North Korea constitutes a breach of the peace,

Having recommended that Members of the United Nations furnish such assistance to the Republic of Korea as may be necessary to repel the armed attack and to restore international peace and security in the area,

1. Welcomes the prompt and vigorous support which governments and peoples of the United Nations have given to its Resolutions of 25 and 27 June 1950 to assist the Republic of Korea in defending itself against armed attack and thus to restore international peace and security in the area;

2. Notes that Members of the United Nations have transmitted to the United Nations offers of assistance for the Republic of Korea;

3. Recommends that all Members providing military forces and other assistance pursuant to the aforesaid Security Council resolutions make such forces and other assistance available to a unified command under the United States;

4. Requests the United States to designate the commander of such forces;

5. Authorizes the unified command at its discretion to use the United Nations flag in the course of operations against North Korean forces concurrently with the flags of the various nations participating;

6. Requests the United States to provide the Security Council with reports as appropriate on the course of action taken under the unified command.

6. *Discussion in the Security Council, 3–11 August 1950.*

SCOR, V, No. 24, pp. 3–14; No. 28, pp. 4–11.

[On 31 July 1950, the United States presented the following draft resolution (S/1653; SCOR, V, No. 21, p. 7):

"The Security Council

"Condemns the North Korean authorities for their continued defiance of the United Nations;

"Calls upon all States to use their influence to prevail upon the authorities of North Korea to cease this defiance;

"Calls upon all States to refrain from assisting or encouraging the North Korean authorities and to refrain from action which might lead to the spread of the Korean conflict to other areas and thereby further endanger international peace and security."

During the discussion of this resolution a few days later, the following exchange of views took place:]

The PRESIDENT [Mr. J. Malik, USSR]: . . . Speaking as the representative of the USSR, I must point out that this is the third meeting which the Security Council has been obliged to spend on the consideration of the procedural question concerning the form in which the Korean question should be included in the agenda.

In the course of the discussion, two diametrically opposed approaches to this question have become apparent: one is that it should be discussed with a view to a peaceful settlement, as the USSR delegation insists; the other, that it should be discussed with a view to continuing military operations in Korea, intensifying the United States Government's armed intervention against the Korean people, and extending the scope of aggression and war. . . .

In pressing for the inclusion of its draft resolution in the Council's agenda and in attempting to give this draft the inaccurate title of "Complaint of aggression upon the Republic of Korea", the United States delegation is attempting to mask its aggression upon the Korean people, to mislead the United Nations and world opinion, to represent the origin and development of events in Korea on the basis of a one-sided United States version, which is known to be false, and to cast the blame for the beginning of events in Korea on the Government of the Korean People's Democratic Republic.

It has, however, been shown on the basis of irrefutable data and facts that the events taking place in Korea began on 25 June as a result of the provocative attack by the forces of the South Korean authorities on frontier areas of the Korean People's Democratic Republic. . . .

After provoking an armed attack by their South Korean puppets on the frontier areas of the Korean People's Democratic Republic, the ruling circles of the United States have hastened to take advantage of this act of provocation in order to justify their long-planned and armed aggression against the Korean people.

It is clear to anyone with a grain of impartiality that a civil war is in progress in Korea between the North and South Koreans. The military operations between the North and South Koreans are of an internal character; they bear the character of a civil war. There is therefore no justification for regarding these military operations as aggression.

Aggression takes place where one State attacks another. The USSR Government has taken this line in defining aggression since 1933, when the delegation of the Soviet Union put forward a definition of aggression in the Committee on Security Questions of the Conference for the reduction and limitation of armaments in Geneva. This definition contains instructions for the guidance of international organs which may be called upon to determine the side guilty of attack, the attacking side, in other words, the aggressor.

As is known, this definition of aggression includes such acts as a declaration of war by a State against another State; invasion of a territory by the armed forces of another State even without a declaration of war; the invasion of the territory of one State by the armed forces of another State and so forth.

According to this definition no political, strategic or economic considerations can justify aggression. Nor can the denial that a territory which is attacked has the specific attributes of statehood serve as a justification for an attack. Nor can a revolutionary or counter-revolutionary movement, or a civil war, serve as a justification, or the establishment or the maintenance of a particular political, economic or social order. . . .

From the standpoint of the standards and definitions of international law set forth in the above definition, the military operations of the United States Government against the Korean people are acts of direct armed aggression, and the United States Government is the attacker or, in other words, the aggressor.

United States armed forces have invaded Korean territory, although without a formal declaration of war. The above-mentioned definition qualifies such action as aggression. United States land, sea and air forces are bombing Korean territory and attacking Korean vessels and aircraft. According to the above-mentioned definition, such acts are acts of aggression, and the United States is the attacking State—the aggressor. United States land, sea and air forces have landed on Korean territory and are carrying on military action there against the Korean people which is at present in a state of domestic civil war. Such acts constitute aggression on the part of the United States. The United States has established a naval blockade of the Korean coast and ports. Such acts constitute aggression in accordance with the definition referred to. . . .

As regards the war between the North and South Koreans, it is a civil war and therefore does not come under the definition of aggression, since it is a war, not between two States, but between two parts of the Korean people temporarily split into two camps under two separate authorities.

The conflict in Korea is thus an internal conflict. Consequently rules relating to aggression are just as inapplicable to the North and South Koreans as the concept of aggression was inapplicable to the northern and southern states of America, when they were fighting a civil war for the unification of their country. We know that the role of aggressor at that time was played by Great Britain, which attempted to intervene in that civil war and to prevent the unification of the North and South in the United States. Similarly, the United Kingdom is now, together with the United States, intervening in the civil war in Korea in the attempt to impede the unification of that country. . . .

As is known, the United Nations Charter also directly prohibits intervention by the United Nations in the domestic affairs of any State when the conflict is an internal one between two groups within a single State and a single nation. Accordingly, the United Nations Charter provides for intervention by the Security Council only in events of an international rather than of an internal nature. . . .

Taking advantage of the absence from the Security Council of . . two permanent members—the USSR and China—and dictating its will in the Council to its military and political allies, the United States has hurriedly forced upon the Council a series of illegal and indeed scandalous resolutions, designed on the one hand to cover up United States aggression in Korea and, on the other, to promote to the furthest possible extent the plans for war in Korea and the Far East by involving other States in this war.

The local conflict within Korea, arising as a result of United States provocation, has been used by the ruling circles of the United States not only as a pretext for military intervention in the internal affairs of Korea, but also as a screen for expanding its aggression over wide regions of Asia, from the shores of Korea and Japan to the Vietnam territory, and for interference in the internal affairs of the Chinese, Vietnamese and Philippine peoples. . . .

The resolutions adopted in the Security Council under the dictate of the United States delegation and in violation of the United Nations Charter have no legal force. They were motivated by the desire of the aggressor to cloak and mask his aggression and are in no way directed towards strengthening the cause of peace.

The Security Council must fulfil the obligations laid upon it by the United Nations Charter to maintain peace and to promote peaceful settlements. It can fulfil these obligations only if immediate steps are taken—without delay—for the settlement of the Korean question. . . .

Mr. AUSTIN (USA): . . . Since the Soviet Union representative takes issue primarily with the position of the United States, I suppose he expects that I should speak to the charges he has raised about the United States. . . .

I am not going to try to prove at this time that the Republic of Korea was not the aggressor; that it did not attack the forces of

North Korea; that the United States is not really the influence that unleashed the Korean war; that there is a United Nations Command in Korea; that we are trying to back and support it in the United Nations; and that fifty-three Members of the United Nations are interested in supporting our flag over there.

We are tired, and I think the whole world is tired, of these obvious and shameless travesties of the realities with which we in this room are supposed to deal. Surely the time for that sort of thing has passed, and surely the matters we are dealing with today are too tragic and too real to be served by any preoccupation with propagandistic distortions which were properly referred to here yesterday as "upside-down" language. In any case, my Government sees no need and feels no desire to attempt today to fill with any more words of its own the immense abyss which lies between the statements of the representative of the USSR Government and the facts of this situation as they are known the world over and as they were reported by the United Nations Commission. . . .

Sir Gladwyn JEBB (UK): . . . The Soviet Union representative's basic intention, as I understand it, is based on the premise that what we are dealing with in Korea is a civil war. . . .

This would all be very obvious were it not for the fact that the Soviet Union representative, in his desire to impress public opinion with the rightness of his cause, has omitted to draw attention to the fact that the Government of the Republic of Korea has already been declared the lawful government by the United Nations; that United Nations observers were stationed on its *de facto* northern frontier; and that, therefore, the whole State was, as it were, existing under the mantle of this great international Organization.

The Government of the Korean Republic was, however, attacked . . . by soldiers coming under the authority of a rival Korean government, not acceptable to the United Nations, and established at Pyongyang. It is quite true that the soldiers I refer to were Koreans, and therefore were, so to speak, blood brothers of the people whom they attacked; but to argue that this fact in itself constitutes a civil war, or that it necessarily in itself puts both sides on an equal footing, is patent nonsense. The President made what he thought were some very telling observations regarding the American Civil War, but they would only have been relevant if he had gone on to show that in 1861 either the northern states or the southern had been recognized by an international organization, which he could not do for the simple reason that no international organization existed at that time.

Moreover, whatever the version of history current in Moscow may now be—and I understand it is rewritten from time to time so as to blot out uncomfortable facts from any public memory—the fact is that England, though it could have done so, did not intervene in the war between the states. Indeed, as is well known, my fellow-countrymen, and particularly the working class, suffered great privations by not intervening.

Quite apart from this, there is absolutely no reason to suppose that wars between people of the same race, even if they do not involve a government which has been set up under the aegis of the United Nations, are necessarily exempt from the decisions of the Security Council. A civil war in certain circumstances might well, under Article 39 of the Charter, constitute a "threat to the peace", or even a "breach of the peace", and if the Security Council so decided, there would be nothing whatever to prevent its taking any action it liked in order to put an end to the incident, even if it should involve two or more portions of the same international entity. Indeed, paragraph 7 of Article 2 of the Charter so provides. . . .

It will be seen that the last few words [of that Article] make it quite clear that the United Nations has full authority to intervene actively in the internal affairs of any country if this is necessary for the purpose of enforcing its decisions as regards the maintenance of international peace and security. I do honestly hope that, for the reasons given, we shall hear no more of this "civil war" argument from the mouth of the Soviet Union spokesman.

It is equally true that, under the Charter, the Security Council might be unlikely to make a recommendation or a decision under Article 39 in regard to another such incident as the present, since such action could and no doubt would be vetoed by the Soviet Union. But when the Security Council very properly decided that the Government of the Republic of Korea should be defended against a brutal attack, and decided on the appropriate measures to that effect, it did so unanimously, and no permanent member present at this table objected in the slightest degree, or even made any reservations. On the contrary, they were all horrified at the outrage which had occurred, and the Council machinery therefore worked smoothly and easily and in entire accord with the purposes and principles of the Charter. Nor can the fact that one of these permanent members represents a government not recognized by a minority of members of the Security Council affect the issue at all. This point can only be decided by a majority; and if this is disputed—as it is disputed—it is difficult to see how the Security Council can function. For how can it decide anything, except by a process of voting?

Finally, it may also be said, and indeed is said by my Soviet Union colleague, that he himself was not present when the decision to resist aggression was made. Perhaps he now regrets the fact that he was not present. That may be. But to maintain that the Security Council must be powerless because one member in a fit of pique simply boycotts it, is really to admit that the Security Council, and indeed the whole of the United Nations, can function only if it functions in accordance with the wish, and even at the behest, of one individual permanent member.

Valid though I myself believe the theory of great Power unity to be—in the sense that the United Nations can never work properly for so long as the great Powers are at loggerheads, and can therefore only proceed in the long run on the basis of unanimity—I cannot conceive that any rational being would admit that the theory ought to be abused in such a way as this, more especially since all the great Powers, along with the small ones, have entered into a solemn obligation to abide by the purposes and principles of the Charter. . . .

[W]hat has happened in Korea simply must not be allowed to occur again. The immediate necessity is, as I think I have said before, for the North Korean authorities who are responsible for the outrage to say that they will do what this Council has told them to do, before they can come to us and put forward any constructive proposals that they may then have for a solution as regards the future of Korea as a whole. . . .

In short, whatever solution is finally established, one thing comes necessarily first and that is, that the invading forces in Korea should go back whence they came. Then there might be a period during which some body representing the United Nations could establish contact with the North Korean authorities and report to the Security Council. Only then, I suggest, could we think of inviting representatives of the North Korean authorities to this table, with the object of enabling the United Nations to consider and carry out a scheme establishing a really independent and democratic Korea, which of course it is in the interest of all of us, including the Soviet Union Government, to achieve.

This is what I would call the United Nations way—a way totally at variance with the solutions based on force which, unfortunately, at present seem to be approved by the Soviet Union. It is in pursuing this way, which discards force except when it is necessary to meet aggression by force, that we can hope to create a world community consisting of free nations, obedient only to law, which must in the final count be based on the will of a majority of the human race. Imperfect though the United Nations undoubtedly still is, slow though the progress towards the ideal must inevitably be, wrong though it may be to precipitate changes too suddenly with consequent risk of chaos and the breakdown of society as such, still it is true that the United Nations provides the only present basis for a possible world community other than some centrally controlled world despotism which must be at variance with all the purposes and principles inscribed in the Charter itself.

NOTE. By various procedural manoeuvers, Mr. Malik (USSR), who was the President of the Security Council during August 1950, prevented the taking of any decisions on the Korean Question during that month. The United States proposal was finally voted on 5 September 1950, but it was not adopted as one permanent member (USSR) voted against it. SCOR, V, No. 38, pp. 18–19. When the General Assembly met in September 1950, it had before it the report of the United Nations Commission on Korea [GAOR, V, Supp. 16 (A/1350), 4 Sept. 1950], and on the basis of that report the General Assembly approved Resolution 376 (V), for the text of which see Document 7, below.

7.   *Resolution 376(V) of the General Assembly, 7 October 1950.*

GAOR, V, Supp. 20 (A/1775), pp. 9–10.

The General Assembly,

Having regard to its resolutions of 14 November 1947 (112(II)), of 12 December 1948 (195(III)) and of 21 October 1949 (293 (IV)),

Having received and considered the report of the United Nations Commission on Korea,

Mindful of the fact that the objectives set forth in the resolutions referred to above have not been fully accomplished and, in particular, that the unification of Korea has not yet been achieved, and that an attempt has been made by an armed attack from North Korea to extinguish by force the Government of the Republic of Korea,

Recalling the General Assembly declaration of 12 December 1948 that there has been established a lawful government (the Government of the Republic of Korea) having effective control and jurisdiction over that part of Korea where the United Nations Temporary Commission on Korea was able to observe and consult and in which the great majority of the people of Korea reside; that this government is based on elections which were a valid expression of the free will of the electorate of that part of Korea and which were observed by the Temporary Commission; and that this is the only such government in Korea,

Having in mind that United Nations armed forces are at present operating in Korea in accordance with the recommendations of the Security Council of 27 June 1950, subsequent to its resolution of 25 June 1950, that Members of the United Nations furnish such assistance to the Republic of Korea as may be necessary to repel the armed attack and to restore international peace and security in the area,

Recalling that the essential objective of the resolutions of the General Assembly referred to above was the establishment of a unified, independent and democratic Government of Korea,

1.   Recommends that

(a) All appropriate steps be taken to ensure conditions of stability throughout Korea;

(b) All constituent acts be taken, including the holding of elections, under the auspices of the United Nations, for the establishment of a unified, independent and democratic government in the sovereign State of Korea;

(c) All sections and representative bodies of the population of Korea, South and North, be invited to co-operate with the organs of

the United Nations in the restoration of peace, in the holding of elections and in the establishment of a unified government;

(d) United Nations forces should not remain in any part of Korea
otherwise than so far as necessary for achieving the objectives specified in sub-paragraphs (a) and (b) above;

(e) All necessary measures be taken to accomplish the economic
rehabilitation of Korea;

2. Resolves that

(a) A Commission consisting of Australia, Chile, Netherlands,
Pakistan, Philippines, Thailand and Turkey, to be known as the
United Nations Commission for the Unification and Rehabilitation of
Korea, be established to (i) assume the functions hitherto exercised
by the present United Nations Commission on Korea; (ii) represent
the United Nations in bringing about the establishment of a unified,
independent and democratic government of all Korea; (iii) exercise
such responsibilities in connexion with relief and rehabilitation in Korea as may be determined by the General Assembly after receiving the
recommendations of the Economic and Social Council. The United
Nations Commission for the Unification and Rehabilitation of Korea
should proceed to Korea and begin to carry out its functions as soon
as possible; . . .

The General Assembly furthermore,

Mindful of the fact that at the end of the present hostilities the task
of rehabilitating the Korean economy will be of great magnitude,

3. Requests the Economic and Social Council, in consultation with
the specialized agencies, to develop plans for relief and rehabilitation
on the termination of hostilities and to report to the General Assembly
within three weeks of the adoption of the present resolution by the
General Assembly;

4. Also recommends the Economic and Social Council to expedite
the study of long-term measures to promote the economic development and social progress of Korea, and meanwhile to draw the attention of the authorities which decide requests for technical assistance
to the urgent and special necessity of affording such assistance to
Korea. . . .

NOTE.—1. This resolution was interpreted at the time as allowing the
United Nations Command to pursue the North Korean troops beyond the
38th parallel. When the United Nations troops approached the Manchurian
border in November 1950, Chinese communist military units, composed allegedly of "volunteers", joined the fighting in large numbers. SCOR, V, No.
60, p. 4. With respect to later developments, see the case relating to the
Chinese intervention in Korea, below pp. 509–527.

2. For comments on various aspects of the Korean Question, see B. BOU-
TROS-GHALI, "L'intervention américaine en Corée et le droit des Nations
Unies," *in* SOCIETÉ ÉGYPTIENNE DE DROIT INTERNATIONAL, La

Corée et les Nations Unies (Cairo, 1951), pp. 9–26; John C. CALDWELL, The Korea Story (Chicago, 1952), 180 pp.; Shiv DAYAL, India's Role in the Korean Question: A Study in the Settlement of International Disputes under the United Nations (Delhi, 1959), 360 pp.; Gamal el DIN ATTIA, Les forces armées des Nations Unies en Corée et au Moyen-Orient (Geneva, 1963), pp. 113–284; Marc FRANKENSTEIN, L'Organisation des Nations Unies devant le conflit coréen (Paris, 1952), 364 pp.; Leland M. GOOD-RICH, "Korea: Collective Measures against Aggression," 494 Int. Conc. (Oct. 1953), pp. 129–192; Leland M. GOODRICH, Korea: A Study of U. S. Policy in the United Nations (New York, 1956), 235 pp.; Leon GOR-DENKER, The United Nations and the Peaceful Unification of Korea: The Politics of Field Operations, 1947–1950 (The Hague, 1959) 306 pp.; L. C. GREEN, "Korea and the United Nations," 4 World Affairs (1950), pp. 414–437; Edwin C. HOYT, "The United States Reaction to the Korean Attack: A Study of the Principles of the United Nations Charter as a Factor in Amer-ican Policy-Making," 55 AJIL (1961), pp. 45–76; D. H. N. JOHNSON, "The Korean Question and the United Nations," 26 NTIR (1956), pp. 25–36; Josef L. KUNZ, "Legality of the Security Council Resolutions of June 25 and 27, 1950," 45 AJIL (1951), pp. 137–142; G. E. LAVAU, "L'Organi-sation des Nations Unies et la guerre de Corée," in SOCIÉTÉ ÉGYP-TIENNE DE DROIT INTERNATIONAL, La Corée et les Nations Unies (Cairo, 1951), pp. 27–49; In-Sang LEE, La Corée et la politique des puis-sances (Geneva-Paris, 1959) 157 pp.; Gene M. LYONS, Military Policy and Economic Aid: The Korean Case, 1950–1953 (Columbus, 1961), 298 pp.; George M. McCUNE and Arthur L. GREY, Jr., Korea Today (Cambridge, Mass., 1950), 372 pp.; Robert T. OLIVER, Why War Came in Korea (New York, 1950), 260 pp.; Normal L. PADELFORD, "The United Nations and Korea: A Political Résumé," 5 Int. Org. (1951), pp. 685–708; Pitman B. POTTER, "Legal Aspects of the Situation in Korea," 44 AJIL (1950), pp. 709–712; SCIHCHIEH CHIHSHIH, A Chronicle of Principal Events Re-lating to the Korean Question, 1945–1954 (Peking, 1954), 93 pp.; SOVIET NEWS, The Soviet Union and the Korean Question (London, 1950), 99 pp.; UN SECRETARIAT, DEPARTMENT OF PUBLIC INFORMATION, Korea and the United Nations (Pub. 1950.I.8), 96 pp.; US, DOS, Korea's Independence (Pub. 2933; Washington, 1947), 60 pp.; US, DOS, Korea, 1945 to 1948 (Pub. 3305; Washington, 1950), 124 pp.; US, DOS, United States Policy in the Korean Crisis (Pub. 3922; Washington, 1950), 68 pp.; US, DOS, United States Policy in the Korean Conflict, 1950–1951 (Pub. 4263; Washington, 1951), 52 pp.; US, DOS, The Record on Korean Unifi-cation, 1943–1960: Narrative Summary with Principal Documents (Pub. 7084; Washington, 1960), 241 pp.; US, DOS, A Historical Summary of United States-Korean Relations: With a Chronology of Important Events, 1834–1962 (Pub. 7446; Washington, 1962), 138 pp.; US SENATE, COM-MITTEE ON FOREIGN RELATIONS, The United States and the Korean Problem: Documents, 1943–1953 (98th Congress, 1st Session, Doc. 74; 30 July 1953), 168 pp.; Quincy WRIGHT, "Collective Security in the Light of the Korean Experience," 45 ASIL Proceedings (1951), pp. 165–181; Tae-Ho YOU, The Korean War and the United Nations: A Legal and Diplomatic Historical Study (Louvain, 1965), 209 pp.

Section 2. Development of New Powers by the United Nations

UNITING FOR PEACE

1. *United States Proposal, 20 September 1950.*

Statement by Mr. Acheson (Secretary of State, USA), 20 September 1950. GAOR,
V, Plenary, pp. 23–4. See also US Note of 20 September 1950, A/1377;
GAOR, Annexes (V) 68, p. 2.

Mr. ACHESON (USA): This session of the General Assembly is a
session of decision. Before us lies opportunity for action which can
save the hope of peace, of security, of well-being and of justice for
generations to come. Before us also lies opportunity for drift, for
irresolution, for effort feebly made. In this direction is disaster.
The choice is ours. It will be made whether we act or whether we do
not act. .   .   .

Article 24 of the Charter gives the Security Council primary responsibility for the maintenance of peace, and this is the way it should
be. But if the Security Council is not able to act because of the ob-.
structive tactics of a permanent member, the Charter does not leave.
the United Nations impotent. The obligation of all Members to take
action to maintain or restore the peace does not disappear because of
a veto. The Charter, in Articles 10, 11 and 14, also vests in the Gen-.
eral Assembly authority and responsibility for matters affecting international peace. The General Assembly can and should organize
itself to discharge its responsibility promptly and decisively if the Security Council is prevented from acting.

To this end, the United States delegation is placing before the
General Assembly a number of recommendations designed to increase the effectiveness of United Nations action against aggression.

This programme will include the following proposals.

First, provision for the calling of an emergency session of the General Assembly upon twenty-four hours' notice if the Security Council
is prevented from acting upon a breach of the peace or an act of aggression.

Secondly, the establishment by the General Assembly of a security
patrol, a peace patrol, to provide immediate and independent observation and reporting from any area in which international conflict
threatens, upon the invitation or with the consent of the State to be
visited.

Thirdly, a plan under which each Member State would designate
within its national armed forces a United Nations unit or units, to be
specially trained and equipped and continuously maintained in readiness for prompt service on behalf of the United Nations. To assist in
the organization, training and equipping of such units, we shall suggest that a United Nations military advisor should be appointed.

Until the forces provided for under Article 43 are made available to the United Nations, the availability of these national units will be an important step toward the development of a world-wide security system.

Fourthly, the establishment by the General Assembly of a committee to study and report on means which the United Nations might use through collective action—including the use of armed force—to carry out the purposes and principles of the Charter.

I shall request that these proposals should be added as an item to the agenda. It is the hope of my delegation that the General Assembly will act on these and other suggestions which may be offered for the strengthening of our collective security system.

2. Discussion in the First Committee of the General Assembly, 9–19 October 1950.

GAOR, V, First C., pp. 63–136.

[After the General Assembly agreed to include the United States proposal on the agenda and referred it to the First Committee, a joint draft resolution was submitted by Canada, France, Philippines, Turkey, UK, USA and Uruguay (A/C.1/576 and Rev. 1; GAOR, Annexes (V) 68, pp. 4–8); this draft resolution, as amended, formed the basis of Resolution 377(V) which may be found in BASIC DOCUMENTS, II, 7.

The following debate preceded the adoption of this resolution:]

Mr. DULLES (USA) said that the authors of the joint draft resolution, of which his country was one, had been inspired by the United Nations action in Korea, which had proved that the Organization could be an effective instrument for suppressing aggression. Nevertheless, if aggressors were to be deterred by fear of the United Nations, certain organizational weaknesses would have to be remedied. It was only thanks to a series of adventitious and favourable circumstances that the United Nations had been able to take action against the aggressors in Korea.

It was doubtful, firstly, whether the Security Council would have acted if at the decisive moment, for extraneous reasons, one of the permanent members had not been absent; secondly, whether, if the General Assembly had not sent a commission to Korea three years ago, the Council would have had the information needed to justify prompt and decisive action; thirdly, whether United Nations forces could have saved the Republic of Korea if the United States had not stationed troops in Japan five years ago to enforce compliance with the terms of the armistice; lastly, whether the aggressor would have failed in Korea except for what amounted to, from his standpoint, extraordinarily bad fortune.

If potential aggressors were to be deprived of all hope of success, a reliable system would have to be created instead of matters being left to chance.

The need for collective resistance to aggression was as imperative today as it had been in March 1939. Then, Generalissimo Stalin had asserted that the non-aggressive States, primarily the United Kingdom, France and the United States of America, had rejected the policy of collective resistance to aggressors in favour of non-intervention and neutrality, thus conniving at aggression and allowing the war to become a world war.

Generalissimo Stalin's prediction had been fulfilled. Since then, however, the peoples had progressed and they expected the United Nations to show them how to promote collective resistance to the aggressors. There were doubtless those who feared that such action would precipitate aggression. The United States, for its part, would not resign itself to tolerate repeated acts of aggression, or to take action outside the United Nations, or to revert to a condition of each for himself and the devil take the hindmost.

Fortunately, the Charter had provided for the three basic security needs: (a) prompt and dependable action; (b) reliable means of information; (c) a backing of adequate power ready for action. In those three respects, the Security Council had what the Charter referred to as "primary responsibility": Firstly, the Council had to ensure "prompt . . . action by the United Nations . . . for the maintenance of international peace and security" (Article 24). Secondly, it had to investigate any "international friction" that was "likely to endanger the maintenance of international peace and security" (Article 34). Thirdly, the Council had to undertake to negotiate "as soon as possible" agreements with the Members of the United Nations, in order that armed force should be held in such "degree of readiness and general location" as would be found appropriate (Article 43).

Five years had elapsed and, while the Security Council had in many respects served admirably the purposes for which it had been set up, experience had shown that it was impossible to rely solely on the Council on the three points referred to above. The right of veto had already been used nearly fifty times; the Security Council had not established an adequate system of observation; it had not taken the initiative required of it in virtue of Article 43. On those three points, the facts were so well known that it was unnecessary to dwell on them.

But the Charter, which gave the Security Council "primary responsibility" for peace and which sanctioned the veto, also gave the General Assembly the right to make recommendations even in cases where the right of veto could be exercised. Apart from Articles 11 and 14, Article 10 gave the Assembly the right to make recommendations to the Members on any matters "within the scope of the present Charter" except in relation to disputes or situations with which the Security Council was dealing.

In fact, at San Francisco the small Powers had only agreed to the power of veto on condition that the General Assembly were granted the power to intervene and to make recommendations within the framework of Chapters VI and VII of the Charter in cases where the Security Council was unable to discharge its primary responsibility. As the delegation of the USSR had objected to the General Assembly having the right to overrule a veto, even by way of a recommendation, the United States had advised the Soviet Union on 19 June 1945 that, in view of the short time which remained before the ceremony of signing the Charter, the United States could wait no longer and that, in order to break the deadlock, it was going to negotiate alone with the small Powers. The following day, the Chairman of the Soviet Union delegation had informed the Secretary of State that his Government agreed to the extension of the scope of Article 10. The time had now come to use the right obtained that day.

Section A of draft resolution A/C.1/576 provided that the General Assembly could promptly make a recommendation if Security Council action were blocked. Obviously, a recommendation by the General Assembly had not the force of a decision of the Security Council taken under the terms of Chapter VII of the Charter. But the history of the Korean question had shown that the voluntary response to a recommendation could be even more effective than obedience to an order; although the Security Council had not exercised its powers of action, fifty-three Members were carrying out its recommendation.

It was doubtless considered in some quarters that an amendment of the rules of procedure of the General Assembly to provide for emergency special sessions, although legally permissible, would be unwise, because the Assembly might be unable to act responsibly, and that if it could not be relied upon to act responsibly, it would be better to abandon all idea of United Nations action.

The United States delegation considered that the responsibility for maintaining peace was not the monopoly of the great Powers and that an informed world opinion was the factor most likely to affect the course of events. There was every reason to believe that the General Assembly, better than any other organ, would reflect world opinion on the question of what was right, in other words, the supremacy of law.

The Security Council, of course, should have the opportunity of exercising its primary responsibility, but in the unfortunate eventuality of its failing to do its duty, it was the right and the duty of the General Assembly to consider the situation without delay. The very fact that the General Assembly would stand ready to act if the Security Council failed to do so would stimulate the members of the Council to co-operate so that that organ might function as was contemplated by the Charter.

Section B of the joint draft resolution dealt with the establishment of a more adequate system of observation; a peace observation commission would be set up, its members to be chosen by the Assembly from among Member States other than the so-called great Powers. That commission, and any subsidiary organs and observers it might have, would be the eyes and ears of the United Nations and it would reduce the danger of aggression. As Generalissimo Stalin had said of the League of Nations in 1939, the existence of a forum in which the aggressors would be exposed might hinder the outbreak of war. If the Security Council—or, failing that, the General Assembly—nevertheless found itself obliged to deal with a breach of the peace, the observation commission would be able to supply prompt and reliable information. It was thus that, in Greece and Korea, commissions of the Assembly had in the one case perhaps prevented open war and in the other case made prompt action possible. In the present state of tension, all those who were innocent of aggressive intentions would welcome a development of the United Nations' system of observation.

Under section C of the draft resolution, certain elements of the armed forces of Member States would be brought into readiness to serve the United Nations. There was no question of binding commitments for the future, or even of the designation of particular forces, and each of the Member States would continue to be able to avail itself of all of its armed forces in virtue of its right of individual or collective self-defence, as recognized in Article 51 of the Charter. Finally, a panel of military experts under the authority of the Secretary-General would be put at the disposal of any Member State which so requested.

Since the Security Council had not taken the initiative prescribed by Article 43, the Member States, which under the Charter had assumed the obligation of putting armed forces at the disposal of the United Nations, should now be invited to undertake some first steps without awaiting further attempts at negotiation by the Security Council. Certain Member States had in fact expressed regret at not having had forces ready to act in Korea, where one nation had had to bear initially a great weight of sacrifice. Without giving orders to anyone, the General Assembly could thus make recommendations on the subject to Member States, which, it would seem, were awaiting such an initiative on the part of the Assembly.

Under section D of the seven-Power draft resolution, a collective measures committee would report to the Security Council and to the General Assembly on the whole problem of collective security.

Subject to further suggestions, the seven-Power draft resolution recommended no objectives or methods that were not in conformity with the Charter, into which new life should be breathed without further delay. For, verbal attacks and threats of violence had been succeeded by civil wars and then by an armed attack which had led many people to believe that a world war was inevitable. The United States of America, while not sharing that view, recognized that fear of war, if not allayed, created the conditions that made war more likely.

The fifth session of the General Assembly should therefore take "effective collective measures for the prevention and removal of threats to the peace" (Article 1, paragraph 1). Already fifty-three Member States had responded in varying degree to the appeal made by the Security Council on 25 and 27 June, and the forces of eighteen Member States were then actually committed to serve in Korea under the United Nations flag, to achieve the aims of the United Nations. For the first time in history, humanity's dream of seeing a world organization repel an aggressor had come true. But now some people were wondering in retrospect whether the action taken in relation to Korea had not been only an accident, and whether aggressors would not still have an opportunity to succeed in the future; while others believed that if a new spirit were to animate the United Nations, it would be possible to avoid such local aggressions, which, as history had shown, were the prelude to general war.

The measures proposed did not involve acceptance of any particular theory as to the causes of the present tension, on which everyone had his own ideas, no doubt, without anyone being wholly right. The proposals were not based upon any finding of past guilt, but upon two general propositions that had been accepted ever since San Francisco: the first, that the dangers of aggression and of world war were ever present, and secondly, that effective collective resistance to aggression was an excellent preventive. . . .

Mr. VYSHINSKY (USSR) . . . said that the USSR delegation agreed to some parts of the joint draft resolution but at the same time had certain amendments to submit and objections to propound regarding some points. However, he wished to analyse some general considerations advanced by the advocates of the joint draft before stating his delegation's views on the draft itself.

According to its sponsors, the joint draft resolution was designed to strengthen the United Nations. Mr. Dulles had stated that the organizational weaknesses of the United Nations must be corrected if it was to be able to halt those who were preparing for aggression. Similar ideas had been expressed by other delegations, including the view that adoption of the joint proposal would be the best method of strengthening the United Nations, raising respect for it, and turning it into a mainstay of peace. Apparently the United Nations was not respected throughout the world and not the mainstay of peace but had to be turned into one. Mr. Vyshinsky said that his delegation must take exception to those premises.

However, the important element in the argument of the proponents of the joint draft resolution was the emphasis placed upon the necessity of strengthening the United Nations and removing organizational weaknesses which were supposed to have come to light. Unfortunately, those were only empty phrases. There could be no question of strengthening the United Nations by weakening the Security Council, which would be the inevitable result of the adoption of proposals like those contained in the joint draft resolution. The purpose of that draft was to relieve the Security Council of its primary responsibility, the maintenance of peace and security as stipulated in Article 24 of the Charter. There could be no strengthening of the United Nations if the cornerstone of the Organization, the organ which under the Charter had the exclusive right and power to fight against aggression, to forestall the threat of aggression, and to call upon forces not available to other organs under the Charter, was to be weakened. The proclaimed purpose of the sponsors of the joint draft resolution— the strengthening of the United Nations—would thus inevitably have a contrary result, through the implementation of measures which would weaken the Security Council.

Mr. Dulles' speech on 9 October had contained four implicit conclusions about the Security Council. They were that the Council was incapable of acting speedily or of acting at all; that the Council could not have the information required for the adoption of quick and decisive actions; that the Security Council, or the United Nations as a whole, could not have armed forces at its disposal; and that the Security Council, or the United Nations as a whole, was incapable of fighting against or forestalling aggression. The reason in each case had been ascribed to the principle of unanimity in the Security Council in connexion with action on non-procedural questions, or, in other words, to the veto. The same spectre of the veto was discerned in every direction and the general conclusion to be drawn was that the principle of unanimity must be liquidated. However, if that was the conclusion reached by the sponsors of the joint draft resolution led by the United States, why was it that the constitutional method provided in the Charter for the revision and amendment of the Charter was not resorted to? If the establishment of a new method of operation to circumvent the Security Council was demanded, why was it that the sponsors of the joint proposal remained silent about the possibility of changing the Charter, which was what was actually proposed? The fact was that the seven-Power draft resolution would explode and crush the Charter.

Of course, it could be contended that the veto was no good; that it was an obstruction; that it doomed the Security Council to a palsied state, that it prevented the Council or the United Nations from taking measures to discharge their responsibilities. If that were so, however, common sense and elementary good faith would require, in accordance with Article 109 of the Charter, that steps be taken to abolish such a provision. But the sponsors of the joint proposal avoided that course, although they attached considerable significance to speeches attacking the principle of unanimity in the Security Council, which was said to be the source of all the sorrows, failures and fiascos which the United Nations had experienced. All that was clear, at least to those members of the Security Council who had firmly and consistently championed the principle of unanimity, without trying to circumvent the Charter and without introducing unconstitutional principles into the work of the Council.

Everything that had been said and that would be said in the future against the principle of unanimity, however, could not withstand criticism from the point of view of the implementation of those principles which formed the basis of a United Nations composed of sovereign States. The principal questions relating to implementation of measures for the maintenance of peace and security had remained unsolved, not because of the veto but because of the position taken in the Security Council by the Anglo-American bloc, which had consistently tried to foist decisions designed for its own benefit, on the Security Council, decisions which consistently failed to take into consideration the interests of the United Nations and were designed to favour the American monopolists. That had been done by dint of the Anglo-American bloc's majority in the Security Council. There was no use in the veto if a majority could always be commanded. The advantage was always on the side of the majority, particularly when it had reached an understanding and had set forth an objective to which all members of the majority must submit, though perhaps not all of them sympathized with it. When a country was completely in debt to another Power, it could not take an independent position. That was the situation in the Security Council.

The majority of delegations in the Security Council belonged to the Anglo-American camp, or the North Atlantic Alliance and other bodies which had put themselves in competition with the United Nations. The majority had repeatedly tried to foist its decisions on the Council on such vital questions as the admission of new Members, the organization of the armed forces of the United Nations in accordance with Article 43 of the Charter, the prohibition of the atomic weapon, the regulation and reduction of armaments and many others. The majority had recklessly endeavoured to put through their proposals at any cost, paying no heed to the will of other States, or to the principle of agreed decision. The Anglo-American bloc did not wish to seek agreed decisions in the international sphere and did not wish to pay heed to the principle that it was impossible in international relations to impose one's will on another State but that one must seek agreement with another State. The Anglo-American camp was not acting in the interests of the United Nations as a whole, but in the interests of groups of Members, principally of one or two States which headed it. That was the situation which underlay the paralysis which was said to have affected the work of the Security Council.

Under such conditions, there might have been many more vetoes than there had been. The veto was a method of self-defence against pressure and dictation by those countries which regarded themselves as powerful, mighty and glorious and therefore entitled to implement their plans. An international organization could hardly have become viable if a sovereign State had been unable to rely on the veto to defend its interests. Such an organization could hardly have failed to become an alliance of groups of States, kept together by their own interests, rather than by the interests of mankind, which had guided the efforts of the States that had sponsored the United Nations five years previously.

Mr. Dulles had been wrong in ascribing the state of affairs in the Security Council to the principle of unanimity. The basis of every international organization was the obligation of each of its members to respect the governmental and national independence and equality of rights of all other members. The root of the evil was the use of the method of imposing one's will at any cost in international relations. Quite apart from the fact that on one issue alone—the admission of new Members—the veto had had to be employed seventeen times because the matter had been brought up repeatedly, Mr. Vyshinsky stated that had there been ten times as many vetoes or occasions for vetoes any self-respecting State would have utilized its veto right, which was the only guarantee of the independence and freedom of action of each State, a fundamental principle in the establishment of the United Nations Organization from the time of the Dumbarton Oaks Conference of 1944. . . .

Mr. Vyshinsky recalled that, on 14 October 1947, his delegation had exposed the tendency of the United States delegation to use all quibbles and excuses to transfer to the Interim Committee as many as possible of the powers and rights of other organs of the United Nations, particularly those belonging to the Security Council. Now that that had failed, it was proposed to endow the General Assembly with functions clearly vested in the Security Council under the Charter. The purpose of that proposal was to get the United Nations to do without the Security Council and allow the General Assembly to act in lieu of the Security Council, thus undermining the very basis of the joint, common and mutual responsibility of the five great Powers for the maintenance of peace. . . .

To give that proposal the cloak of legality, Mr. Vyshinsky said, reference had repeatedly been made to Articles 10, 11 and 14 of the Charter. Those Articles had been cited to prove that the General Assembly had the right to deal with all questions that might be dealt with by any other organ of the United Nations. That was clear to anyone who read the Charter and could not be contested. Nor was it debatable that the General Assembly could submit, to all other organs of the United Nations, and to Member States, recommendations on any questions coming within the competence of the Assembly or of the other organs of the United Nations, within the framework of the Charter, except as provided in Article 12. . . . Article 11, Mr. Vyshinsky explained, made it quite clear that if a recommendation were to involve some action, the General Assembly would have no right to take such action and, consequently, could not recommend what was to be done. In other words, the General Assembly could not arrogate to itself the right to take action that was incumbent on the Security Council. One could not say that the General Assembly must make a recommendation and, therefore, there was a moral obligation for the Security Council, or for any other organ, or for the Members of the United Nations, to act. That would violate the provisions of Article 10, since only the Security Council could take action on questions falling within the scope of Articles 10 and 11. . . . To say that the General Assembly could recommend action under the Charter to forestall aggression would be a flagrant violation of Article 11, paragraph 2, which clearly vested that prerogative in the Security Council. That was a very important prerogative whose fulfillment might be fraught with dire consequences for the peace of the world since it related to the kind of action which required the concurring votes of the five permanent members of the Security Council. Elimination of that requirement was the essential proposal of the seven-Power draft resolution.

Explaining the position of his delegation regarding the joint draft resolution, Mr. Vyshinsky stated that it had no objection to the provision contained in section A calling for extraordinary sessions of the General Assembly. Article 20 of the Charter had directly provided for such special sessions. However, his delegation could not agree to the proposal that such special sessions should be convoked at the request of seven members of the Security Council. According to the Charter, a decision to convoke a special session of the Assembly could not be made by any seven members of the Council; it must be a decision of the Council as legally constituted, which required the concurring votes of the permanent members. Moreover, the delegation of the USSR believed that, since a special session would be called in special circumstances, special preparation would be necessary. Obviously, such preparation would require more than the twenty-four hour period proposed in the joint draft resolution. His delegation was of the opinion that a period of two weeks would be needed to allow Members to send specially prepared and qualified representatives.

Mr. Vyshinsky stated that his delegation also accepted the establishment of the peace observation commission proposed in section B of the joint draft resolution. The General Assembly had the right, under Article 22 of the Charter, to establish such subsidiary organs as it deemed necessary for the performance of its functions. Nevertheless, the USSR delegation wished to draw attention to the fact that the primary issue in connexion with this proposal was the question of the membership of the commission. His delegation believed that such a commission should be a representative organ of the United Nations and not a mere tool in the hands of one group of States.

Section C, as well as some parts of the preamble to the joint draft resolution, contemplated the setting up of armed forces of the United Nations. The USSR delegation could not agree to the proposal because it constituted an attempt to usurp the rights of the Security Council and violated Chapter VII of the Charter, which provided for armed forces to be put under the control not of the General Assembly but of the Security Council through its Military Staff Committee. The proposal would call upon Member States to earmark armed elements to await orders. But whose orders? They would be subject to the orders not of the Security Council, as provided in the Charter, but of the General Assembly. Mr. Dulles had contended that the General Assembly would not order but would merely recommend. Various representatives, however, had pointed out in the Committee that a recommendation, morally speaking, was tantamount to an order. But where did the Charter endow the General Assembly with the function of recommending troop movements? Moreover, it was contended that the General Assembly had the right to recommend anything it wished. Mr. Vyshinsky begged to differ. The Assembly could recommend everything except that which Article 11 stated it could not do. Article 11 stipulated that any question on which action was necessary must be referred to the Security Council. The movement of armed forces obviously would be for the purpose of taking action. Therefore, section C of the joint draft resolution was basically and fundamentally incompatible with the Charter. It short-circuited both the Military Staff Committee and the Security Council. Mr. Vyshinsky also objected to paragraph 9 of the joint draft resolution on the ground that it suggested that military experts and advisers would be under the orders of the Secretary-General.

The representative of the USSR declared that Mr. Dulles and Mr. Acheson had endeavoured to camouflage the question as to what authority would control the proposed armed forces. They had not specified the organ of the United Nations at whose disposal those armed elements would be placed. He would assume that the Security Council would act, in such a case, in the name of the United Nations since that was what the Charter provided under Articles 23, 25, 47 and 48 and under Chapter VII. If that was so, it should be said.

It was further suggested, Mr. Vyshinsky continued, that in case of aggression, some steps preliminary to the measures stipulated in Article 43 should be taken. But the Charter did not leave a vacuum before the agreements referred to in Article 43 were concluded. Article 106 of the Charter stipulated that, pending the coming into force of such agreements, the parties to the Four-Nation Declaration, signed at Moscow on 30 October 1943, and France, should, in accordance with the provisions of paragraph 5 of that Declaration, consult with one another and, as occasion required, with other Members of the United Nations with a view to taking such joint action on behalf of the Organization as might be necessary for the purpose of maintaining international peace and security. Article 106 was in force since no agreements existed under Article 43; but thus far no one had even tried to act in accordance with the provisions of Article 106. The USSR delegation intended to submit a formal proposal in that connexion. There was no reason, therefore, for the establishment of panels of military experts which would encroach upon the exclusive province of the Security Council. Instead, the United Nations should endeavour to implement Chapter VII of the Charter, especially Article 43.

Finally, as to section D of the joint draft resolution calling for the establishment of a collective measures committee, Mr. Vyshinsky said that his delegation was of the opinion that the section was contradictory to Chapters V and VII of the Charter and would encroach upon the functions of the Security Council. The Soviet delegation was therefore opposed to section D.

In conclusion, Mr. Vyshinsky stated that the Security Council was faced with the task of elaborating measures to implement the provisions of Articles 43, 45, 46 and 47 of the Charter. The Council was also acutely faced with the adoption of measures for removing threats to peace, for dealing with aggression, and for the peaceful settlement of disputes likely to endanger the maintenance of international peace and security. It must take measures for the effective functioning of the Military Staff Committee. The Council and, in the first instance, its permanent members, must take all necessary steps to remove the obstacles which thus far had prevented the implementation of those measures, thus discharging the duties vested in them by the Charter of the United Nations. . . .

Mr. UNDEN (Sweden) said that his delegation regarded the joint draft resolution as an effort to find new safeguards for peace through the development of certain principles of the Charter which thus far had not been implemented. . . .

He called attention, however, to the provisions of the draft resolution empowering the General Assembly to set up national armed forces and giving the Assembly competence to recommend enforcement action. The question arose whether those two points were in harmony with the Charter. Regarding the first provision, establishment of military forces to be used in time of crisis, there was no conflict with the Charter. Regarding the second, the competence of the General Assembly to recommend the use of armed forces for enforcement action, it must be recognized that there was some doubt. Article 11, paragraph 2, stated in categorical terms that any question involving the maintenance of peace and security on which action was required must be referred to the Security Council, either before or after discussion by the Assembly. The argument that the Article did not extend to the mere making of recommendations by the Assembly was certainly debatable. Moreover, Swedish experts who had been given the task of submitting their opinion on the Charter to the Swedish Government before its entry into the Organization, had pronounced themselves in the opposite sense.

On the other hand, it had been noted during the past few years that the General Assembly had had the tendency of extending its competence beyond the limits indicated in the Articles of the Charter. The Assembly had, for instance, adopted a resolution [39(I)] in connexion with the question of Franco Spain recommending a type of diplomatic boycott. That action was tantamount to an enforcement measure. In another resolution [193A(III)], the General Assembly had recommended that Member States should not permit the export of [war] materials to the States neighbours to Greece. That again was a recommendation calling for action. That tendency to bolster the position of the General Assembly in the security field by extending its competence was quite natural. The same development had taken place in the League of Nations. The letter of the Charter had, therefore, been exceeded in practice, but this was a felicitous and a happy development of the Organization. Its Charter, like all other constitutions, must develop so that it would not become a dead letter.

Mr. Unden said that it was difficult for his delegation to form an opinion concerning the proposal for the establishment of international military contingents to serve the United Nations without knowing the ideas of the sponsors regarding the implementation of the proposal. If most of the States were to maintain only selective and limited contingents, they could hardly play a considerable role in case of serious warfare. The maintenance by some Member States of a number of limited national contingents could not be of any great significance if none of the great Powers having at their disposal the bulk of arms desired to intervene with all its forces. Nevertheless, limited contributions on the part of a great number of States that might be relatively weak, militarily speaking, might have a considerable moral and psychological significance. That provision of the draft resolution might also constitute a step towards implementing Article 43 of the Charter. . . .

Sir Frank SOSKICE (UK) . . . The United Kingdom delegation attached the greatest importance to the problem of the conformity of the draft resolution with the letter of the Charter. In legal questions, the British were if anything too formalistic, and in the case in point they would not have supported the United States proposals had they not been convinced that they were based on the letter of the Charter. . . .

As Mr. Dulles had indicated, the General Assembly was entitled, under Article 10, to discuss any question or matter within the scope of the Charter with a view to making recommendations, subject, however, to certain restrictions, namely, unless in a given case a provision embodied in another Article applied and precluded the General Assembly from considering the given matter. Specifically, situations which might lead, or had led, to an international dispute or a breach of the peace fell within the scope of the Charter and *prima facie,* therefore, Article 10 authorized the General Assembly to make recommendations on such situations.

With regard to the question of exceptions to the general principle, only Article 11, paragraph 2, and Article 12, paragraph 1, could be regarded as implying certain restrictions. It should therefore be considered whether either of those Articles was drafted in such a way as to bar the General Assembly from studying questions which it had, *a priori,* authority to discuss. . . .

If the principle that Article 10 gave the Assembly general authority to make recommendations in the sphere concerned was accepted, then it was necessary to consider in what circumstances the restrictions placed on its authority by Article 11 or Article 12 would make any eventual action taken by the Assembly illegal and contrary to the Charter.

The last sentence of paragraph 2 of Article 11 set forth a restriction which should be clarified. The word "action" was not defined and it was natural to think that it meant a coercive action which only the Security Council was authorized to take. According to that restrictive interpretation, the last sentence of paragraph 2 of Article 11 would be applicable only in critical situations. However, even if the word were given a wider meaning, the United Kingdom delegation felt that no real difficulty would arise.

If it were assumed that there existed an international dispute or breach of the peace—an assumption which undoubtedly would imply the appropriateness for "action" in the widest sense—what then, precisely, was the requirement contained in the last sentence of paragraph 2? It stipulated that such a question should be submitted, by the appropriate procedural machinery, before or after discussion by the General Assembly, to the Security Council for its consideration with a view, if necessary, for the latter to exercise the powers conferred upon it by Chapters V, VI and VII of the Charter. If it was felt that, under Article 24 of the Charter, the Security Council was primarily but not exclusively responsible for the maintenance of peace, it was only natural that Article 11 should provide that a question of that nature should be submitted to the Council.

The authors of the seven-Power draft resolution all agreed that if a question necessitating action were raised, it should undoubtedly be submitted to the Council, through the appropriate procedure, so as to enable the latter to consider what measures might be taken.

The United Kingdom delegation considered, however, that if that procedure were adopted and if the Security Council did not make use of its powers, Article 11 would not in any way preclude the General Assembly from exercising, in respect of such a situation, the powers conferred upon it by Article 10. That was obvious from the way in which the text was drafted, and even if the wording of the text did not make it clear, there was no doubt that such was the intention of the Charter.

Mr. Younger had stated that the Charter should be so construed as to prevent it from appearing to be wholly ineffective for the purposes for which it was designed. That desire sometimes led jurists to stretch the meaning of its provisions, but the United Kingdom delegation felt that, in the case in point, the draft resolution merely clarified and defined the powers which the letter of the law conferred upon the General Assembly.

Sir Frank Soskice said that he had already mentioned the case where the General Assembly referred a question for action to the Security Council and where the latter, being unable to act, merely shelved the matter. In such circumstances, it was in order for the General Assembly once again to exercise its competence in the question. Once that obstacle had been removed, Article 12 still remained to be considered. But when a question referred to the Security Council had been removed from the Council's agenda, Article 12 could no longer be considered to be an obstacle to a recommendation on the part of the Assembly, since the Security Council no longer fulfilled any function in connexion with that question.

The United Kingdom delegation therefore felt that, under Article 12, the General Assembly had to exercise the powers conferred upon it by the Charter, and that it was entitled to make recommendations once a question had been removed from the Council's agenda.

His delegation recognized that the Charter did not give the General Assembly the power to take coercive action. The Assembly could only make recommendations, but experience had shown that the recommendations of the General Assembly carried great force, in the same way as the Security Council recommendations had done on the Korean question in virtue of Article 39.

If therefore a General Assembly recommendation implied positive action by a Member State, it was perfectly lawful for the Member State to exercise the powers which it already possessed under international law, including the right to defend itself and to assist friendly Powers in the face of unjustified aggression. The Charter did not diminish those rights; it merely provided in Article 51 that when the Security Council intervened, nations had to obey its decisions. But there was also no violation of the Charter when the General Assembly, acting within its power, recommended to governments that they should exercise their right of self-defence, and the latter complied.

With regard to the question whether the provisions of section A for the calling of special sessions were consistent with Article 20 of the Charter, it should be noted that the General Assembly had the right to determine the time of its sessions and the circumstances in which they should be called. With regard to action by the Security Council, that was obviously a procedural matter for which an affirmative vote by seven members would suffice. Whatever doubts might subsist on that point, the fact remained that the provision enabling the Security Council to call special sessions of the General Assembly could not prejudice the Assembly's powers in the matter as defined in the first sentence of Article 20.

Thus, notwithstanding the doubts raised by some delegations, the General Assembly was competent to make recommendations calling upon nations to use force in self-defence, and there was nothing in section A of the seven-Power draft resolution which was contrary to the Charter. . . .

Sir Benegal N. RAU (India) wished to discuss certain points arising from the statement made by Sir Frank Soskice of the United Kingdom.

In order to convey those points by a concrete illustration, Sir Benegal assumed that State "X", not a Member of the United Nations, attacked a Member State, "Y", at a time when the General Assembly was not in session. That situation was brought to the attention of the Security Council under Articles 35 or 99 of the Charter. . . .
Sir Benegal further assumed that the Security Council was then deadlocked and therefore, by a procedural vote of seven members, called the General Assembly into an emergency session and also removed the matter from its agenda, thus removing the bar imposed by Article 12, paragraph 1. The Security Council, in the Korean case, had called for a cessation of hostilities, for the withdrawal of the North Korean forces to the 38th parallel, and later had recommended to all Members of the United Nations to give aid to South Korea to repel the armed attack and restore international peace. Orders to cease hostilities or to withdraw troops could not have been given under Article 10 because the General Assembly could make recommendations only to the Members of the United Nations or the Security Council, or to both, and State "X" was not a Member of the United Nations. Only Article 11, paragraph 2 provided for recommendations "to the State or States concerned", whether Members or not.

As regards the other recommendation to the Members to assist State "Y" to repel the attack, it seemed *prima facie* that both Articles 10 and 11 were applicable, Article 10 being the general provision applying to any matter within the scope of the Charter, and Article 11 being the particular provision, applying to questions relating to the maintenance of international peace. However, according to the canon of interpretation, the particular provision applied in preference to the general one, and the general provisions did not derogate from special provisions. Hence, also the matter had to be dealt with under Article 11, rather than under Article 10. This had been confirmed by Sir Frank Soskice.

Accordingly, after the situation had been brought to the notice of the General Assembly, the Assembly's first duty was to refer it to the Security Council in accordance with the last sentence of Article 11, paragraph 2. That would appear to mean that the case coming before the Assembly from the Security Council had to be referred back to the Council.

The United Kingdom representative had further contended that if the Security Council, owing to the exercise of the veto, failed to deal with the situation, the matter would again go to the General Assembly, at which time the General Assembly would have the competence as well as the duty to exercise the functions conferred upon it by Article 10 of the Charter.

All that meant, presumably, that the question was first taken off the Security Council agenda in order to enable the General Assembly to deal with it under Article 11. The General Assembly referred it back to the Security Council under that Article. The Security Council was then deadlocked once again and the question was again taken off the agenda of the Security Council to enable the General Assembly to deal with it under Article 10.

If that interpretation was correct, the Security Council was to be given a second opportunity of dealing with the situation before the General Assembly proceeded to deal with it under Article 10.

[The First Committee first rejected by 47 votes to 5, with 6 abstentions, the Soviet proposal to delete in paragraph 1 of Section A the words "to making appropriate recommendations to Members for collective measures, including in the case of a breach of the peace or act of aggression the use of armed force, when necessary, to maintain or restore international peace and security" and replace them by the words "to making appropriate recommendations to maintain or restore international peace and security, it being understood that any such question on which action is necessary, shall, in accordance with Article 11 of the Charter, be referred to the Security Council by the General Assembly either before or after discussion". It then approved the draft resolution, as amended, by 50 votes to 5 (Soviet bloc), with 3 abstentions (Argentina, India—which voted in favor of sections A, B, and E only—and Syria). GAOR, V, First C., pp. 156, 160–1. The General Assembly adopted Resolution 377 (V) on 3 November 1950 by 52 votes to 5, with 2 abstentions (Syria now voting in favor). GAOR, V, Plenary, p. 347. For text of the resolution, see BASIC DOCUMENTS, II.7.]

NOTE.—1. In 1951, the *Collective Measures Committee* made a study of the "techniques, machinery and procedures relating to the coordination of national and international action in regard to collective measures." It considered what appropriate steps "can be taken in advance, whether by the United Nations or by individual States, in order that any measures which may eventually be decided upon may be taken with all possible speed and effectiveness." It also studied the "arrangements which might become necessary after the application of collective measures has already been decided upon, in order to co-ordinate the action of the participating States." The Committee, in its reports, discussed in detail various practical and legal problems involved in different types of measures, i.e., political, economic, financial and military. GAOR, VI, Supp. 13 (A/1891), p. 3. The principal recommendations of the Committee were incorporated in the General Assembly's Resolution 503 (VI), of 12 January 1952, on the "methods which might be used to maintain and strengthen international peace and security in accordance with the Purposes and Principles of the Charter." GAOR, VI, Supp. 20 (A/2119), pp. 2–4. At the same time the General Assembly rejected a Soviet proposal to abolish the Collective Measures Committee, and continued the Committee for another year. GAOR, VI, First C., p. 170, and Plenary, p. 826.

2.   In its second report, in 1952, the Committee compiled an arms embargo list and a reference list of strategic materials, studied the problem of equitable sharing of burdens involved in collective measures and the question of economic assistance to States victims of hostile economic pressures, and considered a proposal by the Secretary-General to establish a "United Nations Legion" or a "United Nations Volunteer Reserve." GAOR, VII, Supp. 17 (A/2215). The General Assembly, in Resolution 703 (VII), of 17 March 1953, expressed appreciation of the work done by the Committee and continued it until the ninth session. GAOR, VII, Supp. 20A (A/2361/Add.1), pp. 2–3.

3.   The third report of the Collective Measures Committee dealt rather superficially with the role of regional arrangements and collective self-defense agreements. A/2713 (13 Aug. 1954); GAOR, Annexes (IX) 19, pp. 1–4. The General Assembly noted the report of the Committee and directed it "to remain in a position to pursue such further studies as it may deem desirable." Resolution 809 (IX), 4 Nov. 1954; GAOR, IX, Supp. 21 (A/2890), p. 4.

4.   With respect to the nature and functions of the *Panel of Military Experts*, see the 1951 report of the Collective Measures Committee, GAOR, VI, Supp. 13 (A/1891), pp. 24, 44. The services of the Panel have not yet been requested.

5.   The *Peace Observation Commission* was requested by the General Assembly to establish a Balkan Sub-Commission with authority to "dispatch such observers as it may deem necessary to any area of international tension in the Balkans on the request of any State or States concerned, but only to the territory of States consenting thereto." Resolution 508B (VI), 7 Dec. 1951. GAOR, VI, Supp. 20 (A/2119), p. 9. The Sub-Commission was established on 23 January 1952, and at the request of the Government of Greece it dispatched observers to the frontier areas of Greece. GAOR, VII, Supp. 1 (A/2141), pp. 51–52. For the Observations Manual for these observers, see A/CN.7/SC.1/44 (12 May 1953). The observer group was discontinued on 1 August 1954 in view of the improved relations between Greece and her neighbors. GAOR, IX, Supp. 1 (A/2663), p. 29.

6. The powers of the General Assembly to make recommendations to Members for collective measures were used for the first time in 1951, in the case relating to the Chinese intervention in Korea, and they were also applied in several cases thereafter.

7. For comments on the Uniting for Peace Resolution, see J. ANDRASSY, "Uniting for Peace," 50 AJIL (1956), pp. 563–82; GOODRICH-SIMONS, pp. 406–23, 430–32; H. KELSEN, Recent Trends in the Law of the United Nations (London, 1951), pp. 953–90; Keith S. PETERSEN, "The Uses of the Uniting for Peace Resolution since 1950," 8 Int. Org. (1959), pp. 219–32; André ROSSIGNOL, "Des tentatives effectuées en vue de mettre un nouveau mécanisme de sécurité collective à la disposition de l'Assemblée Générale des Nations Unies et de leur inconstitutionnalité," 58 RGDIP (1954), pp. 94–129; UN, Department of Public Information, Uniting for Peace (Pub. 1952.I.8), 38 pp.; L. H. WOOLSEY, "The 'Uniting for Peace' Resolution of the United Nations," 45 AJIL (1951), pp. 129–37, Piero ZICCARDI, "L'intervento collettivo delle Nazioni Unite e i nuovi poteri dell'Assemblea Generale," 12 Comunitá Internazionale (1957), pp. 221–36, 415–47.

CHINESE INTERVENTION IN KOREA

NOTE.—1. On 6 November 1950, the United States brought to the attention of the Security Council a special report of the United Nations Command in Korea, according to which the United Nations forces were "in hostile military contact with Chinese communist military units." SCOR, V, No. 60, pp. 3–5. A joint draft resolution was submitted by Cuba, Ecuador, France, Norway, the United Kingdom and the United States, in which the Security Council was asked: to note that according to this report "Chinese communist military units are deployed for action against the forces of the United Nations in Korea"; to call upon all states and authorities "to prevent their nationals or individuals or units of their armed forces from giving assistance to North Korean forces and to cause the immediate withdrawal of any such nationals, individuals, or units which may presently be in Korea"; to affirm that "it is the policy of the United Nations to hold the Chinese frontier with Korea inviolate and fully to protect legitimate Chinese and Korean interests in the frontier zone"; and to call attention to "the grave danger which continued intervention by Chinese forces in Korea would entail for the maintenance of such a policy." S/1894 (10 Nov. 1950); SCOR, V, No. 72, pp. 22–23. On the other hand, the Soviet Union presented a Chinese proposal that the Security Council demand "the withdrawal from Korea of the armed forces of the United States of America and all other countries" so that the people of North and South Korea would be left "to settle the domestic affairs of Korea themselves." S/1921 (30 Nov. 1950); SCOR, V, No. 72, p. 22. The Chinese-Soviet proposal was rejected by the Security Council on 30 November 1950, by 9 votes to 1, and the joint draft resolution was vetoed by the Soviet Union. *Idem*, pp. 22, 25.

The six sponsors of the joint draft resolution then asked that the question of "Intervention of the Central People's Government of the People's Republic of China" be included on the agenda of the General Assembly as "an important and urgent question." A/1618 (4 Dec. 1950); GAOR, Annexes (V) 76, p. 2.

2. With respect to the Chinese contention that only volunteers took part in the Korean fighting, see Ian BROWNLIE, "Volunteers and the Law of War and Neutrality", 5 ICLQ (1956), pp. 570–80.

1. *Discussion in the General Committee of the General Assembly, 5 December 1950.*

GAOR, V, General C., pp. 21–27.

Mr. AUSTIN (USA) said that . . . the facts of the case were known throughout the world.   The United Nations forces had been on the point of achieving their objective to repel the aggression against the Republic of Korea when they had encountered intervention by Chinese communist armed forces.   The United Nations was under attack. . . .   Representatives of the six nations which now requested consideration of the question by the General Assembly had submitted a joint draft resolution to the Security Council on 10 November 1950. . . .   On 30 November 1950 the Security Council had voted on the joint draft resolution which was not adopted owing to the negative vote of one of the permanent members, the Union of Soviet Socialist Republics.   As a result of the lack of unanimity among its permanent members, the Security Council had been unable to exercise its primary responsibility for the maintenance of international peace and security.   Since the Security Council had not been able to act in the matter, the six delegations which had sponsored the joint draft resolution now proposed that the General Assembly should consider the question. .   .   .

Mr. VYSHINSKY (USSR) .   .   .   said that he would confine himself to the procedural aspects of the question.   According to the United States representative, the Security Council had already considered the matter.   But since 25 June 1950 the Council had examined a wide variety of questions relating to different aspects of United States intervention in Korea.   Mr. Austin had reminded the Committee that the Security Council had rejected a certain draft resolution on 30 November 1950 because of the negative vote of the USSR representative. That was perfectly true, but the draft resolution in question had an entirely different purpose from the proposal now before the General Committee. .   .   .

The draft resolution which had been rejected dealt with all aspects of the Korean question and made two references to communist China; the first reference, in the third paragraph, stated that "Chinese communist military units are deployed for action against the forces of the United Nations in Korea."   That reference indicated that the Council was not then in a position to consider the question of intervention by the People's Republic of China.   MacArthur's report in fact referred to "communist military units", which might very well have been units composed of volunteers such as, for example, the International Brigade or the detachment of American volunteers who fought on the Republican side in the Spanish Civil War. It would be absurd to claim that those volunteers formed part of the armed forces of the United States and had been sent to Spain by the United States Government.

No one denied the presence of military units from communist China. Those units were, however, exclusively composed of volunteers while the United States representative had referred to the intervention of Chinese Government forces. An entirely different matter was therefore involved.

The third paragraph of the operative part of the draft resolution which had been rejected also mentioned "Chinese forces" but did not specify the forces it referred to. At no time during the eleven meetings, which, according to Mr. Austin, the Security Council had devoted to the question, had reference been made to the intervention of the armed forces of the Central People's Government of the People's Republic of China and that question had never been placed on the Council's agenda. The proposal was in effect a ruse employed by defendants attempting to play the part of the prosecutor. . . .

The USSR delegation felt that if the sponsors of that request wished to submit a complaint, they should address themselves to the Security Council, since they were not entitled to appeal to the General Assembly. Moreover, the General Assembly resolution of 6 November 1950 entitled "Uniting for Peace" laid down a compulsory procedure under which States wishing to lodge a complaint had to approach the Security Council in the first place. The USSR delegation had opposed the adoption of that resolution, but, inasmuch as it had been adopted by a majority of the Assembly, it considered that those who had voted for it less than a month ago should not violate its provisions. In any event, the General Committee should comply with its provisions and reject the proposal before it. . . .

Mr. GUTIERREZ (Cuba) strongly objected to the USSR representative's statement to the effect that the majority of the General Assembly distorted the truth and violated the provisions of the resolution entitled "Uniting for Peace" or the provisions of the Charter. It was not against the majority of the General Assembly, but against Member States which prevented the United Nations from achieving its purposes, that such an accusation should be made.

The facts were well known and had been proclaimed by the Press and radio throughout the world: the armed forces of the People's Republic of China had committed an act of aggression in Korea against the armed forces of the United Nations. According to the USSR representative, only volunteers had intervened in Korea. In fact, there were 800,000 fully-equipped men advancing as a regular army.

The obstructive manoeuvre of the USSR delegation on the occasion of the vote on the draft resolution submitted to the Security Council on 30 November 1950 had led six Member States to request the inclusion of that question on the General Assembly's agenda. The Soviet

Union was against such a move, knowing that its delegation could not paralyse the General Assembly as it paralysed the Security Council; the USSR delegation wanted to submit the question anew to the Security Council and continue to procrastinate whilst thousands of men were dying daily in Korea.

The USSR representative had stated that in including the new question in the General Assembly's agenda the General Committee would be taking an illegal step. He was entirely wrong. Mr. Gutierrez would not discuss the point with the Soviet Union representative for, in his opinion, the question was not whether the Chinese armed forces were or were not composed solely of volunteers. The fact was that the United Nations was now faced with an undeclared war; and Articles 10, 11 and 14 of the Charter, subject to the provisions of Article 12, authorized the General Assembly to deal with a question of that kind.

For all those reasons, the representative of Cuba was in favour of including the new question in the General Assembly's agenda.

Mr. VYSHINSKY (USSR) felt obliged, in view of the remarks just made by the representative of Cuba, to explain in greater detail than he had intended his delegation's views on the matter. . . .

At that juncture, Mr. Vyshinsky thought it necessary to reaffirm the very definite attitude adopted in the matter by his delegation. In spite of the Soviet Union's objections, the General Assembly had adopted a resolution on the question of unity for peace. As it had been adopted, the resolution should be respected by United Nations organs. As the Committee's members were aware, the resolution provided that the General Assembly could only take action if the Security Council, after studying a question, was unable to solve it. But as the Soviet Union representative had already pointed out in previous statements, the question of the intervention of the Central People's Government of the People's Republic of China in Korea had never been examined by the Security Council. The fact that the report of the so-called United Nations Command in Korea, dated 5 November 1950, mentioned the presence in Korea of "Chinese communist military units" or that the draft resolution discussed in the Security Council referred, in more or less veiled terms, to an intervention by Chinese forces in Korea, did not make it permissible to state that the question of the intervention of the Central People's Government of the People's Republic of China in Korea had been examined by the Security Council. . . .

Quoting from the declaration made by the democratic parties of China, Mr. Vyshinsky asserted that it was absolutely false to accuse the Central People's Government of military intervention in Korea. That was merely an effort to distort the meaning of the spontaneous movement that had led Chinese volunteers to lend their assistance to their Korean brethren who were the victims, not the instigators, of aggression—an effort to place on another State the heavy responsi-

bilities incurred by the United States Government. He doubted if anyone could maintain that it was the Korean people who had attacked
the United States and were threatening peace, when the United States
armed forces had invaded Korean territory and the United States fleet
was bombarding that country's coasts. . . .

Certain doubts had been expressed as to whether the Chinese fighting in Korea were actually volunteers . . .   Chinese volunteer action in Korea, however, was not without precedent. Men like La Fayette and Beaumarchais, for example, impelled by their sympathy for
the American people who had just risen against England and were
fighting for their independence, had provided sufficient equipment to
arm 20,000 volunteers, which was a considerable figure for those times.
That being the case, were there any grounds for surprise that Chinese
volunteers, whose country was infinitely closer to Korea than France
was to America, were fighting side by side with the Koreans? If nothing had prevented La Fayette and Beaumarchais from sending well-
trained and well-equipped units to America, why should it be otherwise in the case of the Chinese volunteers? Was there any reason why
China, whose population, infinitely greater than that of France, was
most indignant at the aggression of the United States and that country's policy with regard to China, should not allow its volunteers to
assist the Koreans? As a matter of fact the Central People's Government had with good reason declared that it saw no reason for preventing the departure for Korea of volunteers who wished to participate in the Korean people's struggle for liberation under the command
of the Government of the People's Democratic Republic of Korea.

In so doing, the Central People's Government of the People's Republic of China had in no way violated the provisions of the relevant
international conventions. Mr. Vyshinsky drew the Committee's attention to the Hague Convention (V) of 1907 with respect to the rights
and duties of neutral Powers and persons in case of war on land and
the Hague Convention (XIII) of 1907 concerning the rights and duties
of neutral Powers in naval war. Article 6 of the first of those conventions provided that "The responsibility of a neutral Power is not
engaged by the fact of persons crossing the frontier separately to offer
their services to one of the belligerents" while article 7 provided that
"A neutral Power is not called upon to prevent the export or transport, on behalf of one or other of the belligerents, of arms, munitions
of war, or, in general, of anything which can be of use to an army or a
fleet". Moreover, article 7 of the second of those conventions provided that "A neutral Power is not bound to prevent the export or
transit, for the use of either belligerent, of arms, ammunition, or, in
general, of anything which could be of use to an army or a fleet".

The United States Government should recognize the validity of
those two conventions since it had signed them. That being the case,
how could it possibly object if the Central People's Government of
the People's Republic of China did not prevent Chinese volunteers from

going to the assistance of their Korean brothers? The number of those volunteers in no way altered the legal situation. Moreover, it should not be imagined for one moment that the Chinese people could remain indifferent while the United States forces were in action, at a given moment, on the very frontiers of their country.

Such facts were too self-evident to be ignored. They showed beyond all possible doubt that there had been no intervention of the Central People's Government of the People's Republic of China in Korea but rather the participation in that war of Chinese volunteers who wished to save Korea from the imperialist yoke and defend the security of their own territory. Consequently, there was nothing to justify the inclusion in the General Assembly's agenda of an item entitled "Intervention of the Central People's Government of the People's Republic of China in Korea".

NOTE.—1. Despite Soviet opposition, the General Committee agreed to put the item on the agenda by 10 votes to 2. GAOR, V, General C., p. 27. After further discussion, the General Assembly approved the decision of the General Committee by 51 votes to 5. GAOR, V, Plenary, p. 597.

2. On the proposal of thirteen Asian States, the General Assembly established on 14 December 1950 a committee of three "to determine the basis on which a satisfactory cease-fire in Korea can be arranged." Resolution 384 (V); GAOR, V, Supp. 20 (A/1775), p. 15. The Committee, composed of the President of the General Assembly [Mr. Nasrollah Entezam (Iran)], Mr. Lester B. Pearson (Canada), and Sir Benegal Rau (India), suggested that the objective should be "the achievement, by stages, of the programme outlined below for a cease-fire in Korea, for the establishment of a free and united Korea, and for a peaceful settlement of Far Eastern problems:

"1. In order to prevent needless destruction of life and property, and while other steps are being taken to restore peace, a cease-fire should be immediately arranged. Such an arrangement should contain adequate safeguards for ensuring that it will not be used as a screen for mounting a new offensive.

"2. If and when a cease-fire occurs in Korea, either as a result of a formal arrangement or, indeed, as a result of a lull in hostilities pending some such arrangement, advantage should be taken of it to pursue consideration of further steps to be taken for the restoration of peace.

"3. To permit the carrying out of General Assembly resolution that Korea should be a unified, independent, democratic, sovereign State with a constitution and a government based on free popular elections, all non-Korean armed forces will be withdrawn, by appropriate stages, from Korea, and appropriate arrangements, in accordance with United Nations principles, will be made for the Korean people to express their own free will in respect of their future government.

"4. Pending the completion of the steps referred to in the preceding paragraph, appropriate interim arrangements, in accordance with United Nations principles, will be made for the administration of Korea and the maintenance of peace and security there.

"5. As soon as agreement has been reached on a cease-fire, the General Assembly shall set up an appropriate body which shall include representatives of the Governments of the United Kingdom, the United States of America, the Union of Soviet Socialist Republics and the People's Republic of China, with a view to the achievement of a settlement, in conformity with existing international obligations and the provisions of the United Nations Charter, of Far Eastern problems, including, among others, those of Formosa (Taiwan) and of the representation of China in the United Nations." A/C.1/645 (11 Jan. 1951); GAOR, Annexes (V) 76, p. 13.

3. In its reply, the People's Republic of China contended that the basic point of this proposal was "the arrangement of a cease-fire in Korea first, and the conducting of negotiations among the various countries concerned, afterwards. The purpose of arranging a cease-fire first is merely to give the United States troops a breathing space. Therefore, regardless of what the agenda and subject-matter of the negotiations may be, if a cease-fire comes into effect without first conducting negotiations to fix the conditions therefor, negotiations after the cease-fire may entail endless discussions without solving any problems." It submitted instead the following proposals:

"(a) Negotiations should be held among the countries concerned on the basis of agreement to the withdrawal of all foreign troops from Korea and the settlement of Korean domestic affairs by the Korean people themselves, in order to put an end to the hostilities in Korea at an early date;

"(b) The subject-matter of the negotiations must include the withdrawal of United States armed forces from Taiwan and the Taiwan Straits and Far Eastern related problems;

"(c) The countries to participate in the negotiations should be the following seven countries: the People's Republic of China, the Soviet Union, the United Kingdom, the United States of America, France, India and Egypt, and the rightful place of the Central People's Government of the People's Republic of China in the United Nations should be established as from the beginning of the seven-nation conference;

"(d) The seven-nation conference should be held in China, at a place to be selected." A/C.1/653 (17 Jan. 1951); GAOR, Annexes (V) 76, pp. 14–15.

4. After a few attempts were made by India and Canada to clarify the Chinese proposals (GAOR, V, C.1, pp. 525, 543, 553–55), twelve Asian States proposed the convening of a conference, composed of France, the United Kingdom, the United States of America, the Union of Soviet Socialist Republics, Egypt, India and the People's Republic of China, for the purpose of "securing all necessary elucidations and amplifications" of the Chinese reply, and in order to make "any incidental or consequential arrangements toward a peaceful settlement of the Korean and other Far Eastern problems." They added that as the first step towards this end the conferees should, "at their first meeting, agree upon an appropriate cease-fire arrangement in Korea," and that they should proceed in their deliberations only after the cease-fire has been put into effect. A/C.1/642/Rev.2 (29 Jan. 1951); GAOR, Annexes (V) 76, pp. 5–6. The crucial parts of this proposal, quoted above, were rejected by the Committee by 27 votes to 18, with 14 abstentions, and by 32 votes to 14, with 14 abstentions, respectively. GAOR, V, C.1, p. 601. The Committee then approved a United States draft resolution, which was adopted by the General Assembly by 44 votes to 7 (Soviet bloc, Burma and India) with

9 abstentions (7 Asian states, Sweden and Yugoslavia); for its text see Document 2, below.

To permit this action by the General Assembly, the Security Council, on 31 January 1951, removed from its agenda the item relating to aggression against Korea. SCOR, VI, Mtg. 531, pp. 7–12.

2.   *Resolution 498(V) of the General Assembly, 1 February 1951.*

GAOR, V, Supp. 20A (A/1775/Add. 1), p. 1.

The General Assembly,

Noting that the Security Council, because of lack of unanimity of the permanent members, has failed to exercise its primary responsibility for the maintenance of international peace and security in regard to Chinese Communist intervention in Korea,

Noting that the Central People's Government of the People's Republic of China has not accepted United Nations proposals to bring about a cessation of hostilities in Korea with a view to peaceful settlement and that its armed forces continue their invasion of Korea and their large-scale attacks upon United Nations forces there,

1.   Finds that the Central People's Government of the People's Republic of China, by giving direct aid and assistance to those who were already committing aggression in Korea and by engaging in hostilities against United Nations forces there, has itself engaged in aggression in Korea;

2.   Calls upon the Central People's Government of the People's Republic of China to cause its forces and nationals in Korea to cease hostilities against the United Nations forces and to withdraw from Korea;

3.   Affirms the determination of the United Nations to continue its action in Korea to meet the aggression;

4.   Calls upon all States and authorities to continue to lend every assistance to the United Nations action in Korea;

5.   Calls upon all States and authorities to refrain from giving any assistance to the aggressors in Korea;

6.   Requests a Committee composed of the members of the Collective Measures Committee as a matter of urgency to consider additional measures to be employed to meet this aggression and to report thereon to the General Assembly, it being understood that the Committee is authorized to defer its report if the Good Offices Committee referred to in the following paragraph reports satisfactory progress in its efforts;

7.   Affirms that it continues to be the policy of the United Nations to bring about a cessation of hostilities in Korea and the achievement of United Nations objectives in Korea by peaceful means, and requests the President of the General Assembly to designate forthwith two persons who would meet with him at any suitable opportunity to use their good offices to this end.

NOTE. On the basis of this resolution, the Additional Measures Committee presented a proposal for economic sanctions [A/1799 (14 May 1951); GAOR, Annexes (V) 76, pp. 20–21], which led to the following discussion in the General Assembly with respect to the Assembly's competence.

3. *Discussion in the General Assembly, 18 May 1951.*

GAOR, V, Plenary, pp. 733–42.

Mr. QUEVEDO (Ecuador): . . . What we are concerned with now is to hasten the end of the fighting in Korea, and the question of Korea has already been discussed in the Security Council. We can therefore conclude that, even if this draft resolution is to be considered as one which comes under the last part of paragraph 2 of Article 11 of the Charter, the provisions of that article have already been observed.

The Chinese intervention and aggression in Korea are only one aspect of the aggression committed by the North Korean Communists against the Republic of Korea. The Security Council dealt with that aggression, and it is because the Council did not succeed in taking the new steps which its position of primary responsibility required, that my Government and five other members of the Council several months ago asked the Assembly to deal with the Chinese intervention in Korea by virtue of its statutory powers. The Security Council's basic resolution on the subject was that of 27 June 1950, which recommended "that the Members of the United Nations furnish such assistance to the Republic of Korea as may be necessary to repel the armed attack and to restore international peace and security in the area".

Inasmuch as a contribution has already been made, in the form of armed assistance, to the defence of the independence of the Republic of Korea and the repulse of the aggression committed against it, I cannot see what assistance could be more effective than an embargo on armaments and strategic materials, to ensure that such materials did not benefit the aggressors. In other words, in view of what has already happened, the draft under consideration is legally valid, even apart from the resolution of 27 June. That resolution, however, reinforces the legality of the draft before us and removes all possible reason for criticizing it.

Since, on 27 June, the Security Council adopted a resolution, and since the relevant item was subsequently removed from the Council's agenda, the General Assembly, in proceeding to exercise its duties for the maintenance of security and the restoration of peace, was obviously—given the circumstances—taking steps which were strictly within its own competence. It was acting within its powers because, even assuming that the condition stipulated in paragraph 2 of Article 11 of the Charter must be met, the fact is that it has already been met; the item has been withdrawn from the Council's agenda, in accordance with Article 12. Moreover, the draft resolution under discussion is really in some sort an application or a consequence of the resolution of 27 June.

In my opinion, the fact that the Charter confers certain powers on the Security Council, and the fact that lack of unanimity among the permanent members may in some cases prevent the Council from exercising those powers, does not mean that the broad powers conferred on the General Assembly under Chapter IV of the Charter are thereby nullified. If that were the case, those powers would be illusory, because the General Assembly would not be able to make any recommendation, either on a particular subject with which the Council was dealing, or on a subject with which the Council had not dealt or was not dealing. It could not have been intended at the San Francisco Conference to give the Assembly powers which it could not use and which would have to remain a dead letter in the text of the Charter.

We therefore maintain that the Security Council declared that there had been aggression against the Republic of Korea and asked the Member States of the United Nations to help to repel that aggression. The Council subsequently removed the question from its agenda. The General Assembly then placed the question on its agenda, being fully competent to do so. Later, on 1 February 1951, the Assembly adopted a resolution [*resolution 498 (V)*] which it was also competent to do under the Charter. My delegation therefore believes that the present draft resolution is of undoubted legal validity and that the recommendations it makes are of great moral value.

Unfortunately, the draft resolution has become necessary again precisely because the authorities of North Korea and Peking have rejected the persistent efforts of the United Nations to bring about a peaceful solution of the conflict in order to ensure peace in that part of the Far East. The draft resolution is intended to secure the unification of Korea and guarantees that country true independence and its people the right freely to choose their political régime.

My Government believes that the draft resolution in no way infringes the right of any government to decide in good faith to what exports the embargo applies, to take the necessary measures of control within the framework of its responsibilities and its laws, or to attempt to prevent people, so far as it can, from setting aside the failure of control measures taken by other States. My delegation likewise believes that the States whence the exported materials come cannot be held responsible for infractions of the embargo abroad if the country of origin was assured that the export was not to a forbidden destination. . . .

Mr. MALIK (USSR): . . . Article 24 of the Charter places on the Security Council the primary responsibility for the maintenance of international peace and security. Paragraph 2 of that Article states that the specific powers granted to the Security Council for the discharge of its duties in the maintenance of peace and security are laid down in Chapters VI, VII, VIII and XII of the Charter. The whole question of an embargo comes under Chapter VII of the Charter. The thirteen Articles of Chapter VII of the Charter mention only the Security Council. The General Assembly is not mentioned once. This is an unchallengeable and fundamental provision of the Charter, and however hard the United States representatives try to get out of the difficulty, they will not succeed in proving that the United States draft resolution is compatible with the Charter for that is impossible to prove.

As for the United States representative's attempt to assert that Article 11 of the Charter gives the General Assembly the right to take decisions on such questions as the adoption of economic sanctions, it does not bear scrutiny and is the crudest of falsifications. Paragraph 2 of Article 11 of the Charter actually reads as follows:

"The General Assembly may discuss any questions relating to the maintenance of international peace and security . . . and . . . may make recommendations with regard to any such questions . . . Any such question on which action is necessary shall be referred to the Security Council by the General Assembly either before or after discussion."

Such a question is to be referred to the Security Council for action because the General Assembly has no power to take any action whatsoever. The Assembly may make recommendations but is not authorized to take action: action is for the Security Council, and is its prerogative. That is the fundamental provision of the United Nations Charter, and no attempt to controvert it can succeed. That is what is laid down in Article 11 of the Charter. It must be clear to everyone that the application of economic sanctions against any country, or the imposition of an embargo, involves action. In accordance with the clear and indisputable provisions of paragraph 2 of Article 11 of the Charter, such a question must be referred to the Security Council for its decision. The General Assembly is not entitled to decide on questions of this kind. .   .   .

In order to achieve its aggressive aims, the United States has pushed through the General Assembly and the Security Council a number of illegal and shameful resolutions which are contrary to the Charter. After launching its aggression on 26 June 1950 against the Korean people and China—a fact which has now become officially established as a result of General Marshall's testimony and the interview given by Admiral Martin, Commander of the Seventh Fleet— the United States, on 27 June 1950, forced its illegal resolution on the United Nations *post factum* and is attempting to use it as a screen. The reference which the representative of Ecuador made to that resolution was absurd and unwarranted. The representative of Ecuador was unable to base his argument on the Charter or its provisions; that is why he was obliged to appeal to that illegal resolution.

Subsequently the United States pushed through yet another illegal resolution, this time on the General Assembly. That resolution was hypocritically and demagogically entitled by the United States aggressors "Uniting for peace" [*resolution 377 (V)*], but its real title should have been, "Uniting for the benefit of United States aggression", for that was its real purpose. The shameful United States draft resolution which was subsequently adopted, declaring the People's Republic of China the aggressor, and this new United States draft resolution calling for an embargo, fully confirm the fact that such was indeed the purpose and intention of that resolution. . . .

United States representatives adduce the illegal decision to which I have referred, a decision which was incompatible with the Charter, as a reason for forcing through new decisions which are in flagrant violation of, and obviously contrary to, the Charter. That is precisely the case also with the United States draft resolution concerning an embargo, which is now before the General Assembly. The United States is urging the General Assembly to commit a flagrant violation of the United Nations Charter, to adopt an illegal and shameful resolution. It is forcing the General Assembly to embark on what is in fact the liquidation of the Security Council as the United Nations organ which, under the Charter, bears the primary responsibility for the maintenance of international peace and security, and which hinders the United States aggressors in the execution of their sanguinary misdeeds.

The ruling circles of the United States have adopted a policy which will lead to the collapse of the structure of the United Nations. The responsibility for this incipient disintegration of the United Nations rests primarily on the United States, whose plans for aggression are thwarted by the Organization as it was established at San Francisco, and for which the Charter has become nothing more than a straitjacket to restrain raving aggressors. But the responsibility for the collapse of the United Nations will also be shared by the members of the aggressor bloc in the United Nations; as allies of the United States in various military and aggressive blocs and alliances, they are daily undermining the foundations of the Organization.

The political purposes of the draft resolution concerning an embargo which the United States is endeavouring to push through the General Assembly, in violation of the Charter and without reference to the Security Council, are clear. The purpose of the resolution is not to terminate the war in Korea and arrive at a peaceful settlement of the Korean conflict, but to continue and extend the war. Those are the intentions of the ruling circles of the United States. . . .

For the foregoing reasons the delegation of the Soviet Union did not participate in the discussion or the vote on this question in the

First Committee, and is not taking part in the present discussion and/or vote. This non-participation will not signify abstention from the vote. It means non-participation in the discussion and voting because of the illegality of the question and because the General Assembly has no power to consider it. . . .

Mr. KATZ-SUCHY (Poland): The draft resolution which has been submitted to the General Assembly for adoption envisages sanctions of an economic nature to be directed against the Government of Korea as well as against the Central People's Government of China. Action of such kind is envisaged in Article 41 of the Charter, where it is reserved exclusively to the Security Council. No provision whatsoever under Chapter VII of the Charter makes it possible for any organ other than the Security Council to take any action directed against threats to the peace, breaches of the peace or acts of aggression.

Article 41 reserves to the Security Council exclusively the power to deal with such matters; therefore, if any other organ deals with them, that is contrary to the Charter and such action must be considered illegal. That legal argument has been fully elaborated by all leading commentators on the Charter, as well as in the discussions in the Foreign Relations Committee of the United States Senate during its debate on the Charter. . . . The position was also made quite clear by the former Secretary of State, Edward Stettinius, in his report to the President of the United States on the results of the San Francisco Conference. It is further emphasized by Article 11, paragraph 2, of the Charter, which makes the reservation that any action must be referred to the Security Council either before or after discussion. . . .

Mr. GROSS (USA): I wish to deal with the Soviet Union argument and the argument advanced by the associates of the Soviet Union representative that this draft resolution is beyond the competence of the General Assembly. They say that recommendations of the sort contained in the draft resolution may be made by the Security Council, and only by the Security Council, under Chapter VII of the Charter, in particular, under Article 41. It seems to me to be very late for my USSR colleague to question whether Article 10 of the Charter means what it says. I shall read Article 10:

"The General Assembly may discuss any questions or any matters within the scope of the present Charter or relating to the powers and functions of any organs provided for in the present Charter, and, except as provided in Article 12, may make recommendation to the Members of the United Nations or to the Security Council or to both on any such questions or matters."

The sole exception in Article 10 to the competence of the General Assembly, therefore, is contained in Article 12. Article 12 is not involved in this situation, and it has not been referred to in this regard by the representative of the Soviet Union or by his associates. Of course, the Security Council is not dealing with this question at the present time. It is not doing so because the matter has been removed from the agenda of the Security Council. The representative of the USSR voted for the removal of the matter from the agenda of the Security Council; I should like to point out in passing that he made the following statement—I quote from the record of the Security Council meeting of 31 January 1951:

"Moreover, the delegation of the Soviet Union considers it necessary to affirm the illegality of all decisions adopted on this matter by the Security Council under pressure by the United States."

The USSR representative now wishes this matter to be referred to the Security Council, where he has taken a position that the Security Council may not validly deal with the subject. It is part of the history of the Charter that the Soviet Union sought at San Francisco to limit Article 10, which I have just quoted, so that a veto in the Security Council could bring the United Nations to the end of the road in a particular case, but the Soviet Union effort failed. In the case of Korea, the Security Council was prevented by the USSR veto from making an order under Article 41 of the Charter and from taking any action, as that term is used in the Charter, under Article 11. But although the Soviet Union, by abusing the veto, may frustrate the Security Council, it cannot paralyse the United Nations. On the contrary, the responsibility of the General Assembly becomes all the greater in the essential peace-making functions of the United Nations.

The argument of the Soviet group lacks consistency as well as logic. Today, we heard the representative of Poland—I think I quote his words accurately—say that sanctions of an economic nature, as he described the matter, are reserved entirely to the Security Council. He went on to say that no provisions in the Charter permit any action with respect to breaches of the peace or threats to the peace and that such matters can be dealt with only by the Security Council, not by any other organ. That is what the representative of Poland said today. On 1 November 1946, the Polish delegation put before the General Assembly a draft resolution which, among other things, recommended that each Member of the United Nations should "terminate, forthwith, diplomatic relations with the Franco régime". If this is not a measure of the sort described by the representative of Poland, I am at a loss to know to what measures or actions he referred. . . . . . .

The delegation of the Byelorussian SSR at that time submitted an amendment to the Polish draft resolution, to which I have just referred, recommending that each Member of the United Nations should "terminate diplomatic and economic relations with Franco Spain, such action to include the suspension of communications by rail, sea, air, post and telegraph".

Did the representative of the Soviet Union at that time question the competence of the General Assembly to consider this draft resolution and the amendment of the Byelorussian SSR to which I have referred? No. I should like to quote from the *Official Records of the General Assembly, second part of the first session, First Committee,* page 267. Mr. Gromyko said that:

"It had been claimed in the Security Council that the General Assembly should take action, but now it was being stated in the General Assembly that the matter was within the competence of the Security Council. The General Assembly had the power and right to consider and take a decision on this problem, and a policy of inaction would have grave consequences."

Those were the views of Mr. Gromyko, the representative of the USSR, in regard to this demand for economic sanctions against Spain.

It is not without significance that the delegation of the Soviet Union and its associates have refrained from raising at this meeting, as they did yesterday in the First Committee, a formal point on this matter so that a vote might be taken upon it and the General Assembly might formally express itself on the question. They obviously knew what the sense of the General Assembly would be; they knew that there would be unanimity except for their own votes. Perhaps they would have refrained from participating in that vote as well.

It is possible that there may be genuine differences of opinion from time to time among the Members of the United Nations as to what is within the competence of the General Assembly. Here again, how has the USSR delegation itself suggested that such a question should be determined when it is raised? Let me recall what Mr. Vyshinsky said in the General Assembly on 14 November 1947. Again, I shall read from the *Official Records of the General Assembly, second session, Plenary Meetings, volume II,* page 882. Mr. Vyshinsky said:

"I would remind you of the opinion expressed by the experts of the Preparatory Commission at San Francisco, to the effect that when an organ has to apply the Charter, it must also interpret it. In this connexion it is easy to understand why the Charter does not say that the International Court of Justice may interpret the Charter".

Has the delegation of the Soviet Union proposed that this General Assembly should determine its powers under the Charter in this regard? It has not. It has rested on rhetoric, on appeals to fears, to division, to disunity. It has used blackmail, it has used frustration. It has not used logic; it lacks logic.

In summary, the entire argument on the competence of the General Assembly is old ground being ploughed again. Each organ of the United Nations can be the judge, in the first instance, of its own competence, and I believe the principle is inherent in the Charter that when a majority of the members of that organ vote in favour of a resolution, that vote can be considered as a determination by that body of the competence of the organ concerned in accordance with the principles of the Charter. . . .

Mr. KATZ-SUCHY (Poland): . . . The representative of the United States could have found many other Articles in the Charter in which no limitation of the powers of the General Assembly is given. Why did he refer to Article 10? He could have referred to Article 26, Article 89, or Article 90. There is nothing said in those Articles concerning the limitation of the powers of the General Assembly. Why did he not refer to Article 11, which is the Article relevant in this case and which should be interpreted in the light of Chapter VII of the Charter? He referred to Article 10 because it suited his convenience. With regard to the functions and powers of the General Assembly, the San Francisco Conference found it necessary to establish Articles 10 and 11. Article 11 refers in particular to questions relating to the maintenance of international peace and security, including the principles governing disarmament. This is the Article which is relevant in this case, and no other.

As I said, I can find several other Articles in which no reference is made to a limitation of the powers of the General Assembly with regard to action concerning breaches of the peace and acts of aggression. The relevant Article in this situation is Article 11, paragraph 2, the last sentence of which the representative of the United States prefers to overlook. The last sentence of that paragraph reads as follows: "Any such question on which action is necessary shall be referred to the Security Council by the General Assembly either before or after discussion." That provision is binding on the General Assembly and makes it clear that the action of the United States is illegal, and I am quite sure that the representative of the United States is well aware of the illegality of this action.

My delegation did not press for a vote concerning competence because it believes that this is a matter which cannot be decided by a vote. We cannot decide by means of a vote to suspend Article 11 or to suspend Chapter VII. The representative of the United States would like to create certain precedents. On the next occasion he might put forward a proposal that the Chapter should be replaced by certain rules of procedure of the Committee on Un-American Activities. The representative of the United States knows that he has nothing to be proud of in the fact that, if the question of competence were submitted, the required majority would be found to support his view. This is something which gives no cause for pride. Many who would vote with him would blush as they did so. It shows only the immoral methods of United States foreign policy—the constant violation of the national sovereignty of many Member States and the illegal methods of pressure which are being used.

Also in an attempt to divert attention from, and to distort, the present situation, reference has been made to the action contemplated in the draft resolution concerning relations with Franco Spain which Poland submitted in 1946. This, again, is an attempt to distort the picture and to divert the attention of the General Assembly and of public opinion from relevant to irrelevant facts. In the first place, the action against Franco Spain was taken under special conditions which existed and on the basis of binding international agreements. It was taken on the basis of the Yalta, Potsdam and Moscow agreements which existed and which were binding, since we all adhered to the principle *pacta sunt servanda,* even if the United States found it wise and necessary for its aggressive policy to violate each and every provision of those international agreements with regard to relations between the United Nations and Franco Spain.

But the action against Franco Spain was not being taken under Chapter VII of the Charter. It was not an action with respect to a breach of peace or an act of aggression, and it was not an action envisaged under Article 41. It was an action which could be considered as falling under the provisions for a peaceful adjustment of a situation, and one which could be considered to come within the competence of the General Assembly. I still maintain, therefore, that the whole argument with regard to Franco Spain was invalid, and I am quite sure that it will not deceive anyone as to the fact that the United States is attempting to cover up its aggression in the Far East by phrases representing that aggression as a United Nations action. That argument has failed to deceive the peace-loving nations, and the latest argument of the United States representative will likewise fail to deceive anyone inside or outside this General Assembly.

[The draft resolution was approved by 47 votes to none, with 8 abstentions, but the five Soviet bloc delegations did not participate in the vote.]

4.   *Resolution 500(V) of the General Assembly, 18 May 1951.*

GAOR, V, Supp. 20A (A/1775/Add. 1), p. 2.

The General Assembly,

Noting the report of the Additional Measures Committee dated 14 May 1951,

Recalling its resolution 498 (V) of 1 February 1951,

Noting that:

(a) The Additional Measures Committee established by that resolution has considered additional measures to be employed to meet the aggression in Korea,

(b) The Additional Measures Committee has reported that a number of States have already taken measures designed to deny contributions to the military strength of the forces opposing the United Nations in Korea,

(c) The Additional Measures Committee has also reported that certain economic measures designed further to deny such contributions would support and supplement the military action of the United Nations in Korea and would assist in putting an end to the aggression,

1. Recommends that every State:

(a) Apply an embargo on the shipment to areas under the control of the Central People's Government of the People's Republic of China and of the North Korean authorities of arms, ammunition and implements of war, atomic energy materials, petroleum, transportation materials of strategic value, and items useful in the production of arms, ammunition and implements of war;

(b) Determine which commodities exported from its territory fall within the embargo, and apply controls to give effect to the embargo;

(c) Prevent by all means within its jurisdiction the circumvention of controls on shipments applied by other States pursuant to the present resolution;

(d) Co-operate with other States in carrying out the purposes of this embargo;

(e) Report to the Additional Measures Committee, within thirty days and thereafter at the request of the Committee, on the measures taken in accordance with the present resolution;

2. Requests the Additional Measures Committee:

(a) To report to the General Assembly, with recommendations as appropriate, on the general effectiveness of the embargo and the desirability of continuing, extending or relaxing it;

(b) To continue its consideration of additional measures to be employed to meet the aggression in Korea, and to report thereon further to the General Assembly, it being understood that the Committee is authorized to defer its report if the Good Offices Committee reports satisfactory progress in its efforts;

3. Reaffirms that it continues to be the policy of the United Nations to bring about a cessation of hostilities in Korea, and the achievement of United Nations objectives in Korea by peaceful means, and requests the Good Offices Committee to continue its good offices.

NOTE.—1. A large majority of the Member States and several non-members imposed immediately the necessary restrictions on their trade with Communist China. Annual Report of the Secretary General, 1950–1951 [GAOR, VI, Supp. 1 (A/1844)]; p. 53; A/1841 and Adds. 1–8 (12 July 1951–7 July 1953). Negotiations for an armistice in Korea were initiated in June 1951; they were concluded by the signature of an armistice agreement on 27 July 1953, after a solution had been found to the problem of repatriation of prisoners of war who were unwilling to return to their home country. SCOR, VIII, Supp. for July-Sept. 1953, pp. 9–41; Syed AZIZ

PASHA, "The Repatriation Problem of the Korean Prisoners of War and India's Contribution in Its Solution," 2 Indian JIL 1–47 (1962); R. R. BAXTER, "Asylum to Prisoners of War," 30 BYBIL (1953), pp. 489–98; Jan P. CHARMATZ and Harold M. WIT, "Repatriation of Prisoners of War and the 1949 Geneva Convention," 62 Yale L.J. (1953), pp. 391–415; Maurice FLORY, "Vers une nouvelle conception du prisonnier de guerre," 58 RGDIP (1954), pp. 53–93; Joyce A. C. GUTTERIDGE, "The Repatriation of Prisoners of War," 2 ICLQ (1953), pp. 207–16; Josef L. KUNZ, "Treatment of Prisoners of War," 47 ASIL Procgs. (1953), pp. 99–121; Carl E. LUNDIN, Jr., "Repatriation of Prisoners of War: The Legal and Political Aspects," 39 ABAJ (1953), pp. 559–63; Jaro MAYDA, "The Korean Repatriation Problem and International Law," 47 AJIL (1953), pp. 414–38; William H. VATCHER, Jr., Panmunjom: The Story of the Korean Military Armistice Negotiations (New York, 1958), 322 pp.; William L. WHITE, The Captives of Korea: An Unofficial White Paper on the Treatment of War Prisoners (New York, 1957), 347 pp.

2. On 28 August 1953, the General Assembly noted the armistice agreement "with approval"; reaffirmed that "the objectives of the United Nations remain the achievement by peaceful means of a unified, independent and democratic Korea under a representative form of government and the full restoration of international peace and security in the area"; welcomed the holding of "a political conference of a higher level of both sides   .   .   . to settle through negotiation the questions of the withdrawal of all foreign forces from Korea, the peaceful settlement of the Korean question, etc."; and recommended that "the Union of Soviet Socialist Republics participate in the Korean political conference provided the other side desires it." Resolution 711 (VII); GAOR, VII, Supp. 20B (A/2361/Add.2), p. 1. This political conference was held at Geneva, 26 April-15 June 1954, but no agreement was reached. US, DOS, The Korean Problem at the Geneva Conference (Pub. 5609; Washington, 1954), 193 pp.

3. The General Assembly repeatedly reaffirmed that the objectives of the United Nations in Korea are "to bring about by peaceful means, the establishment of a unified, independent and democratic Korea under a representative form of government, and the full restoration of international peace and security in the area", and the United Nations Commission for the Unification and Rehabilitation of Korea continues to seek a lasting settlement. See, for instance, GA Resolution 2132 (XX), of 21 Dec. 1965 [GAOR, XX, Supp. 14 (A/6014), p. 12]; and the report of the Commission of 19 Aug. 1966 [GAOR, XXI, Supp. 12 (A/6312), pp. 1–2]. With respect to recent statements of the North Korean authorities and of the Soviet bloc, see A/6370 (29 Aug. 1966) and A/6394 (20 Sept. 1966).

EGYPTIAN QUESTION

NOTE.—1. After the conclusion of the armistice agreements between Israel and the Arab States, there were many incidents and grave violations of these agreements, some of which were vigorously condemned by the Security Council. See, e. g. Security Council Resolution 111, 19 Jan. 1956; SCOR, XI, Resolutions and Decisions, 1956 (S/INF/11/Rev.1), pp. 1–3. On request of the Security Council, the Secretary-General visited the countries concerned in April-May 1956, clarified various issues preventing full implementation of the armistice agreements, and presented a number of proposals for ameliorating the situation. For his reports, see S/3594 (2 May 1956) and S/3596 (9 May 1956); SCOR, XI, Supp. for April-June 1956, pp. 27-56. His second report was endorsed by Resolution 114 of the Security Council on 4 June 1956. SCOR, XI, Resolutions and Decisions, 1956 (S/INF/11/Rev.1), pp. 4-5.

2.   The situation in the Middle East was aggravated in July 1956, when Egypt, in retaliation for the United States' refusal to assist in the building of the Aswan dam, nationalized the Suez Canal Company and placed the Canal under Egyptian management. After Egypt rejected the proposals prepared by a conference held at London by the users of the Canal, France and the United Kingdom informed the Security Council that the Egyptian action endangered the free passage of shipping through the Canal and the situation, if allowed to continue, would constitute a manifest danger to peace and security. The Soviet Union declared that the military preparations of the United Kingdom and France for the purpose of exerting pressure on Egypt, were grossly at variance with the Charter and must be considered as an act of aggression against Egypt. Annual Report of the Secretary-General, 1956-1957 [GAOR, XII, Supp. 1 (A/3594)], pp. 4-6. See also US, DOS, The Suez Canal Problem, July 26-Sept. 22, 1956 (Pub. 6392; Washington, 1956), 370 pp. At the end of September both sides submitted the question to the Security Council, which on 13 October 1956 reached unanimous agreement that any settlement of the Suez question should meet the following requirements:

"(1) There should be free and open transit through the Canal without discrimination, overt or covert—this covers both political and technical aspects;

"(2) The sovereignty of Egypt should be respected;

"(3) The operation of the Canal should be insulated from the politics of any country;

"(4) The manner of fixing tolls and charges should be decided by agreement between Egypt and the users;

"(5) A fair proportion of the dues should be allotted to development;

"(6) In case of disputes, unresolved affairs between the Suez Canal Company and the Egyptian Government should be settled by arbitration with suitable terms of reference and suitable provisions for the payment of sums found to be due." SCOR, XI, Resolutions and Decisions, 1956 (S/INF/11/Rev.1), p. 7. An effort by the Secretary-General to implement these requirements led to the acceptance by Egypt of almost all his proposals, but the negotiations were interrupted by the commencement of hostilities in the Middle East. S/3728 (3 Nov. 1956); SCOR, XI, Supp. for Oct.-Dec. 1956, pp. 120-24.

1.   *Discussion in the Security Council, 30-31 October 1956.*

SCOR, XI, 748th-751st Meetings.

[30 October 1956, 11 a.m.]

Mr. LODGE (USA): We have asked for this urgent meeting of the Security Council to consider the critical developments which have

occurred and which are unfortunately still continuing in the Sinai Peninsula as the result of Israel's invasion of that area yesterday.
. . . .

Certain things are clear. The first is that, by their own admission, Israel armed forces moved into Sinai in force to eliminate the Egyptian *fedayeen* bases in the Sinai Peninsula. They have admitted the capture of El Qusaima and Ras el Naqb. Second, reliable reports have placed Israel armed forces near the Suez Canal. Third, Israel has announced that both the Egyptian and Israel armed forces were in action in the desert battle. . . .

These events make the necessity for the urgent consideration of this item all too plain. Failure by the Council to react at this time would be a clear avoidance of its responsibility for the maintenance of international peace and security. The United Nations has a clear and unchallengeable responsibility for the maintenance of the armistice agreements.

The Government of the United States feels that it is imperative that the Council act in the promptest manner to determine that a breach of the peace has occurred, to order that the military action undertaken by Israel cease immediately, and to make clear its view that the Israel armed forces should be immediately withdrawn behind the established armistice lines. Nothing less will suffice.

It is also to be noted that the Chief of Staff of the United Nations Truce Supervision Organization has already issued a cease-fire order on his own authority which Israel has so far ignored. Information has reached us also that military observers of the United Nations Truce Supervision Organization have been prevented by Israel authorities from performing their duties.

We, as members of the Council, accordingly should call upon all Members of the United Nations to render prompt assistance in achieving a withdrawal of Israel forces. All Members, specifically, should refrain from giving any assistance which might continue or prolong the hostilities. No one, certainly should take advantage of this situation for any selfish interest. Each of us here, and every Member of the United Nations, has a clear-cut responsibility to see that the peace and stability of the Palestine area is restored forthwith. Anything less is an invitation to disaster in that part of the world. This is an immediate responsibility which derives from the Council's obligations under its cease-fire orders and the armistice agreements between the Israelis and the Arab States endorsed by this Security Council. It derives, also, of course, from the larger responsibility under the United Nations Charter.

On behalf of the United States Government, I give notice that I intend at the afternoon meeting to introduce a draft resolution whereby the Council will call upon Israel to withdraw and will indicate such steps as will assure that it does. . . .

Mr. SOBOLEV (USSR): The available facts are evidence that Israel has committed aggression against Egypt. Israel has attacked with massed forces in the area of the Sinai Peninsula and penetrated Egyptian territory to a considerable depth. Fighting is now going on.

The Security Council is thus faced with an extremely dangerous situation in the Middle East.

It is plain from everything that is happening that Israel could not have made this attack without encouragement and help from those aggressive circles which are not interested in the preservation of peace in the Middle East and are trying to find some pretext for moving their troops into this area. In this connexion, I am compelled to draw the Council's attention to the following Associated Press report from London which is now being distributed. To save time I will read it in English:

"Britain and France declared today their forces will occupy key positions in the Suez Canal area unless Israeli and Egyptians stop fighting within twelve hours. The two Western Powers sent their warning to both Cairo and Jerusalem. Prime Minister Eden told the House of Commons the Anglo-French operation aims to 'separate the belligerents and guarantee the freedom of passage' through the Suez Canal."

This report makes it quite clear that the intention is to intervene in the events taking place in the Middle East without waiting for United Nations action.

This is not the time for long speeches. The Security Council must act, because it bears primary responsibility for the maintenance of peace and security. In our view, the Council must take effective action to put an end to the aggression committed by Israel against Egypt and to secure the immediate withdrawal of its troops from Egyptian territory. At the same time, the Council must issue a warning that no State has the right to exploit the existing serious situation in its own selfish interests. This applies also to the United Kingdom and France. . . .

Mr. LOUTFI (Egypt): . . . Now is not the time for speeches. The situation is grave. The peace of the world is in jeopardy. The facts speak for themselves and need no commentary. We are faced by an armed unprovoked attack committed by Israel forces on Egyptian territory in violation of the general Armistice Agreement, the Security Council resolutions and the United Nations Charter. This attack, moreover, constitutes a breach of the peace, and a serious act of aggression, which falls within the scope of Chapter VII of the Charter.

We are certain that the Security Council will declare Israel to be an aggressor State and apply the appropriate provisions of Chapter VII of the Charter. We are confident that the Council will also recommend to the General Assembly, under Article 6 of the Charter, that

Israel should be expelled from the United Nations. We are convinced that those Members of the United Nations which have been providing Israel with any economic, technical or military assistance will refrain from doing so and will immediately end such aid. Lastly, we share the hope expressed by the United States representative a few moments ago that no State will exploit the situation to secure political advantages.

Under the Charter, primary responsibility for the maintenance of peace and security rests with the Security Council. Its members must assume their responsibilities.

Mr. EBAN (Israel): I have only a brief preliminary statement at this stage. On Sunday last, three *fedayeen* units from Egypt created the latest breach of the peace by invading the territory of Israel from Egypt. Two of the invading units were captured and are in our hands; the third was repelled. This followed the Amman conference between the Chiefs of Staff of the armed forces of Egypt, Syria and Jordan, at which decisions were reached for the immediate and drastic intensification of aggression against Israel. On the evening of 29 October, Israel took security measures to eliminate the Egyptian *fedayeen* bases in the Sinai Peninsula. . . .

[30 October 1956, 4 p.m.]

Sir Pierson DIXON (UK) . . . In order that the Security Council may have the fullest possible information before it, I shall read out the text of the communication which was handed to the Chargé d'affaires of Israel in London at 4:15 G.M.T. this afternoon by the Permanent Head of the Foreign Office and the French Foreign Minister:

"The Governments of the United Kingdom and France have taken note of the outbreak of hostilities between Israel and Egypt. This event threatens to disrupt the freedom of navigation through the Suez Canal, on which the economic life of many nations depends. The Governments of the United Kingdom and France are resolved to do all in their power to bring about the early cessation of hostilities and to safeguard the free passage of the Canal. They accordingly request the Government of Israel: (a) to stop all warlike action on land, sea and air forthwith, and (b) to withdraw all Israel military forces to a distance of ten miles east of the Canal.

"A communication has been addressed to the Government of Egypt requesting them to cease hostilities and to withdraw their forces from the neighbourhood of the Canal, and to accept the temporary occupation by Anglo-French forces of key positions at Port Said, Ismailia and Suez.

"The United Kingdom and French Governments request an answer to this communication within twelve hours. If at the expiration of that time one or both Governments have not undertaken to comply with the above requirements, United Kingdom and French forces will intervene in whatever strength may be necessary to secure compliance."

At 4:25 p. m., G.M.T., today—ten minutes after the communication was handed to the Chargé d'affaires of Israel—a similar communication was given to the Egyptian Ambassador in London. . . .

Mr. BRILEJ (Yugoslavia): The statement we have heard from the representative of the United Kingdom introduces a new element of the utmost gravity into an already tense and serious situation. While the Security Council, the organ of the United Nations which bears primary responsibility for the maintenance of international peace and security, is considering the action to be taken in the face of Israel aggression against Egypt, two Member States of the United Nations have apparently decided to embark upon what can only be described as the unilateral application of force. They have done so clearly without any kind of authorization from the United Nations and even without any foundation in their own specific treaty commitments, which, in any case, could not prevail over their obligations under the United Nations Charter.

To make matters even more strange, this threat of force is primarily directed against the country which is the victim of aggression. Egypt is being enjoined to waive its inherent right of self-defence as set forth in Article 51 of the United Nations Charter. Egypt is also being summoned to acquiesce in the occupation of part of its territory by two foreign Powers. It is confronted with a rigid time-limit in the worse tradition of what we had hoped had become an obsolete policy of ultimatums.

Such a course of action is clearly contrary to the Charter. It can only endanger still further the peace and security of the world. It is only natural, therefore, that this should be a matter of the most serious concern to the Security Council. . . .

Mr. EBAN (Israel): At this morning's meeting I defined the objective of the security measures which the Israel defence forces have felt bound to take in the Sinai Peninsula in the exercise of our country's inherent right of self-defence. The object of those operations is to eliminate the Egyptian *fedayeen* bases from which armed Egyptian units, under the special care and authority of Mr. Nasser, invade Israel's territory for purposes of murder, sabotage and the creation of permanent insecurity to peaceful life. . . .

In recent months and days the Government of Israel has had to face a tormenting question: Do its obligations under the United Nations Charter require us to resign ourselves to the existence of uninterrupted activity to the south and north and east of our country, of armed units practising open warfare against us and working from their bases in the Sinai Peninsula and elsewhere for the maintenance of carefully regulated invasions of our homes, our lands, and our very lives, or, on the other hand, are we acting in accordance with an inherent right of self-defence when having found no other remedy for over two years, we cross the frontier against those who have no scruple or hesitation in crossing the frontier against us?

Members of the Security Council may be in a better position to evaluate this choice and to identify themselves with this situation if they hear something about the *fedayeen* movement, of its place in the total pattern of Egyptian belligerency, of its extension, under Egyptian direction, to other Arab countries falling under Nasser's sway, and of what would happen if we made no attempt at this time to resist that movement in its drive towards total conflict. The system of waging war against Israel by *fedayeen* units is the product of Mr. Nasser's mind. It is one of his contributions to the international life and morality of our times. After intensive preparation during the spring and summer of 1955, this new weapon was launched in August of that year, breaking a period of relative tranquillity on the Egyptian front, and indeed coming at a time when Egypt and Israel were engaged in hopeful negotiations with the Chief of Staff of the United Nations Truce Supervision Organization looking towards the integral implementation of the 1949 General Armistice Agreement. The Government of Egypt made no secret of these activities or of its responsibility for them. . . .

It cannot be seriously suggested that these activities are not the direct responsibility of the Government of Egypt. In recent months it has become apparent to us that the Arab Governments, and especially Egypt, have come to regard the *fedayeen* weapon as an instrument not for mere harassment but for Israel's destruction. The Commander-in-Chief himself, Mr. Nasser, defined their mission on 28 May of this year when he said:

"The *fedayeen*, the Palestine army, which started as a small force of 1,000 men last year, is today great in number and training and equipment. I believe in the strength, the ability, the loyalty and the courage of this army. Its soldiers will be responsible for taking revenge for their homeland and people."

On 19 June, Mr. Nasser declared, in the context of this *fedayeen* movement:

"We are obliged to be strong in order to liberate the entire Arab land from Morocco to Baghdad and in order to retrieve the rights of Palestine's people."

Having concerted his military plans with Syria and Saudi Arabia, the Commander-in-Chief of the Egyptian army, General Abdel Hakim Amer, spoke as follows:

"Now that the hour is approaching, I and the members of the revolutionary council will be in the front line of battle. In this battle our enemies will be convinced of their weakness, and victory will be yours and that of all Arab States." A little later, the same Commander-in-Chief said: "The Israel danger no longer exists. Egypt has enough strength to wipe Israel off the map."

The Security Council will observe that this was merely the spearhead of Egyptian belligerency. It was a new device for making war, and for making it with safety. The doctrine was that of unilateral belligerency. The Egyptian-Israel frontier is to be a one-way street; it is to be wide open for these armed Egyptian units to penetrate as deeply into Israel as they like, to accomplish their mission and then return; it is to be closed in their favour against any defensive response. . . .

This is the background, and these are the issues which have guided my Government's choice. We have faced them alone, and we made a decision to invoke for this purpose, and no other, our sovereign rights of self-defence. Israel is not out to conquer any new territory, but is determined to wipe out the bases in the Sinai wilderness from which murder and death and destruction are launched against it. . . .

The PRESIDENT [Mr. Bernard Cornut-Gentille, France]: . . . I shall now be speaking as the representative of France.

The speakers who have preceded me have all agreed that the situation is extremely grave. My delegation shares that view. It cannot, however, express a judgment on the events and the responsibilities involved which would imply any condemnation; it believes that any attempt, even, to pass such a judgment or to formulate such a condemnation would pointlessly aggravate a bad situation. . . .

For months, then, and indeed for years, we have been witnesses of a policy whose aims, aims fundamentally incompatible with the United Nations Charter, are openly affirmed: namely, the annihilation of the State of Israel, the expansion of Egyptian imperialism from the Atlantic to the Persian Gulf, open intervention in French internal affairs, direct material assistance to rebellious citizens, and the seizure, in defiance of all treaties and rules of international law, of a waterway which is essential to the life of the nations.

It was inevitable in these circumstances that Israel, faced with a policy so diametrically opposed to the Charter, should at some given moment feel compelled to react.

A recent conference between the Chiefs of Staff of the Egyptian, Jordanian and Syrian armies only heightened the tension by conjuring up the threat of a concerted attack.

Yesterday, three *fedayeen* raids took place near Aqaba. The Israel army struck back hard; it took up their pursuit; and the rest of the story we know.

For all the reasons I have just stated we feel in all fairness that it is not possible to condemn Israel.

Furthermore, the Governments of France and the United Kingdom have taken steps which should remove the danger of hostilities and put an end to the fighting. The French and United Kingdom Governments have asked the Governments of Egypt and Israel to withdraw their respective military forces from the Suez Canal zone. In order to ensure that the cease-fire is effective, the French and United Kingdom Governments have also asked that they should be allowed to move temporarily into key positions in the Canal zone. This request is fully justified by past experience. It is designed to ensure effective separation of the belligerents and also to guarantee freedom of transit through the Canal. These measures should lead to the immediate cessation of hostilities and the establishment of machinery which would make it virtually impossible for fighting to continue.

It is only proper therefore to await the replies which the Governments at Tel Aviv and Cairo should make within a few hours at the most, to the communication they received this morning from the French and United Kingdom Governments. . . .

The French delegation is opposed to the adoption of any resolution before the Governments at Tel Aviv and Cairo have made known their reply to the requests submitted to them by the French and United Kingdom Governments acting in concert.

[The Security Council then voted on the following draft resolution, presented by the United States (SCOR, XI, Mtg. 749, p. 31, n. 2):

"The Security Council,

"Noting that the armed forces of Israel have penetrated deeply into Egyptian territory in violation of the General Armistice Agreement between Egypt and Israel,

"Expressing its grave concern at this violation of the Armistice Agreement,

"1. Calls upon Israel and Egypt immediately to cease fire;

"2. Calls upon Israel immediately to withdraw its armed forces behind the established armistice lines;

"3. Calls upon all Members

"(a) To refrain from the use of force or threat of force in the area in any manner inconsistent with the purposes of the United Nations;

"(b) To assist the United Nations in ensuring the integrity of the armistice agreements;

"(c) To refrain from giving any military, economic or financial assistance to Israel so long as it has not complied with this resolution;

"4. Requests the Secretary-General to keep the Security Council informed on compliance with this resolution and to make whatever recommendations he deems appropriate for the maintenance of international peace and security in the area by the implementation of this and prior resolutions."

The result of the vote was 7 in favour, 2 against (France, UK), with 2 absentions (Australia, Belgium). The draft resolution was, therefore, not adopted, the negative votes being those of permanent members of the Security Council.

Mr. Sobolev (USSR) then proposed a short resolution calling upon Israel "immediately to withdraw its armed forces behind the established armistice lines." To this a provision was later added calling, in the first draft, "upon Israel and Egypt," and, in the second draft, "upon all the parties concerned" immediately to cease fire (S/3173/Rev. 1). At the meeting of the Security Council held at 9 p. m. on 30 October 1956, this draft resolution was also vetoed by France and the United Kingdom.

The Council, having thus taken no action on the item on its agenda dealing with "steps for the immediate cessation of the military action in Egypt", proceeded to the next item on its agenda, the Egyptian complaint against the British-French "ultimatum" (S/3712).]

Mr. LOUTFI (Egypt): You have before you the letter addressed by my Government to the President of the Security Council, expressing the Egyptian view concerning the ultimatum presented to Egypt by France and the United Kingdom.   .   .   .

The United Kingdom and France have twice made use of the veto to avoid being bound by the decisions of the Council, which might be an inconvenience to them in the aggressive designs they have clearly adopted since Israel launched its armed attack against Egypt.   .   .

Egypt has been the victim of aggression; its territory has been invaded; and as I had the honour to inform you this morning, it has been obliged to take the necessary measures and to use force to repel the aggressors invading its territory. But it did not resort to force until the Israel troops had actually entered Egyptian territory in large numbers, equipped with tanks and aircraft.

It is therefore very hard to conceive of a country which has been the victim of armed aggression, in contravention of the United Nations Charter, being presented with an ultimatum by two other Member States of the United Nations, when the question of the armed attack on that country is under examination by the Security Council.

.   .   .

Sir Pierson DIXON (UK):   .   .   .   The position which my Government and the Government of France have taken is this. In violation of the terms of the General Armistice Agreement, Israel forces have entered Egyptian territory. There has been fighting in the Sinai Peninsula within a few miles of the Suez Canal. A threat to the security of the Suez Canal is rapidly developing—the Canal, a waterway which is not only of vital importance to the commerce and the welfare of the whole world, but is also extremely vulnerable.

There are certain objectives which, I think, every member of the Council—or nearly every one—has in common. These are: to stop the fighting, which could, unless arrested, easily develop into a full-scale war; to secure the withdrawal of the Israel forces, and to restore the security of the area of the Canal. Where we differ is in regard to the means of attaining these objectives.

Nearly ten years of experience have taught the lesson that decisions of this Council, weighty as they are, in regard to Israel and its Arab neighbours are slow to take effect. But the situation facing us all is one of the most immediate urgency. Unless action is taken at once—and by "at once", I mean in a very few hours—we believe that the Canal may be put out of operation and that the fighting may spread outside the Sinai Peninsula.

These are the reasons which have impelled my Government and the Government of France to take preventive action of what is certainly a very drastic kind. As I have said repeatedly earlier in the course of today, this action is to be of a purely temporary nature. We have no wish to infringe the sovereignty of Egypt. When the emergency passes, our forces will be withdrawn. This is, I repeat, preventive action, not just selfishly in our own vital interests, but in the interests of all those who use and are dependent on the Canal and are interested in the maintenance of order in the Middle East. .   .   .

Mr. BRILEJ (Yugoslavia): .   .   .   We are faced with a situation in which the Security Council, through the use of the veto, has been rendered powerless, a situation which literally is deteriorating by the minute. The danger to world peace is growing at the same alarming pace. Too much is at stake. We surely cannot let the situation remain that way. We must do something. I should like to suggest to the members of the Council that they might find time to consider the possibility of calling an emergency session of the General Assembly under the terms of General Assembly resolution 377(V), entitled, "Uniting for peace". .   .   .

[31 October 1956, 3 p. m.]

The SECRETARY-GENERAL: Yesterday morning—on the basis of the information then available—I would have used my right to call for an immediate meeting of the Security Council, had not the United States Government in the course of the night taken the initiative.

This afternoon I wish to make the following declaration: The principles of the Charter are, by far, greater than the Organization in which they are embodied, and the aims which they are to safeguard are holier than the policies of any single nation or people. As a servant of the Organization, the Secretary-General has the duty to maintain his usefulness by avoiding public stands on conflicts between Member nations unless and until such an action might help to resolve the conflict. However, the discretion and impartiality thus imposed on the Secretary-General by the character of his immediate task may not degenerate into a policy of expediency. He must also be a servant of the principles of the Charter, and its aims must ultimately determine what for him is right and wrong. For that he must stand. A Secretary-General cannot serve on any other assumption than that—within the necessary limits of human frailty and honest differences of opinion—all Member nations honour their pledge to observe all Articles of the Charter. He should also be able to assume that those organs which are charged with the task of upholding the Charter will be in a position to fulfil their task.

The bearing of what I have just said must be obvious to all without any elaboration from my side. Were the members to consider that another view of the duties of the Secretary-General than the one here stated would better serve the interests of the Organization, it is their obvious right to act accordingly.

[In the course of the ensuing debate, the representatives of the United States, France, USSR, United Kingdom, Australia, Iran, Peru and Yugoslavia expressed their full confidence in the Secretary-General.]

Mr. LOUTFI (Egypt): At the very moment I am speaking before the Council, French and British aircraft have begun to bomb Egypt; the intention being to land armed forces. This is the report contained in a United Press bulletin which I have received and which I should like to take the liberty of reading to you in English:

"An air offensive by bomber aircraft under Allied command is at this moment being launched against military objectives in Egypt.

"British planes carried out an air attack on the city of Cairo at 7 o'clock this evening." . . .

It is evident that the position taken by the Governments of France and the United Kingdom which, as I told you yesterday, wish to settle, by their own means and unilaterally, a question which has been submitted to the Security Council, constitutes a flagrant and wholly unjustifiable violation of the United Nations Charter. My argument is proved by the fact that yesterday, for the first time, these two States resorted to the veto in the Security Council in order to prevent the Council from adopting a resolution one of the clauses of which provided for a cease-fire order. . . .

This unprovoked armed attack, in violation of the United Nations Charter, committed by two permanent members of the Security Council, is a serious attack on the United Nations, on world peace and on all mankind.

The situation is grave; the precedent is dangerous. The Charter has placed upon the Security Council the primary responsibility for the maintenance of international peace and security. I ask the members of the Council to rise to their responsibilities and condemn the aggression. . . .

Mr. BRILEJ (Yugoslavia): At the close of yesterday's night meeting, as the Council stood apparently powerless in the face of a rapidly worsening situation, I suggested the possibility of an emergency session of the General Assembly. The tragic developments that have since taken place have given an added emphasis and a new sense of urgency to the necessity of finding other forms of United Nations action to deal with the deepening crisis. My delegation therefore formally proposes that an emergency special session of the General Assembly be called in accordance with rule 8(b) of the rules of procedure of the General Assembly. The text of the draft resolution which I am submitting to the Council is as follows:

"The Security Council,

"Considering that a grave situation has been created by action undertaken against Egypt,

"Taking into account that the lack of unanimity of its permanent members at the 749th and 750th meetings of the Security Council has prevented it from exercising its primary responsibility for the maintenance of international peace and security,

"Decides to call an emergency special session of the General Assembly, as provided in General Assembly resolution 377A(V) of 3 November 1950, in order to make appropriate recommendations." . . .

Sir Pierson DIXON (UK): The representative of Yugoslavia has just submitted a draft resolution calling for an emergency special session of the General Assembly under General Assembly resolution 377(V) entitled "Uniting for peace".

I submit that the procedure proposed is quite out of order and not in accordance with the clear terms of the "Uniting for peace" resolution itself. I shall explain why.

It is quite clear that the "Uniting for peace" resolution may be invoked only when certain conditions are fulfilled. The relevant passage of the resolution provides for the calling of an emergency special session of the General Assembly:

" . . . if the Security Council, because of lack of unanimity of the permanent members, fails to exercise its primary responsibility for the maintenance of international peace and security in any case where there appears to be a threat to the peace, breach of the peace, or act of aggression . . . ".

Thus, a pre-condition of invoking the procedure is that a lack of unanimity of the permanent members of the Security Council should have prevented the Council from taking a decision.

This clearly presupposes that a draft resolution on the substance of the item before the Council has been submitted, circulated and voted upon, and until that has been done, it cannot be determined that the Security Council has failed to take a decision owing to the lack of unanimity of the permanent members. But no such text has been circulated or voted upon on the item now before the Council, namely, the letter dated 30 October from the representative of Egypt.

Furthermore, the two draft resolutions which we voted upon yesterday under another item are not within the compass of the "Uniting for peace" resolution and, therefore, in my submission they cannot be invoked to support the Yugoslav proposal.

A further consideration in my mind is that it is quite true that two draft resolutions, advanced successively by the United States delegation and then by the Soviet Union delegation, failed yesterday to carry because of the lack of unanimity of the permanent members of the Council, but the reason for that is simple and must be well known to all the members of the Council. It was because my Government and the French Government were and are convinced that action on the lines proposed by the United States delegation would not be an effective method for maintaining international peace and security in the present case. That is very evidently true of the truncated version of the same draft which subsequently was put to the vote at the request of the Soviet delegation. On the contrary, our two Governments believed yesterday and believe today that the action undertaken by them as an emergency temporary measure was then and is a more effective course.

Finally, I would add that in the present circumstances the calling of an emergency special session of the General Assembly on this subject would clearly have serious implications.

Mr. BRILEJ (Yugoslavia): I am sorry, but it is impossible for me to accept the arguments submitted by the representative of the United Kingdom. It seems to me that some of his arguments are not at all relevant to the draft resolution, such as, for instance, the reasons for which the two permanent members of the Security Council used the veto yesterday. They used the veto twice on two draft resolutions calling for a cease-fire.

It seems to me that the representative of the United Kingdom will agree with me that there exists not only a threat to the peace but also a breach of the peace. I hope that he will agree with me that the landing of armed forces on the territory of an independent country and the bombarding of its cities are certainly a breach of the peace. The Security Council failed to agree on that because of the veto.

The third argument the representative of the United Kingdom introduced is that on the item now under discussion no draft resolution has been vetoed, and that, therefore, the "Uniting for peace" resolution cannot be applied. Both aspects of the problem in respect of which we propose that an emergency special session should be convened are covered by the United States draft resolution, which was submitted yesterday. The question of the intervention in Egypt of forces other than Israel forces is covered by paragraph 2(a) [3(a)] of that draft resolution. That was recognized by the representative of Australia yesterday when he said:

"I just wish to explain the Australian vote on item 3 of the provisional agenda." This was the vote on the agenda which we are now discussing. "The Australian delegation abstained on the inclusion of this item because we consider that the substance of the matter has already been before the Council in the statement of the representative of the United Kingdom and that while the views set forth in the letter contained in document S/3712 may no doubt be advanced in the Council, it is not necessary to inscribe this as a separate matter on the agenda."

I also have here the views expressed by the representative of the United Kingdom. He said:

"This letter in fact deals with the substance of a letter which I myself read out to the Council in the course of my intervention earlier today."

We were discussing the first point at that time.

It seems to me, therefore, that the provisions of the General Assembly resolution entitled "Uniting for peace" are in full accordance with the draft resolution which I presented this evening.

Sir Pierson DIXON (UK): I intervene again simply to set forth what I believe to be the correct juridical position in regard to the "Uniting for peace" resolution.

In my submission, this resolution can only be invoked following action under Chapter VII of the Charter. Action under Chapter VII is dependent upon a determination by the Council of the existence of a threat to the peace, a breach of the peace or an act of aggression. The draft resolutions which were before the Council yesterday contained no such finding. This, I think, is all I need say at the moment in response to the counter-arguments advanced by the Yugoslav representative.

The PRESIDENT [Mr. de Guiringaud, France]: I should like to speak as the representative of France.

I cannot agree with Mr. Brilej's interpretation of the juridical background of his draft resolution. I note that this draft resolution does not specify the question which would be brought before the General Assembly. There have been no manifestations today of the lack of unanimity among the permanent members of the Security Council. If the Yugoslav representative is referring to the voting which took place yesterday, I must point out to him that the item to which those votes related, that is to say, the United States complaint, is not on the agenda of this meeting.

Moreover, the resolution entitled "Uniting for peace" provides that the Council may bring before the General Assembly cases of threats to the peace, breaches of the peace or acts of aggression. Now—and I am still speaking of the United States complaint—neither the text of the complaint nor the draft resolutions proposed yesterday by the United States and the Soviet Union delegations respectively came within the terms of the General Assembly resolution, in other words within the terms of Chapter VII of the Charter. A specific decision would have been necessary for that purpose.

For both these reasons, the Yugoslav draft resolution seems to me to be inconsistent with the texts on which it is based.   .   .   .

Mr. BRILEJ (Yugoslavia): I have one brief remark to make. The President, in his capacity as the representative of France, has stated, *inter alia,* that the subject with which we were dealing yesterday was not a question under Chapter VII of the Charter. I should like to recall first the statement made yesterday by the representative of the United States in introducing his draft resolution. He said:

"The Government of the United States feels that it is imperative that the Council act in the promptest manner to determine that a breach of the peace has occurred, to order that the military action undertaken by Israel cease immediately."

It seems to me that, whatever might be the wording of the draft resolutions and questions with which we are dealing, the fact is that yesterday's draft resolution called for the immediate withdrawal of armed forces, expressed grave concern at the violation of the Armistice Agreement and requested a cease-fire. It would seem to me, according to my understanding of the Charter, that all of this is covered by Chapter VII, Articles 40 and 41.   .   .   .

Mr. TSIANG (China): The considerations put before us by the representatives of the United Kingdom and Australia seem to me to be well founded, but I consider those considerations to be of a technical nature. If pressed too far, they would be tantamount to an invitation to put before the Council such a draft resolution, to put it to a vote and then to bring about the failure that would fulfil the technical requirements advanced by Sir Pierson and Mr. Walker. On political grounds, therefore, I hope that the delegations of the United Kingdom and Australia will not press that technical argument too far.   .   .   .

[The Yugoslav draft resolution was adopted by 7 votes to 2 (France, UK) with 2 abstentions (Australia, Belgium), at 7 p. m. on 31 October 1956. France and UK then made reservations regarding the legality of the Council's decision.

The Secretary-General immediately summoned the first emergency session of the General Assembly to meet on 1 November 1956, at 5 p. m.]

2.   *Discussion at the First Emergency Session of the General Assembly, 1–2 November 1956.*

GAOR, ES–I, Plenary, pp. 2–36.

[At the beginning of the session, Mr. de Guiringaud (France) raised again the following objections: that in the debate on the Egyptian complaint in the Security Council "no draft resolution was submitted"; that, therefore, "there was no vote and consequently, no manifestation of the lack of unanimity of the permanent members"; that the "United States complaint on the other hand was clearly within the framework of Chapter VI, not Chapter VII, of the Charter" and did not relate to a case where, as required by the Uniting for Peace Resolution, the Council failed to exercise its responsibility for the maintenance of peace; and that in these circumstances "the Council could not legally bring the Egyptian complaint before the Assembly."

Nevertheless, the Assembly agreed to the inclusion in the agenda of the item "Question considered by the Security Council at its 749th and 750th meetings . . ." by 62 votes to 2, with 7 abstentions.]

Sir Pierson DIXON (UK): Before I enter into the substance of the matter for which this emergency session of the General Assembly has been called, I feel bound to point out, as has already been done by the representative of France, and as I did in the Security Council yesterday, that the procedure under resolution 377 (V) of the General Assembly, "Uniting for peace", has, in our view, been improperly invoked on this occasion. . . .

Her Majesty's Government in the United Kingdom has nevertheless decided to attend this session, for an important reason. It is because it believes that the United Nations can and should do what it can to make effective contributions in the present grave situation in the Middle East. . . .

The immediate situation with which we were confronted was Israel's incursion in force into Egyptian territory, in violation of the Egyptian-Israel General Armistice Agreement, and the ensuing threat to the safety of the Suez Canal.

The threat to the Canal arising from Israel movements in that direction—and I can assure this Assembly that it is only too clear that this threat was very real—introduced a further complication in an already highly explosive situation. If the Israel adventure were allowed to continue as planned, it would undoubtedly have given rise to a threat to ships and cargoes in passage, and to the security of the Canal itself. It would have imperilled free passage through that vital waterway. It was a threat to the vital interests of my country, as well as to those many nations which are dependent on free passage through the Canal.

The Assembly must acknowledge that, by our swift intervention, the Israel advance has already been averted. I do not know of any alternative steps which could have achieved this result. . . .

Between Egypt and Israel the attitude of Her Majesty's Government remains quite impartial. We do not and could not condone this Israel action, which is clearly in violation of the Armistice Agreement and aimed at the occupation of positions in Egyptian territory. It was indeed precisely because of this very serious Israel violation that we judged it necessary ourselves to intervene. It is, of course, our view that Israel should withdraw its forces from its present positions as soon as this can be arranged.

Let me, at this stage, towards the end of my speech, briefly restate the objectives of the Anglo-French intervention. The overriding purposes are: the safeguarding of the Suez Canal and the restoration of peaceful conditions in the Middle East. Let me say with all the emphasis at my command that neither we nor the French Government have any desire whatever that the military action which we have taken should be more than temporary in its duration. It will be terminated as soon as the emergency is over. It is our intention that our action to protect the Canal, to terminate hostilities and to separate the combatants should be as short as possible in duration.

The action taken by my Government and by the Government of France has been called an act of aggression against Egypt. This is a charge which we emphatically deny. There is much debate about what constitutes aggression, but it is certainly not true to say that every armed action constitutes aggression. Every action must clearly be judged in the light of the circumstances in which it has taken place and the motives which have prompted it.

The action of France and the United Kingdom is not aggression. We do not seek the domination of Egypt or of any part of Egyptian territory. Our purpose is peaceful, not warlike. Our aim is to re-establish the rule of law, not to violate it; to protect, and not to destroy. What we have undertaken is a temporary police action necessitated by the turn of events in the Middle East and occasioned by the imperative need not only to protect the vital interests of my own and many other countries, but also to take immediate measures for the restoration of order.

Our action is in no way aimed at the sovereignty of Egypt, and still less at its territorial integrity. It is not of our choice that the police action which we have been obliged to take is occurring on Egyptian territory. We have taken the only action which we could clearly see would be effective in holding the belligerents apart and which would give us a chance to re-establish peace in the area. By entering the Suez Canal area, we would only be seeking to protect a vital waterway, and it is also the only practicable line of division between the combatants. . . .

The first urgent task is to separate Israel and Egypt and to stabilize the position. That is our purpose. If the United Nations were willing to take over the physical task of maintaining peace in the area, no one would be better pleased than we. But police action there must be, to separate the belligerents and to stop the hostilities. . . .

Mr. DULLES (USA): I doubt that any representative ever spoke from this rostrum with as heavy a heart as I have brought here tonight. We speak on a matter of vital importance, where the United States finds itself unable to agree with three nations with which it has ties of deep friendship, of admiration and of respect, and two of which constitute our oldest and most trusted and reliable allies.

The fact that we differ with such friends has led us to reconsider and re-evaluate our position with the utmost care, and that has been done at the highest levels of our Government, but even after that re-evaluation we still find ourselves in disagreement. And, because it seems to us that that disagreement involves principles which far transcend the immediate issue, we feel impelled to make our point of view known to you and, through you, to the world.

This is the first time that this Assembly has met pursuant to the "Uniting for peace" resolution which the General Assembly adopted in 1950. I was a member of the United States delegation and had the primary responsibility for handling that proposal in committee and on the floor of this Assembly. It was then the period of the communist attack upon the Republic of Korea, and at that time surely we little thought that the resolution would be invoked for the first time under the conditions which now prevail.

What are the facts that bring us here? There is, first of all, the fact that there occurred, beginning last Monday, 29 October 1956, a deep penetration of Egypt by Israel forces. Then, quickly following upon that action, there came action by France and the United Kingdom in subjecting Egypt first to a twelve-hour ultimatum, and then to an armed attack, which is now going on from the air with the declared purpose of gaining temporary control of the Suez Canal, presumably to make it more secure. Then there is the third fact that after the matter had been brought to the Security Council, it was sought to deal with it by a draft resolution which was vetoed by the United Kingdom and France, which cast the only dissenting votes against the draft resolution.

Thereupon, under the provisions of the "Uniting for peace" resolution, the matter was brought before the Assembly upon a call from the Secretary-General instituted by a vote of seven members of the Security Council requiring that this Assembly convene in emergency special session within twenty-four hours.

The United States recognizes full well that the facts which I have referred to are not the only facts in this situation. There is a long and sad history of irritations and provocations. There have been armistice violations by Israel and against Israel. There have been violations by Egypt of the Treaty of 1888 governing the Suez Canal, and disregard by Egypt of the Security Council resolution of 1951 calling for the passage through the Canal of Israel ships and cargoes. There has been a heavy rearmament of Egypt in somewhat ominous circumstances. There was the abrupt seizure by Egypt of the Universal Suez Canal Company which, largely under British and French auspices, had been operating that Canal ever since it was opened ninety years ago. There had been repeated expressions of hostility by the Government of Egypt towards other Governments with which it ostensibly had and should have friendly relations.

We are not blind to the fact that what has happened within the last two or three days has emerged from a murky background. We have, however, come to the conclusion that these provocations—serious as they were—cannot justify the resort to armed force which has occurred during these last two or three days and which is continuing tonight.

To be sure, the United Nations has perhaps not done all that it should have done. I have often—and particularly in recent weeks—pointed out that Article 1, paragraph 1, of the United Nations Charter calls for the settlement of these matters in conformity with the principles of justice and international law; that it calls not merely for a peaceful but also for a just solution. The United Nations may have been somewhat laggard, somewhat impotent, in dealing with many injustices inherent in this Middle Eastern situation. I think that we should, and I hope that we shall, give our most earnest thought—perhaps at the next regular session of the General Assembly—to the problem of how we can do more to establish and implement the principles of justice and international law. We have not done all that we should have done in that respect, and on that account part of the responsibility for the present events lies at our doorstep.

If, however, we were to agree that the existence in the world of injustices which this Organization has so far been unable to cure means that the principle of the renunciation of force should no longer be respected, that whenever a nation feels that it has been subjected to injustice it should have the right to resort to force in an attempt to correct that injustice, then I fear that we should be tearing this Charter into shreds, that the world would again be a world of anarchy, that the great hopes placed in this Organization and in our Charter would vanish, and that we should again be where we were at the start of the Second World War, with another tragic failure in place of what we had hoped—as we still can hope—would constitute a barrier to the recurrence of world war, which in the words of the preamble to the Charter, has twice in our lifetime brought untold sorrow to mankind.

. . .

While I should be the last to say that there can never be circumstances where force may not be resorted to, and certainly there can be resort to force for defensive purposes under Article 51 of the Charter, it seems to us that, in the circumstances which I have described the violent armed attack by three Members of the United Nations upon a fourth cannot be treated as anything but a grave error inconsistent with the principles and purposes of the Charter; an error which, if persisted in, would gravely undermine this Organization and its Charter.

The question then is: what shall we do? It seems to us imperative that something should be done, because what has been done, in apparent contravention of our Charter, has not yet gone so far as irretrievably to damage this Organization or to destroy it, and indeed, our "Uniting for peace" resolution was designed to meet just such circumstances as have arisen. It is still possible for the united will of this Organization to have an impact upon the situation and perhaps to make it apparent to the world, not only for the benefit of ourselves but for all posterity, that there is here the beginning of a world order. We do not, any of us, live in a society in which acts of disorder do not occur, but all of us live in societies where, if such acts do occur, something is done by the constituted authority to deal with them.

At the moment, we are the constituted authority, and while, under the Charter, we do not have the power of action, we do have a power of recommendation, a power which, if it reflects the moral judgement of the world community, world opinion, will be influential upon the present situation.

It is animated by such considerations that the United States has introduced a draft resolution which I should like to read out:

"The General Assembly,

"Noting the disregard on many occasions by parties to the Israel-Arab armistice agreements of 1949 of the terms of such agreements and that the armed forces of Israel have penetrated deeply into Egyptian territory in violation of the General Armistice Agreement between Egypt and Israel of 24 February 1949,

"Noting that armed forces of France and the United Kingdom of Great Britain and Northern Ireland are conducting military operations against Egyptian territory,

"Noting that traffic through the Suez Canal is now interrupted to the serious prejudice of many nations,

"Expressing its grave concern over these developments,

"1.   Urges as a matter of priority that all parties now involved in hostilities in the area agree to an immediate cease-fire and, as part thereof, halt the movement of military forces and arms into the area;

"2.   Urges the parties to the armistice agreements promptly to withdraw all forces behind the armistice lines, to desist from raids across the armistice lines into neighbouring territory, and to observe scrupulously the provisions of the armistice agreements;

"3.   Recommends that all Member States refrain from introducing military goods in the area of hostilities and in general refrain from any acts which would delay or prevent the implementation of the present resolution;

"4.   Urges that, upon the cease-fire being effective, steps be taken to reopen the Suez Canal and restore secure freedom of navigation;

"5.   Requests the Secretary-General to observe and promptly report on the compliance with the present resolution to the Security Council and to the General Assembly, for such further action as they may deem appropriate in accordance with the Charter;

"6. Decides to remain in emergency session pending compliance with the present resolution."

I recognize full well that a recommendation which is merely directed towards a cease-fire, to getting back to the armistice lines the foreign land forces in Egypt which, so far as we are aware today, are only those of Israel, to stopping the attacks by air and to preventing the introduction of new belligerent forces in the area, and which puts primary emphasis upon that and upon the opening, as rapidly as possible, of the Suez Canal, is not an adequate and comprehensive treatment of the situation. All of us, I think, would hope that out of this tragedy there should come something better than merely a restoration of the conditions out of which this tragedy arose. There must be something better than that, and surely this Organization has a duty to strive to bring that betterment about. If we should fail to do that, we, too, would be negligent and would have dealt only with one aspect of the problem.

I have said, and I deeply believe, that peace is a coin which has two sides—one is the avoidance of the use of force and the other is the creation of conditions of justice. In the long run you cannot expect one without the other. I do not by the form of this draft resolution want to seem in any way to believe that this situation can be adequately taken care of merely by the steps provided therein. There needs to be something better than the uneasy armistices which have existed now for these eight years between Israel and its Arab neighbours. There needs to be a greater sense of confidence and sense of security in the free and equal operation of the Canal than has existed since three months ago, when President Nasser seized the Universal Suez Canal Company. These things I regard as of the utmost importance.

But if we say that it is all right for the fighting to go on until these difficult and complicated matters are settled, then I fear that such a situation will be created that no settlement will be possible, that the war will have intensified and may have spread, that the world will be divided by new bitterness and that the foundation for peace will be tragically shattered. These things that I speak of need to be done, and I believe that they are in the process of being done because the Security Council is already seized of these matters and has been working upon them in a constructive way.

We must put first things first. I believe that the first thing is to stop the fighting as rapidly as possible, lest it becomes a conflagration which endangers us all—and that is not beyond the realm of possibility. As President Eisenhower said last night, the important thing is to limit and to extinguish the fighting in so far as it is possible and as promptly as possible. I hope, therefore, that this point of view, reflected in the draft resolution, will prevail, because I fear that if we do not act, and act promptly and with sufficient unanimity of opinion so that our recommendations carry real influence, there is great danger that what has started and what has been called a police action may develop into something which is far more grave; and that, even if that does not happen, the apparent impotence of this Organization to deal with this matter may set a precedent which will lead other nations to attempt to take into their own hands the remedying of what they believe to be their injustices. If that happens, the future will be dark indeed.

When we wrote the Charter at San Francisco in 1945, we thought that we had perhaps seen the worst in war and that our task was to prevent a recurrence of what had been. Indeed, what then had been was tragic enough. But now we know that what can be will be infinitely more tragic than what we saw in the Second World War. I believe that at this critical juncture we owe the highest duty to ourselves, to our peoples, and to posterity to take action which will ensure that this fire which has started shall not spread but shall be promptly extinguished; and then to turn with renewed vigour to curing the injustices out of which this trouble has risen. . . .

Mr. EBAN (Israel): On Monday, 29 October 1956, the Israel defence forces took security measures in the Sinai peninsula in the exercise of Israel's inherent right of self-defense. The object of these operations is to eliminate the bases from which armed Egyptian units under the special care and authority of Mr. Nasser invade Israel's territory for purposes of murder, sabotage and the creation of permanent insecurity to peaceful life. These are the only military activities for which the Government of Israel is responsible.

Stretching back far behind the events of this week lies the unique and sombre story of a small people subjected throughout all the years of its national existence to a furious, implacable, comprehensive campaign of hatred and siege for which there is no parallel or precedent in the modern history of nations. Not for one single moment throughout the entire period of its modern national existence has Israel enjoyed that minimal physical security which the United Nations Charter confers on all Member States, and which all other Member States have been able to command. . . .

What we confront tonight is a point of explosion after seven years of illicit belligerency. Belligerency is the key to the understanding of our problem tonight. Egypt has practised belligerency against Israel by land. Egypt has practised belligerency against Israel by sea. Egypt has established belligerency as the juridical basis of its relations with Israel. Egypt has held belligerency to be the spiritual and emotional mainspring of its conduct towards Israel. Out of this four-fold belligerency maintained by Egypt for seven years—but with special vigour and intensity since the rise of the Nasser régime—is born the crisis which the Assembly of the United Nations confronts tonight. . . . .

I will not weary the General Assembly with this sordid chronicle in all its details. Suffice it to say that, during this period of Egyptian belligerency, there had taken place against Israel 435 cases of armed incursion, nearly 2,000 cases of armed robbery and theft, 1,300 cases of armed clashes with Egyptian armed forces, 172 cases of sabotage perpetrated by Egyptian military units and *fedayeen* in Israel. As a result of these activities, 465 of our people have been killed or wounded. In 1956 alone, so far, as a result of this one aspect of Egyptian belligerency, 28 of our people have been killed and 127 have been wounded. . . .

It was with full knowledge of this fact that we have been forced to interpret Article 51 of the Charter as furnishing both a legal and a moral basis for such defensive action as is literally and specifically applicable to the dangers which we face. Under Article 51 of the Charter, the right of self-defence is described as "inherent"; in the French translation it is *"naturel"*. It is something which emerges from the very nature of a State and of humanity. This inherent right of self-defence is conditioned in the Charter by the existence of armed attacks against a Member State.

Can anyone say that this long and uninterrupted series of encroachments did not constitute in its totality the essence and the reality of an armed attack? Can it seriously be suggested that we made no attempt to exhaust peaceful remedies. Time after time at the table of the Security Council and in meetings of the Mixed Armistice Commission efforts were made to bring about tranquillity on this frontier. Yet all of this well-intentioned, enlightened, and, at certain times, hopeful effort ended without making the life or the security of a single citizen of Israel greater than it was before. . . .

Israel has no desire or intention to wield arms beyond the limits of its legitimate defensive mission. But whatever is demanded of us by way of restoring Egypt's rights and respecting Egypt's security under international law must surely be accompanied by equally binding Egyptian undertakings to respect Israel's security and Israel's rights under the identical law. Egypt's obligation to abstain from acts of hostility, to liquidate its commando activities, to abolish its illicit discrimination against Israel shipping in the Suez Canal and in the Gulf of Aqaba, is equal and identical in law to Israel's obligation to respect the established armistice lines. Our signpost is not backward to belligerency, but forward to peace. Whatever Israel is now asked to do for Egypt must have its counterpart in Egypt's reciprocal duty to give Israel the plenitude of its rights.

Beyond the moment when fire will cease, the prospect must not be one of unilateral claims by one party against the other. The horizon must be of peace by agreement, peace without maritime blockades in the Gulf or in the Canal, peace without frontier raids or commando incursions, peace without constant threats to the integrity or independence of any State, peace without military alliances directed against Israel's independence. . . .

Mr. TRUJILLO (Ecuador): . . . I believe that this is one of the gravest and most acute crises in the history of our Organization, because of the nature of the acts committed and of the status of those responsible for committing them. I can explain, though I do not justify, Israel's aggression. From the beginning, Israel's history has been one of struggle. It is surrounded by a group of peoples hostile to it, peoples opposed to it on grounds of religion, language and culture; it has to fight, and it has fought bravely. In Israel, passions are running high; the people are besieged, panic-stricken, and could commit an act of tragic folly.

But what are France and the United Kingdom fighting for? Israel is fighting for its very existence, for all that the mind and muscle of its people have created, but what are these two great Powers fighting for? Simply for a matter of business, the business of the Suez Canal. They are fighting, they say, for the freedom of this vital international waterway; for freedom of passage through the Suez Canal, the canal which is essential to the existence of many European countries and on which the life of half of Europe, and of the United Kingdom and France in particular, depends.

All this is true, but at bottom it is a question only of great economic interests, it is simply a matter of big business; and peoples surely do not go to war to defend the fat dividends of Suez Canal shareholders.

. . .

We shall vote for the draft resolution introduced by the United States delegation; but, applying Mr. Eisenhower's observation that there should be one law for all, I would say that the first and second paragraphs of the preamble should have been drafted in the same form.

In the first, which notes the disregard on many occasions by the parties to the Israel-Arab armistice agreements of 1949 of the terms of such agreements, and the fact that the armed forces of Israel have penetrated deeply into Egyptian territory in violation of the General Armistice Agreement between Egypt and Israel, there is a strong condemnation of Israel. The second paragraph, however, notes only that armed forces of France and the United Kingdom are conducting military operations against Egyptian territory.

These military operations constitute the most flagrant and open aggression, they are a violation of the United Nations Charter and they threaten the downfall of our Organization. But they are referred to in veiled diplomatic and tactful terms, although the act in question violates the United Nations Charter, whereas the other act, which is no more than a breaking of the armistice between a group of countries, is harshly judged.

Are we applying the same law in our judgement of the little State of Israel and the little Arab States, as in our judgement of the great Powers which are at this moment attacking Egypt? I do not think so. I wish merely to draw attention to the fact that the carefully worked out and subtle language used to disguise this bitter pill simply means that the military operations are open and flagrant aggression against a country which had given no cause for it and, even if it had done so, should not have been so attacked. . . .

Mr. DE GUIRINGAUD (France): . . . The French Government did not lightly embark on measures which at first glance might appear to be inconsistent with its traditions. It did so because it felt, in full agreement with the United Kingdom Government, that the tragic and rapid turn of events called for vigorous and immediate decisions.

Who can in all honesty dispute the fact that ten years' work by the United Nations, innumerable resolutions of the General Assembly and the Security Council, and even the noteworthy efforts of our Secretary-General, have been powerless not only to eliminate the danger of war in the Middle East, but even to prevent that danger from increasing to the point where it became a threat to world peace?

In reality, the United Nations has proved powerless to settle the Palestine question, because the action of the Security Council has been paralysed by the veto of one of its permanent members. Two years ago, for the first time, the Soviet Union delegation exercised its right of veto to prevent the condemnation of an Arab stand in the Palestine question. Subsequently it persistently prevented any condemnation, no matter how justified, from being pronounced against any one of Israel's neighbours.

The impunity thus vouchsafed to certain States has intensified the intransigence of some of them. The inability of this Organization to enforce its decisions—or even sometimes to take such decisions—and to induce the parties concerned to conclude a permanent peace, has had the result of giving free rein to inordinate ambitions, based on increasingly modern armaments, the source of which should provide serious cause for concern to those who would regard the situation we are considering today as a mere border incident.

These are not unfounded allegations. There is abundant proof in the writings and statements of Mr. Nasser and his spokesmen, and also in a number of indisputable facts. The United Nations need hardly be reminded of statements to the effect that Israel must be wiped off the map, or appeals made to Islamic solidarity, which, under the guise of strengthening the religious ties of all Moslems—ties which in themselves are worthy of respect—were actually designed to serve Egyptian national interests exclusively since, to quote Mr. Nasser, that solidarity was without a doubt destined to be the gigantic scaffolding of Egyptian power.

In so far as Egypt's African ambitions are concerned, suffice it to recall [that] Mr. Nasser considered that "we cannot forswear the task of expanding Egyptian civilization, even into the heart of the virgin forest". . .

Thus, before our very eyes, day in and day out, notwithstanding our decisions, Egypt has been openly and cynically helping to aggravate the situation and to prepare the way, within a relatively short time, for developments even more serious than those which we are witnessing today.

Could traditional methods prevent this march towards the point of no return? I regret to say that we were no longer able to believe it. When, on the night of 29 October 1956, Israel forces, retaliating against the provocation of the Egyptian death commandos, penetrated into the Sinai area, the French Government considered that this time it would no longer suffice to add to the collection of Security Council resolutions another page containing recommendations which would remain a dead letter. What was called for was action, and swift action. Those who now blame us for that action should recall the continued flouting of the provisions of the Security Council resolution concerning the free passage of Israel's ships through the Suez Canal and the Council's inability to act effectively when, hardly a month ago, the question of the seizure of the Suez Canal in violation of international agreements was placed before it. Precedents of this order left no hope that substantial and lasting results could be expected from recourse to traditional procedures. These procedures have also proved incapable of putting an end to a situation which, as Mr. Dulles remarked earlier in this meeting, has existed for eight years.

France and the United Kingdom then decided to intervene, not in a manner contrary to the purposes of the United Nations as defined during the past few days by the majority of the members of the Security Council, but because it seemed to them essential—as at the time of the Korean situation—that a Power or group of Powers should resolutely take the initiative of facing the real problems. It has been alleged that we have violated international law, and even that we have committed an act of aggression. But as Mr. Mollet, Prime Minister of France, stated on 30 September 1956, "the spirit of the Charter is not a spirit of capitulation; the quest for peaceful solutions cannot mean the acceptance, out of inertia, of *faits accomplis*". It was in that spirit that we felt in duty bound to intervene.

Those were the motives which impelled the French Government to take its decision, jointly with the United Kingdom Government. We are aware that it is in the interests of some people not to understand those motives. But we also know that the majority of the members of this Assembly are convinced that the greatest international catastrophes have been caused by the fact that those who were to be the victims were unable to take the necessary decisions in time. As I have already said, the Franco-British intervention in the Suez Canal zone is designed, in the first place, to call an immediate halt to hostilities between Egyptian and Israel armed forces by setting a screen, as it were, between the belligerent forces, and, in the second place, to protect the Suez Canal and establish lasting peace in the Middle East.

The French Government will not maintain its forces in the Canal area beyond the time required for the fulfilment of the objectives I have just enumerated. This operation in no way jeopardizes Egyptian sovereignty. We affirm that in taking the decisions which have been forced upon us we in no way intended to act in a manner incompatible with the principles of the Charter. The situation facing us today can be properly appraised only in the light of all its elements, historical, geographical and political. It is within this general framework that the decision taken by my Government, in the interests of the free world and of that just peace which Mr. Dulles invoked a short time ago, must be placed.   .   .   .

[The draft resolution presented by the United States was adopted in the early hours of 2 November 1956 by 64 votes to 5 (Australia, France, Israel, New Zealand, UK), with 6 abstentions (Belgium, Canada, Laos, Netherlands, Portugal, and Union of South Africa). Resolution 997 (ES–I); GAOR, ES–I, Supp. 1 (A/3354), p. 2.]

Mr. PEARSON (Canada): I rise not to take part in this debate, because the debate is over; the vote has been taken. But I do wish to explain the abstention of my delegation on that vote.

It is never easy to explain an abstention, and in this case it is particularly difficult, because we are in favour of some parts of this resolution, and also because this resolution deals with such a complicated question.

Because we are in favour of some parts of the resolution, we could not vote against it, especially as, in our opinion, it is a moderate proposal couched in reasonable and objective terms, without unfair or unbalanced condemnation; and also, by referring to violations, by both sides to the armistice agreements, it puts, I think, recent action by the United Kingdom and France—and rightly—against the background of those repeated violations and provocations.

We support the effort being made to bring the fighting to an end. We support it, among other reasons, because we regret that force was used in the circumstances that face us at this time. As my delegation sees it, however, this resolution which the General Assembly has thus adopted in its present form—and there was very little chance to alter that form—is inadequate to achieve the purposes which we have in mind at this session.   .   .   .

This is the first time that action has been taken under the "Uniting for peace" resolution, and I confess to a feeling of sadness, indeed even distress, at not being able to support the position taken by two countries whose ties with my country are and will remain close and intimate; two countries which have contributed so much to man's progress and freedom under law; and two countries which are Canada's mother countries.

I regret the use of military force in the circumstances which we have been discussing, but I regret also that there was not more time, before a vote was taken, for consideration of the best way to bring about that kind of cease-fire which would have enduring and beneficial results. . . .

This resolution does provide for a cease-fire, and I admit that that is of first importance and urgency. But, alongside a cease-fire and a withdrawal of troops, it does not provide for any steps to be taken by the United Nations for a peace settlement, without which a cease-fire will be only of temporary value at best. Surely we should have used this opportunity to link a cease-fire to the absolute necessity of a political settlement in Palestine and for the Suez, and perhaps we might also have been able to recommend a procedure by which this absolutely essential process might begin. . . .

I believe that there is another omission from this resolution, to which attention has also already been directed. The armed forces of Israel and of Egypt are to withdraw or, if you like, to return to the armistice lines, where presumably, if this is done, they will once again face each other in fear and hatred. What then? What then, six months from now? Are we to go through all this again? Are we to return to the *status quo*? Such a return would not be to a position of security, or even a tolerable position, but would be a return to terror, bloodshed, strife, incidents, charges and counter-charges, and ultimately another explosion which the United Nations Truce Supervision Organization would be powerless to prevent and possibly even to investigate.

I therefore would have liked to see a provision in this resolution—and this has been mentioned by previous speakers—authorizing the Secretary-General to begin to make arrangements with Member States for a United Nations force large enough to keep these borders at peace while a political settlement is being worked out. I regret exceedingly that time has not been given to follow up this idea, which was mentioned also by the representative of the United Kingdom in his first speech, and I hope that even now, when action on the resolution has been completed, it may not be too late to give consideration to this matter. My own Government would be glad to recommend Canadian participation in such a United Nations force, a truly international peace and police force.

NOTE.—1. Egypt accepted the resolution of the Assembly "on the condition of course that it could not implement the resolution in case attacking armies continue their aggression". A/3266 (2 Nov. 1956); GAOR, Annexes (ES–I) 5, p. 3.

France and the United Kingdom replied as follows:

"1. The British and French Governments have given careful consideration to the resolution passed by the General Assembly on 2 November. They maintain their view that police action must be carried through urgently to stop the hostilities which are now threatening the Suez Canal, to prevent a resumption of those hostilities and to pave the way for a definitive settlement of the Arab-Israel war which threatens the legitimate interests of so many countries.

"2. They would most willingly stop military action as soon as the following conditions could be satisfied:

"(a) Both the Egyptian and the Israeli Governments agree to accept a United Nations Force to keep the peace;

"(b) The United Nations decides to constitute and maintain such a Force until an Arab-Israel peace settlement is reached and until satisfactory arrangements have been agreed in regard to the Suez Canal, both agreements to be guaranteed by the United Nations;

"(c) In the meantime, until the United Nations Force is constituted, both combatants agree to accept forthwith limited detachments of Anglo-French troops to be stationed between the combatants." A/3268 and A/3269 (3 Nov. 1956); GAOR, Annexes (ES–I)5, pp. 4–5.

Israel agreed to an immediate cease-fire "provided a similar answer is forthcoming from Egypt" (GAOR, ES–I, Plenary, p. 61).

2. In the early morning of 4 November 1956, the General Assembly adopted two resolutions: a resolution presented by Canada, requesting "the Secretary-General to submit to it within forty-eight hours a plan for the setting up, with the consent of the nations concerned, of an emergency international United Nations Force to secure and supervise the cessation of hostilities in accordance with all the terms of the aforementioned resolution"; and a resolution presented by nineteen Afro-Asian Members, authorizing the Secretary-General "immediately to arrange with the parties concerned for the implementation of the cease-fire and the halting of the movement of military forces and arms into the area," and requesting him "to obtain compliance of the withdrawal of all forces behind the armistice lines". Resolutions 998 and 999 (ES–I); GAOR, ES–I, Supp. 1 (A/3354), p. 2.

3. *First Report of the Secretary-General on the Plan for an Emergency International United Nations Force, 4 November 1956.*

A/3289; GAOR, Annexes (ES–I) 5, p. 14.

In the course of the day I consulted the representatives of various Member States in order to explore the possibility of assistance from those countries in the setting up of a United Nations Force. The contacts will be continued, and the Assembly will be informed about the results in my final report. I am, however, in a position to state that, among the representatives so far consulted, the representatives of Colombia and Norway have, on behalf of their Governments, accepted participation in the projected Force. The representative of New Zealand has confirmed the declaration to the same effect that he made in the Assembly debate during the 563rd plenary meeting. Other representatives have submitted the question to their Governments with their recommendations.

In the course of my consideration of the matter I have arrived at the conclusion that a step which should be taken immediately is the setting up of a United Nations Command for the purpose in question. The first elements of such a Command can be drawn from the staff of the United Nations Truce Supervision Organization. If the General Assembly were to decide on the immediate establishment of a United Nations Command, the decision, therefore, could be put partially into effect without any delay.

In accordance with the view just expressed, I submit that the General Assembly, without waiting for my final report, should now decide that a United Nations Command for "an emergency international United Nations Force to secure and supervise the cessation of hostilities in accordance with all the terms" of its resolution 997 (ES–I) of 2 November 1956, be established; that the Assembly should further appoint, on an emergency basis, General Burns, at present Chief of Staff of the United Nations Truce Supervision Organization, to be Chief of the new Command; that General Burns, in that capacity, should be authorized immediately to organize a small staff by recruitment from the observer corps of the Truce Supervision Organization of a limited number of officers, drawn from countries which are not permanent members of the Security Council; that, further, General Burns should be authorized, in consultation with the Secretary-General, to recruit directly from various Member States, with the same limitation, the additional number of officers of which he may be in need; and that the Secretary-General should be authorized to take such administrative measures as would prove necessary for the speedy implementation of this decision.

In the continuing consultations which, in my view, will be considerably facilitated in case the General Assembly should decide immediately on the establishment of a United Nations Command, I would try to determine from which countries the necessary troops might be drawn without delay, as well as from which countries recruitment may be possible for a somewhat later stage. For both stages I would endeavour to develop a plan where, as a matter of principle, troops should not be drawn from countries which are permanent members of the Security Council.

The first of the stages referred to seems in a natural way to coincide with the stage immediately envisaged in resolution 999 (ES–I) of 4 November 1956. The later stage is likely to correspond to a period where the functions would be of a somewhat different nature, and should be viewed in the light of efforts over a longer range. While mentioning this point in the present report I reserve my right to elaborate the considerations, briefly mentioned here, in my final report.

In keeping with the terms of the resolution, the explorations, undertaken in order to establish the requested plan, are concerned only with the situation which would follow from the implementation of General Assembly resolution 997 (ES–I).

4.   *Resolution 1000 (E–I) of the General Assembly, 5 November 1956.*

GAOR, ES–I, Supp. 1 (A/3354), pp. 2–3.

The General Assembly,

Having requested the Secretary-General, in its resolution 998 (ES–I) of 4 November 1956, to submit to it a plan for an emergency international United Nations Force, for the purposes stated,

Noting with satisfaction the first report of the Secretary-General on the plan, and having in mind particularly paragraph 4 of that report,

1.   Establishes a United Nations Command for an emergency international Force to secure and supervise the cessation of hostilities in accordance with all the terms of General Assembly resolution 997 (ES–I) of 2 November 1956;

2.   Appoints on an emergency basis, the Chief of Staff of the United Nations Truce Supervision Organization, Major-General E. L. M. Burns, as Chief of the Command;

3.   Authorizes the Chief of the Command immediately to recruit, from the observer corps of the United Nations Truce Supervision Organization, a limited number of officers who shall be nationals of countries other than those having permanent membership in the Security Council, and further authorizes him, in consultation with the Secretary-General, to undertake the recruitment directly, from various Member States other than the permanent members of the Security Council, of the additional number of officers needed;

4.   Invites the Secretary-General to take such administrative measures as may be necessary for the prompt execution of the actions envisaged in the present resolution.

NOTE.—1.   On 5 November 1956, Israel notified the Secretary-General that it agreed unconditionally to the cease-fire and that all fighting had ceased between Israeli and Egyptian forces. A/3301 (5 Nov. 1956) ; GAOR, Annexes (ES-I) 5, p. 19. France and the United Kingdom welcomed the idea of an international Force to be interposed between Israel and Egypt, but pointed out that the "composition of the staff and contingents of the international Force would be a matter for discussion". While they agreed to cease all military action as soon as the Force is established, they announced the continuance of certain "operations with limited objectives." A/3293 and A/3294 (5 Nov. 1956) ; GAOR, *op.cit.*, pp. 16–17. In fact, on that day the British and French paratroopers landed in Port Said, "bombing being conducted with the utmost consideration for civilians." A/3299 (5 Nov. 1956) ; GAOR, *op.cit.*, p. 19.

2.   On the request of USSR, a meeting of the Security Council was held on 5 November 1956 to consider the noncompliance by the United Kingdom, France and Israel with Resolution 997 of the General Assembly. The Soviet Union suggested that the Security Council adopt a resolution proposing a cease-fire and withdrawal of forces within three days, as well as considering "it essential, in accordance with Article 42 of the United Nations Charter, that all States Members of the United Nations, especially the United States of America and the Union of Soviet Socialist Republics, as permanent members of the Security Council having powerful air and naval forces at their disposal, should give military and other assistance to the Republic of Egypt, which has been the victim of aggression, by sending naval and air forces, military units, volunteers, military instructors and other forms of assistance, if the United Kingdom, France and Israel fail to carry out this resolution within the stated time limits." The Soviet Government also declared its willingness "to contribute to the cause of curbing the aggression . . . by sending to Egypt the air and naval forces necessary for the achievement of this purpose." S/3736 (5 Nov. 1956); SCOR, XI, Supp. for Oct.–Dec. 1956, pp. 128–29.

The Security Council rejected the inclusion of the Soviet item on the agenda, by 4 votes (Australia, France, UK, US) to 3 (Iran, USSR, Yugoslavia), with 4 abstentions (Belgium, China, Cuba, Peru). SCOR, XI, Mtg. 755, p. 4. It was contended that one of the bases of the United Nations "is the avoidance of overlapping competence or double jurisdiction. Just as the General Assembly cannot consider a question of which the Security Council is seized, so the Security Council obviously cannot logically consider a question which is pending before the General Assembly, particularly one referred to it by virtue of a procedural resolution adopted by the Council itself." *Idem,* p. 10.

5.   *Second and Final Report of the Secretary-General on the Plan for an Emergency International United Nations Force, 6 November 1956.*

A/3302; GAOR, Annexes (ES–I) 5, pp. 19–22.

Questions of principle

4.   An emergency international United Nations Force can be developed on the basis of three different concepts:

(a) It can, in the *first* place, be set up on the basis of principles reflected in the constitution of the United Nations itself. This would mean that its chief responsible officer should be appointed by the United Nations and that he, in his functions, should be responsible ultimately to the General Assembly and/or the Security Council. His authority should be so defined as to make him fully independent of the policies of any one nation. His relations to the Secretary-General of the United Nations should correspond to those of the Chief of Staff of the United Nations Truce Supervision Organization;

(b) A *second* possibility is that the United Nations charge a country, or a group of countries, with the responsibility to provide independently for an emergency international Force serving for purposes determined by the United Nations. In this case it would obviously be impossible to achieve the same independence in relation to national policies as would be established through the first approach;

(c) Finally, as a *third* possibility, an emergency international Force may be set up in agreement among a group of nations, later to be brought into an appropriate relationship to the United Nations. This approach is open to the same reservation as the second one, and possibly others.

Variations of form, of course, are possible within a wide range, but the three concepts mentioned seem to circumscribe the problem.

5. In the decision on the establishment of the United Nations Command, on an emergency basis, which the General Assembly took on 5 November 1956, the Assembly chose to follow the first of the three types mentioned in paragraph 4 above. The second type was that followed in the case of the Unified Command in Korea. There is no precedent for the use of the third type, but it would seem to represent one of the possible forms for implementation of the suggestion in the replies of 5 November 1956 of the Governments of France and the United Kingdom (A/3294, A/3293) to my request for a cease-fire. In attempting to work out a plan for setting up an emergency international United Nations Force, I have based my considerations on the legal situation created by the decision in principle of the General Assembly, implied in the request of the Assembly to me to submit within forty-eight hours a plan for such a Force, and in its later decision to establish a United Nations Command, in implementation of this first resolution.

6. In its resolution 1000(ES–I) on the United Nations Command, the General Assembly authorized the Chief of Command, in consultation with the Secretary-General, to recruit officers from the United Nations Truce Supervision Organization, or directly from various Member States other than the permanent members of the Security Council. This recruitment procedure affords an important indication of the character of the Force to be set up. On the one hand, the independence of the Chief of Command in recruiting officers is recognized. On the other hand, the principle is established that the Force should be recruited from Member States other than the permanent members of the Security Council. The first of these elements in the new approach has an important bearing on the interpretation of the status of the Chief of Command. The second point has an equally important bearing on the character of the whole Command. It may in this context be observed that the Franco-British proposal, to which I have already referred, may imply that the question of the composition of the staff and contingents should be subject to agreement by the parties involved, which it would be difficult to reconcile with the development of the international Force along the course already being followed by the General Assembly.

7. Resolution 998(ES–I), in which the General Assembly requests the Secretary-General to submit a plan for the international Force, gives further guidance. Thus, it is said that the Force should be set up on an "emergency" basis. The situation envisaged is more clearly defined in the terms of reference of the Force (resolution 998(ES–I)) which are "to secure and supervise the cessation of hostilities in accordance with all the terms" of the General Assembly resolution of 2 November 1956.

8. A closer analysis of the concept of the emergency international United Nations Force, based on what the General Assembly has stated in its resolution on the matter, indicates that the Assembly intends that the Force should be of a temporary nature, the length of its assignment being determined by the needs arising out of the present conflict. It is further clear that the General Assembly, in its resolution 1000(ES–I) of 5 November 1956, by the reference to its resolution 997(ES–I) of 2 November, has wished to reserve for itself the full determination of the tasks of this emergency Force and of the legal basis on which it must function in fulfilment of its mission. It follows from its terms of reference that there is no intent in the establishment of the Force to influence the military balance in the present conflict and, thereby, the political balance affecting efforts to settle the conflict. By the establishment of the Force, therefore, the General Assembly has not taken a stand in relation to aims other than those clearly and fully indicated in its resolution 997(ES–I) of 2 November 1956.

9. Functioning, as it would, on the basis of a decision reached under the terms of the resolution 337(V) "Uniting for Peace", the Force, if established, would be limited in its operations to the extent that consent of the parties concerned is required under generally recognized international law. While the General Assembly is enabled to *establish* the Force with the consent of those parties which contribute units to the Force, it could not request the Force to be *stationed* or *operate* on the territory of a given country without the consent of the Government of that country. This does not exclude the possibility that the Security Council could use such a Force within the wider margins provided under Chapter VII of the United Nations Charter. I would not for the present consider it necessary to elaborate this point further, since no use of the Force under Chapter VII, with the rights in relation to Member States that this would entail, has been envisaged.

10. The point just made permits the conclusion that the setting up of the Force should not be guided by the needs which would have existed had the measure been considered as part of an enforcement action directed against a Member country. There is an obvious difference between establishing the Force in order to secure the cessation of hostilities, with a withdrawal of forces, and establishing such a Force with the view to enforcing a withdrawal of forces. It follows that

while the Force is different in that, as in many other respects, from
the observers of the United Nations Truce Supervision Organization,
it is, although para-military in nature, not a Force with military objectives.

Questions of functions

11.   The question of determining the functions of the emergency
international United Nations Force has been dealt with in part in the
preceding paragraphs.   It is difficult in the present situation and without further study to discuss it with any degree of precision.   However, the general observations which are possible should at this stage
be sufficient.

12.   In the General Assembly resolution 998(ES–I) the terms of
reference are, as already stated, "to secure   .   .   .   the cessation of
hostilities in accordance with all the terms" of resolution 997 (ES–I)
of 2 November 1956.   This resolution urges that "all parties now involved in hostilities in the area agree to an immediate cease-fire and,
as part thereof, halt the movement of military forces and arms into
the area;" and also "urges the parties to the armistice agreements
promptly to withdraw all forces behind the armistice lines, to desist
from raids across the armistice lines into neighbouring territory, and
to observe scrupulously the provisions of the armistice agreements."
These two provisions combined indicate that the functions of the United Nations Force would be, when a cease-fire is being established, to
enter Egyptian territory with the consent of the Egyptian Government, in order to help maintain quiet during and after the withdrawal
of non-Egyptian troops, and to secure compliance with the other terms
established in the resolution of 2 November 1956.   The Force obviously should have no rights other than those necessary for the execution of its functions, in co-operation with local authorities.   It would
be more than an observers' corps, but in no way a military force temporarily controlling the territory in which it is stationed; nor, moreover, should the Force have military functions exceeding those necessary to secure peaceful conditions on the assumption that the parties
to the conflict take all necessary steps for compliance with the recommendations of the General Assembly.   Its functions can, on this basis,
be assumed to cover an area extending roughly from the Suez Canal to
the armistice demarcation lines established in the armistice agreement
between Egypt and Israel.

Questions of size and organization of the Force

13.   Time has so far not permitted the necessary technical studies.
It is therefore not yet possible to say what should be the size of the
Force.   In my first report, I pointed out that the situation is likely to
involve two stages: the first one when certain immediate tasks have
to be fulfilled, the second one when somewhat different tasks, although
within the framework set out in paragraph 12 above, will fall upon the
Force.   It is likely that the size of the Force will require some adjust-

ment to the development of the tasks. Further study of such matters is required, and I have invited the Chief of the United Nations Command, General Burns, to present his views urgently.

14. It is not possible at this time to make any proposals as to the general organization of the Force beyond those clearly following from resolution 998 (ES–I) of 4 November 1956. General experience seems to indicate that it is desirable that countries participating in the Force should provide self-contained units in order to avoid the loss of time and efficiency which is unavoidable when new units are set up through joining together small groups of different nationalities. The question requires additional study and is obviously closely linked to the condition that various Member States will provide sufficiently large units. The difficulty in presenting a detailed plan of organization need not delay the establishment of the Force. It is likely that during the first period, at all events, the Force would have to be composed of a few units of battalion strength, drawn from countries or groups of countries which can provide such troops without delay. It is my endeavour in the approaches to Governments to build up a panel sufficiently broad to permit such a choice of units as would provide for a balanced composition in the Force. Further planning and decisions on organization will to a large extent have to depend on the judgement of the Chief of Command and his staff.

Questions of financing

15. The question of how the Force should be financed likewise requires further study. A basic rule which, at least, could be applied provisionally, would be that a nation providing a unit would be responsible for all costs for equipment and salaries, while all other costs should be financed outside the normal budget of the United Nations. It is obviously impossible to make any estimate of the costs without a knowledge of the size of the corps and the length of its assignment. The only practical course, therefore, would be for the General Assembly to vote a general authorization for the cost of the Force on the basis of general principles such as those here suggested.

Questions of recruitment

16. Time permitted me to discuss the question of participation in the Force with only a limited number of Member Governments. Offers of assistance in writing so far received are annexed to the present report. In cases other than those covered by the annexed letters, the question of participation is under consideration by the Governments. It is my hope that broader participation will be possible as soon as a plan is approved, so that a more definite judgement may be possible concerning the implications of participation. The reactions so far received lead me to believe that it should be possible to meet quickly at least the most basic need for personnel. The possibilities, as finally established, may call for an adjustment later of the size and organiza-

tion of the Force in relation to what would in principle be the most satisfactory solution.

General questions

17. In my first report it was stated that the later stage in the development to which I referred in paragraph 13 above "is likely to correspond to a period where the functions . . . should be viewed in the light of efforts over a longer range" (A/3289, para. 6). While mentioning this point I reserved my right to elaborate the consideration briefly dealt with. After further reflection, I would not for the present wish to go beyond what I have said on the subject in previous parts of the present report, especially concerning the functions of the Force. It would be premature to express views on problems likely to arise after the immediate crisis is past.

18. On several matters mentioned above it has been necessary to leave the question open. This is explained in part by a lack of time and in part by the need for further study. I suggest that these open matters be submitted to exploration by a small committee of the General Assembly; this body, if established, might also serve as an advisory committee to the Secretary-General for questions relating to the operations. On the other hand, on all points where a decision of significance to the further development of the plan seems possible now, the General Assembly should proceed to action forthwith.

19. I am fully aware of the exploratory character of this plan in many respects. Time is vital and this is some excuse not only for the lack of detail in this first approach but also for decisions by the General Assembly reached in more general terms than is customary. If the Force is to come into being with all the speed indispensable to its success, a margin of confidence must be left to those who will carry the responsibility for putting the decisions of the General Assembly into effect.

6. *Resolution 1001 (ES–I) of the General Assembly, 7 November 1956.*

GAOR, ES–I, Supp. 1 (A/3354), p. 3.

The General Assembly,

Recalling its resolution 997 (ES–I) of 2 November 1956 concerning the cease-fire, withdrawal of troops and other matters related to the military operations in Egyptian territory, as well as its resolution 998 (ES–I) of 4 November 1956 concerning the request to the Secretary-General to submit a plan for an emergency international United Nations Force,

Having established by its resolution 1000 (ES–I) of 5 November 1956 a United Nations Command for an emergency international Force, having appointed the Chief of Staff of the United Nations Truce Supervision Organization as Chief of the Command with authorization to him to begin the recruitment of officers for the Command, and having invited the Secretary-General to take the administrative measures necessary for the prompt execution of that resolution,

Noting with appreciation the second and final report of the Secretary-General on the plan for an emergency international United Nations Force as requested in General Assembly resolution 998 (ES–I), and having examined that plan,

1. Expresses its approval of the guiding principles for the organization and functioning of the emergency international United Nations Force as expounded in paragraphs 6 to 9 of the Secretary-General's report;

2. Concurs in the definition of the functions of the Force as stated in paragraph 12 of the Secretary-General's report;

3. Invites the Secretary-General to continue discussions with Governments of Member States concerning offers of participation in the Force, toward the objective of its balanced composition;

4. Requests the Chief of the Command, in consultation with the Secretary-General as regards size and composition, to proceed forthwith with the full organization of the Force;

5. Approves provisionally the basic rule concerning the financing of the Force laid down in paragraph 15 of the Secretary-General's report;

6. Establishes an Advisory Committee composed of one representative from each of the following countries: Brazil, Canada, Ceylon, Colombia, India, Norway and Pakistan, and requests this Committee, whose Chairman shall be the Secretary-General, to undertake the development of those aspects of the planning for the Force and its operation not already dealt with by the General Assembly and which do not fall within the area of the direct responsibility of the Chief of the Command;

7. Authorizes the Secretary-General to issue all regulations and instructions which may be essential to the effective functioning of the Force, following consultation with the Committee aforementioned, and to take all other necessary administrative and executive action;

8. Determines that, following the fulfilment of the immediate responsibilities defined for it in operative paragraphs 6 and 7 above, the Advisory Committee shall continue to assist the Secretary-General in the responsibilities falling to him under the present and other relevant resolutions;

9. Decides that the Advisory Committee, in the performance of its duties, shall be empowered to request, through the usual procedures, the convening of the General Assembly and to report to the Assembly whenever matters arise which, in its opinion, are of such

urgency and importance as to require consideration by the General Assembly itself;

10.   Requests all Member States to afford assistance as necessary to the United Nations Command in the performance of its functions, including arrangements for passage to and from the area involved.

NOTE.—1.   As soon as this resolution was approved, France and the United Kingdom accepted the cease-fire arrangements. Their troops started withdrawing from Egypt upon the arrival of the UN Emergency Force (UNEF), and they left Egypt completely on 22 December 1956. A/3500 (15 Jan. 1957); GAOR, Annexes (XI) 66, p. 42.

2.   Israeli withdrawal was slower but by 22 January 1957 Israeli troops withdrew from the Sinai peninsula, except from the Sharm el-Sheikh area on the Straits of Tiran. The long negotiations for the withdrawal of Israel from that area, from the islands in the Straits of Tiran and from the Gaza Strip ended on March 8, when the Israeli forces there were replaced by the United Nations Emergency Force. For a summary of the discussions and negotiations which led to these withdrawals, see the Annual Report of the Secretary-General, 1956–1957 [GAOR, XII, Supp. 1 (A/3594)], pp. 8–25. A few important documents are reproduced in Nos. 7–10, below.

3.   On 25 November 1956, by Resolution 1121 (XI), the General Assembly also authorized the Secretary-General to make arrangements for clearing the Suez Canal. GAOR, XI, Supp. 17 (A/3572), p. 61. Between 27 December 1956 and 15 April 1957 forty-five major obstacles to navigation were removed by the United Nations salvage fleet. See the Annual Report of the Secretary-General, op.cit., pp. 24–25; Jean SALMON, "Les opérations internationales de dégagement du Canal de Suez", 3 AFDI (1957), pp. 349–59. On 24 April 1957, Egypt made a "Declaration on the Suez Canal", reaffirming the Convention of 1888, elaborating the basic principles which will govern the Canal in the future, and indicating the arrangements for the operation of the Canal. S/3818 (24 April 1957); SCOR, XII, Supp. for April–June 1957, pp. 8–12. By a supplementary declaration, Egypt accepted the jurisdiction of the International Court of Justice in respect of any dispute relating to the interpretation or application of the main Declaration. S/3818/Add.1 (23 July 1957); SCOR, XII, Supp. for July–Sept. 1957; pp. 1–2. For a comment on the Egyptian Declaration, see Jacques DEHAUSSY, "La déclaration égyptienne de 1957 sur le Canal de Suez", 6 AFDI (1960), pp. 169–84. A settlement of the claims of stockholders of the Suez Canal Company against Egypt was finally reached on 29 April and 13 July 1958. A/3827 and S/4014 (29 May 1958); SCOR, XIII, Supp. for April–June 1958, pp. 39–42; and A/3898 and S/4089 (23 Sept. 1958); SCOR, XIII, Supp. for July–Sept. 1958, pp. 140–48. For a comment on this agreement, see Lazar FOCSANEANU, "L'accord ayant pour objet l'indemnisation de la Compagnie de Suez nationalisée par l'Égypte", 5 AFDI (1959), pp. 161–204. See also E. LAUTERPACHT, ed., The Suez Canal Settlement: A Selection of Documents, 1956–1959 (London, 1960), 82 pp.

7. *Report of the Secretary-General, 24 January 1957.*

A/3512; GAOR, Annexes (XI) 66, pp. 47-50.

To help toward solutions of the pending problems in the area, United Nations actions must be governed by principle and must be in accordance with international law and valid international agreements. For his part, the Secretary-General, in carrying out the policies of the United Nations, must act with scrupulous regard for the decisions of the General Assembly, the Security Council and the other principal organs. It may be useful to note the implications of the foregoing for the actions of the United Nations and of the Secretary-General in the present situation. In this regard, it would seem that the following points are generally recognized as non-controversial in the determination of the limits within which the activities of the United Nations can be properly developed. Within their scope, positive United Nations measures in the present issue, rendered possible by full compliance with the General Assembly resolutions, can be and have to be developed, which would represent effective progress toward the creation of peaceful conditions in the region.

(a) The United Nations cannot condone a change of the *status juris* resulting from military action contrary to the provisions of the Charter. The Organization must, therefore, maintain that the *status juris* existing prior to such military action be re-established by a withdrawal of troops, and by the relinquishment or nullification of rights asserted in territories covered by the military action and depending upon it.

(b) The use of military force by the United Nations other than that under Chapter VII of the Charter requires the consent of the States in which the Force is to operate. Moreover, such use must be undertaken and developed in a manner consistent with the principles mentioned under (a) above. It must, furthermore, be impartial, in the sense that it does not serve as a means to force settlement, in the interest of one party, of political conflicts or legal issues recognized as controversial.

(c) United Nations actions must respect fully the rights of Member Governments recognized in the Charter, and international agreements not contrary to the aims of the Charter, which are concluded in exercise of those rights.

Deployment of the Force in Gaza, under the resolutions of the General Assembly, would have to be on the same basis as its deployment along the armistice line in the Sinai peninsula. Any broader function for it in that area, in view of the terms of the Armistice Agreement and a recognized principle of international law, would require the consent of Egypt. A widening of the United Nations administrative responsibilities in the area, beyond its responsibilities for the refugees, would likewise have to be based on agreement with Egypt. It follows, therefore, that although the United Nations General Assembly would be entitled to recommend the establishment of a United Nations administration and to request negotiations in order to implement such an arrangement, it would lack authority in that recommendation, unilaterally, to require compliance. . . .

The United Nations Emergency Force is deployed at the dividing line between the forces of Israel and Egypt. The General Assembly concurred in paragraph 12 of the Secretary-General's second and final report which specifically referred to the deployment of the Force on only one side of the armistice line. On this basis, the Force would have units in the Gaza area as well as opposite El Auja. With demilitarization of the El Auja zone in accordance with the Armistice Agreement, it might be indicated that the Force should have units stationed also on the Israel side of the armistice demarcation line, at least, in that zone. Such deployment, which would require a new decision by the General Assembly, would have the advantage of the Force being in a position to assume the supervisory duties of the Truce Supervision Organization in all the territory where that Organization now functions under the Armistice Agreement between Egypt and Israel. . . As an arrangement of this kind was not foreseen by the Armistice Agreement, it obviously would require the consent of the two parties to that Agreement. . . .

Israel troops, on their withdrawal from the Sharm el-Sheikh area, would be followed by the United Nations Emergency Force in the same way as in other parts of Sinai. The duties of the Force in respect of the cease-fire and the withdrawal will determine its movements. However, if it is recognized that there is a need for such an arrangement, it may be agreed that units of the Force (or special representatives in the nature of observers) would assist in maintaining quiet in the area beyond what follows from this general principle. In accordance with the general legal principles recognized as decisive for the deployment of the United Nations Emergency Force, the Force should not be used so as to prejudge the solution of the controversial questions involved. The Force, thus, is not to be deployed in such a way as to protect any special position on these questions, although, at least transitionally, it may function in support of mutual restraint in accordance with the foregoing.

8. *Report of the Secretary-General, 11 February 1957.*

A/3527; GAOR, Annexes (XI) 66, pp. 57–59.

The General Assembly on 2 February 1957, adopted two resolutions, resolutions I and II [1124(XI) and 1125(XI)], concerning the Middle Eastern question. In resolution I the General Assembly, deploring "the non-compliance of Israel to complete its withdrawal behind the armistice demarcation line", called upon Israel to complete this withdrawal without further delay. In resolution II the General Assembly, recognizing that withdrawal by Israel must be followed by action which would assure progress towards the creation of peaceful conditions, noted with appreciation the Secretary-General's report and the measures therein "to be carried out upon Israel's complete withdrawal", called upon the Governments concerned scrupulously to observe the Armistice Agreement, and stated that it considered that, after full withdrawal of Israel from the Sharm el-Sheikh and Gaza areas, various measures, as proposed in the Secretary-General's report, would be required for the scrupulous maintenance of the Armistice Agreement. The General Assembly requested the Secretary-General, in consultation with the parties concerned, to take steps to carry out the measures envisaged and to report, as appropriate, to the General Assembly. . . .

The General Assembly, in adopting resolutions I and II [1124(XI) and 1125(XI)], was guided by the need to "assure progress towards the creation of peaceful conditions" in the area. It was recognized that this objective—which was also the theme of the Secretary-General's report on which the debate in the General Assembly was based—required, as an initial step, withdrawal of Israel behind the armistice demarcation line, to be followed by various measures within the framework of the Armistice Agreement. These measures aimed at "a return to the state of affairs envisaged in the Armistice Agreement, and avoidance of the state of affairs into which conditions due to lack of compliance with the Agreement had progressively deteriorated." With this in view, resolution II in its operative paragraph 2 called for scrupulous observance of the Armistice Agreement, which, in its first article, establishes the right of each party to "its security and freedom from fear of attack by the armed forces of the other."

The position of the Secretary-General, in his efforts to secure implementation of the two resolutions, has been based on the following considerations. First, agreement was widespread in the General Assembly, as reflected in the sequence of the two resolutions, that "like the cease-fire, withdrawal is a preliminary and essential phase in a development through which a stable basis may be laid for peaceful conditions in the area". Second, the principle which must guide the United Nations after a change in the *status juris* through military action contrary to the Charter, as stated in the last report of the Secretary-General (A/3512, paragraph 5(a)), is recognized as expressing a basic rule of the Charter, thus giving a high priority to requests based on that principle. The key significance of resolution I, as indicated by these two considerations, is confirmed by the fact that resolution II explicitly states that the measures to which it refers are to be carried out "after full withdrawal of Israel" behind the armistice demarcation line.

The Secretary-General has understood the General Assembly to see in resolution II a formal undertaking with respect to measures to be effected upon withdrawal, in the light of which resolution I should be implemented without delay. This is particularly so, since the United Nations Force is deployed in the region with an assurance from the Government of Egypt that the Government, when exercising its sovereign rights on any matter concerning the presence and functioning of UNEF, will be guided in good faith by its acceptance of the basic General Assembly resolution of 5 November 1956 concerning the Force and its functions.

Beginning with its initial resolution of 2 November 1956 (Resolution 997 (ES–I)) concerning this question, and culminating in its resolution II of 2 February 1957 [1125(XI)], the General Assembly has stressed the key importance it attaches to scrupulous observance by both parties of the terms of the Armistice Agreement between Egypt and Israel. In this regard, the Secretary-General is able to report that the Government of Egypt reaffirms its intent to observe fully the provisions of the Armistice Agreement to which it is a party, as indicated earlier in its acceptance (A/3266) of the 2 November resolution of the General Assembly, on the assumption, of course, that observance will be reciprocal. Attention should be drawn, in this context, to the statement in paragraph 22 of the last report of the Secretary-General (A/3512) reporting the desire of the Government of Egypt to see an end to all raids and incursions across the armistice line, in both directions, with effective assistance from United Nations auxiliary organs to that effect. . . .

The relationship between the two resolutions on withdrawal and on measures to be carried out after withdrawal, affords the possibility of informal explorations of the whole field covered by the resolutions, preparatory to negotiations. Later, the results of such explorations may be used in negotiations through a constructive combination of measures, representing for the two countries concerned parallel progress toward the peaceful conditions sought. However, such explorations cannot be permitted to invert the sequence between withdrawal and other measures, nor to disrupt the evolution of negotiations toward their goal. Progress toward peaceful conditions, following the general policy suggested in the last report to the General Assembly, on which its resolution II is based, has to be achieved gradually. To disregard this would render the process more difficult and might seriously jeopardize the possibility of achieving desired results. In explorations and negotiations, which in this sense necessarily have to proceed step by step, the parties involved must time and again show willingness to accept some risks as a condition for progress.

Peaceful conditions in the Middle East *must* be created in the interest of all countries in the region and of the world community. The basic principles of the Charter *must* be asserted and respected, in the very same interest. Neither one of these imperative demands can be met at the expense of the other. The fulfilment of one will make it easier to meet the other, but to have peace with justice, adherence to principle and law must be given priority and cannot be conditioned. In the present case, efforts to meet the two requirements just stated have so far been frustrated. The United Nations must maintain its position on these requirements and, in doing so, should be entitled to count on the assistance, in the complex process of gradual and sensitive approach to the objectives, in particular of the two Member States directly concerned. If such assistance is not forthcoming, the efforts of the United Nations will be caused to fail, to the detriment of all. In an organization based on voluntary co-operation and respect for the general opinion to which the organization gives expression, the responsibility for such a failure would fall, not on the organization, but on those who had denied it the necessary co-operation. This responsibility extends beyond the immediate issue. It may also, in this case, have to cover difficulties flowing from possible failure of the United Nations to fulfill its vital functions under the Armistice Agreements and of the parties to come to grips with the wider problems which call for such urgent attention.

The Charter has given to the Security Council means of enforcement and the right to take decisions with mandatory effect. No such authority is given to the General Assembly, which can only recommend action to Member Governments, which, in turn, may follow the recommendations or disregard them. This is also true of recommendations adopted by the General Assembly within the framework of the "Uniting for Peace" resolution. However, under that resolution the General Assembly has certain rights otherwise reserved to the Security Council. Thus, it can, under that resolution, recommend collective measures. In this case, also, the recommendation is not compulsory.

It seems, in this context, appropriate to distinguish between recommendations which implement a Charter principle, which in itself is binding on Member States, and recommendations which, although adopted under the Charter, do not implement any such basic provision. A recommendation of the first kind would have behind it the force of the Charter, to which collective measures recommended by the General Assembly could add emphasis, without, however, changing the legal character of the recommendation. A decision on collective measures referring to a recommendation of the second kind, although likewise formally retaining its legal character, would mean that the recommendation is recognized by the General Assembly as being of such significance to the efforts of the United Nations as to assimilate it to a recommendation expressing an obligation established by the Charter. If, in some case, collective measures under the "Uniting for Peace" resolution were to be considered, these and other important questions of principle would require attention; this may also be said of the effect of such steps which, while supporting efforts to achieve peaceful solutions, may perhaps, on the other hand, be introducing new elements of conflict.

9.   *Statement by the Secretary-General, 22 February 1957.*

GAOR, XI, Plenary, pp. 1192–1193.

On 11 February I submitted the report, in pursuance of the resolution of the General Assembly of 2 February. Events since then have not called for a further report, and I have presented none. It is well known, however, that discussions have been carried on outside this house in the continuing resolve to attain the goals defined in the several resolutions of the General Assembly. I have maintained close contact with these activities and have been kept well informed on them. These serious efforts to break through the unfortunate impasse and to unlock the door to constructive endeavor are deserving of warm appreciation.

In so far as United Nations activities and positions are concerned, developments in the interim have given no reason to revise any of the substance of the previous report. However, in the light of some subsequent discussions in which I have engaged, I may make the following statement in the nature of a supplement to that report.

The Secretary-General states with confidence that it is the desire of the Government of Egypt that the take-over of Gaza from the military and civilian control of Israel—which, as has been the case, in the first instance would be exclusively by UNEF—will be orderly and safe, as it has been elsewhere.

It may be added with equal confidence that the Government of Egypt, recognizing the present special problems and complexities of the Gaza area and the long-standing major responsibility of the United Nations there for the assistance of the Arab refugees, and having in mind also the objectives and obligations of the Armistice Agreement, has the willingness and readiness to make special and helpful arrangements with the United Nations and some of its auxiliary bodies, such as the United Nations Relief and Works Agency for Palestine Refugees and UNEF. For example, the arrangement for the use of UNEF in the area should ensure its deployment on the armistice line at the Gaza Strip and the effective interposition of the Force between the armed forces of Egypt and Israel.

Similarly, the assistance of the United Nations and its appropriate auxiliary bodies would be enrolled towards putting a definite end to all incursions and raids across the border from either side.

Furthermore, with reference to the period of transition, such other arrangements with the United Nations may be made as will contribute towards safeguarding life and property in the area by providing efficient and effective police protection; as will guarantee good civilian administration; as will assure maximum assistance to the United Nations refugee programme; and as will protect and foster the economic development of the territory and its people.

10. *Statement by the Israeli Foreign Minister (Mrs. Meir),*
1 March 1957.

GAOR, XI, Plenary, pp. 1275-76.

The Government of Israel is now in a position to announce its plans for full and prompt withdrawal from the Sharm el Sheikh area and the Gaza strip, in compliance with General Assembly resolution 1124 (XI) of 2 February 1957.

We have repeatedly stated that Israel has no interest in the strip of land overlooking the western coast of the Gulf of Aqaba. Our sole purpose has been to ensure that, on the withdrawal of Israel forces, continued freedom of navigation will exist for Israel and international shipping in the Gulf of Aqaba and the Straits of Tiran. Such freedom of navigation is a vital national interest for Israel, but it is also of importance and legitimate concern to the maritime Powers and to many States whose economies depend upon trade and navigation between the Red Sea and the Mediterranean Sea.

There has recently been an increasingly wide recognition that the Gulf of Aqaba comprehends international waters, in which the right of free and innocent passage exists.

On 11 February 1957, the Secretary of State of the United States of America handed to the Ambassador of Israel in Washington a memorandum dealing, among other things, with the subject of the Gulf of Aqaba and the Straits of Tiran. This statement discusses the rights of nations in the Gulf of Aqaba and declares the readiness of the United States to exercise those rights on its own behalf and to join with others in securing general recognition of those rights.

My Government has subsequently learned with gratification that other leading maritime Powers are prepared to subscribe to the doctrine set out in the United States memorandum of 11 February and have a similar intention to exercise their rights of free and innocent passage in the Gulf and the Straits.

General Assembly resolution 1125 (XI) of 2 February 1957 contemplates that units of the United Nations Emergency Force will move into the area of the Straits of Tiran on Israel's withdrawal. It is generally recognized that the function of the United Nations Emergency Force in that area includes the prevention of belligerent acts.

In this connexion, my Government recalls the statements by the representative of the United States in the General Assembly on 28 January 1957 and 2 February, with reference to the function of the United Nations Emergency Force units which are to move into the area of the Straits of Tiran on Israel's withdrawal. The statement of 28 January, repeated on 2 February, said:

". . . It is essential that units of the United Nations Emergency Force be stationed at the Straits of Tiran in order to achieve there the separation of Egyptian and Israel land and sea forces. This separation is essential until it is clear that the non-existence of any claim to belligerent rights has established in practice the peaceful conditions which must govern navigation in waters having such an international interest."

My Government has been concerned with the situation which would arise if the United Nations Emergency Force, having taken up its position in the area of the Straits of Tiran for the purpose of assuring non-belligerency, were to be withdrawn in conditions which might give rise to interference with free and innocent navigation and, therefore, to the renewal of hostilities. Such a premature cessation of the precautionary measures taken by the United Nations for the prevention of belligerent acts would prejudice important international interests and threaten peace and security. My Government has noted the assurance embodied in the Secretary-General's note of 26 February 1957, that any proposal for the withdrawal of the United Nations Emergency Force from the Gulf of Aqaba area would first come to the Advisory Committee on the United Nations Emergency Force, which represents the General Assembly in the implementation of its resolution 997 (ES–I) of 2 November 1956. This procedure will give the General Assembly an opportunity to ensure that no precipitate changes are made which would have the effect of increasing the possibility of belligerent acts. We have reason to believe that in such a discussion many Members of the United Nations would be guided by the view expressed by Mr. Lodge, representative of the United States, on 2 February in favour of maintaining the United Nations Emergency Force in the Straits of Tiran until peaceful conditions were in practice assured.

In the light of these doctrines, policies and arrangements by the United Nations and the maritime Powers, my Government is confident that free and innocent passage for international and Israel shipping will continue to be fully maintained after Israel's withdrawal.

Interference, by armed force, with ships of Israel flag exercising free and innocent passage in the Gulf of Aqaba and through the Straits of Tiran, will be regarded by Israel as an attack entitling it to exercise its inherent right of self-defence under Article 51 of the United Nations Charter and to take all such measures as are necessary to ensure the free and innocent passage of its ships in the Gulf and in the Straits.

We make this announcement in accordance with the accepted principles of international law under which all States have an inherent right to use their forces to protect their ships and their rights against interference by armed force. My Government naturally hopes that this contingency will not occur.

In a public address on 20 February 1957, President Eisenhower stated: "We should not assume that, if Israel withdraws, Egypt will prevent Israel shipping from using the Suez Canal or the Gulf of Aqaba." This declaration has weighed heavily with my Government in determining its action today.

Israel is now prepared to withdraw its forces from the regions of the Gulf of Aqaba and the Straits of Tiran in the confidence that there will be continued freedom of navigation for international and Israel shipping in the Gulf of Aqaba and through the Straits of Tiran.

We propose that a meeting be held immediately between the Chief of Staff of the Israel Defence Army and the Commander of the United Nation Emergency Force in order to arrange for the United Nations to take over its responsibilities in the Sharm el Sheikh area.

The Government of Israel announces that it is making a complete withdrawal from the Gaza strip in accordance with General Assembly resolution 1124 (XI). It makes this announcement on the following assumptions:

(*a*) That on its withdrawal the United Nations forces will be deployed in Gaza and that the take-over of Gaza from the military and civilian control of Israel will be exclusively by the United Nations Emergency Force.

(*b*) It is, further, Israel's expectation that the United Nations will be the agency to be utilized for carrying out the functions enumerated by the Secretary-General, namely:

" . . . safeguarding life and property in the area by providing efficient and effective police protection; as will guarantee good civilian administration; as will assure maximum assistance to the United Nations refugee programme; and as will protect and foster the economic development of the territory and its people."

(*c*) It is, further, Israel's expectation that the aforementioned responsibility of the United Nations in the administration of Gaza will be maintained for a transitory period from the take-over until there is a peace settlement, to be sought as rapidly as possible, or a definitive agreement on the future of the Gaza strip.

It is the position of Israel that, if conditions are created in the Gaza strip which indicate a return to the conditions of deterioration which existed previously, Israel would reserve its freedom to act to defend its rights.

Accordingly, we propose that a meeting be held immediately between the Chief of Staff of the Israel Defence Army and the Commander of the United Nations Emergency Force in order to arrange for the United Nations to take over its responsibilities in the Gaza area.

For many weeks, amidst great difficulty, my Government has sought to ensure that on the withdrawal from the Sharm el Sheikh and the Gaza areas, circumstances would prevail which would prevent the likelihood of belligerent acts. We record with gratitude the sympathetic efforts of many Governments and delegations to help bring about a situation which would end the insecurity prevailing for Israel and its neighbours these many years. In addition to the considerations to which I have referred, we place our trust in the vigilant resolve of the international community that Israel should, equally with all Member States, enjoy its basic rights of freedom from fear of attack, freedom to sail the high seas and international waterways in peace, freedom to pursue its national destiny in tranquillity without the constant peril which has surrounded it in recent years. In this reliance we are embarking upon the course which I have announced today.

May I now add these few words to the States in the Middle East area and, more specifically, to the neighbours of Israel. We all come from an area which is a very ancient one. The hills and the valleys of the region have been witnesses to many wars and many conflicts. But that is not the only thing which characterizes that part of the world from which we come. It is also a part of the world which is of an ancient culture. It is that part of the world which has given to humanity three great religions. It is also that part of the world which has given a code of ethics to all humanity. In our countries, in the entire region, all our peoples are anxious for and in need of a higher standard of living, of great programmes of development and progress.

Can we, from now on—all of us—turn a new leaf and, instead of fighting with each other, can we all, united, fight poverty and disease and illiteracy? Is it possible for us to put all our efforts and all our energy into one single purpose, the betterment and progress and development of all our lands and all our peoples?

I can here pledge the Government and the people of Israel to do their part in this united effort. There is no limit to what we are prepared to contribute so that all of us, together, can live to see a day of happiness for our peoples and see again from that region a great contribution to peace and happiness for all humanity.

NOTE. For comments on the Egyptian Question, see Michael ADAMS, Suez and After: Year of Crisis (Boston, 1958), 225 pp.; Eugene ARONEANU, "Le conflit israélo-égyptien et la justice internationale," 35 RDISDP (1957), pp. 5–14; G. BARRACLOUGH, "Suez," in ROYAL INSTITUTE OF INTERNATIONAL AFFAIRS, Survey of International Affairs, 1956–1958 (London, 1962), pp. 3–71; Suzanne BASTID, "L'action militaire franco-britannique en Egypte et le droit des Nations Unies," in Mélanges en l'honneur de Gilbert Gidel (Paris, 1961), pp. 49–78; Wilbourn E. BENTON, "United Nations Action in the Suez Crisis," 4 Tulane Studies in Political Science (1957), pp. 5–23; B. BOUTROS-GHALI and Youssef CHLALA, Le Canal de Suez, 1854–1957 (Alexandria, 1958), 211 pp.; Merry and Serge BROMBERGER, Les secrets de l'expédition d'Egypte (Paris, 1957), 267 pp.; Bengt BROMS, The Legal Status of the Suez Canal (Vammala, Finland, 1961), pp. 167–205; John C. CAMPBELL, Defense of the Middle East: Problems of American Policy (2d ed., New York, 1960), pp. 80–120; CANADA, DEPARTMENT OF EXTERNAL AFFAIRS, The Crisis in the

Middle East, Oct. 1956–March 1957 (Ottawa, 1957), 2 vols., 29 and 39 pp.; John CONNELL, The Most Important Country: The True Story of the Suez Crisis and the Events Leading to It (London, 1957), 240 pp.; Clyde EAGLE-TON and Francis O. WILCOX, "The United Nations and the Suez Crisis," *in* Philip W. THAYER, Tensions in the Middle East (Baltimore, Md., 1958), pp. 273–96; James EAYRS, ed., The Commonwealth and Suez: A Documentary Survey (London, 1964), 483 pp.; Herbert FEIS, "Suez Scenario: A Lamentable Tale," 38 Foreign Affairs (1960), pp. 598–612; George A. FINCH, "Post-Mortem on the Suez Debacle," 51 AJIL (1957), pp. 376–80; Michael FOOT and Mervyn JONES, Guilty Men, 1957: Suez and Cyprus (New York, 1957), 264 pp.; S. A. GOODHART and Quincy WRIGHT, "Some Legal Aspects of the Suez Situation," *in* Philip W. THAYER, Tensions in the Middle East (Baltimore, Md., 1958), pp. 243–72; L. C. GREEN, "The Double Standard of the United Nations," 11 YBWA (1957), pp. 104–37; Stanley HOFFMAN, "Sisyphus and the Avalanche: The United Nations, Egypt and Hungary," 11 Int. Org. (1957), pp. 446–469; John M. HOWELL, "The Application of the Concepts of Domestic Jurisdiction and Aggression in the Suez Crisis," 4 Tulane Studies in Political Science (1957), pp. 49–61; Paul JOHNSON, The Suez War (London, 1957), 145 pp.; Joseph P. LASH, Dag Hammarskjöld: Custodian of the Brush-Fire Peace (Garden City, New York, 1961), pp. 66–111; William F. LONGGOOD, Suez Story: Key to the Middle East (New York, 1957), 174 pp.; R. St. J. MACDONALD, "Hungary, Egypt and the United Nations," 35 Canadian Bar R. (1957), pp. 38–71; MIDDLE EAST RESEARCH CENTER, British and French Action in Egypt, August-November 1956 (Cairo, 1956), 147 pp.; Richard I. MILLER, Dag Hammarskjöld and Crisis Diplomacy (New York, 1961), pp. 59–125; Sir Leslie Knox MUNRO, "Hungary and Suez: Problems of World Order," 12 Record of the Association of the Bar of the City of New York (1957), pp. 12–29; M. Abou NOUSEIR and others, The Suez Canal: Facts and Documents (Cairo, 1956), 249 pp.; Joseph A. OBIETA, The International Status of the Suez Canal (The Hague, 1960), pp. 18–21, 90–113; David B. PRICE, "The Charter of the United Nations and the Suez War," 1 Int. Rels. (London, 1958), pp. 494–511; Dietrich RAUSCHNING, "Rechtsprobleme der Suez-kanal-Krise," 7 JIR (1957), pp. 257–82 and 8 *idem* (1957–58), pp. 267–76; Terrence ROBERTSON, Crisis: The Inside Story of the Suez Conspiracy (New York, 1965), 349 pp.; Arthur McLean STILLMAN, The United Nations and the Suez Canal (University Microfilms, Ann Arbor, Michigan, 1965), 241 pp.; Albert ULLOA, "El Conflicto del Canal de Suez," 16 Revista peruana de derecho internacional (1956), No. 50, pp. 3–60; US, DOS, The Suez Canal Problem, July 26-Sept. 22, 1956: A Documentary Publication (Pub. 6392; Washington, D.C., 1956), 370 pp.; US, DOS, United States Policy in the Middle East, Sept. 1956-June 1957 (Pub. 6505; Washington, D.C., 1957), 425 pp.; Yves VAN DER MENSBRUGGHE, Les garanties de la liberté de navigation dans le Canal de Suez (Paris, 1964), pp. 87–107, 147–79, 252–304, 361–65; R. F. WALL, "The Middle East," *in* ROYAL INSTI-TUTE OF INTERNATIONAL AFFAIRS, Survey of International Affairs, 1956–1958 (London, 1962), pp. 141–61; Siegbert J. WEINBERGER, "The Suez Canal Issue, 1956," 8 Middle Eastern Affairs (1957), pp. 46–57; Guy WINT and Peter CALVOCORESSI, Middle East Crisis (Baltimore, Md., 1957), 141 pp.; Quincy WRIGHT, "Intervention, 1956," 51 AJIL (1957), pp. 257–76. See also Hugh THOMAS, Suez (New York, 1967), 261 pp.

With respect to the various problems involved in this case, see also Benno AVRAM, The Evolution of the Suez Canal Status from 1809 up to 1956: A Historico-Juridical Study (Geneva, 1958), 170 pp.; Louis Mortimer BLOOM-FIELD, Egypt, Israel and the Gulf of Aqaba in International Law (Toronto, 1957), 240 pp.; Erik BRÜEL, "Die völkerrechtliche Stellung des Suez-kanals und die Nationalisierung der Kanalgesellschaft," 7 AVR (1958–59), pp. 24–67; Erskine B. CHILDERS, The Road to Suez: A Study of Western-Arab Relations (London, 1962), 416 pp.; Robert DELSON, "Nationalization of the Suez Canal Company: Issues of Public and Private International Law," 57 Columbia L.R. (1957), pp. 755–86; Paul DE VISSCHER, "Les aspects juridiques fondamentaux de la question de Suez," 62 RGDIP (1958), pp. 400–43; Simcha DINITZ, "The Legal Aspects of the Egyptian Blockade of the Suez Canal," 45 Georgetown L.J. (1956–57), pp. 169–99; James E. DOUGHERTY, "The Aswan Decision in Perspective," 74 Political Science Q. (1959), pp. 21–45; EGYPT, MINISTRY FOR FOREIGN AFFAIRS, White Paper on the Nationalization of the Suez Maritime Canal Company (Cairo, 1956), 72 pp.; Moustapha EL-HEFNAOUI, Les problèmes contemporains posés par le Canal de Suez (Paris, 1951), 392 pp.; Leo GROSS, "Passage through the Suez Canal of Israel-bound Cargo and Israel Ships", 51 AJIL (1957), pp. 530–68; Thomas T. F. HUANG, "Some International and Legal Aspects of the Suez Canal Question", 51 AJIL (1957), pp. 277–307; Raymond de Gouffre de LA PRADELLE, "L'Egypte a-t-elle violé le droit international en nationalisant la Compagnie Universelle du Canal Maritime de Suez?" 3 IRD (1958), pp. 20–27; LAWYERS COMMITTEE ON BLOCK-ADES, The United Nations and the Egyptian Blockade of the Suez Canal (New York, 1953) 27 pp.; Roger PINTO, "L'affaire de Suez: Problèmes juridiques", 2 AFDI (1956), pp. 20–45; Edmond RABBATH, Mer Rouge et Golfe d'Aqaba dans l'évolution de droit international (Cairo, 1962), 52 pp.; Georges SCELLE, "La nationalisation de Canal de Suez et le droit international", 2 AFDI (1956), pp. 3–19; Hugh J. SCHONFIELD, The Suez Canal in World Affairs (New York Philosophical Library, 1953), 174 pp.; Charles B. SELAK, Jr., "A Consideration of the Legal Status of the Gulf of Aqaba", 52 AJIL (1958), pp. 660–698; SUEZ CANAL COMPANY, The Suez Canal Company and the Decision Taken by the Egyptian Government on 26th July 1956 (Paris, 1956–57), 2 vols., 78 and 125 pp.; NOTE, "Nationalization of the Suez Canal Company", 70 Harvard L.R. 480–90.

---

11. *Letter from the Secretary-General to the States Providing Contingents, 21 June 1957.*

Annex I to A/3943 (9 Oct. 1958); GAOR, Annexes (XIII) 65, p. 33.

1. I have the honour to refer to the resolutions of the General Assembly relating to the United Nations Emergency Force (UNEF) and particularly to resolution 1000 (ES–I) of 5 November 1956 and resolution 1001 (ES–I) of 7 November 1956. I also have the honour to refer to our previous communications concerning the national contingent provided by your Government for service with UNEF.

2. It will be recalled that the guiding principles for the organization and functioning of the Force were set out in paragraphs 6 to 9 of

the "Second and final report of the Secretary-General on the plan for an emergency international United Nations Force" (A/3302). They were approved by the General Assembly in paragraph 1 of resolution 1001 (ES–I). By paragraph 2 of the same resolution the General Assembly concurred in the definition of the functions of the Force as stated in paragraph 12 of the Secretary-General's report.

3.   Paragraph 7 of resolution 1001 (ES–I) authorized the Secretary-General to issue regulations and instructions which may be essential to the effective functioning of the Force, following consultation with the Advisory Committee established by the same resolution, and to take all other necessary administrative and executive actions. Pursuant to this resolution I have, on 8 February 1957, concluded by exchange of letters an Agreement between the United Nations and the Government of Egypt concerning the status of UNEF in Egypt. On the same date I submitted a report (A/3526) on this Agreement to the General Assembly which was noted with approval by resolution 1126 (XI) adopted on 22 February 1957. Following consultation with the Advisory Committee, the participating States, and the Commander of the Force, I have also issued Regulations for the United Nations Emergency Force (ST/SGB/UNEF/1) on 20 February 1957. . . .

4.   The Regulations referred to above affirm the international character of the Force as a subsidiary organ of the General Assembly and define the conditions of service for the members of the Force. National contingents provided for UNEF serve under these Regulations.

5.   The Regulations and the Agreement referred to in paragraph 3 of this letter also secure to the Force and its individual members the privileges and immunities necessary for the independent exercise of its functions. I should like to direct your attention to the provisions of the Regulations and of the Agreement which provide these privileges and immunities and particularly to article 34 of the Regulations and to paragraphs 10, 11 and 12 of my letter to the Minister of Foreign Affairs of Egypt of 8 February 1957 (A/3526). It will be noted that paragraph 11 of this letter states that "Members of the Force shall be subject to the exclusive jurisdiction of their respective national States in respect of any criminal offences which may be committed by them in Egypt". This immunity from the jurisdiction of Egypt is based on the understanding that the authorities of the participating States would exercise such jurisdiction as might be necessary with respect to crimes or offences committed in Egypt by any members of the Force provided from their own military services. It is assumed that the participating States will act accordingly.

6.   I should also like to direct your attention to article 13 of the UNEF Regulations concerning "Good order and discipline". This article provides:

"The Commander of the UNEF shall have general responsibility for the good order of the Force. Responsibility for disciplinary action in national contingents provided for the Force rests with the commanders of the national contingents. Reports concerning disciplinary action shall be communicated to the Commander of the UNEF who may consult with the commander of the national contingent and if necessary the authorities of the Participating State concerned."

7. In view of the considerations set out in paragraphs 5 and 6 above, I should appreciate your assurance that the commander of the national contingent provided by your Government will be in a position to exercise the necessary disciplinary authority. I should also appreciate your assurance that your Government will be prepared to exercise jurisdiction with respect to any crime or offence which might be committed by a Member of such national contingent.

8. The effective functioning of the United Nations Emergency Force requires that some continuity of service of units with the Force be ensured in order that the UNEF Commander may be in a position to plan his operations with knowledge of what units will be available. I should, therefore, appreciate your assurance that the national contingent provided by your Government will not be withdrawn without adequate prior notification to the Secretary-General, so as to avoid the impairment of the ability of the Force to discharge its functions. Likewise, should circumstances render the service of your national contingent with the Force no longer necessary, the Secretary-General undertakes to consult with your Government and to give adequate prior notification concerning its withdrawal.

9. Reference is also made to articles 11 and 12 of the UNEF Regulations which deal with "Command authority" and "Chain of command and delegation of authority". Article 12 provides, *inter alia,* that changes in commanders of national contingents which have been made available by participating Governments should be made in consultation between the Commander of the United Nations Emergency Force and the appropriate authorities of the participating Government.

10. Finally, I suggest that questions involving the allocation of expenses should be dealt with, in the light of relevant resolutions of the General Assembly, in a supplemental agreement. Such other supplementary arrangements concerning the service of your national contingents with the Force may be made as occasion requires.

11. It is the intention that this letter together with your reply accepting the proposals set forth herein shall constitute an agreement between the United Nations and . . ., and shall be deemed to have taken effect from the date that the national contingent provided by your Government departed from its home country to assume duties with UNEF. It is also intended that it shall remain in force until such time as your national contingent may be withdrawn from the Force either in accordance with the terms of paragraph 8 above or in the light of developments affecting the functioning of the Force which

may render its service no longer necessary. The provisions of paragraph 12 relating to the settlement of disputes should remain in force until all outstanding claims have been settled.

12. It is also proposed that all disputes between the United Nations and your Government concerning the interpretation or application of this agreement which are not settled by negotiation or other agreed mode of settlement shall be referred for final settlement to a tribunal of three arbitrators. One of the arbitrators shall be appointed by the Secretary-General of the United Nations, one by your Government, and the umpire shall be chosen jointly by the Secretary-General and your Government. If the two parties fail to agree on the appointment of the umpire within one month of the proposal of arbitration by one of the parties, the President of the International Court of Justice shall be asked by either party to appoint the umpire. Should a vacancy occur for any reason, the vacancy shall be filled within thirty days by the method laid down in this paragraph for the original appointment. The tribunal shall come into existence upon the appointment of the umpire and at least one of the other members of the tribunal. Two members of the tribunal shall constitute a quorum for the performance of its functions, and for all deliberations and decisions of the tribunal a favourable vote of two members shall be sufficient.

NOTE.—Some of the letters from the contributing States imposed certain limitations on the use of their forces. For instance, the letter from the Swedish government, of 5 November 1956, presumed that the task of the Force would be limited to the objectives set forth in the General Assembly resolutions of 4 and 5 November, and that there would be no implication "that the Force should remain on watch duty in the area for an unspecified period of time, or pending the solution of the political questions affecting that area." It presumed further that "the Swedish unit shall not be stationed in foreign territory without the consent of the State concerned, and that the costs involved will, to a considerable extent, be borne by the United Nations in accordance with a specific agreement to be concluded for that purpose with the United Nations." Annex 7 to A/3302 (6 Nov. 1956); GAOR, Annexes (ES–I) 5, pp. 22–23.

The Indian government, on 7 November 1956, noted the following conditions of participation in the Force, as outlined to its representative by the Secretary-General:

"1. The emergency Force is set up in the context of the withdrawal of Anglo-French forces from Egypt and on the basis of the call to Israel to withdraw behind the armistice lines.

"2. The Force is not in any sense a successor to the invading Anglo-French forces, or in any sense to take over its functions.

"3. It is understood the Force may have to function through Egyptian territory. Therefore, there must be Egyptian consent for its establishment.

"4. The Force is a temporary one for an emergency. Its purpose is to separate the combatants, namely, Egypt and Israel, with the latter withdrawing as required by the resolution.

"5. The Force must be a balanced one in its composition." A/3302/Add. 4/Rev.1 (7 Nov. 1956); GAOR, Annexes (ES-I) 5, pp. 23-24.

12.   *Report of the Secretary-General on UNEF Experience, 9 October 1958.*

A/3943; GAOR, Annexes (XIII) 65, pp. 8-33.

1.   In the almost two years of operation of the United Nations Emergency Force (hereinafter referred to as "UNEF" or "the Force"), the United Nations has acquired considerable experience in the establishment, organization and functioning of such an international instrument.   UNEF represents a new and in many ways unique experiment by the United Nations in a type of operation which previously it had not been called upon to conduct.

2.   The Force was created as a temporary measure, its characteristics were determined by the nature of its role, and its functions were defined and limited by decisions of the General Assembly applying to a particular set of circumstances.   .   .   .

CHAPTER I.   POLITICAL AND CONSTITUTIONAL QUESTIONS   .   .   .

Role assigned to the Force by the General Assembly.

8.   The General Assembly, in its resolution 1000 (ES-I) of 5 November 1956, provided that the Force would "secure and supervise the cessation of hostilities in accordance with all the terms" of resolution 997 (ES-I) of 2 November, which would include the withdrawal of non-Egyptian forces from Egyptian territory and the restoration of observance of the provisions of the General Armistice Agreement between Egypt and Israel.   These objectives could not be achieved through an organization similar in kind to UNTSO or to the Egyptian-Israel Mixed Armistice Commission, which had been established in other and different circumstances and were designed to meet different and narrower needs.   The role of UNTSO is to observe and maintain the cease-fire in Palestine ordered by the Security Council.   The Mixed Armistice Commission, serviced by UNTSO, is the bilateral machinery established under the Egyptian-Israel General Armistice Agreement in connexion with the execution of the provisions of that Agreement, exercising such functions as the investigation of incidents and complaints.

9.   Under the conditions prevailing in November 1956, it was clear that a new approach and a new type of operation were required in order to facilitate compliance with the recommendations of the General Assembly relating to the armed interventions in Egypt.

10.   This new instrument was charged with a dual role: initially to secure and supervise the cease-fire and the withdrawal of armed forces from Egyptian territory, and later to maintain peaceful con-

ditions in the area by its deployment along the Egyptian-Israel armistice demarcation line in the Gaza area and to the south along the international frontier. This dual role determined the size, organization, equipment and deployment of the Force.

11. The two reports submitted by the Secretary-General to the Assembly on 4 November (A/3289) and 6 November (A/3302) on the plan for an emergency United Nations Force dealt with these factors and their implications.

12. In the guiding principles set forth by the Secretary-General for the organization and functioning of the Force and approved by the Assembly, it was emphasized that there was "no intent . . . to influence the military balance in the present conflict and, thereby, the political balance affecting efforts to settle the conflict" (A/3302, para. 8). Nor was the Force to be "used so as to prejudge the solution of the controversial questions involved" (A/3512, para. 29). It was felt, moreover, that the creation of peaceful conditions in the area required avoidance of the state of affairs into which conditions had progressively deteriorated in the past as a result of the lack of full implementation of the clauses of the Armistice Agreement. The objective sought was to ensure strict compliance by Egypt and Israel with the letter and spirit of the General Armistice Agreement concluded between them. Towards this end, the General Assembly decided, on 2 February 1957, that:

"the scrupulous maintenance of the Armistice Agreement requires the placing of the United Nations Emergency Force on the Egyptian-Israel armistice demarcation line and the implementation of other measures as proposed in the Secretary-General's report [A/3512], with due regard to the considerations set out therein with a view to assist in achieving situations conducive to the maintenance of peaceful conditions in the area."

The deployment of the Force along the Israel-Egyptian armistice demarcation line and the international frontier south of Gaza, and in the Sharm el Sheikh area, was not meant to and could not effect any change in their prior *status juris;* its sole purpose was to maintain quiet and prevent the recurrence of incidents.

Essential characteristics of UNEF.

13. In its resolution 1000 (ES–I) establishing the United Nations Command and in the recruitment procedure prescribed, the General Assembly indicated that the Force would be set up on the basis of principles reflected in the structure and Charter of the United Nations itself, in that its Commanding Officer would be appointed by and responsible to the United Nations, and that his authority would be so defined as to make him fully independent of the policies or control of any one nation. The status of the "Chief of the Command" (later to be known as "Commander") was illustrated by the authority given

to him, in consultation with the Secretary-General, to recruit for the Force officers from Member States other than the permanent members of the Security Council. At the same time, an important principle was introduced regarding the composition of the Force. The concept of a force established on this basis is basically different from that by which the United Nations might entrust a country, or a group of countries, with the responsibility of providing independently for an international force serving purposes determined by the Organization, as in the case of the Unified Command in Korea. It is also different from the concept, for which there is no precedent in application, of an international force set up by agreement among a group of nations, later to be brought into some appropriate relationship with the United Nations.

14. The functions of the Force are exclusively international in character in that they relate to armed conflict among States, and since the purpose of the Force is to facilitate compliance with resolutions relating to that conflict adopted by the General Assembly, the Force, during its early stages, in some instances had to undertake limited responsibility for administrative and security functions, but this was entirely temporary and incidental to the main tasks assigned to it.

15. The first emergency special session of the General Assembly, at which it was decided to establish an emergency force, had been called into session under the terms of the "Uniting for peace" resolution (resolution 377 (V) of 3 November 1950). Thus, UNEF has been necessarily limited in its operations to the extent that consent of the parties concerned is required under generally recognized international law. It followed that, while the General Assembly could establish the Force, subject only to the concurrence of the States providing contingents, the consent of the Government of the country concerned was required before the Assembly could request the Force to be stationed or to operate on the territory of that country. The Force has no rights other than those necessary for the execution of the functions assigned to it by the General Assembly and agreed to by the country or countries concerned. The Force is paramilitary in character and much more than an observer corps, but it is in no sense a military force exercising, through force of arms, even temporary control over the territory in which it is stationed; nor does it have military objectives, or military functions exceeding those necessary to secure peaceful conditions on the assumption that the parties to the conflict will take all the necessary steps for compliance with the recommendations of the General Assembly.

16. The Force is composed of national contingents accepted for service by the Secretary-General from among those voluntarily offered by Member States. The question of the composition of a force based on national contingents offered for service is a fundamental

one. In the case of UNEF, the policy has been to exclude military personnel belonging to any of the permanent members of the Security Council and from any country which for geographical or other reasons might have a special interest in the conflict. The choice of the contingents for the Force, while subject to the decision of the United Nations alone, is nevertheless of major concern also to the country in which the Force operates. Thus, the United Nations must give most serious consideration to the views of the host Government on such matters without, however, surrendering its right to take a serious difference, should one develop, to the political level for resolution. In the experience of UNEF, this latter course has not been necessary, since no impasse has ever developed in this area. A balanced composition was always sought in the selection of units.

17. The size of component units has been determined by two primary requirements. From the point of view of efficiency, it was necessary that Member States should provide units sufficiently large to be relatively self-contained. From the point of view of balance, it was desirable that the Force should include adequate support elements and that the differences in the size of units should not be so great as to lead to excessive dependence on any one State.

18. In practice, the UNEF operation is an example of fruitful military and civilian collaboration. Matters relating to its administration and finance, communications, maintenance and other services are taken care of within the framework of the United Nations Secretariat. The resolutions of the General Assembly authorize the Secretary-General to take all executive and administrative actions essential to the effective functioning of the Force.

19. The Regulations for the Force (ST/SGB/UNEF/1) affirm its international character as a subsidiary organ of the General Assembly. The Assembly intended that the Force should be a temporary arrangement, whose duration would be determined by the needs created by the emergency, and whose tasks and legal basis could be defined only by the Assembly. .   .   .

Responsibilities entrusted to the Secretary-General
by the General Assembly.

26. The resolutions of the General Assembly, involving decisions on various policy matters, required the Secretary-General to assume important additional responsibilities; he was requested to observe and report on compliance with certain Assembly resolutions, and to implement others by executive and administrative actions. For example, in addition to the general requests for reports on compliance, the Assembly authorized him to arrange with the parties concerned for the implementation of the cease-fire and the halting of the movement of military forces and arms into the area; he was also requested, with the assistance of the Chief of Staff and the military

observers of UNTSO, to obtain the withdrawal of all forces behind the armistice lines (resolution 999 (ES–I)). In another resolution, the Secretary-General was requested to continue his efforts to secure the complete withdrawal of Israel forces and to report on such completion within five days (resolution 1123(XI)). . . .

Advisory Committee on UNEF.

30. In conjunction with the establishment of the Force, the General Assembly decided to create an Advisory Committee composed of seven representatives of Member States, under the chairmanship of the Secretary-General (resolution 1001 (ES–I)). In its advisory capacity, this Committee was to assist the Secretary-General in the planning and operation of the Force. It was empowered to request, through the usual procedures, the convening of the General Assembly and to report to the Assembly, if matters should arise which, in its opinion, were of such urgency and importance as to require consideration by the Assembly itself. It has had no occasion to invoke this authority. Meetings of the Advisory Committee have been held whenever matters have arisen requiring discussion, or whenever the Secretary-General has sought advice, or, at times, only to keep the Committee informed on current developments. The Advisory Committee has been consulted particularly on those questions which the Assembly had indicated should be the subject of consultation between it and the Secretary-General, such as the Regulations for the Force, the policy of the Force with regard to self-defence and the issue of medals. . . .

CHAPTER II. FORMATION AND COMPOSITION OF UNEF . . .

The first phase.

35. There was urgent need to assemble a usable force, as rapidly as possible, and to land it in Egypt. While awaiting the conclusion of arrangements with Egypt for the entry of the Force into that country, it was decided that a staging area near the Mediterranean would be necessary, as it would expedite the flow of troops and matériel to Egypt. Arrangements were quickly made with the Government of Italy for the use of Capodichino airport, Naples, for this purpose. Most of the troops brought to Egypt by air were sent via Naples, others were flown in via Beirut, while others came by sea to Port Said. The small staff in charge of the staging area at Capodichino took care of the incoming (and later outgoing) contingents, dealt with the several authorities in Europe through whom major logistic support was obtained, supervised the air-lift to Egypt and arranged for the surface transport of heavy stores.

36. The initial movements of troops from their home bases to Italy were arranged through United Nations Headquarters. The problems

were mainly transportation and co-ordination. The bulk of the transport to the staging area was provided by the United States Air Force. The representatives of the contributing countries supplied information to United Nations Headquarters concerning the numbers, equipment and state of readiness of their national units, and this was transmitted to the representatives of the United States Air Force designated for this purpose. The latter, in turn, gave notification concerning the precise arrangements for transporting the contingents named, which was transmitted to the appropriate Governments by their military representatives at United Nations Headquarters.

37. A selected group of United Nations military observers, who were detached temporarily from their duties with UNTSO and who commenced planning while still in Jerusalem, served at first as the nucleus of a UNEF headquarters staff. They arrived in Egypt on 12 November 1956, established a temporary headquarters in Cairo and, together with Secretariat officials, arranged for the reception and billeting of the first contingents, and the early procurement, storage and issue of the supplies and equipment required. Through negotiations with the Egyptian Government, an air base at Abu Suweir, near Ismailia, became the arrival depot for the early contingents. As the contingents arrived, their officers took over the duties being performed by the military observers, who were then able to return to their UNTSO duties in Jerusalem.

38. Advance elements of UNEF were moved to Egypt at a time when hostilities had but recently ceased; there were restrictions on the times and lanes of flights, and aircraft transporting contingents had to be of suitable nationalities. The initial air-lift of troops to Abu Suweir was carried out by Swissair. The Naples to Egypt air-lift was subsequently taken over by the Royal Canadian Air Force with some assistance from the Italian Air Force in lifting supplies.

39. Speed was a major reason for initially moving some troops and equipment to Egypt by air, but as ships under some flags could not be used, and as ships proceeding to Port Said at that time were required to be self-sustaining, the immediate possibilities of employing sea transport were in any case severely reduced. The Yugoslav reconnaissance battalion, with all its equipment, was brought to Port Said by sea on 28 November 1956, while the main elements of the Canadian and Brazilian contingents arrived in national naval vessels on 11 January and 2 February 1957, respectively. All heavy equipment for UNEF was brought in by ship.

40. One consequence of having to rely on air transport for the first units and their equipment was an immediate and severe shortage of transport vehicles. This difficulty was aggravated by the fact that several of the contingents had not contemplated bringing most of their vehicular transport with them in any event because of the desert

conditions. The shortage was alleviated by obtaining vehicles from UNRWA, by local purchases and by rental. But, as requirements mounted, these sources became inadequate.

41. A preliminary understanding had been reached in New York on the purchase of vehicles and supplies in Port Said from the British forces as they withdrew, the details of the transaction being worked out on the spot. This procurement was very helpful in facilitating the rapid deployment of UNEF forces in the Sinai Peninsula and in equipping the two transportation platoons used for supplying the forces. Shortly after the formation of the Force, a large order for vehicles was placed with United States military authorities. These vehicles arrived in January 1957 and filled the additional transport requirements.

42. The need to transport UNEF units to positions evacuated by the Anglo-French and Israel forces, to keep them supplied and to provide replacements, required the immediate establishment at Abu Suweir of a dump of petrol, oil and lubricants. The necessary stocks and installations were obtained in the area. Additional storage facilities were obtained in Port Said, and further supply points were established as the operation moved forward.

43. The clear identification of UNEF personnel, beyond the customary United Nations armbands, was an immediate necessity for security and other reasons. Light blue helmet liners with United Nations markings were adopted for this purpose, and were later supplemented by blue berets and desert caps and UNEF badges and insignia. Vehicles and aircraft were painted white with United Nations markings.

National contingents and supporting units.

44. On the basis of the position taken in the General Assembly resolutions—which reflects a principle that is both sound and practical —no units from any of the permanent members of the Security Council have been included in the Force. Nor have any been recruited from countries in the area or from countries which might, for other reasons, be thought to have a special interest in the conflict situation. In selecting contingents, weight was given to such factors as their suitability in terms of the needs of the Force, their size and availability, the extent to which they would be self-contained, the undesirability of too great a variation in ordnance and basic equipment, the problem of transportation, and the goal of balanced composition.

45. In the period November-December 1956, twenty-four Member States offered to provide units. A number of these countries also offered other forms of assistance, as did two other Member States and one non-member. Most of the offers of assistance were of infantry units. The Force, at the peak of its strength totalling about 6,000 officers and men, consisted of contingents from the following coun-

tries; Brazil, Canada, Colombia, Denmark, Finland, India, Indonesia, Norway, Sweden and Yugoslavia.

46.   The extent of the area to be covered by UNEF called for highly mobile reconnaissance. This need was met by Yugoslavia, which provided a complete reconnaissance battalion, and by Canada, which later provided a fully-equipped light armoured squadron.

47.   Supporting units were obtained and assigned with the same urgency as those engaged in patrolling. Experience with the Force soon demonstrated the desirability of limiting the number of countries participating in it, particularly those providing support units, in view of the difficulties in co-ordinating and controlling a number of relatively small units having different arms and equipment, requiring varying diets and speaking different languages. Thus, to simplify the organization in the interest of efficiency, the Indian contingent was given responsibility for the Supply Depot and the Service Institute; Canada and India provided units for Transport, the Provost Marshal and Signals; Norway and Canada covered the medical needs. The Canadian contingent was also made responsible for the Ordnance Depot and Workshop, the Base Post Office, Engineering, the Dental Unit, Movement Control and Air Support.

48.   When the contingents were being accepted, it was impossible to determine or to foresee the duration of the UNEF mission. National terms of military service, the nature of the mission, conditions of weather and terrain, and considerations of morale and efficiency, gave strong support to the principle and practice of rather frequent periodic rotation. The exact rotation policies adopted by contributing Governments, however, have varied somewhat, and in some cases the length of the period of service has been shorter than would be dictated exclusively by considerations of efficiency and economy. Full responsibility for the cost of transportation is accepted by the United Nations.

49.   The schedules of rotation are fixed by the contributing countries in consultation with the Commander, in such a way as to ensure continuity of national participation in the Force and to protect it from being undermanned.

50.   With regard to the withdrawal of contingents from the Force, the contributing Governments agreed with the Secretary-General that, in order to protect the organizational strength of the Force, participating Governments would inform the Secretary-General in advance of a decision to withdraw their contingents. In each of the two cases of withdrawal that have occurred to date, notice was given sufficiently in advance to enable the Force to obtain replacements through increasing the size of one or more of the existing contingents.

CHAPTER III.   OPERATIONS IN THE FIELD   .   .   .

Operations relating to the cessation of hostilities.   .   .   .

53.   In the first stage, the objective of the Force was to secure and supervise the cessation of hostilities. The Force was immediately interposed between the Anglo-French and the Egyptian troops, occupying a buffer zone. Units of the Force also entered Port Said and Port Fuad and, by arrangement with the Anglo-French forces, took responsibility for maintaining order in certain areas, in co-operation with local authorities. The Force also undertook guard duty over some vulnerable installations and other points, but turned over all administrative and policing responsibilities to the Egyptian authorities the day following the Anglo-French evacuation.

54.   In the period of transition when the British and French forces were preparing to leave and were actually leaving, the Force temporarily undertook certain essential administrative functions, such as security, with the co-operation of the Governor and the Police Inspector in Port Said. UNEF personnel took measures to protect civilian life and public and private property. With the sanction of local authorities, they also undertook administrative functions with respect to public services and utilities, arranged for the provisioning of the local population with food-stuffs, and exercised a limited power of detention. During this period, UNEF was called upon to investigate a number of incidents, such as violations of the cease-fire, missing personnel and smuggling.   Incidents involving the cease-fire were reported to the proper authorities, who were urged to prevent any recurrence.

55.   No provision having been made for the establishment of joint machinery whereby incidents could be examined and discussed, UNEF's role was limited to investigating, reporting and, if warranted, lodging protests with the proper authorities.

56.   The Force cleared minefields in the Suez Canal area, and arranged and carried out exchanges of prisoners, detainees and internees between the Egyptian Government and the Anglo-French Command. It guarded the off-loading of UNEF stores and vehicles from ships at Port Said and, in the final stage of the withdrawal of British and French troops from Port Said and Port Fuad, the Force was stationed around the final perimeter of the zone occupied by Anglo-French forces, thus preventing clashes between them and the Egyptians.   .   .   .

59.   On the whole, the functions performed by the Force in the Sinai Peninsula were similar to those undertaken in the Suez Canal area. It was interposed between the forces of Egypt and Israel from 3 December 1956 onwards; it undertook temporarily some local civic responsibilities, including security functions, in a few inhabited areas during the successive stages of the withdrawal of Israel, handing over

all such responsibilities to the Egyptian authorities as soon as they returned to their posts; it arranged and carried out the exchange of prisoners of war between Egypt and Israel; it discharged certain investigatory functions; it cleared minefields in the Sinai Peninsula; and it repaired temporarily portions of damaged roads and tracks crossing the Peninsula, necessary for the conduct of its operations.

*Operations along the armistice demarcation line and
the international frontier.*

60. Two local conditions were of special concern to the Force as it moved into the Gaza Strip. In the first place, it was across the Gaza Strip line that the greatest number of incidents, infiltrations and raids had occurred since the armistice. Secondly, there were a very large number of Palestine Arab refugees, who are assisted by the United Nations through UNRWA, living in the Gaza Strip. The United Nations took no action which in any way affected the *status juris* of the Armistice Agreement or the Gaza Strip, since these matters are subject only to agreement of the parties. .   .   .

67. The population of Gaza was officially informed that the Government of Egypt, as a matter of policy, is opposed to infiltration across the armistice demarcation line, UNEF"s purpose was explained, and the Administrative Governor-General of the Gaza Strip took other effective measures. Gaza inhabitants were notified that they were forbidden to approach the demarcation line within 50–100 metres by day and 500 metres by night. The CID (police) in Gaza were instructed to act vigorously with the object of finding persons responsible for mining and other incidents and to prevent recurrences. The local (Palestine) police co-operate with UNEF in preventing infiltration. In order to be as effective as possible in this sphere, the Force was regrouped so that its battalion boundaries now generally correspond to administrative sub-districts in the Strip. This facilitates police co-operation with UNEF at the battalion level. .   .   .

69. With only an occasional hitch, and this seldom more than minor, UNEF personnel and vehicles have enjoyed freedom of movement in the Gaza Strip and between the Sinai Peninsula posts, the headquarters of UNEF and the units deployed along the demarcation line. This includes freedom of flight over the Sinai Peninsula and the Gaza Strip for UNEF aircraft and the manning of the Gaza airport by UNEF.

70. UNEF troops have a right to fire in self-defence. They are never to take the initiative in the use of arms, but may respond with fire to an armed attack upon them, even though this may result from a refusal on their part to obey an order from the attacking party not to resist; a proper refusal, since they are to take orders only from the Commander. UNEF is authorized to apprehend infiltrators and persons approaching the demarcation line in suspicious circumstances.

In practice, this applies to a zone extending up to 500 metres from the demarcation line; after interrogation, the persons apprehended are handed over to the local police.

71.   The Force is deployed along the demarcation line and the international border, over a length of 273 kilometres in largely rugged terrain.   The perimeter of the Gaza Strip (60 km.) is covered by means of observation posts by day and patrols by night.   There are seventy-six observation posts, the location of which varies according to the nature of the terrain.   The primary purposes of the observation posts and patrols are to prevent any movements across the line and to observe and report incidents.   All troops have received full briefing on their outpost and patrolling duties.   In conjunction with the observation duties, reconnaissance flights by UNEF's light aircraft are carried out in the Sinai Peninsula in order to detect movements along the roads, or elsewhere in the area of the frontier.   In view of the prevailing quiet all along the line, air reconnaissance, which had been carried out on a daily basis, was reduced in August 1957 to three days a week.   .   .   .

CHAPTER IV.   ORGANIZATION AND ADMINISTRATION IN THE FIELD

Organizational structure.

The Commander.

75.   The functioning of UNEF in the field is the direct responsibility of the Commander, who serves both as the director of operations and as the supervisor of all other activities of the Force.

76.   The Commander holds office through appointment by the General Assembly.   He operates under the instructions and guidance of the Secretary-General on the basis of executive responsibility for the operation entrusted to him by the Assembly.   In practice, from the inception of the Force, the Commander has functioned as the principal agent of the Secretary-General in the area of operations, within the limits of his post.

77.   The position of Commander combines leadership of the Force with the role of representative of the United Nations.   Much the same qualities are called for in the Chief of Staff of UNTSO, although the military observers in UNTSO do not form a military organization in the UNEF sense and their functions are quite different.   Both operations, however, combine political and administrative with military functions.

Military staff organization.

78.   The military staff organization of UNEF consists of officers selected from each of the contingents, and is headed by the Chief of Staff.   The Chief of Staff acts for the Commander during his absence. The position of Deputy Commander was tried for a while but was

found to be unnecessary. The Headquarters Staff comprises three sections—(1) Personnel, (2) Operations, and (3) Logistics—and a Special Staff composed of a number of specialized officers who advise and assist the Commander in particular fields and, in some cases, co-ordinate, supervise or carry out functional activities. The physical separation of UNEF headquarters in Gaza from the maintenance area at Rafah results in some inconvenience and perhaps a mild loss of efficiency, but it is unavoidable and there is no practical alternative.

79. The contingents receive their instructions and direction from the Commander, advised and assisted by his Staff. The commanding officers of the units are held responsible by the Commander for the proper functioning and discipline of their personnel. The contingent commanders are free to communicate with their home Governments on all matters affecting their units.

80. It is the practice of those contingents furnishing units for more than one functional task to designate a contingent commander, in addition to commanders for each functional activity. This contributes to clarification of responsibility in those matters affecting personnel which are subject to national authority.

81. Aside from the battalions with clearly defined missions of a military nature, normally involving patrol duties along the armistice demarcation line and the international frontier as well as guard duties, there are a number of units assigned to UNEF which perform administrative and other support tasks. Supporting elements for any force represent a special problem in co-ordination and control. To weld together elements of several different nationalities having similar functions would be very difficult. For this reason, UNEF has tended to rely mainly upon two countries, Canada and India, for its supporting units other than the medical.

82. Some of the contributing Governments designated "liaison officers" to represent their interests on the scene of operations of UNEF and to serve as points of contact for them. These liaison officers, not being under the authority of the Commander, are not members of UNEF. Their status, therefore, is rather anomalous. In practice, the liaison officer function has worked best when the officer concerned was one assigned to a UNEF post having important duties in its own right. Those liaison officers not combining functions in this manner have no direct responsibility to the Commander, yet can scarcely avoid becoming involved in matters of Force administration and operations. Moreover, it is difficult for the Commander and his staff, as well as for the commanders of operating units, to decide when and under what circumstances the liaison officers should be consulted and informed. However, in the early days of the organization of the Force, liaison officers for special purposes performed a useful and necessary function.

83. From the beginning of the Force, it was found useful, even essential, to maintain representation in Cairo for liaison with the appropriate authorities in the host Government. UNEF also has liaison representation in Tel Aviv. Military observers have been seconded from the staff of UNTSO for service with UNEF as its liaison officers. UNEF representation is also maintained at places outside the area of operations where UNEF activities and interests are involved, as in Beirut and Pisa (and earlier in Naples) in connexion with the airlift.

The Secretariat.

84. Administratively, responsibility for UNEF rests with the Secretary-General, in order to ensure that the operation will be executed in a manner consistent with the established practices and administrative principles of the United Nations. The day-to-day responsibilities of administration are exercised by the Commander of the Force, assisted by the senior Secretariat officials assigned by the Secretary-General to the Force, and such military officers having important administrative functions as the Chiefs of Personnel and Logistics. Experience has demonstrated that, by and large, requirements for the administrative servicing of an operation such as UNEF, both at Headquarters and in the field, can be met through existing Secretariat services, modestly expanded in certain sections to permit the absorption of heavier work-loads, together with such administrative assistance from the military side as may be implicit in the nature of the organization.

85. Three categories of Secretariat staff have served and are serving with the Force:

(a) Officers, such as the Chief Administrative Officer, with responsibility for the financial affairs of the Force and for the application of United Nations administrative rules and procedures. The Chief Administrative Officer reports directly to the Commander and works closely with him, but also has a direct reporting link with United Nations Headquarters, as the senior Secretariat official who is designated by the Secretary-General and in that capacity is responsible to him. He is assisted by a Chief Procurement Officer, a Chief Finance Officer and a Personnel Officer;

(b) Officials such as the Legal Adviser and the Public Information Officer, both of whom belong to the staff of the Chief Administrative Officer, but who work directly with the Commander in view of the nature of their duties;

(c) Personnel providing services not readily available from military sources, or requiring special training and knowledge. The Field Operations Service, for example, which assists the operation in many ways, quickly sets up external communications service with skilled personnel, and also provides trained security personnel. .   .   .

Relations with the local population.

99.   The relations of UNEF with the local population have in general been good and no serious incidents have occurred, except for one on 10 March 1957.   The Gaza Strip, with its large refugee population, is a sensitive area where particularly strict standards of behaviour and respect for local customs have been necessary and have been adhered to by members of the Force.   The order issued in November 1957 that troops should carry arms only when on duty has been a factor in good relations.   Along the international frontier, with its sparse and largely nomadic population, a tradition of goodwill and co-operation has also been built up, to the advantage of both parties. At the leave centres—whether in Beirut, Cairo or Alexandria—relations with the local populations have posed no serious problems.
. . .

CHAPTER V.   FINANCIAL ARRANGEMENTS

Apportionment of costs between the United Nations and the participating States.

Expenses incurred by the participating States.

117.   The following formulae for the sharing of costs in respect of troops between the Organization and the participating States were adopted by the General Assembly on 22 November 1957 (resolution 1151 (XII)) based on proposals submitted by the Secretary-General (A/3694, paras. 86, 88 and 91) as a result of many difficulties which had earlier arisen in arriving at equitable and uniform reimbursement arrangements:

(a) For the first six months (i. e., during what might reasonably be regarded as the initial emergency period), the United Nations would reimburse to participating Governments any special allowances, as distinct from basic salaries, paid to members of their contingents as a direct result of their service with UNEF in its area of operations, provided that such allowances could be considered as reasonable.

(b) In the event of a contingent serving beyond the initial six-month period, or of a replacement contingent being made available, the United Nations would assume financial responsibility for all extra and extraordinary costs which a Government was obliged to incur in making such forces available for UNEF service.   Apart from the costs of equipment referred to below, this means, in effect, reimbursement by the United Nations of expenditure incurred in respect of pay and allowances over and above those costs which the Government concerned would have been obliged to meet in any event.

118.   These principles were designed to provide a generally equitable basis upon which a collective United Nations responsibility could be discharged and to avoid the possibility of a few Member States as-

suming a disproportionately heavy financial burden beyond a limited emergency period. But their application in practice has proved difficult. For example, in the case of the formula in sub-paragraph (a) of the preceding paragraph, it has been extremely difficult, in view of widely differing national practices, to define what may be reasonably regarded as a "special allowance". Furthermore, although it had been assumed that national contingents would be composed of regular army personnel who would, in any event, have been in the service of their country, certain Governments organized special volunteer units to serve with UNEF. This was done because national laws precluded the assignment of members of the regular armed forces to service overseas other than in defence of the homeland. In other cases, new units had to be organized within the contributing States to replace regular units dispatched for UNEF duty. In these circumstances, some Governments from the outset assumed additional financial liabilities which they believed should be compensated for by the United Nations. Experience indicates the validity of the view that the most equitable collective arrangement is one which distributes among the membership as a whole those costs which a participating Government would not otherwise have incurred.

119. According to the formula adopted by the General Assembly in resolution 1151 (XII), the United Nations would assume financial responsibility for the replacement of equipment destroyed or worn out and for such deterioration beyond that provided for under normal depreciation schedules as could be assessed at the conclusion of the total period of service of a Government's contingent. It is not specified, however, whether or not the word "equipment" should be interpreted in the wider sense of "equipment, matériel or supplies", and no qualification is made as to the terms under which the items had been made available, i. e., it is not indicated either that they should have been normal and necessary in the circumstances or that they should have saved the United Nations expenditure which it otherwise would have had to incur. Consequently, decisions must be based on interpretations of the formula in the light of the actual circumstances of each particular case.

Expenses borne by the United Nations directly.

120. On the basis of the relevant decisions of the General Assembly, the United Nations assumes the following direct costs, when they are not otherwise provided for:

(a) Billeting, rations and summer clothing for the troops including the rental, reconditioning and maintenance of premises;

(b) Payment to each member of the Force of a daily overseas allowance, equivalent to 86 cents, in accordance with a decision by the Fifth Committee of the General Assembly at its 541st meeting on 3 December 1956;

(c) Costs of the rotation of contingents;

(d) Travel and subsistence allowances of military personnel proceeding on official business to points outside the area of operations;

(e) Operation and maintenance of a suitable leave centre and other welfare expenses, such as rental of films, periodic contracting for live shows for the entertainment of the troops, and postage for personal mail;

(f) Miscellaneous supplies and services such as cobbling, tailoring, laundering and haircutting;

(g) Motor transport and heavy mobile equipment;

(h) Miscellaneous non-expendable operational equipment such as barrack stores, tentage, workshop equipment, water and petroleum cans and generators;

(i) Spare parts, maintenance and petrol, oil and lubricants for motor transport and other mobile equipment;

(j) Stationery, photographic and other miscellaneous supplies;

(k) Payment for the use of Royal Canadian Air Force planes comprising the UNEF Squadron, at specified rates per flying hour.

Other costs assumed by the United Nations are:

(a) Salaries, travel and subsistence and other appropriate staff costs of international staff detailed from Headquarters or other United Nations offices, Field Service personnel, and locally recruited personnel;

(b) Communications services, costs of transporting and issuing supplies, and claims against the United Nations for personal injury, property damage and loss of income arising from traffic accidents and other effects of the operation of the Force;

(c) Costs of external auditors and assistants visiting the mission;

(d) Other miscellaneous supplies and services.

Agreements with Governments relating to financial responsibilities.

121.   UNEF experience indicates that such an operation would be greatly facilitated by a standing provision that the costs falling to the United Nations, including the extra and extraordinary costs incurred by Governments furnishing troops, supplies and equipment, should be met by Member States collectively. Acceptance of this principle would facilitate the preparation and consideration of budget estimates and lead to improved financial and logistic arrangements for any new operation.   Thereafter, once the nature and scope of an operation were clearly established, agreements could be formulated between Governments providing military personnel and the United Nations, in the light of the particular circumstances, which should specify the types of services, accommodation and allowances which would be provided directly at United Nations expense.

122. With respect to extra costs incurred by Governments as a result of their participation in the operation, standard rates on a monthly, quarterly or annual basis could be negotiated for inclusion in an agreement, covering such items as:

(a) Reimbursement for governmental pay and allowances;

(b) Payment for personal equipment or governmental issues (clothing, arms, ammunition etc.) ;

(c) Rental of equipment furnished at the request of the United Nations (with title to pass to the United Nations when full value has been paid as rent).

The agreement could also provide for straight reimbursement of governmental supplies furnished at United Nations request and costs of rotating units and transporting equipment. It would likewise be advisable to include in the agreement provision for the reimbursement to Governments of such costs as they might incur under their own legislation in connexion with compensation payable for the death or disability of their nationals while serving the United Nations.

123. Experience also warrants the assumption that once the nature of the operation is clear, a number of Member States would be prepared to provide assistance to the United Nations in the procurement of vital matériel and services quickly and economically, under arrangements similar to those entered into for the purpose of assuring logistic support to UNEF. .   .   .

CHAPTER VI. LEGAL ASPECTS

Means employed.

125. It was natural, in view of the lack of precedents for UNEF as an international Force, that new legal questions should arise in each phase of its development. Most of these questions are settled on the basis of formal agreements or understandings, and others through mutually acceptable working procedures devised at the local level.

126. Written arrangements or understandings have been effected by means of bilateral agreements entered into by the United Nations, represented by the Secretary-General, on the one hand, and the State concerned, on the other; they have not required ratification, but are legally binding on the parties to them.

Legal character of UNEF; its Regulations.

127. The Force was recognized as a subsidiary organ of the General Assembly, established under the authority of Article 22 of the Charter of the United Nations (regulation 6). A problem of first importance, therefore, was that of harmonizing the international character of the Force with the fact of its being composed of national contingents. This was accomplished through the chain of command and

through definition of the legal status of the Force and of its members. Subject to the resolutions of the General Assembly, the Secretary-General has authority for all executive, administrative and financial matters affecting the Force (regulation 15). The Commander has direct command authority over the Force and its operations. Acting in consultation with the Secretary-General in the exercise of this authority, he remains operationally responsible for the performance of all functions assigned to the Force by the United Nations, and for the deployment and assignment of troops placed at the disposal of the Force (regulations 11 and 16). By designating the chain of command for the Force, through which he is empowered to delegate his authority, the Commander in turn is able to make use of the commanding officers of the national contingents (regulation 12).

128.   This effective marriage of national military service with international function is also reflected in the status of individual members of the Force. Although remaining in their national service, they are, during the period of their assignment with UNEF, international personnel under the authority of the United Nations and subject to the instructions only of the Commander and his chain of command. They discharge exclusively international functions (regulations 6, 29, 31 and 32). The immunities necessary to assure their international character as members of the Force are developed in detail in the Agreement on the status of the Force, discussed below.

129.   As a subsidiary organ, UNEF enjoys the status, privileges and immunities of the Organization as already established by the Convention on the Privileges and Immunities of the United Nations. The independent exercise of the functions of UNEF was thus assured in respect of property supplied by the United Nations, but it was necessary to make provision for supplies and equipment which were the property of the national contingents. It was accordingly established that the relevant terms of the Convention also applied to the property, funds and assets of the participating States used in connexion with UNEF (regulation 10). . . . .

Understanding on the presence and functioning of UNEF

132.   The Government of Egypt had accepted the Force in principle by formally accepting resolution 1000 (ES–I) establishing a United Nations Command, but wished to have certain clarifications before the actual arrival of the Force. The Secretary-General had, therefore, given interpretations of the relevant General Assembly resolutions to the Government of Egypt, reporting in full to the Advisory Committee on the interpretations given. The Advisory Committee had approved these interpretations and recommended that the Secretary-General should start at once the transfer of the Force to Egypt, an action to which the Government of Egypt had consented on the basis of the interpretations given by the Secretary-General.

133.   While this procedure was an adequate basis for the dispatch of the first units to Egypt, the Secretary-General, feeling that some firmer foundation was necessary for the presence and functioning of the Force in that country and for continued co-operation with the Egyptian authorities, visited Cairo from 16 to 18 November for personal discussions on these points with the Egyptian authorities. The questions of principle resolved in these talks were embodied in an "Aide-mémoire on the basis for the presence and functioning of the United Nations Emergency Force in Egypt", which was approved by the Government of Egypt. This aide-mémoire was submitted to the General Assembly on 20 November 1956 (A/3375) and, when noted with approval by that organ on 24 November 1956 (resolution 1121 (XI)), constituted an understanding between the United Nations and Egypt concerning the presence and functioning of UNEF in Egypt. The aide-mémoire, after noting the arrival of advance units of UNEF in Egypt, stated the understanding between the Government of Egypt and the Secretary-General on the basic points for the presence and functioning of UNEF as follows:

"1.   The Government of Egypt declares that, when exercising its sovereign rights on any matter concerning the presence and functioning of UNEF, it will be guided, in good faith, by its acceptance of General Assembly resolution 1000 (ES–I) of 5 November 1956.

"2.   The United Nations takes note of this declaration of the Government of Egypt and declares that the activities of UNEF will be guided, in good faith, by the task established for the Force in the aforementioned resolutions; in particular, the United Nations, understanding this to correspond to the wishes of the Government of Egypt, reaffirms its willingness to maintain UNEF until its task is completed.

"3.   The Government of Egypt and the Secretary-General declare that it is their intention to proceed forthwith, in the light of points 1 and 2 above, to explore jointly concrete aspects of the functioning of UNEF, including its stationing and the question of its lines of communication and supply; the Government of Egypt, confirming its intention to facilitate the functioning of UNEF, and the United Nations are agreed to expedite in co-operation and implementation of guiding principles arrived at as a result of that joint exploration on the basis of the resolutions of the General Assembly."

Agreement on the status of the Force.

134.   The Secretary-General, acting in consultation with the Advisory Committee, negotiated and concluded on 8 February 1957 with the Government of Egypt the Agreement on the status of the Force (hereinafter referred to as "the Agreement").   .   .   .

Jurisdiction.

136.   The question of criminal jurisdiction raised a number of points of basic policy in the establishement of UNEF. It is essential

to the preservation of the independent exercise of the functions of such a force that its members should be immune from the criminal jurisdiction of the host State.   The Agreement accordingly provided that members of the Force should be under the exclusive jurisdiction of their respective national States with regard to any criminal offences committed by them in Egypt (Agreement, para. 11).   Such a policy, obviously, makes easier the decision of States to contribute troops from their armed forces.   At the same time, it was important that this waiving of jurisdiction by the host State should not result in a jurisdictional vacuum, in which a given offence might be subject to prosecution by neither the host State nor the participating State.   For this reason, the agreements between the United Nations and the participating States specify that this "immunity from the jurisdiction of Egypt is based on the understanding that the authorities of the participating States would exercise such jurisdiction as might be necessary with respect to crimes or offences committed in Egypt by any members of the Force provided from their own military services".   The Secretary-General, therefore, sought assurance from each participating Government that it would be prepared to exercise this jurisdiction as to any crime or offence which might be committed by a member of its contingent.

137.   Even so, it was probably inevitable that from time to time a number of difficult legal problems would arise in giving effect to these provisions, involving varied legal systems and terms of military law prevailing in participating States.   Fortunately, the number of acts having possible implications under criminal law committed by members of UNEF have been very few.   The Secretary-General has thought it desirable, none the less, to ask the Governments of participating States to review the position under their laws.   As an indication of the type of problem that could arise, it may be noted that national laws differ in the extent to which they confer on courts martial jurisdiction over civil offences in peacetime, or confer on either military or civil courts jurisdiction over offences committed abroad. Some provide only for trial in the home country, thus posing practical questions about the submission of evidence.

138.   As to civil jurisdiction, members of the Force enjoy immunity from legal process in any matter relating to their official duties; but the same machinery is available for settlement as in the case of claims against the United Nations.   In other civil cases, where jurisdiction over a member of the Force might be exercised in Egypt, there are agreed measures to prevent the proceedings from interfering with the performance of his official duties (Agreement, paras. 12 and 38 (b)).

Discipline.

139.   The disciplinary system in UNEF, from the strictly military point of view, is rather anomalous.   Normally, the commander of a

force has powers both of command and punishment, whereas the Commander of UNEF has powers only of command. Disciplinary authority resides in the commanding officer of each national contingent (regulation 13). To confer such authority upon the Commander would probably require specific legislation in most participating States.

140.   The Agreement authorized the use of military police by the Commander to assure the maintenance of discipline and good order among members of the Force. They police UNEF premises, and perform functions elsewhere only in accordance with specific arrangements made with local police authorities. They have the power of arrest over members of the Force. The Agreement likewise sets out a mutual arrangement by which the UNEF military police can, in certain conditions, take other persons into custody for immediate delivery to the Egyptian authorities, or the Egyptian authorities can take into custody a member of the Force for immediate delivery to UNEF (Agreement, paras. 14–18).

CHAPTER VII.   CONCLUDING OBSERVATIONS AND PRINCIPLES

A.   *Observations.*   .   .   .

149.   UNEF was brought into being to meet a particular situation in which a United Nations force could be interposed between regular, national military forces which were subject to a cease-fire agreed to by the opposing parties. UNEF has continued to function along the "dividing line" between the national forces. It follows that in UNEF there has never been any need for rights and responsibilities other than those necessary for such an interposed force under cease-fire conditions. The Force was not used in any way to enforce withdrawals but, in the successive stages of the withdrawals, followed the withdrawing troops to the "dividing line" of each stage. It is also to be noted that the Force has functioned under a clear-cut mandate which has entirely detached it from involvement in any internal or local problems, and also has enabled it to maintain its neutrality in relation to international political issues. The fact that UNEF was designed to meet the needs of this specific situation largely determined its military components, geographical composition, deployment and status, and also its effectiveness.   .   .   .

151.   Obviously, some of the above-mentioned circumstances are of such a nature that it could not reasonably be expected that they would often be duplicated elsewhere. Nor can it be assumed that they provide a sufficient basis to warrant indiscriminate projection of the UNEF experience in planning for future United Nations operations of this kind.   .   .   .

B.   *Basic principles*

154.   In view of the impossibility of determining beforehand the specific form of a United Nations presence of the type considered in

this report, which would be necessary to meet adequately the requirements of a given situation, a broad decision by the General Assembly should attempt to do no more than endorse certain basic principles and rules which would provide an adaptable framework for later operations that might be found necessary. In a practical sense, it is not feasible in advance of a known situation to do more than to provide for some helpful stand-by arrangements for a force or similar forms of a United Nations presence. In the following paragraphs, certain principles and rules are laid down in the light of the experience gathered in the past years, which, if they were to meet with the approval of the General Assembly, would provide a continuing basis on which useful contacts in a stand-by context might be established with interested Governments, with the aim of being prepared for any requests which might arise from future decisions by the Assembly on a force or similar arrangement to deal with a specific case.

155. As the arrangements discussed in this report do not cover the type of force envisaged under Chapter VII of the Charter, it follows from international law and the Charter that the United Nations cannot undertake to implement them by stationing units on the territory of a Member State without the consent of the Government concerned. It similarly follows from the Charter that the consent of a Member nation is necessary for the United Nations to use its military personnel or matériel. These basic rules have been observed in the recent United Nations operations in the Middle East. They naturally hold valid for all similar operations in the future.

156. The fact that a United Nations operation of the type envisaged requires the consent of the Government on whose territory it takes place creates a problem, as it is normally difficult for the United Nations to engage in such an operation without guarantees against unilateral actions by the host Government which might put the United Nations in a questionable position, either administratively or in relation to contributing Governments.

157. The formula employed in relation to the Government of Egypt for UNEF seems, in the light of experience, to provide an adequate solution to this problem. The Government of Egypt declared that, when exercising its sovereign right with regard to the presence of the Force, it would be guided by good faith in the interpretation of the purposes of the Force. This declaration was balanced by a declaration by the United Nations to the effect that the maintenance of the Force by the United Nations would be determined by similar good faith in the interpretation of the purposes.

158. The consequence of such a bilateral declaration is that, were either side to act unilaterally in refusing continued presence or deciding on withdrawal, and were the other side to find that such action was contrary to a good-faith interpretation of the purposes of the operation, an exchange of views would be called for towards harmonizing

the positions. This does not imply any infringement of the sovereign right of the host Government, nor any restriction of the right of the United Nations to decide on the termination of its own operation whenever it might see fit to do so. But it does mean a mutual recognition of the fact that the operation, being based on collaboration between the host Government and the United Nations, should be carried on in forms natural to such collaboration, and especially so with regard to the questions of presence and maintenance.

159. It is unlikely that any Government in the future would be willing to go beyond the declaration of the Government of Egypt with regard to UNEF. Nor, in my view, should the United Nations commit itself beyond the point established for UNEF in relation to the Government of Egypt. In these circumstances, I consider it reasonable to regard the formula mentioned in paragraph 158 above as a valid basis for future arrangements of a similar kind.

160. Another point of principle which arises in relation to the question of consent refers to the composition of United Nations military elements stationed on the territory of a Member country. While the United Nations must reserve for itself the authority to decide on the composition of such elements, it is obvious that the host country, in giving its consent, cannot be indifferent to the composition of those elements. In order to limit the scope of possible difference of opinion, the United Nations in recent operations has followed two principles: not to include units from any of the permanent members of the Security Council; and not to include units from any country which, because of its geographical position or for other reasons, might be considered as possibly having a special interest in the situation which has called for the operation. I believe that these two principles also should be considered as essential to any stand-by arrangements.

161. Given the two principles mentioned in paragraph 160, in actual practice the area within which conflicting views may be expressed will in all probability be so reduced normally as to facilitate the harmonizing of the rights of the United Nations with the interests of the host country. It would seem desirable to accept the formula applied in the case of UNEF, which is to the effect that, while it is for the United Nations alone to decide on the composition of military elements sent to a country, the United Nations should, in deciding on composition, take fully into account the view of the host Government as one of the most serious factors which should guide the recruitment of the personnel. Usually, this is likely to mean that serious objections by the host country against participation by a specific contributing country in the United Nations operation will determine the action of the Organization. However, were the United Nations for good reasons to find that course inadvisable, it would remain free to pursue its own line, and any resulting conflict would have to be resolved on a political rather than on a legal basis. I would recommend

that the basis thus laid in the case of UNEF be considered as the formula on composition applicable to similar operations in the future.

162.   The principles indicated in the four points discussed above
(paragraphs 155–161 inclusive) were either established by the General
Assembly itself, or elaborated in practice or in negotiations with the
Government of Egypt.   They have served as the basis for a status
Agreement which applies to the United Nations personnel in the Force
in Egypt.   In its entirety, this status Agreement has stood up well to
the test of experience.   Its basic principles should be embodied in
similar agreements in the future, and their recognition, therefore,
would seem necessarily to form part of any stand-by arrangements for
a force.   .   .   .

163.   The most important principle in the status Agreement ensures
that UNEF personnel, when involved in criminal actions, come under
the jurisdiction of the criminal courts of their home countries.   The
establishment of this principle for UNEF, in relation to Egypt, has set
a most valuable precedent.   Experience shows that this principle is
essential to the successful recruitment by the United Nations of military personnel not otherwise under immunity rules, from its Member
countries.   The position established for UNEF should be maintained in
future arrangements.

164.   Another principle in the UNEF status Agreement which
should be retained is that the United Nations activity should have
freedom of movement within its area of operations and all such facilities regarding access to that area and communications as are necessary for successful completion of the task.   This also obviously involves
certain rights of over-flight over the territory of the host country.   .   .
[The application of these principles] requires an agreement on
what is to be considered as the area of operations and as to what
facilities of access and communications are to be considered necessary.   On the assumption that, like UNEF, any similar United Nations
operation in the future would be of assistance to the nation on whose
territory it is stationed, it is not to be expected that the necessary
process of agreement will give rise to any serious complications in
the interpretation of the principle.

165.   Apart from the principles thus established in negotiated
agreements or formal decisions, a series of basic rules has been developed in practice.   Some of these rules would appear to merit general application.   This is true especially of the precept that authority
granted to the United Nations group cannot be exercised within a giv-
en territory either in competition with representatives of the host
Government or in cooperation with them on the basis of any joint
operation.   Thus, a United Nations operation must be separate and
distinct from activities by national authorities.   UNEF experience
indicates how this rule may apply in practice.   A right of detention
which normally would be exercised only by local authorities is extend-

ed to UNEF units. However, this is so only within a limited area where the local authorities voluntarily abstain from exercising similar rights, whether alone or in collaboration with the United Nations. Were the underlying principle of this example not to be applied, United Nations units might run the risk of getting involved in differences with the local authorities or public or in internal conflicts which would be highly detrimental to the effectiveness of the operation and to the relations between the United Nations and the host Government.

166.   A rule closely related to the one last mentioned, and reflecting a basic Charter principle, precludes the employment of United Nations elements in situations of an essentially internal nature. As a matter of course, the United Nations personnel cannot be permitted in any sense to be a party to internal conflicts. Their role must be limited to external aspects of the political situation as, for example, infiltration or other activities affecting international boundaries.

167.   Even in the case of UNEF, where the United Nations itself had taken a stand on decisive elements in the situation which gave rise to the creation of the Force, it was explicitly stated that the Force should not be used to enforce any specific political solution of pending problems or to influence the political balance decisive to such a solution. This precept would clearly impose a serious limitation on the possible use of United Nations elements, were it to be given general application to them whenever they are not created under Chapter VII of the Charter. However, I believe its acceptance to be necessary, if the United Nations is to be in a position to draw on Member countries for contributions in men and matériel to United Nations operations of this kind.

168.   Military personnel employed by the United Nations in paramilitary operations are, of course, not under the same formal obligations in relation to the Organization as staff members of the Secretariat. However, the position must be maintained that the basic rules of the United Nations for international service are applicable also to such personnel, particularly as regards full loyalty to the aims of the Organization and to abstention from acts in relation to their country of origin or to other countries which might deprive the operation of its international character and create a situation of dual loyalty. The observance of this rule is not only vital for good relations with the host country, it is also to the benefit of the contributing countries concerned, as any other attitude might involve them in responsibilities which would be undesirable in the light of the national policies pursued. .   .   .

172.   In full recognition of the wide variety of forms which decisions on a United Nations operation may take in seeking to fit differing situations calling for such an operation, the underlying rule concerning command and authority which has been consistently applied in recent years .   .   . should, in my view, be maintained for the

future. Thus, a United Nations operation should always be under a leadership established by the General Assembly or the Security Council, or on the basis of delegated authority by the Secretary-General, so as to make it directly responsible to one of the main organs of the United Nations, while integrated with the Secretariat in an appropriate form.

173. Were soundings with Member Governments, based on the aforementioned legal and political principles and rules and on the regulations regarding financial responsibilities set out below, to show that a number of Governments in their planning would be willing to take into account the possibility of having to provide promptly—on an emergency basis, in response to a specific appeal from the United Nations—men and matériel to a United Nations operation of the kind envisaged in this report, a question would arise regarding the conditions under which such a desirable standby arrangement could be utilized.

174. Under the Charter, and under the "Uniting for peace" resolution (General Assembly resolution 377 (V)), a formal decision on a United Nations operation must be taken by the General Assembly or by the Security Council. It must be regarded as excluded that the right to take such a decision, in any general terms, could properly be considered as delegated to the Secretary-General. Short of an explicit decision by the General Assembly or the Security Council with a specific authorization, the Secretary-General, thus, cannot be considered as entitled to appeal to a Member nation for military personnel to be dispatched to another Member country in a United Nations operation.

175. The terms of the delegation in each operation thus far have set the limit of the Secretary-General's authority. Thus, for example, as apparent from the description of the new body, the decision relating to UNEF, which was to be implemented by the Secretary-General, qualified the operation as being one of a paramilitary nature, while the absence of an explicit authorization for the Force to take offensive action excluded the organization by the Secretary-General of units for such action, and consequently, the units generally were equipped only with weapons necessary for self-defence. Had there been any remaining doubts in this respect, the legal basis on which the General Assembly took its decision would have made this limitation clear. .   .   .

178. Confirmation by the Assembly of the interpretation of the question of authority given above would be useful. This interpretation would signify that a Member country, in deciding upon a contribution of men or matériel to a United Nations operation on the basis of such stand-by understandings as may have been reached, could rely upon the explicit terms of the executive authority delegated to the Secretary-General in determining the use which could be made of the units provided; it being understood, naturally, that in the types of opera-

tion with which this report is concerned this could never include combat activity. There will always remain, of course, a certain margin of freedom for judgment, as, for example, on the extent and nature of the arming of the units and of their right of self-defence. In the case of UNEF, such questions of interpretation have been solved in consultation with the contributing Governments and with the host Government. The Advisory Committee on UNEF set up by the General Assembly has in this context proved to be of especially great assistance.

179. In the preceding paragraph I have touched upon the extent to which a right of self-defence may be exercised by United Nations units of the type envisaged. It should be generally recognized that such a right exists. However, in certain cases this right should be exercised only under strictly defined conditions. A problem arises in this context because of the fact that a wide interpretation of the right of self-defence might well blur the distinction between operations of the character discussed in this report and combat operations, which would require a decision under Chapter VII of the Charter and an explicit, more far-reaching delegation of authority to the Secretary-General than would be required for any of the operations discussed here. A reasonable definition seems to have been established in the case of UNEF, where the rule is applied that men engaged in the operation may never take the initiative in the use of armed force, but are entitled to respond with force to an attack with arms, including attempts to use force to make them withdraw from positions which they occupy under orders from the Commander, acting under the authority of the Assembly and within the scope of its resolutions. The basic element involved is clearly the prohibition against any *initiative* in the use of armed force. This definition of the limit between self-defence, as permissible for United Nations elements of the kind discussed, and offensive action, which is beyond the competence of such elements, should be approved for future guidance.

NOTE.—1. See also the statement made by the Secretary-General on 5 November 1958; GAOR, XIII, Special Political C., pp. 63–64.

2. For a discussion of the legal problems connected with the establishment of the UNEF, see the Report of the Committee on Study of Legal Problems of the United Nations, in 51 ASIL Procgs. (1957), pp. 205–29. See also Michael ADAMS, Suez and After: Year of Crisis (Boston, Mass., 1958), 225 pp.; Hamilton Fish ARMSTRONG, "The United Nations Experience in Gaza", 35 Foreign Affairs (1957), pp. 600–19; D. W. BOWETT, United Nations Forces: A Legal Study of United Nations Practice (London, 1964), pp. 90–151; E. L. M. BURNS, Between Arab and Israeli (London, 1963), 336 pp.; Dudley H. CHAPMAN, "The United Nations Emergency Force: Legal Status", 57 Michigan L.Rev. (1958), pp. 56–81; Charles CHAUMONT, "La situation juridique des Etats Membres à l'égard de la Force d'urgence des Nations Unies", 4 AFDI (1958), pp. 399–440; Maxwell COHEN, "The United Nations Emergency Force: A Preliminary View", 12 Int.J. (Toronto, 1957), pp. 109–27; Gamal el DIN ATTIA, Les Forces

Armées des Nations Unies en Corée et au Moyen-Orient (Geneva, 1963), 467 pp.; Herman FINER, Dulles over Suez: The Theory and Practice of Diplomacy (Chicago, 1964), 538 pp.; William R. FRYE, A United Nations Peace Force (New York, 1957), 227 pp.; Leland M. GOODRICH and Gabriella E. ROSNER, "The United Nations Emergency Force", 11 Int.Org. (1957), pp. 413–30; John W. HALDERMAN, "Legal Basis for United Nations Armed Forces", 56 AJIL (1962), pp. 971–96; INTERNATIONAL LAW ASSOCIATION, COMMITTEE ON THE CHARTER OF THE UNITED NATIONS, "Report on Problems of a United Nations Force", 49 ILA Report (Hamburg, 1960), pp. 126–52; Zachariah KAY, "The United Nations Force in Korea and Sinai", 2 Int. Rels. (1961), pp. 168–83; E. LAUTERPACHT, ed., The United Nations Emergency Force: Basic Documents (London, 1960), 49 pp.; S. MARTINEZ CARO, "La fuerza de emergencia de las Naciones Unidas", 13 REspDI (1960), pp. 83–150; Henry L. MASON, "The United Nations Emergency Force", 4 Tulane Studies in Political Science (1957), pp. 25–48; Herbert NICHOLAS, "U. N. Peace Forces and the Changing Globe: The Lessons of Suez and Congo", 17 Int.Org. (1963), pp. 321–37; Pierre Poirier, La Force internationale d'urgence (Paris, 1962), 385 pp.; Gabriella ROSNER, The United Nations Emergency Force (New York, 1963), 294 pp.; Georg SCHWARZENBERGER, "Problems of a United Nations Force", 12 Current Legal Problems (1959), pp. 247–68; Finn SEYERSTED, United Nations Forces in the Law of Peace and War (Leyden, 1966), pp. 45–60; Graham SPRY, "Canada, the United Nations Emergency Force, and the Commonwealth", 33 Int. Affairs (London, 1957), pp. 289–300; David W. WAINHOUSE and others, International Peace Observation: A History and Forecast (Baltimore, Md., 1966), pp. 277–93.

12. *Withdrawal of the United Nations Emergency Force.*

Report by the Secretary-General, 26 June 1967.
A/6730/Add. 3.

INTRODUCTION

1.   This report on the withdrawal of the United Nations Emergency Force (UNEF) is submitted because, as indicated in my statement on 20 June 1967 to the fifth emergency special session of the General Assembly (1527th plenary meeting), important questions have been raised concerning the actions taken on the withdrawal of UNEF. These questions merit careful consideration and comment. It is in the interest of the United Nations, I believe, that this report should be full and frank, in view of the questions involved and the numerous statements that have been made, both public and private, which continue to be very damaging to the United Nations and to its peacekeeping role in particular. Despite the explanations already given in the several reports on the subject which have been submitted to the General Assembly and to the Security Council, misunderstandings and what, I fear, are misrepresentations, persist, in official as well as unofficial circles, publicly and behind the scenes.

2.   A report of this kind is not the place to try to explain why there has been so much and such persistent and grossly mistaken judgment

about the withdrawal of UNEF. It suffices to say here that the shattering crisis in the Near East inevitably caused intense shock in many capitals and countries of the world, together with deep frustration over the inability to cope with it. It is, of course, not unusual in such situations to seek easy explanations and excuses. When, however, this tactic involves imputing responsibility for the unleashing of major hostilities, it is, and must be, a cause for sober concern. The objective of this report is to establish an authentic, factual record of actions and their causes.

3. The emphasis here, therefore, will be upon facts. The report is intended to be neither a polemic nor an apologia. Its sole purpose is to present a factually accurate picture of what happened and why. It will serve well the interests of the United Nations, as well as of historical integrity, if this presentation of facts can help to dissipate some of the distortions of the record which, in some places, apparently have emanated from panic, emotion and political bias.

CHRONOLOGY OF RELEVANT ACTIONS

4. Not only events but dates, and even the time of day, have an important bearing on this exposition. The significant events and actions and their dates and times are therefore set forth below.

16 May 1967

5. *2000 hours GMT (2200 hours Gaza local time)*. A message from General Fawzy, Chief of Staff of the United Arab Republic Armed Forces, was received by the Commander of UNEF, Major-General Rikhye, requesting withdrawal of "all UN troops which install OPs along our borders" (A/6730, para. 6, sub-para. 3 (a)). Brigadier Mokhtar, who handed General Fawzy's letter to the Commander of UNEF, told General Rikhye at the time that he must order the immediate withdrawal of United Nations troops from El Sabha and Sharm el Sheikh on the night of 16 May since United Arab Republic armed forces must gain control of these two places that very night. The UNEF Commander correctly replied that he did not have authority to withdraw his troops from these positions on such an order and could do so only on instructions from the Secretary-General; therefore, he must continue with UNEF operations in Sinai as hitherto. Brigadier Mokhtar told the Commander of UNEF that this might lead to conflict on that night (16 May) between United Arab Republic and UNEF troops, and insisted that the Commander issue orders to UNEF troops to remain confined to their camps at El Sabha and Sharm el Sheikh. General Rikhye replied that he could not comply with this request. He did, of course, inform the contingent commanders concerned of these developments. He also informed United Nations Headquarters that he proposed to continue with UNEF activities as established until he received fresh instructions from the Secretary-General.

6. *2130 hours GMT (1730 hours New York time)*. The Secretary-General received at this time the UNEF Commander's cable informing him of the above-mentioned message from General Fawzy. The UNEF Commander was immediately instructed to await further instructions from the Secretary-General and, pending this later word from him, to "be firm in maintaining UNEF position while being as understanding and as diplomatic as possible in your relations with local UAR officials".

7. *2245 hours GMT (1845 hours New York time)*. The Permanent Representative of the United Arab Republic visited the Secretary-General at this time at the latter's urgent request. The Secretary-General requested the Permanent Representative to communicate with his Government with the utmost urgency and to transmit to it his views (A/6730, para. 6, sub-para. 3 (c)). In particular, the Secretary-General requested the Permanent Representative to obtain his Government's clarification of the situation, pointing out that any request for the withdrawal of UNEF must come directly to the Secretary-General from the Government of the United Arab Republic.

8. *2344 hours GMT*. The UNEF Commander further reported at this time that considerable military activity had been observed in the El Arish area since the afternoon of 16 May 1967.

17 May 1967

9. *0800 hours GMT (0400 hours New York time)*. The Commander of UNEF reported then that on the morning of 17 May, thirty soldiers of the Army of the United Arab Republic had occupied El Sabha in Sinai and that United Arab Republic troops were deployed in the immediate vicinity of the UNEF observation post there. Three armoured cars of the United Arab Republic were located near the Yugoslav UNEF camp at El Sabha and detachments of fifteen soldiers each had taken up positions north and south of the Yugoslav contingent's camp at El Amr. All UNEF observation posts along the armistice demarcation line and the international frontier were manned as usual, but in some places United Arab Republic troops were also at the line.

10. *1030 hours GMT (0630 hours New York time)*. The Commander of UNEF reported then that troops of the United Arab Republic had occupied the UNEF observation post at El Sabha and that the Yugoslav UNEF camps at El Quseima and El Sabha were now behind the positions of the army of the United Arab Republic. The Commander of UNEF informed the Chief of the United Arab Republic Liaison Staff of these developments, expressing his serious concern at them. The Chief of the United Arab Republic Liaison Staff agreed to request the immediate evacuation of the observation post at El Sabha by United Arab Republic troops and shortly thereafter reported that orders to this effect had been given by the United

Arab Republic military authorities. He requested, however, that to avoid any future misunderstandings, the Yugoslav observation post at El Sabha should be withdrawn immediately to El Quseima camp. The Commander replied that any such withdrawal would require the authorization of the Secretary-General.

11. *1200 hours GMT (0800 hours New York time).* The Chief of the United Arab Republic Liaison Staff at this time conveyed to the Commander of UNEF a request from General Mohd Fawzy, Chief of Staff of the Armed Forces of the United Arab Republic, for the withdrawal of the Yugoslav detachments of UNEF in the Sinai within twenty-four hours. He added that the UNEF Commander might take "forty-eight hours or so" to withdraw the UNEF detachment from Sharm el Sheikh. The Commander of UNEF replied that any such move required instructions from the Secretary-General.

12. *1330 hours GMT.* The Commander of UNEF then reported that a sizeable detachment of troops of the United Arab Republic was moving into the UNEF area at El Kuntilla.

13. *2000 hours GMT (1600 hours New York time).* The Secretary-General at this date held an informal meeting in his office with the representatives of countries providing contingents to UNEF to inform them of the situation as then known. There was an exchange of views. The Secretary-General gave his opinion on how he should and how he intended to proceed, observing that if a formal request for the withdrawal of UNEF were to be made by the Government of the United Arab Republic, the Secretary-General, in his view, would have to comply with it, since the Force was on United Arab Republic territory only with the consent of the Government and could not remain there without it. Two representatives expressed serious doubts about the consequences of agreeing to a peremptory request for the withdrawal of UNEF and raised the questions of consideration of such a request by the General Assembly and an appeal to the United Arab Republic not to request the withdrawal of UNEF. Two other representatives stated the view that the United Arab Republic was entitled to request the removal of UNEF at any moment and that that request would have to be respected regardless of what the General Assembly might have to say in the matter, since the agreement for UNEF"s presence had been concluded between the then Secretary-General and the Government of Egypt. A clarification of the situation from the United Arab Republic should therefore be awaited.

14. *2150 hours GMT (1750 hours New York time).* The Secretary-General at this time saw the Permanent Representative of the United Arab Republic and handed to him an aide-mémoire, the text of which is contained in paragraph 6 of document A/6730. The Secretary-General also gave to the Permanent Representative of the United Arab Republic an aide-mémoire calling to the attention of his Gov-

ernment the "good faith" accord, the text of which is contained in paragraph 7 of document A/6730.

18 May 1967

15. *1321 hours GMT (0921 hours New York time).* The Commander of UNEF reported at this time that his Liaison Officer in Cairo had been informed by an ambassador of one of the countries providing contingents to UNEF that the Foreign Minister of the United Arab Republic had summoned the representatives of nations with troops in UNEF to the Ministry for Foreign Affairs and informed them that UNEF had terminated its tasks in the United Arab Republic and in the Gaza Strip and must depart from the above territory forthwith. This information was confirmed by representatives of some of these countries at the United Nations.

16. Early on 18 May the UNEF sentries proceeding to man the normal observation post at El Sabha in Sinai were prevented from entering the post and from remaining in the area by United Arab Republic Soldiers. The sentries were then forced to withdraw. They did not resist by use of force since they had no mandate to do so.

17. *1100 hours GMT.* United Arab Republic soldiers at this time forced Yugoslav UNEF sentries out of their observation post on the international frontier in front of El Kuntilla Camp. One hour later, United Arab Republic officers arrived at the water point and asked UNEF soldiers to withdraw the guard.

18. *1220 hours GMT.* At this hour, United Arab Republic soldiers entered the UNEF observation post on the international frontier in front of El Amr Camp and forced the Yugoslav soldiers to withdraw. Later, two United Arab Republic officers visited El Amr Camp and asked the UNEF platoon to withdraw within fifteen minutes.

19. *1210 hours GMT.* United Arab Republic officers then visited the Yugoslav camp at Sharm el Sheikh and informed the Commanding Officer that they had come to take over the camp and the UNEF observation post at Ras Nasrani, demanding a reply within fifteen minutes. The contingent commander replied that he had no instructions to hand over the positions.

20. *1430 hours GMT.* The UNEF Yugoslav detachment at El Quseima camp reported that two artillery shells, apparently ranging rounds from the United Arab Republic artillery, had burst between the UNEF Yugoslav camps at El Quseima and El Sabha.

21. *1030 hours New York time.* The Secretary-General met at this time with the Permanent Representative of Israel who gave his Government's views on the situation, emphasizing that the UNEF withdrawal should not be achieved by a unilateral United Arab Republic request alone and asserting Israel's right to a voice in the matter. The question of stationing UNEF on the Israel side of the line was raised by the Secretary-General and this was declared by the

Permanent Representative of Israel to be entirely unacceptable to his
Government.

22.   *1600 hours GMT (12 noon New York time).* At this hour the
Secretary-General received through the Permanent Representative
of the United Arab Republic the following message from Mr. Mahmoud Riad, Minister of Foreign Affairs of the United Arab Republic:

"The Government of the United Arab Republic has the honour to
inform Your Excellency that it has decided to terminate the presence
of the United Nations Emergency Force from the territory of the
United Arab Republic and Gaza Strip

"Therefore, I request that the necessary steps be taken for the
withdrawal of the Force as soon as possible.

"I avail myself of this opportunity to express to Your Excellency
my gratitude and warm regards."

At the same meeting the Permanent Representative of the United
Arab Republic informed the Secretary-General of the strong feeling
of resentment in Cairo at what was there considered to be attempts
to exert pressure and to make UNEF an "occupation force".   The
Secretary-General expressed deep misgivings about the likely disastrous consequences of the withdrawal of UNEF and indicated his
intention to appeal urgently to President Nasser to reconsider the
decision.   Later in the day, the representative of the United Arab Republic informed the Secretary-General that the Foreign Minister had
asked the Permanent Representative by telephone from Cairo to convey to the Secretary-General his urgent advice that the Secretary-
General should not make an appeal to President Nasser to reconsider
the request for withdrawal of UNEF and that, if he did so, such a
request would be sternly rebuffed.   The Secretary-General raised the
question of a possible visit by him to Cairo and was shortly thereafter informed that such a visit as soon as possible would be welcomed
by the Government of the United Arab Republic.

23.   *1700 hours New York time.* The Secretary-General met with
the UNEF Advisory Committee, set up under the terms of paragraphs
6, 8 and 9 of resolution 1001 (ES–I) of 7 November 1956, and the
representatives of three countries not members of the Advisory Committee but providing contingents to UNEF, to inform them of developments and particularly the United Arab Republic's request for UNEF's
withdrawal, and to consult them for their views on the situation.   At
this meeting, one of the views expressed was that the United Arab
Republic's demand for the immediate withdrawal of UNEF from
United Arab Republic territory was not acceptable and that the ultimate responsibility for the decision to withdraw rested with the United Nations acting through the Security Council or the General Assembly.   The holders of this view therefore urged further discussion
with the Government of the United Arab Republic as well as with
other Governments involved.   Another position was that the Secre-

tary-General had no choice but to comply with the request of the Government of the United Arab Republic, one representative stating that the moment the request for the withdrawal of UNEF was known his Government would comply with it and withdraw its contingent. A similar position had been taken in Cairo by another Government providing a contingent. No proposal was made that the Advisory Committee should exercise the right vested in it by General Assembly resolution 1001 (ES–I) to request the convening of the General Assembly to take up the situation arising from the United Arab Republic communication. At the conclusion of the meeting, it was understood that the Secretary-General had no alternative other than to comply with the United Arab Republic's demand, although some representatives felt the Secretary-General should previously clarify with that Government the meaning in its request that withdrawal should take place "as soon as possible". The Secretary-General informed the Advisory Committee that he intended to reply promptly to the United Arab Republic, and to report to the General Assembly and to the Security Council on the action he had taken. It was for the Member States to decide whether the competent organs should or could take up the matter and to pursue it accordingly.

24. After the meeting of the Advisory Committee, at approximately 1900 hours New York time on 18 May, the Secretary-General replied to the message from the Minister for Foreign Affairs of the United Arab Republic through that Government's Permanent Representative as follows: . . .

"Your message informing me that your Government no longer consents to the presence of the United Nations Emergency Force on the territory of the United Arab Republic, that is to say in Sinai, and in the Gaza Strip, and requesting that the necessary steps be taken for its withdrawal as soon as possible, was delivered to me by the Permanent Representative of the United Arab Republic at noon on 18 May.

"As I have indicated to your Permanent Representative on 16 May, the United Nations Emergency Force entered Egyptian territory with the consent of your Government and in fact can remain there only so long as that consent continues. In view of the message now received from you, therefore, your Government's request will be complied with and I am proceeding to issue instructions for the necessary arrangements to be put in train without delay for the orderly withdrawal of the Force, its vehicles and equipment and for the disposal of all properties pertaining to it. I am, of course, also bringing this development and my actions and intentions to the attention of the UNEF Advisory Committee and to all Governments providing contingents for the Force. A full report covering this development will be submitted promptly by me to the General Assembly, and I consider it necessary to report also to the Security Council about some aspects of the current situation in the area.

"Irrespective of the reasons for the action you have taken, in all frankness, may I advise you that I have serious misgivings about it for, as I have said each year in my annual reports to the General Assembly on UNEF, I believe that this Force has been an important factor in maintaining relative quiet in the area of its deployment during the past ten years and that its withdrawal may have grave implications for peace."

It is to be noted that the decision notified to the Government of the United Arab Republic in this letter was in compliance with the request to withdraw the Force. It did not, however, signify the actual withdrawal of the Force which, in fact, was to remain in the area for several more weeks.

25.   Formal instructions relating to the withdrawal of UNEF were sent to the UNEF Commander by the Secretary-General on the night of 18 May.   [A/6730/Add. 3, Annex.]

26.   Also on the evening of 18 May the Secretary-General submitted his special report to the General Assembly (A/6730).

27.   On 19 May the Secretary-General issued his report to the Security Council on recent developments in the Near East (S/7896).

19 May 1967

28.   *1130 hours New York time.*   The Secretary-General again received the Permanent Representative of Israel who gave him a statement from his Government concerning the withdrawal of UNEF, strongly urging the Secretary-General to avoid condoning any changes in the *status quo* pending the fullest and broadest international consultation.

29.   On the afternoon of 22 May, the Secretary-General departed from New York, arriving in Cairo on the afternoon of 23 May. He left Cairo on the afternoon of 25 May, arriving back in New York on 26 May (see S/7906).   While en route to Cairo during a stop in Paris, the Secretary-General learned that on this day President Nasser had announced his intention to reinstitute the blockade against Israel in the Strait of Tiran.

17 June 1967

30.   The withdrawal of UNEF was completed.   Details of the actual withdrawal and evacuation of UNEF are given in document A/6730/Add.2.

MAIN POINTS AT ISSUE

31.   Comment is called for on some of the main points at issue even prior to the consideration of the background and basis for the stationing of UNEF on United Arab Republic territory.

The causes of the present crisis

32. It has been said rather often in one way or another that the withdrawal of UNEF is a primary cause of the present crisis in the Near East. This is, of course, a superficial and over-simplified approach. As the Secretary-General pointed out in his report of 26 May 1967 to the Security Council (S/7906), this view "ignores the fact that the underlying basis for this and other crisis situations in the Near East is the continuing Arab-Israel conflict which has been present all along and of which the crisis situation created by the unexpected withdrawal of UNEF is the latest expression". The Secretary-General's report to the Security Council of 19 May 1967 (S/7896) described the various elements of the increasingly dangerous situation in the Near East prior to the decision of the Government of the United Arab Republic to terminate its consent for the presence of UNEF on its territory.

33. The United Nations Emergency Force served for more than ten years as a highly valuable instrument in helping to maintain quiet along the line between Israel and the United Arab Republic. Its withdrawal revealed in all its depth and danger the undiminishing conflict between Israel and her Arab neighbours. The withdrawal also made immediately acute the problem of access for Israel to the Gulf of Aqaba through the Strait of Tiran—a problem which had been dormant for over ten years only because of the presence of UNEF. But the presence of UNEF did not touch the basic problem of the Arab-Israel conflict—it merely isolated, immobilized and covered up certain aspects of that conflict. At any time in the last ten years either of the parties could have reactivated the conflict and if they had been determined to do so UNEF's effectiveness would automatically have disappeared. When, in the context of the whole relationship of Israel with her Arab neighbours, the direct confrontation between Israel and the United Arab Republic was revived after a decade by the decision of the United Arab Republic to move its forces up to the line, UNEF at once lost all usefulness. In fact, its effectiveness as a buffer and as a presence had already vanished, as can be seen from the chronology given above, even before the request for its withdrawal had been received by the Secretary-General from the Government of the United Arab Republic. In recognizing the extreme seriousness of the situation thus created, its true cause, the continuing Arab-Israel conflict, must also be recognized. It is entirely unrealistic to maintain that that conflict could have been solved, or its consequences prevented, if a greater effort had been made to maintain UNEF's presence in the area against the will of the Government of the United Arab Republic.

The decision on UNEF's withdrawal

34. The decision to withdraw UNEF has been frequently characterized in various quarters as "hasty", "precipitous", and the like, even, indeed, to the extent of suggesting that it took President Nasser by surprise. The question of the withdrawal of UNEF is by no means a new one. In fact, it was the negotiations on this very question with the Government of Egypt which, after the establishment of UNEF by the General Assembly, delayed its arrival while it waited in a staging area at Capodichino airbase, Naples, Italy, for several days in November 1956. The Government of Egypt, understandably, did not wish to give permission for the arrival on its soil of an international force, unless it was assured that its sovereignty would be respected and a request for withdrawal of the Force would be honoured. Over the years, in discussions with representatives of the United Arab Republic, the subject of the continued presence of UNEF has occasionally come up, and it was invariably taken for granted by United Arab Republic representatives that if their Government officially requested the withdrawal of UNEF the request would be honoured by the Secretary-General. There is no record to indicate that this assumption was ever questioned. Thus, although the request for the withdrawal of UNEF came as a surprise, there was nothing new about the question of principle nor about the procedure to be followed by the Secretary-General. It follows that the decision taken by him on 18 May 1967 to comply with the request for the withdrawal of the Force was seen by him as the only reasonable and sound action that could be taken. The actual withdrawal itself, it should be recalled, was to be carried out in an orderly, dignified, deliberate and not precipitate manner over a period of several weeks. The first troops in fact left the area only on 29 May.

The possibility of delay

35. Opinions have also been frequently expressed that the decision to withdraw UNEF should have been delayed pending consultations of various kinds, or that efforts should have been made to resist the United Arab Republic's request for UNEF's withdrawal, or to bring pressure to bear on the Government of the United Arab Republic to reconsider its decision in this matter. In fact, as the chronology given above makes clear, the effectiveness of UNEF, in the light of the movement of United Arab Republic troops up to the line and into Sharm el Sheikh, had already vanished before the request for withdrawal was received. Furthermore, the Government of the United Arab Republic had made it entirely clear to the Secretary-General that an appeal for reconsideration of the withdrawal decision would encounter a firm rebuff and would be considered as an attempt to impose UNEF as an "army of occupation". Such a reaction, combined with the fact that UNEF positions on the line had already been

effectively taken over by United Arab Republic troops in pursuit of their full right to move up to the line in their own territory, and a deep anxiety for the security of UNEF personnel should an effort be made to keep UNEF in position after its withdrawal had been requested, were powerful arguments in favour of complying with the United Arab Republic request, even supposing there had not been other over-riding reasons for accepting it.

36.   It has been said that the decision to withdraw UNEF precipi-tated other consequences such as the reinstitution of the blockade against Israel in the Strait of Tiran. As can be seen from the chron-ology, the UNEF positions at Sharm el Sheikh on the Strait of Tiran (manned by thirty-two men in all) were in fact rendered ineffective by United Arab Republic troops before the request for withdrawal was received. It is also pertinent to note that in response to a query from the Secretary-General as to why the United Arab Republic had announced its reinstitution of the blockade in the Strait of Tiran while the Secretary-General was actually en route to Cairo on 22 May, President Nasser explained that his Government's decision to resume the blockade had been taken some time before U Thant's de-parture and it was considered preferable to make the announcement before rather than after the Secretary-General's visit to Cairo.

The question of consultations

37.   It has been said also that there was not adequate consultation with the organs of the United Nations concerned or with the Mem-bers before the decision was taken to withdraw the Force. The Secre-tary-General was, and is, firmly of the opinion that the decision for withdrawal of the Force, on the request of the host Government, rest-ed with the Secretary-General after consultation with the Advisory Committee on UNEF, which is the organ established by the General Assembly for consultation regarding such matters. This was made clear by Secretary-General Hammarskjöld, who took the following position on 26 February 1957 in reply to a question about the with-drawal of the Force from Sharm el Sheikh:

"An indicated procedure would be for the Secretary-General to in-form the Advisory Committee on the United Nations Emergency Force, which would determine whether the matter should be brought to the attention of the Assembly." [A/3563, Annex I, B, 2.]

The Secretary-General consulted the Advisory Committee before replying to the letter of 18 May 1967 from the United Arab Republic requesting withdrawal. This consultation took place within a few hours after receipt of the United Arab Republic request, and the Ad-visory Committee was thus quickly informed of the decision which the Secretary-General had in mind to convey in his reply to the For-eign Minister of the United Arab Republic. As indicated in the re-port to the Security Council of 26 May 1967:

"The Committee did not move, as it was its right to do under the terms of paragraph 9 of General Assembly resolution 1001 (ES–I) to request the convening of the General Assembly on the situation which had arisen." (S/7906, para. 4)

38. Before consulting the Advisory Committee on UNEF, the Secretary-General had also consulted the Permanent Representatives of the seven countries providing the contingents of UNEF and informed them of his intentions. This, in fact, was more than was formally required of the Secretary-General in the way of consultation.

39. Obviously, many Governments were concerned about the presence and functioning of UNEF and about the general situation in the area, but it would have been physically impossible to consult all of the interested representatives within any reasonable time. This was an emergency situation requiring urgent action. Moreover, it was perfectly clear that such consultations were sure to produce sharply divided counsel, even if they were limited to the permanent members of the Security Council. Such sharply divided advice would have complicated and exacerbated the situation, and, far from relieving the Secretary-General of the responsibility for the decision to be taken, would have made the decision much more difficult to take.

40. It has been said that the final decision on the withdrawal of UNEF should have been taken only after consideration by the General Assembly. This position is not only incorrect but also unrealistic. In resolution 1000 (ES–I) the General Assembly established a United Nations command for an emergency international force. On the basis of that resolution the Force was quickly recruited and its forward elements flown to the staging area at Naples. Thus, though established, it had to await the permission of the Government of Egypt to enter Egyptian territory. That permission was subsequently given by the Government of Egypt as a result of direct discussions between Secretary-General Hammarskjöld and President Nasser of Egypt. There is no official United Nations document on the basis of which any case could be made that there was any limitation on the authority of the Government of Egypt to rescind that consent at its pleasure, or which would indicate that the United Arab Republic had in any way surrendered its right to ask for and obtain at any time the removal of UNEF from its territory. This point is elaborated later in this report (see paras. 71–80 below).

41. As a practical matter, there would be little point in any case in taking such an issue to the General Assembly unless there would be reasonable certainty that that body could be expected expeditiously to reach a substantive decision. In the prevailing circumstances, the question could have been validly raised as to what decision other than the withdrawal of UNEF could have been reached by the Assembly once United Arab Republic consent for the continued presence of UNEF was withdrawn.

42.   As regards the practical possibility of the Assembly considering the request for UNEF"s withdrawal, it is relevant to observe that the next regular session of the General Assembly was some four months off at the time the withdrawal request was made.   The special session of the General Assembly which was meeting at the time could have considered the question, according to rule 19 of the Assembly's rules of procedure, only if two thirds or eighty-two members voted for the inclusion of the item in the agenda.   It is questionable, to say the least, whether the necessary support could have been mustered for such a controversial item.   There could have been no emergency special session since the issue was not then before the Security Council, and therefore the condition of lack of unanimity did not exist.

43.   As far as consultation with or action by the Security Council was concerned, the Secretary-General reported to the Council on the situation leading up to and created by the withdrawal of UNEF on 19 May 1967 (S/7896).   In that report he characterized the situation in the Near East as "extremely menacing".   The Council met for the first time after this report on 24 May 1967, but took no action.

44.   As has already been stated, the Advisory Committee did not make any move to bring the matter before the General Assembly, and no representative of any Member Government requested a meeting of either the Security Council or the General Assembly immediately following the Secretary-General's reports (A/6730 and S/7896).   In this situation, the Secretary-General himself did not believe that any useful purpose would be served by his seeking a meeting of either organ, nor did he consider that there was basis for him to do so at that time.   Furthermore, the information available to the Secretary-General did not lead him to believe that either the General Assembly or the Security Council would have decided that UNEF should remain on United Arab Republic territory, by force if necessary, despite the request of the Government of the United Arab Republic that it should leave.

Practical factors influencing the decision

45.   Since it is still contended in some quarters that the UNEF operation should somehow have continued after the consent of the Government of the United Arab Republic to its presence was withdrawn, it is necessary to consider the factors, quite apart from constitutional and legal considerations, which would have made such a course of action entirely impracticable.

46.   The consent and active co-operation of the host country is essential to the effective operation and, indeed, to the very existence, of any United Nations peace-keeping operation of the nature of UNEF. The fact is that UNEF had been deployed on Egyptian and Egyptian-controlled territory for over ten and a half years with the consent

and co-operation of the Government of the United Arab Republic. Although it was envisaged in pursuance of General Assembly resolution 1125 (XI) of 2 February 1957 that the Force would be stationed on both sides of the line, Israel exercised its sovereign right to refuse the stationing of UNEF on its side, and the Force throughout its existence was stationed on the United Arab Republic side of the line only.

47. In these circumstances, the true basis for UNEF's effectiveness as a buffer and deterrent to infiltration was, throughout its existence, a voluntary undertaking by local United Arab Republic authorities with UNEF, that United Arab Republic troops would respect a defined buffer zone along the entire length of the line in which only UNEF would operate and from which United Arab Republic troops would be excluded. This undertaking was honoured for more than a decade, and this Egyptian co-operation extended also to Sharm el Sheikh, Ras Nasrani and the Strait of Tiran. This undertaking was honoured although UNEF had no authority to challenge the right of United Arab Republic troops to be present anywhere on their own territory.

48. It may be pointed out in passing that over the years UNEF dealt with numerous infiltrators coming from the Israel as well as from the United Arab Republic side of the line. It would hardly be logical to take the position that because UNEF has successfully maintained quiet along the line for more than ten years, owing in large measure to the co-operation of the United Arab Republic authorities, that Government should then be told that it could not unilaterally seek the removal of the Force and thus in effect be penalized for the long co-operation with the international community it had extended in the interest of peace.

49. There are other practical factors relating to the above-mentioned arrangement which are highly relevant to the withdrawal of UNEF. First, once the United Arab Republic troops moved up to the line to place themselves in direct confrontation with the military forces of Israel, UNEF had, in fact, no further useful function. Secondly, if the Force was no longer welcome, it could not as a practical matter remain in the United Arab Republic, since the friction which would almost inevitably have arisen with that Government, its armed forces and with the local population would have made the situation of the Force both humiliating and untenable. It would even have been impossible to supply it. UNEF clearly had no mandate to try to stop United Arab Republic troops from moving freely about on their own territory. This was a peace-keeping force, not an enforcement action. Its effectiveness was based entirely on voluntary co-operation.

50. Quite apart from its position in the United Arab Republic, the request of that Government for UNEF's withdrawal automatically set off a disintegration of the Force, since two of the Governments pro-

viding contingents quickly let the Secretary-General know that their contingents would be withdrawn, and there can be little doubt that other such notifications would not have been slow in coming if friction had been generated through an unwillingness to comply with the request for withdrawal.

51.   For all the foregoing reasons, the operation, and even the continued existence of UNEF on United Arab Republic territory, after the withdrawal of United Arab Republic consent, would have been impossible, and any attempt to maintain the Force there would without question have had disastrous consequences.

LEGAL AND CONSTITUTIONAL CONSIDERATIONS AND THE QUESTION OF
CONSENT FOR THE STATIONING OF UNEF ON
UNITED ARAB REPUBLIC TERRITORY

52.   Legal and constitutional considerations were, of course, of great importance in determining the Secretary-General's actions in relation to the request of the Government of the United Arab Republic for the withdrawal of UNEF.   Here again, a chronology of the relevant actions in 1956 and 1957 may be helpful.

53.   *4 November 1956.*   The General Assembly, at its first emergency special session in resolution 998 (ES–I), requested "the Secretary-General to submit to it within forty-eight hours a plan for the setting up, with the consent of the nations concerned, of an emergency international United Nations Force to secure and supervise the cessation of hostilities   .   .   .".

54.   *5 November 1956.*   The General Assembly, in its resolution 1000 (ES–I), established a United Nations Command for an emergency international Force, and, *inter alia*, invited the Secretary-General "to take such administrative measures as may be necessary for the prompt execution of the actions envisaged in the present resolution".

55.   *7 November 1956.*   The General Assembly, by its resolution 1001 (ES–I), *inter alia*, approved, the guiding principles for the organization and functioning of the emergency international United Nations Force and authorized the Secretary-General "to take all other necessary administrative and executive action".

56.   *10 November 1956.*   Arrival of advance elements of UNEF at staging area in Naples.

57.   *8–12 November 1956.*   Negotiations between Secretary-General Hammarskjöld and the Government of Egypt on entry of UNEF into Egypt.

58.   *12 November 1956.*   Agreement on UNEF entry into Egypt announced and then postponed, pending clarification, until 14 November.

59. *15 November 1956.* Arrival of advance elements of UNEF in Abu Suweir, Egypt.

60. *16 November to 18 November 1956.* Negotiations between Secretary-General Hammarskjöld and President Nasser in Cairo on the presence and functioning of UNEF in Egypt and co-operation with Egyptian authorities, and conclusion of an "aide-mémoire on the basis for the presence and functioning of UNEF in Egypt" (the so-called "good faith accord"). [A/3375, Annex.]

61. *24 January 1957.* The Secretary-General in a report to the General Assembly [A/3512] suggested that the Force should have units stationed on both sides of the armistice demarcation line and that certain measures should be taken in relation to Sharm el Sheikh. On *2 February 1957*, the General Assembly, by its resolution 1125 (XI), noted with appreciation the Secretary-General's report and considered that "after full withdrawal of Israel from the Sharm el Sheikh and Gaza areas, the scrupulous maintenance of the Armistice Agreement required the placing of the United Nations Emergency Force on the Egyptian-Israel armistice demarcation line and the implementation of other measures as proposed in the Secretary-General's report, with due regard to the consideration set out therein with a view to assist in achieving situations conducive to the maintenance of peaceful conditions in the area".

62. *7 March 1957.* Arrival of UNEF in Gaza.

63. *8 March 1957.* Arrival of UNEF elements at Sharm el Sheikh.

64. In general terms the consent of the host country to the presence and operation of the United Nations peace-keeping machinery is a basic prerequisite of all United Nations peace-keeping operations. The question has been raised whether the United Arab Republic had the right to request unilaterally the withdrawal "as soon as possible" of UNEF from its territory or whether there were limitations on its rights in this respect. An examination of the records of the first emergency special session and the eleventh session of the General Assembly is relevant to this question.

65. It is clear that the General Assembly and the Secretary-General from the very beginning recognized, and in fact emphasized, the need for Egyptian consent in order that UNEF be stationed or operate on Egyptian territory. Thus, the initial resolution 998 (ES–I) of 4 November 1956 requested the Secretary-General to submit a plan for the setting up of an emergency force, "with the consent of the nations concerned". The "nations concerned" obviously included Egypt (now the United Arab Republic), the three countries (France, Israel and the United Kingdom) whose armies were on Egyptian soil and the States contributing contingents to the Force.

66. The Secretary-General, in his report to the General Assembly of 6 November 1956, stated, *inter alia:*

"9.   Functioning, as it would, on the basis of a decision reached under the terms of the resolution 337 (V) 'Uniting for peace', the Force, if established, would be limited in its operations to the extent that consent of the parties concerned is required under generally recognized international law.   While the General Assembly is enabled to *establish* the Force with the consent of those parties which contribute units to the Force, it could not request the Force to be *stationed* or *operate* on the territory of a given country without the consent of the Government of that country."   [A/3302.]

67.   He noted that the foregoing did not exclude the possibility that the Security Council could use such a Force within the wider margins provided under Chapter VII of the United Nations Charter.   He pointed out, however, that it would not be necessary to elaborate this point further, since no use of the Force under Chapter VII, with the rights in relation to Member States that this would entail, had been envisaged.

68.   The General Assembly in its resolution 1001 (ES–I) of 7 November 1956 expressed its approval of the guiding principles for the organization and functioning of the emergency international United Nations Force as expounded in paragraphs 6 to 9 of the Secretary-General's report.   This included the principle of consent embodied in paragraph 9.

69.   The need for Egypt's consent was also stated as a condition or "understanding" by some of the States offering to contribute contingents to the Force.

70.   It was thus a basic legal principle arising from the nature of the Force, and clearly understood by all concerned, that the consent of Egypt was a prerequisite to the stationing of UNEF on Egyptian territory, and it was a practical necessity as well in acquiring contingents for the Force.

The "good faith" aide-mémoire of 20 November 1956

71.   There remains to be examined whether any commitments were made by Egypt which would limit its pre-existing right to withdraw its consent at any time that it chose to do so.   The only basis for asserting such limitation could be the so-called "good faith" aide-mémoire which was set out as an annex to a report of the Secretary-General submitted to the General Assembly on 20 November 1956.

72.   The Secretary-General himself did not offer any interpretation of the "good faith" aide-mémoire to the General Assembly or make any statement questioning the remarks made by the Foreign Minister of Egypt in the General Assembly the following week (see paragraph 74 below).   It would appear, however, that in an exchange of cables he had sought to obtain the express acknowledgement from Egypt that its consent to the presence of the Force would not be withdrawn before the Force had completed its task.   Egypt did not accept this

interpretation but held to the view that if its consent was no longer maintained the Force should be withdrawn. Subsequent discussions between Mr. Hammarskjöld and President Nasser resulted in the "good faith" aide-mémoire.

73.   An interpretative account of these negotiations made by Mr. Hammarskjöld in a personal and private paper entitled "aide-mémoire", dated 5 August 1957, some eight and a half months after the discussions, has recently been made public by a private person who has a copy. It is understood that Mr. Hammarskjöld often prepared private notes concerning significant events under the heading "aide-mémoire". This memorandum is not in any official record of the United Nations nor is it in any of the official files. The General Assembly, the Advisory Committee on UNEF and the Government of Egypt were not informed of its contents or existence. It is not an official paper and has no standing beyond being a purely private memorandum of unknown purpose or value, in which Secretary-General Hammarskjöld seems to record his own impressions and interpretations of his discussions with President Nasser. This paper, therefore, cannot affect in any way the basis for the presence of UNEF on the soil of the United Arab Republic as set out in the official documents, much less supersede those documents.

Position of Egypt

74.   It seems clear that Egypt did not understand the "good faith" aide-mémoire to involve any limitation on its right to withdraw its consent to the continued stationing and operation of UNEF on its territory. The Foreign Minister of Egypt, speaking in the General Assembly on 27 November 1956, one week after the publication of the "good faith" aide-mémoire and three days following its approval by the General Assembly, said:

"We still believe that the General Assembly resolution of 7 November 1956 still stands, together with its endorsement of the principle that the General Assembly could not request the United Nations Emergency Force to be stationed or to operate on the territory of a given country without the consent of the Government of the country. This is the proper basis on which we believe, together with the overwhelming majority of this Assembly, that the United Nations Emergency Force could be stationed or could operate in Egypt. It is the only basis on which Egypt has given its consent in this respect."

He then added:

".   .   .   as must be abundantly clear, this Force has gone to Egypt to help Egypt, with Egypt's consent; and no one here or elsewhere can reasonably or fairly say that a fire brigade, after putting out a fire, would be entitled or expected to claim the right of deciding not to leave the house".   [GAOR, XI, Plenary, Mtg. 597, paras. 48, 50.]

Analysis of the "task" of the Force

75. In the "good faith" aide-mémoire the Government of Egypt declared that, "when exercising its sovereign rights on any matters concerning the presence and functioning of UNEF, it will be guided, in good faith, by its acceptance of General Assembly resolution 1000 (ES–I) of 5 November 1956".

76. The United Nations in turn declared "that the activities of UNEF will be guided, in good faith, by the task established for the Force in the aforementioned resolutions [1000 (ES–I) and 997 (ES–I)]; in particular, the United Nations, understanding this to correspond to the wishes of the Government of Egypt, reaffirms its willingness to maintain UNEF until its task is completed".

77. It must be noted that, while Egypt undertook to be guided in *good faith* by its acceptance of General Assembly resolution 1000 (ES–I), the United Nations also undertook to be guided in *good faith* by the task established for the Force in resolutions 1000 (ES–I) and 997 (ES–I). Resolution 1000 (ES–I), to which the declaration of Egypt referred, established a United Nations Command for the Force "to secure and supervise the cessation of hostilities in accordance with all the terms" of resolution 997 (ES–I). It must be recalled that at this time Israel forces had penetrated deeply into Egyptian territory and that forces of France and the United Kingdom were conducting military operations on Egyptian territory. Resolution 997 (ES–I) urged as a matter of priority that all parties agree to an immediate cease-fire, and halt the movement of military forces and arms into the area. It also urged the parties to the armistice agreements promptly to withdraw all forces behind the armistice lines, to desist from raids across the armistice lines, and to observe scrupulously the provisions of the armistice agreements. It further urged that, upon the cease-fire being effective, steps be taken to reopen the Suez Canal and restore secure freedom of navigation.

78. While the terms of resolution 997 (ES–I) cover a considerable area, the emphasis in resolution 1000 (ES–I) is on *securing and supervising the cessation of hostilities*. Moreover, on 6 November 1956 the Secretary-General, in his second and final report on the plan for an emergency international United Nations Force, noted that "the Assembly intends that the Force should be of a temporary nature, the length of its assignment being determined by the needs arising out of the present conflict". Noting further the terms of resolution 997 (ES–I) he added that "the functions of the United Nations Force would be, when a cease-fire is being established, to enter Egyptian territory with the consent of the Egyptian Government, in order to help maintain quiet during and after the withdrawal of non-Egyptian troops, and to secure compliance with the other terms established in the resolution of 2 November 1956" (997 (ES–I)).

79. In a cable delivered to Foreign Minister Fawzi on 9 or 10 November 1956, in reply to a request for clarification as to how long it was contemplated that the Force should stay in the demarcation line area, the Secretary-General stated: "A definite reply is at present impossible but the emergency character of the Force links it to the immediate crises envisaged in resolution 2 November [997 (ES–I)] and its liquidation." This point was confirmed in a further exchange of cables between the Secretary-General and Dr. Fawzi on 14 November 1956.

80. The Foreign Minister of Egypt (Dr. Fawzi) gave his understanding of the task of the Force in a statement to the General Assembly on 27 November 1956:

"Our clear understanding—and I am sure it is the clear understanding of the Assembly—is that this Force is in Egypt only in relation to the present attack against Egypt by the United Kingdom, France and Israel, and for the purposes directly connected with the incursion of the invading forces into Egyptian territory. The United Nations Emergency Force is in Egypt, not as an occupation force, not as a replacement for the invaders, not to clear the Canal of obstructions, not to resolve any question or settle any problem, be it in relation to the Suez Canal, to Palestine or to any other matter; it is not there to infringe upon Egyptian sovereignty in any fashion or to any extent, but, on the contrary, to give expression to the determination of the United Nations to put an end to the aggression committed against Egypt and to the presence of the invading forces in Egyptian territory."

81. In letters dated 3 November 1956 addressed to the Secretary-General, the representatives of both France and the United Kingdom had proposed very broad functions for UNEF, stating on behalf of their Governments that military action could be stopped if the following conditions were met:

"(a) Both the Egyptian and Israel Governments agree to accept a United Nations Force to keep the peace.

"(b) The United Nations decides to constitute and maintain such a Force until an Arab-Israel peace settlement is reached and until satisfactory arrangements have been agreed in regard to the Suez Canal, both agreements to be guaranteed by the United Nations.

"(c) In the meantime, until the United Nations Force is constituted, both combatants agree to accept forthwith limited detachments of Anglo-French troops to be stationed between the combatants." [A/3268 and A/3269.]

These broad functions for the Force were not acceptable to the General Assembly, however, as was pointed out in telegrams dated 4 November 1956 from Secretary-General Dag Hammarskjöld to the Minister for Foreign Affairs of France and the Secretary of State for Foreign Affairs of the United Kingdom.   [A/3824, Annexes 2 and 4.]

82.   Finally, it is obvious that the task referred to in the "good faith" aide-mémoire could only be the task of the Force as it had been defined in November 1956 when the understanding was concluded. The "good faith" undertaking by the United Nations would preclude it from claiming that the Egyptian agreement was relevant or applicable to functions which the Force was given at a much later date. The stationing of the Force on the armistice demarcation line and at Sharm el Sheikh was only determined in pursuance of General Assembly resolution 1125 (XI) of 2 February 1957.   The Secretary-General, in his reports relating to this decision, made it clear that the further consent of Egypt was essential with respect to these new functions.   Consequently, the understanding recorded in the "good faith" aide-mémoire of 20 November 1956 could not have been, itself, a commitment with respect to functions only determined in February and March 1957.   It is only these later tasks that the Force had been performing during the last ten years—tasks of serving as a buffer and deterring infiltrators which went considerably beyond those of securing and supervising the cessation of hostilities provided in the General Assembly resolutions and referred to in the "good faith" aide-mémoire.

The stationing of UNEF on the armistice demarcation line and at Sharm el Sheikh

83.   There remains to examine whether Egypt made further commitments with respect to the stationing of the Force on the armistice demarcation line and at Sharm el Sheikh.   Israel, of course, sought to obtain such commitments, particularly with respect to the area around Sharm el Sheikh.

84.   For example, in an aide-mémoire of 4 February 1957 [A/3527, Annex I], the Government of Israel sought clarification as to whether units of the United Nations Emergency Force would be stationed along the western shore of the Gulf of Aqaba in order to act as a restraint against hostile acts, and would remain so deployed until another effective means was agreed upon between the parties concerned for ensuring permanent freedom of navigation and the absence of belligerent acts in the Strait of Tiran and the Gulf of Aqaba. The Secretary-General pointed out that such "clarification" would require "Egyptian consent".   He stated:

"The second of the points in the Israel aide-mémoire requests a 'clarification' which, in view of the position of the General Assembly, could go beyond what was stated in the last report only after negotiation with Egypt.   This follows from the statements in the debate in the General Assembly, and the report on which it was based, which make it clear that the stationing of the Force at Sharm el Sheikh, under such terms as those mentioned in the question posed by Israel, would require Egyptian consent."

85.   It is clear from the record that Egypt did not give its consent to Israel's proposition.   The Secretary-General's report of 8 March 1957 recorded "arrangements for the complete and unconditional withdrawal of Israel in accordance with the decision of the General Assembly".   There is no agreement on the part of Egypt to forego its rights with respect to the granting or withdrawing of its consent to the continued stationing of the Force on its territory.   On the contrary, at the 667th plenary meeting of the General Assembly on 4 March 1957, the Foreign Minister of Egypt stated:

"At our previous meeting I stated that the Assembly was unanimous in expecting full and honest implementation of its resolutions calling for immediate and unconditional withdrawal by Israel.   I continue to submit to the Assembly that this position—which is the only position the Assembly can possibly take—remains intact and entire.   Nothing said by anyone here or elsewhere could shake this fact or detract from its reality and its validity, nor could it affect the fullness and the lawfulness of Egypt's rights and those of the Arab people of the Gaza Strip."   [GAOR, XI, Plenary, Mtg. 667.]

86.   The Foreign Minister of Israel, in her statement at the 666th meeting of the General Assembly, on 1 March 1957, asserted that an assurance had been given that any proposal for the withdrawal of UNEF from the Gulf of Aqaba area would come first to the Advisory Committee on UNEF (see paragraphs 95–98 below).

Question of the stationing of UNEF on both sides of the armistice demarcation line

87.   Another point having significance with respect to the undertakings of Egypt is the question of the stationing of UNEF on both sides of the armistice demarcation line.   The Secretary-General, in his report of 24 January 1957 to the General Assembly [A/3512], suggested that the Force should have units stationed also on the Israel side of the armistice demarcation line.   In particular, he suggested that units of the Force should at least be stationed in the El Auja demilitarized zone which had been occupied by the armed forces of Israel.   He indicated that if El Auja were demilitarized in accordance with the Armistice Agreement and units of UNEF were stationed there, a condition of reciprocity would be the Egyptian assurance that Egyptian forces would not take up positions in the area in contravention of the Armistice Agreement.   However, Israel forces were never withdrawn from El Auja and UNEF was not accepted at any point on the Israel side of the line.

88.   Following the Secretary-General's report, the General Assembly on 2 February 1957 adopted resolution 1125 (XI), in which it noted the report with appreciation and considered:

". . . that, after full withdrawal of Israel from the Sharm el Sheikh and Gaza areas, the scrupulous maintenance of the Armistice Agreement requires the placing of the United Nations Emergency Force on the Egyptian-Israel armistice demarcation line and the implementation of other measures as proposed in the Secretary-General's report, with due regard to the considerations set out therein with a view to assist in achieving situations conducive to the maintenance of peaceful conditions in the area."

89. On 11 February 1957, the Secretary-General stated in a report to the General Assembly that, in the light of the implication of Israel's question concerning the stationing of UNEF at Sharm el Sheikh (see paragraph 84 above), he "considered it important . . . to learn whether Israel itself, in principle, consents to a stationing of UNEF units on its territory in implementation of the functions established for the Force in the basic decisions and noted in resolution 1125 (XI) where it was indicated that the Force should be placed 'on the Egyptian-Israel armistice demarcation line'". No affirmative response was ever received from Israel. In fact, already on 7 November 1956 the Prime Minister of Israel, Mr. Ben-Gurion, in a speech to the Knesset, stated, *inter alia*, "On no account will Israel agree to the stationing of a foreign force, no matter how called, in her territory or in any of the territories occupied by her." In a note to correspondents of 12 April 1957 a "United Nations spokesman" stated:

"Final arrangements for the UNEF will have to wait for the response of the Government of Israel to the request by the General Assembly that the Force be deployed also on the Israeli side of the Armistice Demarcation Line."

90. In a report dated 9 October 1957 to the twelfth session of the General Assembly, the Secretary-General stated:

"Resolution 1125 (XI) calls for placing the Force 'on the Egyptian-Israel armistice demarcation line', but no stationing of UNEF on the Israel side has occurred to date through lack of consent by Israel."

91. In the light of Israel's persistent refusal to consent to the stationing and operation of UNEF on its side of the line in spite of General Assembly resolution 1125 (XI) of 2 February 1957 and the efforts of the Secretary-General, it is even less possible to consider that Egypt's "good faith" declaration made in November 1956 could constitute a limitation of its rights with respect to the continued stationing and operation of UNEF on Egyptian territory in accordance with the resolution of 2 February 1957.

92. The representative of Israel stated at the 592nd meeting of the General Assembly, on 23 November 1956:

"If we were to accept one of the proposals made here—namely, that the Force should separate Egyptian and Israel troops for as long as Egypt thought it convenient and should then be withdrawn on Egypt's unilateral request—we would reach a reduction to absurdity.

Egypt would then be in a position to build up, behind the screen of this Force, its full military preparations and, when it felt that those military preparations had reached their desired climax, to dismiss the United Nations Emergency Force and to stand again in close contact and proximity with the territory of Israel. This reduction to absurdity proves how impossible it is to accept in any matter affecting the composition or the functions of the Force the policies of the Egyptian Government as the sole or even the decisive criterion."

93. The answer to this problem which is to be found in resolution 1125 (XI) of 2 February 1957 is not in the form of a binding commitment by Egypt which the record shows was never given, but in the proposal that the Force should be stationed on both sides of the line. Israel in the exercise of its sovereign right did not give its consent to the stationing of UNEF on its territory and Egypt did not forgo its sovereign right to withdraw its consent at any time.

Role of the UNEF Advisory Committee

94. General Assembly resolution 1001 (ES–I) of 7 November 1956, by which the Assembly approved the guiding principles for the organization and functioning of UNEF, established an Advisory Committee on UNEF under the chairmanship of the Secretary-General. The Assembly decided that the Advisory Committee, in the performance of its duties, should be empowered to request, through the usual procedures, the convening of the General Assembly and to report to the Assembly whenever matters arose which, in its opinion, were of such urgency and importance as to require consideration by the General Assembly itself.

95. The memorandum of important points in the discussion between the representative of Israel and the Secretary-General on 25 February 1957 recorded the following question raised by the representative of Israel:

"In connexion with the duration of UNEF's deployment in the Sharm El Sheikh area, would the Secretary-General give notice to the General Assembly of the United Nations before UNEF would be withdrawn from the area, with or without Egyptian insistence, or before the Secretary-General would agree to its withdrawal?"

96. The response of the Secretary-General was recorded as follows:

"On the question of notification to the General Assembly, the Secretary-General wanted to state his view at a later meeting. An indicated procedure would be for the Secretary-General to inform the Advisory Committee on the United Nations Emergency Force, which would determine whether the matter should be brought to the attention of the Assembly."

97. On 1 March 1957 the Foreign Minister of Israel stated at the 666th plenary meeting of the General Assembly:

"My Government has noted the assurance embodied in the Secretary-General's note of 26 February 1957 [A/3363, annex] that any proposal for the withdrawal of the United Nations Emergency Force from the Gulf of Aqaba area would first come to the Advisory Committee on the United Nations Emergency Force, which represents the General Assembly in the implementation of its resolution 997 (ES–I) of 2 November 1956. This procedure will give the General Assembly an opportunity to ensure that no precipitate changes are made which would have the effect of increasing the possibility of belligerent acts."

98. In fact, the 25 February 1957 memorandum does not go as far as the interpretation given by the Foreign Minister of Israel. In any event, however, it gives no indication of any commitment by Egypt, and so far as the Secretary-General is concerned it only indicates that a procedure would be for the Secretary-General to inform the Advisory Committee which would determine whether the matter should be brought to the attention of the General Assembly. This was also the procedure provided in General Assembly resolution 1001 (ES–I). It was, furthermore, the procedure followed by the Secretary-General on the withdrawal of UNEF.

OBSERVATIONS

99. A partial explanation of the misunderstanding about the withdrawal of UNEF is an evident failure to appreciate the essentially fragile nature of the basis for UNEF's operation throughout its existence. UNEF in functioning depended completely on the voluntary co-operation of the host Government. Its basis of existence was the willingness of Governments to provide contingents to serve under an international command and at a minimum of cost to the United Nations. It was a symbolic force, small in size, with only 3,400 men, of whom 1,800 were available to police a line of 295 miles at the time of its withdrawal. It was equipped with light weapons only. It had no mandate of any kind to open fire except in the last resort in self-defence. It had no formal mandate to exercise any authority in the area in which it was stationed. In recent years it experienced an increasingly uncertain basis of financial support, which in turn gave rise to strong annual pressures for reduction in its strength. Its remarkable success for more than a decade, despite these practical weaknesses, may have led to wrong conclusions about its nature, but it has also pointed the way to a unique means of contributing significantly to international peace-keeping.

NOTE.—1. Hostilities in the Middle East started on 5 June 1967, and Israel occupied the Gaza strip, the Sinai peninsula, the Jordanian half of Jerusalem, the Jordanian territory west of the Jordan River and the Syrian heights north and west of the Sea of Galilee.

2. The Security Council on 6 June 1967 called upon the Governments concerned "as a first step to take forthwith all measures for an immediate cease-fire and for a cessation of all military activities in the area"; on 7 June

1967 demanded that these Governments "should as a first step cease fire and discontinue all military activities at 2000 hours GMT on 7 June 1967"; on 9 June 1967 demanded that the only remaining hostilities, those between Syria and Israel, "should cease forthwith"; on 12 June 1967 condemned "any and all violations of the cease fire," and affirmed that "its demand for a cease-fire and discontinuance of all military activities includes a prohibition of any forward military movements subsequent to the cease-fire"; and on 14 June 1967 called upon the Government of Israel "to ensure the safety, welfare and security of the inhabitants of the areas where military operations have taken place and to facilitate the return of those inhabitants who have fled the areas since the outbreak of hostilities," and recommended to the Governments concerned "the scrupulous respect of the humanitarian principles governing the treatment of prisoners of war and the protection of civil persons in time of war, contained in the Geneva Conventions of 12 August 1949." SC Resolutions 233–237 (1967); S/RES/233–237 (7–14 June 1967). But the Security Council failed to adopt a Soviet draft resolution, under which the Council would have vigorously condemned "Israel's aggressive activities and continued occupation of part of the territory of the United Arab Republic, Syria and Jordan," and would have asked Israel to remove all its troops from those States and withdraw them behind the armistice lines. S/7951/Rev.2 (14 June 1967).

3. On 13 June 1967 the Soviet Union asked for the convening of an emergency session of the General Assembly "to consider the question of liquidating the consequences of Israel's aggression against the Arab States and the immediate withdrawal of Israel troops behind the armistice lines." A/6717 (13 June 1967). Despite United States objection that there was no legal basis for such a request [A/6718 (15 June 1967)], the fifth emergency session of the General Assembly opened on 17 June 1967, and considered several resolutions centering, on the one hand, on the withdrawal of Israel forces behind the armistice lines and, on the other hand, on complete termination of belligerency and a negotiated settlement of all the issues. On 4 July 1967, the vote on a Yugoslav draft resolution demanding immediate withdrawal was 53 in favor, 46 against, with 20 abstentions; it thus failed to receive the necessary two-thirds majority. A Latin American resolution linking withdrawal to an end to belligerency similarly could not muster a two-thirds majority; the vote on it was 57 for, 43 against, with 20 abstentions. The General Assembly adopted, however, a Pakistani proposal condemning Israel's attempt to annex the Jordanian half of Jerusalem. The General Assembly expressed its deep concern "at the situation prevailing in Jerusalem as a result of the measures taken by Israel to change the status of the City," considered that these measures were invalid, and called upon Israel "to rescind all measures already taken and to desist forthwith from taking any action which would alter the status of Jerusalem." A/RES/2253 and 2254 (ES–V) (5 and 14 July 1967).

HUNGARIAN QUESTION

NOTE. After the success of the revolt in Poland and the Soviet acceptance of a more nationalistic Gomulka Government, the people of Hungary expressed a desire for a similar change. A full-scale riot started in Budapest when some demonstrators were shot down by the security police. During the night of 23–24 October 1956 the Soviet forces entered Budapest, supposedly on request of the Hungarian Government. While "freedom fighters" attacked the Soviet troops in Budapest, Revolutionary and Workers' Councils were formed throughout the country. On their demand Imre Nagy formed a new government, including both communists and non-communists. The Nagy Government ordered a cease-fire on 28 October and Soviet troops withdrew from Budapest on 30 October. After additional Soviet troops started entering Hungary despite objections by the Nagy Government, Nagy announced on 1 November the withdrawal of Hungary from the Warsaw Pact. On the same day, the Hungarian Government adopted a declaration of neutrality for Hungary and requested the United Nations and the four great powers to defend Hungarian neutrality. After two days of negotiations, during the night of 3–4 November the Hungarian negotiators were arrested at a banquet given in their honor by the Soviet military representatives, and the Soviet troops started an attack on Budapest. At the same time a new government was established by Janos Kádár, a former member of the Nagy Government. Report of the Special Committee on the Problem of Hungary, 7 June 1957; GAOR, XI, Supp. 18 (A/3592), pp. 5–12. For the conclusions of the Committee, see Document 1, below.

1. *Findings of a Special Committee on the Problem of Hungary*

Report of the Committee, 7 June 1957. GAOR, XI, Supp. 18
(A/3592), pp. 137–39.

The terms of reference of the Special Committee covered a broad field, namely to report to the General Assembly of the United Nations after full and objective investigation, its findings on all aspects of the question of Soviet intervention in Hungary by armed force and by other means and the effects of such intervention on the political development of Hungary. The Committee's investigation .   .   . involved the study of copious documentation from various sources and in several languages, as well as the questioning of more than a hundred witnesses, whose testimony fills two thousand pages in the verbatim record. The Committee regrets that the attitude of the Hungarian Government has prevented it from basing its investigation on direct observation in Hungary, as required by the General Assembly resolution.   .   .   .

[The following conclusions were drawn by the Committee from its study of the evidence:]

(i) What took place in Hungary in October and November 1956 was a spontaneous national uprising, due to long-standing grievances which had caused resentment among the people. One of these grievances was the inferior status of Hungary with regard to the USSR; the system of government was in part maintained by the weapon of terror, wielded by the AVH or political police, whose influence was exercised at least until the end of 1955, through a complex network of agents and informers permeating the whole of Hungarian society. In other respects also, Soviet pressure was resented. From the stifling of free speech to the adoption of a Soviet-style uniform for the Hungarian army, an alien influence existed in all walks of life. Hungarians felt no personal animosity towards the individual Soviet soldiers on Hungarian soil, but these armed forces were symbols of something which annoyed a proud people and fed the desire to be free;

(ii) The thesis that the uprising was fomented by reactionary circles in Hungary and that it drew its strength from such circles and from Western "Imperialists" failed to survive the Committee's examination. From start to finish, the uprising was led by students, workers, soldiers and intellectuals, many of whom were Communists or former Communists. The majority of political demands put forward during the revolution included a stipulation that democratic socialism should be the basis of the Hungarian political structure and that such social achievements as the land reform should be safeguarded. At no time was any proposal made for the return to power, or to the Government, of any figure associated with pre-war days. "Fascists" and "saboteurs", heavily armed, could not have succeeded in landing on Hungarian airfields which were under Soviet supervision, or in crossing the Austrian frontier, where a closed zone was shown by the Austrian authorities to the military attachés of France, the United Kingdom, the United States of America and the USSR;

(iii) The uprising was not planned in advance. It was the universal testimony of witnesses examined by the Committee that events took participants by surprise. No single explanation can determine exactly why the outbreak occurred just when it did. Communist spokesmen, including Mr. Kádár and the members of his present Government, have recognized the bitter grievances of the Hungarian people before 23 October. They have spoken of a "broad, popular movement" caused by the "bitterness and indignation" of the masses. Two factors would seem to have brought this resentment to a head. The first of these was the news received on 19 October of a successful move by Poland for greater independence from the USSR. This news was largely instrumental in bringing the Hungarian students together in the meetings of 22 October. The second factor was the acute disappointment felt by the people when Ernó Geró, First Secretary of the Central Committee of the Hungarian Workers' (Communist) Party, in his speech on the evening of 23 October failed to meet any of the popular demands and adopted what was considered a truculent tone towards his hearers;

(iv) Although no evidence exists of advance planning, and although the whole course of the uprising bears the hallmark of continuous improvisation, it would appear that the Soviet authorities had taken steps as early as 20 October to make armed intervention in Hungary possible. Evidence exists of troop movements, or projected troop movements, from that date on. It would appear that plans for action had therefore been laid some time before the students met to discuss their demands. The Committee is not in a position to say whether the Soviet authorities anticipated that the grievances of the Hungarian people, stimulated by events in Poland, could no longer be contained. Signs of opposition were evident before the 23rd; the Hungarian Government had reason to foresee that trouble was brewing. While the evidence shows that Soviet troops from outside Hungary were used even in the first intervention, no clause of the Warsaw Treaty provides for intervention by armed forces of the Soviet Union to dictate political developments within any signatory's frontiers;

(v) The demonstrations on 23 October were at first entirely peaceable. None of the demonstrators appear to have carried arms, and no evidence has been discovered that any of those who voiced the political demands or joined the demonstrators had any intention to resort to force. While disappointment at Mr. Geró's speech may have angered the crowds, it would hardly of itself have sufficed to turn the demonstration into an armed uprising. That this happened was due to the action of the AVH in opening fire on the people outside the radio building. Within a few hours, Soviet tanks were in action against the Hungarians. This appearance of Russian soldiers in their midst not as friendly allies, but as enemies in combat, had the effect of still further uniting the people;

(vi) Obscurity surrounds the invitation alleged to have been issued by the Hungarian Government to the Soviet authorities to assist in quelling the uprising by force. Mr. Nagy has denied, with every appearance of truth, that he issued this invitation or was even aware of it. Since Soviet tanks appeared on the streets of Budapest at about 2 a. m. on 24 October, it would have been impossible for him to have addressed any official message to the Soviet authorities, since he held no government post at the time when the tanks must have received their orders. An invitation may have been made privately by Mr. Geró, First Secretary of the Central Committee of the Communist Party, or Mr. Hegedüs, the Prime Minister. The Committee, however, has had no opportunity of seeing a text of such an invitation, or of considering the exact circumstances in which it may have been issued. Until further information comes to light, it would be wise to suspend judgment as to whether such an invitation was issued at all.

Similar considerations apply to the invitation which is alleged to have been addressed to the Soviet authorities before the second intervention on 4 November. Mr. Kádár had remained a member of Mr. Nagy's Government when the latter was reconstituted on 3 November and the Committee is unaware of his having given any recorded indication of his disapproval of Mr. Nagy's policies. Mr. Kádár's movements at this time are not fully known, and he cannot be considered to have substantiated his own claim to have called, in the name of the Government, for Soviet help. In any event, there is abundant evidence that Soviet preparations for a further intervention, including the movement of troops and armour from abroad, had been under way since the last days of October. Mr. Kádár and his Ministers were absent from Budapest during the first few days after he formed his Government, and administrative instructions to the people of Hungary were issued by the commanders of the Soviet troops;

(vii) When Mr. Nagy became Prime Minister, he was not at first able to exercise the full powers of that office. Only when the grip of the AVH was loosened by the victory of the insurgents was he able to take an independent stand. By this time, the real power in Hungary lay with the Revolutionary and Workers' Councils, which had sprung up spontaneously in different parts of the country and had replaced the collapsing structure of the Communist Party. Mr. Nagy, though himself a Communist of long standing who had lived for many years in the USSR, invited non-Communists into his new Government, and listened to the demands of various Revolutionary and Workers' Councils. It would appear that Mr. Nagy himself, like the country at large, was somewhat taken aback by the pace of developments. However, seeing that his countrymen were united in their desire for other forms of government and the departure of Soviet troops, he threw in his lot with the insurgents. By this action, he obliterated the impression which he had created while still under the domination of the AVH, and he became a symbolic figure in the uprising, although he had not instigated it, and was never its actual leader;

(viii) The few days of freedom enjoyed by the Hungarian people provided abundant evidence of the popular nature of the uprising. A free Press and radio came to life all over Hungary, and the disbanding of the AVH was the signal for general rejoicing, which revealed the degree of unity achieved by the people, once the burden of fear had been lifted from them;

(ix) There were a number of lynchings and beatings by the crowds. These were, in almost all cases, confined to members of the AVH or those who were believed to have co-operated with them;

(x) Steps were taken by the Workers' Councils during this period to give the workers real control of nationalized industrial undertakings and to abolish unpopular institutions, such as the production norms. These were widely resented as being unfair to workers and also a reflection of popularly suspected secret trade agreements with the USSR, which were said to make heavy demands on the Hungarian economy for the benefit of the Soviet Union. During the days of freedom, while negotiations continued with the Soviet authorities for the withdrawal of Russian troops, attempts were made to clear up the streets of Budapest and life was beginning to return to normal. The insurgents had agreed to amalgamate, while maintaining their identity, in a National Guard, which would have been responsible, with the Army and Police, for maintaining order;

(xi) In contrast to the demands for the re-establishment of political rights put forward during the uprising, is the fact that basic human rights of the Hungarian people were violated by the Hungarian Governments prior to 23 October, especially up to the autumn of 1955, and that such violations have been resumed since 4 November. The Committee is convinced that the numerous accounts of inhuman treatment and torture by the AVH are to be accepted as true. On the evidence, it is also convinced that numbers of Hungarians, including some women, were deported to the Soviet Union and that some may not have been returned to their homes. These deportations were designed to break the back of the revolution. Action taken by the Hungarian people in their spontaneous uprising succeeded in ridding them for a few days of the apparatus of police terror. This democratic achievement of a united people was indeed, threatened by a form of "counter-revolution" and it was to this that it succumbed. However, the "counter-revolution" consisted in the setting up by Soviet armed forces of Mr. Kádár and his colleagues in opposition to a Government which enjoyed the overwhelming support of the people of Hungary;

(xii) Following the second Soviet intervention on 4 November, there has been no evidence of popular support for Mr. Kádár's Government. Mr. Kádár has successively abandoned most of the points from the revolutionary programme which he had at first promised to the Hungarian people. On the central question of the withdrawal of Soviet troops, he has moved from complete acceptance of the nation's wishes to a refusal to discuss the subject in present circumstances. Against the workers, he has proceeded step by step to destroy their power and that of the Workers' Councils. Capital punishment is applicable to strike activities. The processes of justice have been distorted by the institution of special police and special courts and by the ignoring of the rights of the accused. The Social Democratic Party has again been forcibly liquidated. General elections have been postponed for two years. Writers and intellectuals are subjected to repressive measures. The Hungarian workers have shown no sign of support for Mr. Kádár's Government or for the prospect of continuous Soviet occupation. Only a small fraction of the 190,000 Hungarians, mostly young people, who fled the country have accepted his invitation to return.

(xiii) In the light of the extent of foreign intervention, consideration of the Hungarian question by the United Nations was legally proper and, moreover, it was requested by a legal Government of Hungary. In the matter of human rights, Hungary has accepted specific international obligations in the Treaty of Peace. Accordingly, the Committee does not regard objections based on paragraph 7 of Article 2 of the Charter as having validity in the present case. A massive armed intervention by one Power on the territory of another, with the avowed intention of interfering with the internal affairs of the country must, by the Soviet's own definition of aggression, be a matter of international concern.

NOTE. On 27 October 1956, France, the UK and the US requested that a meeting of the Security Council be convened to consider "the situation created by the action of foreign military forces in Hungary in violently repressing the rights of the Hungarian people which are secured by the Treaty of Peace of 10 February 1947 to which the Governments of Hungary and the Allied and Associated Powers are parties." S/3690 (27 Oct. 1956); SCOR, Supp. for Oct.-Dec. 1956, p. 100. The representative of Hungary to the United Nations submitted to the Council a declaration of his government containing a protest against the placing on the agenda of the Council of "any question concerning the domestic affairs of Hungary"; it pointed out that "the internal events of the preceding days in Hungary have no effect whatsoever on international peace and security and do not endanger their maintenance." S/3691 (28 Oct. 1956); SCOR, op. cit., p. 101.

2. Discussion in the Security Council, 28 October 1956.

SCOR, XI, Mtg. 746, pp. 1–34.

Mr. SOBOLEV (USSR): The representatives of the United States, the United Kingdom and France are proposing the inclusion in the Security Council's agenda of an item entitled: "The situation in Hungary"; that is, an item on the situation inside a country which is a sovereign State and a Member of the United Nations. The very wording of this item shows in itself that what the United States, the United Kingdom and France have in mind is an attempt, in defiance of the provisions of the United Nations Charter, at gross interference in the domestic affairs of the Hungarian People's Republic.

Article 2, paragraph 7, of the Charter states: "Nothing contained in the present Charter shall authorize the United Nations to intervene in matters which are essentially within the domestic jurisdiction of any State or shall require the Members to submit such matters to settlement under the present Charter . . ."

On what grounds, then, are the Governments of the United States, the United Kingdom and France proposing the inclusion of this item in the Council's agenda? Were they asked to do so by the Government of Hungary, with which, as we know, they maintain diplomatic relations: No, they were not. On the contrary; the Government of the Hungarian People's Republic clearly states, in its declaration of 28 October 1956—of which members of the Council have copies—that it "categorically protests against placing on the agenda the consideration of any question concerning the domestic affairs of Hungary, since the consideration of such questions in the United Nations would mean serious violation of the sovereignty of the Hungarian People's Republic and would obviously be in contradiction with the principles laid down in the Charter of the United Nations."

What then is the true purpose of the United States, United Kingdom and French Governments in raising the question of the internal situa-

tion in Hungary in the Security Council? In our view, the purpose
of their action is to give further encouragement to the armed rebellion which is being conducted by a reactionary underground movement against the legal Government of Hungary. Is such a step consistent with normal diplomatic relations between sovereign Governments? Of course not. The Governments of the United States, the
United Kingdom and France are making an unprecedented attempt
to give United Nations protection to reactionary elements in Hungary which have come out against the great democratic achievements
of the Hungarian workers.

The fact that such an attempt is being made at the present time
is not at all surprising, since support for the reactionary underground
movement against the legal Governments of the eastern European
countries has long been one of the guiding principles of ruling circles in the United States. The United States Congress makes multi-
million dollar appropriations to encourage subversive activities against
the legal Governments of the peoples' democracies, the object being
to overthrow them and replace them by the reactionary regimes driven
out by the workers of the eastern European countries.

I should like to remind you, in this connexion, that as long ago as
1951 the United States Congress passed an act appropriating $100
million to finance subversive activities in the USSR and the countries
of eastern Europe. .   .   .

The measures the Hungarian Government has seen fit to take in
order to put an end to the armed uprising of criminal elements of a
fascist type against the legal Government of Hungary and to maintain law and order in the country are its inalienable prerogative, as
they are the prerogative of the Government of any other sovereign
State. In defence of the democratic people's regime, the Hungarian
Government was compelled to bring its armed forces into action for
the liquidation of the counter-revolutionary uprising, and it appealed
to the Government of the Soviet Union for assistance. It is perfectly clear that all these actions of the Hungarian Government are an
internal affair of the Hungarian State, and the United Nations, including the Security Council, is in no way entitled to interfere in these
matters.

According to the letter, these measures taken against the elements referred to constitute an infringement of human rights, which
are guaranteed under the terms of the Treaty of Peace with Hungary.
This is an obvious attempt to distort the facts. During the years that
have passed since the signing of the peace treaty, a regime has been
established in Hungary on the basis of principles providing for the
democratization of the country. This regime is founded on the will
of the Hungarian workers, who are building a socialist society. It is
founded on the freely expressed democratic will of the Hungarian
workers, and on the historic successes they have achieved in the struggle for the building of a new society.

Certain persons in the capitalist countries are trying, and not for the first time, as we know, to cast doubt upon all these obvious facts. All that these attempts reflect is the endeavour of certain circles in the United States, with the help of some small counter-revolutionary groups inside and outside Hungary, to restore the capitalist regime and rob the Hungarian people of the fruits of their victories in the struggle against fascism.

As the letter shows, attempts are being made to assert that in the course of the recent events in Hungary, breaches of the provisions of the peace treaty and of human rights have been committed. We feel compelled to observe, in this connexion, that these assertions are completely without foundation; indeed, the Hungarian Government, in taking measures to put a stop to the criminal activities of counter-revolutionary elements, was acting entirely in accordance with article 4 of the peace treaty, whereby Hungary undertook not to permit the existence and activities of organizations of a fascist type which had as their aim denial to the people of their democratic rights.

In their proposal for the inclusion of this item in the agenda the three Powers invoke Article 34 of the Charter as grounds for the discussion of this question in the Security Council. But that is entirely unwarranted. In point of fact, Article 34 of the Charter empowers the Security Council to investigate only disputes or situations of an international character, namely, those arising in relationships between States. Accordingly, any situations arising inside a country and not affecting its relations with other States, as in the present instance, do not fall under Article 34. Both in itself, therefore, and in association with the provisions of Article 2, paragraph 7, of the Charter, which I have mentioned, and those of Chapter I of the Charter as a whole, the text of Article 34 makes it quite clear that this is the only possible correct interpretation of the question of the Security Council's competence. The United Nations Charter thus leaves no doubt that the Security Council is not competent to examine questions of this nature.

In the light of these facts it is quite clear that the proposal of the United States, the United Kingdom and France to place an item on "The situation in Hungary" on our agenda is in no way dictated by a desire to uphold the lofty purposes and principles proclaimed in the United Nations Charter. It is a provocative step intended in reality not to maintain international peace and security but to foment criminal activities by elements of a fascist type in Hungary and to exacerbate the international situation.

Accordingly, the delegation of the Soviet Union regards the proposal of the United States, United Kingdom and French delegations that the question of the situation in Hungary should be placed on the agenda as a clear attempt at crude interference in the internal affairs of the sovereign Hungarian State, and will vote against the proposal.

. . .

Sir Pierson DIXON (UK): .   .   .   At this procedural stage of the discussion, I should like to confine myself to making two points.

First, I would—briefly, but categorically—deny the motives which the Soviet Union representative has imputed to my Government and the other two Governments which have joined us in submitting this question to the Council.

Secondly, I should like to say this: Mr. Sobolev has claimed that the Council is not competent to consider the matter raised by the three delegations. He has argued that the matter at issue is one of domestic jurisdiction and that Article 2, paragraph 7, of the Charter debars the Council from intervention. But what is the situation in Hungary which we are asking the Council to consider? The letter from the three representatives makes this quite clear. It is—to quote the letter—"the situation created by the action of foreign military forces in Hungary". Foreign troops are fighting in Hungary. This is obviously a matter of international concern. It seems to me clear beyond any doubt that the Security Council is competent; nor have I any doubt, in view of the gravity of the situation, that it is the Council's duty to consider the situation.

In fact, it seems clear beyond any need of further argument that the Council should adopt its agenda and proceed to an immediate discussion of the item before it. .   .   .

[The agenda was adopted by 9 votes to 1 (USSR), with 1 abstention (Yugoslavia).]

Sir Pierson DIXON (UK): .   .   .   After the Second World War, the Allied and Associated Powers, which of course included the Soviet Union, concluded a peace treaty with Hungary. This treaty was signed at Paris on 10 February 1947. I should like to read article 2, paragraph 1, of the treaty:

"Hungary shall take all measures necessary to secure to all persons under Hungarian jurisdiction, without distinction as to race, sex, language or religion, the enjoyment of human rights and of the fundamental freedoms, including freedom of expression, of Press and publication, of religious worship, of political opinion and of public meeting. .   .   ."

Can there be any doubt that what is being attempted is a repression by force of those very rights of the Hungarian people which are expressly secured by the Treaty of Peace with Hungary, a treaty signed between the Government of Hungary and the Allied and Associated Powers, among them the Government of the Soviet Union and her Majesty's Government in the United Kingdom? As signatories of that treaty we clearly have a responsibility to express our deep concern. But this is not all. The use of the armed forces of one country to restrain the peoples of another country in their domestic struggle for political freedom creates a situation fraught with danger to the community of nations, and is therefore a situation of which this Council clearly should take cognizance under Article 34 of the Charter.

Now I should not be surprised to hear it alleged . . . that the action which has been taken in Hungary is justified under the terms of the Warsaw Pact or, to give it its official title, the "Treaty of Friendship, Co-operation and Mutual Assistance" between the USSR, Albania, Bulgaria, Hungary, East Germany, Poland, Romania and Czechoslovakia, which was signed in Warsaw on 4 May 1955. It will no doubt be argued that, under that treaty, the Soviet Union has a right to station military forces in Hungary. That is as it may be, but does anything in that treaty justify the use of foreign forces in Hungary to repress a popular movement?

The Warsaw Pact purports to provide for collective defence between the members of the Soviet East European bloc against some possible external threat. I can find nothing in it—not that I would be impressed if I could—to permit the use of Soviet military forces in the countries of the other signatories, against the peoples of those countries, and in affairs which are the domestic concern of those people. Indeed, if one can take the wording of the Pact at its face value, special provision was made which would rule out any such thing. Under article 8 of the Pact the contracting parties affirm their adherence to "the principles of respect for each other's independence and sovereignty and of non-intervention in each other's domestic affairs". And yet what we see in the State of Hungary is the use of the armed might of the Soviet Union against the population of that sovereign State.

. . . .

Mr. VAN LANGENHOVE (Belgium): The events in Hungary have roused strong feelings throughout the world. Eye-witnesses have described the harrowing scenes which have occurred in the streets of Budapest and over wide areas of the country: the merciless shooting down of unarmed demonstrators, followed by desperate battles against heavily armed foreign troops. In such tragic circumstances, it is only natural that many people should turn to the United Nations and expect it to give them relief.

We cannot disappoint them. We are an organization dedicated to the maintenance of peace and security. We have promised the peoples of the world that we would devise methods to ensure that use should not be made of armed force, save in the common interest. One of our essential principles is respect for the right of peoples to self-determination, and in the Treaty of Peace with Hungary there is a solemn guarantee that the fundamental freedoms shall be respected. It is quite obvious that the cardinal rules upon which we have based not only international co-operation but our very civilization are at this moment being seriously violated. The Security Council, which holds a prominent place in our Organization and which is the only organ that is always in session, has been seized of this question, which has been brought before it by three of its permanent members through the regular procedure.

The representative of the Soviet Union, like the Hungarian Government, has contended that the item under discussion is a matter within the domestic jurisdiction of a State and that we are accordingly prohibited by the Charter from intervening.

Such an objection raised by the Soviet Union representative seems to me somewhat surprising. The Soviet Union has maintained again and again, both in the Security Council and in the General Assembly, even in cases where such provisions of the Charter could lawfully be invoked, that those provisions should not prevent intervention by the United Nations.

Furthermore, in the present case the letter which laid the matter before the Council refers to the action of foreign military forces in Hungary. On this occasion, it is precisely that element which invalidates the arguments drawn from Article 2, paragraph 7, of the Charter. It is alleged that the Soviet army intervened at the request of the Hungarian Government. But would that Government have been able to maintain itself in power without the support of the Soviet army?

Finally, there is yet another reason why the Soviet Union representative's attitude would seem to be at variance with the position hitherto adopted by his Government. I am referring to the principle which is mainly involved in the events in Hungary: that of the right of peoples to self-determination, a principle with which the Soviet Union has often shown itself strongly concerned in our debates. Are we to conclude that the Soviet Union's devotion to that principle is purely relative and is limited to cases in which that country's own interests are served by it? . . .

The question before us is simple and it cannot fail to have widespread repercussions throughout the world: can a foreign State by force of arms and by profuse bloodshed deprive a people of the right to govern itself freely in accordance with its own wishes? The Belgian delegation joins its voice to all those voices which cry out in reply: No.

NOTE. As no resolution was presented to the Council, the meeting was adjourned without any action. On 1 November 1956, the Nagy Government sent the following telegram to the Secretary-General of the United Nations:

"Reliable reports have reached the Government of the Hungarian People's Republic that further Soviet units are entering into Hungary. The President of the Council of Ministers in his capacity as Minister of Foreign Affairs summoned M. Andropov, Ambassador Extraordinary and Plenipotentiary of the Soviet Union to Hungary, and expressed his strongest protest against the entry of further Soviet troops into Hungary. He demanded the instant and immediate withdrawal of these Soviet forces. He informed the Soviet Ambassador that the Hungarian Government immediately repudiates the Warsaw Treaty and at the same time declares Hungary's neutrality, turns to the United Nations and requests the help of the four great

Powers in defending the country's neutrality. The Government of the Hungarian People's Republic made the declaration of neutrality on 1 November 1956. Therefore I request Your Excellency promptly to put on the agenda of the forthcoming General Assembly of the United Nations the question of Hungary's neutrality and the defence of this neutrality by the four great Powers." A/3251 (1 November 1956); GAOR, Annexes (ES–II) 5, p. 1.

On 2 November, the Hungarian Permanent Mission to the United Nations transmitted to the Secretary-General a letter from Mr. Nagy which confirmed the previous telegram and added the following information and request:

"On 2 of November 1956 further and exact information, mainly military reports, reached the Government of the Hungarian People's Republic, according to which large Soviet military units crossed the border of the country, marching towards Budapest. They occupy railway lines, railway stations and railway safety equipment. Reports also have come about that Soviet military movements of east-west direction are being observed on the territory of Western Hungary. . . .

"I request Your Excellency to call upon the great powers to recognize the neutrality of Hungary and ask the Security Council to instruct the Soviet and Hungarian Governments to start the negotiations immediately." S/3726 (2 November 1956); SCOR, XI, Supp. for Oct.–Dec. 1956, pp. 119–20.

On 2 November 1956, France, the UK and the US requested an urgent meeting of the Security Council in view of the "critical situation in Hungary." S/3723 (2 Nov. 1956); SCOR, *op. cit.*, p. 117. That meeting was held at 5 p. m. After a short dispute about the credentials of the Hungarian representative, the Council proceeded to consider "the situation in Hungary."

3. *Discussion in the Security Council, 2–4 November 1956.*

SCOR, XI, 752nd–754th Meetings.

Mr. LODGE (USA): Only yesterday the General Assembly met in an emergency session to consider the grave crisis in Egypt, and its members demonstrated a remarkable degree of unanimity in calling for a cessation of hostilities there. The danger of this situation has not lessened, and we must continue to give it our close attention, but at the same time the world community cannot afford to ignore the equally urgent and dangerous situation that is developing in Hungary. It cannot stand idly by while the people of Hungary are engaged in a desperate struggle to protect their national life.

The application of the principle of peace with justice cannot be restricted to one geographical area at a time. It is a universal principle that must be upheld in all cases and at all times.

Events in Hungary appear to have moved swiftly since the Council voted last Sunday to place on its agenda the item entitled "The situation in Hungary". We must give honest consideration to what the United Nations can do now to assist the brave Hungarian people in their struggle for freedom. We must now get all the facts, so that whatever we do will be done in a surefooted way and will be really helpful.

Events have moved so fast that we understand that arrangements made the other day to send new representatives to New York to represent Hungary have been cancelled. We believe, however, that the Council could best be assisted in its efforts to help Hungary if a representative of that State participated in our deliberations, and I think we should consider having the Secretary-General communicate with the Hungarian Government with a view to having a representative of the Government of Hungary appear before the Security Council as soon as possible. The situation in Hungary is so confused that it is necessary to comply with all the provisions of the rules in order to protect the interests of Hungary and of the Security Council as regards the representation of that country here. . . .

I therefore think that that should be the next step: to ascertain the facts. In helping the Hungarian people we must, above all, act with knowledge of the facts, and then the action that we take will be constructive and will be in the interests of peace and justice and national independence.

Mr. NUÑEZ PORTUONDO (Cuba): . . . The Cuban delegation believes that a draft resolution should be submitted as soon as possible, stating at least the three basic requirements which must be met. In the first place, it should contain an urgent appeal to the Government of the Soviet Union to withdraw its troops from Hungarian territory; this is in keeping with the provisions of the United Nations Charter. Secondly, it should expressly state, or rather reiterate, that the Hungarian people have the unquestionable right to determine, through free elections, the system of government under which they wish to live. Thirdly, it should provide for the establishment of a Security Council commission to supervise the position and to report on compliance with measures adopted by the Council to ensure the national independence and political freedom of the Hungarian people. . . .

Mr. BELAUNDE (Peru): . . . I have now received specific cabled instructions from the Peruvian Government to the effect that my delegation should maintain the juridical traditions of Peru and support any motion or resolution, either in the Council or in the General Assembly, which would guarantee to Hungary the right of self-determination and the freedom to establish its own structure as an independent nation. . . .

The United Nations Charter repeatedly refers to the right of self-determination. The United Nations is a family of nations. It is not merely a family of "States" but a family of "nations"; the concept of a "nation" is wider than that of a "State", in that it adds the idea of a spiritual community and a moral personality. . . .

The duty of the community of nations is to respect and safeguard the personality of each of its members, whose independent sovereignty, territorial integrity, institutional freedoms and chosen economic structure are the basic requirements for progress. For that reason, the United Nations admitted Hungary as a nation; it regarded Hungary as a moral and international entity, and in admitting Hungary it was thinking not of some particular government or régime representing a government but of the international personality of Hungary. Despite the surprising objections of the Soviet Union, I believe that we cannot contend for one single moment that the United Nations can remain indifferent and declare that it lacks the competence to take up the problem before us. This problem involves no less than the life, independence and freedom of one of the members of the international community to which we all belong. . . .

I therefore consider it essential that we should urgently, though not precipitately, adopt a resolution couched in noble and lofty terms and framed in such a manner that the Soviet Union could object to it only if it were prepared to violate the Charter, morality and, for that matter, common sense. I cling to the hope that no such objection will be forthcoming. If it should be made, we would have to bring the question before the supreme tribunal of the emergency special session of the General Assembly. The word "emergency" implies a provisional character, but momentous decisions may yet be taken and the emergency session may come to be regarded as a milestone in the establishment of lasting peace and justice. . . .

Mr. SOBOLEV (USSR): . . . The situation in Hungary does not warrant this emergency meeting of the Council. The counter-revolutionary uprising against the people's régime in Hungary has been suppressed by the action of the Hungarian authorities. The Soviet troops which had been brought in at the request of the Government of Hungary to assist in combating the uprising have been withdrawn from Budapest at the request of the Government of Hungary; on this point the Soviet Government has issued an official statement, dated 30 October. Let me quote a part of that statement:

". . . At the request of the Hungarian People's Government, the Soviet Government agreed to move Soviet military units into Budapest with a view to assisting the Hungarian People's Army and the Hungarian authorities to restore order in the city. Considering that the continued presence of Soviet military units in Hungary may have the effect of still further aggravating the situation, the Soviet Government has instructed its military command to withdraw Soviet military units from the city of Budapest as soon as this is thought necessary by the Hungarian Government.

"The Soviet Government also declared that it was prepared to enter into suitable negotiations with the Government of the Hungarian People's Republic. In this, the Soviet Government proceeds from the general principle that the troops of any State party to the Warsaw Pact are stationed on the territory of another State party to the Pact by agreement between all the parties thereto, and only with the consent of the State on whose territory such troops are, or are to be, stationed at its request. . . . ” . . .

Yesterday rumours were spread that the Soviet Government was moving additional armed forces into Hungarian territory. These statements, as also the statement made by Mr. Imre Nagy, are utterly unfounded, and in order to refute such fabrications the Soviet Government yesterday, through its Ambassador in Hungary, made a statement declaring that no additional Soviet troops had been brought into Hungary. . . .

In these circumstances, the Security Council has no grounds whatever for considering the situation in Hungary.

[As no resolution was presented to the Council at this meeting, the Council adjourned to 3 November, at 3 p. m. At that meeting the United States presented a draft resolution (S/3730), but no action was taken in view of news from Budapest that negotiations were being conducted for the withdrawal of Soviet troops. In view of the Soviet attack during the night of 3/4 November, a meeting of the Council was held at 3 a. m. on 4 November.]

Mr. LODGE (USA): If ever there was a time when the action of the United Nations could literally be a matter of life and death for a whole nation, this is that time. If ever there was a question which clearly raised a threat to the peace, this is the question. A few minutes ago, we received word of the appeal of the Prime Minister of Hungary for help from the whole world while his capital city is burning. . . .

We can truly say to the Hungarian people, "By your heroic sacrifice you have given the United Nations a brief moment in which to mobilize the conscience of the world on your behalf. We are seizing that moment, and we will not fail you."

[Mr. Lodge then presented to the Council the following draft resolution, revising slightly the text proposed on 3 November 1956 (S/3730/Rev. 1; SCOR, XI, Suppl. for Oct.–Dec. 1956, pp. 125–26):

"The Security Council,

"Considering that the United Nations is based on the principle of the sovereign equality of all its Members,

"Recalling that the enjoyment of human rights and of fundamental freedoms in Hungary was specifically guaranteed by the Peace Treaty between Hungary and the Allied and Associated Powers signed at Paris on 10 February 1947 and that the general principle of these rights and freedoms is affirmed for all peoples in the Charter of the United Nations,

"Convinced that present events in Hungary manifest clearly the desire of the Hungarian people to exercise and to enjoy fully their fundamental rights, freedoms and independence,

"Deploring the use of Soviet military forces to suppress the efforts of the Hungarian people to re-assert their rights,

"Noting moreover the declaration by the Government of the Soviet Union of 30 October 1956, of its avowed policy of non-intervention in the internal affairs of other States,

"Noting the communication of 1 November 1956 of the Government of Hungary to the Secretary-General regarding demands made by that Government to the Government of the Union of Soviet Socialist Republics for 'instant and immediate withdrawal of . . . Soviet forces',

"Noting further the communication of 2 November 1956 of the Government of Hungary to the Secretary-General asking the Security Council "to instruct the Soviet and Hungarian Governments to start the negotiations immediately' on withdrawal of Soviet forces,

"Anxious to see the independence and sovereignty of Hungary respected,

"1. Calls upon the Government of the Union of Soviet Socialist Republics to desist forthwith from any form of intervention, particularly armed intervention, in the internal affairs of Hungary;

"2. Calls upon the Union of Soviet Socialist Republics to cease the introduction of additional armed forces into Hungary and to withdraw all of its forces without delay from Hungarian territory;

"3. Affirms the right of the Hungarian people to a government responsive to its national aspirations and dedicated to its independence and well-being;

"4. Requests the Secretary-General in consultation with the heads of appropriate specialized agencies to explore on an urgent basis the need of the Hungarian people for food, medicine and other similar supplies and to report to the Security Council as soon as possible;

"5. Requests all Members of the United Nations and invites national and international humanitarian organizations to co-operate in making available such supplies as may be required by the Hungarian people."]

Mr. SOBOLEV (USSR): The Soviet delegation has no official information on the reports that have just been circulated about the new developments in Hungary. In these circumstances, the Soviet delegation considers that the more correct course would be for us to postpone consideration of this question until reliable information is available.

However, the majority of the Council members have unfortunately chosen a different course. On the basis of fragmentary, unconfirmed Press and radio reports, certain members of the Council have decided to force a discussion of the situation in Hungary on the Council. . . .

The representatives of the United States, the United Kingdom and France and other members of the Council have referred in their statements to the presence of Soviet forces in Hungary. This compels me to remind them of certain facts. The relations between the Soviet Union and the peoples' democracies are based primarily on the Warsaw Pact, under which the parties assumed certain political and military obligations, including the obligation to take such concerted action as might be necessary to reinforce their defensive strength, in order to defend the peaceful labour of their peoples, guarantee the inviolability of their frontiers and territories and afford protection against possible aggression. Soviet forces have been and remain on Hungarian territory pursuant to the Warsaw Pact. They are helping to put an end to the counter-revolutionary intervention and riots; the presence of Soviet forces in Hungary serves the common interest of the security of all the countries parties to the Pact. It was a measure taken to counter the militarization of Western Germany and the conclusion of military agreements of an aggressive nature between the United Kingdom, France, the United States and Western Germany.

In the light of the foregoing considerations it is quite plain that this question in no way concerns the United Nations or, in particular, the Security Council. Any intervention by the United Nations and the Western Powers in the further course of events in Hungary can only lead to complications, and would in any event be illegal and incompatible with the Charter. The delegation of the Soviet Union feels compelled to warn the Council that the United States, the United Kingdom and France, in placing this question on the Security Council's agenda, must bear full responsibility for such intervention. . . . .

A vote was taken by show of hands.

In favour: Australia, Belgium, China, Cuba, France, Iran, Peru, United Kingdom of Great Britain and Northern Ireland, United States of America.

Against: Union of Soviet Socialist Republics.

Present and not voting: Yugoslavia. [At the 755th meeting the representative of Yugoslavia stated that he wished his vote to be recorded as an abstention.]

The result of the vote was 9 in favour and 1 against.

The draft resolution was not adopted, the negative vote being that of a permanent member of the Council.

Mr. LODGE (USA): The Soviet Union has added another veto to the list of more than eighty by which it has thwarted the Security Council as the main organ for the maintenance of international peace and security. Soviet troops and tanks at this moment are annihilating the patriots of Hungary. We cannot afford to temporize over this cynical and brutal breach of the peace.

I therefore make the following motion to call an emergency special session of the General Assembly in accordance with rule 8(b) of the rules of procedure of the General Assembly:

"The Security Council,

"Considering that a grave situation has been created by the use of Soviet military forces to suppress the efforts of the Hungarian people to reassert their rights,

"Taking into account that because of the lack of unanimity among its permanent members the Security Council has been unable to exercise its primary responsibility for the maintenance of international peace and security,

"Decides to call an emergency special session of the General Assembly, as provided in General Assembly resolution 377A(V) of 3 November 1950, in order to make appropriate recommendations concerning the situation in Hungary."

Mr. SOBOLEV (USSR): We have already stated that any examination of the "situation in Hungary" in the Security Council is totally unjustified and constitutes an act of intervention in the domestic affairs of Hungary. The same criticism also applies to the proposal to refer the question to the General Assembly. The only purpose of the proposal to refer the situation in Hungary to a special session of the General Assembly can be to exacerbate still further a situation which is already difficult enough. It will not help to restore normal conditions, but is intended to fan still higher the flames of the recent disorders.

There is a further purpose behind the proposal to refer this question to a special session of the General Assembly. The Council is aware that a special session is now examining the question of a cease-fire and of the cessation of the hostilities undertaken against Egypt. The authors of this action, those who are chiefly responsible for the aggression committed against Egypt, are understandably feeling somewhat uncomfortable. They need a smoke-screen, and that is the purpose of the proposed discussion on the situation in Hungary.

It will, I believe, be understood why I shall vote against this proposal.

[The draft resolution was adopted by 10 votes to 1.]

4. *Discussion at the Second Emergency Special Session of the General Assembly, 4–10 November 1956.*

GAOR, ES–II, Plenary, pp. 2–7, 20, 41, 61–73.

Mr. SOBOLEV (USSR): The Soviet Union delegation objects to the inclusion in the agenda and to any discussion of the item entitled "The situation in Hungary", on the ground that such a discussion would be a gross breach of Article 2 of the United Nations Charter, which prohibits any intervention by the Organization in the domestic affairs of Member States.

For the same reasons, the Soviet delegation opposed the discussion of this question in the Security Council. It is regrettable that the majority of the members of the Council, acting in contravention of the United Nations Charter, tried to impose a discussion of this question on the Council. And now attempts are being made to impose the discussion of this question on the General Assembly.

It must be pointed out that the Security Council's decision to raise the question of the situation in Hungary was adopted in spite of the statement issued on 28 October 1956 by the legal government of the Hungarian People's Republic, categorically protesting against the discussion of any matters relating to the domestic affairs of Hungary in the United Nations, since the discussion of such questions in the United Nations would be a serious violation of the sovereign rights of the Hungarian People's Republic.

With regard to Mr. Nagy's communications to the United Nations, it must be borne in mind that these were unconstitutional, and are therefore invalid. The Nagy government has in fact collapsed, and a Revolutionary Workers' and Peasants' Government has been formed, which includes several ministers of the Nagy cabinet who have remained loyal servants of the Hungarian people. This Workers' and Peasants' Government has sent the Secretary-General a telegram to the effect that all communications from Mr. Nagy are invalid. The Government of Hungary, this declaration states, objects to any discussion of the situation in Hungary in the United Nations, either in the Security Council or in the General Assembly, since this is a matter within the domestic jurisdiction of Hungary.

Thus, the proposal for placing on the agenda and discussing the question of the situation in Hungary is motivated not by a desire to promote a return to normal conditions in the Hungarian People's Republic but, on the contrary, by a desire to aggravate the situation and to support fascist elements which have risen against the Hungarian people and its lawful government. Nor would such a step contribute in any way to furthering the high purposes and principles proclaimed in the United Nations Charter. This provocative move is really aimed not at the maintenance of international peace and security, in accordance with the Charter, but at aggravating the international situation.

The reasons for the attempt to involve the General Assembly in a discussion of the situation in Hungary just at this particular time are quite clear. The initiative in raising this issue was taken by the United Kingdom and France, which are engaging in open aggression against the Egyptian people, and by the United States, where certain groups have done everything in their power to prepare the way for the criminal attacks of fascist elements against the Hungarian people. By imposing a discussion of the item entitled "The situation in Hungary" on the General Assembly, they are hoping to distract the attention of the United Nations and of world public opinion from the aggressive action undertaken by the United Kingdom and France against Egypt. The Governments of the United Kingdom and France have rejected the General Assembly's cease-fire decision, thus flouting the wishes of the sixty-four States which resolutely supported the demand for the cessation of military operations.

Only yesterday, our Organization adopted a new decision calling for an immediate halt to military action against Egypt. By trying, in contravention of the Charter, to involve the General Assembly in a discussion of the situation in Hungary, the United Kingdom and France, together with the United States, are attempting to gain time and to enable the British-French forces to settle accounts with the Egyptian people.

The Soviet delegation expresses the hope that those who are genuinely concerned for the immediate cessation of British and French aggression against Egypt will refuse to allow the attention of the General Assembly and of our Organization as a whole to be distracted from the necessity of ensuring the implementation of its decision on the cessation of military activities against Egypt, or to authorize United Nations intervention in the domestic affairs of the Hungarian People's Republic. . . .

Mr. WALKER (Australia): This extraordinary session of the General Assembly has been called under the "Uniting for peace" procedure, provided for in resolution 377 (V), to deal with the situation in Hungary. . . .

I intervene at this point because Australia is a country that has always attached very great importance to the very consideration that the Soviet representative raised in his argument as to why this matter should not be dealt with, namely, the restrictions upon the right of the United Nations to deal with matters that are of purely domestic concern. I say that is a consideration that we always take very seriously in Australia, but we have no doubts that, in this particular matter, that objection is not a relevant one. . . .

Under the Treaty of Peace with Hungary of 10 February 1947, to which the Soviet Union, the United Kingdom, the United States and the other Allied and Associated Powers, including Australia, were parties, the Soviet Union was required to withdraw its troops from Hungary when Soviet occupation forces had been withdrawn from Austria. The Soviet forces in fact withdrew from Austria last year.

Article 2 of the political clauses of the Peace Treaty provides that:

"1. Hungary shall take all necessary measures to secure to all persons under Hungarian jurisdiction, without distinction as to race, sex, language or religion, the enjoyment of human rights and of the fundamental freedoms, including freedom of expression, of Press and publication, of religious worship, of political opinion and of public meeting."

These provisions were, of course, plainly inserted for the protection of the Hungarian people, who had and have a perfect right to require that they should be honoured. It is quite clear that in fact these provisions have over the years been substantially disregarded.

In order to circumvent these provisions about the withdrawal of its forces, the Soviet Union entered into a pact with the satellite countries, including Hungary. The Warsaw Pact of May 1955 provided for the use of Soviet troops to repel foreign aggression against the satellites. That this represented an intention to disregard the provisions of the Peace Treaty is now made clear, for it is the Warsaw Pact which the Hungarian Communist leaders have purported to invoke in calling into Hungary Soviet forces to suppress the present popular movement, and it is the Warsaw Pact that has been invoked in the discussions of the Security Council on occasion by the Soviet representative to justify the presence of Soviet troops in Hungary.

It is important to mention these facts in view of the argument advanced by the Soviet representative today.

It is the opinion of the Australian Government that it is quite impossible to contend that so clear a violation of a treaty as is constituted by the use of foreign forces to repress rights established by the Peace Treaty could be regarded as of no concern to the other nations parties to the Treaty. In other words, the setting at nought of a treaty provision does not become a domestic matter simply because the conflicts so engendered take place within the boundaries of one nation. . . .

Mr. SOLE (Union of South Africa): The representative of the Soviet Union, in objecting to the inscription of this item, has invoked the well-known Article 2, paragraph 7, of the Charter. This is an article with which, as members of the Assembly are aware, my delegation in particular is very familiar indeed. The South African delegations, at successive sessions of the General Assembly, have had occasion, I think on practically every occasion we have met in New York, to protest against what we have regarded as intervention in the affairs of South Africa, affairs which we regard as falling essentially within our domestic jurisdiction.

In these circumstances, we would be most careful before deciding to lend our support to any motion which might seem to run contrary to the principles which we have consistently applied since the first session of the General Assembly in 1946, the principles which we have applied even when it has been a most unpopular course to follow. I might recall, for example, that in 1946 South Africa was one of the very few countries which declined to support the resolution adopted by the Assembly in that year on conditions in Franco Spain.

It is against this background that we lend our earnest support to the proposal for the inscription of this item, because we are thoroughly satisfied in our own minds that Article 2, paragraph 7, of the Charter does not apply in this instance. We regret that the item has been designated "situation in Hungary". We feel that it would have been more appropriate to describe it as "external intervention in the internal affairs of Hungary".

We base our support for the inscription of this item not on the terms of the Peace Treaty to which reference has been made by the representative of Australia. They may or may not be relevant. We base our support for the inscription of the item on Article 2, paragraph 4, of the Charter which, *inter alia*, provides:

"All Members shall refrain in their international relations from the threat or use of force against the territorial integrity or political independence of any State."

In our view, the events of the past few hours have demonstrated clearly that both the threat of force and force have been employed against the political independence of Hungary, and we have received from the Soviet delegation no convincing arguments to the contrary.

. . .

The item was included in the agenda by 53 votes to 8, with 7 abstentions. . . .

Mr. LODGE (USA): At dawn this morning, Soviet troops in Hungary opened fire in Budapest and throughout the country. . . .

We must take drastic and decisive action here in this Assembly to answer the appeal of the Hungarian Government. The United States delegation, therefore, is submitting a draft resolution which we believe should be promptly put to the vote and which I would now like to read:

"The General Assembly,

"Considering that the United Nations is based on the principle of the sovereign equality of all its Members,

"Recalling that the enjoyment of human rights and of fundamental freedom in Hungary was specifically guaranteed by the Peace Treaty between Hungary and the Allied and Associated Powers signed at Paris on 10 February 1947 and that the general principle of these rights and this freedom is affirmed for all peoples in the Charter of the United Nations,

"Convinced that recent events in Hungary manifest clearly the desire of the Hungarian people to exercise and to enjoy fully their fundamental rights, freedom and independence,

"Condemning the use of Soviet military forces to suppress the efforts of the Hungarian people to reassert their rights,

"Noting moreover the declaration by the Government of the Union of Soviet Socialist Republics, of 30 October 1956, of its avowed policy of non-intervention in the internal affairs of other States,

"Noting the communication of 1 November 1956 of the Government of Hungary to the Secretary-General regarding demands made by that Government to the Government of the Union of Soviet Socialist Republics for the instant and immediate withdrawal of Soviet forces,

"Noting further the communication of 2 November 1956 from the Government of Hungary to the Secretary-General asking the Security Council to instruct the Government of the Union of Soviet Socialist Republics and the Government of Hungary to start the negotiations immediately on withdrawal of Soviet forces,

"Noting that the intervention of Soviet military forces in Hungary has resulted in grave loss of life and widespread bloodshed among the Hungarian people,

"Taking note of the radio appeal of Prime Minister Imre Nagy of 4 November 1956,

"1.   Calls upon the Government of the Union of Soviet Socialist Republics to desist forthwith from all armed attack on the peoples of Hungary and from any form of intervention, in particular armed intervention, in the internal affairs of Hungary;

"2.   Calls upon the Union of Soviet Socialist Republics to cease the introduction of additional armed forces into Hungary and to withdraw all of its forces without delay from Hungarian territory;

"3.   Affirms the right of the Hungarian people to a government responsive to its national aspirations and dedicated to its independence and well-being;

"4.   Requests the Secretary-General to investigate the situation, to observe directly through representatives named by him the situation in Hungary, and to report thereon to the General Assembly at the earliest moment, and as soon as possible suggest methods to bring an end to the existing situation in Hungary in accordance with the principles of the Charter of the United Nations;

"5.   Calls upon the Government of Hungary and the Government of the Union of Soviet Socialist Republics to permit observers designated by the Secretary-General to enter the territory of Hungary, to travel freely therein, and to report their findings to the Secretary-General;

"6.   Calls upon all Members of the United Nations to co-operate with the Secretary-General and his representatives in the execution of his functions;

"7.   Requests the Secretary-General in consultation with the heads of appropriate specialized agencies to inquire, on an urgent basis, into the needs of the Hungarian people for food, medicine, and other similar supplies, and to report to the General Assembly as soon as possible;

"8. Requests all Members of the United Nations, and invites national and international humanitarian organizations to co-operate in making available such supplies as may be required by the Hungarian people." . . .

Mr. DE GUIRINGAUD (France): I should like operative paragraph 4 of the United States draft resolution to be replaced by the following text:

"Requests the Secretary-General to investigate the situation caused by foreign intervention in Hungary, to observe the situation directly through representatives named by him, and to report thereon to the General Assembly at the earliest moment, and as soon as possible suggest methods to bring an end to the foreign intervention in Hungary in accordance with the principles of the Charter of the United Nations." . . .

Mr. LODGE (USA): Several members have spoken to me about this same amendment which the representative of France has suggested. That is what the language of the draft resolution means. Therefore, in the interests of clarity, I am glad to accept the amendment. I do so because of my extreme sense of urgency about the situation in Hungary. I am extremely anxious that we should act without delay.

[The draft resolution, as amended (Resolution 1004), was adopted on 4 November 1956 by 50 votes to 8 (Soviet bloc), with 15 abstentions (Afghanistan, Burma, Ceylon, Egypt, Finland, India, Indonesia, Iraq, Jordan, Libya, Nepal, Saudi Arabia, Syria, Yemen, Yugoslavia).

On 8 November 1956, the Secretary-General addressed an aide-mémoire to the Hungarian Government asking whether that Government would be willing to permit observers designated by him to enter the territory of Hungary, to travel freely within that country, and to report to him on their findings. A/3315 (8 Nov. 1956); GAOR, Annex (ES–II) 5, p. 3. It may be noted that main fighting ended in Hungary on that day. The General Assembly resumed its discussion on 8–10 November 1956.]

Mr. VITETTI (Italy): The task of the Assembly is too important and too urgent, and its time too precious, for me to make a speech. This is not the moment for eloquence, but the moment for action.

Four days have elapsed since the Assembly adopted resolution 1004 (ES–II) condemning the intervention of Soviet armed forces in Hungary. During those four days the massacres in Hungary have continued. Deaf to the decision of the Assembly and to the humanitarian appeal which came from it, Soviet troops have been fighting and killing Hungarian workers, peasants and students.

The news which comes from Hungary is appalling. Even though Hungary seems blacked out so that the world is kept in the dark about what is really happening, we have sufficient information to understand and realize that the heroic Hungarian people has been resisting with whatever forces it could in face of a violent and bloody repression.

The struggle now seems to be coming to its tragic end. Soviet armed forces are strangling the revolt of the Hungarian people, and now we are told that order has been restored. A Mr. Kádár, who styles himself "Prime Minister of the Revolutionary Workers' and Peasants' Government", has sent the Secretary-General a telegram saying that he objects categorically to any discussion of Hungarian events because that question is within the exclusive jurisdiction of the Hungarian People's Republic.

That telegram is really a tragic farce. It is a farce for the Hungarian Government to style itself "the Workers' and Peasants' Government", when the peasants and workers are massacred in Hungary by the Soviet soldiers, who imposed that government on them. It is a farce to deny the right of the United Nations to discuss events in Hungary when those events represent a brutal, cynical and murderous violation of the Charter. It is a farce to call events in Hungary domestic affairs when there is a foreign army which has taken possession of Hungary and is in complete control of its affairs.

We cannot rely on any statement whatever which comes or may come in the future from the so-called Hungarian Government. That Government has been created under the thunder of Soviet guns and the terror of Soviet invasion. It is not a government: it is a Soviet agency, and its voice is not the voice of the Hungarian people. The voice of the Hungarian people is the voice of the workers, the peasants and the students dying in their desperate struggle. It is not our right, but our duty to ignore the utterances of Mr. Kádár, whoever he is. It is our duty to continue along the road which we have chosen, and on that we must be resolute and firm.

Soviet troops must leave Hungary, and they must leave Hungary immediately. A foreign army which has been committing the crime of decimating the Hungarian population to such an extent that it must be considered an act of genocide can no longer be allowed to remain in Hungary. Hungary must be free. The Hungarian people must be given the right to choose its own government through free elections, as is done in every civilized country. That is what we must demand, and demand now.

On those lines, my delegation together with the delegations of Cuba, Ireland, Pakistan and Peru, has prepared a draft resolution which I shall now read out to the General Assembly:

"The General Assembly,

"Noting with deep concern that the provisions of its resolution 1004 (ES–II) of 4 November 1956 have not as yet been carried out and that the violent repression by the Soviet forces of the efforts of the Hungarian people to achieve freedom and independence continues,

"Convinced that the recent events in Hungary manifest clearly the desire of the Hungarian people to exercise and to enjoy fully their fundamental rights, freedom and independence,

"Considering that foreign intervention in Hungary is an intolerable attempt to deny to the Hungarian people the exercise and the enjoyment of such rights, freedom and independence, and in particular to deny to the Hungarian people the right to a government freely elected and representing their national aspirations,

"Considering that the repression undertaken by the Soviet forces in Hungary constitutes a violation of the Charter of the United Nations, of the Peace Treaty between Hungary and the Allied and Associated Powers and of the Convention on Genocide,

"Considering that the immediate withdrawal of the Soviet forces from Hungarian territory is necessary,

"1.   Calls again upon the Government of the Union of Soviet Socialist Republics to withdraw its forces from Hungary without further delay;

"2.   Considers that free elections should be held in Hungary under United Nations auspices, as soon as law and order have been restored, to enable the people of Hungary to determine for themselves the form of government they wish to establish in their country;

"3.   Reaffirms its request to the Secretary-General to continue to investigate, through representatives named by him, the situation caused by foreign intervention in Hungary and to report at the earliest possible moment to the General Assembly;

"4.   Requests the Secretary-General to report in the shortest possible time to the General Assembly on compliance."

In my opinion, it is imperative that the United Nations should state in a clear, definite and precise way, the necessity for and urgency of the withdrawal of Soviet troops from the scene of their crimes. It is imperative that we should provide for free elections in Hungary. It is imperative that we should help the Hungarian people to reconstruct its free life, to be what it wants to be: a free people among free peoples.

I am not unaware of the grave difficulties which must be met. We shall face them. We shall explore the possibility of further action. The conditions in Hungary are appalling, and the help of the United Nations will be necessary. The Italian delegation considers, above all, that it will be necessary to provide for a United Nations commission to proceed to Hungary, and that it will be necessary, in order to protect peace and order, to establish a United Nations police force. We reserve the right to present, at a later stage, definite proposals on these lines. . . .

Mr. JOJA (Romania): . . . In view of the new draft resolution submitted to the Assembly, I feel bound once again to draw attention to certain aspects of this matter which are becoming increasingly plain. First, it should be emphasized that the rapid succession of texts, each less well founded than its predecessor, shows that the General Assembly of the United Nations is now the scene of persistent efforts to involve the Organization more and more deeply in a problem which is outside its competence and thereby to weaken its authority, to exacerbate and exasperate the international situation and to maintain a state of unrest prejudicial to peace. It is obvious that the sponsors of the draft resolution disregard the principle in law that a people has the right to organize its own system of national representation and elections without any outside interference in violation of that principle.

It is equally obvious that the five-Power draft resolution, regarding the question of the Soviet troops in Hungary which helped the Government to restore order and eliminate the threat to that country's democratic institutions, is in fact directed against the Warsaw Treaty. In other words, it is directed against the right of Hungary and the other countries parties to that Treaty to follow a foreign policy that furthers the interest of peace and their national security and independence.

As is well known Romania is a party to the Warsaw Treaty, whose underlying principle is the defence of the collective security of the European States against the threat of aggression. The Warsaw Treaty was born of the need to defend the peace and security of the peoples of Eastern Europe and, thereby, the security of all the European peoples. It is based on the United Nations Charter, is consistent with the Charter, and is a pillar of world peace.

It is unthinkable that the United Nations should have any right to consider the question of the modification, termination, or even interpretation of a treaty which was freely accepted and is in keeping with the interests of Hungary and the other signatory States. It is obvious that the draft resolution seeks implicitly to attain that objective. Such a position is wholly unwarranted, particularly as some of the States whose delegations sponsored the draft resolution are themselves parties to certain military alliances, such as the Paris Agreements providing for the re-armanent of Western Germany, whose aggressive purposes led to the conclusion of the defensive Warsaw Treaty.

It is clear that intentions such as those expressed in the draft resolution are far-reaching and have nothing to do with the Hungarian people and their interests. The Romanian Government considers that the proper way to solve the Hungarian problem is through the application of the programme of the Revolutionary Workers' and Peasants' Government, which provides for broad measures to restore Hungary's economy and to further its progress on the basis of a freely elected people's democratic régime. My delegation is persuaded that nothing can prevent the Hungarian people from developing socialism.

The situation in Hungary has already improved substantially from every point of view. The Romanian delegation wishes again to state its opinion that it is a grave error and an unacceptable violation of the Charter to attempt to associate the United Nations with the fascist elements who tried to overthrow the democratic régime established by the Hungarian people and to undermine Hungary's security. For these reasons the Romanian delegation will vote against the draft resolution before the Assembly. . . .

Mr. Krishna MENON (India): . . . [M]y delegation desires to submit with respect that we are not giving sufficient thought and attention to the resolving of the problems and the difficulties that exist in Hungary at the present moment. There was no one here who does not appreciate that there has been fighting, suffering and unsettlement and that there is not the stability required. Any decisions that we adopt here must be directed to the improvement of those conditions. Furthermore, my delegation cannot subscribe at any time to any phraseology or proposals before the Assembly which disregard the sovereignty of States represented here. For example, we cannot say that a sovereign Member of this Assembly, admitted after due procedures, can be called upon to submit its elections and everything else to the United Nations without its agreement. Therefore, any approach that we make as though this is a colonial country which is not represented at the United Nations, is not in accordance either with the law or the facts of the position.

With regard to the subject matter, it has disturbed our minds and caused my Government and people a great deal of anxiety; . . . we have, as a Government, as all Governments do, the right to exert what influence we have and make such approaches as are possible to assist in resolving this problem and to bring about a situation where the Hungarian people will be able to settle down to constructive tasks and enjoy their national independence.

I am to say that in the correspondence between the Prime Ministers of the Soviet Union and India, the last part of which was communicated from New Delhi and received here this afternoon, the Soviet Government informed us of a determination to deal with its relationships with their neighbouring socialist States on the principles of mutual respect of their sovereignty, territorial integrity, and friendship, co-operation and non-interference in the internal affairs of each other. This appears in the declaration of the Soviet Government of 30 October, and it is reiterated.

There is the problem of the Soviet troops. The Government of India is informed that Soviet troops are to be withdrawn from Budapest in agreement with the Hungarian Government as soon as order is restored. And the Russian Government intends to start negotiations with the Hungarian Government in regard to Soviet-Hungarian relations in conformity with this declaration.

It is entirely up to the Assembly to make its own decision with re-gard to these matters. As far as our Government is concerned, we have made efforts in this direction with a view to attaining the ends that are put forward in these resolutions. In agreement with Yugo-slavia, Poland and other countries, who are very near to Hungary and whose problems though not identical are of a similar character, we think that we should not do things here merely out of emotion or other reactions or out of our political predilections, forgetting the interests of the Hungarian people and of the Hungarian State. Therefore, any attitude which is taken which will retard this process of the with-drawal of troops and the settling down of the Hungarian people will be contrary to our general purposes.

For those reasons, we think that the five-Power draft resolution is not one which we can support. We consider that it will not assist in the purposes in which the Assembly has interested itself. . . .

Mr. GUNEWARDENE (Ceylon): . . . [We] are able to sup-port very strongly the request made in the previous resolution, as well as in the draft resolution that has been placed before us, for the withdrawal of all foreign forces from Hungary and also that no fur-ther military forces should be brought into Hungary for any purpose whatsoever. . . .

We certainly denounce armed intervention in the affairs of a coun-try, whichever that country may be. I freely admit that there was a Warsaw Treaty, under which Soviet troops had the right to be in Hun-gary, a reason which certainly could not cover the action of the United Kingdom and France in Egypt. If comparisons are being made, how-ever odious it may be, it is sometimes necessary to point out such facts.

My Government holds the view that, whether for reasons of restor-ing order or in the name of peace, we do not want foreign forces to interfere in the internal affairs of a country, whatever pacts there may be. The Government of Ceylon does not believe in military pacts and has always denounced them. These actions are sometimes the results of military pacts. We do not believe in military pacts. I hope that Soviet Russia will not plead the Warsaw Pact in order to keep its forces in Hungary. . . .

As regards the political issues, I state again in categorical language that we are pledged to the upholding of the democratic ideal. We who believe in democracy would like to see the right of self-determination be given to every country of the world. We believe in the freedom of speech, we believe in the freedom of assembly, we believe in the free-dom of the people to vote a government out of office. We believe that it is the right of a people to determine what their future should be.

Therefore, we would always welcome free elections. But in the name of free elections I would certainly not support the five-Power draft resolution because it serves no practical purpose. I certainly would like to have free elections—in the way I think they are free— in Russia, in Poland, in Romania, in Eastern Germany, in Hungary, in all countries of the world, and even in some of those other democratic countries with different political ideologies. There are also others with the name of democracy, with the name of freedom, who do not have the same concept of democracy as I have. There are countries in the world who believe that sometimes the bullet is superior to the ballot. But we who believe in the supremacy of the ballot would like to have seen free elections.

The mere moving of a resolution to the effect that we should like to have free elections in Russia, in Poland, in Hungary, and in these countries will not secure the result. It may have excellent propaganda value, but I am not a party to that business. We are not aligned with any power politics. We are not aligned with any power blocs. We only deal with questions as and when they arise. With regard to the present occasion, the bringing into this resolution something in connexion with elections and asking the United Nations to interfere with the sovereign rights of peoples is a dangerous principle. On the present occasion it may sometimes suit the fancies and the wishes of several Members. But they must visualize the time when such interference may be possible even in the domain of their own affairs.

Therefore, on principle, I would not have the United Nations interfering in elections. How are elections to be held? Surely elections must be held on the basis of a constitution. Did it not take Pakistan eight years to draft a constitution? Are we going to say that elections are to be held pending a constitution? Are we going to wait for eight years for it? No, I certainly do not say so. Elections therefore must be based on a constitution, and a constitution can be drafted only after peoples have expressed their wishes. It is a long process. The mere saying that elections must be held means nothing.

Let us get down to practicalities. It is all very well to talk of free elections. I believe in free elections. My country believes in free elections and all of us believe in free elections. But the mere adoption of a draft resolution in this form does not bring about free elections. Therefore, I have no alternative but to say that I cannot understand how this should be interposed in the draft resolution, asking the United Nations to do something which is impossible of achievement. Of course, I have no doubt that it is also premature, because we have already assigned to the Secretary-General a task of first-class importance, of great magnitude, to survey the position and to submit a report to us. It is only after the observers have gone in, if they do go there—and that must be at the express wish of the Government of the country—and it is only after the submission of a report that we can get down to the practical business of what we should do: whether elections are to be held, what elections should be held, and what should be done next.   It is like putting the cart before the horse.   I am not prepared, therefore, in the name of propaganda, or in the name of revenge, or in the name of anything else, to subscribe to something that is utterly futile.   In those circumstances I have no alternative but to oppose that draft resolution, though with much regret.   .   .   .

U PE KIN (Burma): My delegation has already made its position clear on the question of Soviet intervention in Hungary.   For the benefit of those who may still be in doubt, may I be allowed to repeat that my Government does not see any justification whatever in the course which the Soviet Union has taken in Hungary and has expressed the hope that the Soviet Union would take steps to effect speedy withdrawal of its troops from there.   My delegation also added that the Government of Burma would support any effort of the United Nations which is not incompatible with the Charter or which the people of Hungary will not consider as tantamount to interference in their internal affairs. My delegation reaffirms its adherence to that declaration.

We now have before us a five-Power draft resolution.   It will be recalled that on 4 November a resolution was adopted by the Assembly to deal with the situation in Hungary.   That resolution directed the Secretary-General to take certain actions, one of them being to get in touch with the parties concerned in Hungary.   The Secretary-General has reported to the Assembly that he has addressed an *aide-mémoire* to the Hungarian authorities on the subject and circulated it to the Assembly yesterday.   We have received no further progress report from him and my delegation therefore cannot appreciate the necessity for the draft resolution I have just referred to at this stage.

My delegation does not want to give any impression that it is opposed to the entire draft resolution.   For example, my delegation is perfectly agreeable to the expression of deep concern that the provisions of the previous resolution have not been met.   We support the view that the Hungarian people should enjoy freedom, independence and fundamental rights.   We also consider that the Soviet Union's interference cannot be condoned as it constitutes a violation of the Charter.   We have also expressed the hope that the Soviet Union will withdraw its troops speedily from Hungary.   We also endorse the fact that the Secretary-General should continue to make every endeavour to obtain further particulars on the situation existing in Hungary.

But where does all this repetition of previous resolutions of the Assembly on the subject lead us?   With due respect to the representatives who have sponsored this draft resolution, my delegation could find no constructive contribution in it towards a solution of the problem.   It has only afforded further expressions of feelings of outrage.

Then, there is the question of elections as soon as law and order have been restored.   That, in the opinion of my delegation, is the concern of the Hungarian people, and it is not for us to proffer suggestions. What do we mean by the term "as soon as law and order have been restored"?   My delegation assumes that it envisages a situation following the withdrawal of the Soviet troops, and not before.   Then, it is entirely up to the people of Hungary to say whether they want assistance from the United Nations in holding their elections.

If this contention of my delegation is erroneous, and if the draft resolution envisages a situation while the Soviet Union troops are still in Hungary, then it is impracticable and would remain only a pious wish.

For these reasons, and for no other, my delegation finds it difficult to vote in favour of the draft resolution, but, because it contains, in several other paragraphs, sentiments which we fully share, my delegation will not oppose it.   We shall abstain.

[The five-Power draft resolution was adopted on 9 November 1956, as Resolution 1005 (ES–II), by 48 votes to 11 (Soviet bloc, India and Yugoslavia), with 16 abstentions (Afghanistan, Austria, Burma, Cambodia, Ceylon, Egypt, Finland, Haiti, Indonesia, Jordan, Lebanon, Libya, Nepal, Saudi Arabia, Syria, Yemen).

The General Assembly also adopted Resolutions 1006 (ES–II) and 1007 (ES–II) calling for humanitarian assistance to the people of Hungary and to refugees from Hungary.   GAOR, ES–II, Supp. 1, p. 3.]

5.   *Cablegram from the Ministry of Foreign Affairs of Hungary to the Secretary-General, 12 November 1956.*

A/3341 (12 Nov. 1956); GAOR, Annexes (XI) 67, p. 4.

In connexion with the notifications of the Secretary-General of the United Nations concerning the resolutions of the General Assembly accepted on 4 and 10 November 1956, the Revolutionary Workers and Peasants' Government of the Hungarian Peoples' Republic deems it necessary to state the following:

In the past weeks, mass demonstrations took place in Hungary, the democratic and patriotic demands of which the Revolutionary Workers' and Peasants' Government has accepted as its own.   From the beginning the participants of these demonstrations included organized Fascist elements, and later ordinary criminals also who escaped from prison.   These persons meanwhile gradually took the lead and carried off and murdered hundreds of progressive-minded people and members of their families.

In this situation, the first task was the restoration of law and order, the prevention of the danger of fascism, which task Hungary has, in article 4 of the Treaty of Peace, also undertaken to carry out.

In the serious situation which arose, the Revolutionary Workers' and Peasants' Government could restore law and order only by requesting the aid of Soviet troops.   After the complete restoration of order, the Hungarian Government will immediately begin negotiations with the Government of the Soviet Union for the withdrawal of these troops from Hungary.

On the basis of the foregoing, the Hungarian Government most emphatically states the settlement of the situation which has arisen in Hungary lies exclusively within the internal legal competence of the Hungarian State.   Therefore, any resolution of the General Assembly relating to the internal political situation of Hungary constitutes an interference in Hungarian internal affairs and is in contradiction with the provisions of Article 2, paragraph 7, of the Charter.

Accordingly,

1.   The Hungarian Government and the Soviet Government are exclusively competent to carry on negotiations concerning the withdrawal of the Soviet troops from Hungary, which troops are here only for the purpose of restoring law and order and do not take any measures against the population which are contrary to international law and the principles of humanity.

2.   In view of the fact that Soviet troops are in Hungary at the request of the Hungarian Government, the Hungarian Government is decidedly of the opinion that the sending of representatives to be appointed by the Secretary-General of the United Nations is not warranted.

3.   The holding of elections in Hungary is entirely within the competence of the Hungarian authorities.

In connexion with the resolution on Hungarian refugees, the Hungarian Government states that it will make [it] possible for Hungarian citizens who have fled abroad as a result of the battles to return freely and without harm.

The Hungarian Government accepts with sincere thanks the humane resolutions of the General Assembly which are in conformity with Article 1, paragraph 3, of the United Nations Charter and aim to assist the Hungarian people; and communicates that it will facilitate with every means the receipt and distribution of food and medicine sent for the Hungarian people, and is at present also co-operating with the representatives of the International Red Cross Committee.   The Soviet troops in Hungary do not hinder this relief work in any way.   In carrying out this task, the Hungarian Government is prepared to co-operate most fully with the agencies of the United Nations.

6.   Decisions of the Eleventh Session of the General Assembly, 1956–1957.

NOTE. At the eleventh session of the General Assembly the Soviet bloc raised again objections to the competence of the Assembly to deal with the situation in Hungary, but the Assembly included the item in its agenda on 13 November 1956, by 62 votes to 9, with 8 abstentions.   GAOR, XI, General C., pp. 1–2; *idem*, Plenary, pp. 18–23.

In November and December efforts were made to send observers to Hungary and the Secretary-General sought to visit Budapest in order to discuss the humanitarian assistance by the United Nations to Hungary. In view of the negative attitude of the Hungarian Government, none of these steps could be taken.

During the eleventh session the General Assembly adopted several resolutions on Hungary in which, *inter alia:*

(a) The Assembly recalled "the principles of the Charter of the United Nations, in particular the principle embodied in Article 2, paragraph 4, the obligations assumed by all Member States under Articles 55 and 56 of the Charter, the principles of the Convention on the Prevention and Punishment of the Crime of Genocide, in particular article II(c) and (e), to which Hungary and the Union of Soviet Socialist Republics are parties, and the Treaty of Peace with Hungary, in particular the provisions of article 2"; and urged "the Government of the Union of Soviet Socialist Republics and the Hungarian authorities to take immediate steps to cease the deportation of Hungarian citizens and to return promptly to their homes those who have been deported from Hungarian territory." Resolution 1127 (XI), of 21 Nov. 1956; GAOR, XI, Supp. 17 (A/3572), p. 63. This was adopted by 55 votes to 10, with 14 abstentions.

(b) The Assembly accepted a proposal by Ceylon, India and Indonesia, urging Hungary to accede to the request of the Secretary-General for admission of observers "without prejudice to its sovereignty." Resolution 1128 (XI) of 21 Nov. 1956, adopted by 57 votes to 8, with 14 abstentions (Chile, China, Cuba, Dominican Republic, Egypt, Ethiopia, Jordan, Panama, Paraguay, Poland, Saudi Arabia, Syria, Yemen, Yugoslavia). GAOR, *op. cit.,* p. 63.

(c) After noting "with deep concern that the Government of the Union of Soviet Socialist Republics has failed to comply with the provisions of the United Nations resolutions calling upon it to desist from its intervention in the internal affairs of Hungary, to cease its deportations of Hungarian citizens and to return promptly to their homes those it has already deported, to withdraw its armed forces from Hungary and to cease its repression of the Hungarian people", the Assembly reiterated "its call upon the Government of the Union of Soviet Socialist Republics and the Hungarian authorities to comply with the above resolutions and to permit United Nations observers to enter the territory of Hungary, to travel freely therein and to report their findings to the Secretary-General"; recommended that "the Secretary-General arrange for the immediate dispatch to Hungary, and other countries as appropriate, of observers named by him pursuant to paragraph 4 of General Assembly resolution 1004 (ES–II) of 4 November 1956"; and requested "all Member States to co-operate with the representatives named by the Secretary-General by extending such assistance and providing such facilities as may be necessary for the effective discharge of their responsibilities." Resolution 1130 (XI), of 4 Dec. 1956, adopted by 54 votes to 10, with 14 abstentions. GAOR, *op. cit.,* pp. 63–64.

(d) After considering "that recent events have clearly demonstrated the will of the Hungarian people to recover their liberty and independence" and noting "the overwhelming demand of the Hungarian people for the cessation of intervention of foreign armed forces and the withdrawal of foreign troops", the Assembly declared that, "by using its armed force against the Hungarian people, the Government of the Union of Soviet Socialist Republics is violating the political independence of Hungary"; condemned "the violation of the Charter of the United Nations by the Government of the Union of Soviet Socialist Republics in depriving Hungary of its liberty and independence and the Hungarian people of the exercise of their fundamental rights"; reiterated "its call upon the Government of the Union of Soviet Socialist Republics to desist forthwith from any form of intervention in the internal affairs of Hungary"; called upon the Government of the Union of Soviet Socialist Republics "to make immediate arrangements for the withdrawal, under United Nations observation, of its armed forces from Hungary and to permit the re-establishment of the political independence of Hungary"; and requested "the Secretary-General to take any initiative that he deems helpful in relation to the Hungarian problem, in conformity with the principles of the Charter and the resolutions of the General Assembly." Resolution 1131 (XI), of 12 Dec. 1956, adopted by 55 votes to 8, with 13 abstentions (Afghanistan, Cambodia, Egypt, Finland, India, Indonesia, Jordan, Morocco, Saudi Arabia, Sudan, Syria, Yemen, Yugoslavia). GAOR, *op. cit.*, p. 64.

(e) In order to make available "the fullest and best available information regarding the situation created by the intervention of the Union of Soviet Socialist Republics, through its use of armed force and other means, in the internal affairs of Hungary, as well as regarding developments relating to the recommendations of the General Assembly on this subject", the Assembly established "'a Special Committee composed of representatives of Australia, Ceylon, Denmark, Tunisia and Uruguay, to investigate, and to establish and maintain direct observation in Hungary and elsewhere, taking testimony, collecting evidence and receiving information, as appropriate, in order to report its findings to the General Assembly." Resolution 1133 (XI), of 10 Jan. 1957, adopted by 59 votes to 8, with 10 abstentions (Afghanistan, Cuba, Egypt, Finland, India, Jordan, Saudi Arabia, Sudan, Syria, Yugoslavia). GAOR, *op. cit.*, pp. 64–65.

For a summary of the United Nations efforts to find a constructive solution of the Hungarian problem, see the Annual Report of the Secretary-General, of 25 June 1957; GAOR, XII, Supp. 1 (A/3594), pp. 31–46.

7.   *Possibility of Further Action.*

Statement by Mr. Belaunde (Peru), 9 January 1957.
GAOR, XI, Plenary, pp. 836–38.

The United Nations faces a very serious problem: defiance by one of the great founding Powers of the Organization—after the United States of America the strongest world power—of the resolutions adopted at its second emergency special session by the General Assembly which, and I wish to emphasize these words, deal with matters relating to world peace and were adopted in pursuance and on the basis of explicit provisions of the Charter.

I have emphasized those words because, although it is true that the majority of General Assembly resolutions do not have the character or binding force of decisions of the Security Council, it is also true that

such resolutions are concerned with the general welfare and not with
the actual application of the Charter; they are not resolutions adopted
under the "Uniting for Peace" resolution, as an emergency measure,
when the Security Council is prevented from acting.

This defiance by a great Power, this repeated defiance—not mere
forgetfulness, inattention or ignorance, but open defiance publicly announced from this rostrum—is a fact of the gravest significance; it
constitutes a direct threat and a most serious danger to the existence
of the United Nations.   .   .   .

Is the General Assembly to remain paralysed? Is it to remain, in
the words of a famous Peruvian leader, aggrieved but inactive in the
face of an impotent public opinion? Can we say that it is enough for
us to deplore the failure of the Soviet Union to comply with those resolutions, and to remain unmoved, impassive, and resigned to such a situation? No; for the honour of the Assembly forbids it. Duty, which
is akin to honour, forbids it, duty that is one aspect of honour; indeed, one of its noblest manifestations.

It is the duty of the Assembly to do what it can to secure compliance
with its resolutions; and there is something which it can do: it can
continue to mobilize public opinion, it can continue to express censure.
The cry, *"J'accuse"*, does not fade away because it is shouted only
once; it echoes forever. And the position of the Soviet Union in this
Assembly is an unhappy one: although exercising a right, it is the
object of universal, unanimous censure on the part of the Assembly.
.   .   .

In the case of the defiance by a Member State of specific resolutions
—not the resolutions of the regular type dealing with the general welfare and with economic or cultural co-operation among States, but
specific resolutions dealing with peace and based on the principles of
the Charter. What are the terms of the problem? It is whether the
Assembly is empowered only to make recommendations under Chapter
VI of the Charter, which refers to the pacific settlement of disputes.
Can it not also make recommendations under Chapter VII? We know
it cannot take decisions, because the power to do so is vested in the
Council. Are the powers established under Chapter VII solely confined
to the Security Council? Do they not extend to the Assembly, when
the latter is exercising the functions of the Council in accordance with
the interpretation placed on the Charter by the "Uniting for Peace"
resolution?

We must bear in mind that it is the United Nations as a whole which
is responsible for maintaining peace. It exercises that function either
through recommendations of the General Assembly or through decisions of the Security Council; but nobody believes that the maintenance of peace is the exclusive province of the Security Council. When
we adopted the "Uniting for Peace" resolution, we clearly established
the fact that the relevant Articles of the Charter referred to the United

Nations and not merely to the Council. Consequently, if it is true that
the maintenance of peace, either through recommendations under
Chapter VI or under Chapter VII, is a matter for the United Nations,
and that the Security Council's inability to take action does not mean
that the United Nations remains crippled, hamstrung and powerless,
but rather that the Council's powers are temporarily transferred to
the General Assembly in emergency situations, why, then, cannot the
Assembly exercise the powers provided for in Chapter VII? Why
cannot the Assembly adopt not a decision, but a recommendation, urging certain Member States to break off or reduce or curtail their diplomatic relations with the Soviet Union and the Government of Hungary,
the *de facto* Government of Hungary, the Government in Hungary supported by Soviet tanks? Is there any legal reason—I am not speaking
about the political aspect of the matter—why the Assembly should not
recommend the rupture of economic relations with that great Power
and with the Government of Hungary? Is there any reason why it
should not take that course?

I shall be told that sanctions presuppose an unequivocal and fully
defined legal obligation and not merely a moral obligation. Non-compliance with a moral obligation calls for moral sanctions; non-compliance with a legal obligation requires legal sanctions. An Assembly
recommendation obviously imposed a weighty moral obligation upon
the Soviet Union, but, it will be said, it cannot be claimed that a recommendation acquires a strictly and unequivocally legal character,
simply because it is an Assembly recommendation. We are mobilizing
and bringing into play all the moral forces of the world to censure the
Soviet Union for its failure to comply with its moral obligation; but,
it will be argued, we cannot go beyond that, because then we should be
assuming the existence of a legal obligation.

I venture to disagree with that view for the following reason. I ask
you whether the obligations laid down in the United Nations Charter,
the duties which the United Nations Charter places on the Members of
the United Nations in virtue of the fact that it constitutes a multilateral agreement, whether these obligations represent moral or legal obligations? Will anyone dare to maintain that they are purely moral
obligations? Who will dare affirm that the avoidance of the use of
force contrary to the principles of the Charter or against the independence and sovereignty of a State is a moral obligation? No one. It is
a legal obligation. The principle of non-intervention, which is implied
or expressly stated in the Charter and is moreover a well established
principle of international law, does it impose a moral or a legal obligation? No one can claim that the principle of non-intervention establishes a moral obligation. It establishes a legal obligation.

Thus, the Assembly's directions are legally binding, not only because
the Assembly has assumed a function of the Council, but mainly because it is prescribing simply what the United Nations Charter prescribed, and its resolution merely gives effect to, and interprets, the

Charter in a specific case. Accordingly, no jurist can argue that a resolution adopted on a matter relating to peace at an emergency Assembly session, based expressly on the terms of the Charter, involves nothing more than a moral obligation for the Soviet Union, for the countries allied with it, and for Hungary. It involves a legal obligation.

For these reasons, we would have a perfect right to apply sanctions because of non-compliance with a legal obligation in the present instance, with respect to the failure of the Soviet Union to comply with the United Nations Charter; sanctions proposed by an overwhelming majority of the United Nations.

I would remind you . . . that the resolutions adopted by the General Assembly on Hungary were adopted by an overwhelming majority, and that the abstentions did not represent negative or opposing votes, because the countries which abstained made it clear, either by voting in favour of another resolution or through the statements of their representatives and official spokesmen, that they condemned the Soviet Union's intervention in Hungary and the presence of Soviet troops in Hungarian territory. Thus, with the exception of the countries, at present allied to communism, which understandably adopted an attitude of opposition, the whole world has called upon the Soviet Union to withdraw from Hungary and has reminded Hungary—as the Prime Minister of India did so eloquently—of the Soviet Union's obligation to withdraw its troops.

We are therefore confronted with a clear and conclusive legal case. I should like to state that, with respect to non-compliance with Assembly resolutions based on the Charter, there is no legal bar to our taking all the measures provided for in the Charter to secure compliance with the legal obligations which the Charter has imposed on all Member States. But I shall be told that there is another side to the matter, which rebuts my arguments. Let us look at the rebuttal in the light of logic and with philosophical detachment. If my argument were not valid, if the Assembly possessed only the very limited power to make abstract or moral declarations which might be extremely valuable, but would have no legal force, what would be the position of the other States?

Perhaps, through some significant historical coincidence, two problems have come before the Assembly, the two problems it has dealt with in its emergency special sessions, on which it has adopted resolutions which are not based on Chapter VI alone, because measures for the withdrawal of troops and establishment of a cease-fire come under Article 40, and it will be recalled that Article 40 is part of Chapter VII of the United Nations Charter.

Among the measures to secure peace there is a category intermediate between what we might call peace and coercive action to secure peace—the category of provisional measures which come under Chapter VII. We have already taken such measures. There is thus a legal precedent for the United Nations taking measures which have the practical effect of halting action in a conflict. A cease-fire and the withdrawal of its troops—was this not what we asked of the Soviet Union? We called upon France, the United Kingdom and Israel to institute a cease-fire, and did we not have every justification for requesting the Soviet Union to do likewise? We have called upon it to withdraw its tanks and to desist from slaughtering poor defenceless women, students and children. We have called upon it to withdraw from the territory of Hungary where it had no authority or justification for being. . . .

Let us assume that we have, on the one hand, a moral recommendation with respect to which our only recourse is to mobilize public opinion and, on the other hand, a moral obligation which has been given legal force and has been complied with, having been treated by other Powers as a legal obligation.

If we accept the view that resolutions adopted by the General Assembly on the question of peace involve a moral obligation only, what would be the position of those Powers which have interpreted the obligation imposed by such resolutions as being legal as well as moral and have immediately fulfilled it, thus honouring the pledge they gave when they signed the United Nations Charter? What double standard would we have? We would be dividing countries into those which comply with the law and those that do not. The former would be confronted with the full weight of moral sanctions and the latter with inertia, indulgence and collusion through inaction. No, we cannot accept such a state of affairs. Those countries which have fulfilled the moral and legal obligations deriving from the Charter should be proud of the fact that they have done so and we express our appreciation of their action. Sound indeed is the democratic form of government. A definition of democracy has just occurred to me: it is a form of government in which there is room for the honourable and beneficial rectification of errors. On the strength of this definition, I would tell the Soviet Union that its régime today is one in which there is never room for the honourable, human and beneficial rectification of errors. To err is human. To correct errors is more than human, it is to do honour to mankind. Not to correct errors out of pride, perversity or obstinacy is more than inhuman, it is fiendish.

On the basis of the jurisprudence recently developed, the obligations imposed upon the Soviet Union under General Assembly resolutions are legal obligations, because they are a re-statement of the principles of the Charter and because, if these principles are to be applied, they must clearly be interpreted. If it were left to any Power to interpret the Charter subjectively, its provisions would never be carried into effect.

The Charter is interpreted by the General Assembly. When the Assembly comes to apply the Charter in a specific case when it says to a Power: "Comply with Article 2, paragraph 4, of the United Nations Charter", such an injunction has a two-fold face—the legal force derived from a treaty and the moral force derived from the Assembly's high moral and legal authority. But then I will be told that life is very complex and that there is more to this than the legal aspect. I should have liked this legal aspect to have been studied by a commission so that it could have been laid before the United Nations with greater skill than I possess. I should have liked a committee of legal experts, of representatives with a legal background, assisted by the best experts of the United Nations Office of Legal Affairs and of United States universities, to have made a complete analysis of the binding effect of General Assembly resolutions based on the application of the Charter in specific cases. Perhaps there is still time to carry this idea into effect.

I fully realize that, apart from this clear-cut legal aspect, political issues are also involved which are primarily of concern not to us, but to the countries which can effectively impose the legal sanctions of which I have been speaking. Such sanctions might well give rise to a grave situation; far from resolving the problem, concentration on its theoretical legal aspects might lead to a *de facto* situation conducive to a heightening of international tension and might bring about conditions even more unpropitious to the unfortunate people of Hungary. But that is a political consideration and I do not propose to pursue the legal argument to its conclusion, because the political aspects are a matter not for the small Powers but for the great.

We have faith in the United States. Never has the course followed by the United States been as brilliant and splendid as in recent years. We are proud to share with it the traditions of freedom, the common heritage of democracy and the principles of Christian civilization. I have never been given to flattery. I have spent my life in criticism and condemnation. If in the autumn, I might say, in the winter of my life, I venture to utter words of praise, I do so only out of a profound sense of conviction and duty.

I respect the reserve of the United States at this time and that of the United Kingdom and France, countries with which we have many cultural and political ties. I shall not therefore go into the matter. However, though I may not be in a position to present a definite proposal calling for specific measures, there is no reason why I should not outline the necessary measures with a view to arousing the conscience of mankind; once world public opinion has been mobilized behind an appeal to the Soviet Union to fulfil its moral and legal obligations, circumstances may so change that it may be possible for us to give full effect to the "Uniting for Peace" resolution and to the lofty and unequivocal provisions of the United Nations Charter on non-intervention and respect for the sovereignty and independence of all States.

. . . .

The virtues of diplomacy and of politics are patience and persever-ance. Let us be patient, but with perseverance, with energy, with zeal and above all with unity. The example of Hungary represents a dan-ger for all the peoples of the world; it is a living example given us by Providence of what an extension of the Soviet régime would mean to the other peoples of the world. While it has sometimes been said "Workers of the world, unite"—a union that in many respects has much of fundamental justice and morality—I would say from this ros-trum "Free peoples of the world, unite to impose justice and peace".

NOTE.—1. See also Thomas J. Dodd, "Our Missed Opportunities in Hungary," *in his* Freedom and Foreign Policy (New York, 1926), pp. 31–38.

2. The Committee appointed under the General Assembly Resolution 1132 (XI) presented its report to the General Assembly in June 1957. Some of the findings of the Committee are reproduced in Document 1, above; others are quoted in the General Assembly Resolution 1133 (XI), reproduced in No. 8, below. In discussing the legal basis for Soviet action, the Committee made the following statement:

"The official explanations formulated by the USSR and Kádár Govern-ments for the Soviet military interventions in Hungary . . . were that on 23 October . . ., and again on 4 November, 'anti-democratic ele-ments' brought about serious disturbances of public order and created 'the danger of a non-democratic fascist-type system opposed to social progress coming into being'. Exercising the sovereign right of a State 'to take through its government any measures it considers necessary and proper in the interest of guaranteeing the State order and the peaceful life of the population', the Hungarian Government has 'called for the assistance of Soviet troops stationed in Hungary under the Warsaw Defense Treaty so as to avoid further bloodshed and disorder and to defend the democratic order and people's power. With this step the Government warded off anarchy in Hungary and the creating of a situation which would have seriously im-perilled peace and security'. As to the Nagy Government, it had collapsed and its communications to the United Nations had no legal force. As these occurrences had no effect on international peace and security, and related to events within Hungary, or only to the application of an international treaty 'under the exclusive purview of the Hungarian and Soviet Governments and of the other Member States of the Warsaw Treaty', the United Nations could not intervene or even consider the matter by virtue of paragraph 7 of Article 2 of the Charter.

"While the latter was the only provision of the United Nations Charter mentioned, two provisions of other international instruments were referred to in the statement of the Soviet and the Kádár Governments' position. Firstly, that of article 4 of the Hungarian Peace Treaty which created an obligation for Hungary not to permit in the future 'the existence and ac-tivities of organizations of a fascist-type on Hungarian territory, whether political, military or para-military'; secondly, that of article 5 of the Warsaw Treaty providing for 'concerted action' by the contracting parties 'necessary to reinforce their defensive strength, in order to defend the peaceful labour of their people, guarantee the inviolability of their frontiers and territories and afford protection against possible aggression'.

"In the course of the lengthy debates which the Security Council and the General Assembly devoted to the Hungarian question, these and other arguments were abundantly discussed by representatives of Member States. The provisions of article 2 of the Hungarian Peace Treaty guaranteeing human rights and fundamental freedoms, including political rights, to the Hungarian people; the principles and the character of the Warsaw Treaty as a defensive arrangement against an external aggression; the unacceptability of the position that armed forces stationed in a foreign country by virtue of a defensive alliance against outside aggression might be used to quell popular movements aiming at a change of government or of régime; the protests against the Soviet intervention and demands to the Soviet Union and to the United Nations for the withdrawal of Soviet forces put forward by the properly constituted Government of Imre Nagy; the doubtful constitutional nature of the Kádár Government at the time of its call for Soviet military assistance —all these arguments were invoked against the thesis of the Soviet Government and the Kádár Government, together with the Charter provisions on sovereign equality of Member States, the principles of equal rights and self-determination of peoples and those of paragraph 4 of Article 2 of the Charter prohibiting the threat or use of force against the political independence of any State. All these considerations led to the solemn declaration by the General Assembly in resolution 1131 (XI) of 12 December 1956 that 'by using its armed force against the Hungarian people, the Government of the Union of Soviet Socialist Republics is violating the political independence of Hungary'; and to the condemnation by the same resolution of the 'violation of the Charter of the United Nations by the Government of the Union of Soviet Socialist Republics in depriving Hungary of its liberty and independence and the Hungarian people of the exercise of their fundamental rights'.

"The Committee does not consider it necessary to review these arguments anew. It wishes merely to refer to its findings and conclusions contained in other chapters of this Report which directly bear on the assumption on which are built the Soviet and the Hungarian Governments' legal and political explanations namely, that the uprising was not of a fascist or anti-democratic character as these terms are generally understood; that armed Soviet assistance was sought in all probability before a peaceful demonstration had taken on a violent character and that whether the intervention took place in a regular or irregular manner under the terms of Hungarian constitutional processes is a matter which the Committee was not able to ascertain; that Imre Nagy's Government, whose legitimacy during the events was uncontested, had taken practical steps for re-establishing public order and conditions for a normal pursuit of peaceful activities of the people, and was reconstituting a democratic and parliamentary régime which would have given to all Hungarians the exercise of political and human rights; that the Nagy Government was endeavouring to bring about the withdrawal and not the intervention of the Soviet armed forces, the presence of which it did not find necessary to maintain itself in power; and that Mr. Kádár's Government, on the other hand, not only was established because of the assistance of the Soviet armed forces, but could not under the terms of the Hungarian Constitution claim any but the most doubtful element of legality at the time of its appeal to the Soviet Command for intervention. The Committee's conclusions support, therefore, the assumptions on which were based the resolutions of the General Assembly on the question of Hungary and, in particular, resolution 1131 (XI). . . .

"Leaving aside arguments of a juridical nature, it appeared quite clear to the Committee that the Soviet military intervention had its essential reason in the desire to save a political régime, and retain a military ally within its area of economic dominance. As reported by the Budapest Radio, on 15 November 1956, Mr. Kádár explained to a delegation of the Greater Budapest Workers' Council that 'we were compelled to ask for the intervention of Soviet troops . . . It has been made clear by the events of the past weeks that we were threatened with the immediate danger of the overthrow of the people's power . . . We realized that this whole movement could not be described as a counter-revolution, but we would have been blind if we had ignored that, apart from the deep indignation felt over grave mistakes and the just demands of the workers, there were also counter-revolutionary demands . . . It was in such a situation that some of us reached the conclusion that, first of all and by all means, even with the help of Soviet troops, the counter-revolution must be broken by the people's power consolidated with the help of armed workers . . .' At the sixth session of the USSR Supreme Soviet held in February 1957, Mr. Shepilov stated that 'By assisting the Hungarian people, the USSR did its international duty to the working people of Hungary and other socialist countries, in keeping with the interest of world peace', and in the 'Joint Declaration of the Government of the Soviet Union and the Government of the Hungarian People's Republic', issued upon the conclusion of the negotiations held between the two Governments in Moscow from 20 March to 28 March 1957, it was again stated that 'The participation of Soviet Army units in crushing the fascist rebels was a supreme act of proletarian solidarity'. György Marosán, former First Deputy Chairman of the Council of Ministers in the Hegedüs Government and at present Minister of State in the Kádár Government, speaking in Republic Square in Budapest on 29 March 1957 and recalling that during the night of 23–24 October 1956 he personally had demanded that Soviet troops be called in, seems to have correctly summarized the situation from the point of view of the present rulers of Hungary by saying: 'We know but one legality: the legality of the Revolution.'" GAOR, XI, Supp. 18 (A/3592), pp. 51–52.

8. *Resolution 1133 (XI) of the General Assembly, 14 September 1957.*

GAOR, XI, Supp. 17A (A/3572/Add. 1), p. 1.

The General Assembly,

Recalling its resolution 1132 (XI) of 10 January 1957, establishing a Special Committee, consisting of representatives of Australia, Ceylon, Denmark, Tunisia and Uruguay, to investigate, and to establish and maintain direct observation in Hungary and elsewhere, taking testimony, collecting evidence and receiving information, as appropriate,

Having now received the unanimous report of the Special Committee on the Problem of Hungary,

Regretting that the Union of Soviet Socialist Republics and the present authorities in Hungary have failed to co-operate in any way with the Committee,

1. Expresses its appreciation to the Special Committee on the Problem of Hungary for its work;

2. Endorses the report of the Committee;

3. Notes the conclusion of the Committee that the events which took place in Hungary in October and November of 1956 constituted a spontaneous national uprising;

4. Finds that the conclusions reached by the Committee on the basis of its examination of all available evidence confirm that:

(a) The Union of Soviet Socialist Republics, in violation of the Charter of the United Nations, has deprived Hungary of its liberty and political independence and the Hungarian people of the exercise of their fundamental human rights;

(b) The present Hungarian régime has been imposed on the Hungarian people by the armed intervention of the Union of Soviet Socialist Republics;

(c) The Union of Soviet Socialist Republics has carried out mass deportations of Hungarian citizens to the Union of Soviet Socialist Republics;

(d) The Union of Soviet Socialist Republics has violated its obligations under the Geneva Convention of 1949;

(e) The present authorities in Hungary have violated the human rights and freedoms guaranteed by the Treaty of Peace with Hungary;

5. Condemns these acts and the continued defiance of the resolutions of the General Assembly;

6. Reiterates its concern with the continuing plight of the Hungarian people;

7. Considers that further efforts must be made to achieve the objectives of the United Nations in regard to Hungary in accordance with the Purposes and Principles of the Charter and the pertinent resolutions of the General Assembly;

8. Calls upon the Union of Soviet Socialist Republics and the present authorities in Hungary, in view of evidence contained in the report, to desist from repressive measures against the Hungarian people, to respect the liberty and political independence of Hungary and the Hungarian people's enjoyment of fundamental human rights and freedoms, and to ensure the return to Hungary of those Hungarian citizens who have been deported to the Union of Soviet Socialist Republics;

9. Requests the President of the eleventh session of the General Assembly, H.R.H. Prince Wan Waithayakon, as the General Assembly's special representative on the Hungarian problem, to take such steps as he deems appropriate, in view of the findings of the Committee, to achieve the objectives of the United Nations in accordance with General Assembly resolutions 1004 (ES-II) of 4 November 1956,

1005 (ES-II) of 9 November 1956, 1127 (XI) of 21 November 1956, 1131 (XI) of 12 December 1956 and 1132 (XI) of 10 January 1957, to consult as appropriate with the Committee during the course of his endeavours, and to report and make recommendations as he may deem advisable to the General Assembly;

10. Decides to place the Hungarian item on the provisional agenda of the twelfth session of the General Assembly.

NOTE.—1. A special report of the Special Committee, of 14 July 1958, dealt with the execution of Nagy, Maleter and two associates on 16 June 1958. A/3849; GAOR, Annexes (XIII) 69, pp. 1–5. The execution was denounced by the General Assembly in Resolution 1312 (XIII), of 12 December 1958, which also called upon the USSR and the authorities in Hungary "to desist from repressive measures against the Hungarian people and to respect the liberty and political independence of Hungary," and appointed Sir Leslie Munro "to represent the United Nations for the purpose of reporting . . . . on significant developments relating to the implementation of the Assembly resolutions on Hungary." GAOR, XIII, Supp. 18 (A/4090), pp. 59–60.

2. For the reports of the United Nations Special Representative on the Question of Hungary, see UN Docs. A/4304 (21 Nov. 1959), GAOR, Annexes (XIV) 74, pp. 2–7; A/4606 (1 Dec. 1960); A/4996 (1 Dec. 1961), GAOR, Annexes (XVI) 89, pp. 2–5; and A/5236 (25 Sept. 1962), GAOR, Annexes (XVII) 85, pp. 1–5. On 20 December 1962, the General Assembly decided to discontinue the position of the United Nations Special Representative on Hungary. Resolution 1857 (XVII); GAOR, XVII, Supp. 17 (A/5217), p. 11.

3. For comments on the Hungarian situation, see Samir N. ANABTAWÏ, "The Afro-Asian States and the Hungarian Question," 17 Int.Org. (1963), pp. 872–900; G. BARRACLOUGH, "Poland and Hungary" *in* ROYAL INSTITUTE OF INTERNATIONAL AFFAIRS, Survey of International Affairs, 1956–1958 (London, 1962), pp. 72–138; Neal v. BUHLAR, "The Hungarian Question," in Ernst C. HELMREICH, ed., Hungary (New York, 1957), pp. 352–89; Stanley HOFFMAN, "Sisyphus and the Avalanche: The United Nations, Egypt, and Hungary," 11 Int.Org. (1957), pp. 446–69; HUNGARIAN LAWYERS' ASSOCIATION, Some Comments on the Juristic Aspects of the "Hungarian Question" (Budapest, 1957), 28 pp.; INTERNATIONAL COMMISSION OF JURISTS, The Hungarian Situation and the Rule of Law (The Hague, 1957), 144 pp.; Imre KOVACS, Facts about Hungary (New York, 1958), 280 pp.; Melvin J. LASKY, ed., The Hungarian Revolution: The Story of the October Uprising (New York, 1957), 318 pp.; Dietrich A. LOEBER, "Hungary and the Soviet Definition of Aggression," 2 IRD (1957), pp. 46–58, 78–85; R. St. J. MACDONALD, "Hungary, Egypt and the United Nations," 35 Canadian Bar R. (1957), pp. 38–71; Tibor MERAY, Thirteen Days That Shook the Kremlin (New York, 1959), 290 pp.; Richard I. MILLER, Dag Hammarskjöld and Crisis Diplomacy (New York, 1961), pp. 126–56; Sir Leslie Knox MUNRO, "Hungary and Suez: Problems of World Order," 12 Record of the Association of the Bar of the City of New York (1957), pp. 12–29; Joseph A. SZIKSZOY, The Legal Aspects of the Hungarian Question (Geneva thesis No. 147; Ambilly-Annemase, France, 1963), 218 pp.; Ferenc A. VALI, "The Hungarian Revolution and International Law," 2 Fletcher Review (1959), No. 1, pp. 9–25; Ferenc A. VALI, Rift and Revolt in Hungary: Nationalism versus Com-

munism (Cambridge, Mass., 1961), 590 pp.; David W. WAINHOUSE and others, International Peace Observation: A History and Forecast (Baltimore, Md., 1966), pp. 461–71; Quincy WRIGHT, "Intervention, 1956," 51 AJIL (1957), pp. 257–76; Paul ZINNER, ed., National Communism and Popular Revolt in Eastern Europe: A Selection of Documents on Events in Poland and Hungary (New York, 1957), 563 pp.; Paul E. ZINNER and Christopher EMMET, "Should U. S. Have Helped Hungary More?", 36 Foreign Policy Bull. (1957), pp. 132–35.

LEBANESE QUESTION

NOTE. The Lebanese crisis of 1958 had two aspects: an insurrection supported by foreign elements, and United States intervention to assist the Lebanese Government.

Since the Suez invasion in 1956, the United States was preoccupied with the rising unrest in the Middle East. On 5 January 1957, President Eisenhower addressed a special message to Congress requesting an authorization for providing military assistance to nations in the Middle East which request such aid. A resolution embodying this "Eisenhower Doctrine" was enacted on 9 March 1957. It authorized the President "to undertake, in the general area of the Middle East, military assistance programs with any nation or group of nations of that area desiring such assistance. Furthermore, the United States regards as vital to the national interest and world peace the preservation of the independence and integrity of the nations of the Middle East. To this end, if the President determines the necessity thereof, the United States is prepared to use armed forces to assist any such nation or group of such nations requesting assistance against armed aggression from any country controlled by international communism." Apart from the members of the Baghdad Pact, only Lebanon welcomed the new policy. US, DOS, American Foreign Policy: Current Documents, 1957 (Washington, D.C., 1961), pp. 783–91, 829–31, 835–36. See also John C. CAMPBELL, "From 'Doctrine' to Policy in the Middle East," 35 Foreign Affairs (1957), pp. 441–53; Lazar FOCSANEANU, "La 'doctrine Eisenhower' pour le Proche-Orient," 4 AFDI (1958), pp. 33–111.

A constitutional crisis in Lebanon led in May 1958 to large-scale disturbances and the occupation of parts of Lebanese territory by forces hostile to the Government. On 22 May 1958, Lebanon submitted to the Security Council a complaint charging "the intervention of the United Arab Republic in the internal affairs of Lebanon." S/4007 (23 May 1958); SCOR, XIII, Supp. for April-June 1958, p. 33.

1. *Discussion in the Security Council, 6–11 June 1958.*

SCOR, XIII, Mtgs. 823–24.

Mr. MALIK (Lebanon): . . . Lebanon placed its present complaint first before the League of Arab States. We are a member of that regional organization and we wanted its machinery to deal first with our issue. Then we brought it to the attention of the Security Council. . . .

The Arab League has been in session for six days on this question. It has taken no decision on it. Consequently, the Government of Lebanon is now bound, much to its regret, to press this issue before the Security Council. . . .

The case which we have brought to the attention of the Security Council consists of three claims. The first is that there has been, and there still is, massive, illegal and unprovoked intervention in the affairs of Lebanon by the United Arab Republic. The second is that this intervention aims at undermining, and does in fact threaten, the independence of Lebanon. The third is that the situation created by this intervention which threatens the independence of Lebanon is likely, if continued, to endanger the maintenance of international peace and security. I now proceed to the proof of these three claims.

The actuality of the intervention is proven by adducing six sets of facts concerning:

a. The supply of arms on a large scale from the United Arab Republic to subversive elements in Lebanon;

b. The training in subversion on the territory of the United Arab Republic of elements from Lebanon and the sending back of these elements to Lebanon to subvert their Government;

c. The participation of United Arab Republic civilian nationals residing in or passing into Lebanon in subversive and terrorist activities in Lebanon;

d. The participation of United Arab Republic governmental elements in subversive and terrorist activities and in the direction of rebellion in Lebanon;

e. The violent and utterly unprecedented press campaign conducted by the United Arab Republic against the Government of Lebanon;

f. The violent and utterly unprecedented radio campaign conducted by the United Arab Republic inciting the people of Lebanon to overthrow their Government. . . .

There are several thousand armed men engaged in subversive activities in Lebanon today. Most of these men operate near the Syrian borders in the north of Lebanon, in the Beqaa valley, and in the south. We have no doubt at all, from all the evidence that we have gathered, that all the arms that these men use were supplied them from Syria.
. . .

No region in the whole world is more sensitive than the Near East. Interference by States in one another's affairs in that area is certain to have international repercussions. There is the most delicate balance of forces and powers there; let this balance be but slightly upset and incalculable consequences could ensue. Therefore, a situation like ours, with such possibilities of development, is exactly one with which the Security Council should be concerned. This is what we have done by calling the attention of this Council to our case. . . .

We ask this Council, then, to bring its wisdom into play, to the end that the unprovoked massive intervention stop, that our independence, to which we have every right, be preserved and indeed strengthened, and that as a result the threat to international peace and security inherent in this situation be removed. . . .

Mr. LOUTFI (United Arab Republic): . . . This complaint and the tendentious propaganda surrounding it, which endeavours to make use of the Security Council for the settlement of domestic questions, cannot but impair the prestige of the Council. . . .

According to information I have received today, six States of the Arab League, namely the Sudan, Saudi Arabia, Iraq, Jordan, Libya and Yemen, submitted a resolution, which was unfortunately not accepted by the Lebanese Government. I have before me the text of this resolution which, with your permission, I shall read out:

"The Council of the League of Arab States, at its extraordinary session held at Benghazi, examined the complaint submitted by the Government of the Lebanese Republic against the United Arab Republic.

"Having heard the statements of the delegations of the Lebanese Republic and the United Arab Republic; having noted the wish of both parties to settle their differences in a peaceful manner within the League of Arab States; in accordance with the letter and the spirit of the Pact of the League of Arab States, and desirous of removing anything which disturbs the atmosphere of calm among the brotherly Arab States:

"The Council decides:

"(1) To do all in its power to put an end to anything which may disturb the atmosphere of calm among member States;

"(2) To request the Government of Lebanon to withdraw the complaint it has placed before the Security Council;

"(3) To appeal to the various Lebanese groups to end the disturbances and to take the necessary measures to settle domestic disputes by peaceful and constitutional means;

"(4) To send a committee selected from among the members of the Council to ease the situation and to give effect to the decision of the Council."

This resolution, which we accepted in a spirit of conciliation, was in our view capable of settling the dispute we are discussing today. Unfortunately the Lebanese Government, for reasons of which I am unaware, opposed it. . . .

The disorders now occurring in Lebanon are due mainly to the fact that President Chamoun wishes to continue in office for a second term contrary to the provisions of the Constitution, and proposes to revise the latter so that he may again be a candidate for the presidency of the Republic in the forthcoming elections.

According to statements made by the members of the Opposition, elections held in Lebanon last year are another cause of these disorders: the present Lebanese Government is accused of having manipulated the elections in order to secure the return of the governmental candidates. . . .

In a memorandum submitted to the United States Ambassador at Beirut, the National Front, which consists of the Opposition parties, states that "the present national movement is in no way actuated by any doctrine of foreign origin but is strictly domestic in character." In its closing passages, the memorandum gives an assurance that "the movement is fully aware of the foreign interests in Lebanon, which it will do nothing to injure." (*Le Monde*, 17 May 1958, p. 7.)

Moreover, I should like to recall that, when forming the National Front, the members of the Opposition issued a statement in which they proclaimed as a first principle of their political action the maintenance of Lebanon's independence, sovereignty and defence by every possible means and in whatever circumstances. . . .

According to the Press and to information which has reached us, political parties and Lebanese organizations, including the National Front, notified the Secretary-General of the United Nations of their opposition to the submission of this complaint to the Security Council. The National Front stressed that it regarded the dispute as one of exclusively domestic concern. It protested against such recourse to the Council, urged the need for immediate rejection of the complaint and drew attention to the fallacious character of the points raised, which could not but impair the good neighbourly relations naturally linking two sister countries and dangerously increase the tension prevailing in Lebanon. . . .

Before concluding, I should like to recall a statement made by the President of the United Arab Republic on 16 May 1958: . . .

"In the name of the people of the United Arab Republic I repeat what I have already said: we support and respect the independence of Lebanon and we shall not permit interference in its affairs."

From all the foregoing it is clear that it has not been established that the United Arab Republic has intervened in the domestic affairs of Lebanon. As I have said again and again, the question is a purely domestic concern of Lebanon. The events in Lebanon concern only the Lebanese. It is their duty, and theirs alone, to put an end to them. The international diversion which the present Government of Lebanon is seeking to create by this unjustified complaint could not be a real solution of the problems.

Moreover, this Lebanese domestic problem is not and could not be a threat to international peace. The present situation is the result of political differences which divide the Lebanese themselves and it is for them alone to find the solution. . . .

Mr. SOBOLEV (USSR): . . .   After hearing the statement made by Mr. Malik, the Minister of Foreign Affairs of Lebanon, I must say that my first impression was that Mr. Malik had not submitted convincing evidence of intervention by the United Arab Republic in Lebanon's domestic affairs. . . .

Moreover, the fact that the Lebanese complaint was submitted simultaneously to the Arab League and the Security Council (and it was in fact submitted simultaneously) also gives room for thought. Has the Lebanese Government really made an effort to settle its differences with the neighbouring United Arab Republic through the normal means prescribed by the United Nations Charter, namely, first of all by a bilateral or regional settlement? . . .

Secondly, there is one fact which leads me to take a somewhat guarded view of the information submitted by the Minister of Foreign Affairs of Lebanon. I have before me a statement made by the Lebanese Opposition parties on 22 May 1958, which reads as follows:

"Responsible leaders in Lebanon are seeking to cover up the failure of their regime by bringing charges against the United Arab Republic which are refuted by both the facts and causes underlying events in Lebanon. This is being done in order to give the domestic crisis an international colouring and to justify a demand for foreign intervention and the landing of foreign troops in Lebanese territory." It is clear that the landing of foreign troops mentioned here does not mean forces of Arab origin, but a landing by other troops. . . .

So far as the Soviet Union is concerned, we consider that the solution of questions affecting the Lebanese State is the inalienable prerogative of the Lebanese people and that no other State is entitled to interfere in its affairs. Any attempt to take advantage of domestic events in Lebanon for the purpose of external intervention creates a dangerous situation in the Near East and may have serious consequences not only for the future of the Lebanese State and its independence, but also for peace in the Near and Middle East. . . .

Mr. JARRING (Sweden): In the complaint which is now before the Council a Member State has alleged that another Member State has, by its actions, brought about a situation the continuance of which is likely to endanger the maintenance of international peace and security. Under the Charter, the Security Council may investigate such a situation and, if it so deems appropriate, recommend methods of adjustment. In order to enable the Council to perform this task, the parties must present to the Council detailed information concerning, on the one hand, the evidence which forms the basis of the allegation and, on the other hand, the arguments which may be brought forward in refutation. If this information is considered inadequate, the Council may arrange for an investigation, for instance, by establishing an investigation or observation commission. Such a measure should not be taken, however, unless the complaining party has produced convincing *prima facie* evidence that actions or omissions by the other party have contributed to the creation of the situation and that that situation does in fact endanger the maintenance of international peace and security. Furthermore, experience tends to show that a decision to undertake an investigation can hardly yield a positive result unless both parties have declared themselves willing loyally to co-operate in the investigation.

With regard to the present complaint, the Council is faced in the first place with the question whether the disturbances in Lebanon are caused by internal antagonisms or are provoked by a foreign Power. In the former case, possible action by the Council is greatly restricted, in consequence of the provisions of Article 2, paragraph 7, of the Charter; in the latter case, the Council would be free to act.

The Government of Lebanon has presented strong and precise allegations tending to show that foreign interference has in fact taken place. This interference is said essentially to have taken the form of illegal imports of arms and illegal entry of armed persons into Lebanon, as well as of propaganda in support of the rebels. These allegations have been categorically repudiated by the Government of the United Arab Republic.

My delegation feels that the Security Council has reason to give the statements of the parties serious consideration and to keep a close watch on the situation and its further development. It is evident that foreign interference may contribute to the aggravation of internal antagonisms in Lebanon and make a settlement difficult. If such interference has occurred, it is deeply to be deplored, and every effort should be made to bring about a correction. In these circumstances there may be justification for considering some arrangement of investigation or observation by the Council itself with a view to clarifying the situation. Such a measure might itself further contribute to the creation of a less tense atmosphere in connexion with the Lebanon situation. . . .

The text of the draft resolution that I wish to submit to the Council is the following:

"The Security Council,

"Having heard the charges of the representative of Lebanon concerning interference by the United Arab Republic in the internal affairs of Lebanon and the reply of the representative of the United Arab Republic,

"1. Decides to dispatch urgently an observation group to proceed to Lebanon so as to ensure that there is no illegal infiltration of personnel or supply of arms or other matériel across the Lebanese borders;

"2.   Authorizes the Secretary-General to take the necessary steps to that end;

"3.   Requests the observation group to keep the Security Council currently informed through the Secretary-General."

NOTE.   The Swedish draft resolution was adopted on 11 June 1958, by 10 votes to none.   The USSR abstained in view of the fact that neither the UAR nor Lebanon objected to that resolution, though the Soviet delegation continued to regard the Lebanese complaint as unfounded.   SCOR, XIII, Mtg. 825, pp. 16–17.

The Secretary-General immediately appointed three members of the "United Nations Observation Group in Lebanon" (UNOGIL): Mr. Galo Plaza of Ecuador, Mr. Rajeshwar Dayal of India, and Major-General Odd Bull of Norway.   The latter was in charge of military observers, the first fifteen of which were borrowed from the United Nations Truce Supervision Organization in Palestine.   S/4029 (16 June 1958); SCOR, XIII, Supp. for April-June 1958, pp. 70–71.   From the beginning, the Observation Group was accorded free access to areas under Government control, but gradually it obtained "full freedom of access to all sections of the Lebanese frontier." S/4051 (16 July 1958); SCOR, XIII, Supp. for July-Sept. 1958, p. 33.   The Group pointed out that the "existence of a state of conflict between opposing armed forces in a territory to which an independent body of observers seeks free access throughout imposes upon that body an attitude of discretion and restraint if the express or tacit acceptance of its presence is to be obtained from those exercising authority or effective control on different sides in the conflict.   The Observation Group is fully conscious of the fact that its methods of observation and its use of the information it receives must duly reflect the independent character of its status and its complete objectivity and impartiality in relation to the present conflict."   S/4040 (3 July 1958); SCOR, op. cit., p. 5.

The methods of operation of the Observation Group were as follows (idem, pp. 6–7):

"a.   Regular and frequent patrols of all accessible roads are carried out from dawn to dusk, primarily in the border districts and in the areas adjacent to the zones held by opposition forces.   The patrolling is done by observers travelling in white jeeps marked with 'UN', equipped with two-way radio sets.

"b.   A system of permanent observation posts has been set up, where groups of military observers are stationed.   These posts are in continuous radio communication with headquarters in Beirut, with each other, and with the patrolling jeeps.   There is now a total of ten such observation posts placed at strategic positions all over the country.   Their location has been determined by the need for stations to be as close as possible to the dividing line between the opposing forces, as near the frontier as possible, or at points commanding supposed infiltration routes or distribution centres.   The observers manning these stations attempt to check all reported infiltration in their areas, and to keep track of any suspicious development.

"c.   An emergency reserve of experienced military observers has been formed at headquarters and at the main observation posts; they are available at short notice for the purpose of making inquiries, or they may be detailed to places where particular instances of smuggling of arms may be reported.

"d. An evaluation team has been set up at headquarters, composed of specialized observer personnel, whose task is to analyse, evaluate and co-ordinate all information received from observers and other sources.

"e. Recently a new form of observation has been added, namely, aerial reconnaissance. Two helicopters are already in action; four light planes have just arrived, and another four are expected soon. These will have aerial photography capability, and will be in radio communication with head-quarters and military observers in the field. The aeroplanes will do regular patrol duty, but will also be directed to perform special tasks in co-ordination with the ground personnel, as the need arises.

"f. A special procedure has been established in order to utilize the information which the Lebanese Government possesses about suspected infiltration. The Government thus sends frequent reports about such alleged infiltration to the Group, which immediately deals with each case as conditions require. The majority of these communications contain statements regarding alleged infiltration incidents, routes and methods. Instructions have, wherever appropriate, been issued to the observers for the maintenance of special vigilance within the areas in question. In other cases the Group has requested, through the executive member of the Group, that the military observers inquire into the matter. Either final or preliminary reports have already been received from military observers or are awaited. In some cases the Observation Group has requested further clarification by the Government in order to determine whether useful action by the Observation Group may be taken. Some of the communications refer to events which are said to have taken place before the establishment of the Observation Group and which have no bearing on situations likely to become the object of the Group's proper concern. Others relate to events falling wholly within the framework of the internal conflict between the governmental authorities and opposition groups or supporters, and having no *prima facie* relationship to questions of infiltration."

While the Group noted substantial movements of armed men within the country, it did not find it possible to establish whether they "had infiltrated from outside"; nevertheless, it expressed the view that "the vast majority were in any case Lebanese." *Idem*, p. 9. In a later report, the Group found no evidence of a major build-up, though it did not exclude the possibility of infiltration of a certain amount of arms and ammunition. S/4069 (30 July 1958); SCOR, *op. cit.*, pp. 84, 93.

A coup in Iraq and a landing of United States marines in Lebanon and of British air-borne troops in Jordan caused a new deterioration of the situation in the middle of July 1958.

2. *Discussion in the Security Council, 15–18 July 1958.*

SCOR, XIII, Mtgs. 827, 832, 833.

Mr. LODGE (USA): The Council meets today to confront difficulties as serious as any in its history. The territorial integrity of Lebanon is increasingly threatened by insurrection stimulated and assisted from outside. Plots against the Kingdom of Jordan which have become evident over the past few months are another sign of serious instability in the relations between nations in the Middle East. And now comes the overthrow in an exceptionally brutal and revolting manner of the legally established Government of Iraq. . . .

In all these circumstances, the President of Lebanon has asked, with the unanimous authorization of the Lebanese Government, for the help of friendly Governments so as to preserve Lebanon's integrity and independence. The United States has responded positively and affirmatively to this request in the light of the need for immediate action, and we wish the Security Council to be officially advised hereby of this fact. In addition, the United States Government has under active consideration economic assistance to help Lebanon revive its economy.

Our purpose in coming to the assistance of Lebanon is perfectly clear. As President Eisenhower explained this morning, our forces are not there to engage in hostilities of any kind, much less to fight a war. Their presence is designed for the sole purpose of helping the Government of Lebanon at its request in its efforts to stabilize the situation brought on by the threats from outside, until such time as the United Nations can take the steps necessary to protect the independence and political integrity of Lebanon. They will afford security to the several thousand Americans who reside in that country. That is the total scope and objective of the United States assistance.

Now I need scarcely say that we are the first to admit that the dispatch of United States forces to Lebanon is not an ideal way to solve present problems, and they will be withdrawn as soon as the United Nations can take over. In fact, the United States Government hopes that the United Nations itself will soon be able to assume these responsibilities. We intend to consult with the Secretary-General and with other delegations urgently on a resolution to achieve these objectives. Until then, the presence of United States troops in Lebanon will be a constructive contribution to the objectives the Security Council had in mind when it passed the 11 June resolution dealing with the problem.

Let me now review the recent history of this situation. A little over a month ago, the Government of Lebanon presented a complaint to the Security Council. . . .

At that time, various members of the Council drew special attention to Article 2, paragraph 4 of the Charter of the United Nations which enjoins all Members to "refrain in their international relations from the threat or use of force against the territorial integrity or political independence of any state . . . ." This was one of the fundamental considerations behind the resolution adopted by the Council on 11 June which called for the urgent dispatch of an observation group to proceed to Lebanon so as to ensure that there was no illegal infiltration of personnel or supply of arms or other matériel across the Lebanese borders.

The United Nations Observer Group has thus far been able to achieve limited success. We hope that it will pursue its work in the most effective and energetic way possible. Our forces are being instructed to co-operate with it and to establish liaison immediately upon arrival.

This United Nations Group has helped to reduce interference from across the border. We learn now, however, that with the outbreak of the revolt in Iraq, the infiltration of arms and personnel into Lebanon from the United Arab Republic in an effort to subvert the legally constituted Government has suddenly become much more alarming. This development, coupled with persistent efforts over the past months to subvert the Government of Jordan, must be a cause of grave concern to us all. They place in jeopardy both the independence of Lebanon and that of any Middle Eastern State which seeks to maintain its national integrity free from outside influences and pressures.

. . .

Now we confront here a situation involving outside involvement in an internal revolt against the authorities of the legitimate Government of Lebanon. Under these conditions, the request from the Government of Lebanon to another Member of the United Nations to come to its assistance is entirely consistent with the provisions and purposes of the United Nations Charter. In this situation, therefore, we are proceeding in accordance with the traditional rules of international law, none of which in any way inhibits action of a character which the United States is undertaking in Lebanon.

The United States is acting pursuant to what the United Nations Charter regards as an inherent right, the right of all nations to work together to preserve their independence. The Council should take note that United States forces went to Lebanon at the specific request of the duly constituted Government of Lebanon. Let me also emphasize again what I have said before, that these forces will remain there only until the United Nations itself is able to assume the necessary responsibility for ensuring the continued independence of Lebanon. . . .

I conclude now, and I do so by saying to my colleagues of the Security Council to remember this one more fact. The members of the League of Nations tolerated direct and indirect aggression in Europe, in Asia and in Africa during the 1930's, and the tragic result was to strengthen and stimulate aggressive forces in such a way that World War II became inevitable.

The United States, for its part, is determined that history shall not now be repeated. We hope and believe that the action which we are taking will bring stability and that United States forces now being sent into Lebanon at the request of its Government can be promptly withdrawn. We must, however, be prepared to meet the situation whatever the consequences may be. . . .

The SECRETARY–GENERAL [Mr. Hammarskjöld]: . . . [We] recall that the Security Council passed, on 11 June, a resolution in which it decided to "dispatch urgently an observation group to proceed to Lebanon", and authorized the Secretary-General to take the necessary steps for implementation of the resolution. In the resolution the Security Council stated that the aim of the step it was taking was "to ensure that there is no illegal infiltration of personnel or supply of arms or other matériel across the Lebanese border."

I have in my actions regarding the Lebanese case acted solely with that purpose in view. I have used the tool created for this purpose in the resolution. I have also relied on the authority that the Secretary-General is recognized as having under the Charter.

My actions have had no relation to developments which must be considered as the internal affairs of Lebanon. Nor have I, in my implementation of the resolution, or acting under the Charter, concerned myself with wider international aspects of the problem than those referred to in the resolution. The Secretary-General in this situation obviously is neither an arbiter nor a mediator. However, even with these important restrictions, there has been wide scope for action for the purposes of the resolution, strictly in keeping with United Nations principles and rules.

The Security Council, in deciding to dispatch to Lebanon an "observation group," defined not only the character of the operation but also its scope. It did so by linking the observation to illegal traffic in arms and infiltration, requesting the Group to keep the Council currently informed of its findings. In taking this stand, the Council defined the limits for authority delegated to the Secretary-General in this case.

I have, in the light of the decision, considered myself free to take all steps necessary for an operation, covering illegal traffic in arms and infiltration, as effective as it could be made as a tool towards ensuring against such traffic or infiltration with its basic character of observation maintained. I have had a free hand as to the structure and organization of the operation but have considered myself as barred from an interpretation of the authority granted which would have implied that I changed the policy, laid down by the Council, by my decisions on the scope of the operation and the authority of the observers.

In fact, had I by going beyond the reasonable limits of a "group" charged with "observation," or by deciding on terms of reference exceeding observation, changed the observation operation into some kind of police operation, not only would I have overstepped the resolution but I would also have faced a conflict with principles laid down in

the Charter. In a police operation, the participants would in this case
need the right, if necessary, to take the initiative in the use of force.
Such use of force would, however, have belonged to the sphere of
Chapter VII of the Charter and could have been granted only by the
Security Council itself, directly or by explicit delegation, under con-
ditions spelled out in that chapter.   .   .   .

Mr. AZKOUL (Lebanon): .   .   .   The peril threatening the independence and integrity of Lebanon is today even more imminent, for
the *coup d'état* in Iraq has begun to have serious repercussions in
Lebanon.

In view of this situation, my Government would again appeal to
the Security Council and urge it to take some more effective emergency measure than the one it has already taken, and one more likely
to achieve the Council's purpose: to prevent any illegal infiltration of
personnel or any supply of arms or other matériel across the Lebanese
borders. The Lebanese Government would like to reaffirm here, today, before the Security Council, that it is always anxious to ensure
that the assistance it needs to protect Lebanon's independence and
integrity should be obtained through the United Nations and within
the framework of the United Nations Charter.

It is for this reason that, while making this request of the Security
Council, the Lebanese Government has decided, in view of the immediacy of the threat to Lebanon's independence and to the maintenance
of international peace and security in the Middle East, and while
awaiting the action it has asked the Security Council to take, to rely
on Article 51 of the Charter which recognizes the inherent right of
individual or collective self-defence. Consequently, the Lebanese Government has asked for direct assistance from friendly countries. It is
clearly understood that this assistance is strictly temporary and
will continue only until such time as the measure we have asked of
the Security Council is carried into effect. As soon as such action is
undertaken, the forces of friendly countries which have sent troops
into Lebanon will at once be evacuated from our territory.   .   .   .

Mr. SOBOLEV (USSR): .   .   .   We have just heard the United
States representative's statement about the landing of United States
armed forces in the territory of Lebanon. The fact is that the United
States has decided openly, without taking cover behind any flag, to
intervene with its armed forces in the internal affairs of the Arab
countries and to force to their knees peoples who have risen in defence
of their freedom and independence, not only in Lebanon, but also in
other Arab States.

In an attempt to justify his country's aggressive action, the United
States representative alleges that it was requested by the present
rulers of Lebanon. It is no secret, however, that these rulers are

simply political puppets of the United States and that their requests are inspired by the United States State Department.

In these circumstances, the sending of United States troops to Lebanon is an act of aggression against the peoples of the Arab world and a case of gross intervention in the domestic affairs of the countries of that area. This act is a flagrant violation of the United Nations Charter, which prohibits the use of force as a tool of foreign policy. This act is contrary to the principles and tenets of international law and constitutes a challenge to all freedom-loving people. No reference to Chamoun's requests can justify this act of armed aggression, for these requests were provoked precisely in order to justify United States intervention in the domestic affairs of the countries of the Arab world. But such justification is impossible.

As grounds for its intervention the United States refers to the United Nations Charter. It is true that the Charter provides for the right of individual or collective self-defence if an armed attack occurs against a Member of the United Nations, until the Security Council has taken the measures necessary to maintain international peace and security. But in this case the situation is quite different. The Security Council is taking action in Lebanon. It has taken a decision which makes possible a settlement of the situation in that country. No one has attacked Lebanon and there is no threat of an armed attack against Lebanon. It is obvious that this reference to the Charter has nothing to do with the case and that it is merely a manoeuvre designed to conceal the aggressive nature of the armed intervention of the United States against the Arab peoples. Lebanon is threatened by no one except those who have undertaken armed intervention with a view to crushing a people in revolt. Moreover, the reference to the United Nations Charter also runs counter to the report of the Observation Group sent by the Security Council, which states that there is no threat whatsoever to Lebanon, on the part of the United Arab Republic.

The Soviet Union delegation considers that the attempt of the United States to cover up its armed intervention against the peoples of the Near and Middle East by a reference to self-defence makes a mockery of the United Nations Charter, and of the high purposes and principles on which our Organization is based and which are reflected in the Charter.

The peoples of Lebanon and Iraq have the inalienable right to settle all problems relating to these States. No internal incidents occurring within a country can serve as a pretext for intervention in its domestic affairs. Any armed intervention by the Western Powers is fraught with the most serious consequences, threatens acutely to aggravate the international situation and is liable to plunge the world into the abyss of a new war. . . .

Mr. MATSUDAIRA (Japan): In the light of the new facts revealed by the second interim report of the United Nations Observation Group in Lebanon, I should like . . . to make clear the position of my country.

First of all, it is inappropriate and regrettable indeed that the United States has taken measures to intervene in the dispute in Lebanon by sending its own armed forces to Lebanon while the Security Council is still examining Lebanon's complaint. It is true that the said dispatch of forces was made in response to the request of the Government of Lebanon. However, it cannot be denied that intervention by a State in the disputes of another State could have unfavourable repercussions directly or indirectly, and the Government and the people of my country sincerely hope that the stationing of United States troops in Lebanon will come to an end as soon as possible.

Secondly, a solution to the Lebanese question should be sought only through the machinery of the United Nations. The question of the existence of infiltration into Lebanon or of a threat to the security of Lebanon and the measures to be taken on the basis of the existence of such infiltration or threat [should] be determined by the United Nations; and it is not desirable that one country should take on its own judgement specific measures on these matters without waiting for such determination by the United Nations.

Thirdly, in view of the foregoing, it is necessary that the United Nations should promptly take such practical measures as would enable an early withdrawal of the United States forces which are already in Lebanon. The United Nations should seriously examine the circumstances which have made it necessary for the United States to dispatch its forces to Lebanon and should take such measures as are appropriate to cope with the situation. This would be the only way to prevent deterioration of the present situation. Mere disapproval of the dispatch of forces by the United States would not contribute to a solution of the problem. Speedy and constructive measures arc also required in order to maintain the prestige of the United Nations. . . .

Mr. LOUTFI (UAR): . . . I wish to inform the Council of a message I received today from Cairo:

"On 18 July, at 1:30 a. m., the United States Ambassador in Cairo asked to see Mr. Ali Sabry, the Acting Minister of Foreign Affairs, who received him at 3 a. m. The Ambassador delivered a *note verbale*, the contents of which were as follows:

" 'The landing of United States forces is intended to preserve the independence of Lebanon and to protect American citizens.'

"He also expressed the United States Government's intention to withdraw its forces as soon as circumstances permit:

" 'The troops have no hostile intentions. It was necessary to come to the assistance of Lebanon because of the change of government in

Iraq. The United Arab Republic should realize that if United States forces are attacked by military units of the United Arab Republic or by elements which the United States knows to be under control of the United Arab Republic or ready to carry out its instructions, there will be a danger that the problem may be enlarged and assume major proportions.' "

This last part of the *note verbale* is very serious. It refers to elements known to be under our control or ready to carry out our instructions. We can understand that the United States Government is not prepared to sit back and allow its troops to be attacked by the armed forces of the United Arab Republic. What is important and serious is that the United States wishes to be the judge of which elements are under our control or accept our instructions. In making such a decision, the United States will rely on the unilateral information of their intelligence service. It did so when it decided to intervene in Lebanon, discounting the report of the Observation Group. . . .

We are a small State, we do not have an atomic bomb, and nobody has proved that we have any aggressive designs. The world bears witness to our peaceful intentions. Our policy is one of non-alignment. It may not please everyone, but we will continue to pursue it in cooperation with the United Nations and in accordance with the United Nations Charter, by which we abide. We have proved on several occasions that we are always prepared to co-operate with the United Nations in settling international problems and preserving world peace.

NOTE. On 18 July 1958, the Security Council rejected by 8 votes to 1, with two abstentions (Japan, Sweden), a Soviet draft resolution (S/4047/Rev.1; SCOR, XIII, Mtg. 831, p. 17) which would have called upon the United States and the United Kingdom "to cease armed intervention in the domestic affairs of the Arab States and to remove their troops from the territories of Lebanon and Jordan immediately." The Council also rejected by 9 votes to 2 (Sweden, USSR) a Swedish draft resolution (S/4054; SCOR, XIII, Supp. for July-Sept. 1958, p. 38), which, in view of the action taken by the United States, would have requested the Secretary-General "to suspend the activities of the observers in Lebanon." On the other hand, the Soviet Union vetoed a United States draft resolution (S/4050/Rev.1; SCOR, *op. cit.*, pp. 31–32) which would have requested "the Secretary-General immediately to consult the Government of Lebanon and other Member States as appropriate with a view to making arrangements for additional measures, including the contribution and use of contingents, as may be necessary to protect the territorial integrity and independence of Lebanon and to ensure that there is no illegal infiltration of personnel or supply of arms or other matériel across the Lebanese borders". SCOR, XIII, Mtg. 834, p. 11. On 22 July 1958, the Soviet Union also vetoed a Japanese resolution (S/4055/Rev.1; SCOR, Supp. for July-Sept. 1958, pp. 38–39) which would have requested "the Secretary-General to make arrangements forthwith for such measures, in addition to those envisaged by the resolution of 11 June 1958, as he may consider necessary in the light of the present circumstances, with a view to enabling the United Nations to fulfil the general purposes established in that resolution, and which will, in accordance with the Charter of the United Nations, serve to ensure the territorial integrity and political independence of Lebanon, so as to make possible the withdrawal of United States forces from Lebanon."

The Secretary-General then made the following statement: "The Security Council has just failed to take additional action in the grave emergency facing us. However, the responsibility of the United Nations to make all efforts to live up to the purposes and principles of the Charter remains. . .

"In a statement before this Council on 31 October 1956, I said that the discretion and impartiality imposed on the Secretary-General by the character of his immediate task must not degenerate into a policy of expediency. On a later occasion—it was 26 September 1957—I said in a statement before the General Assembly that I believed it to be the duty of the Secretary-General 'to use his office and, indeed, the machinery of the Organization to its utmost capacity and to the full extent permitted at each stage by practical circumstances.' I added that I believed that it is in keeping with the philosophy of the Charter that the Secretary-General also should be expected to act without any guidance from the Assembly or the Security Council should this appear to him necessary towards helping to fill any vacuum that may appear in the systems which the Charter and traditional diplomacy provide for the safeguarding of peace and security.

"It is my feeling that, in the circumstances, what I stated in those two contexts, on 31 October 1956 and 26 September 1957, now has full application.

"I am sure that I will be acting in accordance with the wishes of the members of the Council if I, therefore, use all opportunities offered to the Secretary-General, within the limits set by the Charter and towards developing the United Nations effort, so as to help to prevent a further deterioration of the situation in the Middle East and to assist in finding a road away from the dangerous point at which we now find ourselves.

"First of all—the continued operation of the United Nations Observation Group in Lebanon being acceptable to all members of the Council—this will mean the further development of the Observation Group so as to give it all the significance it can have, consistent with its basic character as determined by the Security Council in its resolution of 11 June 1958 [S/4023] and the purposes and principles of the Charter.

"The Council will excuse me for not being able to spell out at this moment what it may mean beyond that. However, I am certain that what I may find it possible to do, acting under the provisions of the Charter and solely for the purposes of the Charter, and guided by the views expressed around this table to the extent that they have a direct bearing on the activities of the Secretary-General, will be recognized by you as being in the best interests of the Organization and, therefore, of the cause of peace.

"The Security Council would, of course, be kept fully informed on the steps taken. Were you to disapprove of the way these intentions were to be translated by me into practical steps, I would, of course, accept the consequences of your judgment." SCOR, XIII, Mtg. 837, pp. 3–4.

Nobody challenged this statement of the Secretary-General and he proceeded with the enlarging of the military personnel of the Observation Group in Lebanon to 591, of the number of permanently manned posts to 49, and of the aerial watch to more than 300 sorties per month. S/4114 (17 Nov. 1958); SCOR, XIII, Supp. for Oct.-Dec. 1958, pp. 8–9.

The Observation Group pointed out that "the effect of the landing of United States armed forces on the inhabitants of opposition-held areas where observers were operating, occasioned difficulties and caused setbacks to the task of observation. Not only was the Group prevented from carrying out its plans to establish immediately the permanent posts in opposition-held areas for which it had made arrangements on 15 July, but also its observers had to resume the difficult task of gaining the confidence of the inhabitants of those areas in the impartiality and independence of the observers.

"With a view to emphasizing the independent nature of its task, the Group made the following announcement on 16 July:

" 'The United Nations Observation Group in Lebanon wishes to clarify its position in regard to its relationship with the foreign forces on Lebanon soil. The United Nations Observation Group alone is in Lebanon in pursuance of the mandate contained in the Security Council resolution of 11 June 1958 [S/4023]. The United Nations Observation Group represents the only action taken by the Security Council. There is, therefore, no basis for establishing any contact or working relationship, formal or informal, between the United Nations Observation Group and any non-Lebanese forces in Lebanon beyond what may be strictly required for the independent fulfilment of its mandate from the United Nations Security Council, which cannot be altered without further action by the Council.'

"By dint of their perseverance and tact in dealing with difficult and often dangerous situations, the observers have won back the ground lost after 15 July. In addition, most of the permanent stations in opposition-held areas envisaged in the second interim report of the Group, have already been established and other stations are expected to be established shortly.

"The election of General Chehab as the next President of Lebanon took place on 31 July. Even before the election informal truces had taken effect in Saïda and Soûr; in fact, during the period immediately preceding the election there was a noticeable reduction in tension practically throughout the country and a comparative absence of armed clashes between Government and opposition forces. Since 31 July, there has been a further reduction in tension throughout the country, including the opposition-held areas. There has, in fact, been virtually a nation-wide truce since then with only occasional reports of sporadic firing in some areas.

"On the other hand, there appears to have been a decrease in some areas in the ability of opposition leaders to control their followers, and a noticeable increase in acts of lawlessness. The Group has received frequent reports of holdups, stealing of vehicles, shootings and other acts of terrorism and of kidnapping in pursuit of party feuds or personal vendettas." S/4085 (14 August 1958); SCOR, XIII, Supp. for July-Sept. 1958, pp. 127–28.

In the meantime the Soviet Union asked that the Security Council call an emergency special session of the General Assembly "in order to consider the question of the immediate withdrawal of United States troops from Lebanon and of United Kingdom troops from Jordan." S/4057/Rev.1; SCOR, XIII, Mtg. 838 (7 August 1958), pp. 8–9. After the United States presented a counterproposal, the Security Council unanimously adopted a shortened resolution calling merely for "an emergency special session of the General Assembly," with only an oblique reference to the complaints by Lebanon and Jordan, and without a reference to the Uniting for Peace Resolution. SCOR, *op. cit.*, p. 45.

The Soviet Union presented to the General Assembly a proposal that the General Assembly recommend the withdrawal of United States and United Kingdom troops without delay, and that it instruct the Secretary-General to strengthen UNOGIL and to send an observation group to Jordan "with a view to the supervision of the withdrawal of United States and United Kingdom troops from Lebanon and Jordan, and of the situation along the frontiers of those countries." A/3870 (12 August 1958); GAOR, Annexes (ES-III) 5, pp. 1–2. The Secretary of State of the United States (Mr. Dulles) notified the President of the General Assembly that "United States forces are now in Lebanon in response to an appeal of the duly constituted Government of Lebanon for assistance in maintaining Lebanon's territorial integrity and political independence against danger from without. United States forces will be withdrawn from Lebanon whenever this is requested by the duly constituted Government of Lebanon or whenever, as a result of the further action of the United Nations or otherwise, their presence is no longer required. The United States will in any event abide by a determination of the United Nations General Assembly that action taken or assistance furnished by the United Nations makes the continued presence of United States forces in Lebanon unnecessary for the maintenance of international peace and security." A/3876 (18 August 1958); GAOR, *op. cit.*, p. 2. (See also the speech made by President Eisenhower before the General Assembly on 13 August 1958; GAOR, ES-III, Plenary, pp. 7–10.) On the basis of a proposal by ten Arab States, including Lebanon and the United Arab Republic, the General Assembly adopted unanimously Resolution 1237 (ES-III); for its text, see Document 3, below.

3.   *General Assembly Resolution 1237 (ES–III), 21 August 1958.*

GAOR, ES–III, Supp. 1 (A/3905), p. 1.

The General Assembly,

Having considered the item entitled "Questions considered by the Security Council at its 838th meeting on 7 August 1958",

Noting the Charter aim that States should practise tolerance and live together in peace with one another as good neighbours,

Noting that the Arab States have agreed, in the Pact of the League of Arab States, to strengthen the close relations and numerous ties which link the Arab States, and to support and stabilize these ties upon a basis of respect for the independence and sovereignty of these States, and to direct their efforts toward the common good of all the Arab countries, the improvement of their status, the security of their future and the realization of their aspirations and hopes,

Desiring to relieve international tension,

I

1.   Welcomes the renewed assurances given by the Arab States to observe the provision of article 8 of the Pact of the League of Arab

States that each member State shall respect the systems of government established in the other member States and regard them as exclusive concerns of these States, and that each shall pledge to abstain from any action calculated to change established systems of government;

2.   Calls upon all States Members of the United Nations to act strictly in accordance with the principles of mutual respect for each other's territorial integrity and sovereignty of non-aggression, of strict non-interference in each other's internal affairs, and of equal and mutual benefit, and to ensure that their conduct by word and deed conforms to these principles;

II

Requests the Secretary-General to make forthwith, in consultation with the Governments concerned and in accordance with the Charter, and having in mind section I of this resolution, such practical arrangements as would adequately help in upholding the purposes and principles of the Charter in relation to Lebanon and Jordan in the present circumstances, and thereby facilitate the early withdrawal of the foreign troops from the two countries;

III

Invites the Secretary-General to continue his studies now under way and in this context to consult as appropriate with the Arab countries of the Near East with a view to possible assistance regarding an Arab development institution designed to further economic growth in these countries;

IV

1.   Requests Member States to co-operate fully in carrying out this resolution;

2.   Invites the Secretary-General to report hereunder, as appropriate, the first such report to be made not later than 30 September 1958.

4.   *Report of the Secretary-General, 28 September 1958.*

A/3934/Rev.1 (29 Sept. 1958).

The resolution under which this report is presented notes in the preamble "the Charter aim that States should 'practise tolerance and live together in peace with one another as good neighbours' ". It further notes "that the Arab States have agreed, in the Pact of the

League of Arab States, to 'strengthen the close relations and numerous ties which link the Arab States, and to support and stabilize these ties upon a basis of respect for the independence and sovereignty of these States, and to direct their efforts toward the common good of all the Arab countries, the improvement of their status, the security of their future and the realization of their aspirations and hopes' ".

The first operative part of the resolution should be evaluated in the light of the reference to the "good neighbour policy" established as an aim in the Charter, and likewise in the Pact of the Arab League. It elaborates the Charter aim in calling upon all the Member States of the United Nations "to act strictly in accordance with the principles of mutual respect for each other's territorial integrity and sovereignty, of non-aggression, of strict non-interference in each other's internal affairs, and of equal and mutual benefit, and to ensure that their conduct by word and deed conforms to these principles". In the context of this appeal to all Member States, the resolution "welcomes the renewed assurances given by the Arab States to observe the provision of Article 8 of the Pact of the League of Arab States that 'Each Member State shall respect the systems of government established in the other member States and regard them as exclusive concerns of these States', and that 'Each shall pledge to abstain from any action calculated to change established systems of government' ".

Part I contains the political essence of the resolution. Accepted by a unanimous vote, the principles elaborated in this part may be regarded as a renewed joint pledge of all Member States to pursue a policy of non-interference and non-aggression in relation to each other and to all nations in the region. More specifically, being co-sponsored by the ten Arab States, the principles represent an agreement of the Arab States, in implementation of this pledge, to adhere to a good neighbour policy as set out in Article 8 of the Pact of the Arab League. The other provisions of the resolution flow from the joint undertakings.

The second operative part of the resolution "requests the Secretary-General to make forthwith, in consultation with the Governments concerned and in accordance with the Charter, and having in mind part I of this resolution, such practical arrangements as would adequately help in upholding the purposes and principles of the Charter in relation to Lebanon and Jordan in the present circumstances". It is added that "the practical arrangements" envisaged, in helping to uphold the purposes and principles of the Charter in relation to the two countries mentioned, are expected also to "facilitate the early withdrawal of the foreign troops" from those countries.

The resolution states that the practical arrangements shall be made "having in mind part I" of the resolution. This emphasizes that they are not to be regarded as a substitute for a policy aiming at good neighbourly relations in accordance with part I, but as being made in order to support the general implementation of such a policy in relation to

Lebanon and Jordan, and "thereby" to facilitate the withdrawal as part of a parallel development along the lines of the resolution.

Two limits are set for the arrangements, namely that they should be made in consultation with the Governments concerned, and that they should be in accordance with the Charter. This is a reminder especially of the fact that any arrangement within one of the countries concerned must be with the consent of its Government. It is likewise a reminder of the fact that no measures can be taken which go beyond the limits authorized by the Charter in the case of such a resolution as the one under which action would be taken; the most important consequence of this is that it excludes the setting up of a force with military tasks under Chapter 7 of the Charter. . . . .

The Task of the Secretary-General

As recalled above, the General Assembly in its resolution requests the Secretary-General to make certain practical arrangements for the purposes of the resolution. The scope of this task is obvious in the light of the preceding interpretation of the resolution. It may, however, be useful to define the mandate with somewhat greater precision.

As the task of the Secretary-General is limited to practical arrangements it is, in the first place, clear that it does not cover a mediation or good offices intended to further the implementation among the Arab States of their agreed policy. Were such mediation or good offices needed, it would be more natural to have it undertaken by the joint organ which the Arab States have created in the Arab League, especially as their pledge in the resolution directly refers to the Pact of the Arab League. Alternatively, were such assistance to be considered necessary, it could, on the basis of a direct request from the Arab States, be rendered either by the Secretary-General or by a Government or a group of Governments.

It may be noted, further, that the resolution does not give the Secretary-General a mandate to negotiate with the Arab States regarding additional or more specific assurances with regard to their policies. This, obviously, does not exclude any action which may properly be his under the Charter, or that, in consultations with the Governments concerned, he would seek all the clarification, regarding their intentions with respect to the implementation of the good neighbour policy, which he would consider necessary as a background for decisions on practical arrangements. A clear distinction should, however, be made between such clarifications and any further assurances regarding intentions formally given by one Government to another.

While the resolution does not—as was the case in the Suez question —establish negotiations regarding withdrawals as a task of the Secretary-General, he is, under the resolution, to facilitate "early withdrawal" by the practical arrangements he is requested to make. For that purpose he must inform himself about the intentions of the Governments concerned and consult with them with a view to clarifying the relationship between the practical arrangements to be made and the withdrawals. Likewise, he must maintain contact with Governments so as to be able to respond to the invitation of the General Assembly to him to report on the developments under the resolution also in this respect. These contacts or consultations, however, include responsibilities for him regarding the withdrawals only to the extent which follows from the relationship, established in the resolution, between the implementation of a good neighbour policy, the practical arrangements which the Secretary-General is in a position to make in its support, and the withdrawal.

What emerges as the task of the Secretary-General under the resolution is in the first instance to consult with the Arab Governments concerned regarding their views on the need for, and form of, practical arrangements as envisaged in the resolution. In the second place he has to see how he can relate the various governmental positions, as determined in the course of the consultations, so that they can best serve and support the implementation of a general good neighbour policy, especially in relation to Lebanon and Jordan. In doing so, he must be guided by the desirability of achieving the highest degree of efficiency which respect for the views of the Governments concerned and adherence to the rules of the Charter permit. Were he to consider the measures possible under those conditions to be inadequate, or were the Governments concerned to consider them insufficient, this naturally should be brought to the attention of the General Assembly.

In judging the adequacy of the practical arrangements possible, he must be guided by the interpretation of the resolution set out above. While it cannot be a question for him of evaluating the arrangements as substitutes for the presence of foreign troops, as the arrangements are clearly not intended to be, he should consider them in the context of the withdrawals. This factor forms a part of his general evaluation, which must take into account especially the degree to which the pledges to a good neighbour policy seem to have already been translated into live reality. Were such a policy to be firmly established, no practical arrangements would be needed, while, on the other hand, in its absence, far-reaching and extensive measures would be required. In the period of transition, when it is justified to hope that the Arab nations will succeed in their efforts to establish a good neighbour policy but while frictions and departures from the main line may still be feared, the practical arrangements must in the first instance aim at keeping under review the degree of implementation of the general policy line and provide for means to set straight what may seem to be going wrong. This last mentioned situation appears to come close to the assumptions on which the resolution was based when it regarded the practical arrangements as steps in support of the policy laid down in the first operative part; reference may here again

be made to the explicit statement in the resolution that the practical
arrangements should be made "having in mind part I" of the resolution.

Consultations

Noting the request to work out the practical arrangements in consultation with the Governments concerned, noting further that such
consultations, in order to be fruitful, to all possible extent should be
directly with the Governments in the various countries and noting
that the resolution had been sponsored by all the Governments concerned, I regarded the decision as implying a joint invitation to visit
the capitals of the nations most directly concerned with the problem,
for personal talks. Consequently I went to the region on 25 August
1958. I visited Amman 27–28 August and again 8–9 September. I
visited Cairo 3–5 September and Baghdad 7–8 September. I finally
visited Beirut 10–12 September.

In the consultations, which without exception proved highly useful,
I based my position on the interpretation of the resolution and of the
mandate of the Secretary-General explained above. Thus, I invited the
Governments to present their views on practical arrangements and on
the situation into which they have to be fitted, while abstaining, myself, from presenting any definite proposals for their consideration and
from pressing for the acceptance of any specific line of action of the
United Nations. I further sought an elucidation of the intentions of
the Governments regarding part I of the resolution, and the good
neighbour policy set out therein, with a view to getting as specific
a basis as possible for my decisions regarding practical measures in
support of such a policy in line with the principles explained in the
previous part. It was not within my competence to translate the
elucidations achieved into additional assurances of a formal nature.

.   .   .

Practical Arrangements: General Considerations

The practical arrangements for the purposes mentioned in the resolution, as explained above, must be adjusted to the development of
the good neighbour policy to which Member Governments have pledged
themselves in the resolution. The implementation of the joint pledge
is still at an early stage and it is therefore premature to pass a judgement on the degree of success with which it may meet. From all the
Governments contacted, I have heard firm expressions of an intention to translate the terms of the resolution into a living reality. At
the same time, however, most of the Governments found reasons, although in varying degree, to complain about the way in which, so far,
the joint pledge to a good neighbour policy had been implemented by
others.

It is undoubtedly true that, so far, we have not reached the stage in which mutual confidence is restored and departures from the desirable line of action are such rare occurrences as to make it possible to disregard them. However, it seems reasonable to work on the assumption that the impact of the intention of all Governments to translate the words of the resolution into deeds will increasingly be felt and that, therefore, the implementation of the good neighbour policy will meet with growing success. Regarding developments which have taken place after the consultations, I wish to mention, especially, encouraging contacts about the supply of oil to Jordan through the Syrian region and the supply of oil from Iraq on a commercial basis.

For the present, practical arrangements made by the Secretary-General may be developed on the aforementioned assumption and with a view to strengthening the forces working in the desirable direction. Were the assumption later to prove unwarranted, a reconsideration of the practical arrangements would become necessary. In the ultimate case of a failure of the good neighbour policy they would have to be so developed as to present a more solid guarantee for the line of action which they are intended to support.

On the basis of this assumption it seems reasonable to conclude that the practical arrangements should, on the one hand, provide means for the United Nations to keep the implementation of part I, and the policy it establishes, continuously within its purview and, on the other hand, provide means for the United Nations, in case of departures from a good neighbour policy, as set out in the resolution, to take appropriate diplomatic or political action. The two sets of arrangements, although naturally closely related, should be kept strictly apart so that neither the arrangements for the purview may come to be used also for diplomatic purposes, nor the character of the diplomatic arrangements may be distorted by their being used also for the purpose of the purview. The natural link between the two sets of arrangements is the office of the Secretary-General which would receive reports on the findings, made in the course of the purview, and decide on the political or diplomatic action to be taken through the means created for that purpose. .   .   .

During his stay in Lebanon, the Secretary-General had the privilege of getting the views of the Lebanese authorities on practical arrangements which, in their view, would adequately help in upholding the purposes of the Charter in relation to Lebanon. It was felt that the United Nations Observation Group, set up under a resolution of the Security Council, 11 June 1958, while continuing to serve the general purposes mentioned in that resolution, presents a practical arrangement in the sense of the resolution of the General Assembly, 21 August 1958, and in present circumstances, with the further development of it envisaged, adequately helps in upholding the purposes of the Charter in relation to Lebanon.

It was found unnecessary for the time being to consider any additional practical arrangements under the General Assembly resolution. Decisive significance was, in this context, attached to the successful implementation of part I of the resolution, that is, to the development of the good neighbour policy in the area, to which the Arab Governments have pledged themselves in the resolution. The United Nations operation, now organized in Lebanon, was considered as helpful in the development of such a policy. After the withdrawal of foreign troops from Lebanon, the question of the Observation Group and of alternative or additional practical arrangements under the resolution would have to be considered in the light of the degree of success with which the implementation of part I of the resolution of 21 August 1958 had met. . . .

The Governments of Lebanon and of the United States have been fully informed about the conclusions drawn after my consultations in the region and about the arrangements made or planned regarding the United Nations Observation Group in Lebanon. In view of the information thus conveyed, the Government of Lebanon and the United States Government are at present discussing a schedule for the completion of the withdrawal of the United States forces. I am informed that it is the intention of the two Governments that the total withdrawal of the forces shall begin in the near future and be completed as expeditiously as possible, they hope by the end of October, provided the international security situation with respect to Lebanon continues to improve in the framework of a successful implementation of part I of the resolution of 21 August 1958. The two Governments concerned plan to announce their decision shortly.

NOTE.—1. The new President of Lebanon, General Fouad Chehab, originally nominated by the opposition but elected by a majority which included both government and opposition partisans, assumed his office on 23 September 1958 and a new government was formed on 15 October 1958. The withdrawal of the United States forces was completed without incident on 25 October 1958. The forces of the Lebanese Government obtained control over the whole territory and the opposition disbanded its forces. The Observation Group ceased its operation on December 9. S/4114 (17 Nov. 1958); SCOR, XIII, Supp. for Oct.-Dec. 1958, pp. 7–13; GAOR, XIV, Supp. 1 (A/4132), pp. 21–22.

2. In its final report, the Observation Group made the following assessment of its accomplishments (S/4114; SCOR, XIII, Supp. for Oct.-Dec. 1958, pp. 12–13):

"When the first few observers arrived in Lebanon some five months ago, they found an extremely complex situation, with large groups in different parts of the country in open and armed opposition to the Government, while practically the entire land frontier was open and outside the control of the Government. To enable the function of observation to be performed, it was first necessary to obtain physical access to the areas where such observation would be valuable, namely, along the borders. After patient and persistent efforts, the observers were able to gain access to one part, and then to another of the frontier, so that eventually a string of sub-stations and observation posts came to be established practically throughout the length of the frontier. From these posts and others to the rear, and by means of incessant patrolling, the observers were able to maintain constant vigilance.

"During the five months, the situation in and around Lebanon has undergone big and sometimes dramatic changes, which have inevitably affected the task of observation. Without departing from the mandate of the Group, it has been necessary to vary the approach to the task from time to time. This has involved the taking of timely decisions, while keeping the standing instructions under constant review; what is more, these decisions have had to be communicated promptly to the observers in the field and their execution closely supervised. Considering the complex, and in many respects unprecedented, nature of the Observation Group's operations, it is a matter of some satisfaction that a proper balance was maintained throughout and that the Group's efforts at no point got out of contact with the realities of the changing situation.

"In general, it may be stated that the United Nations Observation Group in Lebanon has been a symbol of the concern of the international community for the welfare and security of Lebanon. Apart from the effects of its mission of observation and reporting, its presence has had a reassuring effect on the population and has influenced the historic events which have taken place. By helping to free the Lebanese situation from its external complications, it has contributed to the creation of conditions under which the Lebanese people themselves could arrive at a peaceful solution of their internal problems.

"In expressing these views, the Group feels it appropriate to pay tribute to the devotion to duty shown by the military observers under its control. The success of an operation such as the present one depends on the application of moral force to circumstances where otherwise only the use of arms would be effective. The military observers, armed only with the moral authority of the United Nations and their own determination and courage, have been able to fulfil their task of peace and have won for themselves the respect of the people in all areas in which they have operated. In doing so they have, even in the recent improved circumstances in Lebanon, repeatedly undergone hardship and dangers, which have been described in detail in this and previous reports.

"The distinctions of national origin have proved to be superficial in relation to the deep significance of the common task which the observers were called upon to perform. Observers from twenty-one countries from different parts of the world have co-operated effectively and in a spirit of comradeship not only in circumstances of danger and under the stimulus of urgent events, but also in the carrying out of routine duties and patrols. If, as it believes, the Group has been able to make a useful contribution to the restoration of more peaceful conditions in Lebanon, it is because it has been able to base its reports on the objective information faithfully supplied to it by its observers on the ground and in the air."

3. For comments on the various aspects of the Lebanese Question, see M. S. AGWANI, ed., The Lebanese Crisis, 1958: A Documentary Study (New York, 1956), 407 pp.; Camille CHAMOUN, Crise au Moyen-Orient (Paris, 1963), 436 pp.; Gerald L. CURTIS, "The United Nations Observation Group

in Lebanon," 18 Int. Org. (1964), pp. 738–65; René-Jean DUPUY, "Agression indirecte et intervention solicitée: A propos de l'affaire libanaise," 5 AFDI (1959), pp. 451–67; George LENCZOWSKI, The Middle East in World Affairs (3rd ed., Ithaca, New York, 1962), pp. 326–44; Richard I. MILLER, Dag Hammarskjöld and Crisis Diplomacy (New York, 1961), pp. 157–210; Pitman B. POTTER, "Legal Aspects of the Beirut Landing," 52 AJIL (1958), pp. 727–30; Fahim I. QUBAIN, Crisis in Lebanon (Washington, D. C., 1961) 243 pp.; Edmond RABBATH, "L'intervention militaire des U.S.A. au Liban au regard de l'art. 51 de la Charte de l'O.N.U.," 8 RDIMO (1959), pp. 1–29; David W. WAINHOUSE and others, International Peace Observation (Baltimore, 1966), pp. 374–86; Quincy WRIGHT, "United States Intervention in the Lebanon," 53 AJIL (1959), pp. 112–25. See also ROYAL INSTITUTE OF INTERNATIONAL AFFAIRS, Survey of International Affairs, 1956–1958 (London, 1962), pp. 369–94.

CONGO QUESTION

NOTE.   On 30 June 1960, the Belgian Congo became an independent State under the name of the Republic of the Congo; it applied immediately for membership in the United Nations, and on 7 July 1960 the Security Council recommended its admission.   S/4361 (1 July 1960), and S/4377 (7 July 1960); SCOR, XV, Supp. for July-Sept. 1960, pp. 2, 9.

After a mutiny of the Congolese army, which led to a collapse of public order, looting and attacks on Europeans, the Belgian Government sent troops to the Congo to restore order and ensure the safety of Europeans.   The Congolese Government then appealed to the United Nations for assistance.

1.   *Cable from the President and the Prime Minister of the Republic of the Congo to the Secretary-General of the United Nations, 12 July 1960.*

S/4382 (13 July 1960), p. 1; SCOR, XV, Supp. for July-Sept. 1960, p. 11.

The Government of the Republic of the Congo requests urgent dispatch by the United Nations of military assistance.   This request is justified by the dispatch to the Congo of metropolitan Belgian troops in violation of the treaty of friendship signed between Belgium and the Republic of the Congo on 29 June 1960.   Under the terms of that treaty, Belgian troops may only intervene on the express request of the Congolese Government.   No such request was ever made by the Government of the Republic of the Congo and we therefore regard the unsolicited Belgian action as an act of aggression against our country.

The real cause of most of the disturbances can be found in colonialist machinations.   We accuse the Belgian Government of having carefully prepared the secession of the Katanga with a view to maintaining a hold on our country.   The Government, supported by the Congolese people, refuses to accept a *fait accompli* resulting from a conspiracy between Belgian imperialists and a small group of Katanga leaders. The overwhelming majority of the Katanga population is opposed to secession, which means the disguised perpetuation of the colonialist regime. The essential purpose of the requested military aid is to protect the national territory of the Congo against the present external aggression which is a threat to international peace. We strongly stress the extremely urgent need for the dispatch of United Nations troops to the Congo.

2. *Cable from the President and the Prime Minister of the Republic of the Congo to the Secretary-General of the United Nations, 13 July 1960.*

S/4382 (13 July 1960), p. 2; SCOR, *op. cit.*, p. 12.

In connexion with military assistance requested of the United Nations by the Republic of the Congo the Chief of State and the Prime Minister of the Congo make the following clarification: (1) the purpose of the aid requested is not to restore internal situation in Congo but rather to protect the national territory against acts of aggression posed by Belgian metropolitan troops. (2) The request for assistance relates only to a United Nations force consisting of military personnel of neutral countries and not of United States as reported by certain radio stations. (3) If requested assistance is not received without delay the Republic of the Congo will be obliged to appeal to the Bandung Treaty Powers. (4) The aid has been requested by the Republic of the Congo in the exercise of its sovereign rights and not in agreement with Belgium as reported.

3. *Letter from the Secretary-General to the President of the Security Council, 13 July 1960.*

S/4381 (13 July 1960); SCOR, *op. cit.*, p. 11.

I wish to inform you that I have to bring to the attention of the Security Council a matter which, in my opinion, may threaten the maintenance of international peace and security. Thus, I request you to call an urgent meeting of the Security Council to hear a report of the Secretary-General on a demand for United Nations action in relation to the Republic of the Congo.

4. *Discussion in the Security Council, 13–14 July 1960.*

SCOR, XV, Mtg. 873, pp. 3–45.

The SECRETARY–GENERAL: The reason for my request, under Article 99, for an immediate meeting of the Security Council is the situation which has arisen in the newly independent Republic of the Congo.

The difficulties which have developed in the Congo are well known to all members of the Council. They are connected with the maintenance of order in the country and the protection of life. But the difficulties have an important international bearing as they are of a nature that cannot be disregarded by other countries.

I have received three communications from the Government of the Congo. . . .

One is a request for urgent technical assistance in the field of administration, aiming especially at assistance in developing the security administration of the country. This request is within the limits of the competence of the Secretary-General and I have sent it informally to the delegates, members of the Security Council, only because of its bearing on the general problem.

The other two communications are both related to a request for military assistance from the United Nations. . . .

It is a matter of course that the only sound and lasting solution to the problem which has arisen is that the regular instruments of the Government, in the first place its security administration, are rendered capable of taking care of the situation. I understand the request for technical assistance to have been sent with this in view. My reaction, already communicated to the Government of the Congo, is entirely positive. A technical assistance office is being established and a resident representative appointed. I will submit to the Government of the Congo today or tomorrow detailed proposals for implementation of my acceptance of the request. In formulating my proposals regarding technical assistance experts in the field of security administration, I have had the advantage of consulting the heads of a number of delegations of African Member States.

Keeping firmly in mind what I have just characterized as the sound and lasting solution, which I hope that we will effectively further through the steps on which I have decided at the request of the Government, we must, on the other hand, realistically recognize that this work will take some time and that therefore there is an intermediary period during which the Government may find it difficult to operate in the security field with all the needed efficiency. Irrespective of what we can do in order to shorten this intermediary or transitional period, we must therefore face the problem of what if anything, should be our assistance to the Government pending satisfactory results on the technical assistance line.

As is well known, the Belgian Government has, in the Congo, troops stated by the Government to be maintained there in protection of life and for the maintenance of order. It is not for the Secretary-General to pronounce himself on this action and its legal and political aspects, but I must conclude from the communications received from the Government of the Congo that the presence of these troops is a source of internal and potentially also of international tension. In these circumstances the presence of the Belgian troops cannot be accepted as a satisfactory stopgap arrangement pending the re-establishment of order through the national security force.

It is in this light I personally wish to see the request for military assistance, which has been addressed to me by the Government of the

Congo. Although I am fully aware of all the problems, difficulties and even risks involved, I find that the stopgap arrangement envisaged by the Government of the Congo is preferable to any other formula. It is, therefore, my conclusion that the United Nations should accede to the request of the Government of the Congo, and, in consequence, I strongly recommend to the Council to authorize the Secretary-General to take the necessary steps, in consultation with the Government of the Congo, to provide the Government with military assistance during the period which may have to pass before, through the efforts of the Government with the technical assistance of the United Nations, the national security forces are able to fully meet their tasks. It would be understood that were the United Nations to act as proposed, the Belgian Government would see its way to a withdrawal.

Were the Security Council to act on my recommendation, I would base my actions on the principles which were set out in my report to the General Assembly on the conclusions drawn from previous experiences in the field. [A/3943.] It follows that the United Nations Force would not be authorized to action beyond self-defence. It follows further that they may not take any action which would make them a party to internal conflicts in the country. Finally, the selection of personnel should be such as to avoid complications because of the nationalities used. In the prevailing situation this does not, in my view, exclude the use of units from African States, while, on the other hand, it does exclude recourse to troops from any of the permanent members of the Security Council. May I add that in fact it would be my intention to get, in the first place, assistance from African nations.

In conclusion, I must invite the Council to act with the utmost speed. A decision in principle reached today would be of the highest value. I would welcome consultations followed by renewed meetings for a fuller elaboration of the mandate which I recommend to the Security Council to give to me now. As a matter of course I would report to the Council as appropriate on any action taken on the basis of the authorization which I hope the Council will give me tonight. . . .

Mr. SLIM (Tunisia): I followed with an interest the Council can well imagine the report which the Secretary-General has just made to us on the situation in the Republic of the Congo and on the difficulties with which this newly-independent African State has been confronted in recent weeks.

With regard to the request to the Secretary-General for technical assistance in the field of administration, my delegation welcomes the rapid action that the Secretary-General has been able to take within the limits of his competence, in response to the express request of the Government of the Congo.

It is undeniable that since last week a situation which is as serious as it is unexpected has developed in the Republic of the Congo. Some units of the Congolese forces which had been instructed and trained by

the Belgian authorities before independence have suddenly mutinied.
They have committed unfortunate acts. The mutiny appears to be
directed against the troops' Belgian officers. In the heat of the mutiny
a number of regrettable acts have been committed against some members of the European population, in particular Belgians.

What in fact drove these Congolese troops to mutiny? My delegation believes that we are not at present in a position to answer that
question with any certainty. It is evident from the information which
the Secretary-General has just given us that the situation is still grave.
For several days, despite the seriousness of the acts committed by these
members of the Congolese forces against their Belgian officers and
members of the European population, there were no deaths and no one
was seriously wounded; there was, understandably enough, general
panic among the European residents, which led them to seek safety
outside the Republic of the Congo.

The Belgian Government, however, felt obliged to intervene in order
to maintain or restore order in the Congo. It sent troops, which landed at various Congolese airfields. These troops intervened against the
Congolese troops, and it was at that point that the casualties began to
occur.

The intervention by Belgian troops does not seem to have contributed to the restoration of order in the Republic of the Congo. On the
contrary, its only effect has been to increase the disorder; it took place
against the wishes of the Congo Government, which duly made the
most strenuous protests against the return of Belgian troops to Congolese national territory; it is a breach of the treaty between Belgium
and the Congo, signed on 29 June 1960, and a violation of the sovereignty and independence of the new Republic solemnly recognized by
Belgium on 30 June 1960. Undeniably, therefore, the intervention constitutes an aggressive act for which there is no justification and which
nothing can, in our view, legitimate.

This violation of the sovereignty and independence of the Congo is
the more serious because it was committed by Belgium, the country
which had long administered the Congo. The danger to which the Belgian population in the Congo was exposed cannot serve to justify the
intervention. How can one explain, for instance, the fact that the
recent disturbances in the Congo were provoked solely by Congolese
police and security forces trained by Belgium prior to independence
and under the command of Belgian officers since independence?

I should like now to make a few factual statements.

First, the recent disturbances in the Congo do not reflect any revolutionary tendency directed against the Government of the Republic of
the Congo with a view to a change in the present régime.

Secondly, the Congolese civilian population has been in no way involved in the movement and has, fortunately, taken no part in it. It

follows that there is no question of any general feeling of xenophobia, which could not indeed exist in an African heart.

Thirdly, there is no indication of discord, dissension, or tribal or regional disagreements among the various elements of the Congolese population. It is true that three days ago a somewhat ill-defined secessionist tendency was shown by the Katanga regional Government. It has, moreover, rapidly disappeared, and the Prime Minister of Katanga has reaffirmed his intention of maintaining complete unity with the whole country, in accordance with the present provisional Constitution of the Congo.

Fourthly, Congolese police and security units mutinied against their Belgian officers in the first place and later, alone and without any direct support from the Congolese population, allowed themselves to be carried away and to commit regrettable acts against some members of the European population, in particular Belgians. I would point out also that in the initial stages of the disturbances there were no casualties and no European-occupied buildings were destroyed. The facts show that casualties occured only after the announcement of intervention by Belgian troops.

The conclusion which logically follows from these facts is that the origin of the disturbances, while a matter of concern, cannot be in any way imputed to the Congolese people or to the desires or will of its Government.

Therefore, as I said at the beginning of my statement, the Belgian intervention is clearly an unwarranted act of aggression. My Government can but regret it, and sincerely hopes that the Belgian Government will withdraw the troops it has sent to the Congo.

I have no intention whatever of wounding the feelings of the Belgian people and Government. I took pleasure in congratulating them warmly when the Council a few days ago considered the application of the Republic of the Congo for admission to membership of the United Nations. With regard to the present question of the intervention of Belgian troops after the independence of the Congo, however, I can only express my profound regret.

I turn now to the situation as it has been described by the Secretary-General and to the Congolese Government's formal request for military assistance. From the information provided it is clear that the Congolese Government is requesting military assistance from the United Nations to enable it to protect the national territory. Those are the very terms used in the telegram sent by the Government of the Congo to the Secretary-General. In my delegation's opinion the Government of the Congo, as the Government of an independent and sovereign State, is the sole judge of the advisability of such assistance. It has just made a formal request. In our view there is nothing to prevent the Security Council, which has the matter before it, from taking a decision making such assistance available rapidly, with the least possible delay. My delegation considers that the troops which the Secretary-General, in agreement with the Government of the Congo, employs in providing such assistance should be selected in a manner which will avoid any irritation of Congolese feelings, so that the troops may contribute, by their presence alone, to the reduction of tension and restoration of calm in the country.

Like all the independent African States, Tunisia has followed developments in the Congo since independence with great anxiety. The situation is a matter of grave concern to peoples and to Governments. The independent African countries, moved solely by an understandable feeling of brotherhood, will, I am certain, not fail to make available to the Secretary-General whatever is needed to provide the assistance which the United Nations must, as an act of general solidarity, give to the newly-independent State in the great task of reorganization and peace. It is understood that this United Nations military assistance will cease on the day that the Congolese Government considers the objectives of the assistance to have been accomplished.

Having thus briefly—because of the urgency of the situation—but clearly explained my Government's position, I should like to say that my delegation has deemed it advisable to submit, in the course of this debate, a draft resolution [S/4383] calling upon the Government of Belgium to withdraw its troops from the territory of the Republic of the Congo and authorizing the Secretary-General to take the necessary steps, in consultation with the Government of the Republic of the Congo, to provide rapidly the military assistance requested of the United Nations. This draft resolution has just been distributed to members of the Security Council. I hope that it reflects the general opinion of the members of the Security Council and that it will therefore receive their approval. . . .

[The draft resolution proposed by Tunisia was as follows:

"The Security Council,

"Considering the report of the Secretary-General on a request for United Nations action in relation to the Republic of the Congo,

"Considering the request for military assistance addressed to the Secretary-General by the President and the Prime Minister of the Republic of the Congo (document S/4382),

"1. Calls upon the Government of Belgium to withdraw their troops from the territory of the Republic of the Congo;

"2. Decides to authorize the Secretary-General to take the necessary steps, in consultation with the Government of the Republic of the Congo, to provide the Government with such military assistance as may be necessary, until, through the efforts of the Congolese Government with the technical assistance of the United Nations, the national security forces may be able, in the opinion of the Government, to meet fully their tasks;

"3.   Requests the Secretary-General to report to the Security Council as appropriate."

Soviet amendments to this resolution (S/4386), calling for immediate withdrawal of Belgian troops, condemning "the armed aggression" of Belgium, and limiting military assistance to African troops, were rejected by the Security Council, and the Tunisian draft resolution was approved by 8 votes, with 3 abstentions (China, France, and the United Kingdom) in the early morning on 14 July 1960. S/4387; SCOR, XV, Supp. for July–Sept. 1950, p. 16.]

5.   *First Report of the Secretary-General, 18 July 1960.*

S/4389 (18 July 1960); SCOR, XV, Supp. for July–Sept. 1950, pp. 16–24.

The Mandate

The resolution of the Security Council was adopted in response to my initial statement to the Council.   Therefore, that statement may be regarded as a basic document on the interpretation of the mandate. In the statement I made clear my view of the main purpose of the introduction of a United Nations Force in the Congo as well as of the relationship between this action and a withdrawal of Belgian troops. I also stated in general terms what legal principles in my view should apply to the operation.

However, even with these explanations of my intentions and of my interpretation of the situation, important points were left open for an interpretation in practice.   In submitting this first progress report, I want not only to bring to the knowledge of the Council what so far has been achieved, but also what lines I have followed concerning the implementation of the authorization.

I indicated as a "sound and lasting solution" to the difficulties which had arisen in the Congo the re-establishment of the instruments of the Government for the maintenance of order.   It was implied in my presentation that it was the breakdown of those instruments which had created a situation which through its consequences represented a threat to peace and security justifying United Nations intervention on the basis of the explicit request of the Government of the Republic of the Congo.   Thus, the two main elements, from the legal point of view, were on the one hand this request and, on the other hand, the implied finding that the circumstances to which I had referred were such as to justify United Nations action under the Charter.   Whether or not it was also held that the United Nations faced a conflict between two parties was, under these circumstances, in my view, legally not essential for the justification of the action.   However, I pointed out that, on the basis of the interpretation I had given, it would be understood that, were the United Nations to act as I proposed, the Belgian Government "would see its way to a withdrawal", and the Council itself called upon the Belgian Government to withdraw their troops.

In order to assist the Government of the Republic of the Congo to re-establish its administration, specifically in the field of security, certain decisions had already been taken by me in response to a general appeal from the Government. However, they could yield results only after a certain time and in the meanwhile there was a need for a stop-gap arrangement, established by the United Nations in consultation with the Government, no preferable alternative arrangements being available for the intermediary period which might have to pass until, in the words of the resolution, "the national security forces might be able, in the opinion of the Government, to meet fully their tasks". Thus, the Force introduced is to be regarded as a temporary security force, present in the Republic of the Congo with the consent of the Government for the time and the purpose indicated.

Although the United Nations Force under the resolution is dispatched to the Congo at the request of the Government and will be present in the Congo with its consent, and although it may be considered as serving as an arm of the Government for the maintenance of order and protection of life—tasks which naturally belong to the national authorities and which will pass to such authorities as soon as, in the view of the Government, they are sufficiently firmly established—the Force is necessarily under the exclusive command of the United Nations, vested in the Secretary-General under the control of the Security Council. This is in accordance with the principles generally applied by the Organization. The Force is thus not under the orders of the Government nor can it, as I pointed out in my statement to the Council, be permitted to become a party to any internal conflict. A departure from this principle would seriously endanger the impartiality of the United Nations and of the operation.

Another principle which I consider as generally applicable and, therefore, as basic also to the present operation, is that, while, on its side, the host Government, when exercising its sovereign right with regard to the presence of the Force, should be guided by good faith in the interpretation of the purpose of the Force, the United Nations, on its side, should be understood to be determined by similar good faith in the interpretation of the purpose when it considers the question of the maintenance of the Force in the host country. This principle is reflected in the final phrase of the resolution authorizing the Secretary-General to provide the Government of the Republic of the Congo with United Nations military assistance.

From this basic understanding regarding the presence of a United Nations Force in the country it follows that the United Nations activity should have freedom of movement within its area of operations and all such facilities regarding access to that area and communications as are necessary for a successful accomplishment of the task. A further elaboration of this rule obviously requires an agreement with the Government, i. e., specifying what is to be considered the area of operations.

Regarding the composition of the Force, there is another general principle which, in the light of previous experience, I find it necessary to apply. In the report to which I referred in my statement to the Security Council, it is stated that "while the United Nations must reserve for itself the authority to decide on the composition of such [military] elements, it is obvious that the host country, in giving its consent, cannot be indifferent to the composition of those elements." The report continues: "In order to limit the scope of possible differences of opinion, the United Nations in recent operations has followed two principles: not to include units from any of the permanent members of the Security Council; and not to include units from any country which, because of its geographical position or for other reasons, might be considered as possibly having a special interest in the situation which has called for the operation. . . . It would seem desirable to accept a formula . . . to the effect that, while it is for the United Nations alone to decide on the composition of military elements sent to a country, the United Nations should, in deciding on composition, take fully into account the viewpoint of the host Government as one of the most serious factors which should guide the recruitment of the personnel. Usually this is likely to mean that serious objections by the host country against participation by a specific contributing country in the United Nations operation will determine the action of the Organization. However, were the United Nations for good reasons to find that course inadvisable, it would remain free to pursue its own line, and any resulting conflict would have to be resolved on a political rather than on a legal basis." [A/3943.] I recommended in the report quoted, that this principle should be considered applicable to all United Nations operations of the present kind. The problem is in this particular case covered by the request for consultations with the Congo Government. In my statement to the Council I pointed out that, while I consider that the aforementioned principle excludes military units in the Force from any of the permanent members of the Security Council, I, in fact, had the "intention to get, in the first place, assistance from African nations."

Among other principles which I consider essential to this operation, I may mention the following.

The authority granted to the United Nations Force cannot be exercised within the Congo either in competition with representatives of the host Government or in co-operation with them in any joint operation. This naturally applies *a fortiori* to representatives and military units of other Governments than the host Government. Thus, the United Nations operation must be separate and distinct from activities by any national authorities.

Likewise, it follows from the rule that the United Nations units must not become parties in internal conflicts, that they cannot be used to enforce any specific political solution of pending problems or to influence the political balance decisive to such a solution. Apart from the general reasons for this principle, there is the specific one, that it is only on this basis that the United Nations can expect to be able to draw on Member countries for contributions in men and material.

To all United Nations personnel used in the present operation the basic rules of the United Nations for international service should be considered as applicable, particularly as regards full loyalty to the aims of the Organization and to abstention from actions in relation to their country of origin which might deprive the operation of its international character and create a situation of dual loyalty.

In my initial statement I recalled the rule applied in previous United Nations operations to the effect that the military units would be entitled to act only in self-defence. In amplification of this statement I would like to quote the following passage from the report to which I referred: " . . . men engaged in the operation may never take the initiative in the use of armed force, but are entitled to respond with force to an attack with arms, including attempts to use force to make them withdraw from positions which they occupy under orders from the Commander", acting under the authority of the Security Council and within the scope of its resolution. "The basic element involved is clearly the prohibition against any *initiative* in the use of armed force."

The Composition of the Force

Before reporting on the steps taken for the building up of the Force and on the agreements reached with a number of Governments regarding contributions to the Force, I wish to make some general observations.

As stated to the Security Council on 13 July 1960, the ultimate solution to the problem that has arisen in the Congo has to be found by the Republic of the Congo itself, with the assistance of the United Nations. In the same spirit I believe that, to the extent that the Republic of the Congo needs international assistance, such assistance should, within the framework of the United Nations, in the first instance be given by its sister African nations, as an act of African solidarity. However, this natural reliance on regional solidarity for the solution of a problem of this kind, should be qualified by an element of universality, natural—and indeed essential—to any United Nations operation. Therefore, while the Force, in my view, should be built around a hard core of military units from African States, it should also, to the extent which might be found practical, include units from other areas which meet the general conditions for the composition of a United Nations Force to which I have referred above.

Thus, in my view, the present operation is, in the first place, a manifestation of the willingness and ability of the African States to help within the framework of the United Nations, of which I have found the most convincing evidence in the course of this effort. Elements from other regions, included in the Force, may be considered as assistance given, in the spirit of the Charter, to the African community of nations by nations of those other regions. With this approach, the present operation should serve to strengthen the African community of nations and to strengthen also their ties, within the United Nations, with the world community. It would be wholly unjustified to interpret the United Nations action in the sense that nations from outside the region step into the Congo situation, using the United Nations as their instrumentality, because of the incapability of the Congo and of the African States themselves to make the basic contribution to the solution of the problem.

My efforts to build up the Force have been guided by this interpretation of the United Nations operation. For that reason I have in the first place, appealed to African States for troops, addressing myself in a second stage to other nations meeting the conditions which are generally applicable, and continuing my efforts to activate further African units to the extent necessary. While the requests for troops so far presented by me, or offers of troops accepted by me, follow the pattern just stated, I have already in the first stage addressed a series of appeals for support in such fields as logistics, signals, material, aircraft and specialized personnel to those countries which are most likely to provide them at very short notice, irrespective of their geographical position.

Apart from being influenced by the factors which I have explained above, I have, naturally, been guided by considerations of availability of troops, language and geographical distribution within the region.

Even before the decision of the Security Council I was informed by the Republic of Ghana that it had responded favourably to an urgent demand from the Government of the Republic of the Congo for military assistance and that it wanted this assistance to be integrated in the general United Nations effort which the Government anticipated, after having been informed of the convening of the Security Council and of my proposals to the Council. Likewise, the Governments of Guinea, Morocco and Tunisia informed me at this early stage of their willingness to put, forthwith, military units at the disposal of the United Nations. These offers have been accepted and the troops have been or will be airlifted to the Congo as quickly as practicable. Some short delays have been unavoidable for logistic reasons or because of the necessity to stagger the airlifts.

Immediately after the end of the meeting of the Security Council, in the morning of 14 July 1960, I addressed appeals for assistance to the Chiefs of State of all African Member nations north of the Congo and of the Federation of Mali, either asking directly for troops, or, where language difficulties could be foreseen, asking for an immediate discussion with their Permanent Representatives at the United Nations about the best form in which the country concerned could render help.

A full account of the results of this appeal and of arrangements made will be given in the following. At this point I wish to state that I immediately accepted an offer of troops also from Ethiopia, thus getting in the first set-up of the Force adequate representation from North Africa, West Africa and East Africa. As will be clear from the detailed report on arrangements made, the five countries specifically mentioned provide the Force with an initial strength of seven battalions, numbering more than 4,000 men.

I have received promises of additional battalions from several African French-speaking countries, as well as from some English-speaking nations in Africa. An offer of the Federation of Mali has been accepted and will be activated at a somewhat later stage. In the light of the general approach to which I referred above, I am activating the other offers as necessary.

Following the pattern which I have previously explained, I have, with the establishment of an initial Force of seven battalions of five African countries, completed a first phase of the building up of the Force. For a second phase I have appealed for assistance in the form of troops from three European, one Asian and one Latin American country, meeting the general conditions applying to a United Nations Force. In one of these cases, Sweden, I have asked for, and received permission on a temporary basis, to transfer the Swedish battalion of the United Nations Emergency Force (UNEF) in Gaza to the Congo by an airlift which is likely to be carried out on Wednesday, 20 July, thus bringing the total strength up to eight battalions.

As regards assistance in other forms, I have reached agreement on the sending of police companies from a number of African States. I have also appealed for aircraft, heavy equipment and specialized personnel from some of the last-mentioned countries. Apart from its other contribution, Ghana has undertaken to provide the Force with two military medical units.

Requests for heavy material and aircraft as well as for signals and other parts of the logistic support have been addressed to a number of non-African States; as regards signals, a special difficulty has been created by the fact that the personnel, if at all possible, should be bilingual, having knowledge of both French and English.

Appeals for assistance with air transport have been addressed to three non-African nations.

The response to all these various appeals has been favourable.

I have appointed Major-General Carl von Horn, Sweden, Supreme Commander of the Force. As Chief of Staff of the United Nations Truce Supervision Organization for three years, General von Horn has already considerable experience as a senior military representative of the United Nations. He will be assisted by a small personal staff of officers drawn from the group under his command in Jerusalem. I have directed a request to India to make available to me a senior officer as military adviser in the Executive Office of the Secretary-General.

In broad outline, this completes the picture of the geographical distribution sought for the Force in implementation of the decision of the Security Council on the basis of the principles outlined above. It reflects my wish to give to the African community of nations the central position which in this case is their due, while maintaining the universal character of a United Nations operation. As the composition of the Force is still not completed, I can in the following stages make such adjustments as the Security Council may find desirable, but I wish to express my hope that the steps so far taken on the basis of the authority given to me by the Council will meet with the approval of the Council. . . .

Withdrawal of Belgian Troops

As recalled above, the resolution of the Security Council refers also to the withdrawal of Belgian troops. Both at Headquarters and in Leopoldville, we remain in close touch with this aspect of the problems covered by the resolution.

I have been informed by my representative in Leopoldville that he has received from the Belgian Ambassador a letter according to which instructions have been given to the Belgian Commander in the Congo to the effect that Belgian military interventions should be limited to what is called for by the security needs of Belgian nationals and that in all other matters the Belgian Command has been advised to abide by the instructions of the military Command of the United Nations forces. The letter further states that in case of grave and imminent danger, the Belgian forces will continue to take "the necessary security measures" but that "in each case they will immediately refer the matter to the military Command of the United Nations". The Belgian Military Command, according to the letter has been "ordered to impose strict discipline upon their forces in the Congo and has been told to cooperate to the greatest extent when any request is made to them by the United Nations".

My representative in Leopoldville has also been informed that "following the arrival of the United Nations Forces, Belgian units amounting to one company and one platoon have left Leopoldville on 17 July 1960. They are kept at the disposal of the Commander of the Belgian metropolitan Forces to answer calls of help where there are no United Nations troops available".

I wish to draw the attention of the Council to the fact that this statement refers to the situation as of 17 July 1960. Discussions are continuing and I shall report separately on the development.

6. *Discussion in the Security Council, 20–21 July 1960.*

SCOR, XV, Mtg. 877.

The SECRETARY-GENERAL: . . . One week has passed since the Security Council adopted its resolution regarding military assistance to the Republic of the Congo and a withdrawal of Belgian troops.

The development up to Monday morning has been covered in my first report to the Council. I have later issued three addenda which indicate, on the one side, that the Force has now been brought up to twelve African battalions and two European battalions, one of which, however, is there only on a temporary basis; I have not specified the other and numerous military units of a smaller size and of specialized character which, thanks to the help of various Member States, we are bringing into the Congo. The addenda also show where we stood as of yesterday regarding the question of Belgian withdrawal. . . .

You find in the report an indication that in due time there will have to be established by agreement with the Government of the Congo, an area of operation for the United Nations Force, as well as certain other conditions for its contribution to the maintenance of satisfactory conditions in the country. On this point, I would like to stress that, in one important respect, there cannot, from my viewpoint, exist any hesitation as regards what is the area of operation. The resolution of the Security Council, in response to the appeal from the Government of the Congo, clearly applies to the whole of the Territory of the Republic as it existed when the Security Council, only a few days earlier, recommended the Congo for admission as a Member of the United Nations. Thus, in my view, the United Nations Force, under the resolution and on the basis of the request of the Government of the Congo, is entitled to access to all parts of the territory in fulfilment of its duties.

I may mention here that, in reply to a communication to me from Mr. Tshombe, President of the Provincial Government of Katanga, I have made it clear that actions of the United Nations through the Secretary-General, in respects covered by the resolution, must in view of the legal circumstances which he has to take into account, be considered by him as actions referring to the Republic of the Congo as an entity.

I should recall that I said both in my initial statement and in my first report that the United Nations Force cannot be a party to any internal conflict nor can the United Nations Force intervene in a domestic conflict.

Although the Security Council did not, as it has done in previous cases, authorize or request the Secretary-General to take specific steps for the implementation of withdrawal—apart, of course, from the establishment of the Force—my representatives in the Congo have taken the initiatives they have found indicated for the co-ordination of the implementation of the Security Council decision on the Force with the implementation of its decision on withdrawal. Although I do not consider it necessary, a clarification of my mandate on this point may be found useful by the Council. Such a clarification, if made, might aim at establishing the substance of my mandate on this point and the aim of the Council as regards the implementation of the call for a withdrawal.

Through the decision of the Security Council of last Wednesday, the United Nations has embarked on its biggest single effort under United Nations colours, organized and directed by the United Nations itself. I already had reason to pay a tribute to Member Governments for what they have done to render the task of the Organization possible. May I say here and now that I will have—as a spokesman for the Security Council and on behalf of the United Nations—to ask for much, much more from Member Nations, in the military field as well as in the civilian field. There should not be any hesitation, because we are at a turn of the road where our attitude will be of decisive significance, I believe, not only for the future of this Organization, but also for the future of Africa. And Africa may well in present circumstances mean the world. I know these are very strong words, but I hope that this Council and the Members of this Organization know that I do not use strong words unless they are supported by strong convictions.

Mr. KANZA (Republic of the Congo): . . . The Congolese Government has instructed me to state to the Council these four points, which in our opinion represent four suggestions amounting almost to decisions if the world wishes that Belgium should be able to win its way once more to the heart of the Congolese—a heart which at the moment is closed to Belgian friendship, but which is ready to open to understanding with Belgium on these lines.

The first point is that an end should be put to the aggressive action of Belgian troops in the Congo. . . .

Over a week ago [873rd meeting], when we were discussing the second point—the evacuation of Belgian troops—we were somewhat trusting and were simply asking that the Belgian troops be evacuated [to] the military bases in the Congo, those of Kamina and Kitona. But our trust has since given way to an unfortunate distrust, and therefore our second point is that these Belgian troops must be evacuated from our national territory as quickly as possible.

The first two points go, so far as we are concerned, a considerable way towards solving the conflict between two friendly countries which are still ready to co-operate in the future. You will have learnt that existing impatience is such that our Head of State, Mr. Joseph Kasa-vubu, and our Prime Minister, Mr. Lumumba, have gone so far as to issue an ultimatum—the first of its kind—to the Secretary-General's representative at Leopoldville. The ultimatum appears in the last paragraph of the letter which they wrote from Stanleyville on 17 July last to Mr. Bunche, the United Nations Under-Secretary, who is at present at Leopoldville. . . . The paragraph reads as follows:

"If the United Nations seems unable to carry out, between now and 19 July 1960 at 12 midnight, the task which we have asked it to accomplish—the evacuation of Belgian troops from the national territory, and the retaking of the positions occupied by the Belgian metropolitan forces—we shall regretfully be compelled to request the Soviet Union to intervene, but"—this is what follows—"we hope that you will be able to avoid such a contingency." . . .

The third point is concerned with the situation prevailing in our sixth province, Katanga. The Congolese Government, which does not idly divulge certain information at its disposal, is aware of the behind-the-scenes manoeuvres designed to bring about the secession of Katanga. . . .

The fourth point concerns general technical assistance. It is painful for us to note the continued existence of a certain amount of panic deliberately created by our Belgian friends. . . .

It is a fact that the Belgians have accomplished in the Congo more than have other countries, that the Belgians have invested more than others in the Congo, and that they have only begun their work there. It would be a regrettable capitulation for them to abandon what they have begun instead of finishing. It is therefore our intention to guarantee the safety of the person and property of every Belgian who wishes to remain in the Congo. . . .

Mr. WIGNY (Belgium): . . . I shall briefly summarize the Belgian Government's position and the principles which guide its actions. . . .

(1) The purpose of Belgian military intervention in the Congo is purely humanitarian.

(2) The intervention had been strictly proportionate to the objective sought, namely the protection of the lives of Belgian nationals.

(3) It is limited in its scope by its objective. It is limited in time since it is conceived as a temporary action.

(4) In intervening, Belgium is not pursuing any political design or seeking to interfere in any way in the domestic politics of the Congo.

(5) So far as we are concerned the independence of the Congo is an accomplished fact. Why would we have granted it only to take it back indirectly a fortnight later? The independence of the Congo is an accomplished fact.

(6) Belgium is gratified that, under the direction of the Secretary-General, the United Nations has undertaken military action to restore order and security in the Congo.

(7) The Belgian authorities will co-operate in the military action undertaken by the United Nations.

(8) Belgium will withdraw its intervening troops as soon as, and to the extent that, the United Nations effectively ensures the maintenance of order and the safety of persons. This principle has already begun to be carried out, particularly in Leopoldville, and we hope that the situation will soon be the same elsewhere.

Mr. KUZNETSOV (USSR): . . . The Security Council has met today at the request of the Soviet Government in order to hear the report of the Secretary-General on the implementation of the Security Council's resolution of 14 July 1960. As is known, one of the most important points in that resolution was the request for the withdrawal of Belgian troops from the territory of the Republic of the Congo—in other words, for the cessation of armed intervention against the Congolese people, who had just attained their national independence.

The urgent need to give prompt consideration to this question is dictated by the fact that the Belgian Government, relying on the support of those Powers which are interested in the preservation of the colonial régime in the Congo, is continuing its armed intervention in that country's domestic affairs. The Belgian Government is continuing an open combat against the legitimate Government of the Republic of the Congo, which has firmly stated its determination to ensure its country's genuine independence and to preserve its territorial integrity.

The Security Council, having examined several days ago the situation in the Congo, unquestionably took useful action when it called upon the Government of Belgium to withdraw Belgian troops from the territory of the Congo. The problem now is to put that constructive decision into effect as quickly as possible. More and more contingents of Belgian troops are arriving in the Congo every day, in which connexion it should be noted that the new Belgian reinforcements are arriving simultaneously with United Nations forces.

Belgian paratroopers have seized a number of Congolese towns and have virtually occupied Leopoldville, the capital of the Congo. The Belgians have the airfields and the main lines of communication and bridges in their hands. According to the latest reports, Belgian aircraft equipped with rocket weapons are being hastened to the Congo and Belgian troops are feverishly erecting fortifications at Leopoldville, which shows that they are preparing for a protracted war. At the same time the occupying forces are broadening the scope of their military operations in the Congo. . . .

We now know that the expansion of military intervention in the Congo is being accompanied by efforts to dismember the young State. As so often in the past, the colonialists are here trying to apply the principle of "divide and rule". They have succeeded in finding a stooge to be used to that end in the person of one Tshombé who, only a few days after the proclamation of the Republic's independence, came out with the idea of separating from the new-born African State one of its most important provinces, namely Katanga.

It is hardly surprising that the activities of Tshombé should have caused the financial and industrial moguls to exult. Behind these attempts to dismember the Congo can easily be discerned the desire of the Western Powers to reserve for themselves the economically valuable areas of the former Belgian colonies, which are among the chief sources of enrichment for the capitalist monopolies.

Not without reason did the delegations of the African States Members of the United Nations, in their statement of 18 July concerning the Congo situation, resolutely condemn any attempt to undermine the Congo's territorial integrity from without. That position is fully shared and whole-heartedly supported by the Soviet Government.

The enemies of the Republic of the Congo are combining their political and military attacks upon it with economic aggression, designed to strangle the young Republic by hunger, the provocation of disorder, and sabotage.

As the colonialists continue their open military intervention in the domestic affairs of the Congo, the situation in that country deteriorates with every passing day. The Government of the Republic has appealed again and again to world opinion, to the United Nations, drawing attention to the mortal danger which threatens the country and asking that urgent measures be taken to put an end to the continuing aggression. First of all it demands the immediate withdrawal of Belgian troops from the Congo. Yet the Belgian authorities continue to ignore these demands by the Government of the Republic of the Congo.

The Security Council, on which is conferred primary responsibility for the maintenance of international peace and security, should without delay extend a helping hand to the victim of imperialist aggression and take effective steps to enable the Congo to consolidate its independence. . . .

In connexion with the situation which has arisen, the Soviet delegation, on instructions from the Soviet Government, submits the following draft resolution [S/4402] to the Security Council for its consideration:

"The Security Council,

"Having heard the report of the Secretary-General of the United Nations on the question of aggression by Belgium against the Republic of the Congo,

"1.   Insists upon the immediate cessation of armed intervention against the Republic of the Congo and the withdrawal from its territory of all troops of the aggressor within a period of three days;

"2.   Calls upon the States Members of the United Nations to respect the territorial integrity of the Republic of the Congo and not to undertake any actions which might violate that integrity."

The Soviet delegation expresses the hope that at this crucial moment the draft resolution which it has submitted will receive the unanimous support of the Security Council's members.

If aggression continues, then, of course, more active measures will have to be taken, both by the United Nations and by peace-loving States which are in sympathy with the Congo's cause. . . .

Mr. LODGE (USA): . . . There have been reports that the Soviet Union might intervene in the Congo directly with troops and before I yield the floor I would just like to say a word about that. The position of the United States Government on this point is unequivocally clear for itself and for others. For, as I have said, despite an official request from the Government of the Congo some days ago for United States troops we insisted that all American help should be channeled through the United Nations. The United Nations effort, we think, offers the best way of restoring order and making possible the speedy withdrawal by stages, of Belgian forces. Obviously, no troops should be introduced into the Congo other than those requested by the Secretary-General pursuant to the Security Council's resolution of 14 July. The United States can, accordingly, be counted on to continue its vigorous support of the United Nations in the Congo. With other United Nations Members we will do whatever may be necessary to prevent the intrusion of any military forces not requested by the United Nations. Such forces, if they were introduced, not only would be in defiance of the United Nations but would seriously jeopardize any effort to bring stability and order to the Congo. . . .

[A joint draft resolution, introduced by Ceylon and Tunisia (S/4404), provided as follows:

"The Security Council,

"Having considered the first report by the Secretary-General on the implementation of Security Council resolution S/4387 of 14 July 1960 (document S/4389),

"Appreciating the work of the Secretary-General and the support so readily and so speedily given to him by all Member States invited by him to give assistance,

"Noting that as stated by the Secretary-General the arrival of the troops of the United Nations force in Leopoldville has already had a salutary effect,

"Recognizing that an urgent need still exists to continue and to increase such efforts,

"Considering that the complete restoration of law and order in the Republic of the Congo would effectively contribute to the maintenance of international peace and security,

"Recognizing that the Security Council recommended the admission of the Republic of the Congo to membership in the United Nations as a unit,

"1. Calls upon the Government of Belgium to implement speedily the Security Council resolution of 14 July 1960, on the withdrawal of their troops and authorizes the Secretary-General to take all necessary action to this effect;

"2. Requests all States to refrain from any action which might tend to impede the restoration of law and order and the exercise by the Government of Congo of its authority and also to refrain from any action which might undermine the territorial integrity and the political independence of the Republic of the Congo;

"3. Decides to authorize the Secretary-General to continue to take such action as may be necessary under the authority given to him by the Security Council dated 14 July 1960, and by this resolution;

"4. Commends the Secretary-General for the prompt action he has taken to carry out resolution S/4387 of the Security Council and his first report;

"5. Invites the specialized agencies of the United Nations to render to the Secretary-General such assistance as he may require;

"6. Requests the Secretary-General to report further to the Security Council as appropriate."

After the deletion of operative paragraph 3, which was considered redundant, the Council adopted unanimously this draft resolution. S/4405 (22 July 1960); SCOR, XV, Supp. for July–Sept. 1960, p. 34.]

7. *Basic Agreement between the United Nations and the Republic of the Congo, 29 July 1960.*

A/4389/Add. 5 (29 July 1960); SCOR, XV, Supp. for July–Sept. 1960, pp. 27–28.

1. The Government of the Republic of the Congo states that, in the exercise of its sovereign rights with respect to any question concerning the presence and functioning of the United Nations Force in the Congo, it will be guided, in good faith, by the fact that it has requested military assistance from the United Nations and by its acceptance of the resolutions of the Security Council of 14 and 22 July 1960; it likewise states that it will ensure the freedom of movement of the Force in the interior of the country and will accord the requisite privileges and immunities to all personnel associated with the activities of the Force.

2. The United Nations takes note of this statement of the Government of the Republic of the Congo and states that, with regard to the

activities of the United Nations Force in the Congo, it will be guided in good faith, by the task assigned to the Force in the aforementioned resolutions; in particular the United Nations reaffirms, considering it to be in accordance with the wishes of the Government of the Republic of the Congo, that it is prepared to maintain the United Nations Force in the Congo until such time as it deems the latter's task to have been fully accomplished.

3.   The Government of the Republic of the Congo and the Secretary-General state their intention to proceed immediately, in the light of paragraphs 1 and 2 above, to explore jointly specific aspects of the functioning of the United Nations Force in the Congo, notably with respect to its deployment, the question of its lines of communication and supply, its lodging and its provisioning; the Government of the Republic of the Congo, confirming its intention to facilitate the functioning of the United Nations Force in the Congo, and the United Nations have agreed to work together to hasten the implementation of the guiding principles laid down in consequence of the work of joint exploration on the basis of the resolutions of the Security Council.

4.   The foregoing provisions shall likewise be applicable, as appropriate, to the non-military aspects of the United Nations operation in the Congo.

NOTE.   On 4 August 1960, the Secretary-General noted that, according to a message from Mr. Tshombe, "the dispatch of United Nations troops to Katanga will be resisted and that the arrival of these troops will set off a general uprising in Katanga." The Secretary-General drew Mr. Tshombe's attention "to Article 25 of the United Nations Charter, as also to Article 49, which Articles confer on the Security Council an authority applicable directly to Governments, and *a fortiori* to subordinate territorial non-governmental authorities of Member nations. The same obligations must be regarded as applicable by analogy to nations which, like the Republic of the Congo, have been recommended for admission to the United Nations. Resistance by a Member Government to a Security Council decision has legal consequences laid down in the Charter. These sanctions necessarily apply also to the subordinate territorial organs of a nation to which the Charter rules apply. The Secretary-General has already transmitted the text of an interpretative statement which he made to the Security Council, which makes it clear that the Security Council's resolutions apply to the entire territory of the Congo. The Secretary-General's position was unanimously approved by the Security Council. The conclusions to be drawn from this and from the Charter rules for the Congo are obvious. The Secretary-General trusts that in the light of these observations the intentions indicated in the message will be considered with full knowledge of their extremely serious character. He hopes also that the situation will be clarified before the arrival of the United Nations troops, in such a way as to provide every assurance that the entry of these military elements does not represent any interference in the internal affairs of the Republic of the Congo, including its provinces, or impede or modify in any way the free exercise of rights to act, in legal and democratic forms, in favour of one or another solution of such constitutional problems as may in due time arise for the Congolese people."

The Secretary-General also pointed out that the following principles apply to any para-military operation of the United Nations: "(i) The troops are under the sole command and the sole control of the United Nations. (ii) The troops are not permitted to interfere in the internal affairs of the country in which they are deployed. They cannot be used in order to impose any particular political solution of pending problems, or to exert any influence on a balance of political forces which may be decisive for such a solution. (iii) United Nations military units are not entitled to act except in self-defence. This rule categorically prohibits the troops participating in the operation from taking the initiative of resorting to armed force, but permits them to reply by force to an armed attack, in particular to any attempts to resort to force which might be made with the object of compelling them to evacuate positions which they occupy on the orders of their commander." S/4417 (6 August 1960); SCOR, XV, Supp. for July-Sept. 1960, p. 45, at 48–49.

After a visit to Katanga by Mr. Bunche, the Special Representative of the Secretary-General in the Congo, confirmed the "unyielding opposition" of the authorities in Katanga to the coming of the United Nations troops, the Secretary-General reported to the Security Council that the aim of the Council's resolutions "cannot be achieved by the use of the United Nations Force, as its mandate has been defined. If the Council, as it is assumed, wishes to maintain its objectives, the Council must, therefore, either change the character of the Force, which appears to me to be impossible, both for constitutional reasons and in view of the commitments to the contributing Governments, or resort to other methods which would enable me to carry through the implementation of its resolution without going beyond my instructions as regards the Force."

He added that the "difficulty which the Council faces in the case of Katanga does not have its root in the Belgian attitude regarding the problem as stated to me, as the Belgian Government acquiesces in the Security Council decisions and therefore undoubtedly will instruct its military elements in the province to act in accordance with the resolutions as implemented by the United Nations Force, if that has not yet been done.

"Nor is the problem a desire on the part of the authorities of the province to secede from the Republic of the Congo. The question is a constitutional one with strong undercurrents of individual and collective political aims. The problem for those resisting the United Nations Force in Katanga may be stated in these terms: Will United Nations participation in security control in Katanga submit the province to the immediate control and authority of the Central Government against its wishes? They consider this seriously to jeopardize their possibility to work for other constitutional solutions than a strictly unitarian one, e.g. some kind of federal structure providing for a higher degree of provincial self-government than now foreseen. The spokesmen for this attitude reject the unitarian formula as incompatible with the interest of the whole Congo people and as imposed from outside.

"This is an internal political problem to which the United Nations as an organization obviously cannot be a party. Nor would the entry of the United Nations Force in Katanga mean any taking of sides in the conflict to which I have just referred. Nor should it be permitted to shift the weights between personalities or groups or schools of thought in a way which would prejudge the solution of the internal political problem. I believe all this can be avoided if the United Nations maintains firmly its aim and acts with clarity and tact, but the question is not one which can be taken lightly. The Security Council may wish to clarify its views on the matter and to lay down such rules for the United Nations operation as would serve to separate effectively questions of a peaceful and democratic development in the constitutional field from any questions relating to the presence of the United Nations Force." *Idem*, pp. 52–53.

In his oral statement to the Security Council on 8 August 1960, the Secretary-General noted that the Katanga authorities "have introduced an unexpected element of organized military opposition by Congolese forces against the entry of the United Nations Force. Such opposition would require military initiative from the United Nations force to which I would not be entitled to resort short of a formal authorization of the Council, even in that case naturally using only contingents representing Governments which would accept such a new stand by the Council." He pointed out that the Belgian Government only promised not to offer active resistance, that the Central Government has shown great impatience and distrust, and that some of the Governments which have contributed forces have been threatening to take matters in their own hands, to break away from the United Nations Force and to pursue a unilateral policy. He expressed his hope for a successful conclusion which he defined as follows:

"By a 'successful conclusion' I mean a conclusion preserving the unity of the Congo people, while protecting the democratic rights of everybody to let his influence bear, in democratic forms, on the final constitution for the Republic to be determined only by the Congolese people themselves.

"I further mean by that term the speediest possible withdrawal of Belgian troops in accordance with the Security Council resolutions, as the presence of those troops now is the main cause of continued danger, a withdrawal that must be complete and unconditional.   .   .   .

"Finally, I mean by a satisfactory solution one which will permit the Congolese people to choose freely its political orientation in our world of today, independent of any foreign elements the presence and role of which would mean that through the Congo we might get conflicts extraneous to the African world introduced on the continent.

"I do not hesitate to say that the speediest possible—I would even say immediate—achievement of such a solution of the Congo problem is a question of peace or war, and when saying peace or war I do not limit my perspective to the Congo. A delay now, hesitation now, efforts to safeguard national or group interests now in a way that would hamper the United Nations effort, would risk values immeasurably greater than any of those which such action may be intended to protect. This applies to all parties, first of all the one to which the Security Council has addressed its appeal.

"The Charter states in several articles the obligations of Member nations in relation to the Organization in a situation like the present one. I have mentioned them in the reply to Mr. Tshombé's 'démarche' which is published in my report, but I want here and now to quote them in full. The first one is Article 25, which says: 'The Members of the United Nations agree to accept and carry out the decisions of the Security Council in accordance with the present Charter.' The other one is Article 49, which says: 'The Members of the United Nations shall join in affording mutual assistance in carrying out the measures decided upon by the Security Council.'

"Could there be a more explicit basis for my hope that we may now count on active support, in the ways which emerge from what I have said, from the Governments directly concerned? Could there be a more explicit basis also for my expectation that local authorities will now adjust themselves to the obligations which their country has incurred?

"However, I want to go one step further and quote also Article 40 of the Charter, which speaks about actions taken by the Security Council in protection of peace and security, first of all, by certain so-called 'provisional measures'. It is stated in the Article: 'Such provisional measures shall be without prejudice to the rights, claims, or position of the parties concerned. The Security Council shall duly take account of failure to comply with such provisional measures.'

"Please, permit me here to remind you also of Article 41: 'The Security Council may decide what measures not involving the use of armed force are to be employed to give effect to its decisions, and it may call upon the Members of the United Nations to apply such measures.'

"The resolutions of the Security Council of 14 July and 22 July were not explicitly adopted under Chapter VII, but they were passed on the basis of an initiative under Article 99. For that reason I have felt entitled to quote three articles under Chapter VII, and I repeat what I have already said in this respect: in a perspective which may well be short rather than long, the problem facing the Congo is one of peace or war—and not only in the Congo.
. . .

"I have held it necessary and in accordance with the intentions of the Council that everywhere in the Congo the withdrawal of Belgian troops should be immediately followed, or even preceded, by the entry of United Nations troops, shouldering the responsibility for the maintenance of security and order. So it has been everywhere outside Katanga.

"In Katanga this principle has led to the development of a vicious circle. The entry of United Nations troops is obstructed and, correspondingly, the withdrawal of the Belgian troops is rendered impossible if the principle is to be maintained that, at the withdrawal, the responsibility for security must be taken over at once by United Nations troops. However, the opposition to the United Nations is raised in the shadow of the continued presence of the Belgian troops.

"This vicious circle must be broken; further delays in the entry of United Nations troops, due to armed opposition, can in my view not any longer be permitted to delay the withdrawal of the Belgian troops. If, at the withdrawal of Belgian troops, the United Nations troops are not in the area because of such opposition, it is for those who oppose the entry of the United Nations troops, or who support or encourage this obstruction, to carry the full responsibility for what may develop in the vacuum which they have forced upon us.

"One final word about the situation of some of those private interests [which] are involved in the present situation. I think of Europeans who work in Katanga. There is no need for me to assure them that the United Nations has not come to the region in order to 'take over' or put others in their place. There should not be any need for me to explain that the United Nations action is their best hope for the future, as their work will have to be in harmony with the interest of the people among whom they live and whom they ultimately serve, and must be under the protection of security, maintained in forms which guarantee the rights of all.

"In a state of emotion irrational reactions are to be expected and we should have understanding and sympathy for those who see themselves as being threatened. However, is it too much to expect that the people to whom I refer may lift themselves above their emotions, see present day realities as they are and see, for that reason, in the United Nations their only valid support if they wish to continue a work to which they have devoted so much of their best efforts? Surely, others who are more remote from the heat of present conflicts—and I think in the first place of the Belgian Government itself—should be able to help in creating the right atmosphere and the right understanding of the United Nations operation; if so, I believe that even the present unrest and worry may be overcome and also that the United Nations will not encounter further resistance in its efforts from those to whom this assistance should bring satisfaction and not fear." SCOR, XV, Mtg. 884, pp. 2–7.

8. *Resolution of the Security Council, 9 August 1960.*

S/4426; SCOR, XV, Supp. for July–Sept. 1960, pp. 91–92.

The Security Council,

Recalling its resolution of 22 July 1960 (S/4405), *inter alia,* calling upon the Government of Belgium to implement speedily the Security Council resolution of 14 July (S/4387) on the withdrawal of its troops and authorizing the Secretary-General to take all necessary action to this effect,

Having noted the second report of the Secretary-General [S/4417] on the implementation of the aforesaid two resolutions and his statement before the Council,

Having considered the statements made by the representatives of Belgium and the Republic of the Congo to this Council at this meeting,

Noting with satisfaction the progress made by the United Nations in carrying out the Security Council resolutions in respect of the territory of the Republic of the Congo other than the province of Katanga,

Noting, however, that the United Nations had been prevented from implementing the aforesaid resolutions in the province of Katanga although it was ready, and in fact attempted, to do so,

Recognizing that the withdrawal of Belgian troops from the province of Katanga will be a positive contribution to and essential for the proper implementation of the Council resolutions,

1. Confirms the authority given to the Secretary-General by the Security Council resolutions of 14 July and 22 July 1960 and requests him to continue to carry out the responsibility placed on him thereby;

2.   Calls upon the Government of Belgium to withdraw immediately its troops from the province of Katanga under speedy modalities determined by the Secretary-General and to assist in every possible way the implementation of the Council's resolutions;

3.   Declares that the entry of the United Nations Force into the province of Katanga is necessary for the full implementation of this resolution;

4.   Reaffirms that the United Nations Force in the Congo will not be a party to or in any way intervene in or be used to influence the outcome of any internal conflict, constitutional or otherwise;

5.   Calls upon all Member States, in accordance with Articles 25 and 49 of the Charter of the United Nations, to accept and carry out the decisions of the Security Council and to afford mutual assistance in carrying out measures decided upon by the Council;

6.   Requests the Secretary-General to implement this resolution and to report further to the Council as appropriate.

NOTE.   After a further exchange of correspondence with Mr. Tshombe, the Secretary-General proceeded to Elizabethville, the capital of Katanga, on 12 August 1960, with his military and civilian advisers and "two companies of the Swedish battalion, all the military to be in uniform but with the understanding that they will be under [his] exclusive personal authority and will have only the right of legitimate self-defence in the event"—which he ruled out as inconceivable—"that they are attacked."   See S/4417/Add.4 (10 Aug. 1960); SCOR, XV, Supp. for July-Sept. 1960, p. 59.   A United Nations presence was thus established in Katanga and the Belgian troops started to withdraw.

Nevertheless, a new dispute arose between the United Nations and the Central Government of the Congo, which led to an exchange of letters which is reproduced in Documents 9 and 10, below.

9.   *Memorandum by the Secretary-General, of 12 August 1960, on the Implementation of the Security Council Resolution of 9 August 1960.*

S/4417/Add. 6 (12 August 1960); SCOR, XV, Supp. for July–Sept. 1960, pp. 64–65, 70–71.

Operative paragraph 4 of the resolution of the Security Council of 9 August reads: "Reaffirms that the United Nations Force in the Congo will not be a party to or in any way intervene in or be used to influence the outcome of any internal conflict, constitutional or otherwise."   The paragraph has to be read together with operative paragraph 3, which reads: "3.   Declares that the entry of the United Nations Force into the Province of Katanga is necessary for the full implementation of this resolution."

Guidance for the interpretation of operative paragraph 4 can be found in the attitudes upheld by the Security Council in previous cases where elements of an external nature and elements of an internal nature have been mixed. The stand of the Security Council in those cases has been consistent. It most clearly emerges from the policy maintained in the case of Lebanon which, therefore, will be analysed here in the first instance.

In the Lebanese question, as considered by the Security Council in the summer of 1958, there was a conflict between the constitutional President, Mr. Chamoun, and a group of insurgents, among them Mr. Karame, later Prime Minister of the Republic. The Government called for United Nations assistance, alleging that a rebellion was fomented from abroad and supported actively by the introduction of volunteers and arms across the border. The request of the Government was in the first place that the United Nations should send observers to report on intervention from abroad; however, no clear distinction was made from the side of the Government between such observation activities and active assistance from the United Nations, by troops aiming at sealing off the border. The Security Council responded by requesting the Secretary-General to dispatch an observer group, which, in fact, at the height of the crisis numbered some 500 officers. This group of observers was deployed on the side held by the Government as well as on the other side. The observers passed freely between the parts into which the country was divided through civil war. It was perfectly clear that the Security Council considered itself as concerned solely with the possibility of intervention from outside in assistance to the rebels. All observation activities were limited to that problem and the question was never raised from the Security Council side of an intervention in support of the constitutional Government, or in support of the other party. It is clear from the record that had the Government side asked for United Nations assistance for protection either in its effort to stop the rebellion or, for example, in an effort to blockade the rebel-held territory, the United Nations would have refused to co-operate. Naturally, the same would have been true of a similar approach from the rebel side in relation to the Government side.

The importance of this example for the interpretation of operative paragraph 4 of the resolution of 9 August is obvious. There is reason to underscore especially the words in the paragraph that the Force will not "in any way . . . be used to influence the outcome of any internal conflict, constitutional or otherwise". This is, in fact, the first expression in a resolution of the Security Council under Chapter VII of the principle applied and approved in the case of Lebanon.

As another example of the doctrine upheld by the Security Council, there may be cited its attitude in the Hungarian case, where decisions were directed solely against the intervention of foreign troops in support of the Government, without any stand being taken on the relationship between the Government and the insurgents.

Applied to the situation in Katanga, this means that the United Nations is directly concerned with the attitude taken by the provincial government of Katanga to the extent that it may be based on the presence of Belgian troops, or as being, for its effectiveness, influenced by that presence. It should, in this context, be noted that the same resolution, of 9 August 1960, which reaffirmed the principle of non-intervention, put the main emphasis on the withdrawal of Belgian troops.   Therefore, in the application of operative paragraph 4, as seen in the light of precedents, it can be concluded that were Belgian troops to be withdrawn, and pending full withdrawal, a Belgian assurance to be given to the Secretary-General that the Belgian troops would in no way "intervene in or be used to influence the outcome of" the conflict between the provincial government and the central Government—that is to say, that they would remain completely inactive during the phasing out—the question between the provincial government and the central Government would be one in which the United Nations would in no sense be a party nor would it be one on which it could in any sense exert influence. It might be held that the United Nations is duty bound to uphold the Fundamental Law as the legal constitution and, therefore, should assist the central Government in exercising its power in Katanga. However, the United Nations has to observe that, *de facto,* the provincial government is in active opposition—once a Belgian assurance of non-intervention and withdrawal has been given—using only its own military means in order to achieve certain political aims.

The view that the United Nations should support the central Government, as it functions under the provisional Fundamental Law, and as it is the party which has asked for assistance, is contradicted by the stand maintained in the case of Lebanon, where both those conditions were met and, yet, the United Nations stood aside and had to stand aside.

Applying the line pursued by the Security Council in the Lebanese case to the interpretation of operative paragraph 4, it follows that the United Nations Force cannot be used on behalf of the central Government to subdue or to force the provincial government to a specific line of action. It further follows that United Nations facilities cannot be used, for example, to transport civilian or military representatives, under the authority of the central Government, to Katanga against the decision of the Katanga provincial government. It further follows that the United Nations Force has no duty, or right, to protect civilian or military personnel, representing the central Government, arriving in Katanga, beyond what follows from its general duty to maintain law and order. It finally follows that the United Nations, naturally, on the other side has no right to forbid the central Government to take any action which by its own means, in accordance with the Purposes and Principles of the Charter, it can carry through in relation to Katanga. All these conclusions necessarily apply, *mutatis mutandis,* as regards the provincial government in its relations with the central Government.

The policy line stated here, in interpretation of operative paragraph 4, represents a unilateral declaration of interpretation by the Secretary-General. It can be contested before the Security Council. And it can be changed by the Security Council through an explanation of its intentions in the resolution of 9 August. The finding is not subject to agreement or negotiation.

The Secretary-General presents his findings, as to the significance of the operative paragraph in question, to the central Government and to the provincial government. If, as expected, the provincial government on the basis of this declaration, were to admit the free deployment of the United Nations force in Katanga, but if, on the other hand, the finding and its consequences were to be challenged before the Security Council by others, and the Council were to disapprove of the finding, this would obviously mean a change of assumptions for the actions of the provincial government which would justify a reconsideration of its stand, having been taken in good faith on the basis of the interpretation given by the Secretary-General.

Were the findings of the Secretary-General, as regards operative paragraph 4, to be challenged either by the central or by the provincial Government, the Secretary-General would immediately report to the Security Council with a request that it consider the interpretation and pronounce itself on its validity. Naturally, the Secretary-General in this context would draw the attention of the Security Council to its previous stand, and strongly recommend its confirmation of this interpretation.

10. *Letter from Mr. Lumumba, Prime Minister of the Republic of the Congo, to the Secretary-General 14 August 1960.*

S/4417/Add. 7 (15 August 1960); SCOR, XV, Supp. for July–Sept. 1960, pp. 71–73.

As it has informed Mr. Bunche, the Government of the Republic of the Congo can in no way agree with your personal interpretation, which is unilateral and erroneous, as the resolution of 14 July 1960 expressly states that the Security Council authorizes you "to provide the Government [of the Republic of the Congo] with such military assistance as may be necessary". This text adds that you are to do so "in consultation with" my Government. It is therefore clear that in its intervention in the Congo the United Nations is not to act as a neutral organization but rather that the Security Council is to place all its resources at the disposal of my Government. From these texts it is clear that, contrary to your personal interpretation, the United Nations Force may be used "to subdue the rebel Government of Katanga", that my Government may call upon the United Nations services to transport civilian and military representatives of the central Government to Katanga in opposition to the provincial Government of Katanga and that the United Nations Force has the duty to protect the civilian and military personnel representing my Government in Katanga. Paragraph 4 of the Security Council's resolution of 9 August 1960, which you invoke in order to challenge this right, cannot be interpreted without reference to the two earlier resolutions. This third resolution which you cite is only a supplement to the two preceding resolutions, which remain intact. The resolution to which you refer confirms the first two. It reads: "Confirms the authority given to the Secretary-General by the Security Council resolutions of 14 July and 22 July 1960 and requests him to continue to carry out the responsibility placed on him thereby".

It follows from the foregoing that paragraph 4 which you invoke cannot be interpreted as nullifying your obligation to "provide the Government with such military assistance as may be necessary" throughout the entire territory of the Republic, including Katanga. On the contrary, it is the particular purpose of this third decision of the Security Council to make it clear that Katanga falls within the scope of the application of the resolution of 14 July 1960.

You base your personal interpretation on precedents such as those of Lebanon and Hungary. This procedure would be acceptable only if the relevant resolutions were identical. Contrary to what you suggest, it is not because the Fundamental Law is now the legal Constitution of the Republic that the United Nations is duty bound to defend it but rather because the Security Council has so decided in its resolution of 14 July 1960.

In its resolution of 22 July 1960 the Security Council formally and explicitly confirmed the provision of the Fundamental Law which had been challenged, namely, the provision concerning the territorial integrity of the Republic. From your interpretation it would have to be concluded that the task of the United Nations was not to restore law and order in the Congo or bring about the pacification of the country, in accordance with my Government's request, but to limit itself solely to ensuring the withdrawal of the Belgian troops.

My Government also takes this opportunity to protest against the fact that upon your return from New York *en route* to Katanga, you did not consult it, as prescribed in the resolution of 14 July 1960, despite the formal request submitted to you by my Government's delegation in New York before your departure and despite my letter replying to your cable on this subject. On the contrary, you have dealt with the rebel Government of Katanga in violation of the Security Council's resolution of 14 July 1960. That resolution does not permit you to deal with the local authorities until after you have consulted with my Government. Yet you are acting as though my Government, which is the repository of legal authority and is alone qualified to deal with the United Nations, did not exist. The manner in which you have acted until now is only retarding the restoration of order in the Republic, particularly in the Province of Katanga, whereas the Security Council has solemnly declared that the purpose of the intervention is the complete restoration of order in the Republic of the Congo (see in particular the resolution of 22 July 1960). Furthermore, the conversations you have just had with Mr. Moise Tshombe, the assurances you have given him and the statements he has just made to the Press are ample evidence that you are making yourself a party to the conflict between the rebel Government of Katanga and the legal Government of the Republic, that you are intervening in this conflict and that you are using the United Nations Force to influence its outcome, which is formally prohibited by the very paragraph which you invoke.

It is incomprehensible to me that you should have sent only Swedish and Irish troops to Katanga, systematically excluding troops from the African States even though some of the latter were the first to be landed at Leopoldville. In this matter you have acted in connivance with the rebel Government of Katanga and at the instigation of the Belgian Government.

In view of the foregoing, I submit to you the following requests:

1. To entrust the task of guarding all the airfields of the Republic to troops of the National Army and the Congolese police in place of United Nations troops.

2. To send immediately to Katanga Moroccan, Guinean, Ghanaian, Ethiopian, Mali, Tunisian, Sudanese, Liberian and Congolese troops.

3. To put aircraft at the disposal of the Government of the Republic for the transportation of Congolese troops and civilians engaged in restoring order throughout the country.

4. To proceed immediately to seize all arms and ammunition distributed by the Belgians in Katanga to the partisans of the rebel Government, whether Congolese or foreign, and to put at the disposal of the Government of the Republic the arms and ammunition so seized, as they are the property of the Government.

5. To withdraw all non-African troops from Katanga immediately.

I hope that you will signify your agreement to the foregoing. If my Government does not receive satisfaction it will be obliged to take other steps.

NOTE.—1. The memorandum of the Secretary-General and the comments of the Congo Government on that memorandum were discussed by the Security Council on 21–22 August 1960. The Secretary-General pointed out that he was not asking the Security Council "to confirm" his interpretation of the functions of the United Nations Force, but if any members of the Council disagreed with it "they may wish to give expression in a draft resolution, to what they consider to be the right interpretation." He added that "in the light of the domestic jurisdiction limitation of the Charter, it must be assumed that the Council would not authorize the Secretary-General to intervene with armed troops in an internal conflict, when the Council had not specifically adopted enforcement measures under Articles 41 and 42 of Chapter VII of the Charter." SCOR, XV, Mtg. 887, pp. 9–10. At the end of the debate a Soviet draft resolution (S/4453; SCOR, XV, Supp. for July-Sept, 1960, p. 116), proposing the establishment of a group to "ensure on the spot and without delay, the execution of decisions of the Security Council," was withdrawn, and the President of the Security Council (Mr. Berard, France) expressed his conviction that, despite different and sometimes conflicting opinions, "the Secretary-General will have found in this debate the clarification which he desired, and that it will assist him in the pursuit of his mission." SCOR, XV, Mtg. 889, p. 29.

2. On 5 September 1960 a grave constitutional crisis arose in the Congo. As reported by the Secretary-General, the facts were as follows: "In a statement broadcast on the national radio the Chief of State proclaimed that the Prime Minister had betrayed his office by plunging the country into a fratricidal civil war and that he was removing him and certain Ministers of his Government from office, with immediate effect. At the same time he instructed Mr. Joseph Ileo, the President of the Senate, to form a new Government and he requested the United Nations to ensure peace and order.

"The Prime Minister, for his part, spoke to the population three times that day on the national radio, declaring that the President was no longer the Chief of State and calling upon the people, the workers and the army to rise.

"That same night, in the face of an imminent breakdown of law and order, ONUC, in the interests of the maintenance of peace, temporarily closed all the major airports to air traffic. The following day it took an emergency step directly related to the foregoing and temporarily closed the Leopoldville radio station.

"On 7 September the Chamber of Representatives decided, by 60 votes to 19, to annul the decisions whereby the Chief of State and the Prime Minister had dismissed each other from office and on 8 September the Senate decided by 41 votes to 2, with 6 abstentions, against the presidential proclamations. The following day President Kasa-Vubu rejected the votes of the Senate and the Chamber, on the grounds that decisions by the Chief of State were not subject to the approval of the two Chambers. Mr. Lumumba, for his part, declared that he himself was now Chief of State and Supreme Commander of the National Army." Annual Report of the Secretary-General, 1960–1961 [GAOR, XVI, Supp. 1 (A/4800)], pp. 10–11. See also the statement of the Secretary-General in the Security Council, 9 Sept. 1960, SCOR, XV, Mtg. 896, pp. 16–17.

3. When the debate was renewed in the Security Council on 9 September 1960, the Soviet Union presented a draft resolution inviting the Secretary-General "to cease forthwith any form of interference in the internal affairs of the Republic of the Congo," and, in particular, "to evacuate armed forces under the control of the United Nations Command from all airports at present occupied by them and to hand over national radio stations to the complete and unrestricted control of the Central Government of the Congo." That resolution would also have instructed the Secretary-General "to remove the present Command of the United Nations Force, whose actions constitute flagrant violations of the Security Council's decisions." S/4519 (15 Sept. 1960); SCOR, XV, Mtg. 903, pp. 16–17. This resolution was re-

jected in the Security Council by 7 votes to 2, with 2 abstentions (Ceylon and Tunisia). A draft resolution presented by Ceylon and Tunisia [S/4523 (16 Sept. 1960); SCOR, XV, Supp. for July-Sept. 1960, pp. 172–73], which would have reaffirmed the power of the United Nations Force "to restore and maintain law and order as necessary for the maintenance of international peace and security," and would have decided that "no assistance for military purposes be sent to the Congo except as part of the United Nations action," was vetoed by the Soviet Union. On proposal of the United States, the Security Council then decided to call an emergency session of the General Assembly. SCOR, XV, Mtg. 906 (17 September 1960), pp. 30–38. The General Assembly immediately adopted a resolution presented by seventeen Afro-Asian States, by a vote of 70 to none, with 11 abstentions (9 members of the Soviet bloc, France and South Africa); for the text of that resolution, see Document 11, below.

4. In the debate preceding the adoption of this resolution it was argued that the Soviet Union had sent to the Congo "hundreds of so-called technicians," some two dozen aircraft and 100 trucks. In reply, it was contended that the Soviet specialists were placed at the disposal of the legitimate Government of the Congo at its request; that the NATO countries were engaged in subversive activities against the Lumumba Government, which "had dared to steer a course independent of the collective colonialism of NATO"; and that the Secretary-General had misused the powers vested in him by the Council. The Secretary-General replied that "no Government could turn the United Nations Force into a national force and use it for its own purposes"; and that the Security Council had not authorized the Secretary-General to take any enforcement action. Annual Report of the Secretary-General, 1960–1961 [GAOR, XVI, Supp. 1 (A/4800)], pp. 14–17.

11. *Resolution 1474 (ES–IV) of the General Assembly,*
20 September 1960.

GAOR, Fourth Emergency Special Session (ES–IV), Suppl. 1 (A/4510), p. 1.

The General Assembly,

Having considered the situation in the Republic of the Congo,

Taking note of the resolutions of 14 July, 22 July and 9 August 1960 of the Security Council,

Taking into account the unsatisfactory economic and political conditions that continue in the Republic of the Congo,

Considering that, with a view to preserving the unity, territorial integrity and political independence of the Congo, to protecting and advancing the welfare of its people, and to safeguarding international peace, it is essential for the United Nations to continue to assist the Central Government of the Congo,

1. Fully supports the resolutions of 14 and 22 July and 9 August 1960 of the Security Council;

2. Requests the Secretary-General to continue to take vigorous action in accordance with the terms of the aforesaid resolutions and to assist the Central Government of the Congo in the restoration and

maintenance of law and order throughout the territory of the Republic of the Congo and to safeguard its unity, territorial integrity and political independence in the interests of international peace and security;

3.   Appeals to all Congolese within the Republic of the Congo to seek a speedy solution by peaceful means of all their internal conflicts for the unity and integrity of the Congo, with the assistance, as appropriate, of Asian and African representatives appointed by the Advisory Committee on the Congo, in consultation with the Secretary-General, for the purpose of conciliation;

4.   Appeals to all Member Governments for urgent voluntary contributions to a United Nations Fund for the Congo to be used under United Nations control and in consultation with the Central Government for the purpose of rendering the fullest possible assistance to achieve the objective mentioned in the preamble;

5.   Requests:

(a) All States to refrain from any action which might tend to impede the restoration of law and order and the exercise by the Government of the Republic of the Congo of its authority and also to refrain from any action which might undermine the unity, territorial integrity and the political independence of the Republic of the Congo;

(b) All Member States, in accordance with Articles 25 and 49 of the Charter of the United Nations, to accept and carry out the decisions of the Security Council and to afford mutual assistance in carrying out measures decided upon by the Security Council;

6.   Without prejudice to the sovereign rights of the Republic of the Congo, calls upon all States to refrain from the direct and indirect provision of arms or other materials of war and military personnel and other assistance for military purposes in the Congo during the temporary period of military assistance through the United Nations, except upon the request of the United Nations through the Secretary-General for carrying out the purposes of this resolution and of the resolutions of 14 and 22 July and 9 August 1960 of the Security Council.

NOTE.—1. On 14 September 1960, Mr. Mobutu, the Chief of Staff of the Army, announced that the Army "was taking power," and on 20 September, with the assistance of the Chief of State, he established a third government in the Congo, "a College of High Commissioners", to "neutralize" the other two governments. The General Assembly admitted the Republic of the Congo (Leopoldville) to membership in the United Nations on 20 September 1960, but a dispute arose immediately as to the Government entitled to represent the new Member in the United Nations. The Credentials Committee recommended that the General Assembly accept the credentials of the delegation appointed by President Kasa-Vubu, the Head of the Congolese State, rather than those of the delegation appointed by Lumumba. This recommendation was approved by the General Assembly on 22 November 1960, by 53 votes to 24, with 19 abstentions. Annual Report of the Secretary-General, 1960–1961 [GAOR, XVI, Supp. 1 (A/4800)], pp. 13–24; GAOR, XV, Plenary, pp. 871–979.

2. Mr. Lumumba, who was threatened with arrest by Mr. Mobutu, was guarded by United Nations troops until 27 November 1960, when he escaped from Leopoldville. He was arrested, however, by Congolese troops on 1 December. The Secretary-General protested against the arbitrary arrest and brutal treatment of Mr. Lumumba and asked that Mr. Lumumba be accorded "proper treatment commensurate with his position and human dignity, in accordance with the requirements of the Universal Declaration of Human Rights." S/4571 (5 Dec. 1960); SCOR, XV, Supp. for Oct.-Dec. 1960, pp. 67–71. The Soviet Union proposed that the Security Council should call on the Secretary-General to secure the immediate release of Mr. Lumumba and his associates; and should request that the United Nations troops in the Congo immediately disarm "the terrorist bands of Mobutu." S/4579 (7 Dec. 1960); SCOR, XV, Mtg. 914, pp. 13–14. The Secretary-General pointed out that there were limits on the power of the Security Council "to decide on the use of military force—that is to say to take military initiative—in order to liberate a person, held on the authority of the Chief of State, or to do the same in order to enforce the convening of a Parliament which should be convened by the Chief of State." He noted that "the Council has never explicitly referred to the Charter Article on the basis of which it took action in the Congo. In particular, it is significant that the Council did not invoke Articles 41 and 42 of Chapter VII, which provide for enforcement measures and which would override the domestic jurisdiction limitation of Article 2(7)." The reference by the Council to Articles 25 and 49 "as the basis for the legal obligation imposed on the States concerned by the Council's action," was "not the same as invoking enforcement measures." It was the Secretary-General's own view that "the resolutions may be considered as implicitly taken under Article 40 and, in that sense, as based on an implicit finding under Article 39." But he emphasized that "neither the Council nor the Assembly has ever endorsed this interpretation, much less put such endorsement in a resolution. What is even more certain is that the Council in no way directed that we go beyond the legal basis of Article 40 and into the coercive action covered by Articles 41 and 42." SCOR, XV, Mtg. 920, pp. 18–22. Both the Soviet draft resolution and a more limited Polish draft resolution were rejected by the Security Council, while a draft resolution by Argentina, Italy, UK and US was vetoed by the Soviet Union. *Idem,* pp. 35–37.

3. On 13 February 1961, the Minister of the Interior of the provincial government of Katanga announced that Mr. Lumumba and two of his associates were killed while attempting to escape. The Soviet Union then proposed the adoption by the Security Council of the following resolution [S/4706 (14 Feb. 1961); SCOR, XVI, Mtg. 934, pp. 23–24]:

"The Security Council,

"Regarding the murder of the Prime Minister of the Republic of the Congo, Patrice Lumumba, and of the outstanding statesmen of the Republic, Okito and Mpolo, as an international crime incompatible with the United Nations Charter and as a flagrant violation of the Declaration on the grant of independence to colonial countries and peoples adopted by the United Nations General Assembly at its fifteenth session,

'"Decisively condemns the actions of Belgium which led to this crime;

"Deems it essential that the sanctions provided under Article 41 of the United Nations Charter should be applied to Belgium as to an aggressor which by its actions is creating a threat to international peace, and calls on the States Members of the United Nations for the immediate application of these sanctions;

"Enjoins the command of the troops that are in the Congo pursuant to the decision of the Security Council immediately to arrest Tshombé and Mobutu in order to deliver them for trial, to disarm all the military units and gendarmerie forces under their control, and to ensure the immediate disarming and removal from the Congo of all Belgian troops and all Belgian personnel;

"Directs that the 'United Nations operation' in the Congo shall be discontinued within one month and all foreign troops withdrawn from there so as to enable the Congolese people to decide its own internal affairs;

"Deems it essential to dismiss D. Hammarskjold from the post of Secretary-General of the United Nations as a participant in and organizer of the violence committed against the leading statesmen of the Republic of the Congo."

4. This draft resolution was rejected by 8 votes to 1, with 2 abstentions (Ceylon and the United Arab Republic). The Security Council then adopted a draft resolution presented by Ceylon, Liberia and the United Arab Republic, by 9 votes with 2 abstentions (France and USSR). SCOR, XVI, Mtg. 942, pp. 18–19. For the text of that resolution, see Document 12, below.

12. *Resolution of the Security Council, 21 February 1961.*

S/4741 (21 Feb. 1961); SCOR, XVI, Supp. for Jan.–March, 1961, pp. 147–48.

A. The Security Council,

Having considered the situation in the Congo,

Having learnt with deep regret the announcement of the killing of the Congolese leaders, Mr. Patrice Lumumba, Mr. Maurice Mpolo and Mr. Joseph Okito,

Deeply concerned at the grave repercussions of these crimes and the danger of wide-spread civil war and bloodshed in the Congo and the threat to international peace and security,

Noting the report of the Secretary-General's Special Representative (S/4691) dated 12 February 1961 bringing to light the development of a serious civil war situation and preparations therefor,

1. Urges that the United Nations take immediately all appropriate measures to prevent the occurrence of civil war in the Congo, including arrangements for cease-fires, the halting of all military operations, the prevention of clashes, and the use of force, if necessary, in the last resort;

2. Urges that measures be taken for the immediate withdrawal and evacuation from the Congo of all Belgian and other foreign military and para-military personnel and political advisers not under the United Nations Command, and mercenaries;

3.   Calls upon all States to take immediate and energetic measures to prevent the departure of such personnel for the Congo from their territories, and for the denial of transit and other facilities to them;

4.   Decides that an immediate and impartial investigation be held in order to ascertain the circumstances of the death of Mr. Lumumba and his colleagues and that the perpetrators of these crimes be punished;

5.   Reaffirms the Security Council resolutions of 14 July, 22 July and 9 August 1960 and the General Assembly resolution 1474 (ES–IV) of 20 September 1960 and reminds all States of their obligation under these resolutions.

B.   The Security Council,

Gravely concerned at the continuing deterioration in the Congo, and the prevalence of conditions which seriously imperil peace and order, and the unity and territorial integrity of the Congo, and threaten international peace and security,

Noting with deep regret and concern the systematic violations of human rights and fundamental freedoms and the general absence of rule of law in the Congo,

Recognizing the imperative necessity of the restoration of parliamentary institutions in the Congo in accordance with the fundamental law of the country, so that the will of the people should be reflected through the freely elected Parliament,

Convinced that the solution of the problem of the Congo lies in the hands of the Congolese people themselves without any interference from outside and that there can be no solution without conciliation,

Convinced further that the imposition of any solution, including the formation of any government not based on genuine conciliation would, far from settling any issues, greatly enhance the dangers of conflict within the Congo and threat to international peace and security,

1.   Urges the convening of the Parliament and the taking of necessary protective measures in that connexion;

2.   Urges that Congolese armed units and personnel should be re-organized and brought under discipline and control, and arrangements be made on impartial and equitable bases to that end and with a view to the elimination of any possibility of interference by such units and personnel in the political life of the Congo;

3.   Calls upon all States to extend their full co-operation and assistance and take such measures as may be necessary on their part, for the implementation of this resolution.

NOTE.—1.   In commenting on this resolution, on 24 February 1961, the Secretary-General of the United Nations made the following observation:

"The latest resolution, adopted by the Security Council, does not seem to me to derogate from the position that United Nations troops should not be-

come parties to armed conflict in the Congo. The basic intention of the resolution is, in my opinion, the taking of all appropriate measures for the purposes mentioned, resort being had to force only when all other efforts such
as negotiation, persuasion or conciliation were to fail. If following such efforts, or measures taken in support of their result, United Nations troops
engaged in defensive action, when attacked while holding positions occupied
to prevent a civil war risk, this would not, in my opinion, mean that they
became a party to a conflict, while the possibility of becoming such a party
would be open, were troops to take the initiative in an armed attack on an organized army group in the Congo." S/4752 (27 Feb. 1961), Annex VII;
SCOR, XVI, Supp. for Jan.-March 1961, p. 176, at 188.

2.   When, in execution of the Security Council resolution of 21 Feb. 1961,
the United Nations troops in Katanga made an attempt to apprehend and
evacuate foreign military and para-military personnel, they were subjected to an attack on 13 September 1961 which continued for several days.
The Secretary-General agreed to meet Mr. Tshombe to arrange for a cease-
fire but his plane crashed on the way, in Rhodesian territory, on 17 September 1961, and the Secretary-General and all his companions died in the wreck.
A cease-fire agreement came into effect on 21 Sept. 1961. Annual Report of
the Secretary-General, 1961–1962 [GAOR, XVII, Supp. 1 (A/5201)], pp. 3–5.
See also Arthur L. GAVSHON, The Mysterious Death of Dag Hammarskjold (New York, 1962), 243 pp.

13.   *Resolution adopted by the Security Council,*
 24 November 1961.

S/5002 (24 Nov. 1961); SCOR, XVI, Supp. for Oct.–Dec. 1961, pp. 148–50.

The Security Council,

Recalling its resolutions S/4387, S/4405, S/4426 and S/4741,

Recalling further General Assembly resolutions 1474 (ES–IV), 1592
(XV), 1599 (XV), 1600 (XV) and 1601 (XV),

Reaffirming the policies and purposes of the United Nations with
respect to the Congo (Leopoldville) as set out in the aforesaid resolutions, namely:

(a) To maintain the territorial integrity and the political independence of the Republic of the Congo;

(b) To assist the Central Government of the Congo in the restoration and maintenance of law and order;

(c) To prevent the occurrence of civil war in the Congo;

(d) To secure the immediate withdrawal and evacuation from the
Congo of all foreign military, paramilitary and advisory personnel
not under the United Nations Command, and all mercenaries; and

(e) To render technical assistance,

Welcoming the restoration of the national Parliament of the Congo
in accordance with the *Loi fondamentale* and the consequent formation
of a Central Government on 2 August 1961,

Deploring all armed action in opposition to the authority of the Government of the Republic of the Congo, specifically secessionist activities and armed action now being carried on by the Provincial Administration of Katanga with the aid of external resources and foreign mercenaries, and completely rejecting the claim that Katanga is a "sovereign independent nation",

Noting with deep regret the recent and past actions of violence against United Nations personnel,

Recognizing the Government of the Republic of the Congo as exclusively responsible for the conduct of the external affairs of the Congo,

Bearing in mind the imperative necessity of speedy and effective action to implement fully the policies and purposes of the United Nations in the Congo to end the unfortunate plight of the Congolese people, necessary both in the interests of world peace and international co-operation, and stability and progress of Africa as a whole,

1.   Strongly deprecates the secessionist activities illegally carried out by the provincial administration of Katanga, with the aid of external resources and manned by foreign mercenaries;

2.   Further deprecates the armed action against United Nations forces and personnel in the pursuit of such activities;

3.   Insists that such activities shall cease forthwith, and calls upon all concerned to desist therefrom;

4.   Authorizes the Secretary-General to take vigorous action, including the use of requisite measure of force, if necessary, for the immediate apprehension, detention pending legal action and/or deportation of all foreign military and paramilitary personnel and political advisers not under the United Nations Command, and mercenaries as laid down in Part A, operative paragraph 2 of the Security Council resolution of 21 February 1961;

5.   Further requests the Secretary-General to take all necessary measures to prevent the entry or return of such elements under whatever guise and also of arms, equipment or other material in support of such activities;

6.   Requests all States to refrain from the supply of arms, equipment or other material which could be used for warlike purposes, and to take the necessary measures to prevent their nationals from doing the same, and also to deny transportation and transit facilities for such supplies across their territories, except in accordance with the decisions, policies and purposes of the United Nations;

7.   Calls upon all Member States to refrain from promoting, condoning, or giving support by acts of omission or commission, directly or indirectly, to activities against the United Nations often resulting in armed hostilities against the United Nations forces and personnel;

8.   Declares that all secessionist activities against the Republic of the Congo are contrary to the *Loi fondamentale* and Security Council

decisions and specifically demands that such activities which are now taking place in Katanga shall cease forthwith;

9. Declares full and firm support for the Central Government of the Congo, and the determination to assist that Government in accordance with the decisions of the United Nations to maintain law and order and national integrity, to provide technical assistance and to implement those decisions;

10. Urges all Member States to lend their support, according to their national procedures, to the Central Government of the Republic of the Congo, in conformity with the Charter and the decisions of the United Nations;

11. Requests all Member States to refrain from any action which may directly or indirectly impede the policies and purposes of the United Nations in the Congo and is contrary to its decisions and the general purpose of the Charter.

14. *Report by the Secretary-General concerning the Implementation of the Security Council Resolutions, 4 February 1963.*

S/5240 (4 Feb. 1963); SCOR, XVIII, Supp. for Jan.–March, 1963, pp. 92–104.

I feel it appropriate . . . at this stage . . . to present an accounting of the extent to which the mandates given to ONUC by the Security Council resolutions have been fulfilled, of the aspects of those mandates that remain to be implemented, and to suggest what a look ahead may indicate as to the tasks to be fulfilled and the resources that will be required for that purpose.

At the beginning of 1962, there was hope, following Mr. Tshombe's declaration at Kitona, that the problem of the secession of Katanga might be speedily settled. That hope was quickly dispelled, however, when Mr. Tshombe, in effect, disavowed his promises as soon as he returned to Katanga. A subsequent six months of dilatory "negotiating" by Mr. Tshombe, for half of that time in the talks with Prime Minister Adoula in Leopoldville, served only to waste time and to raise questions of bad faith. During the entire year from December 1961 to December 1962, the Katangese provincial authorities were evasive on the question of the expulsion of foreign mercenaries and on the issue of freedom of movement for ONUC personnel. Indeed, because of its determination to make all possible efforts toward peaceful reconciliation, ONUC, seeking throughout 1962 to avoid doing anything that might impede those efforts, exercised a considerable restraint in pressing the issues of freedom of movement and elimination of mercenaries. During that year, however, Mr. Tshombe and other Katangese provincial authorities repeatedly avowed that no more mercenaries were engaged in Katanga. We now know positively that this was not the case.

It was imperative that the problem of attempted Katangese secession, which not only caused impoverishment and instability in the rest of the Congo, but also threatened the peace of the African continent, and imposed on the United Nations itself serious political and financial difficulties, be finally settled. I myself, therefore, following consultations with a number of Governments, proposed in August 1962 the Plan of National Reconciliation. This Plan was promptly accepted by Prime Minister Adoula and Mr. Tshombe. It was only a proposal which the parties were entirely free to accept or reject.

The failure of the Katangese provincial authorities, after more than three months, to take any practical steps to implement this Plan, and their continued lack of co-operation with other activities of the United Nations, led me in December 1962 to advance certain measures designed to bring economic pressure to bear on the Katanga provincial authorities and thereby to lead the Katangese problem to an early and peaceful solution.   The Government of Belgium was thus asked to exert every possible influence on the Union Minière du Haut-Katanga, a Belgian corporation, which is part of a powerful international financial complex, to induce it to desist from paying to Katanga province the revenues and taxes due to the Government of the Congo. States which had jurisdiction over territories through which Katangese copper was exported, namely Portugal, the Union of South Africa and the United Kingdom, were requested to take measures to prohibit the shipment of such copper until the question of the payment of UMHK revenues was settled. Other interested Governments were requested by the Central Government of the Congo, with my support, not to permit the import of copper and cobalt from Katanga into their territories. Developments in Katanga since these letters were written have overtaken the requests in them. I do, however, express my special appreciation to those Governments which had already intimated to me their readiness to co-operate with the United Nations in the implementation of my appeals.

On 12 December 1962, Mr. Tshombe offered to permit the UMHK to transfer to the Monetary Council of the Republic of the Congo all foreign exchange generated by Katangese exports, provided that after deduction of the needs of the UMHK, 50 per cent of such exchange would be returned to Katanga. Despite this gesture, for which I expressed my appreciation, there was long delay on the part of the Katanga provincial authorities in arranging for representatives of the Bank of Katanga and of the UMHK to proceed to Leopoldville for discussions on this matter.

Instead of further acts of co-operation by the Katangese provincial authorities, there ensued provocative military action by the Katangese gendarmerie and its mercenary elements, which Mr. Tshombe was unwilling or unable to control. After United Nations troops had been fired at for six days without retaliation, I was obliged, with great reluctance, to authorize the ONUC military actions that began on last December 28th. The successive stages of those actions, culminating in the peaceful entry of ONUC forces into Kolwezi on 21 January 1963, have been detailed in the last report of the Officer-in-Charge (S/5053/ Add.15).

Full freedom of movement for ONUC personnel throughout Katanga has thus been fully and firmly established. ONUC could never hope to discharge the mandates given to it with regard to law and order, prevention of civil war and the elimination of mercenaries, without freedom of movement. It was with this in mind that freedom of movement for ONUC was provided for in the Plan.

It is a matter of very great regret to me that the recent military actions were attended by some loss of life and by some damage to property. Because of the skill and restraint with which these actions were conducted, the casualties and damage were remarkably light. I wish to pay tribute to the courage, skill, devotion to duty, and the forbearance shown by all of those—in both the civilian and military branches of ONUC—who were connected with these events. This tribute applies equally to those many members of the Secretariat at United Nations Headquarters and in other United Nations Offices throughout the world who have been assisting the Congo operation as an extra work load. Nor do I forget the countries and Governments providing contingents to the Force. The actions were highly successful. But I would like to emphasize that the United Nations claims no victory in such situations. Nor does it speak of enemies. It is only too happy that the military action forced upon it last December is over; and it is thankful that this came about with comparatively little fighting. For a peace force, even a little fighting is too much and only a few casualties are too many.

It was my concern at all times during these events to offer every opportunity to Mr. Tshombe and his provincial ministers to give practical evidence of their readiness to accept and put into effect the Plan of National Reconciliation and thus avoid further needless bloodshed. I also found it necessary to warn Mr. Tshombe very seriously against carrying out the threats of massive destruction which he from time to time announced to the Press.

Despite the unnecessary fighting which had occurred since 28 December, it was still my conviction that the only practical course to the reconstruction of a united Congo would be through national reconciliation. Therefore, when on 14 January I received the message of Mr. Tshombe and his ministers indicating that they were ready to proclaim the end of the attempted secession of Katanga, to grant freedom of movement to United Nations troops and to co-operate with the United Nations, I immediately welcomed the statement and commended it to the attention of the President and the Prime Minister of the Congo. It was, indeed, with the Congolese authorities that the final decision rested, since only they could confirm the promise of amnesty which was the one condition which Mr. Tshombe and his ministers attached to their voluntary declaration of a change in course. The replies of Prime Minister Adoula and President Kasavubu confirming that the amnesty proclamation of 26 November 1962 remained valid despite the changed circumstances became available the following day. Their messages, moderate in tone and emphasizing peaceful reconciliation and co-operation in reconstruction, were statesmanlike and encouraging.

The unopposed entry of United Nations troops into Kolwezi on 21 January and the subsequent return of Mr. Tshombe and his provincial ministers to Elisabethville after their reiterated assurances of determination to carry out the Plan of National Reconciliation were significant and hopeful notes. The arrival of Mr. Ileo as Minister Resident of the Central Government in Elisabethville on 23 January symbolizes the restoration of the Central Government's authority in South Katanga. This, taken together with the numerous other concrete measures toward reintegration reported in the Officer-in-Charge's last report (S/5053/Add.15), indicated that the authority of the Central Government was being rapidly restored throughout Katanga. As this report is being written, Mr. Tshombe has communicated the list of names of senior officers of the Katangese gendarmerie, who, under the provisions of the Plan, are to be transported by the United Nations to Leopoldville to take the oath of allegiance to President Kasavubu, thus signalling the integration of the Katangese gendarmerie into the Congolese National Army.

In the light of these events, it is possible now to reach some conclusions about the fulfilment of the mandates laid down by Security Council resolutions on the Congo. This is a record of achievement under extraordinarily difficult conditions in which the United Nations may take pride. There is also so much still to be done that it may be rightly said that we are just at the beginning of a new phase of the Operation, in which a radical change in emphasis and direction will take place.

The policies and purposes of the United Nations with respect to the Republic of the Congo, as set out by the Security Council in its resolutions, are the following:

(a) To maintain the territorial integrity and the political independence of the Republic of the Congo;

(b) To assist the Central Government of the Congo in the restoration and maintenance of law and order;

(c) To prevent the occurrence of civil war in the Congo;

(d) To secure the immediate withdrawal and evacuation from the Congo of all foreign military, paramilitary and advisory personnel not under the United Nations Command, and all mercenaries; and

(e) To render technical assistance.

These are the mandates governing the actions of the United Nations Operation in the Congo.

It may be noted that in the prevention of civil war, the resolution of 21 February 1961 (S/4741) provides for "the use of force, if necessary, in the last resort", while the resolution of 24 November 1961 (S/5002) authorizes "the use of requisite measure of force, if necessary. . ." in the apprehension of mercenaries. In these respects, as in the use of its arms in simple self-defence, ONUC has acted with utmost prudence and restraint. The Force, although heterogeneous in its composition, is well disciplined, well officered and reliable. It is a thoroughly professional body.

The extent to which the above-mentioned mandates have been carried out, under the limitations on action decreed by the Security Council resolutions, may now be briefly reviewed.

(a) *Maintenance of territorial integrity and political independence*

The most serious threat to the territorial integrity of the Republic of the Congo has been the secessionist activity carried on since 11 July 1960 by the provincial authorities of Katanga. The integrity of the Congo was in a symbolic sense restored by the entry, with the consent of Mr. Tshombe, of United Nations troops into Katanga in August 1960. Despite unceasing efforts by the United Nations Force to prevent civil war and to create secure conditions in which the Katanga provincial authorities might enter into discussions with the Central Government for a peaceful reintegration of Katanga into the Republic, the Katanga provincial authorities persisted in their secessionist intrigues and activities. The recklessness of these activities was underscored by the unprovoked attacks of mercenary-led elements of the Katangese gendarmerie on United Nations troops in Elisabethville in September and December 1961 and in December 1962.

It is significant that since its free and peaceful entry into Katanga province in early August 1960, the United Nations Force there has enjoyed, almost without exception, good and friendly relations with the African people of Katanga. In recent months this has been increasingly true also of the non-African populations in Albertville, Elisabethville, Kipushi, Jadotville, Baudoinville and Kolwezi. Moreover, armed clashes between ONUC troops and the gendarmerie have occurred in general only when elements of the gendarmerie have been led by European mercenary officers. Despite frequent statements by Mr. Tshombe that he accepted reintegration, no real progress in that direction was achieved until after the recent military operations in Katanga.

In view of the subsequent public renunciation of secession by Mr. Tshombe and his ministers at Kolwezi; their declaration that they would henceforth co-operate with the United Nations in the full implementation of the Plan of National Reconciliation; the complete freedom of movement achieved by ONUC throughout Katanga; the neutralizing and disarming of the Katanga gendarmerie; the elimination of the Katanga airforce; the flight of the mercenaries; and the new situation as regards Union Minière revenues, it may be reasonably concluded that the attempted secession of Katanga is at an end. Given an absence of alertness or a too rapid withdrawal of the ONUC troops, it is conceivable that it could be revived. There are interests and elements in the Katanga scene which would always favour and flirt with it. There could be a regrouping and rearming of the gendarmerie or parts of it as a new secessionist force. But Katanga secession has never had a firm mass base among the people and it now appears that with most of them its demise has passed virtually unnoticed. Indeed, most of the people of North Katanga have at all times strongly opposed secession and given their full support to the Central Government.

There have been other separatist attempts in the Congo, of course, but none of these has had the importance or financial support of the Katanga pretensions, and they are now more or less quiescent. Happily, there appears to be no direct threat to the independence of the Congo from external sources. Thus it can be asserted that the territorial integrity and political independence mandate of the United Nations Operation has been largely fulfilled, except for a caretaker role.

(b) *Assistance in the restoration and maintenance of law and order*

It was the inability of the national security forces of the Congo, because of their mutiny one week after independence, to carry out their task of maintaining law and order that led indirectly to the decision by the Security Council to launch the United Nations Operation in the Congo. There was a breakdown of administration and of economic life; there were political disputes verging on civil war and inter-tribal differences which often took violent form. For a considerable period, the results of ONUC efforts could at best be palliative, seeking desperately in some areas only to prevent a complete breakdown of law and order. When the new Central Government came into power in August 1961, ONUC was able to co-ordinate its efforts in a much more effective way with those of the Congolese authorities, and from that time on the situation has shown in general a steady improvement. In the former Equateur province, for example, it has not been found necessary to post United Nations troops for a considerable period. In Leopoldville, for quite some time, and more recently in such areas as Stanleyville, Bukavu and Albertville, conditions have become much more settled and secure, and this is reflected in some resumption of economic activity and a return of many foreign nationals.

In Katanga, the continuing pursuit of secessionist policies by the provincial authorities has kept conditions constantly disturbed until very recently. It now appears, however, that law and order have been firmly restored in the main centres of Katanga, and it is expected that ONUC presence will have the same effect in rural areas where fighting has occurred between ANC troops and Katangese gendarmes. In any case, during the transitional period of reintegration of Katanga into the rest of the Republic, the problem of law and order there will be a delicate one. This is recognized by the Central Government, which has tentatively agreed for the present to place its own security forces in South Katanga under United Nations command and has accepted, at least in principle, that the introduction of its armed units into South Katanga should be spread out over a period of time. The transitional period during which the full authority of the Central Government is to be installed in Katanga unavoidably embodies many problems, some of which impose no little strain on the relations between the Central Government and ONUC. As regards the introduction of the ANC into South Katanga, the issues are essentially those of pace and method. The United Nations Operation, in the interest of order, security and public tranquillity, prefers a gradual introduction, based on an orderly plan, and insists for the time being on a single command, to avoid confusion and conflict.

Unfortunately, it appears that inter-tribal differences in the former province of Kasai seem to have been accentuated by the division of that province into smaller provinces more or less along tribal lines. Serious clashes continue to occur between ANC troops and "jeunesse" elements in the province of South Kasai, as well as between tribal elements. An intensified presence of United Nations troops in this area seems to be called for very soon.

The Officer-in-Charge and the Commander of the Force have been asked to consult with Congolese authorities about the extent and approximate length of time of continuing need of the Congolese Government for United Nations military assistance in the maintenance of law and order. It is perhaps an easy and safe guess to make that some United Nations armed troops will be required and will still be in the Congo a year from now. Circumstances, however, could change that picture. The reduction from present strength can and will be very substantial, but there will be much still to be done by ONUC under its law and order mandate, and for some time to come.

(c) *Prevention of the occurrence of civil war in the Congo*

This mandate of ONUC was adopted in February 1961 at a time when there were two sets of competing governmental authorities, one in Leopoldville and one in Stanleyville, each claiming to be the legitimate Government of the Republic of the Congo and each with elements of the ANC under its control. In addition, there were two other administrations, in South Kasai and Katanga, seeking to secede from the Government and the territory of the Congo.

This desperate situation was ameliorated as a result of the formation in August 1961 of a Government of National Unity acceptable to all parties concerned, other than the secessionist authorities of Katanga province.

Clashes occurred subsequently between elements of the ANC and Katanga gendarmerie, the latter supported by mercenaries. While endeavouring to limit these hostilities, in particular by pressing for a peaceful solution, ONUC obviously could not, consistently with decisions of the Security Council calling for the maintenance of the territorial integrity of the Congo and for an immediate end to the secessionist activities in Katanga, regard and deal with such hostilities as "civil war" actions under the terms of its mandate. Now, however, these hostilities, which ONUC always sought to halt but not always successfully, have come finally to an end following the decision by the Katangese provincial authorities to terminate their secessionist activities and the seeming distaste of both mercenaries and gendarmerie for any more fighting.

It may therefore be considered that the mandate of ONUC relating to civil war has been fulfilled in major degree, although an alert and effective watch over the situation will be indispensable for some time.

(d) *The removal of military and paramilitary and advisory personnel and mercenaries*

This aspect of ONUC's mandate was brought into effect by the Security Council resolution of 21 February 1961 at a time when the intervention of such personnel in Congolese affairs and, in particular, the military support given by these hired gunmen to the secessionist efforts of the Katangese provincial authorities, were flagrant and intolerable. A number of mercenaries were apprehended and expelled from the Congo in April 1961 and a further number of political and military advisers of the Katangese authorities were expelled in the succeeding months, However, the co-operation of the Katangese provincial authorities in this matter was altogether ineffective and unreliable, and on 28 August 1961 ONUC undertook action of its own to round up foreign military personnel in Katanga. A considerable number of personnel, particularly those loaned by the Belgian Government to the Katangese provincial authorities, left Katanga in the next few days, but many mercenaries succeeded in escaping and a renewed attempt to proceed with this operation led to the hostilities which began on 13 September 1961. Mercenary elements played a leading role in those hostilities and also in those of December 1961. Following this latter clash, Mr. Tshombe agreed to the evacuation of mercenaries but remained evasive on this point throughout the year 1962. Consequently, there were an estimated 400 mercenaries still in the Katangese gendarmerie at the beginning of the operations of December 1962–January 1963. The successful conclusion of these operations has resulted, it appears, in the flight of most if not all remaining mercenaries from Katanga via Angola, with the exception of a small number now in United Nations custody.

It may, therefore, be concluded that for all practical purposes the mandate relating to mercenaries has been fulfilled. It is, however, open to question whether there may not still be amongst the technicians who serve the Katangese provincial authorities, or amongst the non-Congolese residents of South Katanga, a number of persons who overstepped the limits of legitimate activity and acted as political and possibly military advisers or as mercenaries. The possibility of a number of expulsions on this ground cannot, therefore, be excluded.

(e) *Civilian operations and technical assistance*

The breakdown of law and order and the mass exodus of foreign technicians after the mutiny threatened a collapse in public adminis-tration, public services and in the economy which gave to the technical assistance operations of the United Nations in the Congo a scope and magnitude surpassing by far that ever before considered. ONUC civil-ian operations, involving an impressive collaboration between the United Nations and the specialized agencies, for much of the time under emergency conditions, helped to provide essential public servic-es which the organizations, in large measure, financed. Since the re-establishment of a constitutional government, the emphasis has been increasingly on advisory rather than operative staff. Moreover, the assistance given is limited by the funds available, which consist of voluntary contributions of Governments.

There will continue to be a need for assistance on a massive scale during the ensuing period of reconstruction, following which the pro-gramme of technical assistance to the country could eventually assume a more normal character.

The Prime Minister of the Congo Republic wrote to me on 20 December 1962, requesting assistance in a number of ways in seeking the modernization and training of the Congolese armed forces. I have responded favourably to this appeal and consultations in Leopold-ville between the Prime Minister and the Officer-in-Charge on the procedures to be followed are now under way. . . .

I have opened consultations with the Government of the Congo on the question of the channelling of future aid to the Congo. There will be, of course, a continuation of multilateral or United Nations aid. The question is the extent to which it may now have become advisable and desirable to envisage also an increase in bilateral aid. Although heretofore, the United Nations has been inclined to seek to have all aid to the Congo channelled or at least cleared through the United Nations, it is apparent that the United Nations alone will not have the resources to meet the vast needs of the Congo. The attitude of the Central Government will, of course, be decisive in determining how the aid should be given, and although that attitude is being sought, it is not yet ascertained. Obviously, it will be essential to try to avoid by some means, subjecting the Congo to the dangers of a politically motivated assistance competition among States.

A decisive phase in the United Nations Congo experience has been concluded. That is the phase of active military involvement by United Nations troops. This does not, however, automatically indicate an immediate military disengagement in the Congo by the United Nations. To do that could result in quickly undoing almost everything that has been achieved by the United Nations operation in more than two and one half painful and costly years. It may be that a smaller United Nations armed force in the Congo will be needed for some time, owing to the still inadequate military and police resources of the Central Government in coping with endemic problems of tribal warfare and maintenance of law and order. There will be, however, a progressive reduction in the strength of the Force, and an early disengagement cannot be ruled out. A phasing out schedule is now in process of formulation, in consultation with the Officer-in-Charge and the Commander of the Force, taking into account tasks to be performed, contingent withdrawals and rotation schedules. The first stage of the phasing out will be reached about the end of February and the process will be gradual but steady thereafter. This reduction process, naturally, will find a prompt reflection in substantially reducing the costs of the Operation. This, in turn, will lighten but not eliminate the severe financial strain which the United Nations has been experiencing largely because of its heavy expenditures in the Congo.

It is perhaps still too early to draw any final conclusions from the operation in the Congo. The lines of certain lessons that may be learned from this extensive and intensive experience begin to become apparent, however.

Merely to maintain a huge operation, involving political and military, as well as economic activities, within the territory of a sovereign, independent State is a task of very great complexity and delicacy. There are unavoidable problems in the daily relations with the national government. There are at Headquarters the inevitable problems that spring from the differing attitudes of Member Governments toward the issue and approaches to it. There are the external as well as internal influences at work. To keep the Operation going on an even keel demands very much, both from United Nations Headquarters and in the field, in the way of patience, endurance, forbearance, tact and firmness. The key, no doubt, is to have a clear definition of the basic principles on which the Operation is to rest and to adhere strictly to them. For the Congo Operation, these principles were defined clearly enough by the Security Council resolutions, although inevitably there were differences of viewpoint amongst the Members as to how the principles should be interpreted and applied. There has been, for example, the principle of non-interference in the internal political affairs of the Congo. This principle has been observed and the United Nations has scrupulously avoided any support for or opposition to any Congolese official or candidate, whether in the national or provincial governments. The United Nations has avoided any intervention in the internal politics of the country beyond the opposition to secession in general required by the Security Council resolutions and the constitutional suggestions embodied in the Plan for National Reconciliation which, after all, was only a proposal which each party was free to accept or reject.

The United Nations operation in the Congo has also adhered to the principle of avoiding the use of force for political purposes, although it is true that the very presence and activity of the United Nations Force in the Congo has been an important factor in giving effective weight to United Nations opposition to secession, whether in Katanga, Kasai or elsewhere in the country. It is in the Congo, of course, for this and other purposes, at the specific request of the Government of the country. But the United Nations has never used the arms at its disposal to further the political aims of any group or individual in the country, or to interfere with its political processes. Even with regard to secession, civil war and the elimination of mercenaries, the employment of the Force has been in the most limited manner, with limited objectives, without the Force itself taking any military initiatives, and only then as a last resort.

There are some who have been critical of the policy governing the United Nations Operation in the Congo, either because on the one hand it has used the Force under its command too sparingly and too cautiously, or on the other because of the mere presence of the Force, let alone its use. I am convinced of the wisdom of the course originally ordered by the Security Council resolutions. Quite apart from the profound and possibly shattering implications which would flow from a United Nations policy decision to employ force to regulate the internal political affairs of a country, even at the request of or with the acquiescence of its Government, to have done so in the Congo would have created a most adverse impact on both Congolese and international public opinion, besides inevitably creating some unmeritorious and troublesome martyrs. It seems to me, on the basis of the Congo experience, that the only sound way to inject an international armed force into a situation of that kind is to ensure that it is for clearly defined and restricted purposes, is fully under control of the Organization and always maintains its primary posture of arms for defence.

Quite possibly no activity ever engaged in by the United Nations has suffered so much as the Congo Operation from public misunderstanding of its purposes and activities. Much of this misunderstanding, of course, has been due to the deliberate campaign of the well-financed Katanga propaganda machine, which in some countries has been not inconsiderably aided and abetted by organized special interests with ulterior motives, such as hostility to the United Nations or interests, financial or other, in Katanga. The United Nations, through its Public Information services, has striven valiantly to counteract this propaganda, but has enjoyed only partial success. It is by no means clear how the United Nations, which must always seek to adhere to fact and truth, can fend off the insidious attacks or unscrupulous propaganda. This vital problem will require very careful attention in connexion with any future operation of a kind similar to that undertaken in the Congo.

15. *Final Report of the Secretary-General on the United Nations Operation in the Congo, 29 June 1964.*

S/5784 (29 June 1964); SCOR, XIX, Supp. for April–June 1964, p. 259, at 288–91.

The creation of the United Nations Force in the Congo in July 1960 was a remarkable and dramatic manifestation of world solidarity at that time. Whatever its shortcomings, and whatever the political contentions about it, that Force has proved and extended the ability of the United Nations to meet grave emergency situations. In response to the urgent appeal from the Congolese Government jointly signed by President Kasa-Vubu and Prime Minister Lumumba, the largest operation in the history of the United Nations was set up, or more accurately, improvised, in an incredibly short time, in order to come speedily to the aid and support of a young and struggling nation. In the circumstances in which that appeal was made, the United Nations would have suffered a severe loss of confidence throughout the world had it failed to respond. This was a crucial situation in which rapid historic change had produced problems of such complexity and danger that all Member States agreed that the United Nations, despite its limited authority and resources, offered the only possible hope of keeping the peace and gaining time for a solution to be found. When ONUC began its activities, the Congo was in a desperate situation, its army disrupted by the mutiny, its essential services on the verge of total disintegration, most of its population in a state of panic or despair, its territory threatened with amputation by the attempted secession of its richest province, and much of its area controlled by foreign troops.

During the subsequent four years, thousands of members of the United Nations Force—because of the rotations, a total of more than 93,000—and hundreds of civilians have devoted their best efforts and energies to helping the Congolese rebuild and develop their nation. Many of them, including my predecessor, Mr. Dag Hammarskjöld, have given their very lives toward this end. As a result of these efforts, the Congo situation is now incomparably improved, despite the recent disturbances. Four years have been gained in which the Government and the people of the Congo have had the opportunity to come to grips with their vast problems and to be assisted in meeting some of the worst of them. Four years have been gained in which Congolese public administrators, doctors, professional people, experts of all kinds, and technicians could at least begin their training and begin to gain experience under the guidance and with the expert help of personnel of the United Nations and its specialized agencies. These long-term efforts are now commencing to bear fruit, and they give cause for hope for the future of the Congo.

The United Nations Force in the Congo has afforded the United Nations its broadest experience with an operation of this kind. The conduct of this Force, its leadership and discipline, and its restraint, often under severe provocation, have been notably fine. In many places, units of this Force have been in daily contact with the civilian population and have almost always enjoyed good relations with the people. In fact, the Force never at any time or place encountered hostility from the Congolese people. There have been, naturally, some acts of a criminal nature by individuals in the Force, and there were, on occasion, some unfortunate excesses by individual soldiers, mainly under the emotional stress of sniper fire and harassment. Such instances, although relatively few, have been magnified and exploited by those seeking for one reason or another to discredit the United Nations. Over-all, it may be said that the record of the United Nations Force in the Congo, in all respects, has been distinguished. It has done its difficult job remarkably well. All of those who served in the Force, the countries that provided the contingents or afforded supporting services and money, and all of the civilian staff serving the Congo operation in the field and at Headquarters, are due great credit and appreciation for the valuable service they have rendered. The Congo Advisory Committee has given indispensable assistance and is due much gratitude.

The United Nations Force in the Congo was international in the sense that it was composed of units of troops from a number of different countries which had been placed under United Nations command. But these troops were never fully merged and consolidated, since the national contingents always maintained their separate identity and uniforms, except for United Nations headgear and insignia, used their own arms, and each national contingent had its own commanding officer. The authority of the Commander of the Force did not extend to the discipline of its members, that being left to the commanders of each national contingent. Weaknesses of this nature, in fact, have been common to all of the United Nations peace-keeping forces. There was a typical problem also in the very great variations amongst the contingents in pay and allowances based on national law and practice. This inevitably has implications for the morale and effectiveness of a force.

Maintaining a United Nations Force in a country, especially over an extended period, involves many difficulties in the relations with the Government of the country. Despite this fact, throughout the four years of the presence of the United Nations Force in the Congo, the relations with the Congo Government, and with those authorities in charge during that bleak period when there was no government at all, have been generally good and have weathered the relatively few major crises. There have been disagreements, at times serious, about policy. There have been difficulties on the part of governmental officials in comprehending the mandates and functions of a United Nations Force. There have been instances when the United Nations has had to take a firm stand against a wish or even a caprice of the Government. But these inevitable experiences have never seriously impaired the efforts of the Force or the effectiveness of other aspects of the United Nations Operation in the Congo. At the present time the relations with the Government of the Congo are good.

It was inevitable that over so long a period as four years, in a situation as complex and politically controversial as the Congo, certain impressions, assumptions, and even myths, would have developed, as they have, some of which certainly have had political overtones and no doubt political motivations as well. But they are decisively countered by certain well-documented and firmly established facts. The United Nations intervention in the Congo was directly in response to an urgent appeal from the Government of a newly independent country. The United Nations Operation in the Congo at all times has scrupulously avoided intervention in the internal affairs of that country; it has not taken sides in political or constitutional differences; it has not sought to usurp any governmental authority or ever to act like a government. The United Nations Force in the Congo, from beginning to end, was under strict instructions to use its arms for defensive purposes only, and its record of restraint in this regard had been highly commendable. Other than its successful efforts to eliminate the mercenaries in South Katanga, in pursuance of the Security Council mandate, the Force took no military initiatives involving the use of force; it launched no offensive. The Force, as every United Nations Force must be, was exclusively under United Nations command at all times. The Force, in pursuance of the mandate given it by the Security Council, undertook to assist the Central Government in the restoration and maintenance of law and order, but never permitted itself to become an arm of the Government or to be at its beck and call for political purposes. Violation of these two fundamental principles quite likely would have resulted in the disintegration of the Force through the withdrawal of some or all of its contingents. The presence of the United Nations Force has been the decisive factor in preserving the territorial integrity of the country; it has been solely responsible for the cessation of the activities of the mercenaries in Katanga; and it has been a major factor in preventing widespread civil war in the Congo.

NOTE. The last United Nations troops left the Congo on 30 June 1964. On 9 July 1964, Mr. Tshombe replaced Mr. Adoula as Prime Minister of the new Democratic Republic of the Congo. When the Congo Government was not able to cope with a rebellion in Stanleyville which was threatening the safety of more than a thousand foreigners residing there, it authorized a rescue operation by Belgian paracommandos carried to the Congo by United

States aircraft on 24–29 November 1964. Twenty-two Afro-Asian States complained to the Security Council against this intervention in African affairs which they considered as a flagrant violation of the Charter of the United Nations and a threat to the peace and security of the African continent. On the other hand, the Democratic Republic of the Congo asked the Council to examine the flagrant intervention in Congolese domestic affairs by various countries which were assisting the rebel movement in the Congo. After a prolonged discussion, to which seventeen meetings of the Council were devoted, the Security Council adopted unanimously a comprehensive resolution presented by the Ivory Coast and Morocco, with important amendments by Guinea. Annual Report of the Secretary-General, 1964–1965 [GAOR, XX, Supp. 1 (A/6001)], pp. 1–5. For the text of the resolution, see Document 16, below.

16. *Resolution 199 of the Security Council, 30 December 1964.*

SCOR, XIX, Resolutions and Decisions of the Security Council, 1964 (S/INF/19/Rev.1), pp. 18–19.

The Security Council,

Noting with concern the aggravation of the situation in the Democratic Republic of the Congo,

Deploring the recent events in that country,

Convinced that the solution of the Congolese problem depends on national reconciliation and the restoration of public order,

Recalling the pertinent resolutions of the General Assembly and the Security Council,

Reaffirming the sovereignty and territorial integrity of the Democratic Republic of the Congo,

Taking into consideration the resolution of the Organization of African Unity dated 10 September 1964, in particular paragraph 1 relating to the mercenaries,

Convinced that the Organization of African Unity should be able, in the context of Article 52 of the Charter of the United Nations, to help find a peaceful solution to all the problems and disputes affecting peace and security in the continent of Africa,

Having in mind the efforts of the Organization of African Unity to help the Government of the Democratic Republic of the Congo and the other political factions in the Congo to find a peaceful solution to their dispute,

1. Requests all States to refrain or desist from intervening in the domestic affairs of the Congo;

2. Appeals for a cease-fire in the Congo in accordance with the resolution of the Organization of African Unity dated 10 September 1964;

3. Considers, in accordance with that same resolution, that the mercenaries should as a matter of urgency be withdrawn from the Congo;

4. Encourages the Organization of African Unity to pursue its efforts to help the Government of the Democratic Republic of the Congo to achieve national reconciliation in accordance with the above-mentioned resolution of the Organization of African Unity;

5. Requests all States to assist the Organization of African Unity in the attainment of this objective;

6. Requests the Organization of African Unity, in accordance with Article 54 of the Charter of the United Nations, to keep the Security Council fully informed of any action it may take under the present resolution;

7. Requests the Secretary-General of the United Nations to follow the situation in the Congo and to report to the Security Council at the appropriate time.

NOTE. For comments on the United Nations Operation in the Congo, see D. W. BOWETT and others, United Nations Forces: A Legal Study of United Nations Practice (London, 1964), pp. 152–254; Ralph J. BUNCHE, "The United Nations Operation in the Congo," *in* Andrew W. CORDIER and Wilder FOOT, eds., The Quest for Peace (New York, 1965), pp. 119–38; Arthur Lee BURNS and Nina HEATHCOTE, Peace-Keeping by United Nations Forces: From Suez to Congo (New York, 1963), 256 pp.; Georges DINANT, L'O.N.U. face à la crise congolaise: La politique d'Hammarskjöld (Brussels, 1962), 174 pp.; G.I.A.D. DRAPER, "The Legal Limitations upon the Employment of Weapons by the United Nations Force in the Congo," 12 ICLQ (1963), pp. 387–413; Thomas M. FRANCK, "United Nations Law in Africa: The Congo Operation as a Case Study," 27 Law and Contemporary Problems (1962), pp. 632–52; Thomas M. FRANCK and John CAREY, The Legal Aspects of the United Nations Action in the Congo (Dobbs Ferry, New York, 1963), 137 pp.; King GORDON, The U.N. in the Congo: A Quest for Peace (New York, 1962), 184 pp.; Leo GROSS, "Domestic Jurisdiction, Enforcement Measures and the Congo," 1965 Australian YBIL, pp. 137–58; John W. HALDERMAN, "Legal Basis for United Nations Armed Forces," 56 AJIL (1962), pp. 971–996; Stanley HOFFMANN, "In Search of a Thread: The UN in the Congo Labyrinth," 16 Int.Org. (1962), pp. 331–61; Catherine HOSKYNS, The Congo since Independence, January 1960–December 1961 (New York, 1965), 518 pp.; Harold K. JACOBSON, "ONUC's Civilian Operations: State-Preserving and State-Building," 17 World Politics (1964), pp. 75–107; KATANGESE GOVERNMENT, White Paper on the Events of September and December 1961 (Elisabethville, 1962) 111 pp.; Joseph P. LASH, Dag Hammarskjöld: Custodian of the Brush-Fire Peace (Garden City, New York, 1961), pp. 223–62; Claude LECLERCQ, L'ONU et l'affaire du Congo (Paris, 1964), 367 pp.; Ernest W. LEFEVER, Crisis in the Congo: A United Nations Force in Action (Washington, D.C., 1965), 215 pp.; René LEMARCHAND, "The Limits of Self-Determination: The Case of the Katanga Secession," 56 APSR (1962), pp. 404–16; E. M. MILLER (pseud. for O. SCHACHTER), "Legal Aspects of U.N. Action in the Congo," 55 AJIL (1961), pp. 1–28; Richard I. MILLER, Dag Hammarskjöld and Crisis Diplomacy (New York, 1961), pp. 266–340; Herbert NICHOLAS, "U.N. Peace Forces and the Changing Globe: The Lessons of Suez and Congo," 17 Int. Org. (1963) pp. 321–37; Connor Cruise O'BRIEN, To Katanga and Back: A UN Case History (New York, 1962), 370 pp.; Patrick

O'DONOVAN, "The Precedent of the Congo," 37 Int. Affairs (London, 1961), pp. 181–88; Fouad Abdel Moneim RIAD, "The United Nations Action in the Congo and Its Legal Basis," 17 REgDI (1961), pp. 1–53; Ruth B. RUSSELL, United Nations Experience with Military Forces: Political and Legal Aspects (Washington, D.C., 1964), pp. 86–126; Oscar SCHACHTER, "Preventing the Internationalization of Internal Conflict: A Legal Analysis of the U.N. Congo Experience," 57 ASIL Procgs. (1963), pp. 216–224; Oscar SCHACHTER, "The Uses of Law in International Peace-Keeping," 50 Virginia L.R. (1964), pp. 1096–1114; J. W. SCHNEIDER, "Congo Force and Standing United Nations Force: Legal Experience with ONUC," 4 Indian JIL (1964), pp. 269–300; Finn SEYERSTED, United Nations Forces in the Law of Peace and War (Leyden, 1966), pp. 60–76; UN, The United Nations and the Congo: Some Salient Facts (New York, 1963), 19 pp.; Fernand VAN LANGENHOVE, Le rôle proéminent du Secrétaire Général dans l'opération des Nations Unies au Congo (Bruxelles, 1964), 260 pp.; Michel VIRALLY, "Les Nations Unies et l'affaire du Congo en 1960," 6 AFDI (1960), pp. 557–97; David W. WAINHOUSE and others, International Peace Observation: A History and Forecast (Baltimore, Md., 1966), pp. 405–13; Quincy WRIGHT, "The United Nations and the Congo Crisis," 2 J. of John Bassett Moore Society of International Law (1961–62), pp. 411–55.

See also Victor BERNY, "La sécession du Katanga: Étude juridique et historique (11 juillet 1960–14 janvier 1963)", 19 RJPIC (1965), pp. 563–77; Karl E. BIRNBAUM, "Hammarskjöld und die Funktionen der Vereinten Nationen während der Kongo-Krise," 17 Europa-Archiv (1962), pp. 533–48; Lincoln P. BLOOMFIELD, "Headquarters-Field Relations: Some Notes on the Beginning and End of ONUC," 17 Int. Org. (1963), pp. 377–89; Ritchie CALDER, Agony of the Congo (London, 1961), 160 pp.; M. Donald CARDWELL and others, Congo-Katanga Quest (New York, 1962), 36 pp.; Jules CHOMÉ, La crise congolaise: De l'indépendance a l'intervention militaire belge, 30 juin–9 juillet, (Brussels, 1960), 174 pp.; Jules CHOMÉ, Le gouvernement congolais et l'O.N.U.: Un paradoxe tragique (Brussels, 1961), 208 pp.; Pierre DAVISTER, Katanga enjeu du monde: Récits et documents (Brussels, 1960), 317 pp.; Pierre DAVISTER and P. TOUSSAINT, Croisettes et casques bleus (Brussels, 1962), 268 pp.; W. J. GANSHOF VAN DER MEERSCH, Fin de la souveraineté belge au Congo: Documents et réflexions (Brussels, 1963), 684 pp.; J. GÉRARD-LIBOIS, ed., Congo, 1959 (2d ed., Brussels, 1961), 293 pp.; J. GÉRARD-LIBOIS and Benoit VERHAEGEN, eds., Congo 1960 (2d ed., Brussels, 1961), 3 vols., 1252 pp.; J. GÉRARD-LIBOIS and Benoit VERHAEGEN, eds., Congo 1962 (Brussels, 1963), 453 pp.; J. GÉRARD-LIBOIS, Sécession au Katanga (Brussels, 1963), 363 pp.; Smith HEMPSTONE, Rebels, Mercenaries and Dividends: The Katanga Story (New York, 1962) 250 pp.; Pierre HENRI and Jacques MARRES, L'Etat Belge responsable en droit du désastre congolais? (Brussels, 1960), 179 pp.; Pierre HOUART, La penetration communiste au Congo: Commentaires et documents sur les événements de juin–novembre 1960, 117 pp.; INSTITUT ROYAL DES RELATIONS INTERNATIONALES, "La crise congolaise: Documents," 13 Chronique de politique étrangère (1960), pp. 439–951; 14 *idem* (1961), pp. 565–1135; INSTITUT ROYAL DES RELATIONS INTERNATIONALES, "L'O.N.U. et le Congo," 15 Chronique de politique étrangère (1962), pp. 339–1074; INSTITUT ROYAL DES RELATIONS IN-

TERNATIONALES, "Conclusion de l'opération de l'O.N.U. au Congo," 17 Chronique de politique étrangère (1964), pp. 5–96; Colin LEGUM, Congo Disaster (Baltimore, Md., 1961), 174 pp.; Alan P. MERRIAM, Congo: Background of Conflict (Evanston, Ill., 1961), 368 pp.; Washington A. Julango OKUMU, Lumumba's Congo: Roots of Conflict (New York, 1963), 250 pp.; Jean J. A. SALMON, "L'accord O.N.U.-Congo (Léopoldville du 27 novembre 1961," 68 RGDIP (1964), pp. 60–98; Philippa SCHUYLER, Who Killed the Congo? (New York, 1962) 240 pp.; Benoit VERHAEGEN, Congo 1961 (Brussels, 1962), 691 pp.; Arthur WAUTERS and others, Le monde communisme et la crise du Congo belge (Brussels, 1961), 176 pp.; Pierre WIGNY, "Belgium and the Congo," 37 Int. Affairs (1961), pp. 273–84.

FINANCING PEACE-KEEPING

NOTE. In financing its budget, the United Nations encountered only a few minor difficulties prior to 1956. But several States, including the Soviet Union, refused to pay their share of the expenses of UNEF, and a larger group of States, including not only the Soviet Union but also France, denied their obligation to pay for the expenses of ONUC. A Working Group of Fifteen, established to examine the administrative and budgetary procedures of the United Nations and the methods for covering the cost of peace-keeping operations, could not agree on any principles or recommendations. A/4791 (15 Nov. 1961); GAOR, Annexes (XVI) 62, pp. 1–6. It proved necessary in 1961 to authorize the Secretary-General to issue up to $200 million of bonds to be amortized over twenty-five years. GA Resolution 1739 (XVI), 20 Dec. 1961; GAOR, XVI, Supp. 17 (A/5100), p. 60. On the same day, the General Assembly decided by 52 votes to 11, with 32 abstentions, to ask the International Court of Justice for an advisory opinion on the legal character of its resolutions relating to peace-keeping expenditures. GAOR, XVI, Plenary, pp. 1150–54. With respect to the background of this resolution, see the Report of the Fifth Committee, A/5062 (18 Dec. 1961); GAOR, Annexes (XVI) 62, pp. 11–16.

1.   *Certain Expenses of the United Nations*

International Court of Justice, Advisory Opinion of 20 July 1962.
ICJ Reports, 1962, pp. 151–80.

Resolution 1731 (XVI) by which the General Assembly decided to request an advisory opinion from the Court reads as follows:
"The General Assembly,

"Recognizing its need for authoritative legal guidance as to obligations of Member States under the Charter of the United Nations in the matter of financing the United Nations operations in the Congo and in the Middle East,

"1.   Decides to submit the following question to the International Court of Justice for an advisory opinion:

" 'Do the expenditures authorized in General Assembly resolutions 1583 (XV) and 1590 (XV) of 20 December 1960, 1595 (XV) of 3 April 1961, 1619 (XV) of 21 April 1961 and 1633 (XVI) of 30 October 1961 relating to the United Nations operations in the Congo undertaken in pursuance of the Security Council resolutions of 14 July, 22 July and 9 August 1960, and 21 February and 24 November 1961, and General Assembly resolutions 1474 (ES-IV) of 20 September 1960 and 1599 (XV), 1600 (XV) and 1601 (XV) of 15 April 1961, and the expenditures authorized in General Assembly resolutions 1122 (XI) of 26 November 1956, 1089 (XI) of 21 December 1956, 1090 (XI) of 27 February 1957, 1151 (XII) of 22 November 1957, 1204 (XII) of 13 December 1957, 1337 (XIII) of 13 December 1958, 1441 (XIV) of 5 December 1959 and 1575 (XV) of 20 December 1960 relating to the operations of the United Nations Emergency Force undertaken in pursuance of General Assembly resolutions 997 (ES-I) of 2 November 1956, 998 (ES-I) and 999 (ES-I) of 4 November 1956, 1000 (ES-I) of 5 November 1956, 1001 (ES-I) of 7 November 1956, 1121 (XI) of 24 November 1956 and 1263 (XIII) of 14 November 1958, constitute "expenses of the Organization" within the meaning of Article 17, paragraph 2, of the Charter of the United Nations?'

"2. Requests the Secretary-General, in accordance with Article 65 of the Statute of the International Court of Justice, to transmit the present resolution to the Court, accompanied by all documents likely to throw light upon the question." . . .

Before proceeding to give its opinion on the question put to it, the Court considers it necessary to make the following preliminary remarks:

The power of the Court to give an advisory opinion is derived from Article 65 of the Statute. The power granted is of a discretionary character. In exercising its discretion, the International Court of Justice, like the Permanent Court of International Justice, has always been guided by the principle which the Permanent Court stated in the case concerning the Status of Eastern Carelia on 23 July 1923: "The Court, being a Court of Justice, cannot, even in giving advisory opinions, depart from the essential rules guiding their activity as a Court" (P.C.I.J., Series B, No. 5, p. 29). Therefore, and in accordance with Article 65 of its Statute, the Court can give an advisory opinion only on a legal question. If a question is not a legal one, the Court has no discretion in the matter; it must decline to give the opinion requested. But even if the question is a legal one, which the Court is undoubtedly competent to answer, it may nonetheless decline to do so. As this Court said in its Opinion of 30 March 1950, the permissive character of Article 65 "gives the Court the power to examine whether the circumstances of the case are of such a character as should lead it to decline to answer the Request" (Interpretation of Peace Treaties with Bulgaria, Hungary and Romania (First Phase), I.C.J. Reports 1950, p. 72). But, as the Court also said in the same Opinion, "the reply of the Court, itself an 'organ of the United Nations', represents its participation in the activities of the Organization, and, in principle, should not be refused" (*ibid.*, p. 71). Still more emphatically, in its Opinion of

23 October 1956, the Court said that only "compelling reasons" should lead it to refuse to give a requested advisory opinion (Judgments of the Administrative Tribunal of the I.L.O. upon complaints made against the Unesco, I.C.J. Reports 1956, p. 86).

The Court finds no "compelling reason" why it should not give the advisory opinion which the General Assembly requested by its resolution 1731 (XVI). It has been argued that the question put to the Court is intertwined with political questions, and that for this reason the Court should refuse to give an opinion. It is true that most interpretations of the Charter of the United Nations will have political significance, great or small. In the nature of things it could not be otherwise. The Court, however, cannot attribute a political character to a request which invites it to undertake an essentially judicial task, namely, the interpretation of a treaty provision.

In the preamble to the resolution requesting this opinion, the General Assembly expressed its recognition of "its need for authoritative legal guidance". In its search for such guidance it has put to the Court a legal question—a question of the interpretation of Article 17, paragraph 2, of the Charter of the United Nations. In its Opinion of 28 May 1948, the Court made it clear that as "the principal judicial organ of the United Nations", it was entitled to exercise in regard to an article of the Charter, "a multilateral treaty, an interpretative function which falls within the normal exercise of its judicial powers" (Conditions of Admission of a State to Membership in the United Nations (Article 4 of the Charter), I.C.J. Reports 1947–1948, p. 61).

The Court, therefore, having been asked to give an advisory opinion upon a concrete legal question, will proceed to give its opinion.

The question on which the Court is asked to give its opinion is whether certain expenditures which were authorized by the General Assembly to cover the costs of the United Nations operations in the Congo (hereinafter referred to as ONUC) and of the operations of the United Nations Emergency Force in the Middle East (hereinafter referred to as UNEF), "constitute 'expenses of the Organization' within the meaning of Article 17, paragraph 2, of the Charter of the United Nations".

Before entering upon the detailed aspects of this question, the Court will examine the view that it should take into consideration the circumstance that at the 1086th Plenary Meeting of the General Assembly on 20 December 1961, an amendment was proposed, by the representative of France, to the draft resolution requesting the advisory opinion, and that this amendment was rejected. The amendment would have asked the Court to give an opinion on the question whether the expenditures relating to the indicated operations were "decided on in conformity with the provisions of the Charter" ; if that question were answered in the affirmative, the Court would have been asked to proceed to answer the question which the resolution as adopted actually poses.

If the amendment had been adopted, the Court would have been asked to consider whether the resolutions *authorizing the expenditures* were decided on in conformity with the Charter; the French amendment did not propose to ask the Court whether the resolutions *in pursuance of which the operations in the Middle East and in the Congo were undertaken,* were adopted in conformity with the Charter.

The Court does not find it necessary to expound the extent to which the proceedings of the General Assembly, antecedent to the adoption of a resolution, should be taken into account in interpreting that resolution, but it makes the following comments on the argument based upon the rejection of the French amendment.

The rejection of the French amendment does not constitute a directive to the Court to exclude from its consideration the question whether certain expenditures were "decided on in conformity with the Charter", if the Court finds such consideration appropriate. It is not to be assumed that the General Assembly would thus seek to fetter or hamper the Court in the discharge of its judicial functions; the Court must have full liberty to consider all relevant data available to it in forming an opinion on a question posed to it for an advisory opinion. Nor can the Court agree that the rejection of the French amendment has any bearing upon the question whether the General Assembly sought to preclude the Court from interpreting Article 17 in the light of other articles of the Charter, that is, in the whole context of the treaty. If any deduction is to be made from the debates on this point, the opposite conclusion would be drawn from the clear statements of sponsoring delegations that they took it for granted the Court would consider the Charter as a whole.

Turning to the question which has been posed, the Court observes that it involves an interpretation of Article 17, paragraph 2, of the Charter. On the previous occasions when the Court has had to interpret the Charter of the United Nations, it has followed the principles and rules applicable in general to the interpretation of treaties, since it has recognized that the Charter is a multilateral treaty, albeit a treaty having certain special characteristics. In interpreting Article 4 of the Charter, the Court was led to consider "the structure of the Charter" and "the relations established by it between the General Assembly and the Security Council" ; a comparable problem confronts the Court in the instant matter. The Court sustained its interpretation of Article 4 by considering the manner in which the organs concerned "have consistently interpreted the text" in their practice (Competence of the General Assembly for the Admission of a State to the United Nations, I.C.J. Reports 1950, pp. 8–9).

The text of Article 17 is in part as follows:

"1. The General Assembly shall consider and approve the budget of the Organization.

"2. The expenses of the Organization shall be borne by the Members as apportioned by the General Assembly."

Although the Court will examine Article 17 in itself and in its relation to the rest of the Charter, it should be noted that at least three separate questions might arise in the interpretation of paragraph 2 of this Article. One question is that of identifying what are "the expenses of the Organization" ; a second question might concern apportionment by the General Assembly; while a third question might involve the interpretation of the phrase "shall be borne by the Members". It is the second and third questions which directly involve "the financial obligations of the Members", but it is only the first question which is posed by the request for the advisory opinion. The question put to the Court has to do with a moment logically anterior to apportionment, just as a question of apportionment would be anterior to a question of Members' obligation to pay.

It is true that, as already noted, the preamble of the resolution containing the request refers to the General Assembly's "need for authoritative legal guidance as to obligations of Member States", but it is to be assumed that in the understanding of the General Assembly, it would find such guidance in the advisory opinion which the Court would give on the question whether certain identified expenditures "constitute 'expenses of the Organization' within the meaning of Article 17, paragraph 2, of the Charter". If the Court finds that the indicated expenditures are such "expenses", it is not called upon to consider the manner in which, or the scale by which, they may be apportioned. The amount of what are unquestionably "expenses of the Organization within the meaning of Article 17, paragraph 2" is not in its entirety apportioned by the General Assembly and paid for by the contributions of Member States, since the Organization has other sources of income. A Member State, accordingly, is under no obligation to pay more than the amount apportioned to it; the expenses of the Organization and the total amount in money of the obligations of the Member States may not, in practice, necessarily be identical.

The text of Article 17, paragraph 2, refers to "the expenses of the Organization" without any further explicit definition of such expenses. It would be possible to begin with a general proposition to the effect that the "expenses" of any organization are the amounts paid out to defray the costs of carrying out its purposes, in this case, the political, economic, social, humanitarian and other purposes of the United Nations. The next step would be to examine, as the Court will, whether the resolutions authorizing the operations here in question were intended to carry out the purposes of the United Nations and whether the expenditures were incurred in furthering these operations. Or, it might simply be said that the "expenses" of an organization are those which are provided for in its budget. But the Court has not been asked to give an abstract definition of the words "expenses of the Organization". It has been asked to answer a specific question related to certain identified expenditures which have actually been made, but the Court would not adequately discharge the obligation incumbent on it unless it examined in some detail various problems raised by the question which the General Assembly has asked.

It is perhaps the simple identification of "expenses" with the items included in a budget, which has led certain arguments to link the interpretation of the word "expenses" in paragraph 2 of Article 17, with the word "budget" in paragraph 1 of that Article; in both cases, it is contended, the qualifying adjective "regular" or "administrative" should be understood to be implied. Since no such qualification is expressed in the text of the Charter, it could be read in, only if such qualification must necessarily be implied from the provisions of the Charter considered as a whole, or from some particular provision thereof which makes it unavoidable to do so in order to give effect to the Charter.

In the first place, concerning the word "budget" in paragraph 1 of Article 17, it is clear that the existence of the distinction between "administrative budgets" and "operational budgets" was not absent from the minds of the drafters of the Charter, nor from the consciousness of the Organization even in the early days of its history. In drafting Article 17, the drafters found it suitable to provide in paragraph 1 that "The General Assembly shall consider and approve *the budget* of the Organization". But in dealing with the function of the General Assembly in relation to the specialized agencies, they provided in paragraph 3 that the General Assembly "shall examine the *administrative budgets* of such specialized agencies". If it had been intended that paragraph 1 should be limited to the administrative budget of the United Nations organization itself, the word "administrative" would have been inserted in paragraph 1 as it was in paragraph 3. Moreover, had it been contemplated that the Organization would also have had another budget, different from the one which was to be approved by the General Assembly, the Charter would have included some reference to such other budget and to the organ which was to approve it.

Similarly, at its first session, the General Assembly in drawing up and approving the Constitution of the International Refugee Organization, provided that the budget of that Organization was to be divided under the headings "administrative", "operational" and "large-scale resettlement"; but no such distinctions were introduced into the Financial Regulations of the United Nations which were adopted by unanimous vote in 1950, and which, in this respect, remain unchanged. These regulations speak only of "the budget" and do not provide any distinction between "administrative" and "operational".

In subsequent sessions of the General Assembly, including the sixteenth, there have been numerous references to the idea of distinguishing an "operational" budget; some speakers have advocated such a distinction as a useful book-keeping device; some considered it in connection with the possibility of differing scales of assessment or apportionment; others believed it should mark a differentiation of activities to be financed by voluntary contributions. But these discussions have not resulted in the adoption of two separate budgets based upon such a distinction.

Actually, the practice of the Organization is entirely consistent with the plain meaning of the text. The budget of the Organization has from the outset included items which would not fall within any of the definitions of "administrative budget" which have been advanced in this connection. Thus, for example, prior to the establishment of, and now in addition to, the "Expanded Programme of Technical Assistance" and the "Special Fund", both of which are nourished by voluntary contributions, the annual budget of the Organization contains provision for funds for technical assistance; in the budget for the financial year 1962, the sum of $6,400,000 is included for the technical programmes of economic development, social activities, human rights activities, public administration and narcotic drugs control. Although during the Fifth Committee discussions there was a suggestion that all technical assistance costs should be excluded from the regular budget, the items under these heads were all adopted on second reading in the Fifth Committee without a dissenting vote. The "operational" nature of such activities so budgeted is indicated by the explanations in the budget estimates, e.g. the requests "for the continuation of the operational programme in the field of economic development contemplated in General Assembly resolutions 200 (III) of 4 December 1948 and 304 (IV) of 16 November 1949" ; and "for the continuation of the operational programme in the field of advisory social welfare services as contemplated in General Assembly resolution 418 (V) of 1 December 1950".

It is a consistent practice of the General Assembly to include in the annual budget resolutions, provisions for expenses relating to the maintenance of international peace and security. Annually, since 1947, the General Assembly has made anticipatory provision for "unforeseen and extraordinary expenses" arising in relation to the "maintenance of peace and security". In a Note submitted to the Court by the Controller on the budgetary and financial practices of the United Nations, "extraordinary expenses" are defined as "obligations and expenditures arising as a result of the approval by a council, commission or other competent United Nations body of new programmes and activities not contemplated when the budget appropriations were approved".

The annual resolution designed to provide for extraordinary expenses authorizes the Secretary-General to enter into commitments to meet such expenses with the prior concurrence of the Advisory Committee on Administrative and Budgetary Questions, except that such concurrence is not necessary if the Secretary-General certifies that such commitments relate to the subjects mentioned and the amount does not exceed $2 million. At its fifteenth and sixteenth sessions, the General Assembly resolved "that if, as a result of a decision of the Security Council, commitments relating to the maintenance of peace and security should arise in an estimated total exceeding $10 million" before the General Assembly was due to meet again, a special session should be convened by the Secretary-General to consider the matter. The Secretary-General is regularly authorized to draw on the Working Capital Fund for such expenses but is required to submit supplementary budget estimates to cover amounts so advanced. These annual resolutions on unforeseen and extraordinary expenses were adopted without a dissenting vote in every year from 1947 through 1959, except for 1952, 1953 and 1954, when the adverse votes are attributable to the fact that the resolution included the specification of a controversial item—United Nations Korean war decorations.

It is notable that the 1961 Report of the Working Group of Fifteen on the Examination of the Administrative and Budgetary Procedures of the United Nations, while revealing wide differences of opinion on a variety of propositions, records that the following statement was adopted without opposition:

"22. Investigations and observation operations undertaken by the Organization to prevent possible aggression should be financed as part of the regular budget of the United Nations."

In the light of what has been stated, the Court concludes that there is no justification for reading into the text of Article 17, paragraph 1, any limiting or qualifying word before the word "budget".

Turning to paragraph 2 of Article 17, the Court observes that, on its face, the term "expenses of the Organization" means all the expenses and not just certain types of expenses which might be referred to as "regular expenses". An examination of other parts of the Charter shows the variety of expenses which must inevitably be included within the "expenses of the Organization" just as much as the salaries of staff or the maintenance of buildings.

For example, the text of Chapters IX and X of the Charter with reference to international economic and social cooperation, especially the wording of those articles which specify the functions and powers of the Economic and Social Council, anticipated the numerous and varied circumstances under which expenses of the Organization could be incurred and which have indeed eventuated in practice.

Furthermore, by Article 98 of the Charter, the Secretary-General is obligated to perform such functions as are entrusted to him by the General Assembly, the Security Council, the Economic and Social Council, and the Trusteeship Council. Whether or not expenses incurred in his discharge of this obligation become "expenses of the Organization" cannot depend on whether they be administrative or some other kind of expenses.

The Court does not perceive any basis for challenging the legality of the settled practice of including such expenses as these in the budgetary amounts which the General Assembly apportions among the Members in accordance with the authority which is given to it by Article 17, paragraph 2.

Passing from the text of Article 17 to its place in the general structure and scheme of the Charter, the Court will consider whether in that broad context one finds any basis for implying a limitation upon the budgetary authority of the General Assembly which in turn might limit the meaning of "expenses" in paragraph 2 of that Article.

The general purposes of Article 17 are the vesting of control over the finances of the Organization, and the levying of apportioned amounts of the expenses of the Organization in order to enable it to carry out the functions of the Organization as a whole acting through its principal organs and such subsidiary organs as may be established under the authority of Article 22 or Article 29.

Article 17 is the only article in the Charter which refers to budgetary authority or to the power to apportion expenses, or otherwise to raise revenue, except for Articles 33 and 35, paragraph 3, of the Statute of the Court which have no bearing on the point here under discussion. Nevertheless, it has been argued before the Court that one type of expenses, namely those resulting from operations for the maintenance of international peace and security, are not "expenses of the Organization" within the meaning of Article 17, paragraph 2, of the Charter, inasmuch as they fall to be dealt with exclusively by the Security Council, and more especially through agreements negotiated in accordance with Article 43 of the Charter.

The argument rests in part upon the view that when the maintenance of international peace and security is involved, it is only the Security Council which is authorized to decide on any action relative thereto. It is argued further that since the General Assembly's power is limited to discussing, considering, studying and recommending, it cannot impose an obligation to pay the expenses which result from the implementation of its recommendations. This argument leads to an examination of the respective functions of the General Assembly and of the Security Council under the Charter, particularly with respect to the maintenance of international peace and security.

Article 24 of the Charter provides:

"In order to ensure prompt and effective action by the United Nations, its Members confer on the Security Council primary responsibility for the maintenance of international peace and security . . ."

The responsibility conferred is "primary", not exclusive. This primary responsibility is conferred upon the Security Council, as stated in Article 24, "in order to ensure prompt and effective action". To this end, it is the Security Council which is given a power to impose an explicit obligation of compliance if for example it issues an order or command to an aggressor under Chapter VII. It is only the Security Council which can require enforcement by coercive action against an aggressor.

The Charter makes it abundantly clear, however, that the General Assembly is also to be concerned with international peace and security. Article 14 authorizes the General Assembly to "recommend measures for the peaceful adjustment of any situation, regardless of origin, which it deems likely to impair the general welfare or friendly relations among nations, including situations resulting from a violation of the provisions of the present Charter setting forth the purposes and principles of the United Nations". The word "measures" implies some kind of action, and the only limitation which Article 14 imposes on the General Assembly is the restriction found in Article 12, namely, that the Assembly should not recommend measures while the Security Council is dealing with the same matter unless the Council requests it to do so. Thus while it is the Security Council which, exclusively, may order coercive action, the functions and powers conferred by the Charter on the General Assembly are not confined to discussion, consideration, the initiation of studies and the making of recommendations; they are not merely hortatory. Article 18 deals with *"decisions"* of the General Assembly "on important questions". These "decisions" do indeed include certain recommendations, but others have dispositive force and effect. Among these latter decisions, Article 18 includes suspension of rights and privileges of membership, expulsion of Members, "and budgetary questions". In connection with the suspension of rights and privileges of membership and expulsion from membership under Articles 5 and 6, it is the Security Council which has only the power to recommend and it is the General Assembly which decides and whose decision determines status; but there is a close collaboration between the two organs. Moreover, these powers of decision of the General Assembly under Articles 5 and 6 are specifically related to preventive or enforcement measures.

By Article 17, paragraph 1, the General Assembly is given the power not only to "consider" the budget of the Organization, but also to "approve" it. The decision to "approve" the budget has a close connection with paragraph 2 of Article 17, since thereunder the General Assembly is also given the power to apportion the expenses among the Members and the exercise of the power of apportionment creates the obligation, specifically stated in Article 17, paragraph 2, of each Member to bear that part of the expenses which is apportioned to it by the General Assembly. When those expenses include expenditures for the maintenance of peace and security, which are not otherwise provided for, it is the General Assembly which has the authority to apportion the latter amounts among the Members. The provisions of the Charter which distribute functions and powers to the Security Council and to the General Assembly give no support to the view that such distribution excludes from the powers of the General Assembly the power to provide for the financing of measures designed to maintain peace and security.

The argument supporting a limitation on the budgetary authority of the General Assembly with respect to the maintenance of international peace and security relies especially on the reference to "action" in the last sentence of Article 11, paragraph 2. This paragraph reads as follows:

"The General Assembly may discuss any questions relating to the maintenance of international peace and security brought before it by any Member of the United Nations, or by the Security Council, or by a State which is not a Member of the United Nations in accordance with Article 35, paragraph 2, and, except as provided in Article 12, may make recommendations with regard to any such question to the State or States concerned or to the Security Council, or to both. Any such question on which action is necessary shall be referred to the Security Council by the General Assembly either before or after discussion."

The Court considers that the kind of action referred to in Article 11, paragraph 2, is coercive or enforcement action. This paragraph, which applies not merely to general questions relating to peace and security, but also to specific cases brought before the General Assembly by a State under Article 35, in its first sentence empowers the General Assembly, by means of recommendations to States or to the Security Council, or to both, to organize peace-keeping operations, at the request, or with the consent, of the States concerned. This power of the General Assembly is a special power which in no way derogates from its general powers under Article 10 or Article 14, except as limited by the last sentence of Article 11, paragraph 2. This last sentence says that when "action" is necessary the General Assembly shall refer the question to the Security Council. The word "action" must mean such action as is solely within the province of the Security Council. It cannot refer to recommendations which the Security Council might make, as for instance under Article 38, because the General Assembly under Article 11 has a comparable power. The "action" which is solely within the province of the Security Council is that which is indicated by the title of Chapter VII of the Charter, namely "Action with respect to threats to the peace, breaches of the peace, and acts of aggression". If the word "action" in Article 11, paragraph 2, were interpreted to mean that the General Assembly could make recommendations only of a general character affecting peace and security in the abstract, and not in relation to specific cases, the paragraph would not have provided that the General Assembly may make recommendations on questions brought before it by States or by the Security Council. Accordingly, the last sentence of Article 11, paragraph 2, has no application where the necessary action is not enforcement action.

The practice of the Organization throughout its history bears out the foregoing elucidation of the term "action" in the last sentence of Article 11, paragraph 2. Whether the General Assembly proceeds under Article 11 or under Article 14, the implementation of its recommendations for setting up commissions or other bodies involves organizational activity—action—in connection with the maintenance of international peace and security. Such implementation is a normal feature of the functioning of the United Nations. Such committees, commissions or other bodies or individuals, constitute, in some cases, subsidiary organs established under the authority of Article 22 of the Charter. The functions of the General Assembly for which it may establish such subsidiary organs include, for example, investigation, observation and supervision, but the way in which such subsidiary organs are utilized depends on the consent of the State or States concerned.

The Court accordingly finds that the argument which seeks, by reference to Article 11, paragraph 2, to limit the budgetary authority of the General Assembly in respect to the maintenance of international peace and security, is unfounded.

It has further been argued before the Court that Article 43 of the Charter constitutes a particular rule, a *lex specialis,* which derogates from the general rule in Article 17, whenever an expenditure for the maintenance of international peace and security is involved. Article 43 provides that Members shall negotiate agreements with the Security Council on its initiative, stipulating what "armed forces, assistance and facilities, including rights of passage, necessary for the purpose of maintaining international peace and security", the Member State will make available to the Security Council on its call. According to paragraph 2 of the Article:

"Such agreement or agreements shall govern the numbers and types of forces, their degree of readiness and general location, and the nature of the facilities and assistance to be provided."

The argument is that such agreements were intended to include specifications concerning the allocation of costs of such enforcement actions as might be taken by direction of the Security Council, and that it is only the Security Council which has the authority to arrange for meeting such costs.

With reference to this argument, the Court will state at the outset that, for reasons fully expounded later in this Opinion, the operations known as UNEF and ONUC were not *enforcement* actions within the compass of Chapter VII of the Charter and that therefore Article 43 could not have any applicability to the cases with which the Court is here concerned. However, even if Article 43 were applicable, the Court could not accept this interpretation of its text for the following reasons.

There is nothing in the text of Article 43 which would limit the discretion of the Security Council in negotiating such agreements. It cannot be assumed that in every such agreement the Security Council would insist, or that any Member State would be bound to agree, that such State would bear the entire cost of the "assistance" which it would make available including, for example, transport of forces to the point of operation, complete logistical maintenance in the field, supplies, arms and ammunition, etc. If, during negotiations under the terms of Article 43, a Member State would be entitled (as it would be) to insist, and the Security Council would be entitled (as it would be) to agree, that some part of the expense should be borne by the Organization, then such expense would form part of the expenses of the Organization and would fall to be apportioned by the General Assembly under Article 17. It is difficult to see how it could have been contemplated that all potential expenses could be envisaged in such agreements concluded perhaps long in advance. Indeed, the difficulty or impossibility of anticipating the entire financial impact of enforcement measures on Member States is brought out by the terms of Article 50 which provides that a State, whether a Member of the United Nations or not, "which finds itself confronted with special economic problems arising from the carrying out of those [preventive or enforcement] measures, shall have the right to consult the Security Council with regard to a solution of those problems". Presumably in such a case the Security Council might determine that the overburdened State was entitled to some financial assistance; such financial assistance, if afforded by the Organization, as it might be, would clearly constitute part of the "expenses of the Organization". The economic problems could not have been covered in advance by a negotiated agreement since they would be unknown until after the event and in the case of non-Member States, which are also included in Article 50, no agreement at all would have been negotiated under Article 43.

Moreover, an argument which insists that all measures taken for the maintenance of international peace and security must be financed through agreements concluded under Article 43, would seem to exclude the possibility that the Security Council might act under some other Article of the Charter. The Court cannot accept so limited a view of the powers of the Security Council under the Charter. It cannot be said that the Charter has left the Security Council impotent in the face of an emergency situation when agreements under Article 43 have not been concluded.

Articles of Chapter VII of the Charter speak of "situations" as well as disputes, and it must lie within the power of the Security Council to police a situation even though it does not resort to enforcement action against a State. The costs of actions which the Security Council is authorized to take constitute "expenses of the Organization within the meaning of Article 17, paragraph 2".

The Court has considered the general problem of the interpretation of Article 17, paragraph 2, in the light of the general structure of the Charter and of the respective functions assigned by the Charter to the General Assembly and to the Security Council, with a view to determining the meaning of the phrase "the expenses of the Organization". The Court does not find it necessary to go further in giving a more detailed definition of such expenses. The Court will, therefore, proceed to examine the expenditures enumerated in the request for the advisory opinion. In determining whether the actual expenditures authorized constitute "expenses of the Organization within the meaning of Article 17, paragraph 2, of the Charter", the Court agrees that such expenditures must be tested by their relationship to the purposes of the United Nations in the sense that if an expenditure were made for a purpose which is not one of the purposes of the United Nations, it could not be considered an "expense of the Organization".

The purposes of the United Nations are set forth in Article 1 of the Charter. The first two purposes as stated in paragraphs 1 and 2, may be summarily described as pointing to the goal of international peace and security and friendly relations. The third purpose is the achievement of economic, social, cultural and humanitarian goals and respect for human rights. The fourth and last purpose is: "To be a center for harmonizing the actions of nations in the attainment of these common ends."

The primary place ascribed to international peace and security is natural, since the fulfilment of the other purposes will be dependent upon the attainment of that basic condition. These purposes are broad indeed, but neither they nor the powers conferred to effectuate them are unlimited. Save as they have entrusted the Organization with the attainment of these common ends, the Member States retain their freedom of action. But when the Organization takes action which warrants the assertion that it was appropriate for the fulfilment of one of the stated purposes of the United Nations, the presumption is that such action is not *ultra vires* the Organization.

If it is agreed that the action in question is within the scope of the functions of the Organization but it is alleged that it has been initiated or carried out in a manner not in conformity with the division of functions among the several organs which the Charter prescribes, one moves to the internal plane, to the internal structure of the Organization. If the action was taken by the wrong organ, it was irregular as a matter of that internal structure, but this would not necessarily mean that the expense incurred was not an expense of the Organization. Both national and international law contemplate cases in which the body corporate or politic may be bound, as to third parties, by an *ultra vires* act of an agent.

In the legal systems of States, there is often some procedure for determining the validity of even a legislative or governmental act, but no analogous procedure is to be found in the structure of the United Nations. Proposals made during the drafting of the Charter to place the ultimate authority to interpret the Charter in the International Court of Justice were not accepted; the opinion which the Court is in course of rendering is an *advisory* opinion. As anticipated in 1945, therefore, each organ must, in the first place at least, determine its own jurisdiction. If the Security Council, for example, adopts a resolution purportedly for the maintenance of international peace and security and if, in accordance with a mandate or authorization in such resolution, the Secretary-General incurs financial obligations, these amounts must be presumed to constitute "expenses of the Organization".

The Financial Regulations and Rules of the United Nations, adopted by the General Assembly, provide:

"Regulation 4.1: The appropriations voted by the General Assembly shall constitute an authorization to the Secretary-General to incur obligations and make payments for the purposes for which the appropriations were voted and up to the amounts so voted."

Thus, for example, when the General Assembly in resolution 1619 (XV) included a paragraph reading:

"3. *Decides* to appropriate an amount of $100 million for the operations of the United Nations in the Congo from 1 January to 31 October 1961",

this constituted an authorization to the Secretary-General to incur certain obligations of the United Nations just as clearly as when in resolution 1590 (XV) the General Assembly used this language:

"3. *Authorizes* the Secretary-General   .   .   .   to incur commitments in 1961 for the United Nations operations in the Congo up to the total of $24 million   .   .   ."

On the previous occasion when the Court was called upon to consider Article 17 of the Charter, the Court found that an award of the Administrative Tribunal of the United Nations created an obligation of the Organization and with relation thereto the Court said that:

"the function of approving the budget does not mean that the General Assembly has an absolute power to approve or disapprove the expenditure proposed to it; for some part of that expenditure arises out of obligations already incurred by the Organization, and to this extent the General Assembly has no alternative but to honour these engagements". (Effects of awards of compensation made by the United Nations Administrative Tribunal, I.C.J. Reports 1954, p. 59.)

Similarly, obligations of the Organization may be incurred by the Secretary-General, acting on the authority of the Security Council or of the General Assembly, and the General Assembly "has no alternative but to honour these engagements".

The obligation is one thing: the way in which the obligation is met —that is from what source the funds are secured—is another. The

General Assembly may follow any one of several alternatives: it may apportion the cost of the item according to the ordinary scale of assessment; it may apportion the cost according to some special scale of assessment; it may utilize funds which are voluntarily contributed to the Organization; or it may find some other method or combination of methods for providing the necessary funds. In this context, it is of no legal significance whether, as a matter of book-keeping or accounting, the General Assembly chooses to have the item in question included under one of the standard established sections of the "regular" budget or whether it is separately listed in some special account or fund. The significant fact is that the item is an expense of the Organization and under Article 17, paragraph 2, the General Assembly therefore has authority to apportion it.

The reasoning which has just been developed, applied to the resolutions mentioned in the request for the advisory opinion, might suffice as a basis for the opinion of the Court. The Court finds it appropriate, however, to take into consideration other arguments which have been advanced.

The expenditures enumerated in the request for an advisory opinion may conveniently be examined first with reference to UNEF and then to ONUC. In each case, attention will be paid first to the operations and then to the financing of the operations.

In considering the operations in the Middle East, the Court must analyze the functions of UNEF as set forth in resolutions of the General Assembly. Resolution 998 (ES-I) of 4 November 1956 requested the Secretary-General to submit a plan "for the setting up, with the consent of the nations concerned, of an emergency international United Nations Force to secure and supervise the cessation of hostilities in accordance with all the terms of" the General Assembly's previous resolution 997 (ES-I) of 2 November 1956. The verb "secure" as applied to such matters as halting the movement of military forces and arms into the area and the conclusion of a cease-fire, might suggest measures of enforcement, were it not that the Force was to be set up "with the consent of the nations concerned".

In his first report on the plan for an emergency international Force the Secretary-General used the language of resolution 998 (ES-I) in submitting his proposals. The same terms are used in General Assembly resolution 1000 (ES-I) of 5 November in which operative paragraph 1 reads:

"*Establishes* a United Nations Command for an emergency international Force to secure and supervise the cessation of hostilities in accordance with all the terms of General Assembly resolution 997 (ES-I) of 2 November 1956."

This resolution was adopted without a dissenting vote. In his second and final report on the plan for an emergency international Force of 6 November, the Secretary-General, in paragraphs 9 and 10, stated:

"While the General Assembly is enabled to *establish* the Force with the consent of those parties which contribute units to the Force, it could not request the Force to be *stationed* or *operate* on the territory of a given country without the consent of the Government of that country. This does not exclude the possibility that the Security Council could use such a Force within the wider margins provided under Chapter VII of the United Nations Charter. I would not for the present consider it necessary to elaborate this point further, since no use of the Force under Chapter VII, with the rights in relation to Member States that this would entail, has been envisaged.

"10. The point just made permits the conclusion that the setting up of the Force should not be guided by the needs which would have existed had the measure been considered as part of an enforcement action directed against a Member country. There is an obvious difference between establishing the Force in order to secure the cessation of hostilities, with a withdrawal of forces, and establishing such a Force with a view to enforcing a withdrawal of forces."

Paragraph 12 of the Report is particularly important because in resolution 1001 (ES-I) the General Assembly, again without a dissenting vote, *"Concurs* in the definition of the functions of the Force as stated in paragraph 12 of the Secretary-General's report". Paragraph 12 reads in part as follows:

"the functions of the United Nations Force would be, when a cease-fire is being established, to enter Egyptian territory with the consent of the Egyptian Government, in order to help maintain quiet during and after the withdrawal of non-Egyptian troops, and to secure compliance with the other terms established in the resolution of 2 November 1956. The Force obviously should have no rights other than those necessary for the execution of its functions, in co-operation with local authorities. It would be more than an observers' corps, but in no way a military force temporarily controlling the territory in which it is stationed; nor, moreover, should the Force have military functions exceeding those necessary to secure peaceful conditions on the assumption that the parties to the conflict take all necessary steps for compliance with the recommendations of the General Assembly."

It is not possible to find in this description of the functions of UNEF, as outlined by the Secretary-General and concurred in by the General Assembly without a dissenting vote, any evidence that the Force was to be used for purposes of enforcement. Nor can such evidence be found in the subsequent operations of the Force, operations which did not exceed the scope of the functions ascribed to it.

It could not therefore have been patent on the face of the resolution that the establishment of UNEF was in effect "enforcement action" under Chapter VII which, in accordance with the Charter, could be authorized only by the Security Council.

On the other hand, it is apparent that the operations were undertaken to fulfil a prime purpose of the United Nations, that is, to promote and to maintain a peaceful settlement of the situation. This being true, the Secretary-General properly exercised the authority given him to incur financial obligations of the Organization and expenses resulting from such obligations must be considered "expenses of the Organization within the meaning of Article 17, paragraph 2".

Apropos what has already been said about the meaning of the word "action" in Article 11 of the Charter, attention may be called to the fact that resolution 997 (ES-I), which is chronologically the first of the resolutions concerning the operations in the Middle East mentioned in the request for the advisory opinion, provides in paragraph 5:

"*Requests* the Secretary-General to observe and report promptly on the compliance with the present resolution to the Security Council *and* to the General Assembly, for such further *action as they may deem appropriate in accordance with the Charter.*"

The italicized words reveal an understanding that either of the two organs might take "action" in the premises. Actually, as one knows, the "action" was taken by the General Assembly in adopting two days later without a dissenting vote, resolution 998 (ES-I) and, also without a dissenting vote, within another three days, resolutions 1000 (ES-I) and 1001 (ES-I), all providing for UNEF.

The Court notes that these "actions" may be considered "measures" recommended under Article 14, rather than "action" recommended under Article 11. The powers of the General Assembly stated in Article 14 are not made subject to the provisions of Article 11, but only of Article 12. Furthermore, as the Court has already noted, the word "measures" implies some kind of action. So far as concerns the nature of the situations in the Middle East in 1956, they could be described as "likely to impair . . . friendly relations among nations", just as well as they could be considered to involve "the maintenance of international peace and security". Since the resolutions of the General Assembly in question do not mention upon which article they are based, and since the language used in most of them might imply reference to either Article 14 or Article 11, it cannot be excluded that they were based upon the former rather than the latter article.

The financing of UNEF presented perplexing problems and the debates on these problems have even led to the view that the General Assembly never, either directly or indirectly, regarded the expenses of UNEF as "expenses of the Organization within the meaning of Article 17, paragraph 2, of the Charter". With this interpretation the Court cannot agree. In paragraph 15 of his second and final report on the plan for an emergency international Force of 6 November 1956, the Secretary-General said that this problem required further study. Provisionally, certain costs might be absorbed by a nation providing a unit, "while all other costs should be financed outside the normal budget of the United Nations". Since it was "obviously impossible to make any estimate of the costs without a knowledge of the size of the corps and the length of its assignment", the "only practical course . . . would be for the General Assembly to vote a general authorization for the cost of the Force on the basis of general principles such as those here suggested".

Paragraph 5 of resolution 1001 (ES-I) of 7 November 1956 states that the General Assembly *"Approves provisionally* the basic rule concerning the financing of the Force laid down in paragraph 15 of the Secretary-General's report".

In an oral statement to the plenary meeting of the General Assembly on 26 November 1956, the Secretary-General said:

". . . I wish to make it equally clear that while funds received and payments made with respect to the Force are to be considered as coming outside the regular budget of the Organization, the operation is essentially a United Nations responsibility, and the Special Account to be established must, therefore, be construed as coming within the meaning of Article 17 of the Charter".

At this same meeting, after hearing this statement, the General Assembly in resolution 1122 (XI) noted that it had *"provisionally approved* the recommendations made by the Secretary-General concerning the financing of the Force". It then authorized the Secretary-General "to establish a United Nations Emergency Force Special Account to which funds received by the United Nations, outside the regular budget, for the purpose of meeting the expenses of the Force shall be credited and from which payments for this purpose shall be made". The resolution then provided that the initial amount in the Special Account should be $10 million and authorized the Secretary-General "pending the receipt of funds for the Special Account, to advance from the Working Capital Fund such sums as the Special Account may require to meet any expenses chargeable to it". The establishment of a Special Account does not necessarily mean that the funds in it are not to be derived from contributions of Members as apportioned by the General Assembly.

The next of the resolutions of the General Assembly to be considered is 1089 (XI) of 21 December 1956, which reflects the uncertainties and the conflicting views about financing UNEF. The divergencies are duly noted and there is ample reservation concerning possible future action, but operative paragraph 1 follows the recommendation of the Secretary-General "that the expenses relating to the Force should be apportioned in the same manner as the expenses of the Organization". The language of this paragraph is clearly drawn from Article 17:

"1. *Decides* that the expenses of the United Nations Emergency Force, other than for such pay, equipment, supplies and services as may be furnished without charge by Governments of Member States, shall be borne by the United Nations and shall be apportioned among the Member States, to the extent of $10 million, in accordance with the scale of assessments adopted by the General Assembly for contributions to the annual budget of the Organization for the financial year 1957; . . ."

This resolution, which was adopted by the requisite two-thirds majority, must have rested upon the conclusion that the expenses of UNEF were "expenses of the Organization" since otherwise the General Assembly would have had no authority to decide that they "shall be borne by the United Nations" or to apportion them among the Members. It is further significant that paragraph 3 of this resolution, which established a study committee, charges this committee with the task of examining "the question of the *apportionment* of the expenses of the Force in excess of $10 million . . . and the principle or the formulation of *scales of contributions different from the scale of contributions* by Member States to the ordinary budget for 1957". The italicized words show that it was not contemplated that the Committee would consider any method of meeting these expenses except through some form of apportionment although it was understood that a different *scale* might be suggested.

The report of this study committee again records differences of opinion but the draft resolution which it recommended authorized further expenditures and authorized the Secretary-General to advance funds from the Working Capital Fund and to borrow from other funds if necessary; it was adopted as resolution 1090 (XI) by the requisite two-thirds majority on 27 February 1957. In paragraph 4 of that resolution, the General Assembly decided that it would at its twelfth session "consider the basis for financing any costs of the Force in excess of $10 million not covered by voluntary contributions".

Resolution 1151 (XII) of 22 November 1957, while contemplating the receipt of more voluntary contributions, decided in paragraph 4 that the expenses authorized "shall be borne by the Members of the United Nations in accordance with the scales of assessments adopted by the General Assembly for the financial years 1957 and 1958 respectively".

Almost a year later, on 14 November 1958, in resolution 1263 (XIII) the General Assembly, while *"Noting with satisfaction* the effective way in which the Force continues to carry out its function", requested the Fifth Committee "to recommend such action as may be necessary to finance this continuing operation of the United Nations Emergency Force".

After further study, the provision contained in paragraph 4 of the resolution of 22 November 1957 was adopted in paragraph 4 of resolution 1337 (XIII) of 13 December 1958. Paragraph 5 of that resolution requested "the Secretary-General to consult with the Governments of Member States with respect to their views concerning the manner of financing the Force in the future, and to submit a report together with the replies to the General Assembly at its fourteenth session". Thereafter a new plan was worked out for the utilization of any voluntary contributions, but resolution 1441 (XIV) of 5 December 1959, in paragraph 2: *"Decides* to assess the amount of $20 million against all Members of the United Nations on the basis of the regular scale of assessments" subject to the use of credits drawn from voluntary contributions. Resolution 1575 (XV) of 20 December 1960 is practically identical.

The Court concludes that, from year to year, the expenses of UNEF have been treated by the General Assembly as expenses of the Organization within the meaning of Article 17, paragraph 2, of the Charter.

The operations in the Congo were initially authorized by the Security Council in the resolution of 14 July 1960 which was adopted without a dissenting vote. The resolution, in the light of the appeal from the Government of the Congo, the report of the Secretary-General and the debate in the Security Council, was clearly adopted with a view to maintaining international peace and security. However, it is argued that that resolution has been implemented, in violation of provisions of the Charter inasmuch as under the Charter it is the Security Council that determines which States are to participate in carrying out decisions involving the maintenance of international peace and security, whereas in the case of the Congo the Secretary-General himself determined which States were to participate with their armed forces or otherwise.

By paragraph 2 of the resolution of 14 July 1960 the Security Council *"Decides* to authorize the Secretary-General to take the necessary steps, in consultation with the Government of the Republic of the Congo, to provide the Government with such military assistance as may be necessary". Paragraph 3 requested the Secretary-General "to report to the Security Council as appropriate". The Secretary-General made his first report on 18 July and in it informed the Security Council which States he had asked to contribute forces or matériel, which ones had complied, the size of the units which had already arrived in the Congo (a total of some 3,500 troops), and some detail about further units expected.

On 22 July the Security Council by unanimous vote adopted a further resolution in which the preamble states that it had considered this report of the Secretary-General and appreciated "the work of the Secretary-General and the support so readily and so speedily given to him by all Member States invited by him to give assistance". In operative paragraph 3, the Security Council *"Commends* the Secretary-General for the prompt action he has taken to carry out resolution S/4387 of the Security Council, and for his first report".

On 9 August the Security Council adopted a further resolution without a dissenting vote in which it took note of the second report and of an oral statement of the Secretary-General and in operative paragraph 1: *"Confirms* the authority given to the Secretary-General by the Security Council resolutions of 14 July and 22 July 1960 and requests him to continue to carry out the responsibility placed on him thereby". This emphatic ratification is further supported by operative paragraphs 5 and 6 by which all Member States were called upon "to afford mutual assistance" and the Secretary-General was requested "to implement this resolution and to report further to the Council as appropriate".

The Security Council resolutions of 14 July, 22 July and 9 August 1960 were noted by the General Assembly in its resolution 1474 (ES-IV) of 20 September, adopted without a dissenting vote, in which it "fully supports" these resolutions. Again without a dissenting vote, on 21 February 1961 the Security Council reaffirmed its three previous resolutions "and the General Assembly resolution 1474 (ES-IV) of 20 September 1960" and reminded "all States of their obligations under these resolutions".

Again without a dissenting vote on 24 November 1961 the Security Council, once more recalling the previous resolutions, reaffirmed "the policies and purposes of the United Nations with respect to the Congo (Leopoldville) as set out" in those resolutions. Operative paragraphs 4 and 5 of this resolution renew the authority to the Secretary-General to continue the activities in the Congo.

In the light of such a record of reiterated consideration, confirmation, approval and ratification by the Security Council and by the General Assembly of the actions of the Secretary-General in implementing the resolution of 14 July 1960, it is impossible to reach the conclusion that the operations in question usurped or impinged upon the prerogatives conferred by the Charter on the Security Council. The Charter does not forbid the Security Council to act through instruments of its own choice: under Article 29 it "may establish such subsidiary organs as it deems necessary for the performance of its functions"; under Article 98 it may entrust "other functions" to the Secretary-General.

It is not necessary for the Court to express an opinion as to which article or articles of the Charter were the basis for the resolutions of the Security Council, but it can be said that the operations of ONUC did not include a use of armed force against a State which the Security Council, under Article 39, determined to have committed an act of aggression or to have breached the peace. The armed forces which were utilized in the Congo were not authorized to take military action against any State. The operation did not involve "preventive or enforcement measures" against any State under Chapter VII and therefore did not constitute "action" as that term is used in Article 11.

For the reasons stated, financial obligations which, in accordance with the clear and reiterated authority of both the Security Council and the General Assembly, the Secretary-General incurred on behalf of the United Nations, constitute obligations of the Organization for which the General Assembly was entitled to make provision under the authority of Article 17.

In relation to ONUC, the first action concerning the financing of the operation was taken by the General Assembly on 20 December 1960, after the Security Council had adopted its resolutions of 14 July, 22 July and 9 August, and the General Assembly had adopted its supporting resolution of 20 September. This resolution 1583 (XV) of 20 December referred to the report of the Secretary-General on the estimated cost of the Congo operations from 14 July to 31 December 1960, and to the recommendations of the Advisory Committee on Administrative and Budgetary Questions. It decided to establish an *ad hoc* account for the expenses of the United Nations in the Congo. It also took note of certain waivers of cost claims and then decided to apportion the sum of $48.5 million among the Member States "on the basis of the regular scale of assessment" subject to certain exceptions. It made this decision because in the preamble it had already recognized:

"that the expenses involved in the United Nations operations in the Congo for 1960 constitute 'expenses of the Organization' within the meaning of Article 17, paragraph 2, of the Charter of the United Nations and that the assessment thereof against Member States creates binding legal obligations on such States to pay their assessed shares".

By its further resolution 1590 (XV) of the same day, the General Assembly authorized the Secretary-General "to incur commitments in 1961 for the United Nations operations in the Congo up to the total of $24 million for the period from 1 January to 31 March 1961". On 3 April 1961, the General Assembly authorized the Secretary-General to continue until 21 April "to incur commitments for the United Nations operations in the Congo at a level not to exceed $8 million per month".

Importance has been attached to the statement included in the preamble of General Assembly resolution 1619 (XV) of 21 April 1961 which reads:

"*Bearing in mind* that the extraordinary expenses for the United Nations operations in the Congo are essentially different in nature from the expenses of the Organization under the regular budget and that therefore a procedure different from that applied in the case of the regular budget is required for meeting these extraordinary expenses."

However, the same resolution in operative paragraph 4:

"*Decides further* to apportion as expenses of the Organization the amount of $100 million among the Member States in accordance with the scale of assessment for the regular budget subject to the provisions of paragraph 8 below [paragraph 8 makes certain adjustments for

Member States assessed at the lowest rates or who receive certain designated technical assistance], pending the establishment of a different scale of assessment to defray the extraordinary expenses of the Organization resulting from these operations."

Although it is not mentioned in the resolution requesting the advisory opinion, because it was adopted at the same meeting of the General Assembly, it may be noted that the further resolution 1732 (XVI) of 20 December 1961 contains an identical paragraph in the preamble and a comparable operative paragraph 4 on apportioning $80 million.

The conclusion to be drawn from these paragraphs is that the General Assembly has twice decided that even though certain expenses are "extraordinary" and "essentially different" from those under the "regular budget", they are none the less "expenses of the Organization" to be apportioned in accordance with the power granted to the General Assembly by Article 17, paragraph 2. This conclusion is strengthened by the concluding clause of paragraph 4 of the two resolutions just cited which states that the decision therein to use the scale of assessment already adopted for the regular budget is made "pending the establishment of a *different scale of assessment* to defray the extraordinary expenses". The only alternative—and that means the "different procedure"—contemplated was another *scale* of assessment and not some method other than assessment. "Apportionment" and "assessment" are terms which relate only to the General Assembly's authority under Article 17.

At the outset of this opinion, the Court pointed out that the text of Article 17, paragraph 2, of the Charter could lead to the simple conclusion that "the expenses of the Organization" are the amounts paid out to defray the costs of carrying out the purposes of the Organization. It was further indicated that the Court would examine the resolutions authorizing the expenditures referred to in the request for the advisory opinion in order to ascertain whether they were incurred with that end in view. The Court has made such an examination and finds that they were so incurred. The Court has also analyzed the principal arguments which have been advanced against the conclusion that the expenditures in question should be considered as "expenses of the Organization within the meaning of Article 17, paragraph 2, of the Charter of the United Nations", and has found that these arguments are unfounded. Consequently, the Court arrives at the conclusion that the question submitted to it in General Assembly resolution 1731 (XVI) must be answered in the affirmative.

For these reasons,

THE COURT IS OF OPINION,
by nine votes to five,

that the expenditures authorized in General Assembly resolutions 1583 (XV) and 1590 (XV) of 20 December 1960, 1595 (XV) of 3

April 1961, 1619 (XV) of 21 April 1961 and 1633 (XVI) of 30 October 1961 relating to the United Nations operations in the Congo undertaken in pursuance of the Security Council resolutions of 14 July, 22 July and 9 August 1960 and 21 February and 24 November 1961, and General Assembly resolutions 1474 (ES–IV) of 20 September 1960 and 1599 (XV), 1600 (XV) and 1601 (XV) of 15 April 1961, and the expenditures authorized in General Assembly resolutions 1122 (XI) of 26 November 1956, 1089 (XI) of 21 December 1956, 1090 (XI) of 27 February 1957, 1151 (XII) of 22 November 1957, 1204 (XII) of 13 December 1957, 1337 (XIII) of 13 December 1958, 1441 (XIV) of 5 December 1959 and 1575 (XV) of 20 December 1960 relating to the operations of the United Nations Emergency Force undertaken in pursuance of General Assembly resolutions 997 (ES–I) of 2 November 1956, 998 (ES–I) of 4 November 1956, 1000 (ES–I) of 5 November 1956, 1001 (ES–I) of 7 November 1956, 1121 (XI) of 24 November 1956 and 1263 (XIII) of 14 November 1958, constitute "expenses of the Organization" within the meaning of Article 17, paragraph 2, of the Charter of the United Nations.

[The Court's opinion was approved in its entirety by Vice-President Alfaro and Judges Badawi, Wellington Koo, Tanaka and Jessup. Judges Spender, Fitzmaurice and Morelli filed separate opinions, and Judge Spiropoulos made a separate declaration. President Winiarski and Judges Basdevant, Moreno Quintana, Koretsky and Bustamante y Rivero filed dissenting opinions.]

SEPARATE OPINION OF SIR GERALD FITZMAURICE. . . .
I propose . . . to consider the question whether, if given expenditures are duly expenses of the Organization, an obligation for every Member State to contribute to them as apportioned arises in all circumstances. The core of the difficulty is how to reconcile the obligatory character of the liability to meet the expenses of the Organization with the non-obligatory character of many, indeed most, of the resolutions under which these expenses are incurred. To me, it has not seemed self-evident that Article 17, paragraph 2, on its actual wording, necessarily or automatically disposes of this difficulty; and unless it can be disposed of satisfactorily, the affirmative reply given to the question addressed to the Court must be less convincing than it ought to be.

There is clearly no problem in the case of *decisions* of the Security Council which, under Article 25 of the Charter, are binding on Member States, even on those Members of the Council which voted against them, and equally on those Members of the Assembly which, not being Members of the Council, *ex hypothesi* did not vote at all. Therefore, even in the absence of Article 17, paragraph 2, all these Member States would be obliged to meet the expenses of carrying such decisions out. But many Security Council resolutions only have a recommendatory intention and effect, and this is in principle also the case with most Assembly resolutions. If however a Member State has voted in favour of such a resolution, or, by abstaining, has not manifested opposition to it, it is reasonable to regard either of these attitudes, not indeed as involving any formal obligation for that Member State itself to carry out the resolution, operationally, but as indicating approval of, or at any rate tacit acquiescence in, its being carried out by those Member States which are ready to do so; and also (and quite apart from Article 17, paragraph 2) as implying willingness to contribute to the expenses of carrying it out—although as regards the effect of abstentions, it would be better to put the matter on the basis that a Member State which does not vote *against* a given resolution, can scarcely object if it is called upon to pay its share of the resultant expenses.

Similar considerations can hardly apply to the case of a vote which does go to the length of being cast against the resolution concerned—a resolution which is in any case purely recommendatory. Certainly it would seem at first sight an odd position that a Member State which is not itself bound to carry out such a resolution, and which has manifested disapproval of its being carried out at all by anyone, should nevertheless be legally obliged to contribute to the expenses of executing it. Here therefore is a case in which, in order to justify the conclusion that a Member State in this position is nevertheless bound to contribute its apportioned share, reliance on the inherent obligation of Member States to meet the costs of the Organization might not be sufficient; for that obligation is an obligation of principle only. It would not necessarily extend to or cover every case. A Member State which had voted against a resolution having only a recommendatory effect could, in the absence of express language figuring, or to be deemed to figure, in the Charter itself, very plausibly argue that the obligation did not exist for it in the particular case, especially with reference to certain types of activities. . . . It is therefore important that the records of the San Francisco Conference—even if the language used for the purpose was not particularly felicitous—do indicate that the intention to impose a definite financial obligation on Member States was there. Looking at the matter as a whole, I think that (with the possible exception of the class of case considered . . . below) this intention must be deemed to have extended to covering the payment by Member States of their apportioned shares, irrespective of how their votes were cast on any given occasion, at any rate as regards all the essential activities of the Organization, and even if they have no formal legal obligation to join in carrying out the activities to which the given expenditures relate. . . .

In reaching this conclusion, it is material to take account of the following factor: those who framed the Charter deliberately broke away from the fundamental voting rule of the former League of Nations (unanimity—see Article 5, paragraph 1, of the League Covenant), and they adopted for the United Nations a majority voting rule. In an Organization which has never numbered much less than 50–60 Member States, and now numbers over 100, no other rule than a majority one would be practicable. But a majority voting rule is meaningless unless, although the States of the minority are not formally bound as regards their own action, they at least cannot prevent or impede the action decided on from being carried out *aliunde*. This they obviously could do if they had a species of veto, the exercise of which, through the refusal to contribute financially, would enable them to prevent or seriously impede the action concerned.

The same conclusion can be reached in another way, for if there is, on the one hand, a general position under the Charter according to which certain resolutions have no formally obligatory character—doubly not so for those who vote against them—there is also, on the other hand, a special provision, Article 17, paragraph 2, obliging Member States to contribute to the cost of carrying these resolutions out, in so far as these costs duly rank as expenses of the Organization. To this situation the rule *generalia specialibus non derogant* must apply, so that in spite of the general element of non-obligation under these resolutions, the special obligation to contribute to the expenses incurred in carrying them out prevails, and applies even to Member States voting against. There is in short no substantive conflict.

This position was aptly compared, by one of the representatives of Governments at the oral hearing, to that of a member of the public who cannot be compelled physically to join in constructing a public edifice but can, through the medium of ordinary taxation, be made to contribute to the cost of having it constructed by others. Another comparison, perhaps even closer, would be that of membership of a club. If the Committee or governing body of a club decides to acquire additional premises, or to extend the club's activities, or otherwise to increase expenditure, and this necessitates raising the annual subscription, or in some other manner involves financial liabilities for members, and this decision is ratified by a general meeting of the members, the latter, irrespective of how they voted, must pay accordingly, or resign their membership.

I have mentioned the existence of a class of case to which, possibly, the foregoing considerations would not apply, and regarding which there may be room for some real doubt whether any financial obligation can arise, at least for Member States voting against the resolution concerned in any given case. In the normal case, a resolution provides for certain action to be taken by the Organization, either through such of the Member States as are willing to participate, or through the medium of the Secretary-General or of some other agent or agency. In these cases, despite the obligation to contribute to the resultant expenses, the resolution retains its fundamentally non-obligatory character; for if the Member States are obliged to contribute financially, they are not obliged to participate in the operational carrying out of the substantive activities provided for in the resolution. Where however the "action" to be taken under the resolution consists *solely* of provision for making a payment or financial contribution (e. g. for some purpose of aid or relief), so that the making of this payment or contribution is not merely a means to an end—viz. enabling the resolution to be carried out—but the end itself, and the sole object of the resolution, it is evident that if the payment or contribution concerned is to be treated as one to which even Member States which voted against the resolution must contribute by reason of Article 17, paragraph 2, the resolution acquires in practice a wholly obligatory character— since it does one thing only, and Member States are bound, or would be bound, to do or contribute to doing that one thing. In this connexion, it is significant that the actual *practice* of the Assembly (and the Court has drawn considerable inspiration from this source), has been to finance expenditures falling within this class of case, mainly by calling for *voluntary* contributions from Member States. Examples are the activities (or most of them) for which budgetary provision is made under such heads as those of "Trust Funds" and "Special Accounts"—for instance the U. N. Special Fund, UNKRA, UNSCO, EPTA, UNRWA, UNICEF, the U. N. Fund for the Congo, and the U. N. Congo Famine Fund. No doubt special considerations applied in some of these cases; still, the fact remains that contributions were not claimed as a matter of actual obligation. . . .

There are broadly two main classes of functions which the Organization performs under the Charter—those which it has a duty to carry out, and those which are more or less permissive in character. Peacekeeping, dispute-settling and, indeed, most of the political activities of the Organization would come under the former head; many of what might be called its social and economic activities might come under the latter. Expenses incurred in relation to the first set of activities are therefore true expenses, which the Organization has no choice but to incur in order to carry out a duty, and an essential function which it is bound to perform. Therefore the principle enunciated by the Court in the *Injuries to United Nations Servants* case . . . applies: the Organization "must be deemed to have those powers which, though not expressly provided in the Charter, are conferred upon it by necessary implication as being essential to the performance of its duties" [I.C.J. Reports 1949, at p. 182]. Even without Article 17, paragraph 2, the Organization could require Member States to contribute to these expenses.

It is less clear that any similar power exists to require Member States to meet the costs incurred in performing merely permissive activities carried out under non-binding resolutions. There certainly would be no such power without Article 17, paragraph 2—at least not as regards Member States which voted against the resolution giving rise to the expenditure concerned; and even with the assistance of Article 17, the position is not entirely clear. There is a definite distinction, inasmuch as where the activities involved are such as the Organization has a duty to carry out, non-contribution by a Member State would be fundamentally inconsistent with that State's membership, as being calculated to prevent or gravely impede the performance by the Organization of an essential function. Where the costs of permissive, or non-essential activities are concerned, there is no correspondingly clear-cut inconsistency, and there must remain a question whether, in this type of case, Article 17, paragraph 2, is sufficient to give rise to a financial obligation *for the dissenting voter.* If it is sufficient, then it would follow that, in theory at least, the Assembly could vote enormous expenditures, and thereby place a heavy financial burden even on dissenting States, and as a matter of obligation even in the case of non-essential activities. This would be reading a lot into such a provision as Article 17, paragraph 2. In this connexion, it must be borne in mind that, if a two-thirds majority is required for the adoption of financial resolutions, the present scales of apportionment cause a major part of the resulting contributions to fall on a comparatively small minority of the Member States. As has already been mentioned, the existence here of a genuine difficulty seems to have been recognized in practice within the Organization, inasmuch as the cost of a large part of these permissive activities is met from voluntary contributions.

To set against these considerations, there is the fact that it would not be easy to draw a hard and fast line between necessary, essential and obligatory functions of the Organization, on the one hand, and merely optional, non-essential and permissive ones on the other. Changing concepts also are involved. Today, the humanitarian and aid-giving functions of the Organization are, if less imperative, hardly less important than its political functions, and may well contribute materially, or even be essential, to the success of the latter.

.   .   .

DISSENTING OPINION OF JUDGE KORETSKY. I regret that I cannot agree with the Opinion of Court both (a) as I do not consider that the Court would and should give an opinion on the given question posed to it by the General Assembly of the United Nations, and (b) as the Court, to my mind, did not come to the acceptable conclusion in relation to the question which in substance is a question of financial obligations of Member States in peace-keeping operations.

To give an Advisory Opinion on the question "do the expenditures authorized in General Assembly resolutions [numbered in its request] constitute 'expenses of the Organization' within the meaning of Article 17, paragraph 2, of the Charter of the United Nations?" is impossible without an appraisal, from the point of view of validity, "charterability", of the named resolutions. . . .

The question posed to the Court, in spite of its apparent narrowness, involves more than an interpretation of only one Article and even of one paragraph of that Article (Article 17(2)). As was stated by the Mexican delegate, the problem would not be regarded as basically a budgetary one; there was, rather, a basic constitutional problem. Political issues prevailed over juridical considerations. First and foremost we have there a political question, the question of financial policy in peace-keeping matters and, connected with it, a question of the powers and responsibilities of the principal organs of the United Nations, the political essence of which can hardly be denied. As the political aspect of the question posed to the Court is the prevailing one, the Court, to my mind, ought to avoid giving an answer to the question on the substance and ought not to find unwillingly that its opinion may be used as an instrument of political struggle. I think that there are "compelling reasons" for not giving an answer on the substance of the request of the General Assembly as "the circumstances of the case are of such a character as should lead it to decline to answer the request" (I.C.J.Reports 1950, p. 72).

The Court embarked on a different course. I am obliged therefore to follow the Court and examine also the substance of the posed question. . . .

People say that you cannot have two coachmen in the driver's seat. In the cause of the struggle for international peace and security, in the question of their maintenance or restoration, in questions of "action with respect to threats to the peace, breaches of the peace, and acts of aggression", the organizational confusion would only have been harmful. Therefore the Charter clearly enough delimits the functions of the Security Council and those of the General Assembly.

To place the Security Council, as the Opinion does, beside the General Assembly, considering them as interchangeable in solving and implementing the tasks of maintaining international peace and security, would be objectively to replace the Security Council by the General Assembly, to put the Council aside and thereby undermine the very foundations of the Organization. It does not befit the Court to follow this line. It has been said that you cannot leave one word out of a song. The Charter represents one of the most important international multilateral treaties, from which it is impossible to leave out any of its provisions either directly or through an interpretation that is more artificial than skilful.

The Court's Opinion thus limits the powers of the Security Council and enlarges the sphere of the General Assembly. The Opinion achieves this by (a) converting the recommendations that the General Assembly may make into some kind of "action", and (b) reducing this action, for which the Security Council has the authority, to "enforcement or coercive action", particularly against aggression.

In order to prove that the General Assembly, in the matter of maintaining international peace and security, may not only discuss and make recommendations but take measures and carry out "actions" as well, the Opinion examines Articles 10, 11, 12, 14, 18 and 35 of the Charter.

The Opinion quotes Article 18 in order to show that the Assembly may take decisions. This has never been denied by anyone. But the questions mentioned in Article 18 have nothing in common with the question of maintaining international peace and security. The General Assembly may only discuss the latter and make recommendations.

Article 14 of the Charter, which the Opinion apparently considers to be specially important for purposes of transforming a "recommendation" into an "action" provides that "the General Assembly may recommend measures for the peaceful adjustment of any situation . . .". "To recommend measures" does not mean "to take measures". The General Assembly in fact may recommend *measures* but, as has already been pointed out, it is not the General Assembly that takes these measures but those to whom the recommendations are addressed. Article 11 of the Charter makes it clear to whom the recommendations relating to the maintenance of international peace and security may be addressed. That Article provides that the General Assembly "may make recommendations with regard to such principles to the Members or to the Security Council or to both". Article 10 also provides (apart from the reference to the natural powers of the Assembly to discuss any question of any matters within the scope of the Charter) that "The General Assembly . . . except as provided in Article 12, may *make recommendations* to the Members of the United Nations or to the Security Council or to both on any such questions or matters".

The Opinion of the Court supposes that Article 11 (2) may be interpreted in such a way that it appears that the General Assembly "could make recommendations only of a *general character* affecting peace and security *in the abstract,* and not in relation to specific cases".

I do not consider it proper to make such an interpretation. Article 35, for example, has in view a "special case"; Article 11 refers to "recommendations with regard to any . . . 'questions' ". The recommendations may be, and it is even desirable that they should be, concrete. But the point is that the General Assembly may make *only* recommendations in regard to any questions relating to the maintenance of international peace and security except as provided in Article 12. It may, for example, recommend a cease-fire; but it cannot set up the United Nations Force and decide to bring it into an area of military conflicts in order to provide the implementation of the cease-fire. Article 35 of the Charter deals with the proceedings of the General Assembly in respect of matters brought to its attention concerning any dispute, or any situation which might lead to international friction. But this Article makes a direct reference to Articles 11 and 12, and adds nothing new to our question.

To reach the conclusion, on the basis of the aforementioned Articles, that the Assembly may "organize peace-keeping operations" would, from a logical point of view, mean, to say the least, an anti-Charter encroachment upon the sphere of powers of another organ; while "to organize peace-keeping operations" means no more than "to perform peace-keeping actions".

The Opinion curtails the functions of the Security Council, reducing them, in the question of maintaining international peace and security, to the implementation of enforcement or coercive action. In this connection, the Opinion indicates that the Security Council, as provided in Article 24, has merely the primary but not the exclusive responsibility.

The word "primary" is not used in Article 24 in the sense of an ordinal number (i. e. first, second, etc.), but, one may say, in the hierarchical sense. The French text reads: "la responsabilité *principale*", the Spanish text: "la responsabilidad primordial", and the Russian text: "glavnuju otvjetstvjennostj" (which literally translated means "chief", "main" responsibility).

Of course no single organ of the United Nations has the monopoly in the matter of the maintenance of international peace and security, which is one of the main purposes of the United Nations. But the Organization is a complicated and intricate piece of "international machinery" in which each of the organs, as separate parts, has a specific sphere of operation as provided in the plan, and with regard to the Organization, as provided in its Charter.

Despite all efforts to the contrary, under the Charter only the Security Council may take an action with regard to a question relating to the maintenance of international peace and security. Such is the meaning of Article 11(2). It reads: "Any such question on which action is necessary shall be referred to the Security Council by the General Assemby either before or after discussion."

According to the Opinion the action which the Security Council should take is enforcement or coercive action. It is worth mentioning incidentally that the Security Council may not only take "action" but also make recommendations although they are not "action" as that word is used in the Charter.

But it may be agreed that the Security Council's decisions have a coercitive or (that is almost the same) enforcement character. (This is borne out by Article 25 and by the whole of Chapter VII itself; mention may also be made of Article 94(2) of the Charter.) But the main point in the arguments apparently lies not in this, but in the statement that the Security Council is competent to implement enforcement action directed *against* any of the States "if for example [to use the words of the Opinion] it [the Security Council] issues an order or command to an aggressor under Chapter VII". What is the basis for such an interpretation? If we turn to the first Article of Chapter VII, i. e. to Article 39, we are unable to find there any direct reference to the fact that the measures which, as decided by the Security Council, "shall be taken . . . to maintain or restore international peace and security" should be directed against any of the States. But then the question arises: What prompted the above-mentioned interpretation? It is hardly worth reasoning in the abstract, and losing contact with the real situation that gave rise to the request for an Advisory Opinion and to the above-mentioned interpretation. The matter concerned the procedure for financing operations in the Congo. A number of Member States insisted that the question concerning the financing of these operations should be decided by the Security Council in accordance with Article 43 of the Charter.

The course of reasoning followed by the opponents of such a position may be outlined as follows: the implementation of Article 43 of the Charter might have been necessary, had the aforementioned operations been carried out in compliance with the procedure provided by Chapter VII of the Charter; Chapter VII allegedly provides for enforcement action against any of the States. The operations in the Middle East and in the Congo are allegedly not directed against any of the States. Ergo, the provisions of Article 43 of the Charter cannot be applied to them.

This is motivated in the statements of some delegations and in the Secretary-General's reports. In one of his latest statements (A/C. 5/864), the Secretary-General, summarizing the statements of some delegations, spoke of the inapplicability of Article 43 of the Charter inasmuch as the Security Council's resolutions regarding the Congo could be considered as implicitly taken under Article 40, but certainly did not involve the type of coercitive action directed against Governments envisaged by the enforcement measures of Articles 41 and 42.

This provision has apparently been suggested to their chief by his legal advisers, who had in mind what had been said in literature or what they themselves had published; they did not, however, take into consideration the fact that Article 40 is closely connected with Articles 41 and 42 of the Charter through Article 39. The situation in the Congo was by no means a simple one and all efforts were devoted to preventing an aggravation of the situation. It was not simply a question of "call[ing] upon the parties concerned to comply with such provisional measures as it deems necessary or desirable".

Long before that date, the Security Council had had to take "account of failure to comply with such provisional measures" as provided in its resolutions from July 1960 onwards. And it inevitably had to turn its attention to the other Articles of Chapter VII.

Moreover, the Security Council should, from the very beginning, have acted in compliance with Article 39 of the Charter.

As already noted, the Government of the Republic of the Congo, applying for assistance on 13 July 1960, pointed out that "the purpose of the aid requested is not to restore the internal situation in the Congo but rather to protect the national territory against acts of aggression".

If the Security Council in its resolutions did not call the activity of the Belgian troops an aggression, then this was only for tactical reasons. "We have refrained", said the representative of Tunis (speaking in support of the draft resolution submitted by Ceylon and Tunis) ". . . from using the word 'aggression' or even the term 'aggressive acts' in resolutions, since we are most anxious not to exacerbate the feelings of the Belgian people . . ." But this cannot change the essence of the matter.

The Secretary-General was authorized to take all necessary action and to use force, if necessary, in the last resort. Military contingents were sent. The so-called United Nations Force in the Congo had grown up into an army numbering many thousands. To maintain this army and its operations, millions of dollars have been spent.

The United Nations Force was sent there, not to persuade or to parade, but to carry out military operations. And they did so. If we direct our attention to the last events connected with the blockading of the roads leading to Elizabethville, then we may say that such a blockade can be easily related to the measures provided by Article 41 of the Charter. Thus the whole chain of logical considerations, designed to justify the deviation from Article 43, may be easily torn to pieces on contact with reality.

For less than half a year more than $60 million were spent for the operations in the Congo. This greatly exceeded the expenses for UNEF and even the regular expenses for the United Nations itself.

The amount of the expenses, the character of the operations, the contradictions in the evaluation of the character of the United Nations Organization's activity in the Congo, the methods of implementing the approved resolutions have influenced the contradictory views put forward during the debates on the methods of financing the above-mentioned operations.

There could not have been the same common approach to the methods of financing which characterized budget appropriations.

The report of the Fifth Committee of 19 December 1960 (A/4676), which summed up the methods of financing the operations in the Congo, as proposed by the delegations, has indicated six different methods:

"(*a*) The expenses should be included in the regular budget and apportioned among the Member States in accordance with the 1960 scale of assessments for Members' contributions;

(*b*) The expenses should be entered in a special account and apportioned among the Member States in accordance with the 1960 scale of assessments for Members' contributions to the regular budget; voluntary contributions should be applied, at the request of the Member State concerned, to reduce the assessments of Members with the least capacity to pay;

(*c*) The expenses should be met under special agreements concluded in accordance with Article 43 of the Charter, between the Security Council and the countries providing troops;

(*d*) The expenses should be borne in larger part by the permanent members of the Security Council, as having a major responsibility for the maintenance of peace and security;

(*e*) The expenses should be borne in larger part by the former administering Power;

(*f*) The expenses should be financed entirely out of voluntary contributions."

Having regard to the approach of different groups of States to the methods of financing the operations in the Congo, the only way to reach a proper decision should be strict compliance with the Charter, of which Article 43 was to be regarded as decisive. . . .

At the San Francisco Conference the necessity was at any rate realized of establishing a special procedure for assessment of eventual expenditures for operations of this kind. It is the Security Council which has, first of all, to decide about the financial implications of concrete peace-keeping operations. Article 43 gave directives as to how to arrange financial questions which might arise from these operations. Article 17 has nothing to do with these questions unless the Security Council should ask that necessary measures be taken by the General Assembly.

One cannot consider that decisions of the Security Council regarding the participation of any Member State in concrete peace-keeping operations are not obligatory for a given Member. Its obligation to participate in a decided operation was based on Articles 25 and 48 of the Charter. Agreements envisaged in Article 43 proceed from this general obligation. Article 43 says that all Members undertake to make available to the Security Council *on its call* armed forces, etc. Agreements must (not may) specify the terms of participation, the size of armed forces to be made available, the character of assistance, etc., envisaging all the ensuing financial consequences as well. The General Assembly may only *recommend* measures. Expenses which might arise from such recommendations should not lead to an obligatory apportionment of them among all Members of the United Nations.

That would mean to convert a non-mandatory recommendation of the General Assembly into a mandatory decision; this would be to proceed against the Charter, against logic and even against common sense.

This applies even more to resolutions adopted not in conformity with the Charter. It is not within the power of the General Assembly "to cure" the invalidity of its resolutions enumerated in the Request by approving the financial provisions of these resolutions.

For the reasons given above I am of the opinion that a negative answer must be given to the question put to the Court by the General Assembly.

NOTE.—1. For comments on the opinion of the Court, see C. F. AME-RASINGHE, "The United Nations Expenses Case: A Contribution to the Law of International Organization," 4 Indian JIL (1964), pp. 177–232; William H. BUCHANAN, Jr., "Expenses of the United Nations: Their Limits and the Financial Obligations Created," 5 Harvard Int. L. Club J. (1964), pp. 165–94; Leo GROSS, "Expenses of the United Nations for Peace-Keeping Operations: The Advisory Opinion of the International Court of Justice," 17 Int.Org. (1963), pp. 1–35; James F. HOGG, "Peace-Keeping Costs and Charter Obligations: Implications of the International Court of Justice Decision on Certain Expenses of the United Nations," 62 Columbia L.R. (1962), pp. 1230–63; R. Y. JENNINGS, "International Court of Justice: Advisory Opinion of July 20, 1962: Certain Expenses of the United Nations," 11 ICLQ (1962), pp. 1169–83; Rahmatullah KHAN, "Peace-Keeping Powers of the U.N. General Assembly: Advisory Opinion of the I.C.J.," 6 Int. Studies (Bombay, 1965), pp. 317–32; Riccardo MONACO, "Gli obblighi finanziari degli Stati membri delle Nazioni Unite nel parere della Corte internazionale di Giustizia," 45 RiDI (1962), pp. 605–15; A. Donat PHARAND, "Analysis of the Opinion of the International Court of Justice on Certain Expenses of the United Nations," 1 Canadian YBIL (1963), pp. 272–97; Roger PINTO, "Chronique de jurisprudence de la Cour internationale de Justice: Avis consultatif, relatif à certaines dépenses des Nations Unies'," 40 JDI (1963), pp. 204–15 (French and English); G. S. RAJU, "The Expenses of the United Nations Organisation," 2 Indian JIL (1962), pp. 485–490; T. S. Rama RAO, "The Expenses Judgment of the International Court of Justice: A Critique," 12 Indian YB Int. Affairs (1963), pp. 134–60; S. N. Guha ROY, "The World Court's Advisory Opinion of 20 July 1962 on 'Certain Expenses of the United Nations'," 15 ÖZÖR (1965), pp. 179–269; K. R. SIMMONDS, "The UN Assessments Advisory Opinion," 13 ICLQ (1964) pp. 854–98; S. SLONIM, "Advisory Opinion of the International Court of Justice on Certain Expenses of the United Nations: A Critical Analysis," 10 Howard L.J. (1964), pp. 227–76; Marcello SPATAFORA, "Gli interventi collettivi delle Nazioni Unite e il parere della Corte internazionale di Giustizia," 47 RiDI (1964), pp. 23–49; Hubert THIERRY, "Avis consultatif de la Cour internationale de Justice du 20 juillet 1962: Certaines dépenses des Nations Unies," 8 AFDI (1962), pp. 247–76; J. H. W. VERZIJL, International Court of Justice: Certain Expenses of the United Nations," 10 Nederlands TIR (1963), pp. 1–32.

2. On 19 December 1962, the General Assembly accepted the opinion of the Court, re-established the Working Group on the Examination of the Ad-

ministrative and Budgetary Procedures of the United Nations, and requested it to study "special methods for financing peace-keeping operations of the United Nations involving heavy expenditures, such as those for the Congo and the Middle East, including a possible special scale of assessments." Resolution 1854 (XVII); GAOR, XVII, Supp. 17 (A/5217), pp. 54–55. The Working Group was not able to agree on the future financing methods, and only limited progress on this question was made at a special session of the General Assembly held in the spring of 1963. But the General Assembly agreed on the following guidelines for "the equitable sharing" of the costs of future peace-keeping operations "involving heavy expenditures":

"(a) The financing of such operations is the collective responsibility of all Member States of the United Nations;

"(b) Whereas the economically more developed countries are in a position to make relatively larger contributions, the economically less developed countries have a relatively limited capacity to contribute toward peace-keeping operations involving heavy expenditures;

"(c) Without prejudice to the principle of collective responsibility, every effort should be made to encourage voluntary contributions from Member States;

"(d) The special responsibilities of the permanent members of the Security Council for the maintenance of peace and security should be borne in mind in connexion with their contributions to the financing of peace and security operations;

"(e) Where circumstances warrant, the General Assembly should give special consideration to the situation of any Member States which are victims of, and those which are otherwise involved in, the events or actions leading to a peace-keeping operation." Resolution 1874 (S–IV), 27 June 1963; GAOR, Fourth Special Session, Supp. 1 (A/5441), p. 3.

3. By 1 January 1964, twenty-two Members of the United Nations were sufficiently in arrears to lose their vote in the General Assembly under Article 19 of the Charter. Before the General Assembly convened in December of that year, all these Members, with the exception of the Soviet Union and six Eastern European countries, made payments sufficient to regain the right to vote. On 1 January 1965, France and eight other Members of the United Nations became also subject to Article 19, and only four of these Members made during the year the payments required to restore their voting rights.

2.   *Soviet Memorandum on the Financial Situation of the United Nations, 11 September 1964.*

A/5729 (11 Sept. 1964); GAOR, Annexes (XIX) 21, pp. 6–10.

The financial situation of the United Nations has been attracting universal attention lately. Frequent references are even made to "the financial crisis of the United Nations."

This problem is taking on especial significance for the United Nations, and not only because the financing of the United Nations is important in itself. The main point is that, in this matter as in others, some States are trying to compel the United Nations to violate its

Charter, in order to justify illegal acts which have been committed under the United Nations flag in the past, and in order to make it easier to violate the Charter in the future.

The effectiveness of the United Nations as an instrument of peace and international co-operation can be assured only if individual States, as well as the Organization as a whole, abide by the provisions of the United Nations Charter. Violation of the provisions of the Charter, on the other hand, may have serious adverse consequences for the international situation and may even lead to the collapse of the United Nations.

It is universally known that the existing financial difficulties of the United Nations have been caused by the expenses incurred in maintaining the Emergency Force in the Middle East and the operations in the Congo.

What would the position be with regard to the payment of such expenses if the United Nations Charter was adhered to?

I. *The operations of the United Nations Emergency Force in the Middle East and the United Nations operations in the Congo lay no financial obligations on Members of the United Nations, inasmuch as these operations have been conducted otherwise than in accordance with the requirements of the United Nations Charter.*

The United Nations was established in the same way as other international organizations; namely, through the conclusion of an international treaty—the Charter. This treaty determines, in particular, the competence of United Nations organs, their procedure, and so forth. Under the United Nations Charter, States have assumed certain obligations which cannot be altered without a new agreement among the Members of the Organization. It is perfectly evident— and this situation is universally recognized—that the Charter does not place the United Nations above States, that it does not authorize it to act without regard for the provisions of the Charter.

It is natural, therefore, that financial obligations for the Members of the United Nations can arise only out of such actions of the United Nations as conform to its Charter. As to expenses connected with actions which do not conform to the Charter, such actions cannot give rise to obligations for Member States with regard to the payment of expenses.

It is precisely to this category of expenses that the cost of maintaining the United Nations Emergency Force in the Middle East and the cost of the United Nations operations in the Congo belong.

The United Nations Emergency Force in the Middle East was established on the basis of resolutions 998 (ES–I) of 4 November 1956 and 1000 (ES–I) of 5 November 1956, adopted at the first emergency special session of the General Assembly.

The USSR Government has repeatedly emphasized that the establishment of the Emergency Force in the Middle East was carried out in violation of the United Nations Charter.

In matters relating to the maintenance of international peace and security, the Charter clearly delimits the competence of the Security Council and of the General Assembly. According to the Charter, only the Security Council is empowered to decide questions relating to the taking of action to maintain international peace and security; the establishment of the United Nations Emergency Force in the Middle East falls into this category.

In order to ensure prompt and effective action by the United Nations, the Members of the United Nations have conferred on the Security Council "primary responsibility for the maintenance of international peace and security", and have agreed that "in carrying out its duties under this responsibility the Security Council acts on their behalf" (Article 24 of the Charter). The States Members of the United Nations have assumed an obligation to accept and carry out the decisions of the Security Council (Article 25).

The General Assembly may, as provided in Article 11, "discuss any questions relating to the maintenance of international peace and security" and "may make recommendations with regard to any such question". However, as stated further on in the same Article, "Any such question on which action is necessary shall be referred to the Security Council by the General Assembly either before or after discussion".

Under Article 39, it is specifically the Security Council which "shall determine the existence of any threat to the peace, breach of the peace, or act of aggression, and shall make recommendations, or decide what measures shall be taken in accordance with Articles 41 and 42, to maintain or restore international peace and security". Each succeeding Article of Chapter VII of the Charter contains provisions confirming, reinforcing and crystallizing the proposition that all questions relating to the establishment and use of United Nations armed forces lie within the competence of the Security Council.

Guided by these provisions of the Charter, the USSR representative at the first emergency special session of the General Assembly in 1956 had the following to say about the decision to establish the Emergency Force in the Middle East:

" .   .   . As regards the creation and stationing on Egyptian territory of an international police force, the Soviet delegation is obliged to point out that this Force is being created in violation of the United Nations Charter.

"The General Assembly resolution on the basis of which it is now proposed to form this Force is inconsistent with the Charter. Chapter VII of the Charter empowers the Security Council, and the Security

Council only, not the General Assembly, to set up an international armed force and to take such action as it may deem necessary, including the use of such a force, to maintain or restore international peace and security."

The Government of the Union of Soviet Socialist Republics, in a memorandum concerning the procedure for financing the operations of the United Nations Emergency Force in the Middle East and the United Nations operations in the Congo, transmitted to the International Court of Justice in 1962, drew the following conclusion:

"Thus, since the Emergency Force for the Middle East was set up in violation of the United Nations Charter and in circumvention of the Security Council, its financing cannot be regarded as an obligation devolving on States Members of the United Nations pursuant to the Charter."

The basis for the conduct of the United Nations operations in the Congo was the Security Council resolution of 14 July 1960 (S/4387), which was adopted at the request of Patrice Lumumba's Government in consequence of the Belgian aggression in that country. Thereafter, however, in the course of the operations of the United Nations armed forces in the Congo, both this resolution and the United Nations Charter were grossly violated.

According to the Charter, the Security Council shall determine which States shall take part in carrying out its decisions for the maintenance of international peace and security. Article 48 of the Charter provides that: "The action required to carry out the decisions of the Security Council for the maintenance of international peace and security shall be taken by all the Members of the United Nations or by some of them, as the Security Council may determine". In violation of these provisions of the Charter, the Secretary-General, bypassing the Security Council, himself determined the group of States which were invited to take part, with armed forces or otherwise, in the United Nations operations in the Congo. As early as the Security Council meeting of 20 July 1960 [877th meeting], the USSR representative was compelled to protest against the actions of the Secretary-General, which were undertaken in violation of the Security Council resolution of 14 July.

Furthermore the provisions of the Charter were not observed in relation to the direction of the United Nations operations in the Congo.

The decisive criterion for the legality of the actions of a United Nations armed force in any eventuality is, of course, their consistency with the purposes and principles of the United Nations. It is possible to conceive a situation in which the requirements of the Charter are satisfied as regards the establishment of United Nations armed forces, but the activity of those forces is so directed as to produce results which are diametrically opposed to the purposes set forth in the Charter. This is precisely what happened in the Congo.

The then Secretary-General and the United Nations Command in the Congo, acting in the interest of the colonizers and in flagrant contradiction to the Charter, frustrated the implementation of the Security Council decision of 14 July 1960, which—as was repeatedly pointed out by USSR representatives and as is required by the Charter—should have put an end to interference by the colonizers in the domestic affairs of the Congo and served to strengthen the independence of the new Congolese State. The USSR Government, in its statement of 14 February 1961, roundly condemned the actions of the Secretary-General and proposed the prompt withdrawal of all foreign troops from the Congo so as to enable the Congolese people to settle their domestic affairs themselves.

The sequel to these violations of the Charter was that the Secretary-General, ignoring the Security Council, asked the General Assembly for appropriations to cover the cost of the United Nations operations in the Congo; the General Assembly, in its turn, without being competent to do so under the Charter, took a decision to make an appropriation for these operations and to apportion the cost they entailed among the States Members of the United Nations in accordance with the scale of assessment for the regular budget of the Organization.

Obviously, however, resolutions of the General Assembly cannot make the reimbursement of expenses, incurred on measures carried out otherwise than in accordance with the Charter, into an obligation upon States Members of the United Nations.

II. *Expenditure for United Nations armed forces does not come under Article 17 of the United Nations Charter.*

All questions connected with the establishment and operations of United Nations armed forces, including the question of expenditure for such forces, come under Chapter VII of the Charter and are within the competence of the Security Council.

Article 17 of the Charter reads in part:

"1. The General Assembly shall consider and approve the budget of the Organization.

"2. The expenses of the Organization shall be borne by the Members as apportioned by the General Assembly."

It is perfectly obvious that paragraph 2 of Article 17 is closely linked to paragraph 1 and refers to the budgetary expenses of the Organization. The General Assembly apportions the expenses of the United Nations budget among the Member States and these are required to bear such expenses in accordance with that apportionment.

The phrase "expenses of the Organization" as used in Article 17 of the Charter does not by any means signify "all the expenses of the Organization" but only the expenses under the budget, i. e., the "normal" expenses of the United Nations. The apportionment of such expenses among the Member States is decided by the General Assembly. Expenditure for United Nations armed forces and other matters connected with the establishment and operations of such forces are governed by the provisions of Chapter VII of the Charter and fall within the competence of the Security Council. . . .

The reference in the Committee's report to Articles 49 and 50 of Chapter VII of the Charter also underlines the fact that the expenses of United Nations armed forces were regarded by the Committee as coming under Chapter VII and not under Article 17 of the Charter and, consequently, as falling within the exclusive jurisdiction of the Security Council.

The principle that any United Nations action undertaken on the basis of Chapter VII falls within the exclusive jurisdiction of the Security Council is laid down in the Charter clearly and unequivocally. Chapter VII speaks only of the Security Council and does not even mention the General Assembly. When at the San Francisco Conference the proposal was made by the New Zealand delegation that "in all matters of the application of sanctions, military or economic, the Security Council associate with itself the General Assembly", it was not adopted. During the discussion on the proposal, it was pointed out, in particular by the United States representative, that the General Assembly should not encroach on the Security Council's powers and the Security Council should be the main agency to prevent aggression.

For a long time after the adoption of the United Nations Charter and until the Western Powers, and especially the United States, began their violations of the provisions of the Charter on this matter, no one questioned the fact that under the Charter measures relating to the establishment and operations of United Nations armed forces, including the question of expenditure for such forces, did not come under Article 17 and had no connexion with the "budget" mentioned in that Article. . . .

III. *There can be no question of applying Article 19 of the Charter not only in connexion with the cost of maintaining the Emergency Force in the Middle East and the armed forces in the Congo, but also in cases where United Nations armed forces are created and employed in accordance with the United Nations Charter.*

The question is sometimes raised, in connexion with the cost of maintaining the Emergency Force in the Middle East and the armed forces in the Congo, whether Article 19 of the Charter can be applied against States which are allegedly in arrears in defraying such expenses.

It is obvious, however, that Members of the United Nations can be said to be in arrears only in cases where they are under an obligation to defray the expenses in question. In the present case, no such obligation exists.

There could be no obligation for Members of the United Nations to pay the cost of maintaining the armed forces in the Middle East and the Congo because, in any case, the question of the cost of maintaining United Nations armed forces does not come under Article 17 of the Charter and is within the competence of the Security Council and not of the General Assembly. When it considered matters connected with defraying the cost of maintaining armed forces in the Middle East and the Congo, the General Assembly exceeded its powers (*ultra vires*). Hence, the General Assembly's resolutions on these matters cannot impose any financial obligation on Members of the United Nations.

Article 19 of the Charter provides that a Member of the United Nations which is in arrears beyond a certain amount in the payment of its financial contributions shall have no vote in the General Assembly. The arrears to which this Article refers are arrears in the payment of expenses under Article 17 of the Charter, which, as has already been pointed out, do not include expenditure on the maintenance of United Nations armed forces.

It should be recalled that at the San Francisco Conference Articles 17 and 19 of the Charter were regarded as parts of a whole. The Committee first approved the provisions which later became Article 17 and then approved supplementary provisions which today constitute Article 19.

Article 19 was drafted on the basis of Indian, Netherlands and Norwegian amendments, which were submitted as additions to the present Article 17 and Article 18, paragraph 1. The purpose of these amendments was stated as follows: "It should come under consideration whether the right of voting of Member States which do not pay their contribution should be suspended".

It will be recalled that, in the Committee, Australia introduced an amendment to the present Article 19 for the purpose of extending its application to obligations of Member States under Chapter VII of the Charter. However, that amendment was not incorporated into the Charter.

Thus, it is quite clear that Article 19 of the Charter applies only to the financial obligations of Member States with regard to expenses governed by Article 17. This further bears out the proposition stated above that Article 17 does not apply to the costs of maintaining United Nations armed forces, which are governed by Chapter VII of the Charter.

IV. *Strict compliance with the provisions of the Charter relating to the establishment, employment and financing of United Nations armed forces is of particular importance.*

In its "Memorandum regarding certain measures to strengthen the effectiveness of the United Nations in the safeguarding of international peace and security" [see A/5721], the USSR Government made a number of proposals designed to increase the effectiveness of the United Nations in safeguarding international peace and security. The basic idea of these proposals is, as was emphasized in the memorandum itself, the following:

"The Charter contains the essential principles for peaceful and good-neighbourly relations among States. Therefore, to enhance the effectiveness of the United Nations in keeping the peace means first of all putting an end to violations of the Charter, permanently ridding the Organization of all remnants of the 'cold war' period, creating within the United Nations a situation favourable to the co-operation of all States as equals."

This is particularly important as regards action to maintain international peace and security and, above all, as regards the employment of armed forces.

The employment of United Nations armed forces is an emergency measure which can greatly affect the international situation. At the same time, employment of such forces entails substantial expenditure.

The question of the payment by Member States of expenses connected with such operations must be decided in accordance with the provisions of the United Nations Charter, which, in this as in other matters, are based on the principles that all States enjoy sovereign equality, that the situation and capacities of each State must be taken into account, and that the armed forces must truly be employed for the purpose of maintaining or restoring international peace and security.

In the above-mentioned memorandum, the USSR Government stated that the question of the reimbursement of expenditure required for the execution of emergency measures adopted by the Security Council to deter or repel aggression through the use of United Nations armed forces should be decided in conformity with the generally recognized principle of international law that aggressor States bear political and material responsibility for the aggression they commit and for the material damage caused by that aggression.

The memorandum went on to state:

"Nevertheless, the Soviet Government does not rule out the possibility that situations may arise where, in order to execute the above-mentioned emergency measures of the Security Council, it will be necessary for States Members of the United Nations to take part in defraying the expenditure involved in the maintenance and use of United Nations armed forces established in order to maintain international peace and security. In such future cases when the

Security Council adopts decisions to establish and finance United Nations armed forces in strict compliance with the provisions of the Charter, the Soviet Union will be prepared to take part with other States Members of the United Nations in defraying the expenditure involved in the maintenance of those armed forces."

The question of reimbursing United Nations expenditure on the maintenance of armed forces is tremendously important, and affects the very foundations of the Organization. For that reason, it is of the utmost importance that the provisions of the United Nations Charter should be observed in deciding this question.

Being convinced that compliance with the Charter is essential to the viability of the United Nations and guarantees the effectiveness of its activities in safeguarding peace and developing international co-operation, the Soviet Union does not intend to depart from the provisions of the Charter.

3. *United States Memorandum on the United Nations Financial Crisis, 8 October 1964.*

A/5739 (8 Oct. 1964); GAOR, Annexes (XIX) 21, pp. 10–18.

The United States of America is vitally interested in the survival of the United Nations as an effective institution, and is deeply troubled by the financial crisis facing the Organization.

The crisis is painfully clear. The United Nations has a net deficit of $134 million.

On 30 June 1964 the United Nations had on its books unpaid obligations owed to Governments and other outsiders totalling some $117 million. In addition, it owed to its own Working Capital Fund—which it is supposed to have on hand in order to keep afloat and solvent pending the receipt of assessments—$40 million. Other internal accounts were owed $27 million. Against this total of $183 million of obligations it had $49 million in cash resources, or a net deficit of $134 million.

What does this mean?

It means that the United Nations does not have the money to pay its debts, and that it would be bankrupt today if it were not for the forbearance of the Member Governments to which it owes those debts.

It means that, unless something is done, the United Nations will have to default on its obligations to Member Governments which, in good faith and in reliance on the Organization's promises and good faith, have furnished troops and supplies and services to the United Nations, at its request, for the safeguarding of the peace. In so doing, these Governments incurred substantial additional and extraordinary expenditures which the United Nations agreed to reimburse— an agreement which the Secretary-General referred to in his statement at the opening session of the Working Group of Twenty-one on

9 September 1964 (A/AC.113/29) as "the commitment which the Organization has accepted, in its collective capacity, towards those of its Members who have furnished the men and material for its successive peace-keeping operations." . . .

The crisis has been thrust upon the United Nations by those Members which have refused to pay the assessments for the Middle East (UNEF) and Congo (ONUC) operations as voted by the General Assembly in accordance with the Charter. . . .

Let us now consider the legal arguments which have been made by the USSR. . . .

Every single one of those arguments was specifically rejected in the Court's advisory opinion of 20 July 1962. That Opinion was accepted on 18 December 1962 by the General Assembly [resolution 1854 (XVII)] by the overwhelming vote of 76 to 17, with 8 abstentions, after the Assembly had decisively defeated an amendment which would merely have taken note of the opinion.

Nevertheless, it may be useful to deal briefly with the Soviet contentions.

1. *The claimed "exclusive" peace-keeping rights of the Security Council*

The Soviet position is that the Security Council, and *only* the Security Council, has *any* right to take any action whatsoever with respect to the keeping of the peace, and that the General Assembly has no rights whatsoever in that area.

It should first be noted that this argument has nothing to do with ONUC, which was authorized and reauthorized by the Security Council by repeated resolutions, four out of five of which were voted *for* by the Soviet Union—it abstained on the fifth. Further, it will be remembered that UNEF was recommended by the General Assembly pursuant to the Security Council's referral of the problem to the General Assembly for its recommendations, by a resolution which the Soviet Union voted *for*.

In any event, there is no basis for the contention that the Security Council has exclusive rights as to peace-keeping, and the General Assembly none. Article 24 of the Charter gives the Security Council "primary responsibility for the maintenance of international peace and security", *primary* but not *exclusive* authority. . . .

Few Members of the United Nations would ever agree that, if the Security Council proves itself unable to act in the face of an international emergency, the General Assembly can only stand by, motionless and powerless to take any step for the preservation of the peace.

Certainly the record of recent years shows that the General Assembly can take and has taken appropriate measures in the interest of international peace, and that it has done so with the support of the overwhelming majority of the Members, who believe that such measures are fully within the letter and the spirit of the Charter.

2. *The claimed "exclusive" rights of the Security Council as to peace-keeping expenses*

The Soviet Union also contends that the Security Council has *sole* authority to determine the expenses of a peace-keeping operation, and to assess them on the membership, and that the General Assembly has no such right.

We think it unlikely that many Members would ever agree that the eleven members of the Security Council should be able to assess the other 101 Members without any consent or action on their part—surely taxation without representation.

There is not the slightest justification in the Charter for any such contention. The only reference in the Charter to the Organization's expenses is in Article 17, paragraph 2, which provides that "the expenses of the Organization shall be borne by the Members as apportioned by the General Assembly". The Security Council is never mentioned in the Charter in connexion with any expenses of the United Nations.

3. *The claimed "non-includability" of peace-keeping expenses under Article 17 of the Charter*   .   .   .

It is clear that if the expenses of UNEF and ONUC, as apportioned by the General Assembly, are "expenses of the Organization", they are obligatory on the Members and must be paid.

This is precisely the question which was decided in the affirmative by the International Court of Justice in its Advisory Opinion of 20 July 1962, accepted by the General Assembly.   .   .   .

4. *The claimed "non-applicability" of Article 19 of the Charter*

The first sentence of Article 19 of the Charter reads as follows:

"A Member of the United Nations which is in arrears in the payment of its financial contributions to the Organization shall have no vote in the General Assembly if the amount of its arrears equals or exceeds the amount of the contributions due from it for the preceding two full years."

The Soviet memorandum of 11 September 1964 states in section III that the arrears to which Article 19 refers are arrears in the payment of expenses under Article 17. This is of course true.

But the memorandum contends that since, according to the Soviet claim, UNEF and ONUC expenses are solely within the competence of the Security Council and are not "expenses of the Organization" under Article 17, they cannot be included in the calculation of arrears under Article 19.

But, as the International Court of Justice has held and as the General Assembly confirmed, UNEF and ONUC expenses *are* "expenses of the Organization" under Article 17 and *were* properly apportioned under that Article by the General Assembly. Therefore they *are* to be included in any calculation of arrears under Article 19.

The memorandum refers, also in section III, to an amendment to the present Article 19 proposed at the San Francisco Conference by Australia. The amendment in question would have added to Article 19 a provision that a Member shall have no vote if it has not carried out its obligations under what is now Article 43. In other words, for example, if a Member has agreed with the Security Council under Article 43 to furnish certain troops on the Council's call, and later refuses to do so, it should lose its vote. The proposed amendment would thus have *added* to Article 19, which already provided for loss of vote by a member failing to pay its assessments for United Nations expenses, a provision for loss of vote by a Member failing to comply with its Article 43 obligations. Expenses were not involved in the proposed amendment at all.

In point of fact the proposed amendment was withdrawn by Australia and was never voted on. The proposed amendment and its withdrawal have nothing to do with the fact that Article 19 *does* deprive a member of its vote for failing to pay its assessments for United Nations expenses, and the fact that those expenses include, as the International Court of Justice has held, the UNEF and ONUC peacekeeping expenses incurred by the United Nations itself and duly assessed on all Members by the General Assembly. Those interested in the proposed amendment will find the accurate story in the documents of the United Nations Conference on International Organization, volume 8, pages 470 (II/1/34) and 476 (II/1/35).

So the conclusion is clear that, in the calculation of arrears under Article 19, UNEF and ONUC assessments *are* to be included. . . .

November 10 is the opening of the General Assembly, and November 10 presents the inevitable and inescapable issue of Article 19 unless requisite payments are made before that opening. . . .

The first sentence of Article 19 says in simple and clear terms that a Member subject to its provisions *shall have* no vote in the General Assembly. It does not say that the General Assembly has any discretion with respect to such a Member; it does not say that the General Assembly shall *vote* as to whether the delinquent shall have no vote; it simply says that the delinquent *shall* have no vote. The first sentence of Article 19 in the French text is even more emphatic: it says the delinquent Member *cannot* vote—"*ne peut participer au vote*".

The second sentence of Article 19 *does* provide for a vote; a delinquent Member whose failure to pay is due to conditions beyond its control *may* be permitted by the General Assembly to vote. But there is no discretion as to a delinquent Member whose failure to pay is *not* due to conditions beyond its control, no discretion as to a Member which *refuses* to pay.

The United States hopes that those Members about to be confronted by Article 19 will take the action necessary to avoid the confrontation.

The way to avoid the confrontation is for those subject to the terms of Article 19 to make the necessary payments.

The United States does not seek the confrontation—but if on November 10 the plain and explicit terms of Article 19 do become applicable, there is no alternative to its application.

It is not only that Article 19 means what it says—that the Member shall have no vote—it is that failure to apply the Article would be a violation of the Charter which would have far-reaching consequences.

Failure to apply the Article would break faith with the overwhelming majority of Members who are paying their peace-keeping assessments—often at great sacrifice—as obligations binding under the Charter.

Failure to apply the Article would be a repudiation of the International Court of Justice and of that rule of international law whose continued growth is vital for progress toward peace and disarmament.

Failure to apply the Article would mean the discarding of the *only* sanction which the United Nations has in support of its capacity to collect what its Members owe it.

Failure to apply the Article would undermine the only mandatory power the General Assembly has—the power under Article 17 to assess the expenses of the Organization on the Members.

Failure to apply the Article would tempt Members to pick and choose, with impunity, from among their obligations to the United Nations, refusing to pay for items they dislike even though those items were authorized by the overwhelming vote of the Members. Indeed, the Soviet Union has already said that it will not pay for certain items in the regular budgets. How could any organization function on such a fiscal quicksand?

Failure to apply the Article to a great Power simply because it is a great Power would undermine the constitutional integrity of the United Nations, and could sharply affect the attitude toward the Organization of those who have always been its strongest supporters.

Failure to apply the Article could seriously jeopardize the support of United Nations operations and programmes, not only for the keeping of the peace but for economic and social development.

The consequences of not applying Article 19 would thus be far worse than any conjectured consequences of applying it.

We believe that it is the desire of most Members of the United Nations that the situation *not* arise which makes Article 19 applicable, and therefore we believe that it is up to the membership to see to it that the confrontation is avoided through the means available under the Charter for avoiding it—the making of the necessary payments.

The United Nations financial crisis is not an adversary issue between individual Members; it is an issue between those who refuse to pay and the Organization itself, the Organization as a whole. It is an issue which involves the future capacity of the United Nations as an effective institution. If the United Nations cannot collect what is due from its Members, it cannot pay what it owes; if it cannot collect what is due from its Members, it will have no means of effectively carrying on its peace-keeping functions and its economic and social programmes will be jeopardized.

The issue is one which vitally affects *all* Members of the United Nations.

The United Nations is of particular importance to its developing Members. It is not only a free and open forum where all can defend what they think and urge what they want, it is an institution which, in response to the interests of all—both large and small—can *act*. But it cannot act unless it has the funds to support its acts. And if it cannot get from its Members the funds to support its acts, *all* would be the losers. So it is to *all* countries that the United Nations must look for a solution.

It has sometimes been said that somehow the United States should work out with the Soviet Union a compromise on some of the fundamental issues.

Could the United States—or should it—agree that Member States which are not members of the Security Council should have nothing at all to say about peace-keeping, even in cases in which the Security Council cannot act? And nothing to say about peace-keeping expenses or their assessment?

Could the United States—or should it—agree that Article 19, despite its plain terms, should not be applied against a great Power in support of General Assembly assessments, simply because it is a great Power?

The United States does not see how, without violating the Charter, anyone could or should agree to any of these propositions.

United States efforts to find solutions

The sincere and earnest desire of the United States to find a way out of the United Nations financial crisis, and to avoid confrontation under Article 19, is evidenced by the repeated attempts it has made to reach common ground. . . .

This sincere effort to enter into a dialogue with the Soviet delegation was in the hope that adjustments as to the arrangements for the initiation and financing of future peace-keeping operations could make it easier to reach some solution as to the present and the past. Unfortunately, there has been no Soviet willingness to enter into that dialogue. . . .

None the less, the United States has not given up hope, and it intends to continue its attempts to work out new arrangements in the hope that solutions for the future may make it easier for those in arrears on UNEF and ONUC assessments to clear up in some manner these past arrears. . . .

Accordingly, on 14 September 1964, the United States tabled in the Working Group of Twenty-one, as a basis for discussion, a working paper which sets forth examples of the kinds of new arrangements it has in mind as to peace-keeping operations involving the use of military forces. The following elements were mentioned:

"1. All proposals to initiate such peace-keeping operations would be considered first in the Security Council. The General Assembly would not authorize or assume control of such peace-keeping operations unless the Council had demonstrated that it was unable to take action." [This would be a self-denying ordinance on the part of the General Assembly, emphasizing the *primary* role of the Security Council.]

"2. The General Assembly would establish a standing special finance committee. The composition of this committee should be similar to that of the present Working Group of Twenty-one . . . ." [The committee membership would include the permanent members of the Security Council, who would thus have a position more commensurate with their responsibilities than in the General Assembly.]

"3. In apportioning expenses for such peace-keeping operations, the General Assembly would act only on a recommendation from the committee passed by a two-thirds majority of the committee's membership." [The permanent members of the Security Council would have an influence greater than in the Assembly, but no single Member could frustrate, by a veto, action desired by the overwhelming majority.]

"4. In making recommendations, the committee would rather consider various alternative methods of financing, including direct financing by countries involved in a dispute, voluntary contributions, and assessed contributions. In the event that the Assembly did not accept a particular recommendation, the committee would resume consideration of the matter with a view to recommending an acceptable alternative.

"5. One of the available methods of assessment for peace-keeping operations involving the use of military forces would be a special scale of assessments in which, over a specified amount, States having greater ability to pay would be allocated higher percentages, and States having less ability to pay would be allocated smaller percentages than in the regular scale of assessments." [A/AC.113/30.]

The United States hopes that such ideas may lead to a measure of agreement among Members of the United Nations as to how these operations are to be started and paid for in the future. Arrangements of this kind should go a long way toward giving the Soviet Union and others in a similar position such assurances for the future as should make it easier for them to make their payments relating to the past.

NOTE.—1. When the nineteenth session of the General Assembly opened on 1 December 1964, it was agreed that, to avoid a confrontation with respect to Article 19, the General Assembly would limit itself to the consideration of those issues which "can be disposed of without objection." GAOR, XIX, Plenary, Mtg. 1286, p. 1. Consequently, all the decisions at that session of the General Assembly were made on the basis of consensus, without voting, except for one "procedural" vote on an Albanian appeal against a ruling by the President. GAOR, XIX, Plenary Mtgs. 1327–30.

2. On 18 February 1965, the General Assembly established a Special Committee of Thirty-Three on Peace-Keeping Operations to make "a comprehensive review of the whole question of peace-keeping operations in all their aspects, including ways of overcoming the present financial difficulties of the Organization." Resolution 2006 (XIX); GAOR, XIX, Supp. 15 (A/5815), pp. 7–8. In speaking before this Committee on 16 August 1965, Ambassador Goldberg reversed the position of the United States on Article 19. He noted that "the United States had regretfully concluded that, at the present stage in the development of the United Nations, the General Assembly was not prepared to carry out the relevant provisions of the Charter, that is, to apply the loss-of-vote sanction provided in Article 19. The intransigence of a few Member States and their unwillingness to abide by the rule of law had created that state of affairs, and while the United States continued to maintain that Article 19 was applicable in present circumstances, it recognized that the consensus of opinion in the Assembly was against application of the Article and in favour of having the Assembly proceed normally. The United States would not seek to frustrate that consensus, since it was not in the interest of the world to have the Assembly's work immobilized, particularly in view of present world tensions. It agreed that the Assembly must proceed with its work. At the same time, if any Member State could make an exception to the principle of collective financial responsibility with respect to certain United Nations activities, the United States reserved the same option to make exceptions if, in its view, there were strong and compelling reasons to do so. There could be no double standard among the Members of the Organization." A/5916/Add.1 (30 Sept. 1965); GAOR, Annexes (XIX) 21, p. 86. On the basis of this statement, the Committee agreed:

"(a) That the General Assembly will carry on its work normally in accordance with its rules of procedure;

"(b) That the question of the applicability of Article 19 of the Charter will not be raised with regard to the United Nations Emergency Force and the United Nations Operation in the Congo;

"(c) That the financial difficulties of the Organization should be solved through voluntary contributions by Member States, with the highly developed countries making substantial contributions." A/5916 (31 Aug. 1965); GAOR, Annexes (XIX) 21, p. 85.

3. The General Assembly, at its twentieth session, continued the Committee of 33, and established, in addition, an *Ad Hoc* Committee of Experts

to Examine the Finances of the United Nations and the Specialized Agencies. Resolutions 2049 and 2053 (XX), 13 and 15 Dec. 1965; GAOR, XX, Supp. 14 (A/6014), pp. 16, 72–73. For the comprehensive reports of that Committee, see A/6289 and Add.1 and 2 (28–31 March 1966) and A/6343 (19 July 1966); they were approved by GA Resolution 2150 (XXI) on 4 Nov. 1966.

4. The Committee of 33 considered a variety of proposals in 1966 but again reached no agreement. A/AC.121/SR.22 (29 Sept. 1966), p. 11, annexed to A/6414 (30 Sept. 1966). At the twenty-first session of the General Assembly, the Special Political Committee adopted by 52 votes to 14, with 42 abstentions, a seven-power draft resolution, based on a Canadian proposal, suggesting that the General Assembly should note that "various methods of financing peace-keeping operations may be considered when the need for any such operation arises and that these include:

"(a) Apportionment among the Members of the Organization;

"(b) Special arrangements agreed among the parties involved;

"(c) Voluntary contributions;

"(d) Any combination of these methods."

According to this proposal, the General Assembly should also consider that "if the costs of a particular peace-keeping operation involving heavy expenditures are to be apportioned among the Members of the Organization this should be done in a manner which would provide for the equitable sharing of the above-mentioned costs, due account being taken of:

"(a) The special responsibilities of the permanent members of the Security Council;

"(b) The relatively limited capacity of economically developing countries to contribute towards the costs of such an operation;

"(c) Where circumstances warrant, the need to give special consideration to the situation of any Member States which are victims of, and those which are otherwise involved in, the events or actions leading to a peace-keeping operation."

Finally, under this proposal, "the equitable sharing of the costs of a particular peace-keeping operation involving heavy expenditures might be achieved by means of a special scale which would establish that the economically developing countries would contribute 5 per cent of the total costs, with the balance of the costs to be borne by other Member States." A/6603 (15 Dec. 1966), pp. 17–18.

The Committee also adopted, by 33 votes to 27, with 48 abstentions, a more precise draft resolution, based on a proposal by Ireland, suggesting that

"(a) Peace-keeping expenditure of up to $100 million in any one year which is not otherwise covered by agreed arrangements or by items in the regular budget should be apportioned as follows:

"(i) As to 5 per cent, among the group of economically less developed Member States;

"(ii) As to 25 per cent, among the group of economically developed Member States, other than the permanent members of the Security Council;

"(iii) As to 70 per cent, among the group of permanent members of the Security Council, to be assessed only on those permanent members which vote in favour of the operation, provided, however, that no member shall be assessed for more than 50 per cent of the net cost of the operation and that any balance unassessed by reason of this proviso shall be added to the sum apportioned on the group of Members specified in sub-paragraph (ii) above;

"(b) Expenditure in excess of $100 million in any one year should be assessed *pro rata* on the groups specified in sub-paragraphs (a) (ii) and (a) (iii) above;

"(c) Within each group the amount to be paid by each Member State shall be in proportion to its capacity to contribute relative to the other members of the group as determined by the scale of assessments for the regular budget;

"(d) Any State Member of the United Nations or other State or organization may make voluntary subscriptions to reduce the amount to be assessed on any or all of the groups." *Idem*, pp. 15–16.

The General Assembly, instead of adopting one or both of these resolutions, decided to refer the whole matter to the fifth special session of the General Assembly to be held in April 1967. GA Resolution 2220 (XXI), 19 Dec. 1966. No action was taken at that session, however. For the report of the Special Committee on Peace-Keeping Operations submitted to that session, see A/6654 (17 May 1967), 72 pp.

5. For comments on the financial problems of peacekeeping, see F. A. M. ALTING VON GEUSAU, "Financing United Nations Peace-Keeping Activities," 12 Nederlands TIR (1965), pp. 281–303; Peter V. BISHOP, "Canada's Policy on Financing of U.N. Peace-keeping Operations," 20 Int. J. (Toronto, 1965), pp. 463–86; D. W. BOWETT and others, United Nations Forces: A Legal Study of United Nations Practice (London, 1964), pp. 139–48, 249–54, 468–83; Inis L. CLAUDE, Jr., "The Political Framework of the United Nations' Financial Problems," 17 Int.Org. (1963), pp. 831–59; Andrew CORDIER and others, Report of the Committee on Peacekeeping Operations of the National Citizens' Commission for the White House Conference on International Cooperation (UNA-USA, New York, 1966), 27 pp. [reprinted in part in Richard N. GARDNER, Blueprint for Peace (New York, 1966), pp. 65–73]; Dante B. FASCELL [and M. A. CZARNECKI], United Nations Financial Situation: Background and Consequences of the Article 19 Controversy over the Financing of U.N. Peacekeeping Operations (89th Congress, 2d Session, Committee on Foreign Affairs, 1966), 139 pp.; John H. JACKSON, "The Legal Framework of United Nations Financing: Peacekeeping and Penury," 51 California L.R. (1963), pp. 79–133; Luke T. LEE, "An Alternative Approach to Article 19," 59 AJIL (1965), pp. 872–76; Nathaniel L. NATHANSON, "Constitutional Crisis at the United Nations: The Price of Peacekeeping," 32 University of Chicago L.R. (1965), pp. 621–58; Norman J. PADELFORD, The Financing of Future Peace and Security Operations under the United Nations (Cambridge, Mass., 1962), 87 pp.; Norman J. PADELFORD, "Financing Peacekeeping: Politics and Crisis," 19 Int.Org. (1965), pp. 444–462; Ruth B. RUSSELL, "United Nations Financing and 'the Law of the Charter'," 5 Columbia J. Transnational L. (1966), pp. 68–95; John G. STOESSINGER, "Financing the United Nations," 535 Int.Conc. (Nov. 1961), pp. 1–72; John G. STOESSINGER and others, Financing the United Nations System (Washington, D.C., 1964), pp. 100–90; US, DOS, OFFICE OF THE LEGAL ADVISER, "Article 19 of the

Charter of the United Nations: Memorandum of Law," 58 AJIL (1964), pp. 753–78; US, DOS, "The UN Financial Crisis," 51 DSB (1964), pp. 681–90, reprinted in 59 AJIL (1965), pp. 622–31; Robert L. WEST, "The United Nations and the Congo Financial Crisis: Lessons of the First Year," 15 Int. Org. (1961), pp. 603–17.

6.   For comments on other aspects of peace-keeping and on the problems of a standing United Nations Force, see C. F. AMERASINGHE, "The Use of Armed Force by the United Nations in the Charter *travaux préparatoires*," 5 Indian JIL (1965), pp. 305–333; Lincoln P. BLOOMFIELD, ed., "International Force: A Symposium," 17 Int.Org. (1963), pp. 321–485; Lincoln P. BLOOMFIELD and others, International Military Forces (Boston, 1964), 296 pp.; D. W. BOWETT and others, United Nations Forces: A Legal Study (New York, 1965), 579 pp.; E. L. M. BURNS, "The Role of Peace-keeping Forces in Disarmament," *in* E. LUARD, First Steps to Disarmament (New York, 1965) pp. 186–200; Inis L. CLAUDE, "United Nations Use of Military Force," 7 J. of Conflict Resolution (1963), pp. 117–29; Edwin B. FIRMAGE, "A United Nations Peace Force," 11 Wayne L.R. (1965), pp. 717–38; Maurice FLORY, "L'Organisation des Nations Unies et les opérations de maintien de la paix," 11 AFDI (1965), pp. 446–68; Per FRYDENBERG and others, Peace-Keeping: Experience and Evaluation (Oslo, 1964), 339 pp.; Richard N. GARDNER, "The Development of the Peace-Keeping Capacity of the United Nations," 57 ASIL Procgs. (1963), pp. 224–34; Leland M. GOODRICH, "The Maintenance of International Peace and Security," 19 Int.Org. (1965), pp. 429–443; Ernst B. HAAS, "Types of Collective Security: An Examination of Operational Concepts," 49 APSR (March, 1962), pp. 40–62; Per HAEKKERUP, "Scandinavia's Peace-Keeping Forces for the U.N.," 42 Foreign Affairs (1964), pp. 675–81; Stanley HOFFMANN, "Erewhon or Lilliput?   A Critical View of the Problem [of International Military Forces]," 17 Int.Org. (1963), pp. 404–24; Alan JAMES, "U.N. Action for Peace: I. Barrier Forces, II. Law and Order Forces," 18 The World Today (1962), pp. 478–86, 503–13; Rahmatulla KHAN, "Collective Security versus Preventive Diplomacy: The Role of the United Nations in the Maintenance of World Peace and Security," 4 Indian JIL (1964), pp. 408–427; Hidejiro KOTANI, "Peace-Keeping: Problems for Smaller Countries," 19 Int.J. (Toronto, 1964), pp. 308–25; Shigeru KOZAI, "Japanese Participation in the United Nations Forces: Possibilities and Limitations," 9 Japanese AIL (1965), pp. 10–20; Karl H. KUNZMANN, "Aktuelle Vorschläge für eine Friedenstruppe der Vereinten Nationen," 13 Europa-Archiv (1958), pp. 10811–26; Paul MARTIN, "Peace-Keeping and the United Nations: The Broader View," 40 Int. Affairs (London, 1964), pp. 191–204; Paul MOHN, "Problems of Truce Supervision," 478 Int.Conc. (Feb. 1962), pp. 49–99; Sir Leslie MUNRO, "Can the United Nations Enforce Peace?" 38 Foreign Affairs (1960), pp. 209–18; G. S. MURRAY, "United Nations Peace-Keeping and Problems of Political Control," 18 Int.J. (Toronto, 1963), pp. 442–57; Nathaniel L. NATHANSON, "Constitutional Crisis at the United Nations: The Price of Peace-Keeping," 32 Chicago L.R. (1965), pp. 621–58, and 33 *idem* (1966), pp. 249–313; Alan F. NEIDLE, "Peace-Keeping and Disarmament," 57 AJIL (1963), pp. 46–72; A. C. NUNN, "The Arming of an International Police," 2 J. of Peace Research (1965), pp. 187–191; Lester B. PEARSON, "Force for U.N.," 35 Foreign Affairs (1957), pp. 395–404; Lester B. PEARSON, "Keeping the Peace,"

6 Survival (1964), pp. 150–58; Nikolai PITERSKY, International Security
Forces (Moscow, 1966), 47 pp.; Ruth B. RUSSELL, United Nations Ex-
perience with Military Forces: Political and Legal Aspects (Washington,
1964), 174 pp.; Ruth B. RUSSELL, "Development by the United Nations of
Rules Relating to Peacekeeping," 59 ASIL Procgs. (1965), pp. 53–60; Ul-
rich SCHEUNER, "Eine internationale Sicherungsmacht in Dienste der
Vereinten Nationen," 19 ZaöRV (1958), pp. 389–415; Finn SEYERSTED,
United Nations Forces in the Law of Peace and War (Leyden, 1966), 447 pp.;
Louis B. SOHN, "The Authority of the United Nations to Establish and
Maintain a Permanent United Nations Force," 52 AJIL (1958), pp. 229–240;
Louis B. SOHN, "Some Peacekeeping Proposals," 34 The Correspondent
(1965), pp. 35–40; Y. TANDON, "The Peaceful Settlement of International
Disputes," 2 Int. Relations (1964), pp. 555–587; David W. WAINHOUSE
and others, International Peace Observation: A History and Forecast
(Baltimore, 1966), 663 pp.; Arthur I. WASKOW, Quis Custodiet? Con-
trolling the Police in a Disarmed World (Washington, 1963), 2 vols.;
WORLD VETERANS FEDERATION, The Functioning of Ad Hoc United
Nations Emergency Forces (Helsinki, 1963) 61 pp. See also Carl von HORN,
Soldiering for Peace (New York, 1967), 402 pp.; COMMISSION TO STUDY
THE ORGANIZATION OF PEACE, New Dimensions for the United Na-
tions (Dobbs Ferry, N. Y., 1966), pp. 24–35, 121–34.

VIET-NAM QUESTION

NOTE.—1.   The hostilities in Indochina between the French army and the
guerilla forces of the Viet Minh were terminated on 20 July 1954 by three
separate Geneva Agreements on the cessation of hostilities in Viet-Nam, Laos
and Cambodia. By the agreement relating to Viet-Nam: a "provisional military demarcation line" was fixed, and the Viet Minh forces were to be withdrawn to the north of that line and the French to the south of it (Article 1);
thereafter, no "person, military or civilian, shall be permitted to cross the
provisional military demarcation line unless specifically authorized by the
Joint Commission," composed of an equal number of representatives of the
two parties (Articles 6 and 31); arrangements were made for the civil administration in each regrouping zone, pending "the general elections which
will bring about the unification of Viet-Nam" [Article 14, para. (a)]; each
party undertook "to refrain from any reprisals or discrimination against
persons or organizations on account of their activities during the hostilities
and to guarantee their democratic liberties" [Article 14, para. (c)]; introduction of additional military personnel and arms and munitions into Viet-
Nam was prohibited (Articles 16 and 17); "no military base under the control of a foreign State" was to be established in either zone, the zones were
prohibited to "adhere to any military alliance" and were not to be used "for
the resumption of hostilities or to further an aggressive policy" (Article 19);
the armed forces of each party were to "respect the demilitarized zone and
the territory under the military control of the other party" and were bound
to "commit no act and undertake no operation against the other party" (Article 24); an International Commission for Supervision and Control was established, composed of representatives of Canada, India and Poland (Articles 29 and 34). The Geneva Agreements were accompanied by a Final

Declaration of the Geneva Conference, of 21 July 1954, in which the Conference recognized that, "the essential purpose of the agreement relating to Viet-Nam is to settle military questions with a view to ending hostilities and that the military demarcation line is provisional and should not in any way be interpreted as constituting a political or territorial boundary"; and declared that, "so far as Viet-Nam is concerned, the settlement of political problems, effected on the basis of respect for the principles of independence, unity and territorial integrity, shall permit the Viet-Namese people to enjoy the fundamental freedoms, guaranteed by democratic institutions established as a result of free general elections by secret ballot. In order to ensure that sufficient progress in the restoration of peace has been made, and that all the necessary conditions obtain for free expression of the national will, general elections shall be held in July 1956, under the supervision of an international commission composed of representatives of the Member States of the International Supervisory Commission, referred to in the agreement on the cessation of hostilities." The Government of the United States did not sign this Declaration, as the United States was not a belligerent in the war, but it made a unilateral declaration in which it noted the Geneva Agreements and stated that: "(i) it will refrain from the threat or the use of force to disturb them, in accordance with Article 2(4) of the Charter of the United Nations dealing with the obligation of members to refrain in their international relations from the threat or use of force; and (ii) it would view any renewal of the aggression in violation of the aforesaid agreements with grave concern and as seriously threatening international peace and security." US SENATE, COMMITTEE ON FOREIGN RELATIONS, Background Information Relating to Southeast Asia and Vietnam (89th Congress, 1st Session, 14 Jan. 1965), pp. 28–42, 58–61; US, DOS, American Foreign Policy, 1950–1955 (Washington, D.C., 1957), pp. 750–67, 785–88.

2. Article IV of the Southeast Asia Collective Defense Treaty, signed at Manila on 8 September 1954 by Australia, France, New Zealand, Pakistan, the Philippines, Thailand, UK and US, contains the following provisions:

"1. Each Party recognizes that aggression by means of armed attack in the treaty area against any of the Parties or against any State or territory which the Parties by unanimous agreement may hereafter designate, would endanger its own peace and safety, and agrees that it will in that event act to meet the common danger in accordance with its constitutional processes. Measures taken under this paragraph shall be immediately reported to the Security Council of the United Nations.

"2. If, in the opinion of any of the Parties, the inviolability or the integrity of the territory or the sovereignty or political independence of any Party in the treaty area or of any other State or territory to which the provisions of paragraph 1 of this Article from time to time apply is threatened in any way other than by armed attack or is affected or threatened by any fact or situation which might endanger the peace of the area, the Parties shall consult immediately in order to agree on the measures which should be taken for the common defense.

"3. It is understood that no action on the territory of any State designated by unanimous agreement under paragraph 1 of this Article or on any territory so designated shall be taken except at the invitation or with the consent of the Government concerned."

In a protocol annexed to this Treaty the parties unanimously designated "for the purposes of Article IV of the Treaty the States of Cambodia and Laos and the free territory under the jurisdiction of the State of Vietnam." 209 UNTS (1955), p. 28, at 30, 36.

3.   After an attack on United States vessels in the Gulf of Tonkin by naval units of North Viet-Nam, a Southeast Asia Resolution was adopted by the United States Congress on 10 August 1964, approving and supporting "the determination of the President, as Commander in Chief, to take all necessary measures to repel any armed attack against the forces of the United States and to prevent further aggression."   The Congress declared further that the "United States regards as vital to its national interest and to world peace the maintenance of international peace and security in southeast Asia.   Consonant with the Constitution of the United States and the Charter of the United Nations and in accordance with its obligations under the Southeast Asia Collective Defense Treaty, the United States is, therefore, prepared, as the President determines, to take all necessary steps, including the use of armed force, to assist any member or protocol state of the Southeast Asia Collective Defense Treaty requesting assistance in defense of its freedom."   It added that this Resolution "shall expire when the President shall determine that the peace and security of the area is reasonably assured by international conditions created by action of the United Nations or otherwise, except that it may be terminated earlier by concurrent resolution of the Congress." US SENATE, COMMITTEE ON FOREIGN RELATIONS, Background Information Relating to Southeast Asia and Vietnam (89th Congress, 1st Session, 14 Jan. 1965), p. 128; 78 US Statutes (1964), p. 384.

4.   The Viet-Nam Question raised two basic problems: whether the United States action in Viet-Nam constituted a violation of the United Nations Charter (see Documents 1–3, below), and what role should the United Nations play in this situation (see Documents 4–6, below)?

1.   *Memorandum of Law by Lawyers Committee on American Policy Towards Vietnam, September 1965.*

US Senate, Committee on Foreign Relations, Hearings on S. 2793: Supplemental Foreign Assistance, Fiscal Year 1966—Vietnam (89th Congress, 2nd Session, 1966), pp. 687–713.

The Charter of the United Nations was signed on behalf of the United States on June 26, 1945 by the President of the United States, and was ratified on July 28, 1945, by the Senate.   Thus, the United States became a signatory to the Charter, along with 55 other nations (there are now 114), obligating itself to outlaw war, to refrain from the unilateral use of force against other nations, and to abide by the procedures embodied in the Charter for the settlement of differences between States.   In essence, the obligations assumed by member nations under the United Nations Charter represent the principles of international law which govern the conduct of members of the United Nations and their legal relations.

The Charter of the United Nations is a presently effective treaty binding upon the Government of the United States because it is the "Supreme Law of the Land."   Indeed, the Charter constitutes the cornerstone of a world system of nations which recognize that peaceful relations, devoid of any use of force or threats of force, are the fundamental legal relations between nations.   The following provisions of the Charter are relevant:

(a) *"All members shall refrain in their international relations from the threat or use of force* against the territorial integrity or political independence of any state or in any other manner inconsistent with the purposes of the United Nations" (Chapter I, Article II(4)) (emphasis added).

(b) *"The Security Council shall determine the existence of any threat to the peace, breach of the peace, or act of aggression,* and shall make recommendations or shall decide what measures shall be taken . . . to maintain or restore international peace and security." (Chapter VII, 39) (Italics ours throughout the Memorandum)

It is thus plain that signatory members of the United Nations Charter are barred from resorting to force unilaterally and that only the Security Council is authorized to determine the measures to be taken to maintain or restore international peace (apart from the question as to whether or not the General Assembly has any residual authority by virtue of the "Uniting for Peace" Resolution for this purpose when the Security Council is unable to meet its responsibilities).

It may be recalled that in 1956, Israel justified its attack on the Egyptian forces in the Sinai Peninsula "as security measures to eliminate the Egyptian Fedayeen 'Commando' bases in the Sinai Peninsula from which raids had been launched across the Israeli frontier." Starke, "Introduction to International Law", 4th ed., London, 1958, at p. 83 *et seq.*

When Great Britain and France introduced their troops into the Sinai Peninsula, under claim of a threat to their vital interests, the "preponderant reaction of the rest of the world was to condemn this action as inter alia, a breach of the United Nations Charter." Starke, "Introduction to International Law", 4th ed., London, 1958, at pp. 85–88.

When the Soviet Union suggested a Joint Military Operation with the United States to restore the peace in the Middle East, Secretary of State John Foster Dulles rejected this proposal as "unthinkable" (New York Times, November 6, 1956). Dulles declared:

". . . Any intervention by the United States and/or Russia, or any other action, except by a duly constituted United Nations peace force would be counter to everything the General Assembly and the Secretary-General of the United Nations were charged by the Charter to do in order to secure a United Nations Police Cease Fire."

At a news conference on November 8, 1956, President Eisenhower, answering an announcement of the Soviet Union at that time, declared that the United States would oppose the dispatch of Russian "volunteers" to aid Egypt, saying that it would be the duty of all United Nations Members, including the United States, under the clear mandate of the United Nations Charter to counter any Soviet military intervention in the Middle East. The President said:

"The United Nations is *alone* charged with the responsibility of securing the peace in the Middle East and throughout the world." *United Nations Action in the Suez Crisis.* Tulane Studies in Political Science, Vol. IV entitled "International Law in the Middle East Crisis."

To the fundamental, substantive and procedural requirements and conditions vesting sole authority in the United Nations to authorize utilization of force, there are only two exceptions set forth in the Charter. The first exception is found in Article 51 of Chapter 7:

"Nothing in the present Charter shall impair the inherent right of individual or collective self-defense *if an armed attack occurs against a member of the United Nations*, until the Security Council has taken measures to maintain international peace and security."

Article 51 of the Charter marked a serious restriction on the traditional right of self-defense. As was stated by Professor Philip C. Jessup in his work, "A Modern Law of Nations", published in 1947 (at pp. 165–166):

"Article 51 of the Charter suggests a further limitation on the right of self-defense: it may be exercised only 'if an armed attack occurs'. . . . This restriction in Article 51 very definitely narrows the freedom of action which states had under traditional law. A case could be made out for self-defense under the traditional law where the injury was threatened but no attack had yet taken place. Under the Charter, alarming military preparations by a neighboring state would justify a resort to the Security Council, but would not justify resort to anticipatory force by the state which believed itself threatened."

The traditional right of self-defense, even prior to the adoption of the United Nations Charter, was limited. As stated by Secretary of State Daniel Webster in the Caroline Case, and as adopted in the Nurenberg Judgment in 1945, any resort to armed force in self-defense must be confined to cases in which "the necessity of that self-defense is instant, overwhelming and leaving no choice of means and no moment of deliberation".

In expressly limiting independent military action to instances of *armed attack*, the founding nations explicitly and implicitly rejected the right to the use of force based on the familiar claim of "anticipatory self-defense", or "intervention by subversion", or "pre-emptive armed attack to forestall threatened aggression", and similar rationale. Such concepts were well known to the founding nations if only because most of the wars of history had been fought under banners carrying or suggesting these slogans. . . .

It has been authoritatively said that the exceptional circumstances stipulated in Article 51 are "clear, objective, easy to prove and difficult to misinterpret or to fabricate". The wording was deliberately and carefully chosen.

Hence Article 51 can under no circumstances afford a justification for U. S. intervention in Vietnam, since the Saigon regime is indisputably not a member of the United Nations and, indeed, under the Geneva Accords of 1954, South Vietnam is merely a temporary zone not even qualifying politically as a state (See Section II *infra*), even if it be assumed that an "armed attack", within the meaning of Article 51, has occurred against South Vietnam. For, as has been shown, Article 51 is operative only in the event of "an armed attack *against a member of the United Nations*". Hence, neither the right of *individual* self-defense nor the right of *collective* self-defense can become operative.

It has been claimed that United States intervention in Vietnam is sanctioned under Article 51 on the ground (1) that South Vietnam is an independent state; (2) that South Vietnam had been the victim of an armed attack from North Vietnam and (3) that the United States, with the consent of South Vietnam was engaging in "collective self-defense" of that country, as claimed by the United States in a communication to the United Nations Security Council in March, 1965 (U. N. Chronicle, Vol. 2, p. 22). To sustain this claim, *all* three elements must be satisfied.

This claim is untenable, however, on several grounds. First, South Vietnam was not recognized as an independent state at the 1954 Geneva Conference. Even if it had become a *de facto* state in the course of events since 1954, the infiltrations from North Vietnam cannot be deemed to constitute an "armed attack" within the purview of Article 51.

Since the Geneva Accords recognized all of Vietnam as a *single* state, the conflict whether of the Vietcong or Ho Chi Minh against South Vietnam is "civil strife" and foreign intervention is forbidden, because civil strife is a domestic question—a position insisted upon by the United States in its civil war of 1861. Ho Chi Minh can compare his position in demanding union of Vietnam with that of Lincoln, when Britain and France were threatening to intervenue to assure the independence of the Confederacy (and with the added point that the national elections mandated for 1956 in the Geneva Accords were frustrated by South Vietnam with apparent support of the United States). Nor should it be overlooked that Lincoln had very little sup-port from the people of the South, who generally supported the Confederacy, while Ho Chi Minh has a great deal of support from the people in South Vietnam organized in the National Liberation Front whose military arm is the Vietcong. There is, therefore, a basic issue whether the hostilities in Vietnam constitute external aggression (by

North Vietnam) or "civil strife". Here it should be noted that the
United Nations is authorized to intervene where civil strife threatens
international peace, as the United Nations did in the Congo, in accord
with Article 39 of the Charter—but individual states are not permitted to intervene unilaterally.

The third element requisite for the invocation of the right of *collective* self-defense under Article 51 presupposes that the nations invoking such right are properly members of a regional collective system within the purview of the United Nations Charter. The point
here involved is: Can the United States validly be a genuine member
of a regional system covering Southeast Asia. Article 51 and Article 53, dealing with regional systems, were interrelated amendatory
provisions intended primarily to integrate the inter-American system
with the United Nations organization. . . . The concept that
the United States—a country separated by oceans and thousands
of miles from Southeast Asia and bereft of any historical or ethnic
connection with the peoples of Southeast Asia—could validly be considered a member of a regional system implanted in Southeast Asia
is utterly alien to the regional systems envisaged in the Charter. The
"Southeast Asia Collective Defense Treaty"—connecting the United
States with Southeast Asia, architectured by Secretary of State Dulles,
is a legalistic artificial formulation to circumvent the fundamental
limitations placed by the United Nations Charter on unilateral actions
by individual members. However ingenious—or disingenuous—the
Dulles approach, SEATO is a caricature of the genuine regional systems envisaged by the U.N. Charter. A buffalo cannot be transformed
into a giraffe however elongated its neck may be stretched. The
Dulles approach to collective defense treaties employed legal artifice
to circumvent the exclusive authority vested in the United Nations to
deal with breaches in the peace. Articles 51 and 53 were intended to
make a bona fide integration of regional systems of cooperation with
the world system of international security—but these envisaged regional systems which historically and geographically developed into a
regional community—not contemplating a regional system which
fused a region like Southeast Asia with a country on the North American Continent. SEATO is not a regional agency within the letter or
spirit of the U. N. Charter as to authorize the United States to claim
the right of collective self-defense even if there had been an armed
attack on a member of the United Nations geographically located in
Southeast Asia. If artifices like SEATO were sanctioned, the path
would be open for the emasculation of the United Nations organization and the world system of international security assiduously developed to prevent the scourge of war.

Hence Article 51 cannot be properly invoked for (1) South Viet-
nam does not have the political status of a state; (2) even if South Viet-
nam were deemed a *de facto* state, the infiltrations do not constitute
an "armed attack" within the purview of Article 51; and (3) the Unit-

ed States cannot claim the right of "collective self-defense" in respect of a regional system involving Southeast Asia.

Apart from Article 51 (inapplicable to the situation here), the only other exception to the renunciation of the "threat or use of force" by member states is found in Chapter VIII of the Charter dealing with regional arrangements. Article 53 of said Chapter contains two paragraphs of particular significance:

(a) "The Security Council shall, where appropriate, utilize such regional arrangements or agencies for enforcement action under its authority. *But no enforcement action shall be taken* under regional arrangements or by regional agencies *without the authorization of the Security Council,* with the exception of measures against an enemy state, as defined in paragraph 2 of this Article." (Ch. VIII, Art. 53 (1)).

Paragraph two of that article provides:

(b) "The term enemy state as used in paragraph one of this Article applies to any state which during the Second World War has been an enemy of any signatory of the present Charter."

With respect to regional arrangements therefore, it is clear that no enforcement action may be undertaken without the authorization of the Security Council of the United Nations, save and except in only one instance: against any state which, during World War II, was an enemy of any signatory of the Charter, to wit, Germany, Italy and Japan. Since Vietnam was manifestly not an "enemy state" within the purview of Article 53(b), enforcement action under SEATO is unauthorized and cannot be justified in view of the express restrictions set out under Article 53(a) of the United Nations Charter.

. . .

One other noteworthy Charter provision is Article 103 which subordinates all regional and treaty compacts to the United Nations Charter.

"In the event of a conflict between the obligations of the members of the United Nations under the present Charter and their obligations under any other international agreement, *their obligations under the present Charter shall prevail.*" (Ch. XVI, Art. 103)

This Supremacy clause was drafted to meet the predictable reassertion of dominance by the great powers within their respective geographic zones or hemispheres. Because of the unhappy history of a world fragmented by such "spheres of influence", the Supremacy clause and the restrictions on the use of force under regional agreements emerge as limitations upon the super powers even within their own geographic zones. It is significant that the United States not only accepted these limitations, but actively supported their incorporation within the Charter.

Article 103 makes clear that the obligations of the United Nations Charter prevail vis-a-vis the obligations of the SEATO Treaty. Indeed, Article VI of the SEATO expressly recognizes the supremacy of the United Nations Charter. . . . Moreover the frequent citation by President Johnson of the pledges given by Presidents Eisenhower, Kennedy and himself to aid South Vietnam afford no justification for U. S. intervention in Vietnam. In the first place, these pledges or commitments do not even have the status of treaties, for these Presidential pledges have not been ratified by the Senate. And even if these Presidential pledges had been solemnly ratified by the Senate, any obligations thereunder must yield to the obligations imposed under the United Nations Charter by virtue of the Supremacy clause embodied in Article 103. Nor would the illegality of U. S. intervention in Vietnam be altered by the circumstance that the Saigon regime may have invited the United States to assume its role in the Vietnam conflict. The supremacy clause of the Charter manifestly prevails and cannot be annulled by mutual agreement of third parties. . . .

It appears difficult to escape the conclusion therefore, in the light of the aforesaid, that the action of the United States Government in Vietnam contravenes essential provisions of the United Nations Charter. The United States Government has decided for itself to use armed forces in South Vietnam and to bomb North Vietnam without authorization of the Security Council or the General Assembly of the United Nations. The failure of the United States to honor its obligations under the United Nations Charter is a regrettable but inescapable conclusion which we as lawyers have been compelled to reach. We, as lawyers, urge our President to accept the obligations for international behavior placed upon us by our signature on the United Nations Charter.

2. *Memorandum by Leonard C. Meeker, Legal Adviser, US Department of State, 4 March 1966.*

54 DSB (1966), pp. 474–89.

1. The United States and South Viet-Nam have the Right Under International Law to Participate in the Collective Defense of South Viet-Nam Against Armed Attack.

In response to requests from the Government of South Viet-Nam, the United States has been assisting that country in defending itself against armed attack from the Communist North. This attack has taken the forms of externally supported subversion, clandestine supply of arms, infiltration of armed personnel, and most recently the sending of regular units of the North Vietnamese army into the South.

International law has long recognized the right of individual and collective self-defense against armed attack. South Viet-Nam and the United States are engaging in such collective defense consistently with international law and with United States obligations under the United Nations Charter.

A. South Viet-Nam Is Being Subjected to Armed Attack by Communist North Viet-Nam.

The Geneva accords of 1954 established a demarcation line between North Viet-Nam and South Viet-Nam. They provided for withdrawals of military forces into the respective zones north and south of this line. The accords prohibited the use of either zone for the resumption of hostilities or to "further an aggressive policy."

During the 5 years following the Geneva conference of 1954, the Hanoi regime developed a covert political-military organization in South Viet-Nam based on Communist cadres it had ordered to stay in the South, contrary to the provisions of the Geneva accords. The activities of this covert organization were directed toward the kidnaping and assassination of civilian officials—acts of terrorism that were perpetrated in increasing numbers.

In the 3-year period from 1959 to 1961, the North Viet-Nam regime infiltrated an estimated 10,000 men into the South. It is estimated that 13,000 additional personnel were infiltrated in 1962, and, by the end of 1964, North Viet-Nam may well have moved over 40,000 armed and unarmed guerrillas into South Viet-Nam.

The International Control Commission reported in 1962 the findings of its Legal Committee:

".   .   .   there is evidence to show that arms, armed and unarmed personnel, munitions and other supplies have been sent from the Zone in the North to the Zone in the South with the objective of supporting, organizing and carrying out hostile activities, including armed attacks, directed against the Armed Forces and Administration of the Zone in the South.

".   .   .   there is evidence that the PAVN [People's Army of Viet-Nam] has allowed the Zone in the North to be used for inciting, encouraging and supporting hostile activities in the Zone in the South, aimed at the overthrow of the Administration in the South."

Beginning in 1964, the Communists apparently exhausted their reservoir of Southerners who had gone North. Since then the greater number of men infiltrated into the South have been native-born North Vietnamese. Most recently, Hanoi has begun to infiltrate elements of the North Vietnamese army in increasingly larger numbers. Today, there is evidence that nine regiments of regular North Vietnamese forces are fighting in organized units in the South.

In the guerrilla war in Viet-Nam the external aggression from the North is the critical military element of the insurgency, although it is unacknowledged by North Viet-Nam. In these circumstances, an "armed attack" is not as easily fixed by date and hour as in the case of traditional warfare. However, the infiltration of thousands of armed men clearly constitutes an "armed attack" under any reasonable definition. There may be some question as to the exact date at which North Viet-Nam's aggression grew into an "armed attack," but there can be no doubt that it had occurred before February 1965.

B. International Law Recognizes the Right of Individual and Collective Self-Defense Against Armed Attack.

International law has traditionally recognized the right of self-defense against armed attack. This proposition has been asserted by writers on international law through the several centuries in which the modern law of nations has developed. The proposition has been acted on numerous times by governments throughout modern history. Today the principle of self-defense against armed attack is universally recognized and accepted.

The Charter of the United Nations, concluded at the end of World War II, imposed an important limitation on the use of force by United Nations members. Article 2, paragraph 4, provides:

"All Members shall refrain in their international relations from the threat or use of force against the territorial integrity or political independence of any state, or in any other manner inconsistent with the Purposes of the United Nations."

In addition, the charter embodied a system of international peace-keeping through the organs of the United Nations. Article 24 summarizes these structural arrangements in stating that the United Nations members:

". . . confer on the Security Council primary responsibility for the maintenance of international peace and security, and agree that in carrying out its duties under this responsibility the Security Council acts on their behalf."

However, the charter expressly states in article 51 that the remaining provisions of the charter—including the limitation of article 2, paragraph 4, and the creation of United Nations machinery to keep the peace—in no way diminish the inherent right of self-defense against armed attack. . . . Thus, article 51 restates and preserves, for member states in the situations covered by the article, a long-recognized principle of international law. The article is a "saving clause" designed to make clear that no other provision in the charter shall be interpreted to impair the inherent right of self-defense referred to in article 51.

Three principal objections have been raised against the availability of the right of individual and collective self-defense in the case of Viet-Nam: (1) that this right applies only in the case of an armed attack on a United Nations member; (2) that it does not apply in the case of South Viet-Nam because the latter is not an independent sovereign state; and (3) that collective self-defense may be undertaken only by a regional organization operating under chapter VIII of the

United Nations Charter. These objections will now be considered in turn.

C. *The Right of Individual and Collective Self-Defense Applies in the Case of South Viet-Nam Whether or Not That Country is a Member of the United Nations.*

1. *South Viet-Nam enjoys the right of self-defense.*

The argument that the right of self-defense is available only to members of the United Nations mistakes the nature of the right of self-defense and the relationship of the United Nations Charter to international law in this respect. As already shown, the right of self-defense against armed attack is an inherent right under international law. The right is not conferred by the charter, and, indeed, article 51 expressly recognizes that the right is inherent.

The charter nowhere contains any provision designed to deprive nonmembers of the right of self-defense against armed attack.* Article 2, paragraph 6, does charge the United Nations with responsibility for insuring that nonmember states act in accordance with United Nations "Principles so far as may be necessary for the maintenance of international peace and security." Protection against aggression and self-defense against armed attack are important elements in the whole charter scheme for the maintenance of international peace and security. To deprive nonmembers of their inherent right of self-defense would not accord with the principles of the organization, but would instead be prejudicial to the maintenance of peace. Thus article 2, paragraph 6—and, indeed, the rest of the charter—should certainly not be construed to nullify or diminish the inherent defensive rights of nonmembers.

2. *The United States has the right to assist in the defense of South Viet-Nam although the latter is not a United Nations member.*

The cooperation of two or more international entities in the defense of one or both against armed attack is generally referred to as collective self-defense. United States participation in the defense of South Viet-Nam at the latter's request is an example of collective self-defense.

---

* While nonmembers, such as South Viet-Nam, have not formally undertaken the obligations of the United Nations Charter as their own treaty obligations, it should be recognized that much of the substantive law of the charter has become part of the general law of nations through a very wide acceptance by nations the world over. This is particularly true of the charter provisions bearing on the use of force. Moreover, in the case of South Viet-Nam, the South Vietnamese Government has expressed its ability and willingness to abide by the charter, in applying for United Nations membership. Thus it seems entirely appropriate to appraise the actions of South Viet-Nam in relation to the legal standards set forth in the United Nations Charter.

The United States is entitled to exercise the right of individual or collective self-defense against armed attack, as that right exists in international law, subject only to treaty limitations and obligations undertaken by this country.

It has been urged that the United States has no right to participate in the collective defense of South Viet-Nam because article 51 of the United Nations Charter speaks only of the situation "if an armed attack occurs *against a Member of the United Nations.*" This argument is without substance.

In the first place, article 51 does not impose restrictions or cut down the otherwise available rights of United Nations members. By its own terms, the article preserves an inherent right. It is, therefore, necessary to look elsewhere in the charter for any obligation of members restricting their participation in collective defense of an entity that is not a United Nations member.

Article 2, paragraph 4, is the principal provision of the charter imposing limitations on the use of force by members. It states that they:

" . . . shall refrain in their international relations from the threat or use of force against the territorial integrity or political independence of any state, or in any other manner inconsistent with the Purposes of the United Nations."

Action taken in defense against armed attack cannot be characterized as falling within this proscription. The record of the San Francisco conference makes clear that article 2, paragraph 4, was not intended to restrict the right of self-defense against armed attack.

One will search in vain for any other provision in the charter that would preclude United States participation in the collective defense of a nonmember. The fact that article 51 refers only to armed attack "against a Member of the United Nations" implies no intention to preclude members from participating in the defense of nonmembers. Any such result would have seriously detrimental consequences for international peace and security and would be inconsistent with the purposes of the United Nations as they are set forth in article 1 of the charter. The right of members to participate in the defense of nonmembers is upheld by leading authorities on international law.

D.   The Right of Individual and Collective Self-Defense Applies Whether or Not South Viet-Nam Is Regarded as an Independent Sovereign State.

1.   South Viet-Nam enjoys the right of self-defense.

It has been asserted that the conflict in Viet-Nam is "civil strife" in which foreign intervention is forbidden. Those who make this assertion have gone so far as to compare Ho Chi Minh's actions in Viet-Nam with the efforts of President Lincoln to preserve the Union during the American Civil War. Any such characterization is an entire fiction disregarding the actual situation in Viet-Nam. The Hanoi regime is anything but the legitimate government of a unified country in which the South is rebelling against lawful national authority.

The Geneva accords of 1954 provided for a division of Viet-Nam into two zones at the 17th parallel. Although this line of demarcation was intended to be temporary, it was established by international agreement, which specifically forbade aggression by one zone against the other.

The Republic of Viet-Nam in the South has been recognized as a separate international entity by approximately 60 governments the world over. It has been admitted as a member of a number of the specialized agencies of the United Nations. The United Nations General Assembly in 1957 voted to recommend South Viet-Nam for membership in the organization, and its admission was frustrated only by the veto of the Soviet Union in the Security Council.

In any event there is no warrant for the suggestion that one zone of a temporarily divided state—whether it be Germany, Korea, or Viet-Nam—can be legally overrun by armed forces from the other zone, crossing the internationally recognized line of demarcation between the two. Any such doctrine would subvert the international agreement establishing the line of demarcation, and would pose grave dangers to international peace.

The action of the United Nations in the Korean conflict of 1950 clearly established the principle that there is no greater license for one zone of a temporarily divided state to attack the other zone than there is for one state to attack another state. South Viet-Nam has the same right that South Korea had to defend itself and to organize collective defense against an armed attack from the North. A resolution of the Security Council dated June 25, 1950, noted "with grave concern the armed attack upon the Republic of Korea by forces from North Korea," and determined "that this action constitutes a breach of the peace."

2. *The United States is entitled to participate in the collective defense of South Viet-Nam whether or not the latter is regarded as an independent sovereign state.*

As stated earlier, South Viet-Nam has been recognized as a separate international entity by approximately 60 governments. It has been admitted to membership in a number of the United Nations specialized agencies and has been excluded from the United Nations Organization only by the Soviet veto.

There is nothing in the charter to suggest that United Nations members are precluded from participating in the defense of a recognized international entity against armed attack merely because the entity may lack some of the attributes of an independent sovereign state. Any such result would have a destructive effect on the stability of international engagements such as the Geneva accords of 1954 and on internationally agreed lines of demarcation. Such a result, far from being in accord with the charter and the purposes of the United Nations, would undermine them and would create new dangers to international peace and security.

E.   The United Nations Charter Does Not Limit the Right of Self-Defense to Regional Organizations.

Some have argued that collective self-defense may be undertaken only by a regional arrangement or agency operating under chapter VIII of the United Nations Charter. Such an assertion ignores the structure of the charter and the practice followed in the more than 20 years since the founding of the United Nations.

The basic proposition that rights of self-defense are not impaired by the charter—as expressly stated in article 51—is not conditioned by any charter provision limiting the application of this proposition to collective defense by a regional arrangement or agency. The structure of the charter reinforces this conclusion. Article 51 appears in chapter VII of the charter, entitled "Action With Respect to Threats to the Peace, Breaches of the Peace, and Acts of Aggression," whereas chapter VIII, entitled "Regional Arrangements," begins with article 52 and embraces the two following articles. The records of the San Francisco conference show that article 51 was deliberately placed in chapter VII rather than chapter VIII, "where it would only have a bearing on the regional system."

Under article 51, the right of self-defense is available against any armed attack, whether or not the country attacked is a member of a regional arrangement and regardless of the source of the attack. Chapter VIII, on the other hand, deals with relations among members of a regional arrangement or agency, and authorizes regional action as appropriate for dealing with "local disputes." This distinction has been recognized ever since the founding of the United Nations in 1945.

For example, the North Atlantic Treaty has operated as a collective security arrangement, designed to take common measures in preparation against the eventuality of an armed attack for which collective defense under article 51 would be required. Similarly, the Southeast Asia Treaty Organization was designed as a collective defense arrangement under article 51. Secretary of State Dulles emphasized this in his testimony before the Senate Foreign Relations Committee in 1954.

By contrast, article 1 of the Charter of Bogotá (1948), establishing the Organization of American States, expressly declares that the organization is a regional agency within the United Nations. Indeed, chapter VIII of the United Nations Charter was included primarily to take account of the functioning of the inter-American system.

In sum, there is no basis in the United Nations Charter for contending that the right of self-defense against armed attack is limited to collective defense by a regional organization.

F. The United States Has Fulfilled Its Obligations to the United Nations.

A further argument has been made that the members of the United Nations have conferred on United Nations organs—and, in particular, on the Security Council—exclusive power to act against aggression. Again the express language of article 51 contradicts that assertion. A victim of armed attack is not required to forgo individual or collective defense of its territory until such time as the United Nations organizes collective action and takes appropriate measures. To the contrary, article 51 clearly states that the right of self-defense may be exercised *"until* the Security Council has taken the measures necessary to maintain international peace and security."

As indicated earlier, article 51 is not literally applicable to the Viet-Nam situation since South Viet-Nam is not a member. However, reasoning by analogy from article 51 and adopting its provisions as an appropriate guide for the conduct of members in a case like Viet-Nam, one can only conclude that United States actions are fully in accord with this country's obligations as a member of the United Nations.

Article 51 requires that: "Measures taken by Members in the exercise of this right of self-defense shall be immediately reported to the Security Council and shall not in any way affect the authority and responsibility of the Security Council under the present Charter to take at any time such action as it deems necessary in order to maintain or restore international peace and security."

The United States has reported to the Security Council on measures it has taken in countering the Communist aggression in Viet-Nam. In August 1964 the United States asked the Council to consider the situation created by North Vietnamese attacks on United States destroyers in the Tonkin Gulf. The Council thereafter met to debate the question, but adopted no resolutions. Twice in February 1965 the United States sent additional reports to the Security Council on the conflict in Viet-Nam and on the additional measures taken by the United States in the collective defense of South Viet-Nam. In January 1966 the United States formally submitted the Viet-Nam question to the Security Council for its consideration and introduced a draft resolution calling for discussions looking toward a peaceful settlement on the basis of the Geneva accords.

At no time has the Council taken any action to restore peace and security in Southeast Asia. The Council has not expressed criticism of United States actions. Indeed, since the United States submission of January 1966, members of the Council have been notably reluctant to proceed with any consideration of the Viet-Nam question.

The conclusion is clear that the United States has in no way acted to interfere with United Nations consideration of the conflict in Viet-Nam. On the contrary, the United States has requested United Nations consideration, and the Council has not seen fit to act. . . .

III.   Actions by the United States and South Viet-Nam Are Justi-fied Under the Geneva Accords of 1954. . . .

B.   North Viet-Nam Violated the Accords From the Beginning.

From the very beginning, the North Vietnamese violated the 1954 Geneva accords. Communist military forces and supplies were left in the South in violation of the accords. Other Communist guerrillas were moved north for further training and then were infiltrated into the South in violation of the accords.

C.   The Introduction of United States Military Personnel and Equipment Was Justified.

The accords prohibited the reinforcement of foreign military forces in Viet-Nam and the introduction of new military equipment, but they allowed replacement of existing military personnel and equipment. Prior to late 1961 South Viet-Nam had received considerable military equipment and supplies from the United States, and the United States had gradually enlarged its Military Assistance Advisory Group to slightly less than 900 men. These actions were reported to the ICC and were justified as replacements for equipment in Viet-Nam in 1954 and for French training and advisory personnel who had been with-drawn after 1954.

As the Communist aggression intensified during 1961, with in-creased infiltration and a marked stepping up of Communist terrorism in the South, the United States found it necessary in late 1961 to in-crease substantially the numbers of our military personnel and the amounts and types of equipment introduced by this country into South Viet-Nam. These increases were justified by the international law principle that a material breach of an agreement by one party entitles the other at least to withhold compliance with an equivalent, cor-responding, or related provision until the defaulting party is prepared to honor its obligations.

In accordance with this principle, the systematic violation of the Geneva accords by North Viet-Nam justified South Viet-Nam in sus-pending compliance with the provision controlling entry of foreign military personnel and military equipment.

D.   South Viet-Nam Was Justified in Refusing To Implement the Election Provisions of the Geneva Accords.

The Geneva accords contemplated the reunification of the two parts of Viet-Nam. They contained a provision for general elections to be held in July 1956 in order to obtain a "free expression of the national will." The accords stated that "consultations will be held on this sub-ject between the competent representative authorities of the two zones from 20 July 1955 onwards."

There may be some question whether South Viet-Nam was bound by these election provisions. . . . South Viet-Nam did not sign the cease-fire agreement of 1954, nor did it adhere to the Final Declaration of the Geneva conference. The South Vietnamese Government at that time gave notice of its objection in particular to the election provisions of the accords.

However, even on the premise that these provisions were binding on South Viet-Nam, the South Vietnamese Government's failure to engage in consultations in 1955, with a view to holding elections in 1956, involved no breach of obligation. The conditions in North Viet-Nam during that period were such as to make impossible any free and meaningful expression of popular will.

Some of the facts about conditions in the North were admitted even by the Communist leadership in Hanoi. General Giap, currently Defense Minister of North Viet-Nam, in addressing the Tenth Congress of the North Vietnamese Communist Party in October 1956, publicly acknowledged that the Communist leaders were running a police state where executions, terror, and torture were commonplace. A nation-wide election in these circumstances would have been a travesty. No one in the North would have dared to vote except as directed. With a substantial majority of the Vietnamese people living north of the 17th parallel, such an election would have meant turning the country over to the Communists without regard to the will of the people. The South Vietnamese Government realized these facts and quite properly took the position that consultations for elections in 1956 as contemplated by the accords would be a useless formality. . . .

V. Conclusion.

South Viet-Nam is being subjected to armed attack by Communist North Viet-Nam, through the infiltration of armed personnel, military equipment, and regular combat units. International law recognizes the right of individual and collective self-defense against armed attack. South Viet-Nam, and the United States upon the request of South Viet-Nam, are engaged in such collective defense of the South. Their actions are in conformity with international law and with the Charter of the United Nations. The fact that South Viet-Nam has been precluded by Soviet veto from becoming a member of the United Nations and the fact that South Viet-Nam is a zone of a temporarily divided state in no way diminish the right of collective defense of South Viet-Nam.

The United States has commitments to assist South Viet-Nam in defending itself against Communist aggression from the North. The United States gave undertakings to this effect at the conclusion of the Geneva conference in 1954. Later that year the United States undertook an international obligation in the SEATO treaty to defend South Viet-Nam against Communist armed aggression. And during the past decade the United States has given additional assurances to the South Vietnamese Government.

The Geneva accords of 1954 provided for a cease-fire and regroupment of contending forces, a division of Viet-Nam into two zones, and a prohibition on the use of either zone for the resumption of hostilities or to "further an aggressive policy." From the beginning, North Viet-Nam violated the Geneva accords through a systematic effort to gain control of South Viet-Nam by force. In the light of these progressive North Vietnamese violations, the introduction into South Viet-Nam beginning in late 1961 of substantial United States military equipment and personnel, to assist in the defense of the South, was fully justified; substantial breach of an international agreement by one side permits the other side to suspend performance of corresponding obligations under the agreement. South Viet-Nam was justified in refusing to implement the provisions of the Geneva accords calling for reunification through free elections throughout Viet-Nam since the Communist regime in North Viet-Nam created conditions in the North that made free elections entirely impossible.

5.   *Lawyers Committee Reply to the State Department,*
11 October 1966.

112 Congressional Record (1966), pp. A5801–4.

Examination of the State Department Memorandum of Law ("Department Brief") shows that it is based on untenable arguments. It contains misleading presentations of fact and unconvincing interpretations of law. Some of the major inadequacies of the United States' official legal position are set out below. At stake are not "legalisms" but the norms of behavior essential for world order in our time.

I.   *The Unilateral Military Intervention of the United States in Vietnam Violates the Charter of the United Nations. The Charter's Exceptional Authorization of Individual and Collective Self-Defense "if an Armed Attack Occurs Against a Member of the United Nations" Does Not Apply in the Case of Vietnam.*

The Charter of the United Nations is a treaty that specifically obligates the United States (1) to refrain from the unilateral use or threat of force in international relations (Article 2(4)) and (2) to settle international disputes by peaceful means.

The Charter creates a very narrow exception to the broad prohibition of unilateral force. This exception (Article 51) affirms the "inherent right of individual or collective self-defense if an *armed attack* occurs against a *Member of the United Nations*. . . ."

The Department Brief seizes upon the word "inherent" to argue that prior to the adoption of the United Nations Charter, states possessed a broad right of self-defense; that this right is not diminished by Article 51. Hence, it argues, the exercise of this right of "collective self-defense" by the United States on behalf of South Vietnam is not inconsistent with the Charter.

This contention is fallacious for several reasons:

1.   There Has Been No "Armed Attack" Upon South Vietnam With-in the Meaning of Article 51 of the Charter.

The question crucial for world order is—What kind of grievance permits a state to act in "self-defense"?

The right of self-defense under the Charter exists only if an "armed attack" has occurred. The language of Article 51 is unequivocal. The concrete term "armed attack" was deliberately introduced into the Charter to eliminate the discretion of states to determine for themselves the scope of permissible self-defense—that is, to wage war without *prior* U.N. authorization. A claim for self-defense is permissible only "when the necessity for action is instant, overwhelming, and leaving no choice of means, and no moment for deliberation." This definition of self-defense was stated in classic form by Secretary of State Daniel Webster in the *Caroline Case*, (VII Moore's Digest of International Law, 919) and was affirmed in the Nuremburg judgment, and by unanimous vote of the U.N. General Assembly at its First Session. Res. 95 (I).

The State Department Memorandum acknowledges that a *specific* form of aggression, namely, an *"armed attack"* is an essential condition precedent to the use of force in self-defense, and that a mere allegation of indirect aggression does not entitle a state to wage war by unilateral discretion. However, the Memorandum blurs the essential distinction between the broad and vague *general* concept of aggression and the narrow one of armed attack. Evidently endeavoring to justify the U.S.'s open combat actions against North Vietnam and in South Vietnam which started on February 7, 1965, the State Department merely alleges the occurrence of an armed attack by North Vietnam "before February 1965", without providing a convincing demonstration of why its allegations about the gradual infiltration of North Vietnamese guerrillas over a period of ten years in support of the Vietcong insurgency should be regarded as an armed attack.

The Department Brief quotes selectively from the reports of the International Control Commission to support its claims of subversion and infiltration over the "years." It fails, however, to acknowledge passages in the reports of the ICC that criticize the forbidden, and progressively increasing, military build-up of South Vietnam by the United States that commenced almost immediately after the Geneva Accords of 1954. It is in the context of this gradually increasing American military build-up of South Vietnam and American military presence in South Vietnam that one must assess the contention that the infiltration of 40,000 North Vietnamese between 1954 and 1965 should be viewed as an armed attack.

The Department Brief itself provides the reasoning with which to reject its charge of "armed attack" by North Vietnam. The long-smoldering conditions of unrest, subversion and infiltration in South

Vietnam that it describes is an example of the very opposite of an emergency demanding immediate response "leaving no choice of means, and no moment for deliberation" and justifying a claim of self-defense.   The State Department's argument, if accepted, would broaden Article 51 far beyond either its intended or desirable meaning.   Whereas the Charter limits the use of force by unilateral decision to specific emergencies where there is no time to seek authorization from the Security Council, the State Department's doctrine would grant all states—and even "entities" which are not sovereign states—a dangerous and virtually unlimited discretion to decide when force shall be used.   This is in clear contrast to the letter and spirit of the Charter.

The Department Brief does not even sustain its charge of indirect aggression.   It indicates that prior to 1964 the "infiltrators" were South Vietnamese that had previously moved North after July 1954. Moreover, the lumping together of "40,000 armed and unarmed guerillas" is not meaningful.   How can an unarmed Vietnamese who moves from one zone of his own country to another be classified as a "guerilla" and "infiltrator", contributing to "armed attack"?   Above all, the implication that by 1964 the Southern insurgents had been reinforced by 40,000 guerillas from the North is altogether misleading; for this figure, even if correct, fails to deduct all those who during a whole decade died, became incapacitated, were taken prisoners, deserted, or simply withdrew from or never participated in the insurgency.

The Mansfield Report shows that before 1965 infiltration from the North "was confined primarily to political cadres and military leadership."   On the other hand it notes that by 1962, "United States military advisors and service forces in South Vietnam totalled approximately 10,000 men."   The Report makes plain that significant armed personnel were introduced from the North only *after* the United States had intervened when "total collapse of the Saigon government's authority appeared imminent in the early months of 1965."   It states (at p. 1):

"United States combat troops in strength arrived at that point in response to the appeal of the Saigon authorities.   The Vietcong *counter-response* was to increase their military activity with forces strengthened by intensified *local* recruitment and infiltration of regular North Vietnamese troops.   With the change in the composition of the opposing forces the character of the war also changed sharply."

The Report (p. 3) underscores that significant forces from the North followed and did not precede the direct involvement of the United States.

To summarize this crucial point—self-defense is legally permissible only in response to a particularly grave, immediate emergency—described in international law and the Charter as "armed attack."   The kind of force allegedly employed by North Vietnam in South Vietnam cannot appropriately be regarded as an "armed attack" within the meaning of Article 51. Therefore a claim to act in self-defense is un-available to South Vietnam; and, *a fortiori,* unavailable to the United States as an ally acting in collective self-defense.

2.　The United States Failed to Fulfill its Charter Obligation to Seek a Peaceful Solution in Vietnam.

The State Department also ignores the obligation under the Charter to seek *first of all* a peaceful solution by any method of the disputants' own choice, within or outside the machinery of the United Nations. This legal requirement is elaborated in Article 33(1):

"The parties to any dispute, the continuance of which is likely to endanger the maintenance of international peace and security, shall *first of all,* seek a solution by negotiation, enquiry, mediation, concilia-tion, arbitration, judicial settlement, resort to regional agencies or arrangements, or other peaceful means of their own choice."

The United States has had many years within which to seek a peaceful solution of the Vietnam situation. Indeed, a report prepared for the American Friends Service Committee—"Peace in Vietnam"—discussing "The Negotiation Puzzle", points out that "a careful reading of the *New York Times* shows that the United States has rejected no fewer than seven efforts to negotiate an end to the war" (p. 51), citing efforts by U Thant, President de Gaulle, Hanoi and others, made long before the United States embarked upon an active combat role in Feb-ruary 1965.

Ever since the mid-1950's the reports of the International Control Commission contain many complaints about South Vietnam's de-liberate and systematic sabotage of the machinery created by the Geneva Accords to prevent dangerous developments. The United States has done little to dispel the belief that it has favored a "military solution" to the conflict in Vietnam.

3.　The Doctrine of "Collective Self-Defense" Cannot Justify the United States Military Intervention in the Civil War in South Viet-nam.

If the conflict in South Vietnam is a civil war the intervention of the United States is a violation of the undertaking, fundamental in inter-national law, that one state has no right to intervene in the internal affairs of other countries.

It seems most correct to regard the present conflict in South Viet-nam as essentially a civil war among, what James Reston has described a "tangle of competing individuals, regions, religions and sects . . . [among] a people who have been torn apart by war and dominated and exploited by Saigon for generations." (*New York Times,* April 3, 1966.)

The Charter of the United Nations is silent on the subject of civil war. It has been generally assumed, however, that a civil war is a matter essentially within the domestic jurisdiction of a state (Article

2(7)), and that therefore even the United Nations is obliged to refrain from intervening unless the civil war is identified by a competent organ of the U.N. as a threat to international peace. Certainly if the United Nations must stay aloof from civil wars, then it is even clearer that individual states are likewise obliged to refrain from interfering in civil wars. The weight of opinion among international lawyers lays stress upon a duty of non-intervention in ongoing civil wars.

Even if North Vietnam and South Vietnam are accorded the status of separate entities in international law, approximating the status of independent countries, rather than being "temporary zones" of a single country as decreed by the Geneva Accords, the United States may not respond to the intervention of North Vietnam in the civil war in the South by bombing the North. There is no legal basis for an outside state to respond to an intervention by another state in a civil war with a military attack on the territory of the intervening state. Neither Germany under Hitler nor Italy under Mussolini claimed that their intervention in behalf of Franco during the Spanish Civil War would have vindicated their use of military force upon the territory of the Soviet Union, a state intervening in behalf of the Loyalists. Correspondingly, the Soviet Union, intervening in behalf of Spain's legitimate government, did not claim any right to use military force against Germany or Italy. It is sobering to realize that if the United States was lawfully entitled to bomb North Vietnam in response to North Vietnam's intervention in the Southern civil war, then North Vietnam or any of its allies would have been lawfully entitled to bomb the United States in response to the United States' much more massive intervention in that civil war.

4. The "Request" of the "Government" of South Vietnam Does Not Provide a Legal Basis for "Collective Self-Defense."

The evidence shows that in many respects the present Saigon regime, just as its predecessors since 1954, is a client government of the United States. These governments seem to have been incapable of independent action, as regards either inviting American assistance or requesting modification or termination of American assistance. Furthermore, these regimes have been unable to act on behalf of their people or even to rule effectively the territory under their control.

The present government has no constitutional basis, and is incapable even of achieving stability on its own side in the face of the emergency represented by the ongoing civil war, a factor that normally postpones protest movement until the civil war is settled. The recurring protests of Buddhists, Catholics, business leaders, students, intellectuals, and other civilian groups in South Vietnam are dramatic evidence of the tenuous existence and the repressive quality of Premier Ky's regime.

If the United States were to withdraw from South Vietnam the Ky government would collapse. In what sense, then, is such a regime sufficiently constituted as a government to authorize military intervention of the United States on its own behalf? It is hardly comforting to rely upon the Soviet suppression of the Nagy uprising of 1956 in Hungary as a useful precedent to support what the United States is doing in Vietnam on a far larger and sustained scale.

5. The Korean Precedent Does Not Justify the Unilateral Intervention of the United States in Vietnam

The State Department's reliance upon the Korean precedent to sustain "the right to organize collective defense," is inadequate to establish a legal basis for the unilateral U. S. military intervention in Vietnam. General Ridgeway, among others, has pointed to some of the important differences between Korea and Vietnam (*Look Magazine,* April 5, 1966, p. 82): "In South Korea, we had a workable government . . . We acted in concert with many nations and had been *deputized by the United Nations* to repel the aggressor in its name."

In Korea, a massive invasion (armed attack) from the North had occurred, as attested to by United Nations observers; nevertheless, the United States did not claim a right of "collective self-defense" on behalf of the South, but brought the case before the United Nations Security Council, and thereafter acted in the name of the United Nations.

II. The Military Presence of the United States in Vietnam Violates the Geneva Accords of 1954.

The State Department claims that the U. S. military intervention in Vietnam is compatible with the Geneva Accords of 1954 and, in fact, is based on U. S. assurances made at the time of their signing.

The Geneva Conference dealt with the situation created by the defeat of the French in their 8-year war against the Viet Minh for control over the whole of Vietnam. After the battle at Dien Bien Phu in June 1954, the Viet Minh occupied the major part of the country north of the thirteenth parallel. However, Ho Chi Minh agreed to withdraw his forces to the north of the seventeenth parallel in exchange for two central commitments: (1) the unconditional promise that all foreign military forces in Vietnam would be removed, and (2) that within two years elections would be held under international supervision to unify the country, so that the temporary division of Vietnam into a northern and southern zone would end by July 1956.

The United States pledged on July 21, 1954 not "to disturb" the Geneva Accords. Article 6 of the Final Declaration of the Geneva Conference explicitly stated that "the military demarcation line is provisional and shall not in any way be interpreted as constituting a political or territorial boundary."

It is generally acknowledged that Hanoi initially carried out the central provisions of the Accords and eschewed violence south of the seventeenth parallel because it expected to win the elections and did not wish to alienate those whose electoral support it sought. (See, e.

g., Fourth Interim Report of the International Control Commission, Vietnam No. 3, Command Paper 9654 [1954]). Nevertheless, on July 16, 1955, the Diem regime, with United States backing, announced that it would not participate in the prescribed nation-wide elections and would not even negotiate with Hanoi, as also prescribed in the Accords, about their modalities. The fact that the Accords granted Diem a full year (July 1955–July 1956) to demand any safeguards for fair elections refutes the State Department's assertion that Diem's obstruction of the central provision of the Geneva Settlement—reunification —was justified because the elections would not have been fair in the North.

As late as September 18, 1961, the International Control Commission (ICC) insisted upon compliance with the obligation to hold elections for reunification. In a Special Report of June 2, 1962, the ICC declared that the United States "increased military aid" to South Vietnam and that the United States' "factual military alliance" with South Vietnam violated the Geneva Agreement.

NOTE. While certain peripheral problems relating to Viet-Nam, such as the border incidents on the Cambodian frontier in 1964, and the Tonkin Bay incident in the same year, were considered from time to time by the United Nations, the constantly escalating hostilities were brought to the official attention of the United Nations only on 31 January 1966, when Ambassador Goldberg (USA) requested an urgent meeting of the Security Council "to consider the situation in Vietnam" (Document 4, below).

4. *Letter from Ambassador Goldberg, the US Representative to the United Nations, to the President of the Security Council, 31 January 1966.*

54 DSB (1966), pp. 229–31.

As you know, the United States Government has, time and time again, patiently and tirelessly sought a peaceful settlement of this conflict on the basis of unconditional negotiations and the Geneva Accords of 1954. We have done so both inside and outside the United Nations. . . .

As you are also aware, because my Government was advised by many others that a pause in the bombing of North Vietnam might contribute to the acceptance by its Government of our offer of unconditional negotiations, we did suspend bombing on December 24 and continued that suspension for some thirty-seven days. At the same time, President Johnson dispatched several high-ranking representatives to explain to His Holiness The Pope and to the Chiefs of State or Heads of Government of a number of states our most earnest desire to end the conflict peacefully and promptly. Our views were set forth in fourteen points which were communicated to a very large number of governments and later published and which were summarized in the third paragraph of my letter of January 4, 1966, to the Secretary General.

I should like to repeat that summary to you as follows:

"That the United States is prepared for discussion or negotiations without any prior conditions whatsoever or on the basis of the Geneva Accords of 1954 and 1962, that a reciprocal reduction of hostilities could be envisaged and that a cease-fire might be the first order of business in any discussions or negotiations, that the United States remains prepared to withdraw its forces from South Vietnam as soon as South Vietnam is in a position to determine its own future without external interference, that the United States desires no continuing military presence or bases in Vietnam, that the future political structure in South Vietnam should be determined by the South Vietnamese people themselves through democratic processes, and that the question of the reunification of the two Vietnams should be decided by the free decision of their two peoples."

Subsequently, the President in his State of the Union Address on January 12 reiterated once again our willingness to consider at a conference or in other negotiations any proposals which might be put forward by others. I am authorized to inform the Council that these United States views were transmitted both directly and indirectly to the Government of North Vietnam and were received by that Government.

Unhappily, there has been no affirmative response whatsoever from Hanoi to our efforts to bring the conflict to the negotiating table, to which so many governments lent their sympathy and assistance. Instead, there have been from Hanoi, and of course from Peking as well, merely the familiar charges that our peace offensive, despite the prolonged bombing pause, was merely a "fraud" and a "swindle" deserving no serious consideration. The most recent response seemed to be that set forth in President Ho Chi Minh's letter to certain Heads of State which was broadcast from Hanoi on January 28. In this letter President Ho Chi Minh made quite clear his unwillingness at this time to proceed with unconditional negotiations; on the contrary, he insisted on a number of preconditions which would in effect require the United States to accept Hanoi's solution before negotiations had even begun. This is obviously unacceptable.

Therefore, Mr. President, my Government has concluded that it should now bring this problem with all its implications for peace formally before the Security Council. We are mindful of the discussions over the past months among the members of the Council as to whether a formal meeting could usefully be held in the context of other efforts then in train. We are also aware that it may not be easy for the Council itself, in view of all the obstacles, to take constructive action on this question. We are firmly convinced, however, that in light of its obligations under the Charter to maintain international peace and security and the failure so far of all efforts outside the United Nations to restore peace, the Council should address itself urgently and positively to this situation and exert its most vigorous endeavors and its immense prestige to finding a prompt solution to it.

We hope that the members of the Security Council will agree that our common dedication to peace and our common responsibility for the future of mankind require no less. In this connection, we are mindful of the renewed appeal of His Holiness The Pope only two days ago in which he suggested that "an arbitration of the United Nations confided to neutral nations might tomorrow—we would like to hope even today—resolve this terrible question."

NOTE. On the same day the United States submitted a draft resolution proposing that the Security Council should "call for immediate discussions, without pre-conditions, among the interested Governments to arrange a conference looking towards the application of the Geneva accords of 1954 and 1962 and the establishment of a durable peace in South-East Asia; recommend that the first order of business of such a conference should be arrangements for a cessation of hostilities under effective supervision; offer to assist in achieving the purposes of the resolution by all appropriate means, including the provision of arbitrators or mediators; call on all concerned to co-operate fully in the implementation of the resolution; and request the Secretary-General to assist as appropriate in the implementation of the resolution." S/7106 (31 Jan. 1966).

5. Discussion in the Security Council, 1–2 February 1966.

Summary from the Annual Report of the Secretary-General on the Work of the Organization, 1965–1966 [GAOR, XXI, Supp. 1 (A/6301)], pp. 40–42.

Opening the discussion, the representative of the United States declared that his Government's recourse to the Council signalled not the end of the peace offensive in which it had been engaged, but a new dimension. Despite all the efforts made by the United States and others to bring about negotiations, neither Hanoi nor Peking had shown any sign that they desired to move the problem to the conference table. Nevertheless the United States had suspended the bombing of North Viet-Nam on 24 December 1965.

The purpose of that suspension, which had lasted thirty-seven days, had been to ascertain whether the bombing was in fact a decisive barrier to negotiations and whether Hanoi also desired to reduce the range of armed conflict and to bring about a peaceful settlement.

During the suspension, the United States Government had consulted with more than 115 Governments and had explained its objectives to Hanoi. Unfortunately, its restraint and patience had gone unrewarded. Infiltrations of men and material from the North to the South had gone on; acts of violence in South Viet-Nam had continued at the same rhythm as before.

Finally, on 29 January Hanoi had made public a letter addressed by President Ho Chi Minh to certain Heads of State or Government. That communication laid down three pre-conditions for negotiations: first, that the United States must accept the four-point stand of the Democratic Republic of Viet-Nam; secondly, that the United States must end unconditionally and for good all bombing raids and other acts of war against the Democratic Republic of Viet-Nam; and thirdly, that the United States must recognize the National Front for the Liberation of South Viet-Nam as the sole genuine representative of the people of South Viet-Nam.

In exchange for those demands, President Ho Chi Minh had offered nothing. He rejected flatly the two objectives which the United States had sought to achieve by the prolonged suspension of its bombings and in so doing assumed full responsibility for the United States decision that the suspension of bombing could not be continued beyond thirty-seven days. But the United States wanted to go on seeking a forum and a formula which would permit the beginning of negotiations. Its views on the elements of such a formula had already been stated in the letter sent on 4 January 1966 to the Secretary-General and President Johnson had said on 12 January 1966 that the United States would meet at any conference table, discuss any proposals and consider the views of any group. The United States had finally brought the Viet-Nam situation before the Council because that principal organ of the United Nations for the maintenance of international peace had not yet had the formal opportunity to ascertain whether it could find a new formula which would succeed where others had failed.

The United States would, of course, welcome the reconvening of the Geneva Conference, but it should be noted that a specific request made by the Government of the United Kingdom, one of the co-chairmen of the Conference, to the Government of the Soviet Union, the other co-chairman, had been turned down by the latter. The door to Geneva being momentarily closed, the question was whether the door to the United Nations should also be closed. If it was so decided, what would the people of the world say?

The United States rejected completely the Soviet contention that it had violated the Geneva Agreements. In fact, the International Commission for Supervision and Control in Viet-Nam had stated in its special report of 2 June 1962 to the co-chairmen of the Geneva Conference that it had come to the conclusion that, in specific instances, there was evidence to show that armed and unarmed personnel, arms, munitions and other supplies had been sent from the North to the South, and that the zone in the North had been used for inciting and supporting activities in the South aimed at the overthrow of the Government. Such actions constituted a violation of Articles 10, 19, 24 and 27 of the Agreement on the Cessation of Hostilities in Viet-Nam.

The USSR representative objected to the convening of the Security Council and to the inclusion of the question of Viet-Nam in the agenda, since the question should be settled only within the framework of the Geneva Agreements. Moreover, by bringing the question to the Council simultaneously with the resumption of its barbaric air raids on the Democratic Republic of Viet-Nam, the United States was not aiming at a genuine settlement of the question, but had resorted to a diversionary tactic with a view to covering the expansion of its intervention and aggressive war in Viet-Nam and was using the Council to stage a propaganda show. In fact, the United States was unwilling to revert to a strict compliance with the Geneva Agreements of 1954, since it refused to recognize that the National Liberation Front was the sole genuine representative of the South Viet-Namese people, and the one with which it was necessary to negotiate. While the United States continued to act from a position of brute force, the Government of the Democratic Republic of Viet-Nam had again re- cently demonstrated its readiness to achieve a just settlement by send- ing messages to Heads of States or Governments of many countries stating that, if the Government of the United States was genuinely interested in peaceful settlement, it must recognize the four points of the position taken by the Democratic Republic of Viet-Nam and stop unconditionally and forever the bombing and all other military acts against the territory of the latter.

But the United States had resumed its bombing two days after those messages were sent. On 31 January the Soviet Government had de- clared that such behaviour showed that the United States did not want the war to end and that the so-called United States peace initiative was really aimed at preparing the ground for a further escalation of the war.

Moreover, Mr. Podgorny, Chairman of the Presidium of the USSR, in a reply to President Ho Chi Minh's communication, had stated that the Soviet people resolutely condemned the armed intervention of the United States against the southern portion of his country and against the Democratic Republic of Viet-Nam, a sovereign socialist State. He had also assured President Ho Chi Minh that the Soviet Union would continue to assist its sister democratic republic to strengthen its defenses and to repel all aggression and would support the heroic Viet-Namese people waging a gallant struggle under the leadership of the National Liberation Front.

The Soviet representative also mentioned a message published on 2 February 1966 by the National Liberation Front stating that the Security Council had no right to take any decisions on questions in- volving South Viet-Nam and that it would regard all Council reso- lutions on the issue as null and void. The only possible settlement of the problem must be based on the Geneva accords and be achieved with the participation of all the interested parties, including the Na- tional Liberation Front. While professing to respect the Geneva

Agreements, the United States Government planned to torpedo them through its initiative in convening the Council. It was trying to hide behind the authority and prestige of the Organization.

The position of the Soviet Union as a co-chairman of the Geneva Conference had been misrepresented by the United States representative: in fact, when the Geneva Agreements had been reached, there had not been a single American soldier in Viet-Nam, whereas there were now hundreds of thousands, trying in a bloody operation to repress a people that had risen in defence of its independence.

The Bulgarian representative wondered why the United States had not brought to the United Nations the question whether it should or should not undertake aggression or resume bombing, but had put the question only after the crime had been committed. The United States knew very well that the Council would not have given it permission to resume the bombing, and that was why it had once more presented the Council with a *fait accompli*. The Bulgarian representative opposed the calling of a meeting of the Council for the same reasons which had determined the convening of the Geneva Conference in 1954, that is, the parties concerned could not come to the United Nations or were not yet members of the Organization. The Secretary-General had stated on 20 January 1966 that that was precisely why the parties to the conflict had decided in 1954 to resolve their differences in Geneva, outside the framework of the United Nations.

The United Kingdom and New Zealand representatives supported the United States Government's action in bringing the question to the Security Council and considered that the refusal of the North Vietnamese to negotiate had left the United States no choice but to resume bombing.

The representatives of Argentina, China, Japan and Uruguay favoured consideration of the problem by the Security Council, which had been entrusted with the primary responsibility for the maintenance of international peace and security.

The Netherlands representative observed that under Article 2, paragraph 6, of the Charter, the Organization was to ensure that States not Members of the United Nations respected the principles of the Charter regarding the maintenance of international peace. It did not, therefore, matter that most of the countries involved were not Members of the United Nations; this circumstance could not be regarded as a valid objection to Council consideration of the question. Also, all those concerned could and should be invited to participate in the discussion. The objection that the problem should be solved in the context not of the United Nations, but of the Geneva Conference of 1954, was not justified since the purpose of the discussion was only to arrange a pre-conference looking towards the application of the Geneva Agreements of 1954 and 1962. Recent developments made it all the more necessary to discuss the subject. If events were allowed to run their course, a further escalation of the war seemed inevitable.

The representative of France stated that the United Nations, where only one of the principal parties concerned, the United States, was represented, was not the proper forum for a peaceful solution. Even if the other parties were invited, the discussion could not be held on an equal footing. Moreover, United Nations intervention would only add to the existing confusion, as all parties to the conflict constantly referred to the need for respecting the principles of the Geneva Agreements of 1954 and 1962. France would therefore not support the inclusion of the question of Viet-Nam in the agenda.

The representative of Mali thought that a discussion of the question of Viet-Nam in the Security Council did not seem appropriate in the absence of any of the conditions required for arriving at decisions acceptable to the parties concerned: most of these parties not only were not Members of the Organization, but had explicitly expressed their opposition to any discussion in the Council. Furthermore, because of the existence of the Geneva Agreements, the inclusion of the question of Viet-Nam in the agenda would have political and juridical implications which should be carefully examined. Mali would therefore vote against the adoption of the agenda.

The Nigerian representative felt that the present was not the time to bring the question of Viet-Nam before the Council, since it coincided with the unfortunate resumption of the bombing in North Viet-Nam. Both the representative of Mali and the representative of Nigeria, however, stated that they did not contest the right of any Member State to call for a meeting of the Council if it felt that a situation threatened international peace and security.

The representative of Uganda wondered whether any useful purpose would be served by pushing the inclusion of the question of Viet-Nam in the agenda to the vote. He suggested that the President conclude the debate, summarizing it as best he could, and let the matter rest there. Another alternative was to postpone the meeting and meet at a future date in another place, preferably Geneva. The most important consideration was that all agreed that negotiations were necessary and that a way should be found to resolve the problem.

On a proposal of the representative of Jordan, the decision on the adoption of the agenda was postponed until the following day, 2 February 1966. The representative of Jordan stated he would support the adoption of the agenda when the Security Council met on that date.

On 2 February 1966 the agenda was adopted by 9 votes in favour to 2 against, with 4 abstentions.

Following the vote, the President [Mr. Matsui (Japan)] suggested that informal and private consultations be held in order to decide on the most effective and appropriate way of continuing the debate. The Council adopted this suggestion.

On 26 February 1966, the President of the Council transmitted to the Secretary-General the text of a letter he had sent to the members of the Council. In his letter, the President reported that some members, in conformity with the position they had taken during the debate, had not participated in the consultations he had proposed. Serious differences remained unresolved, especially as to whether consideration of the problem of Viet-Nam in the Council would be useful in the circumstances. These differences had given rise to the feeling that a report in the form of a letter appeared better than a formal meeting of the Council. The President felt that he could detect a certain degree of common feeling among many members of the Council on the points that: (1) there was general concern and growing anxiety over the continuation of hostilities in Viet-Nam and a strong desire for the early cessation of hostilities and a peaceful solution of the Viet-Nam problem; and (2) there appeared also to be a feeling that the termination of the conflict in Viet-Nam should be sought through negotiations in an appropriate forum in order to work out the implementation of the Geneva accords.

Meanwhile, the President concluded, the Security Council remained seized of the Viet-Nam problem.

The representative of France, in a reply to the President of the Council dated 28 February stated that there had been no substantive discussion in the Council and that informal and private consultations clearly could not take the place of such discussions. Therefore, no conclusion should be put forward regarding the feeling of the Council or of any of its members.

On 1 March 1966 the representative of the Soviet Union addressed a letter to the President of the Council in which he stated that the action taken by the latter aroused strong objections since the Security Council had not instructed its President to make any statements and he therefore had no right to send such a letter in his capacity as President. His action went beyond the limits of his competence, violated the Security Council's rules of procedure and could only be regarded as a blatant attempt to support the United States manœuvre. The Soviet Union therefore considered that the President's statement was illegal and had no legal force whatsoever.

In a letter of 2 March addressed to the President of the Council, the representative of Mali entered the most express reservations regarding both the principle and the motivation of the President's letter of 26 February 1966, especially in view of the fact that the meetings held on 1 and 2 February had been devoted to procedural discussions relating solely to the adoption of the agenda. As no discussion had been held on the question, there could be no grounds for drawing any conclusion. The communication dated 26 February 1966 could not constitute a valid precedent in the practice of the Council.

The Bulgarian representative, in a letter to the President of the Security Council dated 3 March, pointed out that the Council's decision to which the President had referred was that informal and private consultations should be held solely to decide on the most appropriate way of continuing the debate in the event that it should prove necessary to have a debate. But the Security Council never entered into a debate on the substance of the question, since the problem could not be solved within the United Nations. Therefore, the Council did not authorize its President to draw conclusions or sum up the feelings of its members in an official document. The Bulgarian delegation refused to be a party to the strange procedure adopted by the President and considered it necessary to return the letter addressed to it by the President on 28 February 1966.

NOTE.—1. During the year 1966, the Secretary-General of the United Nations took an active part in private and informal negotiations and discussions with the parties concerned. On 20 June 1966, he noted, for instance, that he had proposed three steps to bring about a situation congenial for discussions and negotiations: "Firstly, the cessation of the bombing of North Viet-Nam; secondly, the scaling down by all parties of all military activities in South Viet-Nam, which alone could lead to the bringing about of a cease-fire; and thirdly, the willingness by all sides to enter into discussions with those who are actually fighting." 3 UN Monthly Chronicle (1966), No. 7, p. 25.

2. At the same time, the Secretary-General strongly opposed the involvement of the Security Council in the Viet-Nam Question. He pointed out on 1 May 1966 that in 1954, when the Question of Viet-Nam was brought to the attention of the international community, "a lot of thought was given regarding the possibility of the United Nations involvement, in finding a solution to the problem of Viet-Nam, and it was decided, 12 years ago, that among the participants directly involved in the war in Viet-Nam only one—France —was a member of the United Nations. Others were not members. So there was general agreement that the question should be dealt with outside the framework of the United Nations and, thus, the Geneva Conference took place in 1954. He added that among "the parties principally concerned in the conflict in Viet-Nam only one—the United States of America—is a member of the United Nations. Others are not members of the United Nations. So, since there was general agreement in 1954 that the Viet-Nam questions should be dealt with outside the framework of the United Nations," he believed that "the same considerations equally hold true" in 1966. He emphasized that, if "the Security Council is to be usefully involved in finding a solution to any problem threatening international peace and security, one prerequisite is that the Security Council must be in a position to hear both sides of the question." He felt sure "that Peking or the North Vietnamese Government will not, under any circumstances, appear before the Security Council. Not only because of the fact that they are not members of the United Nations, but for another additional reason. Peking, for instance, feels very strongly . . . that there is someone in the Security Council

who is a usurper. As in the case of an accused who had been summoned to appear before a jury and in the view of that particular accused there is some-one among the jury who is inimical to the interests of that particular ac-cused." 3 UN Monthly Chronicle (1966), No. 5, pp. 58–59. See also *ibid*, p. 34.

On 12 May 1966, he considered as an even more basic reason for keeping the situation in Viet-Nam out of the United Nations the disagreement among the big powers with respect to peace-keeping. "Everybody knows that the Soviet Union and France are against United Nations involvement in peace-keeping of any type, of any character, in Viet-Nam. Their attitudes are known to everybody, and I have very good reason to believe that the United Kingdom would be very reluctant to get the United Nations involved in any sort of peace-keeping operation in Viet-Nam. So the situation is much more complex, much more difficult, than the situation the United Nations faced two years ago in the Dominican Republic .   .   .   [One] of the big powers was opposed to United Nations involvement in peace-keeping operations there. Now, in the case of Viet-Nam, more than two big powers will not agree to any type of United Nations involvement by way of peace-keeping operations in that country. I think this is a basic fact." 3 UN Monthly Chronicle (1966), No. 6, p. 31.

3. On 6 January 1967, the Government of North Viet-Nam restated its previous conditions for a peace settlement in the following manner:

"1. Recognition of the independence, sovereignty, unity and territorial integrity of Vietnam and the withdrawal of United States forces from the area pending reunification of Vietnam.

"2. Respect for the military provisions of the 1954 Geneva agreement, in-cluding those barring foreign forces.

"3. Settlement of South Vietnam's internal affairs by the South Viet-namese in accordance with the program of the National Liberation Front.

"4. Peaceful reunification of Vietnam by the peoples of North and South without foreign interference."

The Prime Minister of North Viet-Nam, Mr. Pham Van Dong pointed out in an interview that these four points "constitute the basis for settle-ment of the Vietnam question. These should not be considered 'conditions.' They are merely truths." (New York Times, 8 January 1967).

4. On 27 January 1967, the United States Department of State presented the following elaboration of its "Fourteen Points for Peace in Southeast Asia," which were first made public on 7 January 1966 (in the text repro-duced here, the statements added in 1967 are in square brackets):

"1. The Geneva Agreements on 1954 and 1962 are an adequate basis for peace in Southeast Asia.

"2. We would welcome a conference on Southeast Asia or any part there-of. [We are ready to negotiate a settlement based on a strict observance of the 1954 and 1962 Geneva Agreements, which observance was called for in the declaration on Viet-Nam of the meeting of the Warsaw Pact countries in Bucharest on July 6, 1966. And we will support a reconvening of the Geneva Conference, or an Asian conference, or any other generally ac-ceptable forum.]

"3. We would welcome 'negotiations without preconditions' as called for by 17 nonalined nations in an appeal delivered to Secretary Rusk on April 1, 1965.

"4. We would welcome 'unconditional discussions' as called for by President Johnson on April 7, 1965. [If the other side will not come to a conference, we are prepared to engage in direct discussions or discussions through an intermediary.]

"5. A cessation of hostilities could be the first order of business at a conference or could be the subject of preliminary discussions. [We have attempted, many times, to engage the other side in a discussion of a mutual deescalation of the level of violence, and we remain prepared to engage in such a mutual deescalation. We stand ready to cooperate fully in getting discussions which could lead to a cessation of hostilities started promptly and brought to a successful completion.]

"6. Hanoi's four points could be discussed along with other points which others may wish to propose. [We would be prepared to accept preliminary discussions to reach agreement on a set of points as a basis for negotiations.]

"7. We want no U.S. bases in Southeast Asia. [We are prepared to assist in the conversion of these bases for peaceful uses that will benefit the peoples of the entire area.]

"8. We do not desire to retain U.S. troops in South Viet-Nam after peace is assured. [We seek no permanent military bases, no permanent establishment of troops, no permanent alliances, no permanent American 'presence' of any kind in South Viet-Nam. We have pledged in the Manila Communiqué that 'Allied forces are in the Republic of Vietnam because that country is the object of aggression and its government requested support in the resistance of its people to aggression. They shall be withdrawn, after close consultation, as the other side withdraws its forces to the North, ceases infiltration, and the level of violence thus subsides. Those forces will be withdrawn as soon as possible and not later than six months after the above conditions have been fulfilled.']

"9. We support free elections in South Viet-Nam to give the South Vietnamese a government of their own choice. [We support the development of broadly based democratic institutions in South Viet-Nam. We do not seek to exclude any segment of the South Vietnamese people from peaceful participation in their country's future.]

"10. The question of reunification of Viet-Nam should be determined by the Vietnamese through their own free decision. [It should not be decided by the use of force. We are fully prepared to support the decision of the Vietnamese people.]

"11. The countries of Southeast Asia can be nonalined or neutral if that be their option. [We do not seek to impose a policy of alinement on South Viet-Nam. We support the neutrality policy of the Royal Government of Laos, and we support the neutrality and territorial integrity of Cambodia.]

"12. We would much prefer to use our resources for the economic reconstruction of Southeast Asia than in war. If there is peace, North Viet-Nam could participate in a regional effort to which we would be prepared to contribute at least one billion dollars. [We support the growing efforts by the nations of the area to cooperate in the achievement of their economic and social goals.]

"13.   The President has said 'The Viet Cong would have no difficulty in being represented and having their views presented if Hanoi for a moment decides she wants to cease aggression.   And I would not think that would be an insurmountable problem at all.'

"14.   We have said publicly and privately that we could stop the bombing of North Viet-Nam as a step toward peace although there has not been the slightest hint or suggestion from the other side as to what they would do if the bombing stopped.   [We are prepared to order a cessation of all bombing of North Viet-Nam the moment we are assured—privately or otherwise— that this step will be answered promptly by a corresponding and appropriate deescalation of the other side.   We do not seek the unconditional surrender of North Viet-Nam; what we do seek is to assure for the people of South Viet-Nam the right to decide their own political destiny, free of force.]"   56 DSB (1967), pp. 284–85.

5.   On 28 March 1967, the Secretary-General reasserted "his conviction that a cessation of the bombing of North Vietnam continues to be a vital need, for moral and humanitarian reasons and, also, because it is the step which could lead the way to meaningful talks to end the war."   Nevertheless, he made a new proposal envisaging three steps different from those which he had suggested in 1966 (No. 1, above), i.e.:   "(A) a general standstill truce;   (B) preliminary talks;   (C) reconvening of the Geneva conference." He conceded that "a truce without effective supervision is apt to be breached from time to time by one side or another, but an effective supervision of truce, at least for the moment, seems difficult to envisage as a practical possibility.   If the parties directly involved in the conflict are genuinely motivated by considerations of peace and justice, it is only to be expected that earnest efforts will be exerted to enforce the truce to the best of their ability." N. Y. Times, 29 March 1967, p. 8.   The United States and the Saigon Government promptly accepted this proposal.

6.   *Address by Ambassador Goldberg at Howard University, 19 February 1967.*

56 DSB (1967), pp. 310–16.

Our effort to open the door to peace in Viet-Nam has been continuous.   .   .   .   The United States seeks a political solution in Viet-Nam.   We do not seek the unconditional surrender of our adversaries.   We seek a settlement whose terms will result not from dictation but from genuine negotiations, a settlement whose terms will not sacrifice the vital interest of any party.   In the words of the Manila communique: "   .   .   .   the settlement of the war in Vietnam depends on the readiness and willingness of the parties concerned to explore and work out together a just and reasonable solution."   As President Johnson said a week ago here in Washington: Such a solution "will involve   .   .   .   concessions on both parts."

We are not engaged in a "holy war" against communism.   We do not seek an American sphere of influence in Asia, nor a permanent American "presence" of any kind—military or otherwise—in Viet-Nam, nor the imposition of a military alliance on South Viet-Nam.

We do not seek to do any injury to mainland China nor to threaten any of its legitimate interests.

We seek to assure to the people of South Viet-Nam the affirmative exercise of the right of self-determination, the right to decide their own political destiny free of external interference and force and through democratic processes. In keeping with the announced South Vietnamese Government's policy of national reconciliation, we do not seek to exclude any segment of the South Vietnamese people from peaceful participation in their country's future. We are prepared to accept the results of that decision, whatever it may be. We support the early consummation of a democratic constitutional system in South Viet-Nam and welcome the progress being made to this end.

As regards North Viet-Nam, we have no designs on its territory, and we do not seek to overthrow its government, whatever its ideology. We are prepared fully to respect its sovereignty and territorial integrity and to enter into specific undertakings to that end.

We believe the reunification of Viet-Nam should be decided upon through a free choice by the peoples of both the North and the South without any outside interference; and the results of that choice also will have our full support.

Finally, when peace is restored we are willing to make a major commitment of money, talent, and resources to a multilateral cooperative effort to bring to all of Southeast Asia, including North Viet-Nam, the benefits of economic and social reconstruction and development which that area so sorely needs.

These, then, are the peace aims of the United States. They parallel the objectives stated by the South Vietnamese Government at Manila. Our aims are strictly limited, and we sincerely believe they contain nothing inconsistent with the interests of any party. Our public pronouncements of them—both in Washington and at the United Nations—are solemn commitments by the United States.

Our adversaries have also placed their aims and objectives on the public record over the past 2 years. The major statement of these aims is the well-known four points of Hanoi, which I will summarize without departing too much from their own terminology.

Hanoi's Four Points

The first point calls for recognition of the basic national rights of the Vietnamese people: peace, independence, sovereignty, unity, and territorial integrity. It also calls for the cessation of all acts of war against the North; the ending of United States intervention in the South; the withdrawal of all United States troops, military personnel, and weapons of all kinds; the dismantling of American bases; and the cancellation of what they term the United States "military alliance" with South Viet-Nam.

The United States would not find any essential difficulty with a reasonable interpretation of any of the terms included in this point. Our chief concern is what it does *not* include: namely, that North Viet-Nam also cease its intervention in the South, end all of its acts of war against the South, and withdraw its forces from the South. Such a requirement is obviously essential to the "peace" to which this first point refers.

The second point relates to the military clauses of the Geneva agreements. It provides that, pending the peaceful reunification of Viet-Nam, both the North and the South must refrain from joining any military alliance and that there should be no foreign bases, troops, or military personnel in their respective territories.

Here again, the only real difficulty is the omission of any obligation on the North to withdraw its military forces from the South —although the Geneva accords, which established the demarcation line in Viet-Nam, forbid military interference of any sort by one side in the affairs of the other and even go so far as to forbid civilians to cross the demilitarized zone.

The third point calls for the settlement of the South's internal affairs in accordance with the program of the National Liberation Front for South Viet-Nam. This point, of course, was not a part of the Geneva accords at all. It introduces a new element which I shall discuss later in this analysis.

The fourth point calls for the peaceful reunification of Viet-Nam, to be settled by the people of both zones without any foreign interference. We have no difficulty with this point, as was indicated in my speech to the General Assembly on September 22.

There has apparently been added a fifth point—put forward and repeatedly endorsed by both Hanoi and the National Liberation Front since the enunciation of the four points in April 1965. This fifth point was stated by Ho Chi Minh in January 1966, when he said that if the United States really wants peace, it must recognize the National Liberation Front as the "sole genuine representative" of the people of South Viet-Nam and engage in negotiation with it. This, like the third of the four points, introduces a new element which was not part of the Geneva accords.

Now, from this brief summation of our aims and those declared by Hanoi, it is clear that there are areas of agreement and areas of disagreement. Recent public statements by Hanoi have been helpful in certain aspects, but how great the disagreements are is still uncertain, because the stated aims of Hanoi still contain a number of ambiguities. I would like to discuss some of these ambiguities because they relate to very consequential matters.

Ambiguities in Hanoi's Stated Aims

There is ambiguity, for example, on the role of the National Liberation Front in peace negotiations. I have already noted the statement of Ho Chi Minh and other spokesmen for our adversaries who have said that we must recognize the Front as "the sole genuine representative" of the South Vietnamese people and negotiate with it. If this means that we are asked to cease our recognition of the Government in Saigon and deal only with the Front, insistence on this point would imperil the search for peace. For the Front has not been chosen by any democratic process to represent the people of South Viet-Nam. Nor has the Front been recognized by the world community. It is pertinent to recall that more than 60 nations recognize the Government of the Republic of Viet-Nam in Saigon, whereas none recognizes the National Liberation Front as a government.

On the other hand, some public statements seem to call for the National Liberation Front to be given a place or voice at the negotiating table. If this were the position of our adversaries, the prospects would be brighter; for President Johnson, as long ago as July 1965, said that "The Viet Cong would have no difficulty in being represented and having their views presented if Hanoi for a moment decides she wants to cease aggression." He added that this did not seem to him to be "an insurmountable problem," and that "I think that could be worked out."

A further ambiguity relates to the role of the National Liberation Front in the future political life of South Viet-Nam. Hanoi asks that the affairs of South Viet-Nam be settled "in accordance with the program of the National Liberation Front." Our adversaries, in their various comments on this point, take no notice of the internationally recognized Government of South Viet-Nam or of the steps which the South Vietnamese leaders have taken and have currently under way and the institutions they are now creating for the purpose of providing their country with a constitutional and representative government. Nor would their statements seem to leave any place for the South Vietnamese who have participated in and promoted such steps. Such an interpretation would pose serious obstacles to a settlement.

However, some claim that what the National Liberation Front really seeks is no more than the opportunity to advance its program peacefully along with other elements and groupings in the South in a free political environment.

We have already made it clear that we do not wish to exclude any segment of the South Vietnamese people from peaceful participation in their country's future and that we support a policy of national reconciliation endorsed by the South Vietnamese Government in the Manila communique. Indeed, as Secretary Rusk said in an interview last week, if the Viet Cong were to lay down their arms, ways could be found to permit them to take part in the normal political processes in South Viet-Nam.

Further ambiguities arise concerning the question of foreign troops in South Viet-Nam. What does Hanoi mean by "foreign troops"? They clearly include in this term the forces of the United States and other countries aiding the South, but they have never admitted the presence of their own forces in the South. Of course, a one-sided withdrawal by our side would not lead to an acceptable peace. All external forces must withdraw, those of Hanoi as well as ours, if peace is to be achieved.

There is ambiguity also in Hanoi's position on the timing of the withdrawal of external forces. Do our adversaries consider withdrawal of forces as a precondition to negotiations, as some of their statements imply? If so, this again would raise a serious obstacle to progress. But if they look on withdrawal of forces as a provision to be incorporated in a settlement, this clearly could be worked out. The United States and its allies are already on record in the Manila communique that their forces "shall be withdrawn . . . as the other side withdraws its forces to the North, ceases infiltration, and the level of violence thus subsides. Those forces will be withdrawn as soon as possible and not later than six months after the above conditions have been fulfilled." Further, we have indicated our willingness to join in a phased and supervised withdrawal of forces by both sides.

Next, there is ambiguity in Hanoi's position on the cessation of bombing of North Viet-Nam. At times their public statements have demanded that the bombing be ended unconditionally, without any reference to a possible response from their side. On the other hand, quite recently a spokesman of Hanoi said that "if, after the definitive and unconditional cessation of the bombardments, the American Government proposes to enter into contact with the [North Vietnamese] Government, . . . this proposal will be examined and studied." And just this week we have seen a further statement, in an interview by the North Vietnamese Foreign Minister, that cessation of the bombings "could lead to talks between North Viet Nam and the U. S." Many of their statements insisting that the bombing cease have also contained other expressions, such as that the American military presence in South Viet-Nam be completely withdrawn and that the four points of Hanoi must be recognized and accepted as "the" basis—or possibly as "a" basis—for settlement of the conflict. This creates an additional ambiguity as to whether Hanoi means to add still other prenegotiating conditions.

The position of the United States on this bombing question has been stated by a number of administration spokesmen, including me at the United Nations. The United States remains prepared to take the first step and order a cessation of all bombing of North Viet-Nam the moment we are assured, privately or otherwise, that this step will be answered promptly by a tangible response toward peace from North Viet-Nam. In his letter of February 8 to His Holiness Pope Paul, President Johnson said:

"I know you would not expect us to reduce military action unless the other side is willing to do likewise.

"We are prepared to discuss the balanced reduction in military activity, the cessation of hostilities, or any practical arrangements which could lead to these results.

"We shall continue our efforts for a peaceful and honorable settlement until they are crowned with success."

U. S. Ready To Negotiate in Good Faith

Some analysts contend that our terms of settlement should be more precisely defined. But it is very difficult to be more precise in advance of negotiation and particularly in light of the substantive ambiguities on the other side. But whatever questions may be raised, they should and can best be resolved in discussions between the parties who have the power to resolve them. For our part, we stand ready to negotiate in good faith unconditionally to resolve all outstanding questions.

The United States approach to negotiations is flexible. We and our allies do not ask our adversaries to accept, as a precondition to discussions or negotiations, any point of ours to which they may have objections. Nor do we rule out the discussion of any points of theirs, however difficult they might appear to us. We are willing to discuss and negotiate not only our own points but Hanoi's four points, and points emanating from any other source, including the Secretary-General of the United Nations.

It remains to be seen whether our adversaries share this concept of negotiations. As I have already pointed out, their various public declarations of peace aims have often been coupled with statements that the goals they put forward must, for example, be "accepted" or "recognized" as the "sole basis" or "the most correct basis" or "the only sound basis" or "the basis for the most correct political solution."

Such statements contain still further ambiguity—in one sense the most fundamental of all, since it relates to the concept of negotiation itself. Do these statements mean that Hanoi is willing to enter negotiations only if there is an assurance in advance that the outcome will be on their terms and will, in effect, simply ratify the goals they have already stated? Such an attitude would not be conducive to peace and would make the outlook for a settlement bleak indeed.

If, on the other hand, North Viet-Nam were to say that their points are not preconditions to discussions or negotiations, then the prospects should be more promising.

Our negotiating approach would permit each side to seek clarification of the other side's position. It does not require the acceptance in advance of any points, least of all those whose meaning may be in need of clarification. We do not ask that of Hanoi—and progress toward a settlement will be facilitated if Hanoi does not ask it of us.

In this situation, how can we best move toward a settlement?

One essential early step is to analyze the positions of all parties in order to ascertain whether there is some element or some kernel common to all. Many students of the subject have pointed to one fact which may prove to be such a kernel, namely, the fact that both sides have pointed to the Geneva agreements of 1954 and 1962 as an acceptable basis for a peaceful settlement.

But I must add quickly that this does not necessarily indicate a real meeting of the minds, because of doubts that all sides interpret the Geneva agreements in the same light. Hanoi has said that the essence of the Geneva agreements is contained in its four points. But the four points would not put Hanoi under any restraint or obligations in its hostile activities against the South, which the Geneva accords explicitly prohibit. Besides, as I already pointed out, these points insist that the South's future be regulated in accordance with the program of a group which was not referred to in the Geneva accords and did not even exist when they were written. And in any case, if the Geneva accords were to serve as a basis for settlement, it would obviously be necessary to revitalize the international machinery which they provided for supervision, which is presently operating under severe limitations; to incorporate effective international guarantees; and to update other provisions of the accords which on their face are clearly out of date.

Despite these problems of interpretation, it can be said that if the meaning of the Geneva agreements were accepted as a matter for genuine negotiation, then the constant reference to these agreements by both sides would be more than a verbal similarity; it would be a significant and hopeful sign of the prospects for settlement.

Methods for Seeking a Political Settlement

From all this analysis, there emerges one basic and practical question, and it is this: How are all these apparent obstacles to a settlement to be overcome?

The first and essential prerequisite is the will to resolve them, not by unconditional surrender or by the dictation of terms but through a process of mutual accommodation whereby nobody's vital interests are injured, which would be a political solution. Speaking for the United States Government, I affirm without reservation the willingness of the United States to seek and find a political solution.

The next question, then, is by what procedure such a political settlement can be reached. One well-tested and time-proven way is the conference table. President Johnson has repeatedly stated our readiness to join in a conference in Geneva, in Asia, or in any other suitable place. We remain prepared today to go to the conference table as soon as, and wherever, our adversaries are prepared to join us.

There is also a second procedure by which to pursue a political settlement: namely, private negotiations—either by direct contact or through an intermediary. There is much to be said for this private method, for in a situation as grave as this, with its complex historical background and its present political crosscurrents, it would be exceedingly difficult to negotiate in a goldfish bowl.

I therefore affirm that the United States Government stands ready to take this route also toward a political settlement. And we give our assurance that the secrecy and security of such private explorations would be safeguarded on our side.   .   .   .

Such then is my analysis of the problems involved and the methods to be employed in seeking a negotiated solution of the Vietnamese conflict. Nor should we overlook the possibility that negotiations, private or public, might be preceded or facilitated by the process of mutual deescalation or a scaling down of the conflict without a formally negotiated cease-fire. This, of course, would be welcome on our part.   .   .   .

The great difficulty of achieving peace should serve to remind us that there are substantial conflicting interests at stake which stubbornly resist solution; that peace cannot be bought at any price, nor can real conflicts of purpose be waved away with a magic wand. By the same token, the ferocity of war should not be an incitement to hatred but rather a stern discipline, a reminder of the imperative duty to define responsibly the limited interests for which our soldiers fight and which a peace settlement must protect.

The effort to make such a responsible definition and to carry it through the process of peace negotiations is piled high with difficulty. A genuine meeting of the minds may never be wholly achieved. It is unlikely that terms of settlement for this stubborn conflict can be found which would be wholly pleasing to either side. But it is in our highest national interest that an acceptable, livable solution should be found.

NOTE. For comments on the Viet-Nam Question, see Neil H. ALFORD, Jr., "The Legality of American Military Involvement in Viet Nam: A Broader Perspective," 75 Yale L.J. (1966), pp. 1109–21; AMERICAN FRIENDS SERVICE COMMITTEE, Peace in Viet Nam: A New Approach in Southeast Asia (New York, 1966), 112 pp.; Eberhard P. DEUTSCH, "Legality of the United States Position in Vietnam," 52 ABAJ (1966), pp. 436–42; Richard A. FALK, "International Law and the United States Role in the Viet-Nam War," 75 Yale L.J. (1966), pp. 1122–60; Marvin E. GETTLEMEN, ed., Vietnam: History, Documents, and Opinions on a Major World Crisis (New York, 1965), 448 pp.; Don R. LARSON and Arthur LARSON, Vietnam and Beyond: A New American Foreign Policy and Program (Durham, N.C.,

1965), 42 pp.; Leonard C. MEEKER, "Viet-Nam and the International Law of Self-Defense," 56 DSB (1967), pp. 54–63; John N. MOORE and James L. UNDERWOOD, "The Lawfulness of United States Assistance to the Republic of Vietnam," 112 Congressional Record (14 July 1966), pp. 14943–89; Hans J. MORGENTHAU, Vietnam and the United States (Washington, D.C., 1965), 112 pp.; Daniel G. PARTAN, "Legal Aspects of the Vietnam Conflict," 46 Boston Univ.L.R. (1966), pp. 281–316; Marcus G. RASKIN and Bernard B. FALL, eds., The Viet-Nam Reader: Articles and Documents on American Foreign Policy and the Viet-Nam Crisis (New York, 1965), 415 pp.; SOVIET PEACE COMMITTEE, United States Aggression in Vietnam: Crime Against Peace and Humanity (Moscow, 1966), 227 pp.; William L. STANDARD, "United States Intervention in Vietnam is not Legal," 52 ABAJ (1966), pp. 627–34; Frank N. TRAGER, Why Viet Nam? (New York, 1966), 238 pp.; Ralph K. WHITE, "Misperception and the Vietnam War," 22 J. of Social Issues (1966), No. 3, pp. 1–167; Kenneth T. YOUNG, Jr., and others, The Southeast Asia Crisis (Dobbs Ferry, New York, 1966; Association of the Bar of the City of New York, Hammarskjöld Forums, No. 8), 226 pp.

See also Victor BATOR, Viet-Nam: A Diplomatic Tragedy (Dobbs Ferry, New York, 1965), 271 pp.; Dorothy D. BROMLEY, Washington and Vietnam (Dobbs Ferry, New York, 1966), 128 pp.; Malcolm W. BROWNE, The New Face of War (New York, 1965), 284 pp.; Wilfrid G. BURCHETT, Viet-Nam: Inside Story of the Guerilla War (New York, 1965), 253 pp.; Georges CHAFFARD, Indochine: Dix ans d'indépendance (Paris, 1964), 294 pp.; Oliver E. CLUBB, The United States and the Sino-Soviet Bloc in Southeast Asia (Washington, D. C., 1962), 173 pp.; Allan B. COLE, ed., Conflict in Indo-China and International Repercussions: A Documentary History, 1945–1955 (Ithaca, New York, 1956), 265 pp.; Brian CROZIER, Southeast Asia in Turmoil (Baltimore, Md., 1965), 205 pp.; Bernard B. FALL, Street without Joy: From the Indochina War to the War in Viet-Nam (4th ed., Harrisburg, Pa., 1964), 408 pp.; Bernard B. FALL, The Two Viet-Nams: A Political and Military Analysis (Rev. ed., New York, 1964), 408 pp.; Bernard B. FALL, Vietnam Witness, 1953–66 (New York, 1966), 363 pp.; Russell II. FIFIELD, Southeast Asia in United States Policy (New York, 1963), 488 pp.; Melvin GURTOV, The First Vietnam Crisis (New York, 1967), 228 pp.; David HALBERSTAM, The Making of a Quagmire (New York, 1965), 323 pp.; Ellen J. HAMMER, The Struggle for Indochina (Stanford, Cal., 1954), 342 pp.; William HENDERSON, Southeast Asia: Problems of United States Policy (Cambridge, Mass., 1963), 273 pp.; Wade S. HOOKER, Jr. and David H. SAVASTEN "The Geneva Conventions of 1949: Application in the Vietnamese Conflict," 5 Virginia J. of Int.L. (1965), pp. 243–65; George McT. KAHIN and John W. LEWIS, The United States in Vietnam (New York, 1967), 465 pp.; Jean LACOUTURE, Viet-Nam Between Two Truces (New York, 1966), 295 pp.; Donald LANCASTER, The Emancipation of French Indo-China (London, 1961), 445 pp.; Peter H. LYON, Southeast Asia (London, 1965), 148 pp.; John MECKLIN, Mission in Torment: An Intimate Account of the U. S. Role in Vietnam (New York, 1965), 318 pp.; B. S. N. MURTI, Vietnam Divided: The Unfinished Struggle (New York, 1964), 228 pp.; Norman D. PALMER, South Asia and United States Policy (Boston, 1966), 332 pp.; Douglas PIKE, Viet Cong: The Organization and Techniques of the National Liberation Front of South Vietnam (Cambridge,

Mass., 1967), 490 pp.; Roger PINTO, "Évolution du statut international des États indochinois depuis 1954," *in* Mélanges offerts à Henri Rolin (Paris, 1964), pp. 252–62; Sibnarayan RAY, ed., Vietnam Seen from East and West (New York, 1966), 192 pp.; Robert SCHEER, How the United States Got Involved in Vietnam (Santa Barbara, Cal., 1965), 79 pp.; Arthur M. SCHLESINGER, Jr., The Bitter Heritage: Vietnam and American Democracy, 1941–1966 (Boston, Mass., 1967), 126 pp.; Franz SCHURMANN and others, The Politics of Escalation in Vietnam (Boston, 1966), 160 pp.; Robert SCIGLIANO, South Vietnam: Nation under Stress (Boston, 1963), 227 pp.; Robert SHAPLEN, The Lost Revolution (2d ed., New York, 1966), 406 pp.; Richard W. TREGASKIS, Vietnam Dairy (New York, 1963), 401 pp.; Howard ZINN, Vietnam: The Logic of Withdrawal (Boston, Mass., 1967), 131 pp.

Section 3.   The United Nations and the Organization of American States

COMMENTS ON THE RELATIONSHIP BETWEEN THE UNITED NATIONS AND THE ORGANIZATION OF AMERICAN STATES

NOTE.   With respect to the various questions discussed in this Chapter, see Alonso AGUILAR MONTEVERDE, El Panamericanismo de la Doctrina Monroe a la Doctrina Johnson (Mexico City, 1965), 186 pp.; Manuel CANYES SANTACANA, The Organization of American States and the United Nations (6th ed., Washington, D. C., 1963), 57 pp.; Lilia CLARET DE VOOGT, La O.E.A. y las Naciones Unidas (Buenos Aires, 1956), 219 pp.; Inis L. CLAUDE, Jr., "The OAS, the UN and the US," 547 Int. Conc. (1964), pp. 1–67; Henry P. DE VRIES and José RODRIGUEZ-NOVÁS, The Law of the Americas: An Introduction to the Legal Systems of the American Republics (Dobbs Ferry, New York, 1965), pp. 22–33; G. I. A. D. DRAPER, "Regional Arrangements and Enforcement Action," 20 REgDI (1964), pp. 1–29; John C. DREIER, The Organization of American States and the Hemisphere Crisis (New York, 1962), 145 pp.; R. J. DUPUY, "Organisation internationale et unité politique: La crise de l'Organisation des Etats Américains," 6 AFDI (1960), pp. 185–224; Charles G. FENWICK, The Organization of American States (Washington, D. C., 1963), pp. 246–49, 260–75; INTER-AMERICAN INSTITUTE OF INTERNATIONAL LEGAL STUDIES, The Inter-American System: Its Development and Strengthening (Dobbs Ferry, New York, 1966), pp. 105–208; Eduardo JIMÉNEZ DE ARECHAGA, "La coordination des systémes de l'ONU et de l'Organisation des États Américains pour le réglement pacifique des différends et la sécurité collective," 111 RCADI (1964–I), pp. 423–526; Charles O. LERCHE, Jr., "Development of Rules Relating to Peacekeeping by the Organization of American States," 59 ASIL Procgs. (1965), pp. 60–66; R. St. J. MACDONALD, "The Developing Relationship between Superior and Subordinate Bodies at the International Level: A Note on the Experience of the United Nations and the Organization of American States," 2 Canadian YBIL (1964), pp. 21–54; R. St. J. MACDONALD, "The Organization of American States in Action," 15 Univ. of Toronto L.J. (1963–64), pp. 358–429; William MANGER, Pan America in Crisis: The Future of OAS (Washington, D. C., 1961), 104 pp.; Ilmar Penna MARINHO, O funcionamento do sistema interamericano dentro do sistema mundial (Rio de Janeiro, 1959), 198 pp.; PAN AMERICAN UNION, Inter-American Treaty of Reciprocal Assistance: Applications, 1948–1964 (Washington, D. C., 1964), 2 vols.; Felipe H. PAOLILLO, "Regionalismo y acción coercitiva regional en la Carta de las Naciones Unidas," 1 AUrugDI (1962), pp. 211–45; Felipe H. PAOLILLO, "Nuevas reflexiones en torno a una debatida cuestión: Facultades de las entidades regionales en materia de acción coercitiva," 3 AUrugDI (1964), pp. 173–205; Alberto PEREZ PEREZ, "El concepto de 'medidas coercitivas' en al Articulo 53 de la Carta de las Naciones Unidas," 3 AUrugDI (1964), pp. 207–43; C. Neale RONNING, Law and Politics in Inter-American Diplomacy (New York, 1963), pp. 63–88; José Maria RUDA, "Relaciones de la O.E.A. y la U.N. en cuanto al mantenimiento de la paz y la seguridad internacional," 1961 Revista jurídica de Buenos Aires, Nos. 1–2, pp. 15–76; Ann Van W. THOMAS and A. J. THOMAS, Jr., The Organization of American States (Dallas, Texas, 1963), pp. 249–371; Bryce WOOD and Minerva MORALES M., "Latin America and the United Nations," 19 Int.Org. (1965), pp. 714–27.

GUATEMALAN QUESTION

NOTE.—1. In its Resolution XXXII, the Bogotá Conference of the American States declared in 1948 that, "by its antidemocratic nature and its interventionist tendency, the political activity of international communism or any other totalitarian doctrine is incompatible with the concept of American freedom"; and condemned, in the name of international law, "interference by any foreign power, or by any political organization serving the interests of a foreign power, in the public life of the nations of the American continent." Pan American Union, The International Conferences of American States, 2d Supp., 1942–1954 (Washington, D. C., 1958), pp. 270–71. The Tenth Inter-American Conference, held in Caracas in March 1954, adopted an elaborate "Declaration of Solidarity for the Preservation of the Political Integrity of the American States against the Intervention of International Communism" (Resolution XCIII), in which it condemned the "activities of the international communist movement as constituting intervention in American affairs"; declared that "the domination or control of the political institutions of any American State by the international communist movement, extending to this Hemisphere the political system of an extracontinental power, would constitute a threat to the sovereignty and political independence of the American States, endangering the peace of America, and would call for a Meeting of Consultation to consider the adoption of appropriate action in accordance with existing treaties"; and noted that this "declaration of foreign policy made by the American republics in relation to dangers originating outside this Hemisphere is designed to protect and not to impair the inalienable right of each American State freely to choose its own form of government and economic system and to live its own social and cultural life." *Ibid.*, pp. 433–35.

2. In the summer of 1954, the United States alleged that there was a grave danger of communist take-over in Guatemala. US, DOS, Intervention of International Communism in Guatemala (Pub. 5556; Washington, D. C., 1954), 96 pp. See also Frederick B. PIKE, "Guatemala, the United States, and Communism in the Americas," 17 Review of Politics (1955), pp. 232–61. Be-

fore resort was made, however, to the procedure contemplated by the Caracas Declaration, Guatemala raised a different issue in the Security Council of the United Nations.

1. Cablegram from the Minister for External Affairs of Guatemala, 19 June 1954.

S/3232 (19 June 1954); SCOR, IX, Supp. for April–June 1954, pp. 11–13.

On 1 April 1953 the Government of Guatemala informed the United Nations of the intention of certain international political groups to interfere in the internal affairs of Guatemala . . . There have now occurred events of such gravity that my Government feels obliged to appeal to the United Nations Security Council in order to prevent a disruption of the peace in the American continent. Since the recent arrival in Guatemala of arms for her armed forces, official United States spokesmen have been saying, falsely and tendenciously, that this defense equipment, acquired by my Government in the performance of its sovereign rights, were intended for the purpose of attacking neighbouring Central American countries. Such statements were and are completely false. Guatemala had many times declared that it neither had nor has aggressive intentions. Events have shown that while the Guatemalan Government maintains an unshakable policy of friendship and non-intervention, other governments are pursuing a policy of hostility and aggressiveness towards our country. The first response to the incitement provided by the official United States spokesmen came from the Government of Nicaragua, which unilaterally announced the breaking off of diplomatic relations with Guatemala on 19 May last. The Government of Nicaragua gave explanations which were not only false but which, even if they had been true, would not have justified a rupture of international relations. On 26 May 1954, unidentified aircraft from the direction of Honduras and Nicaragua violated Guatemalan territory by flying over the city of Guatemala and dropping propaganda leaflets inciting the Guatemalan Army to rise against the legitimate and constitutional Government of our country. On 7 June 1954, these planes made another incursion and dropped similar propaganda leaflets over various parts of our territory. On 14 June, the planes did not confine themselves to dropping propaganda leaflets: this time they parachuted arms and ammunition into the area of Tiquisate, Headquarters of the Compania Agricola de Guatemala, which is a subsidiary of the United Fruit Company. These arms appear to be of Soviet and North American make. The Guatemalan Government, reliably informed that expeditionary forces situated in Honduras were preparing to invade Guatemalan territory, made representations to the Government of Honduras through the normal diplomatic channels, requesting it, for the sake of international friendship, to concentrate and control these armed groups. The Honduran Government in reply gave assurances that these elements would be concentrated, but in fact no measure was taken for that purpose, as may easily be proved from statements in the Honduran Press itself. On 15 June the invading aircraft again violated our territory, flying over the same area of Tiquisate and other places. On 16 June there was another violation, apparently for the purpose of carrying out reconnaissance over various parts of the country. On June 17 I appealed directly to the Chancellor of Honduras, and stated that in spite of the assurances given by his Government, the expeditionary forces preparing to invade Guatemala had not been concentrated. I repeated our request in this connexion, and demanded that they should be disarmed in accordance with international law and the agreements in force. The same day the diplomatic representative of Guatemala in Honduras made strong representations to the Government of that country, protesting against the Government's passive attitude towards the preparations being made by the expeditionary forces to invade Guatemala. At the same time we reiterated our desire to maintain the friendliest of relations with that country and to avoid any breach of the peace in Central America. However, notwithstanding the repeated requests which we made in friendly fashion, the expeditionary forces which we had condemned captured the Guatemalan frontier post of El Florido in the Department of Chiquimula, and later advanced about fifteen kilometres inside Guatemalan territory. These forces are still in our territory and we have not ordered that they be repulsed precisely because we do not want to give other pretexts, this time in connexion with frontier incidents. This morning aircraft from the direction of Honduras and Nicaragua have invaded our country, dropping explosive bombs on stocks of fuel in the port of San José and on the city of Retalhuleu. Today at 4:00 p. m. P–47 type planes of United States-make also from the direction of these two countries attacked the city of Guatemala, machine-gunning government buildings and private dwellings and bombing military bases. The same aircraft later attacked the military base at the port of San José. The aggressor Governments and international provocateurs have felt safe in committing such outrages and acts of aggression because they knew that Guatemala pursues a policy of friendly and peaceful relations with her neighbours, and also more particularly, because the policy of encircling and boycotting our country which has been pursued by United States leaders has left us without an air force sufficient to repel repeated acts of aggression. Those Governments probably felt safe too because they have recently signed military agreements with the United States of America, while at the same time the Government of Honduras rejected the pact of friendship and non-aggression offered by my Government to that of Honduras in proof of its friendly and peaceable intentions. The facts we have just cited clearly prove that open aggression has been perpetrated by the Governments of Honduras and Nicaragua at the instigation of certain foreign monopolies whose interests have been affected by the progressive policy of my Government. Guatemala has simply defended her sovereign rights by enacting and applying those laws which seemed to her necessary to promote the country's economic and social progress. For that reason the international crime which has been committed is all the more to be condemned. In view of the foregoing, I would request Your Excellency urgently to convene a meeting of the United Nations Security Council in order that, in accordance with Articles 34, 35 and 39 of the United Nations Charter, it may take the measures necessary to prevent the disruption of peace and international security in this part of Central America and also to put a stop to the aggression in progress against Guatemala.

2.   *Discussion in the Security Council, 20 June 1954.*

SCOR, IX, Mtg. 675, pp. 1–41.

Mr. CASTILLO ARRIOLA (Guatemala): . . . On behalf of my country I wish to declare categorically and publicly that the Republic of Guatemala has been invaded by expeditionary forces forming part of an unlawful international aggression. This international aggression is the outcome of a vast international conspiracy which has been directed against my country for some time and which, let me say for the record, Guatemala reported officially to the United Nations on two occasions. And now, to add to this intensive campaign of defamation intended to convince world public opinion of the justice of these devious plans, we are confronted with an act of criminal aggression against Guatemala, one which has so far gone unpunished. Fortunately, public opinion has not been deceived in a single country; and even though only one side of the picture has been given, people—even people ignorant of the true state of affairs in Guatemala—have felt, have indeed been confident, thanks to the sense of honesty innate in all human beings, that there is another side to the picture, namely justice, independence and democracy, the very features which distinguish my country.

Those who have today conspired to stifle democracy in the name of a false freedom already stand condemned by public opinion and will undoubtedly be condemned by history. They did not try to, nor could they, hide their great joy at hearing that there was war in Guatemala and that Guatemala had been invaded since they were sure that to overcome a small country which had intentionally been left defenceless, they had taken the best measures to achieve their end, which was the destruction of a true democracy in America.

The battle for Guatemala has begun. The battle which has threatened us for so long has started. The people of Guatemala are now undergoing an international invasion masked as a movement of exiles, of whom [there are] only a small number in the expeditionary forces which have violated Guatemala's soil. The expeditionaries are foreign forces.   Nevertheless, as one more demonstration by my country of its love for peace and peaceful international coexistence, the Guatemalan army has not wished to take decisive action to halt the aggression, especially at points near our sister Republic of Honduras, while this Council, and no other organization, is intervening to prevent useless bloodshed.   In this way it would also avoid any accusation of provoking frontier incidents which might be used to justify the aggression.   But the people and Government of Guatemala refuse as one man to tolerate this international attempt to unseat the first democratic government my country has had in this century. It is for this reason that we wished, in strict compliance with our international obligations to the United Nations, to bring this delicate problem before the Security Council so that, in scrupulous and unequivocal compliance with its duties and obligations as laid down categorically in the Charter, the Council might carry out its task of preventing a war which might spread, and of preserving world peace and security.   .   .   .

For some time past the most active and intensive campaign ever conducted against a country like mine has been waged against Guatemala.   This campaign has been based on utterly false and tendentious reports.   Its sole purpose has been to prepare the way for open intervention in the domestic affairs of our country.   This campaign, set on foot by the United Fruit Company and other monopolies operating in the country and encouraged by the United States State Department, has sought to represent Guatemala as an outpost of Soviet communism on the American continent, a tool of Moscow and a spearhead of the Soviet Union against the United States.   Guatemala has also been unjustly accused of being a disturber of the peace in the American continent and a threat to the security of the countries of the Western Hemisphere.   .   .   .

My country did not repel the invading forces, but we are prepared to repel them and not to acquiesce in the invasion.   In obedience to a principle which is innate in us Guatemalans—the observance of our undertakings and obligations—we should like the Security Council to send an observation mission to Guatemala as quickly as possible. This is the first request which I officially make here on behalf of my Government: that an observation commission should be sent to Guatemala to ask questions, to investigate, and to listen to the diplomatic corps.

There are North American journalists in Guatemala who have sent reports on the bombing, on the incidents of the bombing, to their respective periodicals.   Nevertheless, I repeat, my country has not chosen to repel the invaders in the north, although they have already taken three large towns near the Honduran frontier.   It is our desire that the Security Council should in the first place, and with a knowledge of reports which can be obtained, send a warning to the Gov-

ernments of Honduras and Nicaragua, calling upon them to apprehend the exiles and the mercenaries who, for pay, are invading the
territory of Guatemala, and who have operating bases, support bases,
in Nicaragua and Honduras, possibly with assistance, or through people closing their eyes to these actions.

The Ambassador of Guatemala in Honduras lodged a complaint
with the Honduran Ministry of Foreign Affairs in which he denounced
the movements of uniformed mercenary troops by air towards the
frontier of Honduras. We have clear proofs. An observation commission can easily verify what we have stated. The object is clear,
simple and imperative: the Security Council must preserve peace to
avoid the extension of war to this part of the world. This warning
should go forth immediately to these Governments.

My Government's second request is that an observation commission
of the Security Council should be constituted in Guatemala, and in
other countries if necessary, to verify through an examination of
the documentary evidence, the fact that the countries which my
Government accuses have connived at the invasion. .   .   .

To conclude, my country clearly and concretely requests the Security Council's intervention in this matter. The Peace Committee
of the Organization of American States met yesterday. My Government, exercising the option which is open to the Organization's members, this morning officially declined to allow the Organization of
American States and the Peace Committee to concern themselves
with this situation. That is a right embodied in the rules of the
Organization of American States, and I therefore believe that there
would be no purpose in discussing here any proposal by which any
attempt might be made to evade the responsibilities of the Security
Council, which are laid down with the utmost clarity in the United
Nations Charter and which I think it unnecessary to repeat here.
.   .   .

Mr. GOUTHIER (Brazil): .   .   .   It has long been a tradition
among the American States that all disputes and situations which
could threaten or endanger the friendly relations among American
republics should be dealt with by the organization which those republics themselves have set up for that purpose. According to its charter,
the Organization of American States is empowered to deal with and
to solve any problems relating to such disputes or situations. Furthermore, Chapter VIII of the United Nations Charter acknowledges this
principle in Article 52, and I wish to draw the attention of the Council
to paragraph 3 of that Article, which reads as follows:

"The Security Council shall encourage the development of pacific
settlement of local disputes through such regional arrangements or
by such regional agencies either on the initiative of the states concerned or by reference from the Security Council."

I think that the Council should act today according to that very clear provision of our Charter and, without going into the merits of the case, should refer it to the Organization of American States.

For these reasons, and having in mind the traditional way to settle disputes among American republics, my delegation is of the opinion that this matter should be referred to the Organization of American States. Accordingly, I wish to introduce the following draft resolution, which is sponsored by Brazil and Colombia [S/3236]:

"The Security Council,

"Having considered on an urgent basis the communication of the Government of Guatemala to the President of the Security Council,

"Noting that the Government of Guatemala has dispatched a similar communication to the Inter-American Peace Committee, an agency of the Organization of American States,

"Having in mind the provisions of Chapter VIII of the Charter of the United Nations,

"Conscious of the availability of Inter-American machinery which can deal effectively with problems concerning the maintenance of peace and security in the Americas,

"Refers the complaint of the Government of Guatemala to the Organization of American States for urgent consideration;

"Requests the Organization of American States to inform the Security Council as soon as possible, as appropriate, on the measures it has been able to take on the matter."

Mr. ECHEVERRI CORTES (Colombia): It has been a cause of anxiety for my delegation to hear of the violent events in Guatemala related by Mr. Castillo Arriola, the Guatemalan representative, and we hope that there will be an end to any action which might cause shedding of blood. However, my delegation has some comments of a strictly legal nature to make.

Since the San Francisco Conference it has been a concern of the Colombian delegation to avoid any direct appeal to the Security Council without going first to the regional organization, because, in that case, any action taken on this continent to prevent aggression would be at the mercy of the veto. This view was shared by all the American delegations and was expressed in Chapter VIII of the United Nations Charter.

According to Article 33 of the United Nations Charter, the parties to any dispute, the continuation of which is likely to endanger the maintenance of international peace and security, must seek a solution to it and in that connexion mention is made of resort to regional agencies or arrangements. This Article must be taken in conjunction with Article 52, paragraph 2 of which says that every effort must be made to achieve pacific settlement of local disputes through such regional arrangements or agencies before referring them to the Security Council.

I should like to make it quite clear that the provisions of Article 52, paragraph 2, of the United Nations Charter impose on all Members the duty to apply first to the regional organization, which is of necessity the court of first appeal. This is not a right which can be renounced because the States which signed the Charter undertook this obligation. For these legal reasons my delegation has joined the delegation of Brazil in submitting the proposal.

Mr. HOPPENOT (France): At the last meeting of the Security Council, the day before yesterday, [during a discussion of a request by Thailand that the Council consider the situation in Laos,] the President [Mr. Lodge, USA] said:

"The United States was a small country for a long time and still looks at many things from the standpoint of a small country. I hope that I will never live to see the day when a small country comes to the United Nations and asks for protection against war and is simply greeted with the question: What is the hurry?"

When we listened to him then we did not think we should so soon be confronted with the almost academic problem he set. I should like to express, on my own behalf and, I think, on behalf of all the members of the Council, our great appreciation of the trouble the President has taken to convene the Security Council today, despite considerable physical difficulties, in order to enable the Guatemalan representative to lay his request before us as quickly as possible.

As to the substance of the problem before us, it appears a difficult matter for the Council to take a decision at once and without longer consideration. I have examined the draft resolution just submitted by the Brazilian delegation with the support of the Colombian delegation. The French delegation has no objection in principle to voting for this draft resolution. It is right that the Council should have a picture of the whole of the situation referred to it. It can be justly claimed that the Inter-American Peace Committee is qualified to report to us on this subject, comprising as it does a group of countries which have long been accustomed to working together, which are bound one to another by historical and geographical ties, and between which it may prove possible for understanding to be achieved more readily than before an international body of wider scope. I consider that in referring Guatemala's request to the Inter-American Peace Committee as a matter of urgency the Security Council will not be unloading its responsibilities on that committee; for it is requesting the committee to report on the conclusions it reaches after carrying out its enquiry. On those conclusions, in my opinion, it will rest with the Security Council to take its final decision.

There is, however, one immediate responsibility which the Security Council cannot evade without failing in its essential mission: to decide this very day in favour of the immediate cessation of any action involving the loss of human lives, and of all external aid to such action.

It is in this spirit that my delegation proposes to the Council that the following final paragraph should be added to the draft resolution submitted by the Brazilian delegation:

"Without prejudice to such measures as the Organization of American States may take, the Council calls for the immediate termination of any action likely to cause further bloodshed and requests all Members of the United Nations to abstain, in the spirit of the Charter, from giving assistance to any such action."

Needless to say, the French delegation has no particular country in mind in submitting this amendment. It is even less necessary to state that this delegation cannot, so far as it is concerned, attach any credence to the charges levelled by the Guatemalan delegation against the United States; it cannot believe that those charges are well-founded, nor that the United States Government is, either directly or indirectly, the instigator of the events which today plunge the territory of a free and sovereign country into mourning.

What my delegation asks—and believes that it has the right to ask of the Security Council—is simply that it should issue an appeal for the cessation of this bloodshed, so that no more innocent victims may fall today in the city streets and in the countryside of Guatemala, and so that the most tragic consequences of this situation may be ended immediately.

I trust that our Brazilian colleague will be good enough to accept this amendment and join with me in recommending its adoption by the Security Council. . . .

Mr. GOUTHIER (Brazil): I gladly accept the ideas expressed by the representative of France. My delegation shares the views of Mr. Hoppenot, and we sincerely hope that further bloodshed will be avoided. In presenting our proposal we dealt only with the best way of proceeding with the case, taking into account the machinery of the Organization of American States and the principles of the Charter. Keeping within this line of impartiality, we did not prejudge the matter. For my part, I have no objections to the amendment proposed by the representative of France. . . .

Mr. CASTILLO ARRIOLA (Guatemala): . . . I should like to explain to the representative of France that neither my Government nor I, in the course of my remarks, have sought to impute connivance either to the people or to the Government of the United States. I have referred to the United Fruit Company and to certain official groups interested in supporting that company's interests.

After that explanation I must express my thanks to the French representative for his amendment to the Brazilian draft resolution, which closely reflects the anxious feelings of the Guatemalan people

and contains one of the two specific requests I have made this afternoon on behalf of my Government: an appeal to Member States to
abstain from supplying the invading forces with a means of bringing
success to this aggression. I thank the French representative. . . .

From remarks I have heard I understand that the draft resolution
submitted by Brazil and Colombia is based on Articles 33 and 52.
Article 33 says:

"The parties to any dispute, the continuance of which is likely to
endanger the maintenance of international peace and security, shall,
first of all, seek a solution by negotiation, enquiry, mediation, conciliation, arbitration, judicial settlement, resort to regional agencies or
arrangements, or other peaceful means of their own choice."

This article is completely inapplicable to Guatemala's case. The Republic of Guatemala, as can easily be appreciated, has no dispute either with the brother country of Honduras, or with Nicaragua, or
with any other State. Guatemala has no dispute. We have not even
any boundary difficulties. We are in no disagreement about boundaries. Nor is there any question under discussion, of a political, territorial, economic or any other nature. To this day we have enjoyed
excellent diplomatic relations with Honduras. Nicaragua, at its own
wish and for no essential reason, has broken off diplomatic relations
with Guatemala. This Article would be operative in any kind of dispute, but not in the case of an aggression or an invasion; not when open
towns are being machine-gunned, when we have victims among the
innocent civilian population, and when children have been machine-
gunned to create panic. I would ask you to take Article 33 into consideration from this point of view. The Security Council cannot compel the parties to settle their disputes by this means, for in this case
there are no parties and there is no dispute.

In connexion with regional arrangements, Article 52, paragraph 2,
states:

"The Members of the United Nations entering into such arrangements or constituting such agencies shall make every effort to achieve
pacific settlement of local disputes through such regional arrangements or by such regional agencies before referring them to the
Security Council."

For the same reason, this Article is not applicable. We cannot
achieve a pacific settlement with Honduras and Nicaragua because we
have no dispute with them.

On the other hand, if my country's appeal is to be considered from
a legal standpoint, if juridical arguments are to our taste in this hour
of anxiety and aggression, what more weighty juridical argument
could there be than Articles 34, 35 and 39, on which my Government
has based its appeal? My Government considers Articles 33 and 52,
which are perfectly clear, to be irrelevant. We cannot go to a regional
organization to discuss a dispute which does not exist. In view of this

fact I stated that the Guatemalan Embassy in Washington this morning officially renounced on behalf of the Guatemalan Government any intervention by the Organization of American States or the Inter-American Peace Committee in this matter. We are faced with an outright act of aggression. Perhaps at this very moment when it is being proposed to refer the matter to the Inter-American Peace Committee for a subsequent report, aircraft are machine-gunning my country. Under the terms of Article 34 my Government has an unchallengeable right to appeal to the Security Council. That Article reads: "The Security Council may investigate any dispute . . ." Here again, there is reference to a dispute; but we have no dispute. That does not apply to this case. However, the Article goes on as follows: " . . . or any situation which might lead to international friction or give rise to a dispute, in order to determine whether the continuance of the dispute or situation is likely to endanger the maintenance of international peace and security".

Article 35 reads: "Any Member of the United Nations may bring any dispute, or any situation of the nature referred to in Article 34, to the attention of the Security Council or of the General Assembly. A State which is not a Member . . ." and the Article goes on to analyse the other cases. My country is one of the sixty States which originally formed this Organization. Under the Articles I have quoted, the Security Council cannot deny it its right of direct intervention by the Council, not intervention through a regional organization. We recognize the effectiveness of that organization; we have the greatest respect for it and are members of it, but we consider that under Articles 33 and 52, precisely, that organization ceases to be effective when an invasion is already in progress, when aggression has been committed against my country.

I should like to ask you to give your attention to these facts, no aspect of which is such as to allow the Council to avoid direct intervention. . . .

Mr. TSARAPKIN (USSR): The Security Council has before it the protest of the Guatemalan Government against the armed aggression committed by neighbouring States.

As can be seen from the telegram from the Guatemalan Minister for External Relations, which was distributed to the members of the Council as a Security Council document, Guatemala has been the subject of an armed attack by land, sea and air. We are confronted with an absolutely clear and obvious case of aggression—an attack on one of the Central American States, Guatemala, which is a Member of the United Nations.

In these circumstances it is the Council's duty and responsibility to take urgent steps to end the aggression. In the present circumstances and at the present time when the forces of aggression have already been unleashed on the country, the Council cannot refuse to accept this responsibility, and no other body can take its place in this respect at this moment.

A draft resolution on the question has been introduced by Brazil and Colombia. It proposes that the question of the aggression against Guatemala raised in the telegram from the Guatemalan Minister for External Relations should be referred to the Organization of American States. In this case, however, when the forces of aggression are already on Guatemalan territory, a small country which can be crossed in one day's march, we know that Guatemala will be overcome while we refer the question to that organization and allow it time to discuss and decide upon it. Moreover, such a powerful world Power as the United States has already done everything to ensure that this plan will be put into effect.

I have before me the text of a State Department declaration on Guatemala, which says that the most recent outbreak of disorder in Guatemala bears out the point of view previously expressed by the United States concerning possible action against Guatemala by the Organization of American States. Nevertheless, we are now confronted with a draft resolution asking that Guatemala's complaint should be referred to the very Organization of American States which the United States State Department is planning to use to settle its accounts with Guatemala.

Clearly there could be no more ridiculous resolution on this question. At this critical moment when there is not only a threat of aggression against a Member of the United Nations, but when aggression has already occurred, it is intolerable that the Security Council should wish to refuse to take immediate steps to end aggression and to refer the question to the Organization of American States. The United States of America, which dominates the Organization of American States and bends it and controls it at will, has already stated— the State Department said so yesterday—that it wants the question of Guatemala to be referred to the Organization so that its accounts with Guatemala can be settled there. Guatemala's sin has already been explained to the Council by the Guatemalan representative; its sin was to dare to set a limit to the appetites of an American fruit company, the United Fruit Company. .   .   .

It should be noted that the hostile policy of the United States to Guatemala, as the documents show, dates back to 1944. It has been particularly marked since 1952, when, as can be seen from the documents, the Guatemalan Government nationalized vacant and unused lands owned by the United Fruit Company and transferred them to the landless labourers and almost landless peasants. Approximately 100,000 landless labourers and almost landless peasants were given land, land which was not being used at all by the United Fruit Company. The old saying about the dog in the manger would seem to be apt. In view of the fact that the United Fruit Company has such a strong position in the State Department itself and in the United States Senate, it will be seen that that was the last straw. Increasing pressure and influence were brought to bear on Guatemala, and threats directed against Guatemala were to be read daily in the American papers, which stated openly that the time was near when Guatemala would receive the fate she deserved because of her opposition to the United States. There were threats of invasion; and that invasion has been carried out.

We are thus confronted with an open act of aggression against Guatemala, a Member of the United Nations; and we consider that the Security Council should take immediate steps to end this aggression. The Council cannot refer this matter to another body, particularly since, as I have already said, it must be clear, when we remember the State Department announcement to which I have already referred, that Guatemala can expect nothing good from that body. . . .

I should like to say a few more words in opposition to the draft resolution submitted by Brazil and Colombia.

In submitting this draft resolution the representatives of Brazil and of Colombia, and the members of the Council who supported them, referred particularly to Article 52 of the Charter. Article 52, paragraph 2, reads as follows:

"The Members of the United Nations entering into such arrangements [that is, regional arrangements] or constituting such agencies shall make every effort to achieve pacific settlement of local disputes through such regional arrangements or by such regional agencies before referring them to the Security Council."

This paragraph envisages a situation in which no aggression has taken place; a dispute or quarrel exists; the parties are threatening each other, and so forth, but there has been no aggression. We are here confronted with an entirely different situation; the position is quite clear. An act of aggression has been committed against Guatemala.

The Security Council, acting under Article 24 of the Charter, is bound to take steps to end this aggression. Article 24 says: "In order to ensure prompt"—and I would stress the word "prompt"—"and effective action by the United Nations, its Members confer on the Security Council primary responsibility for the maintenance of international peace and security, and agree that in carrying out its duties under this responsibility the Security Council acts on their behalf." On whose behalf? On behalf of the States Members of the United Nations, including the Latin-American States.

Hence there is absolutely no justification for the attempt by Brazil and Colombia to give priority in this matter to the Organization of American States rather than the Security Council. We reject that suggestion; we cannot agree with it. We consider that all the members of the Security Council, acting in the spirit of the Charter, should take a decision in the Council to end the aggression, not to refer the issue to some other body in which accounts with Guatemala will be settled. The intention is to drag Guatemala where the United States will do with that country as it wills. The Council must not allow that.

Secondly, I must draw the attention of the members of the Council to the fact that in referring this dispute to the Organization of American States the attempt is being made to settle the question in a procedural way, to oblige one of the parties to comply with a procedure which it is not willing to accept.

If I understood the interpretation rightly, the Guatemalan representative said that his Government was opposed to Guatemala's complaint of aggression being referred to the Organization of American States. That, I believe, was what he said. But an attempt is now being made to take the opposite decision, a decision which one of the parties does not consider acceptable.

What does Article 36 of the Charter say? Article 36 of the Charter prohibits the adoption of such a decision. Paragraph 2 of that Article states:

"The Security Council should take into consideration any procedures for the settlement of the dispute which have already been adopted by the parties."

But one of the parties has rejected this procedure. That means that adoption of the Brazilian-Colombian draft resolution would be a violation of Article 36, paragraph 2. The Soviet delegation therefore considers that the draft resolution is inadmissible and should not even be put to the vote.

In view of the fact that a situation has arisen which requires that the Security Council should take a decision and do so promptly, we cannot afford to lose time. The Security Council is confronted with an act of aggression against Guatemala, and in view of the fact that the forces of aggression have already invaded Guatemala, it must take immediate action. What action should it take? In the first place, it should decide that all hostilities should cease, that the bloodshed should be ended and that the aggression should stop.

It would be difficult to adopt any complex resolution today, for a certain interval of time has to be maintained between the submission of a draft resolution and the voting on it. We therefore feel that it would be advisable for the Council to limit itself to a text along the following lines:

"The Security Council,

"Having considered on an urgent basis the communication of the Government of Guatemala to the President of the Security Council (S/3232);

"Calls for the immediate termination of any action likely to cause bloodshed and requests all Members of the United Nations to abstain, in the spirit of the Charter, from giving assistance to any such action." . . .

The PRESIDENT: The President will recognize himself for a few minutes in his capacity as representative of the United States of America. . . .

The United States believes in the basic proposition that any Member, large or small, has the right to have an urgent meeting of the Security Council called whenever it feels itself to be in danger. This is so even when, as is sometimes the case, the Security Council may not itself be in the best position to deal directly with the situation.

Guatemala charges that other Governments are pursuing a policy of hostility and aggressiveness against it. These specific Guatemalan allegations involve two of its immediate neighbors, Honduras and Nicaragua, who are charged with disturbing the peace in a particular part of Central America. These charges are indeed serious and certainly warrant urgent examination. But the question arises as to where the situation can be dealt with most expeditiously and most effectively.

The situation appears to the United States Government to be precisely the kind of problem which, in the first instance, should be dealt with on an urgent basis by an appropriate agency of the Organization of American States. The very fact that the Government of Guatemala, as a member of the inter-American system, has already requested that the Organization of American States take action strengthens this view.

It would perhaps be in order for me to inform the Council that while the reports that we receive on the situation in Guatemala are incomplete and fragmentary, the information available to the United States thus far strongly suggests that the situation does not involve aggression but is a revolt of Guatemalans against Guatemalans. The situation in Guatemala, out of which this problem arises, has caused grave concern to the United States Government and to the other members of the Organization of American States. Consequently, the members of the Organization of American States have for some time been conferring intensively among themselves on the Guatemalan situation, with a view to deciding upon what steps should be taken for the maintenance of the peace and security of the continent.

I am very glad that the Guatemalan representative made it crystal clear that he makes no charge whatever against the United States Government because it is certainly true that the United States has no connexion whatever with what is taking place. . . .

The representative of the Soviet Union said that the United States is the master of the Organization of American States. When he says that he is not reflecting on the United States, he is reflecting on himself because it shows that he cannot conceive of any human relationship that is not the relationship of master and servant; he cannot conceive of a relationship in which there is a rule of "live and let live", in which people are equals, in which people can get along by accommodation and by respecting each other. He can only imagine what would happen to somebody who raised his voice against the Soviet Union in Poland or Czechoslovakia, Latvia, Esthonia or one of those countries. Compare that with the way in which representatives of small countries in the United Nations constantly disagree with the United States; and they are welcome to do it. We have no satellites and we do not want any. We do not desire to set up a monolithic structure in the free world.

The Soviet Union representative also said that the United States had prepared this armed intervention. That is flatly untrue; I challenge him to prove it. He cannot do so.   .   .   .

The Soviet Union representative told us that he intends to veto the draft resolution. That will make the second Soviet veto in three days. We had veto No. 59 on Friday, and now we are to have veto No. 60 on Sunday. And what is the Soviet Union vetoing? It is vetoing a move to ask the Organization of American States to try to solve this problem, to try to bind up this wound in the world, and then report back to the Security Council. This draft resolution does not seek to relieve the Security Council of responsibility; it just asks the Organization of American States to see what it can do to be helpful. Paragraph 2 of Article 52 of the Charter states:

"The Members of the United Nations entering into such arrangements"—that is, regional arrangements—"or constituting such agencies shall make every effort to achieve pacific settlement of local disputes through such regional arrangements or by such regional agencies before referring them to the Security Council."

At the very least, that is a harmless provision. It is actually an intelligent provision and it is a constructive provision. Why does the representative of the Soviet Union, a country thousands of miles away from here, undertake to veto a move like that? What is his interest in it? How can this action of his possibly fail to make unbiased observers throughout the world come to the conclusion that the Soviet Union has designs on the American hemisphere?

There is no other explanation, and the articles which have appeared in Pravda and Isvestia during the last two or three days give colour to that assertion. I say to the representative of the Soviet Union, stay out of this hemisphere and do not try to start your plans and your conspiracies over here.

Mr. TSARAPKIN (Union of Soviet Socialist Republics): I feel obliged to reply to the statement which the President has made as representative of the United States of America. Let me point out that no one has quoted the last paragraph of Article 52, wherein it is stated that "This Article in no way impairs the application of Articles 34 and 35"—which Articles impose on the Security Council a definite obligation to act. I leave aside Article 24, which I have already quoted, and which gives the Security Council primary responsibility for the maintenance of international peace and security.

I should now like to reply to another point. The United States representative asked with emotion what was the reason for the Soviet Union's present attitude in the Security Council; why it was interesting itself in the Western Hemisphere. He even voiced the suggestion that the Soviet Union had certain intentions in the Western Hemisphere. That is the usual method of diverting attention from the main issue before the Council.

We are met here today, on a Sunday, to discuss a case of aggression. A Member of the United Nations has been subjected to an armed attack provoked, organized and carried out by the United States of America; and I undertake to show you that that is the case.

I must once again stress that the Soviet Union considers that whether aggression occurs in the Northern or the Southern Hemisphere, the Eastern or the Western Hemisphere, it must be stopped. The Charter binds each Member of the United Nations, and particularly the permanent members of the Security Council, to take all steps in the Council to end aggression even if it occurs in the Western Hemisphere, even if it occurs in Central America against the minute Republic of Guatemala. Tomorrow aggression may be committed against Honduras; the day after tomorrow Nicaragua may be the victim—who knows, the marines may again be sent to that country to lord it there as they once did in the past. Mr. Lodge appears to have forgotten that incident. I could remind him of United States policy towards a number of small States, including Nicaragua itself. Thus aggression is indivisible, whether it takes place in the Western, the Eastern, the Southern or the Northern Hemisphere. Wherever aggression occurs, Mr. Lodge, it must be stopped; territorial and geographical boundaries have no meaning in this connexion; if aggression occurs in the Western Hemisphere then no one is entitled to discuss the question; it must be referred to the Organization of American States. Mr. Lodge failed to mention that yesterday a spokesman for State Department said the United States would settle its accounts with Guatemala in the Organization of American States.

I should like in addition to reply to the charge that while the Soviet Union representative alleged that the aggression had been carried out by the United States he did not prove his allegation. That is not so: I shall prove it. I can cite additional facts later; in the meantime let me draw attention to the following.

The documents which I studied in preparation for this meeting show that when the United States of America had decided on its plan to settle its accounts with Guatemala for the measures taken by that country in connexion with the vacant and unused lands owned by the United Fruit Company, it concluded a special military alliance with Honduras and another with Nicaragua. The facts show, for example, that on 23 April 1954 the Governments of the United States of America and Nicaragua signed a treaty of military assistance and that on 19 May, that is to say three weeks or a month later, Nicaragua broke off diplomatic relations with Guatemala, and was already making political and military preparations to settle its score with Guatemala. The same thing happened in the case of Honduras. On 21 May, almost the same date, the United States signed a treaty of military assistance with Honduras. And when on 27 May Guatemala asked Honduras to sign a treaty of friendship and non-aggression, its proposal was rejected. Thus everything was done to fan the flames and create an atmosphere in which aggression would be easy; and such an atmosphere was in fact created. It was created, first, by the unrestrained, unbridled, hostile propaganda about Guatemala which is familiar to all of us and which we have all read under glaring headlines, and secondly by sending arms to that region.

Let me draw your attention to a despatch from Mr. Wagner, a *Herald Tribune* correspondent. He wrote that it was well known that the United States Government would prefer one of the Latin-American countries to take the initiative in any such action, that is, in launching aggression against Guatemala, and that there were indications that Honduras or Nicaragua may raise the question.

By 23 April, when the treaties of military assistance had been signed between the United States and Nicaragua and the United States and Honduras, everything was ready and the aggression was begun.

Let me add another fact. On one occasion five soldiers were detained (on 25 May the *Daily News* reported that war between Honduras and left-wing Guatemala had seemed near that evening when frontier guards had seized five armed Guatemalans) and the United States immediately sent aircraft loaded with guns, military supplies, vehicles and arms to Honduras and Nicaragua. That is how the United States reacted. Is this really not proof enough for you? You ask for proof. There is as much proof as you want; it is being published daily and quite openly in the American Press.

I could cite still further facts, but I feel that the case is quite clear. The identity of the parties guilty of aggression is an open secret; the United States cannot distort the issue. We shall adduce additional facts at a later stage. At this juncture, and to conclude my reply to the United States representative, I must state that the Soviet Union is taking part in the discussion of this question—and this should be quite clear even to Mr. Lodge—because wherever aggression occurs—in the Western, the Eastern, the Northern or the Southern Hemisphere—it is still aggression; it must be stopped and the Security Council must come to a decision.

Mr. Lodge remarked that he would prefer that the Security Council should refrain from considering aggression when it occurred in the Western Hemisphere, that is, that he wanted the United States to be left alone with all the backward countries in Latin America. But if all those countries are to ignore the Security Council, if they are to be left alone face to face with the United States, the danger to them will be immense. We believe that this should be clear to everyone, and that the introduction of a draft resolution in which it is proposed that the Security Council should not consider a case of aggression in Central America against a Member of the United Nations is an attempt to prevent the Security Council from considering the question.

At this juncture, when an act of aggression has already been committed, when foreign troops have already invaded Guatemala and aircraft are bombing the country, I feel that to refer the question to an organization in which the United States proposes to settle accounts with Guatemala would be not only wrong but contrary to the fundamental purposes and principles of the United Nations.

The Security Council has no right to wash its hands of its primary responsibility for the maintenance of international peace and security. Aggression knows no territorial limits, and wherever it is committed, even in Central America, the Security Council is in duty bound to consider the case and take prompt action to put an end to it. . . .

Mr. CASTILLO ARRIOLA (Guatemala): I should like to refer very briefly to an explanation of the stage reached in the Organization of American States in dealing with the notification of the invasion handed in by Guatemala. First of all, however, I wish to make a few comments on what Mr. Lodge said in his speech. He said that I had not made conclusive accusations; I should like to tell him that I did not, indeed, come here to make accusations or to present any official view of my Government to that effect. One of my Government's requests, its most important request, is that the Council should take steps. Besides, I should like to speak of what Mr. Lodge himself gave as his Government's or his own point of view—that there was no invasion in Guatemala. We, a people who are undergoing bombardment and machine-gunning by civil aircraft, consider that there is an invasion. What could be a better solution than to send a United Nations observation commission to Guatemala and find out which assertion is true? . . .

I should like briefly to explain that my Government has not referred the essential feature of the matter to the Organization of American States. It has merely notified the Peace Committee of the Organization of American States of the invasion, but has asked it to adopt no position until the Security Council has taken action. Thus my country and my Government have renounced the possibility of intervention by that Organization but article 20 of the charter of the Organization of American States binds States to submit to the organization any dispute which may arise between the American States. But, as I said, neither this article nor that of the United Nations Charter is applicable, for we have no dispute with either Honduras, Nicaragua or any other State. This is simply aggression. Hence there is no obligation on the part of my country or my Government to submit this question to the Organization of American States. This right is undeniable and my country cannot be obliged to bring this matter before the Organization of American States. My country has asked the Security Council to act with the authority, and in accordance with the obligations, conferred on it by Articles 34, 35 and 39 of the Charter. In the last analysis, and such being the standpoint of my Government, which has the right to take action, a case of conflict has arisen between the obligations undertaken by Member States of the United Nations under the Charter, and Article 103 must apply. I would ask you to consider this Article, which reads:

"In the event of a conflict between the obligations of the Members of the United Nations under the present Charter and their obligations under any other international agreement, their obligations under the present Charter shall prevail."

It is obvious that in this conflict —if it can be so called, despite the fact that my country has not applied to, but merely notified, the Organization of American States—Articles 34, 35 and 39 of the United Nations Charter must apply. I must also point out in this connexion that Article 52, paragraph 4, lays down that:

"This Article in no way impairs the application of Articles 34 and 35."

Thus, under the Charter, the Security Council is bound by a duty, which it cannot disregard, to investigate this situation which my country, in exercise of the right conferred on it by the Charter, has brought to the notice of the Security Council. I ask you to give thought to this very important aspect of the situation. . . .

The PRESIDENT: We shall now vote on the Brazilian and Colombian draft resolution, as amended [S/3236/Rev. 1].

A vote was taken by show of hands.

In favour: Brazil, China, Colombia, Denmark, France, Lebanon, New Zealand, Turkey, United Kingdom of Great Britain and Northern Ireland, United States of America.

Against: Union of Soviet Socialist Republics.

The result of the vote was 10 in favour and one against.

The PRESIDENT: Anticipating that this issue would come up, I have studied the principles involved and have concluded that, while it is rather a close question in my mind, on balance this is not a procedural question and is, I regret to say, subject to the veto.

The draft resolution was not adopted, the negative vote being that of a permanent member of the Security Council.

Mr. HOPPENOT (France): The French delegation deeply regrets that the Soviet Union delegation has vetoed the Brazilian draft resolution. This veto effectively prevents the Security Council from adopting practical measures which the United Kingdom representative has called reasonable and constructive, and which were worked out by the Brazilian and Colombian representatives to facilitate the peaceful settlement of the situation brought to our notice by the representative of Guatemala.

Once again the veto has paralysed the Council and prevented it from discharging its duty under the Charter. Once again the delegation of the Soviet Union takes on itself a heavy responsibility with regard to the maintenance of peace and international security.

I agree with Mr. Malik [Lebanon], who spoke a few moments ago, that it is highly desirable that the Security Council should not remain in the situation of utter impotence in which it has been placed by the Soviet veto; that, at least on the moral plane, the Council should give expression to its authority and bring the blood-letting to an end; and that the Council, by making a general appeal to that effect, should respond to the feelings of all those free and peace-loving men who have reposed their confidence in us. If the only result of this appeal is that a single human life is spared, that a single innocent victim is saved from joining all those who have already fallen on the battlefields of civil and international wars in the course of so many years, it is still our duty to launch it. Hence I propose to re-introduce as a separate draft resolution the text of the amendment to which all the members of the Council and the representative of Guatemala kindly gave their support.

I wish to make it as clear as possible that there is nothing in this step by the French delegation which can be construed as casting doubt on, or weakening, the competence of the Inter-American Peace Committee or the legitimacy of its action in this matter. On the contrary: the correctness of resort to the machinery provided by the statutes of this organization only gains confirmation from the failure of the Security Council brought about by the Soviet veto. I wish to make quite certain that no doubt remains in the mind of anyone, and particularly in the minds of our Brazilian and Colombian colleagues.

The new draft resolution which I propose to submit will accordingly read as follows:

"The Security Council,

"Having considered on an urgent basis the communication of the Government of Guatemala to the President of the Security Council (S/3232),

"Calls for the immediate termination of any action likely to cause bloodshed and requests all Members of the United Nations to abstain, in the spirit of the Charter, from rendering assistance to any such action."

It is hardly necessary for me to repeat to the Honduran representative that there is absolutely nothing in these general terms, taken from the letter and the spirit of the Charter, which can be construed by anyone to mean that the Government of Honduras, Nicaragua or any other country may have any direct or indirect responsibility for the regrettable events now taking place on Guatemalan territory.

Unless members of the Council ask for this text to be distributed beforehand I would ask the President to be good enough to put it to the vote immediately.

The PRESIDENT: We shall now vote on the draft resolution which has just been proposed by the representative of France.

A vote was taken by show of hands.

The draft resolution was adopted unanimously.

3.   Letter from the Representative of Guatemala to the Secretary-General, 22 June 1954.

S/3241 (23 June 1954); SCOR, IX, Supp. for April–June 1954, pp. 14–15.

I have the honour to request you to inform the Security Council, and the President of the Council, on behalf of the constitutional Government of the Republic of Guatemala, that the resolution adopted by the Council at its 675th meeting, held on 20 June 1954, has not been complied with by those States Members of the United Nations which have acquiesced in or assisted from their territories the acts of aggression suffered by Guatemala, although the resolution is absolutely binding upon them under Article 25 of the Charter.

During the last forty-eight hours, aggressive acts against my country have continued by land, sea and air and have undoubtedly been committed from airfields and centres of operations situated outside Guatemalan territory while the Guatemalan National Army has confined its operations to the defence of the national territory and to repelling the aggressors.

My Government therefore officially requests, through me, that an urgent meeting of the Security Council should be convened so that the Council can use its authority with Honduras and Nicaragua as States Members of the United Nations to secure the cessation of all assistance to, or acquiescence in, the aggressive acts which are being committed by the mercenary forces.

When the Security Council adopted the above-mentioned resolution, it implicitly recognized that some States Members of the United Nations were giving assistance to Guatemala's invaders, and warned them all that they should cease doing so immediately.   The resolution juridically defined the international aggression against Guatemalan soil and must take precedence over any other decision having the character of a personal or unilateral opinion which it may be wished for selfish motives to give against Guatemala.

I reiterate, in the name of my Government, the request that the President of the Security Council should immediately convene a meeting of the Council in virtue of the fact that Guatemala officially gives notice that the resolution adopted on 20 June 1954 by the Security Council has not been complied with by other States Members, thus creating a situation covered by Article 35 of the Charter, which takes precedence over any different unilateral definition.

The Security Council, by adopting the resolution dated 20 June 1954, assumed full jurisdiction in this matter in that it not only called upon the States Members that were giving assistance to commit the aggression against the Guatemalan Republic to abstain from doing so altogether but also rejected the draft resolution submitted by the Brazilian and Colombian delegations [S/3236] which referred examination of the other aspects of the aggression against Guatemala to the Organization of American States. Even in that case, which is juridically impossible, the Security Council of the United Nations retains full jurisdiction in the matter, because Article 52, paragraph 4, of the Charter makes the obligations of the Council under Articles 34, 35 and 39 imperative.

The Organization of American States by strict standards of international law cannot take action because:

(a) The Guatemalan Government which is the victim of aggression has, fully within its rights, expressly requested that that Organization should not deal with this matter;

(b) Under Article 103 of the Charter of the United Nations, in the event of a conflict between the obligations of Guatemala as a Member of the United Nations under the Charter and any obligations it may have towards the Organization of American States, its obligations towards the United Nations prevail;

(c) Although Guatemala might be considered to belong to the Organization, which is the case, as far as this specific instance is concerned, it has not completed the ratifications of the Organization's fundamental agreements of Rio de Janeiro and Bogotá. It follows that neither the Organization of American States itself, nor the Inter-American Peace Committee, which forms part of it, may deal with the aggression against Guatemala; the former for the reason already noted, and the latter because it is only competent to deal with disputes between the Member States, and certainly Guatemala has no dispute of any kind with the neighbouring States of Honduras and Nicaragua.

4. *Discussion in the Security Council, 25 June 1954.*

SCOR, IX, Mtg. 676, pp. 1–34.

The PRESIDENT [Mr. Lodge, USA]: I wish to draw the attention of the members of the Security Council to various communications which have been received on the question before us.

In particular, we have before us a letter from the representative of Guatemala dated 22 June 1954, document S/3241 requesting an urgent meeting of the Security Council.

We also have a letter dated 24 June 1954 from the representative of the Soviet Union, document S/3247, likewise requesting an urgent meeting of the Security Council.

We also have before us a cablegram dated 24 June 1954, from the permanent representative of Nicaragua, document S/3249, stating that a fact-finding commission of the Inter-American Peace Committee will be received in Nicaragua, and that, in the opinion of his Government, the matter before the Council should be referred first to the Inter-American regional organization.

We have also received a cablegram from the Ambassador of Honduras, document S/3250, opposing consideration of this question in the Security Council on the ground that the Inter-American Peace Committee is already acting.

And, finally, we have before us a cablegram dated 23 June 1954 from the Chairman of the Inter-American Peace Committee of the Organization of American States, document S/3245, informing the Security Council that on 23 June the representative of Nicaragua proposed that a commission of inquiry of the Inter-American Peace Committee should be established, to proceed to Guatemala, Honduras and Nicaragua, and that the committee voted unanimously to deal with the question and so informed Guatemala.

Mr. GOUTHIER (Brazil): . . .   The Security Council is aware of a communication addressed to the Secretary-General of the United Nations by the President of the Inter-American Peace Committee in which he referred to the proposal to establish a committee on information composed of the members of the Peace Committee for the purpose of proceeding to Guatemala in order to obtain "the necessary information to enable the committee to establish the facts and to suggest effective methods of achieving a speedy settlement of the dispute".

The President of the Inter-American Peace Committee also stated that this proposal, by unanimous decision of the committee, was sent to the Government of Guatemala, and furthermore that "the committee took the liberty of expressing its hope that the Guatemalan Government would see fit to agree to the proposed procedure".

I was informed unofficially that yesterday the Minister for External Relations of Guatemala had, by direct communication with the President of the Inter-American Peace Committee, agreed to receive a fact-finding committee which was to leave tonight for the area of conflict. However, at the last moment the official communication to that effect had not been received. If it were not for that fact, a commission composed of both diplomats and military men from Argentina, Brazil, Cuba, the United States and Mexico, could leave tonight. The Inter-American Peace Committee issued the following statement after yesterday's meeting:

"The Inter-American Peace Committee met in special session to-night during which it was unanimously decided that, if the Government of Guatemala should accept the proposal which the Inter-American Peace Committee officially transmitted to it yesterday, the Inter-American Peace Committee would immediately proceed to authorize the departure for Guatemala, Honduras and Nicaragua of the fact-finding committee provided for in the proposal."

Nevertheless, even if the Guatemalan Government does not choose to co-operate with the Inter-American Peace Committee, that organization had already been seized of the matter and was bound to go into it in order to fulfil its obligations. As a matter of fact, the fact-finding committee can even now, regardless of any steps taken by Guatemala, go to Nicaragua and Honduras. This could prove very useful since Guatemala has charged these two countries with acts of aggression and has maintained that from the territory of these neighbouring countries planes have been allowed to take off on aggressive missions against Guatemala. Besides this committee of information on the spot, there are several other means provided for in the machinery of the Organization of American States to deal with the problem.

This proves that the Organization of American States can and does act promptly. Their action shows the correctness of our proposal to the Security Council and of the stand we took here on 20 June. The USSR veto only delayed for one or two days the action which otherwise, I feel sure, the Inter-American Peace Committee would have taken at the request of the Security Council. Unfortunately the Soviet veto prevented the Security Council from availing itself of the opportunity to demonstrate the efficacy of the system set forth in the Charter according to which, in certain instances, regional organizations should be put into operation within the larger scope of the world system.

I would like to make it clear, in the name of my Government, that in emphasizing the adequacy of the machinery of the Organization of American States and the appropriateness and competence of a body recognized under the Charter to solve inter-American conflicts and disputes, our stand here can by no means be implied as being against Guatemala, Honduras or Nicaragua.

I do not want to go into the allegations and counter-allegations that have been made. Brazil has always advocated full respect for the sovereign rights of every State—not only of the American States but of any nation—and we never depart from this principle.

I would like to point out that for more than sixty years the Organization of American States has been a useful and efficient instrument for the solution of conflicts, disagreements and strained situations confronting the American republics. The organization has adequate machinery in the many organs and procedures established by it in order to solve such differences. The long record of achievement of the system of the Organization of American States is a flagrant demonstration of its capacity to deal with political situations similar to the one which confronts us. In the Organization of American States all the members have equal rights; whether large or small, each nation has one vote on decisions, and the undemocratic principle of the veto is unknown. . . .

The Inter-American Peace Committee is an organism which is part of the framework of the Organization of American States. It is adequate to deal with the matter. The competence of the Inter-American Peace Committee is stated in articles 6 and 7 of its statutes, adopted 24 May 1950:

"6. The Committee, whose sole purpose is to promote the maintenance of peaceful and amicable relations among the American States, shall have the duty of keeping constant vigilance to insure that the States between which any dispute exists or may arise, of any nature whatsover, may solve it as quickly as possible, and of suggesting, without detriment to the methods adopted by the parties or to the procedures which they may agree upon, the measures and steps which may be conducive to a settlement;

"7. The Committee may take action at the request of any American State, when the recourse of direct negotiation has been exhausted, when none of the other customary procedures of diplomacy or of pacific settlement is in process or when existing circumstances render negotiation impracticable."

Since the adoption of the United Nations Charter, the Inter-American Peace Committee has been requested to act within the limits of its competence in order to resolve differences arising between American States—Cuba and the Dominican Republic (1948), Haiti and the Dominican Republic (1949), Peru and Cuba (1949), in the Caribbean area (1949), again Cuba and the Dominican Republic (1949 and 1951), and then Colombia and Peru (1953–1954).

In view of the action already taken by the Organization of American States, which is acting with commendable expedition, the most reasonable attitude which the Security Council can assume in the matter is to wait for the report of the fact-finding committee. We have already received a first communication from the Inter-American Peace Committee and for that reason are bound to receive another one, after the committee has completed its task. Any action by the Security Council at this stage or even any discussion of the subject without the proper information would not be justified and could only introduce confusion into the present situation. For this reason, the Brazilian delegation is of the opinion that we should not proceed with such a discussion. I would therefore vote against the adoption of the agenda. . . .

Mr. TSARAPKIN (USSR): Point of order.

The PRESIDENT: What is the point of order?

Mr. TSARAPKIN (USSR): I see from the statement which has just been made by the Brazilian representative that the substance of the question is now being discussed before the Council has adopted its agenda and that it is suggested that the Council should take a very serious decision without giving the representative of Guatemala, that is to say, the representative of the country which has been attacked, a chance to participate. I protest against this procedure and request that, since the substantive discussion of the question, of a very serious aspect of the question, has already begun, the Guatemalan representative should be invited to come to the Council table, as it will be very important for us to hear his opinion on this matter.

The PRESIDENT: The Chair will rule on the point of order raised by the representative of the Soviet Union. It is quite true that we are now debating the adoption of the agenda and that speeches should be confined to that subject. In my opinion—and [I] listened very carefully to the speech of the representative of Brazil—everything that the representative of Brazil said was squarely within the limitations imposed by the fact that we are discussing the adoption of the agenda. That is the first point.

The second point concerns inviting the representatives of Guatemala, Nicaragua and Honduras to the Council table. According to the practice that the Council has followed from the beginning, it is not customary to invite non-members of the Security Council to come to the table until after the agenda has been adopted.

The President therefore rules that it is not in order to call these representatives to the table until after the adoption of the agenda. In the meantime, all debates should remain within the limits of the adoption of the agenda. . . .

Mr. TSARAPKIN (USSR): There can be no justification anywhere —either in the Charter or in the rules of procedure—for your objections to my proposal to invite the Guatemalan representative to the Council table.

In the present case we must be guided by the Charter. Article 32 of the United Nations Charter states:

"Any Member of the United Nations which is not a member of the Security Council or any State which is not a Member of the United Nations, if it is a party to a dispute under consideration by the Security Council, shall be invited to participate, without vote, in the discussion relating to the dispute."

The discussion relating to this dispute has already begun. I have quoted word for word the relevant sentence in the Charter. The Brazilian representative has touched on the substance of the question; he has said that the question must be referred to the Organization of American States for consideration, and that the Security Council should postpone its decision, in other words, that it should take no decision. Guatemala, on the other hand, the victim of aggression, requests precisely the opposite, namely, that the Security Council should take immediate steps to put an end to aggression. Yet the Brazilian representative proposes that the Security Council should postpone consideration of the Guatemalan question altogether.

Thus we have two conflicting points of view: the request by the victim of aggression that the Security Council should take immediate action to put an end to aggression and the proposal of the Brazilian representative that this question should not be discussed for a time. Thus we see that the very substance of Guatemala's appeal to the Security Council is at issue. Yet steps are now being taken to prevent the Security Council from dealing with this question at this time, without giving the Guatemalan representative a hearing.

I cannot agree that we are now discussing a procedural question. Everyone present realizes that this is not a procedural question, and the Security Council will not, I believe, be prevented from dealing with the Guatemalan question by a procedural ruse, by various procedural manoeuvres. I maintain that in the present instance it is our duty to extend an invitation to the Guatemalan representative. I challenge the President's ruling, believing that at this stage of the debate, when the substance of the question is already under discussion, the injured party, which has fallen victim to aggression and attack, must participate in the discussion of the question.   .   .   .

The PRESIDENT: The representative of the Soviet Union has challenged my ruling. The ruling is that the Security Council is not involved in a discussion relating to the dispute within the meaning of Article 32 and rule 37 of the rules of procedure until the agenda is adopted. The representative of the Soviet Union has challenged the ruling of the President. Those who are in favour of the challenge by the Soviet representative and opposed to the ruling of the President, please raise their hands.

A vote was taken by a show of hands.

In favour: Union of Soviet Socialist Republics.

Against: Brazil, China, Colombia, Denmark, France, Lebanon, New Zealand, Turkey, United Kingdom of Great Britain and Northern Ireland, United States of America.

The motion was rejected by 10 votes to one.

The President's ruling was maintained.

Mr. ECHEVERRI CORTES (Colombia): The American regional system, which dates back to the hemisphere conference convened by Simón Bolivar and held at Panama in 1824, is the fruit of the most continuous efforts of the countries of the continent and represents its best historical achievements. Ten general conferences—from the conference at Washington in 1889 to the one at Caracas in 1954—four consultative meetings and several special meetings, one of the most important of which was that at Chapultepec in 1945, attest the special and overriding interest which the American countries have placed in the creation, development and perfecting of the regional system.

Conference after conference, endeavour after endeavour, fighting against difficulties of many kinds, the edifice of the inter-American system has risen and has become the most perfect international legal body, because it is the most complete, the most democratic and the most advanced in effective service for peace and security. Resolutions VIII and XI of the Conference on the problems of war and peace which met at Mexico City in 1945 are documents which mark one of the most significant stages in the course of the formation of the system.

As is well known, resolution VIII, entitled the Act of Chapultepec, fixed the bases of the provisions set forth two years later in the Inter-American Treaty of Reciprocal Assistance of Rio de Janeiro and resolution XI laid down the lines for the present Charter of the Organization of American States.

Actuated by the same spirit which has achieved the present vitality of the regional system, the American countries have given full support to the United Nations from its foundation. Accordingly, they attended the San Francisco Conference with convinced faith and at that meeting their main endeavours were to ensure that the Charter of the world organization should harmonize with the intentions defined only a few days previously at Chapultepec in order that their participation in the San Francisco Conference should not impair the success achieved in the regional system and, specifically, that such rules as the unanimity rule concerning decisions of the Security Council should not impede the application of the effective stipulations of reciprocal assistance pledged among the American countries, and thereby put back the international law prevailing in the hemisphere to a stage which had definitively been superseded.

Thanks to those efforts, very important changes were made in the Dumbarton Oaks proposals. Those changes are embodied mainly in Chapters VI, VII and VIII of the United Nations Charter.

In Chapter VI, the outstanding differences between the present text and the original proposal are in Article 33, namely the express inclusion of the reference to regional arrangements or regional agencies.

Among the procedures which parties must adopt to settle disputes likely to endanger the maintenance of international peace and security, Article 36, paragraph 2, provides that the Security Council should take into consideration any procedures for the settlement of disputes which have already been adopted by the parties. Among these procedures are those adopted by the American States; in this connexion, Article 37 provides that when a dispute endangering peace and security is referred to the Security Council, the Council must decide whether to take action under Article 36 which, as has been stated, contains a reference to regional systems, or whether to use another procedure.

There is, however, a fundamental difference in Chapter VII. This is Article 51 of the Charter, which does not occur in the Dumbarton Oaks proposals, and which establishes the inherent right of individual or collective self-defence. This Article enabled the American States to join the United Nations without turning their backs on their Chapultepec agreements on hemispheric security, and this is the basis of the Treaty of Reciprocal Assistance of Rio de Janeiro.

I wish now to quote two articles from the Treaty of Reciprocal Assistance of Rio de Janeiro, which are not widely known:

"Article 1. The High Contracting Parties formally condemn war and undertake in their international relations not to resort to the threat or the use of force in any manner inconsistent with the provisions of the Charter of the United Nations or of this Treaty."

"Article 2. As a consequence of the principle set forth in the preceding article, the High Contracting Parties undertake to submit every controversy which may arise between them to methods of peaceful settlement and to endeavour to settle any such controversy among themselves by means of the procedures in force in the Inter-American system before referring it to the General Assembly or the Security Council of the United Nations."

The amendment in Chapter VIII consisted of adding paragraph 2 of Article 52 which states categorically that Members of the United Nations entering into regional arrangements or agencies shall make every effort to achieve pacific settlement of local disputes through such regional arrangements or by such regional agencies. The most cursory comparison of the texts of the Dumbarton Oaks proposals and the United Nations Charter will suffice to show the value of all these amendments made by the American States at the San Francisco Conference by dint of efforts which will be viewed with admiration in the history of international relations.

It was owing to these changes that the United Nations Charter was reconciled, as I have stated, with the progress of the regional system and that it was possible to sign and put into effect not only the Treaty of Reciprocal Assistance of Rio de Janeiro but also the Pact of Bogotá, the statute of the Organization of American States which guarantees the co-operation of all American States for peace and security and for economic and social progress.   I wish in this connexion to quote a relevant article of the Pact of Bogotá:

"Article 2.   The High Contracting Parties recognize the obligation to solve international controversies by regional pacific procedures before referring them to the Security Council of the United Nations."

As Americans, we are justly proud of the degree of development attained by inter-American law which is one of the great achievements of our peoples.   It is well known that American law is considerably more efficient, more firmly based and more complete than the world system or any other regional system.   The most important fact, however, is that it is the law of the countries themselves, identified with their deepest interests.

Therefore, the American States have at all times been careful to ensure that there shall be no encroachment on the rule of this law. From the outset, the Latin-American States have given their firm and loyal support to the United Nations [but] would do nothing which might be detrimental to the prestige of the regional organization. Therefore, when they are endeavouring to maintain the efficiency, authority and competence of the regional system, they have no trace of any hostile intent towards the universal organization and no wish to create any antagonism between one system and the other.   On the contrary, they base themselves on the principle that the regional system forms part of the world system and are convinced that in inter-American affairs the regional system works more effectively than the world system.   They therefore endeavour to maintain the prestige and functions of the regional system on the understanding that it will redound to the credit of the United Nations of which the inter-American system is merely a branch.

What the American countries could never accept would be that—as the United Nations Charter clearly lays down in Articles 33 and 52 that in settling a dispute likely to endanger peace the parties must first of all use regional arrangements and regional agencies and make every effort to achieve a settlement through them, and as the Charter lays down in Article 36 that the Security Council in considering a dispute of this kind should take into consideration any procedures for its settlement which have already been adopted by the parties, these provisions being the result of efforts for the purpose of avoiding the veto—regional action should be paralysed, since that would allow such a veto to achieve precisely what was feared and obviated in time at San Francisco.

Together with the other American countries, Colombia strove tenaciously and successfully at San Francisco to assure harmony between the world organization and the regional organization. Because of this precedent and its constant interest in perfecting the American system, Colombia today urges the Security Council, without reservations, to abstain from intervening in the activities of the regional agencies.

The President has before him the communication from the chairman of the Inter-American Peace Committee informing him that this agency of the American system has taken the problem under consideration at the request of Honduras and Nicaragua and that in performance of its functions it will send a fact-finding committee to the scene of the conflict.

It should also be remembered that Guatemala too, initially went before this American agency and that it withdrew that request only after the Soviet veto against that system. I do not believe that a country would apply to an agency if it had no faith in its impartiality. The Peace Committee is a body composed of representatives of Argentina, Brazil, Cuba, Mexico and the United States and has acted with wisdom and a high sense of American interests whenever it has been entrusted with missions of promoting peace on the continent. All the governments have acknowledged this, including Guatemala, which has applied to this committee in the past.

The appointment of another commission by the Security Council would be redundant and, we believe, improper and would imply a disauthorization of an American agency; my delegation could not agree to that.

Accordingly, the Colombian delegation considers it its duty to endeavour to prevent the veto or any other outside manoeuvre from impairing the authority and prestige of the regional system, since such manoeuvres would constitute a most inacceptable intervention in American affairs by totalitarian communism.

The Colombian delegation will therefore vote against the adoption of the agenda. .   .   .

Mr. MUNRO (New Zealand): At our 675th meeting, I stated my delegation's view that it was fully consistent with its own over-riding concern for the maintenance of international peace and security for the Council to refer this problem first to the Organization of American States and to ask it to report to the Council at an early date. That is still our position. .   .   .

In the meantime, it does not seem helpful to my delegation for the Council to debate the matter any further. Our preference would be that, following the adoption of the agenda, we should note the action taken by the Organization of American States and then adjourn.

My delegation considers, however, that the Council should not, by any decision it may reach, give the appearance of abdicating the supreme responsibility and authority conferred on it by the Charter.

This, we feel, is a matter of principle and of cardinal importance to small nations like our own. In our view any decision not to proceed today with the discussion of the Guatemalan complaint does not affect this principle and does not prejudice the Council's right to take up the question in the future if events make this necessary. Therefore, we consider, very emphatically, that the Council should not proceed with the substantive debate today but should at the same time maintain its over-riding responsibility.

Mr. DONS MOELLER (Denmark): I am in substantial agreement with the position of the representative of New Zealand which has just been set forth. May I say that this matter, which has been proposed for discussion in the provisional agenda, has created very great interest in the whole world and perhaps even more so in the smaller countries, and not the least in my country, Denmark. There is so much interest that *prima facie* my Government was of the view, as far as I understand it, that it might well have been appropriate for the United Nations itself to investigate this matter, or in some way associate itself with any investigation to be undertaken by other means. However, with a view to the provisions contained in Chapter VIII of the Charter, and considering the firm practice which has developed with regard to the way in which disputes on the American continent are dealt with, we for our part would not wish to oppose a procedure along the lines now suggested by the Inter-American Peace Committee, namely, that the Inter-American Peace Committee should send observers to the countries in question to investigate the facts and that they should submit proposals to the Committee.

The Security Council will thus in no way divest itself of its interest in the matter, because it is clear from Article 54 of the Charter and from the words of the Secretary-General of the Inter-American Peace Committee, that the committee is ready and willing to keep the Security Council fully informed of the results of its procedure. If, therefore, the matter is placed on the agenda of the Security Council, I dare say we would be completely in agreement as to an adjournment, until such time as we know the results of the examination which the Inter-American Peace Committee may undertake, provided that this examination is terminated within a fairly short period of time.

But this does not lead us to the conclusion that we should not adopt the agenda. The procedure that would seem to us to be most correct would be to place the matter on the agenda and hear whether the representative of Guatemala has some new information or new proposals to offer. If nothing new emerges, we would certainly agree to an adjournment and would leave, with full confidence, the examination of the matter in the hands of the Inter-American Peace Committee.

I would like to underline the fact that the position which I have tried to explain here should in no way be taken as a sign of lack of confidence in the Organization of American States or in the delegations which have proposed some other procedure. However, to us it is of prime importance that a Member State who so desires should have a right to be heard, and that only after that should we deal with the actual decisions which the Council might take on the question.

Mr. TSARAPKIN (USSR): I should like to go back to what happened at the beginning of this meeting when the President gave a ruling, which was upheld by ten members of the Security Council against the solitary vote of the Soviet Union representative, concerning the question of issuing an invitation to the representative of the State which is the victim of aggression—the representative of Guatemala—to take a seat at the Council table, in view of the fact that the question is being dealt with in substance here.

Acting in his capacity as President of the Council and of representative of the United States of America, the President prevented such an invitation from being issued and cynically observed that the representative of Guatemala could express his viewpoint after the adoption of the agenda. But it is already apparent that the agenda will not be adopted, that the Security Council will consequently not discuss this question and that the representative of Guatemala will not be given a hearing. Thus, the representative of a State which has been subjected to invasion is being deprived of its right to a hearing in the Security Council under Article 32 of the Charter.

I declare that there has been a violation, through procedural ruses and manoeuvres, of Article 32 of the Charter under the terms of which a State which is the victim of aggression and has referred the question to the Security Council has the right of a hearing. Such is the case and no one can be deceived.

In the second place, reference has been made here to Article 52 of the Charter. Admittedly, Article 52 provides for the consideration of certain disputes between States in regional organizations. It states precisely, however, that such organizations can examine all types of disputes before they are referred to the Security Council— I would emphasize, before they are referred to the Security Council. But this question is now before the Security Council. On Sunday 20 June a decision was taken calling for a halt to aggression and a cease-fire, and requesting States to abstain from giving assistance to the invaders, and so on.

The real subject of discussion, therefore, is the immediate adoption of measures to ensure the fulfilment of this Security Council decision. Moreover, if we are to abide by our established practice and procedure, we cannot permit the issue of including the Guatemalan question on the Security Council's agenda to be settled by means of procedural machinations nor the exclusion of the question from the agenda as a result of such machinations.   .   .   .

Thus the situation is perfectly clear. In spite of the fact that an act of aggression has been committed, that the aggressor is advancing into Guatemala, that at this moment while I am speaking, Guatemala City, the capital of Guatemala is being bombed, procedural ruses are being used here to prevent the Security Council from discussing the question.

I should like to know whether this is in conformity with the spirit, task and purposes of the United Nations. It is said here that the Organization of American States should deal with the matter. Surely, it has never been our practice to transmit questions of aggression to some other organization, particularly the Organization of American States. For all I know, it may be a good organization and Brazil and Colombia may like it, but the procedure of outside settlement cannot be forced upon the Council. Nobody seems to wish to take account of the Article of the Charter to which I have already drawn attention. Article 36, paragraph 2, of the Charter reads:

"The Security Council should take into consideration any procedures for the settlement of the dispute which have already been adopted by the parties."

Guatemala has stated in the Security Council that it does not agree to such a procedure for settling the dispute. Hence, there is a clear violation of Article 36 of the Charter. In spite of the clear provisions of the Charter and the fact that one of the parties—what is more, the victim of aggression—objects to such a procedure of settling the dispute, attempts are being made to do precisely that. And this is consequently illegal.

Thus we see that account is being taken not of the constitutional provisions of the Articles of the Charter, but only of the word of one State which is involved—very seriously involved—as a party, or rather as the organizer of this aggression. . . .

Today Guatemala is the victim of aggression. Tomorrow it may be Honduras, and the day after it may be Colombia, which has previously been the victim of aggression. The representative of Colombia will remember how the Republic of Panama came into existence. I am sure he has not forgotten.

That is what history tells us, and very recent history too, but an attempt has been made here to reproach the Soviet Union with making use of the veto. The reason why the Soviet Union voted against the transfer of the question of an act of aggression to the Organization of American States was that it believes that the question of putting a stop to aggression should be deal with by the Security Council, the body upon which Article 24 of the Charter lays primary responsibility for the maintenance of peace and security. I can read you Article 24 of the Charter:

"In order to ensure prompt and effective action by the United Nations, its Members confer on the Security Council primary responsibility for the maintenance of international peace and security, and agree that in carrying out its duties under this responsibility the Security Council acts on their behalf."

The Security Council, and not some sort of organization of American States, should act on behalf of these States. If some other body is substituted for the Security Council, if the question is transferred to the Organization of American States, it means that the Charter has once more been violated and its principles undermined.

Naturally the Soviet Union could not support the attempt to prevent the Security Council from taking steps to put an end to aggression. The USSR cannot support these attempts to undermine still further the United Nations and in particular the Security Council, one of its principal organs.

I again refer to Article 36 of the Charter, and to the fact that we cannot forcibly adopt a procedure of settlement to which one of the parties objects. Article 36 must be obeyed, and the Security Council should consider, not whether or not to place on the agenda a question which is already there, but what measures it should take to put an end to aggression in Guatemala. Guatemala does not object to an observation commission being sent to the spot, but it wants the Security Council to send there a commission of inquiry which should submit a report and propose measures for restoring peace and putting an end to aggression.

Hence, I again stress that in spite of the demands made here by the Government of Guatemala, the victim of aggression, an attempt is being made to return to the proposal which the Security Council rejected on 20 June; by hook or by crook, as the saying goes, in one way or another, attempts are being made to wrench the question away from the Security Council, to prevent the United Nations and the Security Council from taking a decision on the question and to prevent the adoption of emergency measures to stop aggression. Yet time is passing, and the aggressor is bombing towns and villages. There are already reports that scores of Guatemalan towns and villages are being bombed. . . .

At the 675th meeting Mr. Hoppenot said that the Soviet veto was paralysing the Security Council. But how is that so? Let us take a decision right away. We have enough telegrams from the Guatemalan Minister for External Relations and from the Guatemalan representative here for the Security Council to take an immediate decision to put an end to the aggression. What is the reason for the refusal to take a decision now, and for the attempt to push this question on to the Organization of American States, where the United States, with the support of those who always support it, will settle accounts with Guatemala. This will definitely be the case. Mr. Dulles openly said so on 10 June, and the newspapers write about it with conviction.

Consequently, it is not a matter of preventing the question from being included in the agenda, or of pushing it on to the Organization of American States which is not competent to deal with it, inasmuch as it has already been submitted to the Security Council. Consequently, the Security Council must now deal with the question in accordance with Article 52, paragraph 2, of the Charter. This is my first point.

My second point is that Article 52, paragraph 4, of the Charter stipulates that the Article in no way impairs the application of Articles 34 and 35. Consequently, even in this regard, the provisions of the Charter relating to the prevention of aggression prevail over regional arrangements.

Lastly, I must once again draw attention to Article 36. I dwell on this point because, according to Article 36, the Security Council may adopt only such a procedure for the settlement of a dispute as is acceptable to the two parties. Here we have the victim of aggression, which is really the principal party. We should value its opinion more highly than that of the others; we are bound to take it into account and to help the victim of aggression by restoring peace and security in that country.

This country declared that it did not accept the referral of the dispute to the Organization of American States for consideration, and requested that it should be dealt with by the United Nations through the Security Council. From this point of view, therefore, no procedure can be adopted which would prevent the examination of this question by the Security Council, for that would constitute a violation of Article 36 of the Charter.

In conclusion, I should like to draw the attention of members of the Council to the fact that the attempts which have been made under various guises to pass the whole question over to the Organization of American States represent yet another effort to undermine the United Nations Charter and further to diminish the functions and significance of the Security Council as the principal United Nations body concerned with the restoration of peace and the maintenance of peace and security among States Members of the United Nations.

For all these reasons, the Soviet Union delegation is decidedly opposed to the putting to the vote of the question of including and maintaining on the agenda the request received from the Government of Guatemala, which is at present a victim of aggression. I am opposed to any vote which may actually prevent the discussion of this question by the Security Council. This of course would only serve the aggressor's purpose; it would serve the purpose of those who are against peace, who are against restoring the security of States which have been the victims of aggression in this part of the world.

The demands and machinations which we are witnessing here are aimed at removing the question from the agenda and at preventing

its discussion. These manoeuvres are in line with the statement made
by Mr. Lodge at our last meeting, in which he said in effect "hands
off" and "do not dare to intervene in the Western Hemisphere" and
that it was no concern of the Security Council if any aggression was
taking place in the Western Hemisphere.

Attempts are now being made to uphold this nefarious concept under new pretexts. The USSR delegation firmly protests against it.
It will vote in favour of the inclusion of the question in the agenda;
there can be no doubt that failure to include this question in the
agenda will serve the aggressor's purpose and it will prove that the
Security Council, through the fault of the United States and the countries supporting it, has been unable to stop aggression and to help the
victim of aggression.

The PRESIDENT: Every member of the Council has now spoken
and so the President will recognize himself in his capacity as representative of the United States of America. .   .   .

The Government of the United States joins its colleagues in the
Organization of American States in opposing the adoption of the provisional agenda. We have taken this position only after the most
careful consideration. We believe that there should be great liberality with reference to the consideration of items by either the Security
Council or the General Assembly. But in the present case, we believe
that an issue is involved which is so fundamental that it brings into
question the whole system of international peace and security which
was created by the Charter at San Francisco in 1945. When the
Charter was being drafted, the most critical single issue was that of
the relationship of the United Nations as a universal organization to
regional organizations, notably the already existing organization of
American States. There were a good many days in San Francisco
when it seemed that the whole concept of the United Nations might
fail of realization because of the difficulty of reconciling these two
concepts of universality and regionalism.

Finally, a solution was found in the formula embodied in Articles
51 and 52 of the Charter. Article 51 recognized the inherent right
of individuals to collective self-defence. Article 52, admitted "the
existence of regional arrangements .   .   .   for dealing with such
matters relating to the maintenance of international peace and security as are appropriate for regional action". Article 52 provided
that the Security Council had the inherent right to investigate any
dispute or situation under Article 34 "which might lead to international friction", while "any Member of the United Nations may bring
any dispute, or any situation .   .   .   to the attention of the Security Council" under Article 35. Nevertheless, Members of the
United Nations who had entered into regional arrangements should
"make every effort to achieve pacific settlement of local disputes
through such regional arrangements .   .   .   before referring them

to the Security Council". The Security Council should thus "encourage the development of pacific settlement of local disputes through . . . regional arrangements".

By that formula, a balance was struck between universality, the effect of which was qualified by the veto power, and regional arrangements. The adoption of that formula permitted the Charter of the United Nations to be adopted. Without that formula, there would never have been a United Nations. If the United States Senate in 1946 had thought that the United [Nations] Charter in effect abrogated our inter-American system—and I say this to you as a man with thirteen years' service in the United States Senate—the Charter would not have received the necessary two-thirds vote. In my judgment the American people feel the same way today.

Now, for the first time, the United Nations faces the problem of translating that formula into reality. The problem is as critical as the one which faced the founders at San Francisco in 1945. Let us not delude ourselves. If it is not now possible to make a reality of the formula which made possible the adoption of the Charter, then the United Nations will have destroyed itself in 1954 as it would have been destroyed stillborn in 1945, had not the present formula been devised primarily under the creative effort of the late Senator Vandenberg and the present Secretary of State, Mr. Dulles, working with the Secretary of State at that time, Mr. Stettinius, and other administration leaders. It was this formula which secured bipartisan support in the United States in 1946—and I note that by a completely bipartisan vote, the Senate today declared that the international communist movement must be kept out of this hemisphere.

So much for the United States part in what happened at San Francisco. The great weight of the effort at San Francisco, however, was made by the other American republics, as you have heard Ambassador Gouthier and Ambassador Echeverri Cortes say before me. The representatives of the other American republics were determined that the United Nations should be supplementary to and not a substitute for or impairment of the tried and trusted regional relationships of their own.

The United States, whose representative took such an active part in drafting the Charter provisions in question, soberly believes that if the United Nations Security Council does not respect the right of the Organization of American States to achieve a pacific settlement of the dispute between Guatemala and its neighbours, the result will be a catastrophe of such dimensions as will gravely impair the future effectiveness both of the United Nations itself and of regional organizations such as the Organization of American States. That is precisely what I believe to be the objective of the Soviet Union in this case; otherwise, why is its representative so terribly intent on doing this?

The present Charter provisions were drafted with particular regard for the Organization of American States, which constitutes the oldest, the largest and the most solid regional organization that the world has ever known. The distinctive relationship of the American States dates back to the early part of the last century. Throughout this period of over 130 years, there has been a steady development of ever-closer relations among the twenty-one American republics. They have achieved a relationship which has preserved relative peace and security in this hemisphere and a freedom from the type of wars which has so cruelly devastated the peoples of Europe and Asia.

The Organization of American States is an organization founded upon the freedom-loving traditions of Bolivar, Washington, and Abraham Lincoln. The twenty-one American republics have been bound together by a sense of distinctive destiny and by a determination to prevent the extension to this hemisphere of either the colonial domain of European Powers or the political system of European despotism. They have repeatedly pledged themselves to settle their own disputes among themselves and to oppose the interposition into their midst of non-American influences many of which were abhorrent to the ideals which gave birth to the American republics and which sustained them in their determination to find a better international relationship than has yet been achieved at the universal level.

There has recently been evidence that international communism, in its lust for world domination, has been seeking to gain control of the political institutions of American States in violation of the basic principles which have, from the beginning, inspired them freely to achieve their own destiny and mission in the world. It is our belief that the great bulk of the people of Guatemala are opposed to the imposition upon them of the domination of alien despotism and have manifested their resistance, just as have many other countries which international communism has sought to make its victims.

The Government of Guatemala claims that the fighting now going on there is the result of aggression by Honduras and Nicaragua. It claims that it is a victim; it asks for an investigation. It is entitled to have the facts brought to light; the procedures for doing that are clearly established within the regional Organization of American States. These States have established a permanent Inter-American Peace Committee to handle problems of this nature. Guatemala, Honduras and Nicaragua all applied to that committee for assistance in resolving this problem. The committee has agreed to send a fact-finding committee to the area of controversy for that purpose. Guatemala has attempted to interrupt this wholesome process, first, by withdrawing its petition and, second, by withholding its consent for the fact-finding committee to proceed with its task. Nevertheless, because the members of the committee feel that it is inconceivable that Guatemala will obstruct the very investigation for which it has been clamouring for days, the committee is firmly and vigorously preparing to proceed to the area of controversy.

The Government of Guatemala has regularly exercised the privileges and enjoyed all the advantages of membership in the Organization of American States, including those of attending and voting in its meetings. It is obligated by Article 52, paragraph 2 of the Charter to "make every effort to achieve pacific settlement of local disputes through regional arrangements". Its effort to by-pass the Organization of American States is, in substance, a violation of Article 52, paragraph 2.

We hear today that Guatemala, after years of posing as a member of that organization, now for the first time claims that it is not technically a member thereof. To have claimed and exercised all the privileges of membership for a number of years, and then to disclaim the obligations and responsibilities is an example of duplicity which, surely, the Security Council should not condone. Either Guatemala is a member of the Organization of America States and therefore bound by Article 52, paragraph 2 or else it is guilty of duplicity to such an extent that it cannot come before the Security Council with clean hands. If we adopt the agenda we, in effect, give one State—in this case Guatemala—a veto on the Organization of American States. It is not possible to do both. You do one at the expense of the other in this case.

In any event, the United States is a member of the Organization of American States and, as such, we are clearly bound by Article 52, paragraph 2 of the Charter. The United States is also bound by article 20 of the Charter of the Organization of American States, which provides that:

"All international disputes that may arise between American States shall be submitted to the peaceful procedures set forth in this Charter, before being referred to the Security Council of the United Nations." And that has been so for a long time.

The United States does not deny the propriety of this danger to the peace in Guatemala being brought to the attention of the Security Council in accordance with Article 35 of the Charter. That has been done and . . . I called the meeting the day after I received the message. The United States is, however, both legally and as a matter of honour, bound by its undertakings contained in Article 52, paragraph 2 of the Charter of the United Nations and in article 20 of the charter of the Organization of American States, to oppose consideration by the Security Council of this Guatemalan dispute until the matter has first been dealt with by the Organization of American States which, through its regularly constituted agencies, is dealing actively with the problem now. The United States is, in this matter, moved by more than legal or technical considerations; and I recognize that. We do not lightly oppose consideration of any matter by the

Security Council. We are, however, convinced that a failure by the Security Council to observe the restraints which were spelled out in the Charter will be a grave blow to the entire system of international peace and security which the United Nations was designed to achieve.

The proposal of Guatemala, supported most actively by the Soviet Union—which, in this matter, has already cast its sixtieth veto—is an effort to create international anarchy, rather than international order. International communism seeks to win for itself support by constantly talking about its love of peace and international law and order; in fact, it is the promoter of international disorder.

This Organization is faced with the same challenge which confronted the founders at San Francisco in 1945. The task then was to find the words which would constitute a formula of reconciliation between universality and regionalism, and now the issue is whether those words will be given reality or whether they will be ignored. If they are ignored, the result will be to disturb the delicate, the precious balance between regional and universal organizations and to place one against the other in a controversy which may well be fatal to them both.

The balance struck by the Charter was achieved at San Francisco in the face of the violent opposition of the Soviet Union at that time. It sought from the beginning to secure for the Security Council, where it had the veto power, a monopoly of authority to deal with international disputes. Today international communism uses Guatemala as the tool whereby it can gain for itself the privilege which it was forced to forego at San Francisco. I say with all solemnity that if the Security Council is the victim of that strategy and assumes jurisdiction over disputes which are the proper responsibility of a regional organization of a solid and serious character, then the clock of peace will have been turned back and disorder will replace order. The Guatemalan complaint can be used, as it is being used, as a tool to violate the basic principles of our Charter. It is to prevent that result, which would set in motion a chain of disastrous events, that the United States feels compelled to oppose the adoption of the provisional agenda containing the Guatemalan complaint. My Government appeals to the other members of the Council to join with us in avoiding a step which, under the guise of plausibility and liberality, will in fact engage this Organization in a course so disorderly and so provocative of jurisdictional conflict that the future of both the United Nations and the Organization of American States may be compromised and a grave setback given to the developing processes of international order.

Mr. TSARAPKIN (Union of Soviet Socialist Republics): Generally speaking, as may be seen from the statements which have been made here today, the real question at issue is the following: Is the United Nations to deal with matters relating to the maintenance of peace and

security throughout the world, or is it to be debarred from its rights
with respect to the world as a whole and are its functions with respect
to the struggle against aggression, the termination of aggression and
the strengthening of peace to be restricted, at the mere whim of the
United States of America, to Europe and Asia, with perhaps the addition of Africa.

That is the issue at stake in the discussion that has taken place
today.   That is an undoubted fact, as is shown by the resolution
adopted today in the United States Senate.   The United States Senate
today adopted a resolution the sense of which is that the United Nations and the Security Council should keep their hands off the Western
Hemisphere.   The pretext, of course, is international communism.
These allegations, these cries of international communism are familiar
to us; they bring to mind the proverbial fact that when a thief wishes
to divert the crowd away from himself he shouts "Stop thief!" and
saves himself from capture.

That must be obvious and perfectly clear to all of us. If we ignore
all this propagandist balderdash about international communism and
so forth, and look at things as they are, we shall see that what is being done here marks the beginnings of a dangerous effort to undermine the jurisdiction of the United Nations in matters relating to the
maintenance of peace and security.   That is the first point.

The second point is that the issue here is one of priority, the question being which authority is to be given precedence by the States
Members of the United Nations which are situated in the American
continent.   There are some twenty of these States; yet today we have
heard that all these Latin-American States should give precedence,
in all matters relating to aggression on the American continent, to
the decisions not of the United Nations but of the Organization of
American States; and that the United Nations, and the Security Council, should be debarred from dealing with the matter.

Thus, we are being told that in matters relating to international
peace and security the Latin-American countries—although they are
Members of the United Nations—should act in accordance with concepts, procedures and methods of settlement of disputes entirely different from those governing the remaining Members of the United
Nations.   That is to say that all European States, all Asian States
and all African States will be required to act, in matters relating to
the maintenance of peace, on the basis of the United Nations Charter;
but that the Charter ceases to operate immediately aggression takes
place on the American continent.   That is the interesting theory we
have heard; and the United States representative has even threatened the United Nations with collapse if we demand the application
of the Charter in its entirety to cases of aggression committed on the
American continent also.

That is what the United States representative has told us today. However we understand—and we are confident that every Member of the United Nations understands very clearly—what the real issue is. Either we have a Charter which is binding on all Members of the United Nations, or in actual fact—if the theory propounded by the United States representative and the United States Senate prevails— the United Nations will survive as a mockery, if indeed its days are not numbered.

It is obvious that if the United Nations is to be dealt such serious blows and if entire continents are to be withdrawn from its jurisdiction, the Organization will be reduced to nothing. An organization of that kind will have no authority and no force and will become a mere fiction, not the United Nations. That is what we have heard today. It is to be hoped, however, that things will not turn out like this, that the ideological tint with which the American representative has been trying to colour the whole question will not mislead anyone, for what concerns us here is the struggle against aggression wherever it may occur—in Central America or in other parts of the American continent, in the continents of Europe or Asia or Africa. Wherever it may be, aggression is still aggression, and wherever there is a case of aggression it is for the United Nations and not for some other organization to take energetic measures to put a stop to it.

This principle is indivisible: either it is accepted fully in all its parts or it is utterly destroyed so that there remains not a trace of it.

I believe that all other members of the Security Council and of the United Nations must agree with this interpretation as the only true interpretation, for it lies at the basis of our Charter. Either we have a United Nations Charter, which is binding upon all Members, or we have no Charter, in which case of course the United States representative and the United States Senate are free to do just what they like.

But the United Nations still exists, and therefore this attempt to prevent the Security Council taking steps to put an end to aggression appears to us illogical. We feel obliged to oppose it and fight against it or else, if we make a concession in this direction today, we shall be obliged to make another tomorrow. Tomorrow the United States will feel that the United Nations should not be permitted to take any measures to put a stop to aggression if it should occur on the American continent.

I must repeat once again that what has happened to Guatemala today may happen tomorrow to Honduras, to Costa Rica, to Colombia and to the other States, that there are no limits and no bounds. It is only too clear what the results will be if the United States is left to deal with all the other Latin-American countries. The results of such aggression will be clear to all of us. The United States is powerful enough to subdue any country of Latin America. It must be clear to everyone that those countries of Latin America, and those which share their view are taking a dangerous, reckless course by rejecting now the help of the United Nations and wanting to be left to deal with the United States individually in the Organization of American States.

I think that the situation is sufficiently clear to enable us to choose the right course of action.

The Soviet delegation firmly objects to the proposal not to include the question in the agenda, and not to consider it and maintains that the question should on the contrary be included in the agenda and discussed, and that measures should be taken to put an end to aggression in Central America and in Guatemala.

The PRESIDENT: The question before the Council is the adoption of the agenda.

A vote was taken by show of hands.

In favour: Denmark, Lebanon, New Zealand, Union of Soviet Socialist Republics.

Against: Brazil, China, Colombia, Turkey, United States of America.

Abstaining: France, United Kingdom of Great Britain and Northern Ireland.

The agenda was rejected by 5 votes to 4, with 2 abstentions.

NOTE.—1. While Guatemala refused at first to recognize the jurisdiction of the Inter-American Peace Committee, it invited the Committee on 26 June 1954 to send a fact-finding committee to Guatemala. The Committee decided on 27 June that it itself would leave for Guatemala in the morning of 28 June. But the Government of Guatemala changed during the previous night and by the time the Committee arrived at Mexico City it was informed that mediation had been initiated by the United States and El Salvador between the new Government and the revolutionary forces, and that the Committee should not interfere in these negotiations. On July 2 the three Governments concerned thanked the Committee for its good offices and informed it that "the controversy between them, which was the occasion for the Committee's journey, has ceased to exist." On July 8, the Committee transmitted to the Security Council its report relating its frustrating experience. S/3267 (13 July 1954), pp. 9–19.

2. The Guatemalan question was also discussed in the Council of the Organization of American States. On 26 June 1954 ten American States (including the United States) requested the Council to convoke a Meeting of Ministers of Foreign Affairs under Articles 6 and 11 of the Inter-American Treaty of Reciprocal Assistance, and the Council, by a vote of nineteen to one, decided on 28 June 1954 to convoke such a meeting to be held at Rio de Janeiro on July 7. Following the end of fighting in Guatemala, the Council on 2 July 1954 decided to postpone the meeting *sine die*. By a cablegram dated 9 July 1954, the Minister for External Relations of Guatemala informed the Security Council that peace and order had been restored in his country and that the Government of Guatemala saw no reason why the Guatemalan question should remain on the agenda of the Council. 6 Annals of the Or-

ganization of American States (1954), pp. 159–61; UN Doc. S/3266 (12 July 1954).

3. For comments on this case, see Charles G. FENWICK, "Jurisdictional Questions Involved in the Guatemalan Revolution," 48 AJIL (1954), pp. 597–602; John S. GIBSON, "The Guatemalan Case and Universal-Regional Relationships," 4 Indian Council of World Affairs, Foreign Affairs Reports (1955), No. 1, pp. 1–16; David McK. KEY, "The Organization of American States and the United Nations: Rivals or Partners?", 31 DSB (1954), pp. 115–8; R. St. J. MACDONALD, "The Developing Relationship between Superior and Subordinate Political Bodies at the International Level: A Note on the Experience of the United Nations and the Organization of American States," 2 Canadian YBIL (1964), p. 21, at 24–31; Hellmut SCHATZ-SCHNEIDER, Die neue Phase der Monroedoktrin angesichts der kommunistischen Bedrohung Lateinamerikas unter besonderer Berücksichtigung des Falles Guatemala vor der Organisation Amerikanischer Staaten und den Vereinten Nationen (Göttingen, 1957), 80 pp.; Arthur P. WHITAKER, "Guatemala, OAS and US," 33 Foreign Policy Bull. (1954), No. 24, pp. 4–7. See also comments made at the ninth session of the General Assembly, GAOR, IX, Plenary, pp. 23–4, 98, 147–8, 150, 174–5.

4. The Organization of American States proved more effective by preventing the overthrow of the Costa Rican Government by revolutionary forces which invaded Costa Rica from Nicaragua in 1955. See S/3344, S/3345, S/3347, S/3349, S/3366 and Add.1, S/3395 and S/3438 (12 Jan.–14 Sept. 1955); PAN AMERICAN UNION, Inter-American Treaty of Reciprocal Assistance: Applications (Washington, D.C., 1964), pp. 167–228.

COMPLAINT OF CUBA AGAINST THE UNITED STATES

1. *Letter from the Minister for Foreign Affairs of Cuba*
to the President of the Security Council,
11 July 1960.

S/4378 (11 July 1960); SCOR, XV, Supp. for July–Sept. 1960, pp. 9–10.

On the instructions of the Revolutionary Government of Cuba, I have the honour to inform you of the grave situation which now exists, with manifest danger to international peace and security, as a consequence of the repeated threats, harassments, intrigues, reprisals and aggressive acts to which my country has been subjected by the Government of the United States of America.

This situation began to take concrete shape from the moment when the Revolutionary Government of Cuba, in exercise of the powers devolving from its full sovereignty, adopted measures designed to safeguard the national resources and to raise the standard of living, health and education of the Cuban people. Long before the promulgation of the Agrarian Reform Act—the indispensable precondition for Cuba's future economic, political, social and cultural development and an effective safeguard for the exercise of the fundamental freedoms—there had already been launched, with the object of preparing and promoting plans of intervention conceived almost immediately following the overthrow of the Batista dictatorship and now being openly pursued, a co-ordinated and mounting campaign intended to obscure the national, anti-feudal and democratic character of the Cuban revolution, and seeking to distort its origin, course and purposes.

We have vainly expressed, in keeping with our policy of friendship and co-operation with all nations and peoples of the world, the desire of the Cuban Government and people to live in peace and harmony and to extend, on a basis of equality, mutual respect and reciprocal benefit, their diplomatic and economic relations with the Government and people of the United States of America. What the Government which I represent has been unwilling to do, as it still is and always will be, is to negotiate its disputes with any State which, instead of conforming to the principles of international law, takes up positions of strength.

The protection offered by the Government of the United States to notorious Cuban war criminals, the facilities provided to counter-revolutionary elements for their conspiracies and invasion plans, the frequent violations of Cuban air space, with loss of life and considerable material damage, by aircraft proceeding from United States territory and in some cases piloted by United States pilots, the unconcealed diplomatic pressure, the repeated statements derogatory to our right of self-determination made by leading figures of the three branches of government of the United States, including the President himself, the insulting conduct of the Senate Interior Sub-Committee, which is offensive to human dignity and infringes our sovereignty, the continued threats of economic strangulation which have now been put into effect through the refusal of the oil companies to refine crude oil owned by the Cuban State—an obligation binding on them under the Mineral Fuel Act of 1938—and through the extraordinary powers, now in application, conferred upon the President of the United States to reduce the Cuban sugar quota, and the recent meeting of the National Security Council, at which the future of Cuba was discussed as if that country were a factory or a subject people—these, by any standards, are acts which go to make up a policy of intervention in Cuba's domestic affairs and of economic aggression contrary to the basic terms of the relevant international treaties and agreements and to the fundamental principles of the United Nations Charter.

These acts, which will be described in detail at the appropriate time, have brought about a situation which seriously affects international peace and heightens the tensions brought about by the collapse of the Summit Conference. Accordingly, the Revolutionary Government of Cuba, without prejudice to its right of self-defense, requests Your Excellency to convene the Security Council immediately in order that that body may consider the situation and, after hearing the statements of the undersigned, who is duly accredited for the purpose, may take such measures as it seems fit.

In submitting this question, the Revolutionary Government of Cuba bases itself on Article 52, paragraph 4, and Article 103 of the United Nations Charter which, without invalidating any regional arrangements and agencies, clearly lay down that obligations under the Charter shall prevail over such arrangements.

In submitting this application, the Revolutionary Government of Cuba invokes Articles 24, 34, 35, paragraph 1, and 36 of the Charter, and rule 3 of the provisional rules of procedure of the Security Council.

2.   *Discussion in the Security Council, 18–19 July 1960.*

SCOR, XV, Mtgs. 874–76.

Mr. ROA (Cuba): The right of any State which is a Member of the United Nations to have recourse to the Security Council cannot be questioned. The regional agencies do not take precedence over the obligations of the Charter. They have come into being under the provisions of the Charter, but for the States which belong to them they can never signify one recourse less but rather one recourse more. It is obvious that regional arrangements made under the terms of Article 52 of the Charter entail rights which are of an optional rather than an exclusive character, and that Member States may exercise whichever of those rights they choose.

Cuba is entirely within its rights in coming before the Security Council. Those who invoke in particular Article 52, paragraph 2, of the Charter to support the absurd and non-juridical argument that the cases which States members of the Organization of American States bring before the Security Council should be submitted to that Organization stubbornly ignore paragraph 4 of the Article in question, which reads, "This Article in no way impairs the application of Articles 34 and 35". But that is not all. Let us turn to Article 103 of the Charter, which reads, "In the event of a conflict between the obligations of the Members of the United Nations under the present Charter and their obligations under any other international agreement, their obligations under the present Charter shall prevail". There is nothing here that can be questioned; the juridical meaning of the precept is absolutely clear. As for those who invoke article 20 of the Charter of the Organization of American States, which provides that "all international disputes that may arise between American States shall be submitted to the peaceful procedures set forth in this Charter, before being referred to the Security Council of the United Nations", they too ignore, or pretend to be unaware of, article 102 of the Charter of the Organization of American States, which states categorically that "none of the provisions of this Charter shall be construed as impairing the rights and obligations of the Member States under the Charter of the United Nations".

It is evident that any American State which is a Member of the United Nations can choose between two courses, namely recourse to the Security Council or recourse to the Organization of American States, in the event of a situation or dispute—and I use both terms in order not to enter into a futile legalistic discussion as to whether every dispute implies a situation, since article 20 of the Charter of the Organization of American States refers only to disputes whereas the United Nations Charter, in Article 34, refers to a dispute or situation. The right to choose rests with the Member State and the latter is free to exercise it to the fullest extent. Were it otherwise we should be obliged to reach the sad conclusion that the American States, upon forming a regional agency, suffered an impairment of their rights, that they renounced their rights under the United Nations Charter, whereas there can be no question that what they did was to supplement their rights under the United Nations Charter with those which they enjoy under the regional agency.

This view has been taken and expressed by many representatives of Latin American States. I do not intend to go into the matter exhaustively but I should like to quote a few statements made by Latin American representatives in the general debate which took place during the ninth session of the General Assembly, in September and October 1954, shortly after the Security Council took its regrettable decision to reject the inclusion in the agenda of the second communication sent by the Government of Guatemala.

In the course of that general debate, at the plenary meeting held on 28 September 1954, Francisco Gamarra, former President of the Supreme Court of Justice, speaking as Chairman of the Uruguayan delegation, said:

"In connexion with the case of Guatemala, I should like to draw special attention to, and to support, a point of view which the Secretary-General put forward in his report to the Assembly [A/2663, p. xi], where he says that 'a policy giving full scope to the proper role of regional agencies can and should at the same time fully preserve the right of a Member nation to a hearing under the Charter'.

"My country combines membership in the United Nations with membership in the Organization of American States, in the belief that the principles of the regional system and the safeguards which it offers cannot be invoked in order to prevent States from having direct and immediate access to the jurisdiction of the United Nations or to deprive them, no matter how temporarily, of the protection of the agencies of the world community. The legal protection afforded by both systems should be combined, never substituted for one another."

Mr. José Vicente Trujillo, the representative of Ecuador, made the following statement:

"The precedent established by the Security Council in the case of Guatemala is extremely dangerous inasmuch as it implies distorted interpretations of the Charter and in a way closes its doors to an American State applying to the Security Council for assistance when it feels that its case should be heard by that body. We are members and staunch supporters of the Organization of American States, but we cannot by any means agree that it has exclusive jurisdiction in a dispute such as the one I have just mentioned. My Government took a firm and fundamental position on this question and informed the Security Council accordingly in an official communication [S/3255]. We hope that there will be no more such negative decisions by the Council, lest the prestige of the Organization suffer and one of the fundamental objects of the Charter—protection against attack—become illusory or come too late."

The position which I have set forth and which I am supporting with these quotations is clear and categorical. The boundaries are precise. The problem is simply one of applying certain precepts and it leaves no room for subtle questions of juridical interpretation.

The Revolutionary Government of Cuba—and I proclaim it with pride—has given clear proof of its fidelity to Americanism and has participated, with a clear sense of its duties and responsibilities, in all the activities of the Organization of American States. It has no wish to weaken the regional agency, but it has the right to have recourse to the Security Council when there is justification for doing so.

This is precisely the case here. Without renouncing the right of self-defence in the event of an attack on Cuba, the Revolutionary Government is having recourse to the Security Council to denounce a situation created by the Government of the United States, which, in an attempt to limit Cuba's national self-determination within the harsh framework of the cold war, goes beyond the boundaries of the American continent and is endangering international peace and security. To be more clear and precise, the Government of the United States is trying to conceal its true aims and justify its policy of harassment, retaliation and aggression by deliberately distorting the character, policy and objectives of the Cuban Revolution, representing it now as a Soviet appendage, now as a pawn of "international communism" on the American continent, whichever suits its purposes.

This fraudulent involvement of Cuba in the political, diplomatic and military strategy which the United States Government is applying against the Union of Soviet Socialist Republics has an obvious purpose: to isolate and destroy the Cuban Revolution, as was done in Guatemala in 1954 and on the same pretext. The winning of another "glorious victory" has been the purpose of all its actions, sophistries, pressures and manœuvres ever since its spoiled lackey, that depraved millionaire ex-sergeant named Fulgencio Batista, was swept from power by the invincible might of the Cuban people, who without asking permission or looking to the United States Government for support, won the full exercise of their sovereignty and a unique place for themselves in the true free world, which is not exactly that of the imperialist powers. It is this "bad example" which cannot be pardoned and it is with the purpose of preventing it from being emulated that Cuba is being accused of becoming a Soviet satellite and constituting a "danger" to the security of the United States and the hemisphere. . . .

In the face of the verbal, economic and diplomatic aggression and the growing pressure of United States interests affected by the economic and social reforms undertaken by the revolutionary Government, the threat of armed aggression is becoming increasingly evident to the Cuban people. As this dramatic situation approached a climax, reflected even in the United States Press, there came the statements made on 9 July by the Soviet Premier, Nikita Krushchev. After referring to the demand of the Governor of New York, Nelson Rockefeller, for an even tougher economic policy towards Cuba after the drastic reduction of its sugar quota, the Soviet Premier, in the course of an extempore speech and by way of example, according to the report in *The New York Times* said:

"It should be borne in mind that the United States is now not at such an unattainable distance from the Soviet Union as formerly. Figuratively speaking, if need be, Soviet artillerymen can support the Cuban people with their rocket fire, should the aggressive forces in the Pentagon dare to start intervention against Cuba. And the Pentagon would be well advised not to forget that, as shown by the latest tests, we have rockets which can land precisely in a preset square target 13,000 kilometers away. This, if you want, is a warning to those who would like to solve international problems by force and not by reason."

On Sunday, 10 July, the Prime Minister of Cuba, Dr. Fidel Castro, spoke from his sick-bed to the people in a televised broadcast to inform them of the problems facing Cuba as a result of United States economic aggression. His words, which I shall now quote, are a clear and precise expression of the Cuban point of view:

"At a time when our country is really face to face with the might of the greatest economic empire in the world, with the most powerful oligarchy, which has once again struck out against the peoples of America . . . the Soviet Union has come forward absolutely spontaneously—I must stress that point, for we did not count on Soviet rockets to defend us, we counted on the justice of our cause, we counted on our dignity, we counted on the heroism of our people, on their will to resist . . .

"In response to the statements of the Premier of the Soviet Union, the United States Government has not made the statement the situation calls for. The only logical reply would have been an explicit declaration to the world that the United States has no aggressive plans against Cuba. The United States had the duty to tell the world—a world to which both it and the Soviet Union belong—that it harbours no aggressive intentions against Cuba; to give the world its assurance that it does not propose to attack Cuba."

To date, the only known reaction of the United States Government to the Cuban Prime Minister's invitation—to which it is obliged to reply as a member of the Security Council, the body responsible for the maintenance of international peace and security—has been to dust off, with a defiant air, the Monroe Doctrine, a doctrine continually invoked but never applied to defend the territorial integrity, sovereignty and independence of the Latin American peoples, as we know from the Spanish attack on Tampico in 1829, the Anglo-French invasion of the Plate in 1825, the French blockade of Argentina in 1838, the Anglo-Franco-Spanish intervention in Mexico in 1862, the imposition of Emperor Maximilian on Mexico in 1863, the Spanish bombardment of Chile and Peru in 1866 and the Anglo-Italo-German bombardment and blockade of Venezuela in 1902. .   .   .

Spokesmen for the Department of State have frequently asserted, with the object of deceiving world public opinion, that the Revolutionary Government of Cuba does not show any willingness to negotiate its differences with the United States Government through the diplomatic channel. The facts show that the reverse is true. What the Revolutionary Government has not accepted is the claim that Cuba's national and international policy can be dictated from Washington, as in the past.

In corroboration of what I have just said I should like to read out certain passages from the statement made by Osvaldo Dorticós, President of the Republic of Cuba, on 27 January 1960 in reply to statements made by President Eisenhower:

"The differences of opinion which may exist between the two Governments, being subject to diplomatic negotiation, can in fact be settled by means of such negotiation. The Government of Cuba is entirely willing to discuss all those differences without reservation and to the fullest extent and expressly states that in its view there are no obstacles of any kind which should prevent the carrying out of such negotiations by means of one or another of the methods and instruments traditionally appropriate to that end. The Government of Cuba wishes to maintain and expand its diplomatic and economic relations with the Government and people of the United States on the basis of mutual respect and reciprocal benefits for both countries and considers that on this basis the traditional friendship between the peoples of Cuba and the United States will prove indestructible."

In accordance with this policy, which has consistently guided Cuba's diplomatic relations with the United States, on 22 February 1960, in my capacity as Minister for Foreign Affairs of Cuba, I delivered to the

United States Chargé d'affaires at Havana a note the substantive part of which read as follows:

"The Revolutionary Government of Cuba, in accordance with its expressed proposal to renew through diplomatic channels the negotiations already begun on matters pending between Cuba and the United States of America, has decided to name a commission, qualified for the purpose, which could begin its negotiations in Washington on the date on which the two parties might agree.

"The Revolutionary Government of Cuba wishes to make it clear, however, that the renewal and subsequent development of the said negotiations must necessarily be subject to no measure being adopted, by the Government or the Congress of your country, of a unilateral character which might prejudge the results of the aforementioned negotiations or cause harm to the Cuban economy and people.

"It seems obvious to add that the adherence of your Government to this point of view would not only contribute to the improvement of relations between our respective countries but also reaffirm the spirit of fraternal friendship which has bound and does bind our peoples. It would moreover permit both Governments to examine, in a serene atmosphere and with the broadest scope, the questions which have affected the traditional relations between Cuba and the United States of America."

What was the reaction of the United States Government to this concrete proposal by the Cuban Government, which was both dignified and friendly? It was the following:

"The Government of the United States cannot accept the conditions for the negotiations stated in Your Excellency's note to the effect that no measure of a unilateral character shall be adopted on the part of the Government of the United States affecting the Cuban economy and its people, whether by the legislative or executive branch. As set forth in President Eisenhower's statement of January 26, the Government of the United States must remain free, in the exercise of its own sovereignty, to take whatever steps it deems necessary, fully consistent with its international obligations, in the defense of the legitimate rights and interests of its people."

The unilateral measures had already been decided upon at that time. It had been resolved to strangle the Cuban revolution economically, to put economic aggression into effect, by drastically reducing the sugar quota, a step which constituted a flagrant violation of the tacit agreement undertaken with the Cuban sugar producers, who had made large investments in order to guarantee that the United States market would, as at all times, be adequately supplied.

If a great Power refuses to negotiate and at the same time commits economic aggression against another smaller nation which has no thermonuclear bombs, or guided missiles, can it complain about the diplomatic difficulties which it has itself provoked? In its diplomatic relations the Government of Cuba, the friend of all Governments and all peoples which reciprocate its friendship, asks only genuine respect for its sovereignty and reciprocal treatment on a basis of equality and mutual benefit. The Government of the United States, as the text of the note which I have quoted reveals, writes off the international obligations to which it has subscribed and seeks to negotiate its differences with Cuba from a position of strength, which is intolerable and inadmissible to the dignity of any Government that respects itself and the people whom it represents.

The Revolutionary Government of Cuba therefore reiterates in this universal parliament of nations its readiness to settle its differences with the Government of the United States through normal diplomatic channels, on a footing of equality and in accordance with the international obligations undertaken by both countries. It also wishes to make clear its unshakable determination to resist, in solidarity with the people, any who would dare disembark on our shores in the guise of conquerors. To subjugate or defeat us will not be an easy task. The destiny of my country today is the destiny of all the under-developed peoples of Latin America, Asia and Africa. Cuba is not alone.

Through me the Revolutionary Government of Cuba requests the United Nations Security Council to take action appropriate to the nature of the question before it.

Mr. LODGE (USA): The United States has engaged in no threats, harassments, intrigues, reprisals or aggressive acts against the Government of Cuba.

The Foreign Minister of Cuba has told us that Dr. Castro would like an assurance from the United States that the United States has no aggressive purposes against Cuba. Unnecessary though it most certainly seems to me, let me here and now give him this assurance, heaped up and overflowing: the United States has no aggressive purposes against Cuba.

The United States has consistently exercised restraint in the face of what seems to be a deliberate and concerted effort on the part of the present Government of Cuba to create a grievance with the United States. We can read no other meaning into the recourse of the Cuban Government to the Security Council today. Such recourse is not in harmony with its treaty obligations under the Inter-American Treaty of Reciprocal Assistance signed at Rio de Janeiro on 2 September 1947 and the Charter of the Organization of American States signed at Bogotá on 30 April 1948. Under these treaties the American Republics contracted to resolve their international differences with any other American State first of all through the Organization of American States. The United States believes that the proper forum for the discussion of any controversies between the Government of Cuba and the Governments of other American Republics is the Organization of American States.

The causes of international tensions in the Caribbean area have been under consideration by the Inter-American Peace Committee since the meeting of the American Foreign Ministers in Santiago, Chile, in August of last year, which was called to deal with that problem. Allegations of the kind which the Foreign Minister of Cuba has produced before this body, if they had any validity, could have been considered and dealt with there. At no time has the Cuban Government made any effort to contribute to that Committee's work, despite repeated invitations to all the Governments of the Organization of American States to do so.

On 27 June 1960 the United States Government, after Cuban refusal to engage in direct negotiations, submitted to the Inter-American Peace Committee a memorandum entitled "Provocative Actions of the Government of Cuba against the United States which have served to increase tensions in the Caribbean area" and informed the Committee that it would continue to provide such information as is relevant to the Committee's studies. This memorandum is available to members of the Council in document S/4388.

Consideration of these matters in the Organization of American States has now taken a new dimension, largely as a result of the attempts at intervention by the Soviet Union. On 13 July the Government of Peru requested a meeting of the American Foreign Ministers to consider recent developments which threaten continental solidarity, the defence of the regional system, and American democratic principles. The Council of the Organization of American States met last Saturday and is meeting now. It is expected to call for a Foreign Ministers' meeting to be held in the near future. As a result of the Peruvian initiative, eighteen of the twenty-one members have already expressed support for such a meeting.

In these circumstances, the United States believes that the Security Council should take no action on the Cuban complaint, at least until, as contemplated by the provisions of the inter-American treaties to which I have just referred, such discussions have taken place in the Organization of American States. A solution of these differences should be found by pacific means among the American States in conformity with the Charter of the United Nations and that of the Organization of American States. In the meantime the Council should be alert to outside attempts—notably from the Soviet Union—to aggravate tensions.

Let me say that it is not a question of which is greater or which is less—the Organization of American States or the United Nations. The point is that it makes sense—and the Charter so indicates—to go to the regional organization first and to the United Nations as a place of last resort. There is no question, of course, of replacing the United Nations. . . .

The United States has just been accused by the Foreign Minister of Cuba of harbouring war criminals, providing facilities for counter-revolutionaries, and of frequent violations of Cuban air space. It has also been accused of economic aggression because of the refusal of two private American oil companies to refine Soviet oil and because of the President's decision to reduce the Cuban sugar quota. Let us therefore look at the facts.

First, the provisions for the extradition of persons from the United States are well known to Cuba. Those provisions are set forth in the United States-Cuban Extradition Treaty and in United States statutes, and have been discussed in detail by the Department of State with Cuban Embassy officers. Cuba can file extradition requests in United States courts, furthermore, without even notifying the United States Government. To the best knowledge of the State Department, extradition has never been requested by the Government of Cuba for any of those persons commonly defined by the Government of Cuba as war criminals from the Batista régime.

Second, a number of Cuban nationals have been required by the United States Immigration and Naturalization Service to leave Florida and remain away from any area within 150 miles of the Gulf of Mexico. This was a voluntary and co-operative action by the United States Government to help maintain stability in the Caribbean area, and it never even received an acknowledgement from the Cuban Government.

Third, the United States has taken elaborate precautions in accordance with its obligations under the 1928 Havana Convention on the Duties and Rights of States in the Event of Civil Strife to enforce our domestic laws dealing with the traffic in munitions and implements of war which might be used in revolutionary activities.

Fourth, the United States has instituted the most vigorous and elaborate system of controls ever adopted by the United States Government in time of peace to prevent unauthorized flights in the Caribbean area and has deplored the very few which have taken place in spite of our restrictive actions.   .   .   .

Fifth, among the charges of economic aggression have been all sorts of fanciful charges. President Dorticós, for example, described the withdrawal of United States technical assistance as a "sign of aggression", in a speech in Montevideo in June. On 11 July Dr. Castro referred to the drop in American tourism to Cuba in a context of economic aggression. But surely it is not surprising if Americans do not want to go to a place where they are not wanted and where their country is subjected to a ceaseless stream of abuse. Even the preferential sugar quota and the premium price which Cuba has traditionally enjoyed were described by Guevara in March as meaning "slavery" for the Cuban people.

Sixth, no economic aggression of any sort was involved in the refusal of the American owned oil companies to refine Soviet oil. Those two companies have operated in Cuba for fifty years as law-abiding companies and have made a contribution to the growth of the Cuban economy. Since the revolution, the Cuban Government has allowed those companies to be paid only a small percentage of their cost of importing crude oil from Venezuela to refine in Cuba. At the time of their seizure, the Cuban Government owed them $50 million for oil they continued voluntarily to provide. The law under which Cuba purported to require the companies to refine Soviet oil had never previously been considered to mean that it also required the companies to refine any oil other than that from Cuban soil. The United States believes that the Cuban action in seizing these companies without compensation was arbitrary and illegal. It is further evidence and confirmation of a pattern of relentless efforts to destroy Cuba's traditional investment and trade relations with the free world. To our knowledge, not a single American property-owner in Cuba had been reimbursed for the property taken away—frequently without receipt—from him.

Seventh, the reduction of the Cuban sugar quota was no act of economic aggression, but a justifiable measure of self-protection of the United States to ensure its needed supply of sugar in the face of acts on the part of the Cuban Government which made this supply extremely insecure. The United States was under no obligation under the sugar agreement to purchase raw sugar from Cuba, nor was Cuba obliged to sell. Normally, about one-third of our total sugar supply comes from Cuba. The Government of Cuba is now following a course which raises serious questions as to whether the United States can in the long run continue to rely upon that country for such large quantities of sugar. The arrangement might have continued to be mutually beneficial to both the American and the Cuban peoples if Cuba had not deliberately chosen otherwise, making clear, as the Foreign Minister of Cuba said in Montevideo on 10 June 1960, that Cuba had decided "to break the structure of its commercial relations with the United States"—I believe that is a correct quotation from his speech.

There is no escape from the intent of recent Cuban actions, and the United States regretfully—and very regretfully—has had to protect its own long-range sugar supply accordingly.

We are not frightened by Chairman Khrushchev's threat of rockets, and we will live up to these treaties just as we live up to our obligations in the United Nations.

Now I come to the conclusion of my remarks—and this is a very special question indeed. Let me say this, that when the Foreign Minister of Cuba talks about the United States as a "North American aggressor" and as a "butcher"—I believe that was the word he used this afternoon—and charges us with a number of other offences, I for one am willing to believe that at the moment when he utters these words he actually believes in them. But in the greatest candour I assure him that the United States of America he is talking about does not exist. The United States of America which does exist is the United States of America which helped Cuba to get its independence. It is the United States of America which sprang from the words of Patrick Henry, "Give me liberty or give me death", a rallying-cry which inspired the great Bolívar and the noble José Martí. It is the United States of America of Thomas Jefferson, who wrote in our Declaration of Independence that "all men are created equal" and that they are entitled to "life, liberty and the pursuit of happiness"—happiness as each individual conceives it, and not as somebody tells him that he must have it. It is the United States of America of Abraham Lincoln and the freeing of the slaves, which today inspires our steady progress in the field of civil rights. It is the United States of America of the victory over yellow fever in Panama; of President Franklin D. Roosevelt's Good Neighbor; of President Eisenhower's hopes for economic collaboration; the United States of America by which no one has ever been enslaved. It is the United States of America which is human, of course, and therefore imperfect, but which is always eager to correct its errors. Above all it is the United States of America which wants to be friends with Cuba and which some day, somehow, will be friends again. . . .

The Foreign Minister of Cuba this afternoon has also referred to the Soviet threat of rocket attacks against the United States. So that there may be no mistake at all, let me say that the principles of the Monroe Doctrine—which is another way of saying the prevention of the extension of alien domination of the American continent—are fully alive and will be vigorously defended by the United States. The principles of that Doctrine are now embodied in treaty obligations among the American States, notably in the Charter of the Organization of American States and in the Rio de Janeiro Treaty, which provide means for common action to prevent the establishment of a régime dominated by international communism in the Western Hemisphere.

[After the statements of the parties to the dispute, the following draft resolution [S/4392 and S/4395 (18 and 19 July 1960); SCOR, XV, Supp. for July–Sept. 1960, pp. 29–30] was presented by Argentina and Ecuador, the two Latin American members of the Security Council at that time:

"The Security Council,

"Having heard the statements made by the Foreign Minister of Cuba and by members of the Council,

"Taking into account the provisions of Articles 24, 33, 34, 35, 36, 52 and 103 of the Charter of the United Nations,

"Taking into account also Articles 20 and 102 of the Charter of the Organization of American States of which both Cuba and the United States of America are members,

"Deeply concerned by the situation existing between Cuba and the United States of America,

"Considering that it is the obligation of all Members of the United Nations to settle their international disputes by negotiation and other peaceful means in such a manner that international peace and security and justice are not endangered,

"Noting that this situation is under consideration by the Organization of American States,

"1.   Decides to adjourn the consideration of this question pending the receipt of a report from the Organization of American States;

"2.   Invites the members of the Organization of American States to lend their assistance toward the achievement of a peaceful solution of the present situation in accordance with the purposes and principles of the Charter of the United Nations;

"3.   Urges in the meantime all other States to refrain from any action which might increase the existing tensions between Cuba and the United States of America."]

Mr. AMADEO (Argentina): . . . It has been debated whether a country belonging to the Organization of American States—a regional agency recognized in Article 52 of the Charter of the United Nations—is entitled to bring a dispute with another American State before the United Nations, or should first have recourse to the regional machinery. My delegation, so far as it is concerned, does not think that a theoretical and legal analysis of this question is indispensable. If we look at the matter from a practical standpoint—and since it is generally recognized that no country can be denied access to organizations of which it is a member—we find one circumstance which cannot but affect our decision. That circumstance is that the situation with which we are dealing is already under consideration by the Organization of American States; and this is a fact which we cannot overlook. Accordingly, whatever our individual points of view with regard to the legal aspects of the question may be, we believe that we can all agree on the practical proposition that, since the regional organization has already taken cognizance of the matter, it is desirable to await the results of its action and ascertain its point of view.

That is why the draft resolution submitted by Ecuador and Argentina proposes, in operative paragraph 1, a decision by the Security Council "to adjourn the consideration of this question pending the receipt of a report from the Organization of American States". It should be noted that it is not proposed to deny the Council's competence in the matter, or even to settle the legal question of which organization should act first. What is suggested is a noting of the concrete circumstance that the regional organization is dealing with the question, and a recognition that, for a better evaluation of the issues, it is useful to have before us the considerations at which the regional organization may arrive.

This preliminary measure cannot prevent the Council from making provisions which in procedural law would be described as precautionary, to ensure that the existing situation does not deteriorate before the report of the Organization of American States is transmitted to us. It is in view of these temporary but urgent requirements that operative paragraphs 2 and 3 have been drafted.

As representatives will note, the resolution's recommendations are of two types, according as to whether they are addressed to members or to nonmembers of the Organization of American States. The members of that Organization are parties to binding agreements and therefore have legal commitments which impose on them reciprocal duties of co-operation and assistance. . . . That is why we felt that we could ask the member States of the Organization of American States to co-operate actively and constructively and, as our draft resolution says, to "lend their assistance towards the achievement of a peaceful solution of the present situation." This wording, far from being incompatible with operative paragraph 1, under which consideration of the question by the Council is adjourned, complements it, precisely because it is the co-operation and assistance which we are requesting from the American countries that will make the report of the regional organization useful to us.

The position of countries which are not members of the Organization of American States is different. While many of them are undoubtedly linked to the parties to the dispute by strong emotional ties (I am thinking, for instance, of those countries which were the founders of our nations), they are not bound by legal obligations to co-operate and assist. Accordingly, to them—again in a provisional and precautionary manner—we address a request in negative terms. We urge them to refrain from any action which might increase the existing tensions between Cuba and the United States. We specify no particular country as the object of this request. It is addressed to all States not members of the Organization of American States, because we believe that it is, in the circumstances, the least we can ask of them.

This request to abstain from any action which might aggravate tension, although explicitly made only to countries that are not members of the Organization of American States, also, needless to say, applies to that Organization's members. For if we ask these for the greater contribution—assistance towards a solution of the dispute— it is clear that we must also ask them to make the lesser contribution, namely to refrain from aggravating the situation. If we do not say this explicitly in the text, it is because we regard it as redundant.

Our draft resolution is not addressed to the parties to the dispute, since that would involve a decision of substance incompatible with our proposal that consideration of the question be adjourned. But it seemed to us advisable to include in the preamble a paragraph recalling the obligation of Members of the United Nations to "settle their international disputes by negotiation and other peaceful means in such a manner that international peace and security, and justice, are not endangered." This wording, which is almost identical with that of Article 2, paragraph 3, of the Charter, reminds the parties of the course that they should follow in order to bring their conduct into line with the international rules by which they are bound. It is our hope that these precepts will be duly observed, so that it will be unnecessary for the Security Council to take any further action in this matter. We realize, of course, the gravity of the situation which has arisen between Cuba and the United States. Yet we do not believe that anything irreparable has so far taken place such as to prevent the finding of a mutually acceptable solution. The parties can still usefully resort to direct negotiation, which in this case is the most appropriate course. It is likewise our hope that abusive language will give way to language of moderation, thus making it more possible for the concrete difficulties to be faced in a spirit of calm.

So far as my delegation is concerned, we deem it essential to prevent this distressing conflict from being exploited on behalf of interests foreign to those of the parties in dispute. We have to recognize that opinions in the continent are, on the matter at issue, divided. But the vast majority of our peoples, whatever their standpoint with regard to the dispute may be, would vehemently oppose any extra-continental attempt to use it as a pretext for interference or propaganda. We are sure that the parties, once aware of such intentions, will do everything necessary to thwart them.

The efforts of peoples to attain full political and economic sovereignty deserve all our sympathy. We know that their task is no easy one, and that they do not achieve these aims without a struggle. But we do not believe that they must necessarily be attained in an atmosphere of international violence, at times when such violence can profit only those who seek to destroy our fundamental institutions. If, as we are convinced, countries owning vast material resources have recognized that the protection of their citizens' economic interests abroad must not go an inch beyond what is permitted by law and must in no way serve as a screen for attempts at domination, we are sure that a dispute arising out of a clash of interests can be solved. It is our confident hope that such a solution will be achieved in the case of Cuba and the United States.

All these considerations explain, we believe, the draft resolution now before the Security Council. We hope that it will meet with unanimous approval, which will doubtless contribute to a relaxation of tension, paving the way to that prompt restoration of friendly relations between two sister nations of the American continent which we so earnestly desire. . . .

Sir Claude COREA (Ceylon): It is a matter of deep regret and much concern that the friendly relations that have existed for many years between two neighbouring States, both Members of the United Nations and of the Organization of American States, have become strained and disturbed during recent times. Situations of this kind do arise in relations between Governments, regrettable as that may be, but the path of wisdom appears to us to be to seek a way out and find a sensible solution.

It is the policy of my Government, as a member of the Security Council, to do all we can to promote conciliation and to help in the mutual adjustment of differences by peaceful negotiation. This is also the policy indicated in the Charter of the United Nations. We are all familiar with Article 1 of the Charter, but, lest we forget, I should like to quote a short extract from Article 1. It enjoins us:

"To maintain international peace and security, . . . and to bring about by peaceful means, and in conformity with the principles of justice and international law, adjustment or settlement of international disputes or situations which might lead to a breach of the peace".

The Security Council has a special responsibility regarding the maintenance of international peace and security, and as members of this Council it is our duty, in a situation such as we are faced with, to give effect to the Purposes and Principles of the Charter.

The Foreign Minister of Cuba, in his letter which is before the Security Council, has asked for an urgent meeting of the Council and has set out the reasons which he considers have led to "the grave situation which now exists, with manifest danger to international peace and security, as a consequence of the repeated threats, harassments, intrigues, reprisals and aggressive acts to which my country has been subjected by the Government of the United States of America". Today, in the course of his moderate and detailed statement to this Council, he has set out the acts which, according to his letter, have "brought about a situation which seriously affects international peace and heightens the tensions . . . .".

The representative of the United States, in his statement, which was characterized by much moderation and restraint, endeavoured to refute the charges that have been made by the Foreign Minister of Cuba, and has publicly given two important assurances. In the first place, he has stated categorically, in reply to the Foreign Minister of Cuba, that the United States plans no aggression against Cuba. This is a clear statement made by a responsible official of the United States Government, and must be taken at face value. In the second place, he expressed his desire for the restoration of friendly relations with Cuba.

In these circumstances, my delegation is strongly of the opinion that the way is open to a mutually satisfactory adjustment of the differences that have recently arisen and for the restoration of mutual goodwill and understanding which will enable the two countries to coexist on a peaceful basis. The Charter of the United Nations points out the way for us to establish peace. Article 33, paragraph 1, refers to the pacific settlement of disputes. But is it clear that such attempts as were made in this sense have in this case failed? Very likely, these attempts have not been made as vigorously as they might have been; or, under emotional and other stresses which strained their relationships, the two countries concerned could not use any or all of the means prescribed in that paragraph. It was in these circumstances that the Government of Cuba decided, undoubtedly, to bring the dispute before the Security Council.

The Foreign Minister of Cuba argued at length on the right of his Government to come directly to the Security Council without first going to the regional organization. There can be no doubt that he has the right to choose whether he should put his case before the Security Council or before the regional organization. The Articles of the Charter amply support his contention, with which my delegation fully agrees. It is not necessary to go into this matter at length, as it must be presumed that, when the agenda was adopted without objection, the jurisdiction of the Security Council and the right of Cuba were both admitted. No one has contested this point of view in the course of this discussion. Cuba has, therefore, the right not only to bring its dispute directly before the Security Council, but to ask that its case be fully examined. That is what the Council is now doing. We are engaged in the discussion of the substantive question which has been raised, namely, the acts alleged against the United States which are likely, so it is said, to create tension and endanger world peace and security. At the end of the discussion the Council will reach a decision.

The representatives of Argentina and Ecuador have at this stage suggested what the Council's decision should be, in the draft resolution which they have submitted. The purpose of this draft resolution obviously is, according to its preamble, to make an attempt to employ the peaceful method of negotiation. The draft resolution states that the situation between Cuba and the United States is now under consideration by the Organization of American States, of which Cuba and the United States are members; and it is the view of my delegation that it is not wrong for this Council, in these circumstances, to utilize that organization for the free and full negotiations that are necessary to dispel misunderstanding and create mutual confidence between the parties. Such a course seems to my delegation to be a far more desirable way to bring about conciliation and mutual goodwill than for the Council to proceed to reach a decision here and now on the basis of the statements that have been made by the two parties concerned. It is the restoration of goodwill that is most required. This can be achieved better, especially in the light of the statement made by the representative of the United States on behalf of his Government, by a meeting of the two parties along with the other members of the organization.

In the Organization of American States Cuba enjoys equality of rights, and it is difficult to believe that in that organization there is any one who will interfere with its right to build up its economy in the way best suited to its people, or to deny it the right to maintain good and friendly relations economically, politically and socially with any countries it chooses. On the other hand, all the other member countries will realize, as I am sure Cuba does, how important it is to restore good relations, both in the interests of hemispheric co-operation and development and for the promotion of international goodwill and peace.

The proposal is that we adjourn our further consideration here in the Security Council in order to provide a better opportunity for the restoration of good understanding. This is to be only an interruption of the discussion that is now proceeding in this Council, and in no way can it be interpreted as an attempt to deny to Cuba the right to have its case fully discussed here. As I said before, it must be considered only as an interruption for a purpose, and the purpose, to which I referred earlier, is to make possible the use of a better method for re-creating the understanding and goodwill which prevailed between these two countries in the past. It cannot be construed as an attempt to deny to Cuba the right to have its case heard and decided here. It is not in any sense, therefore, a kind of manoeuvre to put off consideration. The proposal is made only because there exists a forum where an attempt at reconciliation should be tried, with the assurance that if no settlement is reached the issue will be brought back to this Council for a final adjudication. That is implicit in the draft resolution: the wording leaves no doubt on this point. In operative paragraph 1, these important words are used: *"Decides* to adjourn the consideration of this question"—and the word "adjourn" is important in this context—"pending the receipt of a report from the Organization of American States". If to that we add the further consideration, to which I have already referred, that the case is before the Organization of American States at this time, then there can be no denying the conclusion that what is proposed here is an interruption of the debate for the purpose specified.

It is in the interest of all the members of the Organization of American States, including the two parties immediately concerned, to bring about a reasonable settlement and the restoration of goodwill. My delegation is therefore convinced that, having established her undoubted right to come to the Security Council, Cuba should now agree to make use of the good offices of the Organization of American States to obtain a satisfactory settlement; and if Cuba fails to do so she can, as she is quite free to do, once again come to this Council to raise the issue in this Council if she is dissatisfied with the efforts made by the Organization of American States.

Cuba is entitled to the sympathy and support of all freedom-loving countries of the world in its attempt to throw off the yoke of a dictatorial and corrupt government and its endeavour to give to its people a better standard of living by bringing about revolutionary changes in its economic life. In the pursuit of this aim it is inevitable that many measures of reform that are introduced to achieve it will be disliked by those whose personal interests are interfered with. Such interests are often powerful and they will often seek to create ill will and prejudice against a Government. It is our feeling that it is, perhaps, these interests that have used their powerful influence to create misunderstanding between the two Governments.

Especially in this situation, it would serve a useful purpose if such misunderstandings were discussed round the table. Men of goodwill in such circumstances can hardly fail to reach mutual understanding, which is the basis of goodwill and friendly coexistence and good-neighbourly relations. We must, therefore, be most grateful to the representatives of Argentina and Ecuador for the draft resolution they have introduced. They can be assured that if it is accepted by this Council they will be helping both Cuba and the United States, with the assistance of all the other member States of the organization, to re-establish their friendly relations.

Such a result will be beneficial not only to Cuba and the United States, not only to the other Latin American countries, but also to the whole world. My delegation, therefore, supports the draft resolution submitted by Argentina and Ecuador. . . .

Mr. SOBOLEV (USSR): . . . The USSR supports the Cuban people in their struggle for independence. It has declared its sympathy for the objectives of that struggle and its friendship for the Republic of Cuba. It has taken that position because the United States, relying on its might and its wealth, is trying to interfere in Cuba's domestic affairs and impose its will on that country. Mr. N. S. Khrushchev, Chairman of the Council of Ministers of the USSR, stated recently— and I take the liberty of quoting him once more—"If the United States imperialists commit any acts of aggression against the Cuban people who are defending their national independence, we shall support the Cuban people."

The people of the USSR will not remain indifferent if armed intervention is undertaken against Cuba; let no one in the ruling circles of the United States have any illusions on that score. The USSR, relying on its own might, will give the necessary aid to Cuba at the latter's request. Nor will the USSR be alone in so doing. There can be no doubt that Cuba, in its selfless struggle for its freedom and independence, will receive the necessary help from other peaceful States as well. I should make it clear in that connexion that we are not threatening the United States with our rockets, as Mr. Lodge seeks to demonstrate, and we do not intend to make any such threats. We say, "Hands off Cuba;

let it work out its own destiny; do not threaten it with your might, for others have the might to match it". That is the line we are taking.

That is the substance of the USSR's policy towards the Latin American countries and Cuba in particular. Only politicians who feel the ground slipping away from under their feet can assert that such a policy towards Cuba on the part of the USSR constitutes a threat to the United States or any country of the American continent.

The United States' aggressive acts towards Cuba have given rise to a situation constituting a threat to international peace and security. It is precisely for this reason that the Security Council, on which, as we know, the United Nations Charter confers primary responsibility for the maintenance of peace and security, should take steps to halt this aggression and maintain peace.

We should resolutely thwart any attempts to prevent the Security Council from carrying out this responsibility expressly conferred upon it by the Charter. Yet that is precisely the course into which we are being impelled by those who propose that Cuba's complaint should be transferred from the Security Council to the Organization of American States. That proposal means that the question of aggressive acts by the United States would be transferred to a body in which the United States has a predominating influence and could quietly deal with Cuba as it pleased.

In justification of the proposal to transfer Cuba's complaint to the Organization of American States reference is made to Article 52, paragraph 2, of the United Nations Charter and to article 20 of the Charter of the Organization of American States. Let us have a look at the provisions of those instruments.

Article 52, paragraph 2, provides that Members of the United Nations entering into regional arrangements shall make an effort to achieve pacific settlement of local disputes through such regional arrangements or regional agencies before referring them to the Security Council. Article 20 of the Charter of the Organization of American States provides that international disputes that may arise between American States shall be submitted to the peaceful procedures set forth in the Charter of that Organization before being referred to the Security Council.

In the letter dated 11 July 1960 from the Cuban Minister for Foreign Affairs to the President of the Security Council [S/4378], however, it was stated that Cuba's appeal to the Security Council was occasioned by the grave situation which existed as a consequence of the repeated threats, harassments, intrigues, reprisals and aggressive acts of the United States against Cuba and that that situation was giving rise to a threat to international peace. The discussion of the question in the Council has not only confirmed that original statement but has also disclosed new facts demonstrating that we are indeed confronted with a situation the continuation of which constitutes a threat to the maintenance of international peace and security.

How is it possible in the face of all these facts to assert that this situation which endangers world peace should be considered merely a "local dispute" within the meaning of Article 52, paragraph 2, of the United Nations Charter and should, as such, be dealt with by a regional agency? How is it possible to make such an assertion when the subject at issue is not a dispute at all but rather intervention by the United States in the domestic affairs of Cuba, accompanied by a variety of aggressive and other hostile acts directed against that country? Such assertions can be made only by those who, for one reason or another, are seeking to paralyze the Security Council and prevent it from taking prompt and effective measures to put a stop to the aggressive acts of the United States and to preserve world peace.

It is hardly necessary to point out that a threat to peace in any part of the world is far from being a private, local affair concerning only countries in the immediate vicinity. Today peace is indivisible. The fires of war kindled by aggressors in any part of the world threaten all peoples equally. That is why the Security Council, when a threat to peace arises, should act and act without delay, in accordance with the Charter, to put an end to the danger.

This obligation is imposed on it by Article 24 of the Charter, in which it is stated that "In order to ensure prompt and effective action by the United Nations, its Members confer on the Security Council primary responsibility"—and I emphasize the word "primary"—"for the maintenance of international peace and security, and agree that in carrying out its duties under this responsibility the Security Council acts on their behalf"—on behalf of the Members of the Organization. Application of this provision would certainly not mean that the Latin American States would be excluded from participation in the adoption of a decision with regard to the question under consideration. In a case like this the Security Council, as stated in the Charter, acts on behalf of all its Members, which means that it acts on behalf *inter alia* of the American States, some of which are directly represented on the Council.

It should be noted, in particular, that the United Nations Charter includes special provisions stressing the fact that even if a situation threatening international peace has its origin in a local dispute, the Security Council can in no way be deprived of the rights vested in it by the Charter; it cannot decline to consider such a situation on the pretext that the question has not previously been examined by a regional agency and it cannot refuse to take steps to put an end to such a danger.

Article 52 expressly states that the obligation of Members of the Organization to make efforts to achieve a settlement of local disputes within the framework of regional arrangements before referring them to the Security Council in no way impairs the application of Articles 34 and 35 of the Charter, which, as we know, refer to action by the Council in connexion with disputes or situations the continuance of which is likely to endanger the maintenance of international peace and security.

Yet those who are in favour of referring the question before us to the Organization of American States stubbornly disregard this clear and express provision of the Charter. They likewise disregard the fact that the Organization of American States, as a regional agency, is not intended by either the United Nations Charter or its own Charter to be a substitute for the Security Council.

What is more, Article 102 of the Charter of the Organization of American States itself states that "None of the provisions of this Charter shall be construed as impairing the rights and obligations of the Member States under the Charter of the United Nations". Furthermore, it is specifically provided in Article 103 of the United Nations Charter that "In the event of a conflict between the obligations of the Members of the United Nations under the present Charter and their obligations under any other international agreement, their obligations under the present Charter" (that is, the Charter of the United Nations) "shall prevail"—I repeat, "shall prevail". Cuba has acted in accordance with this understanding and interpretation of the Charter, the only possible interpretation, the only one guaranteeing the rights of Members of the United Nations. Cuba chose the Security Council to examine its complaint and it has the right to do so, a right secured by the Charter, secured by international law.

Article 35, paragraph 1, unequivocally provides that: "Any Member of the United Nations may bring any dispute, or any situation of the nature referred to in Article 34, to the attention of the Security Council or of the General Assembly." On the strength of that provision of the Charter alone, the Cuban Government is fully entitled to apply to the Security Council for help and to expect such help from the Council. So far as the Security Council is concerned, the Charter imposes on it the obligation to take the appropriate steps to deal with a situation which threatens peace.

Thus, from the legal standpoint, the proposal to refer the complaint to the Organization of American States is contrary to the United Nations Charter. From the political standpoint, whether or not the sponsors so intend, the effective purpose of the proposal is to prevent the Security Council from taking the requisite effective measures to protect the national independence and political and territorial integrity of Cuba, a purpose that suits the convenience of the United States, which by its actions against Cuba has created a situation threatening universal peace.

The Soviet delegation deems it necessary to emphasize once more that the Security Council has an obligation to discharge the function imposed upon it by the United Nations Charter and to take a decision which will preclude the possibility of continued aggression by the United States against Cuba, facilitate the normalization of the situation in the Caribbean area and the maintenance of international peace and security as a whole.

Let me say a few words concerning the draft resolution submitted for the Council's consideration by the delegations of Argentina and Ecuador.

First of all, let us consider the statement by the Argentine representative that the resolution is a procedural one. What the Council has before it can certainly not be regarded as procedural in any way. It is not a procedural but a substantive resolution. The reference in Article 27 of the Charter to procedure is a reference, as everyone is well aware, to procedural matters relating to the Council's work. What we have in the Argentine and Ecuadorian draft resolution, on the other hand, is an assessment of the situation existing between the United States and Cuba, an assessment of the situation from the standpoint of the Charter; that situation is reflected in the draft resolution.

An assessment of the situation is given. The Security Council, the draft resolution states, is deeply concerned by the situation existing between Cuba and the United States of America. The nature of this situation has been made clear by the statement of the Minister for Foreign Affairs of Cuba and the statement of Mr. Lodge. If we are concerned with the nature of the situation, we are assessing the situation and we are not dealing with a procedural matter relating to our work.

The draft resolution goes on to propose that the consideration of the question should be adjourned pending the receipt of a report from the Organization of American States.

What is the reason for such a proposal? It is based on the fact that the situation is under consideration by the Organization of American States. It would mean that the Security Council, without examining the question itself and not wishing to take any action, would refer the question to the Organization of American States. Is that a procedural matter? No, it is not a procedural matter but a refusal by the Security Council to fulfil its obligation. The Soviet delegation cannot support such a resolution.

We are told that this matter must be referred to the Organization of American States, that we must wait for a report from the Organization of American States. The question is, why? What answer has been given to the question of why we should wait for this? The representative of the United Kingdom has given the reply that it is not for the Security Council to deal with the Cuban question. Mr. Lodge said that the Security Council was not the appropriate organ to deal with it—the same thing in other words. So this question must be referred to the Organization of American States because it is not for the Security Council to deal with it; that is, the Security Council is not competent to deal with it. Is this what the representatives of the United Kingdom and the United States mean? They do not say so in so many words, but when such a proposal is put forward and put to the vote, that is what it means. Whether the sponsors of the resolution wish it or not, that is what the resolution means.

My next point is, why the Organization of American States? One of the reasons we are given is that the Organization of American States has already begun to consider the question. What evidence is there that it has already begun to consider this question? It is a matter of common knowledge that Cuba has raised the question of aggressive actions by the United States in the Security Council and has not brought up the matter in the Organization of American States. Then how can it be said that the Organization of American States has begun to consider this matter?

It is true that the Organization of American States is considering something. The New York Times sheds some light on what it is considering. For once I will pay a tribute to The New York Times and quote what it says in an editorial. This was written before the Security Council meeting, before we had begun to consider this question. On Sunday, 17 July 1960, the paper wrote:

"Tomorrow in the United Nations Security Council, the United States will move to refer a Cuban complaint of United States 'economic aggression' to the twenty-one nation Organization of American States. The Cuban complaint is largely based on the fact that the United States two weeks ago drastically cut Cuba's sugar quota to the United States. . . . Peru, with strong United States encouragement, last Thursday requested an Organization of American States' Foreign Ministers meeting to consider"—to consider what?—"the defense of the regional system and American democratic principles in the face of the threats which might affect them."

The New York Times continues:

"In a bid for Latin American support in the Organization of American States, the United States will submit new economic development programs to an inter-American meeting in Bogotá in September—thus moving to meet one of the Latins' long-standing grievances."

I am not the one who is linking the raising of this matter in the Organization of American States with the promise of assistance for the so-called "economic development" of the American States. The link has been established by the actions of the United States Government. The New York Times continues:

"But New York Times correspondents report that Latin American public opinion does not appear ready for strong collective action against Cuba. There is still much backing for Dr. Castro's social and economic reforms, and a suspicion of the extent to which 'big business' interests (such as the expropriated oil companies and sugar planters) are behind United States policy towards Cuba."

One can readily subscribe to this assessment of the position and of the attitude of public opinion in the Latin American countries to the policy of the United States towards Cuba.

Why do I say this? I say it because in fact the Organization of American States did decide to consider a question, but not the question raised by Cuba. Not that question, but another one. Why then does the resolution propose, on the ground that the situation is already being considered in the Organization of American States, that the Security Council should refrain from acting and should refer the matter to the Organization of American States? Is it not because the United States is counting on being able to deal with Cuba in a quieter, more convenient environment than here in the Security Council, in full view of the whole world, in front of the projectors and television cameras? Is it not because the United States is endeavouring to transfer the question to that Organization?

If we are to believe what The New York Times tells us (and in the present case I have no reason to disbelieve it since these are widely known facts), the United States is drawing a direct connexion between the referral of its disputes to the Organization of American States and the provision of economic help to the Latin American countries. In other words, it is telling them: "If you will support us against Cuba in the Organization of American States, you can count on our help—we promise you." True, it remains to be seen how these promises will be implemented, but at any rate, the existence of such a policy is crystal clear. But what is the role of the Security Council in this? How can we support a policy of this kind?

The Soviet delegation strongly objects to doing so. We therefore consider that the Security Council would be taking the right course if it began by condemning the aggressive actions which the United States has undertaken against Cuba; at all events, it should not renounce its right to consider this question or evade its duty to take active, effective measures to protect the independence of a small country against pressure by a great Power. If the Security Council takes a decision, the least it can do is to refrain from evading its responsibility; it has no right to transfer this question to the Organization of American States in these circumstances.

The Soviet delegation wishes to put forward some amendments [S/4394] to the draft resolution submitted by Argentina and Ecuador. The amendments are to delete from the draft resolution two paragraphs, the one reading: "*Noting* that this situation is under consideration by the Organization of American States;" and the other reading "*Decides* to adjourn the consideration of this question pending the receipt of a report from the Organization of American States". We further propose that in the penultimate paragraph beginning with the words: "*Invites* the members of the Organization of American States to lend their assistance . . . ", the words "Organization of American States" should be replaced by "United Nations".

The Soviet delegation would be prepared to accept this draft resolution if it were thus amended. Why? Because in that case, if the paragraphs I have mentioned regarding the transfer of the question to the Organization of American States were deleted, the Security Council would at least be taking a step, however inadequate, towards discharging its obligations and responsibilities and would be acting in the interests of a small State which has appealed to the Security Council for assistance.

I formally submit these amendments to the draft resolution of Argentina and Ecuador. . . .

[The Soviet amendments were rejected by 8 votes to 2, with 1 abstention (Tunisia). The draft resolution submitted by Argentina and Ecuador was adopted by 9 votes, with 2 abstentions (Poland and USSR).]

Mr. ROA (Cuba) (translated from Spanish): The Revolutionary Government of Cuba had recourse to the Security Council in order to submit for its consideration the situation created by the Government of the United States with manifest danger to international peace and security, and to request the adoption of such measures as were deemed appropriate.

It was thus exercising an optional right granted to it by the Charter of the United Nations, without disparaging or damaging the regional organization to which it belongs, and was prepared in advance to accept the decision taken by the majority of the Council.

The draft resolution just approved, as indeed any other draft resolution which the Council might have adopted, is or would have been something in which the Cuban delegation had no participation whatever. We have not negotiated, nor were we interested in negotiating, any type of resolution; but, faced with the possible alternatives, my Government would have preferred a Council resolution condemning the harassments, reprisals and aggressive acts indulged in by the United States Government against the Government and people of Cuba. At the very least, the situation should have remained exclusively one for consideration by the Council.

The resolution adopted, while maintaining the jurisdiction of the Council, takes it for granted that the situation is under examination by the Organization of American States and accordingly adjourns consideration of the matter pending the receipt of a report from that body.

The position of the Revolutionary Government of Cuba is, briefly, as follows:

(1) It reaffirms its full right to opt for recourse to the Security Council.

(2) It confirms in every detail the charges which it has made.

(3) It denies categorically that the serious situation existing between the United States and Cuba is already under consideration by the Organization of American States. The Revolutionary Government of Cuba appealed to the United Nations and not to the Organization of American States. The memorandum of the United States Government on the acts of provocation which it alleges that the Revolutionary Government of Cuba has committed to the detriment of good relations in the Caribbean was sent to the Inter-American Peace Committee in accordance with a resolution adopted at the Fifth Meeting of Consultation of Foreign Ministers held at Santiago in 1959. It is a memorandum addressed to a collateral body of the Organization of American States, and not a formal charge submitted, as it should have been, to the Council of that Organization.

(4) The Cuban Government accepts the terms of the resolution adopted by the majority and, while continuing to assert its rights before the Security Council as it thinks fit will also uphold those rights with the same zeal and firmness in the Organization of American States.

The Revolutionary Government of Cuba will, in short, reject no international forum that will enable it to defend and uphold the sovereignty, territorial integrity, independence and self-determination of its people.

NOTE. It may be noted that at the San Francisco Conference the Peruvian delegate pointed out that the provision in Article 52 of the Charter referring to the powers of the Security Council under Articles 34 and 35 "might result in practice in the simultaneous handling of a dispute by a regional organization and by the Security Council, or in the failure on the part of the Security Council to rely upon adequate action being taken by the regional organization. The first of these two possibilities would prove inconvenient and the second unacceptable. On behalf of the Peruvian Delegation he affirmed the autonomy of the regional arrangements within the frame of the world Organization. If the regional organs fail to secure peaceful settlement, he said, then, and only then, should the jurisdiction of the Council apply." The Colombian delegate then provided the following explanation: "If a dispute arises between two states which are members of a regional organization, such controversy should be settled by peaceful means established within the said organization. The obligation exists for all states which are members of a regional organization to make every effort to settle the controversy through this agency, and at the same time, the obligation exists for the Security Council to promote these regional peaceful settlements. But the Security Council has the right to investigate in order to determine whether the controversy may constitute a threat to international peace or security, such right of investigation being subject to the reservation expressed in the new article on collective defense, which provides that Articles 1 and 2 of Section A of the same Chapter [Articles 34–35 of the Charter] shall stand in full force.

"Those articles refer to the right of the Security Council to investigate any situation which may threaten peace and security, and to the right of nations to call the attention of the Security Council or of the Assembly to any situation which may threaten international peace or security.

"Under Articles 1 and 2 of Section A, the Council has jurisdiction only to investigate, and the nations, whether or not they are members of the organization, have the right only to ask for an investigation. The Council has jurisdiction to act, to make recommendations, to take precautionary measures other than military measures, and to take military measures, only within the terms of the articles beginning with Article 4 of the said Section A [Article 36 of the Charter] and continuing throughout Section B. There is and, therefore, can be no double jurisdiction or competence as between that of the Security Council, proposing certain peaceful settlements, and that of the regional organization. The Council should limit its action to investigating, either on its own initiative or because any nation so requests, any situation which may threaten peace, and to promoting the regional settlement of the problem; while the states which are members of the regional system have the duty to make every effort to reach a peaceful settlement through their own organization before referring the problem to the Council. This is indicated not only by the articles of the Chapter on regional arrangements but also by Article 3 of Section A, as amended.

"A regional agreement must include, as in the case of the American states, a complete system of peaceful settlements: investigation, direct settlement, mediation, conciliation, arbitration, and recourse to international courts of justice. Any dispute which may arise within a regional system should be acted upon through these regional peaceful means. In accordance with Article 1 of Section A of Chapter VIII, the Security Council, until such action has taken place, and whether on its own initiative, or at the request of any state under Article 2, could only investigate the matter of whether or not there is a situation likely to disturb international peace and security.

"It is evident that if the regional systems for peaceful settlement fail, the Council can intervene, in accordance with Article 5 [Article 37 of the Charter], for the purpose of proposing formulas for settlement.

"But if at any time an armed attack should ensue, that is, an aggression against a state which is a member of the regional group, self-defense, whether individual or collective, exercised as an inherent right, shall operate automatically within the provisions of the Charter, until such time as the Security Council may take the appropriate punitive measures against the aggressor state.

"In the case of the American states, an aggression against one American state constitutes an aggression against all the American states, and all of them exercise their right of legitimate defense by giving support to the state attacked, in order to repel such aggression. This is what is meant by the right of *collective self-defense.*" UNCIO Doc. 576, III/4/9 (25 May 1945); 12 UNCIO Documents, pp. 685–87.

3.   *The Declaration of San José, Costa Rica,*
29 August 1960.

Final Act of the Seventh Meeting of Consultation of Ministers of Foreign
Affairs, pp. 5–6.   OAS Official Records, OEA/SER.F/11.7;
UN Doc. S/4480 (7 Sept. 1960).

The Seventh Meeting of Consultation of Ministers of Foreign Affairs

1.   Condemns emphatically intervention or the threat of intervention, even when conditional, from an extracontinental power in the affairs of the American republics and declares that the acceptance of a threat of extracontinental intervention by any American state jeopardizes American solidarity and security, wherefor the Organization of American States is under obligation to disapprove it and reject it with equal vigor.

2.   Rejects, also, the attempt of the Sino-Soviet powers to make use of the political, economic, or social situation of any American state, inasmuch as that attempt is capable of destroying hemispheric unity and jeopardizing the peace and security of the hemisphere.

3.   Reaffirms the principle of nonintervention by any American state in the internal or external affairs of the other American states, and it reiterates that each state has the right to develop its cultural, political, and economic life freely and naturally, respecting the rights of the individual and the principles of universal morality, and as a consequence, no American state may intervene for the purpose of imposing upon another American state its ideologies or political, economic, or social principles.

4.   Reaffirms that the inter-American system is incompatible with any form of totalitarianism and that democracy will achieve the full scope of its objectives in the hemisphere only when all the American republics conduct themselves in accordance with the principles stated in the Declaration of Santiago, Chile, which was approved at the Fifth Meeting of Consultation of Ministers of Foreign Affairs, the observance of which it recommends as soon as possible.

5.   Proclaims that all member states of the regional organization are under obligation to submit to the discipline of the inter-American system, voluntarily and freely agreed upon, and that the soundest guarantee of their sovereignty and their political independence stems from compliance with the provisions of the Charter of the Organization of American States.

6.   Declares that all controversies between member states should be resolved by the measures for peaceful solution that are contemplated in the inter-American system.

7.   Reaffirms its faith in the regional system and its confidence in the Organization of American States, created to achieve an order of

peace and justice that excludes any possible aggression, to promote solidarity among its members, to strengthen their collaboration, and to defend their sovereignty, their territorial integrity, and their political independence, since it is in this Organization that the members find the best guarantee for their evolution and development.

8.   Resolves that this declaration shall be known as "The Declaration of San José, Costa Rica."

NOTE.—1.   The San José Conference established also an *Ad Hoc* Good Offices Committee, composed of representatives of Venezuela, Mexico, Brazil, Colombia, Chile and Costa Rica, to facilitate, at the request of the governments directly concerned, the settlement of controversies between American Governments "by clarifying the facts and extending its good offices." Final Act of the Seventh Meeting of Ministers of Foreign Affairs, p. 7; OAS Official Records, OEA/SER.F/11.7; UN Doc. S/4480 (7 Sept. 1960). Though the United States proposed that its dispute with Cuba be submitted to that Committee for an examination of facts, Cuba refused its consent to such an examination. UN Docs. S/4559 and S/4565 (10 and 29 Nov. 1960); SCOR, XV, Supp. for Oct.–Dec. 1960, pp. 53–57, 59–65.

2.   On 31 December 1960 and 3 January 1961, Cuba requested the Security Council to consider a threat of military aggression by the United States against Cuba, and the decision of the United States to break off diplomatic relations with Cuba.   The United States justified the decision by hostile attitude of Cuba and denied as false the charges of preparations for an invasion; it pointed out that Cuba refused to accept the Committee of Good Offices of the Organization of American States.   A draft resolution, proposed by Ecuador and Chile, recommending the solution of the differences by the peaceful means provided for in the Charter and urging Member States to refrain from any action which might aggravate the tension was not pressed to a vote.   Report of the Security Council, 1960–61 [GAOR, XVI, Supp. 2 (A/4867)], pp. 64–67.

3.   The attempt of Cuban exiles to land in Cuba on 17 April 1961 was considered by the General Assembly which on 21 April adopted a resolution proposed by seven Latin American States exhorting all Member States "to take such peaceful action as is open to them to remove existing tension"; more far-reaching proposals did not receive a two-thirds vote, and a strong Soviet resolution was not pressed to a vote.   Annual Report of the Secretary-General, 1960–61 [GAOR, XVI, Supp. 1 (A/4800)], pp. 88–90; General Assembly Resolution 1616 (XV), GAOR, XV, Supp. 16A (A/4684/Add. 1), p. 3.

4.   For comments on the problems raised by Cuba in 1960 and 1961, see Adolf A. BERLE, Jr., "The Cuban Crisis: Failure of American Foreign Policy," 39 Foreign Affairs (1960), pp. 40–55; Richard A. FALK, "American Intervention in Cuba and the Rule of Law," 22 Ohio State L.J. (1961), pp. 546–85; Russel H. FITZGIBBON, "The Organization of American States: Time of Ordeal," 5 Orbis (1961), pp. 74–86; Gastón GODOY, El caso cubano y la Organización de Estados Americanos (Madrid, 1961), 110 pp.; D. A. GRABER, "United States Intervention in Latin America," 16 YBWA (1962), pp. 23–50; Karl E. MEYER and Tad SZULC, The Cuban Invasion: The Chronicle of a Disaster (New York, 1962), 160 pp.; Lucien NIZARD, "La question cubaine devant le Conseil de Securité," 66 RGDIP (1962), pp.

486–545; US, DOS, "Cuba," (DOS Pub. 7171; Washington, D.C., 1961), 36 pp.; Quincy WRIGHT, "Intervention and Cuba in 1961," 55 ASIL Procgs. (1961), pp. 2–19.

DOMINICAN REPUBLIC'S ACTS AGAINST VENEZUELA

1. *Resolution I of the Sixth Meeting of Consultation of Ministers of Foreign Affairs, 21 August 1960.*

Final Act of the Meeting, pp. 4–6.   OAS Official Records,
OEA/SER. F/11.6;   UN Doc. S/4476 (1 Sept. 1960).

The Sixth Meeting of Consultation of Ministers of Foreign Affairs Serving as Organ of Consultation in Application of the Inter-American Treaty of Reciprocal Assistance.

Having Seen the Report of the Investigating Committee appointed pursuant to the provisions of the third paragraph of the resolution approved by the Council of the Organization of American States on July 8, 1960, and

Considering

That the Charter of the Organization of American States sets forth the principle that international order consists essentially of respect for the personality, sovereignty and independence of states and the faithful fulfillment of obligations derived from treaties and other sources of international law;

That in connection with the incident denounced by the Government of Venezuela before the Inter-American Peace Committee on November 25, 1959, that organ of the inter-American system reached the conclusion that "the necessary arrangements to carry out the flight from Ciudad Trujillo to Aruba—planned for the purpose of dropping leaflets over a Venezuelan city—and to load these leaflets in Ciudad Trujillo, could not have been carried out without the connivance of the Dominican authorities";

That the Committee of the Council of the Organization of American States acting provisionally as Organ of Consultation that was entrusted with the investigation of the acts denounced by the Government of Venezuela, reached the conclusion that the Government of the Dominican Republic issued diplomatic passports to be used by Venezuelans who participated in the military uprising that took place in April 1960 in San Cristobal, Venezuela;

That the Committee of the Council of the Organization of American States acting provisionally as Organ of Consultation, which was charged with the investigation of the acts denounced by the Government of the Republic of Venezuela, also reached the conclusions that:

1.   The attempt against the life of the President of Venezuela perpetrated on June 24, 1960, was part of a plot intended to overthrow the Government of that country.

2.   The persons implicated in the aforementioned attempt and plot received moral support and material assistance from high officials of the Government of the Dominican Republic.

3.   This assistance consisted principally of providing the persons implicated facilities to travel and to enter and reside in Dominican territory in connection with their subversive plans of having facilitated the two flights of the plane of Venezuelan registry to and from the Military Air Base of San Isidro, Dominican Republic; of providing arms for use in the coup against the Government of Venezuela and the electronic device and the explosives which were used in the attempt; as well as of having instructed the person who caused the explosion in the operation of the electronic device of that explosive and of having demonstrated to him the destructive force of the same.

That the aforementioned actions constitute acts of intervention and aggression against the Republic of Venezuela which affect the sovereignty of that state and endanger the peace of America; and

That in the present case collective action is justified under the provisions of Article 19 of the Charter of the Organization of American States,

Resolves:

To condemn emphatically the participation of the Government of the Dominican Republic in the acts of aggression and intervention against the State of Venezuela that culminated in the attempt on the life of the President of that country, and, as a consequence, in accordance with the provisions of Articles 6 and 8 of the Inter-American Treaty of Reciprocal Assistance;

Agrees:

1.   To apply the following measures:

a.   Breaking of diplomatic relations of all the member states with the Dominican Republic;

b.   Partial interruption of economic relations of all the member states with the Dominican Republic, beginning with the immediate suspension of trade in arms and implements of war of every kind. The Council of the Organization of American States, in accordance with the circumstances and with due consideration for the constitutional or legal limitations of each and every one of the member states, shall study the feasibility and desirability of extending the suspension of trade with the Dominican Republic to other articles.

2.   To authorize the Council of the Organization of American States to discontinue, by a two-thirds affirmative vote of its members, the measures adopted in this resolution, at such time as the Government of the Dominican Republic should cease to constitute a danger to the peace and security of the hemisphere.

3.   To authorize the Secretary General of the Organization of American States to transmit to the Security Council of the United Nations

full information concerning the measures agreed upon in this resolution.

2. Letter from the First Deputy Minister for Foreign Affairs of the USSR to the President of the Security Council, 5 September 1960.

S/4477 (5 Sept. 1960); SCOR, XV, Supp. for July-Sept. 1960, pp. 134–45.

As stated in document S/4476 dated 1 September 1960, the Organization of American States (OAS), at the Meeting of the Ministers of Foreign Affairs of the States members of the OAS held on 20 August 1960, adopted a resolution condemning the acts of aggression and intervention committed against the Republic of Venezuela by the anti-popular Trujillo régime in the Dominican Republic. The resolution provides for the application of enforcement action against this régime including the breaking of diplomatic relations of the member States of the OAS, and partial interruption of economic relations, with the Dominican Republic.

On the basis of Article 53 of the Charter of the United Nations, the Security Council should consider this question and endorse the decision of the Organization of American States, in that it is designed to remove the threat to peace and security created by the actions of the Dominican authorities. Article 53 of the United Nations Charter provides that the Security Council shall utilize "regional arrangements or agencies for enforcement action under its authority" and that "no enforcement action shall be taken under regional arrangements or by regional agencies without the authorization of the Security Council".

In consideration of the foregoing I have the honour to request you, on behalf of the Soviet Government, immediately to convene a meeting of the Security Council for the purpose of considering the decision taken by the Organization of American States concerning the Dominican Republic and with a view to the speedy adoption by the Council of an appropriate resolution.

3. Discussion in the Security Council, 8–9 Sept. 1960.

SCOR, XV, Mtgs. 893–95.

Mr. KUZNETSOV (USSR): The Security Council has before it a resolution of the Sixth Meeting of Consultation of Ministers of Foreign Affairs of the American States in respect of the Dominican Republic, which was brought to the attention of the Security Council in accordance with the provisions of the United Nations Charter. This resolution, adopted at the meeting held at San José, Costa Rica, on 20 August 1960, emphatically condemns the participation of the Government of the Dominican Republic in acts of aggression and intervention against the Republic of Venezuela and provides for the breaking of diplomatic relations of all States members of the Organization of

American States with the reactionary régime of the dictator Trujillo and for the partial interruption of economic relations with the Dominican Republic. . . .

The facts with which the Security Council has been presented leave no doubt that the present Government of the Dominican Republic has committed acts of intervention and aggression against the Republic of Venezuela, has violated the sovereignty of that State and has created a threat to international peace and security. . . .

The Soviet Government, which has invariably supported all measures designed to strengthen the principles of peaceful coexistence in relations between States, regards as right and proper the resolution adopted at the Meeting of Consultation of Ministers of Foreign Affairs of the American States, which condemned the aggressive actions of the Trujillo régime against the Republic of Venezuela. Similarly, the Members of the United Nations can not fail to support the decision of the Organization of American States as to the necessity of taking enforcement action—sanctions—against the Government of the Dominican dictator, including the breaking of the diplomatic relations of all States members of the Organization of American States with the Dominican Republic and the partial interruption of economic relations, beginning with the immediate suspension of trade in arms and implements of war of every kind. The application of such enforcement action is fully in accord with Articles 39 and 41 of the United Nations Charter.

Breaches of the peace and acts of aggression in any part of the world cannot be a matter of indifference to any nation concerned to preserve world peace and tranquillity. And that is quite understandable. For a local conflict may easily spread to other areas, thereby endangering general peace and the security of the peoples.

The United Nations, which was founded in order to stand guard over peace, must take decisive steps to ward off any threat of war, irrespective of the part of the world in which it may arise. The United Nations cannot pass over the aggressive actions of the Trujillo régime, but must do everything in its power to remove the threat to peace which that régime has brought about.

Under the United Nations Charter, as we all know, the primary responsibility for the maintenance of international peace and security rests with the Security Council, which is called upon to conduct all operations designed to halt aggression and restore peace. For that very purpose the founders of the United Nations wrote into the Charter a provision on the utilization by the Security Council of regional arrangements and agencies, of which the Organization of American States is one, for enforcement action under the Council's authority.

Article 53 of the United Nations Charter provides that "no enforcement action shall be taken under regional arrangements or by regional agencies without the authorization of the Security Council".

The Security Council is the only organ empowered to authorize the application of enforcement action by regional organizations against any State. Without authorization from the Security Council, the taking of enforcement action by regional agencies would be contrary to the Charter of the United Nations.

Thus the Security Council, in accordance with the provisions of the Charter, must approve the decision of the Organization of American States, so as to give it legal force and render it more effective. This would mean, in the present case, that the United Nations as a whole would take a stand in support of the decision of the American States, a decision which is aimed at removing the threat to peace and security created by the aggressive actions of the Dominican authorities.

The Soviet delegation has accordingly deemed it necessary to submit, for the consideration of the Security Council, a draft resolution [S/4481/Rev. 1] approving the decision of the Sixth Meeting of Consultation of Ministers of Foreign Affairs in respect of the Dominican Republic. With your permission, I shall now read out the text of this draft resolution:

"The Security Council,

"Having examined resolution I of the Sixth Meeting of Consultation of Ministers of Foreign Affairs of the American States, dated 20 August 1960 (S/4476), in which the acts of aggression and intervention committed against the Republic of Venezuela by the Government of the Dominican Republic are condemned,

"Being guided by Article 53 of the Charter of the United Nations,

"Approves the said resolution of the Meeting of Consultation of Ministers of Foreign Affairs of the American States, dated 20 August 1960."

The Soviet delegation is confident that all the members of the Security Council will support this draft resolution and vote in favour of it. There is no doubt that the adoption of a resolution approving the application of enforcement action against the antipopular Trujillo régime will contribute to the maintenance of peace and security not only in the countries of Latin America, but throughout the world.

. . .

Mr. AMADEO (Argentina): The Soviet Union has asked for this meeting of the Security Council, as its letter says, "for the purpose of considering the decision taken by the Organization of American States concerning the Dominican Republic and with a view to the speedy adoption by the Council of an appropriate resolution".

It is an inflexible rule of conduct for us not to look for any hidden intentions which might lead Members of this Organization to act as they do within it. We must therefore start from the assumption the

Soviet Union made this request simply to the end that the Security Council might confirm and ratify the decision taken in Costa Rica by the Sixth Meeting of Consultation of Ministers of Foreign Affairs of the American States. It is therefore in the light of this interpretation, made in good faith, that we shall consider the matter under discussion.

If we are not mistaken, the Soviet request brings up in the Council, for the first time, the question of the interpretation of Article 53 of the Charter in connexion with steps taken by regional agencies. Both the letter asking for the Council meeting and the Soviet draft resolution before us take this Article as the text on which the Security Council should base its action.

The Soviet view is that, under Article 53 of the Charter, the Security Council is competent to approve the steps recently taken by the Organization of American States with regard to one of its members. At the same time it is clear that, *a contrario sensu,* the Soviet view also implies that the Security Council is entitled to annul or revise these measures if it sees fit.

My delegation does not think this is the juncture at which to take a final decision on this question. All that we can say for the present is that we have great doubts as to whether the Soviet Union's interpretation is the right one. There are weighty reasons to support the argument that measures taken regionally would be subject to the Security Council's ratification only if they called for the use of armed force. In any case, the matter seems open to discussion.

However, we think that this is not the best occasion for a thorough examination of the legal question. For one thing, the sudden calling of this meeting—which we must admit has taken us by surprise—has not allowed us sufficient time for the scrupulous investigation which the matter requires. For another, we do not think that the present international situation is the one most indicated for a discussion of questions of principle. Existing political tensions are such that it would be difficult to conceive of statements not decisively influenced by the conflicting positions and passions characteristic of the world at this period of uncertainty.

In the circumstances, the Argentine delegation thinks that the Council should adopt an attitude to which there can be no valid objection, whether legal or political.

The Meeting of Ministers of Foreign Affairs, in adopting the decisions incorporated in its Final Act, was acting fully within its powers. Those decisions were transmitted to the United Nations by the Secretary-General of the Organization of American States, in accordance with the clear provisions of the Charters of both Organizations. We should therefore officially take note of what has happened. It is well that the Security Council should now take note of what this regional agency has done. This would be a complete demonstration of the co-ordination which should exist between the regional agency and the international Organization. It would also constitute one more proof of the concern which the world Organization—and especially this body, the Security Council—ought to show for problems that have a bearing on international peace and security in every part of the globe.

This is why we agreed that the question should be placed on the agenda and have come to the conclusion that the Council should adopt a resolution. The events which led to the Sixth Meeting of Consultation and the decisions taken there, however much they may pain us States of the American continent, are important enough for cognizance of them to be taken by the Security Council. From this particular standpoint we are glad that the Soviet Union has brought this problem before us.

What I have said is, I think, enough to explain the draft resolution which my delegation has the honour to co-sponsor with the delegations of Ecuador and the United States.

[This draft resolution (S/4484) read as follows:

"The Security Council,

"Having received the report from the Secretary General of the Organization of American States transmitting the Final Act of the Sixth Meeting of Consultation of Ministers of Foreign Affairs of the American Republics (S/4476),

"Takes note of that report and especially of resolution I, approved at the aforesaid Meeting, whereby agreement was reached on the application of measures regarding the Dominican Republic."]

Our text shows the Security Council's interest and concern in matters affecting peace and security, and leaves the door wide open for a constructive interpretation of Article 53 of the Charter in circumstances more favourable than those prevailing at present.

Although we have not taken a stand on the interpretation of Article 53, that cannot prevent us from expressing an idea which is deeply rooted in the Latin American mind—namely, that the geographical region in which we live has in itself the moral values and technical resources required to solve any conflicts which may arise within it.

My country's international conduct has always been based on universalism. We think that the international community, just like the human race, is a single unit and should not be split up into water-tight compartments, completely cut off from one another. Latin America has shown on more than one occasion that it is the first to defend the need to preserve and increase the responsibility and influence of the international world Organization.

But this universalism cannot be carried to the length of denying the reality of regional groups, whose establishment, on the basis of genuine affinities, is possibly the most novel feature of international life in our time. And if we agree that regional groups have an entity of their own, distinct from the world community and from the States of which they are composed, we must acknowledge that they possess certain rights in the matter of regulating the relations between their members and maintaining, within them, peace and the rule of law. This applies particularly to the case now under consideration, since the regional agency—the Organization of American States—has an elaborate legal machinery for guaranteeing observance of the rule of law.

It is therefore our conviction that, however Article 53 of the Charter may be interpreted in the future, legally organized regional groups —not only the American, but also those existing, or to come into being, in other parts of the world—must have sufficient authority to solve problems confined within the limits of the region involved. This will not weaken the world Organization but will, on the contrary, free it from many problems which can and should be handled within a smaller radius.

There can be no doubt whatever that members of this Council who also belong to a regional organization are entitled to a natural right of initiative in matters of this kind. We do not deny to any other members the right, which the Charter gives equally to all, to set the machinery of the system in motion whenever they see fit. But we hope that no one will question our special capacity to act in defence of our rights and to safeguard the international law under which we live.

For all these reasons, the Argentine delegation advocates the adoption of the draft resolution which it submits jointly with Ecuador and the United States of America; and we ask members of the Security Council to vote for it unanimously.

Mr. WADSWORTH (USA): . . . While believing that the Security Council might properly discuss and take note of the resolution of the Sixth Meeting of Consultation, we reject the contention of the USSR that this resolution or action taken pursuant to it requires any endorsement by the Security Council in accordance with Article 53 of the Charter. The United States does not consider that the resolution adopted by the Sixth Meeting requires the endorsement of the Security Council under Article 53.

It is significant that no member of the Organization of American States sought authorization from the Security Council, under Article 53, for the steps taken in connexion with that resolution and that, in specifically deciding that the resolution should be transmitted to the Security Council, only for its full information, the Foreign Ministers were clearly expressing their view that this action required only notification to the United Nations under Article 54.

It is noteworthy that Article 54 clearly envisages the possibility of activities by regional agencies for the maintenance of international peace and security, in regard to which the responsibility of the regional organization to the Security Council is purely that of keeping it informed.

It is also noteworthy that, in the present instance, either of the actions which are being taken collectively by the members of the Organization of American States could be taken individually by any sovereign nation on its own initiative. . . .

In common with the representative of Argentina, I do not propose at this meeting to take up the time of the Council with any discussion as to any motive which might have impelled any other member of the Council to bring this particular subject before a meeting. I believe this to be an unfruitful strategy and I shall not indulge in it. The American Republics, I would remind representatives, however, have within the past month condemned intervention, or the threat of intervention, no matter how phrased, by extra-continental Powers in American Republic affairs. They have rejected specifically any attempt of Communist China or the USSR to make use of the political, economic or social situations of any American State and have reaffirmed that the inter-American system is incompatible with any form of totalitarianism.

The Security Council can best affirm its faith in the inter-American system by the adoption of the draft resolution submitted by the members of the Organization of American States in the Council. We urge that it do so.

Mr. CORREA (Ecuador): . . . [Resolution I] approved by the Sixth Meeting of Consultation is a good example of effective action against aggression and in defence of the sovereignty of a State and the principle of non-intervention, which is essential to an international order based on justice and mutual respect.

It is a source of calm and confidence for those States which base the defence of their sovereignty and integrity on legal and moral forces to know that the doors of the world Organization and of regional agencies are open to them whenever they need the help of such bodies in order to defend their rights and interests. In the present case, the Government of Venezuela chose the way of regional action; and although the facts are very painful for the American Republics, we are none the less glad to see that they have unanimously taken effective steps against aggression and the violation of a State's sovereignty and have thereby defended the principle of non-intervention.

When the Ministers for Foreign Affairs approved the resolution, they took good care to authorize the Secretary-General of the Organization of American States to transmit to the Security Council full information concerning the measures agreed upon, but the resolution of the Meeting of Consultation became effective without authorization from the Security Council and has already been carried out, almost in its entirety, by member States of the Organization of American States. We are therefore dealing with a resolution which is already in force and has already been implemented. At the Meeting of Consultation, the representative of the Dominican Republic did indeed allege, in his defence, that the steps agreed upon would not be valid without the authorization of the Security Council; but the twenty participating States saw fit to instruct the Secretary-General to inform the Security Council, without asking for its authorization.

On this basis, and in conformity with the tradition of the Security Council, the distribution of the text of the Final Act to members of the Council would have been enough. However, the representative of the Soviet Union decided to ask for this meeting so that the Council might take formal note of the communication received from the Organization of American States. We thought it well to comply with this request, out of respect for the right of a member of the Council to bring to its attention a problem which, in that member's view, is of interest to the Council. Naturally, the meeting of the Council to examine the matter in no way affects its right to take any decision it thinks suitable, according to its own interpretation of the Charter and on the merits of the case.

In this connexion I should like to point out that the provisions of the Charter regarding the Security Council's powers, and with respect to the existence and purposes of regional arrangements and agencies, for dealing with such matters relating to the maintenance of international peace and security as are appropriate for regional action, should be considered as a whole; for they establish a delicate system of balances, which might be upset by any attempt to apply a particular provision in isolation, on the basis of some over-simplified and literal interpretation which failed to take into account the spirit of the Charter as a whole and the entire machinery whereby it operates so far as the relations between United Nations bodies and the regional agencies are concerned.

In this delicate matter, we think it essential to pursue a line of conduct which will protect and guarantee the autonomy, the individuality, the structure and the proper and effective working of regional agencies, so that they may deal with situations and disputes which are appropriate for regional action—provided that there is no undermining of the authority of the Security Council or of the Member States' right to appeal to it whenever they consider that the defence of their rights or interests requires such an appeal, or that a particular situation or dispute, even if appropriate for regional action, might endanger international peace and security. We think that the Security Council should not base its decisions in this matter entirely on one provision of Article 53. If we examine this Article in the light of the other provisions and of the spirit of the Charter, we find that it is far from having the clarity which would justify its use in the sense indicated both in the Soviet Union's letter and the Soviet draft resolution.

Several questions may in fact be asked about the scope of paragraph 1 of Article 53—questions to which we find no categorical reply either in the San Francisco discussions, or in the Council's own decisions, or in the context of the relevant Chapters of the Charter.

It is not clear, for example, whether the enforcement action for which the Security Council's authorization is necessary is that which calls for the use of armed force, as provided for in Article 42. Nor is it clear whether the second sentence of Article 53 applies only to action which a regional agency may take in a case which the Security Council has entrusted to it from the beginning. We might also ask whether the Security Council's authorization is necessary only for action which, like the use of force, would be a violation of international law if it were taken without the Council's authorization, but not for action like the breaking of diplomatic relations, which is within the exclusive right of a sovereign State.

I do not wish to burden the Council with an endless series of questions about Article 53. I will simply say this: the questions I have raised are enough to show that this Article cannot and should not be used to make a regional agency's action rigidly dependent upon authorization by the Security Council. On the contrary, the relations between the Council and the regional agencies should be so flexible as to permit these agencies to take effective action for the maintenance of international peace and security in the light of regional conditions and without necessarily bringing regional problems before a world forum.

In the present case, where the Government concerned opted for regional action, we think that the proper course should be for the Security Council simply to take formal note of the approved resolution for the application of certain measures in regard to the Dominican Republic.

The records of the Security Council will undoubtedly constitute, in themselves, an expression of approval for the way in which the Organization of American States has defended the independence of a member State and the principle of non-intervention. However, I would again say that, in order not to create an unnecessary precedent which would not, in our view, be fully in line with the Charter as a whole, the Council should simply take note of the report it has received.

In view of this, the delegations of Ecuador, Argentina and the United States—the three members of the Council who belong to the Organization of American States—have jointly submitted a draft resolution. This draft resolution has just been presented by our Argentine colleague, and we hope that it will receive the Security Council's unanimous approval.

I would also express the hope that the representative of the Soviet Union will not press for a vote on his own draft resolution, to which, for the reasons that I have stated, serious objections of principle might be raised.   .   .   .

Mr. SOSA RODRIGUEZ (Venezuela):   .   .   .   I am sincerely grateful to you for this opportunity because it enables me to raise the voice of the country which has, in its own flesh and in the person of its highest Officer, felt the consequences of the criminal acts which gave rise to the unanimous decision of the American States to impose sanctions and put an end to the activities of a Government which is disturbing the peace of the continent, violating the most fundamental principles of international law and flouting the most elementary standards inherent in the dignity of man as a human being and citizen.   .   .   .

As far as the Government of Venezuela is concerned, the decision of the Organization of American States is wholly in keeping with the principles of inter-American law, which are in essence the principles which govern the United Nations, and that decision is complete in itself and requires, to validate it, no subsequent authorization of the Security Council.

The nature and scope of the measures provided for in resolution I adopted at San José do not, in my Government's opinion, fall within the concept of enforcement action referred to in Article 53 of the United Nations Charter.

It is the Venezuelan Government's view that the authorization of the Security Council would be required only in the case of decisions of regional agencies the implementation of which would involve the use of force, which is not the case with this resolution of the American States.

In the light of these considerations, on which my Government's position with respect to the question under discussion is based, I should like now to comment on the two draft resolutions submitted to the Council.

With regard to the draft resolution submitted by the Soviet Union, we are naturally pleased that part of this draft would have the world Organization recognize the justice and appropriateness of the measures taken by the Organization of American States against the Dominican Republic because of its aggressive acts against Venezuela.

However, the specific reference made in that draft to Article 53 of the Charter would, in our view, create very serious obstacles to the efficient functioning of regional organizations, since it would imply recognition of the need for authorization by the Security Council in order to complete decisions which, as in the present case, are valid and complete in themselves.

With regard to the draft resolution submitted by the delegations of Argentina, Ecuador and the United States, we believe that it is quite in accordance with law; but we would prefer some expression of the Security Council's concern at the serious events which gave rise to the decision taken by the Organization of American States. . . . In point of fact, we are not dealing with trivial happenings which can be brushed aside on grounds, or by arguments, of expediency. We are confronted by events with the most serious political repercussions, which have aroused the unanimous feelings of all the peoples of America. Today's debate in the Security Council will not go unnoticed by all the peoples of the American continent who, in the light of the Security Council's high responsibility for the maintenance of international peace and security, expect not only that it will take note of this decision but that it will in some way assist in the action approved by the inter-American regional organization.

Such a stand by the Council would in no way diminish the force and validity of the regional organization's resolution which, as I have already said, is complete and valid in itself, but it would demonstrate the Security Council's support of and solidarity with the action taken by the regional organization in application of the principles of inter-American law which are, in essence, the principles enshrined in the United Nations Charter. . . .

Mr. BEELEY (UK): Mr. President, when I read the letter addressed to you by the representative of the Soviet Union in which he asked you to convene a meeting of the Security Council immediately to endorse the decision of the Organization of American States with regard to the Dominican Republic, I was somewhat surprised by his action.

In the opinion of the United Kingdom Government, there is no need for the Council to be meeting here this afternoon. We consider that the responsibilities of the Organization of American States towards the United Nations have been adequately discharged by the letter from the Secretary-General of that Organization conveying the Final Act of the meeting at San José to the Security Council, in conformity with Article 54 of the Charter.

The representative of the Soviet Union has argued that the Security Council has responsibilities under Article 53 of the Charter in relation to the recent decisions of the Organization of American States with regard to the Dominican Republic. This opinion is based on the assertion that the measures in question constitute "enforcement action".

The Charter of the United Nations does not define the term "enforcement action". In the opinion of the United Kingdom Government, it is common sense to interpret the use of this term in Article 53 as covering only such actions as would not normally be legitimate except on the basis of a Security Council resolution. There is nothing in international law, in principle, to prevent any State, if it so decides, from breaking off diplomatic relations or instituting a partial interruption of economic relations with any other State. These steps, which are the measures decided upon by the Organization of American States with regard to the Dominican Republic, are acts of policy perfectly within the competence of any sovereign State. It follows, obviously, that they are within the competence of the members of the Organization of American States acting collectively.

In other words, it is the view of my delegation that when Article 53 refers to "enforcement action", it must be contemplating the exercise of force in a manner which would not normally be legitimate for any State or group of States except under the authority of a Security Council resolution. Other pacifying actions under regional arrangements as envisaged in Chapter VIII of the Charter which do not come into this category have simply to be brought to the attention of the Security Council under Article 54. As I said earlier, it is the United Kingdom view that this obligation has been adequately fulfilled by the report already made to the Council by the Organization of American States.

For these reasons, the adoption of a substantive resolution by the Council would, in the United Kingdom view, be improper in the present circumstances. I see no objection, however, to the adoption of the procedural resolution proposed by the representatives of Argentina, Ecuador and the United States of America, which amounts simply to a confirmation of the fact that the members of the Council have been kept appropriately informed of the activities of the Organization of American States. I shall therefore vote in favour of that draft resolution. . . .

Sir Claude COREA (Ceylon): . . . . [The] members of the Organization of American States agreed to apply two measures against the Government of the Dominican Republic: one, to break off diplomatic relations, and two, to interrupt partially economic relations with the Dominican Republic. There can be little doubt that these measures are but two of the several measures not involving the use of armed forces enumerated in Article 41 of the Charter of the United Nations.

The two important points to be borne in mind, in the view of my delegation, are: first, the measures are measures not involving the use of armed force; and second, the measures have been employed not by the Security Council on its own initiative, but by a regional agency as recognized by Article 52.

Now, Article 53, which the First Deputy Foreign Minister of the Soviet Union invoked yesterday in introducing the Soviet draft resolution [S/4481/Rev.1], makes provision for two eventualities: firstly, the Security Council itself may utilize regional arrangements for enforcement of any measures which it may itself decide to employ under Article 41 or Article 42; secondly, where such measures are in the first instance decided on by a regional agency itself, no enforcement action can be taken without the authorization of the Security Council.

In the circumstances of the present case, we need not discuss the first of these eventualities. There is no action proposed by the Security Council on its own initiative. In our view, therefore, we have only the second position to consider, and the second provision to which I have referred does indeed leave room for honest and sincere differences of interpretation.

There are valid arguments to support the view that the enforcement action referred to in Article 53 applies to the measures enumerated in Article 41 as well as in Article 42. On the other hand, there are also important arguments which might be adduced in support of the contention that the enforcement action referred to in Article 53 is restricted to the serious measures referred to in Article 42, namely, measures involving the use of armed force. There is, therefore, a great difficulty in the interpretation of Article 53. This is a matter which we have to face and concede. Much time could usefully be given to the study and serious consideration of this Article in the context of the Charter and the whole field of United Nations jurisprudence. As the representative of Argentina said so eloquently yesterday, this is a matter which requires thought and objectivity. We are, therefore, ourselves reluctant to be over hasty in putting forward an interpretation which, if accepted, will no doubt create a precedent; but, for the purposes of our discussion here, it would not be possible to leave the matter entirely alone.

It would appear to be necessary to say that, in our opinion, Article 53 when it refers to enforcement action, whether taken by the Security Council through the utilization of the regional organization, or by the regional agency with the authority of the Security Council, refers to both kinds of action contemplated in Articles 41 and 42. There is no doubt that such an interpretation is open to the objection—in so far as Article 41 at any rate is concerned—that no enforcement action is required in regard to some of the measures that could be taken under Article 41. For instance, it might be urged that the severance of diplomatic relations does not require any enforcement and, therefore, Article 53 must be construed as referring only to cases where the employment of force is necessary—that is, to cases coming under Article 42.

Such an interpretation would appear to us to be too restrictive and if we examine the Article more carefully we might see that, even in the case just cited—that is, the severance of diplomatic relations—the enforcement action contemplated really means the implementation by the Security Council under its own authority, through the utilization of the regional agency, or by the regional agency itself with the authority of the Security Council. Thus, the reference there is to the implementation; in other words, enforcement action could mean nothing more nor less than the implementation of the action. It would thus appear to be the case that if, by enforcement action, we mean implementation, measures contemplated under Articles 41 and 42 would fall within the scope of Article 53; and any implementation of resolution I of the Final Act should be either by the Security Council through the utilization of the regional agency, or by authorizing the regional agency to take enforcement action.

If this interpretation were valid, the question might be asked whether it would not seriously impair the sovereign rights of individual States. Each member State of the regional organization enjoys sovereign rights, among which would be the right to sever diplomatic relations. Would it be necessary to obtain the authority of the Security Council to do so? If so, would it not curtail its sovereign rights? Undoubtedly it would, if the interpretation which I have placed on Article 53 is correct. There could be no doubt that any member State of the regional organization, however, could, individually, have the fullest right in the exercise of its sovereignty to sever diplomatic relations without authority from anyone else, solely on the strength of its own sovereignty, without the consent even of the Security Council, because I draw a distinction between the individual rights of each State which is a member of the regional organization and the rights of States as members of the organization. I think that there is a real and important difference in the rights and obligations which accrue and must be considered in either case. So I ask, would a State's sovereign right remain the same—the right, for instance, to take measures to sever diplomatic relations—if the State acted as a member of a regional group and brought itself under Chapter VIII of the Charter, and more especially under Article 53? In that case the position might be different. The rights and obligations of the individual State might become merged in the rights and obligations of the regional organization in relation to the Charter.

Thus, while in its individual capacity a State has certain rights, some of these may be subordinated as a result of obligations incurred by another relationship established between the organization and the Charter. I do not, however, as I said earlier, wish to pursue this matter further because it is of such importance as to receive fuller consideration on another occasion.

I have raised it, however, as it certainly appears to be pertinent and indeed important in regard to the matter that we have before us. But so far as a decision on the issue before this Council is concerned, my delegation will be strongly influenced in a matter of this kind not only by the inherent difficulty of interpretation, to which I have referred, but also by the opinion and desires of the representatives of the Latin American countries. I think we should recognize this issue as one which is, though not exclusively, to a very large extent within the competence of the members of the regional group. The Security Council in such cases usually utilizes the regional agency and generally is influenced by the views expressed by the regional agency. I therefore think that we should be guided by their opinion and their advice.

The representatives of Argentina, Ecuador and the United States have suggested, in the draft resolution which they submitted to the Council, that it would be sufficient, for the implementation of the decision taken at the San José Meeting of Consultation, if the Security Council took note of the Final Act. What is more important is that the representative of Venezuela, a party directly concerned, in his able and lucid statement, agreed with the view submitted by the representatives of Argentina, Ecuador and the United States.

For these reasons, I hope that the Council will find it possible to reach a unanimous decision, though I feel constrained to say that the Soviet draft resolution which is also before us certainly adopts a logical attitude and follows the interpretation of Article 53 of the Charter along the lines which appear to us to be a not unreasonable interpretation to be placed on Article 53. But for the reasons I have given, I would submit that it would be preferable on this occasion to accept the viewpoint of those countries which are immediately concerned.

There is further reason why we should on this occasion consider the three-Power draft resolution as acceptable. I would invite the attention of all members of this Council to the operative paragraph of this draft resolution. We are asked to take note not only of the report of the Organization of American States, but especially of resolution I, a resolution which it is stated has been approved at the aforesaid meeting, whereby agreement was reached on the application of measures regarding the Dominican Republic.

My point is that, in reality, I find very little difference, except in wording, between the draft resolution submitted by the Soviet Union and the draft resolution submitted by Argentina, Ecuador and the United States of America, because the meaning one attaches to the three-Power draft resolution is that we are asked to take note of the resolution which had been adopted at the Sixth Meeting of Consultation of Ministers of Foreign Affairs of the American Republics. If we take note of the acceptance of a resolution and take note of it in the very terms of that resolution, it implies that we are not opposed to it. It is not difficult to argue that if one is not opposed to a thing, one more or less concurs in that position.

I place this interpretation on it and I mention it in the hope that it may be possible for all of us to unanimously accept this draft resolution. Even if I am going to be guilty of repetition, I want to say again that if we as a Council take note of resolution I of the Organization of American States, and we do not dissent from the views expressed therein, then this Council, in taking note of it, must be expected to have no objection to it. It must be expected to concur in the terms of that of which we take note.

Undoubtedly, it is not as clear and precise as the wording contained in the Soviet draft resolution: "Approves the said resolution." The difficulty here is that the adoption of the word "Approves" brings into operation the difficulties of interpretation which have been referred to and which our Latin American friends would like to be more fully considered. I think that is a point of view which we might consider favourably. If we take note of that action of the Organization of American States, there may be technical difficulties—I can see legal difficulties in the implementation—but if the Latin American States immediately concerned are satisfied that suitable action can be taken, as perhaps has been taken in the past, without Security Council intervention, then we should leave it to the Latin American States to take such action. If they are satisfied that that action will be a full implementation of the purposes and the spirit of the conference that was held at San José, then I think we could safely leave it at that and leave it to the Latin American countries concerned to get implementation of their resolution in the best way that they think it possible.

. . .

Mr. KUZNETSOV (USSR): The delegation of the Soviet Union deems it necessary to comment on certain observations made here concerning approval by the Security Council, in conformity with Article 53 of the United Nations Charter, of the decision taken by the Organization of American States in respect of the Dominican Republic.

It is common knowledge that Trujillo's antipopular régime has committed acts of aggression against Venezuela, thereby jeopardizing peace and security not merely in South America but throughout the world. Such actions must undoubtedly be condemned, and appropriate steps to halt aggression and prevent its recurrence must be taken without delay. Thus the adoption of enforcement measures—sanctions—against the Trujillo régime, which has infringed the sovereignty of a State Member of the United Nations, is right and proper.

Many members of the Security Council who took the floor yesterday and today have spoken to that effect. At the same time, it cannot be denied that decisions by regional organizations relating to the maintenance of peace and security, and *a fortiori* decisions to take enforcement action, should be carried into effect in strict conformity with the United Nations Charter. As is known, the Charter confers on the Security Council primary responsibility for the maintenance of international peace and security; this is the starting-point for all the provisions in the Charter which determine the Security Council's functions and powers.

Article 53 of the Charter, which is relevant to the issue under consideration, provides that the Security Council can utilize regional arrangements or agencies for enforcement action aimed at removing a threat to peace and security.

As for the substance of Article 53, attention should be drawn to the following fundamental provision in it: " . . . no enforcement action shall be taken under regional arrangements or by regional agencies without the authorization of the Security Council . . ." It follows that all decisions by regional organizations to take enforcement action against any member of such an organization—in the present instance, the decision of the Organization of American States in respect of the Dominican Republic—require approval by the Security Council.

The representatives of some countries, in their statements before the Council, have argued that the measures taken by the Organization of American States against the Trujillo régime are not in the nature of enforcement action and consequently do not come within the scope of Article 53 of the Charter. Such arguments are completely untenable. In fact, what measures against the Dominican Republic were actually approved at the Meeting of the Organization of American States?

Resolution I of 20 August provides for the breaking of diplomatic relations, and for a partial interruption of economic relations, with the Dominican Republic by all States Members of the Organization of American States. It should be pointed out that enforcement measures of this very nature, such as the interruption of economic relations, the severance of diplomatic relations, etc., are specified in Article 41 of the United Nations Charter among measures not involving the use of armed force which can be employed by the Security Council in the event of any threat to the peace, breach of the peace or act of aggression.

As is known, the measures provided for in Article 41 of the Charter are, of their nature, enforcement measures because they are employed by the Security Council for the very purpose of forcing an aggressor to cease acts of aggression against another State and of preventing the recurrence of aggression. How, in the light of this, can one assert that the breaking of diplomatic relations and the interruption of economic relations do not constitute enforcement action?

In this connexion, one may turn to the opinion of many eminent specialists in international law. I shall quote one of them—Professor Kelsen, who, discussing the measures which the Security Council may employ under Chapter VII of the United Nations Charter, writes, in his book The Law of the United Nations:

"There are two kinds of such measures: measures not involving the use of armed force, and measures involving the use of armed force. Both are 'enforcement measures' or 'enforcement actions' as they are sometimes called in the Charter . . . although only the measures determined in Articles 42 to 47 involve the use of 'armed' force. The measures determined in Article 41 are especially: 'complete or partial interruption of economic relations and of rail, sea, air, postal, telegraphic, radio and other means of communication, and the severance of diplomatic relations'." [P. 724.]

Kelsen then goes on to point out that:

"This purpose is defined in Article 41 as follows: 'to give effect to its [the Security Council's] decisions'; that means to enforce the decision upon a recalcitrant State. Hence these measures, too, may be considered to be 'enforcement measures' or 'enforcement actions' referred to in various Articles of the Charter."

Let us take, further, point 2 of the operative part of the Organization of American States' resolution dated 20 August, which says that the Meeting of Ministers authorizes the Council of the Organization of American States "to discontinue . . . the measures adopted in this resolution, at such time as the Government of the Dominican Republic should cease to constitute a danger to the peace and security of the hemisphere" [S/4476].

What does this point mean? It is not hard to understand that its meaning is precisely this: that the purpose of the measures taken is to force the Government of the Dominican Republic to desist from actions which constitute a danger to peace and security. If that were not so, it would be incomprehensible why those measures should be discontinued only when the Council of the Organization of American States had determined that the Dominican Republic no longer constituted a danger to peace and security. . . .

Thus, nobody should have any doubt that, in the light of the nature of the actions provided for in the resolution adopted on 20 August at the Meeting of Ministers of Foreign Affairs of members of the Organization of American States, what is involved is the application of enforcement measures in regard to the Dominican Republic. Accordingly there is no reason why approval by the Security Council of the decision of the Organization of American States regarding the Dominican Republic should be resisted on the pretext that the measures adopted against it are not enforcement measures and are consequently outside the scope of Article 53 of the United Nations Charter.

The United States delegate has opposed such approval of the Organization of American States' decision in the Dominican question on the grounds that the measures against the acts of aggression were being taken by the States—including the United States—individually and unilaterally and did not, therefore, come within the scope of Article 53. This is a clearly artificial objection which merely serves to confirm that the position of those putting forward this argument is unsound.

In actual fact, Article 53 says that "no enforcement action shall be taken under regional arrangements or by regional agencies without the authorization of the Security Council". The situation is in no way altered by the fact that certain measures, such as the severance of diplomatic relations, may be taken by each State only in accordance with its own constitutional provisions—that is, unilaterally.

Undoubtedly, such measures, when applied pursuant to collective decisions by States, assume the character of sanctions. The same is true of measures such as the complete or partial interruption of economic relations, communications, and so forth. In this case, too, each State—including any member of a regional organization—even though it is acting individually, is in fact participating in the application of sanctions.

The United States representative further asserted that only Article 54 of the Charter, which provides that the Security Council shall be kept informed of activities undertaken or in contemplation under regional arrangements or by regional agencies, applied in the present case. Those who argue along these lines obviously wish to assign to the Security Council the role of a passive observer in matters relating to the maintenance of international peace and security. But to treat the Security Council in that way would be clearly contrary to the United Nations Charter, which confers on the Council primary responsibility for the maintenance of international peace and security. All the members must assist the Council in every way in its fulfilment of this noble task, with which the vital interests of all the peoples are bound up. . . .

It follows from all this that the Security Council has every reason for adopting a decision that would express its opinion on the measures which the Meeting of Ministers of Foreign Affairs of the American States has approved in regard to the Dominican Republic. The members of the Security Council understand this perfectly well, and it is therefore no accident that some of them have stated frankly that they are simply not prepared to and cannot, at this juncture, take a more resolute stand in support of the Charter. I think that everybody understands the motives which compel them to act in this particular way.

Approval, by the Security Council, of the Organization of American States' resolution of 20 August 1960, as prescribed in Article 53 of the Charter, not only will give legal force to the resolution but will render it more effective, since the whole of the United Nations will then be supporting the decision of the Organization of the Latin American States aimed at safeguarding international peace and security.

Certain members of the Security Council who object to having the Council approve, as proposed by the Soviet delegation, the resolution on the Dominican question are obviously inspired, not by concern to invest that resolution with legal force and greater effectiveness, but by other motives which have nothing in common with the maintenance of world peace. What other explanation can there be of their opposition to the reinforcement of that resolution by the decision of so authoritative a body as the Security Council, which is acting in the name of all the States Members of the United Nations?

In the Soviet delegation's view it is altogether inadmissible that the Charter of the United Nations should be violated and the Security Council by-passed on an issue involving the employment of enforcement action for the maintenance of peace. The Security Council, in conformity with Article 53 of the Charter, has the duty of approving the decision of the Organization of American States to apply enforcement measures against the Dominican Republic, and of adopting the appropriate decision. The draft resolution submitted by the Soviet delegation conforms with that purpose.

[The draft resolution presented by the three American delegations was adopted on 9 September 1960 by 9 votes, with 2 abstentions (Poland, USSR), and the Soviet Union did not press for a vote on its resolution. SCOR, 895th Meeting, p. 5. For the final text of the resolution, see S/4491 (9 Sept. 1960); SCOR, XV, Supp. for July-Sept.1960, p. 145.]

NOTE.—1. On 21 November 1961 Cuba brought another Dominican question to the Security Council, complaining that the United States was intervening in the Dominican Republic to bolster the Balaguer regime established after the assassination of Trujillo. S/4992 (21 Nov. 1961); SCOR, XVI, Supp. for Oct.–Dec. 1961, pp. 139–41. Mr. Stevenson (USA) replied that the "friendly presence of the United States fleet on the high seas of the Caribbean was undertaken with the full knowledge of the constitutional authorities and the responsible leaders of the Dominican Republic, who were struggling so valiantly to free the nation from the years of the dictatorship. The presence of these units of the United States fleet on the high seas in international waters and air space did not constitute an act of intervention, nor is it contrary to any international agreement." He added that "the real threat to the peace and the security of the Western Hemisphere lies at the door of a Government, aided by the communist bloc, which attempts by any means to frustrate the efforts of the Dominican people to achieve a new democratic life for their country." SCOR, XVI, Mtg. 980, pp. 6–7. While no action was taken by the Security Council, the following statement by Mr. Malalaskera (Ceylon) may be noted (SCOR, XVI, Mtg. 983, p. 2, at 4–6):

"This whole question of intervention has always been, and continues to be, a touchy issue in the OAS—in all of their States. The Organization is going through something of a soul-searching crisis on this issue . . .

"Here are a few questions which arise: Can a regional organization legally decide what kind of governments its members can have? Can a regional organization take sanctions against one of its members only because of the kind of government it has? Can a regional organization set up a police force to carry out such decisions? Can such a police force be given to one of its members? Has the OAS given that power to the United States in respect of the Dominican Republic? Or has the United States Government assumed that it has been given that power by implication? . . .

"I have raised these questions because, if these questions are not raised now, I feel the unmistakable trends of a galloping epidemic of interventions which threatens to engulf the political world with the intensification of the cold war. . . .

"But the greater peril arises not from this general historic trend. The greater danger stems from the attempt to elevate a principle of intervention to a regional status.

"What will happen to the United Nations if this is done? If a single State offends the Charter, the United Nations can deal with it. But if a group of States decides on policing its own part of the world and that group of States has a sizable numerical representation within the United Nations, then how shall the United Nations deal with that kind of a situation?

"The danger is that the United Nations would break into pieces, explode like a hand-grenade from within. . . .

"The time has come for the United Nations to make a complete reappraisal of the relationship of regional security organizations to the United Nations. Such a study could be initiated by the Security Council with its primary responsibility for world security, but if the Council cannot find the strength to do this, it might be done by the General Assembly. It should be done before organized and regional intervention becomes elevated to a juridical concept, and becomes a new type of aggression and the new course of war in a world already rife with too much aggression and with too many causes of war."

2. For a comment on the issues raised by the events in the Dominican Republic, see R. St. J. MACDONALD, "The Developing Relationship between Superior and Subordinate Political Bodies at the International Level: A Note on the Experience of the United Nations and the Organization of American States," 2 Canadian YBIL (1964), p. 21, at 36–41; Jerome SLATER, "The United States, the Organization of American States, and the Dominican Republic, 1961–1963," 18 Int. Org. (1964), pp. 268–91.

CUBA'S EXCLUSION FROM THE INTER–AMERICAN SYSTEM

1. *Resolution VI of the Eighth Meeting of Consultation of Ministers of Foreign Affairs, 31 January 1962.*

Final Act of the Meeting at Punta del Este, OAS Official Records, OEA/SER.F/11.8, pp. 17–19; U.N.Doc. S/5975, pp. 16–18.

Whereas:

The inter-American system is based on consistent adherence by its constituent states to certain objectives and principles of solidarity, set forth in the instruments that govern it;

Among these objectives and principles are those of respect for the freedom of man and preservation of his rights, the full exercise of representative democracy, nonintervention of one state in the internal or external affairs of another, and rejection of alliances and agreements that may lead to intervention in America by extracontinental powers;

The Seventh Meeting of Consultation of Ministers of Foreign Affairs, held in San José, Costa Rica, condemned the intervention or the threat

of intervention of extracontinental communist powers in the hemisphere and reiterated the obligation of the American states to observe
faithfully the principles of the regional organization;

The present Government of Cuba has identified itself with the principles of Marxist-Leninist ideology, has established a political, economic, and social system based on that doctrine, and accepts military assistance from extracontinental communist powers, including even the
threat of military intervention in America on the part of the Soviet
Union;

The Report of the Inter-American Peace Committee to the Eighth
Meeting of Consultation of Ministers of Foreign Affairs establishes
that:

"The present connections of the Government of Cuba with the Sino-
Soviet bloc of countries are evidently incompatible with the principles
and standards that govern the regional system, and particularly with
the collective security established by the Charter of the OAS and the
Inter-American Treaty of Reciprocal Assistance";

The abovementioned Report of the Inter-American Peace Committee
also states that:

"It is evident that the ties of the Cuban Government with the Sino-
Soviet bloc will prevent the said government from fulfilling the obliga-
tions stipulated in the Charter of the Organization and the Treaty of
Reciprocal Assistance";

Such a situation in an American state violates the obligations inherent in membership in the regional system and is incompatible with that
system;

The attitude adopted by the present Government of Cuba and its
acceptance of military assistance offered by extracontinental communist powers breaks down the effective defense of the inter-American
system; and

No member state of the inter-American system can claim the rights
and privileges pertaining thereto if it denies or fails to recognize the
corresponding obligations,

The Eighth Meeting of Consultation of Ministers of Foreign Affairs,
Serving as Organ of Consultation in Application of the Inter-American Treaty of Reciprocal Assistance

Declares:

1. That, as a consequence of repeated acts, the present government
of Cuba has voluntarily placed itself outside the inter-American system.

2. That this situation demands unceasing vigilance on the part of
the member states of the Organization of American States, which shall
report to the Council any fact or situation that could endanger the
peace and security of the hemisphere.

3.   That the American states have a collective interest in strengthening the inter-American system and reuniting it on the basis of respect for human rights and the principles and objectives relative to the exercise of democracy set forth in the Charter of the Organization; and, therefore,

Resolves:

1.   That adherence by any member of the Organization of American States to Marxism-Leninism is incompatible with the inter-American system and the alignment of such a government with the communist bloc breaks the unity and solidarity of the hemisphere.

2.   That the present Government of Cuba, which has officially identified itself as a Marxist-Leninist government, is incompatible with the principles and objectives of the inter-American system.

3.   That this incompatibility excludes the present Government of Cuba from participation in the inter-American system.

4.   That the Council of the Organization of American States and the other organs and organizations of the inter-American system adopt without delay the measures necessary to carry out this resolution.

NOTE.—1.   In addition, in Resolution VIII (on Economic Relations with Cuba) the Organ of Consultation resolved:

"1.   To suspend immediately trade with Cuba in arms and implements of war of every kind.

"2.   To charge the Council of the Organization of American States, in accordance with the circumstances and with due consideration for the constitutional or legal limitations of each and every one of the member states, with studying the feasibility and desirability of extending the suspension of trade to other items, with special attention to items of strategic importance.

"3.   To authorize the Council of the Organization of American States to discontinue, by an affirmative vote of two thirds of its members, the measure or measures adopted pursuant to the preceding paragraphs, at such time as the Government of Cuba demonstrates its compatibility with the purposes and principles of the system."   OAS Official Records, OEA/SER.F/11.8, p. 21.

2.   The Punta del Este resolutions were discussed in the General Assembly in February 1962, but no resolution was adopted by the General Assembly.   A Cuban attempt to include the matter in the agenda of the Security Council was rejected on 27 February.   Annual Report of the Secretary-General, 1961-62 [GAOR, XVII, Supp. 1 (A/5201)], pp. 79-83.

3.   On 8 March 1962, Cuba requested that a meeting of the Security Council be convened without delay so that the Council might request the International Court of Justice, in accordance with Article 96 of the Charter, to give an advisory opinion on certain legal questions related to the resolutions adopted by the Meeting of American Ministers of Foreign Affairs at Punta del Este, Uruguay.   Cuba also requested that the Security Council, under Article 40 of the Charter, and as a provisional measure, call for the suspen-

sion of the agreements which had been adopted by the OAS at Punta del Este, and of such measures as might have been ordered in pursuance of those agreements, because the adoption and execution of those agreements constituted illegal acts and because they involved a threat to international peace and security. S/5086 (8 March 1962); SCOR, XVII, Supp. for Jan.–March 1962, pp. 88–90.

4. On 19 March Cuba presented a draft resolution to the Security Council (S/5095; SCOR, *op. cit.*, pp. 96–97), reformulating slightly the questions to be referred to the International Court of Justice so that they read as follows:

"1. Is the Organization of American States, under the terms of its Charter, a regional agency within the meaning of Chapter VIII of the United Nations Charter and do its activities have to be compatible with the Purposes and Principles of the United Nations?

"2. Under the United Nations Charter, does the Organization of American States have the right as a regional agency to take the enforcement action provided in Article 53 of the United Nations Charter without the authorization of the Security Council?

"3. Can the expression "enforcement action" in Article 53 of the United Nations Charter be considered to include the measures provided for in Article 41 of the United Nations Charter? Is the list of these measures in Article 41 exhaustive?

"4. Does the Charter of the Organization of American States provide for any procedure for expelling a State member of the Organization, in particular because of its social system?

"5. Can the provisions of the Charter of the Organization of American States and the Inter-American Treaty of Reciprocal Assistance be considered to take precedence over the obligations of Member States under the United Nations Charter?

"6. Is one of the main principles of the United Nations Charter that membership in the United Nations is open to States which meet the requirements of Article 4 of the Charter, irrespective of their system?

"7. In the light of the replies to the foregoing questions are, or are not, the resolutions adopted at Punta del Este at the Eighth Meeting of Consultation of American Ministers of Foreign Affairs relating to the expulsion of a State member of the regional agency because of its social system and the taking of other enforcement action against it, without the authorization of the Security Council, consistent with the provisions of the United Nations Charter, the Charter of the Organization of American States and the Treaty of Rio de Janeiro?"

2. *Discussion in the Security Council, 14–23 March 1962.*

SCOR, XVII, Mtgs. 992–98.

Mr. GARCIA INCHAUSTEGUI (Cuba): . . . [At] Punta del Este collective enforcement measures were adopted against Cuba in violation of regional instruments and of the principles of the United Nations Charter. And these illegal decisions have been implemented without the approval of the Security Council, which is required for such measures. In other words, resolutions that are unlawful have been taken and unlawfully put into effect in a twofold violation of the United Nations Charter and international law and of the competence and hierarchical position of this Council. . . .

When we say that the Punta del Este decisions are contrary to the Inter-American Treaty of Reciprocal Assistance signed at Rio de Janeiro on 2 September 1947, under which the meeting was called, contrary to the Charter of the Organization of American States and contrary to the Charter of the United Nations, we base our statement on the following line of reasoning: the Revolutionary Government of Cuba considers that both the decision of the Council of the Organization of American States which resulted in the convocation of the Eighth Meeting of Consultation of Ministers of Foreign Affairs and the Punta del Este decisions are entirely null and void because they run counter to the very purposes, principles, and rules of international law on which they claim to be based. . . .

Let us look more closely into the legal aspect of the problem which we are submitting for the consideration of the Security Council. Article 6 of the Inter-American Treaty of Reciprocal Assistance was the provision which was used to authorize the convening of the Eighth Meeting of Consultation. The article reads as follows:

"If the inviolability or the integrity of the territory or the sovereignty or political independence of any American State should be affected by an aggression which is not an armed attack or by an extracontinental or intracontinental conflict, or by any other fact or situation that might endanger the peace of America, the Organ of Consultation shall meet immediately in order to agree on the measures which must be taken in case of aggression to assist the victim of the aggression or, in any case, the measures which should be taken for the common defence and for the maintenance of the peace and security of the Continent."

The decision taken by the Council of the Organization of American States was directed towards three specific objectives: first, to consider the threats to the peace and political independence of the American States which might arise from the intervention of extracontinental Powers intent upon disturbing American solidarity; secondly, to determine the various types of threats to the peace or specific acts the occurrence of which would justify the application of measures in accordance with the treaties in force; thirdly, to determine what measures should be taken for the maintenance of the peace and security of the continent.

If we examine article 6 of the Inter-American Treaty of Reciprocal Assistance carefully, we shall see that its provisions not only define specific facts and situations, but also that the facts and situations enumerated quite clearly depend grammatically and logically on the conditional proposition with which the article opens. In other words, for a Meeting of Consultation to be held it is essential that there should in fact have occurred one of these three situations: an aggression which is not an armed attack; an extracontinental or intracontinental conflict; any other fact or situation that might endanger the peace of America.

This enumeration is specific and exclusive, not simply demonstrative or declaratory. The provision refers specifically to "an aggression", "a conflict", "any other fact or situation", in other words to events that have occurred in the real world; or, to use the phraseology of the article itself, it is necessary that the American States should have been affected by an aggression, conflict, fact or situation. The article refers to something which has really occurred and not to fantastic suppositions.

Our exegesis of the article does not, however, end here. It will also be observed that each of the situations specifically enumerated depends upon the original proposition, namely, that the "aggression", "conflict", "fact" or "situation" should affect the inviolability or the integrity of the territory or the sovereignty or political independence of an American State. . . .

It must therefore be concluded that the Meeting of Consultation was invalid from the start, because the fundamental prior condition required by the international law in force, namely the occurrence of a fact or a situation which genuinely and effectively threatened the peace or the security of the continent, was lacking. . . .

The concept of collective aggression is clearly set forth in article 24 of the Charter of the Organization of American States, which reads as follows:

"Every act of aggression by a State against the territorial integrity or the inviolability of the territory or against the sovereignty or political independence of an American State shall be considered an act of aggression against the other American States."

Only when the situation defined in that article arises can article 19 of that same Charter be regarded as taking effect, under which the principles of non-intervention and the inviolability of national territory (articles 15 and 17) may be disregarded when the specific purpose is the "maintenance of peace and security".

In other words, collective self-defence is sanctioned in articles 19 and 24. Both articles, however, must be taken in conjunction with Article 51 of the United Nations Charter, which states:

"Nothing in the present Charter shall impair the inherent right of individual or collective self-defence if an armed attack occurs against a Member of the United Nations, until the Security Council has taken measures necessary to maintain international peace and security. . . ."

Only on that assumption of armed attack can the exception provided for in article 19 of the Charter of the Organization of American States take effect.   Otherwise each and every one of the States which are associated in that Organization for geographical reasons is contractually bound by the provisions of articles 15 and 17 of its Charter, which enshrine the principles of non-intervention and the inviolability of the territory of each State.   And here it is necessary to emphasize that, under article 15, the principle of non-intervention "prohibits not only armed force but also any other form of interference or attempted threat against the personality of the State or against its political, economic and cultural elements".

Furthermore, self-defence is a juridical institution that has received ample study in criminal law.   The accepted authorities and current criminal law both lay down as a basic condition for the invoking of self-defence the existence of an unjust act of aggression neither provoked nor purposely sought by the person defending himself.   The first part of that proposition is restricted to any act of assault committed without justifiable reason on another person with a view to causing him harm.   The second part covers what the accepted authorities have called the "pretext of self-defence", in other words the manufacturing of a spurious state of necessity.   In such a case there is, logically, no state of necessity.   It has rightly been said that the person acting in self-defence must behave with a certain candour, which means that the concept of self-defence cannot be extended to the case of an international provoker or to cases in which the provoker is a real aggressor.

The accepted authorities also refer to putative or subjective self-defence and to false self-defence, i. e., when the supposed victim of aggression either imagines in the first case, or falsely pretends, in the second, that he is about to be attacked and so creates a subjective or false, as the case may be, necessity for defence.   .   .   .

[In the present case] we are unquestionably faced with a pretence of self-defence, since an attempt has been made to manufacture a threat of aggression out of hypothetical situations in order to establish grounds for collective self-defence.   The assumption is more or less as follows: if Cuba is socialist, it is a satellite of the "Sino-Soviet system" and therefore constitutes a threat to the peace and security of America.   Such a conclusion is based on two false premises: first, that Cuba is a satellite of the socialist countries; and secondly, that those countries constitute a threat to world peace.

It is also important to remember that existing international law does not recognize putative self-defence, let alone false self-defence.   When a nation is subjected to an armed attack—as was Cuba in April 1961, when we had to defend ourselves against the invading forces sent against our independent Government by the United States Central Intelligence Agency and did so victoriously, thanks to the strength of our people—it has an absolute and unlimited right to defend itself.

When it is threatened by imminent aggression, it can only take preventive action, taking account of the real emergency of the danger; it cannot demand sanctions, since they can only be imposed when aggression has actually taken place.   .   .   .

At the Eighth Meeting of Consultation, the conspirators against Cuba only partially achieved their objectives and to do so they had once again to violate the rules of international law.

In effect, because the Cuban people had made a decision in keeping with its right to self-determination, sovereignty and independence, it was decided to exclude Cuba from the inter-American system, with the qualification, however, that it was the Government of Cuba which was being excluded, as if international law allowed for such an artificial differentiation.

The Cuban State is organized politically in conformity with its fundamental law, and violations of that law are to be determined by the Supreme Court of Justice of Cuba, and not by international organizations. Moreover, the Government is the embodiment of the State, so that by excluding it—despite the fact that it continues to be vested with the political power—they are actually excluding the State which it represents. Under international law, the territory, nation, State and Government all constitute that indivisible entity known as the "member State". Consequently, by their action, the Republic of Cuba was in practice excluded from the Organization of American States as a result of the application of a sanction for which no provision is made in American international law.

Only the United Nations may expel a Member State and it may do so only if the State "has persistently violated the Principles contained in the Charter". And as we shall see later, the United Nations, in adopting that provision, surrounded it with a series of safeguards and guarantees, as is clear from Articles 2 and 6 of the Charter of the United Nations. There is no provision in the legal international instruments of the American continent which excludes a member State on grounds of the political, social and economic system which it may happen to adopt.   .   .   .

The resolution of the Eighth Meeting of Consultation excluding Cuba from the inter-American system goes beyond the limits of the Charters of the Organization of American States and of the United Nations whose precepts have been shamelessly violated, because there is no authority for it and above all because it is based on acts which do not in themselves constitute a violation of the letter or the spirit of these Charters. The resolution constitutes an arbitrary political action which ignores a historical reality covered by international law, and in order to obtain the adoption of the resolution it was necessary to distort basic principles whose strict observance is essential for the peaceful co-existence of nations with different social and political systems.

In a strictly legal sense, the resolution violates the right of peoples to self-determination, recognized in articles 1, 5(b), 6, 9 and 13 of the Charter of the Organization of American States and in Article 2 of the Charter of the United Nations; it violates the right of non-intervention granted to States in the inter-American community by article 15 of the Charter of the Organization of American States and Article 2, paragraph 7, of the United Nations Charter.

The resolution also infringes and ignores Cuba's right to free and active membership in the inter-American system, as stipulated in Article 2 of the Charter of the United Nations and article 9 of the Charter of the Organization of American States. The Charter signed at the Ninth International Conference of American States at Bogotá in 1948 includes no provision which prescribes that member States are obliged to organize themselves in accordance with a specific social system or which forbids their identifying themselves as Marxist-Leninist Governments; on the contrary, the Charter states that they may organize themselves as they see fit. . . .

The resolution adopted at the Eighth Meeting of Consultation also violates and ignores the clear provision in article 102 of the Charter of the OAS to the effect that the provisions which it contains shall not be construed as impairing the rights and obligations of the Member States under the Charter of the United Nations. And this violation is the most unusual aspect of the resolution. The Organization of American States, as a regional agency, is dependent on the United Nations, which is the parent organization. Article 52, paragraph 1, of the United Nations Charter states that:

"Nothing in the present Charter precludes the existence of regional arrangements or agencies for dealing with such matters relating to the maintenance of international peace and security as are appropriate for regional action, provided that such arrangements or agencies and their activities are consistent with the Purposes and Principles of the United Nations."

If a regional agency such as the OAS, in violation of the principles of the United Nations Charter, adopts arrangements or engages in activities contrary to the principles of the international organization, such as expelling a member State because of its social system and applying other enforcement action to it, what organ is responsible for ensuring that the principles of the Charter shall prevail? The text of Article 52, the place this Article is given in the Charter and the type of measures and activities it mentions leave no doubt that this organ is none other than the Security Council. If it were not so, what reason would there be for this Article? Why do we write and sign international charters and treaties if it is not to comply with them and respect them and to see that they are respected? There is all the more reason why we should see that they are respected when a powerful State is arbitrarily using them to attack what a small State holds to be most sacred: its right to independence.

The American States are Members of the United Nations and are obliged to respect the principles of the Charter signed at San Francisco on 26 June 1945. This is also stated in the preamble of the Charter of the Organization of American States when it says that its member States were resolved, in order to constitute it, "to persevere in the noble undertaking that humanity has conferred upon the United Nations, whose principles and purposes they solemnly reaffirm". The most salient and transcendental of these principles is that of peaceful co-existence among States with different political and social systems, which form the very Organization itself. In order to "save succeeding generations from the scourge of war", the nations that met at San Francisco proclaimed that they should unite in order to practise tolerance and live together in peace with one another as good neighbours, and they decided to establish the United Nations.

Under its Charter socialist and capitalist nations were united, thus proclaiming peaceful coexistence. Thus the United Nations is the international forum in which countries with very different social and political systems meet. The American Governments representing States Members of the United Nations, where they coexist peacefully with socialist countries from other continents, in deciding illegally to expel Cuba from the Organization of American States on the grounds that it was "Marxist-Leninist" have violated the fundamental principle that is the basis of the United Nations Charter, which they are obliged to support and respect, and have insulted and outraged nations which have a socialist system of government and nations which, while not having a socialist system, make peaceful coexistence among States with different social systems a principle of their foreign policy.

From the point of view of strictly hierarchical order, the resolution expelling Cuba from the Organization of American States could not be adopted either by the Organ of Consultation or even by the Inter-American Conference, because the power to expel a Member State is vested exclusively in the General Assembly of the United Nations, as laid down in Article 6 of the San Francisco Charter, and for the reasons stated in that Article, as I pointed out earlier.

Thus the Meeting of Consultation seriously exceeded its powers in adopting resolutions which came within the competence of an international organ having greater authority and a higher standing in the juridical community of nations. . . .

In addition to resolution VI concerning exclusion, the Punta del Este Meeting adopted resolution VIII, in which it was resolved, *inter alia*: to suspend immediately trade with Cuba in arms and implements of war of every kind; to charge the Council of the Organization of American States, in accordance with the circumstances and with due consideration for the constitutional or legal limitations of each and every one of the member States, with studying the feasibility and desirability of extending the suspension of trade to other items, with special attention to items of strategic importance. . . .

The breaking-off of relations with Cuba by various countries before and after the Meeting of Consultation were other *de facto* coercive measures applied against Cuba. The breaking-off of relations, like economic sanctions, constitutes a coercive measure within the Inter-American system because the only case in which an American State is permitted to break off diplomatic relations unilaterally is when such a step constitutes a measure of self-defence in the case of an armed attack.   .   .   .

It is obvious that the measures adopted at Punta del Este constitute coercion exerted by a group of member States against another member State because of the social system which that State has adopted and is entitled to adopt in accordance with the principles of the United Nations Charter.

I do not think that anyone here will deny that the social system of a State is a matter essentially within its domestic jurisdiction, whatever its size or geographical position; Article 2, paragraph 7, of the Charter of the United Nations states: "Nothing contained in the present Charter shall authorize the United Nations to intervene in matters which are essentially within the domestic jurisdiction of any State."

At Punta del Este a group of member States, under pressure from the United States Government, excluded Cuba, which is also a member State, for a question which is essentially within its domestic jurisdiction—its social system. If the Punta del Este resolutions were not coercive, they would be no more than empty words; but when they were implemented these resolutions became coercive actions, such as the exclusion of Cuba from the OAS, the economic measures in resolution VIII and the breaking-off of diplomatic relations.   .   .   .

The International Court of Justice is established by the Charter as the principal judicial organ of the United Nations. We have submitted to this Council specific legal questions which are very important for Cuba and for the independence of all Member States which want to defend their sovereignty through the rule of international law but which, should international law not provide them with sufficient protection—[to the disgrace] of international law, of the United Nations and of the Security Council—[would] defend their independence and international legal principles, if necessary with the blood of their own sons.   .   .   .

Mr. MOROZOV (USSR):   .   .   .   The Cuban delegation's specific proposal on this occasion is that the International Court of Justice should be asked for an advisory opinion on a number of important questions of international law. A correct and impartial answer to those questions would largely determine the adoption by the Security Council of the appropriate political decisions which would ensure a radical improvement of the threatening situation in the Caribbean area.   .   .   .

In imposing upon the Punta del Este Meeting decisions which would compel the Organization of American States to become an accomplice in the act of aggression being prepared against Cuba, the United States openly violated the fundamental principles proclaimed by the OAS and the fundamental provisions of its Charter.

In imposing the adoption of the so-called principle of incompatibility between the system prevailing in Cuba and the inter-American system, the United States has violated article 9 of the Charter of the OAS, according to which every one of its member States "has the right . . . to organize itself as it sees fit".

In imposing restrictions on trade with Cuba and a ban on such trade, the United States has violated article 16 of the Charter of the OAS, which says: "No State may use or encourage the use of coercive measures of an economic or political character in order to force the sovereign will of another State and obtain from it advantages of any kind."

In imposing upon the Organization of American States resolutions VI and VII concerning Cuba's expulsion [see S/5075], the United States has again violated the Charter of that Organization since the latter has no provision at all for the expulsion of member States. In this way the United States drove the Punta del Este conference to violate article 111 of the Charter of the Organization of American States, which provides that: "Amendments to the present Charter may be adopted only at an Inter-American Conference convened for that purpose", inasmuch as the expulsion of a member State requires a preliminary amendment of the Charter of the OAS which would make such expulsion possible. . . .

I think that no impartial and objective person who studies the purpose of the questions formulated in the Cuban representative's letter can have any doubt that a serious analysis of these provisions of the Charter and of a number of principles of international law, which Cuba requests the International Court of Justice to take up, is directly relevant to the task now confronting the Council.

In the final question posed in this document, the International Court of Justice is asked to say whether, in the light of replies given to a number of foregoing preliminary questions, the resolutions adopted at Punta del Este by the Eighth Meeting of Consultation of Ministers of Foreign Affairs regarding the expulsion of a State member of the regional agency because of its social system and the adoption of other enforcement action against that State without the authorization of the Security Council are or are not in accordance with the provisions of the Charter of the United Nations, the Charter of the Organization of American States and the Treaty of Rio de Janeiro.

It is clear to everybody that an objective answer to these questions will—and of this we are deeply convinced—make it impossible for the United States of America, and a number of other States which follow it, to continue to use the smoke-screen behind which they are now making political, economic and military preparations for a new attack on Cuba. If this smoke-screen is dispersed, that circumstance will help to put a stop to these insidious plans of the United States directed against a freedom-loving Latin American republic such as Cuba.

We know that attempts may be made here to maintain that the questions which it is proposed to put to the International Court of Justice are political ones. . . .

An impartial observer has only to acquaint himself with the list of questions in the Cuban representative's letter to see that, in the interests of an objective and impartial settlement of this question, Cuba is seeking the arbitration of a body such as the International Court of Justice which is elected by the General Assembly of the United Nations and which most Members of our Organization—though not, apparently, the United States—consider competent to give an impartial and objective reply on the legal points, the points of international law, that govern the just decision, in line with the United Nations Charter, which the Security Council can and must take. . . .

In particular, is the question as to whether the Organization of American States had the right to adopt the said enforcement measures without the sanction of the Security Council of importance for the safeguarding of the principles of the United Nations Charter and of international security? Yes, this question is very important; for Article 53 of the Charter of our Organization explicitly states: ". . . no enforcement action shall be taken under regional arrangements or by regional agencies without the authorization of the Security Council". It is precisely this provision of the Charter, as is evident to all, which was grossly violated by the United States when it impelled the OAS to act without consulting the Security Council. . . .

The Soviet Government drew particular attention to these consequences of the latest actions of the United States, which are so dangerous for the United Nations when in this connexion it said, in its statement of 18 February:

"If we agree with the logic by which United States statesmen are guided with regard to Cuba, that is, if we recognize the right of every State to press for the removal of another State from international organizations merely because it has a different social system, it is easy to see what would become of the United Nations, for instance. The imperialist States would then demand the exclusion of socialist States and the socialist States would demand the exclusion of imperialist States, while the countries with a republican form of government would seek the exclusion of the monarchies and vice versa. Instead of developing co-operation and harmonizing actions, purposes for which over 100 States have joined the United Nations, chaos and lawlessness would prevail there. This would be the end of the United

Nations. It is sufficient to visualize this picture to realize the stupidity and blindness which results from the hatred of Cuba on the part of those statesmen who shape the foreign policy of the United States."

. . .

The Soviet delegation therefore fully supports the proposal of the Republic of Cuba that the Security Council should immediately request the International Court of Justice to give an opinion on the questions listed in document S/5086, suggesting that the Court give priority to the consideration of these questions, and that the Council should suspend the agreements of the regional agency until it has obtained the advisory opinion of the Court and has taken a final decision. . . .

Mr. STEVENSON (USA): . . . The representative of Cuba, has, regrettably, not presented his request for a judicial opinion in a very judicial manner. Rather, by the tone and substance of his speech here yesterday afternoon, it is clear that he is again arguing about a political dispute which his Government has created—a dispute between it, on the one hand, and all of the Republics of the Western Hemisphere, on the other. This time, the attack is against the Organization of American States. But it is clearly aimed at all regional organizations: it is an attempt to subject the activities of all regional organizations to the Soviet veto in the Security Council. Let there be no mistake about the objective. The Cuban letter is camouflaged with legalisms, but the issues it raises are 100 per cent political. The principal issue is whether a regional organization, one which has cooperated fully with the United Nations, has the right to manage its own affairs and to defend itself against a foreign-dominated Government, or whether the Soviet Union is to be allowed to paralyse that organization's activities through the exercise of the veto power in this Council.

We believe that everyone who recognizes the great contributions to the progress of the world which regional organizations have made and can make, whether it be the Organization of American States, the League of Arab States, or some future regional associations of African or Asian States, will join in rejecting this threat to independence and vitality of such regional organizations, and this effort of the Soviet Union to extend its veto over their activities. . . .

Let me review the facts brought out at the Punta del Este conference. It was there clearly shown that the Castro régime, with the assistance of local communist parties, is employing a wide variety of techniques and practices to overthrow the free democratic institutions of Latin America. It is bringing hundreds of Latin American students, labour leaders, intellectuals and dissident political leaders to Cuba for indoctrination and for training to be sent back to their countries for the double purpose of agitating in favour of the Castro régime and undermining their own Governments. It is fostering the establishment in other Latin American countries of so-called "committees of solidarity" with the Cuban revolution. Cuban diplomatic personnel encourage and finance agitation and subversion by dissident elements seeking to overthrow established governments by force.

. . .

What the Organization of American States decided, unanimously, is that Cuba today represents a bridgehead of Sino-Soviet imperialism in the Western Hemisphere and a base for communist aggression, intervention, agitation and subversion against the American republics. The American republics unanimously recognized that this situation is a serious threat to their security and the ability of their peoples to choose freely their own form of government and to pursue freely their goals of economic well-being and of social justice.

In the face of these facts it is absurd to contend that the Punta del Este resolution, excluding not Cuba, but the present Cuban régime from the Organization of American States, constitutes aggression against Cuba, when it is the Cuban régime's own aggression against the Organization of American States which has caused that exclusion. What the Cuban régime has done is to create a condition which makes OAS action necessary, and then appear before this Council to complain of the action made necessary by the very condition they themselves created. Clearly a regional organization can determine for itself the conditions of participation in it. If it could not so decide, it would be incapable of its own defence and therefore have no reason for existence.

Equally clearly such self-exclusion, caused by Cuba's aggressive acts against members of the OAS, is not "enforcement action" within the meaning of Article 53 of the United Nations Charter. Security Council "authorization" cannot be required for regional action—in this case exclusion from participation in a regional organization—as to matters which the Security Council itself cannot possibly act upon, and which are solely within the competence of the regional organization itself.

The Organization of American States is, in the language of Article 52, paragraph 1, of the United Nations Charter, a regional agency for the maintenance of international peace and security. Surely the Organization of American States, like any other regional agency, is and, as an agency for the collective self-defence of the hemisphere, must be entitled to determine who should participate in its proceedings without being subject to a Soviet veto or any other veto in the Security Council. The Council cannot pretend to determine what governments should and should not participate in such a regional agency like the Organization of American States, the League of Arab States, or some future African or Asian regional agency.

It should be noted that the Cuban Government's self-exclusion from the Organization of American States was not based on its "social system", as Cuba alleges. It was based on that Government's violations of the Charter of the OAS to which Cuba had solemnly subscribed. In violation of that Charter, the present Cuban Government has conducted aggressive and subversive activities against its fellow American republics, and in violation of that Charter it has suppressed the fundamental rights of the individual.

Surely it is not a violation of the United Nations Charter to suspend a government for the very aggressive activities which the United Nations Charter is designed to prevent, and surely it is not a violation of the United Nations Charter to suspend a government for suppressing the human rights and fundamental freedoms which the United Nations Charter is designed to uphold. Nor did the framers of the United Nations Charter intend it to protect a government from the consequences of such aggressive activities and such violations of human rights and fundamental freedoms. The Organization of American States is clearly entitled to suspend the participation of a government which deliberately violates basic principles and obligations of the Organization.

The reasoning by which the representative of Cuba has sought to justify his contention that the suspension—or, as he put it, the expulsion—of the Cuban Government from the Organization of American States was unlawful was this: since the OAS Charter, an international treaty, contains no clause expressly authorizing suspension or expulsion, such a right of suspension or expulsion cannot be implied. He claimed that treaties must be interpreted restrictively, and that the principle of restrictive interpretation of treaties in this case prohibited implying a right of suspension.

The Cuban representative is wrong in this regard for three reasons.

First, it is for the Organization of American States to interpret its own Charter. The required majorities of the membership of the OAS have interpreted its Charter to justify this suspension.

Secondly, treaties, including the OAS Charter, are to be interpreted effectively and not restrictively. It is a cardinal rule of the interpretation of treaties that they must be interpreted so as to give effect to their essential purposes. Since the present Cuban Government is doing its best to frustrate the essential purposes of the OAS Charter, effective interpretation of that treaty requires the exclusion of the Cuban Government from the Organization's deliberations.

Thirdly, it is obvious that no regional body can be forced to accept the presence of a government which the members of that regional body determine to be violating the very terms of the charter of that body. In this case, all of the members of the Organization of American States, except Cuba, determined that the Cuban Government is violating the OAS Charter to which Cuba had solemnly subscribed. The independence and effectiveness of regional agencies would be wholly destroyed by a rule that required them to continue in their midst governments that oppose themselves to the organizations' principles and violate their charters.   .   .   .

[As far as Resolution VIII was concerned, it did not constitute aggression or require Security Council authorization.] In the first place, suspension of trade in arms is the very reverse of aggression, and in this instance is a measure of self-defence against aggression. Nor is such suspension an "enforcement action" within the meaning of Article 53 of the Charter. It is a step that any State can properly and legally take, individually or collectively, without authorization from anyone.   .   .   .

There is accordingly no question which merits submission to the International Court of Justice for an advisory opinion.

Furthermore, the issue is one which the Security Council has already thoroughly considered and as to which it has reached a clear-cut decision. I refer, of course, to the decision taken by the Council on 9 September 1960 as to whether the Council considered its authorization to be required for the action that had then been taken by the OAS with respect to the Dominican Republic.   .   .   .

Viewed in the context of the resolutions adopted at Punta del Este, and the square precedent of the Dominican case, the seven questions raised in the letter from the representative of Cuba should be dismissed for lack of substantiality, quite apart from the fact that Cuba comes into court, in the common law phrase, with unclean hands.
.   .   .

Mr. DIAZ CASANUEVA (Chile):   .   .   .   My Government thinks that the question now before the Security Council, while it is undeniably related to the specific case of Cuba, has different and wider legal implications. It tends to cast doubt on the right of a regional agency to take action in regional affairs. Today this applies to the Organization of American States, but tomorrow it may apply to any other regional agency.

Politically, we are considering the question of Cuba. Legally, we are considering the autonomous jurisdiction of a regional organization. We must avoid falling into a confusion which would have unfortunate consequences.

We are not asked to pass a moral or political judgement on the tenor of the decisions of Punta del Este. We are considering whether the Council should approve or disapprove of those decisions or of any others which may be taken in the future, and whether the Council should seek the opinion of the International Court of Justice on the matter.

In 1960 the case of the Dominican Republic was discussed. Today it is the case of Cuba, and tomorrow it may be another. Each case has its own characteristics and its own political implications. Each case may give rise to a new debate, and the Council may put a different interpretation on each decision of the regional Organization, according to varying political standards and according to the shifting ideologies of international life. . . .

It may be useful to warn those who now advocate interfering with the inter-American regional organization that tomorrow other regional organizations founded on the association of States for geographical reasons or for reasons of political, religious or economic identity, may acquire legal form and confront the United Nations. It would be most disturbing if a precedent were set for the interference of the Security Council, where the five great Powers have the right of veto, in the affairs of regional organizations which are entitled to establish themselves by agreement and to impose obligations upon their members, in order to advance regional interests or the principles which determine the attitude of such regional agencies. . . .

My delegation is fully aware that Article 53 of the Charter is the main source of controversies which can reach the highest peaks of legal quibbling.

What is the meaning of the enforcement action referred to in Article 53? The English term "enforcement action" is much stronger than the Spanish term "coacción", which means the use of force or violence. The same is true of the French text: the term "mesures coercitives" comes from the verb "contraindre", which means "to use violence". But at Dumbarton Oaks the more accurate term "acción compulsiva" was being used.

The Charter itself in Articles 41 and 42 makes a distinction between the two types of measures which the Security Council may adopt: those which involve the use of armed force and those which do not. The latter, according to the Charter, include complete or partial interruption of economic relations, etc. The former include action by air, sea, or land forces and also "demonstrations, blockade and other operations by air, sea, or land forces of Members of the United Nations".

Articles 44 and 45 refer explicitly to the use of force. Article 45 relates "international enforcement action" directly to the employment of armed forces. Undoubtedly, therefore, the purpose of Article 53 is to prohibit the "use of armed force"—or physical violence—by regional organizations, without the authorization of the Security Council, with the single exception of individual or collective self-defence.

The identity of meaning between enforcement action and the use of force may also be gathered from the Council's discussion of the question of sanctions against the Dominican Republic in September 1960.

Although at the Eighth Meeting of Consultation my Government did not agree with the expulsion of Cuba from the inter-American system nor with the resolution on economic relations, it must admit that such measures do not amount to enforcement action or the use of force.   .   .   .

My Government does not consider it appropriate that the Security Council should apply to the International Court of Justice for an opinion and regrets that it will have to oppose any move in that direction. Our position is not inspired by political motives; nor is it based on the attitude which we adopted at Punta del Este or the opinion which we have of the Cuban case.

It is determined strictly by legal considerations. It is well known that Chile has always been a zealous—I might almost say a rigid— observer of juridical standards, placing them far above any other considerations, even above its own interests, and we believe that these standards should be applied scrupulously both within individual States and in their international relations.

Our attitude is also based on the conviction that the Council must not establish a precedent that would be disastrous for the existence and development of the inter-American system. This system is not static but is subject to constant evolution and of course can be greatly improved, especially now that the countries of Latin America are beginning to introduce profound economic and social reforms. If reforms had been carried out years ago we would not perhaps be examining the Cuban question today. As President Kennedy pointed out a few days ago: "Those who make peaceful revolution impossible will make violent revolution inevitable."

Our attitude is also determined by the need to safeguard the autonomy of the Organization of American States, or any other regional body, and thus to strengthen its close and harmonious relationship with the United Nations.   .   .   .

Sir Patrick DEAN (UK):   .   .   .   Both in this Council and in the General Assembly, the Government of Cuba has taken many opportunities to voice grievances against the Government of the United States of America. These grievances have been given a very thorough hearing. What is remarkable is that the relevant organs of the United Nations have repeatedly decided to make no recommendation, to take no action on these complaints. This history—and the very recent conclusion of a debate which covered, and dismissed, the whole range of Cuban charges against the United States—led this Council on 27 February [991st meeting] to decide not to adopt its agenda when it was asked to take up these same charges once again. My delegation thinks that this decision was right.

The present series of meetings, however, were set in train by the letter dated 8 March 1962 from the Permanent Representative of Cuba. Reading this letter, it appeared that it was no longer the United States which the Cuban Government sought to place in the dock. Indeed, in their present written complaint the Cuban Government seems implicitly to have accepted the contention of the United States and the other members of the Organization of American States that the quarrel is not bilateral but multilateral. The complaints in the letter before us were directed at the Organization of American States as an organization, and at the decisions which it has recently taken. There was no reiteration in that letter of the familiar accusations of impending United States aggression. Instead, the letter in question proposes that certain questions affecting the Organization of American States as a regional organization should be addressed to the International Court of Justice in the form of a request for an advisory opinion. These questions include the interpretation of certain provisions of the Charter of the United Nations and of the Charter of the Organization of American States. This is a new proposal, and as such, certainly one which it is right that this Council should consider.   .   .   .

Having accepted this, however, I submit that the Council is bound to consider what is the purpose of the present proposal and what are the motives which underlie the questions which it is suggested should be put to the International Court of Justice. In doing this we are helped by internal evidence within the Cuban letter itself. The "specific legal questions" listed in document S/5086 all lead up to the final one, which asks the Court to decide:

"Whether   .   .   .   the resolutions adopted at Punta del Este .   .   .   regarding the expulsion of a State member of the regional agency because of its social system and the adoption of other enforcement action against that State without the authorization of the Security Council are or are not in accordance with the provisions of the Charter of the United Nations, the Charter of the Organization of American States and the Treaty of Rio de Janeiro."

The purpose of this last question is clearly a political one, and accordingly all the questions which lead up to it must be considered as primarily political in both their content and their intent. This conclusion is reinforced by consideration of the penultimate paragraph of document S/5086, which requests the Security Council under Article 40 of the Charter to call for the suspension of the Punta del Este agreements [see S/5075] and of the measures ordered in pursuance of these agreements, pending the opinion of the Court. I think it would be reasonable for the Council to conclude that this proposal represents the crux of the matter.

This internal evidence, together with the history of Cuban complaints in the past and the general character and tone of the speeches made by the representatives of Cuba and the Soviet Union during the present meetings, leaves no doubt whatsoever that although the questions are framed as legal ones, the motives behind the proposal that they should be put to the Court are essentially political, and that the Security Council is, in fact, being asked to put to the Court a question of an essentially political character.

I do not wish to be misunderstood on this point. I am not complaining because the matter before us is political. This is, after all, a political body. My point is simply that we must not be misled by the form in which these proposals are put to us, into thinking that these are purely legal questions, inspired merely by a thirst for legal knowledge. No, they are political questions disguised in a legal form. If they are to be considered at all, they should be considered in that light and on that basis. For this reason I shall not be able to support any proposal to refer the questions set out in document S/5086 to the International Court of Justice.

I now turn to the actual questions posed by the representative of Cuba. These, as I have already indicated, seem to fall into two broad categories: those which concern the interpretation of the Charter of the United Nations, and those which pertain directly to the Organization of American States itself.

As to this latter category, I prefer to accept the views of those more directly concerned and I therefore listened with particular attention to the reasoned, closely argued and persuasive statements of the representatives of Chili and the United States. I would like, however, to comment on one point. The representative of the Soviet Union was eloquent in foreseeing that the expulsion of Cuba from the Organization of American States would lead to the expulsion of most Members from the United Nations. I think he knew that he was letting his imagination run away with him. Had he paused to reflect, he would have seen that his analogy was false. The whole point of the United Nations is that it is a world-wide organization which is open to all States that subscribe to certain basic principles. The whole point of other, less comprehensive, groupings of nations is that these groups allow their members to supplement the relationship enjoyed in the United Nations with other relationships with States with whom they have an especially close identity of views. My delegation is not aware of any provision in the Charter of the United Nations which would justify a claim that this Organization should assume responsibility for ruling upon the membership or qualifications of more limited groups. It would, indeed, be strange if the United Nations, let alone the Security Council, were to have the authority to tell individual States with whom they may associate themselves or on what conditions membership of these groups can be changed. The membership of other and independent organizations is, surely, not a matter upon which the United Nations has any *locus standi* to pronounce.

As to the questions which relate to the interpretation of the Charter of the United Nations, and which principally concern Chapter

VIII of the Charter, I cannot do better than to quote what Sir Harold Beeley said in the Security Council in September 1960:

"The Charter of the United Nations does not define the term 'enforcement action'. In the opinion of the United Kingdom Government, it is common sense to interpret the use of this term in Article 53 as covering only such actions as would not normally be legitimate except on the basis of a Security Council resolution. There is nothing in international law, in principle, to prevent any State, if it so desires, from breaking off diplomatic relations or instituting a partial interruption of economic relations with any other State. These steps .   .   .   are acts of policy perfectly within the competence of any sovereign State. It follows, obviously, that they are within the competence of the members of the Organization of American States acting collectively.

"In other words, it is the view of my delegation that, when Article 53 refers to 'enforcement action', it must be contemplating the exercise of force in a manner which would not normally be legitimate for any State or group of States except under the authority of a Security Council resolution. Other pacifying actions under regional arrangements as envisaged in Chapter VIII of the Charter which do not come into this category have simply to be brought to the attention of the Security Council under Article 54." [893rd meeting, paras. 96 and 97.]

It will be evident from what I have just said that I agree with the interpretation which the representative of Chile, speaking in the Council last Friday [994th meeting], gave to the words "enforcement action" in Article 53 of the Charter. In our view, as in his, that term means coercive action involving the use of physical force. Action of this kind—with the sole exception of legitimate individual or collective defence—requires the authorization of the Security Council under Article 53. The kind of action envisaged in Article 41 of the Charter, that is, "measures not involving the use of armed force", does not require such authorization.   .   .   .

Mr. BERARD (France):   .   .   .   My country thinks there can be no question of refusing a State Member of the United Nations the right to initiate a justified consultation of the International Court of Justice. The French Government is among those which show the greatest loyalty and respect to that high tribunal, which it considers an irreplaceable instrument for the peaceful settlement of disputes. But matters must be laid before the Court in accordance with the provisions which define its competence. What does Article 96 of the United Nations Charter say? It reads: "The General Assembly or the Security Council may request the International Court of Justice to give an advisory opinion on any legal question." Note these words: "on any legal question". But in the matter before us today, is the proposal that the seven questions put by the Cuban Government should be submitted to the Court as they stand really a request for a legal opinion? Is it not rather a device—rather a tendentious one, I am afraid—to raise the essentially political question of the present relations between Cuba and the rest of the Western hemisphere?

By way of example I should like to draw attention to the wording of the fourth question listed by Cuba in its letter of 8 March:

"Whether the Charter of the Organization of American States makes provision for any procedure for the expulsion of a State Member of the Organization, particularly because of its social system".

By deliberately laying stress on the social system of Cuba, this question does not seem to take into account the other aspects of the problem which the OAS considered at Punta del Este and which finally led it to exclude Cuba from the inter-American system. If we re-read the resolutions adopted by Punta del Este, which were circulated in full on 3 February as document S/5075, we perceive that it was not simply the social system of Cuba, as such, which caused its expulsion, but rather certain political aspects of the Castro régime, particularly its subversive attempts to cause disturbances in other countries of the American continent. . . .

Thus it appears that the exclusion of the Cuban Government from the inter-American system is based on something very different from social considerations. In fact it involves a problem of security.

In the circumstances, is there not reason to fear that the Government of Cuba may be trying, behind a screen of legality, to inveigle the International Court of Justice into giving an opinion on questions whose legal nature cannot be separated from their political aspect?

For this reason, my delegation does not think that Article 96 of the Charter can be invoked in support of this request before us. . . .

Mr. GARCIA INCHAUSTEGUI (Cuba): . . . Cuba does not seek to block regional agreements; what Cuba is claiming, in interpreting two Articles as unequivocal as Articles 52 and 53 of the Charter, is that exceptional and extraordinary measures such as enforcement action, and *inter alia*, the exclusion of a State, should not be taken without the Council's approval or in violation of regional instruments and, specifically, of principles of the United Nations Charter. On the other hand, Cuba, which is sure that its position is legally sound, does not wish the Council to prejudge the issue either in favour of its own contentions or in favour of those of its opponent: it merely wishes the International Court of Justice, which is the competent body in the matter, to give an advisory opinion on points which are clearly legal in nature. Cuba has introduced evidence which, far from being refuted, has been confirmed by the statement of the representative of Chile so far as the illegality of the exclusion is concerned; the statements of the Foreign Ministers of Mexico, Brazil, Argentina, Chile, Bolivia and Ecuador also provide evidence that the decision to exclude Cuba is a violation of the Charter of the OAS and of international agreements.

Furthermore, as we have already said, the argument that we are raising political and not legal questions is not in keeping with the facts and its acceptance would render Article 96 of the United Nations Charter virtually inoperative: a State concerned in a case would only have to assert that political questions were involved for the International Court of Justice to be precluded from giving an opinion. All of us who sit in the General Assembly and those who sit around this table as members of the Security Council are politicians; why should we not let the Court answer the legal issues we raise? Is it because we have doubts about the Court? Or do we not want an advisory opinion because the legal arguments are on the side of a small Member State in the war which another powerful Member State has launched against it?

It turns out that the very people who are accusing us of putting political questions to the Court are politicians using political arguments to oppose such a consultation. A paradoxical situation is thus created in which legal questions raised by a Member State concerning important Articles of the Charter are being withheld from the Court by politicians, using political arguments, on the pretext that such questions have a concealed political purpose.

We seem to have heard some member of the Council object to the questions we raised on the ground that they are not "purely legal" and are not prompted by a desire for "legal knowledge", as if the reasons motivating a State in requesting an advisory opinion also had to be legal and as if the International Court of Justice, that modern academy of international law, existed solely to dispel the scientific doubts of those who bring before it legal questions which are "chemically pure"; as if every one of us, every time we came to this Council or engaged in any activity in this house, were not doing so in response to political necessity. If the questions put to the Court are framed in legal terms, objectively legal terms, that should be sufficient and we should refrain from any consideration of their motivation. . . .

Mr. MOROZOV (USSR): . . . While some members of the Council endorsed the need for placing before the International Court of Justice all or some of the questions enumerated in the Cuban draft resolution, others, as we know, objected to that course. We therefore consider it our duty to deal once again with the essence of these objections.

The first is that, although the questions set forth in the Cuban draft resolution are legal in form, they are in fact not legal but political. Consequently, our opponents say, since the questions are political and since Article 96, paragraph 1, of the United Nations Charter states that advisory opinions can be requested from the Court only on legal questions, Article 96 is not applicable to the present case.

It is easy to see that this first argument has itself no legal basis, because it arbitrarily declares *a priori* that the legal questions formulated in the Cuban draft resolution are political ones. It must however be examined, since if we were to assume even for a moment that it was valid, there would then be no need to deal with the other objections.   .   .   .

We know that the Security Council is a political organ of the United Nations. In the last analysis the Council deals only with political questions. But Article 96 specifically states that one of the organs which may request the International Court of Justice to give an advisory opinion is the Security Council. There it is written, in black and white, that the Security Council may request the Court to give an advisory opinion on any legal question. That does not, of course, mean that the Charter makes it incumbent upon the Security Council to decide any purely legal questions not connected with its political functions. Naturally Article 96, paragraph 1, does not add to or alter in any way the competence of the Security Council as defined in Chapters V, VI and VII of the Charter, which deal with the duties of the Council as the organ primarily responsible for the maintenance of international peace and security, i. e., in the last analysis a political organ dealing with political questions. From all this, it follows that the Security Council can and should ask the Court for an advisory opinion only in cases when, while it is dealing with some question within its jurisdiction—namely, a political question—some legal problem arises on the correct solution of which a correct political decision depends.   .   .   .

Thus the legal questions formulated in the Cuban draft resolution can by no means be represented as a kind of legal Trojan horse with a political stuffing, designed to undermine the Security Council's work from within and prevent it from dealing with the question properly. On the contrary, we are insisting that the legal problems be elucidated, because refusal to permit an expert and accurate consideration of the legal problems would be tantamount to complete denial of the bearing of the Charter and other principles of international law on the Security Council's activity.

And here we touch upon an issue which, despite its exceptional significance in relation to the question of Cuba, transcends the particular and very important case at present before us and becomes a matter of the utmost theoretical significance for the activity of the Security Council and that of the United Nations as a whole. For if we were to agree at any juncture with the position of denying the importance of the principles of the Charter and of international law for the solution of political problems in the Security Council—which is the logical result of the stand taken by the United States representative and certain others in the Council—we would be denying that legal problems were of any significance in decisions on political questions in the Security Council. But we cannot break this organic link. It would be tantamount to admitting that anarchy, chaos and arbitrary action reigned in the United Nations.   .   .   .

It is clear that this first argument, according to which the Cuban questions are not legal but political in nature, is incorrect and must be rejected. Even those who put forward this kind of argument are themselves by no means certain that it is at all convincing. That is why, despite an assertion which would seem to exclude the possibility of any legal discussion, there has in fact been, in the Council, a detailed discussion of the legal problems raised in the Cuban draft resolution. This in turn gives us grounds for considering certain important objections put forward during the main debate concerning what are in fact legal problems.

What was the main question around which the discussion centred? It was, of course, the question of whether the measures taken against the Republic of Cuba at Punta del Este constituted enforcement action within the meaning of the United Nations Charter. Everyone understands that this is really the main question, because if at Punta del Este no measures were taken which could be described as enforcement action, it would mean that the decisions of the Organization of American States in that connexion were not subject to authorization by the Security Council. For the only case in which the decisions of a regional organization, although in accordance with the United Nations Charter, still require the approval of the Security Council is the case where, under Article 53 of the Charter, decisions are taken which involve the use of enforcement measures.

Accordingly, if none of us knows what these enforcement measures within the meaning of the United Nations Charter are, we obviously cannot fruitfully discuss that question at the present time.

Do we or do we not know what those enforcement measures within the meaning of the United Nations Charter are?

In the view of the Soviet delegation and a number of other delegations in the Council, the Charter provides a clear answer to this question. In the Soviet delegation's view, enforcement measures according to the Charter are all those measures enumerated in Article 41 of the Charter—and possibly other measures as well—the purpose of which is to make some States submit to the will of other States. As Article 41 says, these measures may include a whole series of measures which are enumerated there in detail and which, in order to save time, I will not repeat here.

If the position were that the whole Council agreed with this view of the Soviet delegation, which has been supported here by certain other delegations, there would be no need to apply to the International Court of Justice. But some members of the Council have put forward at least two objections: they have said, first, that the term "enforce-ment action" covers only measures involving the use of force; and secondly—this was the highly original statement made by the repre-sentative of the United Kingdom—that enforcement measures were something of such a special nature that they could not normally be legitimately undertaken against a State.   True, the United Kingdom representative did not favour us with an indication of what kind of action he had in mind in his—pardon me the expression—fantastic definition of what constitutes enforcement action.   But he hastened to exclude, from the list of enforcement measures, all the measures enumerated in Article 41 of the Charter.   He stated that the measures enumerated in Article 41 of the Charter could not be regarded as enforcement measures, because—as he said—the interruption of eco-nomic relations, the severance of diplomatic relations and the other measures listed in Article 41 could be proceeded to by any State with-out fear of incurring the charge of a breach of international legality with regard to the State against which such action was taken.

That is an entirely fallacious position because—although the action mentioned can indeed be taken by one State against another—when similar action, the same measures, are taken as the result of a decision adopted by an organization of which a number of States are members, their nature is thereby changed.   Such actions, taken collectively become enforcement measures against another State within the meaning of the United Nations Charter, because they constitute political action the scope and consequently the significance of which are completely different from those of actions which may be performed in isolation by one State in regard to another State.   It is perfectly clear that one State cannot blockade all the other States.   The same can be said of the severance of diplomatic relations.   One State may break off diplomatic relations with another State, but it is not in a position to create a political vacuum around that State.   It is a dif-ferent matter if the same action is taken by a group of States, par-ticularly a group organized in a regional or some other organization. That can, of course, lead to quite other and far more serious conse-quences.   This is why the United Nations Charter contains a clause under which, although regional organizations must promote inter-national peace and security in accordance with the principles of the Charter and act freely and without restrictions to that end, they are not entitled to take enforcement action without the authorization of the Security Council.

Nor is there any doubt that even our opponents fully appreciate the weakness of their position.   That is the reason why they put forward an additional argument during the discussion.   When their defences based on the first argument were pierced, and when, as I am now explaining, the defences based on line number two—the argu-ment which I have just now examined concerning the nature of enforcement measures within the meaning of the Charter—were in their turn pierced, we discovered the third and deepest line of defence which had been erected by our esteemed opponents. This third line of defence consists of the additional argument that referring the questions formulated in the Cuban resolution to the International Court of Justice would be equivalent to reviewing or even reversing the decision which was adopted by the Security Council when it considered the question of the application of enforcement measures against the Dominican Republic by the Organization of American States.

The so-called Dominican precedent has been referred to by many members of the Council, and the interpretation of the resolution adopted by the Security Council in connexion with the question of the Dominican Republic which was given by the representative of the Soviet Union in the Council as far back as 1960 is known to all. We are grateful to the delegations that have already reminded the Council of this.

We stated then and repeat now that the Security Council's taking note of the decision of the Organization of American States to apply enforcement measures against the Dominican Republic meant nothing more or less than its approval, and I emphasize the word "approval", of that decision.

If someone takes note of something without making any objections and if, in addition, a formal resolution is adopted in the matter, then the conclusion to be drawn is that what is noted is approved. In the case in point, the assertion that the Security Council was entitled under Article 53 of the Charter not to agree with the adoption of enforcement measures against the Dominican Republic merely strengthens the argument we have just put forward. How, in these circumstances, can it be said that the Council, in noting the decision to take enforcement measures against the Dominican Republic, did not consider the taking of such measures to be valid? Such an assertion is completely inconsistent not only with the text of the formal decision adopted by the Security Council but also with the entire discussion which took place at the time in the Council, since the members expressed no fundamental political divergencies regarding the admissibility of taking enforcement measures against the Dominican Republic. Thus the Council agreed with the decision and sanctioned it. Thus it discharged with respect to these decisions the political function entrusted to it by Article 53 of the Charter.

However, let us try for a moment to put ourselves in the position of our opponents, and to make every allowance for them in this discussion. Let us admit for a moment that the action by the Council in adopting the 1960 decision showed that the Council was more or less indifferent to the question of taking enforcement measures against the Dominican Republic, even though such an admission is inconsistent with the facts, as I have already said. What does this mean in the eyes of those who would like to interpret the Council's decision in that way, although it is incorrect? Even then, it is obvious that the most anyone could assert is that the Council did not establish any precedent in 1960. I repeat that we disagree. A precedent was established, a precedent that can be applied in a positive way to the question we are now examining, the taking of enforcement measures by the same Organization of American States against another Latin American country.

If we have attempted, none the less, to place ourselves in the position of our opponents, this was merely to show that the very most that they can ask for is a re-examination of the whole legal problem arising in connexion with the enforcement measures taken against Cuba. It cannot therefore be said that by referring legal questions to the International Court of Justice, as Cuba asks, the Council would be repealing or altering its decision of 1960.

It is, however, absolutely necessary, as we already pointed out, and as is obvious even to our opponents, to decide the question of what, in the light of the Charter, is meant by Article 53, which speaks of enforcement action. Unless this important question is decided, we cannot make any progress in deciding the other legal questions embodied in the Cuban draft resolution. . . .

To apply to the International Court of Justice for an advisory opinion, as Cuba insists, is fully justified under Article 96, paragraph 1, of the Charter. The attempts to make out that the Court is being asked to reply to political and not legal questions are futile and groundless and contrary to the purposes and principles of the United Nations Charter. They are, in fact, an appeal to set aside international law and to decide questions of international relations on the basis of force and caprice.

At this crucial stage, we again appeal to the members of the Council to show that they are equal to their responsibilities in maintaining international peace and security and to support as a minimum and absolutely essential step at the present time, the consultation of the Court on the questions enumerated in the Cuban draft resolution.
. . .

[On 23 March, the representative of the USSR, in accordance with rule 38 of the provisional rules of procedure, requested that the Cuban draft resolution be put to the vote. At the request of the representative of Ghana, a separate vote was taken on the third paragraph of the draft resolution. Following the rejection of the third paragraph, by a vote of 4 (Ghana, Romania, USSR, United Arab Republic) in favour to 7 against, the representative of Cuba stated that he would not press the remainder of the draft resolution to the vote. However, the United States representative, under rule 35, objected to the withdrawal of the draft resolution. A ruling by the President of the Council to the effect that rule 35 was applicable in this case was challenged by the USSR representative and was upheld by a vote of 7 in favour to 2 against (Romania, USSR), with 2 abstentions (Ghana, United Arab Republic). The draft resolution as amended was rejected by 2 in favour (Romania, USSR), to 7 against, with 1 abstention (United Arab Republic), with Ghana not participating in the vote.]

NOTE. For comments on the decisions taken at Punta del Este and on their aftermath, see Adolf A. BERLE, Jr., Latin America: Diplomacy and Reality (New York, 1962), pp. 97–112; Enrique José BLANCO, De Plaza Girón a Punta del Este (Buenos Aires, 1962), 94 pp.; Gordon CONNELL-SMITH, "The Future of the Organization of American States: Significance of the Punta del Este Conference," 18 The World Today (1962), pp. 112–21; Enrique V. COROMINAS, Cuba en Punta del Este (2d ed., Buenos Aires, 1963), 236 pp.; Enrique V. COROMINAS, Mexico, Cuba y las Organización de los Estados Americanos (Buenos Aires, 1965), 236 pp.; Charles G. FENWICK, "The Issues at Punta del Este: Non-Intervention v. Collective Security," 56 AJIL (1962), pp. 469–74; C. Neale RONNING, Punta del Este: The Limits of Collective Security in a Troubled Hemisphere (New York, 1962), 31 pp.; Louis B. SOHN, "Expulsion or Forced Withdrawal from an International Organization," 77 Harvard L.R. (1964), p. 1381, at 1417–20.

CUBAN MISSILE CRISIS

NOTE. The situation in Cuba became aggravated in September 1962. On 13 September 1962, President Kennedy announced that if "at any time the Communist buildup in Cuba were to endanger or interfere with our security in any way, including our base at Guantanamo, our passage to the Panama Canal, our missile and space activities at Cape Canaveral, or the lives of American citizens in this country, or if Cuba should ever attempt to export its aggressive purposes by force or the threat of force against any nation in this hemisphere, or become an offensive military base of significant capacity for the Soviet Union, then this country will do whatever must be done to protect its own security and that of its allies." 47 DSB (1962), p. 481. In a Joint Resolution, approved on 3 October 1962, the Congress of the United States proclaimed the determination of the United States: "(a) to prevent by whatever means may be necessary, including the use of arms, the Marxist-Leninist regime in Cuba from extending, by force or the threat of force, its aggressive or subversive activities to any part of this hemisphere; (b) to prevent in Cuba the creation or use of an externally supported military capability endangering the security of the United States; and (c) to work with the Organization of American States and with freedom-loving Cubans to support the aspirations of the Cuban people for self-determination." *Ibid.*, at 597. At an informal meeting of the Ministers of Foreign Affairs held at Washington on 2–3 October 1962, it was agreed that the Sino-Soviet intervention in Cuba constituted "an attempt to convert the island into an armed base for communist penetration of the Americas and subversion of the democratic institutions of the Hemisphere"; and that it was desirable "to intensify individual and collective surveillance of the delivery of arms and implements of war and all other items of strategic importance to the communist regime of Cuba, in order to prevent the secret accumulation in the island of arms that can be used for offensive purposes against the Hemisphere." *Ibid.*, pp. 598–60.

1.   *Address by President Kennedy (USA), 22 October 1962.*

47 DSB (1962), pp. 715–20.

This Government, as promised, has maintained the closest surveillance of the Soviet military buildup on the island of Cuba. Within the past week unmistakable evidence has established the fact that a series of offensive missile sites is now in preparation on that imprisoned island. The purpose of these bases can be none other than to provide a nuclear strike capability against the Western Hemisphere.

Upon receiving the first preliminary hard information of this nature last Tuesday morning [October 16] at 9:00 a.m., I directed that our surveillance be stepped up. And having now confirmed and completed our evaluation of the evidence and our decision on a course of action, this Government feels obliged to report this new crisis to you in fullest detail.

The characteristics of these new missile sites indicate two distinct types of installations. Several of them include medium-range ballistic missiles capable of carrying a nuclear warhead for a distance of more than 1,000 nautical miles. Each of these missiles, in short, is capable of striking Washington, D.C., the Panama Canal, Cape Canaveral, Mexico City, or any other city in the southeastern part of the United States, in Central America, or in the Caribbean area.

Additional sites not yet completed appear to be designed for intermediate-range ballistic missiles capable of traveling more than twice as far—and thus capable of striking most of the major cities in the Western Hemisphere, ranging as far north as Hudson Bay, Canada, and as far south as Lima, Peru. In addition, jet bombers, capable of carrying nuclear weapons, are now being uncrated and assembled in Cuba, while the necessary air bases are being prepared.

This urgent transformation of Cuba into an important strategic base—by the presence of these large, long-range, and clearly offensive weapons of sudden mass destruction—constitutes an explicit threat to the peace and security of all the Americas, in flagrant and deliberate defiance of the Rio Pact of 1947, the traditions of this nation and hemisphere, the Joint Resolution of the 87th Congress, the Charter of the United Nations, and my own public warnings to the Soviets on September 4 and 13.

This action also contradicts the repeated assurances of Soviet spokesmen, both publicly and privately delivered, that the arms buildup in Cuba would retain its original defensive character and that the Soviet Union had no need or desire to station strategic missiles on the territory of any other nation.

The size of this undertaking makes clear that it has been planned for some months. Yet only last month, after I had made clear the distinction between any introduction of ground-to-ground missiles and the existence of defensive antiaircraft missiles, the Soviet Government publicly stated on September 11 that, and I quote, "The armaments and military equipment sent to Cuba are designed exclusively for defensive purposes," and, and I quote the Soviet Government, "There is no need for the Soviet Government to shift its weapons for a retaliatory blow to any other country, for instance Cuba," and that, and I quote the Government, "The Soviet Union has so powerful rockets to carry these nuclear warheads that there is no need to search for sites for them beyond the boundaries of the Soviet Union." That statement was false.

Only last Thursday, as evidence of this rapid offensive buildup was already in my hand, Soviet Foreign Minister Gromyko told me in my office that he was instructed to make it clear once again, as he said his Government had already done, that Soviet assistance to Cuba, and I quote, "pursued solely the purpose of contributing to the defense capabilities of Cuba," that, and I quote him, "training by Soviet specialists of Cuban nationals in handling defensive armaments was by no means offensive," and that "if it were otherwise," Mr. Gromyko went on, "the Soviet Government would never become involved in rendering such assistance." That statement also was false.

Neither the United States of America nor the world community of nations can tolerate deliberate deception and offensive threats on the part of any nation, large or small. We no longer live in a world where only the actual firing of weapons represents a sufficient challenge to a nation's security to constitute maximum peril. Nuclear weapons are so destructive and ballistic missiles are so swift that any substantially increased possibility of their use or any sudden change in their deployment may well be regarded as a definite threat to peace.

For many years both the Soviet Union and the United States, recognizing this fact, have deployed strategic nuclear weapons with great care, never upsetting the precarious *status quo* which insured that these weapons would not be used in the absence of some vital challenge. Our own strategic missiles have never been transferred to the territory of any other nation under a cloak of secrecy and deception; and our history, unlike that of the Soviets since the end of World War II, demonstrates that we have no desire to dominate or conquer any other nation or impose our system upon its people. Nevertheless, American citizens have become adjusted to living daily on the bull's eye of Soviet missiles located inside the U.S.S.R. or in submarines.

In that sense missiles in Cuba add to an already clear and present danger—although it should be noted the nations of Latin America have never previously been subjected to a potential nuclear threat.

But this secret, swift, and extraordinary buildup of Communist missiles—in an area well known to have a special and historical relationship to the United States and the nations of the Western Hemisphere, in violation of Soviet assurances, and in defiance of American and hemispheric policy—this sudden, clandestine decision to station strategic weapons for the first time outside of Soviet soil—is a deliberately provocative and unjustified change in the *status quo* which cannot be accepted by this country if our courage and our commitments are ever to be trusted again by either friend or foe.

The 1930's taught us a clear lesson: Aggressive conduct, if allowed to grow unchecked and unchallenged, ultimately leads to war. This nation is opposed to war. We are also true to our word. Our unswerving objective, therefore, must be to prevent the use of these missiles against this or any other country and to secure their withdrawal or elimination from the Western Hemisphere.

Our policy has been one of patience and restraint, as befits a peaceful and powerful nation, which leads a worldwide alliance. We have been determined not to be diverted from our central concerns by mere irritants and fanatics. But now further action is required—and it is underway; and these actions may only be the beginning. We will not prematurely or unnecessarily risk the costs of worldwide nuclear war in which even the fruits of victory would be ashes in our mouth—but neither will we shrink from that risk at any time it must be faced.

Acting, therefore, in the defense of our own security and of the entire Western Hemisphere, and under the authority entrusted to me by the Constitution as endorsed by the resolution of the Congress, I have directed that the following *initial* steps be taken immediately:

First: To halt this offensive buildup, a strict quarantine on all offensive military equipment under shipment to Cuba is being initiated. All ships of any kind bound for Cuba from whatever nation or port will, if found to contain cargoes of offensive weapons, be turned back. This quarantine will be extended, if needed, to other types of cargo and carriers. We are not at this time, however, denying the necessities of life as the Soviets attempted to do in their Berlin blockade of 1948.

Second: I have directed the continued and increased close surveillance of Cuba and its military buildup. The Foreign Ministers of the OAS [Organization of American States] in their communique of October 3 rejected secrecy on such matters in this hemisphere. Should these offensive military preparations continue, thus increasing the threat to the hemisphere, further action will be justified. I have directed the Armed Forces to prepare for any eventualities; and I trust that, in the interest of both the Cuban people and the Soviet technicians at the sites, the hazards to all concerned of continuing this threat will be recognized.

Third: It shall be the policy of this nation to regard any nuclear missile launched from Cuba against any nation in the Western Hemisphere as an attack by the Soviet Union on the United States, requiring a full retaliatory response upon the Soviet Union.

Fourth: As a necessary military precaution I have reinforced our base at Guantanamo, evacuated today the dependents of our personnel there, and ordered additional military units to be on a standby alert basis.

Fifth: We are calling tonight for an immediate meeting of the Organ of Consultation, under the Organization of American States, to consider this threat to hemispheric security and to invoke articles 6 and 8 of the Rio Treaty in support of all necessary action. The United Nations Charter allows for regional security arrangements—and the nations of this hemisphere decided long ago against the military presence of outside powers. Our other allies around the world have also been alerted.

Sixth: Under the Charter of the United Nations, we are asking tonight that an emergency meeting of the Security Council be convoked without delay to take action against this latest Soviet threat to world peace. Our resolution will call for the prompt dismantling and withdrawal of all offensive weapons in Cuba, under the supervision of U.N. observers, before the quarantine can be lifted.

Seventh and finally: I call upon Chairman Khrushchev to halt and eliminate this clandestine, reckless, and provocative threat to world peace and to stable relations between our two nations. I call upon him further to abandon this course of world domination and to join in an historic effort to end the perilous arms race and transform the history of man. He has an opportunity now to move the world back from the abyss of destruction—by returning to his Government's own words that it had no need to station missiles outside its own territory, and withdrawing these weapons from Cuba—by refraining from any action which will widen or deepen the present crisis—and then by participating in a search for peaceful and permanent solutions.

This nation is prepared to present its case against the Soviet threat to peace, and our own proposals for a peaceful world, at any time and in any forum—in the OAS, in the United Nations, or in any other meeting that could be useful—without limiting our freedom of action.

We have in the past made strenuous efforts to limit the spread of nuclear weapons. We have proposed the elimination of all arms and military bases in a fair and effective disarmament treaty. We are prepared to discuss new proposals for the removal of tensions on both sides—including the possibilities of a genuinely independent Cuba, free to determine its own destiny. We have no wish to war with the Soviet Union, for we are a peaceful people who desire to live in peace with all other peoples.

But it is difficult to settle or even discuss these problems in an atmosphere of intimidation. That is why this latest Soviet threat—or any other threat which is made either independently or in response to our actions this week—must and will be met with determination. Any hostile move anywhere in the world against the safety and freedom of peoples to whom we are committed—including in particular the brave people of West Berlin—will be met by whatever action is needed.

Finally, I want to say a few words to the captive people of Cuba, to whom this speech is being directly carried by special radio facilities. I speak to you as a friend, as one who knows of your deep attachment to your fatherland, as one who shares your aspirations for liberty and justice for all. And I have watched and the American people have watched with deep sorrow how your nationalist revolution was betrayed and how your fatherland fell under foreign domination. Now your leaders are no longer Cuban leaders inspired by Cuban ideals. They are puppets and agents of an international conspiracy which has turned Cuba against your friends and neighbors in the Americas— and turned it into the first Latin American country to become a target for nuclear war, the first Latin American country to have these weapons on its soil.

These new weapons are not in your interest. They contribute nothing to your peace and well-being. They can only undermine it. But this country has no wish to cause you to suffer or to impose any system upon you. We know that your lives and land are being used as pawns by those who deny you freedom.

Many times in the past the Cuban people have risen to throw out tyrants who destroyed their liberty. And I have no doubt that most Cubans today look forward to the time when they will be truly free— free from foreign domination, free to choose their own leaders, free to select their own system, free to own their own land, free to speak and write and worship without fear or degradation. And then shall Cuba be welcomed back to the society of free nations and to the associations of this hemisphere.

My fellow citizens, let no one doubt that this is a difficult and dangerous effort on which we have set out. No one can foresee precisely what course it will take or what costs or casualties will be incurred. Many months of sacrifice and self-discipline lie ahead—months in which both our patience and our will will be tested, months in which many threats and denunciations will keep us aware of our dangers. But the greatest danger of all would be to do nothing.

The path we have chosen for the present is full of hazards, as all paths are; but it is the one most consistent with our character and courage as a nation and our commitments around the world. The cost of freedom is always high—but Americans have always paid it. And one path we shall never choose, and that is the path of surrender or submission.

Our goal is not the victory of might but the vindication of right— not peace at the expense of freedom, but both peace *and* freedom, here in this hemisphere and, we hope, around the world. God willing, that goal will be achieved.

2. *Resolution of the Council of the Organization of American States, 23 October 1962.*

OAS Doc. OEA/SER.G/III, C–sa–463; 47 DSB (1962), pp. 722–23.

Whereas:

The Inter-American Treaty of Reciprocal Assistance of 1947 (Rio Treaty) recognizes the obligation of the American Republics to "provide for effective reciprocal assistance to meet armed attacks against any American state and in order to deal with threats of aggression against any of them";

Article 6 of the said Treaty states:

"If the inviolability or the integrity of the territory or the sovereignty or political independence of any American State should be affected by an aggression which is not an armed attack or by an extra-continental or intra-continental conflict, or by any other fact or situation that might endanger the peace of America, the Organ of Consultation shall meet immediately in order to agree on the measures which must be taken in case of aggression to assist the victim of the aggression or, in any case, the measures which should be taken for the common defense and for the maintenance of the peace and security of the Continent."

The Eighth Meeting of Consultation of the Ministers of Foreign Affairs of the American Republics in Punta del Este in January, 1962, agreed in Resolution II "To urge the member states to take those steps that they may consider appropriate for their individual and collective self-defense, and to cooperate, as may be necessary or desirable, to strengthen their capacity to counteract threats or acts of aggression, subversion, or other dangers to peace and security resulting from the continued intervention in this hemisphere of Sino-Soviet powers, in accordance with the obligations established in treaties and agreements such as the Charter of the Organization of American States and the Inter-American Treaty of Reciprocal Assistance" ;

The Ministers of Foreign Affairs of the American Republics meeting informally in Washington, October 2 and 3, 1962, reasserted "the firm intention of the Governments represented and of the peoples of the American Republics to conduct themselves in accordance with the principles of the regional system, staunchly sustaining and consolidating the principles of the Charter of the Organization of American States, and affirmed the will to strengthen the security of the Hemisphere against all aggression from within or outside the Hemisphere and against all developments or situations capable of threatening the peace and security of the Hemisphere through the application of the Inter-American Treaty of Reciprocal Assistance of Rio de Janeiro. It was the view of the Ministers that the existing organizations and bodies of the inter-American system should intensify the carrying out of their respective duties with special and urgent attention to the situation created by the communist regime in Cuba and that they should stand in readiness to consider the matter promptly if the situation requires measures beyond those already authorized" ;

The same meeting "recalled that the Soviet Union's intervention in Cuba threatens the unity of the Americas and its democratic institutions, and that this intervention has special characteristics which, pursuant to paragraph 3 of Resolution II of the Eighth Meeting of Consultation of Ministers of Foreign Affairs, call for the adoption of special measures, both individual and collective" ;

Incontrovertible evidence has appeared that the Government of Cuba, despite repeated warnings, has secretly endangered the peace of the Continent by permitting the Sino-Soviet powers to have intermediate and middle-range missiles on its territory capable of carrying nuclear warheads;

The Council of the Organization of American States Acting
Provisionally as Organ of Consultation

Resolves:

1. To call for the immediate dismantling and withdrawal from Cuba of all missiles and other weapons with any offensive capability.

2. To recommend that the member states, in accordance with Articles 6 and 8 of the Inter-American Treaty of Reciprocal Assistance, take all measures, individually and collectively, including the use of armed force, which they may deem necessary to ensure that the Government of Cuba cannot continue to receive from the Sino-Soviet powers military material and related supplies which may threaten the peace and security of the Continent and to prevent the missiles in Cuba with offensive capability from ever becoming an active threat to the peace and security of the Continent.

3. To inform the Security Council of the United Nations of this resolution in accordance with Article 54 of the Charter of the United Nations, and to express the hope that the Security Council will, in accordance with the Resolution introduced by the United States, dispatch United Nations observers to Cuba at the earliest moment.

4. To continue to serve provisionally as Organ of Consultation and to request the member states to keep the Organ of Consultation duly informed of measures taken by them in accordance with paragraph 2 of this resolution.

3. *US Proclamation Interdicting the Delivery of Offensive Weapons to Cuba, 23 October 1962.*

27 Federal Register (1962), p. 10401 ; 47 DSB (1962), p. 717.

Whereas the peace of the world and the security of the United States and of all American States are endangered by reason of the establishment by the Sino-Soviet powers of an offensive military capability in Cuba, including bases for ballistic missiles with a potential range covering most of North and South America;

Whereas by a Joint Resolution passed by the Congress of the United States and approved on October 3, 1962, it was declared that the United States is determined to prevent by whatever means may be necessary, including the use of arms, the Marxist-Leninist regime in Cuba from extending, by force or the threat of force, its aggressive or subversive activities to any part of this hemisphere, and to prevent in Cuba the creation or use of an externally supported military capability endangering the security of the United States; and

Whereas the Organ of Consultation of the American Republics meeting in Washington on October 23, 1962, recommended that the Member States, in accordance with Articles 6 and 8 of the Inter-American Treaty of Reciprocal Assistance, take all measures, individually and collectively, including the use of armed force, which they may deem necessary to ensure that the Government of Cuba cannot continue to receive from the Sino-Soviet powers military material and related supplies which may threaten the peace and security of the Continent and to prevent the missiles in Cuba with offensive capability from ever becoming an active threat to the peace and security of the Continent:

Now, THEREFORE, I, JOHN F. KENNEDY, President of the United States of America, acting under and by virtue of the authority conferred upon me by the Constitution and statutes of the United States, in accordance with the aforementioned resolutions of the United States Congress and of the Organ of Consultation of the American Republics, and to defend the security of the United States, do hereby proclaim that the forces under my command are ordered, beginning at 2:00 p.m. Greenwich time October 24, 1962, to interdict, subject to the instructions herein contained, the delivery of offensive weapons and associated matériel to Cuba.

For the purposes of this Proclamation, the following are declared to be prohibited matériel:

Surface-to-surface missiles; bomber aircraft; bombs, air-to-surface rockets and guided missiles; warheads for any of the above weapons; mechanical or electronic equipment to support or operate the above items; and any other classes of matériel hereafter designated by the Secretary of Defense for the purpose of effectuating this Proclamation.

To enforce this order, the Secretary of Defense shall take appropriate measures to prevent the delivery of prohibited matériel to Cuba, employing the land, sea and air forces of the United States in cooperation with any forces that may be made available by other American States.

The Secretary of Defense may make such regulations and issue such directives as he deems necessary to ensure the effectiveness of this order, including the designation, within a reasonable distance of Cuba, of prohibited or restricted zones and of prescribed routes.

Any vessel or craft which may be proceeding toward Cuba may be intercepted and may be directed to identify itself, its cargo, equipment and stores and its ports of call, to stop, to lie to, to submit to visit and search, or to proceed as directed. Any vessel or craft which fails or refuses to respond to or comply with directions shall be subject to being taken into custody. Any vessel or craft which it is believed is en route to Cuba and may be carrying prohibited matériel or may itself constitute such matériel shall, wherever possible, be directed to proceed to another destination of its own choice and shall be taken into custody if it fails or refuses to obey such directions. All vessels or craft taken into custody shall be sent into a port of the United States for appropriate disposition.

In carrying out this order, force shall not be used except in case of failure or refusal to comply with directions, or with regulations or directives of the Secretary of Defense issued hereunder, after reasonable efforts have been made to communicate them to the vessel or craft, or in case of self-defense. In any case, force shall be used only to the extent necessary.

4. *Statement by the Soviet Government, 23 October 1962.*

S/5186 (23 Oct. 1962); SCOR, XVII, Supp. for Oct.–Dec. 1962, pp. 149–54.

Last night, 22 October 1962, Mr. Kennedy, the President of the United States of America, announced that he had given orders to the United States Navy to intercept all ships bound for Cuba, to subject them to inspection, and to turn back ships carrying weapons which, in the judgment of the United States authorities, were offensive in character. Orders had also been given for continued and close surveillance of Cuba. Thus the United States Government is in effect placing the Republic of Cuba under naval blockade. At the same time, the landing of additional United States troops at the United States Guantánamo base, situated in the territory of Cuba, has begun, and the United States armed forces are being placed in a state of combat readiness.

The President is endeavouring to justify these unprecedented aggressive acts by arguments to the effect that a threat to the national security of the United States is arising in Cuba.

The Soviet Government has repeatedly drawn the attention of the Governments of all countries and of world public opinion to the serious danger to world peace created by the policy pursued by the United States towards the Republic of Cuba. The statement by the President of the United States shows that the United States imperialist circles will stop at nothing in their attemps to stifle a sovereign State Member of the United Nations. To do this they are prepared to push the world towards the abyss of military catastrophe. The peoples of all countries must clearly realize that, in embarking on such a venture, the United States of America is taking a step towards the unleashing of a world thermonuclear war. Insolently flouting the international rules of conduct for States and the principles of the Charter of the United Nations, the United States has arrogated to itself—and has so announced—the right to attack the vessels of other States on the high seas: in other words, to engage in piracy.

Imperialist circles in the United States are trying to dictate to Cuba what policy it must pursue, what dispositions it is to make at home, and what weapons it must possess for its defence. But who has authorized the United States to assume the role of arbiter of the destinies of other countries and peoples? Why must the Cubans settle the domestic affairs of their own State, not as they see fit, but according to the wishes of the United States? Cuba belongs to the Cuban people, and only they can be masters of their fate.

Under the Charter of the United Nations, all countries, large or small, have the right to organize their lives in their own way, to take such measures as they consider necessary to protect their own security, and to rebuff aggressive forces encroaching on their freedom and independence. To ignore this is to undermine the very basis of existence of the United Nations, to bring jungle law into international practice, and to engender conflicts and wars without end.

In this anxious hour, the Soviet Government considers it its duty to address a serious warning to the United States Government, to advise it that, in carrying out the measures announced by President Kennedy, it is assuming a heavy responsibility for the fate of the world, and recklessly playing with fire.

The United States leaders must at last understand that times have changed completely. Only madmen can now take their stand on "positions of strength" and expect that policy to bring them any success, to allow them to force their own dispositions on other States. While in the past the United States could consider itself the greatest Power on the world scene, there is no foundation for such a view today. There is another force in the world which is no less powerful, and which takes the position that peoples should arrange their life as they please. Today, as never before, statesmen must show calm and prudence, and must not countenance the rattling of weapons.

The Soviet Government emphasizes once again that all weapons in the Soviet Union's possession are serving and will serve the purposes of defence against aggressors. Under existing international conditions, the presence of powerful weapons, including nuclear rocket weapons, in the Soviet Union is acknowledged by all the peoples in the world to be the decisive factor in deterring the aggressive forces of imperialism from unleashing a world war of annihilation. This mission the Soviet Union will continue to discharge with all firmness and consistency.

The President of the United States said in his statement that, if even one nuclear bomb fell on United States territory, the United States would make a retaliatory response. Such an assertion is imbued with hypocrisy, since the Soviet Union has already declared repeatedly that not a single Soviet nuclear bomb will fall either on the United States or on any other country unless aggression has been committed. The nuclear weapons made by the Soviet people are in the people's hands; they will never be used for purposes of aggression. But if the aggressors unleash war, the Soviet Union will inflict the most powerful blow in response.

The Soviet Union has always been true to the principles of the Charter of the United Nations; it has consistently pursued, and still pursues, a policy designed to preserve and strengthen peace. The whole world knows what great efforts the Soviet Union is making to lessen international tension, to eliminate the breeding-grounds of conflict and disputation between States, and to make the principles of peaceful co-existence between States with different social structures a living reality. It is the Soviet Union which has put forward and justified a programme of universal and complete disarmament, the application of which would open real prospects for the establishment of a peace without wars, without weapons. These proposals are gaining ever-increasing support throughout the world; they have fired the imagination of the people; they have become the order of the day. If the cause of disarmament has made no progress so far, the fault lies with the United States of America and its allies in NATO. They fear disarmament; they do not want to part with the big stick with whose help they are trying to dictate their will to other countries.

The United States Government accuses Cuba of creating a threat to the security of the United States. But who is going to believe that Cuba can be a threat to the United States? If we think of the respective size and resources of the two countries, of their armaments, no statesman in his right mind can imagine for one moment that Cuba can be a threat to the United States of America or to any other country. It is hypocritical, to say the least, to say that little Cuba may encroach on the security of the United States of America.

The Cubans wish to secure their homeland, their independence, against the threat emanating from the United States of America. The Government of Cuba is appealing to reason and conscience, and is calling upon the United States to refrain from making threatening passes at Cuba's independence and to establish normal relations with the Cuban State. Is there not a ring of conviction in the official declaration by the Cuban Government concerning its ambition to settle all questions at issue through negotiations with the United States Government?

Only recently, speaking in the General Assembly, Mr. Dorticós, the President of the Republic of Cuba, reiterated that "Cuba has always been prepared to negotiate the differences between the United States and Cuba, through normal diplomatic channels or by any appropriate means". The President of the United States now implies that such statements by the Cuban Government are not enough. But it would be possible to justify any aggressive action, any adventure in this way.

With regard to the Soviet Union's assistance to Cuba, this assistance is exclusively designed to improve Cuba's defensive capacity. As was stated on 3 September 1962 in the joint Soviet-Cuban *communiqué* on the visit to the Soviet Union of a Cuban delegation composed of Mr. E. Guevara and Mr. E. Aragones, the Soviet Government has responded to the Cuban Government's request to help Cuba with arms. The *communiqué* states that such arms and military equipment are intended solely for defensive purposes. The Governments of the two countries still firmly adhere to that position.

Soviet assistance in strengthening Cuba's defences is necessitated by the fact that, from the outset of its existence, the Republic of Cuba has been subjected to continuous threats and acts of provocation by the United States. The United States is stopping at nothing, even going so far as to organize armed intervention in Cuba in April 1961, in order to deprive the Cuban people of the freedom and independence they have won, to bring the country once more under the heel of the United States monopolies and to make Cuba a United States puppet.

The United States is demanding that the military equipment Cuba needs for its own defence should be withdrawn from its territory, a step to which no State prizing its independence can, of course, agree.

The Soviet Union considers that all foreign troops should be withdrawn from the territory of other States and should be brought back within their own national frontiers. If the United States was genuinely concerned to strengthen friendly relations with States and was striving to ensure lasting peace throughout the world, as President Kennedy asserts in his address of 22 October, it should have accepted the Soviet proposal and withdrawn its troops and military equipment and dismantled its military bases that are situated in the territory of other States in various parts of the world.

However, the United States, which has dispersed its armed forces and armaments throughout the world, stubbornly refuses to accept this proposal. It is using these armed forces and armaments for interference in the domestic affairs of other States and for the implementation of its own aggressive designs. It is United States imperialism which has assumed the role of international policeman. The representatives of the United States constantly boast that United States aircraft can attack the Soviet Union at any time, can drop United States bombs on peaceful towns and villages and can deliver heavy blows. Not a day passes without the statesmen, military leaders and the Press of the United States uttering threats that United States submarines, which are ranging through many seas and oceans with

Polaris missiles on board, can launch an atomic attack against the Soviet Union and other peace-loving States. President Kennedy's statement that the United States Government is acting solely in the interests of peace in making its exaggerated demands that Cuba should be deprived of the means of defence rings particularly false in the light of these facts.

The peace-loving States cannot but protest against the piratical operations which the President of the United States has announced against ships bound for Cuban shores, against the institution of control over the ships of sovereign States on the high seas. As we know, United States statesmen like to talk about their adherence to the principles of international law and to dilate upon the need for law and order in the world. But in reality they evidently consider that the laws are written not for the United States, but for other States. The institution by the United States of a virtual blockade of Cuban shores is a provocative act, an unprecedented violation of international law, a challenge to all peace-loving peoples.

It is also obvious that, if the United States is today attempting to prohibit other countries from trading with Cuba and from using their ships to transport goods and cargoes there, United States ruling circles may tomorrow demand that similar action should be taken against any other States whose policy or social system does not suit them.

The United States Government is assuming the right to demand that States should account to it for the way in which they organize their defence, and should notify it of what their ships are carrying on the high seas.

The Soviet Government firmly repudiates such claims. The high-handed acts of United States imperialism may lead to catastrophic consequences for all mankind, which is not desired by any people, including the people of the United States.

In view of the full gravity of the situation which the United States Government has created over Cuba, the Soviet Government has instructed its representative in the United Nations to raise the question of the immediate convening of the Security Council to consider the following question: "The violation of the Charter of the United Nations and the threat to peace by the United States of America".

The Soviet Union appeals to all Governments and peoples to raise their voice in protest against the aggressive acts of the United States of America against Cuba and other States, strongly to condemn such acts and to take steps to prevent the unleashing of a thermonuclear war by the United States Government.

The Soviet Government will do everything in its power to frustrate the aggressive designs of United States imperialist circles and to defend and strengthen peace on earth.

The Soviet Government expresses its firm belief that the Soviet people will still further increase their labour efforts to strengthen the economic and defence capacity of their Soviet fatherland. The Soviet Government is taking all the necessary steps to insure that the country is not taken by surprise and is in a position to mete out an appropriate rebuff to an aggressor.

5. *Discussion in the Security Council, 23–25 October 1962.*

SCOR, XVII, Mtgs. 1022–25.

Mr. STEVENSON (USA): I have asked for an emergency meeting of the Security Council to bring to your attention a grave threat to the Western Hemisphere and to the peace of the world.

Last night, the President of the United States reported the recent alarming military developments in Cuba.　.　.　.

In view of this transformation of Cuba into a base for offensive weapons of sudden mass destruction, the President announced the initiation of a strict quarantine on all offensive military weapons under shipment to Cuba. He did so because, in the view of my Government, the recent developments in Cuba—the importation of the cold war into the heart of the Americas—constitute a threat to the peace of this hemisphere, and, indeed, to the peace of the world.　.　.　.

Let me make it absolutely clear what the issue of Cuba is. It is not an issue of revolution. This hemisphere has seen many revolutions, including the one which gave my own nation its independence.

It is not an issue of reform. My nation has lived happily with other countries which have had thorough-going and fundamental social transformations, like Mexico and Bolivia. The whole point of the Alliance for Progress is to bring about an economic and social revolution in the Americas.

It is not an issue of socialism. As Secretary of State Rusk said in February, "our hemisphere has room for a diversity of economic systems".

It is not an issue of dictatorship. The American Republics have lived with dictators before. If this were his only fault, they could live with Mr. Castro.

The foremost objection of the States of the Americas to the Castro regime is not because it is revolutionary, not because it is socialistic, not because it is dictatorial, not even because Mr. Castro perverted a noble revolution in the interests of a squalid totalitarianism. It is because he has aided and abetted an invasion of this hemisphere—an invasion just at the time when the hemisphere is making a new and unprecedented effort for economic progress and social reform.

The crucial fact is that Cuba has given the Soviet Union a bridgehead and staging area in this hemisphere; that it has invited an extra-continental, anti-democratic and expansionist Power into the bosom of the American family; that it has made itself an accomplice in the communist enterprise of world dominion.

There are those who seek to equate the presence of Soviet bases in Cuba with the presence of NATO bases in parts of the world near the Soviet Union. Let us subject this facile argument to critical consideration.

It is not only that the Soviet action in Cuba has created a new and dangerous situation by sudden and drastic steps which imperil the security of all mankind. It is necessary further to examine the purposes for which these missiles are introduced and these bases established.

Missiles which help a country to defend its independence, which leave the political institutions of the recipient countries intact, which are not designed to subvert the territorial integrity or political independence of other States, which are installed without concealment or deceit—assistance in this form and with these purposes is consistent with the principles of the United Nations. But missiles which introduce a nuclear threat into an area now free of it, which are installed by clandestine means, which result in the most formidable nuclear base in the world outside existing treaty systems—assistance in this form and with these purposes is radically different.

Let me state this point very clearly. The missile sites in NATO countries were established in response to missile sites in the Soviet Union directed at the NATO countries. The NATO States had every right and necessity to respond to the installation of these Soviet missiles by installing missiles of their own. These missiles were designed to deter a process of expansion already in progress. Fortunately, they have helped to do so.

The United States and its Allies established their missile sites after free negotiation, without concealment and without false statements to other Governments. There is, in short, a vast difference between the long-range missile sites established years ago in Europe and the long-range missile sites established by the Soviet Union in Cuba during the last three months.

There is a final significant difference. For a hundred and fifty years the nations of the Americas have laboured painfully to construct a hemisphere of independent and co-operating countries, free from foreign threats. An international system far older than the United Nations—the inter-American system—has been erected on this principle. The principle of the territorial integrity of the Western hemisphere has been woven into the history, the life and the thought of all the people of the Americas. In striking at that principle, the Soviet Union is striking at the strongest and most enduring strain in the policy of this hemisphere. It is disrupting the convictions and aspirations of a century and a half. It is intruding on the firm policies of twenty nations. To allow this challenge to go unanswered would be to undermine a basic and historic pillar of the security of this hemisphere.   .   .   .

In our passion for peace we have forborne greatly. There must, however, be limits to forbearance if forbearance is not to become the diagram for the destruction of this Organization. Mr. Castro transformed Cuba into a totalitarian dictatorship with impunity; he extinguished the rights of political freedom with impunity; he aligned himself with the Soviet bloc with impunity; he accepted defensive weapons from the Soviet Union with impunity; he welcomed thousands of Communists into Cuba with impunity: but when, with cold deliberation, he turns his country over to the Soviet Union for a long-range missile launching base, and thus carries the Soviet programme for aggression into the heart of the Americas, the day of forbearance is past.

If the United States and the other nations of the Western Hemisphere should accept this new phase of aggression we would be delinquent in our obligations to world peace. If the United States and the other nations of the Western Hemisphere should accept this basic disturbance of the world's structure of power we would invite a new surge of aggression at every point along the frontier. If we do not stand firm here our adversaries may think that we will stand firm nowhere—and we guarantee a heightening of the world civil war to new levels of intensity and peril. .   .   .

I am submitting today to the Security Council a draft resolution [S/5182] designed to find a way out of this calamitous situation. It reads as follows:

"The Security Council,

"Having considered the serious threat to the security of the Western Hemisphere and the peace of the world caused by the continuance and acceleration of foreign intervention in the Caribbean,

"Noting with concern that nuclear missiles and other offensive weapons have been secretly introduced into Cuba,

"Noting also that as a consequence a quarantine is being imposed around the country,

"Gravely concerned that further continuance of the Cuban situation may lead to direct conflict,

"1.   Calls as a provisional measure under Article 40 for the immediate dismantling and withdrawal from Cuba of all missiles and other offensive weapons;

"2.   Authorizes and requests the Secretary-General to dispatch to Cuba a United Nations observer corps to assure and report on compliance with this resolution;

"3.   Calls for termination of the measures of quarantine directed against military shipments to Cuba upon United Nations certification of compliance with paragraph 1 above;

"4.   Urgently recommends that the United States of America and the Union of Soviet Socialist Republics confer promptly on measures to remove the existing threat to the security of the Western Hemisphere and the peace of the world, and report thereon to the Security Council." . . .

Mr. GARCIA INCHAUSTEGUI (Cuba): . . . The President of the United States claims, and his representative is repeating it here, that our defensive weapons affect the security of his territory. Now I appeal to the conscience of the members of this Council: do not the military power and the aggressions of the United States constitute a threat to our people?

We do not understand the conception that the United States seems to entertain of the juridical equality of States as laid down in Article 2, paragraph 1, of the Charter. That is to say, that the United States, in its capacity as a military Power and a highly developed country, can promote, encourage and carry out all types of aggression, boycott, sabotage and acts contrary to international law, whereas Cuba, a small but valiant country, may not arm in its own defence.

After so flagrant a violation of law has once been sanctioned, what small country will feel secure in its sovereignty and independence? It will be sufficient for a great Power, neighbouring or otherwise, to decide that the régime of any small State is subversive or that its defences represent a threat to security, for this to constitute a pretext for intervention and for acts of war such as our country is experiencing today. At that rate, no sovereignty will be left intact and only the law of the strongest will prevail in relations between States. . . .

According to the statements made by the representative of the United States, there are two types of military bases and two types of rockets: good military bases and evil military bases, good rockets and evil rockets. And of course the United States Government reserves the right to determine when a rocket is good and when it is evil, or when a base is good or when it is evil. The logic of the United States representative is most convincing . . .

From now onwards, war or peace—the ghastly nuclear war—will depend on what the United States Intelligence Service may see fit to assert. It is as though the international organizations and the Security Council had no reason to exist! As though any State could unilaterally take it upon itself to determine whether certain measures affect its sovereignty! What purpose would be served by your presence here, gentlemen, as representatives in this Security Council, in the light of such an argument and of such a point of view? . . .

What the United States has done now is to adopt a unilateral warlike measure, inspired by its thirst for neo-colonialist domination and control—for such is the naval blockade of Cuba—and thereupon to call on the Security Council and other international organs to sanction that flagrant violation of law. For that at least is the purpose of the United States: it takes a certain step behind the back of the international organization, behind the back of the regional organization, behind the back of international law, and then, by using all sorts of pressure, it tries to get the international organizations to approve what international law and morality repudiate.

To what international body did the United States turn to inform it in advance of its aggressive intentions? Why did it not accuse us before this Council and await its decisions? The United States did not do so because it has not a single legal or moral ground on which to justify the forceful measures taken against our country, measures that have dragged the world to the brink of nuclear war and extermination. . . .

What right has the United States to ask that observers should go to Cuba? The United Nations observers should rather be sent to the United States bases from which the invasions are launched and whence the pirates sally forth to harass a State whose only crime is that of striving to foster the development of its own people. We shall not accept observers of any kind in matters that pertain to our domestic jurisdiction. The manœuvres of imperialism in the Congo will not be repeated in Cuba.

The United Nations has no reason to implicate itself in aggressive and warlike measures adopted unilaterally by a great Power against a small State, without regard to the United Nations. And the United States, which did not arraign Cuba before this international organization but resorted to such measures without the latter's consent, has no right whatsoever to have its violations sanctioned by the latter. Such an endorsement would be a shameful page in the history of this body and would sow the seed of its destruction and of the wholesale destruction of mankind. The United Nations must withstand the pressure and the intimidation that the United States is trying to exercise upon it. Either the United Nations will make the United States abandon its outrageous use of force or the United States will disregard the United Nations and we shall witness a war of extermination in which vast numbers of people, including thousands of North Americans, will be killed.

The naval blockade unilaterally decreed by the United States is an act of war against the sovereignty and independence of our country which our people will resist in every way and by every means. It is moreover an act of desperation on the part of the United States. The latter has failed in all its attempts to destroy our revolution. Now it is trying the ultimate means, namely, war, even though that will imperil the lives of millions throughout the world.

We appeal to the Security Council, in the name of the Charter, in the name of international morality and in the name of the principles of law, for the immediate withdrawal of the aggressive forces of the United States from our coasts and for the cessation of the illegal blockade unilaterally decreed by the Government of the United States in utter contempt of the Charter. We appeal for the immediate withdrawal of all troops, ships and aircraft sent to our coasts and for the cessation of the provocative acts in Guantanamo and of the piratical attacks organized by agents in the service of the United States Government. We appeal for the cessation of all the interventionist measures taken by the United States Government with respect to the domestic affairs of Cuba and for the cessation of the violations of our air space and our waters.   .   .   .

The PRESIDENT [Mr. V. A. Zorin, USSR]: I should now like to make a statement in my capacity as the representative of the UNION OF SOVIET SOCIALIST REPUBLICS.   .   .   .

The Security Council meets today in circumstances which cannot but give rise to the gravest concern for the fate of peace in the Caribbean region and in the whole world. It is not a trivial matter that is involved; it is a matter of the unilateral and arbitrary actions of a great Power, which constitute a direct infringement of the freedom and independence of a small country. It is a matter of a new and very dangerous act of aggression in a chain of acts of aggression which the United States has already committed against Cuba in violation of the most elementary rules and principles of international law, and in violation of the fundamental provisions and of the letter and spirit of the United Nations Charter, of which the United States is also a signatory.   .   .   .

When it announced the introduction of its blockade against Cuba, the United States took a step which is unprecedented in relations between States not formally at war. By its arbitrary and piratical action, the United States menaced the shipping of many countries—including its allies—which do not agree with its reckless and dangerous policy in respect of Cuba. By this aggressive action, which put the whole world under the threat of war, the United States issued a direct challenge to the United Nations and to the Security Council as the principal organ of the United Nations responsible for maintaining international peace and security.

In stating its intention of involving the Organization of American States—which it is already ordering to impose collective sanctions on Cuba—in acts of aggression against Cuba, the United States is openly usurping the prerogatives of the Security Council, which is the only body empowered to take coercive measures.   .   .   .

The United States has no right whatever, either from the point of view of the accepted rules of international law relating to freedom of shipping, or from that of the provisions of the United Nations Charter, to put forward the demands contained in the statements of President Kennedy. No State, no matter how powerful it may be, has any right to rule on the quantities or types of arms which another State considers necessary for its defence. According to the United Nations Charter, each State has the right to defend itself and to possess weapons to ensure its security. The Soviet Union, at the request of the

Cuban Government, is supplying Cuba with armaments intended for defence and only for defence. In so doing, the Soviet Union is not trying to gain any advantage for itself in Cuba, and does not represent a threat to anyone. The Soviet Union is not pursuing any warlike aims at all in this area, just as it has no warlike aims in any other areas of the world. The Soviet Union does not have military bases in thirty-five countries. The Soviet Union is simply making a sincere effort to help the young Cuban Republic to retain and strengthen its sovereignty and independence. .   .   .

The Soviet delegation, fully appreciating the heavy responsibility incumbent on the Security Council at this critical time, considers it essential, as a first priority, that the United States should cease and completely withdraw all the aggressive measures which it has taken against Cuba and other countries.

In view of the pressing need to take these steps, the Soviet delegation, on the instructions of its Government, submits to the Security Council for its consideration the following draft resolution [S/5187] titled "Violation of the United Nations Charter and threat to the peace by the United States of America":

"The Security Council,

"Guided by the need to maintain peace and safeguard security throughout the world,

"Recognizing the right of every State to strengthen its defences,

"Considering inadmissible interference by some States in the internal affairs of other sovereign and independent countries,

"Noting the inadmissibility of violations of the rules governing freedom of navigation on the high seas,

"1.   Condemns the actions of the Government of the United States of America aimed at violating the United Nations Charter and at increasing the threat of war;

"2.   Insists that the Government of the United States shall revoke its decision to inspect ships of other States bound for the Republic of Cuba;

"3.   Proposes to the Government of the United States of America that it shall cease any kind of interference in the internal affairs of the Republic of Cuba and of other States which creates a threat to peace;

"4.   Calls upon the United States of America, the Republic of Cuba and the Union of Soviet Socialist Republics to establish contact and enter into negotiations for the purpose of restoring the situation to normal and thus of removing the threat of an outbreak of war."

It goes without saying that the Soviet delegation will vote against the draft resolution put forward by the United States delegation, [S/5182] which is an absolutely unprecedented attempt not only to justify retrospectively the aggressive actions already undertaken by the United States against Cuba, but also to force the Security Council —the principal organ responsible for maintaining international peace and security—to sanction these actions, which create a most serious threat to the maintenance of world peace. .   .   .

Mr. QUAISON–SACKEY (Ghana): This meeting takes place at a time of serious crisis, the most serious since the Second World War. Upon our words, upon our deeds, hang grave events, events that may well prove decisive for the very survival of humanity. The Council is indeed called upon to shoulder heavy responsibilities, to pronounce on momentous issues. It is therefore incumbent on the Council—on all of us—to proceed, if not along lines of serenity and a lofty sense of responsibility, at least along those of sanity; to tread, if not the road of wisdom, at least that of circumspection. This is the time when wise counsel should prevail to arrest a world catastrophe. .   .   .

The basic contention of the United States, as we understand it, is that a direct threat to peace in this hemisphere is posed by the establishment in Cuba of launching bases and the installation of long-range ballistic missiles capable of carrying thermonuclear warheads to most of North and South America; these steps, it is insisted, are far in excess of any conceivable defence requirements of Cuba, and not only are they offensive in character but they have provided an aggressive extracontinental Power with a bridgehead and staging area in this hemisphere. .   .   .

There is thus a genuine fear that the Western Hemisphere is threatened by Cuba's military build-up, while Cuba is afraid of attack from its neighbours, including the United States—which is the reason for its defence measures.

If my conclusions are correct, then my delegation proposes that the United States should give a written guarantee to the Security Council that it has no intention whatsoever of interfering in the internal affairs of Cuba and taking offensive military action, directly or indirectly, against the Republic of Cuba. Then Cuba should also give a written guarantee to the Security Council that it has no intention whatsoever of interfering in the internal affairs of any country in the Western Hemisphere and taking offensive military action against any country. Although our proposals are long-term palliatives, we are confident that such guarantees would help in the restoration of mutual confidence and respect between Cuba and its neighbours. .   .   .

The representative of the United States has argued, in support of his contention in the matter, that the recent military developments in Cuba introduce a nuclear threat into an area free of it, that they threaten the security and independence of defenceless neighbouring States; that they took place by clandestine means, and constitute a serious blow at the inter-American system.

Having examined, on the basis of objectivity, these assertions, along with the counter-assertions made during the course of this debate, my delegation remains in doubt whether proof has been tendered of Cuba's offensive designs.

That being so, it was with much concern that my Government learnt that the United States Government has initiated measures, including the use of armed force, to quarantine Cuba against imports of military material and related supplies. This in turn has led to a serious warning by the Soviet Union to the United States, which has something of the character of an ultimatum. This, then, is the crisis which . bedevils the peace of the world at this very moment.

In the presentation of his Government's case, the representative of the United States gave the impression that he regarded these measures, as ratified by the Council of the Organization of American States, as falling squarely within the competence of that organization.

My delegation regretfully dissents from this view. As we have said, on an earlier occasion, though regional agencies or arrangements have rights and responsibilities which are recognized by the Charter of the United Nations and which they should not be prevented from exercising fully, these rights and responsibilities do not by any means involve absolute priority in relation to the competence of the United Nations. The flexibility which is desirable in the relations between regional agencies and the United Nations cannot be extended to the point of undermining the Security Council's authority.

In this particular case, if it is recalled that the United States delegation, in previous debates, had expressed the view that enforcement action consists of coercive measures involving the use of air, sea or land forces, of the type falling within the scope of Article 42, then it is clear that the action contemplated by the United States must be regarded as enforcement action, which is inadmissible in terms of Article 53, without the authorization of the Security Council.

That being so, are there grounds for the argument that such action is justified in exercise of the inherent right of self-defence? Can it be contended that there was, in the words of a former American Secretary of State whose reputation as a jurist in this field is widely accepted, "a necessity of self-defence, instant, overwhelming, leaving no choice of means and no moment for deliberation"? My delegation does not think so, for as I have said earlier, incontrovertible proof is not yet available as to the offensive character of military developments in Cuba. Nor can it be argued that the threat was of such a nature as to warrant action on the scale so far taken, prior to a reference to this Council. Even from a strictly juridical point of view my delegation cannot agree that in this particular case self-defence can be invoked to justify the exercise of authority by the United States on the high seas, for the concept of freedom on the open seas, enshrined in numerous international instruments, entails absolute freedom of navigation for vessels of all nations in time of peace.

In conclusion, I must say that the delegation of Ghana cannot apportion blame for this grave crisis. What is important, and what a very large number of Member States of this Organization representing millions of people want now, is that this danger of war should be arrested quickly. Time is of the greatest essence at this momentous moment. We all call upon the leaders of the United States, the Soviet Union and Cuba to understand the yearning of humanity for peace at this critical period.

The responsibility of the Security Council is overwhelming. What is urgently needed is negotiation between the parties concerned to resolve the present crisis on the basis of mutual respect for each other's sovereign rights, and my delegation would urge that this Council authorize the Acting Secretary-General to confer with them immediately with a view to facilitating such negotiations.

It is in the light of these considerations and against the background of two days of consultations with a large number of Member States of the Organization that the draft resolution contained in document S/5190 has been prepared. It is my privilege to present this draft to the Council. The draft resolution is co-sponsored by Ghana and the United Arab Republic and it reads as follows:

"The Security Council,

"Having considered the recent serious developments in the Caribbean,

"Noting with grave concern the threat to international peace and security,

"Having listened to the parties directly concerned,

"1.   Requests the Secretary-General promptly to confer with the parties directly concerned on the immediate steps to be taken to remove the existing threat to world peace, and to normalize the situation in the Caribbean;

"2.   Calls upon the parties concerned to comply forthwith with this resolution and provide every assistance to the Secretary-General in performing his task;

"3.   Requests the Secretary-General to report to the Council on the implementation of paragraph 1 of this resolution;

"4.   Calls upon the parties concerned to refrain meanwhile from any action which may directly or indirectly further aggravate the situation."   .   .   .

The Acting SECRETARY-GENERAL [U Thant]: Today the United Nations faces a moment of grave responsibility. What is at stake is not just the interests of the parties directly involved, nor just the interests of all Member States, but the very fate of mankind. If today the United Nations should prove itself ineffective, it may have proved itself so for all time.

In the circumstances, not only as Acting Secretary-General of the United Nations but as a human being, I would be failing in my duty if I did not express my profound hope and conviction that moderation, self-restraint and good sense will prevail over all other considerations.

In this situation where the very existence of mankind is in the balance, I derive some consolation from the fact that there is some common ground in the draft resolutions introduced in the Council. Irrespective of the fate of those draft resolutions, that common ground remains. It calls for urgent negotiations between the parties directly involved, though, as I said earlier, the rest of the world is also an interested party. In this context, I cannot help expressing the view that some of the measures proposed or already taken, which the Council is called upon to approve, are very unusual and, I might say, even extraordinary except in wartime.

At the request of the permanent representatives of a large number of Member Governments who have discussed the matter amongst themselves and with me, I have sent, through the permanent representatives of the two Governments, the following identically worded message to the President of the United States of America and the Chairman of the Council of Ministers of the USSR:

"I have been asked by the permanent representatives of a large number of Member Governments of the United Nations to address an urgent appeal to you in the present critical situation. These representatives feel that in the interest of international peace and security, all concerned should refrain from any action which may aggravate the situation and bring with it the risk of war.

"In their view it is important that time should be given to enable the parties concerned to get together with a view to resolving the present crisis peacefully and normalizing the situation in the Caribbean. This involves on the one hand the voluntary suspension of all arms shipments to Cuba, and also the voluntary suspension of the quarantine measures involving the searching of ships bound for Cuba. I believe that such voluntary suspension for a period of two to three weeks will greatly ease the situation and give time to the parties concerned to meet and discuss with a view to finding a peaceful solution of the problem. In this context, I shall gladly make myself available to all parties for whatever services I may be able to perform.

"I urgently appeal to your Excellency to give immediate consideration to this message.

"I have sent an identical message to the President of the United States of America/Chairman of the Council of Ministers of the USSR."

I should like also to take this occasion to address an urgent appeal to the President and Prime Minister of the Revolutionary Government of Cuba.   Yesterday [1022nd meeting] Ambassador García Incháustegui of Cuba recalled the words of his President, words which were uttered from the rostrum of the General Assembly just over two weeks ago, and I quote:

"If the United States could give assurances, by word and deed, that it would not commit acts of aggression against our country, we solemnly declare that there would be no need for our weapons and our armies"   .   .   .

Here again I feel that on the basis of discussion some common ground may be found through which a way may be traced out of the present impasse.   I believe it would also contribute greatly to the same end if the construction and development of major military facilities and installations in Cuba could be suspended during the period of negotiations.

I now make a most solemn appeal to the parties concerned to enter into negotiations immediately, even this night, if possible, irrespective of any other procedures which may be available or which could be invoked.   I realize that if my appeal is heeded, the first subject to be discussed will be the modalities, and that all parties concerned will have to agree to comply with those responsibilities which fall on them before any agreement as a whole can become effective.   I hope, however, that the need for such discussion will not deter the parties concerned from undertaking these discussions.   In my view it would be short-sighted for the parties concerned to seek assurances on the end result before the negotiations had even begun.

I have stated in my message to both the President of the United States of America and the Chairman of the Council of Ministers of the USSR that I shall gladly make myself available to all parties for whatever services I may be able to perform.   I repeat that pledge now.

During the seventeen years that have passed since the end of the Second World War, there has never been a more dangerous or closer confrontation of the major Powers.   At a time when the danger to world peace was less immediate, or so it appears by comparison, my distinguished predecessor said:

"The principles of the Charter are, by far, greater than the Organization in which they are embodied, and the aims which they are to safeguard are holier than the policies of any single nation or people."

He went on to say:

" .   .   .   the discretion and impartiality   .   .   .   imposed on the Secretary-General by the character of his immediate task may not degenerate into a policy of expediency   .   .   .   A Secretary-General cannot serve on any other assumption than that—within the necessary limits of human frailty and honest differences of opinion —all Member nations honour their pledge to observe all Articles of the Charter." [751st meeting, para. 4.]

It is after considerable deliberation that I have decided to send the two messages to which I have referred earlier, and likewise I have decided to make this brief intervention tonight before the Security Council including the appeal to the President and Prime Minister of Cuba.

I hope that at this moment, not only in the Council Chamber but in the world outside, good sense and understanding will be placed above the anger of the moment or the pride of nations. The path of negotiation and compromise is the only course by which the peace of the world can be secured at this critical moment. . . .

Mr. STEVENSON (USA): Today we must address our attention to the realities of the situation posed by the build-up of nuclear striking power in Cuba. In this connexion I want to say at the outset that the course adopted by the Soviet Union yesterday to avoid direct confrontations in the zone of quarantine is welcome to my Government. We welcome also the assurance by Chairman Khrushchev in his letter to Earl Russell that the Soviet Union will take no reckless decisions with regard to this crisis. And we welcome most of all the report that Mr. Khrushchev has agreed to the proposals advanced by the Secretary-General.

In the next place, there are some troublesome questions in the minds of Members that are entitled to serious answers. There are those who say that, conceding the fact that the Soviet Union has installed these offensive missiles in Cuba, conceding the fact that this constitutes a grave threat to the peace of the world, why was it necessary for the nations of the Western Hemisphere to act with such speed? Why could not the quarantine against the shipment of offensive weapons have been delayed until the Security Council and the General Assembly had a full opportunity to consider the situation and make recommendations?

Let me remind the Members that the United States was not looking for some pretext to raise the issue of the transformation of Cuba into a military base. On the contrary, the United States made no objection whatever to the shipment of defensive arms by the Soviet Union to Cuba, even though such shipments offended the traditions of this hemisphere. Even after the first hard intelligence reached Washington concerning the change in the character of Soviet military assistance to Cuba, the President of the United States responded by directing an intensification of surveillance, and only after the facts and the magnitude of the build-up had been established beyond all doubt did we begin to take this limited action of barring only those nuclear weapons, equipment and aircraft.

To understand the reasons for this prompt action, it is necessary to understand the nature and the purposes of this operation. It has been marked, above all, by two characteristics: speed and stealth. As the photographic evidence makes clear, the installation of these missiles, the erection of these missile sites, has taken place with extraordinary speed. One entire complex was put up in twenty-four hours. This speed not only demonstrates the methodical organization and the careful planning involved, but it also demonstrates a premeditated attempt to confront this hemisphere with a fait accompli. By quickly completing the whole process of nuclearization of Cuba, the Soviet Union would be in a position to demand that the *status quo* be maintained and left undisturbed—and, if we were to have delayed our counteraction, the nuclearization of Cuba would have been quickly completed.

This is not a risk which this hemisphere is prepared to take. When we first detected the secret and offensive installations, could we reasonably be expected to have notified the Soviet Union in advance, through the process of calling a meeting of the Security Council, that we had discovered its perfidy, and then to have done nothing but wait while we debated, and then have waited further while the Soviet representative in the Security Council vetoed a resolution, as he has already announced he will do? In different circumstances, we would have done so, but today we are dealing with dread realities and not with wishes.

One of the sites, as I have said, was constructed in twenty-four hours. One of these missiles can be armed with its nuclear warhead in the middle of the night, pointed at New York, and landed above this room five minutes after it was fired. No debate in this room could affect in the slightest the urgency of these terrible facts or the immediacy of the threat to peace.

There was only one way to deal with the emergency and with the immediacy, and that was to act, and to act at once, but with the utmost restraint consistent with the urgency of the threat to the peace. We came to the Security Council, I would remind you, immediately and concurrently with the Organization of the American States. We did not even wait for the OAS to meet and to act. We came here at the same time.

We immediately put into process the political machinery that we pray will achieve a solution of this grave crisis, and we did not act until the American Republics had acted to make the quarantine effective. We did not shirk our duties to ourselves, to the hemisphere, to the United Nations or to the rest of the world.

We are now in the Security Council on the initiative of the United States, precisely because having taken the hemispheric action which has been taken, we wish the political machinery, the machinery of the United Nations, to take over to reduce these tensions and to interpose itself to eliminate this aggressive threat to peace and to ensure the removal from this hemisphere of offensive nuclear weapons and the corresponding lifting of the quarantine.

There are those who say that the quarantine is an inappropriate and extreme remedy; that the punishment does not fit the crime. But I would ask those who take this position to put themselves in the position of the Organization of American States and to consider what they would have done in the face of the nuclearization of Cuba. Were we to do nothing until the knife was sharpened? Were we to stand idly by until it was at our throats? What were the alternatives available? On the one hand, the Organization of American States might have sponsored an invasion or destroyed the bases by an air strike, or imposed a total blockade of all imports into Cuba, including medicine and food. On the other hand, the Organization of American States and the United States might have done nothing. Such a course would have confirmed the greatest threat to the peace of the Americas known to history and would have encouraged the Soviet Union in similar adventures in other parts of the world. It would have discredited our will and our determination to live in freedom and to reduce, not increase, the perils of this nuclear age. The course we have chosen seems to me to be perfectly graduated to meet the character of the threat. To have done less would have been to fail in our obligation to peace.

NOTE. No action was taken by the Council upon any of the resolutions before it. On the basis of the appeal of the Secretary-General and after several further exchanges of messages between the President of the United States and the Chairman of the Council of Ministers of the USSR, the Soviet Union removed from Cuba the missiles and bombers which the United States considered as offensive, and the United States terminated the interdiction of deliveries to Cuba. 47 DSB (1962), pp. 740–46, 762, 874–75, 918. On 7 January 1963, the United States and the USSR sent a joint message to the Secretary-General thanking him for his assistance in averting the crisis, and notifying him that "in view of the degree of understanding reached between them on the settlement of the crisis and the extent of progress in the implementation of this understanding, it is not necessary for this item to occupy further the attention of the Security Council at this time." S/5227 (7 Jan. 1963); SCOR, XVIII, Supp. for Jan.–March 1963, p. 85.

6.   *The Legal Case for United States Action in Cuba.*

Statement by Abram Chayes, Legal Adviser, US Department of State, 3 November 1962. 57 DSB (1962), pp. 763–65.

The Cuban crisis is not over yet. It may be a very long time before it is over. And such progress as we have made cannot, on the whole, be attributed to our legal position. The primary elements in the confrontation of the last weeks have been the ability and the will of the United States to deploy the necessary force in the area to establish and enforce the quarantine, and the mobilization of friends and allies—in the hemisphere, in Europe, and elsewhere in the world —in support of our action.

But if it would not have been enough merely to have the law on our side, that is not to say it is wholly irrelevant which side the law was on. The deployment of force, the appeal for world support, to say nothing of the ultimate judgment of history, all depend in some significant degree on the reality and coherence of the case in law for our action.

It is worthwhile I think to set out that legal case and to examine some of its implications.

The question was not, as most of my friends in and out of the press seemed to think, "Is it a legal blockade?" The effort to name and classify things has its place in the law as in other disciplines, but this audience needs no reminder that legal problems are something more than a search for pigeonholes within which to encase living phenomena.

In wartime the establishment of a blockade, of course, with all its classical elements, is justified according to the books. It represents minimal interference with neutral commerce consistent with the necessities of war. But even in the most hallowed of the texts, war is not the sole situation in which such interference is permissible.

It is instructive to examine the rules of blockade. They were developed in the 19th century. They reflect very accurately the problems of the international order—as well as the weapons technology— that then prevailed. The typical subjects of international law were European nation-states. Their relations with each other were episodic and largely bilateral.

The age of total war was only beginning; so the application of force as an instrument of national policy was recognized as legitimate, if not positively beneficial. When force was applied it was, at least in theory, a bilateral affair or, at most, something between small and temporary groupings of nations on each side. The operating legal rules—always nicer and more coherent in retrospect than at the time —had two principal objects: first, to help assure that these affrays were carried out with the smallest disturbance of the normal activities of all concerned; and second, to permit a state to make an unambiguous choice whether to join with one of the belligerents—and so have a chance to share in any political gains—or to remain uninvolved and make its profits commercially, which were in any event likely to be both larger and safer.

International law addresses different problems today and in a different context. Its overriding object is not to regulate the conduct of war but to keep and defend the peace. If nonalinement continues to be a goal for some countries, noninvolvement has become a luxury beyond price. We remember that war in this century has twice engulfed us all, willy-nilly. Paper commitments to right conduct did not stop it. Above all we are burdened with the knowledge and the power to destroy the world. The international landscape today, too, looks quite different than it did a century ago. It is peopled with permanent organizations of states—some more comprehensive, some less, some purely for defense, and some with broader purposes. It is through these organizations that we hope to give reality to our pledges to maintain the peace.

The Soviet Union's threat in Cuba was made in the context of this international system, and it was answered in the same context.

The United States saw its security threatened, but we were not alone. Our quarantine was imposed in accordance with the recommendation of the Organization of American States acting under the Rio Treaty of 1947. This treaty, together with related agreements, constitutes the inter-American system. Twenty-one countries, including Cuba, are parties to that treaty. None has ever disaffirmed it.

The Rio Treaty provides for collective action not only in the case of armed attack but also "if the inviolability or the integrity of the territory or the sovereignty or political independence of any American State should be affected : . . by any . . . fact or situation that might endanger the peace of America. . . ." In such cases, a special body, the Organ of Consultation, is to "meet immediately in order to agree on the measures . . . which should be taken for the common defense and for the maintenance of the peace and security of the Continent." The Organ of Consultation acts only by a two-thirds vote.

The treaty is explicit as to the measures which may be taken "for the maintenance of the peace and security of the Continent." The "use of armed force" is specifically authorized, though "no State shall be required to use armed force without its consent."

On October 23d, the Organ of Consultation met, in accordance with the treaty procedures, and considered the evidence of the secret introduction of Soviet strategic nuclear missiles into Cuba. It concluded that a situation existed which endangered the peace of America. It recommended that member states "take all measures, individually and collectively, including the use of armed force, which they may deem necessary to ensure that the Government of Cuba cannot continue to receive from the Sino-Soviet powers military material and related supplies. . . ." The quarantine was imposed to carry out this recommendation.

Action by regional organizations to keep the peace is not inconsistent with the United Nations Charter. On the contrary, the charter assigns an important role to regional organizations in carrying out the purposes of the United Nations. Article 52(1) prescribes the use of "regional arrangements or agencies for dealing with such matters relating to the maintenance of international peace and security as are appropriate for regional action. . . ." And it is certainly not irrelevant in the present context that provisions dealing with regional organizations were written into the charter at San Francisco at the insistence of the Latin American countries and with the inter-American system specifically in mind.

The activities of regional organizations, of course, must be "consistent with the Purposes and Principles of the United Nations." It may seem self-evident that action to deal with a threat to the peace meets this requirement. But the principles of the United Nations are stated in article 2 of the charter and include the undertaking of all members to "refrain in their international relations from the threat or use of force against the territorial integrity or political independence of any state, or in any other manner inconsistent with the Purposes of the United Nations." The quarantine action involves a use of force and must be squared with this principle.

The promise not to use force is not absolute. One qualification comes readily to mind. Article 51 affirms that nothing in the charter, including article 2(4), impairs "the inherent right of individual or collective self-defense if an armed attack occurs." The quarantine action was designed to deal with an imminent threat to our security. But the President in his speech did not invoke article 51 or the right of self-defense. And the OAS acted not under article 3, covering cases of armed attack, but under article 6, covering threats to the peace other than armed attack.

Self-defense, however, is not the only justifiable use of force under the charter. Obviously, the United Nations itself could sanction the use of force to deal with a threat to the peace. So it did in Korea and in the Congo. We accept use of force in these instances as legitimate for two reasons. First, all the members have constituted the United Nations for these purposes. In signing the charter they have assented to its powers and procedures. Second, the political processes by which the U.N. makes a decision to use force give some assurance that the decision will not be rashly taken.

I submit that the same two factors legitimize use of force in accordance with the OAS resolution dealing with a threat to the peace in the hemisphere. The significance of assent is attested by the fact that, though Cuba is now and has been for some time the object of sanctions and hostility from the OAS and has been suspended from participation in its agencies, she has remained a party to the treaties and a member of the inter-American system, as, in a like case, did the Dominican Republic. The significance of the political processes in the Organization is attested by the fact that, despite the disproportion of power between the United States and its neighbors to the south, it was not until the danger was clear and present that the necessary majority could be mustered to sanction use of armed force. But when that time came, the vote was unanimous.

Some have asked whether we should not first have gone to the Security Council before taking other action to meet the Soviet threat in Cuba. And I suppose that in the original conception of the United Nations, it was thought that the Security Council would be the agency for dealing with situations of this kind. However, the drafters of the charter demonstrated their wisdom by making Security Council responsibility for dealing with threats to the peace "primary" and not "exclusive." For events since 1945 have demonstrated that the Security Council, like our own electoral college, was not a viable institution. The veto has made it substantially useless in keeping the peace.

The withering away of the Security Council has led to a search for alternative peacekeeping institutions. In the United Nations itself the General Assembly and the Secretary-General have filled the void. Regional organizations are another obvious candidate.

Regional organizations, even when they employ agreed processes and procedures, remain subject to check. They are subordinate to the U.N. by the terms of the charter, and in the case of the OAS, by the terms of the relevant inter-American treaties themselves. Like an individual state, it can be called to account for its action in the appropriate agency of the parent organization. In recognition of this relation, the President ordered that the case be put immediately before the Security Council. The U.N., through the Council and the Secretary-General, is, as a result, actively engaged in the effort to develop a permanent solution to the threat to the peace represented by the Soviet nuclear capability in Cuba.

You will not have failed to see that the legal defense of the quarantine I have outlined reflects what I would call an American constitutional lawyer's approach to international law.

There is normative content in the system: "Congress shall make no law   .   .   .   abridging the freedom of speech, or of the press .   .   ."; "Member States shall refrain in their international relations from the threat or use of force." But it recognizes that norms, to be durable, must be subject to growth and development as circumstances change.

For assurance of healthy decision within this range, there must be reliance upon institutional arrangements, checks and balances. And therefore we must worry about the reality of the assent reflected in those arrangements.

There is recognition that in public international law, as in our domestic constitutional system, the membrane that separates law from politics is thin and permeable. And there must therefore be professional vigilance so that law is not corrupted by *raison d'état.*

The consequence of having a system within this kind of "play in the joints" is that we must live without the certainty, provided by more formal systems, that we have done well. Vindication or failure of the work of the lawyer, like that of the politician and other artists, must await the riper judgment of history. I am content to submit our efforts these past weeks to that judgment. I have some confidence, perhaps reflecting my parochial bias, that in the final decision the rigor of the logician will be tempered by the working precepts of the American constitutional lawyer.

NOTE.—1. For comments on the Cuban missile crisis, see James S. CAMPBELL, "The Cuban Crisis and the U.N. Charter: An Analysis of the United States Position," 16 Stanford L.R. (1963), pp. 160–77; Abram CHAYES, "The Legal Case for U.S. Action in Cuba," 47 DSB (1962), pp. 763–65; Abram CHAYES, "Law and the Quarantine of Cuba," 41 Foreign Affairs (1963), pp. 550–57; Carl Q. CHRISTOL and Charles R. DAVIS, "Maritime Quarantine: The Naval Interdiction of Offensive Weapons and Associated Matériel to Cuba, 1962," 57 AJIL (1963), pp. 525–45; James DANIEL and John G. HUBBEL, Strike in the West: The Complete Story of the Cuban Crisis (New York, 1963), 180 pp.; C. G. FENWICK, "The Quarantine Against Cuba: Legal or Illegal?" 57 AJIL (1963), pp. 588–92; FOREIGN POLICY ASSOCIATION, The Cuban Crisis: A Documentary Record (New York, 1963; Headline Series 157), 84 pp.; Thomas FREEMAN (pseud.), The Crisis in Cuba (Derby, Conn., 1963), 159 pp.; Emile GIRAUD, "L'interdiction du recours à la force: La théorie et la pratique des Nations: À propos de l'affaire cubaine: Le 'Quarantaine'," 67 RGDIP (1963), pp. 501–44; John W. HALDERMAN, "Regional Enforcement Measures and the United Nations," 52 Georgetown L.J. (1963), pp. 89–118; Rahmatullah KHAN, "Cuban Quarantine and the Charter of the U.N.," 4 Indian JIL (1964), pp. 107–123; Y. KOROVIN, "International Law through the Pentagon's Prism," 8 Int. Affairs (Moscow, 1962), No. 12, pp. 3–7; David L. LARSON, ed., The "Cuban Crisis" of 1962: Selected Documents and Chronology (Boston, 1963), 333 pp.; Brunson MacCHESNEY, "Some Comments on the 'Quarantine' of Cuba," 57 AJIL (1963), pp. 592–97; Joseph B. McDEVITT, "The U.N. Charter and the Cuban Quarantine," 17 JAG Journal (1963), pp. 71–80; Myres S. McDOUGAL, "The Soviet-Cuban Quarantine and Self-Defense," 57 AJIL (1963), pp. 597–604; W. T. MALLISON, Jr., "Limited Naval Blockade or Quarantine-Interdiction: National and Collective Defense Claims Valid under International Law," 31 George Washington L.R. (1962), pp. 335–98; Leonard C. MEEKER, "Defensive Quarantine and the Law," 57 AJIL (1963), pp. 515–24; Covey OLIVER, "International Law and the Quarantine of Cuba," 57 AJIL (1963), pp. 373–77; Covey OLIVER and others, The Inter-American Security System and the Cuban Crisis (Dobbs Ferry, New York, 1964; Association of the Bar of the City of New York, The Hammarskjöld Forums, No. 3), 96 pp.; Henry M. PACHTER, Collision Course: The Cuban Missile Crisis and Coexistence (New York, 1963), 261 pp.; Daniel G. PARTAN, "The Cuban Quarantine: Some Implications for Self-Defense," 1963 Duke L.J., pp. 696–721; Ruby H. PHILLIPS, The Cuban Dilemma (New York, 1963), 357 pp.; Eustace SELIGMAN, "The Legality of U.S. Quarantine Action under the United Nations Charter," 49 ABAJ (1963), pp. 142–45; Robert F. SMITH, What Happened in Cuba? A Documentary

History (New York, 1963), 360 pp.; US, DOS, American Foreign Policy: Current Documents, 1962 (DOS Pub. 8007; Washington, D.C., 1966), pp. 313–473; G. S. WINDASS, "The Cuban Crisis and World Order," 3 Int. Relations (London, 1966), No. 13, pp. 1–15; Quincy WRIGHT, "The Cuban Quarantine," 57 AJIL (1963), pp. 546–565. See also Arthur M. SCHLE-SINGER, Jr., A Thousand Days (Boston, Mass., 1967), pp. 794–841.

2. On 29 November 1963, Venezuela requested the convocation of a Meeting of Consultation "to consider the measures that should be taken to deal with the acts of intervention and aggression on the part of the Government of Cuba that affect the territorial integrity and the sovereignty of Venezuela, as well as the operation of its democratic institutions." After an investigation of the complaint, the Ninth Meeting of Consultation, which met at Washington, D.C., from 21 to 26 July 1964, resolved [21 DSB (1964), pp. 181–83]:

"1. To declare that the acts verified by the Investigating Committee constitute an aggression and an intervention on the part of the Government of Cuba in the internal affairs of Venezuela, which affects all of the member states.

"2. To condemn emphatically the present Government of Cuba for its acts of aggression and of intervention against the territorial inviolability, the sovereignty, and the political independence of Venezuela.

"3. To apply, in accordance with the provisions of Articles 6 and 8 of the Inter-American Treaty of Reciprocal Assistance, the following measures:

"a. That the governments of the American states not maintain diplomatic or consular relations with the Government of Cuba;

"b. That the governments of the American states suspend all their trade, whether direct or indirect, with Cuba, except in foodstuffs, medicines, and medical equipment that may be sent to Cuba for humanitarian reasons; and

"c. That the governments of the American states suspend all sea transportation between their countries and Cuba, except for such transportation as may be necessary for reasons of a humanitarian nature.

"4. To authorize the Council of the Organization of American States, by an affirmative vote of two thirds of its members, to discontinue the measures adopted in the present resolution at such time as the Government of Cuba shall have ceased to constitute a danger to the peace and security of the hemisphere.

"5. To warn the Government of Cuba that if it should persist in carrying out acts that possess characteristics of aggression and intervention against one or more of the member states of the Organization, the member states shall preserve their essential rights as sovereign states by the use of self-defense in either individual or collective form, which could go so far as resort to armed force, until such time as the Organ of Consultation takes measures to guarantee the peace and security of the hemisphere.

"6. To urge those states not members of the Organization of American States that are animated by the same ideals as the inter-American system to examine the possibility of effectively demonstrating their solidarity in achieving the purposes of this resolution.

"7. To instruct the Secretary General of the Organization of American States to transmit to the United Nations Security Council the text of the present resolution, in accordance with the provisions of Article 54 of the United Nations Charter."

See also PAN AMERICAN UNION, Inter-American Treaty of Reciprocal Assistance: Applications, Vol. II, 1960–1964 (Washington, D.C., 1964), pp. 181–212. For comments, see Enrique V. COROMINAS, Mexico, Cuba y la Organización de los Estados Americanos (Buenos Aires, 1965), pp. 173–201; INTER-AMERICAN INSTITUTE OF INTERNATIONAL LEGAL STUDIES, The Inter-American System: Its Development and Strengthening (Dobbs Ferry, New York, 1966), pp. 166–70; R. St. J. MACDONALD, "The Resort to Economic Coercion by International Political Organizations," 17 Univ. of Toronto L.J. (1967), p. 86, at 141–69.

SITUATION IN THE DOMINICAN REPUBLIC

NOTE.—1. After Rafael Leonidas Trujillo Molina, the dictator of the Dominican Republic was assassinated on 30 May 1961, President Joaquin Balaguer took over. He was replaced, after a military coup and a counter coup, by his Vice President Rafael Bonnelly on 18 January 1962. Juan Bosch was elected President on 20 December 1962 and was inaugurated on 26 February 1963. He was ousted by a military coup on 25 September 1963, which put the government in the hands of a three-man civilian junta, of which J. Donald Reid Cabral became the head on 22 December 1963. US SENATE, COMMITTEE ON FOREIGN RELATIONS, Background Information Relating to the Dominican Republic (89th Congress, 1st Session, 1965), pp. 3–14. The supporters of Juan Bosch staged a military uprising on 24 April 1965 and occupied a large part of the capital city, Santo Domingo. But Gen. Elias Wessin y Wessin staged a counterattack and the leaders of the rebellion sought refuge in foreign embassies. The rebellion revived the next day under new leadership, the fighting grew more severe, and the newly established anti-rebel military junta, with Colonel Pedro Bartolomé Benoit as president, asked for a temporary United States intervention and for assistance in restoring order. President Johnson was informed that the embassy was under machine-gun fire and that United States civilians were in grave danger. Tad SZULC, Dominican Diary (Dell ed., New York, 1966), pp. 13–60; S/6364 (18 May 1965), Annex; SCOR, XX, Supp. for April–June 1965, p. 130, at 137. He ordered the landing of Marines "to give protection to hundreds of Americans who are still in the Dominican Republic and to escort them safely back to the United States," submitted the matter to the Council of the Organization of American States, and notified the United Nations. 52 DSB (1965), pp. 738–39; S/6310 (29 April 1965); SCOR, *op. cit.*, pp. 65–66.

2. On 29 April 1965, the Council of the OAS asked the Papal Nuncio, Msgr. Emmanuel Clarizio, as the Dean of the Diplomatic Corps, to convey to all concerned the Council's "strong desire that all armed action or hostilities be suspended," and requested him to keep the Council informed of the developments. S/6364 (18 May 1965), Annex; SCOR, *op. cit.*, p. 130, at 133. On the next day, the Council convoked a Meeting of Consultation of Ministers of Foreign Affairs to consider the "grave situation created by armed hostilities in the Dominican Republic," and appealed to the parties in conflict to permit the "establishment of an international neutral refuge zone"

near the foreign embassies. S/6315 (30 April 1965); SCOR, *op. cit.*, pp. 68–70. On the same day, the Papal Nuncio succeeded in negotiating a cease-fire agreement between the two factions which included acceptance of arbitration by a commission of the OAS. S/6364 (18 May 1965), Annex; SCOR, *op. cit.*, p. 130, at 133. The Tenth Meeting of Consultation of Ministers of Foreign Affairs of the American Republics met in Washington on 1 May 1965, appointed a special committee, composed of representatives of Argentina, Brazil, Colombia, Guatemala and Panama, and instructed it "to go immediately to the city of Santo Domingo, to do everything possible to obtain the re-establishment of peace and normal conditions, and to give priority to the following two functions:

"(a) To offer its good offices to the Dominican armed groups and political groups and to diplomatic representatives for the purpose of obtaining urgently: (i) a cease-fire; and (ii) the orderly evacuation of the persons who have taken asylum in the embassies and of all foreign citizens who desire to leave the Dominican Republic; and

"(b) To carry out an investigation of all aspects of the situation in the Dominican Republic." *Ibid.*, at 131.

On the same day, the USSR requested the convening of "an urgent meeting of the Security Council to consider the question of the armed interference by the United States in the internal affairs of the Dominican Republic." S/6316 (1 May 1965), SCOR, *op. cit.*, p. 70.

I. *Discussion in the Security Council, 3–4 May 1965.*

SCOR, XX, Mtgs. 1196, 1198.

Mr. FEDORENKO (USSR): . . . The question on the Council's agenda is absolutely clear. It is that of open armed intervention by the United States of America, a permanent member of the Security Council, in the domestic affairs of the Dominican Republic, a sovereign State and a Member of the United Nations. In violation of the fundamental principles of the United Nations Charter and the universally recognized rules of international law, the United States has embarked on armed intervention in the Dominican Republic with openly imperialistic aims.

The Security Council has before it an act of open aggression. United States imperialism is dealing barbarously with the people of a sovereign country who have risen against a bloody dictatorship.

Already, in the last few days, 14,000 United States troops have been put ashore on the territory of the Dominican Republic. The city of Santo Domingo has to all intents and purposes been taken over by the United States occupation troops. . . .

This new act of aggression by United States imperialism—military intervention in the Dominican Republic, is, like the acts of the colonialists in the past, being engaged in on the outworn, false pretext of "protecting American lives". It is self-evident that the invasion of the Dominican Republic by United States Marines and paratroop units constitutes nothing other than an act of direct aggression against the people of that small country, flagrant armed intervention in its domestic affairs, and yet another attempt to maintain in power a reactionary, anti-popular dictatorship which suits the purposes of a foreign Power, the United States of America. It is an attempt to suppress, by the force of foreign bayonets, the desire of the Dominican people for freedom and independence. . . .

Strictly speaking, the United States itself has officially admitted the groundlessness of its false arguments about a rescue mission and, with extreme cynicism and frankness, has recognized the fact that the United States armed invasion of the territory of the Dominican Republic was undertaken in order to preserve a régime acceptable to the United States. The White House no longer makes any secret of the fact that the Americans are nurturing plans to keep United States troops in the Dominican Republic even after "order has been restored" in the country. Already, once again, the holy bogey of anti-communism has been dragged out, as it always is by United States propaganda whenever imperialist forces commit a flagrant outrage which can in no way be justified. . . .

By engaging in this criminal invasion of the territory of another country with the aim of interfering in its domestic affairs, the United States is flagrantly violating the United Nations Charter and in particular the provisions of Article 2, paragraph 4, which reads: "All Members shall refrain in their international relations from the threat or use of force against the territorial integrity or political independence of any state, or in any other manner inconsistent with the Purposes of the United Nations." The United States has also violated Article 2, paragraph 7, of the United Nations Charter, which categorically forbids intervention in the domestic affairs of States.

It is quite obvious that the United States is again, on this occasion, trying to use the OAS for its imperialist and interventionist purposes. But what kind of an Organization of American States can we speak of after United States armed forces, in accordance with the law of the jungle and by the "right" of the strong, have intervened on Dominican soil in order to suppress a rising of the people? According to the statement made by President Bosch on 2 May 1965 on television in New York, the armed intervention of United States troops in the Dominican Republic razed to the ground and demolished the very concept of that organization. It should indeed be said that, by using the OAS for its own ends, the United States has even gone so far as to violate that organization's very charter, article 17 of which reads: "The territory of a State is inviolable; it may not be the object, even temporarily, of military occupation or of other measures of force taken by another State, directly or indirectly, on any grounds whatever. . . ."

And after all this, the United States tries to create the appearance of a legal basis for its intervention by saying that it has taken this action in accordance with agreements and with the obligations it has assumed. What a monstrous fraud!

The international Press testifies to the fact that in the Organization of American States itself voices are heard in protest against the American policy of dictation and coercion. It is also well known that the United States, in sending its troops to the Dominican Republic, did not even bother to ascertain beforehand the opinion of members of the OAS. It presented the whole of that organization with a *fait accompli*, convening the Council of the OAS only after United States marines were already committing their foul deeds in Santo Domingo. . . .

One cannot fail to see that, in proceeding to armed intervention in the Dominican Republic, the United States imperialists are treading a path already well worn by them. As early as July 1950, the State Department published a long list of occasions on which the United States, under various pretexts, had used its land and marine forces on foreign territory in peacetime. The list shows that in the period from 1812 to 1932 alone the United States engaged in armed intervention against other States eighty-five times, using a wide variety of excuses. The United States intervened, for instance, "to protect American life", to demand apologies "for insult to the flag", "to punish natives for the murder of a white man", "to restore order", "to aid in evacuation", and even "to extinguish fire on American property". In short, the United States has not disdained any pretext—even the most ludicrous—in order to achieve, each time, a single purpose: the landing of its troops in one country or another, with a view to imposing upon it the will of American imperialism. . . .

The Soviet delegation considers that in the present situation the Security Council must condemn the armed interference by the United States in the domestic affairs of the Dominican Republic as a breach of international peace and as an action incompatible with the obligations assumed by the United States under the United Nations Charter, and must call upon the United States Government to withdraw its forces from the territory of the Dominican Republic immediately. The Security Council must fulfil its duty and the obligations placed upon it by the United Nations Charter. . . .

Mr. STEVENSON (USA): . . . About a week ago the instability which has plagued the Dominican Republic since the fall of the Trujillo régime erupted and the officials who had governed there for a year and a half were violently forced out. Rival groups strove to capture power; fighting broke out between them and among them; and the Dominican Republic was left without effective government for some days. As the situation deteriorated, certain of the contending forces indiscriminately distributed weapons to civilians; armed bands began to roam the streets of Santo Domingo, looting, burning and sniping; law and order completely broke down. The Embassies of Mexico, Guatemala, Peru, Ecuador and the United States were violated and the Embassy of El Salvador burned.

The great majority of those who joined in this insurgent cause in the Dominican Republic are not Communists. In particular, my Government has never believed that the PRD—the Dominican Revolutionary Party, led by President Bosch—is an extremist party. United States co-operation with President Bosch and his Government during his tenure following the ouster of President Trujillo speaks for itself. But, while the PRD planned and during its first hours led the revolutionary movement against the Government of Reid Cabral, a small group of well-known Communists, consistent with their usual tactics, quickly attempted to seize control of the revolution and of the armed bands in the streets. Quite clearly this group was acting in conformity with directives issued by a Communist conference that met in Havana in late 1964 and printed in Pravda on 18 January 1965. These directives called for assistance and continuing campaigns in support of the so-called "freedom fighters" to be organized "on a permanent basis so that this work will not dwindle to sporadic manifestations or disunited statements". They went on to say: "Active aid should be given to those who are subject at present to cruel repressions—for instance, the freedom fighters in Venezuela, Colombia, Guatemala, Honduras, Paraguay and Haiti."

This deliberate effort to promote subversion and overthrow Governments in flagrant violation of all norms of international conduct is responsible for much of the unrest in the Caribbean area.

In the face of uncontrollable violence, the Government which had replaced the Reid Cabral Government also quickly crumbled in a few days. Many of its leaders, and also others from the initial leadership of the revolt against the Reid Cabral Government, also sought asylum.

In the absence of any governmental authority Dominican law enforcement and military officials informed our Embassy that the situation was completely out of control, that the police and the Government could no longer give any guarantee concerning the safety of Americans or of any foreign nationals and that only an immediate landing of United States forces could safeguard and protect the lives of thousands of Americans and thousands of citizens of some thirty other countries. At that moment, the United States Embassy was under fire; the death toll in the city, according to Red Cross estimates, had reached 400; hospitals were unable to care for the wounded; medical supplies were running out; the power supply had broken down; and a food shortage threatened.

Faced with that emergency, the threat to the lives of its citizens, and a request for assistance from those Dominican authorities still struggling to maintain order, the United States on 28 April dispatched the first of the security forces that we have sent to the island. Since their arrival, nearly 3,000 foreign nationals from thirty countries have been evacuated without loss, although a number of the United States military personnel have been killed or wounded. We have made a full report to the Organization of American States; we have successfully evacuated some 2,000 Americans and about 1,000 persons of other nationalities; we have established the secure zone of refuge called for by the OAS; we have supported the dispatch by the OAS of the Committee which is at present in Santo Domingo; we have proposed that other American States make military forces available to assist in carrying out the mission of that Committee and the OAS is considering such a resolution this afternoon. . . .

However, lawlessness and disorder have by no means been eliminated. It has become clear that communist leaders, many trained in Cuba, have taken increasing control of what was initially a democratic movement, and many of the original leaders of the rebellion, the followers of President Bosch, have taken refuge in foreign embassies.

The American nations will not permit the establishment of another communist government in the Western hemisphere. This was the unanimous view of all the American nations when in January 1962 they declared, "The principles of communism are incompatible with the principles of the inter-American system". This is, and this will be, the common action and the common purpose of the democratic forces of the hemisphere, as President Lyndon B. Johnson has said. For the danger is also a common danger, and the principles are common principles. So we have acted to summon the resources of this entire hemisphere to this task. . . .

The OAS has before it today . . . a resolution which would request Governments of the American States that are capable of doing so to make available to the OAS contingents of their military, naval or air forces, to assist in carrying out the Committee's mission. The same resolution would also provide for the Meeting of Consultation to continue in session in order to take the necessary steps to facilitate the prompt restoration of constitutional government in the Dominican Republic and the withdrawal of foreign forces.

In this connexion, I should like to reaffirm the statement made by Ambassador Ellsworth Bunker, representing the United States, in the OAS meeting on Saturday. He said:

"My Government regrets that there was no inter-American force available to respond to the request of the authorities and the needs of the people of the Dominican Republic, and for the protection of the lives and the safety of other nationals. And my Government would welcome the constitution of such a force as soon as possible."

The efforts of the Organization of American States to deal with this tragic crisis in the Dominican Republic have been carefully considered, prudent and reasonable actions. Heroic efforts to end the bloodshed by cease-fire have been made by the Papal Nuncio. The Secretary General of the OAS is in the island contributing his prestige and abilities to this effort. The Inter-American Commission on Human Rights is also in Santo Domingo and functioning actively.

In the face of these energetic and productive steps, the Soviet effort to exploit the anarchy in the Dominican Republic for its own ends is regrettable, if familiar.

My delegation welcomes the discussion in the Security Council of this situation in the Dominican Republic. Members of the Council are well aware, however, that Article 33 of the United Nations Charter states that efforts should be made to find solutions to disputes first of all by peaceful means, including "resort to regional agencies or arrangements". This, of course, does not derogate from the authority of this Council. It merely prescribes the procedures and priorities envisaged by the authors of the two charters, the Charter of the United Nations and that of the OAS, for dealing with disputes of a local nature, procedures and priorities that have been followed consistently in analogous situations in the past.

In the light of the actions already taken, it would be prudent, it would be constructive and in keeping with the precedents established by this Council to permit the regional organization to continue to deal with this regional problem. The United Nations Charter, in Article 52, specifically recognizes the authority of regional organizations in dealing with regional problems. The Council recognizes the desirability of encouraging regional efforts, and I may add, the confidence of this Council in the abilities of regional organizations to deal with their own problems has been justified by the historical record.

In closing I should like to make two things quite clear. First, the United States Government has no intention of seeking to dictate the political future of the Dominican Republic. We believe that the Dominican people, under the established principle of self-determination, should select their own government through free elections. It is not our intention to impose a military junta or any other government. Our interest lies in the re-establishment of constitutional government and, to that end, to assist in maintaining the stability essential to the expression of the free choice of the Dominican people. This intent is in full accord with the basic democratic tenets of the Organization of American States and the inter-American system, the charter of which calls for the maintenance of systems of political organization "on the basis of the effective exercise of representative democracy".

The United States intends to continue to work with the OAS in assisting the Dominican people to return as soon as possible to constitutional government. With the good will and the sincere support of all parties concerned, we are confident that the Dominican people will ultimately be able to have the democratic and progressive government which they seek, and we feel that the members of this body should encourage such a peaceful and orderly evolution in this small republic which has suffered so long from tyranny and civil strife.

Secondly, as President Johnson has emphasized, the United States will never depart from its commitment to the preservation of the right of all of the free people of this hemisphere to choose their own course without falling prey to international conspiracy from any quarter. Our goal in the Dominican Republic is the goal which has been expressed again and again in the treaties and agreements which make up the fabric of the inter-American system. It is that the people of that country must be permitted freely to choose the path of political democracy, social justice and economic progress. Neither the United States nor any nation can want or permit a return to that brutal and offensive despotism which earned the condemnation and punishment of this hemisphere and of all civilized humanity. We intend to carry on the struggle against tyranny, no matter in what ideology it cloaks itself. This is our mutual responsibility under the agreements that we have signed and the common values which binds us together.

Thirdly, we believe that change comes, and we are glad that it does, and it should come through peaceful process. But revolution in any country is a matter for that country to deal with. It becomes a matter calling for hemispheric action only—and I repeat, only—when the object is the establishment of a communistic dictatorship.

Let me also make clear that we support no single man or single group of men in the Dominican Republic. Our goal is a simple one: we are there to save the lives of our people and to save the lives of all people. Our goal, in keeping with the principles of the American system, is to help prevent another communist State in this hemisphere, and we should like to do this without bloodshed or without large-scale fighting.

The form and the nature of a free Dominican Government, I assure you, is solely a matter for the Dominican People. But we do know what kind of government we hope to see in the Dominican Government, for that is carefully spelled out in the treaties and agreements which make up the fabric of the entire inter-American system. It is expressed time and again in the words of our statesmen and the values and hopes which bind us all together. We hope to see a government freely chosen by the will of all the people. We hope to see a government working every hour of every day feeding the hungry, educating the ignorant, healing the sick, a government whose only concern is the progress, the elevation and the welfare of all the people of that country. . . .

[On 4 May the USSR delegation submitted a draft resolution whereby the Security Council would condemn "the armed intervention by the United States in the domestic affairs of the Dominican Republic as a gross violation of the Charter of the United Nations," and demand "the immediate withdrawal of the armed forces of the United States from the territory of the Dominican Republic." S/6328 (4 May 1965); SCOR, XX, Mtg. 1198, pp. 1–2.]

Mr. VELAQUEZ (Uruguay): .   .   .   With the news of the serious events occurring in the Dominican Republic during the last week of April, and in particular the landing by a force of 400 United States Marines for the declared purpose of carrying out a humanitarian operation of protection and rescue, the Council of the OAS, acting on a proposal by the Government of Venezuela, decided to call a Meeting of Consultation of Ministers of Foreign Affairs of the American States. I should like to point out that this Meeting was not convened under article 6 of the Inter-American Treaty of Reciprocal Assistance (Treaty of Rio de Janeiro), which authorizes the convening of the Organ of Consultation in the event of aggression or any other fact or situation that might endanger the peace of America, but under article 39 of the charter of OAS, that is, "in order to consider problems of an urgent nature and of common interest to the American States". .   .   .

My country opposed the request to convene the Meeting of Consultation, on the ground that the regional organization was not authorized to take action in respect of the civil conflict taking place in the Dominican Republic, since it was a matter that came exclusively within the domestic jurisdiction of that State. The information available at the time gave no reason to consider the situation capable of threatening the peace or security of other States in the continent. Nevertheless, the United States forces having already been landed, Uruguay announced, through its representative in the OAS, the displeasure of the Uruguayan Government, based on the traditional and unalterable principles of its foreign policy, at any intervention of the kind that had taken place, which could not be regarded as authorized or justified under existing international norms. .   .   .

When the meeting was convened, Uruguay first reiterated these fundamental reservations and again repudiated the acts of intervention carried out in contravention of articles 15 and 17 of the OAS charter. It then voted in favour of the draft resolution establishing a mediation commission on the understanding that the inquiry which was to be one of its tasks should not extend into matters which continued to rest within the sole jurisdiction of the Dominican people, but should primarily concern the grave armed situation which had arisen owing to the landing of forces of an American State.

My country's position rests squarely within the strictest juridical tradition of Latin America. The charter of the Organization of American States, adopted in 1948, represents the culmination of a long and sometimes arduous process aimed at formalizing certain basic guarantees without which inter-American comity faced the danger, as history had demonstrated, of falling either into anarchy or under the despotic rule of the strongest. And the very heart of that whole system of guarantees was to be the principle of non-intervention.
.   .   .

As a result of this whole process, therefore, agreement was reached on a text, article 15 of the OAS charter, which prohibits in the most explicit and categorical manner any form of intervention, direct or indirect, by one State or by a group of States, for any reason whatever—let me repeat, for any reason whatever—in the internal or external affairs of any other contracting State. The article goes on to say that this principle prohibits not only armed force, the most visible form of intervention, but also any other form of interference or attempted threat against the personality of the State or against its political, economic and cultural elements.

Article 17, in turn, provides that the territory of an American State is inviolable; it may not be the object, even temporarily, of military occupation or of other measures of force taken by another State, directly or indirectly, on any grounds whatever—I repeat, on any grounds whatever.

The American States agreed that the only situation in which the principle of non-intervention might not be rigidly applied—and hence this is an exceptional rule which must accordingly be subject to restrictive interpretation—relates to measures which, again, are adopted in accordance with existing treaties, that is, which are adopted multilaterally through the Organ of Consultation convened previously and in due form, and only in such cases as are stipulated in article 6 of the Treaty of Rio de Janeiro.

In a message broadcast on the evening of 2 May 1965, the President of the United States explained to his people certain aspects of the situation in the Dominican Republic and offered what I think was implicitly an interpretation of the principles which I mentioned, and to which he referred as the principles of the inter-American system. This Johnson doctrine—as it is now being called—or, if you prefer, this new corollary of the Monroe Doctrine, is not, as indeed President Monroe's doctrine was not, either a strictly legal doctrine or an American doctrine, if we use the word "American" in its original sense, that is, applying to all the peoples of the Western hemisphere. It cannot be regarded as a legal doctrine, for the idea it embodies— that while revolutions are *prima facie* the internal affair of countries and for them alone to deal with, they cease to be so and become matters calling for hemispheric action when their object is to establish a communist dictatorship—seems to go beyond the body of norms existing in the inter-American system and constitutes, in its spirit and letter, a notion which my delegation cannot regard as consistent with the principle of self-determination of peoples.   .   .   .

In the statement made yesterday by the representative of the United States, to which I listened with the attention which his statements always deserve, some reservations were expressed, not perhaps about the competence of the Council, but at any rate about the existence of what we might term an overriding competence of the regional bodies.

While I do not intend to embark on a doctrinaire or theoretical discussion, I wish to state that my delegation has no doubts as to the competence of the Security Council to inquire now and in the future into any dispute or situation the continuation of which may be a threat to the maintenance of peace and international security, even if the dispute is at the time under consideration by a regional body. This authority, which the provisions of Article 52, paragraph 4, and Articles 34 and 35 of the Charter of the United Nations clearly confer upon the Council, is even more appropriate when the situation involved appears prima facie to contravene international law and, in particular, Article 2, paragraphs 4 and 7, of the Charter of the United Nations and articles 15 and 17 of the charter of the Organization of American States. . . .

There are, it is true, a number of precedents; examination of the more recent precedents will show, however, that they are not derived from identical cases. For example, when in July 1960 the Security Council heard a complaint by Cuba against the United States of America, a resolution, under which it was decided to adjourn the consideration of the question pending the receipt of a report from the Organization of American States, was adopted without a dissenting vote. At the same time, the members of that organization were invited to lend their assistance towards the achievement of a peaceful solution and all States were urged in the meantime to refrain from any action which might increase the existing tensions. The two sponsors of the resolution, Argentina and Ecuador, nevertheless made an explicit reservation to the effect that the resolution was not intended either to deny the Security Council's competence to consider the complaint or to settle the legal question of which of the two organs, the world Organization or the regional body, should first take action. The resolution noted that the question was already under consideration by the OAS and that it therefore seemed desirable to hear the latter's views so that the Council might be in a better position to assess the problems under discussion. As the representative of Ecuador said, by taking this action the Council would not only not restrict its competence but would be exercising it.

When a further question raised by the same Government was dealt with in December of the same year, the Latin American members of the Council, Ecuador and Chile, submitted a draft resolution making specific recommendations to the Governments of Cuba and of the United States of America. Although this draft was not voted on, since it did not receive the necessary support from the parties to which it was directly addressed, the view that the Council was fully competent to deal with the matter was reaffirmed.

Finally—and I am now referring to the most recent precedent—in January 1964, following the events and incidents which occurred in the Panama Canal Zone and when the regional organization had already taken direct action, the Security Council accepted without question a suggestion by the representative of Brazil that certain emergency measures should be taken to strengthen the action of the regional organization. The representative of Brazil stated that both the Security Council and OAS should strive to maintain peace and to establish a harmonious and just settlement between the parties. At the conclusion of the debate the Council approved the Brazilian proposal and authorized the President to address an appeal to the Governments of the United States and Panama to bring an end to the exchange of fire and bloodshed.

These precedents and others which undoubtedly exist but which I have not had time to examine are evidence that intervention by the Security Council in exercise of the powers and responsibilities conferred on it by the Charter has never been questioned and that consequently the question before us must be decided solely in the light of practical considerations, that is to say, as a matter of political prudence and not of principle. .   .   .

In the light of what I have said, one possible course of action might be for the Council to request that all unilateral action should cease immediately. Another might be for the Council to lend its moral authority to the cease-fire and to the re-establishment of normal conditions so as to enable the Dominican people, once and for all, to exercise its sovereign right of self-determination fully and freely, without threats or coercion. Another possible and, in my view, desirable course would be to support and continue to support the regional organization in its present efforts and in any legitimate measures it may decide to take in the future. .   .   .

Respect for law and the primacy of the rule of law in the conduct of international affairs represent the only way of safeguarding the ideals of culture, liberty and dignity. There is no civilization without law, as there is no liberty without law. The suggestion that in order to re-establish democracy and liberty we should violate the law and open the door to arbitrary action is therefore both paradoxical and extremely dangerous for the very ideals we are trying to defend. We can only hope that this will be realized in time and that the tragically mistaken course which now looms ahead may be abandoned, so that the cordial relations which have hitherto existed among the countries of the Western hemisphere may continue. .   .   .

Mr. ALVAREZ TABIO (Cuba): .   .   . Article 34 of the Charter confers on the Security Council power to investigate any international dispute or situation which, as in the case of the aggression against the Dominican Republic, clearly represents a threat to every member of the international community. Article 34 does not tell us that a distinction must be drawn between sources of friction which occur in areas in which there is a regional agency and those which occur in regions in which no such agency exists, or that, in the first case, the Council shall not take cognizance of such disputes but may take action only in the second case. This would virtually divest the Council of part of its authority, on which, we repeat, the Charter places no restriction whatsoever. Accordingly, any attempt to deny the Security Council's competence to investigate situations such as this or to make its action contingent upon decisions of the regional agency is both dangerous and presumptuous, since there is no legal basis at all for it. Chapter VIII of the Charter of the United Nations does, however, contain very clear provisions about relations between, and the relative status of, the regional agencies and this principal organ of the United Nations. Our only reason for stressing these provisions is the insistence of the United States on basing its position on Article 52.

Although the Charter states, in Article 52, that none of its provisions precludes the existence of regional agencies, it nowhere acknowledges that they have primary responsibility, much less sole responsibility, for dealing with any threats to international peace and security which may arise in the area concerned. On the contrary, paragraph 4 of Article 52 provides that the Article "in no way impairs the application of Articles 34 and 35", the Articles to which I have already referred.

If this were not considered sufficient, Chapter VIII contains other provisions, such as Articles 53 and 54, which reaffirm the natural and logical subordination of the regional agency to the recommendations and decisions of its superior, the Security Council. The United States. representative mentions reports by the OAS to the Council. In view of possible misinterpretations, it must be stressed that the information which the regional agencies must supply to the Council on activities undertaken or in contemplation for the maintenance of international peace and security, in accordance with Article 54, is not and cannot be an adequate substitute for the Council's direct cognizance of the question, which it may undertake whenever it deems it necessary. In fact, under the provisions of Article 36 of the Charter, the Security Council may take cognizance of a situation or dispute "at any stage" and may "recommend appropriate procedures or methods of adjustment": cases which are under consideration by a regional agency are not excluded. This is made even more clear in the cases referred to in Articles 39, 40, 41 and 42.

There is therefore nothing in the provisions of Chapters VI and VII of the Charter on which the United States delegation can justifiably base a restrictive interpretation of the powers of the Security Council simply on the ground that one of the parties—in this case, as it happens, the aggressor—has had recourse to the regional agency in order to cover up its arbitrary actions. If an aggressor could prevent the United Nations Security Council from being seized of and from taking decisions with regard to its aggressive actions simply by convening the regional agency, the very foundations of this Organization would crumble.

The reference in Article 33 of the Charter to the participation of regional agencies in the pacific settlement of international disputes has been quoted as proof of the wisdom of having recourse to such an agency and awaiting its settlements in the present case. Apart from the fact that this step is recommended as something to which the parties have recourse only if they think it advisable—it should be noted that the Article says "shall . . . seek a solution"—this injunction is contained in the Chapter of the Charter which treats of the unrestricted powers of the Security Council to take cognizance of any situation or dispute which may endanger international peace and security and cannot therefore be considered as limiting the powers of the Council in this case, but rather as reaffirming its competence if, for one reason or another, resort to the regional agency has utterly failed to reduce existing tension or solve the problem of the aggression in question.

The reference made by the United States representative to Article 33 is therefore inconsistent and the only thing he can do is to admit that its provisions do not diminish the authority of the Council. It might be well to state that it is useless to invoke precedents.

To summarize: first, any Member of the United Nations, whether or not it is a member of one of the regional agencies referred to in Article 52 of the Charter, is entitled under Article 35, paragraph 1, of the Charter to bring to the attention of the Security Council any situation likely to endanger the peace and security of the international community, irrespective of whether or not the Member is directly involved in the situation; second, the Council, under Article 34, is fully empowered to take cognizance of such situations at any stage, as provided in Article 36; third, the result of the Council's investigation may be either the recommendations mentioned in Chapter VI or the measures referred to in Chapter VII of the Charter of the United Nations; fourth, the fact that a regional agency has under consideration a situation or dispute as dangerous as the present one must in no way restrict the powers granted by all the Member States to the Security Council under Article 24 of the Charter, which defines the Council as the organ having primary responsibility for the maintenance of international peace and security, which acts on behalf of all—whether or not they are members of regional agencies or are directly involved in the situation in question—in carrying out its duties under this responsibility.

In support of this opinion I should like to quote from the introduction to the Annual Report of the Secretary-General to the ninth session of the General Assembly:

"For example, the importance of regional arrangements in the maintenance of peace is fully recognized in the Charter and the appropriate use of such arrangements is encouraged. But in those cases where resort to such arrangements is chosen in the first instance, that choice should not be permitted to cast any doubt on the ultimate responsibility of the United Nations. Similarly, a policy giving full scope to the proper role of regional agencies can and should at the same time fully preserve the right of a Member nation to a hearing under the Charter." . . .

Once again, I wish to emphasize a point I made yesterday: the only foundation on which the United Nations can stand is unlimited respect for the principles of the sovereign equality of nations, non-intervention in their internal affairs and the self-determination of peoples. If those principles can be violated at will by a great imperialist Power, the United Nations will lose its *raison d'être* and die ingloriously like its predecessor, the League of Nations.

Consequently, in the name of the Revolutionary Government of Cuba, I once again urge the Security Council, as the supreme international organ whose decisions take precedence over those of any regional agency, to condemn in the strongest terms what is occurring in the territory of the Dominican Republic, a sovereign State, a Member of the United Nations, and to demand the immediate withdrawal of United States troops from that country.

NOTE. The Special Committee of the OAS, appointed on 1 May 1965, recommended on 4 May 1965 that "a combined inter-American military force under the Organization of American States" be established; and on 5 May 1965 the Military Junta and the "Constitutional Government" of Col. Francisco Caamaño Deno signed the "Act of Santo Domingo" embodying a comprehensive cease-fire agreement and an undertaking by the parties to recognize the full competence of the Special Committee "for purposes of the faithful observance" of that Act. S/6364 (18 May 1965), Annex; SCOR, XX, Supp. for April–June 1965, p. 130, at 139–41.

2.   *Establishment of an Inter-American Force.*

Resolution of the Tenth Meeting of Consultation of the Ministers of Foreign Affairs, 6 May 1965. Adopted by 15 votes to 5 (Chile, Ecuador, Mexico, Peru, Uruguay), with 1 abstention (Venezuela). 52 DSB (1965), pp. 862–63; SCOR, XX, Mtg. 1202, pp. 7–9.

Whereas:

This Meeting at its session of May 1, established a Committee to proceed to the Dominican Republic to seek the re-establishment of peace and normal conditions in the territory of that republic;

The said resolution requests the American governments and the General Secretariat of the Organization of American States to extend their full cooperation to facilitate the work of the Committee;

The formation of an inter-American force will signify *ipso facto* the transformation of the forces presently in Dominican territory into another force that will not be that of one state or of a group of states but that of the Organization of American States, which Organization is charged with the responsibility of interpreting the democratic will of its members;

The American states being under the obligation to provide reciprocal assistance to each other, the Organization is under greater obligation to safeguard the principles of the Charter and to do everything possible so that in situations such as that prevailing in the Dominican Republic appropriate measures may be taken leading to the re-establishment of peace and normal democratic conditions;

The Organization of American States being competent to assist the member states in the preservation of peace and the re-establishment of normal democratic conditions, it is also competent to provide the means that reality and circumstances require and that prudence counsels as adequate for the accomplishment of such purposes; and

The Committee of the Organization of American States that proceeded to the Dominican Republic, in its second report to this Meeting, advises the formation of an inter-American force to achieve the objectives determined by the Meeting of Consultation.

The Tenth Meeting of Consultation of Ministers of Foreign Affairs Resolves:

1. To request governments of member states that are willing and capable of doing so to make contingents of their land, naval, air or police forces available to the Organization of American States, within their capabilities and to the extent they can do so, to form an inter-American force that will operate under the authority of this Tenth Meeting of Consultation.

2. That this Force will have as its sole purpose, in a spirit of democratic impartiality, that of cooperating in the restoration of normal conditions in the Dominican Republic, in maintaining the security of its inhabitants and the inviolability of human rights, and in the establishment of an atmosphere of peace and conciliation that will permit the functioning of democratic institutions.

3. To request the commanders of the contingents of forces that make up this Force to work out directly among themselves and with a Committee of this Meeting the technical measures necessary to establish a Unified Command of the Organization of American States for the coordinated and effective action of the Inter-American Armed Force. In the composition of this Force, an effort will be made to see that the national contingents shall be progressively equalized.

4. That at such time as the OAS Unified Command shall have determined that the Inter-American Armed Force is adequate for the purposes contemplated by the resolution adopted by this Meeting on May 1, 1965, the full responsibility of meeting these purposes shall be assumed by that Force.

5.   That the withdrawal of the Inter-American Force from the Dominican Republic shall be determined by this Meeting.

6.   To continue in session in order to keep the situation under review, to receive the report and recommendations of the Committee, and in the light thereof to take the necessary steps to facilitate the prompt restoration of democratic order in the Dominican Republic.

7.   To inform the Security Council of the United Nations of the text of this resolution.

3.   *Discussion in the Security Council, 7–11 May 1965.*

SCOR, XX, Mtgs. 1203–4.

Mr. DE BEUS (Netherlands):   .   .   .   The question on which my delegation would like to concentrate its attention is: what organization is competent from the legal point of view, and is most apt from the practical point of view, to bring about a speedy improvement inside the Dominican Republic, and is most able to provide a framework which will allow the Dominican people to arrive freely at a democratic solution safeguarding its rights of self-determination?

It is a long-standing tradition that conflicts arising in the Western hemisphere not involving outside Powers be dealt with primarily by the countries themselves, of that hemisphere, which means, in practice, by the Organization of American States. My country has always respected this tradition and should like to do so again in this case.

That conflicts in the Western hemisphere are primarily handled by the Organization of American States is not only a tradition, but is also in conformity with the stipulations of the Charter of the United Nations. In two places the Charter stipulates that parties to a dispute should first of all seek a peaceful solution through regional agencies or arrangements. One place is Article 33, paragraph 1, which states that parties to any dispute shall, first of all, seek a solution by one of several means, enunciated in that Article, and one of those specifically mentioned is resort to regional agencies or arrangements.

The other place where the Charter says the same thing, but in other words, is Article 52, paragraph 2, which states:

"The Members of the United Nations entering into such arrangements or constituting such agencies shall make every effort to achieve pacific settlement of local disputes through such regional arrangements or by such regional agencies before referring them to the Security Council."

The Charter then goes on to impose upon the Security Council the duty to encourage this specific form of settlement through regional arrangements. In paragraph 3 of Article 52, we read:

"The Security Council shall encourage the development of pacific settlement of local disputes through such regional arrangements or by such regional agencies either on the initiative of the states concerned or by reference from the Security Council."

From Articles 33 and 52 of the Charter it seems clear to us that the first and normal way to try to solve a dispute in the Western hemisphere is through the Organization of American States. This does not mean—and I should like there to be no misunderstanding on this subject—that my delegation denies the competence of the Security Council to take cognizance of such a dispute and to make, if necessary, recommendations in respect thereof. That, we believe, follows from paragraph 4 of Article 52, which reads: "This Article in no way impairs the application of Articles 34 and 35"—which deal with the role of the Security Council.

It is, therefore, perfectly correct that this matter was raised before the Security Council, and that the Council is now discussing it. The Council should, however, in our opinion, keep in mind the self-limitation which follows from both the letter and the spirit of the Charter. The meaning of the Charter, it seems to my delegation, is perfectly clear from the Articles which I quoted; that is, the Security Council is fully competent to consider all disputes which might endanger international peace and security, but a solution of such a dispute should in the first place, as the Charter says, be solved through resort to a regional organization where such an organization exists.

Whilst, therefore, both tradition and the Charter point to the Organization of American States as the body most qualified to handle the present dispute in the Western hemisphere, practical considerations, too, lead to the same conclusion since the OAS has already taken the matter in hand.

A five-man committee of the Organization of American States has been active for almost a week on the island to bring about a cease-fire, and on 5 May 1965 we were informed that, on that very day, a second and definite cease-fire had been concluded in Santo Domingo under the auspices of the OAS.

Furthermore, the Ministers of Foreign Affairs of the Organization of America States, as we have been informed, decided on 6 May 1965:

"To request Governments of member States that are willing and capable of doing so to make contingents of their land, naval, air or police forces available to the Organization of American States . . . to form an inter-American force . . . under the authority of this Tenth Meeting of Consultation."

We have also taken note with satisfaction of the statement made, with the authority of President Johnson, by the United States representative to Organization of American States, declaring that:

" . . . when the unified command of the Organization of American States determines that the Inter-American Armed Force is adequate for the purposes contemplated by the resolution adopted by this body on May 1st and that the United States forces are not needed as part of the Inter-American Armed Force, they will be withdrawn from the Dominican Republic."

These results may not solve the whole matter but they are, all the same, important results achieved by the Organization of American States within the first week; they give hope that that Organization will be able to handle this difficult and extremely explosive situation satisfactorily.

For all these reasons which I have mentioned—tradition, the text of the Charter of the United Nations, and practical considerations— my delegation believes that the Security Council should, in compliance with Article 52, paragraph 3, which I have just quoted, encourage, in the words of the Charter, the settlement of this local dispute through regional arrangements, which means in this case through the Organization of American States.

In the meantime, we believe that the Council should keep the matter on its agenda and could discuss it again if the efforts of the Organization of American States should fail to bring about a satisfactory solution. Furthermore, it would be desirable in our opinion if the Secretary-General of the Organization of American States could, in conformity with Article 54 of the Charter, keep the Security Council informed of the negotiations, the decisions and the progress of the OAS.   .   .   .

Mr. ALVAREZ TABIO (Cuba): I had not intended to speak again in this debate, as I thought it had been concluded. The events which have occurred during the last twenty-four hours, however, introduce new factors which have not yet been considered. I am referring to the recent decisions of the Organ of Consultation of OAS.   .   .   .

Yesterday the OAS, after a painful delivery which called for the use of forceps, gave birth to a monster: nothing more or less than the transformation of the invading United States troops, after the crime was committed, into international peace forces.   .   .   .

The Security Council has to consider and decide three essential questions: first, whether, as the draft resolution submitted by the representative of the Soviet Union asserts, the unilateral action taken by the Government of the United States in landing troops on the territory of a sovereign State and Member of this Organization, constitutes a violation of the principles of the United Nations Charter and is therefore a punishable international crime; second, whether the OAS resolution can confer validity *ex post facto* on an action branded as illegal by the law of nations; third, whether, if the possibility of conferring validity *a posteriori* on an action which was originally illegal and void is admitted for the sake of argument, the OAS acting independently and on its own initiative, can implement decisions which involve the organization of a self-styled regional peace force without the authorization of the Security Council.

Let us consider each of these questions separately. . . .

I should first of all like to quote the opinion of the eminent Czech internationalist, Professor Jaroslav Zourek, former Chairman of the United Nations International Law Commission. Professor Zourek says, in his monograph "The prohibition of the use of force as a national policy in international law":

"Other authors, too, have emerged who, following the example of some delegations at San Francisco in their exaggerated fear that any specific reference to the use of force might have restrictive effects, have attempted to deduce from the wording of this provision of Article 2, paragraph 4, the very dangerous inference that force—and armed force, in particular—may be used in those cases in which the aggressor State is not interested in taking possession of foreign territory and in which the occupation is carried out with the object of securing temporary objectives. . . . This theory is quite wrong and clearly absurd. There can be no doubt that the occupation of even the smallest part of the territory of a State without its consent constitutes an attack on its territorial integrity and on its political independence. . . . The only exception to the rule is self-defence against armed aggression by another State."

The professor continues, in words which are specially relevant to the case under discussion:

"To condone any contrary practice would be tantamount to legalizing aggression whenever the aggressor declares that his intention is not to violate the territorial integrity or political independence of the State attacked. . . . We should have to admit that there was a real possibility that the use of force, even of armed force, is compatible with the purposes and aims of the United Nations." . . .

Can there then be any doubt about the illegality of the actions of the United States Government, whatever its purpose may have been in invading the territory of the Dominican Republic? In penal law, motive does not justify or absolve from guilt. At most, it is a circumstance which extenuates guilt. The person who kills for humanitarian reasons is guilty of a crime, although the court may recognize some extenuating circumstance. In the present case, however, the motive adduced by the United States Government is universally branded as fallacious. The evacuation of United States citizens was an operation which was completed in a few hours. . . .

With regard to the other motive, that of saving Dominican democracy from international communism, we all know this old imperialist trick. In any event, what right has the United States Government to set itself up as judge of which ideology is to predominate in this continent? . . .

I now turn to the second question which the Security Council has to decide: whether the OAS resolution can, *ex post facto,* confer validity on an act which current international law brands as illegal and immoral.

Once again, I feel I must draw attention to another aspect of this question, namely the questionable extrinsic validity of the OAS decisions. In this connexion, I submit that the OAS decisions are extrinsically null and void simply because they were not taken in accordance with the mandatory provisions set forth in that organization's own rules of procedure. Under rule 12 of the rules of procedure concerning consultative meetings, a two-thirds majority is required, which explains the efforts of the United States to obtain the essential "fourteenth vote".

In the voting on the decisions under discussion, the fourteenth vote, the casting-vote, was that of the gentleman who formerly represented the Reid Cabral régime at Washington, the régime which was overthrown over a fortnight ago. How is it possible to claim that that gentleman represents a régime which no longer exists? What credentials authorize that gentleman to be the representative of the Dominican State? Credentials issued by Colonel Wessin, we presume. And what authority can Wessin have but the authority of United States guns? . . .

Let us now consider the substantive aspect of this second question. The decisions of the OAS are also completely null and void so far as their substance is concerned, because they openly violate the most important articles of the charter of Bogota. . . .

Article 1 of the charter of the OAS lays down as one of the basic purposes of the organization that of defending the sovereignty, territorial integrity and independence of the American States; how then can the same organization create a so-called "inter-American force" consisting of the very forces which, by their presence on Dominican soil, have been violating the sovereignty, territorial integrity and independence of a member State? . . .

The force in question, moreover, by reason both of its political objectives and of its composition, is incompatible with respect for the personality, sovereignty and independence of a member State, thus contradicting the specific affirmation of these principles in article 5(b) of the OAS charter as pillars of international order.

This illegally created force obviously represents a flagrant violation of article 5(e) and (f) of the charter, which, in addition to condemning aggressive war, states that an act of aggression against one American State is an act of aggression against all of them. Is it possible to conceive of any greater contempt for international law than when the OAS, instead of condemning the aggressor country—that is to say, the United States of America—assigns to the United States expeditionary forces the task of "the restoration of normal conditions in the Dominican Republic" and of "maintaining the security of its inhabitants and the inviolability of human rights . . . "—the rights of these same Dominicans who have been the victims of United States bullets?

Since, according to articles 7 and 8 of the OAS charter, "Every American State has the duty to respect the rights enjoyed by every other State in accordance with international law", and these "fundamental rights . . . may not be impaired in any manner whatsoever", the resolution . . . is illegal on two counts: in that it assigns the task in question to forces which, for ten days, have been encroaching on the sovereignty and territorial integrity of the Dominican Republic, and also in that the new form which the OAS is attempting to give to this military presence is a violation of the right of self-determination of the Dominican people, which has not had a voice in the decision and has not requested such a military presence.

The violation of article 15 of the Bogotá charter is still more glaring, and baffles all description. In that article, the member States agreed that "No State or group of States"—and I repeat, "group of States"—"has the right to intervene, directly or indirectly, for any reason whatever"—and, I repeat, "for any reason whatever—in the internal or external affairs of any other State."

Thus it is clear that the OAS charter does not authorize any group of its members to do what it prohibits each of them from doing individually. From the point of view of so-called "inter-American law" —if anything remains of it—such intervention covers both the unilateral intervention of the United States and the supposedly collective intervention now being attempted. Perhaps this is the point at which the invalidity of this legal monstrosity of the gentlemen of the OAS is most flagrant.

But this is not all. The inviolability of the territory of a State and the unlawfulness of its military occupation or of other measures of force taken against it, even temporarily, on any grounds whatever, are laid down by the regional organization in article 17 of its charter. It is obvious that the resolution under consideration makes a mockery of this principle, since it not only attempts to justify the earlier unilateral violation of Dominican territory and its military occupation but also proposes that it should be continued indefinitely, or, as is said in operative paragraph 5, until such time as the OAS Meeting shall determine. This is in addition to the absurdity—and it needs to be repeated—that it is still the troops of the aggressor country itself which have to carry out this "continental" assignment.

Let me now quote the text of article 18 of the OAS charter. It reads as follows: "The American States bind themselves in their international relations not to have recourse to the use of force, except in the case of self-defense in accordance with existing treaties or in fulfillment thereof."

There is no doubt as to the interpretation of this provision: the sole exception to the prohibition of the use of force sanctioned by inter-American law is self-defence, which implies, we must presume, that there must have been an earlier armed attack against one or more of the members of the "inter-American community", and it is clear that this did not occur in the case under discussion. In this matter the OAS charter is consistent with the principle embodied in Article 51 of the Charter of the United Nations; and since the regional organization ranks lower than the world Organization, this could not be otherwise.

In providing for an armed presence on the territory of a member State, the resolution adopted yesterday morning at Washington not only violates this cardinal principle of the Bogotá charter but also constitutes a frontal attack on the principles of the United Nations Charter, as I said before.

Leaving aside those principles of the United Nations Charter which, as we pointed out earlier, were violated from the beginning by the presence of United States troops at Santo Domingo, and which therefore must be regarded as violated once again by this would-be "continentalization" of the act of aggression, the resolution adopted yesterday by the OAS seriously challenges the Charter of our Organization.

Operative paragraph 1 of the resolution provides that forces contributed by member States "will operate under the authority of this Tenth Meeting of Consultation", the technical term for the meeting which, to America's shame, has been taking place for some days in the capital of the United States. In addition, as I said before, operative paragraph 5 states that "the withdrawal of the Inter-American Force from the Dominican Republic shall be determined by this Meeting".

The attempt to establish this so-called multilateral operation, and the two paragraphs which we have just cited, create grave dangers for the constitutional order of the United Nations and constitute a permanent threat to the sovereignty of all the States of Latin America.

Let us now consider the third question which I raised. Even if we admit, for the sake of argument, that the Washington decisions are valid from both the formal and the substantive points of view, can the OAS carry out such decisions without the authorization of the Security Council?

The Organization of American States, as a regional organization, is not authorized to decide upon enforcement action, and still less to implement such decisions, without the authorization of the Security Council. The latter is the only international body having authority to use force. I shall not read out Articles 52 and 53 of the United Nations Charter, as they are well known.

The only argument which the United States representative could find in order to deny the applicability of these rules in the present case is indeed a weak one, namely that, in this case, the point at issue is simply the peaceful settlement of a dispute.

In the first place, the so-called dispute was not originally international in character. At the beginning it was a private matter among the Dominican people themselves; it became an international conflict precisely as a result of the arbitrary intervention of the United States armed forces. In the second place, the invasion of the territory of a sovereign country by a foreign State is not simply a dispute or controversy among States which can be settled by *ad hoc* machinery. The provisions of the OAS charter cannot be invoked in support of intervention in an internal problem of a sovereign State; they could only have been invoked in this case in order to condemn the United States Government for its arbitrary action in invading the territory of the Dominican Republic without any justification other than the argument that "might is right".

What doubt can there be that the arbitrary acts of the United States Government in invading the territory of another State, acts on which the OAS is now trying to confer validity, constitute acts of force in the eyes of the law?

The United States Government has played the role of the "hired bully" in this case, except that what we are discussing is not a street brawl but the case of a sovereign State which has not vested the United States with authority to settle its domestic disputes. The United States simply plays the local bully and lords it over its weaker neighbours through brute force and coercion.

When a lawfully constituted authority uses force in any dispute, it is fulfilling a duty under the law. When, however, a third party uses force in a neighbour's house, this is not the exercise of lawful authority but a criminal act. The use of coercion or violence is the exclusive prerogative of the authorities legally constituted for the purpose, and in any case a private domicile may not be entered without the authorization of the occupant or an order from the competent authority.

Neither the United States Government nor the OAS is authorized to use force under codified international law. The former is expressly prohibited from using force in any circumstances by the United Nations Charter, and the latter may not use it without the authorization of the Security Council. The rule is perfectly clear: no enforcement action shall be taken under regional arrangements or by regional agencies without the authorization of the Security Council.

Even if we could agree, which we cannot, that the OAS can decide upon enforcement action against a member State in connexion with a purely internal question—a question which in no way affects international peace and security and is therefore not a matter appropriate for regional action under Article 52 of the Charter—the OAS still could not implement such a decision without the authorization of the Security Council, the only international body vested with authority to use force.

It hardly needs stressing that to categorize the invasion of a sovereign State as a measure for maintaining peace is highly dangerous. The peaceful settlement of a dispute presupposes an agreement entered into voluntarily by the parties to the dispute, parties which must of course be sovereign States. But here the dispute was an internal conflict among Dominicans. The action of the United States first, and then of the OAS, involves the use of armed force and, without a shadow of doubt, constitutes enforcement action for the simple reason that it represents an attempt to impose by force a particular line of conduct on an independent and sovereign State which has not even been accused of aggression. Any State on which particular decisions are imposed is being deprived, against its will, of all the prerogatives normally protected by international law, such as sovereignty, independence, the inviolability of its territory, and freedom to choose whatever political, economic and social system it wishes.

The OAS cannot act in such a way as to impair the rights and obligations of States Members of the United Nations, not only because this is expressly laid down in article 10 of the Treaty of Rio de Janeiro but also because Article 103 of the Charter of the United Nations provides that, in the event of a conflict of obligations, their obligations under the Charter shall prevail. It cannot be contended, therefore, that the OAS, turning its back on the Security Council, can decide upon, much less apply, any coercive measures or enforcement action against an American State, whatever the reason or pretext adduced.

The United States Government, with the assistance of the doubtful majority which it has managed to obtain in the OAS, has tried to use the latter body as a new "Holy Alliance" directed against the self-determination of peoples. It seems that the failure of the "Holy Alliance" of the nineteenth century has not served as a warning to it not to seek to resurrect such an alliance in the middle of the twentieth century.

To sum up and in conclusion, we maintain that the Security Council should take action on the following aspects: (a) the unilateral action of the United States in the Dominican Republic constitutes a flagrant violation of international law and of the sovereignty, independence and inviolability of Dominican territory; (b) the OAS decisions, under a universal rule of law, are null and void *ab initio*, and neither time nor confirmation at a later date can confer validity on what is null and void from the outset; (c) in any case, the OAS decisions cannot be implemented without the authorization of the Security Council; (d) when an act which was completely null and void at the outset has been consummated, in accordance with an old rule with which everyone is familiar, the *status quo antes* must be re-established; (e) the Government of the United States must be ordered to evacuate immediately the military forces under its command which are present in the territory of the Dominican Republic—a sovereign State and a Member of this Organization; (f) the OAS must be ordered to refrain from taking any action in implementation of its resolution without the authorization of the Security Council. . . .

Mr. VELAZQUEZ (Uruguay): After several days of consultations and informal talks, after several days of more mature reflection on the problem before the Council, my delegation, on the instructions of its Government, has decided to submit a draft resolution. . . .

The text of the draft resolution is as follows:

"The Security Council,

"Having considered the situation existing in the Dominican Republic,

"Taking note of the communications dated 29 April, 30 April, 1 May, 3 May and 6 May 1965 from the Organization of American States, reporting on the measures taken by that organization in connexion with the situation existing in the Republic,

"Having regard to Articles 24, 34 and 35, and the relevant provisions of Chapter VIII, of the Charter of the United Nations,

"Reaffirming the principles set forth in Chapter I of the Charter of the United Nations and, in particular, in Article 2, paragraphs 4 and 7,

"Having particular regard also to the provisions of articles 15 and 17 of the charter of the Organization of American States,

"1. Expresses its deep concern at the recent developments in the Dominican Republic;

"2. Reaffirms the right of the people of the Dominican Republic freely to exercise, without coercion of any kind, their sovereign right of self-determination;

"3. Urgently appeals to all contending factions in the Dominican Republic to cease hostilities and to make every possible effort to achieve a peaceful and democratic settlement of their differences;

"4. Invites the Secretary-General to follow closely the events in the Dominican Republic and to take such measures as he may deem appropriate for the purpose of reporting to the Security Council on all aspects of the situation;

"5. Invites the Organization of American States to keep the Security Council promptly and fully informed of the action taken by the Organization of American States with respect to the situation existing in the Dominican Republic;

"6. Also invites the Organization of American States to co-operate with the Secretary-General of the United Nations in the implementation of this resolution."

I shall now briefly explain the contents of the text which I read out.

The first preambular paragraph expresses a concern which is shared by all the members of this Council, without exception.

The second preambular paragraph takes note of the communications received by the Council from the regional organization for the Americas. These documents were transmitted to the Council in accordance with the provisions of Article 54 of the Charter, and all Members are familiar with them.

The third preambular paragraph evokes those Articles of the Charter on which the Council must base its competence. As I have said, our concern is to affirm what is the Council's competence without beginning to determine, discuss, consider or question the competence of regional agencies.

During an earlier debate, one or two representatives considered this problem and mentioned provisions which are not referred to in this draft resolution, particularly Article 33 and paragraph 2 of Article 52. In the view of my delegation, it would be inappropriate to mention those Articles, not only because we are confronted with a situation and not a dispute, but also because the temporary priority which those Articles accord to the regional machinery, and which my delegation naturally does not question, relates solely, as it is clear from the Articles themselves, to the type of international dispute amenable to conciliation and pacific settlement, and not to situations like this one, where charges of aggression have been made.

My delegation thinks that, in these cases, it would be inappropriate to mention temporary priority or an obligatory primary jurisdiction. The primary responsibility rests with the organs of the United Nations; however, we preferred to make no mention of this. I think that we may be able to agree among ourselves that, if we wish to affirm the Council's competence—which no one, I repeat, has questioned—these are the Articles we should cite in the draft resolution. These are the Articles on which the Council's authority is based. I should add that, in a spirit of compromise, I preferred to make simply a general reference to Chapter VIII, without mentioning any particular provision of that Chapter that might give rise to a difference of views which, from every standpoint, I wish to avoid.

The two following paragraphs, the fourth and fifth of the preamble, reaffirm cardinal principles of the United Nations; I do not believe that any State could question them. As for their significance, and in particular that of articles 15 and 17 of the charter of the Organization of American States, I have already mentioned this in my first statement [1198th meeting] and I do not think it is necessary to add anything further.

The only point that I wish to make clear, so that it may appear in the record, is that the prohibition contained in Article 2, paragraph

7, of the Charter of the United Nations—namely, the principle of non-intervention—applies both to the Organization and to every one of its Members individually, and with the same force. This we believe, is clear from the preamble of Article 2, which expressly states that "the Organization and its Members"—I repeat, "and its Members"—shall act in accordance with the principles enumerated in the Article.

In the operative part, I do not think that paragraph 1 requires any further explanation.

Operative paragraph 2 is a reaffirmation which we feel it is essential for the Council to make. The right of self-determination is a natural right of all peoples; it is, as it were, a right inherent in their sovereignty which cannot be subject to any kind of restriction, much less, of course, to pressure or coercion by others.

Under operative paragraph 3, the Council will be exercising one of its essential and highest functions, namely, its peace-keeping function. I do not believe that this appeal can be considered an act of intervention in the affairs of the Dominican Republic, and we are sure that it will be favourably received by those to whom it is addressed.

Operative paragraph 4 requests the Secretary-General to take action with a view to providing the Council with the information it needs in order to come to a final decision. This procedure is not novel and was adopted recently without opposition when the Security Council considered the situation in the Congo at the end of 1964. My delegation does not believe, therefore, that the wording of this paragraph can cause any difficulty. The Secretary-General's ability, competence, tact and prudence are beyond all doubt, as is our confidence in him.

Finally, in the last two operative paragraphs, and again in a form similar to other precedents adopted by the Council without objection, the regional organization is invited to continue to inform the Council of all action taken by it with respect to the situation existing in the Dominican Republic—this, I trust, will dispel the misgivings expressed by some of our colleagues—and also to co-operate with the United Nations in the implementation of this resolution. . . .

Mr. STEVENSON (USA): . . . . I have listened most carefully to the statement made by the representative of Uruguay and to the draft resolution which he read out to the Council. . . . I regret to say that, for our part, we cannot agree that the draft resolution proposed by the representative of Uruguay would be helpful at this point.

The Organization of American States is acting vigorously in this case; I do not believe that there can be any dispute about that. Its authority is fully provided for by the Charter of the United Nations, as well as by the OAS charter. It has adopted many decisions. It is due to the action of the Organization of American States that a cease-

fire has been achieved. It is due to the efforts of that regional organization that an investigation has been undertaken and a commission
of good offices appointed. It is due to the efforts of the OAS that an
inter-American force is being established. The Organization of
American States has reported these decisions to the Security Council,
and more reports will doubtless follow.

The draft resolution proposed by the representative of Uruguay
seeks, I am afraid, to interpose the Security Council into the situation
at this time, just when the regional organization seems to be dealing
with the situation effectively. This is not a question of whether the
Security Council may or may not exercise its authority. That certainly is not at issue in any way. The issue is whether the steps taken
by the Organization of American States have been deficient or satisfactory, and, therefore, whether the Security Council should intervene now.

In our view, there is no doubt that the Organization of American
States has acted promptly, effectively and vigorously, and indeed with
a sense of historical movement. The Charter of the United Nations
provides that a regional solution is one of the methods to be sought
first of all. That solution is well under way. We should not be shirking our responsibilities—indeed, we should be following them—if now,
after this long discussion, we were to conclude that the Security Council did not need to interpose itself. This does not mean, of course, that
it could not do so were the situation different and were regional agencies acting improperly or deficiently; it would thus not deprive the
Security Council, as a matter of its own responsibility, of the possibility of action in other situations at earlier stages, or of resuming
its activities in this case if it became necessary to do so.

I suspect that the adoption of the Uruguayan draft resolution would
tend to complicate the activities of the Organization of American
States by encouraging concurrent and independent considerations and
activities by this Council.

There are also some implications in the preambular language of
the draft resolution which would prejudge the situation, imply conclusions which the Organization of American States has not reached
and introduce substantive concepts which would prove contentious.
We do not believe that that would help the situation; indeed, it could
tend to bring the highly contentious atmosphere of world politics, so
sharply manifested in our debates, back into a situation that is now
moving towards a solution. The harsh, Stalinist approach to the
problem that has been introduced into this Council is not encouraging
in that respect.

I suggest that the adoption of this draft resolution would not be
wise and that it might hamper, rather than promote, a solution in the
Dominican Republic which will allow its people to choose their own

government in conditions permitting them to make a free and un-fettered choice.

Our Charter says that the Security Council should encourage—it uses the word "encourage"—pacific settlement of local disputes through regional arrangements. Our view is that if a resolution of some kind should be adopted in order to manifest the admitted competence and concern of the Security Council, the resolution should have no ambiguity, no inferences—especially inferences that the Security Council is not encouraging the regional organization.

NOTE. On 14 May 1965, the United Nations received the following telegram from Mr. Jottin Cury, "Minister for Foreign Affairs of the Constitutional Government of the Dominican Republic" (SCOR, XX, Mtg. 1208, pp. 1–2):

"At this moment, Santo Domingo is the scene of tragic events and is in imminent danger of destruction. This morning, the United States troops advanced on the city, outside their positions in the so-called 'security zone' set up under the Act of Santo Domingo, thus openly violating this Act, which was signed under the auspices of the OAS. The troops of the Constitutionalist armed forces, after first giving warning to the Special Committee of the OAS and the United States authorities, opened fire on certain of the occupation troops stationed outside the security zone which were threatening and carrying out aggression against the Constitutionalist forces. At two o'clock this afternoon, three P–51 aircraft machine-gunned and dropped incendiary bombs on the Santo Domingo radio station, causing many fatalities and damages. These aircraft are attacking again, taking off from the San Isidro air base, which is controlled by the United States occupation troops; this means that the air attacks have been made at least with the consent of the United States forces or on their orders. They are also concentrating troops, tanks and artillery in various positions within the security zone.

"It must be acknowledged with regret that the Organization of American States has shown that it is incapable of resolving the Dominican situation and of opposing the wishes of the United States. The Special Committee has paid no attention to the requests and complaints made by the Constitutionalist Government, including those which led my Government to request intervention by the United Nations Commission on Human Rights. It has merely sought to bring about impossible and improper arrangements, and events have shown that it has no means of controlling the occupation troops. In these circumstances, and in order to prevent the destruction of the city and the slaughter of its heroic inhabitants, we urge your immediate personal intervention to check the attacks by the United States troops and prevent their advance, thus avoiding a catastrophe. At the same time, we request an emergency meeting of the Security Council with a view to action being taken by the United Nations."

The Council adopted promptly Resolution 203 (1965), proposed by Jordan, Malaysia and the Ivory Coast (*ibid.*, p. 3):

"The Security Council,

"Deeply concerned at the grave events in the Dominican Republic,

"1. Calls for a strict cease-fire;

"2.   Invites the Secretary-General to send, as an urgent measure, a representative to the Dominican Republic for the purpose of reporting to the Security Council on the present situation;

"3.   Calls upon all concerned in the Dominican Republic to co-operate with the representative of the Secretary-General in the carrying out of this task."

4.   *Parallel Activities of the UN and the OAS.*

Annual Report of the Secretary-General of the United Nations, 4 August 1965.
GAOR, XX, Supp. 1 (A/6001), pp. 45–49.

REPORTS OF THE SECRETARY-GENERAL

In a report dated 15 May the Secretary-General informed the Council that, pursuant to resolution 203 (1965), he had appointed Mr. José Antonio Mayobre, Executive Secretary of the Economic Commission for Latin American, as his Representative in the Dominican Republic. An advance party, led by Major-General I. J. Rikhye, had arrived in Santo Domingo earlier that day.

On 18 May the Secretary-General further informed the Council that his Representative, after consultations with him in New York, had left for Santo Domingo on 17 May. His Representative's first and most urgent step had been to notify formally all the parties concerned of the Security Council's call for a strict cease-fire. He had also conveyed to all those involved in the conflict in the Dominican Republic the Secretary-General's most pressing and earnest appeal to heed the Council's call for an immediate cessation of hostilities as an essential step in bringing about a propitious atmosphere in which a solution might be found to the grave difficulties facing the Dominican Republic.

A further report, dated on 19 May, stated, *inter alia*, that the Secretary-General's Representative, after arriving in Santo Domingo, had met with leaders of the two factions engaged in the fighting and had informed them of the Secretary-General's appeal. The leaders, General Imbert, President of the "Government of National Reconstruction", and Colonel Caamaño, President of the "Constitutional Government", had given Mr. Mayobre their views on the situation. Mr. Mayobre had also met with the Secretary General of the OAS, the Papal Nuncio, other members of the diplomatic corps and with Mr. McGeorge Bundy and other United States officials. The Secretary-General further reported that late in the evening of 18 May Mr. Mayobre had advised him by telephone of the very serious fighting that had been going on in the northern section of the capital and of the numerous casualties caused in that fighting. It was his assessment that the Imbert forces would continue to press their attack overnight and particularly during the day of 19 May. It had not been possible to persuade General Imbert to agree to a ceasefire, although he had expressed a willingness to agree to a suspension of hostilities some time on 19 May to facilitate the work of the Red Cross in searching for the dead and wounded. In the light of the situation described by his Representative as "extremely grave", and as recommended by him, the Secretary-General had conveyed the above information to the United States Government and had requested it to use its good offices to urge the opposing forces to heed the call of the Security Council for a strict cease-fire.

APPEAL BY THE PRESIDENT OF THE SECURITY COUNCIL

At the meeting of 19 May, the representative of France stated that the Secretary-General's report had confirmed the gravity of the situation in Santo Domingo and the urgency of putting into effect without further delay the truce called for by the International Red Cross for the purpose of evacuating and administering to the wounded. He would suggest that the Secretary-General should instruct his Representative to concentrate his efforts on that point and that the President, on behalf of the Security Council, might make an urgent appeal for a truce.

In a discussion that followed, the suggestion of the representative of France was supported by all members of the Council. Thereupon, the President, with the agreement of the Council, made a statement in which he requested the Secretary-General, in connexion with resolution 203 (1965) and in accordance with the unanimous desire of the members of the Council, to convey to his Representative in Santo Domingo the Security Council's desire that his urgent efforts should be devoted to securing an immediate suspension of hostilities so that the humanitarian work of the Red Cross in searching for the dead and wounded might be facilitated.

REPORT OF THE OAS

On 19 May the Assistant Secretary General of the OAS transmitted for the information of the Security Council copies of the second report of the Special Committee of the Tenth Meeting of Consultation of Ministers of Foreign Affairs. In the report, after reviewing developments in the Dominican Republic since the adoption of its resolutions of 1 and 6 May, the Special Committee stated that it had made every effort to obtain a meeting between the heads of the two conflicting factions, Colonel Caamaño and General Imbert, hoping that such a meeting might help to iron out differences and lead to the re-establishment of normal conditions in the Dominican Republic. The meeting, however, had not taken place and the Committee had re-issued an appeal to the parties demanding strict compliance with the cease-fire agreement. The report also noted that the adoption of resolution 203 (1965) and the appearance of a new international proceeding in the Dominican Republic at a time when the efforts of the OAS for conciliation were being carried forward had created a factor of such a nature that it had compromised and interfered with the action entrusted to the Special Committee. That impact had been felt immediately. The United Nations presence had had an undeniable political effect not only among the diplomatic corps in Santo Domingo but also in the very attitude of the parties, the attention given to the arrival of the Representative of the Secretary-General indicating that they regarded it as a possible element of negotiation in the Dominican situation. It could be said that with the intervention of the United Nations the progress of the negotiations conducted by the Special Committee had been greatly obstructed. In its conclusions the Special Committee stated that since the primary objectives for which it was established had been fulfilled and since new factors had entered into the problem after the adoption of the 1 May resolution, it considered that its mandate had been completed and suggested that the Tenth Meeting of Consultation make another study of the situation and take such measures as might be necessary for the re-establishment of peace and normality. In order that the OAS might achieve its objective within the principles of the inter-American system, the Special Committee felt it essential to request the Security Council to suspend all action until the regional procedures had been exhausted, as established in Article 52, paragraph 2, of the United Nations Charter, and thus avoid simultaneous action on the part of two international organizations in a way that could delay the establishment of peace and normality in the Dominican Republic.

In a minority report, the representative of Panama on the Special Committee stated that he did not consider that the primary objective assigned to the Special Committee in the resolution of 1 May—to bring about the restoration of peace and normality—had yet been accomplished. He believed, therefore, that the suggestion to dissolve the Special Committee would seriously discredit the OAS because it would imply admission of lack of strength and of capacity to solve a problem of a member State which at that moment was being bled by a civil war. The OAS was called upon to solve precisely that kind of problem satisfactorily.

By a telegram dated 20 May, the Assistant Secretary General of the OAS transmitted the text of a resolution adopted that day by the Tenth Meeting of Consultation of Ministers of Foreign Affairs. Under its terms the Tenth Meeting reiterated its gratitude to the Special Committee for its services and entrusted the Secretary General of the OAS with the task of negotiating a strict cease-fire in accordance with the Act of Santo Domingo and providing his good offices to the parties with a view to the establishment of a climate of peace and reconciliation that would permit the functioning of democratic institutions in the Dominican Republic. It also asked the Secretary General of the OAS to co-ordinate, in so far as relevant, action leading to the attainment of his mission with that which the Representative of the Secretary-General of the United Nations was undertaking.

FURTHER REPORTS OF THE SECRETARY-GENERAL

On 20 May, the Secretary-General reported that he had conveyed to his Representative in the Dominican Republic the President's message of 19 May concerning the Security Council's unanimous desire that urgent efforts be made to secure an immediate suspension of hostilities. The Secretary-General asked his Representative to make all possible efforts for the immediate implementation of that message and to report to him as soon as possible on the results.

The Secretary-General also reported that his Representative, on the morning of 19 May prior to the receipt of the President's message, had met with representatives of the Dominican Red Cross, the International Red Cross and the Pan American Sanitary Bureau and suggested that they meet with the leaders of the two factions engaged in the fighting and request a twelve-hour suspension of hostilities to remove the dead and wounded from the battle area. While the leaders of the two factions had agreed in principle that a twelve-hour cease-fire should be imposed on Friday, 21 May, General Imbert had refused to sign a joint agreement with Colonel Caamaño. Thereupon it was decided to prepare separate identical agreements.

On 21 May the Secretary-General reported that he had received further information from his Representative in Santo Domingo to the effect that the negotiations with the leaders of the two factions for suspension of hostilities had been successfully concluded in pursuance of the message of the President of the Security Council of 19 May 1965. An agreement had been reached for the suspension of hostilities for twenty-four hours to begin on Friday, 21 May, at 1200 hours local time. The Secretary-General added that he had expressed to Mr. Mayobre his personal appreciation of the expeditious and highly capable way in which he had been discharging his responsibilities under the mandates of the Security Council. The Secretary-General also placed on record his appreciation of the humanitarian efforts of the representatives of the Dominican Red Cross, the International Red Cross and the Pan American Sanitary Bureau.

FURTHER CONSIDERATION BY THE SECURITY COUNCIL

On 21 May the United States introduced a draft resolution whereby the Security Council would: (1) note with satisfaction the temporary suspension of hostilities agreed to for humanitarian purposes; (2) call for observance of a strict cessation of hostilities; (3) note that the Tenth Meeting of Consultation of the Ministers of Foreign Affairs of the Organization of American States had appointed its Secretary General to represent it in the Dominican Republic and had entrusted him with carrying out the objectives established by the OAS; (4) urge the OAS to intensify its efforts to establish the basis for the functioning of democratic institutions in the Dominican Republic and in particular to assure observance of the cease-fire agreed upon in the Act of Santo Domingo; and (5) request the Secretary-General's Representative, in carrying out the responsibilities assigned to him by the Security Council, to co-ordinate with the Secretary General of the OAS in the light of the OAS resolution of 20 May 1965.

On the same day the representative of Uruguay submitted a revised text of his draft resolution which added to paragraph 1 the words "and the growing deterioration of the situation" and replaced paragraph 3 by a new text calling for immediate compliance with the cease-fire ordered by the Council in resolution 203 (1965) and paragraph 4 by a new text calling upon all States to refrain from supplying the contending factions, directly or indirectly, with facilities or military assistance of any kind and to refrain from any measure which might prevent the restoration of normal living conditions in the country. In a new paragraph the Secretary-General was invited to continue to watch closely the events in the Dominican Republic.

On the morning of 21 May, the Security Council voted on the draft resolution submitted by the USSR. The preamble received 2 votes in favour and 5 against, with 4 abstentions; paragraph 1 received 1 vote in favour and 6 against, with 4 abstentions; and paragraph 2 received 2 votes in favour and 6 against with 3 abstentions. The draft resolution was therefore not adopted.

On the afternoon of the same day, the Secretary-General informed the Council orally that he had received a message from his Representative in Santo Domingo stating that he had completed a tour of the no-man's land between General Imbert's and Colonel Caamaño's forces. While there had been a few scattered shots fired by both sides, the cease-fire was fully effective. The Red Cross, which had succeeded in starting its work early that morning near the fighting zone, had been fully engaged in its humanitarian task. However, he had been advised by the medical staff of the hospitals he had personally visited that another period of twenty-four hours was necessary to evacuate the sick and wounded to less congested hospitals and he was therefore proceeding immediately to endeavour to obtain such an extension of the truce.

On the morning of 22 May, the USSR submitted revised amendments to the revised draft resolution of Uruguay. They provided for (1) the deletion of the first and third preambular paragraphs and the insertion of a new paragraph reading *"Having considered* the question of the armed intervention of the United States of America in the internal affairs of the Dominican Republic"; (2) the addition to operative paragraph 1 of a condemnation of the armed intervention of the United States in the internal affairs of the Dominican Republic as a gross violation of the Charter; (3) the deletion of operative paragraphs 6 and 7; and (4) the insertion of an operative paragraph de-

manding that the United States immediately withdraw its armed forces
from the territory of the Dominican Republic.

On the same morning the Council voted on the revised draft resolution of Uruguay and the USSR amendments thereto. The six USSR
amendments were rejected in separate votes. The draft resolution of
Uruguay was voted upon as a whole, and was also rejected, receiving 5
votes in favour and 1 against, with 5 abstentions.

RESOLUTION 205 (1965)

Following the rejection of the Uruguayan proposal, the United
Kingdom introduced a draft resolution whereby the Council would (1)
call for a continued and complete cessation of hostilities; and (2) call
upon all concerned to intensify their efforts to that end and to do nothing to prejudice the achievement of that immediate and urgent aim.

France also submitted a draft resolution whereby the Council would
request that the suspension of hostilities in Santo Domingo be transformed into a permanent cease-fire, and invite the Secretary-General
to submit a report to it on the implementation of the resolution.

On the afternoon of 22 May, the representative of the United Kingdom indicated that he would not object to precedence being given to
the French draft resolution. The Council then adopted the French
draft resolution by 10 votes to none, with 1 abstention.

FURTHER REPORT OF THE OAS

By a telegram dated 22 May 1965 the Assistant Secretary General
of the OAS transmitted, for the information of the Security Council,
the text of a resolution adopted that day by the Tenth Meeting of Consultation of Ministers of Foreign Affairs. The resolution called upon
the parties in the Dominican Republic to transform the suspension of
hostilities into a permanent cease-fire in accordance with the Act of
Santo Domingo and with the resolution of the Tenth Meeting of 19 May
1965.

On the same day, the Assistant Secretary General forwarded the
text of another resolution adopted that day by the Tenth Meeting of
Consultation, which, *inter alia,* asked the Secretary General of the
OAS to assume the functions referred to in paragraph 3 of the resolution adopted by the Tenth Meeting on 6 May 1965 concerning the
establishment of a unified command of the OAS; requested the Government of Brazil to designate the Commander of the Inter-American
Armed Force and the Government of the United States to designate the
Deputy Commander of that Force; and appointed a Committee composed of those members designated by the President of the Tenth Meeting of Consultation to study the functioning and maintenance of the
Inter-American Armed Force.

On 24 May the Assistant Secretary General forwarded, for the information of the Security Council, the text of the Constituent Act of

the Inter-American Armed Force, which was signed at Santo Domingo on 23 May 1965.

FURTHER REPORTS OF THE SECRETARY-GENERAL

On 22 May the Secretary-General reported to the Council that according to the information submitted by his Representative in the Dominican Republic just prior to the expiry of the twenty-four hour truce, the cease-fire had been observed with the exception of some firing during the night. The Secretary-General was also informed by his Representative that despite the latter's efforts, General Imbert had refused to agree to extend the truce for an additional twenty-four hours. In this connexion, General Imbert had reportedly said, in a statement to the Press, that the "Government of National Reconstruction" had to have its hand free to repel any warlike action, but that it would abstain from a resumption of fire, unless it was provoked, while discussion with the OAS continued for the purpose of finding a definite solution to the conflict. . . .

On 24 May the Secretary-General reported, on the basis of the latest information received from his Representative, that the general situation in the Dominican Republic as of 23 May at 1820 hours local time seemed to show improvement and the cease-fire had been maintained generally, with the exception of isolated incidents. . . .

FURTHER CONSIDERATION BY THE SECURITY COUNCIL

On 24 May the representative of the United States informed the Council that in pursuance of the OAS resolution of 22 May, the Brazilian Government had designated General Hugo Panasco Alvim as the Commander-in-Chief of the Inter-American Force and that the Act establishing that Force had been signed on the afternoon of 23 May. He also drew attention to the reports of the Secretary-General of 23 and 24 May and pointed out that an investigation of the incidents of 22 May had failed to sustain the allegations of Colonel Caamaño. With regard to the charges that the corridor had been extended three times in the past week, a statement had just been issued in Washington to the effect that the corridor had not been extended and that there would be no such extension except upon request of the OAS and with prior notification by the OAS to both sides. Finally, in the light of recent action by the Security Council and the OAS the United States draft resolution was no longer timely and pertinent. He accordingly withdrew it from the Council's consideration. . . .

On 25 May the President of the Council, noting that a *de facto* cessation of hostilities continued to prevail in Santo Domingo and that the Secretary-General had informed him that there had been no new developments concerning its observance since his last report, and also that information submitted by his Representative on the spot would be made available to the members of the Council, suggested that the Council should adjourn, on the understanding that he could call it into immediate session if necessary.

Between 25 May and 15 June, the Secretary-General submitted four additional reports to the Council.

These reports indicated that the cease-fire in Santo Domingo had in general remained effective except for one serious incident: on 4 June the zone held by the Caamaño forces was hit by a series of explosions which had killed two persons and wounded four others.

On 11 June the Secretary-General also reported to the Council that, after receiving information from various sources about alleged mass executions said to have been carried out by military police elements under General Imbert at the El Haras estate near Santo Domingo, his Representative and four members of his staff had visited the estate on 10 June. They found freshly dug earth and signs of recent burning at several spots and at one of them what appeared to be human bones. They also found several spent cartridges.

In the same period, the OAS addressed to the Secretary-General, for the information of the Council, several messages concerning the activities of its Force in the Dominican Republic, which had been renamed the Inter-American Peace Force on 2 June. An investigation of the incident of 4 June, ordered by General Alvim, led to the conclusion that the shots had not been fired by members of the Force.

On 2 June the OAS advised the Council that the Tenth Meeting of Consultation had decided to appoint an *Ad Hoc* Commission—composed of Brazil, El Salvador and the United States—whose good offices would be made available to all the parties with a view to creating an atmosphere of peace and conciliation, thus enabling the democratic institutions in the Dominican Republic to operate. On the same day, it informed the Council of the impending arrival in Santo Domingo of the Chairman of the Inter-American Commission on Human Rights in response to requests made by both Dominican contending groups. Subsequently, the OAS sent to the Council several reports on the activities of its *Ad Hoc* Commission and its Commission on Human Rights. In this connexion, the OAS also informed the Council that following discoveries which pointed to serious violations of human rights it had dispatched to the Dominican Republic a Commission of Criminologists to investigate those violations.

5. *Discussion in the Security Council, 3–7 June 1965.*

SCOR, XX, Mtgs. 1220–21.

Mr. FEDORENKO (USSR): . . . In connexion with the continuing armed interference by the United States in the internal affairs of the Dominican Republic, which is being conducted under cover of the Organization of American States, the Soviet Government has instructed me to make the following statement:

"The United States, after perpetrating overt military intervention against a sovereign State—the Dominican Republic—and thereby grossly violating very important principles of the United Nations Charter and the generally accepted rules of international law, is using the Organization of American States as a smoke-screen for its aggressive acts. On 6 May 1965, the Meeting of Consultation of Ministers of Foreign Affairs of the States members of the OAS, despite the vehement objections of a number of Latin American States participating in the Meeting, adopted, under direct pressure from the United States of America, a resolution on the formation and the use in the Dominican Republic of a so-called 'Inter-American Force'.

"This resolution of the OAS is in flagrant contradiction with the Charter of the United Nations.

"The OAS resolution violates Article 2 of the United Nations Charter, which prohibits the threat or use of force in international relations 'against the territorial integrity or political independence of any State, or in any other manner inconsistent with the Purposes of the United Nations'.

"The resolution violates Article 39 of the United Nations Charter, which states that the Security Council alone shall determine 'the existence of any threat to the peace, breach of the peace, or act of aggression' and decides what measures shall be taken 'to maintain or restore international peace and security'.

"The OAS resolution is contrary to Article 53 of the Charter, which states that no enforcement action shall be taken under regional arrangements or by regional agencies 'without the authorization of the Security Council'.

"Consequently, the OAS resolution violates fundamental provisions of the United Nations Charter and is therefore illegal.

"The United States has also disregarded the obligations it assumed under the Charter of the OAS and other inter-American agreements. Under article 15 of the charter of the OAS, no State or group of States has the right to intervene, directly or indirectly, for any reason whatever, in the internal or external affairs of any other State.

"Following the formation of the so-called 'Inter-American Force', which is being used for intervention in the internal affairs of the Dominican Republic, the United States is now endeavouring to organize a permanent inter-American force, an endeavour that is fraught with great danger for the other countries of Latin America. It means in practice that the imperialist forces in the United States are trying to arrogate to themselves the right to intervene under the OAS flag in the internal affairs of other Latin American States for the purpose of dealing with Governments that are not to their liking and with the democratic forces that are seeking to strengthen their freedom and independence.

"The Soviet Government deems it essential to draw the attention of the States members of the Security Council and of all States Members of the United Nations to the serious consequences which may result from the actions taken by the United States to make use of the Organization of American States for its aggressive purposes, in violation of the United Nations Charter. . . .

"The Soviet Government calls on the Security Council and all States Members of the United Nations to repulse the attempts to bring about arbitrary rule and lawlessness and high-handedly to violate very important principles of the United Nations Charter. It is essential to put an end to the United States aggression against the Dominican Republic and to bring about the immediate withdrawal of United States armed forces and of all foreign troops from that country. It is essential to prevent further use of the Organization of American States by the United States for the attainment of its imperialist aims and for intervention in the affairs of sovereign States." . . .

Mr. YOST (USA): . . . The representative of the Soviet Union has attacked the establishment of the Inter-American Peace Force. In this connexion I should like to recall that the text of the OAS resolution of 6 May, to which Ambassador Fedorenko referred, makes clear that the Inter-American Force has but one purpose: that purpose is to co-operate in the restoration of normal conditions in the Dominican Republic, in maintaining the security of its inhabitants and the inviolability of human rights, and in the establishment of an atmosphere of peace and conciliation that will permit the functioning of democratic institutions. Following the signing of the Act establishing the Force, the Secretary General of the Organization of American States, Mr. José Mora, said that:

"The purpose of the Inter-American Force is clearly not one of intervention but rather one of rendering assistance to the people of a sister nation. The creation of the Force demonstrates once more the capacity of the Organization of American States to adjust to new conditions and to deal with new problems, problems having characteristics, perhaps, not even envisaged at the time the Charter and the Rio Treaty were ratified. It is clear, however, that the objectives for which the Inter-American Force was created fall within those broad provisions of the Charter which are concerned with matters affecting the peace and security of the Western Hemisphere. Peace, prosperity and justice"—he went on—"are indivisible and interdependent. Where these are lacking in one nation, it must be a matter of concern to all.

"The activities of the Organization of American States in the Dominican Republic are directed towards the fostering of peace and tranquility under conditions which will permit the Dominican people to establish a democratic civil government of their own choosing to heal the wounds and the bitterness of civil strife and to begin the path of relief and reconstruction."

The representative of the Soviet Union has renewed the Soviet assertion that authorization from the Security Council for this force is required. That assertion is evidently based on the proposition that the establishment and the functioning of the Inter-American Force somehow constitute enforcement action within the meaning of Article 53, paragraph 1, of the United Nations Charter. It seems evident to us that the voluntary establishment and functioning of the Inter-American Force are solely for the purposes which I have just cited: that is, of assisting in the restoration of normal conditions in the Dominican Republic and of making it possible for the Dominican people to determine their future and to operate under democratic institutions free from outside interference. Clearly, the Inter-American Force is not designed to act, and is not acting, against the Dominican Republic or the Dominican people. The Inter-American Force is not being employed to force any concession from a Dominican Government or to require a Dominican Government to follow or to abstain from any particular course of action. Indeed, as we all know, there was an entire breakdown of governmental authority in the Dominican Republic at the end of April, and it is the purpose of the Organization of American States now to assist in the restoration of democratic government.

These collective efforts of the regional organization concerned to enable the Dominican people to determine their future government cannot properly be termed enforcement action under Article 53. In these circumstances the requirements of the United Nations Charter are those set forth in Articles 52 and 54 rather than in Article 53.

I think that we might note that the Soviet Government objects to peace-keeping operations under the auspices of the OAS, but it also objects to such operations undertaken at the recommendation of the General Assembly. It insists that only the Security Council, where it has a veto—used over a hundred times—can take action to keep the peace. In short, the Soviet Union is trying to establish a *de facto* situation where international peace-keeping operations can take place only at the pleasure of the Soviet Union. Having in mind the explosive and dangerous Soviet doctrine of so-called wars of liberation, we can imagine how many and what kind of peace-keeping operations would take place under these circumstances. . . .

Turning to a more pleasant subject—what the OAS has actually accomplished since we last met—it might be useful to note the following.

First, the Inter-American Force has been established in Santo Domingo. On the same day, the heads of the two factions, Colonel Caamaño and General Imbert, were formally notified of the establishment of the Force and requested to address any complaints concerning compliance with the Act of Santo Domingo—that is, the cease-fire established by the OAS—to the Unified Command Headquarters of the Inter-American Force.

On 29 May 1965 General Hugo Panasco Alvim of Brazil officially took command of the Force. Brazil, Costa Rica, Nicaragua, Honduras and the United States have thus far contributed contingents to the Force. Inter-American patrols have been instituted throughout the safety zone and along the lines of communication which separate the combatants.

The withdrawal of 600 United States Marines took place on 26 May. Since that time, more than 2,500 additional United States forces have been withdrawn. The United States is prepared to make further withdrawals, as Ambassador Bunker told the Organization of American States, when the Unified Command of the OAS determines that the Inter-American Force is adequate for the purposes contemplated by the resolution adopted by this organization on 1 May and that the United States forces are not needed as part of the Inter-American Force.

This Inter-American Force, standing between the two armed factions, has brought about a cessation of organized hostilities between them. Without this peaceful shield, it is highly likely that there would have been further bloody conflict and great loss of life. . . .

[The President of the Security Council (Mr. De Beus, Netherlands) then read the following letter from thirteen Latin American States (Argentina, Bolivia, Brazil, Colombia, Costa Rica, El Salvador, Guatemala, Haiti, Honduras, Nicaragua, Panama, Paraguay and Peru):

"[Concerned] that our regional agency should fulfil the purposes assigned to it by its charter and by the Charter of the United Nations; and, at the same time, seeking to reaffirm the significance of the OAS as an instrument for the preservation of peace and security on the American continent, [we] venture to place before the Security Council, with respect, the following considerations:

"First: The Organization of American States, in its capacity as a regional agency, should continue to exercise the responsibility for the maintenance of peace and security in the hemisphere which is conferred on it by the charter of the OAS and recognized by the Charter of the United Nations.

"Second: In accordance with Article 52, paragraph 3, of the Charter of the United Nations, which Member States are bound to uphold, every effort should be made to encourage action by regional agencies for the pacific settlement of local disputes.

"Third: The foregoing does not preclude coordination of the action of the United Nations and of the OAS for the maintenance of peace and security as an appropriate procedure for the fulfilment of the high purposes of the Charter of the United Nations and of the charter of the Organization of American States."　SCOR, XX, Mtg. 1220, pp. 23–24.]

Mr. RIFA'I (Jordan):　.　.　.　We firmly believe that the United Nations Charter does not permit a military action of the type which took place in the Dominican Republic, whether this action was unilateral or was given a regional form.　Collective measures in self-defence are permitted under the Charter, but no enforcement action can be taken under regional arrangements without the authorization of the Security Council.

With this, allow me to turn to the letter signed by thirteen of our colleagues and friends from the Latin American States [S/6409] and to make a brief comment.　As far as the OAS is concerned, in its capacity as a regional and Latin American organization, it is highly regarded and duly recognized.　We also admit that the OAS, like other regional organizations, can always be a useful instrument for assisting in the cause of peace.　The question is, however, whether, in this particular problem of the Dominican Republic, the OAS has acted in conformity with the provisions of the United Nations Charter, which should prevail over all international agreements.　.　.　.

Mr. VELAZQUEZ (Uruguay):　.　.　.　[The] "Inter-American Peace Force" was　.　.　.　created under an OAS resolution of 6 May [1965].　.　.　.

[My] delegation considers that the legal considerations which it set forth at length in order to demonstrate the illegality of the action of the United States in the Dominican Republic are equally relevant with regard to the resolution of 6 May.　.　.　.

First, there can be no doubt that the OAS, like any of its members, has an obligation to respect the provisions of articles 15 and 17 of its Charter, which lay down the principles of non-intervention and of the inviolability of the territory of a contracting State.　The illegality of intervention, as everyone knows, does not depend on the number of States which intervene or the nature of the body intervening.　Whether unilateral or multilateral, perpetrated by one State or by a group of States, organically united or otherwise, intervention and the use of force are always contrary to international legality, unless they are justified by other substantive norms, as in the case of Chapter VII of our Charter—expressly mentioned as an exception to the principle of non-intervention—and as in the case of article 19 of the OAS Charter.

In the second place, the only legitimate collective action—that is to say, the only collective action based on a substantive legal norm— is the action which may be taken in accordance with the provisions of the Inter-American Treaty of Reciprocal Assistance (articles 19 and 25 of the OAS Charter), the sole case in which force would not be a violation of the principles of non-intervention and of the territorial integrity of States. The Tenth Meeting of Consultation was not convened under the Treaty of Reciprocal Assistance, nor did it base its resolution of 6 May on the provisions of that Treaty. No collective measures, in the sense which that term has in law, can therefore be taken lawfully by that Meeting—and that naturally includes the creation of this Inter-American Force intended to operate in the territory of a member State.

Thirdly, without taking a position on the problem of so-called "peace-keeping operations", on the nature and legality of which, as is well known, there are major differences of opinion among Members of the United Nations and even among members of this Council, my delegation does not consider that the military intervention in the Dominican Republic can be included in this category of operation, if only because a prerequisite generally regarded as essential is lacking, namely the consent of the interested party. And if the conclusion to be drawn, after a more careful study of this problem, particularly in its constitutional and legal aspects, were that this action should be or could be regarded as enforcement action within the meaning of the Charter, the only consequences which could follow from its "regionalization" would be to make applicable the provisions of Article 53 of the United Nations Charter.

Finally, if we leave the sphere of treaties, there is a general principle of law, reaffirmed by the International Court of Justice on many occasions, which is contained in the codes of all civilized nations. It is that expressed in the maxim *ex injuria jus non oritur*, according to which rights cannot derive from injustice nor legality from illegality. If the original presence of military forces on Dominican soil was illegal, the situation is in no way changed by adding other forces to these forces; the situation is in no way altered either by a change of flag, because the only flag which could lawfully work the miracle is precisely the flag which is not at present flying there. . . .

It is with real concern that we view the possibility that this unfortunate episode in the Dominican Republic may serve as a pretext for the adoption of political formulæ which, sheltering behind an equally vague and imprecise multilateralism, might be used in the future to justify intervention in some other Latin American country. . . .

This new doctrine which, as Uruguay pointed out in the OAS, is also a doctrine of preventive action—a fact which considerably increases its dangerous character—does not even attempt to distinguish —and this should be fundamental—between cases in which the establishment of such régimes is the result of illegal action from outside and those other perfectly legitimate cases in which it represents the culmination of an authentic national revolution. In a continent like Latin America, where the lot which still falls to the majority is that of poverty, oppression and ignorance, the reality, the harsh reality . . . cannot be resolved simply by putting the blame on communism, the generals or nationalism. Any interventionist doctrine such as that which is apparently being developed will inevitably, by force of circumstances, help the cause of reaction, and I greatly fear that it will only serve to destroy forever the hopes of our peoples. . . .

It is also a matter of concern to us, at this date in history, again to hear talk of a system of "international policing" by certain national Powers. I do not know whether those who talk of this have realized the fatal consequences of this old myth of a "manifest destiny". Ideas, alas, have an iron logic. Any kind of national Messianism, since many may be tempted by the idea, would inevitably bring world society back to the state of anarchy which existed at the time when the prevailing theory was that of the balance of power, and would presuppose the division of the world into spheres of influence, in each of which one of the "national Powers" would exercise its policing authority, without conditions or limitations. If there really is a desire to destroy the very foundations of the United Nations, I do not think that any better way could be found of doing so.

6.   *Act of Dominican Reconciliation*

Signed at Santo Domingo, 31 August 1965. S/6655 (3 Sept. 1965) ; SCOR, XX, Supp. for July–Sept. 1965, p. 258, at 262–66.

Convinced of the absolute necessity to restore peace and unity to the Dominican family, to promote the economic recovery of the nation and to re-establish its democratic institutions;

Determined to achieve their high purpose of assuring a climate of peace and conciliation in which all Dominicans can live under a system of freedom and social justice;

The Parties signing below, who declare that they represent respectively, in the capacities indicated, the "Constitutional Government" and the Provisional Government of the Dominican Republic, hereby make it known that they have reached the following agreement as a result of negotiations carried out by the *Ad Hoc* Committee of the Tenth Meeting of Consultation of Ministers of Foreign Affairs, whose members also sign the present Act as further testimony that the Parties have agreed to comply with its terms:

1.   The "Constitutional Government" accepts the Provisional Government presided over by Mr. Hector García Godoy as the sole and sovereign Government of the Dominican Republic. The members of the "Constitutional Government" will offer their fullest co-operation to the Provisional Government in the re-establishment and consolidation of political peace, as well as in the rehabilitation of the national economy.

2.   The Parties accept the Institutional Act resulting from this agreement as the constitutional instrument under which the Provisional Government will exercise its functions. No previous Constitu-

tion will have effect during the existence of the Institutional Act, whose text is annexed to this agreement.

3. The Provisional Government will, on the day it takes office, proclaim a general amnesty provided for in article 11 of the Institutional Act and will take the necessary measures to release all political prisoners.

4. Immediately following the inauguration of the Provisional Government, the contending forces will begin to withdraw their defences from the zones at present under their control.

The Inter-American Peace Force will return to its bases, leaving only the barbed wire and a reduced number of observation posts in the present lines.

Demilitarization and the disarming of civilians will begin immediately within the Constitutionalist zone.

The present check-points will be operated during the period of disarming by units of the Inter-American Peace Force.

The observation posts and check-points of the Inter-American Peace Force will be withdrawn as soon as the demilitarization of the zone and the disarming of civilians have been verified by the Provisional Government.

The Provisional Government will take the necessary steps to verify that the terms of this article have been carried out.

The Provisional President will indicate where the Inter-American Peace Force will be transferred until the date of its departure from the country has been decided.

5. The Provisional Government will have the responsibility for assuring that public order is maintained within the security zone. In discharging this responsibility, it may take whatever steps it deems necessary.

6. The Provisional Government will, as soon as it has taken office, establish special centres for the collection of arms in possession of the civilian population. These centres will be under the direction of persons designated by the Provisional Government, and the Provisional Government shall decide when the arms collected should be returned to the arsenals of the nation.

7. The present "Constitutional Government" will take all necessary measures so that all arms now in the possession of civilians under their jurisdiction are delivered in due course after the installation of the Provisional Government to centres established in accordance with the foregoing article. The Provisional Government will take such measures as may be necessary to recover all arms that have not been surrendered voluntarily.

8. As soon as the Provisional Government has been installed, the armed forces will return to their barracks and place themselves under

the orders of their Commander-in-Chief, the Provisional President. All military personnel who have participated in the present conflict will rejoin the armed forces without discrimination or reprisals.

9.   In accordance with the declaration of general amnesty, no officer or enlisted man of the armed forces will be submitted to court martial or subject to punishment of any kind for acts, except common crimes, committed since 23 April 1965.   Any officer or enlisted man who wishes to retire will be permitted to do so in accordance with the prescribed procedure and corresponding retirement benefits set forth in the organic law of the armed forces.   Any officer or enlisted man who desires to leave the country may do so under appropriate guarantees and with assistance provided by the Provisional Government.

10.   The Provisional Government will immediately initiate negotiations with the Tenth Meeting of Consultation of Ministers of Foreign Affairs relating to the manner and date of the withdrawal of the Inter-American Peace Force from the national territory.

NOTE.—1.   This Act was accompanied by the following reservation by the "Constitutional Government":

"The Constitutional Government, in signing this Act, makes a formal reservation that, contrary to what is contained in article 5 of the resolution of the Tenth Meeting of Consultation of Ministers of Foreign Affairs establishing the Inter-American Peace Force, it considers that it is the exclusive and sovereign right of the Provisional Government to determine the date of the withdrawal of the said Force from Dominican territory.   This reservation shall be maintained until the Tenth Meeting of Consultation of Ministers of Foreign Affairs modifies the above-mentioned resolution which was drawn up before the installation of the Provisional Government."   SCOR, XX, Supp. for July–Sept. 1965, p. 264.

2.   As the "Government of National Reconstruction" refused to sign the Act, it was signed instead by the commanders of all its military and police forces, who made the following declaration:

"In view of the fact that the Government of National Reconstruction decided not to sign the Act of Dominican Reconciliation proposed by the *Ad Hoc* Committee of the Tenth Meeting of Consultation of Ministers of Foreign Affairs, but has expressed intention that 'the Dominican Republic might begin in relative peace the great period of reconstruction it deserves', and faced with the alternative that this end might be thwarted, the Armed Forces and the National Police of the Dominican Republic under our command guarantee to the *Ad Hoc* Committee of the Tenth Meeting of Consultation of Ministers of Foreign Affairs and to the Provisional Government that is to be installed that they will give their resolute support and acceptance both to the Act of Dominican Reconciliation and to the Institutional Act and that they will support Mr. Héctor Garcia Godoy as President of the new Government."   *Ibid.*, at 266.

3.   Héctor Garcia Godoy was installed as the President of the Provisional Government on 3 September 1965, and Joaquin Balaguer was elected President on 1 June 1966, defeating Juan Bosch by 754,409 votes to 517,784. Annual Report of the Secretary-General on the Work of the Organization, 1965–

1966 [GAOR, XXI, Supp. 1 (A/6301)], pp. 34–35. The withdrawal of the Inter-American Peace Force began on 28 June 1966 and was terminated on 21 Sept. 1966. S/7502 (21 Sept. 1966).

4. For comments on the Dominican crisis, see John CAREY and J. Bruce IRVING, "The Dominican Crisis: A Case Study of Law in Action at the Security Council," 9 ABA, Int. & Comp.L.Bull. (1965), No. 3, pp. 23–24; Gordon CONNELL-SMITH, "The OAS and the Dominican Crisis," 21 The World Today (1965), pp. 229–36; Theodore DRAPER, "The Dominican Crisis: A Case Study in American Policy," 40 The Commentary (1965), No. 6, pp. 33–68; René-Jean DUPUY, Les États-Unis, l'O.E.A. et l'O.N.U. à Saint-Domingue," 11 AFDI (1965), pp. 71–110; C. G. FENWICK, "The Dominican Republic: Intervention or Collective Self-Defense," 60 AJIL (1966), pp. 64–67; J. William FULBRIGHT, "Comments on the Dominican Republic," 111 Congressional Record (22 Oct. 1965), pp. 27464–98; L. C. MEEKER, "The Dominican Situation in Perspective of International Law," 53 DSB (1965), pp. 60–65; Ved P. NANDA, "The United States Action in the Dominican Crisis: Impact on World Order," 43 Denver L.J. (1966), pp. 439–79; 44 *idem* (1967), pp. 225–74; John N. PLANK, "The Caribbean: Intervention, When and How," 44 Foreign Affairs (1965), pp. 37–48; Jerome SLATER, A Revaluation of Collective Security: The OAS in Action (Columbus, Ohio, 1965), 56 pp.; Tad SZULC, Dominican Diary (New York, 1965), 306 pp.; A. J. THOMAS, Jr., Ann Van W. THOMAS and others, The Dominican Republic Crisis 1965 (Dodds Ferry, New York, 1967; Association of the Bar of the City of New York, Hammarskjöld Forums, No. 9), 164 pp.; Eduardo WARSCHAVER, The Inter-American Military Force (International Association of Democratic Lawyers, Brussels, 1966), 16 pp.

See also Juan BOSCH, Unfinished Experiment: Democracy in the Dominion Republic (New York, 1965), 239 pp.; Alistair HENNESY, "Background to the Dominican Coup," 21 The World Today (1965), pp. 236–39; Dan KURZMAN, Santo Domingo: Revolt of the Damned (New York, 1965), 310 pp.; J. MALLIN, Caribbean Crisis: Subversion Fails in the Dominican Republic (New York, 1965), 101 pp.; Selden RODMAN, Quisqueya: A History of the Dominican Republic (Seattle, Washington, 1964), 202 pp.

INDEX

References are to Pages

VIET-NAM—Cont'd
North's attack on South, 827–28, 834, 836–38.
Question, 818–62.
United States intervention, 820–42, 846.

VOLUNTEERS
Korea, 510–14.
Middle East, 821–22.
Spain, 510–11.

VOTING
Abstentions, 130–48.
Amendments to resolutions, 235.
Budgetary questions, 235, 269.
Clark-Sohn plan, 259, 282–90.
Corrections, 236.
Council of Europe, Consultative Assembly, 253.
Dual, 254–57, 263–67, 272–73, 281–82.
Dulles proposal, 254–57, 260, 263.
European communities, 279.
Gardner's suggestions, 268–77.
General Assembly, 232–82, 287–90.
International Bank for Reconstruction and Development, 253, 279.
International Development Association, 270, 279.
International Finance Corporation, 270, 279.
International Institute of Agriculture, 252.
International Monetary Fund, 253, 270, 279.
International Sugar Council, 252–53.

VOTING—Cont'd
International Wheat Council, 252.
Security Council,
  Abstention of parties, 130–48.
  Double veto, 148–231, 310, 331.
  Procedural questions, 130–33, 144–45, 148–231.
  Recommendations of General Assembly, 189–97, 206, 212–13, 232–35.
  Report of Interim Committee, 81–82, 139, 190–97, 212.
  San Francisco Statement, 151–52, 157, 163–64, 169–89, 197–213, 219–30.
  For text see **Basic Documents.**
Universal Postal Union, 252.
Weighted, 248–90.
Wilcox suggestions, 248–67.

WAR
  See also *Aggression; Intervention.*
Civil, 483–86, 511, 823–24, 830–31, 839–40, 1033.

WARSAW TREATY
Applicability to Hungary, 637, 644, 648–49, 651, 655, 661, 663, 675–76.
Denunciation of, 635, 645.

WASHINGTON CONFERENCE, 891.

YALTA CONFERENCE
Agreement on Spain, 525.

END OF VOLUME